Effective Small Business Management

An Entrepreneurial Approach
SEVENTH EDITION

Norman M. Scarborough
Presbyterian College

Thomas W. Zimmerer
Saint Leo University

Prentice Hall

Upper Saddle River, New Jersey 07458

Library of Congress Cataloging-in-Publication Data

Scarborough, Norman M.
   Effective small business management: an entrepreneurial approach/Norman M.
  Scarborough, Thomas W. Zimmerer.—7th ed.
      p. cm.
  Includes bibliographical references and index.
  ISBN 0-13-008116-7
    1. Small business—Management. 2. New business enterprises—Management.
  3. Small business—United States—Management. 4. New business enterprises—
  United States—Management. I. Zimmerer, Thomas. II. Title.

HD62.7 .S27 2002
658.02'2—dc21   2002066280

Editor-in-Chief: Jeff Shelstad
Project Manager: Jessica Sabloff
Editorial Assistant: Kevin Glynn
Media Project Manager: Michele Faranda
Marketing Manager: Shannon Moore
Marketing Assistant: Christine Genneken
Managing Editor (Production): John Roberts
Production Editor: Maureen Wilson
Permissions Coordinator: Suzanne Grappi
Associate Director, Manufacturing: Vincent Scelta
Production Manager: Arnold Vila
Manufacturing Buyer: Michelle Klein
Cover Design: Bruce Kenselaar
Cover Illustration/Photo: Getty Images Inc.
Full-Service Project Management and Composition: Rainbow Graphics
Project Manager: Rhonda Peters
Printer/Binder: Courier-Westford

Credits and acknowledgments borrowed from other sources and reproduced, with permission, in this textbook appear on appropriate pages within text.

Pearson Education LTD.
Pearson Education Australia PTY, Limited
Pearson Education Singapore, Pte. Ltd.
Pearson Education North Asia Ltd.
Pearson Education, Canada, Ltd.
Pearson Educación de Mexico, S. A. de C.V.
Pearson Education–Japan
Pearson Education Malaysia, Pte. Ltd.

10 9 8 7
ISBN 0-13-008116-7

In memory of Lannie H. Thornley

To Louise T. Scarborough, Mildred Myers,
and John Scarborough. Your love, support,
and encouragement have made all the difference.

N.M.S.

To my wife, Linda, whose many hours of work on this
project helped make the book a reality, and to Jesse and Minnie
Williams, whose simple life and love of learning will inspire
many generations to come.

T.W.Z.

The ability to learn and translate that learning into action
is the ultimate competitive advantage.
—Jack Welch, Former CEO of General Electric

Brief Contents

CONTENTS

Contents

Contents

SECTION IV: SMALL BUSINESS MARKETING STRATEGIES   287

SECTION VII: MANAGING A SMALL BUSINESS: TECHNIQUES FOR ENHANCING PROFITABILITY   509

PREFACE

The field of entrepreneurship is experiencing incredible rates of growth, not only in the United States but across the world as well. People of all ages, backgrounds, and stations of life are launching businesses of their own and, in the process, are reshaping the global economy. Entrepreneurs are discovering that the natural advantages resulting from their size—speed, flexibility, sensitivity to customers' needs, creativity, a spirit of innovation, and many others—give them the ability to compete successfully with companies many times their size and with budgets to match. As large companies struggle to survive wrenching changes in competitive forces by downsizing, merging, and restructuring, the unseen army of small businesses continues to flourish and to carry the nation's economy on its back. Entrepreneurs willing to assume the risks of the market to gain its rewards are at the heart of capitalism. These men and women, with their bold entrepreneurial spirits, have led our nation into prosperity throughout history. Entrepreneurship is a significant force throughout the world. We need look no farther than those nations that are throwing off decades of control and central planning in favor of capitalism to see where the entrepreneurial process begins. In every case, it is the entrepreneurs creating small companies that lead those nations out of the jungles of economic oppression to higher standards of living and hope for the future.

In the United States, we can be thankful that the small business sector is strong and thriving. Small companies deliver the goods and services we use every day, provide jobs and training for millions of workers, and lead the way in creating the products and services that will make our lives easier and more enjoyable in the future. Small businesses were responsible for introducing to the world the elevator, the airplane, FM radio, the zipper, the personal computer, and a host of other marvelous inventions. Only the imaginations of the next generation of entrepreneurs of which you may be a part can see what other fantastic products and services lie in our future! Whatever those ideas may be, we can be sure of one thing: Small businesses will be there to deliver them.

The purpose of this book is to excite you about the possibilities, the challenges, and the rewards of becoming an entrepreneur and to provide the tools you will need to be successful if you choose the path of the entrepreneur. It is not an easy road to follow, but the rewards—both tangible and intangible—are well worth the risks. Not only may you be rewarded financially for your business idea, but like entrepreneurs the world over, you will be able to work at something you love doing!

This edition of *Effective Small Business Management: An Entrepreneurial Approach* brings to you the material you will need to launch and manage a small business successfully in the hotly competitive environment of the twenty-first century. In writing this edition, we have worked hard to provide you with plenty of practical, "hands-on" tools and techniques to make your business venture a success. Many people launch businesses every year, but only some of them succeed. This book teaches you the *right* way to launch and manage a small business with the staying power to succeed and grow. Perhaps one day we'll be writing about *your* success story in the pages of this book!

Text Features

Effective Small Business Management, Seventh Edition, contains many unique features that make it the ideal book for entrepreneurs who are serious about launching their businesses the right way. These features include the following:

- *A complete chapter on e-commerce and thorough coverage of the World Wide Web (WWW) as a business tool.* One of the most important business tools in existence today is the World Wide Web. Still in its infancy, it is already proving to be a powerful force in reshaping the face of business. *Effective Small Business Management,* Seventh Edition, offers the most comprehensive coverage of e-commerce of any book in the market. In these pages, you'll find many references to the Web, ideas for using the Web as a business tool, and examples of entrepreneurs who have discovered the power of the Web.
- *Text material that is relevant, practical, and key to entrepreneurial success.* You'll also find it easy and interesting to read. This edition offers streamlined coverage of the topics you'll need to know about when you launch your own business without sacrificing the quality or the content of earlier editions.
- *An impressive Web site that both professors and students will find extremely useful.* Locate the Web site for *Effective Small Business Management,* Seventh Edition, at: *http://www.prenhall.com/scarborough*

   The Web site contains features for each chapter that are designed to get you onto the Web to research topics, solve problems, and engage in a variety of other activities that will make you a more "Web-wise" entrepreneur. This site includes a multitude of useful features, including a Business Plan Evaluation Scale, a "Before You Start" checklist, a list of hundreds of links to useful small business sites (organized by chapter). The World Wide Web Activities take students to the World Wide Web where they search for data, research relevant topics, and experience firsthand the power of the Web as a practical tool that will influence the way companies do business in the twenty-first century. The site also includes for students sample multiple-choice questions that help them determine how well they have mastered the subject matter and prepare for tests. Students also can find a sample business plan to use as a guideline in preparing their own plans. For professors, the site contains a full set of PowerPoint slides (prepared by one of the authors and professionally designed for teaching), as well as other support material for their courses.
- *Lots of examples.* Examples help people learn more effectively and efficiently. That's why you'll find plenty of examples in this edition, and they're set off in italics. These illustrations tell how entrepreneurs are using the concepts covered in the text to make their businesses more successful. These examples are also a great way to stimulate creativity.
- *Emphasis on building and using a business plan.* Chapter 6 is devoted to building a business plan, and features in many other chapters reinforce the business planning process.
- *A sample business plan for a business.* Many courses in entrepreneurship and small business management require students to write business plans. Students of entrepreneurship find it helpful to have a model to guide them as they build their own plans, and they can access a sample plan from our Web site. The plan is one written for an actual business start-up called StudentFarm.com, a business that links students to business owners through special projects in which students become consultants and problem solvers.
- *Features in every chapter that help students master the material more readily.* Learning objectives introduce each chapter, and they appear in the text margins at the

appropriate places to keep students' attention focused on what they are learning. Chapter summaries are organized by learning objectives as well. Experiential exercises entitled "Step into the Real World" invite students to learn about the exciting world of entrepreneurship firsthand by giving them interesting assignments that enable them to interact with practicing entrepreneurs.

- *Boxed features in every chapter that follow two important themes:*
  - "In the Footsteps of an Entrepreneur," which offer in-depth, interesting examples of entrepreneurs who are using the concepts covered in the text and which reinforce the learning objectives.
  - "Gaining the Competitive Edge," a "hands-on, how-to" feature designed to offer practical advice on a particular topic that students can use to develop a competitive edge for their businesses.

  Each feature presents thought-provoking issues that will produce lively class discussions and enhance students' learning experiences by asking them to (1) identify, (2) analyze, and (3) evaluate key issues related to entrepreneurship.

- *Updated coverage of important topics such as:*
  - E-commerce
  - Strategic management
  - Guerrilla marketing techniques
  - Finding sources of financing, both equity and debt
  - Conducting business in global markets

Acknowledgments

Working with every author team is a staff of professionals who work extremely hard to bring a book to life. They handle the thousands of details involved in transforming a rough manuscript into the finished product you see before you. Their contributions are immeasurable, and we appreciate all they do to make this book successful. We have been blessed to work with the following outstanding publishing professionals:

Melissa Steffens, acquisitions editor, who always performed her often-difficult job professionally, tirelessly, and cheerfully.

Jessica Sabloff, project manager, who helped keep this book on schedule, managed a seemingly infinite number of details, and coordinated the impressive package of supplements that accompanies this edition.

Maureen Wilson, production editor, who skillfully coordinated the production for this edition.

Susan Cooper, copy editor, who helped us polish the manuscript and transform it into the finished product you see before you.

Kevin Glynn, editorial assistant, who handled so capably the many details involved in putting together this book and who steered our chapters into the right hands in a timely fashion.

Shannon Moore, marketing manager, who gave us many ideas based on her extensive contact with those who count the most: our customers.

Especially important in the development of the seventh edition of this book were the following professors, who reviewed the manuscript and provided valuable input that improved the final product: Jan Feldbauer, Austin Community College; Gita DeSouza, Penn State University; and Judy Dietert, Southwest Texas State University.

We also are grateful to our colleagues who support us in the sometimes grueling process of writing a book: Foard Tarbert, Sam Howell, Jerry Slice, Meredith

Holder, Suzanne Smith, Jody Lipford, George Dupuy, and Debby Young of Presbyterian College and Dr. Arthur F. Kirk, Jr., and Dr. Douglas Astolfi of Saint Leo University.

A very special acknowledgement to Pat Guinn, whose talent in manuscript typing is legendary. Finally, we thank Cindy Scarborough and Linda Zimmerer, for their love, support, and understanding while we worked many long hours to complete *Effective Small Business Management*, Seventh Edition. For them, this project represents a labor of love.

Norman M. Scarborough
Associate Professor of Economics
   and Business Administration
Presbyterian College
Clinton, South Carolina
e-mail: *nmscarb@presby.edu*

Thomas W. Zimmerer
Dean, School of Business
Professor of Management
St. Leo University
Saint Leo, Florida
e-mail: *tom.zimmerer@saintleo.edu*

Chapter

1

Entrepreneurs: The Driving Force Behind Small Business

> *You can't cross the sea merely by standing and staring at the water.*
>
> —RABINDRANATH TAGORE

> *It's not how many times we stumble and fall down that matters. It's how many times we stumble and get back up that counts.*
>
> —MAX CAREY, JR.

Upon completion of this chapter, you will be able to:

1. Define the role of the entrepreneur in the U.S. economy.
2. Describe the entrepreneurial profile.
3. Describe the benefits of owning a small business.
4. Describe the potential drawbacks of owning a small business.
5. Explain the forces that are driving the growth in entrepreneurship.
6. Discuss the role of diversity in small business and entrepreneurship.
7. Describe the contributions small businesses make to the U.S. economy.
8. Explain the reasons small businesses fail.
9. Put business failure into the proper perspective.
10. Explain how small business owners can avoid the major pitfalls of running a business.

1

1. Define the role of the entrepreneur in business.

This is the age of the entrepreneur! Never before have more people been realizing that Great American Dream of owning and operating their own business. A recent study by the National Panel Study of U.S. business start-ups found that 8 million people, or one in 25 adults, were actively engaged in trying to launch a new business.[1] The impact of these entrepreneurs on the nation's economy goes far beyond their numbers, however. The resurgence of the entrepreneurial spirit they are spearheading is the most significant economic development in recent business history. These heroes of the new economy are rekindling an intensely competitive business environment that had once disappeared from the landscape of U.S. business. With amazing vigor, their businesses have introduced innovative products and services, pushed back technological frontiers, created new jobs, opened foreign markets, and, in the process, sparked the U.S. economy into regaining its competitive edge in the world.

Scott Cook, co-founder of Intuit Inc., a highly successful publisher of personal financial software, explains the new attitude towards entrepreneurship and the vital role small businesses play:

> Small business is cool now, and I don't mean that lightly. . . . People are seeing that the stuff that makes our lives better comes from business more often than it comes from government. It used to be that there was an exciting part of big business that attracted people. But today it's the reverse; small companies are the heroes . . . and now the entrepreneurs get the attention.[2]

The past several decades have seen record numbers of entrepreneurs launching businesses. In 1969, entrepreneurs created 274,000 new corporations; today, the number of new incorporations exceeds 800,000 per year![3] One indicator of the continued growth in entrepreneurship is the keen interest expressed by students in creating their own businesses. Increasing numbers of young people are choosing entrepreneurship as a career rather than joining the ranks of the pin-striped masses in major corporations. In a recent survey of college seniors, 49 percent of the men and 31 percent of the women said they were interested in pursuing entrepreneurship when they graduate.[4] In short, the probability that you will become an entrepreneur at some point in your life has never been higher!

Current conditions suggest that we may be on the crest of a new wave of entrepreneurial activity—not only in the United States but across the globe as well. Technology makes it possible for companies to accomplish more with fewer people. America's largest companies have engaged in massive downsizing campaigns, dramatically cutting the number of managers and workers on their payrolls. This flurry of "pink slips" has spawned a new population of entrepreneurs—"castoffs" from large corporations (many of whom thought they would be lifetime ladder-climbers in their companies) with solid management experience and many productive years left before retirement. This downsizing has all but destroyed the long-standing notion of job security in large corporations. As a result, people who once saw launching a business as being too risky now see it as the ideal way to create their own job security!

This downsizing trend among large companies has created a more significant philosophical change. It has ushered in an age in which "small is beautiful." Twenty-five years ago, competitive conditions favored large companies with their hierarchies and layers of management; today, with the pace of change constantly accelerating, fleet-footed, agile, small companies have the competitive advantage. These nimble competitors can dart into and out of niche markets as they emerge and recede; they can move faster to exploit opportunities the market presents; and they can use modern technology to create within a matter of weeks or months products and services that once took years and all of the resources a giant corporation could muster. The balance has tipped in favor of small, entrepreneurial companies.

Entrepreneurship also has become mainstream. Although launching a business is never easy, the resources available today make the job much simpler than ever before. Thousands of colleges and universities offer courses in entrepreneurship, the Internet hosts a sea of information on launching a business, sources of capital that did not exist just a few years ago are now available, and business incubators hatch companies at impressive rates. Once looked down upon as a choice for people unable to hold a job, entrepreneurship is now an accepted and respected part of our culture.

Another significant shift in the bedrock of our nation's economic structure is influencing this swing in favor of small companies. The nation is rapidly moving away from an industrial economy to a knowledge-based one. What matters now is not so much the factors of production but *knowledge* and *information*. The final impact of this shift will be as dramatic as the move from an agricultural economy to an industrial one that occurred 200 years ago in the United States. A knowledge-based economy favors small businesses because the cost of managing and transmitting knowledge and information is very low, and computer and information technology are driving these costs lower still.

No matter why they start their businesses, entrepreneurs continue to embark on one of the most exhilarating—and one of the most frightening—adventures ever known: launching a business. It's never easy, but it can be incredibly rewarding, both financially and emotionally. One successful business owner claims that an entrepreneur is "anyone who wants to experience the deep, dark canyons of uncertainty and ambiguity and wants to walk the breathtaking highlands of success. But I caution: Do not plan to walk the latter until you have experienced the former."[5] True entrepreneurs see owning a business as the real measure of success. Indeed, entrepreneurship often provides the only avenue for success to those who otherwise might have been denied the opportunity.

Who are these entrepreneurs, and what drives them to work so hard with no guarantee of success? What forces lead them to risk so much and to make so many sacrifices in an attempt to achieve an ideal? Why are they willing to give up the security of a steady paycheck working for someone else to become the last person to be paid in their own companies? This chapter will examine the entrepreneur, the driving force behind the American economy.

WHAT IS AN ENTREPRENEUR?

2. Describe the entrepreneurial profile.

Each year, entrepreneurs in the United States start between 3.5 million and 4.5 million businesses.[6] An **entrepreneur** is one who creates a new business in the face of risk and uncertainty for the purpose of achieving profit and growth by identifying opportunities and assembling the necessary resources to capitalize on those opportunities. Entrepreneurs usually start with nothing more than an idea—often a simple one—and then organize the resources necessary to transform that idea into a sustainable business. One business writer says that an entrepreneur is "someone who takes nothing for granted, assumes change is possible, and follows through; someone incapable of confronting reality without thinking about ways to improve it; and for whom action is a natural consequence of thought."[7]

Many people dream of owning their own businesses, but most of them never actually launch a company. Those who do take the entrepreneurial plunge, however, will experience the thrill of creating something grand from nothing; they will also discover the challenges and the difficulties of building a business "from scratch." Whatever their reasons for choosing entrepreneurship (see Figure 1.1), many recognize that true satisfaction comes only from running their own businesses the way they choose.

Researchers have invested a great deal of time and effort over the last decade studying these entrepreneurs and trying to paint a clear picture of "the entrepreneurial personality." Although these studies have produced several characteristics entrepreneurs tend to exhibit, none of them has isolated a set of traits required for success. We now turn to a brief summary of the entrepreneurial profile.[8]

1. *Desire for responsibility.* Entrepreneurs feel a personal responsibility for the outcome of ventures they start. They prefer to be in control of their resources and to use those resources to achieve self-determined goals.

2. *Preference for moderate risk.* Entrepreneurs are not wild risk-takers, but are instead *calculating* risk-takers. Unlike "high-rolling riverboat gamblers," they rarely gamble. Entrepreneurs often have a different perception of the risk involved in a business situation. The goal may appear to be high—even impossible—from others' perspective, but entrepreneurs typically have thought through the situation and believe that their goals are reasonable and attainable. This attitude explains why so many successful entrepreneurs failed many times before finally achieving their dreams. For instance, Milton Hershey, founder of one of the world's largest and most successful chocolate makers, started four candy businesses, all of which failed, before he launched the business that would make him famous. One successful entrepreneur who has launched six companies explains entrepreneurs' view of risk[9]:

Contrary to popular myth, entrepreneurs do not enjoy taking risks. Granted, a certain amount of risk is unavoidable in business, but the thrill

Figure 1.1
Why Entrepreneurs Went into Business
Source: Dun & Bradstreet 19th Annual Small Business Survey, 2000.

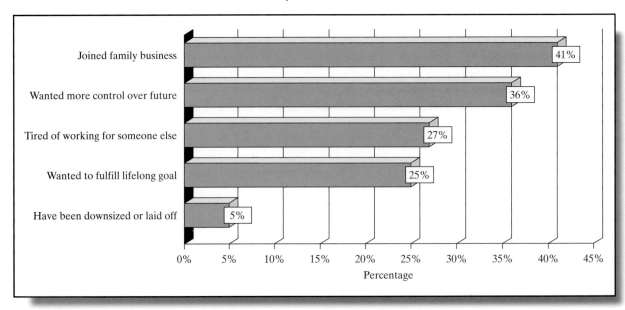

Section I   The Challenge of Entrepreneurship

IN THE FOOTSTEPS OF AN ENTREPRENEUR
From the Ice Age to Outer Space

Two characteristics common to entrepreneurs are creativity and an eye for opportunity. The entrepreneurs in the following stories are living proof!

AN OPPORTUNITY FROM THE ICE AGE

Call it odd or offbeat, but Ronald Stamp has an idea about how to use the 750 or so icebergs that break off from glaciers each year and drift south past Greenland into the Atlantic. Stamp, a former fish wholesaler, is lassoing icebergs and melting them down to make spring water! Recognizing the marketing potential of water made from glacial ice formed in the pristine air of 3000 B.C. (long before any man-made pollution became a concern), Stamp has an eye on tapping into the $30 billion-a-year bottled water business.

The first obstacle Stamp faced was figuring out how to capture icebergs and process them. After several failed attempts, Stamp met Paul Benson, owner of a spring water business, and the two formed Iceberg Industries. In addition to raising $500,000 from investors, Stamp and Benson finally developed a workable method for harvesting icebergs. They purchased a barge with heated tanks onboard (it had once been used to transport molasses) and converted it into a floating water factory. Outfitted with a crane and a hydraulic grapple originally designed to bite chunks out of granite, the barge is towed by a tugboat into the Atlantic each spring, where it spends the next eight months harvesting icebergs. The tugboat lassos the iceberg and pulls it next to the barge, where the grapple bites off a half-ton chunk of ice. Another device equipped with rotating steel teeth crushes the ice before it goes into the heating tanks. There, the ice is melted and filtered. Once the holding tanks are filled, the tug tows the entire barge to Iceberg Industries' processing plant in Newfoundland, where final filtering and bottling takes place. "The result is a bottle of the cleanest, purest fresh water you can get," says the company's promotional literature.

Iceberg Industries went public in 2000, but its two founders still own 15 percent of the company's stock. In addition to its line of bottled water, Iceberg Industries has partnered with other Newfoundland businesses to produce beer (Borealis Iceberg Beer) and vodka (Borealis Iceberg Vodka) with its pure water.

ENTREPRENEURS IN SPACE

Since Congress passed the Commercial Space Act, which legalized private manned space flights, in 1997, entrepreneurs have been vying to develop a safe, inexpensive, and reusable vehicle to carry people into space. One organization, the X PRIZE Foundation, is offering $10 million to the first entrepreneur who can build a spacecraft that carries three people 62 miles into space twice within two weeks. Modeled after the program that inspired Charles Lindbergh to be the first person to cross the Atlantic Ocean alone nonstop in 1927, the award is designed to encourage entrepreneurs to develop low-cost, reusable spacecraft for the space tourism industry. Although no one has qualified for the $10 million prize yet, some entrepreneurs are not waiting to get into the space tourism business. Space Adventures Ltd. is booking passengers on a variety of space-related adventure vacations, ranging from terrestrial tours of Meteor Crater to high-altitude flights in Russian MiG fighter jets. Top Gun wannabes can fly with an experienced pilot at speeds of up to Mach 2.5 (1,850 miles per hour) and altitudes up to 80,000 feet! Airborne thrills don't come cheap, however; prices range from $3,400 up to $13,000. Customers also can experience weightlessness like astronauts in outer space without ever leaving earth's atmosphere on the Russian-built Flying Laboratory (nicknamed the "Vomit Comet"). As the plane flies in a series of parabolic curves, its occupants experience about 25 seconds of zero gravity.

Space Adventures' most ambitious project is a suborbital space flight that will take adventurers 100 kilometers into space. The fact that the company does not yet have a vehicle capable of accomplishing this mission has not slowed down hopeful space travelers. Already, more than 100 people have paid the $6,000 deposit to reserve a spot on the $98,000 two-hour trip into space. The company has agreements with six of the most promising companies working to build reusable space vehicles, so Space Adventures customers will be among the first tourists to travel into space when a vehicle is available. "We imagine that in the next 20 years, [space travel] will become as popu-

(continued)

An artist's rendering of the Reusable Launch Vehicle (RLV) that Space Adventures will use to take passengers on suborbital space trips.

lar as the cruise business," says Bill Bell, Space Adventures' vice-president of sales.

1. Assume that you are a banker and these entrepreneurs approached you with a loan request to start these companies. What questions will you ask them? Would you approve the loan? Explain.

2. Using these business ventures as a source of inspiration, work in a team with two or three of your classmates to generate ideas for unusual business ventures that you could start.

3. Select one idea from those your team generated in question 2. What could you do to convince skeptical lenders or investors to put money into your company and to increase the probability of its success?

Sources: Michele Hatty, "Now on Tap Ice (Age) Water," *USA Weekend,* April 6–8, 2001, p. 17; Nathan Vardi, "It's the Tap of the Iceberg," *Forbes,* September 4, 2000, pp. 114–115; "Iceberg Info," Iceberg Industries, *www.borealisice.com/iceberginfo.htm;* Reed Karaim, "Better Book Your Moon Orbit Now," *USA Weekend,* October 8–10, 1999; Suzanne White, "Blastoff!" *Region Focus,* Fall 2000, pp. 15–19; "Close Up: Space Investor," *Entrepreneur,* September 2000, p. 22; Space Adventures Ltd., *www.spaceadventures.com*

of the start-up doesn't come from defying the odds. It comes from creating a viable company, and you improve your chances of doing that if you keep the level of risk as low as possible.

Good entrepreneurs become risk reducers, and one of the best ways to minimize the risk in any entrepreneurial venture is to create a sound business plan, which is the topic of Chapter 6.

3. *Confidence in their ability to succeed.* Entrepreneurs typically have an abundance of confidence in their ability to succeed. They tend to be optimistic about their chances for success, and usually their optimism is based in reality. One study by the National Federation of Independent Businesses (NFIB) found that one-

third of the entrepreneurs rated their chances of success to be 100 percent![10] Entrepreneurs face many barriers when starting and running their companies, and a healthy dose of optimism can be an important component in their ultimate success.

4. *Desire for immediate feedback.* Entrepreneurs like to know how they are doing and are constantly looking for reinforcement. Tricia Fox, founder of Fox Day Schools, Inc., claims, "I like being independent and successful. Nothing gives you feedback like your own business."[11]

5. *High level of energy.* Entrepreneurs are more energetic than the average person. That energy may be a critical factor given the incredible effort required to launch a start-up company. Long hours—often 60 to 80 hours a week—and hard work are the rule rather than the exception. Building a successful business requires a great deal of stamina.

6. *Future orientation.* Entrepreneurs tend to dream big and then formulate plans to transform those dreams into reality. They have a well-defined sense of searching for opportunities. They look ahead and are less concerned with what they accomplished yesterday than what they can do tomorrow. Ever vigilant for new business opportunities, entrepreneurs *observe* the same events other people do, but they *see* something different.

   Taking this trait to the extreme are **serial entrepreneurs,** those who create multiple companies, often running more than one business simultaneously. *Alan Rothenberg, who at age 36 has already started six successful businesses, is always alert to new business opportunities. His first company was a carpooling service he started in high school. In college, Rothenberg created two business—one selling stereo equipment to fellow students, and the other importing exotic cars from Europe. In the years since college, he has started an art gallery, a high-tech research and development company, and an educational CD-ROM publishing and Web portal company aimed at children.*[12]

7. *Skill at organizing.* Building a company "from scratch" is much like piecing together a giant jigsaw puzzle. Entrepreneurs know how to put the right people and resources together to accomplish a task. Effectively combining people and jobs enables entrepreneurs to bring their visions to reality.

8. *Value of achievement over money.* One of the most common misconceptions about entrepreneurs is that they are driven wholly by the desire to make money. To the contrary, *achievement* seems to be the primary motivating force behind entrepreneurs; money is simply a way of "keeping score" of accomplishments—a *symbol* of achievement. "Money is not the driving motive of most entrepreneurs," says Nick Grouf, the 28-year-old founder of a high-tech company. "It's just a very nice byproduct of the process."[13]

Other characteristics entrepreneurs exhibit include:

- *High degree of commitment.* Launching a company successfully requires total commitment from the entrepreneur. Business founders often immerse themselves completely in their businesses. "The commitment you have to make is tremendous; entrepreneurs usually put everything on the line," says one expert.[14] That commitment helps overcome business-threatening mistakes, obstacles, and pessimism from naysayers, however. An entrepreneur's commitment to her idea and the business it spawns determines how successful her company ultimately becomes.

- *Tolerance for ambiguity.* Entrepreneurs tend to have a high tolerance for ambiguous, ever-changing situations—the environment in which they most often operate. This ability to handle uncertainty is critical since these business builders

Table 1.1
Inside the
Entrepreneurial
Personality.

A recent study of business owners conducted by Yankelovich Partners for Pitney Bowes Inc. identified five different entrepreneurial personalities and described how their tendencies influence the way they run their businesses:

- **Idealists.** With 24% of business owners falling into this category, idealists make up the largest of the five groups. Idealists started their businesses because they had a great idea or wanted to work on something special. Idealists enjoy creative work but are impatient with performing administrative tasks such as financial analysis or legal matters. This group of entrepreneurs and their businesses are most dependent on computers. When making business purchases, idealists tend to focus on price, and they prefer to form relationships with established, reliable suppliers.

- **Optimizers.** Optimizers, which make up 21% of all entrepreneurs, are the second largest category. The benefits of entrepreneurship are most important to them; they enjoy the freedom and flexibility of owning a business and would not be willing to work for someone else. They want their companies to grow, but their focus is on profits rather than on revenues. These business owners are highly knowledgeable about financial issues and use technology to keep costs down and productivity up. They worry less than other business owners because they see themselves as maintaining control over their businesses. They also have learned the secrets of balancing their home and business lives.

- **Hard Workers.** Hard workers make up 20% of the entrepreneurial population. Like optimizers, they love their work and are more likely than any other group to put in extra hours to achieve the targets they have established. They tend to be detail oriented and are the most growth-oriented entrepreneurial group. They are financially aggressive (unafraid to use credit to achieve the growth they desire) and exercise broad control over the details of running their businesses. Hard workers typically have long-term business plans and stick to them.

- **Jugglers.** Jugglers also make up 20% of the entrepreneurial population and are the most involved in the operation of their businesses. They have a difficult time delegating authority and responsibility and prefer to do things themselves to make sure everything meets their high standards. As a result, there never seems to be enough time available for these entrepreneurs. As their name implies, jugglers are highly energetic people who are good at handling multiple tasks simultaneously. They readily embrace technology in their companies and are always looking for ways to improve their businesses. Jugglers feel pressure to maintain positive cash flow in their companies.

- **Sustainers.** The smallest group of entrepreneurs, sustainers comprise 15% of all entrepreneurs. Rather than start their businesses themselves, these entrepreneurs are more likely to have inherited or bought their companies. Of the five groups, they are the least comfortable with technology and prefer to put in more time than to figure out how to apply technology to solve a particular problem. Sustainers are the most conservative group and do not strive to achieve significant levels of growth. The status quo is just fine with them. Maintaining a good balance between business and home life is important to them.

Interested in taking the test yourself? Go to *www.prenhall.com/scarborough*, click on the "Roadmaps to Business Success" survey under Web Activities for Chapter 1, and complete the survey yourself.

constantly make decisions using new, sometimes conflicting information gleaned from a variety of unfamiliar sources.
- *Flexibility.* One hallmark of true entrepreneurs is their ability to adapt to the changing demands of their customers and their businesses. In this rapidly changing world economy, rigidity often leads to failure. As our society, its people, and their tastes change, entrepreneurs also must be willing to adapt their

businesses to meet those changes. *When Bill Hewlett and Dave Packard founded their company in a garage in the late 1930s, they had no clear idea what to make. They knew that they wanted to create a business in the vaguely defined field of electronic engineering. Their company, Hewlett-Packard (now one of the most successful electronics companies in the world), probably survived because of the founders' flexibility. Some of their early product ideas included a clock drive for a telescope, a bowling foul-line indicator, a device to make urinals flush automatically, and a shock machine to make people lose weight!*[15]

- *Tenacity.* Obstacles, obstructions, and defeat typically do not dissuade entrepreneurs from doggedly pursuing their visions. Successful entrepreneurs have the willpower to conquer the barriers that stand in the way of their success.

What conclusion can we draw from the volumes of research conducted on the entrepreneurial personality? Entrepreneurs are not of one mold; no one set of characteristics can predict who will become entrepreneurs and whether or not they will succeed. Indeed, *diversity* seems to be a central characteristic of entrepreneurs. As you can see from the examples in this chapter, *anyone*—regardless of age, race, sex, color, national origin, or any other characteristic—can become an entrepreneur. There are no limitations on this form of economic expression. Entrepreneurship is not a genetic trait; it is a skill that is learned. The editors of *Inc.* magazine claim, "Entrepreneurship is more mundane than it's sometimes portrayed. . . . You don't need to be a person of mythical proportions to be very, very successful in building a company."[16]

Table 1.1 describes the results of an extensive study of entrepreneurs that identified five different types of entrepreneurs and how their tendencies influence the way they run their businesses.

THE BENEFITS OF OWNING A SMALL BUSINESS

3. Describe the benefits of owning a small business.

Surveys show that owners of small businesses believe they work harder, earn more money, and are happier than if they worked for a large company. Before launching any business venture, every potential entrepreneur should consider the benefits and opportunities of small business ownership.

Opportunity to Gain Control Over Your Own Destiny. One of the benefits of owning their own businesses that entrepreneurs cite is controlling their own destinies. Owning a business provides entrepreneurs the independence and the opportunity to achieve what is important to them. Entrepreneurs want to "call the shots" in their lives, and they use their businesses to bring this desire to life. They reap the intrinsic rewards of knowing they are the driving forces behind their businesses.

Opportunity to Make a Difference. Increasingly, entrepreneurs are starting businesses because they see an opportunity to make a difference in a cause that is important to them. Whether it is providing low-cost, sturdy housing for families in developing countries or creating a company that educates young people about preserving the earth's limited resources, entrepreneurs are finding ways to combine their concerns for social issues and their desire to earn a good living. *Josh Knauer founded Greenmarketplace.com, an online retailer selling a wide range of environmentally friendly products, not only with the goal of earning a profit but also with a desire to educate consumers about how the products they buy affect the environment. Greenmarketplace is an offshoot of Envirolink Network, a nonprofit clearinghouse of environmental information Knauer started while he was a freshman at Carnegie Mellon University. Knauer spotted the opportunity for a retail business in the large numbers of Envirolink users who asked for referrals to sellers of environmentally friendly products. "I have* *no smaller goal than to have a positive impact on our planet and to create a positive future for my children and the world,"* says Knauer. *"The success of this business is measured first and foremost by profitability, but also by the health of our employees, our relationships with our manufacturers, and the effect we have on the environment."*[17]

Opportunity to Reach Your Full Potential. Too many people find their work boring, unchallenging, and unexciting. But to most entrepreneurs, there is little difference between work and play; the two are synonymous. Roger Levin, founder of Levin Group, the largest dental practice management consulting firm in the world, says, "When I come to work every day, it's not a job for me. I'm having fun!"[18]

Entrepreneurs' businesses become the instrument for self-expression and self-actualization. Owning a business challenges all of an entrepreneur's skills, abilities,

IN THE FOOTSTEPS OF AN ENTREPRENEUR
The Inca Girl

Stephanie Hirsch started down the path that many young people follow: go to college and then find a good job that eventually will become a career. After graduating from college, Hirsch moved to Los Angeles, where she tried several jobs before taking a job as a fashion stylist in New York. Hirsch enjoyed the fashion business, but she felt stifled working for someone else; an entrepreneurial spring was bubbling up inside her. "I've always wanted to do my own thing so it was difficult for me to be in a job," she says. "I never felt I was being creative enough, and I wanted to be my own boss. I wasn't creating my own destiny."

Hirsch decided to go to Lima, Peru, to visit a friend and to celebrate the new year in South America. On several trips to a festive open-air market in the city, Hirsch was overwhelmed by the colorful fabrics and designs that surrounded her. She also drew inspiration from many churches, cathedrals, and spiritual places she visited. While hiking on the Inca Trail, Hirsch decided to create a business selling fashionable plastic handbags made in the rich, vibrant colors she had seen on her trip. When she returned to New York, Hirsch, then just 24, designed a line of bags, found a manufacturer, and launched Inca Girl Enterprises.

Inca Bags became a tremendous hit, showing up first on the arms of celebrities such as Cameron Diaz, Liv Tyler, Halle Berry, Courtney Cox, Elizabeth Hurley, Cindy Crawford, and many others. Hirsch has expanded Inca Girl's product line to include miniskirts, sarongs, belts, beaded bathing suits, and beach mats. The company received a huge publicity boost when *Sports Illustrated* used Inca Girl swimsuits on some of its models in the magazine's famous "Swimsuit" issue. Inca Girl suits garnered four full pages of coverage in the popular issue.

Hirsch continues to expand her business, selling her products through upscale retail outlets such as Henri Bendel, Saks Fifth Avenue, and Bergdorf Goodman as well as through the company's Web site. She continues to find inspiration for her designs by traveling around the world; some of her favorite locations include Peru, India, Mexico, and Morocco. Hirsch also runs her company with an eye on its social responsibility. Through her business, she supports a variety of charitable organizations, including Hale House and the Doe Fund. Stephanie Hirsch proves that age puts no limit on entrepreneurial ability. Her creativity and hard work have enabled her to guide her company to more than $3 million in sales.

1. In addition to the normal obstacles of starting a business, what other barriers do young entrepreneurs face?

2. What factors do you think contribute to a young person's taking the risk of starting a business?

3. Does Stephanie Hirsch demonstrate the entrepreneurial personality? Explain.

Sources: "She's the Hippest Bag Girl in the World," LifeSMART Solutions, *www.lifesmartsolutions.com/image/incabags.asp;* Amanda C. Kooser, Victoria Neal, Michelle Prather, and Laura Tiffany, "Hot List," *Business Start-Ups,* April 2000, pp. 38–43; "Company Story," Inca Girl Enterprises, *www.incabag.com/company_frameset.html.*

creativity, and determination. The only barriers to success are self-imposed. Entrepreneurs' creativity, determination, and enthusiasm—not limits artificially created by an organization (e.g., the "glass ceiling")—determine how high they can rise.

Opportunity to Reap Unlimited Profits. Although money is *not* the primary force driving most entrepreneurs, the profits their businesses can earn are an important motivating factor in their decisions to launch companies. If accumulating wealth is high on your list of priorities, owning a business is usually the best way to achieve it. Self-employed people are four times as likely to become millionaires than those who work for someone else. In fact, self-employed business owners make up two thirds of the nation's millionaires![19] According to researchers Thomas Stanley and William Danko, the typical American millionaire is first-generation wealthy, owns a small business in a less-than-glamorous industry such as welding, junk yards, or auctioneering, and works between 45 and 55 hours per week.[20]

John Schnatter typifies these entrepreneurial millionaires. In 1984, Schnatter sold his prized Camaro Z28 to purchase some used restaurant equipment, expanded a broom closet in his father's tavern, and began selling $4 pizzas to customers. His business thrived, and within a year, Schnatter, then 22, opened his first official Papa John's restaurant. Since then, Schnatter has transformed Papa John's into the nation's fastest growing pizza chain, with more than 2,800 stores (most of them franchises) in 49 states and 10 foreign countries, generating sales in excess of $2 billion a year. Schnatter has reaped the financial benefits of his hard work; his net worth now stands at more than $500 million![21]

Opportunity to Contribute to Society and Be Recognized for Your Efforts. Often, small business owners are among the most respected—and most trusted—members of their communities. Business deals based on trust and mutual respect are the hallmark of many established small companies. These owners enjoy the trust and the recognition they receive from the customers whom they have served faithfully over the years. Playing a vital role in their local business systems and knowing that the work they do has a significant impact on how smoothly our nation's economy functions is yet another reward for entrepreneurs.

Opportunity to Do What You Enjoy Doing. A common sentiment among small business owners is that their work *really* isn't work. Most successful entrepreneurs choose to enter their particular business fields because they have an interest in them and enjoy those lines of work. They have made their avocations (hobbies) their vocations (work) and are glad they did! These entrepreneurs are living the advice Harvey McKay offers: "Find a job doing what you love, and you'll never have to work a day in your life."

Mike Manclark transformed his passion for airplanes and flying into a lucrative business. In 1984, at age 19, using $3,000 he borrowed from his father, Manclark launched Leading Edge Aviation Services, a company that provides maintenance, inspections, and repairs on aircraft. Leading Edge now generates more than $26 million in annual sales, but owning a business in a field that continues to fascinate him is Manclark's real reward. "I don't do this for the money," he says. "I do it for the love of airplanes."[22]

THE POTENTIAL DRAWBACKS OF ENTREPRENEURSHIP

Although owning a business has many benefits and provides many opportunities, anyone planning to enter the world of entrepreneurship should be aware of its potential drawbacks. "If you aren't 100 percent sure you want to own a business,"

4. Describe the potential drawbacks of owning a small business.

says one business consultant, "there are plenty of demands and mishaps along the way to dissuade you."[23]

Uncertainty of Income. Opening and running a business provides no guarantees that an entrepreneur will earn enough money to survive. Some small businesses barely earn enough to provide the owner–manager with an adequate income. In fact, the median income of small business owners is the same ($30,000) as that of wage and salary workers. (However, business owners are more likely to earn high incomes than wage and salary workers.)[24] In the early days of a business, entrepreneurs often have trouble meeting financial obligations and may have to live on savings. The regularity of income that comes with working for someone else is absent. The owner is always the last one to be paid.

Risk of Losing Your Entire Invested Capital. The small business failure rate is relatively high. According to a study by the Small Business Administration, 34 percent of new businesses fail within two years, and 50 percent shut down within four years. Within six years, 60 percent of new businesses will have folded.

A failed business can be financially and emotionally devastating. Before launching their businesses, entrepreneurs should ask themselves if they can cope financially and psychologically with the consequences of failure. They should consider the risk/reward trade-off before putting their personal assets and their mental well-being at risk:

- What is the worst that could happen if I open my business and it fails?
- How likely is the worst to happen? (Am I truly prepared to launch a business?)
- What can I do to lower the risk of my business failing?
- If my business were to fail, what is my contingency plan for coping?

Long Hours and Hard Work. Business start-ups often demand that owners keep nightmarish schedules. In many start-ups, 10- to 12-hour days and 6- or 7-day workweeks with no paid vacations are the norm. Because they often must do everything themselves, owners experience intense, draining workdays. Many business owners

Figure 1.2
Owner Age at Business Formation

Source: National Federation of Independent Business and Wells Fargo Bank.

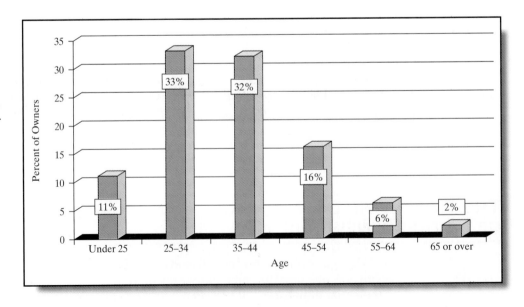

Section I   The Challenge of Entrepreneurship

start down the path of entrepreneurship thinking that they will own a business only to discover later that the business owns them!

Lower Quality of Life Until the Business Gets Established. The long hours and hard work needed to launch a company can take their toll on the remainder of an entrepreneur's life. Business owners often find that their roles as husbands and wives or fathers and mothers take a back seat to their roles as company founders. Marriages and friendships are too often casualties of small business ownership. Part of the problem is that most entrepreneurs launch their businesses between the ages of 25 and 34, just when they start their families (see Figure 1.2). *For Warren Zinn, founder of Hire Point, a temporary labor service company in New York City, the workday starts at 4 A.M. By 5:15 A.M., Zinn is in the office, where he spends the next 13 hours managing and marketing his company's services. Zinn admits that the strain of running the business takes a toll on his relationship with his wife and young son. However, when asked if owning the business is worth all the effort, Zinn quickly replies, "Definitely."*[25]

High Levels of Stress. Launching and running a business can be an extremely rewarding experience, but it also can be a highly stressful one. Most entrepreneurs have made significant investments in their companies, have left behind the safety and security of a steady paycheck, and mortgaged everything they own to get into business. Failure often means total financial ruin as well as a serious psychological blow, and that creates high levels of stress and anxiety.

Complete Responsibility. Owning a business is highly rewarding, but many entrepreneurs find that they must make decisions on issues about which they are not really knowledgeable. When there is no one to ask, pressure can build quickly. The realization that the decisions they make are the cause of success or failure of the business has a devastating effect on some people. Small business owners realize quickly that *they* are the business.

Discouragement. Launching a business requires much dedication, discipline, and tenacity. Along the way to building a successful business, entrepreneurs will run headlong into many obstacles, some of which may appear to be insurmountable. Discouragement and disillusionment can set in, but successful entrepreneurs know that every business encounters rough spots and that perseverance is required to get through them.

WHY THE BOOM: THE FUEL FEEDING THE ENTREPRENEURIAL FIRE

5. Explain the forces that are driving the growth of entrepreneurship.

What forces are driving this entrepreneurial trend in our economy? Which factors have led to this age of entrepreneurship? Some of the most significant ones include:

Entrepreneurs as Heroes. An intangible but very important factor is the attitude that Americans have toward entrepreneurs. As a nation, we have raised them to hero status and have held out their accomplishments as models to follow. Business founders such as Michael Dell (Dell Computers), Lillian Vernon (Lillian Vernon Catalogs), Mary Kay Ash (Mary Kay Cosmetics), and Phil Knight (Nike) are to entrepreneurship what Shaquille O'Neil and Eddie George are to sports.

Entrepreneurial Education. Entrepreneurship is now an extremely popular course of study among students at all levels. One recent poll of students by Junior Achievement found that 80 percent of teenagers want to become entrepreneurs one day.[26] A rapidly growing number of college students see owning a business as an attractive career option, and in addition to signing up for entrepreneurship courses, many of them are launching companies while in school. Today, more than 1,500 colleges and universities offer courses in entrepreneurship and small business to some 15,000 students. Many colleges and universities are having trouble meeting the demand for courses in entrepreneurship and small business management.

Economic and Demographic Factors. Entrepreneurs are most likely to start their businesses between the ages of 25 and 44, and the number of U.S. citizens in that age range stands at more than 82 million! The economic growth that lasted over the past 20 years has created many business opportunities and a significant pool of capital for launching companies to exploit them.

Shift to a Service Economy. The service sector now accounts for about 90 percent of the jobs and 80 percent of the gross domestic product (GDP) in the United States. Because of their relatively low start-up costs, service businesses have been very popular with entrepreneurs. The booming service sector has provided entrepreneurs with many business opportunities, from hotels and health care to translation services and computer maintenance.

While enrolled at New York University, Liz Alting and Paul Shawe started TransPerfect Translations, Inc., a translation service aimed at businesses. The partners spent many hours marketing their new business from their dorm rooms, but their hard work paid off as their client list and number of repeat customers grew. Today, TransPerfect Translations is one of *the largest translation firms in the world with 14 offices on three continents, a network of 3,300 translators, and $15 million in sales!*[27]

Technological Advancements. With the help of modern business machines—personal computers, laptop computers, fax machines, copiers, color printers, answering machines, and voice mail—even one person working at home can look like a big business. At one time, the high cost of such technological wizardry made it impossible for small businesses to compete with larger companies that could afford the hardware. Although entrepreneurs may not be able to manufacture heavy equipment in their spare bedrooms, they can run a service- or information-based company from their homes very effectively and look like any *Fortune* 500 company to customers and clients. *For example, Scott Adams, creator of the Dilbert cartoon strip that appears in more than 2,000 newspapers worldwide, runs his entire business from a home office that resembles nothing of the cubicles in which his cartoon characters exist. His custom-made desk ("the world's coolest desk" according to Adams) and a host of high-tech gadgetry allow Adams to manage his cartoon strip, his books, and many Dilbert-related products as well as to stay in touch with Dilbert fans via e-mail. (Scott gets several hundred e-mails each day.)*[28]

Independent Lifestyle. Entrepreneurship fits the way Americans want to live—independently and self-sustainingly. Increasingly, entrepreneurs are starting businesses for lifestyle reasons. They want the freedom to choose where they live, the hours they work, and what they do. Although financial security remains an important goal for most entrepreneurs, lifestyle issues such as more time with family and friends, more leisure time, and more control over work-related stress are also important. In a recent study by Hilton Hotels, 77 percent of adults surveyed listed spending more time with family and friends as their top priority; 66 percent wanted more free time. Making money ranked a lowly fifth place, and spending money on material possessions came in last.[29]

E-Commerce and the World Wide Web (WWW). The proliferation of the **World Wide Web,** the vast network that links computers around the globe via the Internet and opens up endless oceans of information to its users, has spawned thousands of entrepreneurial ventures since its beginning in 1993. Experts estimate that the volume of electronic commerce has grown from $518 million in 1996 to $6.8 trillion in 2004.[30] A recent survey of small companies with fewer than 50 employees found that just 27 percent have Web sites. Fifty-five percent of these businesses say that their sites have either broken even or earned a profit.[31] *Myriam Zaoui and Eric Malka, cofounders of The Art of Shaving, a chain of retail stores selling shaving products, recently invested $40,000 and eight months developing a Web site* (www.artofshaving.com) *for their business. The site has attracted new customers and generated new sales, and Zaoui and Malka say that the increased business the site brought in the first Christmas more than covered their original investment. The site reflects the same attention to detail and level of customer service customers get in the chain's retail shops and includes not only a wide range of products but also helpful shaving tips. Web sales now account for 15 percent of The Art of Shaving's sales.*[32]

International Opportunities. No longer are small businesses limited to pursuing customers within their own borders. The dramatic shift to a global economy has opened the door to tremendous business opportunities for those entrepreneurs willing to reach across the globe. Although the United States is an attractive market for entrepreneurs, approximately 95 percent of the world's population lives outside its borders. With so many opportunities in international markets, even the smallest businesses can sell globally. Small businesses account for 96 percent of all exporters; however, they account for just 20 percent of total exports. Most small businesses do not take advantage of exporting opportunities; only 13 percent of small companies engage in exporting.[33] As business becomes increasingly global in nature, international opportunities for small businesses will continue to grow rapidly in the twenty-first century.

Although "going global" can be fraught with dangers and problems, especially for small companies, many entrepreneurs are discovering that selling their products and services in foreign markets is not really as difficult as they originally thought. *After graduating from college, Richard Allred took $110,000 in savings and family investments and launched a company that produces surf-related clothing and apparel. Toes on the Nose Corporation domestic sales grew quickly, but Allred also saw opportunities to sell his products in foreign markets such as Australia, Canada, Great Britain, and Japan. "The whole world is accessible to everyone now, and we're trying to take advantage of that," he says.*[34]

THE CULTURAL DIVERSITY OF ENTREPRENEURSHIP

6. Discuss the role of diversity in small business and entrepreneurship.

As we have seen, virtually anyone has the potential to become an entrepreneur. The entrepreneurial sector of the United States consists of a rich blend of people of all races, ages, backgrounds, and cultures. It is this cultural diversity that is one of entrepreneurship's greatest strengths. We turn our attention to those who make up this diverse fabric we call entrepreneurship.

Young Entrepreneurs. Young people are setting the pace in entrepreneurship. Disenchanted with their prospects in corporate America and willing to take a chance at controlling their own destinies, scores of young people are choosing entrepreneurship as their primary career path. Generation X, made up of those people born between 1965 and 1980, is the most entrepreneurial generation in history. Members of this generation are responsible for 70 percent of all business start-ups![35] There is no slowdown in sight as this generation flexes its entrepreneurial muscle. Recent surveys have found that 60 percent of 18- to 29-year-olds say they hope to launch their own businesses.[36] "Generation X" might be more appropriately called "Generation E."

Women Entrepreneurs. Despite years of legislative effort, women still face discrimination in the workforce. However, small business has been a leader in offering women opportunities for economic expression through employment and entrepreneurship. Increasing numbers of women are discovering that the best way to break the "glass ceiling" that prevents them from rising to the top of many organizations is to start their own companies (see Figure 1.3). In fact, women are opening businesses at a rate twice that of the national average, and they are launching businesses in fields that traditionally have been male dominated.[37] Women entrepreneurs have even broken through the comic strip barrier. Blondie Bumstead, long a typical suburban housewife married to Dagwood, now owns her own catering business with her best friend and neighbor, Tootsie Woodly!

Although the businesses women start tend to be smaller than those men start, their impact is anything but small. The 9.1 million women-owned companies across the United States employ 27.5 million workers, about 20 percent of all company workers in the country. Women own about 38 percent of all businesses, and these companies generate approximately $3.7 trillion in sales each year.[38]

Recalling the importance of their joint makeup sessions in maintaining their social bond with one another, sisters Sara, Allison, and Jennifer Jaqua created a company with $15,000 they raised from family members and friends to sell their Beauty Parlor Night Kit.

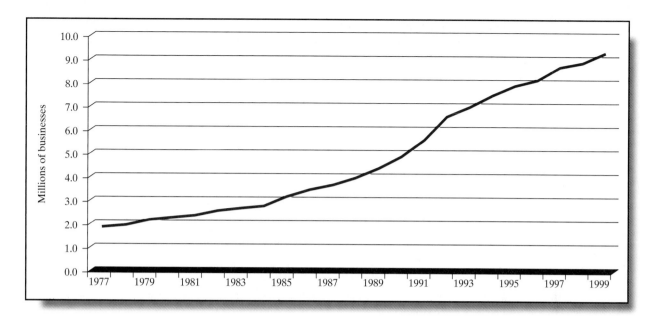

Figure 1.3
Women-Owned Businesses

Source: National Association of Women Business Owners.

The kit, cleverly packaged in a one-gallon paint can, includes ingredients for six women or girls to create their own beauty nights, including naturally botanical manicure, pedicure, and facial ingredient, all the "tools for a night of bonding, fun, and rejuvenation." When their first big order came in from Nordstrom, the three sisters worked in Sara's garage, packaging cans and attaching labels. Jaqua Girls Inc. now sells a variety of kits, including a Traditional Japanese Bath Kit and a Passion Ration Kit for romantic evenings. Sales recently topped $6 million.[39]

Minority Enterprises. Like women, minorities also are choosing entrepreneurship more often than ever before. Asians, Hispanics, and African Americans, respectively, are most likely to become entrepreneurs. Like women, minorities cite discrimination as a principal reason for their limited access to the world of entrepreneurship. Minority-owned businesses have come a long way in the past decade, however. Increasingly, minorities are finding ways to overcome the barriers to business ownership. Studies show that the nation's minority entrepreneurs own 3.2 million businesses that generate $495 billion in revenues and employ nearly 4 million workers.[40] The future is promising for this new generation of minority entrepreneurs who are better educated, have more business experience, and are better prepared for business ownership than their predecessors.

Immigrant Entrepreneurs. The United States has always been a "melting pot" of diverse cultures, and many immigrants have been lured to this nation by its economic freedom. Unlike the unskilled "huddled masses" of the past, today's immigrants arrive with more education and experience. Although many of them come to the United States with few assets, their dedication and desire to succeed enable them to achieve their entrepreneurial dreams. *Mik Kvitchko and Michael Markov, former Russian computer programmers, emigrated from their native country to the United States in the 1980s in search of a better life. In 1992, a mutual friend introduced Kvitchko and Markov, and within months, the partners started a business based on a program they had written to* *help financial advisers evaluate the quality of investments. Today, Markov Processes International generates more than $1 million in sales and counts among its clients some of the biggest names on Wall Street.*[41]

Part-Time Entrepreneurs. Starting a part-time business is a popular gateway to entrepreneurship. Part-timers have the best of both worlds. They can ease into a business without sacrificing the security of a steady paycheck. Nearly 16 million Americans are self-employed part time. A major advantage of going into business part time is the lower risk in case the venture flops. Many part-timers are "testing the entrepreneurial waters" to see whether their business ideas will work and whether they enjoy being self-employed. As they grow, many part-time enterprises absorb more of the entrepreneur's time until they become full-time businesses.

For more than a decade, Charles Manning, Jr., ran a part-time business in an unusual niche: accident investigation, a skill he learned while serving in the Air Force during the Korean War. Manning investigated the causes of everything from plane crashes and auto accidents to train derailments and medical accidents. In 1980, Manning's son, Charles III, convinced him to make Accident Reconstruction Analysis a full-time business. Their company has worked on such high-profile cases as the Challenger space shuttle and ValuJet explosions and generates annual revenues of $3.6 million.[42]

Home-Based Business Owners. Home-based businesses are booming! Fifty-three percent of all businesses are home based, but about 80 percent of them are very small with no employees. However, one study reported more than 55,000 home-based businesses generating sales of more than $1 million per year.[43] The biggest advantage home-based businesses offer entrepreneurs is the cost savings of not having to lease or buy an external location. Home-based entrepreneurs also enjoy the benefits of flexible work and lifestyles.

In the past, home-based businesses tended to be rather unexciting cottage industries such as crafts or sewing. Today's home-based businesses are more diverse; modern home-based entrepreneurs are more likely to be running high-tech or service companies with millions of dollars in sales. The average home-based entrepreneur works 61 hours a week and earns an income of just over $50,000.[44] Studies by Link Resources Corporation, a research and consulting firm, suggest that the success rate for home-based businesses is high: 85 percent of these businesses are still in operation after three years.[45] Less costly and more powerful technology, which is transforming many ordinary homes into "electronic cottages," will continue to drive the growth of home-based businesses.

Dorn Kennison launched his business, DMK Productions, a company that creates 3-D computer animations and sound effects for a variety of applications, from his kitchen table. "It was a way to keep costs down during the time my new venture was taking form—and it sure was handy for snacks," he says. As a set designer and visual effects expert in the movie industry, Kennison saw plenty of opportunities for a business creating special effects and animations for movies as well as for architects needing 3-D graphics of the buildings they designed. His first step was to create a business plan, and then he began calling on prospective clients. Although Kennison's business has experienced tremendous growth, he still runs the company from his home in Simi Valley, California.[46]

Table 1.2 offers 18 guidelines home-based entrepreneurs should follow to be successful.

Family Business Owners. A **family-owned business** is one that includes two or more members of a family with financial control of the company. They are an integral part of our economy. Of the 25.5 million businesses in the United States, 90 percent are family owned and managed. These companies account for 60 percent of total

Table 1.2
Managing a Successful Home-Based Business

Eighty-five percent of home-based entrepreneurs are satisfied with their working arrangement. Yet, working from home poses several unique challenges, including feelings of isolation and learning to separate work and home life. How do those who succeed do it? They follow these guidelines.

1. *Do your homework.* Much of a home-based business's potential for success depends on how much preparation an entrepreneur makes *before ever opening for business.* The library is an excellent source for research on customers, industries, competitors, and the like.

2. *Find out what your zoning restrictions are.* In some areas, local zoning laws make running a business from home illegal. Avoid headaches by checking these laws first. You can always request a variance from the local zoning commission.

3. *Choose the most efficient location for your office.* About half of all home-based entrepreneurs operate out of spare bedrooms. The best way to determine the ideal office location is to examine the nature of your business and your clients. Avoid locating your business in your bedroom or your family room.

4. *Focus your home-based business idea.* Avoid the tendency to be "all things to all people." Most successful home-based businesses focus on a particular customer group or in some specialty.

5. *Discuss your business rules with your family.* Running a business from your home means you can spend more time with your family . . . and that your family can spend more time with you. Establish the rules for interruptions up front.

6. *Select an appropriate business name.* Your first marketing decision is your company's name, so make it a good one! Using your own name is convenient, but it's not likely to help you sell your product or service.

7. *Buy the right equipment.* Modern technology allows a home-based entrepreneur to give the appearance of any *Fortune* 500 company—but only if you buy the right equipment. A well-equipped home office should have a separate telephone line, a computer, a laser or inkjet printer, a fax machine (or board), a copier, a scanner, and an answering machine (or voice mail), but realize that you don't have to have everything from day one.

8. *Dress appropriately.* Being an "open-collar worker" is one of the joys of working at home. But, when you need to dress up (to meet a client, make a sale, meet your banker, close a deal), do it! Avoid the tendency to lounge around in your bathrobe all day.

9. *Learn to deal with distractions.* The best way to fend off the distractions of working at home is to create a business that truly interests you. Budget your time wisely. Avoid leaving your office except for prescheduled breaks. Your productivity determines your company's success.

10. *Realize that your phone can be your best friend or your worst enemy.* As a home-based entrepreneur, you'll spend lots of time on the phone. Be sure you use it productively. Install a separate phone line for the exclusive use of your business.

11. *Be firm with friends and neighbors.* Sometimes friends and neighbors get the mistaken impression that because you're at home, you're not working. If one drops by to chat while you're working, tactfully ask him or her to come back "after work."

12. *Take advantage of tax breaks.* Although a 1993 Supreme Court decision tightened considerably the standards for business deductions for an office at home, many home-based entrepreneurs still qualify for special tax deductions on everything from computers to cars. Check with your accountant.

13. *Make sure you have adequate insurance coverage.* Many homeowner's policies provide minimal coverage for business-related equipment, leaving many home-based entrepreneurs with inadequate coverage on their business assets. Ask your agent about a business owner's policy (BOP), which may cost as little as $300 to $500 per year.

14. *Understand the special circumstances under which you can hire outside employees.* Sometimes zoning laws allow in-home businesses, but they prohibit hiring employees. Check zoning laws carefully.

15. *Be prepared if your business requires clients to come to your home.* Dress appropriately (no pajamas!). Make sure your office presents a professional image.

16. *Get a post office box.* With burglaries and robberies on the rise, you're better off using a "P.O. Box" address rather than your specific home address. Otherwise, you may be inviting crime.

17. *Network, network, network.* Isolation can be a problem for home-based entrepreneurs, and one of the best ways to combat it is to network. It's also a great way to market your business.

18. *Be proud of your home-based business.* Merely a decade ago there was a stigma attached to working at home. Today, home-based entrepreneurs and their businesses command respect. Be proud of your company!

Sources: Susan Biddle Jaffe, "Balancing Your Home Business," *Nation's Business,* April 1997, pp. 56–58; Ronaleen Roha, "Home Alone," *Kiplinger's Personal Finance Magazine,* May 1997, pp. 85–89; Lynn Beresford, Janean Chun, Cynthia E. Griffin, Heather Page, and Debra Phillips, "Homeward Bound," *Entrepreneur,* September 1995, pp. 116–118; Jenean Huber, "House Rules," *Entrepreneur,* March 1993, pp. 89–95; Hal Morris, "Home-Based Businesses Need Extra Insurance," *AARP Bulletin,* November 1994, p. 16; Stephanie N. Mehta, "What You Need," *Wall Street Journal,* October 14, 1994, p. R10.

employment in the United States and generate more than 50 percent of the U.S. GDP. Not all of them are small; 37 percent of the *Fortune* 500 companies are family businesses.[47]

"When it works right," says one writer, "nothing succeeds like a family firm. The roots run deep, embedded in family values. The flash of the fast buck is replaced with long-term plans. Tradition counts."[48] Despite their magnitude, family businesses face a major threat—a threat from within: management succession. Only 33 percent of family businesses survive to the second generation; just 12 percent make it to the third generation; and only 3 percent survive to the fourth generation and beyond.[49] Business periodicals are full of stories describing bitter disputes among family members that have crippled or destroyed once-thriving businesses, usually because the founder failed to create a succession plan. To avoid the senseless destruction of valuable assets, founders of family businesses should develop plans for management succession long before retirement looms before them. We will discuss family businesses and management succession in more detail in Chapter 20, Management Succession and Risk Management.

Copreneurs. "Copreneurs" are entrepreneurial couples who work together as co-owners of their businesses. Unlike the traditional "Mom & Pop" (Pop as "boss" and Mom as "subordinate"), copreneurs divide their business responsibilities on the basis of their skills, experience, and abilities rather than on gender. Studies suggest that companies co-owned by spouses represent one of the fastest growing business sectors.

Managing a small business with a spouse may appear to be a recipe for divorce, but most copreneurs say not. "There are days when you want to kill each other," says Mary Duty, who has operated Poppa Rollo's Pizza with her husband for 20 years. "But there's nothing better than working side-by-side with the [person] you love."[50] Successful copreneurs learn to build the foundation for a successful working relationship *before* they ever launch their companies. Some of the characteristics they rely on include:

- An assessment of how well their personalities will mesh in a business setting
- Mutual respect for each other and one another's talents
- Compatible business and life goals—a common "vision"
- A view that they are full and equal partners, not a superior and a subordinate
- Complementary business skills that each acknowledges in the other and that lead to a unique business identity for each spouse
- The ability to keep lines of communication open, talking and listening to each other about personal as well as business issues
- A clear division of roles and authority—ideally based on each partner's skills and abilities—to minimize conflict and power struggles
- The ability to encourage each other and to "lift up" a disillusioned partner
- Separate work spaces that allow them to "escape" when the need arises
- Boundaries between their business life and their personal life so that one doesn't consume the other
- A sense of humor
- An understanding that not every couple can work together

Although copreneuring isn't for everyone, it works extremely well for many couples and often leads to successful businesses. *After the birth of their daughter, Sheryl and David Drozen launched Uproar Entertainment, a home-based company that produces comedy CDs. When Uproar's sales took off, the Drozens struggled to balance their work and personal lives. They finally corralled their company into a spare bedroom and agreed to work there only between 7 A.M. and 6 P.M. The Drozens say their business and family lives are stronger than ever; sales of Uproar's CDs have climbed 50 percent a year for the past several years.*[51]

Corporate Castoffs. Concentrating on trying to operate more efficiently, corporations have been downsizing, shedding their excess bulk and slashing employment at all levels in the organization. These "corporate castoffs" have become an important source of entrepreneurial activity. Skittish about experiencing more downsizing at other large companies, many of these castoffs are choosing instead to create their own job security by launching their own businesses. They have decided that the best defense against future job insecurity is an entrepreneurial offense. Armed with years of experience, a tidy severance package, a working knowledge of their industries, and a network of connections, these former managers are setting out to start companies of their own. Some 20 percent of these discharged corporate managers become entrepreneurs, and many of those left behind in corporate America would like to join them. A study by Accountemps found that nearly half of the executives surveyed believed their peers would take the entrepreneurial plunge—if they only had the money to do so.[52]

Corporate "Dropouts." The dramatic downsizing of corporate America has created another effect among the employees left after restructuring: a trust gap. The result of this trust gap is a growing number of "dropouts" from the corporate structure who then become entrepreneurs. Although their workdays may grow longer and their incomes may shrink, those who strike out on their own often find their work more rewarding and more satisfying because they are doing what they enjoy and they are in control. *When one dropout left his corporate post, he invited his former co-workers to a bonfire in the parking lot—fueled by a pile of his expensive business suits! He happily passed out marshmallows to everyone who came. Today, he and his wife run an artists' gallery in California's wine country.*[53]

Because they often have college degrees, a working knowledge of business, and years of management experience, both corporate dropouts and castoffs may ultimately increase the small business survival rate. Better trained, more experienced entrepreneurs are less likely to fail in business. *Whit Alexander and Richard Tait are two such dropouts. In 1997, Alexander and Tait decided to leave their jobs at Microsoft to launch Cranium, a unique board game that Tait had dreamed up. When their market research revealed a gap in the board game market for their product, the entrepreneurs assembled an editorial advisory board to help develop the concept, which was done all via e-mail. Cranium has become the fastest-selling board game in history, and Alexander and Tait credit much of their success to the managerial and problem-solving skills they learned at Microsoft.*[54]

THE CONTRIBUTIONS OF SMALL BUSINESSES

7. Describe the contributions small businesses make to the U.S. economy.

Of the 25.5 million businesses in the United States today, approximately 25.1 million, or 98.5 percent, can be considered "small." Although there is no universal definition of a **small business,** a common delineation of a small business is one that employs fewer than 100 people. They thrive in virtually every industry, although the majority of small companies are concentrated in the service and retail industries (see Figure 1.4). Their contributions to the economy are as numerous as the businesses themselves. For example, small companies employ 52 percent of the nation's private sector workforce, even though they possess less than one fourth of total business assets.[55] In addition, because they are primarily labor intensive, small busi-

Figure 1.4
A Profile of Small Business by Industry

Source: Small Business Administration.

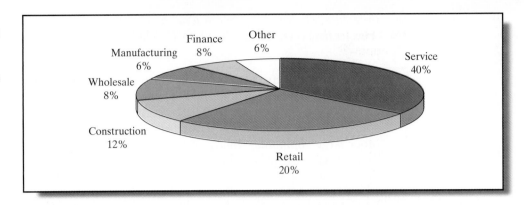

nesses actually create more jobs than do big businesses. The Small Business Administration (SBA) estimates that small companies created 75.8 percent of the nation's net new jobs.[56] David Birch, president of the research firm Cognetics, says that the ability to create jobs is not distributed evenly across the small business sector, however. His research shows that just 6 percent of these small companies created 70 percent of the net new jobs, and they did so across all industry sectors— not just in "hot" industries. Birch calls these job-creating small companies "gazelles," those growing at 20 percent or more per year with at least $100,000 in annual sales. His research also identified "mice," small companies that never grow much and don't create many jobs. The majority of small companies are "mice." Birch tabbed the country's largest job-shedding businesses "elephants," which continued to cut jobs through the 1990s.[57]

Not only do small companies lead the way in creating jobs, but they also bear the brunt of training workers for them. Small businesses provide 67 percent of workers with their first jobs and basic job training. Small companies offer more general skills instruction and training than large ones, and their employees receive more benefits from the training than do those in larger firms. Although their training programs tend to be informal, in-house, and on-the-job, small companies teach employees valuable skills—from written communication to computer literacy.[58]

Small businesses also produce 51 percent of the country's private-sector GDP and account for 47 percent of business sales.[59] In fact, the U.S small business sector is the world's third largest economy, trailing only the economies of the United States and Japan.[60] Small businesses also play an integral role in creating new products, services, and processes. Research conducted for the National Science Foundation concluded that small firms create four times more innovations per research and development (R&D) dollar than medium-sized firms and 24 times as many as large companies. In another study of the most important technological innovations introduced into the U.S. market, researchers found that, on average, smaller companies contributed 20 percent more of these innovations per employee than did large companies.[61] Many important inventions trace their roots to an entrepreneur; for example, the zipper, the personal computer, FM radio, air conditioning, the escalator, the light bulb, and the automatic transmission all originated in small businesses. Entrepreneurs continue to create innovations in many important areas, ranging from energy to communications. Earthfirst Technologies has developed a system that produces both a clean-burning fuel called MagneGas from contaminated water or sewage and irrigation-quality water.[62] ActiveSky Inc. is developing a compression technology that squeezes data down to a size that can be sent to a multitude of wireless portable devices such as cell phones, personal digital assistants, and others. Users will be able to receive video and multimedia images practically anywhere in the world![63]

IN THE FOOTSTEPS OF AN ENTREPRENEUR
Monopoly's Inventor

Throughout history, entrepreneurs have exhibited persistence, determination, and courage in the face of adversity. Although the setting may be different, the challenges and obstacles modern entrepreneurs face resemble in many ways those of entrepreneurs in the past. Consider the following entrepreneur's story.

In 1934, Americans were suffering from the devastating effects of the Great Depression, which had caused so many businesses to fail and the unemployment rate to peak at 25 percent. Charles Darrow of Germantown, Pennsylvania, had lost his job as a heating equipment salesman in 1930 and had worked at odd jobs to support his family. In the evenings, Darrow would listen to the radio, trying to think of an invention that would make him rich. He realized that people in the United States needed a diversion from the worries of everyday living that the Depression had imposed on them. Drawing on his memories of a happy vacation he and his wife had taken to Atlantic City, New Jersey, before the Depression, Darrow, sitting at his kitchen table, developed a board game that allowed players to wheel and deal like the real millionaires of the period. Players rolled the dice and moved game pieces around a board, landing on properties (named after streets in Atlantic City) on which they could build hotels or houses or could buy, sell, or mortgage. Players who went bankrupt were eliminated from the game until only one winner was left. Darrow called the game "Monopoly" and, unable to finance its production and marketing on his own, he took it to Parker Brothers, one of the nation's oldest and best-known game makers. Parker Brothers reviewed the game but rejected it, citing "52 design errors" and concluding that it was too complex and time-consuming to have mass appeal.

Undaunted, Darrow managed to borrow a small amount of money and, with the help of a friend who was a printer, constructed a few hand-made game sets, which he peddled from store to store. Wanamaker's Department Store in Philadelphia placed a consignment order for 5,000 games. They sold quickly, and Monopoly was soon the rage among residents of the city. The popularity of the game caused Parker Brothers to reconsider its decision, and in 1935, the company purchased from Darrow the rights to the game. Demand for the game was so strong that Parker Brothers could not manufacture enough game sets to meet it even though the company was turning out 20,000 sets a week. To date, more than 200 million Monopoly sets have been sold worldwide, making it one of the most popular games ever created. The game has been printed in 26 different languages. Charles Darrow never invented another game, but his legacy lives on through the game that more than 500 million people have played. Darrow became a millionaire from the royalties he received on the sales of Monopoly, and in 1970, Atlantic City erected a commemorative plaque in his honor near the intersection of Boardwalk and Park Place.

1. Explain how Charles Darrow exhibits the "entrepreneurial spirit."

2. Is Darrow's story of continuing to try in the face of failure typical of successful entrepreneurs? Explain.

Sources: "Monopoly, Monopoly," About Boardgames, *www.inventors.about.com/library/weekly/aa121997.htm;* Robert Sobel and David B. Sicilia, "Charles B. Darrow: Playing at the American Dream," *The Entrepreneurs: An American Adventure* (Boston: Houghton Mifflin Company, 1986), pp. 28–31; "History: The Monopoly Story," Hasbro Corporation, *www.monopoly.com/default.asp?x=history.*

THE TEN DEADLY MISTAKES OF ENTREPRENEURSHIP

The median age of U.S. companies is 12 years, and nearly half of the companies in the United States have been in business for at least 15 years.[64] Many businesses don't last that long, however. Studies by the SBA suggest that 60 percent of new businesses will have failed within six years. Because of their limited resources, inexperienced

8. Explain the reasons small businesses fail.

management, and lack of financial stability, small businesses suffer a mortality rate significantly higher than that of larger, established businesses. Exploring the causes of business failure may help you avoid it.

Management Incompetence. In most small businesses, management inexperience or poor decision-making ability is the chief problem of the failing enterprise. Sometimes the manager of the small business does not have the capacity to operate it successfully. The owner lacks the leadership ability and knowledge necessary to make the business work. Many managers simply do not have what it takes to run a small enterprise. *Andrew Kay was a pioneer in the earliest days of the portable computer with his Kaypro model (which in 1981 weighed in at a hefty 25 pounds and had 64 KB of RAM, hardly a laptop by modern standards!). Unfortunately, he had no experience in running a high-tech start-up, and, despite the popularity of his computer, Kay made a series of managerial blunders that ultimately forced the company into bankruptcy.*[65]

Lack of Experience. Small business managers need to have experience in the field they want to enter. For example, if a person wants to open a retail clothing business, he should first work in a retail clothing store. This will give him practical experience as well as help him learn the nature of the business. This type of experience can spell the difference between failure and success. *One West Coast entrepreneur had always wanted to own a restaurant, but he had no experience in the restaurant business. He later admitted that he thought that running a restaurant consisted primarily of dressing up in black tie, greeting his regular customers at the door, and showing them to his best tables. He invested $150,000 of his own money and found a partner to put up more capital and to help manage the restaurant. They opened and immediately ran into trouble because they knew nothing about running a restaurant. Eventually, the restaurant closed, and the partners lost their original investments, their homes, and their cars; they also spent the next several years paying off back taxes.*[66]

Ideally, a prospective entrepreneur should have adequate technical ability; a working knowledge of the physical operations of the business; sufficient conceptual ability; the power to visualize, coordinate, and integrate the various operations of the business into a synergistic whole; and the skill to manage the people in the organization and motivate them to higher levels of performance.

Undercapitalization. Sound management is the key to a small company's success, and effective managers realize that any successful business venture requires proper financial control. The margin for error in managing finances is especially small for most small businesses, and neglecting to install proper financial controls is a recipe for disaster. Two pitfalls affecting small business's financial health are common: undercapitalization and poor cash management. Many small business owners make the mistake of beginning their businesses on a "shoestring," which is a fatal error leading to business failure. Entrepreneurs tend to be overly optimistic and often underestimate the financial requirements of launching a business or the amount of time required for the company to become self-sustaining. As a result, they start off undercapitalized and can never seem to catch up financially as their companies consume increasing amounts of cash to fuel their growth.

Poor Cash Management. Insufficient cash flow due to poor cash management is a common cause of business failure. Many entrepreneurs believe that profit is what matters most in a new venture, but cash is the most important financial resource a business owns. Companies need adequate cash flow to thrive; without it, a company is out of business. Maintaining adequate cash flow to pay bills in a timely fashion is a constant challenge for small companies, especially those in the turbulent start-up phase or more established companies experiencing rapid growth. Fast-growing companies devour cash fast! Poor credit and collection practices on accounts receivable, sloppy accounts payable practices that exert undue pressure on a company's cash balance, and uncontrolled spending are common to many small business bankruptcies. When it comes to managing expenses, one experienced business owner advises entrepreneurs to "throw nickels around like manhole covers."[67]

The founders of Boo.com, a highly publicized Internet clothing retailer, failed to establish adequate financial controls in the business, and it ultimately caused the company to run out of cash and fold. Boo.com had little trouble attracting capital, but its founders were careless in their spending habits, pouring large millions into a complex Web site that launched late and failed to meet customer expectations. Although the company's sales reached $1.1 million per month, its expenses were running 10 times that amount! The company's cash drained away, and by the time the company went into bankruptcy, it had burned through more than $135 million of investors' capital and had become one of the highest profile failures in the "dot.com" crash.[68]

Lack of Strategic Management. Too many small business managers neglect the process of strategic management because they think that it is something that only benefits large companies. "I don't have the time" or "We're too small to develop a strategic plan," they rationalize. Failure to plan, however, usually results in failure to survive. Without a clearly defined strategy, a business has no sustainable basis for creating and maintaining a competitive edge in the marketplace.

Building a strategic plan forces an entrepreneur to assess *realistically* the proposed business's potential. Is it something customers are willing and able to purchase? Who is the target customer? How will the business attract and keep those customers? What is the company's basis for serving customers' needs better than existing companies? We will explore these and other vital issues in Chapter 2, "Strategic Management: Gaining a Competitive Edge."

Weak Marketing Effort. Sometimes entrepreneurs make the classic *"Field of Dreams* mistake."* Like Kevin Costner's character in the movie, they believe that if they "build it," customers automatically "will come." Although the idea makes for a great movie plot, in business, it almost never happens. *Stephen Mason and Alan Davis, co-founders of Catamount Brewery, one of New England's first microbreweries, discovered the importance of marketing the hard way. Early on, customers, intrigued by the romance and mystique of microbreweries, flocked to Catamount's unique beers. The company's marketing efforts amounted to no more than Davis "getting in a car and calling on [customer] accounts. Within six years, Catamount's production had climbed from 3,500 barrels a year to 12,000 barrels a year. Unfortunately, its marketing efforts did not keep pace. Sales slipped as customers drifted away, and the company could not generate enough cash to repay the debt it took on to expand its plant, forcing it into bankruptcy.[69]*

Business success requires a sustained, creative marketing effort to draw a base of customers and to keep them coming back. This is *especially* true for start-up companies. As you will see in Chapter 7, Creating a Guerrilla Marketing Plan, that does *not* mean that entrepreneurs must spend vast amounts of money on costly marketing and advertising campaigns. Creative entrepreneurs find ways to market their businesses effectively to their target customers without breaking the bank.

Uncontrolled Growth. Growth is a natural, healthy, and desirable part of any business enterprise, but it must be planned and controlled. Management expert Peter Drucker says that start-up companies can expect to outgrow their capital bases each time sales increase 40 to 50 percent.[70] Ideally, entrepreneurs finance the expansion of their companies by the profits they generate ("retained earnings") or by capital contributions from the owner(s), but most businesses wind up borrowing at least a portion of the capital investment.

Expansion usually requires major changes in organizational structure, business practices such as inventory and financial control procedures, personnel assignments, and other areas. But the most important change occurs in managerial expertise. As the business increases in size and complexity, problems tend to increase in proportion, and the manager must learn to deal with this. Sometimes entrepreneurs encourage rapid growth, and the business outstrips their ability to manage it. *Shortly after Lyle Bowlin launched his Web-based bookstore, Positively You, his home-based business was featured in the* New York Times *and* Time *magazine and on* Good Morning America *and* Fox News. *Almost overnight, sales skyrocketed from $2,000 a month to more than $50,000 a month. Bowlin and his small staff were overwhelmed by the sales volume, and the company lacked the capital base and the cash flow to finance the unplanned growth. Even worse, Bowlin's lack of experience in running a growing business left a leadership void. "Nobody knew who was in charge or who answered to whom," says one former employee. Within months, Positively You had become just another business failure statistic.*[71]

Poor Location. For any business, choosing the right location is partly an art and partly a science. Too often, entrepreneurs select their locations without adequate research and investigation. Some beginning owners choose a particular location just because they noticed a vacant building. But the location question is much too critical to leave to chance. Especially for retailers, the choice of a location influences heavily the lifeblood of the business—sales. One small merchandiser located in a rural area was heavily dependent on the customers of a nearby restaurant for her clientele. Because of the inconvenience of this location, sales suffered and the business failed.

Another factor to consider in selecting location is the rental rate. Although it is prudent not to pay an excessive amount for rent, business owners should weigh the cost against the location's effect on sales. Location has two important features: what it costs and what it generates in sales volume.

Lack of Inventory Control. Normally, the largest investment the small business manager must make is in inventory; yet, inventory control is one of the most neglected of all the managerial responsibilities. Insufficient inventory levels result in shortages and stockouts, causing customers to become disillusioned and not return. A more common situation is that the manager not only has too much inventory but also too much of the wrong type of inventory. Many small firms have an excessive amount of working capital tied up in an accumulation of needless inventory. We will discuss both purchasing and inventory control techniques in Section VII, "Managing a Small Business: Techniques for Enhancing Profitability."

Inability to Make the "Entrepreneurial Transition." If a business fails, it is most likely to do so in its first five years of life. Making it over the "entrepreneurial start-up hump," however, is no guarantee of business success. After the start-up, growth usually requires a radically different style of leadership and management. Many businesses fail when their founders are unable to make the transition from entrepreneur to manager and are unwilling to bring in a professional management team. The very abilities that make an entrepreneur successful often lead to *managerial* ineffectiveness. Growth requires entrepreneurs to delegate authority and to relinquish hands-on control of daily operations, something many entrepreneurs simply can't do. Their business's success requires that they avoid micromanaging and become preservers and promoters of their companies' vision, values, and culture.

Joe Kraus, along with five friends and a $15,000 loan from their parents, launched the Internet portal Excite (now Excite at Home) shortly after graduating from college. Kraus *became Excite's first chief executive officer, but as the company grew, Kraus, just 23, recognized his limitations as a manager. He and his co-founders decided that Excite needed experienced, professional management to guide its rapid growth and hired George Bell, a top manager at a large magazine publishing company to run the company. Hiring an experienced manager proved to be a wise move for Excite and for Kraus, who is now senior vice-president of content for the company.*[72]

PUTTING FAILURE INTO PERSPECTIVE

9. Put business failure into proper perspective.

Because they are building businesses in an environment filled with uncertainty and shaped by rapid change, entrepreneurs recognize that failure is likely to be a part of their lives; yet, they are not paralyzed by that fear. "The excitement of building a new business from scratch is far greater than the fear of failure," says one entrepreneur who failed in business several times before finally succeeding.[73] Instead, they use their failures as a rallying point and as a means of defining their companies' reason for being more clearly. They see failure for what it really is: an opportunity to learn what doesn't work! Successful entrepreneurs have the attitude that failures are simply stepping stones along the path to success. Walt Disney was fired from a newspaper job because, according to his boss, he "lacked ideas." Disney also went bankrupt several times before he created Disneyland.

Failure is a natural part of the creative process. The only people who never fail are those who never do anything or never attempt anything new. Baseball fans know that Babe Ruth held the record for career home runs (714) for many years, but how many know that he also held the record for strikeouts (1,330)? Successful entrepreneurs realize that hitting an entrepreneurial home run requires a few strikeouts along the way, and they are willing to accept that. Lillian Vernon, who started her mail-order company with $2,000 in wedding present money, says, "Everybody stumbles. . . . The true test is how well you pick yourself up and move on, and whether you're willing to learn from that."[74]

One hallmark of successful entrepreneurs is the ability to fail *intelligently*, learning why they failed so that they can avoid making the same mistake again. They know that business success does not depend on their ability to avoid making mistakes but to be open to the lessons each mistake brings. They learn from their failures and use them as fuel to push themselves closer to their ultimate target. Entrepreneurs are less worried about what they might lose if they try something and fail than about what they miss if they fail to try.

Entrepreneurial success requires both persistence and resilience, the ability to bounce back from failures. Thomas Edison discovered about 1,800 ways *not* to build a light bulb before hitting upon a design that worked—and would revolutionize the world. Entrepreneur Bryn Kaufman explains this "don't quit" attitude, "If you are truly an entrepreneur, giving up is not an option."[75]

HOW TO AVOID THE PITFALLS

As valuable as failure can be to the entrepreneurial process, no one sets out to fail. We have seen some of the most common reasons behind small business failures. Now we must examine the ways to avoid becoming another failure statistic and gain insight into what makes a start-up successful. Entrepreneurial success requires much more than just a good idea for a product or service. It also takes a solid plan of execution, adequate resources (including capital and people), the ability to assemble and

IN THE FOOTSTEPS OF AN ENTREPRENEUR
Tea Time

While in graduate school at Yale University, Seth Goldman and his classmates discussed a case on the beverage industry. One of the topics in Professor Barry Nalebuff's class that day was which Products were missing in the crowded beverage market. "There were too many sweet drinks and too many bland drinks," recalls Goldman. After class, Professor Nalebuff and Goldman spent time discussing the types of drinks that might find a profitable niche in the industry.

At the end of the semester, Goldman moved to Bethesda, Maryland, and took a job with a large mutual fund. A few years later, while visiting in New York, Goldman and an old track teammate went for a run in Central Park. They were very thirsty when they finished their run, but when they tried to buy something to drink, they once again ran into the void in the drink market. Neither syrupy sweet drinks nor plain bottled water appealed to them. On his way home, Goldman recalled the after-class conversation he and Nalebuff had engaged in years earlier at Yale. He e-mailed Nalebuff the next day, asking if he would be interested in discussing the possibility of building a company that would market a drink aimed at filling this niche in the beverage market.

Goldman's timing could not have been better. Nalebuff had just returned from a trip to India, where he had researched material for a case study on the tea industry. Goldman, who had spent time teaching in Russia and China, two cultures in which tea plays an important role, had learned a great deal about tea in his travels. He knew that tea was the second most popular drink in the world behind water. Goldman, who had won a business plan competition while at Yale, was "ready to take the plunge" and start a tea business. Nalebuff came up with the perfect name for the company, Honest Tea. The partners selected five teas for their initial product line and financed the company with $250,000 of their own money and another $257,000 from family and friends (giving them "equitea" in the business, according to Goldman.) Honest Tea's products are brewed with real tea leaves in spring water and with little sugar, making them a much lower calorie count than competing drinks.

Goldman, who is the company's "TeaEO," and Nalebuff have since raised an additional $2.7 million in capital, mostly from enthusiastic customers. Marketing and distribution continue to present challenges to the small company, however. Honest Tea focuses on selling its teas through health food stores, gourmet food shops, and restaurants, although some supermarket chains such as Wegmans and Grand Union also carry its products. In fact, the company's first big sale was to the Fresh Fields/Whole Foods grocery chain, which sells all-natural products. Goldman brewed up a batch of tea and took a thermos full of Honest Tea on the sales call. "They loved it and ordered 15,000 bottles," he recalls.

The company's marketing efforts have been modest, but Goldman and Nalebuff have relied on a strong public relations effort to generate publicity for their small business. Offering free samples, a common marketing ploy for many small companies, has proved to be successful, but building name recognition that way can be extremely slow. Although some beverage industry observers wonder if Honest Tea can build enough market share to become a viable company in the long run, Goldman and Nalebuff are optimistic. "We saw an opportunity that the bigger companies did not see," says Goldman. Plus, we have been a nimble company that can adjust to our customers' needs." What's next for Honest Tea? "We want to be a national brand," explains Goldman.

1. Describe the opportunities and the threats facing Honest Tea.

2. On a scale of 1 to 10, how would you rank Honest Tea's long-term chances of success? Would you be willing to invest in the company? Explain.

3. What advantages do Honest Tea's larger competitors have over the small company? What advantages does Honest Tea have over its larger rivals? How can the company exploit those advantages?

Sources: Thomas Melville, "Throwing a Tea Party," *Success*, September 2000, pp. 38–39; "Company Information," Honest Tea, *www.honesttea.com*; Constance L. Hays, Management: Tea by Two," *New York Times*, August 2, 2000, reprinted; "Brewed at Yale, Honest Tea Thirsts for Success," *Fortune*, July 10, 2000, reprinted.

10. Explain how small business owners can avoid the pitfalls of running a business.

manage those resources, and perseverance. The following suggestions for success follow naturally from the causes of business failures.

Know Your Business in Depth. We have already emphasized the need for the right type of experience in the business. Get the best education in your business area you possibly can *before* you set out on your own. Read everything you can—trade journals, business periodicals, books, Web pages—relating to your industry. Personal contact with suppliers, customers, trade associations, and others in the same industry is another excellent way to get important knowledge.

Before she launched Stephanie Anne Room to Grow, a chain of stores selling upscale furniture for babies and children, Stephanie Anne Kantis had career stints at a major department store and a small interior design/furniture store. In both jobs, she picked up many valuable tips on everything from how to check in merchandise to establishing employee policy manuals and identified the key factors required for success in her industry.[76]

Like Stephanie Anne Kantis, successful entrepreneurs are like sponges, soaking up as much knowledge as they can from a variety of sources, and they continue to learn about their businesses, markets, and customers as long as they are in business.

Prepare a Business Plan. To wise entrepreneurs, a well-written business plan is a crucial ingredient in business success. Without a sound business plan, a company merely drifts along without any real direction and often stalls out when it faces its first challenge. Yet, entrepreneurs, who tend to be people of action, too often jump right into a business venture without taking time to prepare a written plan outlining the essence of the business. "Most entrepreneurs don't have a solid business plan," says one business owner. "But a thorough business plan and timely financial information are critical. They help you make the important decisions about your business; you constantly have to monitor what you're doing against your plan."[77]

Although uncertainty is a part of any business start-up, preparing a business plan allows entrepreneurs to replace "I think" with "I know" in many important areas of a business. In many cases, entrepreneurs attempt to build businesses on faulty assumptions such as "I think there are enough customers in town to support a health food shop." Experienced entrepreneurs investigate these assumptions and replace them with facts before making the decision to go into business. We will discuss the process of developing a business plan in Chapter 6, "Crafting a Winning Business Plan."

Manage Financial Resources. The best defense against financial problems is developing a practical financial information system and then using this information to make business decisions. No entrepreneur can maintain control over a business unless he or she is able to judge its financial health.

The first step in managing financial resources effectively is to have adequate start-up capital. Too many entrepreneurs begin their businesses with too little capital. One experienced business owner advises, "Estimate how much capital you need to get the business going and then double that figure." His point is well taken; it almost always costs more to launch a business than *any* entrepreneur expects. Establishing a relationship early on with at least one reliable lender who understands your business is a good way to gain access to financing when a company needs capital for growth or expansion.

The most valuable financial resource to any small business is *cash;* successful entrepreneurs learn early on to manage it carefully. While earning a profit is essential to its long-term survival, a business must have an adequate supply of cash to pay its bills and obligations. Some entrepreneurs count on growing sales to supply their company's cash needs, but it almost never happens. Growing companies usually consume more cash than they generate; and the faster they grow, the more cash they gobble up! We will discuss cash management techniques in Chapter 9, Managing Cash Flow.

Understand Financial Statements. Every business owner must depend on records and financial statements to know the condition of his or her business. All too often, these records are used only for tax purposes and are not employed as vital control devices. To truly understand what is going on in the business, an owner must have at least a basic understanding of accounting and finance.

When analyzed and interpreted properly, these financial statements are reliable indicators of a small firm's health. They can be quite helpful in signaling potential problems. For example, declining sales, slipping profits, rising debt, and deteriorating working capital are all symptoms of potentially lethal problems that require immediate attention. We will discuss financial statement analysis in Chapter 8, "Creating a Solid Financial Plan."

Learn to Manage People Effectively. No matter what kind of business you launch, you must learn to manage people. Every business depends on a foundation of well-trained, motivated employees. No business owner can do everything alone. The people an entrepreneur hires ultimately determine the heights to which the company can climb—or the depths to which it can plunge. Attracting and retaining a corps of quality employees is no easy task, however; it remains a challenge for every small business owner. One entrepreneur destroyed his company by failing to share any information with his employees and alienated his workers by setting up cameras inside and outside his building to monitor them.[78] Successful entrepreneurs value their employees and constantly find ways to show it. We will discuss the techniques of managing and motivating people effectively in Chapter 19, "Staffing and Leading a Growing Company."

Set Your Business Apart from the Competition. The formula for almost certain business failure involves becoming a "me-too business"—merely copying whatever the competition is doing. Most successful entrepreneurs find a way to convince their customers that their companies are superior to their competitors even if they sell similar products or services. It is especially important for small companies going up against larger, more powerful rivals with greater financial resources. Ideally, the basis for differentiating a company from its competitors is founded in what it does best. For small companies, that basis often is customer service, convenience, speed, quality, or whatever else is important to attracting and keeping happy customers. We will discuss the strategies for creating a unique footprint in the marketplace in Chapter 7, "Creating a Guerrilla Marketing Plan."

Keep in Tune with Yourself. "Starting a business is like running a marathon. If you're not physically and mentally in shape, you'd better do something else," says one business consultant.[79] Managing a successful business, especially in the early days, requires *lots* of energy and enthusiasm. Therefore, good health is essential. Stress is a primary problem for many entrepreneurs, especially if it is not kept in check.

Achieving business success also requires an entrepreneur to maintain a positive mental attitude toward business and the discipline to stick with it. Successful entrepreneurs recognize that their most valuable resource is their time, and they learn to manage it effectively to make themselves and their companies more productive. None of this, of course, is possible without passion—passion for their businesses, their products or services, their customers, their communities. Passion is what enables a failed business owner to get back up, try again, and make it to the top! One business writer says that growing a successful business requires entrepreneurs to have great faith in themselves and their ideas, great doubt concerning the challenges and inevitable obstacles they will face as they build their businesses, and great effort—lots of hard work—to make their dreams become reality.[80]

As you can see, entrepreneurship lies at the heart of this nation's free enterprise system; small companies truly are the backbone of our economy. Their contributions are as many and as diverse as the businesses themselves. Indeed, diversity is one of the strengths of the U.S. small business sector. Although there are no secrets to becoming a successful entrepreneur, there are steps that entrepreneurs can take to enhance the probability of their success. The remainder of this book will explore those steps.

CHAPTER SUMMARY

1. Define the role of the entrepreneur in business.
   - Record numbers of people have launched companies over the past decade. The boom in entrepreneurship is not limited solely to the United States; many nations across the globe are seeing similar growth in the small business sector. A variety of competitive, economic, and demographic shifts have created a world in which "small is beautiful."
   - Society depends on entrepreneurs to provide the drive and risk-taking necessary for the business system to supply people with the goods and services they need.

2. Describe the entrepreneurial profile.
   - Entrepreneurs have some common characteristics, including a desire for responsibility, a preference for moderate risk, confidence in their ability to succeed, desire for immediate feedback, a high energy level, a future orientation, skill at organizing, and a value of achievement over money. In a phrase, they are high achievers.

3. Describe the benefits of owning a small business.
   - Driven by these personal characteristics, entrepreneurs establish and manage small businesses to gain control over their lives, become self-fulfilled, reap unlimited profits, contribute to society, and do what they enjoy doing.

4. Describe the potential drawbacks of owning a small business.
   - Small business ownership has some potential drawbacks. There are no guarantees that the business will make a profit or even survive. The time and energy required to manage a new business may have dire effects on the owner and family members.

5. Explain the forces that are driving the growth in entrepreneurship.
   - Several factors are driving the boom in entrepreneurship, including entrepreneurs portrayed as heroes, better entrepreneurial education, economic and demographic factors, a shift to a service economy, technological advancements, more independent lifestyles, and increased international opportunities.

6. Discuss the role of diversity in small business and entrepreneurship.
   - Several groups are leading the nation's drive toward entrepreneurship—women, minorities, immigrants, "part-timers," home-based business owners, family business owners, copreneurs, corporate castoffs, and corporate dropouts.

7. Describe the contributions small businesses make to the U.S. economy.
   - The small business sector's contributions are many. They make up 99 percent of all businesses, employ 52 percent of the private sector workforce, create 75.8 percent of the new jobs in the economy, produce 51 percent of the country's private gross domestic product (GDP), and account for 47 percent of business sales.

8. Explain the reasons small businesses fail.
   - The failure rate for small businesses is higher than for big businesses, and profits fluctuate with general economic conditions. SBA statistics show that 60 percent of new busi-

nesses will have failed within six years. The primary cause of business failure is incompetent management. Other reasons include poor financial control, failure to plan, inappropriate location, lack of inventory control, improper managerial attitudes, and inability to make the "entrepreneurial transition."

9. Put business failure into the proper perspective.
   - Because they are building businesses in an environment filled with uncertainty and shaped by rapid change, entrepreneurs recognize that failure is likely to be a part of their lives; yet, they are not paralyzed by that fear. Successful entrepreneurs have the attitude that failures are simply stepping stones along the path to success.

10. Explain how small business owners can avoid the major pitfalls of running a business.
    - There are several general tactics the small business owner can employ to avoid failure. Entrepreneurs should know the business in depth, develop a solid business plan, manage financial resources effectively, understand financial statements, learn to manage people effectively, set the business apart from the competition, and keep in tune with themselves.

DISCUSSION QUESTIONS

1. What forces have led to the boom in entrepreneurship in the United States?
2. What is an entrepreneur? Give a brief description of the entrepreneurial profile.
3. *Inc.* magazine claims, "Entrepreneurship is more mundane than it's sometimes portrayed . . . you don't need to be a person of mythical proportions to be very, very successful in building a company." Do you agree? Explain.
4. What are the major benefits of business ownership?
5. Which of the potential drawbacks to business ownership are most critical?
6. Briefly describe the role of the following groups in entrepreneurship: women, minorities, immigrants, "part-timers," home-based business owners, family business owners, copreneurs, corporate castoffs, and corporate dropouts.
7. What contributions do small businesses make to our economy?
8. Describe the small business failure rate.
9. Outline the causes of business failure. Which problems cause most business failures?
10. How can the small business owner avoid the common pitfalls that often lead to business failures?
11. Why is it important to study the small business failure rate?
12. Explain the typical entrepreneur's attitude toward failure.
13. One entrepreneur says that too many people "don't see that by spending their lives afraid of failure, they *become* failures. But when you go out there and risk as I have, you'll have failures along the way, but eventually the result is great success if you are willing to keep risking . . . For every big "yes" in life, there will be 199 "nos." Do you agree? Explain.
14. What advice would you offer an entrepreneurial friend who has just suffered a business failure?
15. Noting the growing trend among collegiate entrepreneurs launching businesses while still in school, one educator says, "A student whose main activity on campus is running a business is missing the basic reason for being here, which is to get an education." Do you agree? Explain.

STEP INTO THE REAL WORLD

1. Choose an entrepreneur in your community and interview him or her. What's the "story" behind the business? What advantages and disadvantages does the owner see in owning a business? What advice would he or she offer to someone considering launching a business?

2. Search through recent business publications (especially those focusing on small companies, such as *Inc., Entrepreneur, Business Start-Ups,* or *FSB*) or the Internet and find an example of an entrepreneur—past or present—who exhibits the entrepreneurial spirit of striving

for success in the face of failure. Prepare a brief report for your class.

3. Select one of the categories under the section "The Cultural Diversity of Entrepreneurship" in this chapter and research it in more detail. Find examples of that entrepreneurial profile. Prepare a brief report for your class.

4. Interview a local banker who has experience lending to small companies. What factors does he or she believe are important to a small company's success? What factors has he or she seen cause business failures? What

does the lender want to see in a business start-up before agreeing to lend any money?

5. Rent the film *Startup.com* and answer the following questions: On a scale of 1 to 10, how would you rate the creativity of their business idea? On the same scale, how would you rate the practicality of their idea? What mistakes did co-founders Tuzman and Herman make as they launched their company? What factors led to the company's failure? What were the results of the company's failure?

TAKE IT TO THE NET

Visit the Scarborough/Zimmerer home page at **www.prenhall.com/scarborough** for updated information, online resources, Web-based exercises, and sample business plan.

ENDNOTES

1. Paul D. Reynolds, "National Panel Study of U.S. Business Startups: First Annual Overview," Entrepreneurial Research Consortium, Babson College, Wellesley, Massachusetts, 1999.
2. "Small Business Is Cool Now," *Inc. Special Report: The State of Small Business 1996*, p. 17.
3. *The State of Small Business: A Report of the President* (Washington, DC: U.S. Government Printing Office, 1999), p. 28.
4. Lynn Beresford, "Dream Job," *Inc.*, January 1997, p. 13.
5. Jeffry A. Timmons, "An Obsession with Opportunity," *Nation's Business*, March 1985, p. 68.
6. *NFIB Small Business Policy Guide* (Washington, DC: NFIB Education Foundation, 2000), p. 15.
7. Jerry Useem, "The Risk-Taker Returns," *FSB*, May 2001, p. 70.
8. David McClellan, *The Achieving Society* (Princeton, NJ: Van Nostrand, 1961), p. 16.
9. Norm Brodsky, "The Road Not Taken," *Inc.*, March 2000, p. 43.
10. Martha E. Mangelsdorf, "Insider," *Inc.*, June 1988, p. 14.
11. Sabin Russell, "Being Your Own Boss in America," *Venture*, May 1984, p. 40.
12. Geoff Williams, "There Ought to Be a Law," *Entrepreneur*, February 2000, pp. 104–109.
13. Stephanie N. Mehta, "Young Entrepreneurs Are Starting Business After Business," *Wall Street Journal*, March 19, 1997, p. B2.
14. Roger Rickleffs and Udayan Gupta, "Traumas of a New Entrepreneur," *Wall Street Journal*, May 10, 1989, p. B1.

15. "Company Information," Hewlett Packard Company, *www.hp.com/hpinfo/abouthp/main.htm*; James C. Collins, "Sometimes a Great Notion," *Inc.*, July 1993, pp. 90–91; Andrew E. Serwer, "Lessons from America's Fastest Growing Companies," *Fortune*, August 8, 1994, pp. 42–62.
16. John Case, "The Origins of Entrepreneurship," *Inc.*, June 1989, p. 52.
17. "Simplicity," NFIB Toolbox, National Federation of Independent Businesses, May 5, 2001 *nfib.org/cgi-bin/NFIB.dll/public/toolsAndTips/ toolsAndTips Display.jsp?BV_SessionID=@@@@1402402229.099721 0063@@@@&BV_EngineID=dcalljddmlgebemgcfkm-cfchfi.0&contentId 73447*
18. Roger P. Levin, "You've Got to Love It or Leave It," *Success,* December 2000/January 2001, p. 22.
19. Tom Fetzer, "Never Say Die," *Success,* December 2000/January 2001, p. 60.
20. Mary Diebel, "4.6 Million Americans Are Millionaires," *The Sacramento Bee,* July 16, 2001, *24hour.sacbee.com/24hour/business/story/632161p-678117c.html*; Sheryl Nance, "You Can Be a Millionaire," *Your Company,* June/July 1997, pp. 26–33.
21. "The Papa John's Story," Papa John's International, *www.papajohns.com/pj_story/index.htm*; Alynda Wheat, "Striking It Rich the Low-Tech Way," *Fortune,* September 27, 1999, p. 86.
22. Victoria Neal, Michelle Prather, Karen E. Spaeder, and Laura Tiffany, "Young Millionaires," *Entrepreneur,* November 1999, pp. 82–98.
23. Gayle Sato-Stodder, "Never Say Die," *Entrepreneur,* December 1990, p. 95.

24. *NFIB Small Business Policy Guide* (Washington, DC: NFIB Education Foundation, 2000), p. 22.

25. Michelle Prather, "Sacrificial Rites," *Entrepreneur,* February 2001, pp. 75–78.

26. "Entrepreneurship 2000: America's Young Entrepreneurs," Interprise Poll, Junior Achievement, December 2000, *www.ja.org/aboutJA/whatsnew/interprise/entrepreneurship.html;* "Youth Movement," *Success,* April 2001, p. 12.

27. Neal, Prather, Spaeder, and Tiffany, "Young Millionaires."

28. Anne Stuart, "A World of His Own," *Inc. Technology 2001,* No. 2, pp. 33–36.

29. Lisa Silver, "Getting Down to Business," *Success,* December 1996, pp. 58–62.

30. "Internet Commerce," Forrester Findings, Forrester Research Inc., *www.forrester.com/ER/Press/ForrFind/0,1768,0,00.html.*

31. George Mannes, "Don't Give Up on the Web," *FSB,* February 2001, pp. 45–53.

32. Ibid.

33. Cynthia E. Griffin, "Brave New World," *Entrepreneur,* April 1999, p. 49; "Exports by Firm Size," U.S. Small Business Administration Office of Advocacy, 1998, p. 2.

34. Neal, Prather, Spaeder, and Tiffany, "Young Millionaires."

35. Meredith Bagby, "Generation X," *Success,* September 1998, pp. 22–23; Debra Phillips, "Great X-Pectations," *Business Start-Ups,* January 1999, pp. 31–33.

36. Phillips, " Great X-Pectations," pp. 31–33; Geoff Williams, "The Deliberate Entrepreneur," *Business Start-Ups,* May 1999, pp. 37–43.

37. "Key Facts," National Federation of Women Business Owners, *www.nfwbo.org/key.html;* "Women-Owned Businesses Continue to Expand Faster than the Economy," National Federation of Women Business Owners, April 4, 2001.

38. "Today's Self-Employed American," *Inc. Special Report: The State of Small Business, 2001,* pp. 45–48; "Key Facts," National Federation of Women Business Owners, *www.nfwbo.org/key.html;* Marci McDonald, "A Start-Up of Her Own," *U.S. News & World Report,* May 15, 2000, pp. 34–42.

39. "About Us," Jaqua Girls, *www.jaquagirls.com/jaqua/about_us.asp;* Adrienne Sanders, "The Three Sisters," *Forbes,* December 13, 1999, p. 314.

40. *Minorities in Business* (Washington, DC: U.S. Small Business Administration Office of Advocacy, 1999), p. 1.

41. Geoff Williams, "Marx Against Them," *Entrepreneur,* November 1999, pp. 174–177.

42. Debra Phillips, Cynthia E. Griffin, Heather Page, Lynn Beresford, Holly Celeste Fisk, and Charlotte Mulhern, "Entrepreneurial Superstars," *Entrepreneur,* April 1997, pp. 108–139.

43. *NFIB Small Business Policy Guide* (Washington, DC: NFIB Education Foundation, 2000), p. 20; Joanne H. Pratt, "Small Business Research Summary, Home-based Business: The Hidden Economy," U.S. Small Business Administration Office of Advocacy, No. 194, March 2000, pp. 1–2.

44. Eleena De Lisser and Dan Morse, "More Men Work at Home Than Women, Study Shows," *Wall Street Journal,* May 18, 1999, p. B2; Ronaleen Roha, "Home Alone," *Kiplinger's Personal Finance Magazine,* May 1997, pp. 85–89.

45. Pratt, "Small Business Research Summary, Home-based Business: The Hidden Economy,"p. 2.; "QuickStats," *Home Business News Report,* Fall 1994, p.1.

46. Jim Woodward, "Kitchen Table Start-Ups," *E-Merging Business,* Fall/Winter 2000, pp. 226–229.

47. "Facts and Perspectives on Family Business in the U.S.," The Family Firm Institute, *www.ffi.org/looking/fbfacts_us.pdf*

48. Erick Calonius, "Blood and Money," *Newsweek,* Special Issue, p. 82.

49. Facts and Perspectives on Family Business in the U.S.," The Family Firm Institute, *www.ffi.org/looking/fbfacts_us.pdf*

50. "Love and the Bottom Line: Couples in Business Find High Rewards and Risks," *Nando Times News, archive.nandotimes.com/newsroom/nt/0212bizcpl.html.*

51. Michael Kaplan, "Till Death (or Bankruptcy) Do Us Part," *FSB,* April 2001, pp. 92–98.

52. "Going Places," *Entrepreneur,* June 1994, p. 14.

53. Donna Kato, "Changing Course, Burning Suits," *Greenville News,* June 6, 1993, p. 1D.

54. Julie Vallone, "Jump Ship," *Start-Ups,* November 2000, pp. 46–48; Laura Tiffany, "All the Right Moves," *Business Start-Ups,* December 1999, pp. 10–11.

55. "Small Business FAQ," U.S. Small Business Administration, Office of Advocacy, December 2000, p. 1; *NFIB Small Business Policy Guide* (Washington, DC: NFIB Education Foundation, 2000), p. 25.

56. "The Job Factory," *Inc Special Report: The State of Small Business 2001,* pp. 40–43.

57. *NFIB Small Business Policy Guide* (Washington, DC: NFIB Education Foundation, 2000), p. 30; "Help Wanted," *Inc. Special Report: The State of Small Business 1997,* pp. 35–41; "The Job Factory," *Inc. Special Report: The State of Small Business 2001,* pp. 40–43; "The Gazelle Theory," *Inc. Special Report: The State of Small Business 2001,* pp. 28–29.

58. Preston McLaurin, "Small Businesses Are Winners," *S.C. Business Journal,* May 2000, p. 10; Erskine

Bowles, "Training Ground," *Entrepreneur,* March 1994, p. 168.

59. *NFIB Small Business Policy Guide* (Washington, DC: NFIB Education Foundation, 2000), p. 33; "Small Business FAQ," U.S. Small Business Administration, Office of Advocacy, December 2000, p. 1; McLaurin, "Small Businesses Are Winners."

60. *NFIB Small Business Policy Guide* (Washington, DC: NFIB Education Foundation, 2000), p. 33.

61. John LaFalce, "The Driving Force," *Entrepreneur,* February 1990, pp. 161–166.

62. "Opportunity Knocks," *Inc. Special Report: The State of Small Business 2001,* pp. 94–99.

63. Lee Smith, "The Innovators," *FSB,* May 2001, pp. 43–68.

64. "Middle-Aged Spread," *Inc. Special Report: The State of Small Business 2001,* p. 54.

65. David Taymond, "Famous Flops," *Forbes ASAP,* June 2, 1997, pp. 101–103.

66. Ray Hoopes, "Mind Your Own Business," *Modern Maturity,* February–March 1991, pp. 26–33.

67. George Gendron, "The Failure Myth," *Inc.,* January 2001, p. 13.

68. Christopher Cooper and Erik Portanger, "Money Men Liked Boo and Boo Liked Money; Then It All Went Poof," *Wall Street Journal,* June 27, 2000, pp. A1, A8.

69. Rifka Rosenwein, "Despite Ale's Success, Brewery Loses Out," *Inc.,* October 2000, p. 37.

70. Eugene Carlson, "Spreading Your Wings," *Wall Street Journal,* October 16, 1992, p. R2.

71. Julia Angwin, "Anatomy of a Net Bookseller's Rapid Rise and Fall," *Wall Street Journal,* March 2, 2000, pp. B1, B4.

72. Hal Lancaster, "Web Winner Discovers Key to New Successes Is Knowing His Limits," *Wall Street Journal,* October 12, 1999, p. B1.

73. Michael Warshaw, "Great Comebacks," *Success,* July/August 1995, p. 43.

74. Michael Barrier, "Entrepreneurs Who Excel," *Nation's Business,* August 1996, p. 28.

75. Clint Willis, "Try, Try Again," *Forbes ASAP,* June 2, 1997, p. 63.

76. Geoff Williams, "I Quit," *Start-Ups,* December 2000, pp. 47–49.

77. Stephanie Barlow, "Hang On!" *Entrepreneur,* September 1992, p. 156.

78. Lee Patterson, "Tanking It Five Ways," *Forbes ASAP,* June 2, 1997, pp. 75–76.

79. Kirsten Von Kriesler-Bomben, "The Obstacle Course," *Entrepreneur,* July 1990, p. 175.

80. Rhonda Abrams, "Building Blocks of Business: Great Faith, Great Doubt, Great Effort," *Business,* March 4, 2001, p. 2.

Chapter

2

Strategic Management and the Entrepreneur

> *Those who dream by day are cognizant of many things that escape those who dream only by night.*

—EDGAR ALLEN POE

> *I cannot give you the formula for success, but I can give you the formula for failure—which is: Try to please everybody.*

—HERBERT B. SWOPE

Upon completion of this chapter, you will be able to:

1. Understand the importance of strategic management to a small business.
2. Explain why and how a small business must create a competitive advantage in the market.
3. Develop a strategic plan for a business using the 10 steps in the strategic planning process.
4. Discuss the characteristics of three basic strategies: cost leadership, differentiation, and focus.
5. Understand the importance of controls such as the balanced scorecard in the planning process.

1. Understand the importance of strategic management to a small business.

Few activities in the life of a business are as vital—or as overlooked—as that of developing a strategy for success. Too often, entrepreneurs brimming with optimism and enthusiasm launch businesses destined for failure because their founders never stop to define a workable strategy that sets them apart from their competition. Because they tend to be people of action, entrepreneurs often find the process of developing a strategy dull and unnecessary. Their tendency is to start a business, try several approaches, and see what works. Without a cohesive plan of action, however, these entrepreneurs have as much chance of building a successful business as a defense contractor attempting to build a jet fighter without blueprints. Companies lacking clear strategies may achieve some success in the short run, but as soon as competitive conditions stiffen or an unanticipated threat arises, they usually "hit the wall" and fold. Without a basis for differentiating itself from a pack of similar competitors, the best a company can hope for is mediocrity in the marketplace.

In today's global competitive environment, any business, large or small, that is not thinking and acting strategically is extremely vulnerable. Every business is exposed to the forces of a rapidly changing competitive environment, and in the future small business executives can expect even greater change and uncertainty. From sweeping political changes around the planet and rapid technological advances to more intense competition and newly emerging global markets, the business environment has become more turbulent and challenging to business owners. Although this market turbulence creates many challenges for small businesses, it also creates opportunities for those companies that have in place strategies to capitalize on them. Historically important, entrepreneurs' willingness to create change, to experiment with new business models, and to break traditional rules has become more important than ever.

Perhaps the biggest change business owners face is unfolding now: the shift in the world's economy from a base of *financial to intellectual* capital. "Knowledge is no longer just a factor of production," says futurist Alvin Toffler. "It is the *critical* factor of production."[1] Today, a company's intellectual capital is likely to be the source of its competitive advantage in the marketplace. **Intellectual capital** is comprised of three components[2]:

1. *Human capital*—the talents, skills, and abilities of a company's workforce.
2. *Structural capital*—the accumulated knowledge and experience that a company possesses. It can take many forms, including processes, software, patents, copyrights, and, perhaps most importantly, the knowledge and experience of the people in a company.
3. *Customer capital*—the established customer base, positive reputation, ongoing relationships, and goodwill a company builds up over time with its customers.

Increasingly, entrepreneurs are recognizing that the capital stored in these three areas forms the foundation of their ability to compete effectively and that they must manage this intangible capital base carefully. Every business uses all three components in its strategy, but the emphasis they place on each component varies.

This knowledge shift will create as much change in the world's business systems as the Industrial Revolution did in the agricultural-based economies of the 1800s. The Knowledge Revolution will spell disaster for companies that are not prepared for it, but it will spawn tremendous opportunities for entrepreneurs equipped with the strategies to exploit these opportunities. Management legend Jack Welch, who masterfully guided General Electric for many years, says, "Intellectual capital is what it's all about. Releasing the ideas of people is what we've got to do if we are going to win."[3] However, in practice, releasing people's ideas is much more difficult than it appears. The key is to encourage employees to generate a large volume of ideas, recognizing that only a few (the best) will survive. According to Gary Hamel, author of *Inside the Revolution*, "If you want to find a few ideas with the power to enthrall customers, foil competitors, and thrill investors, you must first generate hundreds and potentially thousands of unconventional strategic ideas. Put simply, you have to crush a lot of rock to find a diamond."[4]

In short, the rules of the competitive game of business have changed dramatically. To be successful, entrepreneurs can no longer do things in the way they've always done them. Fortunately, successful entrepreneurs have at their disposal a powerful weapon to cope with such a hostile environment: the process of strategic management. **Strategic management** involves developing a game plan to guide the company as it strives to accomplish its vision, mission, goals, and objectives and to keep it from straying off its desired course. The idea is to give the owner a blueprint for matching the company's strengths and weaknesses to the opportunities and threats in the environment.

BUILDING A COMPETITIVE ADVANTAGE

2. Explain why and how a small business must create a competitive advantage in the market.

The goal of developing a strategic plan is to create for the small company a **competitive advantage**—the aggregation of factors that sets the small business apart from its competitors and gives it a unique position in the market. From a strategic perspective, the key to business success is to develop a unique competitive advantage, one that creates value for customers and is difficult for competitors to duplicate. No business can be everything to everyone. In fact, one of the biggest pitfalls many entrepreneurs stumble into is failing to differentiate their companies from the crowd of competitors. Entrepreneurs often face the challenge of setting their companies apart from their larger, more powerful competitors (who can easily outspend them) by using their creativity and the special abilities their businesses offer customers. *For instance, when Spencer Newman opened his mail-order business specializing in adventure travel books in 1994, he focused on selling the best titles from 100 different publishers. His one-stop shopping approach was a hit with customers in the niche he was targeting, and in 1995 Newman took his business, Adventurous Traveler Bookstore (ATB) online, becoming one of the early adopters of the Internet as a marketing tool. Sales grew rapidly, but in 1998, a previously unknown competitor, Amazon.com, began cutting heavily into ATB's sales. Evaluating Amazon's strategy, Newman realized that he could not compete for customers on price and survive, so he assessed the strengths of his company and the weakness of his new competitor. Newman realized that his staff's knowledge and experience in adventure travel was the key to competing successfully with Amazon. Customers might be able to purchase* Hiking Mount St. Helens *for a few cents less at Amazon, but ATB customers can call or e-mail the company and talk to a staff member who has not only read the book but also has made the hike! He focused on providing superb customer service, on deepening relationships with customers, and on stocking books that were hard to get or that Amazon did not carry. He began publishing an online newsletter twice a month, offering foreign language courses; providing maps, videos, and autographed posters on ATB's Web site; and producing online book reviews from his staff. With ATB's competitive strategy of becoming a travel resource for customers, both catalog and Web sales (which now account for the majority of ATB's revenues) have climbed rapidly. More importantly, Newman has found a way to compete successfully with a much larger rival.*[5]

In the long run, a company gains a sustainable competitive advantage through its ability to develop a set of core competencies that enable it to serve its selected target customers better than its rivals. **Core competencies** are a unique set of capabilities that a company develops in key areas, such as superior quality, customer service, innovation, team building, flexibility, responsiveness, and others that allow it to vault past competitors. Typically, a company is likely to build core competencies in no more than five or six (sometimes fewer) areas. These core competencies become the nucleus of a company's competitive advantage and are usually quite enduring over time. Markets, customers, and competitors may change, but a company's core competencies are more durable, forming the building blocks for everything a company does. To be effective, these competencies should be difficult for competitors to duplicate, and they must provide customers with some kind of perceived benefit. Small companies' core competencies often have to do with the advantages of their size—agility, speed, closeness to their customers, superior service, ability to innovate. In short, their smallness is an advantage, allowing them to do things that their larger rivals cannot. The key to success is building these core competencies (or identifying the ones a company already has) and then concentrating them on providing superior service and value for its target customers.

Developing core competences does *not* necessarily require a company to spend a great deal of money. It does, however, require an entrepreneur to use creativity, imagination, and vision to identify those things that it does best and that are most important to its target customers. Building a company's strategy around its core competences allows the business to gain a sustainable competitive edge over its rivals and to ride its strategy to victory. *For example, Fastenal Company, a supplier of fasteners such as nuts and bolts, has achieved an impressive annual growth rate in excess of 20 percent for the past 18 years by focusing on its core competencies and the value they offer customers. Founded in 1967 by Bob Kierlin and four friends, Fastenal targets factories, builders, and others with a complete line of fasteners and tools. Kierlin recognized that even though fasteners literally are "nuts and bolts" items, their absence can cause a multimillion-dollar factory or construction project to grind to a halt. As a result, Fastenal maintains a vast fleet of delivery trucks that can supply materials on short notice—a highly valuable service to customers. Capitalizing on its mastery of controlling inventories of vast number of small parts, Fastenal offers to manage customers' hardware parts inventory as well. Fastenal relies on yet another core competency it has developed over time: its efficient purchasing process that uses electronic data interchange (EDI) and makes buying its products simple, convenient, and inexpensive for its customers.*[6]

When it comes to developing a strategy for establishing a competitive advantage, small companies have a variety of natural advantages over their larger competitors. The typical small business has fewer product lines, a more well-defined customer base, and a specific geographic market area. Entrepreneurs usually are in close contact with their markets, giving them valuable knowledge on how to best serve their customers' needs and wants. Because of the simplicity of their organization structures, small business owners are in touch with employees daily, often working side-by-side with them, allowing them to communicate strategic moves firsthand. Consequently, small businesses find that strategic management comes more naturally to them than to larger companies with their layers of bureaucracy and far-flung operations.

Strategic management can increase a small company's effectiveness, but entrepreneurs first must have a process designed to meet their needs and their business's special characteristics. It is a mistake to attempt to apply a big business's strategic development techniques to a small business because a small business is not a little big business. Because of their size and their particular characteristics—resource poverty, a flexible managerial style, an informal organizational structure, and adaptability to change—small businesses need a different approach to the strategic management process. The strategic management procedure for a small business should include the following features:

- Use a relatively short planning horizon—two years or less for most small companies.
- Be informal and not overly structured; a shirt-sleeve approach is ideal.
- Encourage the participation of employees and outside parties to improve the reliability and creativity of the resulting plan.
- Do not begin with setting objectives, as extensive objective-setting early on may interfere with the creative process of strategic management.
- Maintain flexibility; competitive conditions change too rapidly for any plan to be considered permanent.
- Focus on strategic *thinking,* not just planning by linking long-range goals to day-to-day operations.

THE STRATEGIC MANAGEMENT PROCESS

3. Develop a strategic plan for a business using the nine steps on the strategic planning process.

Strategic planning is a continuous process that consists of nine steps:

Step 1. Develop a clear vision and translate it into a meaningful mission statement.
Step 2. Assess the company's strengths and weaknesses.
Step 3. Scan the environment for significant opportunities and threats facing the business.
Step 4. Identify the key factors for success in the business.
Step 5. Analyze the competition.
Step 6. Create company goals and objectives.
Step 7. Formulate strategic options and select the appropriate strategies.
Step 8. Translate strategic plans into action plans.
Step 9. Establish accurate controls.

Step 1: Develop a Clear Vision and Translate It into a Meaningful Mission Statement

Vision. Throughout history, the greatest political and business leaders have been visionaries. Whether the vision is as grand as Martin Luther King, Jr.'s "I have a dream" speech or as simple as Ray Kroc's devotion to quality, service, cleanliness, and value at McDonald's, the purpose is the same: to focus everyone's attention and efforts on the same target. The vision touches everyone associated with the company—employees, investors, lenders, customers, the community. It is an expression of what entrepreneurs believe in and the values on which they build their businesses. A vision statement addresses the questions, "What do we stand for?" and "What do we want to become?" In his book, *Daring Visionaries: How Entrepreneurs Build Companies, Inspire Allegiance, and Create Wealth,* Ray Smilor describes the importance of vision[7]:

> Vision is the organizational sixth sense that tells us why we make a difference in the world. It is the real but unseen fabric of connections that nurture and sustain values. It is the pulse of the organizational body that reaffirms relationships and directs behavior.

Highly successful entrepreneurs are able to communicate their vision and their enthusiasm about that vision to those around them. One study of more than 500 "hidden champions"—little-known superperforming companies that hold worldwide market shares of at least 50 percent—identified the presence of a clear vision as an important factor in the competitive edge these companies had established. The founders of these companies adhere strongly to their own fundamental vision and purpose, while giving employees the freedom to handle daily activities within the context of that vision.[8]

Vision is based on an entrepreneur's values. Successful entrepreneurs build their businesses around a set of three to six core values, which might range from respect for the individual and encouraging innovation to creating satisfied customers and making the world a better place. Indeed, truly visionary entrepreneurs see their companies' primary purpose as more than just "making money." One writer explains, "Almost all workers are making decisions, not just filling out weekly sales reports or tightening screws. They will do what they think best. If you want them to do as the company thinks best too, then you must [see to it that] they have an inner gyroscope aligned with the corporate compass."[9] That gyroscope alignment depends on the entrepreneur's values and how well she transmits them throughout the company.

The best way to put values into action is to create a written mission statement that communicates those values to everyone the company touches.

Mission Statement. A mission statement addresses the first question of any business venture: "What business am I in?" Establishing the purpose of the business in writing must come first in order to give the company a sense of direction. "If you don't reduce [your company's purpose] to paper, it just doesn't stick," says the owner of an architectural firm. "Reducing it to paper really forces you to think about what you are doing."[10] The mission is the mechanism for making it clear to everyone the company touches "why we are here" and "where we are going." It helps create an emotional bond between a company and its stakeholders, especially its employees and its customers. Without a concise, meaningful mission statement, a small business risks wandering aimlessly in the marketplace, with no idea of where to go or how to get there. The mission statement essentially sets the tone for the entire company and guides the decisions its people make.

Tom's of Maine, a successful small company that sells all-natural consumer products, such as toothpaste, deodorant, and soap, has relied heavily on its mission statement (which was written collaboratively by employees and owners in 1989) as a strategic and ethical compass. The statement expresses the importance of earning a profit while meeting the company's social responsibility. When Tom's of Maine modified one of its deodorants, the company discovered that the new formula did not work. When deciding how to handle the problem, Tom Chappell and his employees turned to the mission statement for guidance. They decided to contact every customer who had purchased the deodorant and replace it with a newly formulated one. "We [made the decision] because our mission statement says that we will serve customers with safe, effective, and natural products," says Chappell.[11]

Elements of a Mission Statement. A sound mission statement need not be lengthy to be effective. Some of the key issues an entrepreneur and his employees should address as they develop a mission statement for the company include:

- What are the basic beliefs and values of the organization? What do we stand for?
- Who are the company's target customers?
- What are our basic products and services? What customer needs and wants do they satisfy?
- How can we better satisfy these needs and wants?
- Why should customers do business with us rather than the competitor down the street (or across town, on the other coast, on the other side of the globe)?

- What constitutes value to our customers? How can we offer them better value?
- What is our competitive advantage? What is its source?
- In which markets (or market segments) will we choose to compete?
- Who are the key stakeholders in our company, and what effect do they have on it?
- What benefits should we be providing our customers five years from now?
- What business do we want to be in five years from now?

By answering these basic questions, a company will have a much clearer picture of what it is and what it wants to be.

A firm's mission statement may be the most essential and basic communication that it puts forward. If the people on the plant, shop, retail, or warehouse floor don't know what a company's mission is, then, for all practical purposes, it does not have one! The mission statement expresses the firm's character, identity, and scope of operations, but writing it is only half the battle, at best. The most difficult part is living that mission every day. *That's* how employees decide what really matters. To be effective, a mission statement must become a natural part of the organization, embodied in the minds, habits, attitudes, and decisions of everyone in the company every day. Consider the mission statement of Fetzer Vineyards—a vineyard whose own acreage is 100 percent organic, with no chemical pesticides, herbicides, fungicides, or fertilizers—and the message it sends to company stakeholders:

> We are an environmentally and socially conscious grower, producer, and marketer of wines of the highest quality and value.
>
> Working in harmony with respect for the human spirit, we are committed to sharing information about the enjoyment of food and wine in a lifestyle of moderation and responsibility.
>
> We are dedicated to the continuous growth and development of our people and our business.[12]

A company may have a powerful competitive advantage, but it is wasted unless (1) the owner has communicated that advantage to workers, who, in turn, are working hard to communicate it to customers and potential customers, and (2) customers are recommending the company to their friends because they understand the benefits they are getting from it that they cannot get elsewhere. *That's* the real power of a mission statement.

Step 2: Assess the Company's Strengths and Weaknesses

Having defined the vision and the mission of the business, entrepreneurs can turn their attention to assessing company strengths and weaknesses. Competing successfully demands that a business create a competitive strategy that magnifies its strengths and overcomes or compensates for its weaknesses. **Strengths** are positive internal factors that contribute to the accomplishment of a company's mission, goals, and objectives. **Weaknesses** are negative internal factors that inhibit the accomplishment of its mission, goals, and objectives.

Identifying strengths and weaknesses helps entrepreneurs understand their business as it exists (or will exist). An organization's strengths should originate in its core competencies because they are essential to its ability to remain competitive in each of the market segments in which it competes. The key to building a successful strategy is using the company's underlying strengths as its foundation and matching those strengths against competitors' weaknesses.

Table 2.1
Identifying
Company
Strengths and
Weaknesses

STRENGTHS (POSITIVE INTERNAL FACTORS)	WEAKNESSES (NEGATIVE INTERNAL FACTORS)

One effective technique for taking this strategic inventory is to prepare a balance sheet of the company's strengths and weaknesses (see Table 2.1). The positive side should reflect important skills, knowledge, or resources that contribute to the firm's success. The negative side should record honestly any limitations that detract from the company's ability to compete. This balance sheet should analyze all key performance areas of the business—personnel, finance, production, marketing, product development, organization, and others. This analysis should give owners a more realistic perspective of their business, pointing out foundations on which they can build future strengths and obstacles that they must remove for business progress. This exercise can help owners move from their current position to future actions.

Step 3: Scan the Environment for Significant Opportunities and Threats Facing the Business

Opportunities. Once entrepreneurs have taken an internal inventory of company strengths and weaknesses, they must turn to the external environment to identify any opportunities and threats that might have a significant impact on the business. **Opportunities** are positive external options that the firm could employ to accomplish its objectives. The number of potential opportunities is limitless, so managers need analyze only factors significant to the business (probably two or three at most). Otherwise, they may jeopardize their core business by losing focus and trying to do too much at once.

When identifying opportunities, entrepreneurs must pay close attention to new potential markets. Are competitors overlooking a niche in the market? Is there a better way to reach customers? Have environmental changes created new markets? *After the dispute over the 2000 presidential election in which the reliability of paper voting ballots came into question, many small companies that make electronic voting machines saw an opportunity to boost their sales. Legislators in many states began considering election reform bills that required the purchase of new electronic voting machines. Jim Adler, president of VoteHere, a company that makes electronic voting machines that resemble bank automated teller machines, moved quickly to take advantage of the opportunity for his company. Adler has formed alliances with Compaq Computer Corporation and Cisco Systems and has seen his company climb rapidly.*[13]

Threats. **Threats** are negative external forces that inhibit the firm's ability to achieve its objectives. Threats to the business can take a variety of forms, such as new competitors entering the local market, a government mandate regulating a business activity, an economic recession, rising interest rates, technological advances making a company's product obsolete, and many others. *For instance, owners of traditional travel agencies are facing threats from many sides, including the World Wide Web. Travelers* *easily circumvent travel agents by booking their own flights and making their own travel arrangements through a multitude of online services such as Travelocity, Expedia, Biztravel, and others. Another serious threat to travel agents' revenue comes from the caps that many major airlines have placed on agents' commissions for booking flights. After agents' commission on domestic round-trip flights was cut to just $20, the American Society of Travel Agents condemned the action, saying that the airlines were using their "power as the 900-pound gorilla in the industry to attempt to eliminate travel agencies as viable competitors in the marketplace."*[14] Although they cannot control these threats, owners must prepare a strategic plan that will shield their businesses from such threats.

Figure 2.1 illustrates that opportunities and threats are products of the interactions of forces, trends, and events outside the direct control of the business. These external forces will have a direct impact on the behavior of the markets in which the business operates, the behavior of competitors, and the behavior of customers. By monitoring demographic trends as well as trends in their particular industries, entrepreneurs can sharpen their ability to spot most opportunities and threats well in advance, giving themselves time to prepare for them. *Christian Martin, sixth-generation president of C.F. Martin and Company, a famous maker of high-quality acoustic guitars for 170 years, made an important strategic decision after observing the rapid growth in the low end of the guitar market. Martin's specialty has always been luxury guitars. Guitars in the under-$900 price range now account for about 65 percent of acoustic guitar sales, but C.F. Martin, whose guitars normally sell for $1,500 to $50,000, had no guitars in the lower price range. Martin decided to enhance his company's product line by introducing the X series of guitars that starts at $600. The challenge for Martin is to boost sales in the low end of the market without diluting its reputation for quality among customers in the luxury end of the market.*[15]

Table 2.2 on page 46 provides a form that allows business owners to take a strategic inventory of the opportunities and threats facing their companies.

Step 4: Identify the Key Factors for Success in the Business

Key Success Factors. Every business is characterized by controllable variables that determine the relative success of market participants. Identifying and manipulating

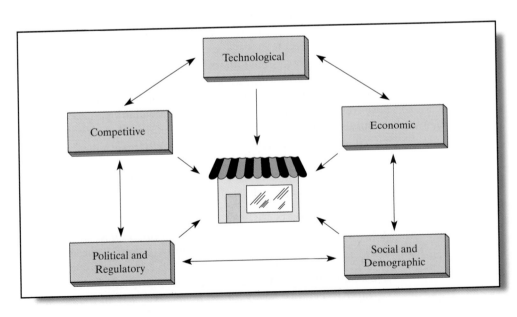

Figure 2.1
External Market
Forces

Section II   Building the Business Plan: Beginning Considerations

IN THE FOOTSTEPS OF AN ENTREPRENEUR
A High-Flying Entrepreneur

In the 1990s, several entrepreneurs took the bold step of launching airlines; unfortunately, almost all of them fell victim to intense competition, escalating fuel and labor prices, and a turbulent business environment. "They either had the wrong equipment, route strategy, or they were weak in management," says one industry analyst. Despite a reputation for being one of the toughest industries for start-ups to survive in, the airline industry continues to attract entrepreneurs. One of the most promising entrants is David Neeleman, founder of JetBlue Airways. JetBlue is Neeleman's third successful business startup in the airline industry. In the early 1990s, he launched Morris Air, a Salt Lake City, Utah–based company that offered passengers innovative, high-quality service coupled with low fares. Morris Air attracted a loyal base of satisfied customers, and Neeleman, just 33, sold the company to Southwest Airlines in 1993. Neeleman's next venture was in Canada, where he helped launch another airline, WestJet. He also transformed the electronic ticketing system he had created at Morris Air into another business, OpenSkies, which he later sold to Hewlett-Packard. "He's a genius entrepreneur," says a friend who is also an airline industry analyst. "He has an uncanny knack for knowing when an opportunity is right."

Drawing on his knowledge of and experience in the airline business, Neeleman decided to try his hand at another start-up, applying the same formula that had worked at Morris Air and WestJet to the world's largest aviation market, New York City. Learning from the mistakes of past airline start-ups, Neeleman carefully crafted his strategy for success. Rather than fly out of LaGuardia or Newark airports, both of which are incredibly expensive for airlines to use, he decided to use New York's Kennedy Airport, which many airlines spurn. Although not as popular, Kennedy offers much lower rates to airlines and is just eight miles away from LaGuardia. Knowing that Kennedy was subject to congestion from international flights at certain times of the day, Neeleman carefully scheduled JetBlue's flights to avoid aggravating delays for passengers. Unlike most aviation start-ups, which buy a hodge-podge of used, inexpensive airplanes, Neeleman decided that JetBlue would use all new jets and that they would be identical. Choosing Airbus A320s enables the company to keep its maintenance costs much lower than airlines using a variety of airplanes.

Neeleman's strategy is to keep operating costs low, maintain fast turnaround times on the ground, and offer customers superior service and "extras" they don't get at other airlines. Neeleman is no stranger to technology, and he uses it extensively throughout the company to keep costs low. Neeleman says that JetBlue's electronic ticketing system, its unified ticketing and accounting systems, and its high-tech virtual call center allow it to operate at half the cost of a typical airline. JetBlue serves no on-board meals and lets passengers pick their own seats. It also offers leather seats throughout its planes and provides free satellite television at every seat. The start-up airline also incurs a lower labor cost than its more established and much larger rivals. Taking a lesson from many failed start-ups that simply ran out of cash, Neeleman raised a sizeable amount of start-up capital—$130 million—to start JetBlue. The company also keeps a low profile against stronger competitors by flying to secondary markets such as Buffalo, New York; Orlando, Florida; and Oakland, California. Neeleman's strategy has worked well so far. JetBlue's costs per passenger mile are the lowest in the industry, and the company became profitable shortly after its launch.

Neeleman's plans for JetBlue are ambitious. The airline will continue to add routes and cities to its schedule, again focusing on secondary markets. It also plans to add new jets to its fleet at a rate of one every five weeks until 2008. In addition to his goal of carrying seven million passengers a year in and out of Kennedy airport, Neeleman wants to transform the substandard reputation of the airline industry. "With our friendly service and hassle-free technology, we're going to bring humanity back to air travel," he says.

1. List the core competencies on which Neeleman has built JetBlue. (You may want to use the Web to learn more about the company.)

2. Evaluate Neeleman's strategy for JetBlue. What future do you predict for the company? Explain.

(continued)

3. Using the World Wide Web and other resources, develop a profile of the airline industry. Create a list of opportunities and threats JetBlue is likely to face in the near future.

Sources: Eryn Brown, "A Smokeless Herb," *Fortune*, May 28, 2001, pp. 78–79; Melanie Trottman, "Now Available on Start-Up Airlines: Leather Seats, Wine, Satellite TV," *Wall Street Journal*, October 25, 2000, pp. B1, B4; JetBlue Airways, *www.jetblue.com/LearnMore/index.html*.

these variables is how a small business gains a competitive advantage. By focusing efforts to maximize their companies' performance on these key success factors, entrepreneurs can achieve dramatic market advantages over their competitors. Companies that understand these key success factors tend to be leaders of the pack, whereas those who fail to recognize them become also-rans.

Key success factors come in a variety of different patterns depending on the industry. Simply stated, they are relationships between a controllable variable (e.g., plant size, size of sales force, business location, distribution system, product packaging) and a critical factor influencing the firm's ability to compete in the market. Many of these sources of competitive advantages are based on cost factors such as manufacturing cost per unit, distribution cost per unit, or development cost per unit. Some are less tangible and less obvious, but are just as important, such as product quality, services offered, store location, and customer credit. For example, one restaurant owner identified the following key success factors for his business:

> Tight cost control (labor, 15 to 18 percent of sales and food costs, 35 to 40 percent of sales)
> Trained, dependable, honest in-store managers
> Close monitoring of waste
> Convenient location
> Maintenance of food quality
> Consistency
> Cleanliness
> Friendly and attentive service from a well-trained wait staff

These controllable variables determine the ability of any restaurant in his market segment to compete. Restaurants lacking these key success factors are not likely to survive, whereas those who build their strategies with these factors in mind will prosper. However, before any small business owner can build a strategy on the foundation of the industry's key success factors, she must identify them. Table 2.3 pre-

Table 2.2
Identifying Opportunities and Threats

OPPORTUNITIES (POSITIVE EXTERNAL FACTORS)	THREATS (NEGATIVE EXTERNAL FACTORS)

Section II   Building the Business Plan: Beginning Considerations

Table 2.3
Identifying Key
Success Factors

List the key success factors that your business must possess if it is to be successful in its market segment.

KEY SUCCESS FACTOR	HOW YOUR COMPANY RATES . . .
1	Low 1 2 3 4 5 6 7 8 9 10 High
2	Low 1 2 3 4 5 6 7 8 9 10 High
3	Low 1 2 3 4 5 6 7 8 9 10 High
4	Low 1 2 3 4 5 6 7 8 9 10 High
5	Low 1 2 3 4 5 6 7 8 9 10 High

Conclusions:

sents a form to help the owner identify the most important success factors and their implications for the company.

Entrepreneurs must use the information gathered to analyze their businesses, their competitors, and their industries to isolate these sources of competitive advantage. They must then determine how well their companies meet these criteria for successfully competing in the market. Highly successful companies know and understand these relationships, but marginal competitors are mystified by which factors determine success in that particular business. For example, a small manufacturer of cosmetics may discover that shelf space, brand recognition, innovative products, efficient distribution, and high quality are crucial to business success. On the other hand, a small retail chain owner may find that broad product lines, available customer credit, personalized service, capable store management, and a high-volume location determine success in his business.

Step 5: Analyze the Competition

When one survey asked small business owners to identify the greatest challenge they faced in the upcoming year, the overwhelming response was *competition*.[16] As these business owners recognize, keeping tabs on rivals' movements through competitive intelligence programs is a vital strategic activity. "Business is like any battlefield. If you want to win the war, you have to know who you're up against," says one small business consultant.[17] The primary goals of a competitive intelligence program include:

- Avoiding surprises from existing competitors' new strategies and tactics
- Identifying potential new competitors
- Improving reaction time to competitors' actions
- Anticipating rivals' next strategic moves

Unfortunately, many small companies fail to gather competitive intelligence because their owners mistakenly assume that it is too costly or simply unnecessary. In reality, the cost of collecting information about competitors typically is minimal, but it does require discipline.

Competitor Analysis. Sizing up the competition gives a business owner a more realistic view of the market and his or her position in it. A competitive intelligence exercise enables entrepreneurs to update their knowledge of competitors by answering the following questions:

- Who are your major competitors and where are they located? Bob Dickinson, president of Carnival Cruise Lines, considers his company's main competition to be land-based theme parks and casinos rather than other cruise lines. Why? Because 89 percent of American adults have never been on a cruise![18]
- What distinctive competencies have they developed?
- How do their cost structures compare to yours? Their financial resources?
- How do they market their products and services?
- What do customers say about them? How do customers describe their products or services; their way of doing business; the additional services they might supply?
- What are their key strategies?
- What are their strengths? How can your company surpass them?
- What are their primary weaknesses? How can your company capitalize on them?
- Are new competitors entering the market?

A small business owner can collect a great deal of information about competitors through low-cost methods including the following:

- Read industry trade publications for announcements from competitors.
- Ask questions of customers and suppliers on what they hear competitors may be doing. In many cases, this information is easy to gather because some people love to gossip.
- Talk to employees, especially sales representatives and purchasing agents. Experts estimate that 70 to 90 percent of the competitive information a company needs already resides with employees who collect it in their routine dealings with suppliers, customers, and other industry contacts.[19]
- Attend trade shows and collect the competitors' sales literature.
- If appropriate, buy the competitors' products and assess their quality and features. Benchmark their products against yours. The owner of an online gift-basket company periodically places orders with his primary competitors and compares their packaging, pricing, service, and quality to his own.[20]
- Obtain credit reports from firms such as Dun & Bradstreet on each of your major competitors to evaluate their financial condition.
- Check out the resources of your local library, including articles, computerized databases, and online searches. For local competitors, review back issues of the area newspaper for articles on and advertisements by competitors.
- Use the vast resources of the World Wide Web to learn more about your competitors. The Web enables entrepreneurs to gather valuable competitive information at little or no cost.
- Visit competing businesses periodically to observe their operations.

Using the information gathered, a business owner can set up teams of managers and employees to evaluate key competitors and make recommendations on specific strategic actions that will improve the firm's competitive position against each one.

Entrepreneurs can use the results of the competitor intelligence analysis to construct a competitive profile matrix for each market segment in which the firm operates. A **competitive profile matrix** allows an entrepreneur to evaluate his or her firm against the major competitor on the key success factors for that market segment (refer to Table 2.4). The first step is to list the key success factors identified in Step 4

Section II Building the Business Plan: Beginning Considerations

Table 2.4
Sample
Competitive
Profile Matrix

Key Success Factors (From Step 5)		Your Business			Competitor 1		Competitor 2	
	Weight	Rating	Weighted Score	Rating	Weighted Score	Rating	Weighted Score	
Market Share	0.10	3	0.30	2	0.20	3	0.30
Price Competitiveness	0.20	1	0.20	3	0.60	4	0.80
Financial Strength	0.10	2	0.20	3	0.30	2	0.20
Product Quality	0.40	4	1.60	2	0.80	1	0.40
Customer Loyalty	0.20	3	0.60	3	0.60	2	0.40
Total	1.00		2.90		2.50		2.10

of the strategic planning process and to attach weights to them reflecting their relative importance. (For simplicity, the weights in this matrix sum add up to 1.00). In this example, notice that product quality is weighted twice as heavily (twice as important) as price competitiveness.

The next step is to identify the company's major competitors and to rate each one (and your company) on each of the key success factors:

IF FACTOR IS A:	RATING IS:
Major weakness	1
Minor weakness	2
Minor strength	3
Major strength	4

Once the rating is completed, the owner simply multiplies the weight by the rating for each factor to get a weighted score, and then adds up each competitor's weighted scores to get a total weighted score. Table 2.4 shows a sample competitive profile matrix for a small company. The results will show which company is strongest, which is weakest, and which of the key success factors each one is best and worst at meeting. By carefully studying and interpreting the results, small business owners can begin to envision the ideal strategy for building a competitive edge in their market segment.

Knowledge Management. Unfortunately, many small companies fail to gather competitive intelligence because their owners mistakenly assume that it is too costly or simply unnecessary. In reality, the cost of collecting information about competitors and the competitive environment typically is minimal, but it does require discipline. The key is learning how to manage the knowledge a company accumulates. **Knowledge management** is the practice of gathering, organizing, and disseminating the collective wisdom and experience of a company's employees for the purpose of strengthening its competitive position. "Organizations that harness knowledge and put it to good use are able to gain a clear competitive advantage," says Eric Lesser, a consultant at IBM's Institute for Knowledge Management.[21] Knowledge management enables companies to get more innovative products to market faster, respond to customers' needs faster, and solve (or avoid altogether) problems more efficiently. Because of their size and simplicity, small businesses have an advantage over large companies when it comes to managing knowledge. Knowledge management requires that a small company identify what its workers know, incorporate that knowledge into the business and distribute it where it is needed, and leverage it into more useful knowledge.

The first step in creating a knowledge management program is to take an inventory of the special knowledge a company possesses that gives it a competitive advantage. This involves assessing the knowledge bank that employees have compiled over time. One of the most valuable assets available to companies is their customer databases, information that, when analyzed properly, can give amazing insight into customers' likes, dislikes, and buying habits and patterns. The second step in knowledge management is to organize the essential knowledge and disseminate it throughout the company to those who need it. High-tech solutions such as e-mail, computerized databases, and software that allows many different employees to work on a project simultaneously are important tools, but low-tech methods such as whiteboards, Post-it notes, and face-to-face meetings can be just as effective in small companies. The final step in creating a knowledge management program is to continue to add to the knowledge base the company has asembled.

Heather Hesketh, owner of hesketh.com, a Web-consulting firm, realized that a knowledge management program was essential to her fast-growing company's success. Not only is Hesketh hiring a new employee every two months, but she also is selling her employees' collective knowledge to her clients! When employees left the company, Hesketh realized that a valuable base of information went out the door with them. To avoid this brain drain, she created a constantly growing database of employees' knowledge on the company intranet, where it is available to any employee at any time. She claims it is her way of preserving the company's past and preparing for its future.[22]

Step 6: Create Company Goals and Objectives

Before an entrepreneur can build a comprehensive set of strategies, he must first establish business goals and objectives, which give him targets to aim for and provide a basis for evaluating his company's performance. Without them, an entrepreneur cannot know where the business is going or how well it is performing. Creating goals and objectives is an essential part of the strategic management process.

Goals. Goals are the broad, long-range attributes that a business seeks to accomplish; they tend to be general and sometimes even abstract. Goals are not intended to be specific enough for a manager to act on, but simply state the general level of accomplishment sought. Do you want to boost your market share? Does your cash balance need strengthening? Would you like to enter a new market or increase sales in a current one? What return on your investment do you seek? Researchers Jim Collins and Jerry Porras studied a large group of businesses and determined that one of the factors that set apart successful companies from unsuccessful ones was the formulation of very ambitious, clear, and inspiring long-term goals. Collins and Porras called them BHAGs ("Big Audacious Hairy Goals," pronounced "bee-hags") and say that their main benefit is to inspire and focus a company on important actions that are consistent with its overall mission.[23]

Addressing these broad issues will help you focus on the next phase—developing specific, realistic objectives.

Objectives. Objectives are more specific targets of performance. Common objectives address profitability, productivity, growth, efficiency, markets, financial resources, physical facilities, organizational structure, employee welfare, and social responsibility. Because some of these objectives might conflict with one another, entrepreneurs must establish priorities. Which objectives are most important? Which are least important? Arranging objectives in a hierarchy according to their priority can help business owners resolve conflicts when they arise. Well-written objectives have the following characteristics:

- *They are specific.* Objectives should be quantifiable and precise. For example, "to achieve a healthy growth in sales" is not a meaningful objective; but "to increase retail sales by 12 percent and wholesale by 10 percent in the next fiscal year" is precise and spells out exactly what management wants to accomplish.
- *They are measurable.* Managers should be able to plot the organization's progress toward its objectives; this requires a well-defined reference point from which to start and a scale for measuring progress.
- *They are assignable.* Unless an entrepreneur assigns responsibility for an objective to an individual, it is unlikely that the company will ever achieve it. Creating objectives without giving someone responsibility for accomplishing it is futile.
- *They are realistic, yet challenging.* Objectives must be within the reach of the organization or motivation will disappear. In any case, managerial expectations must remain high. In other words, the more challenging an objective is (within realistic limits), the higher the performance will be. Set objectives that will challenge your business and its employees.
- *They are timely.* Objectives must specify not only what is to be accomplished but also when it is to be accomplished. A time frame for achievement is important.
- *They are written down.* This writing process does not have to be complex; in fact, the manager should make the number of objectives relatively small, from 5 to 15.

The strategic planning process works best when managers and employees are actively involved jointly in setting objectives. Developing a plan is top management's responsibility, but executing it falls to managers and employees; therefore, encouraging them to participate broadens the plan's perspective and increases the motivation to make the plan work. In addition, managers and employees know a great deal about the organization and usually are willing to share this knowledge.

Step 7: Formulate Strategic Options and Select the Appropriate Strategies

4. Discuss the characteristics of three basic strategies: cost leadership, differentiation, and focus.

By now, an entrepreneur should have a clear picture of what her business does best and what its competitive advantages are. Similarly, she should know her firm's weaknesses and limitations as well as those of its competitors. The next step is to evaluate strategic options and then prepare a game plan designed to achieve the business's objectives.

Strategy. A **strategy** is a road map an entrepreneur draws up of the actions necessary to fulfill a firm's mission, goals, and objectives. In other words, the mission, goals, and objectives spell out the ends, and the strategy defines the means for reaching them. A strategy is the master plan that covers all of the major parts of the organization and ties them together into a unified whole. The plan must be action oriented—that is, it should breathe life into the entire planning process. An entrepreneur must build a sound strategy based on the preceding steps that uses the company's core competencies as the springboard to success. Joseph Picken and Gregory Dess, authors of *Mission Critical: The 7 Strategic Traps that Derail Even the Smartest Companies*, write, "A flawed strategy—no matter how brilliant the leadership, no matter how effective the implementation—is doomed to fail. A sound strategy, implemented without error, wins every time."[24]

A successful strategy is comprehensive and well integrated, focusing on establishing the key success factors that the manager identified in Step 4. For instance, if maximum shelf space is a key success factor for a small manufacturer's product, the strategy must identify techniques for gaining more in-store shelf space (e.g., offering

Many people pick up a good book, looking to escape the pressures of life for just a few hours by traveling to a world of fantasy. For the people who sell those books, however, escaping the competitive pressures of real life is a fantasy they know they are not likely to live out. Across the country, the explosion of book superstores and Web-based booksellers such as Amazon.com has put intense pressure on small, independent booksellers, threatening to squeeze them out of existence. The number of bookstore failures has increased in the past 10 years, as independents' share of the market has slipped from 33 percent to 15 percent. Superstores such as Borders and Barnes & Noble, already with outlets numbering in the hundreds, are adding more each year. They offer a wide selection of titles (150,000 or more) and discount prices and bill themselves as "destination stores" that customers are willing to seek out. That can make it tough for some small, independent booksellers to remain competitive.

Yet, many are doing just that—and more; they are thriving in the face of the giants. A variety of well-planned, well-executed strategies give these independent bookstores the ability to retain a base of loyal customers and to increase sales and profits. According to the American Booksellers Association, an association representing small, independent bookstores, the most successful independents are analyzing their larger competitors to identify their weaknesses and then are focusing their resources in those areas. For instance, chain stores often have a more difficult time adapting their inventories to suit local tastes and culture, something that independent bookstores have always done. Because they are locally owned and operated, small bookstores are better at stocking books that are unique to a particular community or region. Superstores, whose inventories are usually managed from a headquarters that may be thousands of miles away, are not as responsive to individual communities' needs and interests. Other independents are settling successfully into niches, such as cookbooks, children's books, science fiction, mystery, or travel. By focusing on just one category of book titles, these stores can offer their customers a wide selection of books of interest to them.

Virtually every small bookstore has at its disposal a powerful competitive weapon that often turns out to be a dandy giant slayer: customer service and lots of little "extras" that keep customers coming back. At The Open Book in Greenville, South Carolina, owner Tom Gower says that for titles he doesn't normally stock, he can fill an order much faster than a superstore (a day or two compared to as much as 4 to 6 weeks at a chain store) by relying on his network of publishers and book brokers. In nearby Spartanburg, South Carolina, Jane Hughes, owner of Pic-A-Book, keeps customers coming back with in-store book signings, readings, and workshops featuring well-known local authors.

Workshops and classes—as many as 40 per year—have boosted sales at Book Passage, a small shop in Corte Madera, California. Because their nearest competitor is a superstore just a few yard away, owners Bill and Elaine Petrocelli decided to draw customers by offering short courses and workshops on everything from beginning Italian to mystery writing. Book Passage also publishes a stylish, informative newsletter chock-full of useful information to customers. "You can't sell books like corn flakes," says Elaine. "We're really trying to make the store the cultural center of our area."

Corn flakes or not, underestimating the power of a great marketing idea can be a mistake. Booksmith, a San Francisco store, recently hired science fiction writer Harlan Ellison to sit in its window at his typewriter and compose a short story. Several years ago, the store began printing "author trading cards" that, like baseball cards, include pictures, autographs, and publishing "statistics."

Powell's City of Books, a landmark in Portland, Oregon, takes on the chains and Amazon.com by focusing on everything that its larger competitors are not. Stocking more than 1.6 million volumes, Powell's, the largest independent bookstore in the country, sells new and used books, paperbacks and hardbacks, mainstream titles and obscure ones from tiny publishing houses from its downtown location in Portland. However, Powell's niche remains in used books, which carry a higher profit margin than new ones. It also sells books from its Web site, *www.powells.com*,
(continued)

which it started a year before Amazon.com went online. Despite the fact that Amazon's advertising budget of $1.6 million dwarfs the $200,000 Powell's spends on advertising, the online giant has not made a dent in Powell's loyal base of customers, who prefer dealing with an independent bookseller with friendly, knowledgeable employees who know their subject matter. "You can make a bookstore a destination by having a wonderful atmosphere, a good café, and great service," says Powell.

1. What advice would you offer the owner of a small bookstore located in a town where one of the book superstores has just announced it will open an outlet?

2. Visit Amazon.com's World Wide Web site at *www.amazon.com,* Barnes & Noble's site at *www.barnesandnoble.com,* and Powell's City of Books at *www.powells.com.* What benefits do these companies' Web sites offer customers? What weaknesses do booksellers on the Web experience?

3. What advice would you offer the owner of a small bookstore about conducting business on the World Wide Web?

Sources: David G. Propson, "We Stand United," *Small Business Computing,* July 2001, pp. 28–33; Adam Penenberg, "Crossing Amazon," *Forbes,* April 17, 2000, pp. 168–170; Charles C. Mann, Volume Business, *Inc. Technology 1997,* No. 2, pp. 54–61; Dierdre Donahue, "Bookstores May Be on the Upswing, but Book Sales Are Down," *USA Today,* July 31, 1997, p. 5D; Barbara Carton, "Bookstore Survival Stunts Have Scant Literary Merit," *Wall Street Journal,* June 3, 1997, pp. B1, B8; Patrick M. Reilly, "Booksellers Prepare to Do Battle in Cyberspace," *Wall Street Journal,* January 28, 1997, pp. B1, B8; Ed O'Donoghue, "Reading the Market," *Upstate Business,* July 20, 1997, pp. 1, 6–7; David D. Kirkpatrick, "Small Bookstores End Fight, Dropping Suit Against Chains," *New York Times,* April 20, 2001, *www.nytimes.com/2001/04/20/business/20BOOK.html.*

higher margins to distributors and brokers than competitors do, assisting retailers with in-store displays, or redesigning a wider, more attractive package). When building their strategies, successful companies avoid going toe-to-toe with more powerful rivals, choosing instead to be the dominant player in a specific market segment. They focus their resources on serving the customers in their corner of the market better than anyone else rather than try to compete for market leadership with companies that are much stronger.

Three Strategic Options. The number of strategies from which entrepreneurs can choose is infinite. When all the glitter is stripped away, however, three basic strategies remain. In his classic book, *Competitive Strategy,* Michael Porter defines these strategies: (1) cost leadership, (2) differentiation, and (3) focus.

Cost Leadership. A company pursuing a **cost leadership strategy** strives to be the lowest-cost producer relative to its competitors in the industry. Low-cost leaders have a competitive advantage in reaching buyers whose primary purchase criterion is price, and they have the power to set the industry's price floor. Such a strategy works well when buyers are sensitive to price changes, when competing firms sell the same commodity products, and when companies can benefit from economies of scale. Not only is a low-cost leader in the best position to defend itself in a price war, but it also can use its power to attack competitors with the lowest price in the industry. "You have to be the lowest-cost producer in your patch," says the president of a company that sells the classic commodity product—cement.[25]

There are many ways to build a low-cost strategy, but the most successful cost leaders know where they have cost advantages over their competitors, and they use these as the foundation for their strategies. For example, a small, nonunion airline is likely to have a significant advantage in labor costs, but not in fuel costs, over its larger, unionized competitors. *Papa Murphy's has become the nation's seventh largest pizza chain by relentlessly pursuing a low-cost strategy. Unlike its larger rivals in the pizza business, the Vancouver, Washington–based chain provides no space for diners to eat, no delivery, and no cooking! Papa Murphy's sells made-to-order, uncooked pizzas that customers* *pick up and cook at home, a strategy that enables it to keep its operating costs extremely low. Most of its 615 tiny stores are located in suburban strip malls where rents are low and are staffed by just three people who assemble the pizzas. Papa Murphy's no-frills, take-and-bake strategy enables it to sell a 16-inch pepperoni pizza for just $6, about half the price its full-service competitors charge. Customers are responding; company sales are climbing 20 percent a year.*[26]

Of course, there are dangers in following a cost leadership strategy. Sometimes, a company focuses exclusively on lower manufacturing costs, without considering the impact of purchasing, distribution, or overhead costs. Another danger is misunderstanding the firm's true cost drivers. For instance, one furniture manufacturer drastically underestimated its overhead costs and, as a result, was selling its products at a loss. Finally, a company may pursue a low-cost leadership strategy so zealously that it essentially locks itself out of other strategic choices.

Differentiation. A company following a **differentiation strategy** seeks to build customer loyalty by positioning its goods or services in a unique or different fashion. In other words, a company strives to be better than its competitors at something that customers value. The primary benefit of successful differentiation is the ability to generate higher profit margins because of customers' heightened brand loyalty and reduced price sensitivity. There are many ways to create a differentiation strategy, but the key concept is to be special at something that is important to the customer such as quality, convenience, performance, or style. "You'd better be on top of what it is your customers value and continually improve your offerings to better deliver that value," advises Jill Griffin, a strategic marketing consultant.[27] If a small company can improve a product's or service's performance, reduce the customer's risk of purchasing it, or both, it has the potential to differentiate. *For example, Chicago's luxurious East Bank Club is not the typical health club. In addition to its spacious exercise rooms lined with banks of exercise machines to prevent patrons from waiting or dealing with time limits, the East Bank Club offers amenities typically found in a five-star resort. Guests can get a haircut, a massage, and a pedicure in the salon, eat at the full-service bar and restaurant, and drop their children off at the child-care center while they exercise or participate in yoga or aerobics classes. Locker rooms are plush, complete with carpet, marble sinks, and an army of attendants. Not only do these additional services generate significant revenues for the East Bank Club (they account for 47 percent of total revenue), but they also keep pampered customers coming back. East Bank customers are so loyal that even during economic recessions the company's sales remain strong.*[28]

The key to a successful differentiation strategy is to build it on a *distinctive competence*—something the small company is uniquely good at doing in comparison to its competitors. Common bases for differentiation include superior customer service, special product features, complete product lines, instantaneous parts availability, absolute product reliability, supreme product quality, and extensive product knowledge. To be successful, a differentiation strategy must create the perception of value in the customer's eyes. No customer will purchase a good or service that fails to produce its perceived value, no matter how real that value may be. One business consultant advises, "Make sure you tell your customers and prospects what it is about your business that makes you different. Make sure that difference is in the form of a true benefit to the customer."[29]

There are risks in pursuing a differentiation strategy. One danger is trying to differentiate a product or service on the basis of something that does not boost its performance or lower its cost to the buyer. Another pitfall is overdifferentiating and charging so much that a company prices its products out of its target customers' reach. The final risk is focusing only on the physical characteristics of a product or service and ignoring important psychological factors—status, prestige, image, and style. For many successful companies, psychological factors are key elements in differentiating their products and services from those of competitors.

Focus. A **focus strategy** recognizes that not all markets are homogeneous. In fact, in any given market, there are many different customer segments, each having different needs, wants, and characteristics. The principal idea of this strategy is to select one (or more) segment(s); identify customers' special needs, wants, and interests; and approach them with a good or service designed to excel in meeting these needs, wants, and interests. Focus strategies build on *differences* among market segments.

A successful focus strategy depends on a small company's ability to identify the changing needs of its targeted customer group and to develop the skills required to serve them. That means the owner and everyone in the organization must have a clear understanding of how to add value to the product or service for the customer. How does the product or service meet the customer's needs at each stage—from raw material to final sale?

Rather than attempting to serve the total market, a company pursuing a focus strategy specializes in serving a specific target segment or niche that larger companies are overlooking or underestimating. A focus strategy is ideally suited to many small businesses, which often lack the resources to reach a national market. Their goal is to serve their narrow target markets more effectively and efficiently than do competitors that pound away at the broad market. Common bases for building a focus strategy include zeroing in on a small geographic area, targeting a group of customers with similar needs or interests (e.g., left-handed people), or specializing in a specific product or service (e.g., petite clothing). *For example, Wayne and Marty Scott, owners of Clown Shoes & Props, have captured about 20 percent of the U.S. market for clown shoes! The copreneurs learned their craft while working at the Ringling Brothers Circus in the 1960s, and now*

Wayne and Marty Scott, owners of Clown Shoes & Props, have built a successful business by focusing on a unique niche—custom-made clown shoes!

fill orders from across the country for wingtips that are two feet long. The Scotts offer nine basic clown shoe styles, each a shoe within a shoe, and add accessories such as squirting flowers, trains, and mouths that open and close with each step. Making clown shoes is serious business for the Scotts, however; the average pair sells for $225. Before making a pair of shoes, the Scotts insist on a description of the clown's character and a picture of the clown in costume. "A clown isn't complete without the right shoes," says Peggy Williams, a former clown and now a manager at Ringling Brothers, "and you can't get these at the mall."[30]

Like the Scotts, the most successful focusers build a competitive edge by concentrating on specific market niches and serving them better than any other competitor can. Essentially, this strategy depends on creating value for the customer either by being the lowest-cost producer or by differentiating the product or service in a unique fashion, but doing so in a narrow target segment. Speedy service, a unique product or service, superior customer service, and convenience are important strengths for companies using focus strategies. Consider the following examples of small companies competing successfully in small, yet profitable, niches:

- Doug Kidd, owner of Border States Leatherworks, sells authentic reproductions of military saddles and leather goods to Civil War reenactors. Traveling from one reenactment site to another, Kidd sets up his tent in "sutler's row" with other merchants selling supplies to participants in one of the fastest-growing and most expensive hobbies in the country—military reenactments. To pass muster with reenactors, sutlers' goods must be true to the original equipment used in the 1860s, down to the number of stitches per square inch and the type of thread used (on saddles, linen cord coated with rosin, never just cotton).[31]
- Frank J. Zamboni and Company dominates the market for ice resurfacing machines with a famous product that bears the founder's name. Every hockey fan knows the Zamboni comes out to resurface the ice between periods! The small company sells about 200 machines a year at a price of about $60,000 each.[32]
- Ray Giesse, owner of the American Whistle Company, sells more than one million whistles each year to police departments, the Boy Scouts and Girl Scouts, the National Football League, and Wal-Mart. The company is the only maker of metal whistles in the United States.[33]

The rewards of dominating a niche can be huge, but pursuing a focus strategy does carry risk. Companies sometimes must struggle to capture a large enough share of a small market to be profitable. A niche must be big enough for a company to generate a profit. A successful focus strategy also brings with it a threat. If a small company is successful in its niche, there is the danger of larger competitors entering the market and eroding or controlling it. Sometimes a company with a successful niche strategy gets distracted by its success and tries to branch out into other areas. As it drifts farther away from its core strategy, it loses its competitive edge and runs the risk of confusing or alienating its customers. Muddying its image with customers puts a company in danger of losing its identity.

An effective strategic plan identifies a complete set of success factors—financial, operating, and marketing—that, taken together, produce a competitive advantage for the small business. The resulting action plan distinguishes the firm from its competitors by exploiting its competitive advantage. The focal point of this entire strategic plan is the customer. The customer is the nucleus of any business, so a competitive strategy will succeed only if it is aimed at serving customers better than the competitors do. An effective strategy draws out the competitive advantage in a small company by building on its strengths and by making the customer its focal point. It also designates methods for overcoming the firm's weaknesses, and it identifies opportunities and threats that demand action.

Section II   Building the Business Plan: Beginning Considerations

Step 8: Translate Strategic Plans into Action Plans

No strategic plan is complete until it is put into action. The small business manager must convert strategic plans into operating plans that guide the company on a daily basis and become a visible, active part of the business. No small business can benefit from a strategic plan sitting on a shelf collecting dust.

IN THE FOOTSTEPS OF AN ENTREPRENEUR
A "Beary" Successful Business

After working for May Department Stores for 25 years, Maxine Cook took what she had learned in retail and launched her own unique business, Build-A-Bear Workshop, where children of all ages can go to design and build their own teddy bears. For her efforts, Clark, the self-described Chief Executive Bear (CEB) of the company, has been named the retail innovator of the year by the National Retail Federation and the Entrepreneur of the Year in St. Louis, where the company is based. With more than 70 locations nationwide (mostly in malls), the company generates more than $100 million in revenues, twice the national average of a typical mall store. "My strength is in merchandising and marketing, and I knew that kids require you to be creative," says Clark. "I loved retailing and wanted to try something different."

As children enter a Build-A-Bear Workshop, they become Guest Bear Builders, and their first stop is the "Choose Me" station, where they select the unstuffed skin that will become their teddy bear (or monkey, frog, bunny, or other animal). The next stop is the "Hear Me" area, where the children pick the sounds their animals will make. The message can be prerecorded, or the children can record the sounds themselves. Next, guests go to the "Stuff Me" station, where with help of an employee (a Master Bear Builder), they fill their animals to just the right volume on a machine that resembles a large popcorn popper. Each child then picks a tiny pillowy heart to be inserted before the stuffed animal is stitched up. Kids groom their creations into just the right shape at the "Fluff Me" station before moving on to a row of computers where they name their animals and complete a birth certificate for them. Prices for each bear

range from $10 to $25, but kids can choose from an assortment of clothing options—from argyle sweaters to athletic shoes—for their stuffed animals at prices ranging from $2 to $15. Just as in any clothing store, new styles arrive regularly. At the cash register, each Guest receives a printed birth certificate signed by "Maxine Clark, C.E.B." The child's new friend is packed safely into a house-shaped box, ready for the journey to its new home.

To make sure her company continues to meet her young customers' expectations, Clark has formed the Cub Advisory Board, which is made up of 20 children, aged 6 to 14, from the St. Louis area. Clark says that some of the most valuable advice she has gotten for her business has come from these young advisors. Clark gets their input on everything from the selection of animals to carry to the location of new stores. "If they don't like it, we don't do it," she declared.

In addition to its retail stores, Build-A-Bear Workshops has a Web site (*www.buildabear.com*), a monthly newsletter (*Bearly Newsworthy*) and complementary items such as CDs. The company recently started hosting bear-building birthday parties and is considering designing its new stores with a room dedicated to that purpose. Clark's goal is to make Build-A-Bear Workshops a global company within 10 years.

1. Which of the three types of strategies described in this chapter is Build-A-Bear Workshops following? Explain.

2. What competitive advantages does Build-A-Bear have? What possible threats might the company face?

Sources: Sharon Nelton, "Building an Empire One Smile at a Time," *Success*, September 2000, pp. 34–37; Teresa F. Lindeman, "Former Payless Chief Hits Pay Dirt with Build-A-Bear," *Post-Gazette.com, www.post-gazette.com/businessnews/20010803bears0803bnp1.asp.*

Implement the Strategy. To make the plan workable, the business owner should divide the plan into projects, carefully defining each one by the following:

Purpose. What is the project designed to accomplish?

Scope. Which areas of the company will be involved in the project?

Contribution. How does the project relate to other projects and to the overall strategic plan?

Resource requirements. What human and financial resources are needed to complete the project successfully?

Timing. Which schedules and deadlines will ensure project completion?

Once managers assign priorities to these projects, they can begin to implement the strategic plan. Involving employees and delegating adequate authority to them is essential since these projects affect them most directly.

If an organization's people have been involved in the strategic management process to this point, they will have a better grasp of the steps they must take to achieve the organization's goals as well as their own professional goals. Early involvement of the total workforce in the strategic management process is a luxury that larger businesses cannot achieve. Commitment to achieve the objectives of the firm is a powerful force for success, but involvement is a prerequisite for achieving total employee commitment. Without a committed, dedicated team of employees working together to implement strategy, a company's strategy, no matter how well planned, usually fails.

When putting their strategic plans into action, small companies must exploit all of the competitive advantages of their size by:

- Responding quickly to customers' needs
- Remaining flexible and willing to change
- Continually searching for new emerging market segments
- Building and defending market niches
- Erecting "switching costs" through personal service and special attention
- Remaining entrepreneurial and willing to take risks
- Acting with lightning speed to move into and out of markets as they ebb and flow
- Constantly innovating

Step 9: Establish Accurate Controls

5. Understand the importance of controls such as the balanced scorecard in the planning process.

So far, the planning process has created company objectives and has developed a strategy for reaching them, but rarely, if ever, will the company's actual performance match stated objectives. Entrepreneurs quickly realize the need to control actual results that deviate from plans.

Controlling the Strategy. Planning without control has little operational value, and so a sound planning program requires a practical control process. The plans created in this process become the standards against which actual performance is measured. It is important for everyone in the organization to understand—and to be involved in—the planning and controlling process.

Controlling projects and keeping them on schedule means that the owner must identify and track key performance indicators. The source of these indicators is the operating data from the company's normal business activity; they are the guideposts for detecting deviations from established standards. Accounting, production, sales, inventory, and other operating records are primary sources of data the manager can use for controlling activities. For example, on a customer service project, performance indicators might include customer complaints, orders returned, on-time shipments, and order accuracy.

To evaluate the effectiveness of their strategies, some companies are developing **balanced scorecards,** a set of measurements unique to a company that includes both financial and operational measures and gives managers a quick yet comprehensive picture of the company's total performance. One writer says that a balanced scorecard is:

> a sophisticated business model that helps a company understand what's really driving its success. It acts a bit like the control panel on a spaceship—the business equivalent of a flight speedometer, odometer, and temperature gauge all rolled into one. It keeps track of many things, including financial progress and softer measurements—everything from customer satisfaction to return on investment—that need to be managed to reach the final destination: profitable growth.[34]

Rather than sticking solely to the traditional financial measures of a company's performance, the balanced scorecard gives managers a comprehensive view from *both a financial and an operational perspective.* The premise behind such a scorecard is that relying on any single measure of company performance is dangerous. Just as a pilot in command of a jet cannot fly safely by focusing on a single instrument, an entrepreneur cannot manage a company by concentrating on a single measurement. The complexity of managing a business demands that an entrepreneur be able to see performance measures in several areas simultaneously.

Properly used, an entrepreneur can trace the elements on the company's balanced scorecard back to its vision and mission. When creating a balanced scorecard for a company, the key is to establish goals for each critical indicator of company performance and then create meaningful measures for each one. Although some elements will apply to many businesses, a company's scorecard should be unique. The balanced scorecard looks at a business from four important perspectives (see Figure 2.3)[35]:

1. *Customer perspective.* How do customers see us? Customers judge companies by at least four standards: time (how long it takes the company to deliver a good or service), quality (how well a company's product or service performs in terms of reliability, durability, and accuracy), performance (the extent to which a good or service performs as expected), and service (how well a company meets or exceeds customers' expectations of value). Because customer-related goals are external, managers must translate them into measures of what the company must do to meet customers' expectations.
2. *Internal business perspective.* What must we excel at? The internal factors that managers should focus on are those that have the greatest impact on customer satisfaction and retention and on company effectiveness and efficiency. Developing goals and measures for factors such as quality, cycle time, productivity, costs, and others that employees directly influence is essential.
3. *Innovation and learning perspective.* Can we continue to improve and create value? This view of a company recognizes that the targets required for success are never static; they are constantly changing. If a company wants to continue its pattern of success, it cannot stand still; it must continuously improve. A company's ability to innovate, learn, and improve determines its future. These goals and measures emphasize the importance of continuous improvement in customer satisfaction and internal business operations.
4. *Financial perspective.* How do we look to shareholders? The most traditional performance measures, financial standards, tell how much the company's over-

Figure 2.3
The Balanced
Scorecard Links
Performance
Measures

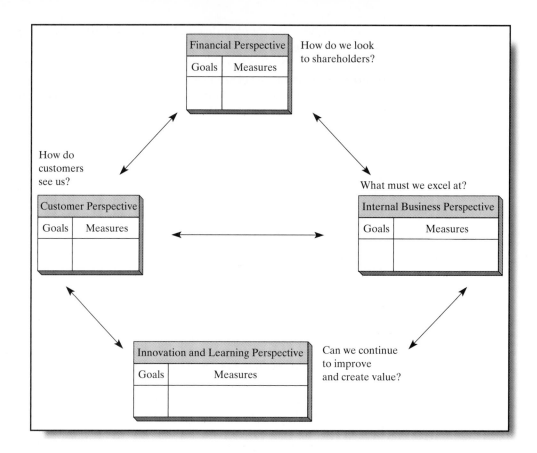

all strategy and its execution are contributing to its bottom line. These measures focus on such factors as profitability, growth, and shareholder value. On balanced scorecards, companies often break their financial goals into three categories: survival, success, and growth.

Although the balanced scorecard is a vital tool that helps managers keep their companies on track, it is also an important tool for changing behavior in an organization and for keeping everyone focused on what really matters. As conditions change, managers must make corrections in performances, policies, strategies, and objectives to get performance back on track. A practical control system is also economical to operate. Most small businesses have no need for a sophisticated, expensive control system. The system should be so practical that it becomes a natural part of the management process.

CONCLUSION

The strategic planning process does *not* end with the nine steps outlined here; it is an ongoing procedure that the small business owner must repeat. With each round, he or she gains experience, and the steps become much easier. The planning process outlined here is designed to be as simple as possible. No small business should be burdened with an elaborate, detailed formal planning process that it cannot easily use. Such programs require excessive amounts of time to operate, and they generate a sea of paperwork. The small business manager needs neither.

What does this strategic planning process lead to? It teaches entrepreneurs a degree of discipline that is important to their business's survival. It helps them to learn about their business, their competitors, and, most important, their customers. It forces them to recognize and evaluate their company's strengths and weaknesses as well as the opportunities and threats facing it. It also encourages entrepreneurs to define how they will set their business apart from the competition. Although strategic planning cannot guarantee success, it does dramatically increase the small firm's chances of survival in a hostile business environment. Unfortunately, most business owners forgo the benefits of strategic planning. A recent survey of family businesses by Arthur Andersen Consulting and MassMutual Life Insurance Company found that just 30 percent of the companies had a written strategic plan.[36] Don't let that happen to you!

CHAPTER SUMMARY

1. Understand the importance of strategic management to a small business.
   - Strategic planning, often ignored by small companies, is a crucial ingredient in business success. The planning process forces potential entrepreneurs to subject their ideas to an objective evaluation in the competitive market.
2. Explain why and how a small business must create a competitive advantage in the market.
   - The goal of developing a strategic plan is to create for the small company a competitive advantage—the aggregation of factors that sets the small business apart from its competitors and gives it a unique position in the market. Every small firm must establish a plan for creating a unique image in the minds of its potential customers.
3. Develop a strategic plan for a business using the nine steps in the strategic planning process.
   - Small businesses need a strategic planning process designed to suit their particular needs. It should be relatively short, be informal and not structured, encourage the participation of employees, and not begin with extensive objective setting. Linking the purposeful action of strategic planning to an entrepreneur's little ideas can produce results that shape the future.

   Step 1. Develop a clear vision and translate it into a meaningful mission statement. Highly successful entrepreneurs are able to communicate their vision to those around them. The firm's mission statement answers the first question of any venture: What business am I in? The mission statement sets the tone for the entire company.

   Step 2: Assess the company's strengths and weaknesses. Strengths are positive internal factors; weaknesses are negative internal factors.

   Step 3: Scan the environment for significant opportunities and threats facing the business. Opportunities are positive external options; threats are negative external forces.

   Step 4: Identify the key factors for success in the business. In every business, key factors that determine the success of the firms in it, and so they must be an integral part of a company's strategy. Key success factors are relationships between a controllable variable (e.g., plant size, size of sales force, advertising expenditures, product packaging) and a critical factor influencing the firm's ability to compete in the market.

   Step 5: Analyze the competition. Business owners should know their competitors' business almost as well as they know their own. A competitive profile matrix is a helpful tool for analyzing competitors' strengths and weaknesses.

   Step 6: Create company goals and objectives. Goals are the broad, long-range attributes that the firm seeks to accomplish. Objectives are quantifiable and more precise; they should be specific, measurable, assignable, realistic, timely, and written down. The process works best when subor-

dinate managers and employees are actively involved.

Step 7: Formulate strategic options and select the appropriate strategies. A strategy is the game plan the firm plans to use to achieve its objectives and mission. It must center on establishing for the firm the key success factors identified earlier.

Step 8: Translate strategic plans into action plans. No strategic plan is complete until the owner puts it into action.

Step 9: Establish accurate controls. Actual performance rarely, if ever, matches plans exactly. Operating data from the business serve as guideposts for detecting deviations from plans. Such information is helpful when plotting future strategies.

The strategic planning process does not end with these nine steps; rather, it is an ongoing process that the owner will repeat.

4. Discuss the characteristics of three basic strategies: leadership cost, differentiation, and focus.
   • Three basic strategic options are cost leadership, differentiation, and focus. A company pursuing a cost leadership strategy strives to be the lowest-cost producer relative to its competitors in the industry.

A company following a differentiation strategy seeks to build customer loyalty by positioning its goods or services in a unique or different fashion. In other words, the firm strives to be better than its competitors at something that customers value.

A focus strategy recognizes that not all markets are homogeneous. The principal idea of this strategy is to select one (or more) segment(s); identify customers' special needs, wants, and interests; and approach them with a good or service designed to excel in meeting these needs, wants, and interests. Focus strategies build on differences among market segments.

5. Understand the importance of controls such as the balanced scorecard in the planning process.
   • Just as a pilot in command of a jet cannot fly safely by focusing on a single instrument, an entrepreneur cannot manage a company by concentrating on a single measurement. The balanced scorecard is a set of measurements unique to a company that includes both financial and operational measures and gives managers a quick yet comprehensive picture of the company's total performance.

DISCUSSION QUESTIONS

1. Why is strategic planning important to a small company?
2. What is a competitive advantage? Why is it important for a small business to establish one?
3. What are the steps in the strategic management process?
4. What are strengths, weaknesses, opportunities, and threats? Give an example of each.
5. What is knowledge management? What benefits does it offer a small company?
6. Explain the characteristics of effective objectives. Why is setting objectives important?

7. What are business strategies? Explain the three basic strategies from which entrepreneurs can choose. Give an example of each one.
8. Describe the three basic strategies available to small companies. Under what conditions is each most successful?
9. How is the controlling process related to the planning process?
10. What is a balanced scorecard? What value does it offer entrepreneurs who are evaluating the success of their current strategies?

STEP INTO THE REAL WORLD

1. Choose an entrepreneur in your community and interview him or her. Does the company have a strategic plan? A mission statement? Why or why not? What does the owner con-

sider the company's strengths and weaknesses to be? What opportunities and threats does the owner perceive? What image is the owner trying to create for the business? Has the effort been successful? (Do you agree?) Which of the generic competitive strategies is the company following? Who are the company's primary competitors? How does the owner rate his or her chances for success in the future (use a low [1] to high [10] scale).

2. Using the resources on your campus or in your community, find an example of a company using each of the three basic strategies described in this chapter: cost leadership, differentiation, and focus. Prepare a brief report on each company explaining how well its strategy is working. What strategic recommendations would you make to each business owner?

3. Contact a local entrepreneur and help him or her devise a balanced scorecard for his or her company. What goals did you and the owner establish in each of the four perspectives?

What measures did you use to judge progress towards those goals?

4. Contact the owner of a small business that competes directly with an industry giant (such as Home Depot, Wal-Mart, Barnes & Noble, or others). What does the owner see as his or her competitive advantage? How does the business communicate this advantage to its customers? What competitive strategy is the owner using? How successful is it? What changes would you suggest the owner make?

5. Use the strategic tools provided in this chapter to help a local small business owner discover his or her firm's strengths, weaknesses, opportunities, and threats; identify the relevant key success factors; and analyze its competitors. Help the owner devise a strategy for success for his or her business.

TAKE IT TO THE NET

Visit the Scarborough/Zimmerer home page at **www.prenhall.com/scarborough** for updated information, online resources, Web-based exercises, and sample business plan.

ENDNOTES

1. Alvin Toffler, "Shocking Truths About the Future," *Journal of Business Strategy*, July/August 1996, p. 6.
2. Thomas A. Stewart, "You Think Your Company's So Smart? Prove It," *Fortune*, April 30, 2001, p. 188.
3. Thomas A. Stewart, "Intellectual Capital: Ten Years Later, How Far We've Come," *Fortune*, May 28, 2001, p. 188.
4. Gary Hamel, "Innovation's New Math," *Fortune*, July 9, 2001, p. 130.
5. Donna Fenn, "Niche Picking," *Inc.*, October 1999, pp. 97–98; Adventurous Traveler, *www.adventurous-traveler.com/*.
6. Dan Morse, "Hardware Distributor Sticks to Nuts-and-Bolts Strategy," *Wall Street Journal*, July 3, 2001, p. B2; Fastenal Company Overview, *www.fastenal.com/inside/overview.asp*.
7. Ray Smilor, *Daring Visionaries: How Entrepreneurs Build Companies, Inspire Allegiance, and Create Wealth* (Avon, MA: Adams Media Corporation, 2001), pp. 12–13.
8. Hermann Simon, "The World's Best Unknown Companies," *Wall Street Journal*, May 20, 1996, p. A18.
9. Thomas A. Stewart, "Why Values Statements Don't Work," *Fortune*, June 10, 1996, p. 137.
10. Michael Barrier, "Back from the Brink," *Nation's Business*, September 1995, p. 21.
11. Tom Chappell, "Heart, Soul, and Toothpaste," *Your Company*, September 1999, pp. 64–68; Tom's of Maine, *www.tomsofmaine.com/*.
12. Miriam Shulman, "Winery with a Mission," *Ethics*, Spring 1996, p. 14.
13. Joshua Kurlantzick, "Finding Profit in Chad," *U.S. News & World Report*, March 5, 2001, p. 45; Jackie Calmes, "Talk of Voting Machine Overhauls Is Heating Up a Niche Market," *Wall Street Journal*, April 30, 2001, p. A20; VoteHere, *www.votehere.com*.
14. American Society of Travel Agents, ASTANet News, *www.astanet.com/news/index.asp#commissioncut*.
15. Stephanie Fitch, "Stringing Them Along," *Forbes*, July 26, 1999, pp. 90–91; C.F. Martin and Company, *www.cfmartin.com/*.
16. Stephanie Gruner, "What Worries CEOs," *Inc.*, February 1997, p. 98; Janean Chun, "Mighty Morphing," *Entrepreneur*, November 1996, p. 16.
17. Carolyn Z. Lawrence, "Know Your Competition," *Business Startups*, April 1997, p. 51.
18. Martha Brannigan, "Cruise Lines Look to the Land to Get Boomers on Board," *Wall Street Journal*, December 6, 1999, p. B.4.

19. Shari Caudron, "I Spy, You Spy," *Industry Week,* October 3, 1994, p. 36.
20. Dan Brekke, "What You Don't Know Can Hurt You," *Smart Business,* March 2001, pp. 64–76.
21. Samuel Greenguard, "Knowledge Management Can Turbocharge Your Company," *Beyond Computing,* November/December 2000, p. 28.
22. Chris Penttila, "Who Knows?" *Entrepreneur,* April 2000, pp. 138–143.
23. Mark Henricks, "In the BHAG," *Entrepreneur,* August 1999, pp. 65–67.
24. Joseph C. Picken and Gregory Dess, "The Seven Traps of Strategic Planning," *Inc.,* November 1996, p. 99.
25. Kambiz Foroohar, "Step Ahead—and Avoid Fads," *Forbes,* November 4, 1996, pp. 172–176.
26. Dorothy Pomerantz. "Raw Deal," *Forbes,* December 25, 2000, pp. 238–239.
27. Debra Phillips, "Leaders of the Pack," *Entrepreneur,* September 1996, p. 127.
28. Kevin Helliker, "How Hardy Are Upscale Gyms?" *Wall Street Journal,* February 9, 2001, pp. B1, B6.
29. Phillips, "Leaders of the Pack."
30. Robert Johnson, "This Pair of Shoes Are Soles of Indiscretion; That's the Point," *Wall Street Journal,* February 25, 2000, pp. A1, A4.
31. Jerry Useem, "New Business, Old War," *FSB,* December 1999/January 2000, pp. 70–74.
32. Mark Borden, "The Monopolists," *FSB,* May 2001, pp. 85–89.
33. Borden, "The Monopolists."
34. Joel Kurtzman, "Is Your Company Off Course? Now You Can Find Out Why," *Fortune,* February 17, 1997, p. 128.
35. Robert S. Kaplan and David P. Norton, "The Balanced Scorecard—Measures That Drive Performance," *Harvard Business Review,* January–February 1992, pp. 71–79.
36. Patricia Schiff Estes, "Survival Training," *Entrepreneur,* September 1997, pp. 78–81.

Chapter 3

Choosing a Form of Ownership

> *Nothing in fine print is ever good.*

—Anonymous

> *It's just paper—all I own is a pickup truck and a little Wal-Mart stock.*

—Sam Walton

Upon completion of this chapter, you will be able to:

1. Describe the advantages and disadvantages of the sole proprietorship.
2. Describe the advantages and disadvantages of the partnership.
3. Describe the advantages and disadvantages of the corporation.
4. Describe the features of the alternative forms of ownership such as the S corporation, the limited liability company, and the joint venture.

Choosing a form of ownership involves making a legal decision with implications that can be far-reaching. For that reason, it is important not to assume you know all the legal issues but to read this chapter carefully and then consult an attorney or accountant to verify whether your choice of ownership best addresses your specific needs. Although any choice is not irreversible, changing the form of ownership can be expensive and often complicated.

Each form of ownership has its own unique set of advantages and disadvantages. The key to choosing the "right" form of ownership is the ability to understand the characteristics of each and knowing how they affect an entrepreneur's business and personal circumstances. Before we examine the more typical legal forms of ownership, the following are the issues the entrepreneur should consider in the evaluation process:

- *Tax considerations.* Because of the graduated tax rates under each form of ownership, the government's constant tinkering with the tax code, and the year-to-year fluctuations in a company's income, an entrepreneur should calculate the firm's tax bill under each ownership option every year.
- *Liability exposure.* Certain forms of ownership offer business owners greater protection from personal liability due to financial problems, faulty products, and a host of other difficulties. Entrepreneurs must weigh the potential for legal and financial liabilities and decide the extent to which they are willing to assume personal responsibility for their companies' obligations.
- *Start-up and future capital requirements.* The form of ownership can impact an entrepreneur's ability to raise start-up capital. Depending on how much capital is needed and the source from which it is to be obtained, some forms of ownership are better when obtaining start-up capital. Also, as a business grows, capital requirements increase, and some forms of ownership make it easier to attract outside financing.
- *Control.* By choosing certain forms of ownership, an entrepreneur automatically gives up some control over the company. Each individual must decide early on how much control he or she is willing to sacrifice in exchange for help from other people or organizations. *For example, the founder of an Internet health portal site diligently labored for over a year to build the operational "skeleton" of a very impressive Web site. This work was done utilizing existing resources and volunteer labor from a large medical organization, but stopped once the existing resources were exhausted. The reason: The founder did not want to give up control to investors who were willing to financially back the venture!*
- *Managerial ability.* Entrepreneurs must assess their own ability to manage their company successfully. If they lack skill or experience in certain areas, they may need to select a form of ownership that allows them to bring individuals who possess those needed skills or experience into the company. *The decline and failure of many high-profile Internet companies during the 2001 economic downturn can in many cases be directly linked to the lack of managerial skills resulting in a series of bad business decisions.*
- *Business goals.* How big and how profitable an entrepreneur plans for the business to become will influence the form of ownership chosen. Businesses often evolve into a different form of ownership as they grow, but moving from some formats can be complex and expensive. For instance, switching from a corporation to a limited liability company can be daunting in the face of current tax laws. *"That conversion gets taxed as though the entire company was liquidated and sold off,"* says tax attorney Jeffery Hart, *"which entails such an exorbitant tax bill that it's not worth doing."* [1]
- *Management succession plans.* When choosing a form of ownership, business owners must look ahead to the day when they will pass their companies on to the next generation or to a buyer. Some forms of ownership make this transition easier. In other cases, when the owner dies—so does the business.
- *Cost of formation.* Some forms of ownership are much more costly and complex to create. Entrepreneurs must weigh carefully the benefits and the costs of the particular form they choose.

Figure 3.1
Forms of U.S.
Businesses by
Percentage of
Number of
Businesses, Sales,
and Net Income,
1997

Source: Internal
Revenue Service, 1997.

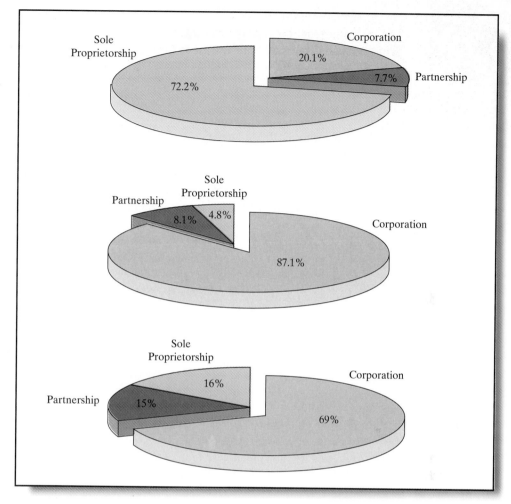

Business owners have traditionally had three major forms of ownership from which to choose: the sole proprietorship, the partnership, and the corporation. See Figure 3.1 for a breakdown of the major forms of ownership. In recent years, various hybrid forms of business ownership have emerged. This chapter will outline the key features of the forms of ownership, beginning with the three most common forms and then moving on to the hybrid forms, including the S corporation, the limited liability company, and the joint venture.

THE SOLE PROPRIETORSHIP

1. Describe the advantages and disadvantages of the sole proprietorship.

The sole proprietorship is a business owned and managed by one individual. Because of its simplicity and ease of formation, this is by far the most popular form of ownership in the United States.

Advantages of a Sole Proprietorship

Simple to Create. One attractive feature of a proprietorship is the ease and speed of its formation. If an entrepreneur wants to form a business under her own name (e.g., J. Allen Financial Consulting), she obtains the necessary business licenses from state,

GAINING THE COMPETITIVE EDGE
What Does the Name of Your Business Convey to Potential Customers?

For some people, something as simple as naming the business seems totally irrelevant. But for one company in Stamford, Connecticut, the choice of a name became the company's worst enemy. GHB Marketing Communications started getting numerous e-mails and phone calls requesting a certain product. Sounds harmless. Right? Wrong! The product that individuals were seeking was GHB—an illegal drug known as ecstasy. "Imagine having a 30-year-old company named LSD, Inc., in the late 60s," says company President Mark Bruce. "Then you can begin to understand what we went through." The new name (HiTechPR) cost the owners $20,000.

Choosing a memorable name can be one of the most fun—and most challenging—aspects of starting a business. Larger companies spend hundreds of thousands of dollars researching names. While small businesses do not normally have unlimited resources at their disposal, you can use the same tools and development process that larger companies use to catch the customer's eye.

Look at your name from your potential customer's perspective. The customer may want to be reassured (Gentle Dentistry) or they may prefer a bit of humor (The Barking Lot Dog Grooming). Other choices might be to convey an image to your customers that is compatible with your business strategy, for example, Discount Hair Products, Quality Muffler, or Pay Less Auto Detailing. In addition, most of us are familiar with the really upscale practice of including foreign phrases (especially French) to convey an exclusive image. La Petite Day Care sounds more up scale than the Small Day Care.

Whatever the image you wish to communicate to an audience of potential customers, the process of choosing the "perfect" name involves a series of steps.

1. Decide the most appropriate single quality of the business that you wish to convey. Avoid sending a mixed or inappropriate message. Remember: A name is the single most visible attribute of your company. It will be displayed on all of your advertising and printed material, it portrays a personality, stands out in a crowd, and sticks in the minds of consumers if done properly.

2. Avoid names that are hard to spell, pronounce, or remember. This is especially true if your business is an Internet company or if you plan on having a Web site. Try typing in posiesbythedozenandthensomefromrosie.com a few times before you decide this is the name for your online flower store!

3. Attempt to select a name that is short, attention getting, and memorable. The name can be your initial marketing tool to attract new customers. Rosiesposies.com may be a better choice than the above example.

4. Be creative, but in good taste!

5. Make sure your choice of a name won't get dated quickly. Big Stiff Hair Salon might have been a great name in the 50s, but it would have died a horrible death in the 60s as long, straight locks became the norm.

6. Be careful that the name, while catchy and cute, doesn't create a negative image. Ask yourself: Does Rent-a-Wreck attract you because you think you'll save money on a car rental or does the name put you off because you question the reliability of their cars?

7. Once you have selected a suitable name, practice using it for a few days. Try it out on friends and family. "Hello, I am the CEO of FlubberDuds" may get on your nerves after the first few times.

8. Finally, after all is said and done and you are comfortable with your choice, conduct a name search to make sure that no one else in your jurisdiction has already claimed the name. This is an especially tedious chore if you are starting an Internet company. Registering a domain name can be daunting because quite often you will find that your brilliant idea is already taken—but it just might be available for the tiny sum of 1.9 million dollars!

There are millions of names in the marketplace. Coming up with the one that is just right for your business can help greatly in creating a brand image for your business. Choosing a name that is distinctive, memorable, and positive can go a long way toward helping you achieve success in your business venture. What's in a name? Everything!

Sources: Elizabeth Weinstein, "GHB Marketing Finds Its Name Is One Thing It Doesn't Want to Plug," *Wall Street Journal*, June 7, 2001; Andrew Raskin, "The Name of the Game," *Inc.*, February 2000, pp. 31–32; Rhonda Adams, "Sometimes Business Success Is All in the Name," *Business*, July 23, 2000, p. 3; Thomas Edmark, "What's in a Name?" *Entrepreneur*, October 1999, pp. 163–165.

county, and/or local governments and begins operation. In most cases, an entrepreneur can complete all of the necessary paperwork in a single day!

Least Costly Form of Ownership to Establish. In addition to being quick and easy to establish, the proprietorship is generally the least expensive form of ownership to establish. There is no need to create and file the legal documents that are recommended for partnerships and are required for corporations. An entrepreneur simply goes to the city or county government, states the nature of the business he or she will start, and pays the appropriate fees and license costs. Paying these fees and license costs gives the entrepreneur the right to conduct business in that particular jurisdiction.

In many jurisdictions, entrepreneurs planning to conduct business under a trade name are usually required to acquire a Certificate of Doing Business under an Assumed Name from the secretary of state. The fee for the certificate is usually nominal. Acquiring this certificate involves conducting a search to determine that the name chosen for the business is not already registered as a trademark or service mark with the secretary of state. Filing this certificate also notifies the state of who owns the business. In a proprietorship, the owner *is* the business. *As an example, Ben Johnson thought that his last name was too common and could be confused with another*

The vast majority of small businesses in the United States are family owned and operated.

restaurant using the Johnson name. Ben opted to use the trade name Zachary O'Riley because it was unique and no competitor had a similar name.

Profit Incentive. One major advantage of the proprietorship is that once the owner has paid all of the company's expenses, he or she can keep the remaining profits (less taxes, of course). The profit incentive is a powerful one, and profits represent an excellent way of "keeping score" in the game of the business.

Total Decision-Making Authority. Because the sole proprietor is in total control of operations, she can respond quickly to changes. The ability to respond quickly is an asset in a rapidly shifting market, so the freedom to set the company's course of action is a major motivational force. For people who thrive on seeking new opportunities, the freedom of fast, flexible decision making is vital.

No Special Legal Restrictions. The proprietorship is the least regulated form of business ownership. In a time when government requests for information seem never-ending, this feature has much merit.

Easy to Discontinue. If the entrepreneur decides to discontinue operations, he can terminate the business quickly, even though he will still be liable for all of the business's outstanding debts and obligations. Although these advantages of a proprietorship are extremely attractive to most individuals contemplating starting a new business, it is important to recognize that this form of ownership has some significant disadvantages.

Disadvantages of a Sole Proprietorship

Unlimited Personal Liability. Probably the greatest disadvantage of a sole proprietorship is the unlimited personal liability of the owner; the sole proprietor is per-

IN THE FOOTSTEPS OF AN ENTREPRENEUR
A Brief History

Many environmental factors must be analyzed when trying to decide which form of ownership is best. Over the past two decades, fluctuating tax rates and changes in the legal environment have had a significant impact on the "popularity" of certain forms of ownership. For example, prior to 1981, maximum individual marginal tax rates exceeded the maximum rates for C corporations. This made C corporations an appealing choice from a tax standpoint. However, the 1981 Tax Act lowered the maximum individual tax rate from 70 percent to 50 percent. At the same time, the maximum corporate rate decreased from 48 percent to 46 percent. Then, in 1986, the Tax Reform Act (TRA 86) established a maximum rate for individuals that was lower than the tax rate for C corporations. The maximum individual rate became 28 percent, compared to the maximum corporate rate of 34 percent. TRA 86 led to an increased popularity of conduit entities such as partnerships and S corporations, vis-à-vis C corporations. Today, the individual rate once again exceeds the corporate rate, though not at the magnitude prior to 1981.

In addition to the impact of changing tax law on the choice of form of ownership, liability or limiting exposure has become a major factor in business planning. Many accounting firms learned a bitter lesson about personal liability in the early 1980s. Accounting firms organized as general partnerships were devastated by their legal responsibility for the savings and loan crisis. Plaintiffs attached the personal assets of partners regardless of direct responsibility for malfeasance. As a result, the S corporation became a viable choice as owners sought to limit their personal legal liability. However, restraints on ownership and capital structure limited the usefulness of the S corporation. Demand rose for a more "hybrid" form of ownership that would offer more flexibility to maximize individual taxpayers' advantage and, at the same time, increase liability protection for owners. In 1988,

the IRS issued Revenue Ruling 88-76, which provided a guide for states to follow the lead of Wyoming (adopted the first LLC statute in 1977) and develop their own LLC law. Then, in 1991, Texas enacted the first LLP statute. Many states initially restricted the use of LLCs by professionals such as physicians and attorneys. LLPs filled this void and provided better liability protection than general partnerships, but somewhat less than LLCs.

For many entrepreneurs, the taxation and personal liability concerns often cloud their reasoning when deciding on a form of ownership. The following are a series of business conditions that are unique to Jody Jeffers and her potential business. You have been asked to evaluate these specific conditions and make a recommendation to her about the most appropriate form of ownership. The conditions are:

1. Three years ago Ms. Jeffers inherited a large sum of money, and, although invested, her earnings place her in the highest federal tax bracket.

2. Ms. Jeffers plans to use the invested funds as collateral to borrow 20 percent of what she needs to start a new business venture.

3. Ms. Jeffers has eight close friends who indicate that they are each willing to invest in the business to cover the remaining 80 percent of financial capital requirements.

4. The business will involve a fleet of automobiles on the road 10 to 15 hours each day.

5. A legal question exists as to whether the drivers are company employees or contract workers.

6. Because this new venture is a dramatic new concept, there is honest debate as to its economic viability.

7. In the event the business fails, an issue to the ownership of some of the firm's inventory would be in question.

Source: Adapted from "C Corporation, LLC, or Sole Proprietorship: What Form Is Best for Your Business?" *Management Accounting Quarterly*, Spring 2000.

sonally liable for all of the business's debts. Remember, in a proprietorship, the owner is the business. The proprietor owns all the business's assets, and if the business fails, creditors can force the sale of those assets to cover its debts. If unpaid business debts remain, creditors can also force the sale of the proprietor's *personal* assets to cover repayment. In short, the company's debts are the owner's debts. Laws vary from one state to another, but most states require creditors to leave the failed business owner a minimum amount of equity in a home, a car, and some personal items. The reality: *Failure of the business can ruin the sole proprietor financially.*

Limited Access to Capital. If the business is to grow and expand, a sole proprietor often needs additional financial resources. However, many proprietors have already put all they have into their business and have used their personal resources as collateral on existing loans, so it is difficult for them to borrow additional funds. A sole proprietorship is limited to whatever capital the owner can contribute and whatever money he can borrow. In short, proprietors, unless they have great personal wealth, find it difficult to raise additional money while maintaining sole ownership. Most banks and other lending institutions have well-defined formulas for determining a borrower's eligibility. Unfortunately, many sole proprietors cannot meet those borrowing requirements, especially in the early days of business. *Retiree Mildred Bostic wanted to own a small business to occupy her time and as a means of increasing her monthly income. To her astonishment, the business grew very rapidly. She was faced with expenses for inventory and expansion that caught her in a "cash crisis." She was too high risk for the bank and too small for major venture capital funding. Her opportunity to expand was frustrated by a lack of access to necessary capital.*

Limited Skills and Abilities. A sole proprietor may not have the wide range of skills running a successful business requires. Each of us has areas in which our education, training, and work experiences have taught us a great deal; yet there are other areas in which our decision-making ability is weak. Many business failures occur because owners lack skills, knowledge, and experience in areas that are vital to business success. Owners tend to push aside problems they do not understand or do not feel comfortable with in favor of those they can solve more easily. Unfortunately, the problems they set aside seldom solve themselves. By the time an owner decides to ask for help in addressing these problems, it may be too late to save the company.

Feelings of Isolation. Running a business alone allows an entrepreneur maximum flexibility, but it also creates feelings of isolation; there is no one to turn to for help in solving problems or getting feedback on a new idea. Most small business owners report that they sometimes feel alone and frightened when they must make decisions knowing that they have nowhere to turn for advice or guidance. The weight of each critical decision rests solely on the proprietor's shoulders. Lee Gardner, the sole proprietor of a company that arranges sponsorships for sporting events, says, "After I set up my company, I realized I was all by myself and responsible for everything. Building a business brick by brick, alone, is not easy."[2]

Lack of Continuity for the Business. Lack of continuity is inherent in a sole proprietorship. If the proprietor dies, retires, or becomes incapacitated, the business automatically terminates. Unless a family member or employee can take over, the business could be in jeopardy. Because people look for secure employment and an opportunity for advancement, proprietorships, being small, often have trouble recruiting and retaining good employees. If no one is trained to run the business, creditors can petition the court to liquidate the assets of the dissolved business to pay outstanding debts.

For founders who have no intention of ultimately creating a large, complex business, a sole proprietorship may be ideal. Some entrepreneurs, however, find that forming partnerships is one way to overcome the disadvantages of the sole proprietorship. For instance, a person who lacks specific managerial skills or has insufficient access to needed capital can compensate for those weaknesses by forming a partnership with someone who has complementary management skills or money to invest.

THE PARTNERSHIP

2. Describe the advantages and disadvantages of the partnership.

A **partnership** is an association of two or more people who co-own a business for the purpose of making a profit. In a partnership the co-owners (partners) share a business's assets, liabilities, and profits according to the terms of a previously established partnership agreement.

The law does not require a written partnership agreement (also known as the articles of partnership), but it is wise to work with an attorney to develop one that spells out the exact status and responsibility of each partner. All too often, the parties think they know what they are agreeing to, only to find later that no real meeting of the minds took place. The **partnership agreement** is a document that states in writing all of the terms of operating the partnership for the protection of each partner involved. Every partnership should be based on a written agreement. Although many do not believe they need such an agreement, when problems arise between partners, the written document becomes invaluable.[3]

When no partnership agreement exists, the Uniform Partner Act (discussed below) governs the partnership, but its provisions may not be as favorable as a specific agreement hammered out among the partners. Creating a partnership agreement is not costly. In most cases, the partners can discuss each of the provisions in advance. Once they have reached an agreement, an attorney can draft the formal document. Banks will often want to see a copy of the partnership agreement before lending the business money. Probably the most important feature of the partnership agreement is that it addresses in advance sources of conflict that could result in partnership battles and the dissolution of a business that could have been successful. Spelling out details—especially sticky ones such as profit splits, contributions, workloads, decision-making authority, dispute resolution, and others—at the outset will help avoid tension in a partnership that could lead to business "divorce." Business divorces, like marital ones, are almost always costly and unpleasant for everyone involved.[4]

A partnership agreement can include any terms the partners want (unless they are illegal). The standard partnership agreement will likely include the following:

1. Name of the partnership.
2. Purpose of the business. What is the reason the partners created the business?
3. Domicile of the business. Where will the business be located?
4. Duration of the partnership. How long will the partnership last?
5. Names of the partners and their legal addresses.
6. Contributions of each partner to the business, at the creation of the partnership and later. This would include each partner's investment in the business. In some situations a partner may contribute assets that are not likely to appear on the balance sheet. Experience, sales contracts, or a good reputation in the community may be some reasons for asking a person to join a partnership.
7. Agreement on how the profits or losses will be distributed.
8. Agreement on salaries or drawing rights against profits for each partner.
9. Procedure for expansion through the addition of new partners.
10. Distribution of the partnership's assets if the partners voluntarily dissolve the partnership.
11. Sale of the partnership interest. How can partners sell their interests in the business?
12. Absence or disability of one of the partners. If a partner is absent or disabled for an extended period of time, should the partnership continue? Will the absent or disabled partner receive the same share of profits as she did before

her absence or disability? Should the absent or disabled partner be held responsible for debts incurred while unable to participate?

13. Voting rights. In many partnerships, partners have unequal voting power. The partners may base their voting rights on their financial or managerial contributions to the business.

14. Decision-making authority. When can partners make decisions on their own, and when must other partners be involved?

15. Financial authority. Which partners are authorized to sign checks, and how many signatures are required to authorize bank transactions?

16. Handling tax matters. The Internal Revenue Service requires partnerships to designate one person to be responsible for handling the partnership's tax matters.

17. Alterations or modifications of the partnership agreement. No document is written to last forever. Partnership agreements should contain provisions for alterations or modifications. As a business grows and changes, partners often find it necessary to update their original agreement. As stated before, in the event there is no written partnership agreement and a dispute arises, the courts will apply the body of law entitled the Uniform Partnership Act.

The Uniform Partnership Act

The **Uniform Partnership Act (UPA)** codifies the body of law dealing with partnerships in the United States. Under the UPA, the three key elements of any partnership are common ownership interest in a business, sharing the business's profits and losses, and the right to participate in managing the operation of the partnership. Under the act, each partner has the right to:

1. Share in the management and operations of the business
2. Share in any profits the business might earn from operations
3. Receive interest on additional advances made to the business
4. Be compensated for expenses incurred in the name of the partnership
5. Have access to the business's books and records
6. Receive a formal accounting of the partnership's business affairs

The UPA also sets forth the partners' general obligation. Each partner is obligated to:

1. Share in any losses sustained by the business
2. Work for the partnership without salary
3. Submit differences that may arise in the conduct of the business to majority vote or arbitration
4. Give the other partner complete information about all business affairs
5. Give a formal accounting of the partnership's business affairs

Beyond what the law prescribes, a partnership is based above all else on mutual trust and respect. Any partnership missing those elements is destined to fail. Like sole proprietorships, partnerships have advantages and disadvantages.

Advantages of the Partnership

Easy to Establish. Like the proprietorship, the partnership is easy and inexpensive to establish. The owners must obtain the necessary business license and submit a minimal number of forms. In most states, partners must file a Certificate for Conducting Business as Partners if the business is run under a trade name.

Complementary Skills. In a sole proprietorship, the owner must wear lots of different hats, and not all of them fit well. In successful partnerships, the parties' skills and abilities complement one another, strengthening the company's managerial foundation. For example, what attracted James Biber to close his practice and join a partnership can be captured in a single phrase—"make work better."[5] Pentagram, a partnership of designers that grows by attracting stars, has created an organization "in which even Biber and his ilk can find more fulfilling work than they could find on their own."

The synergistic effect of partners of equal skill and creativity with whom to collaborate results in outcomes that reflect the contributions of all involved. When it comes to the many new technology-oriented businesses, it is beneficial if at least one of the partners has knowledge and experience at operating a business. Understanding the technological aspects of building a large Internet site or creating an Internet storefront must be supported by a sound understanding of the principles that govern marketing, commerce, business liability, logistics, and a myriad of other factors. Many technology-based firms fail because they lack basic business skills, even though they may otherwise have the technological expertise to succeed.

Division of Profits. There are no restrictions on how partners distribute the company's profits as long as they are consistent with the partnership agreement and do not violate the rights of any partner. The partnership agreement should articulate the nature of each partner's contribution and proportional share of profits. If the partners fail to create an agreement, the UPA says that the partners share equally in the partnership's profits, even if their original capital contributions are unequal.

Larger Pool of Capital. The partnership form of ownership can significantly broaden the pool of capital available to a business. Each partner's asset base will support a larger borrowing capacity than either partner would have had alone. Undercapitalization is a common cause of business failures.

Ability to Attract Limited Partners. Not every partner takes an active role in the operation of a business. Partners who take an active role in managing a company and who share in its rewards, liabilities, and responsibilities are **general partners.** Every partnership must have at least one general partner (although there is no limit on the number of general partners a business can have). General partners have unlimited personal liability for the company's debts and obligations and are expected to take an active role in managing the business.

Limited partners, on the other hand, cannot take an active role in the operation of the company. They have limited personal liability for the company's debts and obligations. If the business fails, they lose only what they have invested in it and no more. Essentially, limited partners are financial investors who do not want to participate in the day-to-day affairs of the partnership. If limited partners are "materially and actively" involved in a business (defined as spending more than 500 hours a year in the company), they will be treated as general partners and will lose their limited liability protection. Silent partners and dormant partners are special types of limited partners. **Silent partners** are not active in a business but generally are known to be members of the partnership. **Dormant partners** are neither active nor generally known to be associated with the business.

A limited partnership can attract many investors by offering them limited liability and the potential to realize a substantial return on their investments if the business is successful. Many individuals find it very profitable to invest in high-potential small businesses, but only if they avoid the disadvantages of unlimited liability while doing so. Limited partnerships will be discussed in greater detail later in this chapter.

Little Governmental Regulation. Like the proprietorship, the partnership form of operation is not burdened with red tape.

Flexibility. Although not as flexible as sole proprietorships, partnerships can generally react quickly to changing market conditions because no giant organization stifles quick and creative responses to new opportunities. In large partnerships, however, getting all partners' approval on key decisions can slow down a company's strategic actions.

Taxation. The partnership itself is not subject to federal taxation. It serves as a conduit for the profit or losses it earns or incurs; its net income or losses are passed through the individual partners as personal income, and the partners, not the business, pay income tax on their distributive shares. The partnership, like the proprietorship, avoids the "double taxation" disadvantage associated with the corporate form of ownership.

Disadvantages of the Partnership

Unlimited Liability of at Least One Partner. At least one member of every partnership must be a general partner. The general partner has unlimited personal liability, even though he or she is often the partner with the fewest personal resources. In most states, certain property belonging to a proprietor or a general partner is exempt from attachment by creditors of a failed business. The most common is the homestead exemption, which allows the debtor's home to be sold to satisfy debt but stipulates that a certain dollar amount be reserved to allow the debtor to find other shelter. Some states require that the debtor have a family before the homestead exemption is allowed. Also, state laws normally exempt certain personal property items from attachments by creditors. For example, household furniture (up to a specified amount), clothing and personal possessions, government or military pensions, and bonuses are protected and cannot be taken to satisfy an outstanding business debt.

Capital Accumulation. Although the partnership form of ownership is superior to the proprietorship to attract capital, it is generally not as effective as the corporate form of ownership, which can raise capital by selling shares of ownership to outside investors.

Difficulty in Disposing of Partnership Interest Without Dissolving the Partnership. Most partnership agreements restrict how partners can dispose of their shares of the business. Often, a partner is required to sell his or her interest to the remaining partner. Even if the original agreement contains such a requirement and clearly delineates how the value of each partner's ownership will be determined, there is no guarantee that other partners will have the financial resources to buy the seller's interest. For example, if the money is not available to purchase a partner's interest, the other partner may be forced to either accept a new partner or to dissolve the partnership, distribute the remaining assets, and begin again. If a partner withdraws from the partnership, the partnership ceases to exist unless there are specific provisions in the partnership agreement for a smooth transition. In the event a general partner dies, becomes incompetent, or withdraws from the business, the partnership automatically dissolves, although it may not terminate (the difference is discussed below). Even when there are numerous partners, if one wishes to disassociate his or her name from the business, the remaining partners will probably form a new partnership.

Lack of Continuity. If one partner dies, significant complications arise. Partnership interest is often nontransferable through inheritance because remaining partners may not want to be in a partnership with the person who inherits the deceased partner's interest. Partners can make provisions in the partnership agreement to avoid dissolution due to death only if all parties agree to accept as partners those who inherit the deceased's interest.

Potential for Personality and Authority Conflicts. Being in a partnership is much like being married. Making sure partners' work habits, goals, ethics, and general business philosophy are compatible is an important step in avoiding a nasty business divorce. Still, as in a marriage, friction among partners is inevitable and can be difficult to control. The key is having a mechanism such as a partnership agreement and open lines of communication for controlling it. The demise of many partnerships can often be traced to interpersonal conflicts and the lack of a partnership agreement for resolving those conflicts.[6] Consider how much conflict could be created when there is a fundamental difference of opinion between partners on one or more critical business decisions.

Partners Are Bound by the Law of Agency. A partner is like a spouse in that decisions made by one, in the name of the partnership, bind all. Each partner is an agent for the business and can legally bind the other partners to a business agreement. Because of this agency power, all partners must exercise good faith and reasonable care in performing their responsibilities. *Consider the case of a partner who dramatically increased the cost of the business when, in the name of the company, she signed a three-year lease for a business jet. Decisions like these ultimately forced the partners to file for bankruptcy.*

Some partnerships survive a lifetime; others experience the difficulties described above. In a general partnership, the continued exposure to personal liability for partners' actions can wear an entrepreneur down. Knowing that they could lose their personal assets because of a partner's bad business decision is a fact of life in partnerships. Conflicts between or among partners could force a business to close. Few partnerships ever put into place a mutually agreed upon means for conflict resolution. The result is that disagreements can escalate to the point where the partnership is dissolved and the business ceases to operate.

Dissolution and Termination of a Partnership

Partnership dissolution is not the same as partnership termination. **Dissolution** occurs when a general partner ceases to be associated with the business. **Termination** is the final act of winding up the partnership as a business. Termination occurs after the partners have expressed their intent to cease operations and all affairs of the partnership have been concluded. In other words, dissolution ends the partnership as a business; termination winds up its affairs. Dissolution occurs as a result of one or more of the following events:

- Expiration of a time period or completion of the project undertaken as delineated in the partnership agreement
- Expressed wish of any general partner to cease operation
- Expulsion of a partner under the provisions of the agreement
- Withdrawal, retirement, insanity, or death of a general partner (except when the partnership agreement provides a method of continuation)
- Bankruptcy of the partnership or of any general partner
- Admission of a new partner resulting in the dissolution of the old partnership and establishment of a new partnership
- A judicial decree that a general partner is insane or permanently incapacitated, making performance or responsibility under the partnership agreement impossible

- Mounting losses that make it impractical for the business to continue
- Impropriety or improper behavior of any general partner that reflects negatively on the business

Limited Partnerships

A **limited partnership,** which is a modification of a general partnership, is composed of at least one general partner and at least one limited partner. In a limited partnership the general partner is treated, under law, exactly as in a general partnership. Limited partners are treated as investors in the business venture, and they have limited liability. They can lose only the amount they have invested in the business.

Most states have ratified the Revised Uniform Partnership Act. To form a limited partnership, the partners must file a Certificate of Limited Partnership in the state in which the partnership plans to conduct business. The Certificate of Limited Partnership should include the following information:

- The name of the limited partnership
- The general character of its business
- The address of the office of the firm's agent authorized to receive summonses or other legal notices
- The name and business address of each partner, specifying which ones are general partners and which are limited partners
- The amount of cash contributions actually made, and agreed to be made in the future, by each partner
- A description of the value of noncash contributions made or to be made by each partner
- The times at which additional contributions are to be made by any of the partners
- Whether and under what conditions a limited partner has the right to grant a limited partner status to an assignee of his or her interest in the partnership
- If agreed upon, the time or the circumstances when a partner may withdraw from the firm (unlike the withdrawal of a general partner, the withdrawal of a limited partner does not automatically dissolve a limited partnership)
- If agreed upon, the amount of, or the method of determining, the funds to be received by a withdrawing partner
- Any right of a partner to receive distributions of cash or other property from the firm, and the circumstances for such distributions
- The time or circumstances when the limited partnership is to be dissolved
- The rights of the remaining general partners to continue the business after the withdrawal of a general partner
- Any other matters the partners want to include

Although limited partners do not have the right to take an active role in managing the business; they can make management suggestions to general partners, inspect the business, and make copies of business records. A limited partner is, of course, entitled to a share of the business's profits as agreed on and specified in the Certificate of Limited Partnership. The primary disadvantage of limited partnerships is the complexity and cost of establishing them.

Master Limited Partnerships

A relatively new form of business structure, **master limited partnerships (MLPs),** are just like regular limited partnerships, except their shares are traded on stock exchanges. They provide most of the same advantages to investors as a corpora-

The honeymoon phase between business owners often is short lived. A failure to address the most important issues in running the business is why conflicts between partners (and often friends), can quickly arise. Business disputes can normally be traced to one or more of the following:

1. The lack of a written agreement between or among all involved that spell out the duties, privileges, and obligations of all owners

2. The incompatibility of the owners as to the ultimate goals of the business

3. The failure to reach agreement on what role each party will play in the decision-making process

The causes of failure serve to reinforce the need to make every effort to obtain a meeting of the minds of all involved on all relevant strategic and operational issues and to commit the agreement to writing. Because all businesses are dynamic and circum-stances change, it is important to include an agreement on how conflicts between co-owners will be resolved.

Some co-owners have established regularly scheduled meeting times to openly discuss the operation of the business and any issues that are producing conflict. These open issue meetings encourage all partners involved to put the facts about the business on the table. These facts would include the current financial statements as well as any documented evaluations of the firm's operations. Sharing and discussing these facts provide a common focus for the owners. Issues that are causing conflict can be dealt with openly and all involved can work together to find workable solutions. Just like in a successful marriage, honesty, openness, and a willingness to deal with issues causing conflict are critical elements in long-term success in a business.

tion—including limited liability. A master limited partnership behaves like a corporation and trades on major stock exchanges like a corporation.[7] Congress originally allowed MLPs to be taxed as partnerships. However, in 1987, it ruled that any MLP not involved in natural resources or real estate would be taxed as a corporation, eliminating their ability to avoid the double taxation disadvantage. Master limited partnership profits typically must be divided among thousands of partners.

Limited Liability Partnerships

Many states now recognize **limited liability partnerships (LLPs)** in which all partners in the business are limited partners, having only limited liability for the debts and obligations of the partnership. Most states restrict LLPs to certain types of professionals such as attorneys, physicians, dentists, accountants, and others. Just as with any limited partnership, the partners must file a Certificate of Limited Partnership in the state in which the partnership plans to conduct business. Also, like every partnership, an LLP does not pay taxes; its income is passed through to the limited partners, who pay taxes on their shares of the company's net income.

THE CORPORATION

The **corporation** is the most complex of the three major forms of business ownership. Corporations make up slightly over 20 percent of the three major forms of ownership (see Figure 3.1 on page 67). However, they are responsible for more than 87 percent of sales and 69 percent of the income gained from the three major forms of owner-

3. Describe the advantages and disadvantages of the corporation.

ship (see Figure 3.1). It is a separate entity apart from most of its owners and may engage in business, make contracts, sue and be sued, and pay taxes. The Supreme Court has defined a corporation as "an artificial being, invisible, intangible, and existing only in contemplation of the law."[8] Because the life of the corporation is independent of its owners, the shareholders can sell their interest in the business.

Corporations (also known as C corporations) are creations of the state. When a corporation is founded, it accepts the regulations and restrictions of the state in which it is incorporated and any other state in which it chooses to do business. A corporation that conducts business in the state in which it is incorporated is a **domestic corporation.** When a corporation conducts business in another state, that state considers it to be a **foreign corporation.** Corporations that are formed in other countries but do business in the United States are **alien corporations.**

Corporations have the power to raise large amounts of capital by selling shares of ownership to outside investors, but many corporations have only a handful of shareholders. **Publicly held corporations** have a large number of shareholders, and their stock is usually traded on one of the large stock exchanges. **Closely held corporations** have shares that are controlled by a relatively small number of people, often family members, relatives, or friends. Their stock is not traded on any stock exchange but instead is passed from one generation to the next. Many small corporations are closely held.

In general, a corporation must report annually its financial operations to its home state's attorney general. These financial reports become public record. If the corporation's stock is sold in more than one state, the corporation must comply with federal regulations governing the sale of corporate securities. There are substantially more reporting requirements for a corporation than for the other forms of ownership.

Requirements for Incorporation

Most states allow entrepreneurs to incorporate without the assistance of an attorney. Some states even provide incorporation kits to help in the incorporation process. Although it is cheaper for entrepreneurs to complete the process themselves, it is not always the best idea.[9] In some states, the application process is complex, and the required forms are confusing. Unless the incorporation process is extremely complicated, an entrepreneur can usually employ an attorney to incorporate their business for a nominal fee. Most new corporations are a great deal less complex than their larger "cousins." Obtaining the advice of a qualified professional is a wise decision for all entrepreneurs to consider when creating or expanding a business.

Once the owners decide to form a corporation, they must choose the state in which to incorporate. If the business will operate in a single state, it usually makes sense to incorporate in that state. States differ—sometimes dramatically—in the requirements they place on the corporations they charter and in how they treat corporations chartered in other states. They also differ in the tax rate imposed on corporations, the restrictions placed on their activities, the capital required to incorporate, and the fees or organization tax charged to incorporate.

Every state requires a Certificate of Incorporation or charter to be filed with the secretary of state. The following information is generally required to be in the Certificate of Incorporation:

- *The corporation's name.* The corporation must choose a name that is not so similar to that of another firm in that state that it causes confusion or lends itself to deception. It must also include a term such as *corporation, incorporated, company,* or *limited* to notify the public that they are dealing with a corporation.

- *The corporation's statement of purpose.* The incorporators must state in general terms the intended nature of the business. The purpose must, of course, be lawful. An illustration might be "to engage in the sale of office furniture and fixtures." The purpose should be broad enough to allow for some expansion in the activities of the business as it develops.
- *The company's time horizon.* Most corporations are formed with no specific termination date; they are formed "for perpetuity." However, it is possible to incorporate for a specific duration (e.g., 50 years).
- *Names and addresses of the incorporators.* The incorporators must be identified in the articles of incorporation and are liable under the law to attest that all information in the articles of incorporation is correct. In some states, one or more of the incorporators must reside in the state in which the corporation is being created.
- *Place of business.* The post office address of the corporation's principal office must be listed. This address, for a domestic corporation, must be in the state in which incorporation takes place.
- *Capital stock authorization.* The articles of incorporation must include the amount and class (or type) of capital stock the corporation wants to be authorized to issue. This is not the number of shares it must issue; a corporation must also define the different classification of stock and any special rights, preferences, or limits each class has.
- *Capital required at the time of incorporation.* Some states require a newly formed corporation to deposit in a bank a specific percentage of the stock's par value before incorporating.
- *Provisions for preemptive rights*, if any, that are granted to stockholders.
- *Restrictions on transferring shares.* Many closely held corporations—those owned by a few shareholders, often family members—require shareholders interested in selling their stocks to offer it first to the corporation. (Shares the corporation itself owns are called **treasury stock.**) To maintain control over their ownership, many closely held corporations exercise this right, known as the **right of first refusal.**
- *Names and addresses of the officers and directors of the corporation.*
- *Rules under which the corporation will operate.* **Bylaws** are the rules and regulations the officers and directors establish for the corporation's internal management and operation.

Once the attorney general of the incorporating state has approved a request for incorporation and the corporation pays its fees, the approved articles of incorporation become its charter. With the charter in hand, the next order of business is to hold an organizational meeting for the stockholders to formally elect directors, who, in turn, will appoint the corporate officers. Corporations may dominate sales and profitability in our economy, but, like the preceding forms of ownership, they have advantages and disadvantages.

Advantages of the Corporation

Limited Liability of Stockholders. The primary reason most entrepreneurs choose to incorporate is to gain the benefit of limited liability, which means that investors can limit their liability to the total amount of their investment. This legal protection of personal assets beyond the business is of critical concern to many potential investors. The shield of limited liability may not be impenetrable, however. Because start-up companies are so risky, lenders and other creditors require the owners to *personally* guarantee loans made to the corporation. Robert Morris Associates, a national organization of bank loan officers, estimates that 95 percent of small business owners have to sign personal guarantees to get the financing they need. By making these guarantees, owners are putting their personal assets at risk (just as in a proprietorship) despite choosing the corporate form of ownership.

Court decisions have extended the personal liability of small corporation owners beyond the financial guarantees that banks and other lenders require, "piercing the corporate veil" much more than ever before. Courts are increasingly holding entrepreneurs personally liable for environmental, pension, and legal claims against their corporations—much to the surprise of owners, who chose the corporate form of ownership to shield themselves from liability.[10] Courts will pierce the corporate veil and hold owners liable for the company's debts and obligations if the owners deliberately commit criminal or negligent acts when handling corporate business. Corporate shareholders most commonly lose their liability protection, however, because owners and officers have commingled corporate funds with their own personal funds. Failing to keep corporate and personal funds separate is most often a problem in closely held corporations.[11] Positive steps that should be taken to avoid legal difficulties include the following:

- *File all of the reports and pay all of the necessary fees required by the state in a timely manner.* Most states require corporations to file reports with the secretary of state on an annual basis. Failing to do so will jeopardize the validity of your corporation and will open the door for personal liability problems for its shareholders.
- *Hold annual meetings to elect officers and directors.* In a closely held corporation, the officers elected may *be* the shareholders, but that does not matter. Corporations formed by an individual are not required to hold meetings, but the sole shareholder must file a written consent form.
- *Keep minutes of every meeting of the officers and directors, even if it takes place in the living room of the founders.* It is a good idea to elect a secretary who is responsible for recording the minutes.
- *Make sure that the corporation's board of directors makes all major decisions.* Problems arise in closely held corporations when one owner makes key decisions alone without consulting the elected board.
- *Make it clear that the business is a corporation by having all officers sign contracts, loan agreements, purchase orders, and other legal documents in the corporation's name rather than their own names.* Failing to designate their status as agents of the corporation can result in the officers' being held personally liable for agreements they think they are signing on the corporation's behalf.
- *Keep corporate assets and the personal assets of the owners separate.* Few things make courts more willing to hold shareholders personally liable for a corporation's debts than commingling corporate and personal assets. In some closely held corporations, owners have been known to use corporate assets to pay their personal expenses (or vice versa) or to mix their personal funds with corporate funds into a single bank account. Don't do it! Protect the corporation's identity by keeping it completely separate from the owners' personal identities.

Despite a more complicated process of initial establishment, corporations have many advantages that have made them both popular and successful in the business world.

Ability to Attract Capital. Because of the protection of limited liability, corporations have proved to be the most effective form of ownership for accumulating large amounts of capital. Limited only by the number of shares authorized in its charter (which can be amended), the corporation can raise money to begin business and expand as opportunity dictates by selling shares of its stock to investors. A corporation can sell its stock to a limited number of private investors (a private placement) or to the public (a public offering).

Ability to Continue Indefinitely. Unless limited by its charter, a corporation is a separate legal entity and can continue indefinitely. Unlike a proprietorship or partnership, in which the death of a founder ends the business, the corporation lives beyond the lives of those who gave it life. This perpetual life gives rise to the next major advantage—transferable ownership.

Transferable Ownership. If stockholders in a corporation are displeased with the business's progress, they can sell their shares to someone else. Millions of shares of stock representing ownership in companies are traded daily on the world's stock exchanges. Shareholders can also transfer their stock through inheritance to a new generation of owners. During all of these transfers of ownership, the corporation continues to conduct business as usual.

Unlike that of large corporations, whose shares are traded on organized stock exchanges, the stock of many small corporations is held by a small number of people ("closely held"), often company founders, family members, or employees. Because only a small number of people hold the stock, the resale market for shares is limited, so the transfer of ownership might be difficult.

Disadvantages of the Corporation

Cost and Time Involved in the Incorporation Process. Corporations can be costly and time consuming to establish. The owners are giving birth to an artificial legal entity, and the gestation period can be prolonged for the novice. In some states, an attorney must handle incorporation, but in most states entrepreneurs can complete all of the required forms alone. However, an owner must exercise great caution when incorporating without the help of an attorney. Also, incorporating a business requires fees that are not applicable to proprietorships or partnerships. Creating a corporation can cost between $500 and $2,500, typically averaging around $1,000.

Double Taxation. Because a corporation is a separate legal entity, it must pay taxes on its net income to the federal, most state, and local governments. Before stockholders receive a penny of its net income as dividends, a corporation must pay these taxes at the corporate tax rate. Then, stockholders must pay taxes on the dividends they receive from these same profits at the individual tax rate. Thus, a corporation's profits are taxed twice—once at the corporate level and again at the individual level. This **double taxation** is a distinct disadvantage of the corporate form of ownership.

Potential for Diminished Managerial Incentives. As corporations grow, they often require additional managerial expertise beyond that which the founder can provide. Because they created their companies and often have most of their personal wealth tied up in them, entrepreneurs have an intense interest in ensuring their success and are willing to make sacrifices for their businesses. Professional managers an entrepreneur brings in to help run the business as it grows do not always have the same degree of interest or loyalty to the company. As a result, the business may suffer without the founder's energy, care, and devotion. One way to minimize this potential problem is to link managers' (and even employees') compensation to the company's financial performance through a profit-sharing or bonus plan. Corporations can also stimulate managers' and employees' incentive on the job by creating an employee stock ownership plan (ESOP) in which managers and employees become shareholders in the company.

Legal Requirements and Regulatory Red Tape. Corporations are subject to more legal and financial requirements than other forms of ownership. Entrepreneurs must resist the temptation to commingle their personal funds with those of the corporation and must meet more stringent requirements for recording and reporting business transactions. They must also hold annual meetings and consult the board of directors about major decisions that are beyond day-to-day operations. Managers may be required to submit some major decisions to the stockholders for approval. Corporations that are publicly held must file quarterly and annual reports with the Securities and Exchange Commission (SEC).

Potential Loss of Control by the Founders. When entrepreneurs sell shares of ownership in their companies, they relinquish some control. Especially when they need large capital infusions for start-up growth, entrepreneurs may have to give up significant amounts of control, so much, in fact, that they become minority shareholders. Losing majority ownership—and therefore control—in their companies leaves founders in a precarious position. They no longer have the power to determine the company's direction; "outsiders" do. In some cases, founders' shares have been so diluted that majority shareholders actually vote them out of their jobs!

The Professional Corporation

A **professional corporation** is designed to offer professionals such as lawyers, doctors, dentists, accountants, and others the advantage of the corporate form of ownership. Corporate ownership is ideally suited for licensed professionals, who must always be concerned about malpractice lawsuits, because it offers limited liability. For example, if three doctors formed a professional corporation, none of them would be liable for the malpractice of the other. (Of course, each would be liable for his or her own actions.) Professional corporations are created in the same way as regular corporations. They often are identified by the abbreviation PC (professional corporation), PA (professional association), or SC (service corporation).

ALTERNATIVE FORMS OF OWNERSHIP

4. Describe the features of the alernative forms of ownership such as the S corporation, the limited liability company, and the joint venture.

In addition to the sole proprietorship, the partnership, and the corporation, entrepreneurs can choose other forms of ownership, including the S corporation, the limited liability company, and the joint venture.

The S Corporation

In 1954, the Internal Revenue Service Code created the Subchapter S corporation. In recent years the IRS has changed the title to S corporation and has made a few modifications in its qualifications. An S corporation is a distinction that is made only for federal income tax purposes and is, in terms of legal characteristics, no different from any other corporation. In 1996, Congress passed legislation to simplify or eliminate some of the restrictive rules and requirements for S corporations so that businesses seeking "S" status must meet the following criteria:

1. It must be a domestic (U.S.) corporation.
2. It cannot have a nonresident alien as a shareholder.
3. It can issue only one class of common stock, which means that all shares must carry the same rights (e.g., the right to dividends or liquidation rights). The

exception is voting rights, which may differ. In other words, an S corporation can issue voting and nonvoting common stock.

4. It cannot have more than 75 shareholders (increased from 35).

By increasing the number of shareholders allowed in S corporations to 75, the new law makes succession planning easier for business owners. Aging founders now can pass their stock on to their children and grandchildren without worrying about exceeding the maximum allowable number of owners. The larger number of shareholders also granted S corporations a greater ability to raise capital by attracting more investors. The new law includes another provision that enables S corporations to raise money more readily. It permits them to sell shares of their stock to certain tax-exempt organizations such as pension funds. (Previous rules limited ownership strictly to individuals, estates, and certain trusts.)

The new law also allows S corporations to own subsidiary companies. Previously, the owners of S corporations had to establish separate businesses if they wanted to launch new ventures, even those closely related to the S corporation. This change is especially beneficial to entrepreneurs with several businesses in related fields. They can establish an S corporation as the "parent" company and then set up multiple subsidiaries as either C or S corporations as "offspring" under it. Because they are separate corporations, the liabilities of one business cannot spill over and destroy the assets of another.

Violating any of the requirements for an S corporation automatically terminates a company's S statues. If a corporation satisfies the definition for an S corporation, the owners must actually elect to be treated as one. The election is made by filing IRS Form 2553 (within the first 75 days of the tax year), and all shareholders must consent to have the corporation treated as an S corporation.

Advantages of an S Corporation. S corporations retain all of the advantages of a regular corporation, such as continuity of existence, transferability of ownership, and limited personal liability for its owners. The most notable provision of the S corporation is that it passes all of its profits or losses through to the individual shareholders and its income is taxed only once at the individual tax rate. Thus, electing S corporation status avoids a primary disadvantage of the regular (or C) corporation—double taxation. In essence, the tax treatment of an S corporation is exactly like that of a partnership; its owners report their proportional shares of the company's profits on their individual income tax returns and pay taxes on those profits at the individual rate (even if they never take the money out of the business). Like the C corporation, the S corporation can serve to bring together the "critical mass" of talent necessary to make a new venture successful. *Applied Science Fiction of Austin, Texas, is a business that combined the talents and skills of principals that Mary Summers describes in her article, "Ménage à Trois," as "a dreamer, a doer, and a schmoozer." Each key player has contributed to the success of the venture.*[12]

Another advantage of the S corporation is that it avoids the tax that C corporations pay on the assets that have appreciated in value and are sold. Also, owners of S corporations enjoy the ability to make year-end payouts to themselves if profits are high. In a C corporation, owners have no such luxury because the IRS watches for excessive compensation to owners and managers.

Disadvantages of an S Corporation. When the 2001 tax legislation was enacted, it restructured individual tax rates, and many business owners switched to S corporations to lower their tax bills. For the first time since Congress enacted the federal income tax in 1913, the maximum individual rate was lower than the maximum corporate rate. However, in 1993, Congress realigned the tax structure by raising the maximum personal tax rate to 39.6 percent from 31 percent. This new rate was 4.6 percent *higher* than the maximum corporate tax rate of 35 percent.

Although these changes make S corporation status much less attractive than before, entrepreneurs considering switching to C corporation status must consider the total impact of such a change on their companies, especially if they pay out a significant amount of earnings to owners. In addition to the tax implications of making the switch from an S corporation, owners should consider the size of the company's net profits, the tax rates of its shareholders, plans (and their timing) to sell the company, and the impact of the C corporation's double taxation penalty on income distributed as dividends. These recent reductions in the upper personal tax rate may alter the calculation used in deciding if the S corporation has an advantage when compared to the standard C corporation.

When Is an S Corporation a Wise Choice? Choosing S corporation status is usually beneficial to start-up companies anticipating net losses and to highly profitable firms with substantial dividends to pay out to shareholders. In these cases, the owner can use the loss to offset other income or is in a lower tax bracket than the corporation, thus saving money in the long run. Companies that plan to reinvest most of their earnings to finance growth also find S corporation status favorable. Small business owners who intend to sell their companies in the near future will prefer S over C status because the taxable gains on the sale of an S corporation are generally lower than those on the sale of a C corporation.

On the other hand, small companies with the following characteristics are *not* likely to benefit from S corporation status:

- Highly profitable personal-service companies with large numbers of shareholders, in which most of the profits are passed on to shareholders as compensation or retirement benefits
- Fast-growing companies that must retain most of their earnings to finance growth and capital spending
- Corporations in which the loss of fringe benefits to shareholders exceeds tax savings
- Corporations in which the income before any compensation to shareholders is less than $100,000 a year
- Corporations with sizeable net operating losses that cannot be used against S corporation earnings

The Limited Liability Company (LLC)

A relatively new creation, the limited liability company (LLC) is, like an S corporation, a cross between a partnership and a corporation. Originating in Wyoming in 1977, LLCs are gaining in popularity because, like S corporations, they combine many of the benefits of the partnership and the corporate forms of ownership but are not subject to many of the restrictions imposed on S corporations. For example, S corporations cannot have more than 75 shareholders, and they are limited to only one class of stock. Those restrictions do not apply to LLCs. Although an LLC can have one owner, most have multiple owners (called members). An LLC offers its owners limited liability without imposing any requirements on their characteristics or any ceiling on their numbers.[13] Unlike a limited partnership, which prohibits limited partners from participating in day-to-day management of the business, an LLC does not restrict its members' ability to become involved in managing the company.

In addition to offering its members the advantage of limited liability, LLCs also avoid the double taxation imposed on C corporations. Like an S corporation, an LLC does not pay income taxes; its income flows through to the members, who are responsible for paying income taxes on their shares of the LLC's net income. Because they are not subject to the many restrictions imposed on other forms of ownership, LLCs offer entrepreneurs another significant advantage: flexibility. Like a partnership, an LLC permits its members to divide income (and thus tax liability) as they see fit.

These advantages make the LLC an ideal form of ownership for small companies in many diverse industries. Moviegoers will recognize the production company, Dream Works SKG. The SKG represents Steven Spielberg, Jeffery Katzenberg, and David Geffen. Dream Works SKG was formed as a limited liability company.

Creating an LLC is much like creating a corporation. Forming an LLC requires an entrepreneur to file two documents with the secretary of state: the articles of organization and the operating agreement. The LLC's **articles of organization,** similar to the corporation's articles of incorporation, establish the company's name, its method of management (board managed or member managed), its duration, and the names and addresses of each organizer. In most states, the company's name must contain the words *limited liability company, limited company,* or the letters LLC or LC. Unlike a corporation, an LLC does not have perpetual life; in most states, an LLC's charter may not exceed 30 years. However, the same factors that would cause a partnership to dissolve would also cause an LLC to dissolve before its charter expired.

The **operating agreement,** similar to a corporation's bylaws, outlines the provisions governing the way the LLC will conduct business. To ensure that their LLCs are classified as partnerships for tax purposes, entrepreneurs must draft the operating agreement carefully. The operating agreement must create an LLC that has more characteristics of a partnership than of a corporation to maintain this favorable tax treatment. Specifically, an LLC cannot have any more than two of the following four corporate characteristics:

1. *Limited liability.* Limited liability exists if no member of the LLC is personally liable for the debts or claims against the company. Because entrepreneurs choosing this form of ownership usually get limited liability protection, the operating agreement almost always contains this characteristic.
2. *Continuity of life.* Continuity of life exists if the company continues to exist despite changes in stock ownership. To avoid continuity of life, any LLC member must have the power to dissolve the company. Most entrepreneurs choose to omit this characteristic from their LLC's operating agreements. Thus, if one member of an LLC resigns, dies, or declares bankruptcy, the LLC automatically dissolves, and all remaining members must vote to keep the company going.
3. *Free transferability of interest.* Free transferability of interest exists if each LLC member has the power to transfer his ownership to another person without the consent of other members. To avoid this characteristic, the operating agreement must state that the recipient of a member's LLC stock cannot become a substitute member without the consent of the remaining members.
4. *Centralized management.* Centralized management exists if a group that does not include all LLC members has the authority to make management decisions and to conduct company business. To avoid this characteristic, the operating agreement must state that the company elects to be "member managed."

Despite their universal appeal to entrepreneurs, LLCs have some disadvantages. For example, they can be expensive to create. Although an LLC may be ideally suited for an entrepreneur launching a new company, it may pose problems for business owners who are considering converting an existing business to an LLC. Switching to an LLC from a general partnership, a limited partnership, or a sole proprietorship reorganizing to bring in new owners is usually not a problem. However, owners of corporations and S corporations would incur large tax obligations if they converted their companies to LLCs.

Table 3.1
Characteristics of the Major Forms of Ownership

FEATURE	SOLE PROPRIETORSHIP	PARTNERSHIP	C CORPORATION	S CORPORATION	LIMITED LIABILITY COMPANY
Owner's personal liability	Unlimited	Unlimited for general partners Limited for limited partners	Limited	Limited	Limited
Number of owners	1	2 or more (at least 1 general partner required)	Any number	Maximum of 75 (with restriction on who they are)	2 or more
Tax liability	Single tax: proprietor pays at individual rate	Single tax: partners pay on their proportional shares at individual rate	Double tax: corporation pays tax and shareholders pay tax on dividends distributed	Single tax: owners pay on their proportional shares at individual rate	Single tax: members pay on their proportional shares at individual rate
Maximum tax rate	39.6%	39.6%	35% (39.6% on distributed dividends)	39.6%	39.6%
Transferability of ownership	Fully transferable through sale or transfer of company assets	May require consent of all partners	Fully transferable	Transferable (but transfer may affect S status)	Usually requires consent of all members
Continuity of business	Ends on death or insanity of proprietor or upon termination by proprietor	Dissolves upon death, insanity, or retirement of a general partner (business may continue)	Perpetual life	Perpetual life	Perpetual life
Cost of formation	Low	Moderate	High	High	High
Liquidity of owner's investment in business	Poor to average	Poor to average	High	High	High
Complexity of formation	Extremely low	Moderate	High	High	High
Ability to raise capital	Low	Moderate	Very high	Moderate to high	High
Formation procedure	No special steps required other than buying necessary licenses	No written partnership agreements required (but highly advisable)	Must meet formal requirements specified by state law	Must follow same procedures as C corporation, then elect S status with IRS	Must meet formal requirements specified by state law

Section II   Building the Business Plan: Beginning Considerations

The Joint Venture

The **joint venture** is very much like a partnership, except that it is formed for a specific, limited purpose. For instance, suppose that you have a 500-acre tract of land 60 miles from Chicago. This land has been cleared and is normally used for farming. One of your friends has solid contacts among major musical groups and would like to put on a concert. You expect prices for your agricultural products to be low this summer, so you and your friend form a joint venture for the specific purpose of staging a three-day concert. Your contribution will be the exclusive use of the land for one month, and your friend will provide all the performers, as well as the technicians, facilities, and equipment. All costs will be paid out of receipts, and the net profits will be split, with you receiving 20 percent for the use of your land. When the concert is over, the facilities removed, and the accounting for all costs completed, you and your friend will split the profits 20–80, and the joint venture will terminate. The "partners" form a new joint venture for each new project they undertake. The income derived from a joint venture is taxed as if it had arisen from a partnership.

In any endeavor in which neither party can effectively achieve the purpose alone; a joint venture becomes the common form of ownership. That's why joint ventures have become increasingly popular in global business dealings. For instance, a small business in the United States may manufacture a product that is in demand in Brazil, but the U.S. firm has no knowledge of how to do business in Brazil. Forming a joint venture with a Brazilian firm that knows the customs and laws of the country, has an established distribution network, and can promote the product effectively could result in a mutually beneficial joint venture.

SUMMARY OF THE MAJOR FORMS OF OWNERSHIP

Table 3.1 summarizes the key features of the sole proprietorship, the partnership, the C corporation, the S corporation, and the limited liability company.

CHAPTER SUMMARY

1. Describe the advantages and disadvantages of the sole proprietorship.
   - A sole proprietorship is a business owned and managed by one individual and is the most popular form of ownership.
   - Sole proprietorships offer these advantages:
     - Simple to create
     - Least costly form to begin
     - Owner has total decision making authority
     - No special legal restrictions
     - Easy to discontinue
   - Sole proprietorships suffer from these disadvantages:
     - Unlimited personal liability of owner
     - Limited managerial skills and capabilities
     - Limited access to capital
     - Lack of continuity

2. Describe the advantages and disadvantages of the partnership.
   - A partnership is an association of two or more people who co-own a business for the purpose of making a profit.
   - Partnerships offer these advantages:
     - Easy to establish
     - Complementary skills of partners
     - Division of profits
     - Larger pool of capital available
     - Ability to attract limited partners
     - Little government regulation
     - Flexibility
     - Tax advantages
   - Partnerships suffer from these disadvantages:
     - Unlimited liability of at least one partner

- Difficulty in disposing of partnership interest
- Lack of continuity
- Potential for personality and authority conflicts
- Partners are bound by the law of agency

3. A limited partnership operates like any other partnership except that it allows limited partners (primary investors that cannot take an active role in managing the business) to become owners without subjecting themselves to unlimited personal liability for the company's debts.
4. Describe the advantages and disadvantages of the corporation.
   - A corporation, the most complex of the three basic forms of ownership, is a separate legal entity. To form a corporation, an entrepreneur must file the articles of incorporation with the state in which the company will incorporate.
   - Corporations offer these advantages:
     - Limited liability of stockholders
     - Ability to attract capital
     - Ability to continue indefinitely
     - Transferable ownership

- Corporations suffer from these disadvantages:
  - Cost and time in incorporating
  - Double taxation
  - Potential for diminished managerial incentives
  - Legal requirements and regulatory red tape
  - Potential loss of control by the founders

5. Describe the advantages and disadvantages of the alternative forms of ownership such as the S corporation, the limited liability company, and the joint venture.
   - An S corporation offers its owners limited liability protection, but avoids the double taxation of C corporations.
   - A limited liability company, like an S corporation, is a cross between a partnership and a corporation. However, it operates without the restrictions imposed on an S corporation. To create a LLC, an entrepreneur must file the articles of organization and the operating agreement with the secretary of state.
   - A joint venture is like a partnership, except that it is formed for a specific purpose.

DISCUSSION QUESTIONS

1. What factors should an entrepreneur consider before choosing a form of ownership?
2. Why are sole proprietorships so popular as a form of ownership?
3. How does personal conflict affect partnerships? How can co-owners avoid personal conflict?
4. What issues should the articles of partnership address? Why are the articles important to a successful partnership?
5. Can one partner commit another to a business deal without the other's consent? Why?
6. Explain the differences between a domestic corporation, a foreign corporation, and an alien corporation.
7. What issues should the Certificate of Incorporation cover?
8. How does an S corporation differ from a regular corporation?
9. How does a joint venture differ from a partnership?
10. What role do limited partners play in a partnership? What will happen if a limited partner takes an active role in managing the business?
11. What advantages does a limited liability company offer over an S corporation? Over a sole proprietorship?
12. How is an LLC created?
13. What criteria must an LLC meet to avoid double taxation?

STEP INTO THE REAL WORLD

1. Interview five local small business owners. What form of ownership did they choose? Why? Prepare a brief report summarizing your findings, and explain advantages and disadvantages those owners face because of their choices.

2. Contact the secretary of state to determine the status of limited liability companies in your state. Are they recognized? How does an entrepreneur create one? What requirements must an LLC meet? Report your findings to the class.

3. Invite entrepreneurs who operate as partners to your classroom. Do they have written partnership agreements? Are their skills complementary? How do they divide the responsibility for running their company? What do they do when disputes and disagreements arise?

4. Find in the Yellow Pages of your local telephone book the names of four businesses that you think are effective marketing tools. Also find four companies whose names do little or nothing to help market their products or services. Explain the reasons for your choices. Select a business with the "wrong" name and work with a team of your classmates to brainstorm a better name.

5. Find three local small businesses that are utilizing the Internet to reach their target audience. Interview the owners to determine their level of online involvement for marketing their product/services regionally and/or nationally. Also, determine from these individuals how they obtained the necessary information for starting a small business (e.g., Small Business Administration, Internet, family, legal counsel, etc). Have them discuss the pros and cons of their choice for information.

Take It to the Net

Visit the Scarborough/Zimmerer home page at **www.prenhall.com/scarborough** for updated information, online resources, Web-based exercises, and sample business plan.

Endnotes

1. Jill Andresky Fraser, "Perfect Form," *Inc.,* December 1997, pp. 155–158.
2. Barbara Bucholz and Margaret Crane, "One-Man Bands," *Your Company,* Summer 1993, p. 24.
3. Jacquelyn Lynn, "Partnership Procedures," *Business Start-Ups,* June 1996, p. 73.
4. Frances Huffman, "Irreconcilable Differences," *Entrepreneur,* February 1992, p. 108.
5. Emily Barker, "The Pentagram Papers," *Inc.,* September 1999, pp. 58–64.
6. Tom McGrath, "How to Fire Your Partner," *Success,* February 1998, p. 49.
7. Manuel Schiffres, "Partnerships with a Plus," *Changing Times,* October 1989, p. 49.
8. Jacquelyn Lynn, "Your Business Inc.," *Business Start-Ups,* July 1996, p. 52.
9. *Kinney Shoe Corporation v. Polan,* 939 D. 2d 209 (4th Cir. 1991).
10. Joan Szabo, "Good News," *Entrepreneur,* January, 1997, pp. 60–62.
11. Kylo-Patrick Hart, "Step 4: Decide Your Legal Structure," *Business Start-Ups,* August 1996, p. 64.
12. Mary Summers, "Ménage à Trois," *Forbes,* October 4, 1999, p. 84.
13. Deborah L. Jacobs, "Choosing a Business Structure," *Your Company,* Winter 1993, pp. 36–41.

Chapter 4

Franchising and the Entrepreneur

> *No mistakes, no experience; no experience, no wisdom.*
>
> —STANLEY GOLDSTEIN

> *The big print giveth, the fine print taketh away.*
>
> —BISHOP FULTON J. SHEEN

Upon completion of this chapter, you will be able to:

1. Explain the importance of franchising in the U.S. economy.
2. Define the concept of franchising and describe the different types of franchises.
3. Describe the benefits and limitations of buying a franchise.
4. Describe the legal aspects of franchising, including the protection offered by the Federal Trade Commission's Trade Regulation Rule.
5. Explain the right way to buy a franchise.
6. Describe a typical franchise contract and some of its provisions.
7. Explain current trends shaping franchising.

1. Explain the role of franchising in the U.S. economy.

Franchising is booming! Much of its popularity arises from its ability to offer those who lack business experience the chance to own and operate a business with a high probability of success. Franchising's growth in recent years has been phenomenal, reaching far beyond the traditional auto dealerships and fast food outlets. Through franchised businesses, consumers can buy nearly every good or service imaginable—from singing telegrams and home cleaning services to waste-eating microbes and tax preparation services. "Franchising is the most successful marketing concept ever created," says trend-tracker John Naisbitt.[1]

Today, some 5,000 franchisors operate more than 600,000 franchise outlets throughout the world, and more are opening at an incredibly fast pace. A new franchise opens somewhere in the United States every 8 minutes and somewhere in the world every 6.5 minutes![2] Because of the many benefits it offers both franchisors and franchisees, franchising has experienced exponential growth rates in the United States and abroad. Franchises now account for 50 percent of all retail sales, totaling more than $1 trillion, and they employ more than 8 million people in more than 100 major industries.[3] Franchising has become an important part of both the American economy and its culture.

WHAT IS FRANCHISING?

2. Define the concept of franchising.

Franchising can be traced to Civil War times when Isaac M. Singer devised a more efficient, less expensive way to sell his Singer sewing machines through franchised outlets. From this meager beginning as a distribution system, franchising has become a major force in the U.S. economy, expanding into a broad range of retail and service businesses. The concept has reached beyond its traditional fast-food roots (which still accounts for about 40 percent of all the goods sold by franchisees) into businesses as diverse as diamond jewelry, on-site furniture repair, in-home pet care, and management training for executives. Retail outlets dominate franchising, accounting for about 85 percent of all franchise sales. However, increasing demand for consumer and business services is producing a boom among service-oriented franchises.

In **franchising,** semi-independent business owners (franchisees) pay fees and royalties to a parent company (franchisor) in return for the right to sell its products or services under the franchisor's trade name and often to use its business format and system. Franchisees do not establish their own autonomous businesses; instead, they buy a "success package" from the franchiser, who shows them how to use it. Ulf Schaefer, who operates a highly successful Play It Again Sports franchise with partner T.J. Western, says, "Buying a franchise is like buying a cookbook: The recipe is there, but you have to do the cooking yourself. But a good franchisor gives you a system—advertising support, group buying power, continuing training, market research and so on. That support . . . is like a little insurance policy."[4]

Franchisees, unlike independent business owners, don't have the freedom to change the way they run their businesses—for example, shifting advertising strategies or adjusting product lines—but they do have a formula for success that the franchisor has worked out. "In fact," says one writer, "the secret to success in franchising is following the formula precisely. . . . Successful franchisors claim that neglecting to follow the formula is one of the chief reasons that franchisees fail."[5] Franchisors develop the business systems their franchisees use to create a standard level of quality and service. This standardization lies at the core of franchising's success as a method of distribution. One writer explains:

> The science of franchising is an exacting one; products and services are
> delivered according to tightly-wrapped operating formulas. There is no

Chapter 4 Franchising and the Entrepreneur

variance. A product is developed and honed under the watchful eye of the franchisor, then offered by franchisees under strict quality standards. The result: a democratization of products and services. Hamburgers that taste as good in Boston as in Beijing. Quick lubes available to everyone, whether they drive a Toyota or a Treblinka.[6]

TYPES OF FRANCHISING

2B. Describe the different types of franchises.

There are three basic types of franchising: trade-name franchising, product distribution franchising, and pure franchising. **Trade-name franchising** involves a brand name such as True Value Hardware or Western Auto. Here, the franchise purchases the right to become identified with the franchisor's trade name without distributing particular products exclusively under the manufacturer's name. **Product distribution franchising** involves licensing the franchisee to sell specific products under the manufacturer's brand name and trademark through a selective, limited distribution network. This system is commonly used to market automobiles (Chevrolet, Chrysler), gasoline products (Exxon, Sunoco, Texaco), soft drinks (Pepsi-Cola, Coca-Cola), bicycles (Schwinn), appliances, cosmetics, and other products. Both of these forms of franchising allow franchisees to acquire some of the parent company's identity.

    Pure (or **comprehensive** or **business format**) **franchising** involves providing the franchisee with a complete business format, including a license for a trade name, the products or services to be sold, the physical plant, the methods of operation, a marketing strategy plan, a quality control process, a two-way communications system, and the necessary business services. The franchisee purchases the right to use all the elements of a fully integrated business operation. Pure franchising is the most rapidly growing of all types of franchising and is common among fast-food restaurants, hotels, business service firms, car rental agencies, educational institutions, beauty aid retailers, and many others.

THE BENEFITS OF BUYING A FRANCHISE

3A. Describe the benefits of buying a franchise.

Perhaps the most important reason franchising has been so successful is the mutual benefits it offers franchisors and franchisees. In a franchising relationship, each party depends on the other for support. The ideal franchising relationship is a partnership based on trust and a willingness to work together for mutual success. Over the long run, the most successful franchisors are those that see their franchisees as partners. They know that *their* success depends on their *franchisees'* success.

    Franchisees get the opportunity to own a small business relatively quickly, and, because of the identification with an established product and brand name, a franchise often reaches the break-even point faster than an independent business would. Still, most new franchise outlets don't break even for at least 6 to 18 months.

    Franchisees also benefit from the franchisor's business experience. In fact, experience is the essence of what a franchisee is buying from a franchisor. Many entrepreneurs go into business by themselves and make many costly mistakes. Given the thin margin for error in the typical start-up, a new business owner cannot afford to make many mistakes. In a franchising arrangement, the franchisor already has worked out the kinks in the system, often by trial and error, and franchisees benefit from that experience. Franchisors have climbed up the learning curve and can share with franchisees the secrets of success they have discovered in the industry. For fran-

IN THE FOOTSTEPS OF AN ENTREPRENEUR
America's First Business Format Franchise

Martha Matilda Harper probably never knew that the word *franchising* is derived from the French word that means "to free from servitude," yet this determined, visionary woman who had spent 25 years as a domestic servant created the first business format franchise in the United States. Born in 1857 in Ontario, Canada, and hired out as a servant at age 7, Harper never had the opportunity to be formally educated, but she quickly learned the skills required for entrepreneurial success. As a young woman, Harper emigrated to Rochester, New York, bringing with her a secret formula for a special shampoo (known as hair tonic in those days) and the lessons learned from years of caring for the hair of the women for whom she had worked.

In 1888, with her life savings of $360, Harper opened Rochester's first hair- and skin-care salon in the most prestigious building in town. A woman opening a business was a major accomplishment in the Victorian era, and the fact that Harper had spent most of her life as a servant made her entrepreneurial move all the more remarkable. (She had to hire an attorney to negotiate the lease after the building's owner refused to deal with her because she was a woman.) Despite stringent Victorian standards that encouraged women to have their hair done in the pri-

Martha Matilda Harper used her wavy floor-length hair as an effective advertising tool for her beauty salons.

vacy of their homes, Harper's salon was highly successful. One of her most effective marketing tools was her own hair, which flowed in beautiful waves to the floor! Superior customer service, something Harper learned during her years of domestic work, became a hallmark of her company. "Base everything on customer service," she preached.

As her business's reputation grew, Harper saw the opportunity to expand her business as out-of-town customers begged her to open salons in their hometowns. Harper encouraged these satisfied customers to recruit other potential clients before she would consider opening a shop in their towns. Knowing that her new shops had to maintain the same standards as the one in Rochester and recognizing that she could not manage each one herself, Harper came up with a new way to do business: franchising! By franchising her salons, she would be able to expand rapidly without draining the capital from her existing business and she could change the destinies of other women as well, helping them get into business for themselves. Harper wanted women who would follow precisely the formula for success she had worked out in her Rochester, New York salon, so she targeted former domestic servants as her franchisees. She understood that high standards that guaranteed customers consistency and quality were keys to expanding her business empire. Her system became known as the Harper Method.

In 1891, the first franchise opened in Buffalo, New York, followed by another in Chicago's Marshall Field department store. Franchisees not only sold the hair- and skin-care products Harper manufactured, but they also attended her beauty training schools that sprang up in cities ranging from Calgary, Canada, to Atlanta, Georgia. Harper also taught her franchisees how to collect information from their customers and to use it to create effective direct-mail advertising campaigns. Harper encouraged her franchisees to establish child-care centers in their salons so that customers could relax and enjoy their visits. She also saw the centers as a way to recruit the children as future customers! Harper's customer-focused business practices paid off, and her list of clients grew to include many famous people of the day, including

(continued)

Chapter 4   Franchising and the Entrepreneur

Susan B. Anthony and first ladies Wilson and Coolidge. Even during the Great Depression, customers continued to visit Harper's franchises, and every one of her salons survived the economic downturn. When she died in 1950, Harper had more than 500 salons bearing her name in the United States, Canada, South America, and Europe.

Martha Matilda Harper truly was a woman ahead of her time, creating a method of doing business that has become one of the most successful in the world!

1. How does business format franchising work?

2. How important was standardization and consistent quality to Harper's franchises? How important are these factors to modern franchisors?

3. What can franchisors do to ensure standardization and consistent quality? What impact do these steps have on franchisees?

Sources: Adapted from Jane R. Plitt, *Martha Matilda Harper and the American Dream: How One Woman Changed the Face of Modern Business* (Syracuse, NY: Syracuse University Press, 2000), p. 120.

chisees, the ability to draw on the franchisor's experience is like having a safety net under them as they build their businesses.

Franchisees also earn a great deal of satisfaction from their work. According to a recent Gallup survey of franchise owners, 71 percent of franchisees said their franchises either met or exceeded their expectations. Plus, 65 percent said they would purchase their franchises again if given the opportunity (compared to just 39 percent of Americans who say they would choose the same job or business again).[7]

Before jumping at a franchise opportunity, an entrepreneur should consider carefully the question: "What can a franchise do for me that I cannot do for myself?" The answer to the question will depend on one's particular situation and is just as important as a systematic evaluation of any franchise opportunity. After careful deliberation, a potential franchisee may conclude that a franchise offers nothing that she could not do on her own; on the other hand, it may turn out that the franchise is the key to success as a business owner.

Let us investigate the specific advantages of buying a franchise.

Management Training and Support. Recall from Chapter 1 that a leading cause of business failure is incompetent management. Franchisors are well aware of this, and, in an attempt to reduce the number of franchise casualties, offer managerial training programs to franchisees prior to opening a new outlet. Many franchisors, especially the well-established ones, also provide follow-up training and counseling services. This service is vital since most franchisors do not require a franchisee to have experience in the business. "Just putting a person in business, giving him a trademark, patting him on the [back], and saying 'Good luck,' is not sufficient," says one franchise consultant.[8]

Training programs often involve both classroom and on-site instruction to teach franchisees the basic operations of the business—from producing and selling the good or service to purchasing raw materials and completing paperwork. Before beginning operations, Subway franchisees take a 55-hour course and then spend an additional 34 hours in on-the-job training at Subways near company headquarters in Milford, Connecticut. Toward the end of their training, franchisees manage a store by themselves, and they must pass a final exam before Subway gives them final approval to become franchisees.[9] Franchisees at Golden Corral learn how to manage a restaurant as well as how to perform every job in a typical 100-employee location, while Dunkin' Donuts trains franchisees for as long as five weeks in everything from accounting to dough making. Although these training programs are beneficial to successfully operating a franchise, franchisees should not expect a two- to five-week program to make them management experts. Management is much too complex to learn in any single crash course.

To ensure franchisees' continued success, many franchisors supplement their start-up training programs with ongoing instruction and support. Franchisors commonly provide field support to franchisees in customer service, quality control, inventory management, and general management. Some franchisors assign field consultants to guide new franchisees through the first week or two of operation after the grand opening. Franchisors offer this support because they realize that their ultimate success depends on the franchisee's success. Because the level of field support provided is one of the most common causes of franchisee–franchisor lawsuits, prospective franchisees should know exactly what the franchise contract says about the nature, extent, and frequency of field support they can expect.

Despite the positive features of training, inherent dangers exist in the trainer–trainee relationship. Every would-be franchisee should be aware that, in some cases, "assistance" from the franchisor tends to drift into "control" over the franchisee's business. Also, some franchisors charge fees for their training services, so the franchisee should know exactly what she is agreeing to, and what it costs.

Brand Name Appeal. Franchisees purchase the right to use a nationally known and advertised brand name for a product or service, giving them the advantage of identifying their businesses with a widely recognized name, which provides a great deal of drawing power. Customers recognize the identifying trademark, the standard symbols, the store design, and the products of an established franchise. Jeff McCoy, who converted his independent electronics store into a Radio Shack franchise, explains, "Name recognition means a lot because it brings in customers who know what they're going to get as soon as they walk through the door."[10] Indeed, one of franchising's basic tenets is cloning the franchisor's success. Nearly everyone is familiar with the golden arches of McDonald's or the red roof of the Red Roof Inn, and the standard products and quality offered at each. A customer is confident that the quality and content of a meal at McDonald's in Fort Lauderdale will be consistent with a meal at a San Francisco McDonald's. One franchising expert explains, "The day you open a McDonald's franchise, you have instant customers. If you choose to open [an independent] hamburger restaurant, . . . you'd have to spend a fortune on advertising and promotion before you'd attract customers."[11]

Standardized Quality of Goods and Services. Because a franchisee purchases a license to sell the franchisor's product or service and the privilege of using the associated brand name, the quality of the goods or service sold determines the franchisor's reputation. Building a sound reputation in business is not achieved quickly, although destroying a good reputation takes no time at all. If some franchisees were allowed to operate at substandard levels, the image of the entire chain would suffer irreparable damage; therefore, franchisors normally demand compliance with uniform standards of quality and service throughout the entire chain. In many cases, the franchisor conducts periodic inspections of local facilities to assist in maintaining acceptable levels of performance. Maintaining quality is so important that most franchisors retain the right to terminate the franchise contract and to repurchase the outlet if the franchisee fails to comply with established standards.

National Advertising Programs. An effective advertising program is essential to the success of virtually all franchise operations. Marketing a brand name product or service over a wide geographic area requires a far-reaching advertising campaign. A regional or national advertising program benefits all franchisees. Normally, such an advertising campaign is organized and controlled by the franchisor. It is financed by each franchisee's contribution of a percentage of monthly sales, usually 1 to 5 percent or a flat monthly fee, into an advertising pool. For example, Subway franchisees pay 3.5 percent of gross revenues to the Subway national advertising program. The franchisor uses this pool of funds to create a cooperative advertising program, which has more impact than if the franchisees spent the same amount of money separately.

Most franchisors also require franchisees to spend a minimum amount on local advertising. To supplement their national advertising efforts, both Wendy's and Burger King require franchisees to spend at least 3 percent of gross sales on local advertising. Some franchisors assist franchisees in designing and producing their local ads. Many companies help franchisees create promotional plans and provide press releases, advertisements, and special materials such as signs and banners for grand openings and special promotions.

Financial Assistance. Because they rely on their franchisees' money to grow their businesses, franchisors typically do not provide any extensive financial help for franchisees. Franchisors rarely make loans to enable franchisees to pay the initial franchise fee. However, once a franchisor locates a suitable prospective franchisee, it may offer the qualified candidate direct financial assistance in specific areas, such as purchasing equipment, inventory, or even the franchise fee. Because the total start-up costs of some franchises are already at breathtaking levels, some franchisors find that they must offer direct financial assistance. *For example, Valvoline Instant Oil Change Franchising Inc., with more than 500 outlets across the United States, offers 100 percent financing to franchisees who lease their land and buildings. Valvoline also offers a mortgage-based financing program for franchisees who choose to purchase rather than lease their franchises' fixed assets, which cost an average of $500,000. The company-sponsored financing programs translate into much lower up-front costs for franchisees. "We've found that financing is a big motivator because it gives our franchisees more options. Financing allows them to expand at the pace they want."*[12]

Nearly half of the International Franchise Association's members indicate that they offer some type of financial assistance to their franchises; however, only one fourth offer direct financial assistance. In most instances, financial assistance takes a form other than direct loans, leases, or short-term credit. Many franchisors offer to help franchisees prepare a business plan or apply for a loan from a bank, the Small Business Administration, or another lender. Franchisors usually are willing to assist qualified franchisees in establishing relationships with banks, private investors, and other sources of funds. Some franchisors have established alliances with lenders to make it easier for their franchisees to get financing. For instance, Dunkin' Donuts has created an arrangement with two national small business lending programs in which its franchisees can qualify for up to 75 percent of the cost of a franchise. Through this preferred lender relationship, Dunkin' Donut franchisees can obtain loans to cover the initial franchise fee, fixtures, vehicles, working capital, and equipment purchases.[13] Support from the franchiser enhances the franchisee's chances of getting the financing they seek because most lenders recognize the lower failure rate among reputable franchises.

Proven Products and Business Formats. What a franchisee essentially is purchasing is the franchisor's experience, expertise, and products. A franchise owner does not have to build the business from scratch. Instead of being forced to rely solely on personal ability to establish a business and attract a clientele, the franchisee can depend on the methods and techniques of an established business. These standardized procedures and operations greatly enhance the franchisee's chances of success and avoid the most inefficient type of learning—trial and error. "When we say 'Do things our way,'" says an executive at Subway Sandwiches & Salads, "it's not just an ego thing on the part of the franchisor. We've proven it works."[14]

Also, franchisees do not have to struggle for recognition in the local marketplace as much as an independent owner might. *Concerned that an independent pet shop would have difficulty competing with much larger stores with greater visibility and name recognition, Stephen Adams decided to take the franchising route into business. After researching their options, Adams and his wife purchased a Pet Valu franchise and are extremely pleased with the results. The business became profitable just a few months after they launched it, and sales are growing at 46 percent a year!*[15]

Reputable franchisors also invest resources in researching and developing new products and services (or improvements on existing ones) and in tracking market trends that influence the success of its product line. In fact, many franchisees cite this as one of the primary benefits of the franchising arrangement.

Centralized Buying Power. A significant advantage a franchisee has over the independent small business owner is participation in the franchisor's centralized and large-volume buying power. If franchisors sell goods and materials to franchisees (not all do), they may pass on to franchisees any cost savings from quantity discounts they earn by buying in volume. For example, it is unlikely that a small, independent ice cream parlor could match the buying power of Baskin-Robbins with its 3,000 retail ice cream stores. In many instances, economies of scale simply preclude the independent owner from competing head-to-head with a franchise operation.

Site Selection and Territorial Protection. A proper location is critical to the success of any small business, and franchises are no exception. In fact, franchise experts consider the three most important factors in franchising to be location, location, and location. Becoming affiliated with a franchisor may be the best way to get into prime locations. McDonald's, for example, is well known for its ability to obtain prime locations in high-traffic areas. Although choosing a location is the franchisee's responsibility, the franchisor usually reserves the right to approve the final site. Many franchisors will make an extensive location analysis for each new outlet (for a fee), including studies of traffic patterns, zoning ordinances, accessibility, and population density. Even if the franchisor does not conduct a site analysis, the franchisee must. A thorough demographic and statistical analysis of potential locations is essential to selecting the site that offers the greatest potential for success. We will discuss these topics in more detail in Chapter 7, Creating a Guerrilla Marketing Plan, and Chapter 16, Location, Layout, and Physical Facilities.

Franchisors also may offer a franchisee territorial protection, which gives the franchisee the right to exclusive distribution of brand name goods or services within a particular geographic area. Under such an agreement, a franchisor agrees not to sell another franchised outlet or to open a company-owned unit within the franchisee's assigned territory. The size of a franchisee's territory varies from company to company. For example, one fast-food restaurant agrees not to license another franchisee within 1.5 miles of existing locations. One soft-serve ice cream and yogurt franchisor defines its franchisees' territories on the basis of zip code designations. The purpose of this protection is to prevent an invasion of existing franchisees' territories and the accompanying dilution of sales. Unfortunately for franchisees, fewer franchisors now offer their franchisees territorial protection.

As the competition for top locations has escalated over the past decade, disputes over the placement of new franchise outlets has become a source of friction between franchisors and franchisees. Existing franchisees charge that franchisors are encroaching on their territories by granting new franchises in such close proximity that their sales are diluted. According to Susan Kezios, president of the American Franchisee Association, territorial encroachment is "the number one problem" for the organization's 7,000 members.[16] Although the new outlets that franchisors grant lie outside the boundaries of existing franchisees' territories, their market coverage and reach overlap those of existing territories, causing sales and profits to decline. A ruling by a court of appeals in California has given franchisees greater protection from encroachment. *When Naugles Inc., a Mexican restaurant chain, opened a company-owned outlet within 1.5 miles of an existing franchisee's location, the franchisee, Vylene Enterprises, charged that Naugles's opening of the new restaurant breached the franchise agreement and violated the implied requirement of fair dealing. Vylene testified that the new outlet caused a 35 percent sales decline at its store. Even though the franchise agreement did not grant Vylene an exclusive territory, the court ruled in Vylene's favor, stating that "Naugles's construction of a competing restaurant within a mile and a half of Vylene's restaurant was a breach of the covenant of good faith and fair dealing."*[17]

Greater Chance for Success. Investing in a franchise is not risk free. Between 200 and 300 new franchise companies enter the market each year, and many of them do not survive. Studies show that nearly 75 percent of new franchisors do not last as many as 10 years.[18] Still, available statistics suggest that franchising is less risky than building a business from the ground up. Approximately 24 percent of new businesses fail by the second year of operation; in contrast, only about 7 to 10 percent of all franchises will fail by the second year. After five years, about 85 percent of franchises are still in business compared to less than 50 percent of independent businesses.[19] This impressive success rate for franchises is attributed to the broad range of services, assistance, and guidance franchisors provide. These statistics must be interpreted carefully, however, because when a franchise is in danger of failing, the franchisor often repurchases or relocates the outlet and does not report it as a failure. According to the American Bar Association's Franchise Committee, one third of the franchisees in a typical franchise system are making a decent profit, one third are breaking even, and one third are losing money.[20]

The risk of purchasing a franchise is two pronged: Success—or failure—depends on an entrepreneur's managerial skills and motivation and the franchisor's business experience and system. "Don't think that because you become a franchisee you'll automatically be successful," warns one franchise consultant. "The franchisor is only providing the tools; the rest is up to you."[21] Many owners are convinced that franchising has been a crucial part of their success. "The business system they get serves as a safety net when launching a business. Many franchisees say that buying a franchise is like going into business *for* yourself but not *by* yourself.

DRAWBACKS OF BUYING A FRANCHISE

Obviously, the benefits of franchising can mean the difference between success and failure for a small business. However, franchisees must sacrifice some freedom to the franchisor. Prospective franchisees must explore other limitations of franchising before buying into this business system. Thoroughly researching potential franchise opportunities is the only way an entrepreneur can find a franchise that is a good match with his or her personality, likes, and dislikes.

3B. Describe the limitations of buying a franchise.

Franchise Fees and Profit Sharing. Virtually all franchisors impose some type of fees and demand a share of the franchisee's sales revenues in return for the use of the franchisor's name, products or services, and business system. Franchise fees and initial capital requirements vary among the different franchisors. The Commerce Department reports that total investments for franchises range from $1,000 for business services up to $10 million for hotel and motel franchises. For example, Jani-King, a home-based commercial cleaning business, sells franchises for $8,200 to $33,500, depending on the territory's size; a Mail Boxes Etc. franchise sells for a total investment of $113,000 to $210,000; and McDonald's requires an investment of $478,000 to $1,400,000 (but McDonald's owns the land and the building). The average start-up cost for a franchise is between $150,000 and $200,000.[22]

Start-up costs for franchises often include numerous additional fees. Most franchisors impose a franchise fee ranging from $5,000 to $50,000 up front for the right to use the company name. Molly Maid, for example, charges a franchise fee of $6,900, and McDonald's up-front franchise fee is $45,000. Other additional start-up costs might include site purchase and preparation, construction, signs, fixtures, equipment, management assistance, and training. Some franchise fees include these costs while others do not. Before signing any contract, a prospective franchisee should determine the total cost of a franchise, something every franchisor is required to disclose in item 10 of its Uniform Franchise Offering Circular (see "Franchising and the Law" on pages 103–106).

Franchisors also impose ongoing royalty fees as profit-sharing devices. The royalty usually involves a percentage of gross sales with a required minimum, or a flat fee levied on the franchise. Royalty fees typically range from 1 percent to 12 percent of sales, although most franchisors assess a rate between 3 and 7 percent. Subway Sandwiches and Salads charges franchisees a royalty of 8 percent, payable weekly. These fees can increase a franchisee's overhead expenses significantly. Because franchisors' royalties and fees are calculated as a percentage of a franchisee's sales, they get paid—even if the franchisee fails to earn a profit. Sometimes unprepared franchisees discover (too late) that the franchisor's royalties and fees are about what the normal profit margin is for a franchise. To avoid such problems, a prospective franchisee should find out which fees are required (some are merely recommended) and then determine what services and benefits the fees cover. One of the best ways to do this is to itemize what you are getting for your money, and then determine whether the cost is reasonable. Be sure to get the details on all expenses—amount, time of payment, and financing arrangements; find out which items, if any, are included in the initial franchise fee and which ones are extra.

Strict Adherence to Standardized Operations. Although franchisees own their businesses, they do not have the autonomy of independent owners. The terms of the franchise agreement govern the franchisor–franchisee relationship. That agreement requires franchisees to operate their outlets according to the principles spelled out in the franchisor's operations manual. Typical topics covered in the manual include operating hours, dress codes, operating policies and procedures, product or service specifications, and confidentiality requirements.

To protect their public image, franchisors require their franchisees to maintain certain operating standards. If a franchise constantly fails to meet the minimum standards established for the business, the franchisor may terminate its license. Determining compliance with standards is usually accomplished by periodic inspections. At times, strict adherence to franchise standards may become a burden to the franchisee.

Restrictions on Purchasing. In the interest of maintaining quality standards, franchisors sometimes require franchisees to purchase products, supplies, or special equipment from the franchisor or from an approved supplier. For example, Kentucky Fried Chicken requires that franchisees use only seasonings blended by a particular company. A poor image for the entire franchise could result from some franchisees using inferior products to cut costs. Franchisees at some chains have filed antitrust suits alleging that franchisors overcharge their outlets for supplies and equipment and eliminate competition by failing to approve alternative suppliers. A franchisor can legally set the prices paid for the products it sells to franchisees but cannot establish the retail prices franchisees charge. Franchisors may suggest retail prices but cannot force the franchisee to abide by them.

Limited Product Line. In most cases, the franchise agreement stipulates that the franchise can sell only those products approved by the franchisor. Unless they are willing to risk license cancellation, franchisees must avoid selling any unapproved products through their outlets. Franchisors strive for standardization in their product lines so that customers, wherever they may be, know what to expect. Some companies allow franchisees to modify their product or service offerings to suit regional or local tastes, but only with the franchisor's approval.

A franchise may be required to carry an unpopular product or be prevented from introducing a desirable one by the franchise agreement. A franchisee's freedom to adapt a product line to local market conditions is restricted. However, some franchisors solicit product suggestions from their franchisees. *In fact, a McDonald's franchisee, Herb Peterson, created the highly successful Egg McMuffin while experimenting with a Teflon-coated egg ring that gave fried eggs rounded corners and a poached appearance. Peterson put his round eggs on English muffins, adorned them with Canadian bacon and melted cheese, and showed his creation to McDonald's chief, Ray Kroc. Kroc devoured two of them and was sold on the idea when Peterson's wife suggested the catchy name. In 1975, McDonald's became the first fast-food franchise to open its doors for breakfast, and the Egg McMuffin became a staple on the breakfast menu.*[23]

Unsatisfactory Training Programs. Every would-be franchisee must be wary of unscrupulous franchisors who promise extensive services, advice, and assistance but deliver nothing. For example, one owner relied on a franchisor to provide what had been described as an "extensive, rigorous training program" after paying a handsome technical assistance fee. The program was nothing but a set of pamphlets and do-it-yourself study guides. Common prey for dishonest franchisors are those impatient entrepreneurs who purchase franchises without investigating the business and never hear from the franchisor again. Although disclosure rules have reduced the severity of the problem, dishonest characters still thrive on unprepared prospective franchisees.

Market Saturation. As the owners of many fast-food and yogurt and ice cream franchises have discovered, market saturation is a very real danger. Although some franchisors offer franchisees territorial protection, many do not. Territorial encroachment has become a hotly contested issue in franchising as growth-seeking franchisors have exhausted most of the prime locations and are now setting up new franchises in close proximity to existing ones. The biggest challenge to the growth potential of franchising is the lack of satisfactory locations. In some areas of the country, franchisees are upset, claiming that their markets are oversaturated and their sales are suffering.

Another challenge to territorial protection for franchisees is the Internet. Increasingly, franchisors are setting up Web sites, which some franchisees say are taking sales from their outlets and are in violation of their exclusive territory agreements. Franchisees of one drug store chain recently filed arbitration claims to block the franchisor from competing with them by selling products over its Web site. The

Table 4.1
A Franchise
Evaluation Quiz

Taking the emotion out of buying a franchise is the goal of this self-test developed by Franchise Solutions, Inc., a franchise consulting company in Portsmouth, New Hampshire. Circle the number that reflects your degree of certainty or positive feelings for each of the following 12 statements: 1 is low; 5 is high.

	Low				High
1. I would really enjoy being in this kind of business.	1	2	3	4	5
2. This franchise will meet or exceed my income goals.	1	2	3	4	5
3. My people-handling skills are sufficient for this franchise.	1	2	3	4	5
4. I understand fully my greatest challenge in this franchise, and I feel comfortable with my abilities.	1	2	3	4	5
5. I have met with the company management and feel compatible.	1	2	3	4	5
6. I understand the risks with this business and am prepared to accept them.	1	2	3	4	5
7. I have researched the competition in my area and feel comfortable with the potential market.	1	2	3	4	5
8. My family and friends think this is a great opportunity for me.	1	2	3	4	5
9. I have had an adviser review the disclosure documents and the franchise agreement.	1	2	3	4	5
10. I have contacted a representative number of the existing franchisees; they were overwhelmingly positive.	1	2	3	4	5
11. I have researched this industry and feel comfortable about the long-term growth potential.	1	2	3	4	5
12. My background and experience make franchise an ideal choice.	1	2	3	4	5

The maximum score on the quiz is 60. A score of 45 or below means that either the franchise opportunity is unsuitable or that you need to do more research on the franchise you are considering.

Source: Roberta Maynard, "Choosing a Franchise," *Nation's Business,* October 1996, p. 57.

franchisor denied that its Web site was cannibalizing sales of its franchised outlets and claimed that the site would promote the entire company's brand.[24]

Less Freedom. When franchisees purchase their franchises and sign the contract, they agree to sell the franchisor's product or service by following its prescribed formula. When McDonald's rolls out a new national product, for instance, all franchisees put it on their menus. Franchisors want to ensure success, and most monitor their franchisees' performances closely. Strict uniformity is the rule rather than the exception. Entrepreneurs who want to be their own bosses and to avoid being subject to the control of others will most likely be frustrated as franchisees. Highly independent, "go-my-own-way" individuals probably should not choose the franchise route to business ownership. Table 4.1 offers a Franchise Evaluation Quiz designed to help potential franchisees decide whether or not a franchise is right for them.

FRANCHISING AND THE LAW

The franchising boom spearheaded by McDonald's in the late 1950s brought with it many prime investment opportunities. However, the explosion of legitimate franchises also ushered in with it several fly-by-night franchisors who defrauded their franchisees. In response to these specific incidents and to the potential for deception inherent in a franchise relationship, California in 1971 enacted the first Franchise Investment Law. The law (and those of 13 other states* that have since passed similar laws) requires franchisors to register a **Uniform Franchise Offering Circular (UFOC)** and deliver a copy to prospective franchisees before any offer or sale of a franchise. The UFOC establishes full disclosure guidelines for the franchising company and gives potential franchisees the ability to protect themselves from unscrupulous franchisors running fly-by-night operations.

In October 1979, the Federal Trade Commission (FTC) enacted the **Trade Regulation Rule,** requiring all franchisors to disclose detailed information on their operations at the first personal meeting or at least 10 days before a franchise contract is signed or any money is paid. The FTC rule covers all franchisers, even those in the 36 states lacking franchise disclosure laws. The purpose of the regulation is to assist the potential franchisee's investigation of the franchise deal and to introduce consistency into the franchisor's disclosure statements. In 1994, the FTC modified the requirements for the UFOC, making more information available to prospective franchisees and making the document easier to read and understand. The FTC's philosophy is not so much to prosecute abusers as to provide information to prospective franchisees and help them make intelligent decisions. Although the FTC requires each franchisor to provide a potential franchisee with this information, it does not verify its accuracy. Prospective franchisees should use these data only as a starting point for the investigation. The Trade Regulation Rule requires a franchisor to include in its disclosure statement a sample franchise contract, audited financial statements for three years, and information on the following 23 major topics:

1. Information identifying the franchisor and its affiliates, and describing their business experience and the franchises being sold.
2. Information identifying and describing the business experience of each of the franchisor's officers, directors, and management personnel responsible for the franchise program.
3. A description of the lawsuits in which the franchisor and its officers, directors, and managers have been involved.
4. Information about any bankruptcies in which the franchisor and its officers, directors, and managers have been involved.
5. Information about the initial franchise fee and other payments required to obtain the franchise, including the intended use of the fees.
6. A description of any other continuing payments franchisees are required to make after start-up, including royalties, service fees, training fees, lease payments, advertising charges, and others.
7. A detailed description of the payments a franchisee must make to fulfill the initial investment requirement and how and to whom they are made. The categories covered are initial franchise fee, equipment, opening inventory, initial advertising fee, signs, training, real estate, working capital, legal, accounting and utilities.
8. Information about quality restrictions on goods and services used in the franchise and where they may be purchased, including restricted purchases from the franchises.

---

* The 14 states requiring franchise registration are: California, Hawaii, Illinois, Indiana, Iowa, Maryland, Minnesota, New York, North Dakota, Rhode Island, South Dakota, Virginia, Washington, and Wisconsin.

Section II   Building the Business Plan: Beginning Considerations

9. Information covering requirements to purchase goods, services, equipment, supplies, inventory, and other items from approved suppliers (including the franchisor).
10. A description of any financial assistance available from the franchisor in the purchase of the franchise.
11. A description of all obligations the franchisor must fulfill in helping a franchisee prepare to open and then open and operate a unit, plus information covering location selection methods and the training program provided to franchisees.
12. A description of any territorial protection that will be granted to the franchise and a statement as to whether the franchisor may locate a company-owned store or other outlet in that territory.
13. All relevant information about the franchisor's trademarks, service marks, trade names, logos, and commercial symbols, including where they are registered.
14. Similar information on any patents and copyrights the franchisor owns, and the rights to these transferred to franchisees.
15. A description of the extent to which franchisees must participate personally in the operation of the franchise.
16. A description of any restrictions on the goods or services franchises are permitted to sell and with whom franchisees may deal.
17. A description of the conditions under which the franchise may be repurchased or refused renewal by the franchisor, transferred to a third party by the franchisee, and terminated or modified by either party.
18. A description of the involvement of celebrities and public figures in the franchise.
19. A complete statement of the basis for any earnings claims made to the franchisee, including the percentage of existing franchises that have actually achieved the results that are claimed. New rules put two requirements on franchisers making earnings claims: (1) Any earnings claim must be included in the UFOC, and (2) the claim must "have a reasonable basis at the time it is made." However, franchisors are not required to make any earnings claims at all; in fact, 80 percent of franchisors don't make earnings claims in their circulars, primarily because of liability concerns about committing such numbers to paper.[25]
20. Statistical information about the present number of franchises; the number of franchises projected for the future; the number of franchises terminated; the number the franchisor has not renewed; the number repurchased in the past; and a list of the names and addresses of other franchises.
21. The financial statements of the franchisors.
22. A copy of all franchise and other contracts (leases, purchase agreements, etc.) the franchisee will be required to sign.
23. A standardized, detachable "receipt" to prove that the prospective franchisee received a copy of the UFOC.

The typical UFOC is about 100 pages long, but every potential franchisee should take the time to read and understand it. Unfortunately, most do not, which often results in unpleasant surprises for uninformed franchisees. The information contained in the UFOC does not fully protect potential franchisees from deception, nor does it guarantee success. It does, however, provide enough information to begin a thorough investigation of the franchisor and the franchise deal. Many experts recommend that potential franchisees have an experienced franchise attorney or consultant review a company's UFOC before they invest. The UFOC is a valuable tool for prospective franchisees, giving them the information they need to make informed decisions, saving them time, and providing them with more complete information about a franchise.

HOW TO BUY A FRANCHISE

6. Explain the right way to buy a franchise.

If used, the UFOC can help potential franchisees avoid dishonest franchisors. The best defenses a prospective entrepreneur has against unscrupulous franchisors are preparation, common sense, and patience. By investigating thoroughly before investing in a franchise, potential franchisees eliminate the risk of being hoodwinked into a nonexistent business. Asking the right questions and resisting the urge to rush into an investment decision helps a potential franchisee avoid unscrupulous franchisors.

The president of a franchise consulting firm estimates that 5 to 10 percent of franchisors are dishonest—"the rogue elephants of franchising." Potential franchisees must beware. Franchise fraud has become a major growth market in the United States in recent years. Because dishonest franchisors tend to follow certain patterns, well-prepared franchisees can avoid getting burned. The following clues should arouse the suspicion of an entrepreneur about to invest in a franchise:

- Claims that the franchise contract is a standard one and that "you don't need to read it"
- A franchisor who fails to give you a copy of the required disclosure document at your first face-to-face meeting
- A marginally successful prototype store or no prototype at all
- A poorly prepared operations manual outlining the franchise system or no manual (or system) at all
- Oral promises of future earnings without written documentation
- A high franchisee turnover rate or a high termination rate
- An unusual amount of litigation brought against the franchisor
- Attempts to discourage you from allowing an attorney to evaluate the franchise contract before you sign it
- No written documentation to support claims and promises
- A high-pressure sale—sign the contract now or lose the opportunity
- Claiming to be exempt from federal laws requiring complete disclosure of franchise details
- "Get-rich-quick schemes," promises of huge profits with only minimum effort
- Reluctance to provide a list of present franchisees for you to interview
- Evasive, vague answers to your questions about the franchise and its operation

Not every franchise "horror story" is the result of dishonest franchisors. More often than not, the problems that arise in franchising have more to do with franchisees who buy legitimate franchises without proper research and analysis. They end up in businesses they don't enjoy and that they are not well suited to operate. The following steps will help any franchisee make the right choice.

Evaluate Yourself. Henry David Thoreau's advice to "Know thyself" is excellent advice for prospective franchisees. Before looking at any franchise, entrepreneurs should study their own personalities, experiences, likes, dislikes, goals, and expectations. Will you be comfortable working in a structured environment? What kinds of franchises fit your desired lifestyle? Do you want to sell a product or a service? Do you want to work with the public? Do you enjoy selling? What hours do you expect to work? Do you mind getting dirty? Do you want to work with people or do you prefer to work alone? Which franchise concepts mesh best with your past work experience? What activities and hobbies do you enjoy? What income do you expect a franchise to generate? How much can you afford to invest in a franchise? Will you be happy with the daily routine of operating the franchise? Most franchise contracts run for 10 years or more, making it imperative that prospective franchisees conduct a complete inventory of their interests, likes, dislikes, and abilities before buying a franchise.

Research the Market. Before shopping for a franchise, entrepreneurs should research the market in the areas they plan to serve. How fast is the overall area growing? In which areas is that growth occurring fastest? Is the market for the franchise's product or service growing or declining? Investing some time in the library or on the World Wide Web developing a profile of the customers in the target area is essential; otherwise, the potential franchisee is flying blindly. Who are your potential customers? What are their characteristics? What are their income and education levels? What kinds of products and services do they buy? What gaps exist in the market? These gaps represent potential franchise opportunities for you.

Solid market research should tell a prospective franchisee whether or not a particular franchise is merely a passing fad. Steering clear of fads and into long-term trends is a key to sustained success in franchising. The secret to distinguishing between a fad that will soon fizzle and a meaningful trend that offers genuine opportunity is finding products or services that are consistent with fundamental demographic and lifestyle patterns of the population. That requires sound market research that focuses not only on local market opportunities but also on the "big picture." For instance, the prevalence of dual-career couples, available disposable income, and hectic schedules is creating a booming business for maid service and home improvement and repair franchises.

Consider Your Franchise Options. Tracking down information on prospective franchise systems is easier now than ever before. The International Franchise Association publishes the Franchise Opportunities Guide, which lists its members and some basic information about them. Many cities host franchise trade shows throughout the year, where hundreds of franchisors gather to sell their franchises. Many business magazines, such as *Entrepreneur, Inc., Fortune Small Business,* and others, devote at least one issue to franchising, in which they often list hundreds of franchises. Plus, most franchisors now publish information about their systems on the World Wide Web. These listings can help potential franchisees find a suitable franchise within their price ranges.

Get a Copy of the Franchisor's UFOC and Study It. Once you narrow down your franchise choices, you should contact each franchise and get a copy of its UFOC. Then read it! This document is an important tool in your search for the right franchise, and you should make the most of it. When evaluating a franchise opportunity, what should a potential franchisee look for? Although there's never a guarantee of success, the following characteristics make a franchise stand out:

- *A unique concept or marketing approach.* "Me-too" franchises are no more successful than "me-too" independent businesses. Pizza franchisor Papa John's has achieved an impressive growth rate by emphasizing the quality of its ingredients, while Domino's is known for its fast delivery.
- *Profitability.* A franchisor should have a track record of profitability and so should its franchisees. If a franchisor is not profitable, its franchisees are not likely to be either. Franchisees who follow the business format should expect to earn a reasonable rate of return.

- *A registered trademark.* Name recognition is difficult to achieve without a well-known and protected trademark.
- *A business system that works.* A franchisor should have in place a system that is efficient and is well documented in its manuals.
- *A solid training program.* One of the most valuable components of a franchise system is the training it offers franchisees. The system should be relatively easy to teach.
- *Affordability.* A franchisee should not have to take on an excessive amount of debt to purchase a franchise. Being forced to borrow too much money to open a franchise outlet can doom a business from the outset. Respectable franchisors verify prospective franchisees' financial qualifications as part of the screening process.
- *A positive relationship with franchisees.* The most successful franchises are those that see their franchisees as partners—and treat them accordingly.

The UFOC covers the 23 items discussed in the previous section and includes a copy of the company's franchise agreement and any contracts accompanying it. Although the law requires a UFOC to be written in plain English rather than "legalese," it is best to have an attorney experienced in franchising review the UFOC and discuss its provisions with you. The franchise contract summarizes the details that will govern the franchisor–franchisee relationship over its life. It outlines exactly the rights and the obligations of each party and sets the guidelines that govern the franchise relationship. Franchise contracts typically are long term; 50 percent run for 15 years or more, so it is extremely important for prospective franchisees to understand their terms before they sign them.

Particular items in the UFOC that entrepreneurs should focus on include the franchisor's experience (items 1 and 2), the current and past litigation against the franchisor (item 3), the fees and total investment (items 5, 6, and 7), and the franchisee turnover rate for the past three years (item 20). The **franchisee turnover rate,** the rate at which franchisees leave the system, is one of the most revealing items in the UFOC. If the turnover rate is less than 5 percent, the franchise is probably sound. However, a rate approaching 20 percent is a sign of serious, underlying problems in a franchise. Although virtually every franchisor has been involved in lawsuits, an excessive amount of litigation against a franchisor should also alert a prospective franchisee to potential problems down the road. Determining what the cases were about and whether or not they have been resolved is important.

Talk to Existing Franchisees. Although the UFOC contains much valuable information, it is only the starting point for researching a franchise opportunity thoroughly. Perhaps the best way to evaluate the reputation of a franchisor is to interview (in person) several franchise owners who have been in business at least one year about the positive and the negative features of the agreement and whether the franchisor delivered what it promised. Knowing what they know now, would they buy the franchise again? *After investment banker Todd Recknagel narrowed the field of franchises he was considering, he spent time interviewing several franchisees about their experiences with the franchisors. Based on his findings, Recknagel decided to purchase a Blimpie Subs and Salads franchise. Recknagel's research paid off; in less than six years, he has built eight outlets and was named Franchisee of the Year both by Blimpie and the International Franchise Association.*[26] Item 20 of the UFOC lists all of a company's franchisees and their addresses by state, making it easy for potential franchisees to contact them.

It is also wise to interview past franchisees to get their perspectives on the franchisor–franchisee relationship. (UFOC item 20 also lists those franchisees who have left the system within the past fiscal year.) Why did they leave? Franchisees of some

Table 4.2
Questions to Ask Existing Franchisees

A key ingredient in any prospective franchisee's evaluation of a franchise opportunity is to visit existing franchisees and ask them questions about their relationship with the franchisor. The following questions will reveal how well the franchisor supports its franchisees and the nature of the franchisor–franchisee relationship.

- How much did it cost to start your franchise?
- How much training did you receive at the outset? How helpful was it? Did it prepare you to run your franchise?
- Does the franchisor provide you with adequate ongoing support? How much? Are you pleased with the level of support you receive? What is the nature of this support?
- Is the company available to answer your questions? How often do you contact the company? What is the typical response?
- How much marketing assistance does the franchisor provide? Is it effective? How can you tell?
- Do franchisees have input into the development of new products or services?
- Which of your expectations has the franchisor met? Failed to meet?
- How often does someone from the franchise check on your operation? What is the purpose of those visits?
- What is a "typical day" like for you? How do you spend most of your time?
- Which day-to-day tasks do you enjoy performing most? Least?
- How much did your franchise gross last year? How much do you expect to gross this year? What has been the pattern of your outlet's sales since you started?
- Is your franchise making a profit? If so, how much? What is your net profit margin?
- How long did you operate before your outlet began to earn a profit? Is your outlet consistently profitable?
- What is your franchise's break-even point?
- Has your franchise met your expectations for return on investment (ROI)?
- Is this business seasonal? If so, how do you get through the off season?
- Is there a franchisee association? Do you belong to it? What is its primary function?
- Does the franchisor sponsor system-wide meetings? Do you attend? Why?
- Does the franchisor listen to franchisees?
- What changes would you recommend the franchisor make in its business system?
- Where do you purchase supplies, equipment, and products for your franchise?
- How much freedom do you have to run your business?
- Does the franchisor encourage franchisees to apply their creativity to running their businesses, or does it frown on innovation in the system?
- Has the franchisor given you the tools you need to compete effectively?
- How much are your royalty payments and franchise fees? What do you get in exchange for your royalty payments? Do you consider it to be a good value?
- Are you planning to purchase additional territories or franchises? Why?
- Has the franchisor lived up to its promises?
- Looking back, what portions of the franchise contract would you change?
- What are communications with the franchisor like?
- How would you describe franchisees' relationship with the franchisor? How would you describe your relationship with the franchisor?
- Are most franchisees happy with the franchise system? With the franchisor?
- What advice would you give to someone considering purchasing a franchise from this franchisor?
- Knowing what you know now, would you buy this franchise again?

Sources: Adapted from Andrew A. Caffey, "Analyze This," *Entrepreneur*, January 2000, pp. 163–167; Roger Brown, "Ask More Questions of More People Before Deciding, Then Plan to Work Very Hard," *Small Business Forum*, Winter 1996/1997, pp. 91–93; Roberta Maynard, "Choosing a Franchise," *Nation's Business*, October 1996, pp. 56–63; Andrew A. Caffey, "The Buying Game," *Entrepreneur*, January 1997, pp. 174–177; Julie Bawden Davis, "A Perfect Match," *Business Start-Ups*, July 1997, pp. 44–49.

companies have formed associations, which might provide prospective franchisees with valuable information. Other sources of information include the American Association of Franchisees and Dealers, the American Franchise Association, and the International Franchise Association. Table 4.2 offers some important questions to ask existing franchisees.

Ask the Franchisor Some Tough Questions. Take the time to visit the franchisor's headquarters and ask plenty of questions about the company and its relationship with its franchisees. You will be in this relationship a long time, and you need to know as much about it as you possibly can beforehand. What is its philosophy concerning the relationship? What is the company culture like? How much input do franchisees have into the system? What are the franchisor's future expansion plans? How will they affect your franchise? What kind of profits can you expect? (If the franchisor made no earnings claims in item 19 of the UFOC, why not?) Does the franchisor have a well-formulated strategic plan?

Make Your Choice. The first lesson in franchising is "Do your homework before you get out your checkbook." Once you have done your research, you can make an informed choice about which franchise is right for you. Then it is time to put together a solid business plan that will serve as your road map to success in the franchise you have selected. The plan is also a valuable tool to use as you arrange the financing for your franchise. We will discuss the components of a business plan in Chapter 9.

FRANCHISE CONTRACTS

7. Describe a typical franchise contract and some of its provisions.

The amount of franchisor–franchisee litigation has risen steadily over the past decade. A common source of much of this litigation is the interpretation of the franchise contract's terms. Most often, difficulties arise after the agreement is in operation. Typically, because the franchisor's attorney prepares franchise contracts, the provisions favor the franchisor. Courts have relatively little statutory law and few precedents on which to base decisions in franchise disputes, resulting in minimal protection for franchisees. The problem stems from the tremendous growth of franchising, which has outstripped the growth of franchise law.

The contract summarizes the details that will govern the franchisor–franchisee relationship over its life. It outlines exactly the rights and the obligations of each party and sets the guidelines that govern the franchise relationship. To protect potential franchisees from having to rush into a contract without clearly understanding it, the Federal Trade Commission requires that the franchisee receive the completed contract with all revisions at least five business days before it is signed. Despite such protection, one study by the FTC suggests that 40 percent of new franchisees sign contracts *without reading them!*[27]

Every potential franchisee should have an attorney evaluate the franchise contract and review it with the investor before he signs anything. Too many franchisors don't discover unfavorable terms in their contracts until *after* they have invested in a franchise. By then, however, it's too late to negotiate changes. Although most large, established franchisors are not willing to negotiate the franchise contract's terms, many smaller franchises will, especially for highly qualified candidates. Although franchise contracts cover everything from initial fees and continuing payments to training programs and territorial protection, three terms are responsible for most franchisor–franchisee disputes: termination of the contract, contract renewal, and transfer and buyback provisions.

As sales growth in franchise outlets in the United States have flattened over the past several years, more franchisors are looking to foreign markets to fuel their growth. In fact, many companies are taking their standardized products, services, and business systems on a global jaunt with a vengeance. For instance, KFC (Kentucky Fried Chicken) Corporation is moving into China, where a population of 1.3 billion people offers a huge potential market. KFC, the first foreign fast-food chain allowed to open outlets in China, has established itself as the most recognizable foreign brand in China. Customers in China flock to KFC outlets despite the fact that a meal costs the equivalent of six hours' work for the average person. The company has 500 stores there and is planning to have 5,000 outlets open within 20 years. Negotiating the labyrinth of government regulations and red tape can be challenging and time consuming, but KFC officials have learned to be patient and persistent.

The leader in global franchising, however, is McDonald's, which serves customers on every continent on the globe except Antarctica! The company has more than 28,000 restaurants in 121 countries. Just how does McDonald's export the key to its success around the globe? By following several simple strategies:

- Gather people together often for face-to-face meetings to learn from each other.
- Put employees through arduous and repetitive management training.
- Develop long-term relationships with the best suppliers.
- Understand a country's culture before locating there.
- Hire local employees whenever possible.
- Maximize workers' autonomy.
- Tweak the standard menu only slightly to adapt it to local tastes.
- Keep prices low to build market share; profits will follow.

McDonald's also adds to its global success by blanketing the world with advertising and promotion. The McDonald's name is the single most advertised brand in the world, with a $1.4 billion annual global advertising budget behind it. That explains how the company's signature character, Ronald McDonald, has become the most recognized figure in the world, surpassing even Santa Claus! "The company is an army with one objective that has never strayed," says one board member of McDonald's incredible focus.

Top managers at McDonald's know that sustaining the company's phenomenal growth record forever will be no easy task, so they have placed a premium on innovation and are scouring the globe for new ideas. Many are coming from McDonald's foreign franchisees. The Dutch have developed a prefab modular store that can be moved over a weekend. The Swedes came up with an improved meat freezer. High-rent Singapore invented the concept of satellite "mini-McDonald's" stores.

Much of a franchise's success in global markets comes from its intense preparation before entering a foreign market. For instance, before opening its first store in Poland, McDonald's planned for 18 months, working out in advance locations, real estate, construction, legal issues, and government regulation. (One official told managers they would have to change "that silly logo with those arches." They convinced him to change his mind.) Bureaucracy and foot-dragging officials often create barriers, but McDonald's officials somehow manage to negotiate what they need. For the head of a McDonald's operation in Poland, one problem was convincing local customers not to bring in vodka to drink with their Big Macs since McDonald's is a family restaurant.

Finding reliable, high-quality suppliers in some countries where free enterprise is a new concept has proved to be a challenge. When McDonald's first enters a country, it often has to import its supplies. Then, it tries to shift as quickly as possible to local sources, which it often plays a key role in developing to ensure that supplies meet McDonald's rigid global quality standards. Before it opened its first store in Russia, McDonald's brought in potatoes from Idaho to be transplanted in Russian fields and even imported bull semen to upgrade the quality of the local cattle herds!

Going global can pose risks for any company, especially those stepping into foreign markets for the

(continued)

McDonald's has exported its franchises successfully to markets all across the globe.

first time. Burger King recently pulled out of the Japanese market, and other franchises have struggled to establish their brand names in foreign countries. However, in this global economy, failing to expand into foreign markets may pose an even greater risk in the long run.

1. What advantages does McDonald's global strategy provide for the company?

2. What risks does global expansion entail for franchises?

Sources: Adapted from "Fight for Fast-Food Big Bucks Heats Up," CBNet, August 31, 2001; Andrew E. Serwer, "McDonald's Conquers the World," *Fortune*, October 17, 1994, pp. 103–116; McDonald's Corporation, *www.mcdonalds.com*; KFC Inc., *www.kfc.com*; Evelyn Iritani, "Ruling the Roost in China," *Los Angeles Times*, September 10, 2001, Part A, p.1.

Termination. Probably the most litigated subject of a franchise agreement is the termination of the contract by either party. Most contracts prohibit termination "without just cause." However, prospective franchisees must be sure they know exactly when and under what conditions they—and the franchisor—can terminate the contract. Generally, the franchisor has the right to cancel a contract if a franchisee declares bankruptcy, fails to make required payments on time, or fails to maintain quality standards.

Terminations usually are costly to both parties and are seldom surrounded by a sense of goodwill. Most attorneys encourage franchisees to avoid conditions for termination or to use alternative routes to resolve disputes, such as formal complaints through franchise associations, arbitration, or ultimately selling the franchise.

Renewal. Franchisors usually retain the right to renew or refuse to renew franchisees' contracts. If a franchisee fails to make payments on schedule or does not maintain quality standards, the franchisor has the right to refuse renewal. In some cases, the franchisor has no obligation to offer contract renewal to the franchisee when the contract expires.

When a franchisor grants renewal, the two parties must draw up a new contract. Frequently, the franchisee must pay a renewal fee and may be required to fix any deficiencies of the outlet or to modernize and upgrade it. The FTC's Trade Regulation Rule requires the franchisor to disclose these terms before any contracts are signed.

Transfer and Buybacks. At any given time, about 10 percent of the franchisees in a system have their outlets up for sale.[28] Franchisees typically are not free to sell their businesses to just anyone, however. Under most franchise contracts, a franchisee cannot sell his franchise to a third party or will it to a relative without the franchisor's approval. In most instances, franchisors do approve a franchisee's request to sell an outlet to another person. *American Leak Detection, a system with more than 300 franchisees, lists the company's resale opportunities on its World Wide Web site. That's how Jim Dickson found the two Florida-based territories he purchased when he decided to leave his job in corporate America to operate a business of his own. After finding the franchises listed for sale on the Web, Dickson began his research in earnest, poring over the company's financial records and operating history. "I . . . knew there was no way the [previous owner] was tapping the potential of the franchise," he says.*[29]

Most franchisors retain the right of first refusal in franchise transfers, which means the franchisee must offer the franchise to the franchisor first. For example, McDonald's Corporation recently repurchased 13 restaurants under its first refusal clause from a franchisee wanting to retire. If the franchisor refuses to buy the outlet, the franchisee may sell it to a third party who meets franchisor's approval (essentially the same standards buyers of new franchisees must meet).

TRENDS IN FRANCHISING

8. Explain current trends shaping franchising.

Franchising has experienced three major growth waves since its beginning. The first wave occurred in the early 1970s when fast-food restaurants used the concept to grow rapidly. The fast-food industry was one of the first to discover the power of franchising, but other businesses soon took notice and adapted the franchising concept to their industries. The second wave took place in the mid-1980s as our nation's economy shifted heavily toward the service sector. Franchises followed suit, springing up in every service business imaginable—from maid services and copy centers to mailing services and real estate. The third wave began in the early 1990s and continues today. It is characterized by new, low-cost franchises that focus on specific market niches. In the wake of major corporate downsizing and the burgeoning costs of traditional franchises, these new franchises allow would-be entrepreneurs to get into proven businesses faster and at lower costs. These companies feature start-up costs in the $2,000 to $250,000 range and span a variety of industries—from leak detection in homes and auto detailing to day care and tile glazing.

Other significant trends affecting franchising are discussed next.

International Opportunities. Currently, one of the hottest trends in franchising is the globalization of American franchise systems. Increasingly, franchising is becoming a major export industry for the United States. For most franchisors, markets outside the borders of the United States offer the greatest potential for growth. Faced with extremely competitive conditions in domestic markets that are already saturated, a rapidly rising number of franchises are moving into international markets to boost sales and profits. Others are taking their franchise systems abroad simply because they

GAINING A COMPETITIVE EDGE
Choosing the Right Franchise

AN EXPENSIVE LESSON

As an attorney for Pearle Vision Centers, Todd Maddocks worked with the financial statements of the company's franchised operations and was extremely impressed with what he saw. "Stanley Pearle helped create a lot of millionaires," he says. Maddocks realized that franchising could be an excellent path to entrepreneurship and the many benefits it offered. "These franchisees were living the dream," he remembers thinking. "They had their freedom, which is exactly what I wanted."

Maddocks and his wife Kathy spent six months studying franchise opportunities, searching for one they could afford. They finally settled on a small, young franchise called Auto Exam that had recently started offering franchises in their hometown of Dallas. The franchise, which helped customers distinguish great used cars from lemons, seemed to be ideal for the Maddocks because it was low cost and home based. Before signing on, however, the Maddockses interviewed several existing Auto Exam franchisees and were encouraged by their responses. Looking back, Maddocks says, "We failed to ask them one key question: Are you making any money?"

The couple plunged into running their new franchise, and because of their limited funds, they promoted it with guerrilla marketing techniques such as a booth at a local fair, discount coupons in a school coupon booklet, and flyers stuck on car windshields. "We did what the franchisor told us to do," says Maddocks, "and our sales were climbing, but most of our business came from the Yellow Pages ad placed by the franchisor." The Maddocks's outlet soon became the sales leader for the young franchise, but the couple was still having to plow their own money into the company to cover expenses. Then came an alarming wake-up call: A fellow franchisee closed his business because he could not exist on the meager income it was generating. Other franchisees soon closed their doors, and the management team at Auto Exam split up, leaving only the company's founder to manage the operation. The final blow for the Maddockses came when the franchisor missed the deadline for a new Yellow Pages ad. When the telephone directory was published, there was no ad for the Maddocks's Auto Exam franchise. Predictably, sales dried up, and the Maddockses decided to let go their one employee and close their franchise. Although the failure did not destroy the couple financially, Maddocks says, "We learned an expensive lesson."

THE RIGHT CHOICE

Karen Hoecherl had grown extremely dissatisfied with her job as assistant manager at a bank, leading her to consider franchising as a route to owning her own business. She began to evaluate various franchise opportunities, focusing at first on the fast food industry. Comparing the type of work the industry required to her talents and interests, Hoecherl quickly dismissed fast-food as a possibility. Several years before, while working at the bank, Hoecherl began to notice more people taking an interest in nutrition and health supplements. She began researching the industry and the franchises available and discovered the GNC franchise.

Hoecherl spent several months analyzing the GNC operation, talking to existing franchisees, and learning everything she could about the business. She even went to work for an existing GNC franchise to learn the daily routine of the business. Satisfied that GNC's business concept had the potential for rapid growth and that the business was compatible with her interests, Hoecherl opened a franchise in Howard Beach, New York. She cites GNC's management support and advertising campaign as key reasons for sales at her store growing so rapidly. Hoecherl is confident that she made the right decision to buy the GNC franchise. "I went into an industry that I didn't know much about and with some hard work, I've succeeded," she says. "That's one of the most rewarding things that's come from becoming a franchise operator."

Finding the right franchise is no easy task, but the results are well worth the effort. Franchisees who have made both wise and ill-advised franchise purchases offer the following advice:

- Start by evaluating your own personal and business interests. What activities do you enjoy? Which ones do you dislike?

(continued)

- Establish a budget. Know how much you can afford to spend before you ever go shopping for a franchise.

- Do your research. Study broad trends to determine which franchise concepts are likely to be most successful in the future.

- Identify potential franchise candidates. Create a profile of the most promising franchises that best fit both your interests and market trends.

- Review candidates' marketing literature and narrow your search to the top five or six.

- Get these companies' UFOCs and review them thoroughly. Get an experienced attorney to review the "fine print" in each UFOC.

- Visit existing franchisees and ask them *lots* of questions about the franchise system, the franchisor, and the franchisor–franchisee relationship.

- Study your local market. Use what you learned from existing franchisees to determine whether or not the concept would be successful in the area you are considering. Don't forget to evaluate the level of competition present.

- Meet with company officials to discuss the details of buying a franchise. Look for depth and experience in the management team.

- Complete negotiations with the franchiser and close the deal.

1. Develop a list of the mistakes franchisees commonly make when selecting and purchasing their outlets.

2. What steps can a franchisee take to avoid making these mistakes?

3. Use the World Wide Web and your local library to compile a list of resources that would help potential franchisees as they evaluate franchise opportunities.

Sources: Adapted from Todd D. Maddocks, "Write the Wrong," *Entrepreneur's Be Your Own Boss*, January 2001, pp. 152–155; Kerry Pipes, "Franchisee Lifestyles, Franchise UPDATE, *www.franchise-update.com/fuadmin/articles/article_FranchiseeLifestyles5.htm.*

see tremendous growth potential there. According to a report by Arthur Andersen, 44 percent of U.S. franchisors have international locations, up from 34 percent in 1989. International expansion is a relatively new phenomenon in franchising, however; approximately 75 percent of franchisors established their first foreign outlet within the past 10 years.[30] Canada is the primary market for U.S. franchisors, with Mexico, Japan, and Europe following. These markets are most attractive to franchisors because they are similar to the U.S. market—rising personal incomes, strong demand for consumer goods, growing service economies, and spreading urbanization. However, most franchisors recognize the difficulties of developing franchises in foreign markets and start slowly. According to Arthur Andersen, 79 percent of franchisors doing business internationally have fewer than 100 outlets in foreign countries.[31]

As they move into foreign markets, franchisors have learned that adaptation is one key to success. Although they keep their basic systems intact, franchises that are successful in foreign markets quickly learn how to change their concepts to adjust to local cultures and to appeal to local tastes. For instance, fast-food chains in other countries often must make adjustments to their menus to please locals' palates. In Venezuela, diners prefer mayonnaise with their french fries, and in Chile, customers want avocado on their hamburgers. In Japan, McDonald's (known as "Makudonarudo") outlets sell teriyaki burgers, rice burgers, seaweed soup, and katsu burgers (cheese wrapped in a roast pork cutlet topped with katsu sauce and shredded cabbage) in addition to their traditional American fare. In the Philippines, the McDonald's menu includes a spicy Filipino-style burger, spaghetti, and chicken with rice.

Smaller, Nontraditional Locations. As the high cost of building full-scale locations continues to climb, more franchisors are searching out nontraditional locations in which to build smaller, less expensive outlets. Based on the principle of **intercept marketing,** the idea is to put a franchise's products or services directly in the paths of potential customers, wherever that may be. Franchises are putting scaled-down outlets on college campuses, in sports arenas, in hospitals, on airline flights, and in zoos. Today, customers are likely to find a mini-Wendy's inside the convenience store at a Mobil gas station, a Dunkin' Donuts outlet in the airport, or a Mail Boxes Etc. store on a college campus. *Auntie Anne's Pretzels has begun locating outlets inside Wal-Mart stores, and the 7,000-member Brentwood Baptist Church in Houston recently opened a McDonald's franchise in its lifelong learning center. The church co-owns the franchise with one of its members, who owns six McDonald's franchises.*[32] Many franchisees have discovered that smaller outlets in these nontraditional locations generate nearly the same sales volume as full-sized outlets at just a fraction of the cost. Establishing outlets in innovative locations will be a key to continued franchise growth in the domestic market. One franchise expert explains, "Years ago, we never dreamed you could purchase pizza over the Internet or be served a McDonald's hamburger on an airplane. There are so many ways of franchising now, there's no telling what the future might bring."[33]

Conversion Franchising. The trend toward **conversion franchising,** in which owners of independent businesses become franchisees to gain the advantage of name recognition, will continue. In a franchise conversion, the franchiser gets immediate entry into new markets and experienced operators; franchisees get increased visibility and often a big sales boost. In fact, the average sales gain in the first year for converted franchisees is 20 percent.[34] *Michael Lawrence, with his wife Dee, launched the Cafe Manhatten Bagel Shop in New York in 1988. When the Manhattan Bagel Company approached him about becoming one of their franchisees, he studied the opportunity and decided to take it. He knew his two locations would benefit from the franchise's name recognition and that the franchisor's system would improve the efficiency of his operation. Manhattan Bagel waived the usual franchise fee for Lawrence, but he still invested a total of $100,000 upgrading his stores to franchise standards. The conversion has been extremely successful; sales and profits at both locations have made impressive gains.*[35]

Multiple-Unit Franchising. Multiple-unit franchising (MUF) became extremely popular in the early 1990s, and the trend has accelerated rapidly since then. According to the International Franchise Association, 34 percent of franchisees own multiple outlets.[36] In multiple-unit franchising, a franchisee opens more than one unit in a territory within a specific time period. In recent years, franchising has attracted more professional, experienced, and sophisticated entrepreneurs who have access to more capital—and who have their sights set on big goals that owning a single outlet cannot meet. Twenty-five years ago, a franchisee owning 10 or more outlets was rare; today, it is becoming increasingly common for a single franchisee to own 50 or more outlets. The typical multiunit franchisee owns between three and six outlets, but some franchisees own many more units.

For franchisers, multiple-unit franchising is an efficient way to expand quickly. Multiple-unit franchising is especially effective for franchisors targeting foreign markets, where having a local representative who knows the territory is essential. For franchisees, multiple-unit franchising offers the opportunity for rapid growth without leaving the safety net of the franchise. Also, because franchisors usually offer discounts of about 25 percent off their standard fees on multiple units, franchisees can get fast-growing companies for a bargain. *Daniel Del Prete bought his first Dunkin' Donuts franchise as a way to make a living; then he saw the potential owning multiple units offered. Nearly three decades later, Del Prete owns 18 Dunkin' Donut units and three Blimpie franchises.*[37]

Master Franchising. A **master franchise** (or **subfranchise** or **area developer**) gives a franchisee the right to create a semi-independent organization in a particular territory to recruit, sell, and support other franchisees. A master franchisee buys the right to develop subfranchises within a broad geographic area or, sometimes, an entire country. Like multiunit franchising, subfranchising "turbocharges" a franchisor's growth. *After founding five companies of his own, Tom Watson decided to become an area developer for Steak Out, a delivery and take-out restaurant. Using master franchising, Watson plans to create 102 new stores in his area within five years.*[38]

Many franchisors use master franchising to open outlets in international markets because the master franchisees understand local laws and the nuances of selling in local markets. *One master franchisee with TCBY International, a yogurt franchise, has opened 21 stores in China and in Hong Kong. Based on his success in these markets, the company has sold him the master franchise in India.*[39]

Piggybacking (or Combination Franchising). Some franchisors also are discovering new ways to reach customers by teaming up with other franchisors selling complementary products or services. A growing number of companies are **piggybacking** (or **co-branding**) outlets—combining two or more distinct franchises under one roof. This "buddy system" approach works best when the two franchise ideas are compatible and appeal to similar customers. At one location, a Texaco gasoline station, a Pizza Hut restaurant, and a Dunkin' Donuts—all owned by the same franchisee—work together in a piggyback arrangement to draw customers. Doughnut franchisor Dunkin' Donuts, ice cream franchisor Baskin-Robbins, and sandwich shop Togo's are working together to build hundreds of combination outlets, a concept that has proved to be highly successful.[40] Properly planned, piggybacked franchises can magnify many times over the sales and profits of individual, self-standing outlets.

Serving Aging Baby Boomers. Now that dual-career couples have become the norm, especially among baby boomers, the market for franchises offering convenience and time-saving services is booming. Customers are willing to pay for products and services that will save them time or trouble, and franchises are ready to provide them. Franchisees of Around Your Neck go into the homes and offices of busy male executives to sell men's apparel and accessories ranging from shirts and ties to custom-made suits. Other segments in which franchising is experiencing rapid growth include home delivery of meals, housecleaning and repair services, continuing education (especially computer and business training), leisure activities (crafts, hobbies, health spas, and travel-related activities), products and services aimed at home-based businesses, and health care (ranging from fitness and diet products and services to in-home elder care and medical services).

CONCLUSION

Franchising has proved its viability in the U.S. economy and has become a key part of the small business sector because it offers many would-be entrepreneurs the opportunity to own and operate a business with a greater chance for success. Despite its impressive growth rate to date, the franchising industry still has a great deal of room left to grow, especially globally. Describing the future of franchising, one expert says, "Franchising has not yet come close to reaching its full potential in the American marketplace."[41]

CHAPTER SUMMARY

1. Explain the importance of franchising in the U.S. economy.
   - Through franchised businesses, consumers can buy nearly every good or service imaginable—from singing telegrams and computer training to tax services and waste-eating microbes.
   - A new franchise opens somewhere in the United States every 8 minutes and somewhere in the world every 6.5 minutes! Franchises account for more than 50 percent of all retail sales, totaling more than $1 trillion, and they employ more than 8 million people in more than 100 major industries.
2. Define the concept of franchising and describe the different types of franchises.
   - Franchising is a method of doing business involving a continuous relationship between a franchisor and a franchisee. The franchisor retains control of the distribution system, while the franchisee assumes all of the normal daily operating functions of the business.
   - There are three types of franchising: trade-name franchising, in which the franchisee purchases only the right to use a brand name; product distribution franchising, which involves a license to sell specific products under a brand name; and pure franchising, which provides a franchisee with a complete business system.
3. Describe the benefits and limitations of buying a franchise.
   - The franchisor has the benefits of expanding his business on limited capital and growing without developing key managers internally. The franchisee also receives many key benefits: management training and counseling, customer appeal of a brand name; standardized quality of goods and services, national advertising programs, financial assistance, proven products and business formats, centralized buying power, territorial protection, and greater chances for success.

- Potential franchisees should be aware of the disadvantages involved in buying a franchise: franchise fees and profit sharing, strict adherence to standardized operations, restrictions on purchasing, limited product lines, possible ineffective training programs, and less freedom.
4. Describe the legal aspects of franchising, including the protection offered by the FTC's Trade Regulation Rule.
   - The FTC's Trade Regulation Rule is designed to help the franchisee evaluate a franchising package. It requires each franchisor to disclose information covering 23 topics at least 10 days before accepting payment from a potential franchisee. This document, the Uniform Franchise Offering Circular (UFOC) is a valuable source of information for anyone considering investing in a franchise.
5. Explain the right way to buy a franchise.
   - To buy a franchise the right way requires that you evaluate yourself, research your market, consider your franchise options, get a copy of the franchisor's UFOC and study it, talk to existing franchisees, ask the franchisor some tough questions, and make your choice.
6. Describe a typical franchise contract and some of its provisions.
   - The amount of franchisor–franchisee litigation has risen steadily over the past decade. Three terms are responsible for most franchisor–franchisee disputes: termination of the contract, contract renewal, and transfer and buy-back provisions.
7. Explain current trends shaping franchising.
   - Trends influencing franchising include international opportunities; the emergence of smaller, nontraditional locations; conversion franchising; multiple-unit franchising; master franchising; piggyback franchising (or co-branding); and products and services targeting aging baby boomers.

DISCUSSION QUESTIONS

1. What is franchising?

2. Describe the three types of franchising and give an example of each.

3. How does franchising benefit the franchisor?
4. Discuss the advantages and the disadvantages of franchising for the franchisee.
5. How beneficial to franchisees is a quality training program? Explain.
6. Compare the failure rates for franchises with those of independent businesses.
7. Why might an independent entrepreneur be dissatisfied with a franchising arrangement?
8. What are the clues in detecting an unreliable franchisor?
9. Should a prospective franchisee investigate before investing in a franchise? If so, how and in what areas?
10. What is the function of the FTC's Trade Regulation Rule?
11. Outline the rights the Trade Regulation Rule gives all prospective franchisees.
12. What is the source of most franchisor–franchisee litigation? Whom does the standard franchise contract favor?
13. Describe the current trends affecting franchising.
14. One franchisee says, "Franchising is helpful because it gives you somebody (the franchisor] to get you going, nurture you, and shove you along a little. But, the franchisor won't make you successful. That depends on what you bring to the business, how hard you are prepared to work, and how committed you are to finding the right franchise for you." Do you agree? Explain.

STEP INTO THE REAL WORLD

1. Set up an appointment to visit the owner of a local franchise operation. Is it a trade name, product distribution, or pure franchise? To what extent did the franchisee investigate before investing? What assistance does the franchisor provide? Is the franchisee pleased with the franchising relationship?
2. a. Use the Web to research and then contact several franchisors in a particular business category and ask for their franchise packages. Write a report comparing their treatment of the topics covered by the Trade Regulation Rule.
   b. Analyze the terms of their franchise contracts. What are the major differences? Are some terms more favorable than others? If you were about to invest in the franchise, which terms would you want to change?
3. Invite a local franchisee to lead a class discussion on franchising, its benefits, and its limitations.
4. Contact the International Franchise Association (1350 New York Avenue, NW, Suite 900, Washington, D.C., 20005-4709 [202] 628-8000) for a copy of *Investigate Before Investing*. Also search the resources on the World Wide Web for information on franchising. Prepare a report describing what steps a prospective franchisee should take before buying a franchise.
5. Working with several of your classmates, select a franchise concept with which you are familiar. Conduct a brainstorming session in which your goal is to identify as many nontraditional locations for franchised outlets as possible. Prepare a short report on your ideas and the justification for them.

TAKE IT TO THE NET

Visit the Scarborough/Zimmerer home page at **www.prenhall.com/scarborough** for updated information, online resources, Web-based exercises, and sample business plan.

ENDNOTES

1. Janean Huber, "Franchise Forecast," *Entrepreneur*, January 1993, p. 72.
2. Jane R. Plitt, "Ahead of Her Time," *Success*, July/August 2000, pp. 84–87.
3. Jane Shealy, "Franchising Serves Up Slices of the American Dream," *Success*, October 2000, pp. 80–84; Ellen Paris, "A Franchise of Her Own," *Entrepreneur's Be Your Own Boss*, June 2000, pp. 163–166.

4. Ronaleen R. Roha, "Making It: Franchise Style," *Kiplinger's Personal Finance Magazine,* July 1996, pp. 71–72.

5. Barbara Rudolph, "Franchising Is BIG Business for Small Business," *Your Company,* Spring 1992, p. 44.

6. Gregory Matusky, "The Franchise Hall of Fame," *Inc.,* April 1994, pp. 86–89.

7. "Portrait of an 'Average' Franchisee," The Franchise Store, *www.thefranchisestore.com/portrait_of_an_average_franchisee.htm;* "Gallup Survey of Franchise Owners Finds 92 Percent Successful," *The Info Franchise Newsletter,* April 1998, *www.infonews.com/newsletters/apr98.html*

8. Janean Huber, "The Buddy System," *Entrepreneur,* January 1993, p. 96.

9. Richard Landesberg, "A New Career for You Might Start at Franchise U." *Success,* July/August 2000, pp. 82–83.

10. Bob Weinstein, "Survival of the Biggest," *Entrepreneur,* August 1999, p. 141.

11. Huber, "Franchise Forecast," *Entrepreneur,* January 1993, p. 73.

12. Julie Bawden Davis, "Financing Your Franchise," *Business Start-Ups,* September 1997, pp. 106–110; Valvoline Instant Oil Change, *www.viocfranchise.com/.*

13. Davis, "Financing Your Franchise"; *www.dunkin-baskin-togos.com/*

14. Stephanie Barlow, "Sub-Stantial Success," *Entrepreneur,* January 1993, p. 126.

15. Weinstein, "Survival of the Biggest," pp. 138–141.

16. Richard Gibson, "Court Decides Franchisees Get Elbow Room," *Wall Street Journal,* August 14, 1996, pp. B1, B4.

17. *Vylene Enterprises vs. Naugles,* FindLaw, *http://caselaw.lp.findlaw.com/cgi-bin/getcase.pl?court=9th&navby=case&no=9456470;* Nicole Harris and Mike France, "Franchisees Get Feisty," *Business Week, www.businessweek.com/1997/08/b351592.htm;* Richard Gibson, "Court Decides Franchisees Get Elbow Room," *Franchise Law Update,* Luce, Forward, Hamilton, & Scripps LLP. vol. 1, No. 6, (October 1996), *www.lice.com/publicat/flu_16-3.html*

18. "McBusiness," *Inc. Special Report: State of Small Business, 2001,* pp. 34–35.

19. Glen Weisman, "The Choice Is Yours," *Business Start-Ups,* May 1997, pp. 24–30; Dan Morse and Jeffrey Tannenbaum, "Poll on High Success Rate for Franchises Raises Eyebrows," *Wall Street Journal,* March 17, 1998, p. B2; "McBusiness," pp. 34–35.

20. Kirk Shivell and Kent Banning, "What Every Prospective Franchisee Should Know," *Small Business Forum,* Winter 1996/1997, pp. 33–42.

21. Julie Bawden Davis, "A Perfect Match," *Business Start-Ups,* July 1997, p. 45.

22. Glen Weisman, "The Choice Is Yours," *Business Start-Ups,* May 1997, pp. 24–30; Anne P. Thrower, "Beneath the Golden Arches," *Upstate Business,* June 14, 1998, pp. 1, 10–11.

23. "Notable Franchise Facts," McDonald's, *www.mcdonalds.com/corporate/franchise/facts/index.html;* Matusky, "The Franchise Hall of Fame," pp. 86–89.

24. Dan Morse, "Individual Owners Set Up Own E-Commerce Sites," *Wall Street Journal,* March 28, 2000, p. B2.

25. Catherine Siskos, "Franchises May Have to Tell All," *Kiplinger's Personal Finance Magazine,* March 1997, p. 16.

26. Echo Montgomery Garrett, "Multi-Unit Moguls," *Inc.,* October 1999, pp. 105–111.

27. Jeannie Ralston, "Before You Bet Your Buns," *Venture,* March 1988, p. 57.

28. Roberta Maynard, "Rejuvenated Sales," *Nation's Business,* July 1997, pp. 49–54.

29. Janean Chun, "Global Warming," *Entrepreneur,* April 1997, p. 156.

30. Asia Pacific Economic Cooperation, "Consultative Survey on Franchising in APEC Member Economies," *www.strategis.ic.gc.ca/SSG/ae00275e.html.*

31. Asia Pacific Economic Cooperation, "Consultative Survey on Franchising in APEC Member Economies," *www.strategis.ic.gc.ca/SSG/ae00275e.html*

32. Zaheera Wahid, "Twist and Shout," *Business Start-Ups,* February 2000, p. 85; Elizabeth Bernstein, "Holy Frappuccino," *Wall Street Journal,* August 31, 2001, pp. W1, W8; "Holy Fries," ABC13.com, *http://abclocal.go.com/ktrk/news/020601_sn_holyfries.html*

33. Janean Chun, "Franchise Frenzy," *Entrepreneur,* January 1997, p. 162.

34. Carol Steinberg, "Instant Growth," *Success,* July/August 1996, pp. 77–83.

35. Ibid.

36. "McBusiness," pp. 34–35.

37. Janean Chun, "Power of One," *Entrepreneur,* December 1996, *www.entrepreneur.com/Magazines/MA_SegArticle/0,1539,226686----1-,00.html*

38. Garrett, "Multi-Unit Moguls."

39. Roberta Maynard, "Why Franchisees Look Abroad," *Nation's Business,* October 1995, pp. 65–72.

40. Dunkin Donuts/Baskin-Robbins/Togo's Franchise Opportunities, *www.dunkin-baskin-togos.com/.*

41. Janean Huber, "What's Next?" *Entrepreneur,* September 1994, p. 151.

Chapter 5

Buying an Existing Business

> *Not everything that can be counted counts, and not everything that counts can be counted.*

—ALBERT EINSTEIN

> *If I were two-faced, would I be wearing this one?*

—ABRAHAM LINCOLN

Upon completion of this chapter, you will be able to:

1. Understand the advantages and disadvantages of buying an existing business.
2. Define the steps involved in the *right way* to buy a business.
3. Explain the process of evaluating an existing business.
4. Describe the various ways of determining the value of a business.
5. Understand the seller's side of the buyout decision and how to structure the deal.
6. Understand how the negotiation process works and identify the factors that affect it.

For many entrepreneurs the quickest way to enter a market is to purchase an existing business. Yet, the attraction of "fast entry" can be a big mistake. Buying an existing business requires a great deal of analysis and evaluation to ensure that what you are purchasing really meets your needs. Don't rush—be sure that you know absolutely everything that can be learned about the business before you buy. If vital information, such as audited financial statements and legal clearances are not available, be especially diligent. Be patient and do your homework before you even begin to negotiate a purchase price. For starters, be sure that you have considered answers to each of the following questions:

- Is this the type of business you would like to operate? Do you know the negative aspects of this business?
- Is this the best market for this business?
- Do you know the critical factors that must exist for this business to be successful?
- Do you have the experience required to operate this type of business? If not, will the current owner be willing to "stay-on" for three to six months to teach you the "ropes"?
- Will you need to make any changes to the business or its operating procedures to be successful, and, if so, at what expense?
- If the business is currently in a decline, do you have a plan to return the business to profitability?
- If the business is profitable, why does the current owner(s) want to sell? Does their reason given for selling the business make sense to you? If not, can you verify the reason given?
- Have you examined other similar businesses that are currently for sale or that have sold recently to determine what a "fair market price" should be?

Many of these questions ask you to be honest with yourself about your ability to operate the business successfully. It's one thing to watch others manage a business successfully, and another to know why they make the decision they do and the actions they take. Chapter 1 highlighted the reasons for business failure. Before making any decision to purchase an existing business, review the primary reasons for failure and assure yourself that you have taken all the steps to reduce the risk of failure. Whatever time and energy you invest in the evaluation of the business opportunity will earn significant dividends if you acquire a business that becomes successful or avoid purchasing a business that will fail.

BUYING AN EXISTING BUSINESS

Advantages of Buying an Existing Business

1. Understand the advantages and disadvantages of buying an existing business.

The following are a few of the factors that can make the purchase of an existing business an advantage.

An Established Successful Business May Continue to Be Successful. A business that has been profitable for some time may reflect an owner who has established a solid customer base, developed successful relationships with critical suppliers, and mastered the day-to-day operational components of the business. In such cases, it is important to make changes slowly and to take extra care to retain the relationship with customers, suppliers, and staff that has made the business a success. This advantage often goes hand-in-hand with the second advantage, using the experience of the previous owner.

Section II   Building the Business Plan: Beginning Considerations

How do you determine if this business is a viable investment?

The New Owner Can Use the Experience of the Previous Owner. In many cases in which the business has a long history of success, you may negotiate with the current owner to stay on for a short time to introduce you to the customers or clients, the vendors or suppliers, and to show you how the policies and procedures they developed actually operate. Additionally, the previous owner can be very helpful in unmasking the unwritten rules of business in the area: whom to trust, expected business behavior, and many other critical intangibles. Most owners who have built a successful business want you to succeed. Hiring the previous owner as a consultant for the first few months can be a valuable investment. When this option is not possible, at a minimum, review with the owner the key financial records to ensure that you can recognize the relationships between expenses and revenues.

The New Business Owner Hits the Ground Running. Buying a business is one of the fastest pathways to entrepreneurship. The entrepreneur who purchases an existing business saves the time, costs, and energy required to plan and launch a new business. The buyer gets a business that is already generating cash and sometimes profits. The day he takes over the ongoing business is the day his revenues begin. In this way, he earns while he learns.

An Existing Business May Already Have the Best Location. When the location of the business is critical to its success, it may be wise to purchase a business that is already in the right place. Opening a second-choice location and hoping to draw customers often proves fruitless. In fact, the existing business's greatest asset may be its location. If this advantage cannot be matched in other locations, an entrepreneur may have little choice but to buy instead of build.

Employees and Suppliers Are Already in Place. An existing business already has experienced employees who can help the company earn money while the new owner learns the business. In addition, an existing business has an established set of suppliers with a history of business transactions. The vendors can continue to supply the business while the new owner assesses the products and services of other vendors.

Thus, the new owner is not pressured to choose suppliers quickly without thorough investigation.

Equipment Is Installed and Productive Capacity Is Known. Acquiring and installing new equipment exerts a tremendous strain on a fledgling company's financial resources. In an existing business, a potential buyer can determine the condition of the plant and equipment and its capacity before he or she buys. The previous owner may have established an efficient production operation through trial and error, although the new owner may need to make modifications to improve it. In many cases, the entrepreneur can purchase physical facilities and equipment at prices significantly below replacement costs.

Inventories Are in Place and Trade Credit Has Been Established. The proper amount of inventory is essential to both cost control and sales volume. If the business has too little inventory, it will not have the quantity and variety of products to satisfy customer demand. But if the business has too much inventory, it is tying up excessive capital, increasing costs, reducing profitability, and increasing the danger of cash flow problems. Many successful, established businesses have learned a balance between these extremes. Previous owners also have established trade credit relationships of which the new owner can take advantage. The business's proven track record gives the new owner leverage in negotiating favorable trade credit terms. No supplier wants to lose a good customer.

Finding Financing Usually Is Easier. Because the risk associated with buying an existing business is lower than that of a start-up, financing for the purchase is easier. A buyer can point to the existing company's track record and to the plans he or she has for improving it to convince potential lenders to finance the purchase. Also, in many buy–sell agreements, the buyer uses a "built-in" source of financing: the seller!

It's a Bargain. Some existing businesses may be real bargains. If the current owners want to sell quickly, they may sell the business at a low price. The more specialized the business is, the greater the likelihood is that a buyer will find a bargain. Any special skills or training required to operate the business limit the number of potential buyers. If the owner wants a substantial down payment or the entire selling price in cash, there may be few qualified buyers; those who do qualify may be able to negotiate a good deal.

Disadvantages of Buying an Existing Business

It's a Loser. A business may be for sale because it has never been profitable. Such a situation may be disguised; owners can use various creative accounting techniques that make the firm's financial picture appear much brighter than it really is. The reason that a business is for sale will seldom be stated honestly as "It's losing money." If there is an area of business in which the maxim "let the buyer beware" still prevails, it is in the sale of a business. Any buyer unprepared to do a thorough analysis of the business may be stuck with a real loser.

Although buying a money-losing business is risky, it is not necessarily taboo. If your analysis of a company indicates that it is poorly managed or suffering from neglect, you may be able to turn it around. However, buying a struggling business without a well-defined plan for solving the problems it faces is an invitation to disaster.

The Previous Owner May Have Created Ill Will. Just as proper business dealings create goodwill, improper business behavior or unethical practices create ill will. The business may look great on the surface, but customers, suppliers, creditors, or employees may have extremely negative feelings about it. Too many business buyers discover (after the sale) that they have inherited undisclosed credit problems, poor supplier relationships, soon-to-expire leases, lawsuits, building code violations, and other problems caused by the previous owner. Vital business relationships may have begun to deteriorate, but their long-term effects may not yet be reflected in the business's financial statements. Ill will can permeate a business for years. The only way to avoid these problems is to investigate a prospective purchase target thoroughly *before* moving forward in the negotiation process.

Current Employees May Not Be Suitable. If the new owner plans to make changes in a business, the present employees may not suit his or her needs. Some workers may have a difficult time adapting to the new owner's management style and vision for the company. Previous managers may have kept marginal employees because they were close friends or because they started off with the company. The new owner, therefore, may have to make some very unpopular termination decisions. For this reason, employees often do not welcome a new owner because they feel threatened. Further, employees who may have wanted to buy the business themselves but could not afford it are likely to see the new owner as the person who stole their opportunity. Bitter employees are not likely to be productive workers.

The Business Location May Have Become Unsatisfactory. What was once an ideal location may be in the process of becoming obsolete as market and demographic trends change. Large shopping malls, new competitors, or highway reroutings can spell disaster for a small retail shop. Prospective buyers should always evaluate the existing market in the area surrounding an existing business as well as its potential for future growth and expansion.

Equipment and Facilities May Be Obsolete or Inefficient. Potential buyers sometimes neglect to have an expert evaluate a company's building and equipment before they purchase it. Only after it's too late do they discover that the equipment is obsolete and inefficient, pushing operating expenses to excessively high levels. Modernizing equipment and facilities is seldom inexpensive.

Change and Innovation Are Difficult to Implement. It is easier to plan for change than it is to implement it. Methods and procedures the previous owner used created precedents that can be difficult or awkward for a new owner to change. For example, if the previous owner granted a 10 percent discount to customers purchasing 100 or more units in a single order, it may be impossible to eliminate that discount without losing some of those customers. The previous owner's policies, even those that are unwise, can influence the changes the new owner can make. Implementing changes to reverse a downward sales trend in a turnaround business can be just as difficult as eliminating unprofitable procedures. Convincing alienated customers to return can be an expensive and laborious process that may take years.

Inventory May Be Obsolete. Inventory is valuable only if it is salable. Too many potential owners make the mistake of trusting a company's balance sheet to provide them with the value of its inventory. The inventory value reported on a company's balance sheet is seldom an accurate refection of its real market value. In some cases, a company's inventory may actually appreciate during periods of rapid inflation, but more likely it has depreciated in value. The value reported on the balance sheet reflects the original cost of the inventory, not its actual market value. Most businesses for sale include inventory and other assets that are absolutely worthless because they are outdated and obsolete! It is the buyer's responsibility to discover the real value of the assets before negotiating a purchase price.

Table 5.1

Valuing Accounts Receivable

A prospective buyer asked the current owner of a business about the value of her accounts receivable. The owner's business records showed $101,000 in receivables. But when the prospective buyer aged them and then multiplied the resulting totals by his estimated probabilities of collection, he discovered their *real* value.

AGE OF ACCOUNTS (DAYS)	AMOUNT	PROBABILITY OF COLLECTION	VALUE
0–30	$ 40,000	.95	$38,000
31–60	$ 25,000	.88	$22,000
61–90	$ 14,000	.70	$ 9,800
91–120	$ 10,000	.40	$ 4,000
121–150	$ 7,000	.25	$ 1,750
151+	$ 5,000	.10	$ 500
Total	$101,000		$76,050

Had he blindly accepted the "book value" of these accounts receivable, this prospective buyer would have overpaid by nearly $25,000 for them!

Accounts Receivable May Be Worth Less Than Face Value. Like inventory, accounts receivable rarely are worth their face value. The prospective buyer should age the accounts receivable to determine their collectibility. The older the receivables are, the less likely they are to be collected, and, consequently, the lower their value is. Table 5.1 shows a simple but effective method of evaluating accounts receivable once the buyer ages them.

The Business May Be Overpriced. Most business sales are asset purchases rather than stock purchases, and a buyer must be sure that he or she knows which assets are included in the deal and what their real value is. Each year, many people purchase businesses at prices far in excess of their value. A buyer who correctly values a business's accounts receivable, inventories, and other assets will be in a good position to negotiate a price that will allow the business to be profitable. Making payments on a business that was overpriced is a millstone around the new owner's neck; it will be difficult to carry this excess weight and keep the business afloat.

HOW TO BUY A BUSINESS

2. Define the steps involved in the *right* way to buy a business.

Although it may sound easy, purchasing an existing business is a time-consuming process, and often difficult. Repeated studies report that more than half of all business acquisitions fail to meet the buyer's expectations. This statistic alone should provide a warning about the need to conduct a systematic and thorough analysis prior to closing the deal. The process that is generally recommended includes the following steps:

1. Look first at yourself; objectively analyze your skills, abilities, and personal interest to determine the type(s) of business for which you are best suited.
2. Based on the self-analysis in step 1, develop a list of the criteria that defines your "ideal business."
3. Seek the help of others in the development of a list of potential candidates for acquisitions that meet the criteria developed above.
4. Thoroughly investigate the potential acquisition targets that best meet your criteria.

5. When the most acceptable candidate is selected, begin the negotiation process with the existing owner.
6. Explore a variety of financing options that are beneficial to the creation of a profitable business.
7. Finally, when the deal is completed, be careful to ensure a smooth transition of ownership.

Let's briefly expand on each of these steps.

Self-Analysis of Our Skills, Abilities, and Interests

The first step in buying a business is conducting a self-audit to determine the ideal business for you. Consider, for example, how the following questions could produce a valuable insight into the best type of business for you:

- What business activities do you enjoy most? Least?
- Which industries interest you most? Least? Why?
- What kind of business do you want to buy?
- What kinds of businesses do you want to *avoid?*
- In what geographic area do you want to live and work?
- What do you expect to get out of the business?
- How much can you put into the business—in both time and money?
- What business skills and experience do you have? Which ones do you lack?
- How easily can you transfer your existing skills and experience to other types of businesses? In what kinds of businesses would that transfer be easiest?
- How much risk are you willing to take?
- What size company do you want to buy?

Answering those and other questions *beforehand* will allow you to develop a list of criteria that a company must meet before you will consider it to be a purchase candidate.

Develop a List of Criteria

The next step is to develop a list of criteria that a potential business acquisition must meet. Looking at every business you find for sale is a terrific waste of time. The goal is to identify the characteristics of the "ideal business" for you. Addressing these issues early in your search will save a great deal of time and trouble as you wade through a multitude of business opportunities. These criteria will provide you, and anyone helping you, with specific parameters against which potential acquisition candidates can be evaluated.

Prepare a List of Potential Candidates

Once you know the criteria and parameters for the ideal candidate, you can begin your search. One technique is to start at the macro level and work down. Drawing on the resources in the library, the World Wide Web, government publications, and industry trade associations and reports, buyers can discover which industries are growing fastest and offer the greatest potential in the future. For entrepreneurs with a well-defined idea of what they are looking for, another effective approach is to begin searching in an industry in which they have experience or one they understand well. *For example, to narrow the field of businesses he and his partners would consider, Mitchell Mondy conducted extensive research on a variety of industries that met the criteria they had* *established. He discovered that many of the fastest-growing industries were in high-tech areas (something the group was not interested in), but his research also showed that the staffing industry was growing rapidly and had very bright projections. Focusing on the staffing industry, Mondy and his partners soon found four companies that met their purchase criteria. They purchased all four businesses and merged them into one. Their staffing company, Teamplayers, based in Birmingham, Michigan, generates $9 million in annual revenues.*[1]

Typical sources for identifying potential acquisition candidates include the following:

- Business brokers
- Bankers
- Accountants
- Investment bankers
- Industry contacts: suppliers, distributors, customers, and others
- Knocking on the doors of businesses you would like to buy (even if they're not advertised "for sale")
- Newspaper and trade journal listings of businesses for sale (e.g., the Business Opportunities section of the *Wall Street Journal*)
- Trade associations
- The World Wide Web, where several sites include listings of companies for sale
- "Networking": social and business contact with friends and relatives

Buyers should consider every business that meets their criteria, even those that may not be listed for sale. Just because a business does not have a "for sale" sign in the window does not mean it is not for sale. In fact, the hidden market of companies that might be for sale but are not advertised as such is one of the richest sources of top-quality businesses. By letting the word out that you are seeking a specific type of business, you are often presented with opportunities that must be negotiated in complete confidence. The existing owner may not wish anyone to know that he or she is considering the sale of the business.

Investigate and Evaluate the Most Likely Acquisition Candidates

The next step is to investigate the candidates in more detail through a process known as due diligence. Due diligence involves studying, reviewing, and verifying all of the relevant information concerning your top acquisition candidates. The goal is to discover exactly what you will be buying and to avoid any unpleasant surprises after the deal is closed. Thoroughly exploring a company's character and condition through the Better Business Bureau, credit-reporting agencies, the company's banker, its vendors and suppliers, your accountant, your attorney, and other resources is a vital part of making sure you get a good deal on a business with the capacity to succeed. Additional important questions to investigate include:

- What are the company's strengths? Weaknesses?
- What major threats is the company facing? Are there hidden threats you don't yet know about?
- Is the company profitable? What is its overall financial condition?
- What growth rate can you expect from the company in the near future?
- What is its cash flow cycle?
- Who are its major competitors?
- How large is the company's customer base? Is it growing or shrinking? Are the current employees suitable? Will they stay?

- Will the seller stay on as a consultant to help you make a smooth transition?
- What is the physical condition of the business, its equipment, and its inventory?
- What is the company's reputation in the community and among customers and vendors?

Determining the answers to these (and other questions addressed in this chapter) will make the task of valuing the business much easier.

Conducting a thorough analysis of a potential acquisition candidate usually requires an entrepreneur to assemble a team of advisers. Finding a suitable business, structuring a deal, and negotiating the final bargain involves many complex legal, financial, tax, and business issues, and good advice can be a valuable tool. Many entrepreneurs bring in an accountant, an attorney, an insurance agent, a banker, and a business broker to serve as consultants during the due-diligence process.

Negotiate the Deal

Placing a value on an existing business represents a major hurdle for many would-be entrepreneurs. (We will discuss valuation techniques later in this chapter.) Once an entrepreneur has a realistic value for the business, the next challenge in making a successful purchase is negotiating a suitable deal. Although most buyers do not realize it, the price they pay for a company typically is not as crucial to its continued success as the terms on which they make the purchase. In other words, *the structure of the deal is more important than the actual price the seller agrees to pay.* Of course, wise business buyers will try to negotiate a reasonable price, but they are much more focused on negotiating favorable terms: how much cash they must pay out and when, how much of the price the seller is willing to finance and for how long, the interest rate at which the deal is financed, which liabilities they will assume, and other such terms. The buyer's primary concern should be to make sure that the deal does not endanger the company's financial future and that it preserves the company's cash flow.

Explore Financing Options

Ideally, a buyer has already begun to explore the options available for financing the purchase. (Recall that many entrepreneurs include bankers on their teams of advisers.) Traditional lenders often shy away from deals involving the purchase of an existing business. Those who are willing to finance business purchases normally lend only a portion of the value of the assets, so buyers often find themselves searching for alternative sources of funds. Fortunately, most business buyers discover an important source of financing built into the deal: the seller. Typically, a deal is structured so that the buyer makes a down payment to the seller, who then finances a note for the balance. The buyer makes regular principal and interest payments over time, perhaps with a larger balloon payment at the end, until the note is paid off. In most business sales, the seller is willing to finance 40 percent to 70 percent of the purchase price over time, usually 3 to 10 years. The terms and conditions of such a loan are vital to both buyer and seller. They cannot be so burdensome that they threaten the company's continued existence; that is, the buyer must be able to make the payments to the seller out of the company's cash flow. Defining reasonable terms is the result of the negotiation process between the buyer and the seller.

Ensure a Smooth Transition

Once the parties have negotiated a deal, the challenge of making a smooth transition immediately arises. No matter how well planned the sale is, there are always sur-

Figure 5.1
Steps in the Acquisition Process

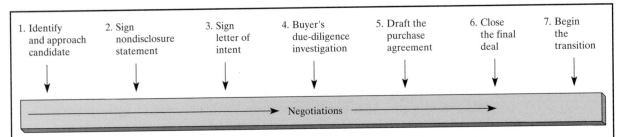

1. Identify and approach candidate
2. Sign nondisclosure statement
3. Sign letter of intent
4. Buyer's due-diligence investigation
5. Draft the purchase agreement
6. Close the final deal
7. Begin the transition

→ Negotiations →

Step 1: Approach the candidate company. If a business is advertised for sale, the proper approach is through the channel defined in the ad. Sometimes, buyers will contact business brokers to help them locate potential target companies. If you have targeted a company in the "hidden market," an introduction from a banker, accountant, or lawyer often is the best approach. During this phase, the seller checks out the buyer's qualifications, and the buyer begins to judge the quality of the company.

Step 2: Sign a nondisclosure document. If the buyer and the seller are satisfied with the results of their preliminary research, they are ready to begin serious negotiations. Throughout the negotiation process, the seller expects the buyer to maintain strict confidentiality of all of the records, documents, and information he receives during the investigation and negotiation process. The nondisclosure document is a legally binding contract that ensures the secrecy of the parties' negotiations.

Step 3: Sign a letter of intent. Before a buyer makes a legal offer to buy the company, he typically will ask the seller to sign a letter of intent. The letter of intent is a nonbinding document that says that the buyer and the seller have reached a sufficient "meeting of the minds" to justify the time and expense of negotiating a final agreement. The letter should state clearly that it is nonbinding, giving either party the right to walk away from the deal. It should also contain a clause calling for "good-faith negotiations" between the parties. A typical letter of intent addresses terms such as price, payment terms, categories of assets to be sold, and a deadline for closing the final deal. Typically, a letter of intent includes a "no-shop" clause. This clause states that the seller cannot use the deal that you are negotiating as leverage to raise the offer from other potential buyers for a given time frame, usually 90 days.

Step 4: Conduct buyer's due diligence. While negotiations are continuing, the buyer is busy studying the business and evaluating its strengths and weaknesses. In short, the buyer must do his homework to make sure that the business is a good value. He should obtain an independent valuation of the business and conduct a detailed review of all company records, employment agreements, leases, pending litigation, and even current or past compliance with federal, state, and local regulations.

Step 5: Draft the purchase agreement. The purchase agreement spells out the parties' final deal. It sets forth all of the details of the agreement and is the final product of the negotiation process. Typical purchase agreement provisions include:

- Definitions for terms in the agreement.
- Description of assets (property) and timing of payment.
- Purchase price.
- Special conditions that the parties must satisfy to close the deal.
- Allocation of purchase price to specific assets.
- Whether the purchaser assumes any liabilities and, if so, which ones.
- Lease transfers and their terms.
- Warranties, representations, and agreements.
- A clause addressing bulk transfer provisions, if appropriate.
- Conduct of the business between the date of the purchase agreement and the closing date.
- Conditions necessary to close the deal.
- Provisions specifying procedures for resolving postclosing disputes and breaches of seller's warranties and representations.
- Covenants restricting competition.
- Miscellaneous matters regarding escrows, payment of broker commissions, and various legal and regulatory provisions.
- Time and place of closing.

Step 6: Close the final deal. Once the parties have drafted the purchase agreement, all that remains to make the deal "official" is the closing. Both buyer and seller sign the necessary documents to make the sale final. The buyer delivers the required money, and the seller turns the company over to the buyer.

Step 7: Begin the transition. For the buyer, the real challenge now begins: Making the transition to a successful business owner!

Sources: Adapted from *The Buying and Selling a Company Handbook* (New York: Price Waterhouse, 1993), pp. 38–42; "Small Business Practices: How to . . . Buy a Business, Edgeonline, *www.edgeonline.com/malnlbizbuilders/ BIZ/Sm_business/buybus.shtml;* "Buying a Business," *www.ptbo.igs.net/~lbk/bab.htm;* Ronaleen R. Roha, "Don't Start It, Buy It," *Kiplinger's Personal Finance Magazine,* July 1997, pp. 74–78.

prises. For instance, the new owner may have ideas for changing the business—perhaps radically—that cause a great deal of stress and anxiety among employees and the previous owner. Charged with such emotion and uncertainty, the transition phase is always difficult and frustrating—and sometimes painful. To avoid a bumpy transition, a business buyer should do the following:

- Concentrate on communicating with employees. Business sales are fraught with uncertainty and anxiety, and employees need reassurance. Take the time to explain your plans for the company.
- Be honest with employees. Avoid telling them only what they want to hear.
- Listen to employees. They have intimate knowledge of the business and its strengths and weaknesses and usually can offer valuable suggestions.
- Devote time to selling your vision for the company to its key stakeholders, including major customers, suppliers, bankers, and others.
- Consider asking the seller to serve as a consultant until the transition is complete. The previous owner can be a valuable resource.

Figure 5.1 sets forth the detailed sequence of events in a successful acquisition negotiation process.

EVALUATING AN EXISTING BUSINESS: UNCOVERING THE TRUTH

3. Explain the process of evaluating an existing business.

The best protection entrepreneurs have against buying a business ill-suited for them is performing the due diligence on potential candidates. That requires time, effort, and the support of the advisory team described earlier. With his or her advisory team assembled, the potential buyer is ready to explore the business opportunity by examining five critical areas:

1. Why does the owner want to sell?
2. What is the physical condition of the business?
3. What is the potential for the company's products or services?
4. What legal aspects are important?
5. Is the business financially sound?

Why Does the Owner Want to Sell?

Every prospective business owner should investigate the *real* reason the business owner wants to sell. One of the most common reasons that owners of small and medium-sized businesses gave for selling were boredom and burnout.[2] Others decided to cash in their business investments and diversify into other types of assets.

Other less obvious reasons that a business owner might have for selling his venture include a major competitor's moving into the market, highway rerouting, frequent burglaries and robberies, expiring lease agreements, cash flow problems, and a declining customer base. Every prospective buyer should investigate *thoroughly* any reason the seller gives for selling the business.

Businesses do not last forever, and most owners know when the time has come to sell. Some owners think ethical behavior requires only not making false or misleading statements, but they may not disclose the whole story. In most business sales, the buyer bears the responsibility of determining whether the business is a good value. Visiting local business owners may reveal general patterns about the area and its overall vitality. The local chamber of commerce also may have useful information.

Suppliers and competitors may be able to shed light on why the business is up for sale. By combining this information with an analysis of the company's financial records, a potential buyer should be able to develop a clear picture of the business and its real value.

What Is the Physical Condition of the Business?

A prospective buyer should evaluate the business's assets to determine their value. Are they reasonably priced? Are they obsolete? Will they need to be replaced soon? Do they operate efficiently? The potential buyer should check the condition of both the equipment and the building. It may be necessary to hire a professional to evaluate the major components of the building: its structure and its plumbing, electrical, and heating and cooling systems. Renovations are rarely inexpensive or simple. Unexpected renovations can punch a gaping hole in a buyer's budget.

How fresh is the firm's inventory? Is it consistent with the image the new owner wants to project? How much of it would the buyer have to sell at a loss? A potential buyer may need to get an independent appraisal to determine the value of the firm's inventory and other assets because the current owner may have priced them far above their actual value. These items typically constitute the largest portion of a business's value, and a potential buyer should not accept the seller's asking price blindly. Remember: *Book value is not the same as market value.* Usually, a buyer can purchase equipment and fixtures at substantially lower prices than book value. Value is determined in the market, not on a balance sheet.

Other important factors that the potential buyer should investigate include the following.

Accounts Receivable. If the sale includes accounts receivable, the buyer should check their quality before purchasing them. How creditworthy are the accounts? What portion of them is past due? By aging the accounts receivable, the buyer can judge their quality and determine their value. (Refer to Table 5.1.)

Lease Arrangements. Is the lease included in the sale? When does it expire? What restrictions does it have on renovation or expansion? The buyer should determine *beforehand* what restrictions the landlord has placed on the lease and should negotiate any change before purchasing the business.

Business Records. Well-kept business records can be a valuable source of information and can tell a prospective buyer a lot about the company's pattern of success (or lack of it). Unfortunately, many business owners are sloppy record keepers. Consequently, the potential buyer and his team may have to reconstruct some critical records. It is important to verify as much information about the business as possible. For instance, does the owner have customer or mailing lists? These can be a valuable marketing tool for a new business owner.

Intangible Assets. Does the sale include any intangible assets such as trademarks, patents, copyrights, or goodwill? Determining the value of such intangibles is much more difficult than computing the value of the tangible assets, yet intangible assets can be one of the most valuable parts of a business acquisition.

Location and Appearance. The location and the overall appearance of the building are important. What had been an outstanding location in the past may be totally unacceptable today. Even if the building and equipment are in good condition and are fairly priced, the business may be located in a declining area. What kinds of busi-

IN THE FOOTSTEPS OF AN ENTREPRENEUR
In Search of the Perfect Business: Part 1

After becoming a victim of corporate downsizing, Hendrix Neimann decided to buy an existing business rather than start one from scratch. At the time, his wife, Judi, was expecting their third child, and Neimann did not want to risk all of the family's personal assets or to commit to the time and emotional demands of a start-up company. He had no idea what kind of business he was looking for, but he believed he would know the right company when he found it. "When I started looking for a company," he says, "I decided that I'd be very clever and find one to buy *before* anyone knew it was on the market."

For months, Neimann found nothing, so he began calling business brokers. As the weeks slipped by and the end of his severance pay approached, Neimann became discouraged and nervous. "Is this what I should be doing?" he asked himself. Then he found a promising company through a blind ad in the *Wall Street Journal*: an access control and security company with sales of nearly $2 million whose owner was retiring. He met with the owner, Peter Klosky, and the broker, Lauren Finberg. In their initial meeting, Klosky told Neimann that there was nothing wrong with the company that a little salesmanship and marketing muscle wouldn't cure. He thought his employees would stay on if he asked them to, and he promised to tell Neimann everything he wanted to know.

On his first visit to Automatic Door Specialists (ADS), Neimann was shocked. "I had never seen such a dirty building," he recalls. "The walls were filthy, and inventory, files, and notebooks were stacked everywhere." His first thought: "This is a mistake." Still, the business intrigued him. The price was affordable, and Neimann's severance pay was about to run out.

Klosky sent Neimann a proposal showing how he could buy ADS with 100 percent financing, while keeping the debt service at manageable levels and taking out 75 percent of what his previous salary was. The deal appealed to Neimann, and he and Klosky signed a letter of intent that, although not legally binding, indicated that they had a serious deal in the works.

The next step was for Neimann to meet with ADS employees. What they told him was unsettling: The company was going downhill *fast*. Neimann asked the employees if they thought he should go ahead with the deal. Their response: "Yes, but only if the price is rock-bottom." Neimann's accountant brought more bad news: ADS was losing money, and there were scads of bad accounts receivable on the books; nearly half were more than 90 days old. Also, the accountant told him, after paying the debts from the purchase, there would be *nothing* left for Neimann's salary! "I was despondent," says Neimann. "And furious. And scared."

Despite his reservations, Neimann went ahead with the purchase, but only after offering Klosky just 50 percent of the amount stated in the letter of intent. Klosky accepted the offer the next day. The final step was the actual closing, which was scheduled to occur three days after Neimann's severance pay ended. Neimann was astonished when Klosky and his attorney suddenly wanted to rewrite the entire deal at the closing. Both Neimann and Klosky came close to walking out, but seven hours—and more negotiations—later, they signed the deal. Hendrix Neimann had bought himself a business.

1. Critique the way in which Neimann went about buying Automatic Door Specialists.

2. Suppose that Neimann is a friend of yours and that he has come to you for advice about whether to purchase ADS. What will you tell him? Explain.

Source: Adapted from Hendrix F. C. Neimann, "Buying a Business," *Inc.*, February 1990, pp. 28–38.

nesses are in the area? Every buyer should consider the location's suitability several years into the future.

The potential buyer should also check local zoning laws to ensure that any changes he or she wants to make are legal. In some areas, zoning laws are very difficult to change and, as a result, can restrict the business's growth.

What Is the Potential for the Company's Products or Services?

No one wants to buy a business with a dying market. A thorough market analysis can lead to an accurate and realistic sales forecast. This research should tell a buyer whether he or she should consider a particular business and help define the trend in the business's sales and customer base.

Customer Characteristics and Composition. Before purchasing an existing business, a business owner should analyze both the existing and potential customers. Discovering why customers buy from the business and developing a profile of the entire customer base can help the buyer identify a company's strengths and weaknesses. The entrepreneur should determine the answers to the following questions:

- Who are my customers in terms of race, age, gender, and income level?
- What do the customers want the business to do for them? What needs are they satisfying?
- How often do customers buy? Do they buy in seasonal patterns?
- How loyal are present customers?
- Will it be practical to attract new customers? If so, will the new customers be significantly different from existing customers?
- Does the business have a well-defined customer base? Is it growing or shrinking? Do these customers come from a large geographic area, or do they all live near the business?

Analyzing the answers to those questions can help the potential owner implement a marketing plan. He will most likely try to keep the business attractive to existing customers but also change some features of its advertising plan to attract new customers.

Competitor Analysis. A potential buyer must identify the company's direct competition: the businesses in the immediate area that sell the same or similar products or services. The potential profitability and survival of the business may well depend on the behavior of these competitors.

In addition to analyzing direct competitors, the buyer should identify businesses that compete indirectly. For example, supermarkets and chain retail stores often carry a basic product line of automobile supplies (oil, spark plugs, and tune-up kits), competing with full-line auto parts stores. These chains often purchase bulk quantities at significant price reductions and do not incur the expense of carrying a full line of parts and supplies. As a result, they may be able to sell such basic products at lower prices. Even though these chains are not direct competitors, they may have a significant impact on local auto parts stores. Indirect competitors frequently limit their product lines to the most profitable segments of the market, and, by concentrating on high-volume or high-profit items, they can pose a serious threat to other businesses.

A potential buyer should also evaluate the trend in the competition. How many similar businesses have entered the market in the past five years? How many similar businesses have closed in the past five years? What caused these failures? Has the market already reached the saturation point? Being a late comer in an already saturated market is not the path to long-term success.

When evaluating the competitive environment, the prospective buyer should answer other questions:

- Which competitors have survived, and what characteristics have led to the success of each?

- How do the competitors' sales volumes compare with those of the business the entrepreneur is considering?
- What unique services do the competitors offer?
- How well organized and coordinated are the marketing efforts of competitors?
- What are the competitors' reputations?
- What are the strengths and weaknesses of the competitors?
- How can you gain market share in this competitive environment?

What Legal Aspects Are Important?

Business buyers face myriad legal pitfalls. The most significant legal issues involve liens, bulk transfers, contract assignments, covenants not to compete, and ongoing legal liabilities.

Liens. The key legal issue in the sale of any asset is typically the proper transfer of good title from seller to buyer. However, because most business sales involve a collection of assorted assets, the transfer of a good title is complex. Some business assets may have liens (creditors' claims) against them, and unless those liens are satisfied before the sale, the buyer must assume them and become financially responsible for them. One way to reduce this potential problem is to include a clause in the sales contract stating that any liability not shown on the balance sheet at the time of sale remains the responsibility of the seller. A prospective buyer should have an attorney thoroughly investigate all of the assets for sale and their lien status before buying any business.

Bulk Transfers. A **bulk transfer** is a transaction in which a buyer purchases all or most of a business's inventory (as in a business sale). To protect against surprise claims from the seller's creditors after purchasing a business, the buyer should meet the requirements of a bulk transfer under Section 6 of the Uniform Commercial Code. Suppose that an owner owing many creditors sells his business to a buyer. The seller, however, does not use the proceeds of the sale to pay his debts to business creditors. Instead, he "skips town," leaving his creditors unpaid. Without the protection of a bulk transfer, those creditors could make claim (within six months) to the assets that the buyer purchased in order to satisfy the previous owner's debts.

To be effective, a bulk transfer must meet the following criteria:

- The seller must give the buyer a sworn list of existing creditors.
- The buyer and the seller must prepare a list of the property included in the sale.
- The buyer must keep the list of creditors and the list of property for six months.
- The buyer must give notice of the sale to each creditor at least 10 days before he takes possession of the goods or pays for them (whichever is first).

State laws differ on the specific actions required to ensure free and clear title to the assets so an attorney should review all aspects of the transaction to ensure compliance with the law.

Contract Assignments. A buyer must investigate the rights and the obligations he or she would assume under existing contracts with suppliers, customers, employees, lessors, and others. To continue the smooth operation of the business, the buyer must assume the rights of the seller under existing contracts. For example, the current owner may have 4 years left on a 10-year lease and so will need to assign this contract to the buyer. In general, the seller can assign any contractual right, unless the contract specifically prohibits the assignment or the contract is personal in nature. For instance, loan contracts sometimes prohibit assignments with **due-on-sale**

clauses. These clauses require the buyer to pay the full amount of the remaining loan balance or to finance the balance at prevailing interest rates. Thus, the buyer cannot assume the seller's loan at a lower interest rate. Also, a seller usually cannot assign his credit arrangements with suppliers to the buyer because they are based on the seller's business reputation and are personal in nature. If such contracts are crucial to the business operation and cannot be assigned, the buyer must negotiate new contracts.

The prospective buyer also should evaluate the terms of any other contracts the seller has, including the following:

- Patent, trademark, or copyright registrations
- Exclusive agent or distributor contracts
- Real estate leases
- Insurance contracts
- Financing and loan arrangements
- Union contracts

Covenants Not to Compete. One of the most important and most often overlooked legal considerations for a prospective buyer is negotiating a **covenant not to compete** (or a **restrictive covenant**) with the seller. Under a restrictive covenant, the seller agrees not to open a new competing store within a specific time period and geographic area of the existing one. (The covenant should be negotiated with the owner, not the corporation, because if the corporation signs the agreement, the owner may not be bound.) However, the covenant must be a part of a business sale and must be reasonable in scope in order to be enforceable. Without such protection, a buyer may find his new business eroding beneath his feet.

Ongoing Legal Liabilities. Finally, the potential buyer must look for any potential legal liabilities the purchase might expose. These typically arise from three sources: (1) physical premises, (2) product liability claims, and (3) labor relations. First, the buyer must examine the physical premises for safety. Is the employees' health at risk because of asbestos or some other hazardous material? If a manufacturing environment is involved, does it meet Occupational Safety and Health Administration (OSHA) and other regulatory agency requirements?

Second, the buyer must consider whether the product contains defects that could result in **product liability lawsuits,** which claim that a company is liable for damages and injuries caused by the products or services it sells. Existing lawsuits might be an omen of more to follow. In addition, the buyer must explore products that the company has discontinued, for he or she might be liable for them if they prove to be defective. The final bargain between the parties should require the seller to guarantee that the company is not involved in any product liability lawsuits.

Third, what is the relationship between management and employees? Does a union represent employees in a collective bargaining agreement? The time to discover sour management–labor relations is before the purchase, not after.

The existence of such liabilities does not necessarily eliminate the business from consideration. Insurance coverage can shift such risks from the potential buyer, but the buyer should check to see whether the insurance covers lawsuits resulting from actions taken before the purchase. Despite conducting a thorough search, a buyer may purchase a business only to discover later the presence of hidden liabilities such as unpaid back taxes or delinquent bills, unpaid pension fund contributions, undisclosed lawsuits, or others. Including a clause in the purchase agreement that imposes the responsibility for such hidden liabilities on the seller can protect a buyer from unpleasant surprises after the sale.

Is the Business Financially Sound?

The prospective buyer must analyze the financial records of the business to determine its health. He shouldn't be afraid to ask an accountant for help. Accounting systems and methods can vary tremendously from one type of business to another and can be quite confusing to a novice. Current profits can be inflated by changes in the accounting procedure or in the method for recording sales. For the buyer, the most dependable financial records are audited statements, those prepared by a certified public accountant in accordance with generally accepted accounting principles (GAAP). Any investment in a company should produce a reasonable salary for the owner and a healthy return on the money invested. Otherwise, it makes no sense to purchase the business.

A buyer also must remember that he or she is purchasing the future profit potential of an existing business. To evaluate the firm's profit potential, a buyer should review past sales, operating expenses, and profits as well as the assets used to generate those profits. He or she must compare current balance sheets and income statements with previous ones and then develop pro forma statements for the next two or three years. Sales tax records, income tax returns, and financial statements are valuable sources of information.

Are profits consistent over the years, or are they erratic? Is this pattern typical in the industry, or is it a result of unique circumstances or poor management? Can the business survive with such a serious fluctuation in revenues, costs, and profits? If these fluctuations are caused by poor management, can a new manager turn the business around? Some of the financial records that a potential buyer should examine include the following.

Income Statements and Balance Sheets for the Past Three to Five Years. It is important to review data from several years because creative accounting techniques can distort financial data in any single year. Even though buyers are purchasing the future profits of a business, they must remember that many businesses intentionally show low profits in order to minimize the owners' tax bills. Low profits should prompt a buyer to investigate their causes.

Income Tax Returns for the Past Three to Five Years. Comparing basic financial statements with tax returns can reveal discrepancies of which the buyer should be aware. Some small business owners "skim" from their businesses; that is, they take money from sales without reporting it as income. Owners who skim will claim their businesses are more profitable than their tax returns show. However, buyers should not pay for "phantom profits."

Owner's Compensation (and That of Relatives). The owner's compensation is especially important in small companies; and the smaller the company is, the more important it will be. Although many companies do not pay their owners what they are worth, others compensate their owners lavishly. Buyers must consider the impact of fringe benefits—company cars, insurance contracts, country club memberships, and the like. It is important to adjust the company's income statements for the salary and fringe benefits that the seller has paid himself and others.

Cash Flow. Most buyers understand the importance of evaluating a company's profit history, but few recognize the need to analyze its cash flow. They assume that if profits are adequate, there will be sufficient cash to pay all of the bills and to fund an adequate salary for themselves. *That is not necessarily the case!* Before closing any deal, a buyer should sit down with an accountant and convert the target company's financial statements into a cash flow forecast. This forecast must take into account

Table 5.2
The Records
a Business
Buyer Should
Review Before
Committing to
a Deal

1. Balance sheets and income statements from the previous three to five years
2. Income tax returns for the previous three to five years
3. Cash flow analysis and forecasts
4. Records of accounts receivable (preferably aged)
5. Records of accounts payable
6. Loan agreements with banks and other lenders
7. Existing contracts with major suppliers and customers
8. Contracts or leases on real estate
9. Repair and maintenance records on equipment, machinery, and fixtures
10. Insurance policies, including workers' compensation coverage
11. Documentation on existing patents, trademarks, or copyrights
12. Individual employees' labor contracts or union (collective bargaining) contracts
13. Copies of business licenses
14. Articles of incorporation (if incorporated) or articles of organization and operating agreement (if a limited liability company)
15. Details of any lawsuits the company is currently involved in

Source: Adapted from Joseph Anthony, "Maybe You Should Buy a Business," *Kiplinger's Personal Finance Magazine,* May 1993, p. 84.

not only existing debts and obligations but also any modifications or additional debts the buyer plans to make in the business. It should reflect the repayment of financing the buyer arranges to purchase the company. The telling question is: Can the company generate sufficient cash to be self-supporting? How much cash will it generate for the buyer?

A potential buyer must look for suspicious deviations from the average (in either direction) for sales, expenses, profits, assets, and liabilities. Have sales been increasing or decreasing? Is the equipment really as valuable as it is listed on the balance sheet? Is advertising expense unusually high? How is depreciation reflected in the financial statements?

This financial information gives the buyer the opportunity to verify the seller's claims about the business's performance. Sometimes, however, an owner will take short-term actions that produce a healthy financial statement but weaken the firm's long-term health and profit potential. For example, a seller might lower costs by gradually eliminating equipment maintenance or might boost sales by selling to marginal businesses that will never pay their bills. Such techniques can artificially inflate assets and profits, but a well-prepared buyer should be able to see through them.

Finally, a potential buyer should always be wary of purchasing a business if the present owner refuses to disclose his financial records. Table 5.2 lists the records that a potential buyer should review before making a final decision about buying a business.

METHODS FOR DETERMINING THE VALUE OF A BUSINESS

Business valuation is partly an art and partly a science. What makes establishing a reasonable price for a privately owned business so difficult is the wide variety of factors that influence its value. These include the nature of the business itself, its posi-

4. Describe the various ways of determining the value of a business.

tion in the market or industry, the outlook for the market or industry, the company's financial status and stability, its earning capacity, any intangible assets it may own (e.g., patents, trademarks, and copyrights), the value of other similar companies that are publicly owned, and many other factors.

Computing the value of the company's tangible assets normally poses no major problem, but assigning a price to the intangibles, such as goodwill, almost always creates controversy. The seller expects goodwill to reflect the hard work and long hours invested in building the business. The buyer, however, is willing to pay extra only for those intangible assets that produce exceptional income. So how can the buyer and the seller arrive at a fair price? There are few hard-and-fast rules in establishing the value of a business, but the following guidelines can help:

- There is no single best method for determining a business's worth, because each business sale is unique. The wisest approach is to compute a company's value using several techniques and then to choose the one that makes the most sense.
- The deal must be financially feasible for both parties. The seller must be satisfied with the price received for the business, but the buyer cannot pay an excessively high price that would require heavy borrowing and would strain his or her cash flows from the outset.
- Both the buyer and the seller should have access to the business records.
- Valuations should be based on facts, not fiction.
- The two parties should deal with one another honestly and in good faith.

The main reason that buyers purchase existing businesses is to capture the firm's earnings potential. The second most common reason is to obtain an established asset base. It is often much easier to buy assets than to build them. Although evaluation methods should take these characteristics into consideration, too many business sellers and buyers depend on rules of thumb that ignore the unique features of many small companies. For example, there is no "rule of thumb" or universal valuation method that fits every type of business.

This section describes three basic techniques—the balance sheet method, the earnings approach, and the market approach—and several variations on them for determining the value of a hypothetical business, Lewis Electronics.

Balance Sheet Method:
Net Worth = Assets − Liabilities

Balance Sheet Technique. The **balance sheet technique** is one of the most commonly used methods of evaluating a business, although it is not highly recommended because it oversimplifies the valuation process. This method computes the book value of a company's **net worth,** or **owner's equity** (net worth = assets − liabilities) and uses this figure as the value. The problem with this technique is that it fails to recognize reality: Most small businesses have market values that exceed their reported book values.

The first step is to determine which assets are included in the sale. In most cases, the owner has some personal assets that he does not want to sell. Professional business brokers can help the buyer and the seller arrive at a reasonable value for the collection of assets included in the deal. Remember that net worth on a financial statement will likely differ significantly from actual net worth in the market. Figure 5.2 shows the balance sheet for Lewis Electronics. Based on this balance sheet, the company's net worth is $151,766 ($266,091 − $114,325).

Two years after purchasing Automatic Door Specialists (ADS), Hendrix Neimann was well aware of the dark side of buying a business. "Never, but never, had an owner known so little about his business," he says, "or been so totally at the mercy of his employees. What's more, I barely even knew what business we were in. I had always thought we were in the security/access control industry. It turned out we were a subset of the construction industry. I had never had any desire to be in construction or anything remotely resembling construction," he says.

Neimann discovered that a substantial portion of ADS sales came from government contracts, wherein the lowest bidder got the job. Under Neimann, however, ADS was focusing on quality product lines and full installation and service practices. Unfortunately, Neimann also discovered that potential customers saw ADS's products as commodities and made their purchase decisions on the basis of price, not quality and service. "I couldn't, or wouldn't, do business that way," says Neimann. As government jobs became more scarce, competition became more intense. Sales slumped, and ADS lost $53,000 in Neimann's first year.

Neimann's attempts to change the company's culture met with no more success than did his marketing strategies. He tried all of the latest management philosophies, but they never seemed to work. "The staff nodded, smiled, asked a few questions—and then proceeded to ignore everything I had said and go about their business," he says. Several long-time employees decided to leave what they saw as a sinking ship.

As in many small companies, cash flow was a constant problem. On two occasions, Neimann barely made payroll—with $37 to spare one week and $95 the other. "We just couldn't seem to develop any momentum," Neimann says. Slipping into panic, he took virtually all decision-making authority away from his workers, further alienating them. Paying creditors soon became a problem, and Neimann was forced to juggle the company's bills. Unpaid telephone bills, vendor invoices, even the payments to former owner Peter Klosky were piling up.

Looking back on his purchase of ADS, Neimann says, "Before I bought the business, I never really, truly assembled enough information to tell if I was actually going to like what I was doing. I got so caught up in the details of negotiating the deal and in checking out all the facts that I didn't take enough time to figure out if I'd be happy. It took a year for me to admit that I didn't like the industry I had joined or what I had to do to be successful in it." Neimann felt trapped. "Here I was," he says, "not having any fun, in fact hating a lot of what I was doing, with every personal asset on the line, and unable to get out. That's as trapped as you get."

1. Review the sections in this chapter entitled "How to Buy a Business" and "In Search of the Perfect Business: Part 1." Which steps did Neimann violate?

2. What could Neimann have done to avoid the problems at ADS?

3. What is your forecast for ADS and Hendrix's future?

Source: Adapted from Hendrix F. C. Neimann, "How to Buy a Business," *Inc.*, October 1991, pp. 38–46.

Variation: Adjusted Balance Sheet Technique. A more realistic method for determining a company's value is to adjust the book value of net worth to reflect the actual market value. The values reported on a company's books may either overstate or understate the true value of assets and liabilities. Typical assets in a business sale include notes and accounts receivable, inventories, supplies, and fixtures. If a buyer purchases notes and accounts receivable, he should estimate the likelihood of their collection and adjust their value accordingly (refer to Table 5.1). In manufacturing, wholesale, and retail businesses, inventory is usually the largest single asset in the sale. Taking a physical inventory count is the best way to determine accurately the quantity of goods to be transferred. The sale may include three types of inventory,

Figure 5.2
Balance Sheet for
Lewis Electronics,
June 30, 200X

Assets

Current Assets

Cash	$11,655	
Accounts receivable	15,876	
Inventory	56,523	
Supplies	8,574	
Prepaid insurance	5,587	
Total current assets		$98,215

Fixed Assets

Land		$24,000	
Buildings	$141,000		
less accumulated depreciation	51,500	89,500	
Office equipment	$ 12,760		
less accumulated depreciation	7,159	5,601	
Factory equipment	$ 59,085		
less accumulated depreciation	27,850	31,235	
Trucks and autos	$ 28,730		
less accumulated depreciation	11,190	17,540	
Total fixed assets			$167,876
Total Assets			$266,091

Liabilities

Current Liabilities

Accounts payable	$19,497	
Mortgage payable	5,215	
Salaries payable	3,671	
Not payable	10,000	
Total current liabilities		$38,383

Long-Term Liabilities

Mortgage payable	$54,542	
Note payable	21,400	
Total long-term liabilities		$ 75,942
Total Liabilities		$114,325

Owner's Equity

Owner's Equity (net worth)	$151,766
Total Liabilities + Owner's Equity	$266,091

each having its own method of valuation: raw materials, work-in-process, and finished goods.

The buyer and the seller must arrive at a method for evaluating the inventory. First-in–first-out (FIFO), last-in–first-out (LIFO), and average costing are three frequently used techniques, but the most common methods use the cost of last purchase and the replacement value of the inventory. Before accepting any inventory value, the buyer should evaluate the condition of the goods.

To avoid such problems, some buyers insist on having a knowledgeable representative on an inventory team to count the inventory and check its condition. Nearly every sale involves merchandise that cannot be sold, but by taking this precaution, a buyer minimizes the chance of being stuck with worthless inventory. Fixed assets transferred in a sale might include land, buildings, equipment, and fixtures. Business owners frequently carry real estate and buildings on their books at prices well below their actual market value. Equipment and fixtures, depending on their condition and usefulness, may increase or decrease the true value of the business. Appraisals of these assets on insurance policies are helpful guidelines for establishing market value. Also, business brokers can be useful in determining the current value of fixed assets. Some brokers use an estimate of what it would cost to replace a company's physical assets (less a reasonable allowance for depreciation) to determine value. For Lewis Electronics, the adjusted net worth is $274,638 − $114,325 = $160,313 (see the adjusted balance sheet in Figure 5.3), indicating that some of the entries on its books did not accurately reflect market value.

Business evaluations based on balance sheet methods suffer one major drawback: They do not consider the future earnings potential of the business. These techniques value assets at current prices and do not consider them as tools for creating future profits. The next method for computing the value of a business is based on its expected future earnings.

Earnings Approach

The buyer of an existing business is essentially purchasing its future income. The **earnings approach** is more refined than the balance sheet method because it considers the future income potential of the business.

Variation 1: Excess Earnings Method. This method combines both the value of the firm's existing assets (over its liabilities) and an estimate of its future earnings potential to determine a business's selling price. One advantage of the **excess earnings method** is that it offers an estimate of goodwill. Goodwill is an intangible asset that often creates problems in a business sale. In fact, the most common method of valuing a business is to compute its tangible net worth and then to add an often arbitrary adjustment for goodwill. In essence, goodwill is the difference between an established, successful business and one that has yet to prove itself. It is based on the company's reputation and its ability to attract customers. A buyer should not accept blindly the seller's arbitrary adjustment for goodwill because it is likely to be inflated.

The excess earnings method provides a fairly consistent and realistic approach for determining the value of goodwill. It measures goodwill by the amount of profit the business earns above that of the average firm in the same industry. It also assumes that the owner is entitled to a reasonable return on the firm's adjusted tangible net worth.

Step 1: Compute Adjusted Tangible Net Worth. Using the previous method of valuation, the buyer should compute the firm's adjusted tangible net worth. Total tangible assets (adjusted for market value) minus total liabilities yields adjusted tangible net worth. In the Lewis Electronics example, adjusted tangible net worth is $274,638 − $114,325 = $160,313 (refer to Figure 5.3).

Step 2: Calculate the Opportunity Costs of Investing in the Business. **Opportunity costs** represent the cost of forgoing a choice. If the buyer chooses to purchase the

Figure 5.3
Balance Sheet for
Lewis Electronics
Adjusted to
Reflect Market
Value, June 30,
200X

Assets

Current Assets

Cash	$11,655	
Accounts receivable	10,051	
Inventory	39,261	
Supplies	7,492	
Prepaid insurance	5,587	
Total current assets		$74,046

Fixed Assets

Land		$36,900	
Buildings	$177,000		
less accumulated depreciation	51,500	125,500	
Office equipment	$ 11,645		
less accumulated depreciation	7,159	4,486	
Factory equipment	$ 50,196		
less accumulated depreciation	27,850	22,346	
Trucks and autos	$ 22,550		
less accumulated depreciation	11,190	11,360	
Total fixed assets			$200,592
Total Assets			$274,638

Liabilities

Current Liabilities

Accounts payable	$19,497	
Mortgage payable	5,215	
Salaries payable	3,671	
Note payable	10,000	
Total current liabilities		$38,383

Long-Term Liabilities

Mortgage payable	$54,542	
Note payable	21,400	
Total long-term liabilities		$ 75,942
Total Liabilities		$114,325

Owner's Equity

Owner's Equity (net worth)	$160,313
Total Liabilities + Owner's Equity	$274,638

assets of a business, he cannot invest his money elsewhere. Therefore, the opportunity cost of the purchase would be the amount that the buyer could have earned by investing the same amount in a similar risk investment.

There are three components in the rate of return used to value a business: (1) the basic, risk-free return, (2) an inflation premium, and (3) the risk allowance for investing in the particular business. The basic, risk-free return and the inflation premium are reflected in investments such as U.S. Treasury bonds. To determine the appropriate rate of return for investing in a business, the buyer must add to this base rate a factor reflecting the risk of purchasing the company. The greater the risk is, the higher the rate of return will be. A normal-risk business typically indicates a 25 percent rate of return. In the Lewis Electronics example, the opportunity cost of the investment is $160,313 \times 25\% - \$40,078$.

The second part of the buyer's opportunity cost is the salary that she could have earned working for someone else. For the Lewis Electronics example, if the buyer purchases the business, she must forgo the $25,000 that she could have earned working elsewhere. Adding these amounts yields a total opportunity cost of $65,078.

Step 3: Project Net Earnings. The buyer must estimate the company's net earnings for the upcoming year before subtracting the owner's salary. Averages can be misleading, so the buyer must be sure to investigate the trend of net earnings. Have they risen steadily over the past five years, dropped significantly, remained relatively constant, or fluctuated wildly? Past income statements provide useful guidelines for estimating earnings. In the Lewis Electronics example, the buyer and an accountant project net earnings to be $74,000.

Step 4: Compute Extra Earning Power. A company's extra earning power is the difference between forecasted earnings (step 3) and total opportunity costs (step 2). Many small businesses that are for sale do not have extra earning power (i.e., excess earnings) and they show marginal or no profits. The extra earning power of Lewis Electronics is $74,000 - \$65,078 = \$8,922$.

Step 5: Estimate the Value of Intangibles. The owner can use the business's extra earning power to estimate the value of its intangible assets: that is, its goodwill. Multiplying the extra earning power by a years-of-profit figure yields an estimate of the intangible assets' value. The years-of-profit figure for a normal-risk business ranges from three to four. A very high-risk business may have a years-of-profit figure of one, whereas a well-established firm might use a figure of seven. For Lewis Electronics, the value of intangibles (assuming normal risk) would be $8,922 \times 3 = \$26,766$.

Step 6: Determine the Value of the Business. To determine the value of the business, the buyer simply adds together the adjusted tangible net worth (step 1) and the value of the intangibles (step 5). Using this method, the value of Lewis Electronics is $160,313 + \$26,766 = \$187,079$.

Both the buyer and seller should consider the tax implications of transferring goodwill. The amount that the seller receives for goodwill is taxed as ordinary income. The buyer cannot count this amount as a deduction because goodwill is a capital asset that cannot be depreciated or amortized for tax purposes. Instead, the buyer would be better off paying the seller for signing a covenant not to compete because its value is fully tax deductible. The success of this approach depends on the accuracy of the buyer's estimates of net earnings and risk, but it does offer a systematic method for assigning a value to goodwill.

Variation 2: Capitalized Earnings Approach. Another earnings approach capitalizes expected net profits to determine the value of a business. The buyer should prepare his own pro forma income statement and should ask the seller to prepare one also. Many appraisers use a five-year weighted average of past sales (with the greatest weights assigned to the most recent years) to estimate sales for the upcoming year.

Once again, the buyer must evaluate the risk of purchasing the business to determine the appropriate rate of return on the investment. The greater the perceived risk, the higher the return the buyer will require. Risk determination is always somewhat subjective, but it is necessary for proper evaluation.

The **capitalized earnings approach** divides estimated net earnings (after subtracting the owner's reasonable salary) by the rate of return that reflects the risk level. For Lewis Electronics, the capitalized value (assuming a reasonable salary of $25,000) is:

$$\frac{\text{Net earnings (after deducting owner's salary)}}{\text{Rate of return}} = \frac{\$74,000 - \$25,000}{25\%} = \$196,000 \quad \text{(1)}$$

Clearly, firms with lower risk factors are more valuable (a 10 percent rate of return would have yielded a value of $499,000) than are those with higher risk factors (a 50 percent rate of return would have yielded a value of $99,800). Most normal-risk businesses use a rate-of-return factor ranging from 25 to 33 percent. The lowest risk factor that most buyers would accept for any business ranges from 15 to 20 percent.

Variation 3: Discounted Future Earnings Approach. This variation of the earnings approach assumes that a dollar earned in the future will be worth less than that same dollar today. Therefore, using the **discounted future earnings approach,** the buyer estimates the company's net income for several years into the future and then discounts these future earnings back to their present value. The resulting present value is an estimate of the company's worth.

The reduced value of future dollars has nothing to do with inflation. Instead, present value represents the cost of the buyers' giving up the opportunity to earn a reasonable rate of return by receiving income in the future instead of today. To visualize the importance of the time value of money, consider two $1 million sweepstakes winners. Rob wins $1 million in a sweepstakes, and he receives it in $50,000 installments over 20 years. If Rob invests every installment at 15 percent interest, he will have accumulated $5,890,505.98 at the end of 20 years. Lisa wins $1 million in another sweepstakes, but she collects her winnings in one lump sum. If Lisa invests her $1 million today at 15 percent, she will have accumulated $16,366,537.39 at the end of 20 years. The difference in their wealth is the result of the time value of money.

The discounted future earnings approach has five steps:

Step 1: Project Earnings for Five Years into the Future. One way is to assume that earnings will grow by a constant amount over the next five years. Perhaps a better method is to develop three forecasts—an optimistic, a pessimistic, and a most likely—for each year and then find a weighted average using the following formula:

$$\begin{array}{c} \text{Forecasted} \\ \text{earnings} \\ \text{for year } i \end{array} = \frac{\begin{array}{c}\text{Optimistic} \\ \text{earnings} \\ \text{for year } i\end{array} + \begin{array}{c}(\text{Most likely} \\ \text{earnings for} \\ \text{year } i \times 4)\end{array} + \begin{array}{c}\text{Pessimistic} \\ \text{earnings} \\ \text{for year } i\end{array}}{6} \quad \text{(2)}$$

For Lewis Electronics, the buyer's forecasts are:

Year	Pessimistic	Most Likely	Optimistic	Weighted Average
XXX1	$65,000	$ 74,000	$ 92,000	$ 75,500
XXX2	74,000	90,000	101,000	89,167
XXX3	82,000	100,000	112,000	99,000
XXX4	88,000	109,000	120,000	107,333
XXX5	88,000	115,000	122,000	111,667

The buyer must remember that the further into the future he forecasts, the less reliable the estimates will be.

Step 2: Discount These Future Earnings Using the Appropriate Present Value Factor. The appropriate present value factor can be found by looking in published present value tables, by using modern calculators or computers, or by solving the equation $1/(1 + k)^t$, where k = rate of return and t = time (year 1, 2, 3 . . . n). The rate that the buyer selects should reflect the rate he could earn on a similar risk investment. Because Lewis Electronics is a normal-risk business, the buyer chooses 25 percent.

Year	Income Forecast (Weighted Average)	Present Value Factor (at 25 percent)	Net Present Value
XXX1	$ 75,500	0.8000	$ 60,400
XXX2	$ 89,167	0.6400	57,067
XXX3	$ 99,000	0.5120	50,688
XXX4	$107,333	0.4096	43,964
XXX5	$111,667	0.3277	36,593
Total			$248,712

Step 3: Estimate the Income Stream Beyond Five Years. One technique suggests multiplying the fifth-year income by $1/$(rate of return). For Lewis Electronics, the estimate is:

$$\text{Income beyond year 5} = \$111,667 \times (1 / 25\%) = \$446,668 \qquad \text{(3)}$$

Step 4: Discount the Income Estimate Beyond Five Years Using the Present Value Factor for the Sixth Year. For Lewis Electronics:

$$\text{Present value of income beyond year 5} = \$446,668 \times 0.2622 = \$117,116 \qquad \text{(4)}$$

Step 5: Compute the Total Value of the Business

$$\text{Total value} = \$248,712 + \$117,116 = \$365,828 \qquad \text{(5)}$$

The primary advantage of this technique is that it evaluates a business solely on the basis of its future earnings potential, but its reliability depends on making forecasts of future earnings and on choosing a realistic present value factor. The discounted future earnings approach is especially well-suited for valuing service businesses (whose asset bases are often small) and for companies experiencing high growth rates.

Market Approach

The **market** (or **price/earnings**) **approach** uses the price/earnings ratios of similar businesses to establish the value of a company. The buyer must use businesses whose stocks are publicly traded in order to get a meaningful comparison. A company's **price/earnings ratio** (or **P/E ratio**) is the price of one share of its common stock in the market divided by its earnings per share (after deducting preferred stock dividends). To get a representative P/E ratio, the buyer should average the P/Es of as many similar businesses as possible.

To compute the company's value, the buyer multiplies the average P/E ratio by the private company's estimated earnings. For example, suppose that the buyer found four companies comparable to Lewis Electronics but whose stock is publicly traded. Their P/E ratios are:

Section II   Building the Business Plan: Beginning Considerations

Company 1	3.3
Company 2	3.8
Company 3	4.7
Company 4	4.1
Average	3.975

Using this average P/E ratio produces a value of $294,150:

$$\text{Value} = \text{Average P/E ratio} \times \text{Estimated net earnings} \tag{6}$$
$$\text{Value} = 3.975 \times \$74{,}000 = \$294{,}150$$

The biggest advantage of the market approach is its simplicity. But this method does have several disadvantages, including the following:

- *Necessary comparisons between publicly traded and privately owned companies.* The stock of privately owned companies is illiquid, and, therefore, the P/E ratio used is often subjective and lower than that of publicly held companies.
- *Unrepresentative earnings estimates.* The private company's net earnings may not realistically reflect its true earnings potential. To minimize taxes, owners usually attempt to keep profits low and rely on fringe benefits to make up the difference.
- *Finding similar companies for comparison.* Often, it is extremely difficult for a buyer to find comparable publicly held companies when estimating the appropriate P/E ratio.
- *Applying the after-tax earnings of a private company to determine its value.*

Despite its drawbacks, the market approach is useful as a general guideline to establishing a company's value.

Is There a Best Method?

Which of these methods is best for determining the value of a small business? Simply stated, there is no single best method. These techniques will yield a range of values. Buyers should look for values that might cluster together and then use their best judgment to determine their offering price.

UNDERSTANDING THE SELLER'S SIDE

5. Understand the seller's side of the buy-out decision and how to structure the deal.

Few events are more anticipated—and emotional—than selling your business. For many entrepreneurs, it has produced vast personal wealth and a completely new lifestyle, and in turn, freedom and the opportunity to catch up on all the things the owners missed out on while building the business. Yet, many entrepreneurs who sell out experience a tremendous void in their lives. After they sell, they discover that their businesses were not only the focal point of their lives for many years but also an essential element in their identities. Letting go is not easy, and putting a price on what they have worked most of their lives to build is even more difficult.

The sale of a business which, in many cases, you gave birth to and developed to what it is today, generally produces a feeling that the enterprise is very valuable. In many cases, the entrepreneur has an unrealistically high expectation of the value of the business. Consequently, negotiations may take some time to complete and a great deal of factual valuation methods are normally needed to create a reasonable price range.

GAINING THE COMPETITIVE EDGE
Preparing to Sell Your Business

The following are actions business owners should take before putting the "For Sale" sign in front of their business:

1. Have a qualified professional conduct a valuation of your business.

2. Have your financial statements up to date and in order.

3. Have the financial statements reflect the true profitability of the business. If you have been charging personal expenses to the business, you are reducing the profitability of the business and, although you may have avoided some taxes, the value of the business as a multiple of profitability has been reduced.

4. Work with a financial advisor to determine which financial structure of the sale of the business is most advantageous in your tax and estate situation.

5. Clean up the appearance of your business. Beauty might only be skin deep—but that outer layer is important when trying to entice potential buyers. Get rid of unnecessary clutter, use a little fresh paint here and there, and remember—first impressions count!

6. Organize your legal papers to reduce confusion at the time of the sale.

7. Consider all aspects of management succession and have a workable plan in place.

8. Write down the reasons why you want to sell and then question the assumptions behind each reason. Once the sale is complete, it's too late to play "what if." It's best to do this up front.

9. Work with your advisory board to ensure that you have not missed any critical aspects of your plan. If you do not have a formal advisory board, seek the help of associates who have successfully sold their business or professionals that get paid to guide sellers through the process.

10. Be sure that the business remains profitable while you are attempting to sell it. You have a better chance to get your asking price when profits are up.

Based on your readings and experience, discuss any other steps that a seller could take to create an environment conducive to a successful sale of a business.

Source: Loraine McDonald, "Preparing to Sell Your Business," *Entrepreneur*, May 7, 2001.

For the Seller, Timing of the Sale Is Important

Selling a business is no simple task. Done properly, it takes time, patience, and preparation to locate a suitable buyer, strike a deal, and make the transition. Too often, business owners put off the selling process until the last minute: at retirement age or when a business crisis looms. Such a "fire sale" approach rarely yields the maximum price for a business. Advance planning and maintaining accurate financial records are keys to a successful sale.

Before selling a business, an entrepreneur must address some important questions: When these questions are satisfactorily addressed by the seller, the negotiation process will move more smoothly. The following are some of the critical questions that the seller needs to answer for herself:

- Do I want to continue my involvement with the business if the new owner asks me to stay on?
- If I decide to stay on to help in the transition, how involved do I wish to be, especially if the new owner has plans to make significant change?
- Before I sell this business and lose my source of income, how much must this business sell for to earn me a comparable income?

- Before I sell to an outside individual, are there internal candidates who both want to purchase the business and can afford to do so? Do I want my children or others to take over the business?
- What professionals (attorneys, accountants, business brokers, etc.) do I need to assemble as a team to help me sell the business?
- What financial terms and conditions do I prefer? What financial terms or conditions are unacceptable?
- Do I feel any pressure to sell in a specific time frame?

Plot an Exit Strategy and Structure the Deal

Once a business owner decides to sell the business, the focus shifts to structuring the most beneficial deal. Next to picking the right buyer, planning the structure of the deal is the most important decision a seller can make. Entrepreneurs who sell their companies without considering the tax implications of the deal can wind up paying as much as 70 percent of the proceeds in the form of capital gains and other taxes![3] A skilled tax adviser or financial planner can help business sellers legally minimize the bite various taxes take out of the proceeds of a sale.

Straight Business Sale. A straight business sale may be best for entrepreneurs who want to step down and turn over the reins of the company to someone else. A recent study of small business sales in 60 categories found that 94 percent were asset sales; the remaining 6 percent involved the sale of stock. About 22 percent were for cash, and 75 percent included a down payment with a note carried by the seller. The remaining 3 percent relied on a note from the seller with no down payment. When the deal included a down payment, it averaged 33 percent of the purchase price. Only 40 percent of the business sales studied included covenants not to compete.

Although selling a business outright is often the safest exit path for an entrepreneur, it is usually the most expensive one. Sellers who want cash and take the money up front face an oppressive tax burden. They must pay a capital gains tax on the sale price less their investments in the company. Nor is a straight sale an attractive exit strategy for those who want to stay on with the company or for those who want to surrender control of the company gradually rather than all at once.

Form a Family Limited Partnership. Entrepreneurs who want to pass their businesses on to their children should consider forming a family limited partnership. Using this exit strategy, an entrepreneur can transfer her business to her children without sacrificing control over it. The owner takes the role of general partner while her children become limited partners. The general partner keeps just 1 percent of the company, but the partnership agreement gives her total control over the business. The children own 99 percent of the company but have little or no say over how to run the business. Until the founder decides to step down and turn the reins of the company over to the next generation, she continues to run the business and sets up significant tax savings for the ultimate transfer of power.

Sell Controlling Interest. Sometimes, business owners sell the majority interest in their companies to investors, competitors, suppliers, or large companies with an agreement that they will stay on after the sale. In this way, a potential buyer might feel more confident abut the acquisition if they know the owner will commit to an intermediate-term (two to four years) management contract. Additionally, for the seller who does not wish to retire or start a new business, the management contract can be an excellent source of income. This type of flexibility by the seller may result in negotiating a more lucrative final deal.

Restructure the Company. Another way for business owners to cash out gradually is to replace the existing corporation with a new one, formed with other investors. The owner essentially is performing a leveraged buyout of his or her own company. For example, assume that you own a company worth $15 million. You form a new corporation with $12 million borrowed from a bank and $3 million in equity: $1.5 million of your own equity and $1.5 million in equity from an investor who wants you to stay on with the business. The new company buys your company for $15 million. You net $13.5 in cash ($15 million – your $1.5 million equity investment) and still own 50 percent of the new leveraged business. For a medium-sized business whose financial statement can justify a significant bank loan, this is an excellent option. This can be an option in cases in which both parties agree that the seller should remain involved in the business.

Use a Two-Step Sale. For owners wanting the security of a sales contract now but not wanting to step down from the company's helm for several years, a two-step sale may be ideal. The buyer purchases the business in two phases, getting 20 to 70 percent today and agreeing to buy the remainder within a specific time period. Until the final transaction takes place, the entrepreneur retains at least partial control of the company.

Establish an Employee Stock Ownership Plan (ESOP). Some owners cash out by selling to their employees through an employee stock ownership plan (ESOP). An ESOP is a form of employee benefit plan in which a trust created for employees purchases their employer's stock. Here's how an ESOP works: The company transfers shares of its stock to the ESOP trust, and the trust uses the stock as collateral to borrow enough money to purchase the shares from the company. The company guarantees payment of the loan principal and interest and makes tax-deductible contributions to the trust to repay the loan (see Figure 5.4). The company then distributes the stock to employees' accounts on the basis of a predetermined formula. In addition to the tax benefits an ESOP offers, the plan permits the owner to transfer all or part of the company to employees as gradually or as suddenly as preferred.

To use an ESOP successfully, a small business should be profitable (with pretax profits exceeding $100,000) and should have a payroll of more than $500,000 a year. In general, companies with fewer than 15 to 20 employees do not find ESOPs beneficial. For companies that prepare properly, however, ESOPs offer significant financial and managerial benefits. The owner gets to sell off his stock at whatever annual

Figure 5.4
A Typical Employee Stock Ownership Plan (ESOP)

Source: Corey Rosen, "Sharing Ownership with Employees," *Small Business Reports*, December 1990, p. 63.

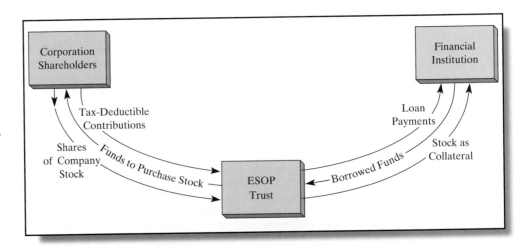

Section II   Building the Business Plan: Beginning Considerations

pace appeals to him. There's no cost to the employees, who eventually get to take over the company. And for the company the cost of the buyout is fully deductible.

Sell to an International Buyer. In an increasingly global marketplace, small U.S. businesses have become attractive buyout targets for foreign companies. Foreign buyers—mostly European—buy more than 1,000 U.S. businesses each year. England leads the list of nations acquiring U.S. companies. Small business owners are receptive to international offers. In our global economy, many business owners may have the opportunity to sell to an international buyer.

In most instances, foreign companies buy U.S. businesses to gain access to a lucrative, growing market. They look for a team of capable managers, whom they typically retain for a given time period. They also want companies that are profitable, stable, and growing.

Selling to foreign buyers can have disadvantages, however. They typically purchase 100 percent of a company, thereby making the previous owner merely an employee. Relationships with foreign owners also can be difficult to manage. Studies report that U.S. executives at foreign-owned businesses stated that they didn't understand what motivated their bosses and that their new owners and relationships generally got worse over time.[4]

NEGOTIATING THE DEAL

6. Understand how the negotiation process works and identify the factors that affect it.

Although determining the value of a business for sale is an important step in buying a business, it is not the final one. The buyer and the seller must sit down to negotiate the actual selling price for the business, and, more important, the terms of the deal. The final deal the parties strike depends, in large part, on their negotiating skills. In a business sale, the party who is the better bargainer usually comes out on top. In a business sale, the seller is looking to:

- Get the highest price possible for the company.
- Sever all responsibility for the company's liabilities.
- Avoid unreasonable contract terms that might limit his or her future opportunities.
- Maximize the cash he or she gets from the deal.
- Minimize the tax burden from the sale.
- Make sure the buyer will make all future payments.

The buyer seeks to:

- Get the business at the lowest price possible.
- Negotiate favorable payment terms, preferably over time.
- Get assurances that he or she is buying the business he thinks he is getting.
- Avoid enabling the seller to open a competing business.
- Minimize the amount of cash paid up front.

Factors Affecting the Negotiation Process

Before beginning negotiations, a buyer should take stock of some basic issues. How strong is the seller's desire to sell? Is the seller willing to finance part of the purchase price? What terms does the buyer suggest? Which ones are most important to him? Is it urgent that the seller close the deal quickly? What deal structure best suits your needs? What are the tax consequences for both parties? Will the seller sign a restric-

Buyers may differ in many regards, but when it comes to your financials—expect the potential buyer to analyze the following numbers:

1. *Cash flow*: Cash flow should be able to cover the current operating expenses plus:
   The salaries that the new owners want to earn,
   Projected annual financing costs to cover borrowing for the purchase, and
   An annual return on their cash investment.

2. *Profitability*: Profitability must be high enough to exceed what could be earned with little or no business risk. If the profitability and cash flow doesn't support the price you are asking for the business, expect few serious buyers.

   What steps can be taken by an owner who plans to sell three years in the future to improve the measures of profitability and cash flow?

Source: Jill Andresky Fraser, "What Do Buyers Really Want?" *Inc.*, July 1999.

tive covenant? Is the seller willing to stay on with the company for a time as a consultant? What general economic conditions exist in the industry at the time of the sale? Sellers tend to have the upper hand in good economic times, and buyers will have an advantage during recessionary periods in an industry.

The Negotiation Process

On the surface, the negotiation process appears to be strictly adversarial. Although each party may be trying to accomplish objectives that are at odds with those of the opposing party, the negotiation process does not have to turn into a nasty battle with overtones of "If you win, then I lose." The negotiation process will go much more smoothly and much faster if the two parties work to establish a cooperative relationship based on honesty and trust from the outset. A successful deal requires both parties to examine and articulate their respective positions while trying to understand the other party's position. Recognizing that neither of them will benefit without a deal, both parties must work to achieve their objectives while making certain concessions to keep the negotiations alive. To avoid a stalled deal, both buyer and seller should go into the negotiation with a list of objectives ranked in order of priority. Prioritizing increases the likelihood that both parties will get most of what they want from the bargain. Knowing which terms are most important (and which are least important) to them enables the parties to make concessions without "giving away the farm" and without getting bogged down in nit-picking. If, for instance, the seller insists on a term that the buyer cannot agree to, he can explain why he cannot concede on that term and then offer to give up something in exchange. The following negotiating tips can help parties reach a mutually satisfying deal[5]:

- *Know what you want to have when you walk away from the table.* What will it take to reach your business objectives? What would the perfect deal be? Although it may not be possible to achieve the perfect deal, defining it helps you identify which issues are most important to you.
- *Develop a negotiation strategy.* Once you know where you want to finish, decide where you will start—and remember to leave some room to give. Try not to be the first one to mention price. Let the other party do that; then negotiate from there.

"How could I possibly have been so foolish?" asks Hendrix Neimann. "I thought I had done a decent job of checking out [Automatic Door Specialists] during the summer-long due-diligence process." After Neimann and his accountant discovered the unpaid bills, inflated inventory values, and past-due accounts receivable, they discounted heavily the price they offered Peter Klosky for the company. "The good news is that I didn't pay much," says Neimann. "The bad news is that I didn't get much."

Yet he went ahead with the deal and, in the process, put all of his family's personal assets at risk. Looking back, Neimann says, "I really thought I was a smart, talented, hardworking guy and that I could fix whatever was wrong with the company. Never mind that I didn't have a technical bone in my body and that this was a technical business in a technical industry. Never mind that the company turned out to be struggling and, in fact, losing money when I bought it. I, Neimann the Great, could do it."

But he couldn't. On February 12, 1997, Neimann closed the company, now called ADS Systems, that he had purchased nearly eight years before. He contacted the company's banker and its creditors and told them that he was ceasing operations. Preparing a summary of the company's financial position shone a spotlight on just how bleak the situation was. ADS had $473,000 in debt and accounts payable and only $142,000 in assets and receivables. Neimann explained to his creditors that he did not want to declare bankruptcy and that he intended to pay everything he owed, even if it took years. The bank stood first in line and had the right to claim all of the company's assets and, if those were insufficient (and they were), to claim the Neimanns' personal assets (including their home and personal bank accounts) as well.

For Neimann, the next few months were a nightmare. "[The banker] called me daily (sometimes twice daily) for no particular reason other than to let me know he was there and, unlike a bad dream, was not going to go away. Creditors called every day by the dozen." Concerned customers called wanting to know who would finish their jobs and who would service the equipment ADS had already installed. The landlord served notice that ADS would be evicted on March 24. The telephone and electric bills were more than two months past due, and the utility companies were threatening to shut off service.

From the time Neimann had bought ADS, the company was struggling financially and was never able to recover. The company was constantly in a cash flow bind, was usually behind in paying its bills, and rarely had a payables-to-receivables ratio of less than 2.5 to 1. When the company fell behind on employee withholding taxes, the Internal Revenue Services swept its bank account, taking out the $7,200 it owed.

To raise as much cash as possible to pay off some of the company's debts, Neimann advertised a business liquidation sale in the local newspaper. As friends and family pitched in to organize the sale, Neimann reflected on the path that had brought him to this point. Looking around at the condition he had allowed his company to degenerate into, Neimann was embarrassed. "Like the former owner, I no longer had noticed the dirt, the grease, the grime, the disorganization. I had allowed the men's offices, their desks, their vans to become no better than the inside of garbage cans. I had let the shop remain in a state of chaos since we had moved in there. The technicians and I never connected—ever. My lack of technical experience and knowledge grated on them—and rightly so. But the worst part of the seven and a half years was the overwhelming sense of hopelessness, of fearing that I would never, ever be able to dig out of the hole. I hated the business, hated the industry, hated the job. Yet I would not, could not, give up or in. My house was the ultimate collateral for the loan I'd taken out to buy the business. Therefore, lose the business, lose the house. I was trapped."

Finally, on March 24, 1997, with the building completely cleared out and all of ADS's assets sold off, Neimann's wife Judi unplugged the office clock at exactly 5 P.M. and took it off the wall. "We were finished," says Neimann.

1. Using Hendrix Neimann's experience with ADS, develop a list of "red flags" that should alert a buyer that a particular business is not for him or her.

2. Looking back at Neimann's experience, what advice would you give to someone who is considering buying a business?

Source: Adapted from Hendrix F. C. Neimann, "The End of the Story," *Inc.*, October 1997, pp. 68–77.

- *Recognize the other party's needs.* For a bargain to result, both parties must believe that they have met at least some of their goals. Asking open-ended questions can clue you in to the other side's position and why it's important.
- *Be an empathetic listener.* To truly understand what the other party's position is, you must listen attentively.
- *Focus on the problem, not on the person.* If the negotiation reaches an impasse, a natural tendency is to attack the other party. Resist! Instead, focus on developing a workable solution.
- *Avoid seeing the other side as "the enemy."* Such an attitude reduces the negotiation to an "I win, you lose" mentality that only hinders the process.
- *Educate; don't intimidate.* Rather than trying to bully the other party into accepting your point of view, try explaining your reasoning and the logic behind your proposal.
- *Be patient.* Resist the tendency to become angry and insulted at the proposals the other party makes. Similarly, don't be in such a hurry to close the deal that you give in on crucial points.
- *Remember that "no deal" is an option.* What would happen if the negotiations failed to produce a deal? In most negotiations, walking away from the table is an option. In some cases, it may be the best option.
- *Be flexible and creative.* Always have a fall-back position: an alternative that, although not ideal, satisfies you and is acceptable to the other party.

CHAPTER SUMMARY

1. Understand the advantages and disadvantages of buying an existing business.
   - The *advantages* of buying an existing business include: A successful business may continue to be successful; the business may already have the best location; employees and suppliers are already established; equipment is installed and its productive capacity known; inventory is in place and trade credit established; the owner hits the ground running; the buyer can use the expertise of the previous owner; and the business may be a bargain.
   - The *disadvantages* of buying an existing business include: An existing business may be for sale because it is deteriorating; the previous owner may have created ill will; employees inherited with the business may not be suitable; its location may have become unsuitable; equipment and facilities may be obsolete; change and innovation are hard to implement; inventory may be outdated; accounts receivable may be worth less than face value; and the business may be overpriced.

2. Define the steps involved in the *right* way to buy a business.
   - Buying a business can be a treacherous experience unless the buyer is well prepared. The right way to buy a business *is*: Analyze your skills, abilities, and interests to determine the ideal business for you; prepare a list of potential candidates, including those that might be in the "hidden market"; investigate and evaluate candidate businesses and evaluate the best one; explore financing options before you actually need the money; and, finally, ensure a smooth transition.

3. Explain the process of evaluating an existing business.
   - Rushing into a deal can be the biggest mistake a business buyer can make. Before closing a deal, every business buyer should investigate five critical areas: (1) Why does the owner wish to sell? Look for the *real* reason. (2) Determine the physical condition of the business. Consider both the building and its location. (3) Conduct a thorough analysis of the market for your products or

services. Who are the present and potential customers? Conduct an equally thorough analysis of competitors, both direct and indirect. How do they operate and why do customers prefer them? (4) Consider all of the legal aspects that might constrain the expansion and growth of the business. Did you comply with the provisions of a bulk transfer? Negotiate a restrictive covenant? Consider ongoing legal liabilities?

(5) Analyze the financial condition of the business, looking at financial statements, income tax returns, and especially cash flow.

4. Describe the various ways of determining the value of a business.
   - Placing a value on a business is partly an art and partly a science. There is no single best method for determining the value of a business. The following techniques (with several variations) are useful: the balance sheet technique (adjusted balance sheet technique); the earnings approach (excess earnings method, capitalized earnings approach, and discounted future earnings approach); and the market approach.

5. Understand the seller's side of the buyout decision and how to structure the deal.
   - Selling a business takes time, patience, and preparation to locate a suitable buyer, strike a deal, and make the transition. Sellers must always structure the deal with tax consequences in mind. Common exit strategies include a straight business sale, forming a family limited partnership, selling a controlling interest in the business, restructuring the company, selling to an international buyer, using a two-step sale, and establishing an employee stock ownership plan (ESOP).

6. Understand how the negotiation process works and identify the factors that affect it.
   - The first rule of negotiating is never confuse price with value. In a business sale, the party who is the better negotiator usually comes out on top. Before beginning negotiations, a buyer should identify the factors that are affecting the negotiations and then develop a negotiating strategy. The best deals are the result of a cooperative relationship based on trust.

DISCUSSION QUESTIONS

1. What advantages can an entrepreneur who buys a business gain over one who starts a business from scratch?
2. How would you go about determining the value of the assets of a business if you were unfamiliar with them?
3. Why do so many entrepreneurs run into trouble when they buy an existing business? Outline the steps involved in the *right* way to buy a business.
4. When evaluating an existing business that is for sale, what areas should an entrepreneur consider? Briefly summarize the key elements of each area.
5. How should a buyer evaluate a business's goodwill?
6. What is a restrictive covenant? Is it fair to ask the seller of a travel agency located in a small town to sign a restrictive covenant for one year covering a 20-square-mile area? Explain.
7. How much negative information can you expect the seller to give you about the business? How can a prospective buyer find out such information?
8. Why is it so difficult for buyers and sellers to agree on a price for a business?
9. Which method of valuing a business is best? Why?
10. Outline the different exit strategies available to a seller.
11. Explain the buyer's position in a typical negotiation for a business. Explain the seller's position. What tips would you offer a buyer about to begin negotiating the purchase of a business?

STEP INTO THE REAL WORLD

1. Ask several new owners who purchased existing businesses the following questions:

   a. How did you determine the value of the business?

b. How close was the price paid for the business to the value assessed before purchase?

c. What percentage of the accounts receivable was collectible?

d. How accurate were the projections concerning customers (especially sales volume and number of customers)?

e. Did you encounter any surprises after buying the business?

f. If you were negotiating the deal again, what would you do differently?

2. Visit a business broker and ask him how he brings a buyer and seller together. What does he do to facilitate the sale? What methods does he use to determine the value of a business?

3. Ask a local attorney about the legal aspects of buying a business. What recommendations does she have for someone considering the purchase of an existing business? What negotiating tips can she offer? Prepare a brief report on what you learned for your class.

4. Use some of the following resources on the World Wide Web (or conduct your own search) to locate two businesses for sale that interest you:

BizQuest   *www.bizQuest.com*
BizBuySell   *www.bizbuysell.com/*
Be The Boss   *www.betheboss.corul*
Internet Business
   Multiple Listing Site *www.bbn-net.com/*

Write a brief synopsis of these businesses and explain why they interest you. Create a plan outlining the steps you would take to actually evaluate and purchase one of these companies.

TAKE IT TO THE NET

Visit the Scarborough/Zimmerer home page at **www.prenhall.com/scarborough** for updated information, online resources, Web-based exercises, and sample business plan.

ENDNOTES

1. Gianna Jacobson, "Misson: Acquisition," *Success,* October 1997, pp. 62–66.
2. John Case, "Buy Now—Avoid the Rush," *Inc.,* February 1991, p. 38.
3. Peter Nulty, "Smart Ways to Sell Your Business," *Fortune,* March 17, 1996, pp. 97–98.
4. "Problems With Foreign Owners," *Small Business Reports,* May 1991, p. 11.
5. Laura M. Litvan, "Selling Off, Staying On," *Nation's Business,* August 1995, pp. 29–30.

Chapter 6

Crafting a Winning Business Plan

The best way to predict the future is to invent it.

—ALAN KAY

You can't direct the wind, but you can adjust the sails.

—ANONYMOUS

Upon completion of this chapter, you will be able to:

1. Explain why every entrepreneur should create a business plan.
2. Describe the elements of a solid business plan.
3. Explain the three tests every business plan must pass.
4. Understand the keys to making an effective business plan presentation.
5. Explain the "5 Cs of Credit" and why they are important to potential lenders and investors reading business plans.

Starting a business requires lots of planning, and one of the most important activities an entrepreneur should undertake before launching a company is building a solid business plan. It is the best insurance against becoming just another business failure statistic. A large body of evidence suggests that, whatever their size, companies that engage in business planning outperform those who do not. For entrepreneurs, a business plan is:

- A systematic, realistic evaluation of a venture's chances for success in the market
- A way to determine the principal risks facing the venture
- A game plan for managing the business successfully
- A tool for comparing actual results against targeted performance
- An important tool for attracting capital in the challenging hunt for money

This chapter describes how to build and use this vital business document, and it will help entrepreneurs create business plans that will guide them on their entrepreneurial journey and will help them attract the capital they need to launch and grow their businesses.

WHY DEVELOP A BUSINESS PLAN?

1. Explain why every entrepreneur should create a business plan.

A **business plan** is a written summary of an entrepreneur's proposed business venture, its operational and financial details, its marketing opportunities and strategy, and its managers' skills and abilities. There is no substitute for a well-prepared business plan, and there are no shortcuts to creating one. The plan serves as an entrepreneur's road map on the journey toward building a successful business. It describes the direction the company is taking, what its goals are, where it wants to be, and how it's going to get there. The plan is written proof that an entrepreneur has performed the necessary research and has studied the business opportunity adequately. In short, the business plan is the entrepreneur's best insurance against launching a business destined to fail or mismanaging a potentially successful company.

The business plan serves two essential functions. First and most important, it guides the company's operations by charting its future course and devising a strategy for following it. The plan provides a battery of tools—a mission statement, goals, objectives, budgets, financial forecasts, target markets, and strategies—to help managers lead the company successfully. It gives managers and employees a sense of direction, but only if everyone is involved in creating or updating it. As more team members become committed to making the plan work, it takes on special meaning. It gives everyone targets to shoot for, and it provides a yardstick for measuring actual performance against those targets, especially in the crucial and chaotic start-up phase. Plus, writing a plan requires entrepreneurs to get an in-depth understanding of the industries in which they plan to compete and how their companies fit into them. Finally, creating a plan forces entrepreneurs to subject their ideas to the test of reality: Can this business actually produce a profit?

The greatest waste of a completed business plan is to let it sit unused on a shelf collecting dust. When properly done, a plan becomes an integral and natural part of a company. In other words, successful entrepreneurs actually use their business plans to help them build strong companies. For instance, Judy Proudfoot, owner of Proudfoot Wearable Art, a home-based business that sells unique, hand-painted clothing, uses the business plan she wrote to keep her company focused and competitive. "I refer to it monthly," says Proudfoot. "It lets me compare projections to reality and discover what works well and what needs to be changed."[1]

The second function of the business plan is to attract lenders and investors. Too often, small business owners approach potential lenders and investors without having prepared to sell themselves and their business concept. "Lenders [and investors] want to see solid, incisive business plans that clearly demonstrate an entrepreneur's creditworthiness and his ability to build and manage a profitable company," says a partner in a venture capital firm.[2] Simply scribbling a few rough figures on a note pad to support a loan application is not enough. Applying for loans or attempting to attract investors without a solid business plan rarely attracts needed capital. The best way to secure the necessary capital is to prepare a sound business plan. The quality of the firm's business plan weighs heavily in the decision to lend or invest funds. It is also potential lenders' and investors' first impression of the company and its managers. Therefore, the finished product should be highly polished and professional in both form and content.

William Hyman, owner of Comprehensive Automotive Reclamation Services (CARS), the largest auto salvage yard in the nation, used a detailed business plan to attract $24 million in capital to purchase and install the equipment he needed to create his one-of-a-kind salvage operation. Hyman's plan showed the special equipment his business would need, how much it would cost, and the unique advantages his design would give the company. The CARS "disassembly line" can dismantle up to 30,000 vehicles a year, compared to about 600 at the average junkyard, and can reclaim 99 percent of the material in them, compared to just 75 percent at a typical salvage operation. After reviewing Hyman's business plan and meeting the entrepreneur, a top manager at one large company was so impressed with the company's competitive edge that he invested $2 million![3]

A plan is a reflection of its creator. It should demonstrate that an entrepreneur has thought seriously about the venture and what will make it succeed. Preparing a solid plan demonstrates that an entrepreneur has taken the time to conduct the necessary research and to commit the idea to paper. Building a plan also forces an entrepreneur to consider both the positive and the negative aspects of the business. A detailed and thoughtfully developed business plan makes a positive first impression on those who read it. In most cases, potential lenders and investors read a business plan before they ever meet with the entrepreneur behind it. Sophisticated investors will not take the time to meet with an entrepreneur whose business plan fails to reflect a serious investment of time and energy in defining a promising business opportunity. They know that an entrepreneur who lacks the discipline to develop a good business plan likely lacks the discipline to run a business.

Entrepreneurs should not allow others to prepare a business plan for them because outsiders cannot understand the business nor envision the proposed company as well as they can. Entrepreneurs are the driving force behind their business ideas and are the ones who can best convey the vision and the enthusiasm they have for transforming those ideas into a successful business. Also, because entrepreneurs will make the presentation to potential lenders and investors, they must understand every detail of the business plan. Otherwise, an entrepreneur cannot present it convincingly and in most cases the financial institution or investor will reject it. Answering the often difficult questions potential lenders and investors ask requires that entrepreneurs completely understand the details of their plans. Alice Medrich, cofounder of Cocolat, a manufacturer of specialty candies and desserts, recalls her first attempt at presenting her business plan:

> First of all, I went to the bank, and I was so ill-prepared and so insecure about what I was asking about . . . I was extremely insecure with a banker. I didn't know how to describe what I was doing with any confidence. I did not know how to present a business plan. And, he was condescending to

Entrepreneur Rob Ryan learned two valuable lessons after starting his first company, Softcom, which he sold to a larger competitor when he ran out of money. "First, never start a company without a great team," he says. "Second, raise a lot of money." He put those lessons into practice with his second company, Ascend Communications, which he co-founded with three partners in 1989 and $2.5 million in venture capital financing. Ascend, a maker of remote networking equipment, was successful and went public in 1994. After undergoing extensive back surgery, Ryan stepped down as Ascend's CEO and chairman and at age 46 found himself a very rich man with not much to do.

Rather than retire, Ryan decided to devote his life to helping other entrepreneurs become successful. He established Entrepreneur America, a business boot camp for budding entrepreneurs housed on his 1,200-acre Roaring Lion Ranch on the outskirts of Hamilton, Montana. His guests must pay their own fare to Montana, but once there, Ryan houses them, feeds them, and puts them through the wringer as he helps them refine their ideas and hone their business plans. Occasionally, he even saddles them up on some of his horses and takes them out into the breathtaking beauty of the Bitterroot Mountains. "If I could grow one great company a year, a really great company, that would be a great contribution to mankind," reflects Ryan. Ryan has coached several companies that have become hugely successful businesses, including search-engine company LookSmart, and Silicon Spice, a computer chip and software maker that was recently sold for $1.2 billion.

Ian Eslick, founder of Silicon Spice, sought Ryan's help when preparing his business plan. After working through Ryan's business plan boot camp, Eslick secured financing for his start-up venture from New Enterprise Associates (NEA), one of the premier venture capital firms in the world. Obviously impressed with the quality of the founders' business plan and their presentation of it, one NEA partner says, "[Rob Ryan] taught them how to orchestrate a business presentation and highlight key things." Eslick is quick to give Ryan credit for much of his company's success.

Out of the 1,000 or so entrepreneurs who apply to attend Entrepreneur America each year, Ryan selects about 20 to attend, mostly founders of start-ups with hot new technologies but few management skills. Every three weeks, a new batch of entrepreneurs arrives to face the challenge of their business lives. As tactful as a drill sergeant, Ryan challenges the entrepreneurs under his tutelage, questioning the assumptions underlying their plans, criticizing their business models, and cajoling them into improving the quality of their business plans. His style can be blistering, but his philosophy is basic: Create a successful business by building a strong management team, keeping costs low, maintaining focus on the right target market, and growing slowly. An experienced fund raiser with connections throughout the financial industry, Ryan also teaches his students how to decipher the language of venture capital and how to create a powerful presentation designed to impress potential lenders and investors.

Although it sounds harsh to outsiders, entrepreneurs love Ryan's tough, straightforward style. In response to one of Ryan's blistering assaults, one entrepreneur practicing his business plan presentation exclaimed, "This is good. It's making my head hurt, which is why I came here." Ryan's entrepreneurial students sense that Ryan's tough talk is designed to help them, and they don't resent it. "Once you realize he's being intimidating because you're up to the challenge, it's very motivating," says one.

Another of Ryan's students who has launched a highly successful technology company says, "There is a saying, 'There is no progress without the unreasonable man.' Unless you're absolutely unreasonable, things become the status quo. That's really the definition of Rob. You have to ask for the impossible. Certainly, Rob challenges people to do that."

1. What benefits does Rob Ryan's entrepreneurial boot camp offer aspiring entrepreneurs?

2. Critique the confrontational style that Ryan uses with his entrepreneurial students. What benefits does it give them?

3. Use the resources in the library and on the World Wide Web to develop a list of suggestions and advice for entrepreneurs presenting their business plans to lenders and investors.

Sources: Adapted from Beth Kwon, "You Call This Work?" *FSB*, October 2000, pp. 59–66; Susan Beck, "Out of Business," *Inc.*, May 1997, pp. 73–80.

me. Looking back on it, I can understand why: I wasn't prepared. . . . We didn't get the loan.[4]

Investors want to feel confident that an entrepreneur has realistically evaluated the risk involved in the new venture and has a strategy for addressing it. They also want to see proof that a business will become profitable and produce a reasonable return on their investment.

Perhaps the best way to understand the need for a business plan is to recognize the validity of the "two thirds rule," which says that only two thirds of the entrepreneurs with a sound and viable new business venture will find financial backing. Those who do find financial backing will get only two thirds of what they initially requested, and it will take them two thirds longer to get the financing than they anticipated.[5] The most effective strategy for avoiding the two thirds rule is to build a business plan!

Sometimes the greatest service a business plan provides an entrepreneur is the realization that "it just won't work." The time to find out that a business idea won't succeed is in the planning stages, *before* an entrepreneur commits significant money, time, and effort to the venture. It is much less expensive to make mistakes on paper than in reality. In other cases, a business plan reveals important problems to overcome before launching a company. Exposing these flaws and then addressing them enhances the chances of a venture's success.

The real value in preparing a plan is not as much in the plan itself as it is in the process the entrepreneur goes through to create the plan. Although the finished product is useful, the process of building the plan requires entrepreneurs to subject their ideas to an objective, critical evaluation. What entrepreneurs learn about their industries, target markets, financial requirements, competition, and other factors is essential to making their ventures successful. Simply put, building a business plan reduces the risk and uncertainty of launching a company by teaching an entrepreneur to do it the right way!

Table 6.1 describes the four bases every business plan should cover.

THE ELEMENTS OF A BUSINESS PLAN

2. Describe the elements of a solid business plan.

Smart entrepreneurs recognize that every business plan is unique and must be tailor-made. They avoid the off-the-shelf, "cookie-cutter" approach that produces look-alike plans. The elements of a business plan may be standard, but how entrepreneurs tell their story should be unique and reflect their personal excitement about the new venture. If this is a first attempt at writing a business plan, it may be very helpful to seek the advice of individuals with experience in this process. Consultants with Small Business Development Centers, accountants, business professors, business planning professionals, and attorneys can be excellent sources of advice in refining a business plan. Remember, however, not to allow someone else to write your plan!

Initially, the prospect of writing a business plan may appear to be overwhelming. Many entrepreneurs would rather launch their companies and "see what happens" than invest the necessary time and energy defining and researching their target markets, defining their strategies, and mapping out their finances. After all, building a plan is hard work! However, it is hard work that pays many dividends, and not all of them are immediately apparent. Entrepreneurs who invest their time and energy building plans are better prepared to face the hostile environment in which their companies will compete than those who do not. Earlier, we said that a business plan is like a road map that guides an entrepreneur on the journey to build-

Table 6.1
Covering the
Bases in a
Business Plan

What do potential lenders and investors look for in a business plan? Although there's no sure-fire method for satisfying every lender or investor, entrepreneurs who emphasize the following four points will cover their bases:

1. **Key people.** Potential lenders and investors want to see proof of the experience, skills, and abilities of a venture's key players. Even though the company may be new, it helps for potential lenders and investors to see that it's not being run by a bunch of amateurs.

2. **Promising opportunity.** A basic ingredient in the success of any business venture is the presence of a real market opportunity. The best way to show that such an opportunity exists is with facts. Smart entrepreneurs use the results of market research and an industry analysis to prove that the market for a business is rapidly expanding or that it is already large enough to support a niche profitably. It is also important to show how a venture will gain a competitive advantage in its market segment.

3. **Business context.** A business plan should also demonstrate that an entrepreneur understands how macroeconomic factors such as inflation and interest rates affect the business. Another important issue for many businesses is the role that government regulation plays.

4. **Risks and rewards.** A business plan should cover the risks a venture faces without dwelling on them. Investors and lenders like to see plans that describe the most serious threats to a venture and how entrepreneurs will deal with them. A plan should address the rewards investors can expect from the company's success. That means defining lender's and investor's exit paths. How will the company repay lenders and "cash out" investors? Is an initial public offering in the future? A sale to a larger company?

Source: Adapted from Brent Pollock, "Remember the Investor," *Success*, October 1997, p. 24.

ing a successful business. If you were making a journey to a particular destination through unfamiliar, harsh, and dangerous territory, would you rather ride with someone equipped with a road map and a trip itinerary or with someone who didn't believe in road maps or in planning trips, destinations, and layovers? Although building a business plan does not guarantee success, it does raise an entrepreneur's chances of succeeding in business.

A business plan typically ranges from 25 to 50 pages in length. Shorter plans usually are too sketchy to be of any value, and those much longer than this run the risk of never getting used or read! This section explains the most common elements of a business plan. However, entrepreneurs must recognize that, like every business venture, every business plan is unique. Entrepreneurs should view the following elements as a starting point for building a plan and should modify them as needed to better tell the story of their new venture.

The Executive Summary. To summarize the presentation to each potential financial institution or investors, the entrepreneur should write an executive summary. It should be concise—a maximum of two pages—and should summarize all of the relevant points of the proposed deal. After reading the executive summary, anyone should be able to understand the entire business concept and what differentiates the company from the competition. The executive summary is a synopsis of the entire plan, capturing its essence in a capsulized form. It should explain the basic business model and the problem the business will solve for customers, and briefly describe the owners and key employees, target market(s), financial highlights (e.g., sales and earnings projections, the dollar amount requested, how the funds will be used, and how and when any loans will be repaid), and the company's competitive advantage.

The executive summary is a written version of what is known as "the elevator pitch." Imagine yourself on an elevator with a potential lender or investor. Only the two of you are on the elevator, and you have that person's undivided attention for the duration of the ride, but the building is not very tall! To convince the investor that your business idea is a great investment, you must boil your message down to its essence—key points that you can communicate in a matter of one or two minutes.

The executive summary is designed to capture the reader's attention. If it misses, the chances of the remainder of the plan being read are minimal. A well-developed, coherent summary introducing the financial proposal establishes a favorable first impression of the entrepreneur and the business and can go a long way toward obtaining financing. Although the executive summary is the first part of the business plan, it should be the last section written.

Mission Statement. As you learned in Chapter 2, a mission statement expresses an entrepreneur's vision for what his or her company is, what it is to become, and what it stands for. It is the broadest expression of a company's purpose and defines the direction in which it will move. It serves as the thesis statement for the entire business plan.

Company History. The manager of an existing small business should prepare a brief history of the operation, highlighting the significant financial and operational events in the company's life. This section should describe when and why the company was formed, how it has evolved over time, and what the owner envisions for the future. It should highlight the successful accomplishment of past objectives and should convey the firm's image in the marketplace.

Business and Industry Profile. To acquaint lenders and investors with the nature of the business, the owner should describe it in the business plan. This section should begin with a statement of the company's general business goals and a narrower definition of its immediate objectives. Together, they should spell out what the business plans to accomplish, how, when, and who will do it. **Goals** are broad, long-range statements of what a company plans to do in the distant future that guide its overall direction and express its *raison d'être*. In other words, they answer the question: "Why am I in business?" Answering such a basic question appears to be obvious, but, in fact, many entrepreneurs cannot define the basis of their businesses.

Objectives are short-term, specific performance targets that are attainable, measurable, and controllable. Every objective should reflect some general business goal and include a technique for measuring progress toward its accomplishment. To be meaningful, an objective must have a time frame for achievement. Both goals and objectives should relate to the company's basic mission. In other words, accomplishing each objective should move a business closer to achieving its goals, which, in turn, should move it closer to its mission.

When summarizing the small company's background, entrepreneurs should describe the present state of the art in the industry and what they will need to succeed in the market segment in which their businesses compete. They should then identify the current applications of the product or service in the market and include projections for future applications.

This section should provide the reader with an overview of the industry or market segment in which the new venture will operate. Industry data such as market size, growth trends, and the relative economic and competitive strength of the major firms in the industry all set the stage for a better understanding of the viability of the new product or service. Strategic issues such as ease of market entry and exit, the ability to achieve economies of scale or scope, and the existence of cyclical or seasonal economic trends further help the reader evaluate the new venture. This part of the plan also should describe significant industry trends and an overall outlook for its future. Information about the evolution of the industry helps the reader comprehend its competitive dynamics. The *U.S. Industrial Outlook Handbook* is an excellent reference that profiles a variety of industries and offers projections for future trends in them. Another useful resource of industry and economic information is the *Summary of Commentary on Current Economic Conditions,* more commonly known as the Beige Book. Published eight times a year by the Federal Reserve, it provides detailed statistics and trends in key business sectors and in the overall economy. The Beige Book offers valuable information on topics ranging from tourism and housing starts to consumer spending and wage rates, and it is available on the World Wide Web.

The industry analysis should also focus on the existing and anticipated profitability of the firms in the targeted market segment. Any significant entry or exit of firms or consolidations and mergers should be discussed in terms of their impact on the competitive behavior of the market. The entrepreneur also should mention any events that have significantly altered the industry in the past 10 years.

Business Strategy. An even more important part of the business plan is the owner's view of the strategy needed to meet—and beat—the competition. In the previous section, entrepreneurs defined where they want to take their business by establishing goals and objectives. This section addresses the question of how to get there—business strategy. Here, entrepreneurs must explain how they plan to gain a competitive edge in the market and what sets their business apart from the competition. They should comment on how they plan to achieve business goals and objectives in the face of competition and government regulation and should identify the image the business will project. An important theme in this section is what makes the company unique in the eyes of its customers. One of the quickest routes to business failure is trying to sell "me-too" products or services that offer customers nothing newer, better, bigger, faster, or different. The foundation for this part of the business plan comes from the material in Chapter 2, "Strategic Management: Gaining a Competitive Edge."

This section of the business plan should outline the methods the company can use to meet the key success factors cited earlier. If, for example, a strong, well-trained sales force is considered critical to success, an entrepreneur must devise a plan of action for assembling one.

Description of Firm's Product/Service. An entrepreneur should describe the company's overall product line, giving an overview of how customers use its goods or services. Drawings, diagrams, and illustrations may be required if the product is highly technical. It is best to write product and service descriptions so that laypeople can understand them. A statement of a product's position in the product life cycle might also be helpful. An entrepreneur should include a summary of any patents, trademarks, or copyrights protecting the product or service from infringement by competitors. Finally, the plan should include an honest comparison of the company's product or service with those of competitors, citing specific advantages or improvements that make its goods or services unique and indicating plans for creating the next generation of goods and services that will evolve from the present product line. What competitive advantage does the venture's product or service offer? Ideally, a product or service offers high-value benefits to customers and is difficult for competitors to duplicate.

One danger entrepreneurs must avoid in this part of the plan is the tendency to dwell excessively on the features of their products or services. This problem is the result of the "fall-in-love-with-your-product" syndrome, which often afflicts inventors. Customers, lenders, and investors care less about how much work, genius, and creativity went into a product or service than about what it will do for them. The emphasis of this section should be on defining the benefits customers get by purchasing the company's products or services, rather than on just a "nuts-and-bolts" description of the features of those products or services. A **feature** is a descriptive fact about a product or service ("An ergonomically designed, more comfortable handle"). A **benefit** is what the customer gains from the product or service feature ("Fewer problems with carpal tunnel syndrome and increased productivity"). Advertising legend Leo Burnett once said, "Don't tell the people how good you make the goods; tell them how good your goods make them."[6] This part of the plan must describe how a business will transform tangible product or service features into important, but often intangible, customer benefits—for example, lower energy bills, faster access to the Internet, less time writing checks to pay monthly bills, greater flexibility in building floating structures, shorter time required to learn a foreign language, and so on. Remember: *Customers buy benefits, not product or service features.* Table 6.2 offers an easy exercise designed to help entrepreneurs translate their products' or services' features into meaningful customer benefits.

Adam Rizika, his brother Bob, and friend Scott Brazina found the basis for their business in a product that Adam's employer had rejected. The product was based on a new type of reflective technology that allowed fabrics to be coated with a material that reflects light. An improvement on traditional reflective garments that rely on light-reflecting stripes, the new fabric, called illumiNITE, provides a full reflective silhouette of the person wearing it, making it ideal for runners, cyclists, children, highway workers, firefighters, and others. After forming their company, Reflective Technologies, and applying for a patent, the entrepreneurs

Table 6.2
Transforming Features into Meaningful Benefits

> For many entrepreneurs, there's a big gap between what a business is selling and what its customers are buying. The worksheet below is designed to eliminate that gap.
>
> First, develop a list of the features your company's product or service offers. List as many as you can think of, which may be 25 or more. Consider features that relate to price, performance, convenience, location, customer service, delivery, reputation, reliability, quality, features, and other aspects.
>
> Next, group features with similar themes together by circling them with the same color ink. Then, translate those groups of features into specific benefits to your customers by addressing the question "What's in it for me?" from the customer's perspective. *Note*: It usually is a good idea to ask actual customers why they buy from you. (They usually give reasons that you never thought of.) As many as six or eight product or service (or even company) features may translate into a single customer benefit, such as saving money or time or making life safer. Don't ignore intangible benefits such as increased status; they can be more important than tangible benefits.
>
> Finally, combine all of the benefits you identify into a single sentence or paragraph. Use this statement as a key point in your business plan and to guide your company's marketing strategy.
>
> | FEATURES | BENEFITS |
> |---|---|
> | | |
> | | |
> | | |
>
> Benefit Statement:
>
> *Source*: Adapted from Kim T. Gordon, "Position for Profits," *Business Start-Ups*, February 1998, pp. 18–20.

focused on marketing their unique material. They spent a year preparing their business plan, and their first step was to develop a matrix that highlighted the advantages illumiNITE offered over existing products and the customer benefits it provided. "New technology isn't a plus if it doesn't translate into a consumer benefit," says Adam Rizika.[7]

Manufacturers should describe their production process, strategic raw materials required, sources of supply they will use, and their costs. They should also summarize the production method and illustrate the plant layout. If the product is based on a patented or proprietary process, a description (including diagrams, if necessary) of its unique market advantages is helpful. It is also helpful to explain the company's environmental impact and how the entrepreneur plans to mitigate any negative environmental consequences the process may produce.

Marketing Strategy. One of the most important tasks a business plan must fulfill is proving that a real market exists for a company's goods or services (or showing the entrepreneur that one does not exist and that launching a business would be a mistake). A business plan must identify and describe the company's target customers and their characteristics and habits. Defining the target audience and its potential is one of the most important—and most challenging—parts of building a business plan. Creating a successful business depends on an entrepreneur's ability to attract real customers who are willing and able to spend real money to buy its products or services. Perhaps the worst marketing error entrepreneurs can commit is failing to define their target market and trying to make their business "everything to everybody." Small companies usually are much more successful focusing on a specific market niche where they can excel at meeting customers' special needs or wants.

Howard and Edna Schwartz have focused their business on a specific target audience: gamblers. The Schwartzes own the Gambler's Book Shop (also known as the Gambler's Book Club), located in Las Vegas (where else?) just two miles off the Strip, where dozens of casinos lure millions of gamblers a year, each hoping to hit the jackpot. Gambler's Book Shop carries more than 1,000 titles, all devoted to gambling and 10 percent of them published by Gambler's Book Shop itself. Shoppers can browse through a multitude of gambling how-to books as well as titles such as Going for Broke: The Depiction of Compulsive Gambling in Film, Losing Your Shirt, *and* The Pool Hustler's Handbook. *Mail-order and Internet sales account for two thirds of the company's annual revenues of just over $1 million, but Schwartz says that sometimes gamblers will call him from the gambling table, wanting advice on how to bet a particular hand! Defining a company's target market involves using the techniques described in Chapter 7, "Creating a Guerrilla Marketing Plan."*[8]

Successful entrepreneurs know that a solid understanding of their target markets is the first step in building an effective marketing strategy. Indeed, every other aspect of marketing depends on their having a clear picture of their customers and their unique needs and wants. Proving that a profitable market exists involves two steps: showing customer interest and documenting market claims.

Showing Customer Interest. Entrepreneurs must be able to prove that their target customers need or want their goods or services and are willing to pay for them. Venture capitalist Kathryn Gould, who has reviewed thousands of business plans, says that she looks for plans that focus on "target customers with a compelling reason to buy. The product must be a 'must-have.'"[9] Proving that a viable market exists for a product or service is relatively straightforward for a company already in business but can be quite difficult for an entrepreneur with only an idea or a prototype. In this case the entrepreneur might offer the prototype to several potential customers in order to get written testimonials and evaluations to show to investors, or the owner could sell the product to several customers at a discount. This would prove that there are potential customers for the product and would allow demonstrations of the product in operation. Getting a product into customers' hands is also an excellent way to get valuable feedback that can lead to significant design improvements and increased sales down the road.

Documenting Market Claims. Too many business plans rely on vague generalizations such as, "This market is so huge that if we get just one percent of it, we will break even in eight months." Such statements usually reflect nothing more than an entrepreneur's unbridled optimism, and in most cases, they are also unrealistic! *When Dave and Dan Hanlon relaunched the Excelsior-Henderson motorcycle brand in 1993, they hoped to carve a profitable niche in a market dominated by Harley-Davidson. With their business plan, the Hanlons raised $15 million in venture capital before making an initial public offering that brought in an additional $28 million. Despite rave reviews about their motorcycles, Excelsior-Henderson filed for bankruptcy after seven years of development and eight months of production. One industry expert says the company failed because the Hanlons "overestimated the market, and they didn't do enough market research to determine the styling, the performance elements, and the price points that would stand the best chance [of success]."*[10]

Entrepreneurs must support claims of market size and growth rates with facts, and that requires market research. Results of market surveys, customer questionnaires, and demographic studies lend credibility of an entrepreneur's frequently optimistic sales projections. (Refer to the market research techniques and resources in Chapter 7.) Quantitative market data are important because they form the basis for all of the company's financial projections in the business plan. One technique involves **business prototyping,** in which entrepreneurs test their business models on a small scale before committing serious resources to a business that might not work. Business prototyping recognizes that every business idea is a hypothesis that needs to be tested before an entrepreneur takes it to full scale. If the test supports the hypothesis and its accompanying assumptions, it is time to launch a company. If the prototype flops, the entrepreneur scraps the business idea with only minimal losses and turns to the next idea.

The World Wide Web makes business prototyping practical, fast, and easy. *In late 1998, when Scott Painter and Bill Gross came up with the idea of selling new cars online, they had no idea if people would be willing to buy cars over the Web, and, even if they would, how profitable each sale would be. To test their business model, Painter and Gross set up a basic Web site and posted banner ads on a popular search engine. They had no inventory of cars, so if a customer actually ordered a car, they would have to buy it from a local dealer and sell it at a loss. Their goal, however, was not to make money but to test their business model. Within one month, Painter and Gross had the answers to their questions. More than 5,000 people visited the site, and 11 actually ordered cars. The entrepreneurs were able to estimate that each sale would generate a profit of $250 to $1,000, and they quickly transformed CarsDirect.com into a real company!*[11]

One of the main purposes of the marketing section of the plan is to lay the foundation for financial forecasts that follow. Sales, profit, and cash forecasts must be founded on more than wishful thinking. An effective market analysis should identify the following:

Target Market. Who are the company's target customers? How many of them are in the company's trading area? What are their characteristics (age, gender, educational level, income, and others)? What do they buy? Why do they buy? When do they buy? What expectations do they have about the product or service? Will the business focus on a niche? How does the company seek to position itself in the market(s) it will pursue? Knowing my customers needs, wants, and habits, what should be the basis for differentiating my business in their minds?

Advertising and Promotion. Once entrepreneurs define their company's target market, they can design a promotion and advertising campaign to reach those customers most effectively and efficiently. Which media are most effective in reaching the target market? How will they be used? How much will the promotional campaign cost? How will the promotional campaign position your company's products or services? How can the company benefit from publicity? How large is the company's promotional budget?

Market Size and Trends. How large is the potential market? Is it growing or shrinking? Why? Are the customer's needs changing? Are sales seasonal? Is demand tied to another product or service?

Location. For many businesses, choosing the right location is a key success factor. For retailers, wholesalers, and service companies, the best location usually is one that is most convenient to their target customers. Using census data and other market research, entrepreneurs can determine the sites with the greatest concentrations of their customers and locate there. Which specific sites put the company in the path of its target customers? Do zoning regulations restrict the use of the site? For manufacturers, the location issue often centers on finding a site near its key raw materials or near its major customers. Using demographic reports and market research to screen potential sites takes the guesswork out of choosing the "right" location for a business.

Pricing. What does the product or service cost to produce or deliver? What is the company's overall pricing strategy? What image is the company trying to create in the market? Will the planned price support the company's strategy and desired image (see Figure 6.1)? Can it produce a profit? How does the planned price compare to those of similar products or services? Are customers willing to pay it? What price tiers exist in the market? How sensitive are customers to price changes? Will the business sell to customers on credit? Will it accept credit cards? Will the company offer discounts? If so, what kinds and how much?

Distribution. How will the product or service be distributed? Will distribution be extensive, selective, or exclusive? What is the average sale? How large will the sales staff be? How will the company compensate its sales force? What are the incentives for salespeople? How many sales calls does it take to close a sale? What can the company do to make it as easy as possible for customers to buy?

This portion of the plan also should describe the channels of distribution that the business will use (mail, in-house sales force, sales agent, retailers, or others). An entrepreneur should summarize the firm's overall pricing strategies and its warranties and guarantees for its products and services.

Figure 6.1
The Link Between Pricing, Perceived Quality, and Company Image

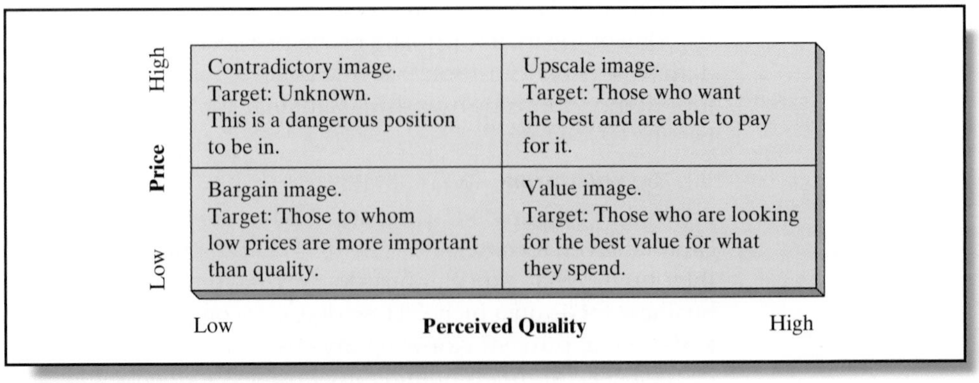

	Low Perceived Quality	High Perceived Quality
High Price	Contradictory image. Target: Unknown. This is a dangerous position to be in.	Upscale image. Target: Those who want the best and are able to pay for it.
Low Price	Bargain image. Target: Those to whom low prices are more important than quality.	Value image. Target: Those who are looking for the best value for what they spend.

Competitor Analysis. Entrepreneurs should assess honestly their new ventures' competition. Failing to assess competitors realistically makes entrepreneurs appear to be poorly prepared, naive, or dishonest. Gathering information on competitors' market shares, products, and strategies is usually not difficult. Trade associations, customers, industry journals, sales representatives, and sales literature are valuable sources of data. This section of the plan should focus on demonstrating that the entrepreneur's company has an advantage over its competitors. Who are the company's key competitors? What are their strengths and weaknesses? What are their strategies? What images do they have in the marketplace? How successful are they? What distinguishes the entrepreneur's product or service from others already on the market, and how will these differences produce a competitive edge?

When Tonya Davis was developing a business plan for the day care center she planned to launch, she visited other day care centers to determine their strengths and weaknesses. She was also able to assess the competition's pricing policies and the range of services they offered, which helped her differentiate her company in the minds of her target customers.[12]

Owners' and Managers' Résumés. The most important factor in the success of a business venture is its management, and financial officers and investors weight heavily the ability and experience of the firm's managers in financing decisions. A plan should include the résumés of business officers, key directors, and any person with at least 20 percent ownership in the company. This is the section of the plan where entrepreneurs have the chance to sell the qualifications and the experience of their management team. Remember: *Lenders and investors prefer experienced managers.* Ideally, they look for managers with at least two years of operating experience in the industry they are targeting.

A résumé should summarize each individual's education, work history (emphasizing managerial responsibilities and duties), and relevant business experience. When compiling a personal profile, an entrepreneur should review the primary reasons for small business failure (refer to Chapter 1) and show how the management team will use its skills and experience to avoid them. Lenders and investors look for the experience, talent, and integrity of the people who will breathe life into the plan. This portion of the plan should show that the company has the right people organized in the right fashion for success. One experienced private investor advises entrepreneurs to remember the following:

- Ideas and products don't succeed; people do. Show the strength of your management team. A top-notch management team with a variety of proven skills is crucial.
- Show the strength of key employees and how you will retain them. Most small companies cannot pay salaries that match those at large businesses, but stock options and other incentives can improve employee retention.
- Show the strength of key employees and how you will retain them. A board of directors or advisers consisting of industry experts lends credibility and can enhance the value of the management team.

Plan of Operation. To complete the description of the business, an entrepreneur should construct an organizational chart identifying the business's key positions and the people occupying them. Assembling a management team with the right stuff is difficult, but keeping it together until the company is established may be harder. Thus, the entrepreneur should describe briefly the steps taken to encourage important officers to remain with the company. Employment contracts, shares of ownership, and perks are commonly used to keep and motivate key employees.

Finally, a description of the form of ownership (partnership, joint venture, S corporation, limited liability company) and of any leases, contracts, and other relevant agreements pertaining to the operation is helpful.

Financial Forecasts. To potential lenders and investors, one of the most important sections of the business plan is financial forecasts an entrepreneur makes. Lenders and investors use past financial statements to judge the health of an existing small company and its ability to repay loans or generate adequate returns. A business owner should supply copies of the firm's major financial statements from the past three years. Ideally, these statements should be audited by a certified public accountant because most financial institutions prefer that extra reliability, although a financial review of the statements by an accountant sometimes may be acceptable.

Preparing financial forecasts for a proposed business is more challenging, but with the help of published industry statistics, information from trade associations, and discussions with industry experts or existing business owners in other locations, entrepreneurs can develop reliable forecasts for start-up companies. We will discuss the techniques involved in developing financial forecasts from these and other resources in Chapter 8, "Creating a Solid Financial Plan."

Whether assembling a plan for an existing business or a start-up, an entrepreneur should carefully prepare monthly projected (or pro forma) financial statements for the venture for one year and by quarter for the next two to three years using past operating data, published statistics, and judgment to derive three sets of forecasts of the income statement, balance sheet, cash budget, and schedule of planned capital expenditures. The first stop for most potential lenders and investors is the income statement, which shows the company's revenues, expenses, and the resulting profit. Although they recognize that start-ups often lose money in their early stages, investors and lenders expect to see positive trends in earnings. They also look to see if the gross-, operating-, and net-income margins on the forecasted income statements are consistent with industry averages. From there, investors typically move on to the cash flow statement to judge whether or not the company is viable over time. Earnings are important, but staying in business requires a company to generate positive cash flow. Entrepreneurs must make sure that they have accumulated enough capital to carry the company until it generates enough cash to support itself. Finally, potential lenders and investors examine the balance sheet, where they see the company's assets (everything it owns), its liabilities (everything it owes), and its net worth (the difference in assets and liabilities). They view intangible assets somewhat suspiciously, especially in start-up companies, and look for potential problems with inventory, which can absorb a company's cash.

There should be forecasts under pessimistic, most likely, and optimistic conditions to reflect the uncertainty of the future. Preparing an extensive set of financial forecasts can be a daunting task for an inexperienced entrepreneur, but spreadsheets can make the job much easier. Entrepreneurs who lack financial aptitude should not hesitate to get help from accountants or consultants when preparing their financial analysis. Tonya Davis did not have a financial background and was having difficulty creating realistic financial projections for her proposed day care center. She worked with a local accountant to develop financial statements based on most likely, pessimistic, and optimistic sales forecasts.[13]

It is essential that all three sets of forecasts be realistic. Entrepreneurs must avoid the tendency to "fudge the numbers" just to make their businesses look good. Financial officers compare these projections against published industry standards and can detect unreasonable forecasts. In fact, some venture capitalists automatically discount an entrepreneur's financial projections by as much as 50 percent. Upon completing these forecasts, an entrepreneur should perform a break-even analysis and a ratio analysis on the projected figures.

Finally, it is also important to include a statement of the assumptions on which these financial projections are based. Potential lenders and investors want to know how the entrepreneur derived forecasts for sales, cost of goods sold, operating expenses, accounts receivable, collections, inventory, and other such items. Spelling out such assumptions gives a plan more credibility. In addition to providing valuable information to potential lenders and investors, these projected financial statements help entrepreneurs run their businesses more effectively and more efficiently. They establish important targets for financial performance and make it easier for an entrepreneur to maintain control over routine expenses and capital expenditures.

The Request for Funds. The loan proposal section of the business plan should state the purpose of the loan or investment, the amount requested, and the plans for repayment or cash-out. One important by-product of preparing a business plan is discovering how much money it will take to launch the business. When describing the purpose of the loan, entrepreneurs must specify the planned use of the funds. "You'd be surprised how many people request a loan for a specific amount but can't articulate what they would use the money for," says one banker.[14] General requests for funds using terms such as *for modernization, working capital,* or *expansion* are unlikely to win approval. Instead, descriptions such as "to modernize production facilities by purchasing five new, more efficient looms that will boost productivity by 12 percent" or "to rebuild merchandise inventory for fall sales peak, beginning in early summer" are much more likely to win approval. Entrepreneurs should state the precise amount of money they are requesting and include relevant backup data, such as vendor estimates of costs or past production levels. They should not hesitate to request the amount of money needed; however, inflating the amount of a loan request in anticipation of the financial officer trying to "talk them down" is a mistake. Remember: *Lenders and investors are familiar with industry cost structures.*

Another important element of the loan or investment proposal is the repayment schedule and exit strategy. A lender's main consideration in granting a loan is the reassurance that the applicant will repay, whereas an investor's major concern is earning a satisfactory rate of return. Financial projections must reflect the firm's ability to repay loans to lenders and to produce adequate yields for investors. Without this proof, a request for funding stands little chance of being accepted. It is necessary for an entrepreneur to produce tangible evidence showing the ability to repay loans or to generate attractive returns. The plan should propose an exit strategy for investors—how they will get their money back (plus an attractive return on their investment), perhaps by selling the company to a larger business or by making an initial public offering.

It is beneficial to include an evaluation of the risks of a new venture. Evaluating risk in a business plan requires an entrepreneur to walk a fine line. Dwelling too much on everything that can go wrong will discourage potential lenders and investors from financing the venture. Ignoring a project's risks makes those who evaluate the plan tend to believe the entrepreneur to be either naive, dishonest, or unprepared. The best strategy is to identify the most significant risks the venture faces and then to describe the plans the entrepreneur has developed to avoid them altogether or to overcome the negative outcome if the event does occur.

Finally, an entrepreneur should have a timetable for implementing the plan. He should present a schedule showing the estimated start-up date for the project and noting any significant milestones along the way. Entrepreneurs tend to be optimistic, so it is important that the timetable of events is realistic.

GAINING THE COMPETITIVE EDGE
The Right Way to Build a Business Plan

Too many entrepreneurs see the task of writing a business plan as an onerous task they must undertake only if they are seeking outside capital. However, those who do take the time to develop a well-thought-out plan say that the experience was an enlightening exercise for everyone involved and made their companies stronger. Building a plan forces entrepreneurs to ask—and to answer—questions that are vitally important to their companies' ultimate success. Building a solid plan is an essential part of launching a business whether or not an entrepreneur is seeking outside financing. How can you create a plan that will help your business become more successful? By integrating the following 10 characteristics into your plan:

1. *Detailed market research.* Prove that you know your target customers and the problems your product or service solves for them. At whom are you aiming your product or service? How can you best reach your target audience? How big is the potential market? How fast is it growing? What competitive advantage does your product or service offer? "The 'better mousetrap' idea, where the public beats a path to your door is passé," says one investor. "We're more cynical than that. It's the marketing that counts. It doesn't matter how great the product is."

2. *Clear and realistic financial projections.* Potential lenders and investors often start and end their investigation of a business here. They want to see summaries of a company's financial performance to date (if it is an existing business) and realistic forecasts for the future. Every business plan should contain forecasted balance sheets, income statements, and cash flow statements. Plus, it helps to include the assumptions on which the entrepreneur has built those forecasts and notes explaining all significant line items.

3. *A detailed competitor analysis.* A business plan that omits an analysis of competitors immediately raises a red flag to potential lenders and investors. Every business has competitors, and a plan should show that an entrepreneur understands the competition and its strengths and weaknesses.

4. *A description of the management team.* If there is one universal factor that potential lenders and investors look for, it is a sound management team. Lenders and investors know that poor management will kill even the best product or service idea. At "the top of the list for a successful business plan is management experience in the field," says one small business advisor. Use the plan to show your management team's breadth and depth of experience and how that will translate into success for the business.

5. *A distinct vision.* Entrepreneurs who have a clear vision of what they want their companies to stand for and to accomplish create a sense of excitement among investors. Your plan should demonstrate a detailed knowledge of the industry, your customers, your products or services, and how your company's offering is different from (and superior to) the competition. It must paint a clear picture of where the company is going and how it intends to get there.

6. *An understanding of financial options.* A plan should explain why a company needs financing, how much money it needs, how it will use the money, and how it will repay lenders or investors. That means entrepreneurs must understand which types of financing best suit their companies. Those seeking loans need rock-solid cash flows to prove their ability to repay their debts. Companies in search of equity investments must prove their growth potential and show investors how they can "cash out."

7. *Proper format and a flowing writing style.* "The first requisite of a business plan is that it be interesting to read, well written, and smooth flowing," says one investor. "The second is that it be well organized, so I can look at the table of contents and find what I need." No one is going to read a plan that is boring, unorganized, or riddled with spelling, grammatical, or typographical errors.

8. *Crisp.* Business plans must include enough detail to answer potetial lenders' and investors' questions without overloading them with

(continued)

unnecessary clutter. It's a fine line for an entrepreneur to walk. Plans that are too short beg to be rejected, and those that are too long never get read.

9. *A killer summary.* The executive summary may be the toughest part of a business plan to write. It's the section almost every potential lender or investor reads first. If the executive summary fails to capture their interest or attention, the odds are that they will not bother to read the rest of the plan. A good executive summary captures the essence of the plan, and piques the reader's interest—all in no more than two pages.

10. *Customized.* The hundreds of books on how to write a business plan and software packages designed to actually create plans can be valuable sources of help for entrepreneurs facing the challenge of writing a business plan. Be careful, however, to avoid the "cookie cutter" look to your plan. Use those guides and resources as a starting point for your plan. After all, no two business ventures are exactly alike, so no two business plans should be exactly alike. Make sure your plan presents your company in the most favorable way. Don't hire someone to write the plan for you, either. Getting help and feedback from others is an excellent idea, but you should always create the plan yourself first.

Sources: Adapted from Ronaleen Roha, "Business Plans That Work," *Kiplinger's Personal Finance Magazine,* June 2000, p. 94; Linda Elkins, "Tips for Preparing a Business Plan," *Nation's Business,* June 1996, pp. 60R–61R; Paul Gallagher, "Getting Down to Business," *Success,* April 2001, pp. 50–53; David R. Evanson and Art Beroff, "Keep It Real," *Entrepreneur,* May 2001, pp. 457–459.

There is a difference between a working business plan—one the entrepreneur is using to guide his or her business—and the presentation business plan—the one the entrepreneur is using to attract capital. Although coffee rings and penciled-in changes in a working plan don't matter (in fact, they're a good sign that the entrepreneur is actually using the plan), they have no place on a plan going to someone outside the company. A business plan is usually the tool that an entrepreneur uses to make a first impression on potential lenders and investors. To make sure that impression is a favorable one, an entrepreneur should follow these tips:

- Make sure the plan is free of spelling and grammatical errors and "typos." It is a professional document and should look like one.
- Make it visually appealing. Use color charts, figures, and diagrams to illustrate key points. Don't get carried away, however, and end up with a "comic book" plan.
- Leave ample "white space" in margins.
- Create an attractive (but not extravagant) cover that includes the company's name and logo.
- Include a table of contents to allow readers to navigate the plan easily.
- Write in a flowing, conversational style and use "bullets" to itemize points in lists.
- Support claims with facts and avoid generalizations.
- Avoid overusing industry jargon and acronyms with which readers may not be familiar.
- Make it interesting. Boring plans seldom get read.
- Use computer spreadsheets to generate financial forecasts. They allow entrepreneurs to perform valuable "what if" (sensitivity) analysis in just seconds.
- Always include cash flow projections. Entrepreneurs sometimes focus excessively on their proposed venture's profit forecasts and ignore cash flow projections. Although profitability is important, lenders and investors are much more interested in cash flow because they know that's where the money to pay them back or to cash them out comes from.

- The ideal plan is "crisp"—long enough to say what it should but not so long that it is a chore to read.
- Tell the truth. Absolute honesty is always critical in preparing a business plan.

CAN YOUR PLAN PASS THESE TESTS?

3. Explain the three tests every business plan must pass.

Preparing a sound business plan clearly requires time and effort, but the benefits greatly exceed the costs. Building the plan forces potential entrepreneurs to look at their business ideas in the harsh light of reality. It also requires the owner to assess the venture's chances of success more objectively. A well-assembled plan helps prove to outsiders that a business idea can be successful. To get external financing, an entrepreneur's plan must pass three tests with potential lenders and investors: the reality test, the competitive test, and the value test.[15] The first two tests have both an external and an internal component:

Reality Test. The external component of the reality test revolves around proving that a market for the product or service really does exist. It focuses on industry attractiveness, market niches, potential customers, market size, degree of competition, and similar factors. Entrepreneurs who pass this part of the reality test prove in the marketing portion of their business plans that there is strong demand for their business idea.

The internal component of the reality test focuses on the product or service itself. Can the company really build it for the cost estimates in the business plan? Is it truly

different from what competitors are already selling? Does it offer customers something of value?

Competitive Test. The external part of the competitive test evaluates the company's relative position to its key competitors. How do the company's strengths and weaknesses match up with those of the competition? How are existing competitors likely to react when the new business enters the market? Do these reactions threaten the new company's success and survival?

The internal competitive test focuses on management's ability to create a company that will gain an edge over existing rivals. To pass this part of the competitive test, a plan must prove the quality of the venture's management team. What other resources does the company have that can give it a competitive edge in the market?

Value Test. To convince lenders and investors to put their money into the venture, a business plan must prove to them that it offers a high probability of repayment or an attractive rate of return. Entrepreneurs usually see their businesses as good investments because they consider the intangibles of owning a business—gaining control over their own destinies, freedom to do what they enjoy, and others; lenders and investors, however, look at a venture in colder terms: dollar-for-dollar returns. A plan must convince lenders and investors that they will earn an attractive return on their money.

The Web site accompanying this book <http:www.prenhall.com/scarborough> contains a sample business plan for a company.

MAKING THE BUSINESS PLAN PRESENTATION

4. Explain the keys to making an effective business plan presentation.

Lenders and investors are favorably impressed by entrepreneurs who are informed and prepared when requesting a loan or investment. When entrepreneurs try to secure funding from lenders or investors, the written business plan almost always precedes the opportunity to meet face-to-face. The written plan must first pass muster before an entrepreneur gets the opportunity to present the plan in person. Usually, the time for presenting a business opportunity is short, often no more than just a few minutes. (When presenting a plan to a venture capital forum, the allotted time is usually 15 to 20 minutes, 30 minutes at the maximum.) When the opportunity arises, an entrepreneur must be well prepared. It is important to rehearse, rehearse, and then rehearse more. It is a mistake to begin by leading the audience into a long-winded explanation about the technology on which the product or service is based. Within minutes, most of the audience will be lost; and so is any chance the entrepreneur has of obtaining the necessary financing for the new venture. A business plan presentation should cover five basic areas:

1. The company's background and its products or services
2. A market analysis and a description of the opportunities it presents
3. The company's competitive edge and the marketing strategies it will use to promote that edge
4. The management team and its members' qualifications and experience
5. A financial analysis that shows lenders and investors an attractive payback or payoff

No matter how good a written business plan is, entrepreneurs who muff the presentation to potential lenders and investors will blow the deal. *For example, the founder of an Internet company wanted to show a group of potential investors how cutting edge his business was by conducting a live demonstration of his company's product on a portable computer and a projection system. Initially, the presentation went well until the computer failed to make the connection to the Internet. That caused the presentation program to lock up, forcing the entrepreneur to reboot the entire system while trying to hold the audience's attention and get the presentation back on track. The technological glitch occurred at the most crucial part of the entrepreneur's presentation, making his company look like a minor league player in a major league industry. His company's prospects for an initial public offering failed to connect to his audience the second his computer failed to connect to the Internet![16]*

Entrepreneurs who are successful in raising the capital their companies need to grow have solid business plans and make convincing presentations of them. Some helpful tips for making a business plan presentation to potential lenders and investors include:

- Prepare. Good presenters prepare their presentations well in advance and know the points they want to get across to their audiences.
- Demonstrate enthusiasm about the business, but don't be overemotional.
- Fight the temptation to launch immediately into a lengthy discourse about the details of your product or service or how much work it took to develop it. Focus instead on communicating the dynamic opportunity your idea offers and how you plan to capitalize on it. Otherwise, you'll never have the chance to describe the details to lenders and investors.
- "Hook" investors quickly with an up-front explanation of the new venture, its opportunities, and the anticipated benefits to them.
- Use visual aids. They make it easier for people to follow your presentation. Don't make the mistake of relying on visuals to communicate the entire message. Visual aids should punctuate your spoken message and focus the audience's attention on what you are saying.
- Hit the highlights; specific questions will bring out the details later. Don't get caught up in too much detail in early meetings with lenders and investors.
- Keep the presentation "crisp" just like your business plan. Otherwise, says one experienced investor, "information that might have caused an investor to bite gets lost in the endless drone."[17]
- Avoid the use of technological terms that will likely be above most of the audience. Do at least one rehearsal before someone who has no special technical training. Tell him to stop you anytime he does not understand what you are talking about. When this occurs (and it likely will), rewrite that portion of your presentation.
- Remember that every potential lender and investor you talk to is thinking "What's in it for me?" Be sure to answer that question in your presentation.
- Close by reinforcing the nature of the opportunity. Be sure you have sold the benefits the investors will realize when the business is a success.
- Be prepared for questions. In many cases, there is seldom time for a long "Q&A" session, but interested investors may want to get you aside to discuss the details of the plan.
- Anticipate the questions the audience is most likely to ask and prepare for them in advance.
- Be sensitive to the issues that are most important to lenders and investors by "reading" the pattern of their questions. Focus your answers accordingly. For instance, some investors may be interested in the quality of the management team while others are more interested in marketing strategies. Be prepared to offer details on either.
- Follow up with every investor you make a presentation to. Don't sit back and wait; be proactive. They have what you need—investment capital. Demonstrate that you have confidence in your plan and have the initiative necessary to run a business successfully.

WHAT LENDERS AND INVESTORS LOOK FOR IN A BUSINESS PLAN

5. Explain the "five Cs of credit" and why they are important to potential lenders and investors.

To increase their chances of success when using their business plans to attract capital, entrepreneurs must be aware of the criteria lenders and investors use to evaluate the creditworthiness of entrepreneurs seeking financing. Lenders and investors refer to these criteria as the **five Cs of credit:** capital, capacity, collateral, character, and conditions.

Capital. A small business must have a stable capital base before any lender will grant a loan. Otherwise, the lender would be making, in effect, a capital investment in the business. Most banks refuse to make loans that are capital investments because the potential for return on the investment is limited strictly to the interest on the loan, and the potential loss would probably exceed the reward. In fact, the most common reasons that banks give for rejecting small business loan applications are undercapitalization or too much debt. Investors also want to make sure that entrepreneurs have invested enough of their own money into the business to survive the tenuous start-up period.

Capacity. A synonym for capacity is cash flow. Lenders and investors must be convinced of the firm's ability to meet its regular financial obligations and to repay a bank loan, and that takes cash. In Chapter 8, you will see that more small businesses fail from lack of cash than from lack of profit. It is possible for a company to be showing a profit and still have no cash—that is, to be technically bankrupt. Lenders expect a business to pass the test of liquidity, especially for short-term loans. Banks study closely a small company's cash flow position to decide whether it meets the capacity required.

Collateral. Collateral includes any assets an entrepreneur pledges to a lender as security for repayment of the loan. If the company defaults on the loan, the bank has the right to sell the collateral and use the proceeds to satisfy the loan. Typically, banks make very few unsecured loans (those not backed by collateral) to business start-ups. Bankers view the owner's willingness to pledge collateral (personal or business assets) as an indication of dedication to making the venture a success. A sound business plan can improve a banker's attitude toward the venture.

Character. Before putting money into a small business, lenders and investors must be satisfied with the owner's character. An evaluation of character frequently is based on intangible factors such as honesty, competence, polish, determination, intelligence, and ability. Although the qualities so judged are abstract, this evaluation plays a critical role in the lender's or investor's decision.

Lenders and investors know that most small businesses fail because of incompetent management, and so they try to avoid extending loans to high-risk entrepreneurs. A solid business plan and a polished presentation can go far in convincing potential lenders and investors of an entrepreneur's ability to manage a company successfully.

Conditions. The conditions surrounding a loan request also affect the owner's chance of receiving funds. Banks consider factors relating to the business operation such as potential growth in the market, competition, location, form of ownership, and loan purpose. Again, the owner should provide this relevant information in an organized format in the business plan. Another important condition influencing the banker's decision is the shape of the overall economy, including interest rate levels, inflation rate, and demand for money. Although these factors are beyond an entrepreneur's control, they still are an important component in a banker's decision.

For years, students of all ages have attended summer camps to hone their outdoor skills. Now, many of them are going off to camp to master a different set of skills: preparing a business plan. For instance, at Camp $tart-UP in Wellesley, Massachusetts, young women between the ages of 13 and 17 work in teams to develop business plans for businesses they hope to launch. In addition to learning the details of writing business plans, these aspiring entrepreneurs also have a chance to network with women entrepreneurs. Like the participants in Camp $tart-UP, college students across the United States are creating business plans for companies they hope to start, or, in some cases, have already launched. For some, more than just a good grade is at stake. They are competing for real start-up funding and valuable feedback from experienced judges in business plan competitions.

Many colleges and universities sponsor these competitions, but one of the best known is the Moot Corporation competition at the University of Texas in Austin. How rugged is the judging and how intense is the competition? A journalist who judged a recent competition offers insight:

Friday 7:30 A.M. An orientation for the judges begins. Five panels of judges will hear presentations from five student teams of entrepreneurs from colleges and universities all over the world. Each team has 20 minutes to deliver its presentation, followed by a 20-minute question-and-answer session. The winners from each division will face off tomorrow before a different panel of judges in the finals.

8:30 A.M. The first team, Capital Mining from Oxford University in the United Kingdom, presents its plan. The company intends to find untapped veins of iron ore in Australia and then collect royalties from mining companies and is seeking $3.5 million in seed capital. The team leader hands each judge a rock and a box shaped like a bar of gold. "I hope this gets your attention," he says. It doesn't.

9:15 A.M. Getoutdoors.com, a team from the University of Illinois at Chicago, present their plan to create an online store where customers planning backpacking or rock-climbing trips can buy gear and get valuable advice. The judges believe that the idea is a good one, but the team's plan and presentation lack the necessary detail. One key to their plan is partner-ing with climbing clubs across the United States, but they have not yet forged any relationships.

10:00 A.M. The team leader for J. H. Reid Corporation shows off the chair he has spent eight years developing. It is a wood-frame, crate-style chair with no legs and a cushion that looks like a futon designed to allow the user to sit on the floor (this is a customer benefit?) to watch television. The plan withers when a judge points out how easy it would be for competitors to work around the design's patent protection.

10:40 A.M. The Granos Inka team from Peru struggles to overcome the language barrier in its presentation. Capitalizing on changes in the Peruvian government's land policies, the team plans to purchase lush farmland and replace coca and illegal drugs with a domestic corn crop. The team leader plans to invest $5.2 million of her own money in the venture. The plan fails to meet the judges' basic criteria: Would I invest my money in the venture?

11:15 A.M. The last team, Vusion Inc., is a "home team" from the University of Texas. Their plan is to market to pharmaceutical companies a cartridge-based system called the Electronic Tongue that detects pollutants and other undesirable substances in chemical fluids. As their presentation progresses, it becomes clear to the judges that the technology is not yet fully developed, and the company does not yet own the rights to the product—both red flags for potential investors. Their smooth presentation and the product's potential lead the judges to send them on to the finals, however.

Saturday 1 P.M. to 5 P.M. The five finalists making presentations are:

- JetFan Technology, a company from Queensland, Australia, with an improved version of the cooling fan used in computers and other electronic devices.

- Regents Park Healthcare from the London Business School, a team of two British doctors who plan to run cardiothoracic centers for hospitals. A question from one judge, "Why would a hospital transfer management to you?" sends the team down in flames.

- Vusion Inc., the team promoting the Electronic Tongue, runs into trouble when the judges zero in on the same holes in the plan that the first-round judges spotted.

- Home Dreams from Fundacao, Getulio Vargas, Brazil, is developing a real estate Web site that will advertise homes for sale in Sao Paulo, Brazil. The judges learn that the Internet is booming in Brazil and that the country has no multiple listing real estate service.

- Fabrica Company Ltd., from Thammasat University in Thailand, introduces a unique loom that makes fabric samples for textile manufacturers. The loom could significantly lower the cost of producing samples. Although the loom is too bulky to bring to the competition, team members hand out plenty of samples created by the 16 looms already in use. They seek $490,000 in financing.

9:25 P.M. Tension mounts in the banquet hall as the time to announce the winners approaches. Second runner-up and winner of $1,000 is JetFan Technology. First runner-up and winner of $2,000 is Vusion Inc. The winner of the Moot Corporation competition and

recipient of $15,000 is Fabrica Company Ltd. from Thailand. In the end, the combination of a rich opportunity, proprietary technology that had proved to be successful, and the team members' charm and quality presentation won the judges over.

1. If your school does not already have a business plan competition, work with a team of your classmates in a brainstorming session to develop ideas for creating one. What would you offer as a prize? How would you finance the competition? Whom would you invite to judge it? How would you structure the competition?

2. Use the World Wide Web to research business plan competitions at other colleges and universities across the nation. Using the competitions at these schools as benchmarks and the ideas you generated in question 1, develop a format for a business plan competition at your school.

3. Assume that you are a member of a team of entrepreneurial students entered in a prestigious business plan competition. Outline your team's strategy for winning the competition.

Sources: Adapted from Art Popham, "BizCamp 2001," *The News Tribune* (online edition), August 20, 2001; Toddi Gutnerhers, "No Arts, No Crafts, All Business," *Business Week* (online edition), September 3, 2001, p. 94; Michael Warshaw, "The Best Business Plan on the Planet," *Inc.*, August 1999, pp. 80–90.

The higher a small business scores on these five Cs, the greater its chance will be of receiving a loan or an investment. Wise entrepreneurs keep this in mind when preparing their business plans and presentations.

CONCLUSION

Although there is no guarantee of success when launching a business, the best way to ensure against failure is to create a business plan. A good plan serves as a strategic compass that keeps a business on course as it travels into an uncertain future. Also, a solid plan is essential to raising the capital needed to start a business; lenders and investors demand it. "There may be no easier way for an entrepreneur to sabotage his or her request for capital than by failing to produce a comprehensive, well-researched, and, above all, credible business plan," says one small business expert.[18] Of course, building a plan is just one step along the path to launching a business. Creating a successful business requires entrepreneurs to put the plan into action. The remaining chapters in this book focus on putting your business plan to work.

SUGGESTED BUSINESS PLAN FORMAT

Although every company's business plan will be unique, reflecting its individual circumstances, certain elements are universal. The following outline summarizes these components:

I. Executive Summary (not to exceed two pages)
   A. Company name, address, and phone number
   B. Name(s), addresses, and phone number(s) of all key people
   C. Brief description of the business, its products and services, and the customer problems they solve
   D. Brief overview of the market for your products and services
   E. Brief overview of the strategies that will make your firm a success
   F. Brief description of the managerial and technical experience of key people
   G. Brief statement of the financial request and how the money will be used
   H. Charts or tables showing highlights of financial forecasts

II. Vision and Mission Statement
   A. Entrepreneur's vision for the company
   B. "What business are we in?"
   C. Values and principles on which the business stands
   D. What makes the business unique? What is the source of its competitive advantage?

III. Company History (for existing businesses only)
   A. Company founding
   B. Financial and operational highlights
   C. Significant achievements

IV. Business and Industry Profile
   A. Stage of growth (start-up, growth, maturity)
   B. Company goals and objectives
      1. Operational
      2. Financial
      3. Other
   C. Industry analysis
      1. Industry background and overview
      2. Significant trends
      3. Growth rate
      4. Key success factors in the industry
      5. Outlook for the future

V. Business Strategy
   A. Desired image and position in market
   B. SWOT analysis
      1. Strengths
      2. Weaknesses
      3. Opportunities
      4. Threats
   C. Competitive strategy
      1. Cost leadership
      2. Differentiation
      3. Focus

VI. Company Products and Services
   A. Description
      1. Product or service features

      2. Customer benefits

      3. Warranties and guarantees

      4. Uniqueness

   B. Patent or trademark protection

   C. Description of production process (if applicable)

      1. Raw materials

      2. Costs

      3. Key suppliers

   D. Future product or service offerings

VII. Marketing Strategy

   A. Target market

      1. Complete demographic profile

      2. Other significant customer characteristics

   B. Customers' motivation to buy

   C. Market size and trends

      1. How large is the market?

      2. Is it growing or shrinking? How fast?

   D. Advertising and promotion

      1. Media used—reader, viewer, listener profiles

      2. Media costs

      3. Frequency of usage

      4. Plans for generating publicity

   E. Pricing

      1. Cost structure

         a. Fixed

         b. Variable

      2. Desired image in market

      3. Comparison against competitors' prices

   F. Distribution strategy

      1. Channels of distribution used

      2. Sales techniques and incentives

VIII. Location and Layout

   A. Location

      1. Demographic analysis of location versus target customer profile

      2. Traffic count

      3. Lease/Rental rates

      4. Labor needs and supply

      5. Wage rates

   B. Layout

      1. Size requirements

      2. Americans with Disabilities Act compliance

      3. Ergonomic issues

      4. Layout plan (suitable for an appendix)

IX. Competitor Analysis

   A. Existing competitors

      1. Who are they? Create a competitive profile matrix.

      2. Strengths

      3. Weaknesses

   B. Potential competitors: Companies that might enter the market

      1. Who are they?

      2. Impact on your business if they enter

X. Description of Management Team
    A. Key managers and employees
        1. Their backgrounds
        2. Experience, skills, and know-how they bring to the company
    B. Résumés of key managers and employees (suitable for an appendix)
XI. Plan of Operation
    A. Form of ownership chosen and reasoning
    B. Company structure (organization chart)
    C. Decision-making authority
    D. Compensation and benefits packages
XII. Financial Forecasts (suitable for an appendix)
    A. Financial statements
        1. Income statement
        2. Balance sheet
        3. Cash flow statement
    B. Breakeven analysis
    C. Ratio analysis with comparison to industry standards (most applicable to existing businesses)
XIII. Loan or Investment Proposal
    A. Amount requested
    B. Purpose and uses of funds
    C. Repayment or "cash out" schedule (exit strategy)
    D. Timetable for implementing plan and launching the business
XIV. Appendices—Supporting documentation, including market research, financial statements, organization charts, résumés, and other items

CHAPTER SUMMARY

1. Explain why every entrepreneur should create a business plan.
   - A business plan serves two essential functions. First and most important, it guides the company's operations by charting its future course and devising a strategy for following it. The second function of the business plan is to attract lenders and investors. Applying for loans or attempting to attract investors without a solid business plan rarely attracts needed capital. Rather, the best way to secure the necessary capital is to prepare a sound business plan.

2. Describe the elements of a solid business plan.
   - Although a business plan should be unique and tailor-made to suit the particular needs of a small company, it should cover these basic elements: an executive summary, a mission statement, a company history, a business and industry profile, a description of the company's business strategy, a profile of its products or services, a statement explaining its marketing strategy, a competitor analysis, owners' and officers' résumés, a plan of operation, financial data, and the loan or investment proposal.

3. Explain the benefits of preparing a plan.
   - Preparing a sound business plan clearly requires time and effort, but the benefits greatly exceed the costs. Building the plan forces potential entrepreneurs to look at their business ideas in the harsh light of reality. It also requires the owner to assess the venture's chances of success more objectively. A well-assembled plan helps prove to outsiders that a business idea can be successful.
   - The real value in preparing a business plan is not so much in the plan itself as it is in the process the entrepreneur goes through to create the plan. Although the finished product is useful, the process of building a plan requires entrepreneurs to subject their ideas to an objective, critical evaluation.

What entrepreneurs learn about their company, its target market, its financial requirements, and other factors can be essential to making the venture a success.

4. Understand the keys to making an effective business plan presentation.
   - Lenders and investors are favorably impressed by entrepreneurs who are informed and prepared when requesting a loan or investment.
   - Tips include: Demonstrate enthusiasm about the venture, but don't be overemotional; "hook" investors quickly with an up-front explanation of the new venture, its opportunities, and the anticipated benefits to them; use visual aids; hit the highlights of your venture; don't get caught up in too much detail in early meetings with lenders and investors; avoid the use of technological terms that will likely be above most of the audience; rehearse your presentation before giving it; close by reinforcing the nature of the opportunity; and be prepared for questions.

5. Explain the "5 Cs of credit" and why they are important to potential lenders and investors reading business plans.

- Small business owners need to be aware of the criteria bankers use in evaluating the creditworthiness of loan applicants—the five Cs of credit: capital, capacity, collateral, character, and conditions.
- Capital: Lenders expect small businesses to have an equity base of investment by the owner(s) that will help support the venture during times of financial strain.
- Capacity: A synonym for capacity is cash flow. The bank must be convinced of the firm's ability to meet its regular financial obligations and to repay the bank loan, and that takes cash.
- Collateral: Collateral includes any assets the owner pledges to the bank as security for repayment of the loan.
- Character: Before approving a loan to a small business, the banker must be satisfied with the owner's character.
- Conditions: The conditions—interest rates, the health of the nation's economy, industry growth rates, and the like—surrounding a loan request also affect the owner's chance of receiving funds.

DISCUSSION QUESTIONS

1. Why should an entrepreneur develop a business plan?
2. Why do entrepreneurs who are not seeking external financing need to prepare business plans?
3. Describe the major components of a business plan.
4. How can an entrepreneur seeking funds to launch a business convince potential lenders and investors that a market for the product or service really does exist?
5. How would you prepare to make a formal presentation of your business plan to a venture capital forum?
6. What are the 5 Cs of credit? How do lenders and investors use them when evaluating a request for financing?

STEP INTO THE REAL WORLD

1. Interview a local banker or investor who has experience in making loans to or investments in small businesses. Ask him or her the following questions:
   a. How important is a well-prepared business plan?
   b. How important is a smooth presentation?
   c. How do you evaluate the owner's character?
   d. How heavily do you weigh the five Cs of credit?
   e. What percentage of small business owners are well prepared to request a loan or investment?
   f. What mistakes do entrepreneurs most commonly make when creating their business plans? When presenting them?
   g. What are the major reasons for rejecting a business plan?

2. Interview a small business owner who has requested a bank loan or an equity investment from external sources. Ask him or her these questions:
   a. Did you prepare a written business plan before approaching the financial officer?
   b. If the answer is "yes" to part a, did you have outside or professional help in preparing it?
   c. How many times have your requests for additional funds been rejected? What reasons were given for the rejection?

TAKE IT TO THE NET

Visit the Scarborough/Zimmerer home page at **www.prenhall.com/scarborough** for updated information, online resources, Web-based exercises, and sample business plan.

ENDNOTES

1. Kylo-Patrick Hart, "Step 6: Compose a Winning Business Plan," *Business Start-Ups,* December 1996, p. 70.
2. Greg Sands, "The Return of the Business Plan," *FSB,* April 2001, p. 31.
3. Chandrani Ghosh, "Junkyard Dog," *Forbes,* April 16, 2001, pp. 34–36.
4. Paul Hawken, "Money," *Growing a Business,* KQED, San Francisco, 1988.
5. Steve Marshall Cohen, "Money Rules," *Business Start-Ups,* July 1995, p. 79.
6. "Advice from the Great Ones, *Communication Briefings,* January 1992, p. 5.
7. Don Debelak, "The Next Big Product," *Entrepreneur's Be Your Own Boss,* October 2000, pp. 163–164.
8. Ed Engel, "The Odds Are Stacked," *Inc.,* March 2002, p. 34.
9. Edward Clendaniel, "The Professor and the Practitioner," *Forbes ASAP,* May 28, 2001, p. 57.
10. Anne Marie Borrego, "Big Plans," *Inc.,* January 2001, pp. 77–85.
11. Jerry Useem, "Will Your Web Business Work? Take It for a Test Drive," *ecompany,* May 2001, pp. 101–104.
12. C. J. Prince, "The Ultimate Business Plan," *Success,* January 2000, pp. 44–49.
13. Ibid.
14. Lynn H. Colwell, "Mapping Your Route," *Business Start-Ups,* December 1996, p. 44.
15. "Prepping Yourself for Credit," *Your Company,* April/May 1997, p. 9.
16. David R. Evanson, "Capital Pitches That Succeed," *Nation's Business,* May 1997, pp. 40–41.
17. Ibid., p. 41.
18. Jill Andresky Fraser, "Who Can Help Out with a Business Plan?" *Inc.,* June 1999, p. 115.

Chapter

Building a Guerrilla Marketing Plan

> *Customer satisfaction is when you sell something that does not return to someone who does.*

—STANLEY MARCUS, CO-FOUNDER, NEIMAN MARCUS

> *There is less to fear from outside competition than from inside inefficiency, discourtesy, and bad service.*

—ANONYMOUS

Upon completion of this chapter, you will be able to:

1. Describe the components of a guerrilla marketing plan and explain the benefits of preparing one.

2. Explain how small businesses can pinpoint their target markets.

3. Explain how to determine customer needs through market research and the steps in the market research process.

4. Describe the guerrilla marketing strategies on which a small business can build a competitive edge in the marketplace.

5. Discuss marketing opportunities the World Wide Web offers and how entrepreneurs can take advantage of them.

6. Discuss the "four Ps" of marketing—product, place, price, and promotion—and their role in building a successful marketing strategy.

Too often, business plans describe in great detail what the entrepreneur intends to accomplish (e.g., "the financials") and pay little, if any, attention to the strategies to achieve those targets. Others fail miserably because they are not willing to invest the time and energy to identify and research their target markets and to assemble a business plan. These entrepreneurs squander enormous effort pulling together capital, staff, products, and services because they neglect to determine what it will take to attract and retain a profitable customer base. To be effective, a solid business plan must contain both a financial plan and a marketing plan. Like the financial plan, an effective marketing plan projects numbers and analyzes them, but from a different perspective. Rather than focus on cash flow, net profits, and owner's equity, the marketing plan concentrates on the customer.

This chapter is devoted to creating an effective marketing plan, which is an integral part of a total business plan. Before producing reams of computer-generated spreadsheets of financial projections, entrepreneurs must determine what to sell, to whom and how often, on what terms and at what price, and how to get the product or service to the customer. In short, a marketing plan identifies a company's target customers and describes how it will attract and keep them.

CREATING A GUERRILLA MARKETING PLAN

1. Describe the components of a guerrilla marketing plan and explain the benefits of preparing one.

Marketing is the process of creating and delivering desired goods and services to customers and involves all of the activities associated with winning and retaining loyal customers. The secret to successful marketing is to understand what the company's target customers' needs, demands, and wants are before competitors can; to offer them the products and services that will satisfy those needs, demands, and wants; and to provide those customers with quality, service, convenience, and value so that they will keep coming back. The marketing function cuts across the entire organization, affecting every aspect of its operation—from finance and production to hiring and purchasing. As the global business environment becomes more turbulent, small business owners must understand the importance of developing relevant marketing strategies; they are not just for megacorporations competing in international markets. Though they may be small in size and cannot match their larger rivals' marketing budgets, entrepreneurial companies are not powerless when it comes to developing effective marketing strategies. By building a guerrilla marketing plan using unconventional, low-cost, creative techniques, small companies can wring as much or more "bang" from their marketing bucks. *Facing industry giants Coca-Cola and Pepsi-Cola as well as a host of other competitors in the beverage industry, tiny Jones Soda has relied on a guerrilla marketing strategy since Peter van Stolk founded the company in 1996. When Jones Soda had trouble landing shelf space from traditional beverage outlets, Van Stolk turned to what he calls "an alternative distribution strategy" for his company's uniquely flavored drinks that carry names such as Blue Bubble Gum and Green Apple. The company lured customers by stocking its colorful drinks (neon-bright reds, yellows, blues, purples, and greens) with their retro long-necked bottles and unusual labels in nontraditional venues such as surf, skate, and snowboarding shops, music stores, tattoo parlors, and clothing stores—all places where Jones Soda's target customers were likely to be. Once customers started requesting the products, more traditional beverage outlets were willing to stock the company's drinks. Convenience stores and supermarket chains such as Safeway and Albertson's now sell Jones Soda products. To keep demand strong, the company has signed an array of extreme athletes, including BMX rider Matt Hoffman, surfer Kahea Hart, and skateboarder Willie Santos, to promote its line of drinks. Employees also travel through cities in recreational vehicles handing out Jones Sodas and talking up the product line among customers. Van Stolk keeps customers interested in his*

Jones Soda Company founder Peter Van Stolk uses a guerrilla marketing strategy to sell unique drinks in the hotly competitive beverage industry.

brand with the help of a contest that encourages them to send in pictures of themselves for use on its products' labels! With its innovative guerrilla strategy, Jones Soda has built a brand with cult status among its customer base.[1]

Developing a winning marketing strategy requires a business to master three vital resources: people, information, and technology. People are the most important ingredient in formulating a successful marketing strategy. Hiring and retaining creative, talented, well-trained people to develop and implement a marketing strategy is the first step. Just as in sports, implementing a successful marketing strategy relies on an entrepreneur's ability to recruit people with the talent to do the job and to teach them to work together as a team.

In today's more sophisticated and competitive markets, successful marketing relies on a company's ability to capture data and transform it into useful, meaningful information. Information is the fuel that feeds the marketing engine. Without it, a marketing strategy soon sputters and stops. Collecting more data than competitors, putting it into a meaningful form faster, and disseminating it to everyone in the business, especially those who deal with customers, can give a company a huge competitive edge. Unfortunately, too many small business owners fail to see the importance of capturing the information needed to drive a successful marketing strategy.

Technology has proved to be a powerful marketing weapon; yet, technology alone is not the key to marketing success. Competitors may duplicate or exceed the investment a small business makes in technology, but that may not guarantee their marketing success. The way a company integrates the use of technology into its overall marketing strategy is what matters most. *For instance, Thomas Neckel, owner of Sumerset Custom Houseboats, installed a Webcam feature on its Web site to allow customers to monitor progress on the construction of their luxury houseboats. Based on what they see online, customers can make changes to their houseboats as construction progresses. The Webcam feature not only has increased the company's percentage of repeat customers from 40 percent to 60 percent, but it also has attracted new customers. Sumerset's Webcam generates 25,000 page views each day!*[2]

A marketing plan focuses the company's attention on the customer and recognizes that satisfying the customer is the foundation of every business. Its purpose is to build a strategy of success for a business—but from the customer's point of view. Indeed, the customer is the central player in the cast of every business venture. According to marketing expert Theodore Levitt, the primary purpose of a business is not to earn a profit; instead, it is "to create and keep a customer. The rest, given reasonable good sense, will take care of itself."[3] Every area of the business must practice putting the customer first in planning and actions. A **guerrilla marketing plan** should accomplish four objectives:

1. It should pinpoint the target markets the small company will serve.
2. It should determine customer needs, wants, and characteristics through market research.
3. It should analyze a company's competitive advantages and build a marketing strategy around them.
4. It should help create a marketing mix that meets customer needs and wants.

This chapter will focus on building a customer orientation into these four objectives of the small company's marketing plan.

MARKET DIVERSITY: PINPOINTING THE TARGET MARKET

2. Explain how small businesses can pinpoint their target markets.

One of the first steps in building a marketing plan is identifying a small company's **target market,** the group of customers at whom the company aims its products and services. The more a business learns from market research about its local markets, its customers and their buying habits and preferences, the more precisely it can focus its marketing efforts on the group(s) of prospective and existing customers who are most likely to buy its products or services. *Blane Nordahl, one of the most successful cat burglars ever (until he was caught), specialized in stealing only the finest sterling silver. What made Nordahl so difficult for police to catch was his meticulous market research that allowed him to target* exactly *the right homes to rob. Nordahl used local libraries and publications such as the* duPont Registry *and* Sotheby's Previews *to identify and learn about upscale neighborhoods. Then he would go out and scout out the most likely "old money" homes in those neighborhoods, carefully selecting his targets to maximize his take and to minimize the likelihood of getting caught. Nordahl's systematic approach to selecting his target market worked for more than 15 years, netting him millions of dollars' worth of ill-gotten gain before a footprint left in a hasty exit allowed police to nab him. "Of all the burglars I've ever gone up against," says one police officer, "he is absolutely the best."*[4]

Although Nordahl used a creative marketing approach to achieve illegal gain, small businesses can use a similar approach to make their businesses more successful. Unfortunately, most marketing experts contend that the greatest marketing mistake small businesses make is failing to define clearly the target market to be served. In other words, most small businesses follow a "shotgun approach" to marketing, firing marketing blasts at every customer they see, hoping to capture just some of them. Most small companies simply cannot use shotgun marketing to compete successfully with larger rivals and their deep pockets. These small businesses develop new products that do not sell because they failed to target them at a specific audience's needs; they broadcast ads that attempt to reach everyone and end up reaching no one; they spend precious resources trying to reach customer who are not the most

"I heard that The Gap is opening a
new store for middle-aged men.
It's called The Gut."

profitable; and, many of the customers they manage to attract leave because they don't know what the company stands for.

Failing to pinpoint their target markets is especially ironic since small firms are ideally suited to reaching market segments that their larger rivals overlook or consider too small to be profitable. Why, then, is the shotgun approach so popular? Because it is easy and does not require market research or a marketing plan! The problem is that the shotgun approach is a sales-driven rather than a customer-driven strategy. To be customer driven, an effective marketing program must be based on a clear, concise definition of the firm's targeted customers.

A "one-size-fits-all" approach to marketing no longer works because the mass market is rapidly disappearing. The population of the United States, like that of many countries, is becoming increasingly diverse. The mass market that dominated the business world of 25 years ago has been replaced by an increasingly fragmented market of multicultural customers including Hispanic, African American, Asian Pacific, Native American, and many other populations. In fact, by 2010, Hispanics, African Americans, Asian Americans, and other minorities will account for one third of the nation's population. To be successful, businesses must be in tune with the multicultural nature of the modern marketplace. Small businesses that take the time to recognize, understand, and cater to the unique needs, experiences, and preferences of these multicultural markets (and their submarkets) will reap immense rewards.

The nation's increasingly diverse population offers businesses of all sizes tremendous marketing opportunities if they target specific customers, learn how to reach them, and offer goods and services designed specifically for them. The key to success is understanding those target customers' unique needs, wants, and preferences. The fastest growing sector in the United States today is the Hispanic population, which showed an increase of 60 percent from 1990 to 2000. The more than 35 million Hispanic Americans now comprise the nation's single largest minority group, edging out African Americans. With $400 billion in purchasing power, the Hispanic American population is an extremely attractive target market for many entrepreneurs selling everything from groceries and perfumes to houses and entertainment.[5] *When Ruben and Rosalinda Montalvo moved to the United States from Mexico, they noted the rapidly rising Hispanic population in their area and left their corporate jobs to launch a string of businesses aimed at serving this market. In addition to their small chain of authentic Mexican restaurants, the Montalvos launched Salsatheque, a nightclub aimed specifically at young, upscale Hispanic professionals. The club's music, food, drinks, décor, and ambience are designed to appeal to the Montalvos' target customers, whom they know well because of their firsthand experience and their market research.*[6]

Like Salsatheque, the most successful businesses have well-defined portraits of the customers they are seeking to attract. From market research, they know their customers' income levels, lifestyles, buying patterns, likes and dislikes, and even their psychological profiles. The target customer permeates the entire business—from the merchandise purchased to the layout and décor of the store. They have an advantage over their rivals because the images they have created for their companies appeal to their target customers, and that's why they prosper. Without a clear picture of its target market, a small company will try to reach almost everyone and usually ends up appealing to almost no one.

DETERMINING CUSTOMER NEEDS AND WANTS THROUGH MARKET RESEARCH

3A. Explain how to determine customer needs through market research.

The changing nature of the U.S. population is a potent force altering the landscape of business. Shifting patterns in age, income, education, race, and other population characteristics (which are the subject of demographics) will have a major impact on companies, their customers, and the way they do business with those customers. Businesses that ignore demographic trends and fail to adjust their strategies accordingly run the risk of becoming competitively obsolete.

A demographic trend is like a train; an entrepreneur must find out early on where it's going and decide whether or not to get on board. Waiting until the train is roaring down the tracks and gaining speed means it's too late to get on board. However, by checking the schedule early and planning ahead, an entrepreneur may find himself at the train's controls wearing the engineer's hat! Similarly, small companies that spot demographic trends early and act on them can gain a distinctive edge in the market. An entrepreneur's goal should be to align her business with as many demographic, social, and cultural trends as possible. Staying on trend means staying in synchronization with the market as it shifts and changes over time. The more trends a business converges with, the more likely it is to be successful. Conversely, a business moving away from significant trends in society is in danger of losing its customer base.

Trends are powerful forces and can be a business owner's greatest friend or greatest enemy. *Arthur Landry purchased the Dydee Diaper Company in 1960 and ran it as a family business for the next 28 years before turning it over to his son Steven. Founded in 1933, Dydee Diapers was one of the country's oldest diaper services. For each of its customers, Dydee kept about 200 diapers in cycle—half with the customer, half being laundered by its four industrial washing machines. The company's 20 trucks delivered diapers to customers' doorsteps on a regular schedule. The business grew steadily until the early 1990s, when the major disposable diaper makers began an advertising blitz touting the convenience and the health benefits of their products. Busy baby boomers switched their babies over to disposables, and Dydee Diapers' business fell by 20 percent (as did sales for diaper services nationwide). The slide continued as diaper services continued to fall out of favor with a new generation of parents, and Dydee Diapers was forced to file for bankruptcy.*[7]

By performing some basic market research, entrepreneurs can detect key demographic, social, and cultural trends and zero in on the needs, wants, preferences, and desires of its target customers. Indeed, every business can benefit from a better understanding of its market, customers, and competitors. **Market research** is the vehicle for gathering the information that serves as the foundation for the marketing plan. It involves systematically collecting, analyzing, and interpreting data pertaining to the small company's market, customers, and competitors. Businesses face the challenge of reaching the highly fragmented markets that have emerged today, and market research can help them. Market research allows entrepreneurs to answer such questions as: Who are my customers and potential customers? What is their gender? To which age group(s) do they belong? What is their income level? What kind of people are they? Where do they live? Do they rent or own their own homes? What are they looking for in the products or services I sell? How often do they buy these products or services? What models, styles, colors, or flavors do they prefer? Why do or don't they buy from my store? How do the strengths of my product or service serve their needs and wants? What hours do they prefer to shop? How do they perceive my business? Which advertising media are most likely to reach them? How do customers perceive my business versus competitors? This information is an integral part of developing an effective marketing plan.

When marketing its goods and services, a small company must avoid mistakes because there is no margin for error when funds are scarce and budgets are tight. Small businesses simply cannot afford to miss their target markets, and market research can help them zero in on the bull's-eye. That usually requires conducting market research up front, *before* launching a company. One of the worst—and most common—mistakes entrepreneurs make is *assuming* that a market exists for their products or services. The time to find out if customers are likely to buy a product or a service is before investing thousands of dollars to launch it! Market research can tell entrepreneurs whether or not a sufficient customer base exists and how likely those customers are to buy their products and services. In addition to collecting and analyzing demographic data about their target customers, entrepreneurs can learn a great deal by actually observing, mingling with, and interviewing customers as they shop. *For instance, researchers for Maker's Mark, a Kentucky bourbon distillery, have gathered some of their most meaningful data while talking to customers and potential customers in bars across the country. Their up-close-and-personal approach allows them to get a handle on customers' attitudes and behavior in a way that more traditional techniques cannot.*[8] Other companies are videotaping their customers while they are shopping to get a clear picture of their buying habits. This hands-on market research allows entrepreneurs to get past the barriers that customers often put up and to uncover their true preferences and hidden thoughts.

Many entrepreneurs are discovering the speed, the convenience, and the low cost of conducting market research over the World Wide Web. Online surveys, customer opinion polls, and other research projects are easy to conduct, cost virtually nothing, and help companies connect with their customers. With Web-based surveys, businesses can get real-time feedback from customers, often using surveys they have designed themselves.

Market research does *not* have to be time consuming, complex, or expensive to be useful. *At Newbury Comics, a 21-year-old chain of music and novelty stores in New England, managers see the necessity of keeping up with the rapidly changing tastes of their young target customers who are typically in their twenties. To stay plugged in, the company hosts small groups of customers at informal dinners of hamburgers and beer, where managers learn what their customers are thinking. Based on feedback from these meetings, Newbury Comics has shifted its advertising from newspapers and radio to transit ads and movie theater advertising.* Market research for a small business can be informal; it does not have to be highly sophisticated nor expensive to be valuable.

How to Conduct Market Research

3B. Outline the market research process.

The goal of market research is to reduce the risks associated with making business decisions. It can replace misinformation and assumptions with facts. Opinion and hearsay are not viable foundations on which to build a solid marketing strategy. Successful market research consists of four steps:

Step 1: Define the Objective. The first, and most crucial, step in market research is defining the research objective clearly and concisely. A common flaw at this stage is to confuse a symptom with the true problem. For example, dwindling sales is not a problem—it is a symptom. To get to the heart of the matter, an entrepreneur must consider all the possible factors that could have caused it. Is there new competition? Are the firm's sales representatives impolite or unknowledgeable? Have customer tastes changed? Is the product line too narrow? Do customers have trouble finding what they want? In other cases, an owner may be interested in researching a specific type of question. What are the characteristics of my customers? What are their income levels? What radio stations do they listen to? Why do they shop here? What factors are most important to their buying decisions? What impact do in-store displays have on their purchasing patterns? Do they enjoy their shopping experience? If so, why? If not, why not? What would they like to see the store do differently?

Business owners also can use market research to uncover new market opportunities as well. For example, when the owner of a fitness center surveyed his customers, he discovered that many had an interest in aerobic exercises. He added an aerobics program, and within a year his revenues had grown by 25 percent.

Step 2: Collect the Data. The marketing approach that companies of all sizes strive to achieve is **individualized (or one-to-one) marketing,** a system of gathering data on individual customers and then developing a marketing plan designed specifically to appeal to their needs, tastes, and preferences. Its goal is not only to attract customers but also to keep them and to increase their purchases. In a society in which people feel so isolated and transactions are so impersonal, one-to-one marketing gives a business a competitive advantage. Companies following this approach know their customers, understand how to give them the value they want, and perhaps most important, know how to make them feel special and important. The goal is to treat each customer as an individual.

Individualized marketing requires business owners to gather and assimilate detailed information about their customers, however. Fortunately, owners of even the smallest businesses now have access to affordable technology that creates and manages computerized databases, allowing them to develop close, one-to-one relationships with their customers. Much like gold nuggets waiting to be discovered, significant amounts of valuable information about customers and their buying habits is hidden *inside* many small businesses, tucked away in computerized databases. For most business owners, collecting useful information about their customers and potential new products and markets is simply a matter of sorting and organizing data that is already floating around somewhere in their companies. "Most companies are data rich and information poor," claims one marketing expert.[9] The key is to mine those data and turn it into useful information that allows the company to "court" its customers with special products, services, ads, and offers that appeal most to them.

Thanks to advances in computer hardware and software, data mining, once available only to large companies with vast computer power, is now possible for even very small businesses. **Data mining** is a process in which computer software

From the exterior, Green Hills Farms, a small 67-year-old grocery store in Syracuse, New York, does not look like the type of business that national chain stores would seek advice from on how to build a customer loyalty program. Yet, this fourth-generation family business has created one of the best customer retention programs in the entire industry. What's the secret? CEO Gary Hawkins really understands his customers and does everything he can to court and to keep the best and most profitable ones. In an industry known for its razor-thin profit margins, Green Hills Farms not only earns above-average profits but also beats its much larger, wealthier rivals, one of which is located at the other end of the parking lot.

In the quest to keep customers, Hawkins began by giving away free Thanksgiving turkeys to customers who spent a certain amount in the store in the weeks before the holidays. The promotion was a money-losing venture for the store and did nothing to increase customer retention. "There has to be a better way," Hawkins thought. In 1993, he launched Green Hills Farms' frequent buyer program using the bar-coded cards that gave customers discounts and produced reams of data about each customer's purchasing patterns. Within two years, 70 percent of the store's customers were using the cards, and Hawkins had volumes of data; unfortunately, he didn't know what to do with it. That's when Hawkins got serious about analyzing the data the frequent buyer program was generating. Managers began to drill into the company's database to identify the store's best customers, and the results were surprising. "There were people spending lots of money whom I didn't know, and 'regular' customers who weren't high spenders," says one manager.

To understand customer loyalty, managers studied how often, when, and what people were buying. Soon, Hawkins and his staff had identified four levels of Green Hills Farms customers, and they named them based on their value to the company: Diamond (at the top of the spending scale), Ruby, Pearl, and Opal. They discovered that of their roughly 15,000 customers, only about 300 customers are Diamonds, those spending at least $100 a week, and about 1,000 customers qualify as Rubies, those spending on average $50 to $99 a week. Hawkins decided to focus his customer loyalty efforts on his most valuable customers, the Diamonds and the Rubies. Once he knew what these customers were like, he even threw a black-tie party to bring in more of them, and 200 people attended.

Although most grocery stores have frequent buyer programs, Green Hills Farms has revamped its program to reflect the value of each level of customer to the store. When customers join, they get $15 back for spending $100 and a personalized tour of the store with their "new customer manager." Those who become Diamonds not only get free Thanksgiving turkeys (fresh, not frozen), but also a free 7-foot Christmas tree, a 25 percent discount in the garden shop every spring, discount coupons during the year, and a host of other benefits. Managers and employees, most of whom have worked for the store for many years, can call hundreds of customers by name. In short, Green Hills Farms takes really good care of its best customers.

Hawkins says he has learned the difference between "deal loyalty" and "relationship loyalty" with his customers. Deal loyalty means a store "buys" a customer for a time, but it is short term, usually just the length of the special promotion. The problem is that these customers simply move on to the next "deal" when it appears. However, customers who continue to buy from a business for reasons other than special promotions and prizes demonstrate relationship loyalty. They are the ones that are most valuable to a business and should be the focus of any retention program.

The approach works. When two new competitors opened stores (bringing the total number of rivals nearby to six), Hawkins generated a list of Green Hills Farms' best customers based on which products they bought most often. Director of Information Services Lisa Piron sent each one a letter thanking them for their business and included a gift certificate for a gift basket customized for their individual preferences. Not only did the store not lose sales to its new rivals, but it actually gained sales and a few new customers! Now that it understands the real value of its customers, Green Hills Farms retains more than 96 percent of its Diamond customers each year, and the

(continued)

company boasts an overall customer retention rate of 80 percent, much higher than the industry average. Also, because the store no longer wastes time and money chasing customers who are looking only for a good deal, its profit margins have climbed. "At the end of the day," says Hawkins, "the goal of any loyalty program is to improve the bottom line."

1. What benefits does increased customer retention offer a small business?

2. Does size matter when it comes to customer loyalty and retention? Explain.

3. What lessons could other businesses, including those in other industries, learn from Green Hills Farms' philosophy of customer retention?

Source: Adapted from Susan Greco, "The Best Little Grocery Store in America," *Inc.*, June 2001, pp. 54–61.

---

that uses statistical analysis, database technology, and artificial intelligence finds hidden patterns, trends, and connections in data so that business owners can make better marketing decisions and predictions about customer's behavior. Finding relationships among the many components of a data set, identifying clusters of customers with similar buying habits, and predicting customers' buying patterns, data mining gives entrepreneurs incredible marketing power. Popular data mining software packages include ACT!, Clementine, DataScope Pro, GoldMine, MineSet, Nuggets, and many others.

For an effective individualized marketing campaign to be successful, business owners must collect and mine three types of information:

1. *Geographic.* Where are my customers located? Do they tend to be concentrated in one geographic region?
2. *Demographic.* What are the characteristics of my customers (age, education levels, income, sex, marital status, and many other features)?
3. *Psychographic.* What drives my customers' buying behavior? Are they receptive to new products or are they among the last to accept them? What values are most important to them?

Harrah's Entertainment Inc., which operates 21 casinos around the United States, uses data mining to develop sophisticated demographic and psychographic profiles of its customers. Using its Total Gold frequent gambler card (much like the cards supermarkets distribute to shoppers) to collect information about its customers and their gambling habits, ranging from which games they play to how fast they play them, Harrah's was able to pinpoint its best customers, whom managers dubbed "avid experienced players," and to develop individual marketing strategies for them. Unlike many casinos that court "high rollers," wealthy gamblers that gamble hundreds of thousands of dollars at a time, with expensive "comps" such as free airfare and luxury suites, Harrah's best and most profitable customers are low rollers with modest incomes who spend between $100 and $499 per trip. With the help of its data mining system, Harrah's targets individual customers with promotional offers, ranging from free meals and show tickets to cash vouchers and free rooms, designed to get them back into the casino. The payoff has been exceptional; Harrah's sales, profits, market share, and customer response rate to promotions have climbed dramatically.[10]

Figure 7.1 explains how to become an effective individualized marketer.

Step 3: Analyze and Interpret the Data. The results of market research alone do not provide a solution to the problem; the owner must attach some meaning to them. What do the facts mean? Is there a common thread running through the responses? Do the results suggest any changes needed in the way the business is run? Are there new opportunities the owner can take advantage of? There are no hard-and-fast

Figure 7.1
How to Become an Effective One-to-One Marketer

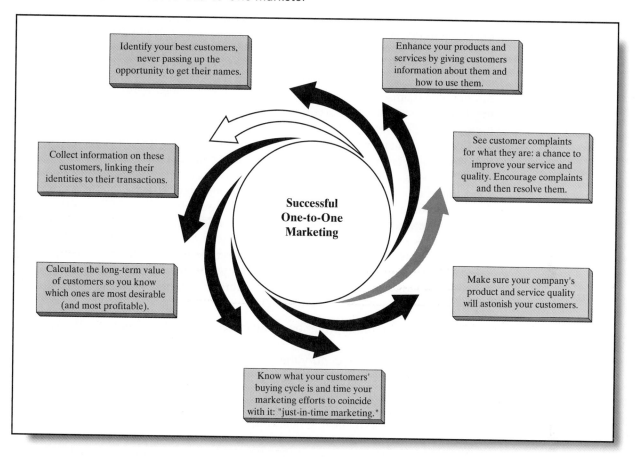

Identify your best customers, never passing up the opportunity to get their names.

Enhance your products and services by giving customers information about them and how to use them.

Collect information on these customers, linking their identities to their transactions.

See customer complaints for what they are: a chance to improve your service and quality. Encourage complaints and then resolve them.

Successful One-to-One Marketing

Calculate the long-term value of customers so you know which ones are most desirable (and most profitable).

Make sure your company's product and service quality will astonish your customers.

Know what your customers' buying cycle is and time your marketing efforts to coincide with it: "just-in-time marketing."

Source: Adapted from Susan Greco, "The Road to One-to-One Marketing," *Inc.*, October 1995, pp. 56–66.

rules for interpreting market research results; the owner must use judgment and common sense to determine what the numbers mean.

Step 4: Draw Conclusions. The market research process is not complete until the business owner acts on the information collected. In many cases, the conclusion is obvious once entrepreneurs interpret the results of their market research. Based on their understanding of what the facts really mean, owners must then decide how to use the information in their business. For example, the owner of a retail shop discovered from a survey that her customers preferred evening shopping hours over early morning hours. She made the schedule adjustment, and sales began to climb.

PLOTTING A GUERRILLA MARKETING STRATEGY: BUILDING A COMPETITIVE EDGE

A competitive edge is crucial for business success. A small business has a competitive edge when customers perceive that the company and its products or services are superior to those of its competitors. The right marketing strategy, not size or financial resources, is a key determinant of how successful a business is at achieving a

4. Describe the guerrilla marketing strategies on which a small business can build a competitive edge.

competitive advantage. Although they may be smaller and lack the marketing budgets of their larger rivals, small companies can gain a competitive advantage using creative, low-cost guerrilla marketing strategies that hit home with their target customers. Independent bookstores have discovered that large chains use their buying power to get volume discounts and undercut the independents' prices. Individual shop owners are finding new ways, such as special ordering, adult reading groups, children's story hours, newsletters, autograph parties, and targeting unique niches to differentiate themselves and to retain loyal customers. These entrepreneurs are finding that the best way to gain a competitive advantage is to create value by giving customers what they really want that they cannot get elsewhere.

Successful businesses often use the special advantages they have to build a competitive edge over their larger rivals. Their close contact with the customer, personal attention, focus on service, and organizational and managerial flexibility provide a solid foundation from which to build a towering competitive edge in the market. Small companies can exploit their size to become more effective than their larger rivals at **relationship marketing** or **customer relationship management (CRM)**—developing, maintaining, and managing long-term relationships with customers so that they will want to keep coming back to make repeat purchases. CRM puts the customer at the center of a company's thinking, planning, and action and shifts the focus from a product or service to customers and their needs and wants. CRM requires business owners to take the following steps:

- Collect meaningful information about existing customers and compile it in a database.
- Mine the database to identify the company's best and most profitable customers, their needs, and their buying habits. In most companies, a small percentage of customers account for the majority of sales and profits. These are the customers on whom a business should focus its attention and efforts.
- Focus on developing lasting relationships with these customers. This often requires entrepreneurs to "fire" some customers that require more attention, time, and expense than they generate in revenue for the business. Failing to do so, however, reduces a company's return on its CRM effort.
- Attract more customers that fit the profile of the company's best customers.

To build long-term relationships with customers and achieve the highest level of customer satisfaction, many small businesses rely on 10 guerrilla marketing strategies to develop a competitive edge: niche-picking, entertailing, emphasizing their uniqueness, connecting with their customers, focusing on customers' needs, emphasizing quality; paying attention to convenience, concentrating on innovation; dedicating themselves to service; and emphasizing speed.

Guerrilla Marketing Principles

To be successful guerrilla marketers, entrepreneurs must be as innovative in creating their marketing strategies as they are in developing new product and service ideas. The following principles can help business owners create powerful, effective guerrilla marketing strategies.

Find a Niche and Fill It. As we saw in Chapter 2, "Strategic Management: Gaining a Competitive Edge," many successful small companies choose their niches carefully and defend them fiercely rather than compete head-to-head with larger rivals. A niche strategy allows a small company to maximize the advantages of its smallness and to compete effectively even in industries dominated by giants. Focusing on niches that are too small to be attractive to large companies is a common recipe for success among thriving small companies. *As the name of her business implies, Phyllis Stoller, founder of the Women's Travel Club, has targeted that portion of the market that accounts for 41 percent of all travel. Market research told Stoller that women travelers are more interested in safety and sanitary conditions than are men, and she plans every club trip with these factors in mind. Stoller also discovered that women are more interested in experiencing everyday life than typical tourist activities when they are traveling in foreign lands. Rather than offer the traditional vacation getaways her competitors sell, Stoller specializes in tours that offer plenty of opportunities for cultural exchanges. Because she knows that women want more information than men do before they make a significant purchase, Stoller publishes a monthly newsletter describing upcoming trips in rich detail, focusing on historical attractions, unusual tourist destinations, and local shopping and dining options. The Women's Travel Club Web site also offers information on every trip, including photos and diaries from past trips.*[11] "Small business is uniquely positioned for niche marketing," says marketing expert Philip Kotler. "If a small business sits down and follows the principles of targeting, segmenting, and differentiating, it doesn't have to collapse to larger companies."[12]

Don't Just Sell; Entertain. Numerous surveys have shown that consumers are bored with shopping and that they are less inclined to spend their scarce leisure time shopping than ever before. Winning customers today requires more than low prices and wide merchandise selection; increasingly, businesses are adopting strategies based on **entertailing,** the notion of drawing customers into a store by creating a kaleidoscope of sights, sounds, smells, and activities, all designed to entertain—and, of course, sell (think Disney). The primary goal of entertailing is to catch customers' attention and engage them in some kind of entertaining experience so that they shop longer and buy more goods or services. Entertailing involves "making [shopping] more fun, more educational, more interactive," says one retail consultant.[13] Research supports the benefits of entertailing's hands-on, interactive, educational, approach to selling; one study found that, when making a purchase, 34 percent of consumers are driven more by emotional factors such as fun and excitement than by logical factors such as price and convenience.[14]

Entertailing's goal, of course, is not only to entertain but also to sell. *One small company that has successfully blended show business with the retail business is Jordan's Furniture, a small chain of furniture stores in the Boston area. Barry and Eliot Tatelman, the third generation to operate this highly successful retail operation founded in 1928 by their grandfather, follow a simple business philosophy: "There is no business that's not show business." In addition to their extensive selection of quality furniture, the Tatelmans offer customers fun and entertainment as part of their shopping trips. Recently, in their newest 130,000-square-foot store, the brothers created an elaborate display recreating a New Orleans Mardis Gras scene, complete with a theme-park version of Bourbon Street and animatronic re-creations of Elvis Presley, Louis Armstrong, the Beatles, and a fortuneteller that pop out of shuttered rooms to entertain guests. Shoppers bring their families to see the attraction and, not coincidentally, to stroll through rooms of beautifully decorated furniture displays. The Tatelmans apply "the Las Vegas theory of marketing" to their business. "We bring people to a furniture store for something other than furniture and make them walk through the whole store," explains Eliot. Once they went to a convention for amusement park owners, where they purchased for $2.5 million a laser-enhanced thrill ride through motion picture images and installed it in their Avon, Massachusetts store. Customers waited for an hour and a half to get in to the store. The Tatelman's unique brand of entertailing has made Jordan's Furniture incredibly successful!*[15]

Strive to Be Unique. One of the most effective guerrilla marketing tactics is to create an image of uniqueness for your business. Entrepreneurs can achieve a unique

Barry and Eliot Tatelman, owners of Jordan's Furniture, combine entertainment and retailing to create what *Home Furnishings Daily* calls "the most unusual furniture store in the world."

place in the market in a variety of ways, including through the products and services they offer, the marketing and promotional campaigns they use, the store layouts they design, and the business strategies they employ. The goal is to stand out from the crowd; few things are as uninspiring to customers as a "me-too" business that offers nothing unique.

Connect with Customers on an Emotional Level. Some of the most powerful marketers are those companies that have a clear sense of who they are, what they stand for, and why they exist. Defining their vision for their companies in a meaningful way is one of the most challenging tasks facing entrepreneurs. As we learned in Chapter 2, that vision stems from the beliefs and values of the entrepreneur and is reflected in a company's culture, ethics, and business strategy. Although it is intangible, this vision is a crucial ingredient in a successful guerrilla marketing campaign. Once this vision is firmly planted, guerrilla marketers can use it to connect with their customers. Companies that establish a deeper relationship with their customers than one based merely on making a sale have the capacity to be exceptional guerrilla marketers. These businesses win because customers receive an emotional boost every time they buy the company's product or service. Companies connect with their customers emotionally by supporting causes that are important to their customer base, taking exceptional care of their customers, and making it fun and enjoyable to do business with them.

Focus on the Customer. Too many companies have lost sight of the most important component of every business: the customer. Research shows that the average American company loses about half of its customer base every five years, and many of those defections are the result of companies failing to take care of their customers.[16] Businesses are just beginning to discover the true costs of poor customer relations. For instance:

- Sixty-seven percent of customers who stop patronizing a particular store do so because an indifferent employee treated them poorly.[17]

- Customers are five times more likely to leave because of poor service than they are for product quality or price.[18]
- Ninety-six percent of dissatisfied customers never complain about rude or discourteous service, but . . .
- Ninety-one percent will not buy from the business again.
- One hundred percent of those unhappy customers will tell their "horror stories" to at least nine other people.
- Thirteen percent of those unhappy customers will tell their stories to at least 20 other people.[19]

According to the authors of "Keeping Customers for Life," "The nasty result of this customer indifference costs the average company from 15 to 30 percent of gross sales."[20] Because 70 percent of the average company's sales come from existing customers, few can afford to alienate any customers. In fact, the typical business loses 20 percent of its customers each year. But a recent study by the consulting firm Bain & Company shows that businesses that retain just 5 percent more customers experience profit increases of at least 25 percent, and in some cases, as much as 95 percent![21] Increasing a company's retention rate by just 2 percent has the same impact as cutting expenses by 10 percent![22] Studies by the Boston Consulting Group also show that companies with high customer retention rates produce above-average profits and superior growth in market share.[23]

Because about 20 to 30 percent of a typical company's customers account for about 70 to 80 percent of its sales, it makes more sense to focus resources on keeping the best (and most profitable) customers than to spend them trying to chase "fair weather" customers who will defect to any better deal that comes along. Suppose that a company increases its customer base by 20 percent each year, but it retains only 85 percent of its existing customers. Its effective growth rate is just 5 percent per year [20% - (100% - 85%) = 5%]. If this same company can raise its customer retention rate to 95 percent, its net growth rate *triples* to 15 percent [20% - (100% - 95%) = 15%].[24] Shrewd entrepreneurs recognize that the greatest opportunity for new business often comes from existing customers.

Although winning new customers keeps a company growing, keeping existing ones is essential to success. Attracting a new customer actually costs five times as much as keeping an existing one. Table 7.1 shows the high cost of lost customers.

Table 7.1
The High Cost of Lost Customers

IF YOU LOSE . . .	SPENDING $5 WEEKLY	SPENDING $10 WEEKLY	SPENDING $50 WEEKLY	SPENDING $100 WEEKLY	SPENDING $200 WEEKLY	SPENDING $300 WEEKLY
1 customer a day	$ 94,900	$ 189,800	$ 949,000	$ 1,898,000	$ 3,796,000	$ 5,694,000
2 customers a day	189,800	379,600	1,898,000	3,796,000	7,592,000	11,388,000
5 customers a day	474,500	949,000	4,745,000	9,490,000	18,980,000	28,470,000
10 customers a day	949,000	1,898,000	9,490,000	18,980,000	37,960,000	56,940,000
20 customers a day	1,898,000	3,796,000	18,980,000	37,960,000	75,920,000	113,880,000
50 customers a day	4,745,000	9,490,000	47,450,000	94,900,000	189,800,000	284,700,000
100 customers a day	9,490,000	18,980,000	94,900,000	189,800,000	379,600,000	569,400,000

Given these statistics, small business owners would be better off asking "How can we improve customer value and service to encourage our existing customers to do more business with us?" rather than "How can we increase our market share by 10 percent?" *When Rick Davis, Lynn Graham, and Randy Vanstory saw a survey showing that consumers hated taking their cars in for repairs more than any other task, they saw a business opportunity. The founders of Joeauto.com believed they could achieve customer service and retention by building their business on trust and convenience. At Joeauto.com, customers can schedule car repairs on the company's Web site and when they drop their cars off or have them picked up, they get a cellular phone that gives them a direct link to their repair technician. Also from the Web site, customers can watch their cars being repaired via Webcams located in each service bay. Joeauto.com, whose slogan is "Invented to not waste your time," can e-mail customers to tell them which parts need repair, the cost of repairs, and when they can pick up their cars. The company also provides a complete personalized electronic file of repair history on each customer's car.*[25]

The most successful small businesses have developed a customer orientation and have instilled a customer satisfaction attitude throughout the company. Companies with world-class customer attitudes set themselves apart by paying attention to little things. For example, at one dentist's office, staff members take photos on a patient's first visit. The photo, placed in the patient's file, allows everyone in the office to call him by name on subsequent visits. A small flower shop offers a special service for customers who forget that special event. The shop will insert a card reading, "Please forgive us! Being short-handed this week, we were unable to deliver this gift on time. We hope the sender's thoughtfulness will not be less appreciated because of our error. Again, we apologize."[26]

How do these companies focus so intently on their customers? They follow basic principles:

- When you create a dissatisfied customer, fix the problem fast. One study found that, given the chance to complain, 95 percent of customers will buy again if a business handles their complaints promptly and effectively.[27] The worst way to handle a complaint is to ignore it, to pass it off to a subordinate, or to let a lot of time slip by before dealing with it.
- Encourage customer complaints. You can't fix something if you don't know it's broken. Table 7.2 describes seven ways to turn complaints into satisfied customers.
- Ask employees for feedback on improving customer service. A study by Technical Assistance Research Programs (TARP), a customer service research firm, found that front-line service workers can predict nearly 90 percent of the cases that produce customer complaints.[28] Emphasize that *everyone* is part of the customer satisfaction team.
- Get total commitment to superior customer service from top managers—and allocate resources appropriately.
- Allow managers to wait on customers occasionally. It's a great dose of reality. The founder of a small robot manufacturer credits such a strategy with saving his company. "We now require every officer of this company—including myself—to meet with customers at least four times a month," he says.[29]
- Develop a service theme that communicates your attitude toward customers. Customers want to feel they are getting something special.
- Reward employees "caught" providing exceptional service to customers. At ScriptSave, a company that manages prescription drug benefit programs, managers hand out Bravo Bucks that are redeemable for gifts to employees who excel in providing superior customer service.[30]

Table 7.2
Ways to Turn
Complaints into
Satisfied
Customers

When faced with a complaining customer, business owners naturally defend their companies. Don't do it! Here are eight ways to turn disgruntled buyers into loyal customers.

1. Let unhappy customers vent their feelings; don't interrupt; maintain eye contact and listen to them.
2. Remain objective; avoid labeling customers' emotions or passing judgment on them.
3. Promptly apologize and accept responsibility for the problem.
4. See the complaint for what it is. The customer is upset about something; zero in on what it is.
5. Wait until the customer finishes expressing a complaint and then respond with a solution.
6. Thank the customer; let him or her know you appreciate being told about the situation. Listen for suggestions they might have about resolving the complaint. Try to win a friend, not an argument.
7. Follow up with the customer. Tell him or her what you're doing about the problem.
8. Ask yourself, "What changes do I need to make to our business system so this complaint does not occur again with this customer or other customers in similar situations?"

Sources: Adapted from Shirley Bednarz, "Fine Whine," *Entrepreneur*, February 1999, pp. 103–105; "Five Ways to Turn Complaints into Satisfied Customers," *Personal Selling Power*, April 1991, p. 53; "Handling Disgruntled Customers," *Your Company*, Spring 1993, p. 5.

- Carefully select and train everyone who will deal with customers. *Never* let rude employees work with customers. Charlie Horn, CEO of ScriptSave, requires every customer service representative to go through three weeks of training before taking their first telephone call from a customer. Each representative also gets an additional 60 hours of classroom training in customer service techniques.[31]

Devotion to Quality. In this intensely competitive global business environment, quality goods and services are a prerequisite for success—and even survival. According to one marketing axiom, the worst of all marketing catastrophes is to have great advertising and a poor-quality product. Customers have come to expect and demand quality goods and services, and those businesses that provide them consistently have a distinct competitive advantage.

Today, quality is more than just a slogan posted on the company bulletin board; world-class companies treat quality as a strategic objective—an integral part of the company culture. This philosophy is called **total quality management (TQM)**— quality not just in the product or service itself but in *every* aspect of the business and its relationship with the customer and continuous improvement in the quality delivered to customers. Companies achieve continuous improvement by using statistical techniques to discover problems, determine their causes, and solve them; then, they must incorporate what they have learned into improving the process. It is a never-ending system of improvement that relies on the "DMAIC" process shown in Figure 7.2.

Companies on the cutting edge of the quality movement are developing new ways to measure quality. Manufacturers were the first to apply TQM techniques, but retail, wholesale, and service organizations have seen the benefits of becoming champions of quality. They are tracking customer complaints, contacting "lost" customers, and finding new ways to track the cost of quality and their return on quality (ROQ). ROQ recognizes that although any improvement in quality may improve a

Figure 7.2
The Quality
DMAIC Process

Adapted from Walter
H. Ettinger, MD, "Six
Sigma," *Trustee,*
September 2001, p. 14.

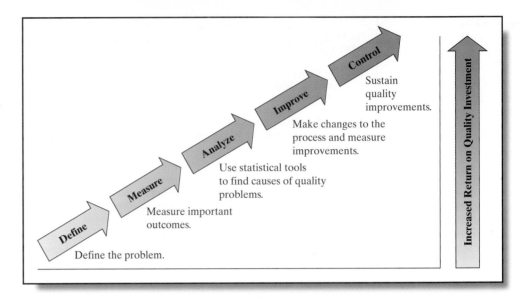

company's competitive ability, only those improvements that produce a reasonable rate of return are worthwhile. In essence, ROQ requires managers to ensure that the quality improvements they implement will more than pay for themselves.

Dean Dunaway, president of Capweld Inc., a small gas distributor in Jackson, Mississippi, turned to a TQM philosophy known as poka-yoke (which comes from two Japanese words meaning "avoid errors") when the cost of lost gas tanks began to cause the company's profits to decline. When Capweld sells $20 worth of oxygen, it is delivered in a $200 tank. Although all of Capwell's tanks are numbered, keeping up with 15,000 to 20,000 transactions each month was difficult and inevitably led to missing tanks. Losing just one tank erased the profits on a huge number of sales. Putting together a team of employees to study the causes of the problem revealed that employees misreading tanks' identification numbers was the source of many lost tanks. The quality team suggested a computerized solution to solve the lost tank problem. Capweld now uses a computerized database to track the location of every one of its 40,000 tanks and has attached scannable microchips to them to avoid employee input errors. The company's poka-yoke efforts have more than paid for themselves by significantly lowering the number of lost tanks. Dunaway, who hopes to keep whittling away at the small errors that have a big impact at Capweld, says, "It's just hundreds of little bitty things."[32]

The key to developing a successful TQM philosophy is seeing the world from the customer's point of view. In other words, quality must reflect the needs and wants of the customer. How do customers define quality? According to one survey, Americans rank quality components in this order: reliability (average time between failures), durability (how long it lasts), ease of use, a known or trusted brand name, and, last, a low price.[33] In services, customers are likely to look for similar characteristics: tangibles (equipment, facilities, and people), reliability (doing what you say you will do), responsiveness (promptness in helping customers), and assurance and empathy (conveying a caring attitude). Companies successful in capturing a reputation for top-quality products and services follow certain guidelines to "get it right the first time":

- Build quality into the process; don't rely on inspection to obtain quality.
- Emphasize simplicity in the design of products and processes; it reduces the opportunity for errors to sneak in.

- Foster teamwork and dismantle the barriers that divide disparate departments.
- Establish long-term ties with select suppliers; don't award contracts on low price alone.
- Provide managers and employees the training needed to participate fully in the quality improvement program.
- Empower workers at all levels of the organization; give them authority and responsibility for making decisions that determine quality.
- Get managers' commitment to the quality philosophy. Otherwise, the program is doomed. Describing his role in his company's TQM philosophy, one CEO says, "People look to see if you just talk about it or actually do it."[34]
- Rethink the processes the company uses now to get its products or services to customers. Employees at Analog Devices redesigned its production process and significantly lowered the defect rate on its silicon chips and saved $1.2 million a year.[35]
- Reward employees for quality work. Ideally, workers' compensation is linked clearly and directly to key measures of quality and customer satisfaction.
- Develop a company-wide strategy for constant improvement of product and service quality.

The goal of these procedures is to achieve 100 percent quality. Table 7.3 offers insight into why 99.9 percent quality simply isn't good enough.

Attention to Convenience. Ask customers what they want from the businesses they deal with and one of the most common responses is "convenience." In this busy, fast-paced world of dual-career couples and lengthy commutes to and from work, consumers have more disposable income, but less time in which to enjoy it. Anything a

Table 7.3
Is 99.9 Percent Quality Good Enough?

In the battle for quality, companies quickly discover just how difficult zero defects are to achieve. Isn't 99.9 percent defect free good enough? Consider the following consequences of 99.9 percent quality and then decide:

- 1 hour of unsafe drinking water every month
- 730 unsafe landings at Chicago's O'Hare Airport each year
- 16,000 pieces of mail lost by the U.S. Postal Service every hour
- 20,000 incorrect drug prescriptions processed each year
- 500 incorrect surgical procedures each week
- 22,000 checks deducted from the wrong bank accounts each hour
- 2 million documents lost by the IRS in a typical year
- 12 babies delivered to the wrong parents each day
- 1,314 telephone calls misrouted every minute
- 2,488,200 magazines published with the wrong covers each year
- 5,517,200 cases of soft drinks produced without any snap, sparkle, or fizz each year

Most entrepreneurs would love for their companies to operate at the 99.9 percent level of quality. However, unless business leaders and their companies continuously strive for 100 percent quality, there is little chance that they will ever achieve 99.9 percent quality. The goal, says one quality expert, "is to move away from the toleration of failure to the idea that we're going to be as perfect as we can be."

Sources: Adapted from Mark Henricks, "Is It Greek to You?" *Entrepreneur*, July 1999, p. 67; Sal Marino, "Is 'Good Enough' Good Enough?" *Industry Week*, February 3, 1997, p. 22; "Why 99.9% Just Won't Do," *Inc.*, April 1989, p. 276.

business can do to enhance convenience for its customers will give it an edge. Several studies have found that customers rank easy access to goods and services at the top of their purchase criteria. Unfortunately, too few businesses deliver adequate levels of convenience, and they fail to attract and retain customers. One print and framing shop, for instance, alienated many potential customers with its abbreviated business hours—9 to 5 daily, except for Wednesday afternoons, Saturday, and Sunday when the shop was closed! Other companies make it a chore to do business with them. In an effort to defend themselves against unscrupulous customers, these businesses have created elaborate procedures for exchanges, refunds, writing checks, and other basic transactions.

Successful companies go out of their way to make it easy for customers to do business with them. *Payam Zamani, founder of Purple Tie, built his company on the concept of customer convenience. Customers can log onto the company's Web site at any time, where they can arrange for one of Zamani's delivery vans to pick up or deliver their dry cleaning at a prearranged time. Purple Tie, which uses only environmentally friendly cleaning agents, has been so successful in San Francisco that Zamani is opening locations in 24 other major markets across the country.*[36]

Many small companies have had success by finding simple ways to make it easier for customers to do business with them. How can entrepreneurs boost the convenience levels of their businesses? By conducting a "convenience audit" from the customer's point of view to get an idea of its ETDBW ("Easy to Do Business With") index:

- Is your business located near your customers? Does it provide easy access?
- Are your business hours suitable to your customers? Should you be open evenings and weekends to serve them better?
- Would customers appreciate on-site or pickup and delivery services? Oil Butler International, an automobile service franchise, offers customers quick oil changes and lube jobs on-site so customers don't have to take their cars into a garage to be serviced.[37]
- Does your company make it easy for customers to purchase on credit or with credit cards?
- Are your employees trained to handle business transactions quickly, efficiently, and politely? Waiting while rude, incompetent employees fumble through routine transactions destroys customer goodwill.
- Does your company handle telephone calls quickly and efficiently? Long waits "on hold," transfers from one office to another, and too many rings before answering signal to customers that they are not important.

Concentration on Innovation. Innovation is the key to future success. Markets change too quickly and competitors move too fast for a small company to stand still and remain competitive. Because of their organizational and managerial flexibility, small businesses often can detect and act on new opportunities faster than large companies. Innovation is one of the greatest strengths of the entrepreneur, and it shows up in the new products, unique techniques, and unusual approaches they introduce. One study of companies with revenues less than $50 million by Coopers and Lybrand showed that nearly two thirds of their CEOs believe their ability to develop new products represents a major competitive advantage.[38]

Despite financial constraints, small businesses frequently are leaders in innovation. For instance, small companies accounted for every significant breakthrough in the computer industry—including handhelds (Palm), microcomputers (Apple Computer), and minicomputers (Digital). Start-up businesses also led the way in developing each generation of computer disk drives. Even in the hotly competitive pharmaceutical industry, the dominant drugs in many markets were discovered by small companies rather than the industry giants like Merck or GlaxoSmithKline with their multimillion-dollar research and development (R&D) budgets.

Although product and service innovation has never been more important to small companies' success, it has never been more challenging. Companies of all sizes are feeling the pressure to develop new products and get them to market faster than ever before. More intense competition, often from across the globe, as well as rapid changes in technology and improvements in communication have made innovation more crucial to business success. "Today's innovation is tomorrow's imitation is next month's commodity," says one business writer.[39] One survey of U.S. companies found that executives expected new products to account for 39 percent of profits in the next five years compared to just 25 percent in the previous five.[40] Ely Callaway, founder of Callaway Golf, the company that makes the famous Big Bertha club, claimed that innovation was his "No. 1 priority and a core value outlined in the company's mission statement. That's because Callaway Golf's long-term success depends on satisfying our customers with a constant stream of innovative new products."[41]

There is more to innovation than spending megadollars on R&D. How do small businesses manage to maintain their leadership role in innovating new products and services? They use their size to their advantage, maintaining their speed and flexibility much like a martial arts expert does against a larger opponent. Their closeness to their customers enables them to read subtle shifts in the market and to anticipate trends as they unfold. Their ability to concentrate their efforts and attention in one area also gives small businesses an edge in innovation. "Small companies have an advantage: a dedicated management team focused solely on a new product or market," says one venture capitalist.[42] *The founders of Molecular Electronics are developing the successor to the integrated circuit that serves as the brains of most modern electronics, from cell phones to computers. Their innovation is a transistor made up of a single molecule that can be switched on and off with a trickle of electric current. The transistors' on–off response mimics the digital zeroes and ones of computer language, but because they are composed of just a single molecule, the transistors are thousands of times smaller than today's silicon chips.*[43]

To be an effective innovator, an entrepreneur should:

- Make innovation a priority in the company by devoting management time and energy to it.
- Measure the company's innovative ability. Tracking the number of new products or services introduced and the proportion of sales products less than five years old generate can be useful measures of a company's ability to innovate.
- Set goals and objectives for innovation. Establishing targets and then rewarding employees for achieving them can produce amazing results.
- Encourage new product and service ideas among employees. Workers have many incredible ideas, but they will lead to new products or services only if someone takes the time to listen to them.
- Always be on the lookout for new product and service ideas. They can come to you (or to anyone in the company) when you least expect it.
- Keep a steady stream of new products and services coming. Even before sales of her safety-handle children's toothbrush took off, Millie Thomas, founder of RGT Enterprises, had developed other children's products using the same triangular-shaped handle, including a crayon holder, paintbrushes, and fingernail brushes.[44]

Dedication to Service and Customer Satisfaction. In the new economy, companies are discovering that unexpected innovative, customized service can be a powerful strategic weapon. Small companies that lack the financial resources of their larger rivals have discovered that offering exceptional customer service is one of the most effective ways to differentiate themselves and to attract and maintain a growing customer base. "It doesn't take money to [provide] good customer service," says the head of one retail company. "It takes a commitment."[45] Unfortunately, the level of service in most companies is poor. Businesses that are not able to improve the quality of their service to customers will fail, while those that can create superior customer service will excel.

Mark Soderstrom, founder of Southstream Seafoods, a small importer and wholesaler of frozen seafood, discovered early on that his business would have to set itself apart with superb customer service in order to thrive in an extremely competitive business. Rapid swings in fish prices can create both opportunities and problems for Southstream's customers, so Soderstrom began using a customer relationship management (CRM) software package to give customers updated information about changes in market prices so they could make good business decisions at purchase time. With the system, Southstream sends anywhere from 500 to 1,000 "customized" faxes a week with pricing information on products each customer is interested in. Customers find the information to be extremely valuable. "Knowledge is power," says Soderstrom, "and we're the people providing them with that power." Soderstrom credits his company's superior customer service as a major source of his company's success and growth, up from sales of $4 million to more than $60 million in just 10 years![46]

Successful businesses recognize that superior customer service is only an intermediate step toward the goal of customer satisfaction. These companies seek to go beyond customer satisfaction, striving for *customer astonishment!* They concentrate on providing customers with quality, convenience, and service as their customers define those terms. Certainly, the least expensive—and the most effective—way to achieve customer satisfaction is through friendly, personal service. Numerous surveys of customers in a wide diversity of industries, from manufacturing and services to banking and high tech, conclude that the most important element of service is "the personal touch." Calling customers by name; making attentive, friendly contact; and truly caring about customers' needs and wants are more essential than any other factor, even convenience, quality, and speed!

How can a company achieve stellar customer service and satisfaction?

Listen to Customers. The best companies constantly listen to their customers and respond to what they hear! This allows them to keep up with customers' changing needs and expectations. The only way to find out what customers really want and value is to ask them. Businesses rely on a number of techniques, including surveys, focus groups, telephone interviews, comment cards, suggestion boxes, toll-free hot lines, and regular one-on-one conversations with customers (perhaps the best technique). Starbucks founder Howard Schultz resisted using skim milk in the company's Italian lattes until he spent time working in a Starbucks outlet and listening to customers repeatedly ask for it.[47]

Define Superior Service. Based on what customers say, managers and employees must decide exactly what "superior service" means in the company. Such a statement should: (1) be a strong statement of intent, (2) differentiate the company from others, and (3) have value to customers. Deluxe Corporation, a printer of personal checks, defines superior service quite simply: "Forty-eight hour turnaround; zero defects."

Set Standards and Measure Performance. To be able to deliver on its promise of superior service, a business must establish specific standards and measure overall performance against them. Satisfied customers should exhibit at least one of three behaviors: loyalty (increased customer retention rate), increased purchases (climbing sales and sales per customer), and resistance to rivals' attempts to lure them away with lower prices (market share and price tolerance).[48] Companies must track performance on these and other service standards and reward employees accordingly.

Examine Your Company's Service Cycle. What steps must a customer go through to get your product or service? Business owners often are surprised at the complexity that has seeped into their customer service systems as they have evolved over time. One of the most effective techniques is to work with employees to flowchart each component in the company's service cycle, including everything a customer has to do to get your product or service. The goal is to look for steps and procedures that are unnecessary, redundant, or unreasonable and then to eliminate them.

Hire the Right Employees. The key ingredient in the superior service equation is *people*. There is no substitute for friendly, courteous sales and service representatives. A customer service attitude requires hiring employees who believe in and embrace customer service.

Train Employees to Deliver Superior Service. Successful businesses train every employee who deals directly with customers; they don't leave the art of customer service to chance. Superior service companies devote 1 to 5 percent of their employees' work hours to training, concentrating on how to meet, greet, and serve customers. "Employees need to be trained to instinctively provide good service," says John Tschol, founder of the Service Quality Institute.[49]

Empower Employees to Offer Superior Service. One of the biggest single variables determining whether or not employees deliver superior service is whether or not they perceive they have permission to do so. The goal is to push decision making down the organization to the employees who have contact with customers. This includes giving them the freedom to circumvent company policy if it means improving customer satisfaction. If front-line workers don't have this power to solve disgruntled customers' problems, they quickly become frustrated and the superior service cycle breaks down. To be empowered, employees need knowledge and information, adequate resources, and managerial support.

Use Technology to Provide Improved Service. The role of technology is not to create a rigid bureaucracy but to free employees from routine clerical tasks, giving them more time and better tools to serve customers more effectively. Ideally, technology gives workers the information they need to help their customers and the time to serve them. Mike Schapansky, owner of Pure-Chem, a pool maintenance company in Austin, Texas, equips his service technicians with handheld computers to boost customer service. Technicians use the Palm Pilots to record pool readings that are fed into a database at the end of each day. The system allows Pure-Chem to monitor customers' pools more closely and to respond to service calls more quickly.[50]

Reward Superior Service. What gets rewarded gets done. Companies that want employees to provide stellar service must offer rewards for doing so. One National Science Foundation study concluded that when pay is linked to performance, employees' motivation and productivity climb by as much as 63 percent.[51]

Get Top Managers' Support. The drive toward superior customer service will fall far short of its target unless top managers support it fully. Success requires more than just a verbal commitment; it calls for managers' involvement and dedication. Periodically, managers should spend time in customer service positions to maintain contact with customers, front-line employees, and the challenges of providing good service.

Emphasis on Speed. We live in a world of instantaneous expectations. Technology that produces immediate results at the click of a mouse and allows for real-time communication has altered our sense of time and space. Speed reigns. Customers now expect companies to serve them at the speed of light! In such a world, speed has become a major competitive weapon. World-class companies recognize that reduc-

IN THE FOOTSTEPS OF AN ENTREPRENEUR
Taking on the Giants

Amilya Antonetti's business, Soapworks, was born from a labor of love. When her infant son became ill, doctors were at a loss to pinpoint the cause of the problem. With the tenacity only a mother could muster, Antonetti traced her son's health problems to the chemicals in the household cleaning products she used every day. She turned to her grandmother for help, asking how her generation cleaned their houses before all of the chemically enhanced products sold today were available. She learned that many of the products used in her grandmother's day were all-natural, often relying on citrus products and other natural cleaning agents. Although her son's was an extreme case of sensitivity, Antonetti was convinced that other mothers faced the same problem and that there was a market for all-natural, hypoallergenic cleaners.

Before launching her business, Antonetti conducted much of her market research in the aisles of grocery stores, talking with shoppers. Seeing an opportunity, she and her husband sold their home and took out a loan to open Soapworks in San Leandro, California. "There was very clearly a niche that was not being served," she says. "Our customers fit into a niche that was not being served by Tide and Cheer and All." But landing her products on some store shelves proved to be a daunting task. Store buyers laughed at her initially, pointing out powerful brands such as Tide and Clorox. That's when Antonetti enlisted her loyal base of customers to help her. Soapworks products have a "cult following," says one store manager, and their loyalty stems not only from the company's products but also from Antonetti's devotion to her customers and the values the company stands for. "Customers are buying into the concept and the message of the company as much as they are the product," says one industry expert and loyal Soapworks customer.

Antonetti has positioned Soapworks' products as empowering, all-natural, safe alternatives aimed at female shoppers who are tired of the advertising hype pushed on them by large companies. Soapworks' advertising budget is minuscule, just $60,000 a year, compared to the millions of dollars her larger rivals spend, so Antonetti counts on guerrilla marketing techniques to succeed. She recently co-sponsored a back-to-school bash with a local family-oriented radio station that proved to be a huge success. She purchased $6,500 worth of airtime and served as her company's spokesperson to reach the station's 250,000 listeners. The audience responded so well to the woman they saw as equal parts CEO and mom that she became a regular guest on one of the station's weekly talk shows, where she answers callers' questions and offers useful tips. To stir up support for her company and its products, Antonetti hands out lots of free samples in children's hospital wards and in women's shelters. She also relies on the power of publicity. Her story has been featured in several national magazines and on both local and national television shows. Soapworks has doubled its sales every year since its launch, and, like the owner of any fast-growing business, Antonetti constantly struggles with cash flow problems. She and her husband have decided that the business must bring in outside investors, but they have to be the *right* investors, and Antonetti has not yet found them.

1. Which of the guerrilla marketing strategies discussed in this chapter is Amilya Antonetti using in her business?

2. Form a team with a few of your classmates to brainstorm ways that Antonetti can market her business.

Source: Adapted from D. M. Osborne, "Taking on Procter & Gamble," *Inc.*, October 2000, pp. 67–72.

ing the time it takes to develop, design, manufacture, and distribute a product reduces costs, increases quality, and boosts market share. One study by McKinsey and Company found that high-tech products that come to market on budget but six months late will earn 33 percent less profit over five years. Bringing the product out on time but 50 percent over budget cuts profits just 4 percent![52] Service companies also know that they must build speed into their business systems if they are to satisfy their impatient, time-sensitive customers.

This philosophy of speed is called **time compression management (TCM),** and it involves three aspects: (1) speeding new products to market, (2) shortening customer response time in manufacturing and delivery, and (3) reducing the administrative time required to fill an order. Studies show plenty of room for improvement; most businesses waste 85 to 99 percent of the time it takes to produce products or services without ever realizing it![53] Although speeding up the manufacturing process is a common goal, companies using TCM have learned that manufacturing takes only 5 to 10 percent of the total time between an order and getting the product into the customer's hands. The rest is consumed by clerical and administrative tasks. The primary opportunity for TCM lies in its application to the administrative process.

Companies relying on TCM to help them turn speed into a competitive edge should:

- "Reengineer" the entire process rather than attempt to do the same things in the same way, only faster.
- Create cross-functional teams of workers and give them the power to attack and solve problems. In world-class companies, product teams include engineers, manufacturers, salespeople, quality experts—even customers.
- Share information and ideas across the company. Easy access to meaningful information can speed a company's customer response time.
- Set aggressive goals for time reduction and stick to the schedule. Some companies using TCM have been able to reduce cycle time from several weeks to just a few hours!
- Instill speed in the culture. At Domino's Pizza, kitchen workers watch videos of the fastest pizza makers in the country.
- Use technology to find shortcuts wherever possible. Rather than build costly, time-consuming prototypes, many time-sensitive businesses use computer-aided design and computer-assisted manufacturing (CAD/CAM) to speed product design and testing.

Zara, a Spanish clothing manufacturer and retailer, uses speed to gain a competitive advantage in the fashion market, where tastes can change extremely quickly. Using a high-tech system that collects sales information real time and funnels it to computerized manufacturing facilities, Zara is able to design and manufacture a new fashion collection in just four to five weeks. Most of its competitors require nine months to accomplish the same task. Zara can deliver current merchandise to its stores twice a week, something most competitors only dream about. The result of Zara's speed advantage: the ability to capitalize on the latest fashion trends and to avoid being stuck with large inventories of out-of-style merchandise.[54]

MARKETING ON THE WORLD WIDE WEB

Much like the telephone, the fax machine, and home shopping networks, the World Wide Web promises to become a revolutionary business tool. Although most entrepreneurs have heard about the **World Wide Web,** the vast network that links computers around the globe via the Internet and opens up endless oceans of information

5. Discuss marketing opportunities the World Wide Web offers and how entrepreneurs can take advantage of them.

to its users, the majority of them are still struggling to understand what it is, how it can work for them, and how they can establish a presence on it. Businesses get on the Web by using one of thousands of "electronic gateways" to set up an address (called a Universal Resource Locator, or URL) there. By establishing a creative, attractive Web site, the electronic storefront for a company on the Web, even the smallest companies can market their products and services to customers across the globe. With its ability to display colorful graphics, sound, animation, and video as well as text, the Web allows small companies to equal or even surpass their larger rivals' Web presence. Although small companies cannot match the marketing efforts of their larger competitors, a creative Web page can be "the Great Equalizer" in a small company's marketing program, giving it access to markets all across the globe. The Web gives small businesses the power to broaden their scope to unbelievable proportions. Web-based businesses are open around the clock seven days a week and can reach customers anywhere in the world. Dean Talbert, owner of the 10,000-acre Alice L Ranch in California, now uses the Web to buy and sell cattle, a big change from the face-to-face traditional methods still used by most ranchers. "I'm selling to people back east, places I've never sold to before the Internet," he says.[55]

The Web has become a mainstream marketing medium, one that small business owners cannot afford to ignore, primarily because of its impressive power as a marketing tool. In 1999, 45 percent of all U.S. households were online; by 2005, experts estimate that 74 percent of all U.S. households will be online, representing a huge opportunity for businesses that are Web savvy.[56] Unfortunately, most small businesses are not taking advantage of this marketing potential; 43 percent of small companies are not online at all, and only about 35 percent have Web sites.[57] The most common reasons small business owners cite for not creating a Web presence are business security concerns, the inability to support a site, and the fear that the site would not draw customers.[58] The result is a disproportionately small impact of small companies on the Web. According to Forrester Research, although small businesses make nearly 50 percent of all retail sales in the United States, they account for just 6 percent of all *online* sales![59]

Small companies that have established well-designed Web sites understand the Web's power as a marketing tool and are reaping the benefits of e-commerce. These entrepreneurs know that they must learn how to sell online before their competitors do even if a return on their investment may be one or two years away. Small companies that have had the greatest success selling on the Web have marketing strategies that emphasize their existing strengths and core competencies. Their Web marketing strategies reflect their "brick-and-mortar" marketing strategies, often focusing on building relationships with their customers rather than merely scouting for a sale. These companies understand their target customers and know how to reach them using the Web. They create Web sites that provide meaningful information to their customers, that customize themselves based on each customer's interests, and that make it easy for customers to find what they want. In short, their Web sites create the same sense of trust and personal attention customers get when dealing with a local small business.

Using the Web as a marketing tool allows entrepreneurs to provide both existing and potential customers with meaningful information in an interactive rather than a passive setting. Well-designed Web sites include interactive features that allow customers to access information about a company, its products and services, its history, and other features such as question-and-answer sessions with experts or the ability to conduct e-mail or on-line conversations with company officials. A recent survey by International Customer Service Association and e-Satisfy Ltd. found that just four percent of Web sites use live, online chats even though other studies show that the inability to talk with a salesperson is the reason that 94 percent of visitors to Web sites never buy.[60] An online chat feature on the company's Web site has allowed John Moore, owner of Spill 911 Inc., a small industrial product supplier, to reduce the number of customers abandoning their shopping carts by 60 percent. Moore says the chat feature allows customers to ask specific questions and reassures them that they are dealing with a reputable company.

The Web allows business owners to link their companies' home pages to other related Web sites, which advertisements in other media cannot offer. For instance, a company selling cookware might include hypertext links on its Web page to other pages containing recipes, cookbooks, foods, and other cooking resources. This allows small business owners to engage in cross-marketing with companies on the Web selling complementary products or services. The Web also magnifies a company's ability to provide superior customer service at minimal cost. An innovative Web site allows customers to gather information about a product or service, have their questions answered, download diagrams and photographs, or track the progress of their orders. *Tom Kohley and Kevin Toohill, founders of Beartooth Mapping, launched their company to provide topographic maps for government agencies but soon discovered a huge market for their detailed maps among outdoor enthusiasts. From the company's Web site, customers can create their own customized maps for any location in the continental United States, which are then shipped out from company headquarters in tiny Red Lodge, Montana.*[61]

Just as in any marketing venture, the key to successful marketing on the World Wide Web is selling the right product or service at the right price to the right target audience. Entrepreneurs on the Web, however, also have two additional challenges: attracting Web users to their Web sites and converting them into paying customers. That requires setting up an electronic storefront that is inviting, easy to navigate, interactive, and offers more than a monotonous laundry list of items. Companies that do so are selling everything from wine and vacations to jewelry and electronics successfully on the Web. So far, the top-selling items on the Web are computers and computer-related products, books, travel services, clothing, and recorded music.[62]

We will discuss using the Web as a business tool in Chapter 13, "E-Commerce and Entrepreneurship."

THE MARKETING MIX

6. Explain the "four Ps" of marketing—product, place, price, and promotion—and their role in building a successful marketing strategy.

The major elements of a marketing strategy are the four Ps of marketing—product, place, price, and promotion. These four elements are self-reinforcing, and when coordinated, increase the sales appeal of a product or service. Small business managers must integrate these elements to maximize the impact of their product or service on the consumer. All four Ps must reinforce the image of the product or service the company presents to the potential customer. One long-time retailer claims, "None of the modern marvels of computerized inventory control and point-of-sale telecommunications have replaced the need for the entrepreneur who understands the customer and can translate that into the appropriate merchandise mix."[63]

Product

The product itself is an essential element in marketing. Products can have form and shape, or they can be services with no physical form. Products travel through various stages of development. The **product life cycle** (see Figure 7.3) measures these stages of growth, and these measurements enable the company's management to

Figure 7.3
Product Life Cycle

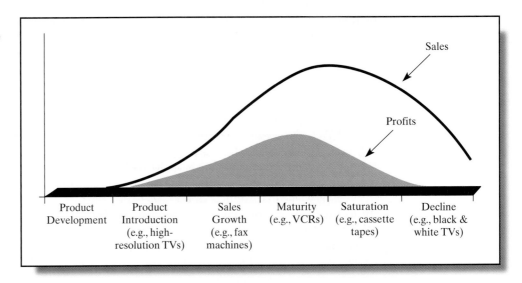

make decisions about whether to continue selling the product and when to introduce new follow-up products.

In the *introductory stage,* the marketers present their product to the potential consumers. Initial high levels of acceptance are rare. Generally, new products must break into existing markets and compete with established products. Advertising and promotion help the new product be more quickly recognized. Potential customers must get information about the product and the needs it can satisfy. The cost of marketing a product at this level of the life cycle is usually high. The small company must overcome customer resistance and inertia. Thus, profits are generally low, or even negative, at the introductory stage.

After the introductory stage, the product enters the *growth and acceptance stage.* In the growth stage, consumers begin to compare the product in large enough numbers for sales to rise and profits to increase. Products that reach this stage, however, do not necessarily become successful. If in the introductory or the growth stage the product fails to meet consumer needs, it does not sell and eventually disappears from the marketplace. For successful products, sales and profit margins continue to rise through the growth stage.

In the *maturity and competition stage,* sales volume continues to rise, but profit margins peak and then begin to fall as competitors enter the market. Normally, this causes reduction in the product's selling price to meet competition and to hold its share of the market.

Sales peak in the *market saturation stage* of the product life cycle and give the marketer fair warning that it is time to begin product innovation.

The final stage of the product life cycle is the *product decline stage.* Sales continue to drop, and profit margins fall drastically. However, when a product reaches this stage of the cycle, it does not mean that it is doomed to failure. Products that have remained popular are always being revised. No firm can maintain its sales position without product innovation and change. Even the maker of Silly Putty, first introduced at the 1950 International Toy Fair (with lifetime sales of more than 300 million "eggs") recently introduced new Day-Glo and glow-in-the-dark colors. These innovations have caused the classic toy's sales to surge by more than 60 percent.[64]

The time span of the stages in the product life cycle depends on the type of products involved. High-fashion and fad clothing have a short product life cycle, lasting for only four to six weeks. Products that are more stable may take years to complete

Figure 7.4
Time Between
Introduction of
Products

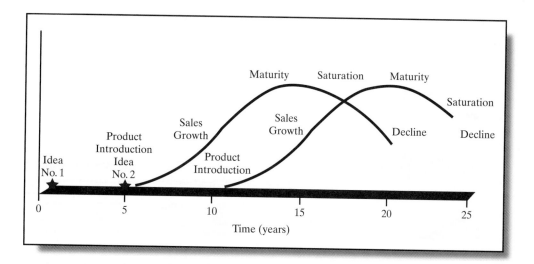

a life cycle. Research conducted by the Massachusetts Institute of Technology (MIT) suggests that the typical product's life cycle lasts 10 to 14 years.

Understanding the product life cycle can help a business owner plan the introduction of new products to the company's product line. Too often, companies wait too late into the life cycle of one product to introduce another. The result is that they are totally unprepared when a competitor produces a " better mousetrap" and their sales decline. The ideal time to develop new products is early on in the life cycle of the current product (see Figure 7.4). Waiting until the current product is in the saturation or decline stages is like living on borrowed time.

Place

Place (or method of distribution) has grown in importance as customers expect greater service and more convenience from businesses. Because of this trend, mail-order houses, home shopping channels, and the World Wide Web, offering the ultimate in convenience—shopping at home—have experienced booming sales in the last decade. In addition, many traditionally stationary businesses have added wheels, becoming mobile animal clinics, computer shops, and dentist offices.

Any activity involving movement of goods to the point of consumer purchase provides place utility. Place utility is directly affected by the marketing channels of distribution, the path that goods or services and their titles take in moving from producer to consumer. Channels typically involve a number of intermediaries who perform specialized functions that add valuable utility to the goods or service. Specifically, these intermediaries provide time utility (making the product available when customers want to buy it) and place utility (making the product available where customers want to buy it).

For consumer goods, there are four common channels of distribution (see Figure 7.5).

1. *Manufacturer to Consumer.* In some markets, producers sell their goods or services directly to consumers. Services, by nature, follow this channel of distribution. Dental care and haircuts, for example, go directly from creator to consumer.
2. *Manufacturer to Retailer to Consumer.* Another common channel involves a retailer as an intermediary. Many clothing items, books, shoes, and other consumer products are distributed in this manner.

Figure 7.5
Channels of Distribution: Consumer Goods

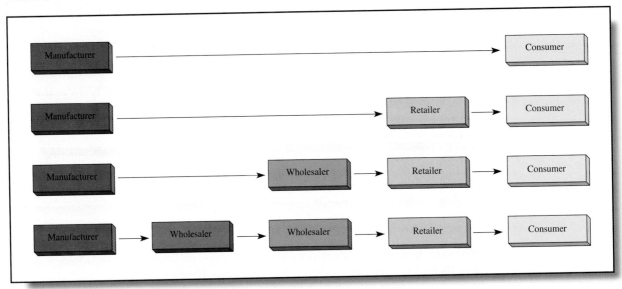

3. *Manufacturer to Wholesaler to Retailer to Consumer.* This is the most common channel of distribution. Prepackaged food products, hardware, toys, and other items are commonly distributed through this channel.
4. *Manufacturer to Wholesaler to Wholesaler to Consumer.* A few consumer goods (e.g., agricultural goods and electrical components) follow this pattern of distribution

Two channels of distribution are common for industrial goods (see Figure 7.6):

1. *Manufacturer to Industrial User.* The majority of industrial goods are distributed directly from manufacturers to users. In some cases, the goods or services are designed to meet the user's specifications.
2. *Manufacturer to Wholesaler to Industrial User.* Most expense items (paper clips, paper, rubber bands, cleaning fluids) that firms commonly use are distributed through wholesalers. For most small manufacturers, distributing goods through established wholesalers and agents is often the most effective route. With their limited resources, entrepreneurs sometimes have to rely on non-

Figure 7.6
Channels of Distribution: Industrial Goods

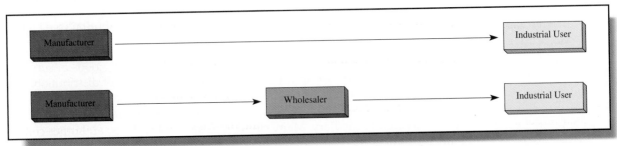

traditional distribution channels and use their creativity to get their products into customers' hands.

Price

Almost everyone agrees that the price of the product or service is a key factor in the decision to buy. Price affects both sales volume and profits, and without the right price, both sales and profits will suffer. As we will see in Chapter 10, "Pricing and Credit Strategies," the right price for a product or service depends on three factors: (1) a small company's cost structure, (2) an assessment of what the market will bear, and (3) the desired image the company wants to create in its customers' minds.

For many small businesses, nonprice competition, focusing on factors other than price, is a more effective strategy than trying to beat larger competitors in a price war. Nonprice competition, such as free trial offers, free delivery, lengthy warranties, and money-back guarantees, intends to play down the product's price and stress its durability, quality, reputation, or special features.

Promotion

Promotion involves both advertising and personal selling. Advertising communicates to potential customers through some mass medium the benefits of a good or service. Personal selling involves the art of persuasive sales on a one-to-one basis.

The goals of a small company's promotional efforts are to create a brand image, to persuade customers to buy, and to develop brand loyalty. Promotion can take many forms and is put before the public through a variety of media. Entrepreneurs often must find ways to use low-cost guerrilla tactics to create promotions that get their companies noticed by both local and national media. Chapter 11, "Creative Use of Advertising and Promotion," is devoted to creating an effective advertising and promotion campaign for a small company.

CHAPTER SUMMARY

1. Describe the components of a guerrilla marketing plan and explain the benefits of preparing one.
   - A major part of the entrepreneur's business plan is the marketing plan, which focuses on a company's target customers and how best to satisfy their needs and wants. A solid marketing plan should pinpoint the specific target markets the company will serve; determine customer needs and wants through market research; analyze the firm's competitive advantages and build a marketing strategy around them; and create a marketing mix that meets customer needs and wants.

2. Explain how small businesses can pinpoint their target markets.
   - Sound market research helps the owner

pinpoint his target market. The most successful businesses have well-defined portraits of the customers they are seeking to attract.

3. Explain how to determine customer needs through market research and the steps in the market research process.
   - Market research is the vehicle for gathering the information that serves as the foundation of the marketing plan. Good research does not have to be complex and expensive to be useful. The steps in conducting market research include: defining the problem—"What do you want to know?"; collecting the data from either primary or secondary sources; analyzing and interpreting the data; and drawing conclusions and acting on them.

4. Describe the guerrilla marketing strategies on which a small business can build a competitive edge in the marketplace.
   - When plotting a marketing strategy, owners must strive to achieve a competitive advantage, some way to make their companies different from and better than the competition. Successful small businesses rely on 10 guerrilla marketing strategies to develop a competitive edge: niche-picking, entertailing, emphasizing their uniqueness, connecting with their customers, focusing on customers' needs, emphasizing quality, paying attention to convenience, concentrating on innovation, dedicating themselves to service, and emphasizing speed.
5. Discuss the marketing opportunities the World Wide Web offers and how entrepreneurs can best take advantage of them.
   - The Web offers small business owners tremendous marketing potential on par with their larger rivals. Entrepreneurs are just beginning to uncover the Web's profit potential, which is growing rapidly. Successful Web sites are attractive, inviting, easy to navigate, interactive, and offers users something of value.
6. Explain the "four Ps" of marketing—product, place, price, and promotion—and their role in building a successful marketing strategy.
   - The marketing mix consists of the "4 Ps":
   Product. Entrepreneurs should understand where in the product life cycle their products are.
   Place. The focus here is on choosing the appropriate channel of distribution and using it most efficiently.
   Price. Price is an important factor in customers' purchase decisions, but many small businesses find that nonprice competition can be profitable.
   Promotion. Promotion involves both advertising and personal selling.

DISCUSSION QUESTIONS

1. What is a marketing plan? What lies at its center?
2. What objectives should a marketing plan accomplish?
3. How can market research benefit a small business owner? List some possible sources of market information.
4. Does market research have to be expensive and sophisticated to be valuable? Explain.
5. Why is it important for small business owners to define their target markets as part of their marketing strategies?
6. What is a competitive edge? How might a small company gain a competitive edge?
7. Describe how a small business owner could use the following sources of a competitive advantage: niche-picking, entertailing, emphasizing their uniqueness, connecting with their customers, focusing on customers' needs, emphasizing quality, paying attention to convenience, concentrating on innovation; dedicating themselves to service; and emphasizing speed.
8. What is the World Wide Web? Describe its marketing potential for small businesses.
9. Explain the concept of the marketing mix. What are the four Ps?
10. List and explain the stages in the product life cycle. How can a small firm extend its product's life?
11. With a 70 percent customer retention rate (average for most U.S. firms according to the American Management Association), every $1 million of business in 1995 will grow to more than $4 million by the year 2005. If you retain 80 percent of your customers, the $1 million will grow to a little over $6 million. If you can keep 90 percent of your customers, that $1 million will grow to more than $9.5 million. What can the typical small business do to increase its customer retention rate?

BEYOND THE CLASSROOM

1. Interview the owner of a local restaurant about its marketing strategy. From how large a geographic region does the restaurant draw its clientele? What is the firm's target market?

What are its characteristics? Does the restaurant have a competitive edge?

2. Select a local small manufacturing operation and evaluate its primary product. What stage of the product life cycle is it in? What channels of distribution does the product follow after leaving the manufacturer?

3. Research current business periodicals such as *Inc., Inc. Technology, Fortune, Fortune Small Business, Forbes,* and others to determine how small companies are using the World Wide Web to market their products and services more effectively. Find at least one example of a company effectively using the Web as a marketing tool and describe its approach.

4. Using one of the search engines on the World Wide Web, research the current demographic profile of Web users. What is the growth rate for Web users? Prepare a brief report on your findings. What implications do your conclusions have for entrepreneurs considering setting up Web sites?

5. Contact three local small business owners and ask them about their marketing strategies. How have they achieved a competitive edge? Develop a series of questions to judge the sources of their competitive edge: niche-picking, entertailing, emphasizing their uniqueness, connecting with their customers, focusing on customers' needs, emphasizing quality, paying attention to convenience, concentrating on innovation, dedicating themselves to service; and emphasizing speed. How do the businesses compare?

TAKE IT TO THE NET

Visit the Scarborough/Zimmerer home page at **www.prenhall.com/scarborough** for updated information, online resources, Web-based exercises, and sample business plan.

ENDNOTES

1. Melanie Wells, "Cult Brands," *Forbes,* April 16, 2001, pp. 198–205; Victoria Neal, "Gourmet Bubbly," *Entrepreneur,* September 1999, *www.entrepreneur.com/Magazines/MA_SegArticle/0,15 39,230624——1-,00.html* ; "The Jones Soda Story," Jones Soda Company, *www.jonessoda.com/stockstuff/story.html* .

2. Chana R. Schoenberger, "Candid Camera," *Forbes,* September 16, 2000, p. 234.

3. Howard Fana Shaw, "Customer Care Checklist," *In Business,* September/October 1987, p. 28.

4. Lynn Rosellini, "The High Life of Crime," *U.S. News & World Report,* November 20, 2000, pp. 76–77.

5. Marci McDonald, "Madison Avenue's New Latin Beat," *U.S. News & World Report,* June 4, 2001, p. 42; James Kuhnhenn, "Mexican Influence Is Here to Stay," *Greenville News,* September 9, 2001, p. 1G; Eric Schmitt, "Census Figures Show Hispanics Pulling Even with Blacks," *New York Times,* March 8, 2001, *www.nytimes.com/2001/03/08/naional/ 08CENS.html* ; Frank Solis, "The Next Big Market," *Success,* October 2000, pp. 36–38.

6. Rudolph Bell, "Mexico Natives Find Love, Success in Greenville," *Upstate Business,* November 26, 2000, pp. 1, 6–7.

7. Phaedra Hise, "Industry Bottoms Out, Disposes of Diaper Service," *Inc.,* June 1997, p. 32.

8. Kimberly L. McCall, "Fielding Questions," *Entrepreneur,* September 2001, pp. 14–15.

9. Shari Caudron, "Right on Target," *Industry Week,* September 2, 1996, p. 45.

10. Christina Binkley, "Lucky Numbers: Casino Chain Mines Data on Its Gamblers and Strikes Pay Dirt," *Wall Street Journal,* May 4, 2000, pp. A1, A10.

11. Lester A. Picker, "Selling to Women," *Your Company,* April/May 1996, pp. 32–38.

12. Roberta Maynard, "Rich Niches," *Nation's Business,* November 1993, p. 41.

13. Dale D. Buss, "Entertailing," *Nation's Business,* December 1997, p. 18.

14. Ibid., pp. 12–18.

15. Arthur Lubow, "Wowing Warren," *Inc.,* March 2000, pp. 72–84.

16. Joseph R. Garber, "Know Your Customer," *Forbes,* February 10, 1997, p. 128.

17. "Deadly Game of Losing Customers," *In Business,* May 1988, p. 189.

18. Jenny C. McCune, "Becoming a Customer-Driven Company," *Beyond Computing,* May 2000, pp. 18–24.

19. David J. Wallace, "e=crm^2," *Small Business Computing,* November 2000, pp. 55–57.

20. "Keeping Customers for Life," *Communication Briefings,* September 1990, p. 3.
21. Rahul Jacob, "Why Some Customers Are More Equal Than Others," *Fortune,* September 19, 1994, pp. 215–224.
22. Robert B. Tucker, "Earn Your Customers' Loyalty," Economics Press Techniques, Strategies, and Inspiration for the Sales Professional, *www.epic.co/SALES/selltips.htm#earn_loyalty.*
23. Patricia Sellers, "Companies That Serve You Best," *Fortune,* May 31, 1993, p. 75.
24. Willian A. Sherden, "The Tools of Retention," *Small Business Reports,* November 1994, pp. 43–47.
25. "Our Vision," Joeauto.com, *www.joeauto.com/our_story.asp*; Wallace, "e=crm^2."
26. "Ways and Means," *Reader's Digest,* January 1993, p. 56.
27. "Encourage Customers to Complain," *Small Business Reports,* June 1990, p. 7.
28. Dave Zielinski, "Improving Service Doesn't Require a Big Investment," *Small Business Reports,* February 1991, p. 20.
29. John H. Sheridan, "Out of the Isolation Booth," *Industry Week,* June 19, 1989, pp. 18–19.
30. Susan Greco, "Fanatics," *Inc.,* April 2001, pp. 36–48.
31. Ibid.
32. Mark Henricks, "Make No Mistake," *Entrepreneur,* October 1996, pp. 86–89.
33. Faye Rice, "How to Deal with Tougher Customers," *Fortune,* December 3, 1990, pp. 39–40.
34. Rahul Jacobs, "TQM: More Than a Dying Fad," *Fortune,* October 18, 1993, p. 67.
35. Ibid.
36. Pamela Rohland, "Dry Heat," *Start-Ups,* December 2000, p. 65.
37. Bob Weinstein, "Easy Does It," *Entrepreneur,* December 1999, pp. 160–163.
38. Roberta Maynard, "The Heat Is On," *Nation's Business,* October 1997, pp. 14–23.
39. Michael Schrage, "Getting Beyond the Innovation Fetish," *Fortune,* November 13, 2000, p. 230.
40. Maynard, "The Heat Is On," p. 16.
41. Joseph R. Mancuso, "How Callaway Runs His Idea Factory," *Your Company,* April/May 1997, p. 72.
42. Alan Deutschman, "America's Fastest Risers," *Fortune,* October 7, 1991, p. 58.
43. Gene Bylinsky, "Look Who's Doing R&D," *Fortune,* November 27, 2000, pp. 232[C]–232[F].
44. Maynard, "The Heat Is On."
45. Greco, "Fanatics," p. 38.
46. Angela R. Garber, "Hook, Line, and Sinker," *Small Business Computing,* February 2000, pp. 41–42.
47. Chris Penttila, "Brand Awareness," *Entrepreneur,* September 2001, pp. 49–51.
48. Thomas A. Stewart, "After All You've Done for Your Customers, Why Are They Still NOT HAPPY?" *Fortune,* December 11, 1995, pp. 178–182; Gile Gerretsen, "Special Tools Are Used by Super Markets," *Upstate Business,* June 14, 1998, p. 4.
49. Debbie Salinsky, "Insanely Great Customer Service," *Success,* September 2000, p. 61.
50. William C. Gillis, "Pool Sharks," *Small Business Computing,* September 2001, p. 25.
51. Ron Zemke and Dick Schaaf, "The Service Edge," *Small Business Reports,* July 1990, p. 60.
52. Brian Dumaine, "How Managers Can Succeed Through Speed," *Fortune,* February 13, 1989, pp. 54–59.
53. Mark Henricks, "Time Is Money," *Entrepreneur,* February 1993, p. 44.
54. Carlta Vitzthum, "Just-in-Time Fashion," *Wall Street Journal,* May 18, 2001, pp. B1, B4.
55. John Galvin, "Home, Home on the Web," *Smart Business,* February 2001, pp. 58–60.
56. "Internet at a Glance," *Business 2.0,* December 12, 2000, p. 282.
57. "Small Businesses Not Making Full Use of Web," *USA Today,* August 29, 2001, *www.infobeat.com/articles/fin_story_2_82901.html.*
58. Ibid.; "Work Week," *Wall Street Journal,* October 26, 1999, p. A1.
59. David G. Propson, "Small Biz Gets Small Piece of the Pie," *Small Business Computing,* November 1999, p. 24.
60. Greco, "Fanatics," p. 42; Bonny L. Georgia, "Make Your Customers Love You," *PC Computing,* January 2000, pp. 105–112.
61. Jamie McAfee, "Over Hill and Dale," *Small Business Computing,* December 2000, p. 31; Beartooth Mapping, Inc., *www.mytopo.com/*
62. "Starting an E-Commerce Business," 2iTrade Resource, August 10, 2001, *www.infobeat.com/stories/fin_story_10_82001.html.*
63. Stanley J. Winkelman, "Why Big Name Stores Are Losing Out," *Fortune,* May 8, 1989, pp. 14–15.
64. Deanna Hodgin, "A War Baby Bounces Back in Trendy Style," *Insight,* April 1, 1991, p. 44.

Chapter 8

Creating a Solid Financial Plan

> *You can't tell who's swimming naked until after the tide goes out.*
>
> —DAVID DARST

> *To know is to control.*
>
> —SCOTT REED

Upon completion of this chapter, you will be able to:

1. Understand the importance of preparing a financial plan.
2. Describe how to prepare financial statements and use them to manage a small business.
3. Create pro forma financial statements.
4. Understand the basic financial statement through ratio analysis.
5. Explain how to interpret financial ratios.
6. Conduct a breakeven analysis for a small company.

1. Understand the importance of preparing a financial plan.

One of the most important steps in launching a new business venture is fashioning a well-designed, logical financial plan. Potential lenders and investors demand such a plan before putting their money into a start-up company. More importantly, a financial plan can be a vital tool that helps entrepreneurs manage their businesses more effectively, steering their way around the pitfalls that cause failures. Entrepreneurs who ignore the financial aspects of their businesses run the risk of watching their companies become just another failure statistic. One financial expert says of small companies, "Those that don't establish sound controls at the start are setting themselves up to fail."[1] Still, according to one survey, one third of all entrepreneurs run their companies without any kind of financial plan.[2] Another study found that only 11 percent of small business owners analyzed their financial statements as part of the managerial planning and decision-making process.[3] To reach profit objectives, entrepreneurs must be aware of their firms' overall financial position and the changes in financial status that occur over time.

This chapter focuses on some very practical tools that will help entrepreneurs develop workable financial plans, keep them focused on their company's financial plan, and enable them to plan for profit. They can use these tools to anticipate changes and plot an appropriate profit strategy to meet them head on. These profit-planning techniques are not difficult to master, nor are they overly time consuming. We will discuss the techniques involved in preparing projected (pro forma) financial statements, conducting ratio analysis, and performing breakeven analysis.

BASIC FINANCIAL REPORTS

2. Describe how to prepare financial statements and use them to manage a small business.

Before we begin building projected financial statements, it would be helpful to review the basic financial reports that measure a company's financial position: the balance sheet, the income statement, and the statement of cash flows. Studies show that the level of financial reporting among small businesses is high; some 81 percent of the companies in one survey regularly produced summary financial information, almost all of it in the form of these traditional financial statements.[4]

The Balance Sheet

The balance sheet takes a "snapshot" of a business, providing owners with an estimate of the firm's worth on a given date. Its two major sections show the assets a business owns and the claims creditors and owners have against those assets. The balance sheet is usually prepared on the last day of the month. Figure 8.1 shows the balance sheet for Sam's Appliance Shop for the year ended December 31, 200X.

The balance sheet is built on the fundamental accounting equation: Assets = Liabilities + Owner's Equity. Any increase or decrease on one side of the equation must be offset by an equal increase or decrease on the other side; hence, the name *balance sheet*. It provides a baseline from which to measure future changes in assets, liabilities, and equity (or net worth). The first section of the balance sheet lists the firm's **assets** (valued at cost, not actual market value) and shows the total value of everything the business owns. **Current assets** consist of cash and items to be converted into cash within one year or within the normal operating cycle of the company, whichever is longer, such as accounts receivable and inventory, and **fixed assets** are those acquired for long-term use in the business. **Intangible assets** include items that, although valuable, do not have tangible value, such as goodwill, copyrights, and patents.

Figure 8.1
Balance Sheet,
Sam's Appliance
Shop

Assets			
Current Assets			
Cash		$ 49,855	
Accounts receivable	$179,225		
Less allowance for doubtful accounts	$ 6,000	$173,225	
Inventory		$455,455	
Prepaid expenses		$ 8,450	
Total Current Assets			$686,985
Fixed Assets			
Land		$59,150	
Buildings	$74,650		
Less accumulated depreciation	$ 7,050	$67,600	
Equipment	$22,375		
Less accumulated depreciation	$ 1,250	$21,125	
Furniture and fixtures	$10,295		
Less accumulated depreciation	$ 1,000	$ 9,295	
Total Fixed Assets			$ 157,70
Intangibles (goodwill)			$ 3,500
Total Assets			$847,655
Liabilities			
Current Liabilities			
Accounts payable		$152,580	
Notes payable		$ 83,920	
Accrued wages and salaries payable		$ 38,150	
Accrued interest payable		$ 42,380	
Accrued taxes payable		$ 50,820	
Total Current Liabilities			$367,850
Long-Term Liabilities			
Mortgage		$127,150	
Note payable		$ 85,000	
Total Long-Term Liabilities			$212,150
Owner's Equity			
Sam Lloyd, capital			$267,655
Total Liabilities + Owner's Equity			$847,655

The second section shows the business's **liabilities**—the creditors' claims against the firm's assets. **Current liabilities** are those debts that must be paid within one year or within the normal operating cycle of the company, whichever is longer, and **long-term liabilities** are those that come due after one year. This section of the balance sheet also shows the **owner's equity,** the value of the owner's investment in the business. It is the balancing factor on the balance sheet, representing all of the owner's capital contributions to the business plus all accumulated earnings not distributed to the owner(s).

The Income Statement

The **income statement** (or profit and loss statement [P&L]) compares expenses against revenue over a certain period of time to show the firm's net income or loss. The income statement is a "moving picture" of the firm's profitability over time. The annual P&L statement reports the bottom line of the business over the fiscal or calendar year. Figure 8.2 shows the income statement for Sam's Appliance Shop for the year ended December 31, 200X.

To calculate net income or loss, the owner records sales revenues for the year, which includes all income that flows into the business from the sale of goods and services. Income from other sources (rent, investments, interest) also must be included in the revenue section of the income statement. To determine net sales revenue, owners subtract the value of returned items and refunds from gross revenue. **Cost of goods sold** represents the total cost, including shipping, of the merchandise sold during the year. Most wholesalers and retailers calculate cost of goods sold by adding purchases to beginning inventory and subtracting ending inventory. Service companies typically have no cost of goods sold. Subtracting the cost of goods sold from net sales revenue results in a company's **gross profit.** Allowing the cost of goods sold to get out of control will whittle away gross profit, virtually guaranteeing a net loss on the income statement. Dividing gross profit by net sales revenue produces the **gross profit margin,** a percentage that every business owner should watch closely. If a company's gross profit margin slips too low, it is likely that it will operate at a loss (negative net income). Many business owners whose companies are losing money mistakenly believe that the problem is inadequate sales volume; therefore, they focus on pumping up sales at any cost. In many cases, however, the losses are due to an inadequate gross profit margin, and pumping up sales only deepens their losses! Repairing a poor gross profit margin requires a company to raise prices, cut manufacturing or purchasing costs, refuse orders with low profit margins, or add new products with more attractive profit margins. Monitoring the gross profit margin over time and comparing it to those of other companies in the same industry are important steps to maintaining a company's long-term profitability.

Operating expenses include those costs that contribute directly to the manufacture and distribution of goods. General expenses are indirect costs incurred in operating the business. "Other expenses" is a catch-all category covering all other expenses that don't fit into the other two categories. Total revenue minus total expenses gives the company's **net income (or loss).**

The Statement of Cash Flows

The **statement of cash flows** shows the changes in the firm's working capital since the beginning of the year by listing the sources of funds and the uses of these funds. Many small businesses never need such a statement; instead, they rely on a cash budget, a less formal managerial tool that tracks the flow of cash into and out of a company over time. (We will discuss cash budgets in Chapter 9.) Sometimes, however, creditors, lenders, investors, or business buyers may require this information.

To prepare the statement, the owner must assemble the balance sheets and the income statements summarizing the present year's operations. She begins with the company's net income for the accounting period (from the income statement). Then

Figure 8.2
Income
Statement, Sam's
Appliance Shop

Net Sales Revenue		$1,870,841
Cost of Goods Sold		
Beginning Inventory, 1/1/XX	$ 805,745	
+ Purchases	$ 939,827	
Goods Available for Sale	$1,745,572	
– Ending Inventory, 12/31/XX	$ 455,455	
Total Cost of Goods Sold		$1,290,117
Gross Profit		$ 580,724
Operating Expenses		
Advertising	$139,670	
Insurance	$ 46,125	
Depreciation		
Building	$ 18,700	
Equipment	$ 9,000	
Salaries	$224,500	
Travel	$ 4,000	
Entertainment	$ 2,500	
Total Operating Expenses		$ 444,495
General Expenses		
Utilities	$ 5,300	
Telephone	$ 2,500	
Postage	$ 1,200	
Payroll Taxes	$25,000	
Total General Expenses		$ 34,000
Other Expenses		
Interest Expense	$39,850	
Bad Check Expense	$ 1,750	
Total Other Expenses		$ 41,600
Total Expenses		$ 520,095
Net Income		$ 60,629

she adds the sources of funds—borrowed funds, owner contributions, decreases in accounts payable, decreases in inventory, depreciation, and any others. Depreciation is listed as a source of funds because it is a noncash expense that is deducted as a cost of doing business. Because the owner has already paid for the item being depreciated, its depreciation is a source of funds. Next, the owner subtracts the uses of these funds—plan and equipment purchases, dividends to owners, repayment of debt, increases in accounts receivable, decreases in accounts payable, increases in inventory, and so on. The difference between the total sources and the total uses of funds is the increase or decrease in working capital. By investigating the changes in the firm's working capital and the reasons for them, owners can create a more practical financial plan of action for the future of the enterprise.

These statements are more than just complex documents used only by accountants and financial officers. When used in conjunction with the analytical tools described in the following sections, they can help small business managers map their firms' financial future and actively plan for profit. Merely preparing these statements is not enough, however; entrepreneurs and their employees must *understand and use* the information contained in them to make the business more effective and efficient.

CREATING PROJECTED FINANCIAL STATEMENTS

3. Create projected financial statements.

Creating projected financial statements via the budgeting process helps the small business owner transform business goals into reality. Once developed, a budget will answer such questions as: What profit can the business expect to earn? If the owner's profit objective is x dollars, what sales level must she achieve? What fixed and variable expenses can she expect at that level of sales? The answers to these and other questions are critical in formulating a successful financial plan for the small business.

This section focuses on creating projected income statements and balance sheets for the small business. These projected (or pro forma) statements estimate the profitability and the overall financial condition of the business for future months. They are an integral part of convincing potential lenders and investors to provide the financing needed to get the company off the ground. Also, because these statements project the firm's financial position through the end of the forecasted period, they help the owner plan the route to improved financial strength and healthy business growth.

Because an established business has a history of operating data from which to construct projected financial statements, the task is not nearly as difficult as it is for a brand new business. When creating projected financial statements for a business start-up, entrepreneurs typically rely on published statistics summarizing the operation of similar-size companies in the same industry. These statistics are available from a number of sources (described later), but this section draws on information found in Robert Morris Associates' (RMA's) *Annual Statement Studies,* a compilation of financial data on thousands of companies across hundreds of industries (organized by Standard Industrial Classification [SIC] Code). Because conditions and markets change so rapidly, entrepreneurs developing financial forecasts for start-ups should focus on creating projections for two years into the future. Investors mainly want to see that entrepreneurs have realistic expectations about their income and expenses and when they can expect to start earning a profit.

Pro Forma Statements for the Small Business

One of the most important tasks confronting the entrepreneur launching a new enterprise is to determine the funds needed to begin operation as well as those required to keep going through the initial growth period. The amount of money needed to begin a business depends on the type of operation, its location, inventory requirements, sales volume, and other factors. But every new firm must have enough capital to cover all start-up costs, including funds to rent or buy plant, equipment, and tools, as well as to pay for advertising, licenses, utilities, and other expenses. In addition, the owner must maintain a reserve of capital to carry the company until it begins to make a profit. Too often, entrepreneurs are overly optimistic in their financial plans and fail to recognize that expenses initially exceed income for most small firms. This period of net losses is normal and may last from just a few months to several years. Owners must be able to meet payrolls, maintain adequate inventory, take advantage of cash discounts, grant customer credit, and meet personal obligations during this time.

The Projected Income Statement. When creating a projected income statement, an entrepreneur has two options: to develop a sales forecast and work down or set a profit target and work up. Most businesses employ the latter method—the owner targets a profit figure and then determines what sales level he must achieve to reach it. Of course, it is important to compare this sales target against the results of the marketing plan to determine whether or not it is realistic. Although they are projections, financial forecasts must be based in reality; otherwise, they are nothing more than a hopeless dream. The next step is to estimate the expenses the business will incur in securing those sales. In any small business, the annual profit must be large enough to produce a return for time the owners spend operating the business, plus a return on their investment in the business.

An entrepreneur who earns less in his own business than he could earn working for someone else must weigh carefully the advantages and disadvantages of choosing the path of entrepreneurship. Why be exposed to all of the risks, sacrifices, and hard work of beginning and operating a small business if the rewards are less than those of remaining in the secure employment of another? Ideally, the firm's net income after taxes should be at least as much as the owner could earn by working for someone else.

An adequate profit must also include a reasonable return on the owner's total investment in the business. The owner's total investment is the amount contributed to the company at its inception plus any retained earnings (profits from previous years funneled back into the operation). If a would-be owner has $70,000 to invest and can invest it in securities and earn 10 percent, he or she should not consider investing it in a small business that would yield only 3 percent.

An entrepreneur's target income is the sum of a reasonable salary for the time spent running the business and a normal return on the amount invested in the firm. Determining how much this should be is the first step in creating the pro forma income statement.

The next step is to translate this target profit into a net sales figure for the forecasted period. To calculate net sales from a target profit, the owner needs published statistics for this type of business. Suppose an entrepreneur wants to launch a small retail bookstore and has determined that his target income is $29,000 annually. Statistics gathered from RMA's *Annual Statement Studies* show that the typical bookstore's net profit margin (net profit/net sales) is 9.3 percent. Using this information, he can compute the sales level required to produce a net profit of $29,000:

$$\text{Net profit margin} = \frac{\text{Net profit}}{\text{Net sales (annual)}}$$

$$9.3\% = \frac{\$29,000}{\text{Net sales (annual)}} \tag{1}$$

$$\text{Net sales} = \frac{\$29,000}{0.093}$$

$$= \$311,828$$

Now the entrepreneur knows that to make a net profit of $29,000 (before taxes), he must achieve annual sales of $311,828. To complete the projected income statement, he simply applies the appropriate statistics from RMA's *Annual Statement Studies* to the annual sales figure. Because the statistics for each income statement item are expressed as percentages of net sales, he merely multiplies the proper statistic by the annual sales figure to obtain the desired value. For example, cost of goods sold usually comprises 61.4 percent of net sales for the typical small bookstore. So the owner of this new bookstore expects his cost of goods sold to be the following:

$$\text{Cost of goods sold} = \$311,828 \times 0.614 = \$191,462 \qquad \textbf{(2)}$$

The bookstore's complete projected income statement is shown as follows:

Net sales	(100%)	$311,828
– Cost of goods sold	(61.4%)	191,462
Gross profit margin	(38.6%)	$120,366
– Operating expenses	(29.3%)	91,366
Net income (before taxes)	(9.3%)	$ 29,000

At this point, the business appears to be a lucrative venture. But remember: This income statement represents a goal that the entrepreneur may not be able to attain. The next step is to determine whether this required sales volume is reasonable. One useful technique is to break down the required annual sales volume into daily sales figures. Assuming the store will be open six days per week for 52 weeks (312 days), the owner must average $999 per day in sales:

$$\text{Average daily sales} = \frac{\$311,828}{312 \text{ days}} \qquad \textbf{(3)}$$

$$= \$999/\text{day}$$

This calculation gives the owner a better perspective of the sales required to yield an annual profit of $29,000.

To determine whether the profit expected from the business will meet or exceed the entrepreneur's target income, the prospective owner should create an income statement based on a realistic sales estimate. The previous analysis showed this entrepreneur what sales level is needed to reach his desired profit. But what happens if sales are lower or higher? To answer that question, he must develop a reliable sales forecast using the market research techniques described in Chapter 7.

Suppose that after conducting a marketing survey of local customers and talking with nearby business owners, the prospective bookstore owner projects annual sales for the proposed business to be only $285,000. He must take this expected sales figure and develop a pro forma income statement.

Net sales	(100%)	$285,000
– Cost of goods sold	(61.4%)	174,990
Gross profit margin	(38.6%)	110,010
– Operating expenses	(29.3%)	83,505
Net income (before taxes)	(9.3%)	$26,505

Based on sales of $285,000, this entrepreneur should expect a net profit (before taxes) of $26,505. If this amount is acceptable as a return on the investment of time and money in the business, he should proceed with his planning.

At this stage in developing the financial plan, the owner should create a more detailed picture of the firm's expected operating expenses. One common method is to use the operating statistics found in Dun & Bradstreet's *Cost of Doing Business* reports. These booklets document typical selected operating expenses (expressed as a percentage of net sales) for 190 different lines of businesses.

To ensure that they have overlooked no business expenses in preparing their business plans, entrepreneurs should list all of the initial expenses they will incur and have an accountant review the list. Figures 8.3 and 8.4 show two useful forms designed to help assign dollar values to anticipated expenses. Totals derived from this list of expenses should approximate the total expense figures calculated from published statistics. Naturally, an entrepreneur should be more confident of the total from his own list of expenses since this reflects his particular set of circumstances.

Entrepreneurs who follow the top-down approach to building an income state-ment—developing a sales forecast and working down to net income—must be care-ful to avoid falling into the trap of excessive optimism. Many entrepreneurs using this method overestimate their anticipated revenues and underestimate their actual expenses, and the result is disastrous. To avoid this problem, some experts advise entrepreneurs to use the rule that many venture capitalists apply when they evalu-ate business start-ups: Divide revenues by two, multiply expenses by two, and if the business can still make it, it's a winner!

The Pro Forma Balance Sheet. In addition to projecting the small firm's net profit or loss, the entrepreneur must develop a pro forma balance sheet outlining the fledg-ling firm's assets and liabilities. Most entrepreneurs' primary focus is on the poten-tial profitability of their businesses, but the assets their businesses use to generate profits are no less important. In many cases, small companies begin life on weak financial footing because their owners fail to determine their firms' total asset requirements. To prevent this major oversight, the owner should prepare a projected balance sheet listing every asset the business will need and all the claims against these assets.

Assets. Cash is one of the most useful assets the business owns; it is highly liquid and can quickly be converted into other tangible assets. But how much cash should a small business have at its inception? Obviously, there is no single dollar figure that fits the needs of every small firm. One practical rule of thumb, however, suggests that the company's cash balance should cover its operating expenses (less deprecia-tion, a noncash expense) for one inventory turnover period. Using this rule, we can calculate the cash balance for the small bookstore as follows:

Operating expenses = $83,250 (from projected income statement)
Less: Depreciation (0.9% of annual sales) of $2,565 (a noncash expense)
Equals: Cash expenses (annual) = $80,940

$$\text{Cash requirement} = \frac{\text{Cash expenses}}{\text{Average inventory turnover}} \qquad \textbf{(4)}$$

$$= \frac{80,940}{3.5^*}$$

$$= \$23,126$$

---

* From RMA Annual Statement Studies.

Figure 8.3
Anticipated Expenses

Worksheet No. 2

Estimated Monthly Expenses	Your estimate of monthly expenses based on sales of $_____ per year	Your estimate of how much cash you need to start your business (See column 3.)	What to put in column 2 (These figures are typical for one kind of business. You will have to decide how many months to allow for in your business.)
Item			
	Column 1	Column 2	Column 3
Salary of owner–manager	$	$	2 times column 1
All other salaries and wages			3 times column 1
Rent			3 times column 1
Advertising			3 times column 1
Delivery expense			3 times column 1
Supplies			3 times column 1
Telephone and telegraph			3 times column 1
Other utilities			3 times column 1
Insurance			Payment required by insurance company
Taxes, including Social Security			4 times column 1
Interest			3 times column 1
Maintenance			3 times column 1
Legal and other professional fees			3 times column 1
Miscellaneous			3 times column 1
Starting costs you have to pay only once			Leave column 2 blank
Fixtures and equipment			Fill in worksheet 3 and put the total here
Decorating and remodeling			Talk it over with a contractor
Installation of fixtures and equipment			Talk to suppliers from whom you buy these
Starting inventory			Suppliers will probably help you estimate this
Deposits with public utilities			Find out from utilities companies
Legal and professional fees			Lawyer, accountant, and so on
Licenses and permits			Find out from city offices what you have to have
Advertising and promotion for opening			Estimate what you'll use
Accounts receivable			What you need to buy more stock until credit customers pay
Cash			For unexpected expenses or losses, special purchases, etc.
Other			Make a separate list and enter total
Total Estimated Cash You Need to Start		$	Add up all the numbers in column 2

Source: U.S. Small Business Administration, *Checklist for Going into Business*, Small Marketers Aid No. 71 (Washington, D.C.: GPO, 1982), pp. 6–7.

Figure 8.4
Anticipated Expenditures for Fixtures and Equipment

Worksheet No. 3
List of Furniture, Fixtures, and Equipment

Leave out or add items to suit your business. Use separate sheets to list exactly what you need for each of the items below.	If you plan to pay cash in full, enter the full amount below and in the last column.	If you are going to pay by installments, fill out the columns below. Enter in the last column your down payment plus at least one installment.			Estimate of the cash you need for furniture, fixtures, and equipment.
		Price	Down payment	Amount of each installment	
Counters	$	$	$	$	$
Storage shelves and cabinets					
Display stands, shelves, tables					
Cash register					
Safe					
Window display fixtures					
Special lighting					
Outside sign					
Delivery equipment if needed					
Total Furniture, Fixtures, and Equipment (Enter this figure also in worksheet 2 under "Starting Costs You Have to Pay Only Once.")					$

Source: U.S. Small Business Administration, *Checklist for Going into Business,* Small Marketers Aid No. 71 (Washington, D.C.: GPO, 1982), p. 12.

Notice the inverse relationship between the small firm's average inventory turnover ratio and its cash requirements.

Inventory. Another decision facing the entrepreneur is how much inventory the business should carry. An estimate of the inventory needed can be calculated from the information found on the projected income statement and from published statistics:

Cost of goods sold = $174,990 (from projected income statement)

$$\text{Average inventory turnover} = \frac{\text{Cost of goods sold}}{\text{Inventory level}}$$

$$= 3.5 \text{ times/year}$$

Substituting, (5)

$$3.5 \text{ times/year} = \frac{\$174,990}{\text{Inventory level}}$$

Solving algebraically,

$$\text{Inventory level} = \$49,997$$

The entrepreneur also includes $1,800 in miscellaneous current assets.
Suppose the estimate of fixed assets is as follows:

Fixtures	$ 17,500
Office equipment	2,850
Computers/Cash register	3,125
Signs	3,200
Miscellaneous	1,500
Total	**$28,175**

Liabilities. To complete the projected balance sheet, the owner must record all of the small firm's liabilities, the claims against the assets. The bookstore owner was able to finance 50 percent of inventory and fixtures through suppliers. The only other major claim against the firm's assets is a note payable to the entrepreneur's father-in-law for $20,000.

The final step is to compile all of these items into a projected balance sheet, as shown in Figure 8.5.

Figure 8.5
Projected Balance
Sheet for a Small
Bookstore

ASSETS	
Current Assets:	
Cash	$ 23,126.00
Inventory	49,997.00
Miscellaneous	1,800.00
TOTAL CURRENT ASSETS	$ 74,923.00
Fixed Assets:	
Fixtures	$ 17,500.00
Office Equipment	2,850.00
Computers/Cash Register	3,125.00
Signs	3,200.00
Miscellaneous	1,500.00
TOTAL FIXED ASSETS	$ 28,175.00
TOTAL ASSETS	$103,098.00
LIABILITIES & OWNER'S EQUITY	
Current Liabilities:	
Accounts Payable	$ 24,998.00
Note Payable	3,750.00
TOTAL CURRENT LIABILITIES	$ 28,748.00
Long-Term Liabilities:	
Note Payable	$ 30,000.00
Total Liabilities	$ 58,748.00
Owner's Equity	$ 44,350.00
TOTAL LIABILITIES AND OWNER'S EQUITY	$103,098.00

Ratio Analysis

4. Understand the basic financial statements through ratio analysis.

Would you be willing to drive a car on an extended trip without being able to see the dashboard displays showing fuel level, engine temperature, oil pressure, battery status, or the speed at which you were traveling? Not many people would! Yet, many small business owners run their companies exactly that way. They never take the time to check the vital signs of their businesses using their "financial dashboards." The result: Their companies develop engine trouble, fail, and leave them stranded along the road to successful entrepreneurship.

Smart entrepreneurs know that once they have their businesses up and running with the help of a solid financial plan, the next step is to keep the company moving in the right direction with the help of proper financial controls. Establishing these controls—and using them consistently—is one of the keys to keeping a business vibrant and healthy. Business owners who don't may be shocked to learn that their companies are in serious financial trouble and they never knew it.

A smoothly functioning system of financial controls is essential to achieving business success. Such a system can serve as an early warning device for underlying problems that could destroy a young business. They allow an entrepreneur to step back and see the big picture and to make adjustments in the company's direction when necessary. According to one writer:

A company's financial accounting and reporting system will provide signals, through comparative analysis, of impending trouble, such as:

- Decreasing sales and falling profit bargains
- Increasing corporate overheads
- Growing inventories and accounts receivable

These are all signals of declining cash flows from operations, the lifeblood of every business. As cash flows decrease, the squeeze begins:

- Payments to vendors become slower.
- Maintenance on production equipment lags.
- Raw material shortages appear.
- Equipment breakdowns occur.

All of these begin to have a negative impact on productivity. Now the downward spiral has begun in earnest. The key is hearing and focusing on the signals.[5]

What are these signals, and how does an entrepreneur go about hearing and focusing on them? One extremely helpful tool is ratio analysis. **Ratio analysis,** a method of expressing the relationships between any two accounting elements, provides a convenient technique for performing financial analysis. When analyzed properly, ratios serve as barometers of a company's financial health. These comparisons allow the small business manager to determine if the firm is carrying excessive inventory, experiencing heavy operating expenses, overextending credit, managing to pay its debts on time, and to answer other questions relating to the efficient operation of the firm. Unfortunately, few business owners actually use ratio analysis; one study discovered that just 2 percent of all entrepreneurs compute financial ratios and use them in managing their businesses![6]

Clever business owners use financial ratio analysis to identify problems in their businesses while they are still problems, not business-threatening crises. Tracking these ratios over time permits an owner to spot a variety of "red flags" that are indi-

IN THE FOOTSTEPS OF AN ENTREPRENEUR
A Challenging Turnaround

Jon Chait decided to buy Louise's Trattoria, a 15-store chain of Italian restaurants in California with a following of customers in trendy areas such as Santa Monica, Brentwood, and Beverly Hills. The chain's popularity had not translated into profits, however. Chait's first move was to hire Fred LeFranc, a 22-year veteran of the restaurant business, as CEO. Even before he had a chance to tour all 15 restaurants, LeFranc saw the company plunged into a severe crisis: The state of California froze Louise's bank accounts, seeking $225,000 for the previous owners' failure to pay sales tax. On LeFranc's ninth day at work, Louise's filed for chapter 11 bankruptcy, unable to pay its bills. He called a meeting to discuss the company's situation with employees and then went on the road to reestablish credit terms with the chain's suppliers.

The typical restaurant's net profit margin is 6 percent of sales, and LeFranc knew it would be a battle to return Louise's to profitability in the face of bankruptcy and intense competition, but he was determined to do it. The company had run into trouble after it began expanding too rapidly, "building restaurants and spending money faster than it was coming in," says Chait. Complicating matters was the chain's bankruptcy settlement, which required a $68,000 monthly payment to pay off creditors, stretching Louise's already tenuous financial position. LeFranc quickly closed four restaurants on the East Coast and went on a focused cost-cutting, cost-controlling binge. "You need to be aware of costs and build it into your daily discipline," he says.

LeFranc knew that turning Louise's around would require detailed information about each restaurant's operations and costs, including everything from the costs of individual food items and staffing schedules to average check sizes and profit margins on each menu item. Unfortunately, because of the chaos created by the bankruptcy filing, LeFranc had access to almost none of the information he needed. LeFranc hired a friend with extensive experience in the restaurant industry as controller, and after three months the two had created enough order out of the chaos to create an income statement. That was the good news; the bad news was that Louise's was losing $157,000 every month.

LeFranc's next job was to track down the causes of the company's losses. He started by examining the company commissary, which made the chain's sauces, salad dressings, and pastas by hand. The commissary charged the restaurants in the chain what appeared to be reasonable prices that pegged their food costs at 28 percent of sales. Then, in December, the commissary introduced a huge price increase to make up the losses it had been incurring by selling its food products below their costs all year! The restaurants' food costs jumped to 50 percent of sales, plunging their income statements into the red. Further study of the commissary and its cost structure led LeFranc to shut it down and outsource the company's basic ingredients such as sauces, dressings, and pasta to lower-cost suppliers. He also reduced the number of weekly deliveries suppliers made from six to three, cutting both transportation costs and the expenses associated with paying accounts receivable. (The number of invoices dropped from 20,000 to just 3,000 a year.) He even moved Louise's headquarters closer to the restaurants, cutting rent by nearly half.

These cost-cutting moves and some changes to the menu brought food costs down to 25.5 percent of sales, and just 11 months after declaring bankruptcy, Louise's was cash-flow positive. LeFranc's next move was to empower the managers of each restaurant to act like CEOs of their locations, which meant training them to collect, analyze, and use information about their operations. He taught them how to read and analyze the information on their income statements and set up an incentive program to improve performance. Many managers quit, but those who stayed responded.

LeFranc also discovered Roger Oritz, who had worked in the commissary and was a self-taught whiz in Excel spreadsheets. LeFranc trained Oritz and promoted him to financial analyst. He provided each restaurant manager with a personal computer so they could e-mail information such as revenues, expenses, and guest counts directly to Oritz at headquarters, who then compiled an Excel report on every phase of each restaurant's operation. LeFranc started monthly meetings where managers met to describe and discuss their financial and operating results. Over time, *(continued)* each location's financial statements became stronger, thanks to the hundreds of small improvements LeFranc and the managers implemented. Louise's has returned to profitability, and based on the numbers, LeFranc says that he can open five more locations without increasing the company's overhead expenses, meaning that the cash flow from those new restaurants would go straight to the company's bottom line.

1. How difficult would it be to turn around a restaurant chain in bankruptcy? Explain.

2. What role did LeFranc's establishing tight financial controls and reporting play in turning around Louise's Trattoria?

3. How important was involving the managers of the individual restaurants in the turnaround process? Why?

Source: Adapted from Samuel Fromartz, "The Mystery of the Blood Red Ledger," *Inc.*, April 2001, pp. 72–80.

cations of these problem areas. This is critical to business success because entrepreneurs cannot solve problems they do not know exist! Business owners also can use ratio analysis to increase the likelihood of obtaining bank loans. By analyzing their financial statements with ratios, owners can anticipate potential problems and identify important strengths in advance. When evaluating a business plan or a loan request, lenders often rely on ratio analysis to determine how well managed a company is and how solid its financial footing is.

But how many ratios should a small business manager monitor to maintain adequate financial control over the firm? The number of ratios that could be calculated is limited only by the number of accounts recorded on the firm's financial statements. However, tracking too many ratios only creates confusion and saps the meaning from an entrepreneur's financial analysis. The secret to successful ratio analysis is simplicity, focusing on just enough ratios to provide a clear picture of a company's financial standing.

Twelve Key Ratios

In keeping with the idea of simplicity, we will describe 12 key ratios that will enable most business owners to monitor their firms' financial position without becoming bogged down in financial details. This chapter presents explanations of these ratios and examples based on the balance sheet and the income statement for Sam's Appliance Shop shown in Figures 8.1 and 8.2. We will group them into four categories: liquidity ratios, leverage ratios, operating ratios, and profitability ratios.

Liquidity Ratios. **Liquidity ratios** tell whether a small business will be able to meet its maturing obligations as they come due. A small company with solid liquidity not only is able to pay its bills on time, but it also is in a position to take advantage of attractive business opportunities as they arise. The two most common measures of liquidity are the current ratio and the quick ratio.

Current Ratio. The **current ratio** measures the small firm's solvency by indicating its ability to pay current liabilities from current assets. It is calculated in the following manner:

$$\text{Current ratio} = \frac{\text{Current assets}}{\text{Current liabilities}}$$

$$= \frac{\$686,985}{\$367,850} \tag{6}$$

$$= 1.87:1$$

Sam's Appliance Shop has $1.87 in current assets for every $1 it has in current liabilities. Current assets are those that the entrepreneur expects to convert into cash in the ordinary business cycle, and normally include cash, notes/accounts receivable, inventory, and any other short-term marketable securities. Current liabilities are those short-term obligations that come due within one year, and include notes/accounts payable, taxes payable, and accruals.

The current ratio is sometimes called the working capital ratio and is the most commonly used measure of short-term solvency. Typically, financial analysts suggest that a small business maintain a current ratio of at least 2:1 (i.e., $2 of current assets for every $1 of current liabilities) to maintain a comfortable cushion of working capital. Generally, the higher the firm's current ratio, the stronger its financial position; but a high current ratio does not guarantee that the firm's assets are being used in the most profitable manner. For example, a business maintaining excessive balances of idle cash or overinvesting in inventory would likely have a high current ratio.

With its current ratio of 1.87:1, Sam's Appliance Shop could liquidate its current assets at 53.5% (1 ÷ 1.87 = 53.5%) of book value and still manage to pay its current creditors in full.

Quick Ratio. The current ratio can sometimes be misleading because it does not show the quality of a company's current assets. For instance, a company with a large number of past-due receivables and stale inventory could boast an impressive current ratio and still be on the verge of financial collapse. The **quick ratio** (or the **acid test ratio**) is a more conservative measure of a firm's liquidity because it shows the extent to which its most liquid assets cover its current liabilities. It is calculated as follows:

$$\text{Quick ratio} = \frac{\text{Quick assets}}{\text{Current liabilities}}$$

$$= \frac{\$686{,}985 - \$455{,}455}{\$367{,}850} \tag{7}$$

$$= 0.63{:}1$$

Quick assets include cash, readily marketable securities, and notes/accounts receivables—those assets that a company can convert into cash immediately if needed. Most small firms determine quick assets by subtracting inventory from current assets because inventory cannot be converted into cash quickly. Also, inventories are the assets on which losses are most likely to occur in case of liquidation.

The quick ratio is a more specific measure of a firm's ability to meet its short-term obligations and is a more rigorous test of its liquidity. It expresses the capacity to repay current debts if all sales income ceased immediately. Generally, a quick ratio of 1:1 is considered satisfactory. A ratio of less than 1:1 indicates that the small firm is overly dependent on inventory and on future sales to satisfy short-term debt. A quick ratio of more than 1.1 indicates a greater degree of financial security.

Leverage Ratios. **Leverage ratios** measure the financing supplied by the firm's owners against that supplied by its creditors; they are a gauge of the depth of a company's debt. These ratios show the extent to which an entrepreneur relies on debt capital (rather than equity capital) to finance operating expenses, capital expenditures, and expansion costs. As such, it is a measure of the degree of financial risk in a company. Generally, small businesses with low leverage ratios are less affected by economic downturns, but the returns for these firms are lower during economic booms. Conversely, small firms with high leverage ratios are more vulnerable to economic slides because their debt loads demolish cash flow; however, they have greater potential for large profits. "Leverage is a double-edged sword," says one financial expert. If it works for you, you can really build something. If you borrow too much, it can drag a business down faster than anything."[7] The following ratios will help entrepreneurs keep their debt levels manageable.

Debt Ratio. The small firm's **debt ratio** measures the percentage of total assets financed by its creditors. The debt ratio is calculated as follows:

$$\text{Debt ratio} = \frac{\text{Total debt (or liabilities)}}{\text{Total assets}} \qquad \textbf{(8)}$$

$$= \frac{\$367,850 + \$212,150}{847,655}$$

$$= 0.68:1$$

Total debt includes all current liabilities and any outstanding long-term notes and bonds. Total assets represent the sum of the firm's current assets, fixed assets, and intangible assets. A high debt ratio means that creditors provide a large percentage of the firm's total financing. Owners generally prefer a high leverage ratio; otherwise, business funds must come either from the owners' personal assets or from taking on new owners, which means giving up more control over the business. Also, with a greater portion of the firm's assets financed by creditors, the owner is able to generate profits with a smaller personal investment. However, creditors typically prefer moderate debt ratios since a lower debt ratio indicates a smaller chance of creditor losses in case of liquidation. To lenders and creditors, high debt ratios mean a high risk of default.

Debt to Net Worth Ratio. The small firm's **debt to net worth ratio** also expresses the relationship between the capital contributions from creditors and those from owners. This ratio compares what the business "owes" to what it "owns." It is a measure of the small firm's ability to meet both its creditor and owner obligations in case of liquidation. The debt to net worth ratio is calculated as follows:

$$\text{Debt-to-net worth ratio} = \frac{\text{Total debt (or liabilities)}}{\text{tangible net worth}}$$

$$= \frac{\$367,850 + \$212,150}{\$267,655 - \$3,500} \qquad \textbf{(9)}$$

$$= 2.20:1$$

Total debt is the sum of current liabilities and long-term liabilities, and tangible net worth represents the owners' investment in the business (capital + capital stock + earned surplus + retained earnings) less any intangible assets (e.g., goodwill) the firm owns.

The higher this ratio, the lower the degree of protection afforded creditors if the business should fail. Also, a higher debt to net worth ratio means that the firm has less capacity to borrow; lenders and creditors see the firm as being "borrowed up." Conversely, a low ratio typically is associated with a higher level of financial security, giving the business greater borrowing potential. As a firm's debt-to-net worth ratio approaches 1:1, the creditors' interest in the business approaches that of the owners'. If the ratio is greater than 1:1, the creditors' claims exceed those of the owners', and the business may be undercapitalized. In other words, the owner has not supplied an adequate amount of capital, forcing the business to be overextended in terms of debt.

Times Interest Earned Ratio. The **times interest earned ratio** is a measure of the small firm's ability to make the interest payments on its debt. It tells how many times the company's earnings cover the interest payments on the debt it is carrying. The times interest earned ratio is calculated as follows:

$$\text{Times interest earned} = \frac{\text{Earnings before interest and taxes (or EBIT)}}{\text{Total interest expense}}$$

$$= \frac{\$60,629 + 39,850}{\$39,850} \qquad \textbf{(10)}$$

$$= 2.52:1$$

EBIT is the firm's net income (earnings) *before* deducting interest expense and taxes; the denominator measures the amount the business paid in interest over the accounting period.

A high ratio suggests that the company would have little difficulty meeting the interest payments on its loans; creditors would see this as a sign of safety for future loans. Conversely, a low ratio is an indication that the company is overextended in its debts; earnings will not be able to cover its debt service if this ratio is less than one. "I look for a [times interest earned] ratio of higher than three-to-one," says one financial analyst, "which indicates that management has considerable breathing room to make its debt payments. When the ratio drops below one-to-one, it clearly indicates management is under tremendous pressure to raise cash. The risk of default or bankruptcy is very high."[8] Many creditors look for a times interest earned ratio of at least 4:1 to 6:1 before pronouncing a company a good credit risk.

Debt is a powerful financial tool, but companies must handle it carefully—just as a demolitionist handles dynamite. And, like dynamite, too much debt can be dangerous. Trouble looms on the horizon for companies whose debt loads are so heavy that they must starve critical operations such as research and development, customer service, and others just to pay interest on the debt. Because their interest payments are so large, highly leveraged companies find that they are restricted when it comes to spending cash, whether on normal operations, an acquisition, or capital expenditures. Unfortunately, some companies have gone on borrowing binges, pushing their debt loads beyond the safety barrier (see Figure 8.6) and are struggling to survive.

Some entrepreneurs are so averse to debt that they run their companies with a minimum amount of borrowing, relying instead on their business's cash flow to finance growth. Jerry Edwards, president of Chef's Expressions, a small catering company, manages to generate annual sales of $2 million with just a $20,000 line of credit. "We've always funded our growth out of cash flow," says Edwards. "I had a credit line that I didn't dip into for 10 years!"[9] Growth may be slower for these companies, but their owners do not have to contend with the dangers of debt. Managed carefully, however, debt can boost a company's performance and improve its productivity. Its treatment in the tax code also makes debt a much cheaper means of financial growth than equity. When companies with AA financial ratings borrow at 10 percent, the after-tax cost is just 7.2 percent (because interest payments to lenders are tax deductible); equity financing costs more than twice that.

Operating Ratios. Operating ratios help the owner evaluate the small firm's performance and indicate how effectively the business employs its resources. The more effectively its resources are used, the less capital a small business will require. These five operating ratios are designed to help entrepreneurs spot those areas they must improve if their businesses are to remain competitive.

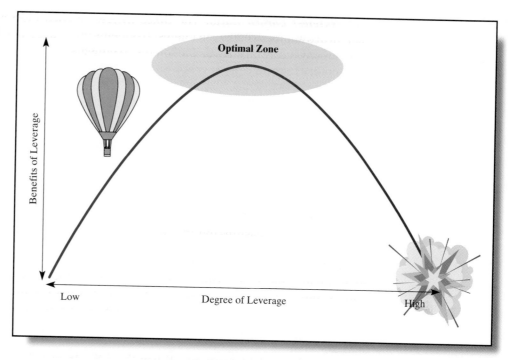

Figure 8.6
The Right Amount of Debt Is a Balancing Act

Optimal Zone

Benefits of Leverage

Low   Degree of Leverage   High

Average Inventory Turnover Ratio. A small company's **average inventory turnover ratio** measures the number of times its average inventory is sold out, or turned over, during the accounting period. This ratio tells the owner whether the firm's inventory is being managed properly. It apprises the owner of whether the business inventory is understocked, overstocked, or obsolete. The average inventory turnover ratio is calculated as follows:

$$\text{Average inventory turnover ratio} = \frac{\text{Cost of goods sold}}{\text{Average inventory}}$$

(11)

$$= \frac{\$1,290,117}{(\$805,745 + \$455,455) \div 2}$$

$$= 2.05 \text{ times/year}$$

Average inventory is found by adding a firm's inventory at the beginning of the accounting period to the ending inventory and dividing the result by 2.

This ratio tells an entrepreneur how fast the merchandise is moving through the business and helps to balance the company on the fine line between oversupply and undersupply. To determine the average number of days units remain in inventory, the owner can divide the average inventory turnover ratio into the number of days in the accounting period (e.g., 365 ÷ average inventory turnover ratio). The result is called **days' inventory** (or **average age of inventory**). Auto dealerships often use average age of inventory as a measure of performance.

An above-average inventory turnover indicates that the small business has a healthy, salable, and liquid inventory and a supply of quality merchandise supported by sound pricing policies. A below average inventory turnover suggests an illiquid inventory characterized by obsolescence, overstocking, stale merchandise, and poor purchasing procedures.

Businesses that turn their inventories more rapidly require a smaller inventory investment to produce a particular sales volume. That means that these companies tie up less cash in inventory that idly sits on shelves. For instance, if Sam's could turn its inventory four times each year instead of just two, the company would require an average inventory of just $322,529 instead of the current level of $630,600 to generate sales of $1,870,841. Increasing the number of inventory turns would free up more than $308,000 currently tied up in excess inventory! Sam's would benefit from improved cash flow and higher profits.

The inventory turnover ratio can be misleading, however. For example, an excessively high ratio could mean the firm has a shortage of inventory and is experiencing stockouts. Similarly, a low ratio could be the result of planned inventory stockpiling to meet seasonal peak demand. Another problem is that the ratio is based on an inventory balance calculated from two days out of the entire accounting period. Thus, inventory fluctuations due to seasonal demand patterns are ignored, which may bias the resulting ratio. There is no universal, ideal inventory turnover ratio. Financial analysts suggest that a favorable turnover ratio depends on the type of business, its size, its profitability, its method of inventory valuation, and other relevant factors. The most meaningful basis for comparison is other companies of similar size in the same industry (more on this later).

Average Collection Period Ratio. The small firm's **average collection period ratio** (or **day's sales outstanding [DSO]**) tells the average number of days it takes to collect accounts receivable. To compute the average collection period ratio, you must first calculate the firm's receivables turnover. If Sam's credit sales for the year were $1,309,589, then the receivables turnover ratio would be as follows:

$$\text{Receivables turnover ratio} = \frac{\text{Credit sales (or net sales)}}{\text{Accounts receivable}}$$

$$= \frac{\$1,309,589}{\$179,225} \tag{12}$$

$$= 7.31 \text{ times/year}$$

This ratio measures the number of times the firm's accounts receivable turn over during the accounting period. Sam's Appliance Shop turns over its receivables 7.31 times per year. The higher the firm's receivables turnover ratio, the shorter the time lag between making a sale and collecting the cash from it.

Use the following to calculate the firm's average collection period ratio:

$$\text{Average collection period ratio} = \frac{\text{Days in accounting period}}{\text{Receivables turnover ratio}}$$

$$= \frac{365 \text{ days}}{7.31} \tag{13}$$

$$= 50.0 \text{ days}$$

Sam's Appliance Shop's accounts and notes receivable are outstanding for an average of 50 days. Typically, the higher a firm's average collection period ratio, the greater is its chance of bad debt losses.

One of the most useful applications of the collection period ratio is to compare it to the industry average and to the firm's credit terms. Such a comparison will indicate the degree of the small company's control over its credit sales and collection techniques. One rule of thumb suggests that the firm's collection period ratio should

Section III   Building the Business Plan: Marketing and Financial Matters

Table 8.1
How Lowering Your Average Collection Period Can Save You Money

Too often, entrepreneurs fail to recognize the importance of collecting their accounts receivable on time. After all, collecting accounts is not as glamorous or as much fun as generating sales. Lowering a company's average collection period ratio, however, can produce tangible—and often significant—savings. The following formula shows how to convert an improvement in a company's average collection period ratio into dollar savings:

$$\text{Annual savings} = \frac{(\text{Credit sales} \times \text{annual interest rate} \times \text{number of days average collection period is lowered})}{365}$$

Where

Credit sales = company's annual credit sales in $

Annual interest rate = the interest rate at which the company borrows money

Number of days average collection period is lowered = the difference between the previous year's average collection period ratio and the current one

Example:

Sam's Appliance Shop's average collection period ratio is 50 days. Suppose that the previous year's average collection period ratio was 56 days, a six-day improvement. The company's credit sales for the most recent year were $1,309,589. If Sam borrows money at 10.25%, this six-day improvement has generated savings for Sam's Appliance Shop of:

$$\text{Savings} = \frac{\$1,309,589 \times 10.25\% \times 6 \text{ days}}{365 \text{ days}} = \$2,207$$

By collecting his accounts receivable just six days faster on the average, Sam has saved his business more than $2,200! Of course, if a company's average collection period ratio rises, the same calculation will tell the owner how much that costs.

Source: "Days Saved, Thousands Earned," *Inc.,* November 1995, p. 98.

be no more than one-third greater than its credit terms. For example, if a small company's credit terms are "net 30," its average collection period ratio should be no more than 40 days. A ratio greater than 40 days would indicate poor collection procedures, such as sloppy record keeping or failure to send invoices promptly. *Nick Ypsilantis, CEO of AccuFile, a company that provides library staff and services to businesses, has learned the importance of sending invoices promptly. Before the company tightened its accounts receivable procedures, cash flow was a constant problem, forcing Ypsilantis to borrow money on its line of credit. By sending invoices sooner and following up promptly on past-due accounts, AccuFile has reduced its average collection period to 41 days and has not had to use its credit line at all.*[10]

Just as Nick Ypsilantis has learned, slow payers represent great risk to many small businesses. Many entrepreneurs proudly point to rapidly rising sales only to find that they must borrow money to keep their companies going because credit customers are paying their bills in 45, 60, or even 90 days instead of 30. Slow receivables often lead to a cash crisis that can cripple a business. Table 8.1 shows how lowering the average collection period ratio can save a company money.

Average Payable Period Ratio. The converse of the average collection period ratio, the **average payable period ratio,** tells the average number of days it takes a company to pay its accounts payable. Like the average collection period, it is measured in days. To compute this ratio, first calculate the payables turnover ratio. Sam's payables turnover ratio is as follows:

$$\text{Payables turnover ratio} = \frac{\text{Purchases}}{\text{Accounts payable}}$$

$$= \frac{\$939,827}{\$152,580} \tag{14}$$

$$= 6.16 \text{ times/year}$$

To find the average payable period, use the following computation:

$$\text{Average payable period ratio} = \frac{\text{Days in accounting period}}{\text{Payables turnover ratio}}$$

$$= \frac{365 \text{ days}}{6.16} \tag{15}$$

$$= 59.3 \text{ days}$$

Sam's Appliance Shop takes an average of 59 days to pay its accounts with suppliers.

An excessively high average payable period ratio indicates the presence of a significant amount of past-due accounts payable. Although sound cash management calls for a business owners to keep their cash as long as possible, slowing payables too drastically can severely damage a company's credit rating. Ideally, the average payable period would match (or exceed) the time it takes to convert inventory into sales and ultimately into cash. In this case, the company's vendors would be financing its inventory and its credit sales.

One of the most meaningful comparisons for this ratio is against the credit terms offered by suppliers (or an average of the credit terms offered). If the average payable ratio slips beyond vendors' credit terms, it is an indication that the company is suffering from cash shortages or a sloppy accounts payable procedure and its credit rating is in danger. If this ratio is significantly lower than vendors' credit terms, it may be a sign that a business is not using its cash most effectively.

Net Sales to Total Assets. A small company's **net sales to total assets ratio** (also called the **total assets turnover ratio**) is a general measure of its ability to generate sales in relation to its assets. It describes how productively the firm employs its assets to produce sales revenue. The total assets turnover ratio is calculated as follows:

$$\text{Total assets turnover ratio} = \frac{\text{Net sales}}{\text{Net total assets}}$$

$$= \frac{\$1,870,841}{\$847,655} \tag{16}$$

$$= 2.21:1$$

The denominator of this ratio, net total assets, is the sum of all of the firm's assets (cash, inventory, land, buildings, equipment, tools, everything owned) less depreciation. This ratio is meaningful only when compared to that of similar firms in the same industry category. A total assets turnover ratio below the industry average may indicate that the small firm is not generating an adequate sales volume for its asset size.

Net Sales to Working Capital. The **net sales to working capital ratio** measures how many dollars in sales the business generates for every dollar of working capital (working capital = current assets − current liabilities). Also called the **turnover of**

working capital ratio, this proportion tells the owner how efficiently working capital is being used to generate sales. It is calculated as follows:

$$\text{Net sales to working capital ratio} = \frac{\text{Net sales}}{\text{Current assets} - \text{Current liabilities}}$$

$$= \frac{\$1,870,841}{\$686,985 - \$367,850} \tag{17}$$

$$= 5.86:1$$

An excessively low net sales to working capital ratio indicates that the small firm is not employing its working capital efficiently or profitably. On the other hand, an extremely high ratio points to an inadequate level of working capital to maintain a suitable level of sales, which puts creditors in a more vulnerable position. This ratio is very helpful in maintaining sufficient working capital as the small business grows. It is critical for the small firm to keep a satisfactory level of working capital to nourish its expansion, and the net sales to working capital ratio helps define the level of working capital required to support higher sales volume.

Profitability Ratios. Profitability ratios indicate how efficiently a small firm is being managed. They provide the owner with information about the company's ability to generate a profit; in other words, they describe how successfully the firm is conducting business.

Net Profit on Sales Ratio. The **net profit on sales ratio** (also called the **profit margin on sales**) measures the firm's profit per dollar of sales. The computed percentage shows the number of cents of each sales dollar remaining after deducting all expenses and income taxes. The profit margin on sales is calculated as follows:

$$\text{Net profit on sales ratio} = \frac{\text{Net income}}{\text{Net sales}}$$

$$= \frac{\$60,629}{\$1,870,841} \tag{18}$$

$$= 3.24\%$$

Most small business owners believe that a high profit margin on sales is necessary for a successful business operation, but this is a myth. To evaluate this ratio properly, the owner must consider the firm's asset value, its inventory and receivables turnover ratios, and its total capitalization. For example, the typical small supermarket earns an average net profit of only one or two cents on each dollar of sales, but its inventory may turn over as many as 20 times a year. If the firm's profit margin on sales is below the industry average, it may be a sign that its prices are relatively low or that its costs are excessively high, or both.

If a company's net profit on sales ratio is excessively low, the owner should check the gross profit margin (net sales minus cost of goods sold expressed as a percentage of net sales). Of course, a reasonable gross profit margin varies from industry to industry. For instance, a service company may have a gross profit margin of 75 percent, while a manufacturer's may be 35 percent. If this margin slips too low, it puts the company's future in immediate jeopardy.

Net Profit to Equity. The **net profit to equity ratio** (or the **return on net worth ratio**) measures the owners' rate of return on investment. Because it reports the percentage of the owner's investment in the business that is being returned through profits annually, it is one of the most important indicators of the firm's profitability or a management's efficiency. The net profit to equity ratio is computed as follows:

$$\text{Net profit to equity ratio} = \frac{\text{Net income}}{\text{Owner's equity (or net worth)}}$$

$$= \frac{\$60,629}{\$267,655} \tag{19}$$

$$= 22.65\%$$

This ratio compares profits earned during the accounting period with the amount the owner has invested in the business during that time. If this interest rate on the owner's investment is excessively low, some of this capital might be better employed elsewhere.

INTERPRETING BUSINESS RATIOS

5. Explain how to interpret financial ratios.

Ratios are useful yardsticks in measuring the small firm's performance and can point out potential problems before they develop into serious crises. But calculating these ratios is not enough to ensure proper financial control. In addition to knowing how to calculate these ratios, the owner must understand how to interpret them and apply them to managing the business more effectively and efficiently.

Not every business measures its success with the same ratios. In fact, key performance ratios vary dramatically across industries and even within different segments of the same industry. Entrepreneurs must know and understand which ratios are most crucial to their companies' success and focus on monitoring and controlling those. Many successful entrepreneurs identify or develop "critical numbers," ratios that are unique to their own operations, to help them achieve success. *For instance, when sales at Petra Group, a small computer systems integrator, flattened, founder Greg Smith found his company losing money for the first time in its history. Smith suspected that the losses were due to more than slow sales, but he didn't know how to pinpoint the problem areas. A local accounting firm helped Smith prepare a ratio analysis for Petra Group and then compare the results with industry averages. The results were quite revealing and valuable. Smith discovered that the company had taken on too much short-term debt but that it was doing an excellent job of managing its accounts receivable, collecting them twice as fast as the industry norm. Smith also identified several critical numbers for his business, one of which was the ratio of payroll expenses to sales. For Petra Group, this ratio exceeded the benchmark of 60 percent, which meant the company was not likely to earn a profit. Smith reduced his workforce by two, and the company quickly returned to profitability.*[11]

As Smith's experience proves, one of the most valuable ways to utilize ratios is to compare them with those of similar businesses in the same industry. By comparing the company's financial statistics to industry averages, the owner is able to locate problem areas and maintain adequate financial controls. "By themselves, these numbers are not that meaningful," says one financial expert of ratios, "but when you compare them to [those of] other businesses in your industry, they suddenly come alive because they put your operation in perspective."[12]

The principle behind calculating these ratios and comparing them to industry norms is the same as that of most medical tests in the healthcare profession. Just as a healthy person's blood pressure and cholesterol levels should fall within a range of normal values, so should a financially healthy company's ratios. A company cannot deviate too far from these normal values and remain successful for long. When deviations from "normal" do occur (and they will), a business owner should focus on determining the cause of the deviations. In some cases, such deviations are the result of sound business decisions, such as taking on inventory in preparation for the busy season, investing heavily in new technology, and others. In other instances, however, ratios that are out of the normal range for a particular type of business are indicators of what could become serious problems for a company. When comparing a company's ratios to industry standards, entrepreneurs should ask the following questions:

- Is there a significant difference in my company's ratio and the industry average?
- If so, is this a *meaningful* difference?
- Is the difference good or bad?
- What are the possible causes of this difference? What is the most likely cause?
- Does this cause require that I take action?
- What action should I take to correct the problem?

Properly used, ratio analysis can help owners identify potential problem areas in their businesses early on—*before* they become crises that threaten their very survival. Several organizations regularly compile and publish operating statistics, including key ratios, summarizing the financial performance of many businesses across a wide range of industries. The local library should subscribe to most of these publications:

Robert Morris Associates. Established in 1914, Robert Morris Associates publishes its *Annual Statement Studies,* showing ratios and other financial data for more than 650 different industrial, wholesale, retail, and service categories.

Dun & Bradstreet, Inc. Since 1932, Dun & Bradstreet has published *Key Business Ratios,* which covers 22 retail, 32 wholesale, and 71 industrial business categories. Dun & Bradstreet also publishes *Cost of Doing Business,* a series of operating ratios compiled from the IRS's *Statistics of Income.*

Vest Pocket Guide to Financial Ratios. This handy guide, published by Prentice Hall, gives key ratios and financial data for a wide variety of industries.

Industry trade associations. Virtually every type of business is represented by a national trade association, which publishes detailed financial data compiled from its membership. For example, the owner of a small supermarket could contact the National Association of Retail Grocers or the *Progressive Grocer,* its trade publication, for financial statistics relevant to his operation.

Government agencies. Several government agencies (the Federal Trade Commission, Interstate Commerce Commission, Department of Commerce, Department of Agriculture, and Securities and Exchange Commission) offer a great deal of financial operating data on a variety of industries, although the categories are more general. In addition, the IRS annually publishes *Statistics of Income,* which includes income statement and balance sheet statistics compiled from income tax returns. The IRS also publishes the *Census of Business* that gives a limited amount of ratio information.

What Do All of These Numbers Mean?

Learning to interpret financial ratios just takes a little practice! This section will show you how it's done by comparing the ratios from the operating data already computed for Sam's to those taken from RMA's *Annual Statement Studies*. (The industry median is the ratio falling exactly in the middle when sample elements are arranged in ascending or descending order.)

Sam's Appliance Shop	**Industry Median**

Liquidity ratios tell whether or not the small business will be able to meet its maturing obligations as they come due.

1. Current Ratio = 1.87:1   1.50:1
   Sam's Appliance Shop falls short of the rule of thumb of 2:1, but its current ratio is above the industry median by a significant amount. Sam's should have no problem meeting its short-term debts as they come due. By this measure, the company's liquidity is solid.

2. Quick Ratio = 0.63:1   0.50:1
   Again, Sam's is below the rule of thumb of 1:1, but the company passes this test of liquidity when measured against industry standards. Sam's relies on selling inventory to satisfy short-term debt (as do most appliance shops). If sales slump, the result could be liquidity problems for Sam's.

   Leverage ratios measure the financing supplied by the firm's owners against that supplied by its creditors and serve as a gauge of the depth of a company's debt.

3. Debt Ratio = 0.68:1   0.64:1
   Creditors provide 68 percent of Sam's total assets, very close to the industry median of 64 percent. Although Sam's does not appear to be overburdened with debt, the company might have difficulty borrowing additional money, especially from conservative lenders.

4. Debt to Net Worth Ratio = 2.20:1   1.90:1
   Sam's Appliance Shop owes $2.20 to creditors for every $1 the owners have invested in the business (compared to $1.90 in debt to every $1 in equity for the typical business). Although this is not an exorbitant amount of debt, many lenders and creditors will see Sam's as "borrowed up." Borrowing capacity is somewhat limited because creditors' claims against the business are more than twice those of the owners.

5. Times Interest Earned = 2.52:1   2.0:1
   Sam's earnings are high enough to cover the interest payments on its debt by a factor of 2.52, slightly better than the typical firm in the industry, whose earnings cover its interest payments just two times. Sam's Appliance Shop has a cushion (although a small one) in meeting its interest payments.

   Operating ratios evaluate the firm's overall performance and show how effectively it is putting its resources to work.

6. Average Inventory Turnover Ratio = 2.05 times/year   4.0 times/year
   Inventory is moving through Sam's at a very slow pace, *half* that of the industry median. The company has a problem with slow-moving items in its inventory and, perhaps, too much inventory. Which items are they, and why are they slow-moving? Does Sam's need to drop some product lines?

7. Average Collection Period Ratio = 50.0 days   19.3 days
   Sam's Appliance Shop collects the average accounts receivable after 50 days, compared with the industry median of 19 days, more than two and a half times longer. A more meaningful comparison is against Sam's credit terms;

if credit terms are net 30 (or anywhere close to that), Sam's has a dangerous collection problem, one that drains cash and profits and demands *immediate* attention!

8. Average Payable Period Ratio = 59.3 days   43 days
   Sam's payables are nearly 40 percent slower than those of the typical firm in the industry. Stretching payables too far could seriously damage the company's credit rating, causing suppliers to cut off future trade credit. This could be a sign of cash flow problems or a sloppy accounts payable procedure. This problem also demands *immediate* attention.

9. Net Sales to Total Assets Ratio = 2.21:1   2.7:1
   Sam's Appliance Shop is not generating enough sales, given the size of its asset base. This could be the result of a number of factors—improper inventory, inappropriate pricing, poor location, poorly trained sales personnel, and many others. The key is to find the cause *fast!*

10. Net Sales to Working Capital Ratio = 5.86:1   10.8:1
    Sam's generates just $5.86 in sales for every $1 in working capital, just over half of what the typical firm in the industry does. Given the previous ratio, the message is clear: Sam's simply is not producing an adequate level of sales. Improving the number of inventory turns will boost this ratio; otherwise, Sam's is likely to experience a working capital shortage soon.

    Profitability ratios measure how efficiently the firm is operating and offer information about its bottom line.

11. Net Profit on Sales Ratio = 3.24%   7.6%
    After deducting all expenses, 3.24 cents of each sales dollar remains as profit for Sam's—less than half the industry median. Sam's should check his company's gross profit margin and investigate its operating expenses, checking them against industry standards and looking for those that are out of balance.

12. Net Profit to Equity Ratio = 22.65%   12.6%
    Sam's Appliance Shop's owners are earning 22.65 percent on the money they have invested in the business. This yield is nearly twice that of the industry median, and, given the previous ratio, is more a result of the owners' relatively low investment in the business than an indication of its superior profitability. The owners are using OPM (other people's money) to generate a profit.

When comparing ratios for their individual businesses to published statistics, entrepreneurs must remember that the comparison is made against averages. Owners should strive to achieve ratios that are at least as good as these average figures. The goal should be to manage the business so that its financial performance is better than the industry average. As owners compare financial performance to those covered in the published statistics, they inevitably will discern differences between them. They should note those items that are substantially out of line from the industry average. However, a ratio that varies from the average does not necessarily mean that a small business is in financial jeopardy. Instead of making drastic changes in financial policy, entrepreneurs must explore why the figures are out of line. Steve Cowan, co-owner of Professional Salon Concepts, a wholesale beauty products distributor, routinely performs such an analysis on his company's financial statements. "I need to know whether the variances for expenses and revenues for a certain

Critical numbers are key financial and operational indicators that determine a company's success. Although they vary from one industry to another and even from one company to another, when these critical numbers are moving in the right direction, a business is on track to achieve its objectives. Entrepreneurs must be sure to identify the right critical numbers and to track them *daily*. Ron Friedman, head of the accounting firm Stonefield Josephson, studies his company's critical numbers every day. "Every morning by 9:30, I receive a printed report that tracks certain key results from the day before," he says. "That's a tremendous management advantage. I can respond immediately to any problem signals."

A company's critical numbers will depend on the business it is in. "Key numbers might be how much was sold each day, how much was shipped, how big your backlog is, and how much was collected," says Friedman. For instance, an airline's basic critical number might be its load factor, the percentage of seats it fills with passengers. A small manufacturer's basic critical number might be revenue per labor hour. At Flywire, a small company that provides Internet services, founder Mark Troy monitors the "utilization ratio," billable hours as a percentage of total hours worked. His target utilization ratio is 80 percent, a number he arrived at from studying industry standards and from his experience in the business. A utilization rate below 80 percent means that too many employees are idle, and a rate above 80 percent means that they are overworked. Hitting his company's critical number keeps Flywire profitable and minimizes employee turnover. Flywire has lost just three workers out of a staff of 40 in two years, an impressively turnover low rate by industry standards. Examples of critical numbers at other companies include:

- The call abandonment rate and the number of calls per paid hour at a toll-free caller service company

- The gross profit margin at a manufacturer of pallets

- Sales per labor hour at a supermarket

- Percentage of rework at a photo processor (Because the percentage of rework is an impor-

tant determinant of profitability, this processor graphs this critical number and posts it weekly).

How can entrepreneurs make critical numbers work for them? The first step is to conduct an analysis to determine the company's critical numbers. Asking managers and employees for input, studying industry standards, and using the management team's experience in the business are the most effective ways to determine the right critical numbers. Simplicity is the key. A company might have just one critical number, or several numbers may be important. Four critical numbers is probably the maximum.

Once managers determine their critical numbers, the next step is to set objectives for the numbers. Where should the numbers be at the end of the month, each quarter, and a year?

Managers also must derive reliable and meaningful ways of measuring critical numbers. Whatever measure is appropriate, it must clearly link employees' actions to the critical numbers. For critical numbers to have an impact, everyone in the company must be able to see how their performance on the job affects the critical numbers. That means the method for measuring the critical numbers must be simple enough for everyone to understand. At one plant of printer R. R. Donnelley and Sons, press efficiency, a measure of output that also incorporates quality, is the critical number, and everyone understands how to measure it.

Finally, managers must give employees an incentive to move critical numbers in the right direction. One California retail chain established daily customer count and average sale per customer as their critical numbers. The company organized a monthly contest with prizes and posted charts tracking each store's performance. Soon, employees were working hard to improve their stores' performances over the previous year and to outdo other stores in the chain. The healthy rivalry among stores boosted the company's performance significantly.

Focusing on critical numbers means keeping a company focused on what is essential for its success. Jack Clegg, CEO of Nobel Learning Communities, a for-profit company that operates 162 schools in 15

(continued)

states, relies on three critical numbers to make sure his business achieves its goal of providing a quality education to children in grades K through 12. Nobel creates clusters of small, uniformly designed schools to maximize efficiency and emphasizes small class sizes and teaching flexibility. At Nobel, maximum enrollment in a single school is 300, and class size is limited to 22 students. The three critical numbers Clegg uses to manage Nobel Learning Communities are general and administrative (G&A) expenses as a percentage of gross tuition; the school occupancy rate, and school personnel cost as a percentage of gross tuition. Maintaining control over these three numbers supports the company's overall strategy and, unlike many of its competitors, enables it to earn an attractive profit in a very challenging business. Every

Friday morning, Clegg convenes a meeting to review a "flash report" of these numbers for each school and to compare them against the objectives stated in Nobel's business plan. "That means that every single week I know how every single school is doing," says Clegg. "This allows us to make adjustments *within* the month, not after it."

1. What role do critical numbers play in running a business successfully?

2. How can business owners use critical numbers to make their businesses more successful?

3. Interview a local entrepreneur who has been in business for at least five years. Explain the concept of critical numbers and then ask him or her to identify the critical numbers in his or her business.

Sources: Adapted from Ilan Mochari, "When to Say When," *Inc.*, February 2001, p. 104; "A Daily Dose of Numbers," *Inc.*, January 1, 1998, *www2.inc.com/search/10147.html*; John Case, "Swipe These Critical Numbers!" *Inc.*, December 11, 1999, *www2.inc.com/search/15982.html*; George Gendron, "FYI: Critical Numbers," *Inc.*, December 1, 2000, *www2.inc.com/search/21103.html*; John Case, "Figuring Out Your Critical Number," *Inc.*, July 24, 1996, *www2.inc.com/search/13200.html*; Edward O. Welles, "The ABCs of Profit," *Inc.*, December 1, 2000, *www2.inc.com/search21116.html*; John Case, "Critical Numbers in Action," *Inc.*, January 21, 2000, *www2.inc.com/search/15981.html*; John Case, "Boosting Performance with Critical Numbers," *Inc.*, December 11, 1999, *www2.inc.com/search/15978-print.html*; John Case, "Troubleshooting Your Critical Numbers," *Inc.*, December 13, 1999, *www2.inc.com/search/15980.html*.

period are similar," he says. "If they're not, are the differences explainable? Is an expense category up just because of a decision to spend more, or were we just sloppy?"[13]

In addition to comparing ratios to industry averages, owners should analyze their firms' financial ratios over time. By themselves, these ratios are "snapshots" of the firm's finances at a single instant; but by examining these trends over time, the owner can detect gradual shifts that otherwise might go unnoticed until a financial crisis is looming (see Figure 8.7).

BREAKEVEN ANALYSIS

6. Conduct a breakeven analysis for a small company.

Another key component of every sound financial plan is a breakeven analysis (or cost–volume–profit analysis). A small firm's **breakeven point** is the level of operation (sales dollars or production quantity) at which it neither earns a profit nor incurs a loss. At this level of activity, sales revenue equals expenses—that is, the firm "breaks even." By analyzing costs and expenses, an owner can calculate the minimum level of activity required to keep the firm in operation. These techniques can then be refined to project the sales needed to generate the desired profit. Most potential lenders and investors will require the potential owner to prepare a breakeven analysis to assist them in evaluating the earning potential of the new business. In addition to its being a simple, useful screening device for financial institutions, breakeven analysis can also serve as a planning device for the small business owner. It occasionally will show a poorly prepared entrepreneur just how unprofitable a proposed business venture is likely to be.

Figure 8.7
Trend Analysis
of Ratios

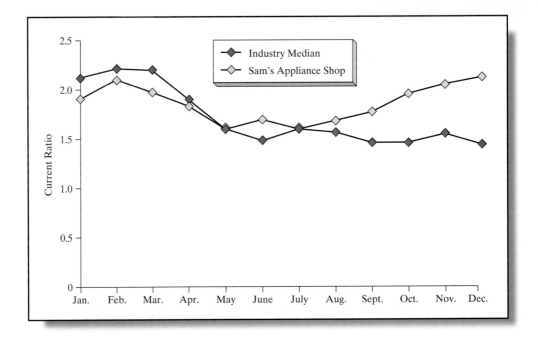

Calculating the Breakeven Point. A small business owner can calculate a firm's breakeven point by using a simple mathematical formula. To begin the analysis, the owner must determine fixed costs and variable costs. **Fixed expenses** are those that do not vary with changes in the volume of sales or production (e.g., rent, depreciation expense, interest payments). **Variable expenses,** on the other hand, vary directly with changes in the volume of sales or production (e.g., raw material costs, sales commissions).

Some expenses cannot be neatly categorized as fixed or variable because they contain elements of both. These semivariable expenses change, although not proportionately, with changes in the level of sales or production (electricity would be one example). These costs remain constant up to a particular production or sales volume, and then climb as that volume is exceeded. To calculate the breakeven point, the owner must separate these expenses into their fixed and variable components. A number of techniques can be used (which are beyond the scope of this text), but a good cost accounting system can provide the desired results.

Here are the steps an entrepreneur must take to compute the breakeven point using an example of a typical small business, the Magic Shop:

Step 1. Determine the expenses the business can expect to incur. With the help of a budget an entrepreneur can develop estimates of sales revenue, cost of goods sold, and expenses for the upcoming accounting period. The Magic Shop expects net sales of $950,000 in the upcoming year, with a cost of goods sold of $646,000 and total expenses of $236,500.

Step 2. Categorize the expenses estimated in step 1 into fixed expenses and variable expenses and separate semivariable expenses into their component parts. From the budget, the owner anticipates variable expenses (including the cost of goods sold) of $705,125 and fixed expenses of $177,375.

Step 3. Calculate the ratio of variable expenses to net sales. For the Magic Shop, this percentage is $705,125 ÷ $950,000 = 74 percent. So the Magic Shop uses $0.74 out of every sales dollar to cover variable expenses, leaving $0.26 as a contribution margin to cover fixed costs and make a profit.

Step 4. Compute the breakeven point by inserting this information into the following formula:

$$\text{Breakeven sales (\$)} = \frac{\text{Total fixed cost}}{\text{Contribution margin expressed as a percentage of sales}} \qquad \textbf{(20)}$$

For the Magic Shop,

$$\text{Breakeven sales} = \frac{\$177,375}{0.26} \qquad \textbf{(21)}$$

$$= \$682,212$$

The same breakeven point will result from solving the following equation algebraically:

Breakeven sales = fixed expense + variable expenses expressed as a percentage of sales

$$S = \$177,375 + 0.74S$$

$$S = \$682,212$$

Thus, the Magic Shop will break even with sales of $682,212. At this point, sales revenue generated will just cover total fixed and variable expense. The Magic Shop will earn no profit and will incur no loss. To verify this, make the following calculations:

Sales at breakeven point	$682,212
− Variable expenses (74% of sales)	−504,837
Contribution margin	177,375
− Fixed expenses	−177,375
Net income (or net loss)	$ 0

Adding in a Profit. What if the Magic Shop's owner wants to do *better* than just break even? His analysis can be adjusted to consider such a possibility. Suppose the owner expects a reasonable profit (before taxes) of $80,000. What level of sales must the Magic Shop achieve to generate this? He can calculate this by treating the desired profit as if it were a fixed cost. In other words, he modifies the formula to include the desired net income:

$$\text{Sales (\$)} = \frac{\text{Total fixed expenses} + \text{desired net income}}{\text{Contribution margin expressed as a percentage of sales}}$$

$$= \frac{\$177,375 + \$80,000}{0.26} \qquad \textbf{(23)}$$

$$= \$989,904$$

To achieve a net profit of $80,000 (before taxes), the Magic Shop must generate net sales of $989,904.

Breakeven Point in Units. Some small businesses may prefer to express the breakeven point in units produced or sold instead of in dollars. Manufacturers often find this approach particularly useful. The following formula computes the breakeven point in units:

$$\text{Breakeven volume} = \frac{\text{Total fixed costs}}{\text{Sales price per unit} - \text{Variable cost per unit}} \qquad \textbf{(24)}$$

For example, suppose that Trilex Manufacturing Company estimates its fixed costs for producing its line of small appliances at $390,000. The variable costs (including materials, direct labor, and factor overhead) amount to $12.10 per unit, and the selling price per unit is $17.50. So, Trilex computes its contribution margin this way:

$$\text{Contribution margin} = \text{Price per unit} - \text{Variable cost per unit}$$

$$= \$17.50 \text{ per unit} - \$12.10 \text{ per unit} \qquad \textbf{(25)}$$

$$= \$5.40 \text{ per unit}$$

So, Trilex's breakeven volume is as follows:

$$\frac{\text{Breakeven}}{\text{volume (units)}} = \frac{\text{Total fixed costs}}{\text{(Per unit contribution margin)}}$$

$$= \frac{\$390,000}{\$5.40 \text{ per unit}} \qquad \textbf{(26)}$$

$$= 72,222 \text{ units}$$

To convert this number of units to breakeven sales dollars, Trilex simply multiplies it by the selling price per unit:

$$\text{Breakeven sales} = 72,222 \text{ units} \times \$17.50 = \$1,263,889 \qquad \textbf{(27)}$$

Trilex could compute the sales required to produce a desired profit by treating the profit as if it were a fixed cost:

$$\text{Sales (units)} = \frac{\text{Total fixed costs} + \text{Desired net income}}{\text{Per unit contribution margin}} \qquad \textbf{(28)}$$

For example, if Trilex wanted to earn a $60,000 profit, its required sales would be:

$$\text{Sales (units)} = \frac{\$390,000 + \$60,000}{5.40} = 83,333 \text{ units} \qquad \textbf{(29)}$$

Constructing a Breakeven Chart. The following outlines the procedure for constructing a graph that visually portrays the firm's breakeven point (that point where revenues equal expenses):

Step 1. On the horizontal axis, mark a scale measuring sales volume in dollars (or in units sold or some other measure of volume). The breakeven chart for the Magic Shop shown in Figure 8.8 uses sales volume in dollars because it applies to all types of businesses, departments, and products.

Step 2. On the vertical axis, mark a scale measuring income and expenses in dollars.

Step 3. Draw a fixed expense line intersecting the vertical axis at the proper dollar level parallel to the horizontal axis. The area between this line and the horizontal axis represents the firm's fixed expenses. On the breakeven chart for the Magic Shop shown in Figure 8.8, the fixed expense line is drawn horizontally beginning at $177,375 (point A). Because this line is parallel to the horizontal axis, it indicates that fixed expenses remain constant at all levels of activity.

Step 4. Draw a total expense line that slopes upward beginning at the point where the fixed cost line intersects the vertical axis. The precise location of the total expense line is determined by plotting the total cost incurred at a particular sales volume. The total cost for a given sales level is found by the following formula:

$$\text{Total expenses} = \text{Fixed expenses} +$$
$$\text{Variable expenses expressed as a percentage of sales} \times \text{Sales level} \qquad \textbf{(30)}$$

Figure 8.8
Breakeven Chart,
the Magic Shop

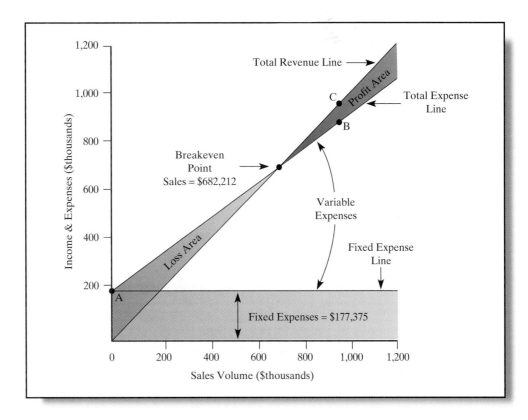

Arbitrarily choosing a sales level of $950,000, the Magic Shop's total costs would be as follows:

$$\text{Total expenses} = \$177,375 + (0.74 \times \$950,000)$$

(31)

$$= \$880,375$$

Thus, the Magic Shop's total cost is $880,375 at a net sales level of $950,000 (point B). The variable cost line is drawn by connecting points A and B. The area between the total cost line and the horizontal axis measures the total costs the Magic Shop incurs at various levels of sales. For example, if the Magic Shop's sales are $850,000, its total costs will be $806,375.

Step 5. Beginning at the graph's origin, draw a 45-degree revenue line showing where total sales volume equals total income. For the Magic Shop, point C shows that sales = income = $950,000.

Step 6. Locate the breakeven point by finding the intersection of the total expense line and the revenue line. If the Magic Shop operates at a sales volume to the left of the breakeven point, it will incur a loss because the expense line is higher than the revenue line over this range. This is shown by the triangular section labeled "Loss Area." On the other hand, if the firm operates at a sales volume to the right of the breakeven point, it will earn a profit because the revenue line lies above the expense line over this range. This is shown by the triangular section labeled "Profit Area."

Using Breakeven Analysis. Breakeven analysis is a useful planning tool for the potential small business owner, especially when approaching potential lenders and investors for funds. It provides an opportunity for integrated analysis of sales volume, expenses, income, and other relevant factors. Breakeven analysis is a simple, preliminary screening device for the entrepreneur faced with the business start-up decision. It is easy to understand and use. With just a few calculations, an entrepreneur can determine the minimum level of sales needed to stay in business as well as the effects of various financial strategies on the business. It is a helpful tool for evaluating the impact of changes in investments and expenditures. *For instance, before Steve Wynn opened the $630 million dollar Mirage, an opulent casino–hotel complex in Las Vegas, a cost-revenue analysis showed that the complex needed revenues of $365 million a year—$1 million a day—just to break even! Although many people doubted the casino–hotel's ability to generate that level of revenue, the Mirage has done so consistently. In its first year of operation, the Mirage brought in an average of $1.97 million each day!*[14] Although few small companies have breakeven points as high as the Mirage's (much to the relief of entrepreneurs!), the breakeven point can be just as useful. Greg Smith, for instance, knows that Petra Group's breakeven point is $23,000 per week, and he compares sales to that figure every week.[15]

Breakeven analysis does have certain limitations. It is too simple to use as a final screening device because it ignores the importance of cash flows. Also, the accuracy of the analysis depends on the accuracy of the revenue and expense estimates. Finally, the assumptions pertaining to breakeven analysis may not be realistic for some businesses. Breakeven calculations assume the following: fixed expenses remain constant for all levels of sales volume; variable expenses change in direct proportion to changes in sales volume; and changes in sales volume have no effect on unit sales price. Relaxing these assumptions does not render this tool useless, however. For example, the owner could employ nonlinear breakeven analysis using a graphical approach.

CHAPTER SUMMARY

1. Understand the importance of preparing a financial plan.
   - Launching a successful business requires an entrepreneur to create a solid financial plan. Not only is such a plan an important tool in raising the capital needed to get a company off the ground, but it also is an essential ingredient in managing a growing business.
   - Earning a profit does not occur by accident; it takes planning.
2. Describe how to prepare the basic financial statements and use them to manage the small business.
   - Entrepreneurs rely on three basic financial statements to understand the financial conditions of their companies:
     - *The balance sheet.* Built on the accounting equation: Assets = Liabilities + Owner's Equity (Capital), it provides an estimate of the company's value on a particular date.
     - *The income statement.* This statement compares the firm's revenues against its expenses to determine its net income (or

loss). It provides information about the company's bottom line.
     - *The statement of cash flows.* This statement shows the change in the company's working capital over the accounting period by listing the sources and the uses of funds.
3. Create pro forma financial statements.
   - Projected financial statements are a basic component of a sound financial plan. They help the manager plot the company's financial future by setting operating objectives and by analyzing the reasons for variations from targeted results. Also, the small business in search of start-up funds will need these pro forma statements to present to prospective lenders and investors. They also assist in determining the amount of cash, inventory, fixtures, and other assets the business will need to begin operation.
4. Understand the basic financial statements through ratio analysis.
   - The 12 key ratios described in this chapter are divided into four major categories: liquidity ratios, which show the small firm's

ability to meet its current obligations; leverage ratios, which tell how much of the company's financing is provided by owners and how much by creditors; operating ratios, which show how effectively the firm uses its resources; and profitability ratios, which disclose the company's profitability.

- Many agencies and organizations regularly publish such statistics. If there is a discrepancy between the small firm's ratios and those of the typical business, the owner should investigate the reason for the difference. A below-average ratio does not necessarily mean that the business is in trouble.

5. Explain how to interpret financial ratios.
   - To benefit from ratio analysis, the small company should compare its ratios to those of other companies in the same line of business and look for trends over time.

- When business owners detect deviations in their companies' ratios from industry standards, they should determine the cause of the deviations. In some cases, such deviations are the result of sound business decisions; in other instances, however, ratios that are out of the normal range for a particular type of business are indicators of what could become serious problems for a company.

6. Conduct a breakeven analysis for a small company.
   - Business owners should know their firm's breakeven point, the level of operations at which total revenues equal total costs; it is the point at which companies neither earn a profit nor incur a loss. Although just a simple screening device, breakeven analysis is a useful planning and decision-making tool.

DISCUSSION QUESTIONS

1. Why is it important for entrepreneurs to develop financial plans for their companies?
2. How should a small business manager use the ratios discussed in this chapter?
3. Outline the key points of the 12 ratios discussed in this chapter. What signals does each give a business owner?
4. Describe the method for building a projected income statement and a projected balance sheet for a beginning business.
5. Why are pro forma financial statements important to the financial planning process?
6. How can breakeven analysis help an entrepreneur planning to launch a business? What information does it give an entrepreneur?

STEP INTO THE REAL WORLD

1. Ask the owner of a small business to provide your class with copies of the firm's financial statements (current or past) or go to the SEC's EDGAR file at *www.freeedgar.com* or to the 10K Wizard at *www.10kwizard.com/* to find the financial statements of a publicly held company that interests you.
   a. Using these statements, compute the twelve key ratios described in this chapter.
   b. Compare the firm's ratios with those of the typical firm in this line of business.
   c. Interpret the ratios and make suggestions for operating improvements.
   d. Prepare a breakeven analysis for the business.
2. Use the World Wide Web to research the retail grocery industry and to develop a set of interview questions for the owner or manager of a local grocery store. What is the store's net profit margin? What techniques is the store using to enhance its profits? What are the primary financial challenges in this business? Prepare a brief report on your findings for your class.
3. Interview a local entrepreneur about his or her business. Is he/she pleased with the company's financial performance? Does the company have financial objectives? What challenges does the company face when meeting its financial targets? Which costs are most difficult to control? Why? What are the company's critical numbers? Does the owner track them? If so, how often?

TAKE IT TO THE NET

Visit the Scarborough/Zimmerer home page at **www.prenhall.com/scarborough** for updated information, online resources, Web-based exercises, and sample business plan.

ENDNOTES

1. Eileen Davis, "Dodging the Bullet," *Venture,* December 1988, p. 78.
2. "Odds and Ends," *Wall Street Journal,* July 25, 1990, p. B1.
3. Richard G.P. McMahon and Scott Holmes, "Small Business Financial Management Practices in North America: A Literature Review," *Journal of Small Business Management,* April 1991, p. 21.
4. Daniel Kehrer, "Big Ideas for Your Small Business," *Changing Times,* November 1989, p. 57.
5. Diedrich Von Soosten, "The Roots of Financial Destruction," *Industry Week,* April 5, 1993, pp. 33–34.
6. McMahon and Holmes, "Small Business Financial Management Practices in North America: A Literature Review."
7. Lori Ioannou, "He's Preaching the Power of Thrift," *Fortune,* October 30, 2000, p. 208[P].
8. "Analyzing Creditworthiness," *Inc.,* November 1991, p. 196.
9. Jill Andresky Fraser, "Giving Credit to Debt," *Inc.,* November 2000, p. 125.
10. Ilan Mochari, "Give Credit to the Small Business Owner," *Inc.,* March 2001, p. 88.
11. Ilan Mochari, "Significant Figures," *Inc.,* July 1, 2000, p. 128; www2.inc.com/search/ 19690.html
12. William F. Doescher, "Taking Stock," *Entrepreneur,* November 1994, p. 64.
13. Ibid.
14. Robert Macy, "Mirage Megaresort Changed Face and Fortunes of Las Vegas," *Greenville News,* November 25, 1999, p. 22A.
15. Mochari, "Significant Figures," p. 128.

Chapter 9

Managing Cash Flow

Upon completion of this chapter, you will be able to:

1. Explain the importance of cash management to the success of a small business.
2. Differentiate between cash and profits.
3. Understand the five steps in creating a cash budget and use them to build a cash budget.
4. Describe fundamental principles involved in managing the "Big Three" of cash management: accounts receivable, accounts payable, and inventory.
5. Explain the techniques for avoiding a cash crunch in a small company.

Cash—a four-letter word that has become a curse for many small businesses. Lack of this valuable asset has driven countless small companies into bankruptcy. Unfortunately, many more firms will become failure statistics because their owners have neglected the principles of cash management that can spell the difference between success and failure. One small business owner compares a small company's cash to oxygen on a space trip[1]:

> Astronauts who take off on a long space flight must take along plenty of food and water (their "healthy balance sheet"). But if they happen to run out of oxygen any time between takeoff and landing, all that food and water is of no use to them; they will perish. Cash is like oxygen to a business. When it's there, it's easily taken for granted. When it's not, death can come quickly.

Developing a cash forecast is essential for new businesses because early sales levels usually do not generate sufficient cash to keep the company afloat. Too often, entrepreneurs launch their companies with insufficient cash to cover their start-up costs and the cash flow gap that results while expenses outstrip revenues. The result is business failure.

Controlling the financial aspects of a business with the profit-planning techniques described in the previous chapter is immensely important; however, by themselves, these techniques are insufficient to achieve business success. Entrepreneurs are prone to focus on their companies' income statements—particularly sales and profits. The balance sheet and the income statement, of course, show an important part of a company's financial picture, but it is just that: only part of the total picture. It is entirely possible for a business to have a solid balance sheet and to make a profit and still go out of business by *running out of cash*. Managing cash effectively requires an entrepreneur to look beyond the "bottom line" and focus on what it takes to keep a company going—cash.

CASH MANAGEMENT

1. Explain the importance of cash management to the success of a small business.

Cash management involves forecasting, collecting, disbursing, investing, and planning for the cash a company needs to operate smoothly. Managing cash is an important task because cash is the most important yet least productive asset that a small business owns. A business must have enough cash to meet its obligations as they come due or it will be declared bankrupt. Creditors, employees, and lenders expect to be paid on time, and cash is the required medium of exchange. But some firms retain an excessive amount of cash to meet any unexpected circumstances that might arise. These dormant dollars have an income-earning potential that the owners are ignoring, and this restricts the firm's growth and lowers its profitability. Proper cash management permits entrepreneurs to adequately meet the cash demands of their businesses, to avoid retaining unnecessarily large cash balances, and to stretch the profit-generating power of each dollar their companies own.

One survey asking small business owners to identify their "greatest financial obstacle" found that the most common response was "uneven cash flow."[2] Managing cash flow is an acute problem especially for young, rapidly growing businesses. Fast-track companies are most likely to suffer cash shortages because they act like "cash sponges," soaking up every available dollar and then some. A study of successful business owners conducted by Geneva Business Bank found that the greatest potential threat to cash flow occurs when a company is experiencing rapid growth.[3] *Aliza Sherman learned about the cash problems that rapid growth can bring about in her second year of business. "My partner pulled me into his office one day and announced, 'If we don't get a check in by Friday, we won't make payroll,'" she recalls. "That couldn't be possible! We had a* *slew of clients, a ton of work in production." Then she discovered that the company had $250,000 in accounts receivable but less than $10,000 in available cash. "Whatever money came in immediately went to paying bills that had accumulated from several months back. No matter how much revenue we generated, we could never get ahead." Fortunately for Sherman and her partner, a check did arrive in time for them to meet payroll, and the partners began focusing more on cash flow management to avoid similar problems in the future.*[4]

Unfortunately, many small business owners do not engage in cash planning. One study of 2,200 small businesses found that 68 percent performed no cash flow analysis at all![5] The result is that many successful, growing, and profitable businesses fail because they become insolvent; they do not have adequate cash to meet the needs of a growing business with a booming sales volume. If a company's sales are up, the owner also must hire more employees, expand plant capacity, increase the sales force, build inventory, and incur other drains on the firm's cash supply. The head of the National Federation of Independent Businesses says that many small business owners "wake up one day to find that the price of success is no cash on hand. They don't understand that if they're successful, inventory and receivables will increase faster than profits can fund them."[6] The resulting cash crisis may force the owner to lose equity control of the business or, ultimately, declare bankruptcy and close.

Table 9.1 describes the five key cash management roles every entrepreneur must fill.

The first step in managing cash more effectively is to understand the company's **cash flow cycle**—the time lag between paying suppliers for merchandise and receiving payment from customers (see Figure 9.1). The longer this cash flow cycle, the more likely the business owner is to encounter a cash crisis. Preparing a cash forecast that recognizes this cycle, however, will help avoid a crisis.

John Fernsell recognizes the importance of cash management because of the length of his company's cash flow cycle. Fernsell, a former stockbroker, is the founder of Ibex Outdoor Clothing, a company that makes outdoor clothing from high-quality European wool. Ibex's sales

Table 9.1

Five Cash Management Roles of the Entrepreneur

Role 1: Cash Finder. This is the entrepreneur's first and foremost responsibility. You must make sure there is enough capital to pay all present (and future) bills. This is not a one-time task; it is an on-going job.

Role 2: Cash Planner. As cash planner, an entrepreneur makes sure the company's cash is used properly and efficiently. You must keep track of its cash, make sure it is available to pay bills, and plan for its future use. Planning requires you to forecast the company's cash inflows and outflows for the months ahead with the help of a cash budget (discussed later in this chapter).

Role 3: Cash Distributor. This role requires you to control the cash needed to pay the company's bills and the priority and the timing of those payments. Forecasting cash disbursements accurately and making sure the cash is available when payments come due is essential to keeping the business solvent.

Role 4: Cash Collector. As cash collector, your job is to make sure your customers pay their bills on time. Too often, entrepreneurs focus on pumping up sales, while neglecting to collect the cash from those sales. Having someone in your company responsible for collecting accounts receivable is essential. Uncollected accounts drain a small company's pool of cash very quickly.

Role 5: Cash Conserver. This role requires you to make sure your company gets maximum value for the dollars it spends. Whether you are buying inventory to resell or computers to keep track of what you sell, it is important to get the most for your money. Avoiding unnecessary expenditures is an important part of this task. The goal is to spend cash so it will produce a return for the company.

Source: Adapted from Bruce J. Blechman, "Quick Change Artist," *Entrepreneur,* January 1994, pp. 18–21.

Figure 9.1
The Cash Flow Cycle

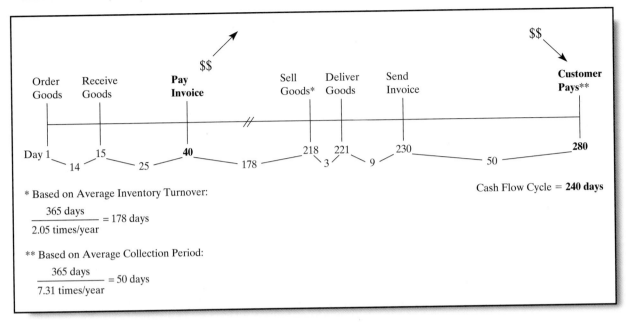

* Based on Average Inventory Turnover:

$$\frac{365 \text{ days}}{2.05 \text{ times/year}} = 178 \text{ days}$$

** Based on Average Collection Period:

$$\frac{365 \text{ days}}{7.31 \text{ times/year}} = 50 \text{ days}$$

Cash Flow Cycle = **240 days**

are growing rapidly, but cash is a constant problem because of its lengthy cash flow cycle. Fernsell orders wool from his European suppliers in February and pays for it in June. The wool then goes to garment makers in California, who ship finished clothing to Ibex in July and August, when Fernsell pays for the finished goods. Ibex ships the clothing to retailers in September and October but does not get paid until November, December, and sometimes January! Ibex's major cash outflows are from June to August, but its cash inflows during those months are virtually nil, making it essential for Fernsell to manage the company's cash balances carefully.[7]

The next step in effective cash management is to begin cutting down the length of the cash flow cycle. Reducing the cycle from 240 days to, say, 150 days would free up incredible amounts of cash that this company could use to finance growth and dramatically reduce its borrowing costs. What steps would you suggest the owner of the business whose cash flow cycle is illustrated in Figure 9.1 take to reduce the cycle's length?

CASH AND PROFITS ARE NOT THE SAME

2. Differentiate between cash and profits.

When analyzing cash flow, a small business manager must understand that cash and profits are not the same. Profit (or net income) is the difference between a company's total revenue and its total expenses. It measures how efficiently the business is operating. Cash is the money that is readily available to use in a business. **Cash flow** measures a company's liquidity and its ability to pay its bills and other financial obligations on time by tracking the flow of cash into and goes out of the business over a period of time. Figure 9.2 shows the flow of cash through a typical small business. Decreases in cash occur when a business purchases, on credit or for cash, goods for inventory or materials for use in production. The resulting inventory is sold either for cash or on credit. When cash is taken in or when accounts receivable are collected, the firm's cash balance increases. Notice that purchases for inventory and production *lead* sales; that is, these bills typically must be paid *before* sales are generated. But, col-

Section III   Building the Business Plan: Marketing and Financial Matters

Figure 9.2
Cash Flow

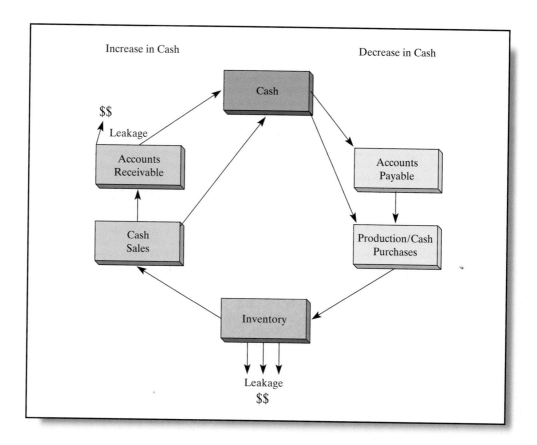

lection of accounts receivable *lags* behind sales; that is, customers who purchase goods on credit may not pay until a month or more later.

As important as earning a profit is, no business owner can pay creditors, employees, and lenders in profits; that requires *cash!* Although profits are tied up in many forms, such as inventory, computers, or machinery, cash is the money that flows through a business in a continuous cycle without being tied up in any other asset. A company can operate in the short run at a negative profit, but if its cash flow is negative, the business is in trouble. It can no longer pay suppliers, meet payroll, pay its taxes, or any other bills. In short, the business is headed for extinction.

THE CASH BUDGET

The need for a cash budget arises because in every business the cash flowing in is rarely "in sync" with the cash flowing out. This uneven flow of cash creates periodic cash surpluses and shortages, making it necessary for entrepreneurs to track the flow of cash through their businesses so they can project realistically the cash available throughout the year. Many owners operate their businesses without knowing the pattern of their cash flows, believing that the process is too complex or time consuming. In reality, entrepreneurs simply cannot afford to disregard the process of cash management. They must ensure that an adequate, but not excessive, supply of cash is on hand to meet their companies' operating needs.

How much cash is enough? What is suitable for one business may be totally inadequate for another, depending on each firm's size, nature, and particular situation. The small business manager should prepare a **cash budget,** which is nothing more than a "cash map," showing the amount and timing of the cash receipts and the cash disbursements day-by-day, week-by-week, or month-by-month. It is used to predict the amount of cash the firm will need to operate smoothly over a specific period of time, and it is a valuable tool in managing a company successfully.

PREPARING A CASH BUDGET

3. Understand the five steps in creating a cash budget and use them to build a cash budget.

Typically, a small business should prepare a projected monthly cash budget for at least one year and quarterly estimates one or two years beyond that. To be effective, a cash budget must cover all seasonal sales fluctuations. The more variable the firm's sales pattern, the shorter its planning horizon should be. For example, a firm whose sales fluctuate widely over a relatively short time frame might require a weekly cash budget. The key to managing cash flow successfully is to monitor not only the amount of cash flowing into and out of a company but also the *timing* of those cash flows.

Regardless of the time frame selected, a cash budget must be in writing for the small business owner to properly visualize the firms' cash position. Creating a written cash plan is not an excessively time-consuming task and can help the owner avoid unexpected cash shortages, a situation that can cause a business to fail. One financial consultant describes "a client who won't be able to make the payroll this month. His bank agreed to meet the payroll for him—but banks don't like to be surprised like that," he adds.[8] Preparing a cash budget will help business owners avoid such adverse surprises. It will also let the owner know if he is keeping excessively high amounts of cash on hand. Computer spreadsheets such as Excel and Lotus 1-2-3 make the job fast and easy to complete and allow for instant changes.

The cash budget is based on the cash method of accounting, which means that cash receipts and cash disbursements are recorded in the forecast only when the cash transaction is expected to take place. For example, credit sales to customers are not reported until the company expects to receive the cash from them. Similarly, purchases made on credit are not recorded until the owner expects to pay them. Because depreciation, bad debt expense, and other noncash items involve no cash transfers, they are omitted entirely from the cash budget.

A cash budget is nothing more than a forecast of the firm's cash inflows and outflows for a specific time period, and it will never be completely accurate. But it does give the small business manager a clear picture of the firm's estimated cash balance for the period, pointing out where external cash infusions may be required or where surplus cash balances may be available for investing. Also, by comparing actual cash flows with projections, the owner can revise his forecast so that future cash budgets will be more accurate. *Michael Koss, president and CEO of Koss Corporation, a manufacturer of stereo headphones, now emphasizes cash flow management after his company's brush with failure. In the 1980s, Koss Corporation expanded rapidly—so rapidly, in fact, that its cash flow couldn't keep pace. Debt climbed, and the company filed for reorganization under chapter 11 bankruptcy. Emergency actions saved the business, and today Koss manages with the determination never to repeat the same mistakes. "I look at cash every single day," he says. "That is absolutely critical."[9]*

Formats for preparing a cash budget vary depending on the pattern of a company's cash flow. Table 9.2 shows a monthly cash budget for a small department store over a four-month period. Each monthly column should be divided into two sections—estimated and actual (not shown)—so that each succeeding cash forecast

Table 9.2
Cash Budget for Small Department Store

Assumptions:

Cash balance on December 31 = $12,000

Minimum cash balance desired = $10,000

Sales are 75% credit and 25% cash.

Credit sales are collected in the following manner:

- 60% collected in the first month after the sale
- 30% collected in the second month after the sale
- 5% collected in the third month after the sale
- 5% are never collected.

SALES FORECASTS ARE AS FOLLOWS:	PESSIMISTIC	MOST LIKELY	OPTIMISTIC
October (actual)		$300,000	
November (actual)		350,000	
December (actual)		400,000	
January	$120,000	150,000	$175,000
February	160,000	200,000	250,000
March	160,000	200,000	250,000
April	250,000	300,000	340,000

The store pays 70% of sales price for merchandise purchased and pays for each month's anticipated sales in the preceding month.

Rent is $2,000 per month.

An interest payment of $7,500 is due in March.

A tax prepayment of $50,000 must be made in March.

A capital addition payment of $130,000 is due in February.

Utilities expenses amount to $850 per month.

Miscellaneous expenses are $70 per month.

Interest income of $200 will be received in February.

Wages and salaries are estimated to be

   January—$30,000

   February—$40,000

   March—$45,000

   April—$50,000

Cash Budget—Pessimistic Sales Forecast

	OCT.	NOV.	DEC.	JAN.	FEB.	MAR.	APR.
Cast Receipts:							
Sales	$300,000	$350,000	$400,000	$120,000	$160,000	$160,000	$250,000
Credit Sales	225,000	262,500	300,000	90,000	120,000	120,000	187,500
Collections:							
60%—1st month after sale				$180,000	$ 54,000	$ 72,000	$ 72,000
30%—2nd month after sale				78,750	90,000	27,000	36,000
5%—3rd month after sale				11,250	13,125	15,000	4,500
Cash Sales				30,000	40,000	40,000	62,500
Interest				0	200	0	0
Total Cash Receipts				$300,000	$197,325	$154,000	$175,000

(continued)

Table 9.2
Cash Budget for Small Department Store *(continued)*

Cash Budget—Pessimistic Sales Forecast *(continued)*

Cash Disbursements:

Purchases	$112,000	$112,000	$175,000	$133,000
Rent	2,000	2,000	2,000	2,000
Utilities	850	850	850	850
Interest	0	0	7,500	0
Tax Prepayment	0	0	50,000	0
Capital Addition	0	130,000	0	0
Miscellaneous	70	70	70	70
Wages/Salaries	30,000	40,000	45,000	50,000
Total Cash Disbursements	$144,920	$284,920	$280,420	$185,920

End-of-Month Balance:

Cash (beginning of month)	$ 12,000	$167,080	$79,485	$ 10,000
+ Cash Receipts	300,000	197,325	154,000	175,000
– Cash Disbursements	144,920	284,920	280,420	185,920
Cash (end of month)	167,080	79,485	(46,935)	(920)
Borrowing/Repayment	0	0	56,935	10,920
Cash (end of month [after borrowing])	$167,080	$ 79,485	$ 10,000	$ 10,000

Cash Budget—Most Likely Sales Forecast

	Oct.	Nov.	Dec.	Jan.	Feb.	Mar.	Apr.
Cash Receipts:							
Sales	$300,000	$350,000	$400,000	$ 150,000	$ 200,000	$ 200,000	$ 300,000
Credit Sales	225,000	262,500	300,000	112,000	150,000	150,000	225,000
Collections:							
60%—1st month after sale				$180,000	$ 67,500	$ 90,000	$ 90,000
30%—2nd month after sale				78,750	90,000	33,750	45,000
5%—3rd month after sale				11,250	13,125	15,000	5,625
Cash Sales				37,500	50,000	50,000	75,000
Interest				0	200	0	0
Total Cash Receipts				$307,500	$220,825	$188,750	$215,625
Cash Disbursements:							
Purchases				$140,000	$140,000	$210,000	$175,000
Rent				2,000	2,000	2,000	2,000
Utilities				850	850	850	850
Interest				0	0	7,500	0
Tax Prepayment				0	0	50,000	0
Capital Addition				0	130,000	0	0
Miscellaneous				70	70	70	70
Wages/Salaries				30,000	40,000	45,000	50,000
Total Cash Disbursements				$172,920	$312,920	$315,420	$227,920

Cash Budget—Most Likely Sales Forecast *(continued)*

End-of-Month Balance:

Cash [beginning of month]	$ 12,000	$146,580	$ 54,485	$ 10,000
+ Cash Receipts	307,500	220,825	188,750	215,625
– Cash Disbursements	172,920	312,920	315,420	227,920
Cash (end of month)	146,580	54,485	(72,185)	(2,295)
Borrowing/Repayment	0	0	82,185	12,295
Cash (end of month [after borrowing])	$146,580	$ 54,485	$ 10,000	$ 10,000

Cash Budget—Optimistic Sales Forecast

	Oct.	Nov.	Dec.	Jan.	Feb.	Mar.	Apr.
Cash Receipts:							
Sales	$300,000	$350,000	$400,000	$175,000	$250,000	$250,000	$340,000
Credit Sales	225,000	262,500	300,000	131,250	187,500	187,500	255,000
Collections:							
60%—1st month after sale				$180,000	$ 78,750	$112,500	$112,500
30%—2nd month after sale				78,750	90,000	39,375	56,250
5%—3rd month after sale				11,250	13,125	15,000	6,563
Cash Sales				43,750	62,500	62,500	85,000
Interest				0	200	0	0
Total Cash Receipts				$313,750	$244,575	$229,375	$260,313
Cash Disbursements:							
Purchases				$175,000	$175,000	$238,000	$217,000
Rent				2,000	2,000	2,000	2,000
Utilities				850	850	850	850
Interest				0	0	7,500	0
Tax Prepayment				0	0	50,000	0
Capital Addition				0	130,000	0	0
Miscellaneous				70	70	70	70
Wages/Salaries				30,000	40,000	45,000	50,000
Total Cash Disbursements				$207,920	$347,920	$343,420	$269,920
End-of-Month Balance:							
Cash [beginning of month]				$ 12,000	$117,830	$ 14,485	$ 10,000
+ Cash Receipts				313,750	244,575	229,375	296,125
– Cash Disbursements				207,920	317,920	343,120	269,920
Cash (end of month)				117,830	14,485	(99,560)	36,205
Borrowing/Repayment				0	0	109,560	0
Cash (end of month [after borrowing])				$117,830	$ 14,485	$ 10,000	$ 36,205

can be updated according to actual cash transactions. There are five basic steps in completing a cash budget:

1. Determining an adequate minimum cash balance
2. Forecasting sales
3. Forecasting cash receipts
4. Forecasting cash disbursements
5. Determining the end-of-month cash balance

Step 1: Determining an Adequate Minimum Cash Balance

What is considered an excessive cash balance for one small business may be inadequate for another, even though the two firms are in the same trade. Some suggest that a firm's cash balance should equal at least one-fourth of its current debts, but this clearly will not work for all small businesses. The most reliable method of deciding cash balance is based on past experience. Past operating records should indicate the proper cash cushion needed to cover any unexpected expenses after all normal cash outlays are deducted from the month's cash receipts. For example, past records may indicate that it is desirable to maintain a cash balance equal to five days' sales. Seasonal fluctuations may cause the firm's minimum cash balance to change. For example, the desired cash balance for a retailer in December may be greater than in June.

Step 2: Forecasting Sales

The heart of the cash budget is the sales forecast. It is the central factor in creating an accurate picture of the firm's cash position because sales ultimately are transformed into cash receipts and cash disbursements. For most businesses, sales constitute the major source of the cash flowing into the business. Similarly, sales of merchandise require that cash be used to replenish inventory. As a result, the cash budget is only as accurate as the sales forecast from which it is derived.

For the established business, the sales forecast can be based on past sales, but the owner must be careful not to be excessively optimistic in projecting sales. Economic swings, increased competition, fluctuations in demand, and other factors can drastically alter sales patterns.

Several quantitative techniques, which are beyond the scope of this text (e.g., linear regression, multiple regression, time series analysis, exponential smoothing), are available to the owner of an existing business with an established sales pattern for forecasting sales. These methods enable the small business owner to extrapolate past and present sales trends to arrive at a fairly accurate sales forecast.

The task of forecasting sales for a new firm is difficult but not impossible. For example, an entrepreneur might conduct research on similar firms and their sales patterns in the first year of operation to come up with a forecast. The local Chamber of Commerce and trade associations in the various industries also collect such information. Marketing research is another source of information that may be used to estimate annual sales for the fledgling firm. Other potential sources that may help predict sales include census reports, newspapers, radio and television customer profiles, polls and surveys, and local government statistics. Table 9.3 gives an example of how one entrepreneur used such marketing information to derive a sales forecast for his first year of operation.

No matter what techniques the small business manager employs, he must recognize even the best sales estimate will be wrong. Many financial analysts suggest

Table 9.3
Forecasting Sales
for a Business
Start-Up

Robert Adler wants to open a repair shop for imported cars. The trade association for automotive garages estimates that the owner of an imported car spends an average of $485 per year on repairs and maintenance. The typical garage attracts its clientele from a trading zone (the area from which a business draws its customers) with a 20-mile radius. Census reports show that the families within a 20-mile radius of Robert's proposed location own 84,000 cars, of which 24 percent are imports. Based on a local market consultant's research, Robert believes he can capture 9.9 percent of the market this year. Robert's estimate of his company's first year's sales are as follows:

Number of cars in trading zone	84,000 autos
× Percent of imports	× 24%
= Number of imported cars in trading zone	20,160 imports
Number of imports in trading zone	20,160
× Average expenditure on repairs and maintenance	× $485
= Total import repair potential	$9,777,600
Total import repair sales potential	$9,777,600
× Estimated share of market	× 9.9%
= Sales estimate	$967,982

Now Robert Adler can convert this annual sales estimate of $967,982 into monthly sales estimates for use in his company's cash budget.

that the owner create *three estimates*—an optimistic, a pessimistic, and a most likely sales estimate—and then make a separate cash budget for each forecast (a very simple task with a computer spreadsheet). This dynamic forecast enables an entrepreneur to determine the range within which his sales and cash flows will likely be as the year progresses.

Step 3: Forecasting Cash Receipts

As noted earlier, sales constitute the major source of cash receipts. When a firm sells goods and services on credit, the cash budget must count for the delay between the sale and the actual collection of the proceeds. Remember: You cannot spend cash you haven't collected yet! For instance, proceeds for appliances sold in February might not be collected until March or April, and the cash budget must reflect this delay. To project accurately a firm's cash receipts, an entrepreneur must analyze the accounts receivable to determine the collection pattern. For example, past records may indicate that 20 percent of sales are for cash, 50 percent are paid in the month following the sale, 20 percent are paid two months after the sale, 7 percent after three months, and 3 percent are never collected. In addition to cash and credit sales, a cash budget must include any other cash the company receives—interest income, rental income, dividends, and others.

Some small business owners never discover the hidden danger in accounts receivable until it is too late for their companies. Receivables act as cash sponges, tying up valuable dollars until an entrepreneur collects them. *When Mary and Phil Baechler started Baby Jogger Company in 1983 to make strollers that would enable parents to take their babies along on their daily runs, Mary was in charge of the financial aspects of the business and watched its cash flow closely. As the company grew, the couple created an accounting department to handle its financial affairs. Unfortunately, the financial management system could not keep up with the company's rapid growth and failed to provide the nec-*

Selling globally is an excellent strategy for boosting sales and profits, but only if you get paid for what you sell! Collecting bills from foreign customers is more difficult than collecting from customers next door. For instance, collecting accounts receivable from U.S. companies takes an average of 42 days. Collecting payment from foreign customers usually takes a good deal longer, however. For example, the countries with the worst payment records include Iran (310 days), Syria (175 days), Chile (109 days), and Ecuador (107 days).

The head of one European debt-collection operation says, "On average, all payments [in Europe] are made 15 days late for domestic trade and 16 days late for exports." Late-paying customers put pressure on companies' cash flow. One study of European companies reported that late payments mean higher interest costs for 80 percent of businesses. In addition, 60 percent reported liquidity problems.

Uniform laws giving businesses the right to pursue late payers and to add interest charges to their accounts do not exist across Europe. "U.S. companies make a big mistake when they assume that they can deal with problem foreign accounts the same way they do [in the United States]," says the head of an international collection agency. "No way. In countries like Mexico, for example, the legal process involved in chasing after a problem payer is very, very complicated." As a result, some companies have developed some rather unusual strategies for encouraging their customers to pay their bills on time. In Venezuela, one debt collection agency shows up at delinquent businesses in a hot-rod truck with a siren wailing. Out pops a man in a devil costume carrying a briefcase with "Deadbeat Collections" printed on it. His entourage includes a woman in a red miniskirt, a large Great Dane, and a lawyer. Many embarrassed business owners pay up on the spot!

Before they send thousands of dollars of merchandise halfway around the world, U.S. entrepreneurs must take some basic precautions to make sure their foreign customers will pay their bills. The following techniques have worked for many small businesses:

Require cash in advance. To eliminate the risk of not getting paid, Jean-Luc Berne, president of Plein Air Inc., an exporter of automotive parts, required his foreign customers to pay cash in advance. Such terms can make it hard to sell in the global market, however.

Purchase export credit insurance. After his company's sales began to slip, Berne changed tactics. Now, he buys credit insurance from Eximbank, a government agency that provides export assistance, to protect his receivables.

Secure a letter of credit. For some small companies, the cost of export credit insurance is prohibitive. Perhaps the easiest and safest way to guarantee payment from a foreign customer is to secure a letter of credit from its bank. If the customer defaults, then the bank issuing the letter of credit must make the payment. Because letters of credit have expiration dates, business owners must process their paperwork promptly.

Research a country's payment norms and creditor protection laws before shipping goods. The International Trade Association (*www.ita.doc.gov*) and the Export–Import Bank (*www.exim.gov/*) are excellent sources of this information. It is also a good idea to keep abreast of the political and economic conditions in countries where major customers are located. The U.S. Department of Commerce offers a variety of publications and several "country desks" that track such information.

Conduct thorough credit checks on all prospective foreign customers. Many of the credit-checking services mentioned in this chapter also offer international evaluations. Some services specialize in international credit reports, which range in price from $47 to $275, depending on the level of detail:

> Graydon America (*www.graydonamerica.com*)
> Veritas (*www.veritas-usa.com/index_eng.html*)
> Whitehall Consultants (*www.whitehallusa.com/*)

In addition, for a reasonable fee, the International Trade Administration at the U.S. Department of Commerce will prepare World Traders Data Reports that provide information on the reliability and the financial status of overseas companies.

Bill only in American dollars and insist on payment in American currency. This will shield against losses

(continued)

due to fluctuations in currency exchange rates. "A lot of exporters are shocked to learn that they could lose 25 percent of the value of their receivables overnight" to currency fluctuations, says one expert.

Sources: Adapted from Marc Lifsher, "In Venezuela, If You Don't Pay Bills, a Devil Might Pay You a Visit," *Wall Street Journal*, June 25, 2001, pp. A1, A8; Karby Legget, "Chinese Deadbeats Cringe at the Sound of Mr. Li's Gong," *Wall Street Journal*, September 21, 2000, pp. A1, A16; "Risky Business," *Small Business Reports*, January 1994, p. 7; "Risky Business," *Small Business Reports*, November 1992, p. 8; Heidi Jacobs, "Payments from Afar," *Small Business Reports*, May 1993, pp. 21–25; Nigel Dudley, "Creative Debt Collecting," *Profiles*, August 1994, p. 19; *www.ita.doc.gov/how_to_export/finance.html*; Vivian Pospisil, "Cross-Border Collections," *Industry Week*, January 20, 1997, p. 6; Jill Andresky Fraser, "Around the World in 180 Days," *Inc.*, April 1997, pp. 107–108.

essary information to keep its finances under control. As inventory and accounts receivable ballooned, the company headed for a cash crisis. To ensure Baby Jogger's survival, the Baechlers were forced to reduce their workforce by half. Then, they turned their attention to the accounts receivable and discovered that customers owed the business almost $700,000! In addition, most of the accounts were past due. Focusing on collecting the money owed their company, the Baechlers were able to steer clear of a cash crisis and get Baby Jogger back on track.[10]

Figure 9.3 demonstrates how vital it is to act promptly once an account becomes past due. Notice how the probability of collecting an outstanding account diminishes the longer the account is delinquent. Table 9.4 illustrates the high cost of failing to collect accounts receivable on time.

Step 4: Forecasting Cash Disbursements

Most owners of established businesses have a clear picture of the firm's pattern of cash disbursements. In fact, many cash payments, such as rent, loan repayment, and

Figure 9.3
Collecting Delinquent Accounts

Source: Commercial Collection Agency Section of the Commercial Law League of America.

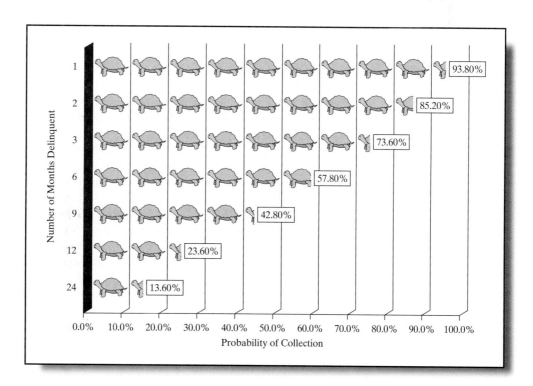

Table 9.4
Managing
Accounts
Receivable

Are your customers who purchase on credit paying late? If so, these outstanding accounts receivable probably represent a significant leak in your company's profits. Regaining control of these late payers will likely improve your company's profits and cash flow.

Slow-paying customers, in effect, are borrowing money from your business interest free! They are using your money without penalty while you forgo opportunities to place it in interest-bearing investments. Exactly how much are poor credit practices costing you? The answer may surprise you.

The first step is to compute the company's average collection period ratio (see the "Operating Ratios" section in Chapter 8), which tells the number of days required to collect the typical account receivable. Then, you compare this number to your company's credit terms. The following example shows how to calculate the cost of past-due receivables for a company whose credit terms are "net 30":

Average collection period	65 days
Less: credit terms	30 days
Excess in accounts receivable	35 days
Average daily sales of $21,500 × 35 days excess[*]	$752,500
Normal rate of return on investment	10%
Annual cost of excess	$ 75,250

If your business is highly seasonal, quarterly or monthly figures may be more meaningful than annual ones.

[*] $\text{Average daily sales} = \dfrac{\text{Annual sales}}{365} = \dfrac{\$7,487,500}{365} = \$21,500$

interest, are fixed amounts due on specified dates. The key factor in forecasting disbursements for a cash budget is to *record them in the month in which they will be paid, not when the debt or obligation is incurred.* Of course, the number of cash disbursements varies with each particular business, but the following disbursement categories are standard: purchases of inventory or raw materials; wages and salaries; rent, taxes, loans, and interest; selling expenses; overhead expenses; and miscellaneous expenses.

A common tendency is to underestimate cash disbursements, which can result in a cash crisis. To prevent this, wise entrepreneurs cushion their cash disbursement account, assuming it will be higher than expected. This is particularly important for entrepreneurs opening new businesses. In fact, some financial analysts recommend that a new owner estimate cash disbursements as best he can and then add on another 25 to 50 percent of the total. When setting up his company's cash budget, one entrepreneur included a line called "Murphy," an additional amount each month to account for Murphy's Law ("What can go wrong, will go wrong"). Whatever forecasting technique an entrepreneur uses, the key is to avoid underestimating cash disbursements, which may lead to severe cash shortages and possibly bankruptcy.

Sometimes, business owners have difficulty developing initial forecasts of cash receipts and cash disbursements. One of the most effective techniques for overcoming the "I don't know where to begin" hurdle is to make a *daily* list of the items that generated cash (receipts) and those that consumed it (disbursements). *Susan Bowen, CEO of Champion Awards, a $9 million T-shirt screen printer, monitors cash flow by tracking the cash that flows into and out of her company every day. Focusing on keeping the process simple, Bowen sets aside a few minutes each morning to track updates from the previous day on four key numbers:*

Accounts receivable: (1) What was billed yesterday? (2) How much was actually collected?
Accounts payable: (3) What invoices were received yesterday? (4) How much in total was paid out?

If Bowen observes the wrong trend—more new bills than new sales or more money going out than coming in—she makes immediate adjustments to protect her cash flow. The benefits produced (not the least of which is the peace of mind knowing no cash crisis is looming) more than outweigh the 10 minutes she invests in the process every day. "I've tried to balance my books every single day since I started my company in 1970," says Bowen.[11]

Step 5: Estimating the End-of-Month Cash Balance

To estimate a firm's cash balance for each month, an entrepreneur first must determine the cash balance at the beginning of each month. The beginning cash balance includes cash on hand as well as cash in checking and savings accounts. As development of the cash budget progresses, the cash balance at the end of a month becomes the beginning balance for the following month. Next, the owner simply adds total cash receipts and subtracts total cash disbursements to obtain the end-of-month balance before any borrowing takes place. A positive amount indicates that the firm has a cash surplus for the month while a negative amount shows a cash shortage will occur unless the manager is able to collect or borrow additional funds.

Normally, a firm's cash balance fluctuates from month to month, reflecting seasonal sales patterns. Such fluctuations are normal, but entrepreneurs must watch closely any increases and decreases in the cash balance over time. A trend of increases indicates that the small firm has ample cash that could be placed in some income-earning investment. On the other hand, a pattern of cash decreases should alert the owner that the business is approaching a cash crisis. A cash budget not only illustrates the flow of cash into and out of the small business, but it also allows the owner to anticipate cash shortages and cash surpluses. By planning cash needs ahead of time, an entrepreneur is able to do the following:

- Increase the amount and the speed of cash flowing into the company.
- Reduce the amount and the speed of cash flowing out of the company.
- Develop a sound borrowing and repayment program.
- Impress lenders and investors with its ability to plan for and repay loans.
- Reduce borrowing costs by borrowing only when necessary.
- Take advantage of money-saving opportunities, such as economic order quantities and cash discounts.
- Make the most efficient use of the cash available.
- Finance seasonal business needs.
- Provide funds for expansion.
- Plan for investing surplus cash.

The message is simple: Managing cash flow means survival for a business. Businesses tend to succeed when their owners manage cash effectively. Those who neglect cash flow management techniques are likely to see their companies fold.

THE "BIG THREE" OF CASH MANAGEMENT

It is unrealistic for business owners to expect to trace the flow of every dollar through their businesses. However, by concentrating on the three primary causes of cash flow problems, they can dramatically lower the likelihood of experiencing a devastating

IN THE FOOTSTEPS OF AN ENTREPRENEUR
Rowena's Cash Budget

Rowena Rowdy had been in business for slightly more than two years, but she had never taken the time to develop a cash budget for her company. Based on a series of recent events, however, she knew the time had come to start paying more attention to her company's cash flow. The business was growing fast, with sales more than tripling from the previous year, and profits were rising. However, Rowena often found it difficult to pay all of the company's bills on time. She didn't know why exactly, but she knew that the company's fast growth was requiring her to incur higher levels of expenses.

Last night, Rowena attended a workshop on managing cash flow sponsored by the local chamber of commerce. Much of what the presenter said hit home with Rowena. "This fellow must have taken a look at my company's financial records before he came here tonight," she said to a friend during a break in the presentation. On her way home from the workshop, Rowena decided that she would take the presenter's advice and develop a cash budget for her business. After all, she was planning to approach her banker about a loan for her company, and she knew that creating a cash budget would be an essential part of her loan request. She started digging for the necessary information, and this is what she came up with:

Current cash balance	$10,685
Sales pattern	63% on credit and 37% in cash
Collections of credit sales	61% in 1 to 30 days;
	27% in 31 to 60 days;
	8% in 61 to 90 days;
	4% never collected (bad debts).

Sales forecasts:

	Pessimistic	Most Likely	Optimistic
January (actual)	—	$24,780	—
February (actual)	—	$20,900	—
March (actual)	—	$21,630	—
April	$19,100	$23,550	$25,750
May	$21,300	$24,900	$27,300
June	$23,300	$29,870	$30,000
July	$23,900	$27,500	$29,100
August	$20,500	$25,800	$28,800
September	$18,500	$21,500	$23,900

Utilities expenses	$950 per month
Rent	$2,250 per month
Truck loan	$427 per month

The company's wages and salaries (including payroll taxes) estimates are:

April	$3,550
May	$4,125
June	$5,450
July	$6,255
August	$6,060
September	$3,525

(continued)

The company pays 66 percent of the sales price for the inventory it purchases, an amount that it actually pays in the following month. (Rowena has negotiated "net 30" credit terms with his suppliers.)

Other expenses include:

Insurance premiums	$1,200, payable in April and September
Office supplies	$125 per month
Maintenance	$75 per month
Uniforms/cleaning	$80 per month
Office cleaning service	$85 per month
Internet and computer service	$225 per month
Computer supplies	$75 per month
Advertising	$450 per month
Legal and accounting fees	$250 per month
Miscellaneous expenses	$95 per month

A tax payment of $3,140 is due in June.

Rowena has established a minimum cash balance of $1,500.

If Rowena must borrow money, she uses her line of credit at the bank which charges interest at an annual rate of 10.25%. Any money that Rowena borrows must be repaid the next month.

1. Help Rowena put together a cash budget for the six months beginning in April.

2. Does it appear that Rowena's business will remain solvent, or could the company be heading for a cash crisis?

3. What suggestions can you make to help Rowena improve her company's cash flow?

---

4. Describe the fundamental principles involved in managing the "big three" of cash management: accounts receivable, accounts payable, and inventory.

cash crisis. The "big three" of cash management are accounts receivable, accounts payable, and inventory. A firm should always try to accelerate a firm's receivables and to stretch out its payables. As one company's chief financial officer states, the idea is to "get the cash in the door as fast as you can, cut costs, and pay people as late as possible."[12] Business owners also must monitor inventory carefully to avoid tying up valuable cash in an excessive stock of inventory.

Accounts Receivable

Selling merchandise and services on credit is a necessary evil for most small businesses. Many customers expect to buy on credit, so business owners extend it to avoid losing customers to competitors. However, selling to customers on credit is expensive; it requires more paperwork, more staff, and more cash to service accounts receivable. Also, because extending credit is, in essence, lending money, the risk involved is higher. Every business owner who sells on credit will encounter customers who pay late or, worst of all, who never pay at all.

Selling on credit is a common practice in business. Experts estimate that 90 percent of industrial and wholesale sales are on credit and that 40 percent of retail sales are on account. One survey of small businesses across a variety of industries reported that 77 percent extend credit to their customers.[13] Because credit sales are so prevalent, an assertive collection program is essential to managing a company's cash flow. A credit policy that is too lenient can destroy a business's cash flow, attracting nothing but slow-paying and "deadbeat" customers. On the other hand, a carefully designed policy can be a powerful selling tool, attracting customers and boosting cash flow. "A sale is not a sale until you collect the money," warns the head of the National Association of Credit Management. "Receivables are the second most important item on the balance sheet. The first is cash. If you don't turn those receivables into cash, you're not going to be in business very long."[14]

Valerie Lichman admits that when she launched her marketing and public relations firm, she was too soft on collecting accounts receivable. Her new company suffered when one client never reimbursed her for $28,000 worth of ads she had purchased for him and another failed to pay for a month's worth of work. Today a more seasoned business owner, Lichman is much more assertive at collecting accounts receivable. She always requests an up-front payment before she begins a job, and if a payment is 30 days late, she stops work completely. The system has paid off; both her company's cash balance and its profits are rising.[15]

How to Establish a Credit and Collection Policy. The first step in establishing a workable credit policy that preserves a company's cash flow is to screen customers carefully before granting credit. Unfortunately, few small businesses conduct any kind of credit investigation before selling to a new customer. According to one survey, nearly 95 percent of small firms that sell on credit sell to anyone who wants to buy.[16] If a debt becomes past due and a business owner has gathered no information about the customer, the odds of collecting the account are virtually nil.

The first line of defense against bad debt losses is a detailed credit application. Before selling to any customer on credit, a business owner should have the customer fill out a customized application designed to provide the information needed to judge his creditworthiness. At a minimum, this credit profile should include the following information about customers:

- Name, address, Social Security number, and telephone number
- Form of ownership (proprietorship, S corporation, limited liability company, corporation, etc.) and number of years in business
- Credit references (e.g., other suppliers), including contact names, addresses, and telephone numbers
- Bank and credit card references

After collecting this information, the business owner should use it by checking the potential customer's credit references! The World Wide Web is a great place to start. On the Web, entrepreneurs can gain access to potential customers' credit information at many sites including the Securities and Exchange Commission's (SEC's) EDGAR database of corporate information, the NASDAQ stock market, the New York Stock Exchange, Dun & Bradstreet, Equifax Credit Reporting, TransUnion, and Experian. The savings from lower bad debt expenses can more than offset the cost of using a credit reporting service such as TransUnion, Equifax, Experian, or Dun & Bradstreet. The National Association of Credit Management (NACM) is another important source of credit information because it collects information on many small businesses that other reporting services ignore. The cost to check a potential customer's credit at reporting services such as these ranges from $10 to several hundred, a small price to pay when considering selling thousands of dollars worth of goods or services to a new customer. Unfortunately, few small businesses take the time to conduct a credit check; in one study, just one third of the businesses protected themselves by checking potential customers' credit.[17] One retailer of large appliances advertised, "Good credit, bad credit, no credit at all! Come see us!" His sales volume was high, but his extremely low collection rate forced him out of business.

The next step involves establishing a firm written credit policy and letting every customer know in advance the company's credit terms. The credit agreement should specify each customer's credit limit (which usually varies from one customer to another, depending on their credit ratings) and any deposits required (often stated as a percentage of the purchase price). It should state clearly all the terms the business will enforce if the account goes bad, including interest, late charges, attorney's fees, and others. Failure to specify these terms in the contract means they cannot be added later after problems arise. When will you invoice? How soon is payment due: immediately, 30 days, 60 days? Will you offer early-payment discounts? Will you add a late charge? If so, how much? The credit policies should be as tight as possible and within federal and state credit laws. According to the American Collectors Association, if a business is writing off more than 5 percent of sales as bad debts, the owner should tighten its credit and collection policy.[18]

The third step in an effective credit policy is to send invoices promptly since customers rarely pay before they receive their bills. The sooner a company sends out invoices, the sooner the customer will send payment. Manufacturers should make sure the invoice is en route to the customer as soon as the shipment goes out the door (if not before). Service companies should keep track of billable hours daily or weekly and bill as often as the contract or agreement with the client permits. Some businesses use **cycle billing,** in which a company bills a portion of its credit customers each day of the month, to smooth out uneven cash receipts.

Small business owners can take several steps to encourage prompt payment of invoices:

- Ensure that all invoices are clear, accurate, and timely.
- State clearly a description of the goods or services purchased and an account number, if possible.
- Make sure that prices on invoices agree with the price quotations on purchase orders or contracts.
- Highlight the terms of sale (e.g., "net 30") on all invoices. One study by Xerox Corporation found that highlighting the "balance due" section of invoices increased the speed of collection by 30 percent.[19]
- Include a telephone number and a contact person in your organization in case the customer has a question or a dispute.
- Respond quickly and accurately to customers' questions about their bills.

Invoices that are well-organized, easy to read, and allow customers to identify what is being billed are much more likely to get paid than those that are not. The key to creating "user-friendly" invoices is to design them from the customer's perspective.

Bob Dempster, co-founder of American Imaging Inc., a distributor of x-ray tubes, once handled receivables the same way most entrepreneurs do: When customers ignored the "net 30" terms on invoices, he would call them around the 45th day to ask what the problem was. Payments usually would trickle in within the next two weeks, but by then 60 days had elapsed, and American Imaging's cash flow was always strained. Then, Dempster decided to try a different approach. Now, he makes a "customer relations call" on the twentieth day of the billing period to determine if the customer is satisfied with the company's performance on the order. Before closing, he reminds the customer of the invoice due date and asks if there will be any problems meeting it. Dempster's proactive approach to collecting receivables has cut his company's average collection period by at least 15 days, improved cash flow, and increased customer satisfaction![20]

When an account becomes overdue, the small business owner must take immediate action. The longer an account is past due, the lower is the probability of collecting it. As soon as an account becomes overdue, many business owners send a "second notice" letter requesting immediate payment. If that fails to produce results, the next step is a telephone call. A better system is to call the customer the day after the payment is due to request payment. If the customer still refuses to pay the bill after 30 days, collection experts recommend the following:

- Send a letter from the company's attorney.
- Turn the account over to a collection agency.
- Hire a collection attorney.

Although collection agencies and attorneys will take a portion of any accounts they collect (typically around 30 percent), they are often worth the price paid. According to the American Collector's Association, only five percent of accounts over 90 days delinquent will be paid voluntarily.[21]

Business owners must be sure to abide by the provisions of the federal Fair Debt Collection Practices Act, which prohibits any kind of harassment when collecting debts (e.g., telephoning repeatedly, issuing threats of violence, telling third parties about the debt, or using abusive language). When collecting past-due accounts, the primary rule in dealing with past-due accounts is, "Never lose your cool." Even if the debtor launches into an X-rated tirade when questioned about an overdue bill, the *worst* thing a collector can do is respond out of anger. Keep the call strictly business, and begin by identifying yourself, your company, and the amount of the debt. Ask the creditor what he or she intends to do about the past-due bill. Table 9.5 describes a proactive collection system that really works.

Techniques for Accelerating Accounts Receivable. Small business owners can rely on a variety of techniques to speed cash inflow from accounts receivable:

- Speed up orders by having customers fax them to you.
- Send invoices when goods are shipped rather than a day or a week later; consider faxing or e-mailing invoices to reduce "in transit" time to a minimum.
- Indicate in conspicuous print or color the invoice due date and any late payment penalties. (Check with an attorney to be sure all finance charges comply with state laws.)
- Restrict the customer's credit until past-due bills are paid.
- Deposit customer checks and credit card receipts daily.
- Identify the top 20 percent of your customers (by sales volume), create a separate file system for them, and monitor them closely. Twenty percent of the typical company's customers generate 80 percent of all accounts receivable.
- Ask customers to pay a portion of the purchase price up front.
- Watch for signs that a customer may be about to declare bankruptcy. If that happens, creditors typically collect only a small fraction, on average just 10 percent, of the debt owed.[22] If a customer does file for bankruptcy, the bankruptcy court notifies all creditors with a "Notice of Filing" document. Upon receipt of this notice, the wise creditor creates a file to track the events surrounding the bankruptcy and takes action immediately. To have a valid claim against the debtor's assets, a creditor must file a proof-of-claim form with the bankruptcy court within a specified time, often 90 days. (The actual time depends on which form of bankruptcy the debtor declares.) If, after paying the debtor's secured creditors, any assets remain, the court will distribute the proceeds to unsecured creditors who have legitimate proof-of-claim.
- Consider using a bank's lockbox collection service (located near customers) to reduce mail time on collections. In a **lockbox** arrangement, customers send payments to a post office box the bank maintains. The bank collects the payments several times each day and deposits them immediately into the company account. The procedure sharply reduces processing and clearing times from the usual two to three days to just hours, especially if the lockboxes are located

Table 9.5
Designing a
Collection System
That Really Works

A collection system that meets the business owner's cash flow requirements and deals fairly with customers can make collecting accounts receivable on time much easier. The best approach is a proactive one that seeks to avoid past-due accounts. Review your collection system and consider these questions:

- Do you perform credit checks on new customers by contacting credit-rating services, analyzing their financial statements, or checking their credit references?
- Have you established a credit policy that spells out your company's expected payment terms and internal procedures for dealing with slow- or non-paying customers?
- Have you circulated that policy to all employees, especially salespeople?
- Do you routinely send a copy of your credit policy to new cusotmers? Do you ask them to sign and return a copy of the policy?
- Have you segmented your customer base into high- and low-risk customers? Do employees know which customers fall into which categories?
- Does your policy include a mechanism for handling high- and low-risk customers differently?
- Do you and other managers in the company receive a weekly accounts receivable update that shows an aging of the company's accounts receivable?
- Do your sales and financial management staffs work together to collect past-due payments from customers?
- Do sales representatives earn commissions on sales whether or not the company actually receives payment?
- Does your credit policy establish clear trigger points that tell you when to turn an account over to a collection agency or attorney and when to stop doing business with delinquent customers?

Even the best collection system produces some past-due accounts. One collection expert describes four stages in the past-due debt collection process: the notification or polite reminder, the discussion, the "push" or firm demand, and the bitter end.

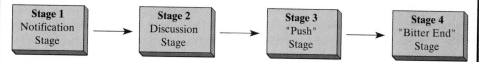

In the *notification or polite reminder stage,* the best approach is an upbeat, positive one. It should begin immediately after an invoice is past due. "Our records show that this bill is still unpaid. Can you check on it?"

During the *discussion stage,* the goal is to motivate the customer to pay the past-due account. Generally, it is not productive to explore the reasons behind the late payment; instead, the focus should be on the business at hand: getting the customer to make a firm commitment to pay by a specific deadline.

If the debt reaches the *push stage,* a business must take a stronger approach to collecting the outstanding debt. Experts recommend limiting this stage to no more than 10 days.

Once a debt reaches the *bitter end stage,* the company usually has few options but to turn the account over to a collection agency or an attorney or to file suit in small claims court. By this stage, the relationship with the customer has soured, and the company is no longer willing to do business with that customer.

One expert recommends persistence when dealing with past-due accounts. "Remember," she says, "it's your money, and you don't make money until you're paid."

Sources: Adapted from Jill Adresky Fraser, "Get Paid Promptly," *Inc.,* November 1996, p. 87; Jacquelyn Lynn, "You Owe It to Yourself," *Business Start-Ups,* October 1996, pp. 54–60.

close to the firm's biggest customers' business addresses. The system can be expensive to operate (typically $55 to $100 per month plus a 30-cent to 40-cent charge for each check) and is most economical for companies with a high volume of large checks (at least 200 checks each month).

- Track the results of the company's collection efforts. Managers and key employees should receive a weekly report on the status of the company's outstanding accounts receivable.

Combining a lockbox with other cash management services from banks—such as zero balance accounts (ZBAs) and sweep accounts—can dramatically improve a small firm's ability to get the most out of its available cash. A **zero balance account** is a checking account that technically never has funds in it but is tied to another master account like payroll. The company keeps the funds in the master account (where they earn interest), but it writes checks on the ZBA. At the end of each day, checks drawn on the ZBA are funded; then, all activity is posted against the master account. The ZBA allows the company to keep more cash working during the float period, the time between a check's being issued to its being cashed. By combining the zero balance account with a **sweep account,** which "sweeps" all funds above a predetermined minimum into an interest-bearing account, the company keeps otherwise idle cash invested until it is needed to cover checks.

Accounts Payable

The second element of the "big three" of cash management is accounts payable. The timing of payables is just as crucial to proper cash management as the timing of receivables, but the objective is exactly the opposite. An entrepreneur should strive to stretch out payables as long as possible *without damaging the company's credit rating.* Paying late could cause suppliers to begin demanding prepayment or cash on delivery (COD) terms, which severely impair the company's cash flow. Small business owners should regulate their payments to vendors and suppliers to their companies' advantage. Efficient cash managers set up a payment calendar each month that allows them to pay their bills on time and to take advantage of cash discounts for early payment.

Nancy Dunis, CEO of Dunis & Associates, a Portland, Oregon marketing firm, recognizes the importance of controlling accounts payable. "Our payables must be functioning just right to keep our cash flow running smoothly," says Dunis. She has set up a simple five-point accounts payable system[23]:

1. Set scheduling goals. *Dunis strives to pay her company's bills 45 days after receiving them and to collect all her receivables within 30 days. Even though "it doesn't always work that way," her goal is to make the most of her cash flow.*
2. Keep paperwork organized. *Dunis dates every invoice she receives and carefully files it according to her payment plan. "This helps us remember when to cut the check," she says, and, "it helps us stagger our payments over days or weeks," significantly improving the company's cash flow.*
3. Prioritize. *Dunis cannot stretch out all of her company's creditors for 45 days; some demand payment sooner. Those suppliers are at the top of the accounts payable list.*
4. Be consistent. *"Companies want consistent customers," says Dunis. "With a few exceptions," she explains, "most businesses will be happy to accept 45-day payments, so long as they know you'll always pay your full obligation at that point."*
5. Look for warning signs. *Dunis sees her accounts payable as an early warning system for cash flow problems. "The first indication I get that cash flow is in trouble is when I see I'm getting low on cash and could have trouble paying my bills according to my staggered filing system," she says.*

Business owners should verify all invoices before paying them. Some unscrupulous vendors will send out invoices for goods they never shipped, knowing that many business owners will simply pay the bill without checking its authenticity. Someone in the company—for instance, the accounts payable clerk—should have the responsibility of verifying every invoice received. One small company caught a bogus invoice for $322 worth of copier paper and toner it never ordered nor received.[24]

Generally, it is a good idea for owners to take advantage of cash discounts vendors offer. A cash discount (e.g., "2/10, net 30"—take a 2 percent discount if you pay the invoice within 10 days; otherwise, total payment is due in 30 days) offers a price reduction if the owner pays an invoice early. Chris Zane, owner of Zane's Cycles, a highly successful bicycle shop in Connecticut, makes taking cash discounts a regular practice in his business. "I make my salary on the discounts we get from paying our vendors early," he says.[25]

Clever cash managers also negotiate the best possible credit terms with their suppliers. Almost all vendors grant their customers trade credit, and entrepreneurs should take advantage of it. However, because trade credit is so easy to get, entrepreneurs must be careful not to abuse it, putting their businesses in a precarious financial position. Favorable credit terms can make a tremendous difference in a firm's cash flow. Table 9.6 shows the same most likely cash budget (from Table 9.2) with one exception: instead of purchasing on COD terms (Table 9.2), the owner has negotiated "net 30" payment terms (Table 9.6). Notice the drastic improvement in the company's cash flow resulting from improved credit terms.

If owners do find themselves financially strapped when payment to a vendor is due, they should avoid making empty promises that "the check is in the mail." Instead, they should discuss openly the situation with the vendor. Most suppliers are willing to work out payment terms for extended credit. One small business owner who was experiencing a cash crisis claims:

> One day things got so bad I just called up a supplier and said, 'I need your stuff, but I'm going through a tough period and simply can't pay you right now.' They said they wanted to keep me as a customer, and they asked if it was okay to bill me in three months. I was dumbfounded: They didn't even charge me interest.[26]

Small business owners also can improve their firms' cash flow by scheduling controllable cash disbursements so that they do not come due at the same time. For example, paying employees every two weeks (or every month) rather than every week reduces administrative costs and gives the business more time to use its cash. Owners of fledgling businesses may be able to conserve cash by hiring part-time employees or by using freelance workers rather than full-time, permanent workers. Scheduling insurance premiums monthly or quarterly rather than annually also improves cash flow.

Inventory

Inventory is a significant investment for many small businesses and can create a severe strain on cash flow. Although inventory represents the largest capital investment for most businesses, few owners use any formal methods for managing it. As a result, the typical small business not only has too much inventory but also too much of the wrong kind of inventory! Because inventory is illiquid, it can quickly siphon off a company's pool of available cash. Small businesses need cash to grow and to survive, which is difficult to do if they have money tied up in excess inventory,

Table 9.6

Cash Budget,[a] Most Likely Sales Forecast

	JAN.	FEB.	MAR.	APR.
Cash Receipts:				
Sales	$150,000	$200,000	$200,000	$300,000
Credit Sales	112,500	150,000	150,000	225,000
Collections:				
60%—1st month after sale	$180,000	$ 67,500	$ 90,000	$ 90,000
30%—2nd month after sale	78,750	90,000	33,750	45,000
5%—3rd month after sale	11,250	13,125	15,000	5,625
Cash Sales	37,500	50,000	50,000	75,000
Interest	0	200	0	0
Total Cash Receipts	$307,500	$220,825	$188,750	$215,625
Cash Disbursements:				
Purchases[a]	$105,000	$140,000	$140,000	$210,000
Rent	2,000	2,000	2,000	2,000
Utilities	850	850	850	850
Interest	0	0	7,500	0
Tax Prepayment	0	0	50,000	0
Capital Addition	0	130,000	3	0
Miscellaneous	70	70	70	70
Wage/Salaries	30,000	40,000	45,000	50,000
Total Cash Disbursements[a]	$137,920	$312,920	$245,420	$262,920
End-of-Month Balance:				
Cash (beginning of month)[a]	$ 12,000	$181,580	$ 89,485	$ 32,815
+ Cash Receipts	307,500	220,825	188,750	215,625
− Cash Disbursements[a]	137,920	312,920	245,420	262,920
Cash (end of month)[a]	181,580	89,485	32,815	(14,480)
Borrowing	0	0	0	24,480
Cash (end of month [after borrowing])[a]	$181,580	$ 89,485	$ 32,815	$ 10,000

[a] After negotiating "net 30" trade credit terms.

which yields a zero rate of return. "The cost of carrying inventory is expensive," says one small business consultant. "A typical manufacturing company pays 25 percent to 30 percent of the value of the inventory for the cost of borrowed money, warehouse space, materials handling, staff, lift-truck expenses, and fixed costs. This shocks a lot of people. Once they realize it, they look at inventory differently."[27]

Marking down items that don't sell will keep inventory lean and allow it to turn over frequently. Even though volume discounts lower inventory costs, large purchases may tie up the company's valuable cash. Wise business owners avoid overbuying inventory, recognizing that excess inventory ties up valuable cash unproductively. In fact, only 20 percent of a typical business' inventory turns over quickly, so owners must watch constantly for stale items.[28] Carrying unsold inventory costs U.S. businesses an estimated $332 billion a year.[29]

Carrying too much inventory increases the chances that a business will run out of cash. *For example, when Tom Meredith joined Dell Computer Corporation as its chief*

Section III   Building the Business Plan: Marketing and Financial Matters

IN THE FOOTSTEPS OF AN ENTREPRENEUR
A Cash Flow Dilemma

Lance Redmond stared out the window of his office and into the park along the river below. It was a beautiful fall day, and the sun reflected off of the water, creating a beautiful hue of colors that magnified the brilliant reds, yellows, and oranges of the trees' leaves. One question stuck in Redmond's mind: What should he do with the check he had just received as an up-front payment from a large customer for a job the customer wanted Redmond's company to do? In light of the fact that Redmond's company, Stallion Manufacturing, a maker of industrial equipment, did not have the cash to meet a payroll due in just 20 days, the answer seemed simple: Cash the check.

The situation was much more complex than that, however. Redmond knew that his company was not capable of doing the job the customer was requesting. The scope of the job required engineering skills, equipment, and financing that Stallion Manufacturing simply did not have. Yet, here was the answer to his company's latest cash flow crisis. Redmond had never missed a payroll before, although he had come close on several occasions. He knew that if he could not give his 41 employees their paychecks on time, some of them would very likely leave the company to work elsewhere. With sales at the four-year-old company growing so fast, he could not afford to lose any of his most skilled, experienced employees.

If he cashed the check, he could use the money to meet payroll, and none of his employees would be aware that the company had narrowly escaped another cash crisis. He could even talk with managers from the company that wanted the work, pretending to consider the opportunity to complete the job. Of course, he'd eventually have to return the $42,000 check to the customer, but this would buy him enough time to collect other accounts customers owed Stallion.

Redmond called a meeting to talk about the situation with his top managers. The chief financial officer, Sandy Camanetti, suggested they cash the check, meet with the managers from the company, and bluff, pretending to consider accepting the job.

"But we *know* we can't do the job," said Jill Sanchez, Stallion's Director of Marketing. "What if they find out? Do we want to risk losing a large, valuable customer we've had for a long time?"

Later that evening at dinner, Redmond happened to see an old friend who also ran his own business and whose opinion he respected. "Got a minute?" Redmond asked his friend, pulling back a chair at the table. "I have a situation I'd like to discuss with you. I need your input."

"Sure," his friend said. "Have a seat. What's up?"

Redmond explained the scenario, pushed back from table, and said, "There you have it. What should I do?"

1. Assume the role of Lance Redmond's friend. What advice would you offer him? Explain your reasoning.

2. Explain the ethical dimensions of Redmond's situation.

3. What other recommendations can you make to Redmond for resolving this problem? Develop a list of at least three suggestions that would help Redmond manage his company's cash flow more effectively.

---

financial officer, he quickly discovered that excessive inventory was a major source of the cash flow problems the company was experiencing. Because the company was focusing on growth, it held large inventories of costly computer components to make sure it could meet every sales opportunity. Meredith's top priority in his first few months at Dell was to cut inventory levels. "Low inventory equals high profit; high inventory equals low profit," he declares. Because the inventory that Dell carries becomes technologically obsolete so rapidly, losing 1 percent of its value each week, high inventory levels increase the likelihood of wasted cash.[30] Plus, the activities required to purchase, store, and control inventory are themselves costly. Efficient cash management calls for a business to commit just enough cash to inventory to meet demand. Scheduling inventory deliveries at the latest possible date will prevent premature payment of invoices. Finally, given goods of comparable quality and price, entrepreneurs should purchase goods from the fastest suppliers to keep inventory levels low.

Monitoring the big three of cash management can help every business owner avoid a cash crisis while making the best use of available cash. According to one expert, maximizing cash flow involves "getting money from customers sooner; paying bills at the last moment possible; consolidating money in a single bank account; managing accounts payable, accounts receivable, and inventory more effectively; and squeezing every penny out of your daily business."[31]

AVOIDING THE CASH CRUNCH

5. Explain the techniques for avoiding a cash crunch in a small company.

Nearly every small business has the potential to improve its cash position with little or no investment. The key is to make an objective evaluation of the company's financial policies, searching for inefficiency in its cash flow and ways to squeeze more cash out of their operations. Young firms cannot afford to waste resources, especially one as vital as cash. By utilizing these tools, the small business manager can get maximum benefit from the company's pool of cash.

Bartering

Bartering, the exchange of goods and services for other goods and services, is an effective way to conserve cash. An ancient concept, bartering began to regain popularity during recent recessions. More than 700 barter exchanges operate across the United States, catering primarily to small and medium-sized businesses and many of them operating on the World Wide Web. Some 475,000 companies, most of them small, engage in more than $12 billion worth of barter each year.[32] Every day, entrepreneurs across the nation use bartering to buy much needed materials, equipment, and supplies—*without using cash*. The president of one barter exchange estimates that business owners can save "between $5,000 and $150,000 in yearly business costs."[33] In addition to conserving cash, companies using bartering can transform slow-moving and excess inventory into much-needed goods and services. Often, business owners who join barter exchanges find new customers for the products and services they sell.

Of course, there is a cost associated with bartering, but the real benefit is that entrepreneurs "pay" for products and services at their wholesale cost of doing business and get credit in the barter exchange for the retail price. In a typical arrangement, businesses accumulate trade credits when they offer goods or services through the exchange. Then, they can use their trade credits to purchase other goods and services from other members of the exchange. *When Scott Floman needed an attorney to help him with a trademark issue for his growing catering company, Big Screen Cuisine, he turned to a barter exchange rather than spend real cash. Through the exchange, Floman, whose company caters meals for the casts of many popular television shows, found an attorney who resolved his trademark issue. In exchange, Floman catered a lunch for a member of the barter exchange. The whole process was simple and saved Floman a $500 cash outlay for legal services.*[34]

The typical exchange charges a $500 membership fee and a 10 percent transaction fee (5 percent from the buyer and 5 percent from the seller) on every deal. The exchange tracks the balance in each member's account and typically sends a monthly statement summarizing account activity. Rather than join a barter exchange, many enterprising entrepreneurs choose to barter on an individual basis. The place to start is with the vendors, suppliers, and customers with whom a company normally does business.

Trimming Overhead Costs

High overhead expenses can strain small firm's cash supply to the breaking point. Frugal small business owners can trim their overhead in a number of ways:

When Practical, Lease Instead of Buy. By leasing automobiles, computers, office equipment, machinery, and other assets rather than buying them, entrepreneurs can conserve valuable cash. The value of such assets is not in *owning* them but in *using* them. Leasing is popular among entrepreneurs because of its beneficial effects on a company's cash flow; 85 percent of U.S. companies use leasing as a cash management strategy.[35] *PWS Foods, Inc., a 75-employee supplier of ice cream and frozen desserts for restaurants, recently gave up the battle to keep its fleet of trucks updated and in good repair and began leasing trucks from a leasing company. "We were able to get a whole new fleet," says Arnold O. Felner, a top manager at PWS. Keeping a modern fleet of trucks in good condition is crucial to the company's ability to deliver frozen desserts in the warm climate of Texas. "There's no way that a company our size could invest in vehicles and have enough capital [left] to run a business," says Felner.[36]*

Although total lease payments often are greater than those for a conventional loan, most leases offer 100 percent financing, which means the owner avoids the large capital outlays required as down payments on most loans. Also, leasing is an "off-the-balance-sheet" method of financing; the lease is considered an operating expense on the income statement, not a liability on the balance sheet. Thus, leasing conserves a company's borrowing capacity. Leasing companies typically allow businesses to stretch payments over a longer time period than those of a conventional loan. Lease agreements also are flexible; entrepreneurs can customize their lease payments to coincide with the seasonal fluctuations in their companies' cash balances. Leasing gives entrepreneurs access to equipment even when they cannot borrow the money to buy it. After his bank rejected his loan request for a $250,000 coffee roaster for Horizon Food Group, CFO Lee Rucker decided to lease the equipment. He filled out a simple online application at Capital.com, a Web-based lease broker, and soon the roaster was in place.[37]

Entrepreneurs can choose from two basic types of leases: operating leases and capital leases. At the end of an **operating lease,** a business turns the equipment back over to the leasing company with no further obligation. Businesses often lease computer and telecommunications equipment through operating leases because it becomes obsolete so quickly. At the end of a **capital lease,** a business may exercise an option to purchase the equipment, usually for a nominal sum.

Avoid Nonessential Outlays. By forgoing costly ego indulgences like ostentatious office equipment, first-class travel, and flashy company cars, business owners can make efficient use of the company's cash. Before putting scarce cash into an asset, every business owner should put the decision to the acid test "What will this purchase add to the company's ability to compete and to become more successful?" Making across-the-board spending cuts to conserve cash is dangerous, however, because the owner runs the risk of cutting expenditures that literally drive the business. One common mistake during business slowdowns is cutting marketing and advertising expenditures. "As competitors pull back," says one advisor, "smart marketers will keep their ad budgets on an even keel, which is sufficient to bring increased attention to their products."[38] The secret to success is cutting nonessential expenditures. "If the lifeblood of your company is marketing, cut it less," advises one advertising executive. "If it is customer service, that is the last thing you want to cut back on. Cut from areas that are not essential to business growth."[39]

Negotiate Fixed Loan Payments to Coincide with Your Company's Cash Flow Cycle. Many banks allow businesses to structure loans so that they can skip specific payments when their cash flow ebbs to its lowest point. Negotiating such terms gives businesses the opportunity to customize their loan repayments to their cash flow cycles. For example, Ted Zoli, president of Torrington Industries, a construction-materials supplier and contracting business, consistently uses "skipped payment loans" in his highly seasonal business. "Every time we buy a piece of construction machinery," he says, "we set it up so that we're making payments for eight or nine months, and then skipping three or four months during the winter."[40]

Buy Used or Reconditioned Equipment, Especially If It Is "Behind-the-Scenes" Machinery. Many shrewd entrepreneurs purchase their office furniture at flea markets and garage sales! One restaurateur saved significant amounts of cash in the startup phase of his business by purchasing used equipment from a restaurant equipment broker.

Look for Simple Ways to Cut Costs. Smart entrepreneurs are always on the lookout for ways to cut the cost of operating their businesses every day. Techniques might range from installing more energy-efficient equipment to adding more fuel-efficient cars to the company fleet. *Gerry Houlihan, owner of Daniel's Restaurant in Tuckahoe, New York, recently switched from incandescent lighting to compact fluorescent lighting and installed more efficient heating and air conditioning units to cut energy costs.*[41] Mark Troy, CEO of Flywire, a Web-design company, went a step farther and hired a financial expert to conduct an expense audit to find ways to lower the company's operating expenses. By switching law firms, shutting down equipment at night, consolidating business trips, and other simple techniques, Troy estimates that the savings to his company is between $13,450 and $17,200 per month![42]

Hire Part-Time Employees and Freelance Specialists Whenever Possible. Hiring part-timers and freelancers rather than full-time workers saves on both the cost of salaries and employee benefits. Robert Ross, president of Xante Corporation, a maker of laser printer products, hires local college students for telemarketing and customer support positions, keeping his recruiting, benefits, and insurance costs down.

Control Employee Advances and Loans. A manager should grant only those advances and loans that are necessary, and should keep accurate records on payments and balances.

Establish an Internal Security and Control System. Too many owners encourage employee theft by failing to establish a system of controls. Reconciling the bank statement monthly and requiring special approval for checks over a specific amount, say $1,000, will help minimize losses. Separating record-keeping and check-writing responsibilities, rather than assigning them to a single employee, offers more protection.

Develop a System to Battle Check Fraud. Customers write about 70 billion checks a year, and merchants lose more than $13 billion in bad checks a year.[43] About 70 percent of all "bounced" checks occur because nine out of ten customers fail to keep their checkbooks balanced; the remaining 30 percent of bad checks are the result of fraud.[44] The most effective way to battle bad checks is to subscribe to an electronic, check approval service. The service works at the cash register, and approval takes about a minute. The fee a small business pays to use the service depends on the volume of checks. For most small companies, charges range from a base of $25 to $100 plus a percentage of the cleared checks' value.

Change Your Shipping Terms. Changing the firm's shipping terms from "FOB (free on board) buyer," in which the seller pays the cost of freight, to "FOB seller," in which the buyer absorbs all shipping costs, will improve cash flow.

Switch to Zero-Based Budgeting. Zero-based budgeting (ZBB) primarily is a shift in the philosophy of budgeting. Rather than build the current year budget on increases from the previous year's budget, ZBB starts from a budget of zero and evaluates the necessity of every item. The idea is to start the budget at zero and review all expenses, asking whether each one is necessary.

Keep Your Business Plan Current. Before approaching any potential lender or investor, a business owner must prepare a solid business plan. Smart owners keep their plans up-to-date in case an unexpected cash crisis forces them to seek emergency financing. Revising the plan annually also forces the owner to focus on managing the business more effectively.

Investing Surplus Cash

Because of the uneven flow of receipts and disbursements, a company will often temporarily have more cash than it needs—for a week, a month, a quarter, or longer. When this happens, most small business owners simply ignore the surplus because they are not sure how soon they will need it. They believe that relatively small amounts of cash sitting around for just a few days or weeks are not worth investing. However, this is not always the case. Entrepreneurs who put surplus cash to work immediately rather than allowing it to sit idle soon discover that the yield adds up to a significant amount over time. This money can help ease the daily cash crunch during business troughs. The goal is to identify every dollar the business does not need to pay today's bills and to invest that money to improve cash flow. However, when investing surplus cash, an entrepreneur's primary objective should not be to earn the maximum yield (which usually carries with it maximum risk); instead, the focus should be on the safety and the liquidity of the investments. The need to minimize risk and to have ready access to the cash restricts the small business owner's investment options to just a few.

Asset-management accounts, which integrate checking, borrowing, and investing services under one umbrella and were once available only to large businesses, now help small companies conserve cash. *Stanley Grossbard, president of RCDC Corporation, a diamond-cutting and -wholesale business in New York City, estimates that opening an asset-management account through a brokerage firm has earned his company several thousand dollars in interest and has saved $7,000 in interest paid. RCDC, with annual sales of $10 million, has a $1 million line of credit, which means the company borrows only what it needs exactly when it needs it, eliminating unnecessary interest expense. The account automatically moves the company's cash where it will earn—or save—the most money by either sweeping excess cash into interest-bearing accounts or applying it to the company's outstanding loan balance.*[45]

CONCLUSION

Successful owners run their businesses "lean and mean." Trimming wasteful expenditures, investing surplus funds, and carefully planning and managing the company's cash flow enables them to compete effectively in a hostile market. The simple but effective techniques covered in this chapter can improve every small company's cash position. One business writer says, "In the day-to-day course of running a company, other people's capital flows past an imaginative CEO as opportunity. By looking forward and keeping an analytical eye on your cash account as events unfold (remembering that if there's no real cash there when you need it, you're history), you can generate leverage as surely as if that capital were yours to keep."[46]

CHAPTER SUMMARY

1. Explain the importance of cash management to a small business's success.
   - Cash is the most important but least productive asset the small business has. The manager must maintain enough cash to meet the firm's normal requirements (plus a reserve for emergencies) without retaining excessively large, unproductive cash balances.
   - Without adequate cash, a small business will fail.

2. Differentiate between cash and profits.
   - Cash and profits are not the same. More businesses fail for lack of cash than for lack of profits.
   - Profits, the difference between total revenue and total expenses, are an accounting concept. Cash flow represents the flow of actual cash (the only thing businesses can use to pay bills) through a business in a continuous cycle. A business can be earning a profit and be forced out of business because it runs out of cash.

3. Understand the five steps in creating a cash budget and use them to build a cash budget.
   - The cash budgeting procedure outlined in this chapter tracks the flow of cash through the business and enables the owner to project cash surpluses and cash deficits at specific intervals.
   - The five steps in creating a cash budget are as follows: forecasting sales, forecasting cash receipts, forecasting cash disbursements, and determining the end-of-month cash balance.

4. Describe fundamental principles involved in managing the "Big Three" of cash management: accounts receivable, accounts payable, and inventory.
   - Controlling accounts receivable requires business owners to establish clear, firm credit and collection policies and to screen customers before granting them credit. Sending invoices promptly and acting on past-due accounts quickly also improve cash flow. The goal is to collect cash from receivables as quickly as possible.
   - When managing accounts payable, a manager's goal is to stretch out payables as long as possible without damaging the company's credit rating. Other techniques include verifying invoices before paying them, taking advantage of cash discounts, and negotiating the best possible credit terms.
   - Inventory frequently causes cash headaches for small business managers. Excess inventory earns a zero rate of return and ties up a company's cash unnecessarily. Owners must watch for stale merchandise.

5. Explain the techniques for avoiding a cash crunch in a small company.
   - Trimming overhead costs by bartering, leasing assets, avoiding nonessential outlays, using zero-based budgeting, and implementing an internal control system boost a firm's cash flow position.
   - Also, investing surplus cash maximizes the firm's earning power. The primary criteria for investing surplus cash are security and liquidity.

DISCUSSION QUESTIONS

1. Why must small business owners concentrate on effective cash flow management?
2. Explain the difference between cash and profit.
3. Outline the steps involved in developing a cash budget.
4. How can an entrepreneur launching a new business forecast sales?
5. Outline the basic principles of managing a small firm's receivables, payables, and inventory.
6. How can bartering improve a company's cash position?

7. Alan Ferguson, owner of Nupremis, Inc., a Web-based application service provider, says, "We lease our equipment and technology because our core business is deploying it, not owning it." What does he mean? Is leasing a wise cash management strategy for small businesses? Explain.

8. What steps should business owners take to conserve cash in their companies?
9. What should be a small business owner's primary concern when investing surplus cash?

STEP INTO THE REAL WORLD

1. Ask several local small business owners about their cash management policies. Do they know how much cash their businesses have during the month? How do they track their cash flows? Do they use some type of cash budget? If not, ask if you can help the owner develop one. Does the owner invest surplus cash?

2. Volunteer to help a small business owner develop a cash budget for his or her company. What patterns do you detect? What recommendations can you make for improving the company's cash management system?

3. Use the resources available in your local library and on the World Wide Web to prepare a brief report on bartering. What benefits does barter offer business owners? How does the typical barter exchange operate? What fees are involved? How are barter transactions taxed? A useful source of information is the International Reciprocal Trade Association's Web site at *www.irta.com.*

4. Interview several local business owners about their policies on accepting payments by check. How much do they typically lose in a year's time to bad checks? What safeguards do they use to combat check fraud? Contact the American Collectors Association at P.O. Box 39106, Minneapolis, Minnesota 55439-0106 or access the ACA's Web site at *www.collector.com/.* How prevalent is check fraud? What can business owners do to prevent it? Using these resources and those in your local library, develop a set of recommendations for the owners you interviewed to reduce their losses to check fraud.

TAKE IT TO THE NET

Visit the Scarborough/Zimmerer home page at **www.prenhall.com/scarborough** for updated information, online resources, Web-based exercises, and sample business plan.

ENDNOTES

1. John Mariotti, "Cash Is Like Oxygen," *Industry Week,* April 21, 1997, p. 42.
2. "What Is Your Greatest Financial Obstacle?" *Inc.,* September 1990, p. 130.
3. Paul DeCeglie, "8 Common Mistakes Entrepreneurs Make with Their Money," *Business Start-Ups,* July 1999, p. 106.
4. Aliza Sherman, "I Got the Blues," *Start-Ups,* September 2000, p. 37.
5. "Are You Ready for the Major Leagues?" *Inc.,* February 2001, p. 106.
6. Daniel Kehrer, "Big Ideas for Your Small Business," *Changing Times,* November 1989, p. 58.
7. Daniel Lyons, "Wool Gatherer," *Forbes,* April 16, 2001, p. 310.
8. Douglas Bartholomew, "4 Common Financial Mistakes . . . And How to Avoid Them," *Your Company,* Fall 1991, p. 9.
9. Karen M. Kroll, "Ca\$h Wears the Crown," *Industry Week,* May 6, 1996, pp. 16–18.
10. Bartholomew, "4 Common Financial Mistakes . . . And How to Avoid Them."
11. Jill Andresky Fraser, "Monitoring Daily Cash Trends," *Inc.,* October 1992, p. 49.
12. George Anders, "Truckers Trials: How One Firm Fights to Save Every Penny As Its Profits

Plummet," *Wall Street Journal,* April 13, 1982, pp. 1, 22.

13. William Bak, "Make 'Em Pay," *Entrepreneur,* November 1992, p. 64.

14. Michael Selz, "Big Customers' Late Bills Choke Small Suppliers," *Wall Street Journal,* June 22, 1994, p. B1.

15. Ilan Mochari, "Wisdom for First-Time Founders," *Inc.,* January 2001, p. 103.

16. Richard G.P. McMahon and Scott Holmes, "Small Business Financial Practices in North America: A Literature Review," *Journal of Small Business Management,* April 1991, p. 21.

17. "The Check Isn't in the Mail," *Small Business Reports,* October 1991, p. 6.

18. Howard Muson, "Collecting Overdue Accounts," *Your Company,* Spring 1993, p. 4.

19. Elaine Pofeldt, "Collect Calls," *Success,* March 1998, pp. 22–24.

20. Kimberly Stansell, "Tend to the Business of Collecting Your Money," *Inc.,* March 2, 2000, *www2.inc.com/search/17568.html;* Frances Huffman, "Calling to Collect," *Entrepreneur,* September 1993, p. 50.

21. "Time Shrinks Value of Debts," *Collection,* Winter 1992, p. 1.

22. John Gorham, "Revenge of the Lightweight," *Forbes,* March 6, 2000, p. 54.

23. Jill Andresky Fraser, "How to Get Paid," *Inc.,* March 1992, p. 105.

24. "Protect Your Business from Phony Invoices," *GSA Business,* December 4, 2000, p. 28.

25. Donna Fenn, "A Bigger Wheel," *Inc.,* November 2000, p. 88.

26. William G. Shepherd, Jr., "Internal Financial Strategies," *Venture,* September 1985, p. 68.

27. Roberta Maynard, "Can You Benefit from Barter?" *Nation's Business,* July 1994, p. 6.

28. "33 Ways to Increase Your Cash Flow and Manage Cash Balances," *The Business Owner,* February 1988, p. 8.

29. Carol Pickering, "The Price of Excess," *Business 2.0,* February 6, 2001, pp. 38–42.

30. Kroll, "Ca\$h Wears the Crown"; Lynn Cook, "Requiem for a Business Model," Forbes, July 24, 2000, pp. 60–63.

31. Jeffrey Lant, "Cash Is King," *Small Business Reports,* May 1991, p. 49.

32. "Statistics," International Reciprocal Trade Association, *www.irta.com/.*

33. Richard J. Maturi, "Collection Dues and Don'ts," *Entrepreneur,* January 1992, p. 328.

34. Carlye Adler, "The Web Exchange," *FSB,* July/August 2000, p. 40.

35. Juan Hovey, "The Most for the Leased," *Emerging Business,* Summer 2001, pp. 171–178.

36. Julie Candler, "Leasing Passes the Road Test," *Nation's Business,* May 1997, p. 54.

37. Tim Reason, "New Life on Lease," *CFO,* November 2000, pp. 123–126.

38. Roger Thompson, "Business Copes with the Recession," *Nation's Business,* January 1991, p. 20.

39. Ibid.

40. Bruce G. Posner, "Skipped Loan Payments," *Inc.,* September 1992, p. 40.

41. Tom Dinome, "Power Plays," *Small Business Computing,* September 2001, pp. 29–34.

42. Ilam Mochari, Cost-Control Diet," *Inc.,* August 2001, p. 74.

43. "Statistics on Checks," ACA International, *www.collector.com/content/press/industrystats/check.html;* "Fraud Statistics," FraudBAN Community, *www.financialgo.net/fraud-statistics.html*

44. "How to Win the Battle of Bad Checks," *Collection,* Fall 1990, p. 3.

45. Randy Myers, "Asset Accounts Keep Cash Working," *Nation's Business,* July 1997, pp. 30–32.

46. Robert A. Mamis, "Money In, Money Out," *Inc.,* March 1993, p. 98.

Chapter

10

Pricing and Credit Strategies

> *The price is what you pay; the value is what you receive.*

—ANONYMOUS

Upon completion of this chapter, you will be able to:

1. Describe effective pricing techniques for both new and existing products and services.
2. Discuss the links among pricing, image, and competition.
3. Explain the pricing techniques used by retailers.
4. Explain the pricing techniques used by manufacturers.
5. Explain the pricing techniques used by service firms.
6. Describe the impact of credit on pricing.

If you would like to become an instant business legend, simply develop a method for pricing products or services that results in maximum net revenue. Pricing is almost always one of the entrepreneur's greatest challenges. If the price of your products or services is perceived to be too high, sales may not reach an adequate level for the business to become profitable. In the opposite extreme, pricing products or services too low may convey an image of inferior quality. Even if sales do occur, the lower price may not result in an adequate profit margin. A serious "side effect" of pricing too low is the reaction of customers when you attempt to adjust prices upward. Your customers will remember the initial low price and they may even feel that their loyalty is being taken advantage of. For example, when the price of gasoline rises significantly, do you feel that the price increase is due to actual availability and cost? Or do you sometimes feel that the increase is due to price gouging or peak demand?

In reality, the pricing process is somewhere between an exact science based on logical factors and an intuitive insight based on gut feeling. Determining the most appropriate price for a product or service requires an entrepreneur to consider how each of the following factors will interact with one another:

- Product or service costs
- Market factors: supply and demand
- Sales volume
- Competitors' prices
- The company's competitive advantage
- Economic conditions
- Business location
- Seasonal fluctuations
- Psychological factors
- Credit terms and purchase discounts
- Customers' price sensitivity
- Desired image

In academic terms, price is the monetary value of a good or service. Price is a measure of what a customer is required to give up to obtain a good or service. For an individual, price is a reflection of value. We, as individuals, pay no more than what we believe the good or service to be worth. In the total marketplace, all potential customers evaluate the available goods and services and establish the demand for each. Value, like beauty, is in the eye of the beholder. The process of setting the price for any good or service must involve an analysis of how the market views the value of that product or service.

Entrepreneurs must develop a keen sensitivity to the psychological and economic thinking of their customers. Without being "in tune" to the customer's psychological and economic motivators and the resultant most likely buying behavior, it is possible to price the good or service incorrectly. This needed customer orientation is an important nonquantitative factor in a successful pricing process. What the process achieves is seldom an "ideal" price, but a price range. This price range can be described as the area between the **price ceiling,** which is the most the target group would be willing to pay, and the **price floor.** The price floor is established by the firm's total cost to produce the product or provide the service.

The price ceiling can be determined only by serious ongoing market research and analysis, and the price floor by an equally competent understanding of the financial operations of the business. Small companies with effective pricing policies tend to have a clear picture of who their customers are and how their companies' products or services fit into their customers' perception of value. They also know with exceptional accuracy the cost associated with the production and delivery of their products or services.

The final price that business owners set depends on the desired image they want to create for their products or services: discount (bargain), middle-of-the-road (value), or prestige (upscale). "There is a direct and strong relationship between the prices you charge and the image of your company," says one expert.[1] A prestige pricing strategy is not necessarily better or more effective than a no-frills, value pricing strategy. What matters most is that the company's pricing strategy enhances the image the owner wants to create for it.

A globally recognized product that conveys the image of exclusivity and high price.

For instance, one career consultant was having trouble attracting clients, even though he had considerable experience in the field. After more than a year of networking and advertising, his consulting business was stagnant. At an industry conference, he discussed his problem with several very successful career consultants, all of whom advised him to raise his prices. *Figuring he had nothing to lose, he took their advice. To his delight, his sales rose dramatically. "I finally realized that what I was selling was knowledge, experience, and information," he says. "Most of my clients are well-paid professionals who want quality in everything they purchase. When my consulting services were priced so low, potential clients perceived them as being of low value. As my prices went up, so did potential clients' perceived value of my services. Sales soon went in the same direction."*[2] Not every business has the good fortune of raising prices and experiencing a sales increase; however, this consultant's experience proves the powerful link between price and perception.

Business owners must walk a fine line when pricing their products and services, setting their prices high enough to cover costs and earn a reasonable profit but low enough to attract customers and generate an adequate sales volume. Furthermore, the right price today may be completely inappropriate tomorrow because of changing market and competitive conditions. For instance, companies often find themselves in a pricing dilemma because of rapidly rising raw materials costs. If they raise their prices to cover the increased materials cost, they run the risk of losing customers, perhaps forever. If they absorb the additional costs themselves, their profits shrink, which can threaten the long-term viability of the company.

That's the situation Danny O'Neill, owner of The Roasterie, a wholesale coffee business that sells to upscale restaurants, coffee houses, and supermarkets, found himself in when coffee prices nearly doubled in just three months.[3] Businesses faced with rapidly rising raw materials costs should consider the following strategies:

- *Communicate with customers.* Let your customers know what's happening. *The Roasterie's O'Neill was able to pass along the rising costs of his company's raw material to customers without losing a single one. He sent his customers a six-page letter and copies of newspaper articles about the increases in coffee prices. The approach gave The Roasterie credibility and helped show customers that the necessary price increases were beyond his control.*

- *Focus on improving efficiency everywhere in the company.* Although raw materials costs may be beyond a business owner's control, other costs within the company are not. One way to dampen the effects of a rapid increase in costs is to find ways to cut costs and to improve efficiency in other areas. These improvements may not totally offset higher raw materials costs, but they can dampen their impact.

- *Consider absorbing cost increases to save accounts with long-term importance to the company.* Saving a large account might be more important than keeping pace with rising costs.

- *Emphasize the value your company provides to customers.* Unless a company reminds them, customers can forget the benefits and value its products offer. When some casinos balked at paying premium prices ($2,000 to $2,600) for his company's portable carts that dispense change to slot machine players, Russell Pike, owner of Advanced Cart Technology, emphasized to casino managers the value his carts offer. He showed them how the convenient carts would pay for themselves in a single weekend by letting casinos use them for two weeks free of charge. He then showed them how his prices compared with their increased profits. "Even though our prices are high," says Pitt, "they are not high for what we are doing for them."[4]

- *Anticipate rising materials costs and try to lock in prices early.* It pays to keep tabs on raw materials prices and be able to predict cycles of inflation.

PRICING STRATEGIES AND TACTICS

There is no limit to the number of variations in pricing strategies and tactics. The wide variety of options is exactly what allows entrepreneurs to be so creative with their pricing. This section will examine some of the more commonly used tactics under a variety of conditions. Pricing always plays a critical role in a firm's overall strategy; pricing policies must be compatible with a company's total marketing plan.

1. Describe effective pricing techniques for both new and existing products and services.

New Products: Penetration, Skimming, or Sliding

Most entrepreneurs approach setting the price of a new product with a great deal of apprehension because they have no precedent on which to base their decision. If the new product's price is excessively high, it is in danger of failing because of low sales volume. However, if its price is too low, the product's sales revenue might not cover costs. When pricing any new product, the owner should try to satisfy three objectives:

1. *Get the product accepted.* No matter how unusual a product is, its price must be acceptable to the firm's potential customers.
2. *Maintain market share as competition grows.* If a new product is successful, competitors will enter the market, and the small company must work to expand or at least maintain its market share. Continuously reappraising the product's price in conjunction with special advertising and promotion techniques helps the firm acquire and retain a satisfactory market share.
3. *Earn a profit.* Obviously, a small firm must establish a price for the new product that is higher than its cost. Managers should not introduce a new product at a price below cost because it is much easier to lower the price than to increase it once the product is on the market. Pricing their products too low is a common and often fatal mistake for new businesses; entrepreneurs are tempted to underprice their products and services when they enter a new market to ensure its acceptance.

When Judy Proudfoot, founder of Proudfoot Wearable Art, launched her company, she made the mistake of underpricing the hand-painted clothing she designs and sells. To determine her prices, Proudfoot says she 'figured out how much I would pay for each type of clothing item. Then, I simply added $15 for my design and painting time and another $3 to cover overhead. What I soon found out, however was that I significantly underpriced my offerings by following this approach." Only after several customers expressed amazement at her low prices did Proudfoot begin to compare her prices with competitors'. After visiting numerous stores selling similar merchandise, Proud-foot raised her prices to be more in line with those at other specialty clothing businesses. "The funny thing about this whole experience," she says, "is that my clothing items have actually sold better since I significantly raised my prices."[5]

Entrepreneurs have three basic strategies to choose from in establishing a new product's price: penetration, skimming, and sliding down the demand curve.

Penetration. If a small business introduces a product into a highly competitive market in which a large number of similar products are competing for acceptance, the product must penetrate the market to be successful. To gain quick acceptance and extensive distribution in the mass market, a company introduces the product at a low price. In other words, it sets the price just above total unit cost to develop a wedge in the market and quickly achieve a high volume of sales. The resulting low profit margins may discourage other competitors from entering the market with similar products.

In most cases, a penetration pricing strategy is used to introduce relatively low-priced goods into a market where no elite segment and little opportunity for differentiation exists. The introduction is usually accompanied by heavy advertising and promotional techniques, special sales, and discounts. Entrepreneurs must recognize that penetration pricing is a long-range strategy; until a company achieves customer acceptance for the product, profits are likely to be small. Another danger of a penetration pricing strategy is that it attracts customers who know no brand loyalty. Companies that attract customers by offering low introductory prices must wonder what will become of their customer bases if they increase their prices or if a competitor undercuts them. If a penetration pricing strategy works, however, and the product achieves mass-market penetration, sales volume will increase, and the company will earn adequate profits. The objective of the penetration strategy is to achieve quick access to the market in order to realize high sales volume as soon as possible.

Skimming. A skimming pricing strategy often is used when a company introduces a new product into a market with little or no competition. Sometimes a company uses this tactic when introducing a product into a competitive market that contains an elite group that is able to pay a premium price. The firm uses a higher-than-normal price in an effort to quickly recover the initial developmental and promotional costs of the product. Product development or start-up costs usually are substantial owing to intensive promotional expenses and high initial costs. The idea is to set a price well above the total unit cost and to promote the product heavily to appeal to the segment of the market that is not sensitive to price. This pricing tactic often reinforces the unique, prestigious image of a store and projects a quality picture of the product. *For instance, Cartier, the famous upscale jeweler, offers its Pasha Golf watch, which keeps both time and up to four golfers' scores for $79,300 (the watch does come with 342 diamonds, and each score-keeping button is adorned with a different gemstone)!*[6] Another advantage of a skimming pricing strategy is that business owners can correct pricing mistakes quickly and easily. If a company sets a price that is too low under a penetration strategy, raising the price can be very difficult. But if a business using a skimming strategy sets a price too high to generate sufficient volume, it can always lower the price.

Sliding Down the Demand Curve. One variation of the skimming pricing strategy is called sliding down the demand curve. Using this tactic, the small company introduces a product at a high price. Then, technological advancements enable the firm to lower its costs quickly and to reduce the product's price sooner than its competition can. By beating other businesses in a price decline, the small company discourages competitors and, over time, becomes a high-volume producer. Computers are a prime example of a product introduced at a high price that quickly cascaded downward as companies forged important technological advances.

Sliding is a short-term pricing strategy that assumes that competition will eventually emerge. But even if no competition arises, the small business almost always lowers the product's price to attract a larger segment of the market. Yet, the initial high price contributes to a rapid return of start-up costs and generates a pool of funds to finance expansion and technological advances.

Established Goods and Services

Each of the following pricing techniques can become part of the toolbox of pricing tactics entrepreneurs can use to set prices of established goods and services.

Odd Pricing. Although studies of consumer reactions to prices are mixed and generally inconclusive, many small business managers use the technique known as **odd pricing.** They set prices that end in odd numbers (frequently 5, 7, 9) because they believe that an item selling for $12.95 appears to be much cheaper than an item selling for $13. Psychological techniques such as odd pricing are designed to appeal to certain customer interests, but their effectiveness remains to be proved.

Price Lining. Price lining is a technique that greatly simplifies the pricing function. Under this system, the manager stocks merchandise in several different price ranges or price lines. Each category of merchandise contains items that are similar in appearance, quality, cost, performance, or other features. For example, most music stores use price lines for their tapes and CDs to make it easier for customers to select items and to simplify stock planning. Most lined products appear in sets of three—good, better, and best—at prices designed to satisfy different market segment needs and incomes.

Leader Pricing. Leader pricing is a technique in which the small retailer marks down the customary price (i.e., the price consumers are accustomed to paying) of a popular item in an attempt to attract more customers. The company earns a much smaller profit on each unit because the markup is lower, but purchases of other merchandise by customers seeking the leader item often boost sales and profits. In other words, the incidental purchases that consumers make when shopping for the leader item boosts sales revenue enough to offset a lower profit margin on the leader.

In the personal computer (PC) industry, the war is on. A price war that industry giant Lou Gerstner of IBM termed "really dumb." Yet, the industry aggressor, Michael Dell of Dell Computers is playing the price leader role because he feels that his business model has achieved the lowest cost in the industry. Michael Dell is attempting to raise the stakes and see if his competitors in the PC industry are willing to follow his lead. More accurately, maybe the expression "afford" to follow his lead is more appropriate. Dell believes that operational efficiency will permit this pricing strategy to result in his firm capturing an even larger market share.[7]

Geographic Pricing. Small businesses whose pricing decisions are greatly affected by the costs of shipping merchandise to customers across a wide range of geographic regions frequently employ one of the **geographic pricing** techniques. For these companies, freight expenses constitute a substantial portion of the cost of doing business and often cut deeply into already narrow profit margins. One type of geographic pricing is **zone pricing,** in which a small company sells its merchandise at different prices to customers located in different territories. For example, a manufacturer might sell at one price to customers east of the Mississippi and at another to those west of the Mississippi. The U.S. Postal Service's parcel post charges are a good example of zone pricing. The small business must be able to show a legitimate basis (e.g., difference in selling or transportation costs) for the price discrimination or risk violating Section 2 of the Clayton Act.

Another variation of geographic pricing is the **uniform delivered pricing,** a technique in which the firm charges all of its customers the same price regardless of their location, even though the cost of selling or transporting merchandise varies. The firm calculates the proper freight charges for each region and combines them into a uniform fee. The result is that local customers subsidize the firm's charge for shipping merchandise to distant customers.

A final variation of geographic pricing is **FOB factory,** in which the small company sells its merchandise to customers on the condition that they pay all shipping costs. In this way, the company can set a uniform price for its product and let each customer cover the freight cost

Opportunistic Pricing. When products or services are in short supply, customers are willing to pay more for products they need. Some businesses use such circumstances to maximize short-term profits by engaging in price gouging. Many customers have little choice but to pay the higher prices. Opportunistic pricing may backfire, however, because customers know that a company that charges unreasonably high prices is exploiting them. *For instance, after a recent hurricane, one convenience store jacked up prices on virtually every item, selling packs of batteries for $10 each. Neighborhood residents* *had little choice but to pay the higher prices. After the incident, customers remembered the store's price gouging and began to shop elsewhere. The convenience store's sales never recovered and the store eventually went out of business.*

Discounts. Many small businesses use **discounts,** or **markdowns,** reductions from normal list prices, to move stale, outdated, damaged, or slow-moving merchandise. A seasonal discount is a price reduction designed to encourage shoppers to purchase merchandise before an upcoming season. For instance, many retail clothiers offer special sales on winter coats in midsummer. Some firms grant purchase discounts to special groups of customers, such as senior citizens or students, to establish a faithful clientele and to generate repeat business. *For example, it is very common to find merchants located near large universities offer a student discount on all purchases. Such a strategy can be quite successful in developing a large volume of student business.*

Multiple Pricing. Multiple pricing is a promotional technique that offers customers discounts if they purchase in quantity. Many products, especially those with a relatively low unit value, are sold using multiple pricing. For example, instead of selling an item for 50 cents, a small company might offer five for $2.

Bundling. Many small businesses have discovered the marketing benefits of **bundling,** grouping together several products or services, or both, into a package

IN THE FOOTSTEPS OF AN ENTREPENEUR
Nine Steps to Maximizing Profits Through Optimal Pricing

1. Compare your prices with those of competitors.
2. Check with associations who conduct pricing studies.
3. Attempt to develop a formula for setting prices that is specifically relevant to your business. An example would be Judy and Doug Johnson, the owners of Huckleberry Mountain Company (specialty candies and preserves), who multiply the cost of all ingredients by 2 and then add 20 percent.
4. For service companies, one method is to calculate backward. Start with the income you need or want, and divide by the number of hours you believe you can reasonably work to earn a desired income. For example, if you would like to earn $75,000 per year and you believe it is possible to bill clients for 1,000 hours, your price per hour would need to be set at $75.
5. Set a price that includes the time you provide that cannot normally be charged to the client. As an example, a professional who charges by the hour may charge an extra 10 percent above the

normal rate for a five-minute question and answer session.
6. Attempt to find what is termed "a magic number." Although your pricing formulas produce a retail price of $30.95, you may discover that the volume you can sell is priced at $29.95 more than compensates for the $1 reduction. Your goal is to maximize total net revenue and the $29.95 price may significantly increase sales volume.
7. Price shrinking may allow a new firm to set a higher-than-normal price initially and then lower the price later. It is easier to explain a price reduction than a price increase.
8. Charge what the market will bear. Customer willingness to buy sets the price ceiling for your product or service. Attempt to continue to add value in the eyes of your customers.
9. Charge what you're worth. If the service you provide or the product you sell is unique or a product of your special skills, don't be embarrassed to charge what you're worth.

Source: Adapted from "How to Set Prices," Jan Norman, *Business Start-Ups*, December 1998, pp. 42–45.

that offers customers extra value at a special price. For instance, many software manufacturers bundle several computer programs (such as a word processor, spreadsheet, database, presentation graphics, and Web browser) into "suites" that offer customers a discount over purchasing the same packages separately. The tourism industry has discovered a large market for travelers who want their entire vacation bundled into a one-price experience. For example, Funjet Vacations can include airfare, ground transport, hotel accommodations, and discounts on local attractions all in one reasonably priced package.

Suggested Retail Prices. Many manufacturers print suggested retail prices on their products or include them on invoices or in wholesale catalogs. Small business owners frequently follow these suggested retail prices because doing so eliminates the need to make a pricing decision. Nonetheless, following prices established by a distant manufacturer may create problems for the small firm. For example, a haberdasher may try to create a high-quality, exclusive image through a prestige pricing policy, but manufacturers may suggest discount outlet prices that are incompatible with the small firm's image. Another danger of accepting the manufacturer's suggested price is that it does not take into consideration the small firm's cost structure or competitive situation. A manufacturer cannot force a business to accept a suggested retail price or require a business to agree not to resell merchandise below a stated price because such practices violate the Sherman Antitrust Act and other legislation.

TWO POTENT PRICING FORCES: IMAGE AND COMPETITION

Price Conveys Image

2. Discuss the links among pricing, image, and competition.

Company pricing policies offer potential customers important information about its overall image (see Figure 9.1). For example, the prices charged by upscale men's clothing stores reflect a completely different image from those charged by factory outlets. Customers look at prices to determine what type of store they are dealing with. High prices frequently convey the idea of quality, prestige, and uniqueness. Accordingly, when developing a marketing approach to pricing, business owners must establish prices that are compatible with what their customers expect and are willing to pay. Too often, small business owners *underprice* their goods and services, believing that low prices are the only way they can achieve a competitive advantage. They fail to identify the extra value, convenience, service, and quality they give their customers—all things many customers are willing to pay for. These companies fall into the trap of trying to compete solely on the basis of price when they lack the sales volume—and hence, the lower costs—of their larger rivals. It is a recipe for failure.

Business owners must recognize that the prices they set for their company's goods and services send clear signals to customers about quality and value. We find that for some customers, a higher price equals higher quality and greater perceived value. Assume you are in a country where the quality of the local water supply is not always consistent. You decide to purchase bottled water and find two competing products. Product A is a world-renowned internationally marketed product priced at $2.50 per bottle, while Product B is an unknown product with "pure" and "safe" clearly stated on the bottle. Product B sells for 75 cents per bottle. Which would you purchase? Some travelers may equate the higher price with a guarantee of safety and quality.

Competition and Prices

An important part of setting appropriate prices is tracking competitors' prices regularly; however, what the competition is charging is just one variable in the pricing mix. When setting prices, business owners should take into account their competitors' prices, but they should not automatically match or beat them. Businesses that offer customers extra quality, value, service, or convenience can charge higher prices as long as customers recognize the "extras" they are getting. *For instance, when an upscale maker of wooden jigsaw puzzles retired, Steve Richardson, CEO of Stave Puzzles, saw an opportunity to enter the puzzle business. Richardson has positioned his company to appeal to the segment of serious puzzle collectors who appreciate quality and customer service and are willing to pay for them. He offers his upscale target customers high-quality puzzles made from exotic woods, customized puzzles ranging from just 44 pieces in complex puzzles with multiple solutions to 1,000 pieces in a traditional landscape scene, and lots of individual attention. Stave Puzzles' satisfied customers don't think twice about paying prices that range from $75 to $10,000 per puzzle. At those prices, these puzzles are not made for kids!*[8]

Steve Richardson, CEO of Stave Puzzles, targets upscale customers with his company's unique, high-quality jigsaw puzzles made from exotic woods. Stave's puzzles sell at prices ranging from $75 to $10,000.

Two factors are vital to studying the effects of competition on the small firm's pricing policies: the location of the competitors and the nature of the competing goods. In most cases, unless a company can differentiate the quality and the quantity of extras it provides, it must match the prices charged by nearby competitors for identical items, For example, if a self-service station charges a nickel more for a gallon of gasoline than the self-service station across the street charges, customers will simply go across the street to buy. Without the advantage of a unique business image—quality of goods sold, value of service provided, convenient location, favorable credit terms—a small company must match local competitors' prices or lose sales. Although the prices that distant competitors charge are not nearly as critical to the small business as are those of local competitors, it can be helpful to know them and to use them as reference points.

Before matching any competitor's price change, however, the small business owner should consider the rival's motives. The competition may be establishing its price structure on the basis of a unique set of criteria and a totally different strategy.

The nature of competitors' goods also influences the small firm's pricing policies. The manager must recognize which products are substitutes for those he sells and then strive to keep prices in line with them. For example, the local sandwich shop should consider the hamburger restaurant, the taco shop, and the roast beef shop as competitors because they all serve fast foods. Although none of them offer the identical menu of the sandwich shop, they're all competing for the same quick-meal dollar. Of course, if a company can differentiate its product by creating a distinctive image in the consumer's mind, it may be able to set higher prices for its food. The issue in this example may hinge on how much the average customer is willing to spend. An entrepreneur may have a superior sandwich, but its price is beyond what the market is willing to spend.

In general, the small business manager should avoid head-to-head price competition with other firms that can more easily achieve lower prices through lower cost structures. Most locally owned drugstores cannot compete with the prices of large national drug chains. However, many local drugstores operate successfully by using nonprice competition; these stores offer more personal service, free delivery, credit sales, and other extras that the chains have eliminated. Nonprice competition can be an effective strategy for a small business in the face of larger, more powerful enterprises, especially because there are many dangers in experimenting with prices. For instance, price shifts cause fluctuations in sales volume that the small firm may not be able to tolerate. Also, frequent price changes may damage the company's image and its customer relations.

One of the deadliest games a small business can get into with competitors is a price war. Price wars can eradicate companies' profit margins and scar an entire industry for years. Price wars usually begin when one competitor believes that they can achieve a higher volume through lower price, or they believe they can exert enough pressure on competitor's profits to drive them out of business. In most cases, entrepreneurs overestimate the power of price cuts to increase sales sufficiently to improve net profitability. Even corporate giants have made this mistake; consider the McDonald's "Campaign 55," in which it planned to lower to 55 cents the price of a different sandwich each month. The 55-cent price was a throwback to the prices in 1955, the year McDonald's was founded. The company kicked off the campaign by selling Big Macs (which cost around 40 cents to make) for 55 cents and hoped to increase store traffic and boost sales on other menu items enough to offset the lower margin on the sandwich. Unfortunately, the increased traffic never materialized and same-store sales fell 6 percent from the year before. In less than two months, McDonald's abandoned the promotion.[9]

In a price war, a company may cut its prices so severely that it is impossible to achieve the volume necessary to offset the lower profit margins. If you have a 25 percent gross (profit) margin, and you cut your price 10 percent, you have to roughly triple your sales volume just to break even. Even when price cuts work, their effects are often temporary. Customers lured by the lowest price usually have almost no loyalty to a business. The lesson: The best way to survive a price war is to stay out of it by emphasizing the unique features, benefits, and value your company offers its customers!

The underlying forces that dictate how a business prices its goods or services vary greatly among industries. In many instances, the nature of the business itself has unique factors that determine a firm's pricing strategy. The next three sections will investigate pricing techniques used in retailing, manufacturing, and service firms.

PRICING TECHNIQUES FOR RETAILERS

3. Explain the pricing techniques used by retailers.

As retail customers have become more price conscious, retailers have changed their pricing strategies to emphasize value. This value–price relationship allows for a wide variety of highly creative pricing and marketing practices. Delivering high levels of recognized value in products and services is one key to retail customer loyalty. To justify paying a higher price than those charged by competitors, customers must perceive a company's products or services are giving them greater value.

Markup

The basic premise of a successful business operation is selling a good or service for more than it costs to produce it. The difference between the cost of a product or service and its selling price is called **markup** (or **markon**). Markup can be expressed in dollars or as a percentage of either cost or selling price:

$$\text{Dollar markup} = \text{Retail price} - \text{Cost of the merchandise}$$

$$\text{Percentage (of retail price) markup} = \frac{\text{Dollar markup}}{\text{Retail price}} \qquad \textbf{(1)}$$

$$\text{Percentage (of cost) markup} = \frac{\text{Dollar markup}}{\text{Cost of unit}}$$

It may sound silly to remind business owners that they need to raise prices when they experience cost increases. Norm Brodsky's advice is to increase prices in small increments that reflect increased costs of doing business. When business owners fail to increase their prices in this fashion, they eventually discover that big increases are a shock to customers. Even when the new prices are in line with those of competitors, the entrepreneur may lose customers.

Even in a period of low inflation, costs do rise, maybe 2.7 percent per year. If the costs are not reflected in higher prices, the compound effect of even 2 percent over five years can take a significant bite out of overall profits.

Source: Adapted from Norm Brodsky, "The Cure for Higher Prices," *Inc.*, May 2000, pp. 33–34.

For example, if a man's shirt costs $15, and the manager plans to sell it for $25, markup would be as follows:

$$\text{Dollar markup} = \$25 - \$15 = \$10$$

$$\text{Percentage (of retail price) markup} = \frac{\$10}{\$25}$$

$$= 0.40 = 40\% \qquad \textbf{(2)}$$

$$\text{Percentage (of cost) markup} = \frac{\$10}{\$15}$$

$$= 0.6667 = 66.67\%$$

The cost of merchandise used in computing markup includes not only the wholesale price of the merchandise but also any incidental costs (e.g., selling or transportation charges) that the retailer incurs and a profit minus any discounts (quantity, cash) that the wholesaler offers.

Once business owners have a financial plan in place, including sales estimates and anticipated expenses, they can compute the firm's initial markup. The **initial markup** is the *average* markup required on all merchandise to cover the cost of the items, all incidental expenses, and a reasonable profit:

$$\text{Initial dollar markup} = \frac{\text{Operating expenses} + \text{Reductions} + \text{Profits}}{\text{Net sales} + \text{Reductions}} \qquad \textbf{(3)}$$

Operating expenses are the cost of doing business, such as rent, utilities, and depreciation; reductions include employee and customer discounts, markdowns, special sales, and the cost of stockouts. For example, if a small retailer forecasts sales of $380,000, expenses of $140,000, and $24,000 in reductions, and he or she expects a profit of $38,000, the initial markup percentage will be:

$$\text{Initial markup percentage} = \frac{\$140,000 + \$24,000 + \$38,000}{\$380,000 + \$24,000} \qquad \textbf{(4)}$$

$$= 50\%$$

This retailer thus knows that an average markup of 50 percent is required to cover costs and generate an adequate profit.

Some businesses use a standard markup on all of their merchandise. This technique, which is usually used in retail stores carrying related products, applies a standard percentage markup to all merchandise. Most stores find it much more practical to use a flexible markup, which assigns various markup percentages to different types of products. Because of the wide range of prices and types of merchandise they sell, department stores frequently rely on a flexible markup. It would be impractical for them to use a standard markup on all items because they have such a divergent cost and volume range. For instance, the markup percentage for socks is not likely to be suitable as a markup for washing machines.

Once owners determine the desired markup percentage, they can compute the appropriate retail price. Knowing that the markup of a particular item represents 40 percent of the retail price:

$$\text{Cost} = \text{Retail price markup}$$

$$= 100\% - 40\% \tag{5}$$

$$= 60\% \text{ of retail price}$$

and assuming that the cost of the item is $18.00, the retailer can rearrange the percentage (of retail price) markup formula:

$$\text{Retail price} = \frac{\text{Dollar cost}}{\text{Percentage cost}} \tag{6}$$

Solving for retail price, the retailer computes a price of the following:

$$\text{Retail price} = \frac{\$18.00}{0.60} = \$30.00 \tag{7}$$

Thus, the owner establishes a retail price of $30.00 for the item using a 40 percent markup.

Finally, retailers must verify that the computed retail price is consistent with their planned initial markup percentage. Will it cover costs and generate the desired profit? Is it congruent with the firm's overall price image? Is the final price in line with the company's strategy? Is it within an acceptable price range? How does it compare with the prices charged by competitors? And, perhaps most important, are the customers willing and able to pay this price?

Follow-the-Leader Pricing

Some small companies make no effort to be price leaders in their immediate geographic areas and simply follow the prices that their competitors establish. Managers wisely monitor their competitors pricing policies and individual prices by reviewing their advertisements or by hiring part-time or full-time comparison shoppers. But then these retailers use this information to establish a "me too" pricing policy, which eradicates any opportunity to create a special price image for their businesses. Although many retailers must match competitors' prices on identical items, maintaining a follow-the-leader pricing policy may not be healthy for a small business because it robs the company of the opportunity to create a distinctive image in its customers' eyes.

Below-Market Pricing

Some small businesses choose to create a discount image in the market by offering goods at below-market prices. By setting prices below those of their competitors, these firms hope to attract a sufficient level of volume to offset the lower profit margins. Many retailers using a below-market pricing strategy eliminate most of the extra services that their above-market pricing competitors offer. For instance, these businesses trim operating costs by cutting out services such as delivery, installation, credit granting, and sales assistance. Below-market pricing strategies can be risky for small companies because they require them to constantly achieve high sales volume to remain competitive.

PRICING TECHNIQUES FOR MANUFACTURERS

4. Explain the pricing techniques used by manufacturers.

For manufacturers, the pricing decision requires the support of accurate, timely accounting records. The most commonly used pricing technique for manufacturers is cost-plus pricing. Using this method, manufacturers establish a price composed of direct materials, direct labor, factory overhead, selling and administrative costs, plus the desired profit margin.

The main advantage of the cost-plus pricing method is its simplicity. Given the proper cost accounting data, computing a product's final selling price is relatively easy. Also, because it adds a profit onto the top of the firm's costs, the manufacturer is guaranteed the desired profit margin. This process, however, does not encourage the manufacturer to use its resources efficiently. Even if the company fails to use its resources in the most effective manner, it will still earn a reasonable profit, and thus, there is no motivation to conserve resources in the manufacturing process. Finally, because manufacturers' cost structures vary so greatly, cost-plus pricing fails to consider the competition sufficiently. But, despite its drawbacks, the cost-plus method of establishing prices remains prominent in many industries such as construction and printing

Direct Costing and Price Formulation

One requisite for a successful pricing policy in manufacturing is a reliable cost accounting system that can generate timely reports to determine the costs of processing raw materials into finished goods. The traditional method of product costing is called **absorption costing** because all manufacturing and overhead costs are absorbed into the finished product's total cost. Absorption costing includes direct materials and direct labor, plus a portion of fixed and variable factory overhead costs, in each unit manufactured. Full-absorption financial statements, used in published annual reports and in tax reports, are very useful in performing financial analysis. But full-absorption statements are of little help to a manufacturer when determining prices or the impact of price changes.

A more useful technique for managerial decision making is **variable** (or **direct**) **costing,** in which the cost of the products manufactured includes only those costs that vary directly with the quantity produced. In other words, variable costing encompasses direct materials, direct labor, and factory overhead costs that vary with the level of the firm's output of finished goods. Factory overhead costs that are fixed (e.g., rent, depreciation, and insurance) are *not* included in the costs of finished items. Instead, they are considered to be expenses of the period.

A manufacturer's goal in establishing prices is to discover the cost combination of selling price and sales volume that exceeds the variable costs of producing a product and contributes enough to cover fixed costs and earn a profit. The problem with using full-absorption costing is that it clouds the true relationships among price, volume, and costs by including fixed expenses in unit cost. Using a direct-costing basis yields a constant unit cost of the product no matter what the volume of production is. The result is a clearer picture of the price–volume–costs relationship. The starting point for establishing product prices is the direct-cost income statement. As Table 10.1 indicates, the direct-cost statement yields the same net profit as does the full-absorption income statement. The only difference between the two statements is the format. The full-absorption statement allocates costs such as advertising, rent, and utilities according to the activity that caused them, but the direct-cost income statement separates expenses into fixed and variable costs. Fixed expenses remain constant regardless of the production level, but variable expenses fluctuate according to production volume.

When variable costs are subtracted from total revenues, the result is the manufacturer's **contribution margin,** the amount remaining that contributes to covering fixed expenses and earning a profit. Expressing this contribution margin as a percentage of total revenue yields the firm's contribution percentage. Computing the

Table 10.1
A Full-Absorption versus a Direct-Cost Income Statement

Full-Absorption Income Statement		
Revenues		$790,000
Cost of goods sold:		
Materials	250,500	
Direct labor	190,200	
Factory overhead	120,200	560,900
Gross Profit		229,100
Operating expenses:		
General & administrative	66,100	
Selling	112,000	
Other	11,000	
Total Expenses		189,100
Net Profit (before taxes)		$ 40,000
Direct-Cost Income Statement		
Revenues (100%)		$790,000
Variable costs:		
Materials	250,500	
Direct labor	190,200	
Variable factory overhead	13,200	
Variable selling expenses	48,100	
Total Variable Costs (63.54%)		502,000
Contribution Margin (36.46%)		288,000
Fixed Costs		
Fixed factory overhead	107,000	
Fixed selling expenses	63,900	
General & administrative	66,100	
Other	11,000	
Total Fixed Costs		248,000
Net Profit (before taxes)		$ 40,000

contribution percentage is a critical step in establishing prices through the direct-costing method. This manufacturer's contribution percentage is 36.5 percent, which is calculated as:

$$\text{Contribution percentage} = \frac{1 - \text{Variable expenses}}{\text{Revenues}}$$

$$= \frac{1 - \$502,000}{\$790,000} = 36.5\%$$

(8)

Computing a Breakeven Selling Price

A manufacturer's contribution percentage tells what portion of total revenue remains after covering variable costs to contribute toward meeting fixed expenses and earning a profit. This manufacturer's contribution percentage is 36.5 percent, which means that variable costs absorb 63.5 percent of total revenues. In other words, variable costs represent 63.5 percent $(1.00 - 0.365 = 0.635)$ of the product's selling price. Suppose that this manufacturer's variable costs include the following:

Material	$2.08/unit
Direct labor	$4.12/unit
Variable factory overhead	$0.78/unit
Total variable cost	$6.98/unit

The minimum price at which the manufacturer would sell the item is $6.98. Any price below that would not cover variable costs. To compute the breakeven selling price for this product, find the selling price using the following equation:

$$\text{Profit} = \frac{\left(\begin{array}{c}\text{Selling} \\ \text{price}\end{array} \times \begin{array}{c}\text{Quantity} \\ \text{produced}\end{array}\right) + \left(\begin{array}{c}\text{Variable cost} \\ \text{per unit}\end{array} \times \begin{array}{c}\text{Quantity} \\ \text{produced}\end{array}\right) + \begin{array}{c}\text{Total} \\ \text{fixed cost}\end{array}}{\text{Quantity produced}}$$

(9)

which becomes:

$$\text{Breakeven selling price} = \frac{\text{Profit} + \left(\begin{array}{c}\text{Variable cost} \\ \text{per unit}\end{array} \times \begin{array}{c}\text{Quantity} \\ \text{produced}\end{array}\right) + \begin{array}{c}\text{Total} \\ \text{fixed cost}\end{array}}{\text{Quantity produced}}$$

(10)

To break even, the manufacturer assumes $0 profit. Suppose that its plans are to produce 50,000 units of the product and that fixed costs will be $110,000. The breakeven setting price is as follows:

$$\text{Breakeven selling price} = \frac{\$0 + (\$6.98/\text{unit} \times 50,000 \text{ units}) + \$110,000}{50,000 \text{ units}}$$

$$= \frac{\$459,000}{50,000 \text{ units}}$$

(11)

$$= \$9.18 \text{ per unit}$$

Thus, $2.20 ($9.18/unit – $6.98/unit) of the $9.18 breakeven price goes toward meeting fixed production costs. But suppose the manufacturer wants to earn a $50,000 profit. There the required selling price is:

Section IV   Small Business Marketing Strategies

$$\text{Selling price} = \frac{\$50,000 + (\$6.98/\text{unit} \times 50,000 \text{ units}) + \$110,000}{50,000 \text{ units}}$$

$$= \frac{\$509,000}{50,000 \text{ units}} \qquad\qquad\qquad\qquad \textbf{(12)}$$

$$= \$10.18/\text{unit}$$

Now the manufacturer must decide whether customers will purchase 50,000 units at $10.18. If it thinks they won't, it must decide either to produce a different, more profitable product or to lower the selling price by lowering either its cost or its profit target. Any price above $9.18 will generate some profit, although less than that desired. In the short run, the manufacturer could sell the product for less than $9.18 if competitive factors so dictate, but not below $6.98 because a price below $6.98 would not cover the variable costs of production.

Because the manufacturer's capacity in the short run is fixed, pricing decisions should be aimed at using its resources most efficiently. The fixed cost of operating the plant cannot be avoided, and the variable costs can be eliminated only if the firm ceases to offer the product. Therefore, the selling price must be at least equal to the variable costs (per unit) of making the product. Any price above that amount contributes to covering fixed costs and providing a reasonable profit.

Of course, over the long run, the manufacturer cannot sell below total costs and continue to survive. So selling price must cover total product costs—both fixed and variable—and generate a reasonable profit.

PRICING TECHNIQUES FOR SERVICE FIRMS

5. Explain the pricing techniques used by service firms.

Service businesses must establish their prices on the basis of the materials used to provide the service, the labor employed, an allowance for overhead, and a profit. As in a manufacturing operation, a service firm must have a reliable, accurate accounting system to keep a tally of the total costs of providing the service. Most service firms base their prices on an hourly rate, usually the actual number of hours required to perform the service. Some companies, however, base their fees on a standard number of hours, determined by the average number of hours needed to perform the service. For most firms, labor and materials constitute the largest portion of the cost of the service. To establish a reasonable, profitable price for service, the small business owner must know the cost of materials, direct labor, and overhead for each unit of service. Using these basic cost data and a desired profit margin, the owner of the small service firm can determine the appropriate price for the service.

Consider a simple example for pricing a common service—television repair. Jerry's TV Repair Shop uses the direct-costing method to prepare an income statement for exercising managerial control (see Table 10.2). Ned estimates that he and his employees spend about 12,800 hours in the actual production of television repair service. So total cost per productive hour for Jerry's TV Repair Shop comes to the following:

$$\text{Total cost per hour} = \frac{\$172,000}{12,800 \text{ hours}} = \$13.44/\text{hour} \qquad \textbf{(13)}$$

Table 10.2

Direct Cost Income
Statement, Ned's
TV Repair Shop

Sales Revenue		$199,000
Variable Expenses:		
Labor	52,000	
Materials	40,500	
Variable factor overhead	11,500	
Total	104,000	
Fixed Expenses:		
Rent	2,500	
Salaries	38,500	
Fixed overhead	27,000	
Total	68,000	
Total Costs		172,000
Net Income		$ 27,000

Now Jerry must add in an amount for his desired profit. He expects a net operating profit margin of 18 percent on sales. To compute the final price he uses this equation:

$$\text{Price per hour} = \text{Total cost per productive hour} \times \frac{1.00}{(1.00 - \text{Net profit target as \% of sales})}$$

$$= \$13.44 \times 1.219$$

$$= \$16.38/\text{hour} \qquad \textbf{(14)}$$

A price of $16.38 per hour will cover Jerry's costs and generate the desired profit. Smart service shop owners compute the cost per production hour at regular intervals throughout the year because they know that rising costs can eat into their profit margins very quickly. Rapidly rising labor costs and materials prices dictate that the service firm's price per hour be computed even more frequently. As in the case of the retailer and the manufacturer, Jerry must evaluate the pricing policies of competitors and decide whether his price is consistent with his firm's image.

Of course, the price of $16.38 per hour assumes that all jobs require the same amount of materials. If this is not a valid assumption, Jerry must recompute the price per hour without including the cost of materials:

$$\text{Cost per productive hour} = \frac{172,000 - 40,500}{12,800 \text{ hours}} \qquad \textbf{(15)}$$

$$= \$10.27/\text{hour}$$

Adding in the desired 18 percent net operating profit on sales yields:

$$\text{Price per hour} = \$10.27/\text{hour} \times \frac{1.00}{(1.00 - 0.18)}$$

$$= \$10.27/\text{hour} \times 1.219 \qquad \textbf{(16)}$$

$$= \$12.52/\text{hour}$$

Under these conditions Jerry would charge $12.52 per hour plus the actual cost of materials used and any markup on the cost of materials. For instance, a repair job that takes four hours to complete would have the following price:

Section IV   Small Business Marketing Strategies

Cost of service (4 hours × 12.52/hour)	$50.08
Cost of materials	$21.00
Markup on materials	$ 2.10
Total price	$73.18

THE IMPACT OF CREDIT ON PRICING

Credit Strategies

6. Describe the impact of credit on pricing.

In today's business environment, it has become essential to link the firm's pricing strategy with its credit strategy. In excess of 8 million American households have credit cards and the estimate of the number of credit cards per person is between four and five. The average personal credit line is approximately $20,000, and we are quickly replacing cash with plastic for many of our transactions. Studies conducted by J. D. Powers and Associates and Bankrate.com have identified regional usage of credit cards. Individuals on the Eastern Seaboard have more credit cards and the highest credit limits. In contrast, the most conservative credit card users were located in the Midwest. Interest payments on credit card balances have now become a significant part of our monthly budget. As of the start of the twenty-first century, American consumers have racked up $462 billion in bank and credit card debt and an additional $88 billion in retail credit card debt.[10]

The plastic in our wallet or purse has, for some individuals, altered the perception of the purchasing decision. Today's entrepreneur needs to take all of the steps necessary to be compliant with the customer's desire to buy now and pay later.

The convenience of credit cards is not free to business owners, however, Companies must pay to use the system, typically 1 to 6 percent of the company's total credit card charges, which they must factor into the prices of their products or services. They also pay a transaction fee of 5 to 50 cents per charge and must purchase or lease equipment to process transactions. Given customer expectations, small businesses find it difficult to refuse major cards, even when the big card companies raise the fees that merchants must pay. Fees operate on a multistep process. On a $100 Visa or MasterCard purchase at a typical business, a processing bank buys the credit card slip from the retailer for $97.44. Then, that bank sells the slip to the bank that issued the card for about $98.80. The remaining $1.20 discount is called the interchange fee, which is what the processing bank passes along to the issuing bank. Before it can accept credit cards, a business must obtain merchant status from either a bank or an **independent sales organization (ISO).** The accompanying *Gaining the Competitive Edge* feature describes how a small company can obtain merchant status.

More small businesses also are equipping their stores to handle debit-card transactions, which act as electronic checks, automatically deducting the purchase amount from a customer's checking account. The equipment is easy to install and to set up, and the cost to the company is negligible. The payoff can be big, however, in the form of increased sales.

Although it has become an essential element of business, credit card sales have many associated fees. Not all merchant account providers charge all of these fees, but expect to see some of these: (a) application fee (usually waived), (b) equipment fee, (c) licensing fee, (d) transaction fee, and (e) holdbacks and chargebacks. Each of these fees are added to the discount rate discussed above.

Acquiring merchant status enables a small business to accept credit card payments for goods and services. Offering customers the convenience of paying with credit cards enhances a company's reputation and translates directly into higher sales. Qualifying for merchant status is not easy for many small companies, however, because banks view it in the same manner as making a loan to a business. "When we give you the ability to accept credit cards," explains one banker, "we are giving you the use of funds before we get them." Although small storefront businesses with short operating histories many have difficulty qualifying for merchant status, home-based businesses and mail-order companies or entrepreneurs doing business over the World Wide Web typically have the greatest difficulty convincing banks to set them up with credit card accounts.

For instance, when Steve and Shelly Bloom, owners of Crystal Collection, a small glass art importer, applied for merchant status, their bank denied their request because their company is home based. The Blooms then turned to an ISO the bank recommended, and the ISO helped them get merchant status through another bank. Because their business represents a higher-than-normal risk to credit card–issuing banks, the Blooms pay higher fees than small storefront companies. Their fees include either 2.5 percent of their monthly credit card transactions or $25 (whichever is higher), a 20 cent per transaction handling fee, a $15 monthly fee, and $32 per month to rent the point-of-sale terminal to process credit card transactions.

What can business owners do to increase their chances of gaining merchant status so that they can accept customers without driving their costs sky-high? Try these tips:

- *Recognize that business start-ups and companies that have been in business less than three years face the greatest obstacles in gaining merchant status.* Entrepreneurs just starting out in business should consider applying for merchant status when they approach a bank for start-up capital. Existing companies can boost their chances of success by preparing a package to present to the bank—credit references, financial statements, business description, and an overview of the company's marketing plan, including a detailed customer profile.

- *Apply with your own bank first.* The best place to begin the application process is with your own bank. "When we look at an application," says one banker, "we consider three critical things: the principal, the product, and the process. In other words, we need to know about you, what you are selling, and how you are selling it." If your banker cannot set up a credit card account for your business, ask for a referral to an ISO that might be interested.

- *Know what information the bank or ISO is looking for and be prepared to provide it.* Before granting merchant status, banks and ISOs want to make sure that a business is a good credit risk. Treat the application process in the same way you would an application for a loan—because, in essence, it is. In addition to the package mentioned above, business owners should be able to estimate their companies' credit card volume and their average transaction size.

- *Make sure you understand the costs involved.* When merchants accept credit cards, they do not receive the total amount of the sale; they must pay a transaction charge to the bank. Costs typically include start-up fees ranging from $50 to $200; transaction fees of 5 cents to 50 cents per purchase; the discount rate, which is a percentage of the actual sales amount and usually ranges from 1 to 6 percent; monthly statement fees of $4 to $20; equipment rental or purchase costs, which can range from $250 to $1,500 or more; and miscellaneous fees. Because the cost of accepting credit cards can be substantial, business owners must be sure that accepting them will produce valuable benefits.

- *Shop around.* Too often, business owners take the first deal offered to them, only to regret it later. "One of the problems is that merchants are forced by society to give people credit, and they get panicky if they can't take credit cards," says one expert. "So they make a pact with the devil and
(continued)

don't do their due diligence before signing [the merchant status agreement]."

- *Have a knowledgeable attorney to look over your contract before you sign it.* Otherwise, you may not discover clauses that work a hardship on your business until it's too late.

Accepting credit cards is not important for every business, but for those whose customers expect that convenience, acquiring merchant status can spell the difference between making a sale and losing it.

1. Use the World Wide Web to research how businesses on the Web conduct credit card transactions. How do they secure the privacy of these transactions?

Sources: Adapted from Charles Gajeway, "Finished Business," *Small Business Computing,* January 2001, pp. 58–59, Johanna S. Billings, "Taking Charge," *Business Start-Ups,* November 1997, pp. 16–18; Lin Grensing-Pophal, "Let Them Use Plastic," *Business Start-Ups,* May 1996, pp. 16–18; Cynthia E. Griffin, "Charging Ahead," *Entrepreneur,* April 1997, pp. 54–57; Frances Cerra Whittelsey, "The Minefield of Merchant Status," *Nation's Business,* January 1997, pp. 38–40; Charles Gajeway, "Finished Business," *Small Business Computing,* January 2001, pp. 58–59.

E-Business and Credit Cards

When it comes to online business transactions, currently the most common way to make a payment is via credit cards. Although credit and charge cards are the most common ways to pay for purchases online, debit cards—which authorize merchants to electronically debit your bank account—are also being used. Your debit card may be your automated teller machine (ATM) card and may require you to use a personal identification number (PIN). It may be a card that requires only some form of signature or other identification; or it may have a combination of these features. While using a debit card is similar to using a credit card, there is one important difference: When you use a debit card, the money for the purchase is transferred almost immediately from your bank account to the merchant's account.

The Internet is a dynamic environment and forms of payment are rapidly evolving. So it's no wonder that a number of electronic payment systems—sometimes referred to as "electronic money"—are under development for simplifying purchases online. For example, "stored-value" cards allow consumers to transfer cash value to the card. Some stored value cards work offline (e.g., to buy a snack at a vending machine); others work online (to buy goods from a Web site); or they may have both features. Some stored value cards contain computer chips that make them "smart" cards: They can act like a credit card as well as a debit card, and can also contain stored value.

Some new Internet-based payment systems would allow value to be transmitted through computers. Consumers can use them to make "micropayments." Micropayments are extremely small payments—for an item like a sheet of music or a short article. When consumers use electronic money to make a purchase, they decrease the balance on their card or computer by the amount of the purchase. Some cards can be "reloaded" with additional value, say, at a cash machine; other cards are "disposable"—you can throw them away after you use them. Internet vendors are constantly challenged by the need to provide secure ways to transact business in a safe environment. Many potential consumers are hesitant about online transactions for reasons of security and privacy. In a recent study conducted by CyberDialogue, an online customer intelligence firm, 60 percent of online users still feel that submitting information is riskier than by telephone, and more than one third feel that it is an invasion of privacy.[11] Because of merchant and consumer vulnerability, credit card processing companies have developed a variety of ways to compensate for the exposure to risk. *For example, one E-entrepreneur who sells men's cosmetic skin care products online uses a credit card processing service called Internet Secure. The entrepreneur states that, "For a $500 start-up fee, the company (Internet Secure) now accepts Master Card, Visa, American Express, and Discover for $24.95 a month plus a discount rate of 2 to 3 percent, depending on the card. Internet Secure holds 10 percent of sales each month in case there are chargebacks."*[12]

E-commerce requires the business to integrate a variety of electronic services into a seamless shopping experience. While this is not currently a perfected process, nor is it one without inherent hassles for the merchant, the payoff of a small local entrepreneur being able to tap into a global market is often well worth the trouble.

Installment Credit

Small companies that sell big-ticket consumer durables—major appliances, cars, and boats—frequently rely on installment credit. Because very few customers can purchase such items in a single lump-sum payment, small businesses finance them over an extended time. The time horizon may range from just a few months up to 30 or more years. Most companies require the customer to make an initial down payment for the merchandise and then finance the balance for the life of the loan. The customer repays the loan principal plus interest on the loan. One advantage of installment loans for a small business is that the owner retains a security interest as collateral on the loan. If the customer defaults on the loan, the owner still holds the title to the merchandise. Because installment credit absorbs a small company's cash, many rely on financial institutions such as banks and credit unions to provide the installment credit. When a business has the financial strength to "carry its own paper," the interest income from the installment loan contract often yields more than the initial profit on the sale of the product. For some businesses, such as furniture stores, this has traditionally been a major source of income.

Trade Credit

Companies that sell small-ticket items frequently offer their customers trade credit; that is, they create customer charge accounts. The typical small business bills its credit customers each month. To speed collections, some offer cash discounts if customers pay their balances early; others impose penalties on late payers. Before deciding to use credit as a competitive weapon, the small business owner must make sure that the firm's cash position is strong enough to support that additional pressure.

For manufacturers and wholesalers, trade credit is traditional. Chapter 8 showed how the potential problems of being unable to adequately control the amount of accounts payable outstanding is a major cause of lost profitability and even total failure. In reality, trade credit is a two-edged sword. Small businesses must be willing to grant credit to purchasers in order to get, and keep, their business; they must work extremely hard, and often be very tough, with debtors who do not pay as they agreed to.

CHAPTER SUMMARY

1. Describe effective pricing techniques for both new and existing products and services.
   - Pricing a new product is often difficult for the small business manager, but it should accomplish three objectives: getting the product accepted; maintaining market share as the competition grows; and earning a profit.
   - There are three major pricing strategies generally used to introduce new products into the market: penetration, skimming, and sliding down the demand curve.
   - Pricing techniques for existing products and services include odd pricing, price lining, leader pricing, geographic pricing, opportunistic pricing, discounts, multiple pricing, bundling, and suggested retail pricing.

2. Discuss the links among pricing, image, and competition.
   - Company pricing policies offer potential customers important information about the firm's overall image. Accordingly, when developing a marketing approach to pricing, business owners must establish prices that are compatible with what their customers expect and are willing to pay. Too often, small business owners *underprice* their goods and services, believing that low prices are the only way they can achieve a competitive advantage. They fail to identify the extra value, convenience, service, and quality they give their customers—all things many customers are willing to pay for.
   - An important part of setting appropriate prices is tracking competitors' prices regularly; however, what the competition is charging is just one variable in the pricing mix. When setting prices, business owners should take into account their competitors' prices, but they should not automatically match or beat them. Businesses that offer customers extra quality, value, service, or convenience can charge higher prices as long as customers recognize the "extras" they are getting. Two factors are vital to studying the effects of competition on the small firm's pricing policies: the location of the competitors and the nature of the competing goods.

3. Explain the pricing techniques used by retailers.
   - Pricing for the retailer means pricing to move merchandise. Markup is the difference between the cost of a product or service and its selling price.
   - Age of retail price, but some retailers put a standard markup on all their merchandise; more frequently, they use a flexible markup.

4. Explain the pricing techniques used by manufacturers.
   - A manufacturer's pricing decision depends on the support of accurate cost accounting records. The most common technique is cost-plus pricing, in which the manufacturer charges a price that covers the cost of producing a product plus a reasonable profit. Every manufacturer should calculate a product's breakeven price, the price that produces neither a profit nor a loss.

5. Explain the pricing techniques used by service firms.
   - Service firms often suffer from the effects of vague, unfounded pricing procedures and frequently charge the going rate without any idea of their costs. A service firm must set a price based on the cost of materials used, labor involved, overhead, and a profit. The proper price reflects the total cost of providing a unit of service.

6. Describe the impact of credit on pricing.
   - Offering consumer credit enhances a small company's reputation and increases the probability, speed, and magnitude of customers' purchases. Small firms offer three types of consumer credit: credit cards, installment credit, and trade credit (charge accounts).

DISCUSSION QUESTIONS

1. What does the price of a good or service represent to the customer? Why is a customer orientation to pricing important?
2. How does pricing affect a small firm's image?
3. What competitive factors must the small firm consider when establishing prices?

4. Describe the strategies a small business could use in setting the price of a new product. What objectives should the strategy seek to achieve?
5. Define the following pricing techniques: odd pricing, price lining, leader pricing, geographic pricing, and discounts.
6. Why do many small businesses use the manufacturer's suggested retail price? What are the disadvantages of this technique?
7. What is a markup? How is it used to determine prices?
8. What is a standard markup? A flexible markup?
9. What is follow-the-leader pricing? Why is it risky?
10. What is cost-plus pricing? Why do so many manufacturers use it? What are the disadvantages of using it?
11. Explain the difference between full-absorption costing and direct costing. How does absorp-

tion costing help a manufacturer determine a reasonable price?
12. Explain the techniques for a small service firm setting an hourly price.
13. What is the relevant price range for a product or service?
14. What advantages and disadvantages does offering trade credit provide to a small business?
15. What are the most commonly used methods to purchase online using credit? What reasons can you give for consumer uncertainty when giving credit card information online as opposed to via the telephone?
16. What advantages does accepting credit cards provide a small business? What costs are involved?
17. What steps should a small business owner take to earn merchant status?

STEP INTO THE REAL WORLD

1. Interview two successful small retailers in your area and ask the following questions: Do you seek a specific image through your prices? What role do your competitors play in pricing? Do you use specific pricing techniques such as odd pricing, price lining, leader pricing, or geographic pricing? How are discounts calculated? What markup percentage does the firm use? What is your cost structure?
2. Select an industry that has several competing small firms in your area. Contact these firms and compare their approaches to determining prices. Do prices on identical or similar items differ? Why?
3. Contact two local small businesses: one that does accept credit cards and one that doesn't.

Ask the owner of the business that does accept credit cards why he or she does. What role do customers' expectations play? Does the owner believe that accepting credit cards leads to increased sales? What does it cost the owner to accept credit cards? How difficult was it to gain merchant status? Does the business sell products to consumers or other businesses online? If so, what method of payment is used and how satisfied is the owner with this method? Ask the owner of the business that does not accept credit cards why he or she does not. Has the business lost sales because it does not accept credit cards? What would it take and how much would it cost for the owner to be able to accept credit cards?

TAKE IT TO THE NET

Visit the Scarborough/Zimmerer home page at **www.prenhall.com/scarborough** for updated information, online resources, Web-based exercises, and sample business plan.

ENDNOTES

1. Jacquelyn Lynn, "The Middle of the Road," *Business Start-Ups*, December 1996, p. 33.
2. Susan Greco, "Are Your Prices Right'?" *Inc.,* January 1998, pp. 88–89.
3. Roberta Maynard, "Take Guesswork Out of Pricing," *Nation's Business*, December 1997, pp. 27–30.
4. Jeannie Mandelker, "Pricing Right from the Start," *Profit*, September/October 1996, p. 20.
5. Kylo-Patrick Hart, "Step 10: Set Your Price," *Business Start-Ups*, March 1997, pp. 72–74.
6. Ed Brown, "$79K—And It Keeps Score!" *Fortune*, March 3, 1997, p. 42.
7. Edwin Starr, "Why Dell's War Isn't Dumb," *Fortune*, July 9, 2001, pp. 134–136; Gary Williams, "How Dell Fine Tunes Its Pricing to Gain Edge in a Slow Market," *Wall Street Journal*, June 8, 2001, p. 1.
8. Peter Nulty, "Make Certain Your Price Is Right," *Your Company, Forecast*, 1997, pp. 15–16.
9. Richard Gibson, "Big Price Cut at McDonald's Seems a McFlop," *Wall Street Journal*, May 9, 1997, pp. B1, B2; Richard Gibson, "Prices Tumble on Big Macs, But Fries Rise," April 25, 1997, *Wall Street Journal,* pp. B1, B2; Cliff Edwards, ""Some McDonalds Franchises Quietly Boosting Prices to Offset Cost of Promotion," *Greenville News*, April 26, 1997, p. 8D.
10. Lucy Lazarony, "What Your Address Says About How You Use Credit Cards," *Bankrate.com*, available at *www.bankrate.com/brm/news/cc/19990816.asp.;* "Consumer Information: Credit Card Stats," *Consumer Credit Counseling, Inc.,* available at *www.consumercredit.com/cardstats.htm;* Bridgette Craney, "Plastic Credit Turns 50," *Regional Focus*, Summer 2000, p. 11.
11. "Privacy Policy," *CyberDialogue White Paper,* available at *http://www.cyberdialogue.com.*
12. Tom DiNome, "Ace in the Hole," *Small Business Computing*, July 2001.

Chapter 11

Creative Use of Advertising and Promotion

> *The only reason a great many American families don't own elephants is that they have never been offered an elephant for a dollar down and easy weekly payments.*

—MAD MAGAZINE

> *Advertising is the "wonder" in Wonder Bread.*

—JEFF I. RICHARDS

Upon completion of this chapter, you will be able to:

1. Describe the steps in developing an advertising strategy.
2. Explain the differences among promotion, publicity, personal selling, and advertising.
3. Describe the advantages and disadvantages of the various advertising media.
4. Identify four basic methods for preparing an advertising budget.
5. Explain practical methods for stretching a small business's advertising budget.

Failing to advertise your products or services would be like preparing a great party but forgetting to invite the guests. Making your potential customers aware of your business and how your products and services can meet their needs is an absolute essential element of a business. Advertising and promotion are not "luxuries" but essential components of any business plan. For the entrepreneurial business, advertising must normally be achieved with fewer financial resources and a higher degree of creativity to get the most effective customer responses possible.

DEVELOPING AN ADVERTISING STRATEGY

1. Describe the steps in developing an advertising strategy.

Every small business needs an advertising strategy to insure that it does not waste the money it spends on advertising. A well-developed strategy does not guarantee advertising success, but it does increase the likelihood of good results. For advertising to work, it must fit into your company's overall marketing strategy.

The first step is to define the purpose of the company's advertising program by creating specific, measurable objectives. In other words, entrepreneurs must decide, "What do I want to accomplish with my advertising?" Some ads are designed to stimulate immediate responses by encouraging customers to purchase a particular product in the immediate future. The object is to trigger a purchase decision. Other ads seek to build name recognition among potential customers and the general public. These ads try to create goodwill by keeping the firm's name in the public's memory so that customers will recall the small firm's name when they decide to purchase a product or service. Although measuring the success of name-recognition ads is more difficult than measuring purchasing results, successful campaigns should produce increased sales within six to nine months. Still other ads strive to draw new customers, build mailing lists, increase foot traffic in a store, or introduce a company or a product into a new territory.

The next step in developing an advertising strategy is to identify the company's target customers. Entrepreneurs who do not know who their advertising targets are cannot reach them! Before considering either the advertising message or the media by which to send it, business owners must understand their target customers. The idea is to match both the message and the media to the target audience. Entrepreneurs should address the following questions:

- What business are we in?
- What image do we want to project?
- Who are our target customers and what are their characteristics?
- Where can we best reach them?
- What do my customers *really* purchase from us?
- What benefits can the customer derive from our goods or services?
- How do I want to position our company in the market?
- What advertising approach do our competitors take?

Each of these questions requires a serious investment of time and mental energy, but without the specific knowledge obtained through answering these questions, an advertising strategy will not achieve the results expected. Through the process of answering these questions, the entrepreneur better defines the business, builds a profile of their customers, and focuses their advertising messages for maximum effectiveness.

Jackie Lent's Inward Bound Adventures, a travel tour service, targets one of the nation's fastest-growing markets: the elderly. By the year 2030, the already sizable population of people over 65 will nearly double, and their spending power will extend into the hundreds of billions of dollars. Recognizing the market potential of this growing market and its abundance of leisure time led Lent to begin designing travel tours for senior citizens looking for unique destinations and activities catering to their needs and interests. Inward Bound tours avoid the typical "tourist destinations," favoring instead quaint, out-of-the-way spots that let visitors see what life in that location is really like. "My goal was to have my customers experience the place rather than just see it," says Lent. All of Inward Bound Adventures' promotions are aimed specifically at Lent's target audience and emphasize the details that elderly leisure travelers want.[1]

Once the small business owner has defined her target audience, she can design an advertising message and choose the media for transmitting it. At this stage, the owner decides what to say and how to say it.

Owners should build their ads around a **unique selling proposition (USP),** a key customer benefit of a product or service that sets it apart from its competition. To be effective, a USP must be unique—something the competition does not (or cannot) provide—and strong enough to encourage the customer to buy. A successful USP answers the critical question every customer asks: "What's in it for me?" It should express in 10 words or less exactly what a business can do for its customers. The USP becomes the heart of the advertising message. *For instance, the owner of a quaint New England bed and breakfast came up with a four-word USP that captures the essence of the escape her business offers guests from their busy lives: "Delicious beds; delicious breakfasts." Sheila Paterson, co-founder of Macro International, a marketing consulting firm, says her company's USP is "Creative solutions for impossible marketing problems."*[2]

Sometimes, the most powerful USPs are the *intangible* or *psychological* benefits a product or service offers customers, for example, safety, security, acceptance, or status. An advertiser must be careful, however, to avoid stressing minuscule differences that are irrelevant to customers. Table 11.1 describes a six-sentence advertising strategy designed to create powerful ads that focus on a USP. The best way to identify a meaningful USP is to describe the primary benefit your product or service offers customers and then to list secondary benefits it provides. By focusing on the most criti-

Table 11.1
A Six-Sentence
Advertising
Strategy

Does your advertising deliver the message you want to the audience you are targeting? If not, try stating your strategy in six sentences:

- **Primary purpose.** What is the primary purpose of this ad? "The purpose of Rainbow Tours' ads is to get people to call or write for a free video brochure."
- **Primary benefit.** What USP can you offer customers? "We will stress the unique and exciting places our customers can visit."
- **Secondary benefits.** What other key benefits support your USP? "We will also stress the convenience and value of our tours and the skill of our tour guides."
- **Target audience.** At whom are we aiming the ad? "We will aim our ads at adventurous male and female singles and couples, 21 to 34, who can afford our tours."
- **Audience reaction.** What response do you want from your target audience? "We expect our audience to call or write to request our video brochure."
- **Company personality.** What image do we want to convey in our ads? "Our ads will reflect our innovation, excitement, and conscientiousness and our warm, caring attitude toward our customers."

Source: Adapted from Jay Conrad Levirison, "The Six-Sentence Strategy," *Communication Briefings*, December 1994, p. 4.

GAINING THE COMPETITIVE EDGE
Making Your USP a Force in the Success of the Business

The goal of any business is to have it perceived as superior, in the minds of its customers, from all competitors. The process begins with an objective and critical evaluation of how your products and/or services generate superior value for those customers. A firm's USP must be tailored to the customer's critical buying criteria. These criteria can be either rational or emotional, or both. When you are confident that you know what the market wants, build an appeal to those identified needs. The following are a few steps to maximizing the effectiveness of your firm's USP:

- Communicate your firm's USP in a simple, concise statement. Use words like *you, your,* and *yours* instead of *I, we, me,* or *our.*

- Be absolutely sure your actions match the promises incorporated in your USP.

- Make your USP the focal point for all advertising. Build all advertising around the USP that has been created.

- Be willing to back up the claims in your USP with generous warranties or money-back guarantees.

- If it's working, keep the pressure on.

Sources: Sid Davis, "Finding Your Competitive Edge," *Emerging Business,* Summer 2001, pp. 116–120; Kim Gordon, "Slogan's Heroes," *Entrepreneur,* July 2001, pp. 89–90.

cal USPs and providing supporting facts, the ads can spell out for the customer the specific benefits they will receive.

With the elements of the message clarified, the next step is determining the most effective advertising media to use.

A company's target audience and the nature of its message determines the advertising media it will use. Some messages are much more powerful in some media than in others.

The process does not end with creating and broadcasting an ad. The final step involves evaluating the ad campaign's effectiveness. Did it accomplish the objectives it was designed to accomplish? Immediate-response ads can be evaluated in a number of ways. For instance, managers can include coupons that customers redeem to get price reductions on products and services. Dated coupons identify customer responses over certain time periods. Some firms use hidden offers, statements hidden somewhere in an ad that offer customers special deals if they make a special request.

A business owner can also gauge an ad's effectiveness by measuring the volume of store traffic generated. Effective advertising should increase store traffic; higher traffic boosts sales of both advertised and nonadvertised items. Of course, if an advertisement promotes a particular bargain item, the manager can judge its effectiveness by comparing sales of that item with preadvertising sales. Remember: The ultimate test of an ad is whether it increases sales!

Ad tests can help determine the most effective methods of reaching potential customers. Owners can design two different ads (or use two different media or broadcast times) that are coded for identification and see which one produces more responses. For example, the manager can use a split run of two different ads in a local newspaper. That is, he can place one ad in part of the paper's press run and another ad in the remainder of the run. Then he can measure the response level to each ad. Table 11.2 offers 12 tips for creating an effective advertising campaign.

Table 11.2

Twelve Tips for Effective Advertising

1. *Plan more than one advertisement at a time.* An advertising campaign is likely to be more effective if it is developed from a comprehensive plan for a specific time period. A piecemeal approach produces ads that lack continuity and a unified theme.

2. *Set long-run advertising objectives.* One cause of inadequate planning is the failure to establish specific objectives for the advertising program. If what is expected from advertising hasn't been defined, the program is likely to lack a sense of direction.

3. *Use advertisements, themes, and vehicles that appeal to diverse groups of people.* Although personal judgment influences every business decision, you cannot afford to let bias interfere with advertising decisions. For example, you should not use a particular radio station just because you like it.

4. *View advertising expenditures as investments, not as expenses.* In an accounting sense, advertising is a business expense, but money spent on ads tends to produce sales and profits over time that might not be possible without advertising. An effective advertising program generates more sales than it costs. You must ask, "Can I afford *not* to advertise?"

5. *Use advertising that is different from your competitors' advertising.* Some managers tend to "follow the advertising crowd" because they fear being different from their competitors. "Me too" advertising frequently is ineffective because it fails to create a unique image for the firm. Don't be afraid to be different!

6. *Choose the media vehicle that is best for your business even if it's not number one.* It is not uncommon for several media within the same geographic region to claim to be "number one": Different media offer certain advantages and disadvantages. The manager should evaluate each according to its ability to reach his target audience effectively

7. *Consider using someone else as the spokesperson on your TV and radio commercials.* Although being your own spokesperson may lend a personal touch to your ads, the commercial may be seen as nonprofessional or "homemade." The ad may detract from the firm's image rather than improve it.

8. *Limit the content of each ad.* Some small business owners think that to get the most for their advertising dollar, they must pack their ads full of facts and illustrations. But overcrowded ads confuse customers and are often ignored. Simple, well-designed ads that focus on your USP are much more effective.

9. *Devise ways of measuring your ad's effectiveness that don't depend on just two or three customers' responses.* Measuring the effectiveness of advertising is an elusive art at best. But the opinions of a small sample of customers, whose opinions may be biased, is not a reliable gauge of an ad's effectiveness. The techniques described earlier offer a more objective measurement of an ad's ability to produce results.

10. *Stop the ad if something does not happen immediately.* Some ads are designed to produce immediate results, but many ads require more time because of the lag effect they experience. One of advertising's rules is: It's not the size; it's the frequency. The head of one advertising agency claims, "The biggest waste of money is stop-and-start advertising."

11. *Emphasize the benefits that the product or service provides to the customer.* Too often, ads emphasize only the features of the products or services a company offers without mentioning the benefits they provide customers. Customers really don't care about a product's or service's "bells and whistles"; they are much more interested in the *benefits* those features can give them! Their primary concern is "How can this solve my problem?"

12. *Evaluate the cost of different advertising medium.* Remember the difference between the absolute and relative cost of an ad. The medium that has a low absolute cost may actually offer a high relative cost if it does not reach your intended target audience. Evaluate the cost of different media by looking at the cost per thousand customers reached. Remember: No medium is a bargain if it fails to connect you with your intended customers. You must be patient, giving the advertising campaign a reasonable time to produce results. One recent study concluded that sales increases are most noticeable four to six months after an advertising campaign begins. One advertising expert claims that successful advertisers "are not capricious ad-by-ad makers; they're consistent ad campaigners."

Sources: Adapted from Sue Clayton, "Advertising" *Business Start-Ups*, December 1995, pp. 6–7; *Marketing for Small Business*, The University of Georgia Small Business Development Center: Athens, Georgia, 1992, p. 69; "Advertising Leads to Sales," *Small Business Reports*, April 1988, p. 14; Shelly Meinhardt, "Put It in Print," *Entrepreneur*, January 1989, p. 54; Danny R. Arnold and Robert H. Solomon, "Ten 'Don'ts' in Bank Advertising;" *Burroughs Clearing House*, vol. 16, no. 12, September 1980, pp. 20–24, 42–43; Howard Dana Shaw, "Success with Ads," *In Business*, November/December 1991, pp. 48–49; Jan Alexander and Aimee L. Stern, "Avoid the Deadly Sins in Advertising," *Your Company*, August/September 1997, p. 22.

ADVERTISING VERSUS PROMOTION

2. Explain the differences among promotion, publicity, personal selling, and advertising.

The terms *advertising* and *promotion* are often confused. **Promotion** is any form of persuasive communication designed to inform consumers about a product or service and to influence them to purchase these goods or services. It includes publicity, personal selling, and advertising.

Publicity

Publicity is any commercial news covered by the media that boosts sales but for which the small business does not pay. Publicity is obtained by allowing someone, normally a newspaper or magazine writer, to tell a positive story about your business, its people, or its products or services. Publicity can be a powerful influence on how customers view your business. The following are a few tactics that can help an entrepreneur stimulate positive publicity for the firm:

- *Write an article that will interest your customers or potential customers.* One investment adviser writes a monthly column for the local newspaper on timely topics such as "retirement planning," "minimizing your tax bill," and "investing strategies for the next century." Not only do the articles help build her credibility as an expert; they also have attracted new customers to her business.
- *Contact local TV and radio stations and offer to be interviewed.* Many local news or talk shows are looking for guests to talk about topics of interest to their audiences (especially in January and February). Even local shows can reach new customers.
- *Publish a newsletter.* With a personal computer and desktop publishing software, any entrepreneur can publish a professional-looking newsletter. Freelancers can offer design and editing advice. Use the newsletter to reach present and potential customers.
- *Contact local business and civic organizations and offer to speak to them.* A powerful, informative presentation can win new business. (Be sure your public speaking skills are up to par first! If they aren't, consider joining Toastmasters.)
- *Offer or sponsor a seminar.* Teaching people about a subject you know a great deal about builds confidence and goodwill among potential customers. The owner of a landscaping service and nursery offers a short course in landscape architecture and always sees sales climb afterward.
- *Write news releases and fax them to the media.* The key to having a news release picked up and printed is finding a unique angle on your business or industry that would interest an editor. Keep it short, simple, and interesting.
- *Volunteer to serve on community and industry boards and committees.* You can make your town a better place to live and work and raise your company's visibility at the same time.
- *Sponsor a community project or support a nonprofit organization or charity.* Not only will you be giving something back to the community, but you will also gain recognition, goodwill, and, perhaps, customers for your business. *Each year, Martha Morgan, owner of Morgan's of Delaware Avenue, a women's apparel store, sponsors a clothing drive for low-income working women with the local YWCA. Morgan offers customers who donate secondhand clothing to the YWCA a receipt for their donations (for tax purposes) and a $25 gift certificate on their next purchase of $125 or more in her store. Morgan says that the drive not only has provided needed clothing for deserving women, but it also has boosted her company's sales by more than $40,000.*[3]

- *Promote a cause.* What started out as a socially responsible act has turned into a successful public relations campaign for one entrepreneur. *Joseph Crilley, owner of Crilley's Circle Tavern, was concerned about the dangers of drinking and driving, so he renovated an old school bus and began offering his customers a free shuttle service. Not only has his service made the roads safer; but it also has boosted his business. During off-peak hours, Crilley uses the bus to shuttle school kids on field trips and senior citizens around town to run errands.*[4]

Sometimes publicity is a matter of knowing a celebrity or, as in the case of Drake Bakeries, having a celebrity who knows and loves your product. *Drake Bakeries, founded in Brooklyn, New York, in 1900 by two brothers, makes a variety of snack cakes that native New Yorkers, including talk-show star Rosie O'Donnell, have loved for decades. O'Donnell, who describes Drake's products as "heaven in a foil wrapper," has promoted the snack cakes on her television show. She has interviewed the company's president, Jack Gallagher, and has even managed to convince supermodel Cindy Crawford to eat a Ring Ding (a cream-filled chocolate cake) on the air! With the help of O'Donnell's publicity, Drake Bakeries' sales climbed 100 percent.*[5]

Personal Selling

Personal selling is the personal contact between salespeople and potential customers resulting from sales efforts. Effective personal selling can give the small company a definite advantage over its larger competitors by creating a feeling of personal attention. Personal selling deals with the salesperson's ability to match customer needs to the firm's goods and services. Individuals who are successful at personal selling often display the following common characteristics:

- *Enthusiasm and alertness to new opportunities.* Star sales representatives demonstrate deep concentration, high energy, and drive.

IN THE FOOTSTEPS OF AN ENTREPRENEUR
CEO and Head Salesman—Knowing What It Takes to Drive the Business

Most people would get tired just reading about the daily schedule of Pat Cavanaugh because he is up at 4:00 A.M. to exercise and in the office by 6:30 A.M. Pat runs his life, and those of his sales staff from his well-worn day-timer. On a recent sales blitz in Cleveland, Ohio, for his firm, Cavanaugh Promotions, he and five sales reps covered 114 appointments in two days. Pat Cavanaugh's sales skills have resulted in a 2,000 percent company growth in 5 years.

One could have predicted that Pat would be a success in sales. At the age of 10, he began his sales career selling flower seeds door to door. He next switched to shoe sales and was so effective that the manufacturer asked if he would consider being the Pennsylvania state sales manager; they didn't expect Pat to be a 10 year old. Today, he runs at a pace that is the inspiration to his sales staff. His efforts produce results, and he normally outsells the typical sales rep by four or five to one.

Recently, Pat has hired key people to help him run the business. What position will Pat hold? He will be the CEO *and* the firm's leading salesperson.

1. Pat Cavanaugh is an absolutely exceptional salesman who has personally driven the company's revenues to new heights. In your opinion, can he continue to grow the firm or should he concentrate on being the CEO?

Source: Susan Greco, "The Nonstop, 24–7 CEO Salesman," *Inc*, August 2000, pp. 92–103.

- *Concentration on selected accounts.* They focus on customers with the greatest sales potential, bypassing lukewarm prospects.
- *Thorough planning.* On every sales call, the best representatives act with a purpose to close the sale.
- *Direct approach.* They get right to the point with customers.
- *Work from the customer's perspective.* They know their customers' businesses and their needs.
- *Spend 60 to 70 percent of a sales call letting the customer talk while they listen.* They know that the best way to solve customers' problems and overcome their objections is to learn what they are.
- *See customers' objections for what they really are—a source of valuable information.* Objections give salespeople the chance to hear what customers are worried about. Once they know that, they can develop a strategy for overcoming the objections. "Sales objections are not a negative, but positive and necessary parts of a successful sale," says one expert.
- *Focus on building a rapport with prospects before attempting to sell them anything.*
- *Don't offer product or service recommendations until 40 percent or more of the time in the sales call has elapsed.*
- *Emphasize customer benefits, not product or service features, when selling.*
- *Use "past success stories."* They encourage customers to express their problems and then present solutions using examples of past successes.
- *Leave sales material with clients.* The material gives the customer the opportunity to study company and product literature in more detail.
- *See themselves as problem solvers, not just vendors.*
- *Measure their success not just by sales volume but also by customer satisfaction.*

Sales is not a profession that is suited to everyone. It is easy to see from the list of personal characteristics above that sales requires discipline, persistence, empathy, and a sincere desire to sell the products and services that will benefit the customer. Salespersons must be capable of coping with rejection. Very few potential customers buy on the first few visits or sales calls. Salespersons must be relentless, resilient, and very resourceful to become successful.

Closing the sale in today's competitive marketplace is aided by some new high-tech tools used as *Win*[2], a computer software program designed to assist the user with the formulation of optimum negotiating strategies. Another software aid is *Sales Proposal-Architect,* which assists the salesperson in analyzing potential customers' needs and objectives. Other sales-assist software or Web-based tools include *Salesforce.com, Hot Office,* and *Hot Data.*[6]

Whatever the new technology will provide to support the front-line salesperson the basic job must still be done. For this reason, most firms develop a "selling system" that is unique to their market. Generalizable elements of a selling system include the following:

- How to initiate contact with the potential customer's. When does the customer wish to entertain salespersons? What is the customer's buying cycle?
- Encourage the prospect. Explain in detail what they need in the way of products and/or services.
- Request an invitation to demonstrate your products or ask when the prospect can visit your facilities, depending on which is most appropriate.
- Demonstrate in ways important to the prospect your product or services superiority.
- Provide tangible proof of that superiority.

- Begin the sales negotiation process. Address each of the prospects stated requirements and deal with their objections. Remain professional and focused on a win–win resolution.
- *Ask* for the customer's business and complete the financial and operational components of the negotiations.

Any system can be improved over time and no system is appropriate for every potential client. Salespersons need to be encouraged to be creative. Before making a sales call, a salesperson should set three objectives:

1. *The primary objective.* The most reasonable outcome expected from the meeting. It may be to get an order or to learn more about a prospect's needs.
2. *The minimum objective.* The very least the salesperson will leave with. It may be to set another meeting or to identify the prospect's primary objections.
3. *The visionary objective.* The most optimistic outcome of the meeting. This objective forces the salesperson to be open-minded and to shoot for the top.

The entrepreneur and each member of the sales staff should be in agreement on the expected sales volume and the appropriate profit margin to be earned. Regular meetings should report on the results achieved by each salesperson, as well as the techniques that are proving to be most effective. The sales process in continuous and consequently positive feedback on customer satisfaction sets the stage for the next sales cycle.

Advertising

Advertising is any sales presentation that is nonpersonal in nature and is paid for by an identified sponsor. Advertising is a billion-dollar industry whose function is to inform customers of their choices and influence their buying decisions. Because of its importance to the long-term success of a business, the remainder of this chapter will address the specifics of selecting the best advertising media; and developing an advertising budget.

SELECTING ADVERTISING MEDIA

3. Describe the advantages and disadvantages of the various advertising media.

Up to this point, the entrepreneur has defined the benefits of its product and/or services, and analyzed the critical purchasing decision criteria of its target market. The message of the advertisement is determined, and what remain are the media that will best deliver that message. The advertising media blend chosen by a firm needs to both have impact and be reinforcing.

Understanding the qualities of the various media available can simplify an owner's decision. Before selecting the vehicle for the message, the owner should consider several questions:

- *How large is my firm's trading area?* How big is the geographic region from which the firm will draw its customers? The size of this area clearly influences the choice of media.
- *Who are my target customers, and what are their characteristics?* A customer profile often points to the appropriate medium to get the message across most effectively.
- *Which media are my target customers most likely to watch, listen to, or read?* Until he knows who his target audience is, a business owner cannot select the proper advertising media to reach it.

- *What budget limitations do I face?* Every business owner must direct the firm's advertising program within the restrictions of its operating budget. Certain advertising media cost more than others.
- *What media do my competitors use?* It is helpful for the small business manager to know the media his competitors use, although he should not automatically assume that they are the best. An approach that differs from the traditional one may produce better results.
- *How important are repetition and continuity of my advertising message?* In general, an ad becomes effective only after it is repeated several times, and many ads must be continued for some time before they produce results.
- *What does the advertising medium cost?* Entrepreneurs must consider both absolute cost and relative cost. **Absolute cost** is the actual dollar outlay a business owner must make to place an ad in a particular medium for a specific time period. An even more important measure is an ad's **relative cost,** the ad's cost per potential customer reached.

Media Options

Entrepreneurs quickly discover that there is a wide array of advertising media options: newspapers, magazines, radio, television, direct mail, and the World Wide Web, as well as many specialty media. Each of the media options have both advantages and disadvantages, as well as cost per contact concentrations to calculate as your advertising strategy is implemented. The relative effectiveness of each media depends on its ability to inform and influence the customers of your target market. The pros and cons of each advertising medium can be evaluated only in light of the firm's advertising strategy (see Figures 11.1 and 11.2).

Figure 11.1
Advertising Expenditures by Medium

Source: McCann-Erickson, Inc.

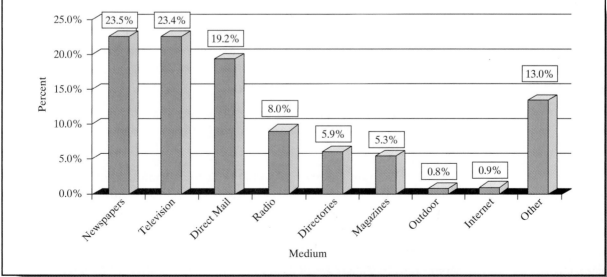

Figure 11.2
Advertising
Expenditures
by Medium

MEDIUM	1998 $	1998 %	1999 $	1999 %
Newspapers	$ 48,524	24.1%	$ 50,563	23.5%
Television	$ 47,474	23.5%	$ 50,440	23.4%
Direct Mail	$ 39,620	19.7%	$ 41,403	19.2%
Radio	$ 15,073	7.5%	$ 17,215	8.0%
Directories	$ 11,990	5.9%	$ 12,652	5.9%
Magazines	$ 10,518	5.2%	$ 11,433	5.3%
Outdoor	$ 1,576	0.8%	$ 1,725	0.8%
Internet	$ 1,050	0.5%	$ 1,940	0.9%
Other	$ 25,769	12.8%	$ 27,930	13.0%
	$201,594	100.0%	$215,301	100.0%
	for 1998		for 1999	

Source: Statistical Abstract of the U.S. New York: McCann-Erickson, Inc. 1999.

Newspapers. Traditionally, the local newspaper has been the medium that most advertisers rely on to get their messages across to customers. Although the number of newspapers in the United States has declined since 1960, this medium still attracts a large percentage of the advertising dollars nationwide.

Newspapers provide several *advantages* to the small business advertiser:

Selected geographic coverage. Newspapers are geared to a specific geographic region, and they reach potential customers in all demographic classes. In general, they provide extensive coverage in a firm's immediate trading area.

Flexibility. Newspaper advertisements can be changed readily on very short notice. The owner can select the size of the ad, its location in the paper, and the days on which it runs. For instance, garages often advertise their tune-up specials in the sports section on weekends; party shops display their ads in the entertainment section.

Timeliness. Papers almost always have very short closing times or publication deadlines. Many papers permit advertisers to submit their copy as late as 24 hours before the ad runs.

Communication potential. Newspaper ads can convey a great deal of information by employing attractive graphics and copy. Properly designed, they can be very effective in attracting attention and persuading readers to buy.

Low costs. Newspapers normally offer advertising space at a low absolute cost and, because of their blanket coverage of a geographic area, at a low relative cost as well.

Prompt responses. Newspaper ads typically produce relatively quick customer responses. A newspaper ad is likely to generate sales the very next day. This advantage makes newspapers an ideal medium for promoting special events such as sales, grand openings, or the arrival of a new product.

Of course, newspaper advertisements also have *disadvantages:*

Wasted readership. Because newspapers reach such a variety of people, at least a portion of an ad's coverage will be wasted on those who are not potential customers. This nonselective coverage makes it more difficult for newspapers to reach specific target markets than ads in other media.

Reproduction limitations. The quality of reproduction in newspapers is limited, especially when it is compared with that of magazines and direct mail. Recent technological advances, however, are improving the quality of reproduction in newspaper ads.

Lack of prominence. One frequently cited drawback of newspapers is that they carry so many ads that a small company's message might be lost in the crowd. The typical newspaper is 65 percent advertising. This disadvantage can be overcome by increasing the size of the ad or by adding color to it. Color can increase the reading of ads by as much as 80 percent over black-and-white ads. Studies show that two-color ads do "pull" better than black-and-white ones but only by a small margin. The *real* increase in ad recall and response comes from using full four-color ads. Bold headlines, illustrations, and photographs also increase an ad's prominence.

Proper ad placement in the newspaper can increase an ad's effectiveness. The best locations are on a right-hand page, near the right margin, above the half-page mark, or next to editorial articles. The most-read sections in the typical newspaper are the main news section and the comics!

Declining readership. Newspaper circulation as a percentage of U.S. households has dropped from 98 percent in 1970 to less than 70 percent today. Newspaper ads are more effective with older adults and those with higher education and income. They are less effective with younger adults.

Short ad life. The typical newspaper is soon discarded and, as a result, an ad's life is extremely short. Business owners can increase the effectiveness of their ads by giving them greater continuity. Spot ads can produce results, but maintaining a steady flow of business requires some degree of continuity in advertising.

Buying Newspaper Space. Newspapers typically sell ad space by lines and columns or inches and columns. For instance, a 4-column by 100-line ad occupies four columns and 100 lines of space (14 lines are equal to 1 column-inch). For this ad, the small business owner would pay the rate for 400 lines. Most papers offer discounts for bulk, long-term, and frequency contracts and for full-page ads. Advertising rates vary from one paper to another, depending on such factors as circulation and focus. A small business owner would do well to investigate the circulation statements, advertising rates, and reader profiles of the various newspapers available before selecting one.

Radio. Newspapers offer blanket advertising coverage of a region, but radio permits advertisers to appeal to specific audiences over large geographic areas. By choosing the appropriate station, program, and time for an ad, a small company can reach virtually any target market.

Radio advertising offers several *advantages*:

Universal infiltration. The radio's nearly universal presence gives advertisements in this medium a major advantage. Virtually every home and car in the United States is equipped with a radio, which means that radio ads receive a tremendous amount of exposure in the target market.

According to the Radio Advertising Bureau, radio reaches 77 percent of all customers each day and 95 percent of customers each week![7]

Market segmentation. Radio advertising is flexible and efficient because advertisers can choose stations directed toward a specific market within a broad geographic region. Radio stations design their formats to appeal to specific types of audiences. (Ever notice how the stations you listen to are not the same ones your parents listen to?) AM stations, which once ruled the airways, now specialize mainly in "talk formats" such as call-in, news, religion, sports, and automotive shows. On the FM dial, country, top 40, rap, easy listening, modern rock, rhythm and blues, Spanish, and "golden oldies" stations have listener profiles that give entrepreneurs the ability to pinpoint virtually any advertising target.

Flexibility and timeliness. Radio commercials have short closing times and can be changed quickly. Small firms dealing in seasonal merchandise or advertising special sales or events can change their ads on short notice to match changing market conditions.

Friendliness. Radio ads are more "active" than ads in printed media because they use the spoken word to influence customers. Vocal subtleties used in radio ads are impossible to convey through printed media. Spoken ads can suggest emotions and urgency, and they lend a personalized tone to the message. Table 11.3 offers a guide to producing effective radio copy.

Radio advertisements also have some *disadvantages*:

Poor listening. Radio's intrusiveness into the public life almost guarantees that customers will hear ads, but they may not listen to them. Listeners are often engaged in other activities while the radio is on and may ignore the message.

Need for repetition. Listeners usually do not respond to radio ads after a single exposure to them. Radio ads must be broadcast repeatedly to be effective. Consistency in radio ads is the key to success.

Limited message. Radio ads are limited to one minute or less, so small business owners must keep their messages simple, covering only one or two points. Also, radio spots do not allow advertisers to demonstrate their products or services. Although listeners can hear the engine purr, they can't see the car; spoken messages can only describe the product or service.

Buying Radio Time. The small business owner can zero in on a specific advertising target by using the appropriate radio station. Stations follow various formats—from rap to rhapsodies—to appeal to specific audiences. Radio advertising time usually sells in 10-second, 20-second, 30-second, and 60-second increments, with the last being the most common. *Fixed spots* are guaranteed to be broadcast at the times specified in the owner's contract with the station. *Preemptible spots* are cheaper than fixed spots, but the advertiser risks being preempted by an advertiser willing to pay the fixed rate for a time slot. *Floating spots* are the least expensive, but the advertiser has no control over broadcast times. Many stations offer package plans, using flexible combinations of fixed, preemptible, and floating spots.

Radio rates vary depending on the time of day they are broadcast, and, like television, there are prime time slots known as drive-time spots. Although exact hours may differ from station to station, the following classifications are common:

Table 11.3
Guidelines for
Effective Radio
Copy

- *Mention the business often.* This is the single most important and inflexible rule in radio advertising. Also make sure listeners know how to find your business. If the address is complicated, use landmarks.
- *Stress the benefit to the listener.* Don't say "Bryson's has new fall fashions"; say "Bryson's fall fashions make you look fabulous."
- *Use attention-getters.* Radio has a whole battery of attention-getters: music, sound effects, unusual voices. Crack the customer-resistance barrier with sound.
- *Zero in on your audience.* Know who you're selling to. Radio's selectivity attracts the right audience. It is up to you to communicate in the right language.
- *Keep the copy simple and to the point.* Don't try to impress listeners with vocabulary. "To be or not to be" may be the best-known phrase in the language, and the longest word has just three letters.
- *Sell early and often.* Don't back into the selling message. At most, you've got 60 seconds. Make the most of them. Don't be subtle.
- *Write for the ear.* Write conversationally.
- *Prepare your copy.* Underline words you want to emphasize.
- *Triple space.* Type clean, legible copy. Make the announcer rehearse.
- *Convey a sense of urgency.* Use words such as now and today, particularly when you're writing copy for a sale. Radio has qualities of urgency and immediacy. Take advantage of them by including a time limit or the date the sale ends.
- *Put the listener in the picture.* Radio's "theater of the mind" enables you to put the listener behind the wheel of a new car with sounds and music.
- *Focus the spot on getting a response.* Make it clear what you want the listener to do. Don't try to get a mail response. Use phone numbers only, and repeat the number three times. End the spot with the phone number.
- *Don't stay with a loser.* Direct response ads produce results right away or not at all. Don't stick with a radio spot that is not generating sales. Change it.

Source: Radio Basics, Radio Advertising Bureau, *www.rab.com.*

Class AA: Morning drive time—6 A.M. to 10 A.M.
Class A: Evening drive time—4 P.M. to 7 P.M.
Class B: Home worker time—10 A.M. to 4 P.M.
Class C: Evening time—7 P.M. to midnight
Class D: Nighttime—midnight to 6 A.M.

Some stations may also have different rates for weekend time slots.

Television. Although the cost of national TV ads precludes their use by most small businesses, local spots on cable stations can be an extremely effective means of broadcasting a small company's message. A 30-second commercial on network television may cost well over $500,000 (30-second spots during the Super Bowl now go for more than $2.3 million), but a 30-second spot on a local cable station may go for $200 or less.

Television advertising has some distinct *advantages*:

Broad coverage. Television ads provide extensive coverage of a sizable region, and they reach a significant portion of the population. About 9 percent of the homes in any area will have a television, and those sets are on an average of 7 hours and 8 minutes each day. Therefore, television ads can reach a large number of people in a short amount of time.

The nation's 200-plus cable channels now draw more than 50 percent of television viewership. As the number of cable channels continues to increase, television exposure time will also rise. Because many channels focus their broadcasting in topical areas—from home and garden or food to science or cartoons—cable television offers advertisers the ability to reach specific target markets much as radio ads do. Because there is an inverse relationship between time spent in television viewing and education level, television ads overall are more likely to reach people with lower educational levels.

Visual advantage. The primary benefit of television is its capacity to present the advertiser's product or service visually. Research shows that 46 percent of television ads result in long-term sales increases and that 70 percent of campaigns boost sales immediately.[8] With TV ads, entrepreneurs are not limited to mere descriptions of a product or service; instead, they can demonstrate their uses and show firsthand their advantages. For instance, a specialty shop selling a hydraulic log splitter can design a television commercial to show how easily the machine works. The ability to use sight, sound, and motion makes TV ads a powerful selling tool.

Flexibility. Television ads can be modified quickly to meet the rapidly changing conditions in the marketplace. Advertising on TV is a close substitute for personal selling. Like a sales representative's call, television commercials can use "hard-sell" techniques, attempt to convince through logic, appeal to viewers' emotions, persuade through subtle influence, or use any number of other strategies. In addition, advertisers can choose the length of the spot (30-second ads are most common), its time slot, and even the program during which to broadcast the ad.

Design assistance. Few entrepreneurs have the skills to prepare an effective television commercial. Although professional production firms might easily charge $50,000 to produce a commercial, the television station from which a manager purchases the air time often is willing to help design and produce the ad very inexpensively.

Television advertising also has several *disadvantages*:

Brief exposure. Most television ads are on the screen for only a short time and require substantial repetition to achieve the desired effect. One of the realities is that television viewers often avoid or ignore the commercial messages. The commercial is the time to get up and do whatever needs to be done before the program returns.

Clutter. The typical person sees 1,500 advertising messages a day, and more ads are on the way! With so many ads beaming across the airwaves, a small business's advertising message could easily become lost in the shuffle.

"Zapping." **"Zappers,"** television viewers who flash from one channel to another, especially during commercials, pose a real threat to TV advertisers. Remote controls invite zapping, which can cut deeply into an ad's target audience. Zapping prevents TV advertisers from reaching the audiences they hope to reach.

Cost. TV commercials can be expensive to create. A 30-second ad can cost several thousand dollars to develop, even before the owner purchases airtime. Advertising agencies and professional design firms offer design assistance—sometimes at hefty prices—so many small business owners hire less expensive freelance ad designers or turn to the stations on which they buy air time for help with their ads. Table 11.4 offers some suggestions for developing creative television commercials.

The World Wide Web. The newest and fastest growing medium business owners have in their advertising arsenal is the World Wide Web. The Web draws customers with attractive demographic profiles—young, educated, and wealthy. Businesses of all sizes may find that advertising online is more effective with the incorporation of larger "virtual" billboards. The Internet Advertising Bureau recently unveiled seven new standardized ad formats. These ad formats are intended to supplement the traditional 5-inch wide by 1-inch high banner ad. The small, rectangular banner ad may be too small to deliver a more complex marketing message. Current research indicates that as little as one half of 1 percent of viewers click on banner ads. The new larger formats include "skyscrapers" that run the length of the page on one side, and rectangles that are up to 3.5-inches wide by 3-inches high. The images are more dynamic than the traditional click-through banners, and hopefully they will build increased sales down the line for companies using them.[9]

Advertising experts agree that the World Wide Web will become an increasingly popular advertising medium, with anticipated spending eclipsing $15 billion in 2005 and an increased share of all advertising spending to approximately 8 percent.[10]

In addition to the banner ads, the Web has cookies, full-page ads, and push technology ads. **Cookies** are small programs that attach to users' computers when they visit a Web site. They track the locations users visit while in the site and use this electronic footprint to send pop-up ads that would be of interest to the user. **Full-page ads** are those that download to Web users' screens before they can access certain Web sites. They are common on popular game sites that sustain high volumes of Web traffic. **Push technology ads** appear on users' screens when they download information such as news, sports, or entertainment from another site. For instance, a Web user downloading sports information might receive an ad for ath-

Table 11.4
Guidelines for Creative TV Ads

- *Keep it simple.* Avoid confusing the viewer. Stick to a simple concept.
- *Have one basic idea.* The message should focus on a single, important benefit to the customer. Why should people buy from your business?
- *Make your point clear.* The customer benefit should be obvious and easy to understand.
- *Make your ad unique to get viewer attention.* To be effective, a television ad must grab the viewer's attention. Unless viewers watch the ad, its effect is lost.
- *Involve the viewer.* To be most effective, an ad should portray a situation the viewer can relate to. Common, everyday experiences are easiest for people to identify with.
- *Use emotion.* The most effective ads evoke an emotion from the viewer: a laugh, a tear, or a pleasant memory.
- *Consider production values.* Television offers vivid sights, colors, motions, and sounds. Use them!
- *Prove the benefit.* Television enables an advertiser to prove a product's or service's customer benefit by actually demonstrating it.
- *Identify your company clearly and often.* Make sure your store's name, location, and product line stand out. The ad should reflect your company's image.

Source: Adapted from *How to Make a Creative Television Commercial,* Television Bureau of Advertising, Inc.

letic shoes or T-shirts with the information. Table 11.5 offers guideline for Internet ad campaigns.

Some firms have been successful employing direct e-mail advertising. **Direct e-mail** can be either solicited, where an individual asked to be placed on an e-mail list, or unsolicited. Internet users are beginning to view unsolicited e-mail (spam) as intrusive and even unethical. On the other hand, "solicited mailers are gaining momentum, and unlike other Web advertising mediums, customer response seems to be strong. Direct e-mail is said to be 5 times more cost effective than traditional direct mail and 20 times more cost efficient than banner ads."[11] Another study reported that "drawing on studies from Forrester Research and the Direct Marketing Association, a recent issue of Internet marketing newsletter *Iconocast* reported that banner ads have an average cost per sale of about $100. For direct-mail pieces sent through the post, that cost declines to about $71. For opt-in e-mail campaigns, in which consumers agree to accept messages, the figure plummets to $2."[12]

Magazines. Another advertising medium available to the small business owner is magazines. Some 1,800 nontrade magazines are in circulation across the United

Table 11.5
Guidelines for Internet Ad Campaigns

- *Use active messages and techniques.* There's another site just a mouse click away. You must grab visitors' attention *immediately.*
- *Avoid slow download.* Although a site or an ad must capture Web surfers' attention instantly, it cannot be so complex that it requires a long time to download. Otherwise, the audience will never see it. A recent study discovered that speed—or lack of it—was Web users' most common complaint. Slow download will kill even the most captivating Web site or most brilliant ad.
- *Change content often.* Visitors get bored if a Web site looks exactly the same every time they visit. If you cannot revise your site or ad at least monthly, include a section that you can change more frequently such as a quotation of the day or a photograph.
- *Run ads about your company's Web site in ads in other advertising media.* To draw traffic to your Web site, you have to let people know it's there. Include your Web site's address in print ads, in broadcast commercials, on your product packaging, and anywhere else customers will see it.
- *Offer visitors something of interest and of value.* Let customers know up front what benefits your site or ad will offer them. Otherwise, they may not stick around long enough to find it. Establishing links to other sites of interest gives Web surfers more reason to visit your site.
- *Go for the hard sell.* Use your Web site or ad to actually sell something. If you are making a special offer, discount, or sale to Web customers, highlight it on the opening page and make it highly visible. "Soft-sell" techniques do not work on the Web!
- *Assure customers that paying online is secure.* One concern customers have about doing business online is making sure that their credit card information is safe from hackers and thieves. Entrepreneurs serious about doing business on the Web will install the necessary security software to ensure the safety of their customers' credit card information.
- *Respond to customers' requests and inquiries quickly.* The fastest way to lose Web customers is to ignore them or to provide them with poor service. Companies that fill orders or respond to requests the same day have an edge over those that do not.

Source: Adapted from "Rules for Internet Selling," *Communication Briefings*, December 1997, p. 6; Jennifer Sucov, "Me and My Website," *Your Company*, June/July 1997, pp. 36–41; Sandra E. Eddy, "A Lasting Impression," *Business Start-Ups*, May 1997, pp. 14–16.

States. Magazines have a wide reach; today, nearly 9 out of 10 adults read an average of seven magazines each month. The average magazine attracts 6 hours and 3 minutes of total adult reading time, and studies show that the reader is exposed to 89 percent of the ads in the average issue.[13]

Magazines offer several *advantages* for advertisers:

Long life spans. Magazines have a long reading life because readers tend to keep them longer than other printed media. Few people read an entire magazine at one sitting. Instead, most pick it up, read it at intervals, and come back to it later. The result is that each magazine ad has a good chance of being seen several times.

Multiple readership. The average magazine has a readership of 3.9 adult readers, and each reader spends about one hour and 33 minutes with each copy. Many magazines have a high "pass-along" rate; they are handed down from reader to reader. For instance, the in-flight magazines on jets reach many readers in their lifetimes.

Target marketing. By selecting the appropriate special-interest periodical, small business owners can reach those customers with a high degree of interest in their goods or service. Once business owners define their target markets, they can select magazines whose readers most closely match their customer profiles. For instance, *Modern Bride* magazine reaches a very different audience than *Rolling Stone*.

Ad quality. Magazine ads usually are of high quality. Photographs and drawings can be reproduced very effectively, and color ads are readily available. Advertisers can also choose the location of their ads in a magazine and can design creative ads that capture readers' attention.

Magazines also have several *disadvantages*:

Costs. Magazine advertising rates vary according to their circulation rates; the higher the circulation, the higher the rate. Thus, local magazines, whose rates are often comparable to newspaper rates, may be the best bargain for small businesses.

Long closing times. Another disadvantage of magazines is the relatively long closing times they require. For a weekly periodical, the closing date for an ad may be several weeks before the actual publication date. Long lead times and the time needed to plan and design magazine ads reduce the timeliness of this medium.

Lack of prominence. Another disadvantage of magazine ads arises from their popularity as an advertising vehicle. The effectiveness of a single ad may be reduced because of a lack of prominence. Proper ad positioning, therefore, is critical to an ad's success. Research shows that readers "tune out" right-hand pages and look mainly at left-hand pages.

Direct Mail. Direct mail has long been a popular method of small business advertising and includes such tools as letters, postcards, catalogs, discount coupons, brochures, computer disks, and videotapes mailed to homes or businesses. The earliest known catalogs were printed by fifteenth-century printers. Today, direct mail marketers sell virtually every kind of product imaginable, from Christmas trees and lobsters to furniture and clothing (the most popular mail-order purchase). Direct mail marketers spend almost 200 billion each year to reach their varied markets. For decades, the process has been less than sophisticated. Today, a Russian-born computer scientist, Yuri Galperin, is marketing a mathematical method for optimizing direct-marketing campaigns. His model applies probability theory to historical data regarding previous response rates to unsolicited direct mail campaigns, customer age and other demographic data. *Data mining,* as it is termed, holds great promise. In the future, you may no longer receive mailers to purchase items for which you have no use.[14] As much as we complain about the volume of "junk mail" it has proven to be an effective advertising medium.

Direct mail offers a number of distinct *advantages* to small business owners:

Selectivity. The greatest strength of direct mail advertising is its ability to target a specific audience to receive the message. Depending on mailing list quality, an owner can select an audience with virtually any set of characteristics. Small business owners can develop, rent, or purchase a mailing list of prospective residential, commercial, or industrial customers.

Flexibility. Another advantage of direct mail is its capacity to tailor the message to the target. The advertiser's presentation to the customer can be as simple or as elaborate as necessary. *For instance, one custom tailor shop achieved a great deal of success with fliers it mailed to customers on its mailing list when it included a swatch of material from the fabric for the upcoming season's suits.* With direct mail, the tone of the message can be personal, creating a positive psychological effect. In addition, the advertiser controls the timing of the campaign; she can send the ad when it is most appropriate.

Reader attention. With direct mail, an advertiser's message does not have to compete with other ads for the reader's attention. People enjoy getting mail, and more than half of us open and read what we receive. For at least a moment, direct mail gets the recipient's undivided attention. If the message is on the mark and sent to the right audience, direct mail ads can be a powerful advertising tool. Table 11.6 describes common categories of direct mail campaigns with examples of each.

Rapid feedback. Direct mail advertisements produce quick results. In most cases, the ad will generate sales within three or four days after customers receive it. Business owners should know whether a mailing has produced results within a relatively short time period.

Measurable results and testable strategies. Because they control their mailing lists, direct marketers can readily measure the results their ads produce. Also, direct mail allows advertisers to test different ad layouts, designs, and strategies (often within the same "run") to see which one "pulls" the greatest response. The best direct marketers are always fine-tuning their ads to make them more effective. Table 11.7 offers guidelines for creating direct mail ads that really work.

Direct mail ads also suffer from several *disadvantages:*

Inaccurate mailing lists. The key to the success of the entire mailing is the accuracy of the customer list. If mailing lists are inaccurate or incomplete, advertisers will be addressing the wrong audiences and risk alienating their customers with misspelled names.

High relative costs. Direct mail has a higher cost per thousand (cpm) than any other advertising medium. Relative to the size of the audience reached, the cost of designing, producing, and mailing a direct mail advertisement is high. Figure 11.3 shows the breakdown of costs for a typical 3,000 piece mailing. But if the mailing is well planned and

Table 11.6

Categories of Direct Mail Campaigns

CATEGORY	DEFINITION	EXAMPLES
Package insert programs	Inserts ride along in merchandise shipments.	Fingerhut Lillian Vernon Hanover House
Statement insert programs	Inserts ride along in customer invoices or statements.	Visa MasterCard U.S. Cable Network *Family Circle* Books
Billing or renewal insert programs	Inserts accompany magazines' billing or renewal efforts mailed to active prospective subscribers.	*McCalls* *Hachette* *Parenting*
Ride-along programs	Inserts are carried in "other" direct mail marketers' own prospecting or negative option mailings.	BMG Music/Video Columbia House Doubleday
National co-op mailings	Direct mail packages contain a mix of direct response inserts and customer product coupons.	Carol Wright Jane Tucker Select & Save
Local co-op mailings	Direct mail packages contain a mix of direct response inserts and local retail coupons.	Money Mailer On Target Trimark
On-the-pack invoices	Inserts ride along in invoices affixed to the outside of merchandise book shipments.	Field Publications Weekly Reader Books McCalls Cooking School
Premium insert programs	Inserts are carried in free gift shipments sent to new and renewing magazine subscribers.	*Money* magazine *Yankee* magazine *Organic Gardening*
Card packs	Inserts or postcards are commingled in polywraps and mailed to targeted audiences.	*Business Week* Direct Response Deck WG&L Real Estate Action Cards Exec-Cards
Catalog bind-ins	Postcards or inserts are bound into catalogs mailed to customers and targeted prospects.	Gardener's Choice Gander Mountain Gurney Seed
Take-one displays	Inserts or brochures are placed on racks in high-visibility locations.	Good Neighbor College Take-Ones Tourist/Business Traveler Take-Ones

Source: Reprinted with permission of *Sales & Marketing Strategies & News*, January 1992, p. 27. © by Hughes Communications, Inc.

properly executed, it can produce a high percentage of returns, making direct mail one of the least expensive advertising methods in terms of results.

Rising postal rates. One of the primary causes of the high costs of direct mail ads is postage costs, which continue to rise.

High throwaway rate. The average family receives numerous pieces of direct mail each week, and much of that ends up in the trash. Often called junk mail, direct mail ads become "junk" when an advertiser selects the wrong audience or broadcasts the wrong message.

Table 11.7

Guidelines for Creating Direct Mail Ads That *Really* Work

Successful direct mail advertisements require copy that catches readers' attention. Try these proven techniques:

- Promise readers your most important benefits in the headline or first paragraph.
- Use a postscript (P.S.) *always*, they are the most often read part of a printed page.
- Use short "action" words and paragraphs.
- Make the copy easy to read; leave lots of white space.
- Use eye-catching words such as *free, you, save, guarantee, new, profit, benefit, improve,* and others.
- Write as if you were speaking to the reader.
- Repeat the offer three or more times in various ways.
- Back up claims and statements with endorsements whenever possible.
- Get right to the point. Make it easy for readers to see why they should respond to your offer.
- Ask for the order or a response.
- Ask questions such as "Would you like to lower your home's energy costs?"
- Use high-quality paper and envelopes (those with windows are best; envelopes that resemble bills always get opened) because they stand a better chance of being opened and read.
- Address the envelope to an individual, not "Occupant."
- Include a separate order form that passes the following "easy" test:

  Easy to find. Consider using brightly colored paper or a unique shape.

  Easy to understand. Make sure the offer is easy for readers to understand. Marketing expert Paul Goldberg says, "Confuse 'em and you lose 'em."

  Easy to complete. Keep the order form simple and unconfusing.

  Easy to pay. Direct mail ads should give customers the option to pay by whatever means is most convenient.

  Easy to return. Including a postage-paid return envelope (or at a minimum a return envelope) will increase the response rate.

- Build and maintain a quality mailing list over time. The right mailing list is the key to a successful direct mail campaign. You may have to rent lists to get started, but once you are in business, use every opportunity to capture information about your customers. Constantly focus on improving the quality of your mailing list.

Sources: Adapted from "Five Easy Order Form Results," *Communication Briefings,* November 1997, p. 3; Howard Scott, "Targeting Prospects with Direct Mail," *Nation's Business,* September 1997, p. 52; Paul Hughes, "Profits Due," *Entrepreneur,* February 1994, pp. 74–78; "Why They Open Direct Mail," *Communication Briefings,* December 1993, p. 5; Teri Lammers, "The Elements of Perfect Pitch," *Inc.,* March 1992, pp. 53–55; "Special Delivery," *Small Business Reports,* February 1993, p. 6; Gloria Green and James W. Peltier, "How to Develop a Direct Mail Program," *Small Business Forum,* Winter 1993/1994, pp. 30–45; Carolyn Campbell, "A Direct Hit," *Business Start-Ups,* August 1997, pp. 8–10.

Creative entrepreneurs have found other ways to boost their direct mail response rates, including three-dimensional mailers, computer diskettes, and compact discs. *Mike Friedman, owner of three pizza restaurants, found a way to make the coupons he mailed to customers stand out by switching from standard coupons to self-adhesive ones that look like Post-It notes. The initial mailing generated a 30 percent response. "It was phenomenal," says Friedman. "In this business, a 1 to 3 percent response is considered good. A year later the Post-It coupons were still drawing a 20 percent response rate.*[15]

"High-Tech" Direct Mail. Sending out ads on computer diskettes is an excellent way to reach upscale households and businesses. Not only do computer-based ads give

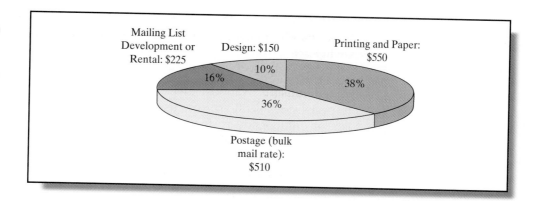

Figure 11.3
Cost Breakdown
of a 3,000-Piece
Direct Mailing.

Source: John Horton,
Horton Associates,
Providence, RI.

Mailing List
Development or
Rental: $225

Design: $150

Printing and Paper:
$550

16%

10%

38%

36%

Postage (bulk
mail rate):
$510

advertisers the power to create flashy, attention-grabbing designs, but they also hold the audience's attention.

Compact discs (CDs) offer advertisers the same benefits as computer disks with one extra—more space to do it in. Companies are using CDs with interactive ads to sell everything from cars to computers. The ads usually contain videos, computer games, quizzes, animation, music, graphics, and other features to engage more of their audiences' senses. In a world where U.S. households receive *3.7 million tons* of paper each year in the form of direct mail ads, multimedia ads can offer a distinct advantage: They get noticed.

How to Use Direct Mail. The key to a direct mailing's success is the right mailing list. Even the best direct mail ad will fail if sent to the "wrong" customers. Owners can develop lists themselves, using customer accounts, telephone books, city and

IN THE FOOTSTEPS OF AN ENTREPRENEUR
You Can Find It in the Catalog

Who would have predicted that the carved wooden figures of Robert DuLong would be such a success? In reality, these products produced by DuLong's Phoenix, New York company, Woodendipity, are perfect for the catalog marketplace. To be successful, you need a product that is catalog ready. The product needs to be unique and invoke an "isn't that neat" response from those who see it. Second, get noticed by the catalog companies. This can be accomplished through exhibiting at trade shows; hiring a manufacture rep with contacts in the catalog industry; attempt to get some positive attention for your product in the media; and, if all else fails, try cold calling the catalogs you believe best fit your product. In every case, you must have the capability to produce the product in sufficient quantity to satisfy demand and it must be

priced in a way for both you and the catalog company to earn a reasonable profit. Finally, cultivate a positive relationship with the catalog company. Recognize that this is now your marketing operation. Treat your catalog partner in a way that encourages a lasting business relationship. Once you build a mutually beneficial relationship with a catalog company, future products have a better chance at being accepted.

1. What type of products do you purchase from catalogs? How confident are you about the quality of the products sold in catalogs?

2. What are the most effective advertising techniques employed by the successful catalog companies?

Source: Victoria Clayton-Alexander, "Catalog Crazy," *Emerging Business,* Summer, 2001, pp. 84–87

trade directories, and other sources. Other sources for mailing lists include companies selling complementary, but not competing products; professional organizations' membership lists; business or professional magazines' subscription lists; and mailing list brokers who sell lists for practically any need.

Outdoor Advertising. National advertisers have long used outdoor ads, and small firms (especially retailers) are now using this medium. Very few small businesses rely solely on outdoor advertising; instead, they supplement other advertising media with billboards. With a creative outdoor campaign, a small company can make a big impact, even on a small budget. *South of the Border, a unique tourist complex with a Mexican theme sitting on 350 acres near tiny Dillon, South Carolina, uses more than 200 billboards along Interstate 95 from Philadelphia to Daytona Beach, Florida, to lure visitors. During the busy summer travel season, as many as 50,000 people a day stop to satisfy the curiosity that the company's billboards create. As they pull into the main gate, visitors are greeted by a 97-foot sign featuring Pedro, the official mascot of South of the Border. Once inside, guests can stay in the complex's hotels or campgrounds and enjoy amusement rides, miniature golf, poker arcades, and restaurants. Owners credit much of their company's success to their creative outdoor advertising campaign.*[16]

Outdoor advertising offers certain *advantages* to the small business:

High exposure. Outdoor advertising offers a high-frequency exposure; studies suggest that the typical billboard reaches an adult 29 to 31 times each month. Most people tend to follow the same routes in their daily traveling, and billboards are there waiting for them when they pass by. Also, when located near the advertiser's business, billboards can be effective as last-minute reminders.

Broad reach. The nature of outdoor ads makes them effective devices for reaching a large number of potential customers within a specific area. The people outdoor ads reach tend to be younger, wealthier, and better educated than the average person.

Attention-getting. The introduction of new technology such as 3-D, fiber optics, and other creative special effects to outdoor advertising has transformed billboards from flat, passive signs to innovative, attention-grabbing promotions that passers-by cannot help but notice.

Flexibility. Advertisers can buy outdoor advertising units separately or in a number of packages. Through its variety of graphics, design, and unique features, outdoor advertising enables the small advertiser to match his message to the particular audience. Modern computer and printing technology have given outdoor ads a design facelift. A decade ago, only 5 percent of billboards actually used such technology; today, about 80 percent of billboards rely on some kind of computer technology. Not only does this technology make billboards look better, but its speed allows advertisers to change boards more frequently at lower costs.[17]

Cost efficiency. Outdoor advertising offers one of the lowest costs per thousand customers reached of all the advertising media.

Outdoor ads also have several *disadvantages*:

Brief exposure. Because billboards are immobile, the reader is exposed to the advertiser's message for only a short time, typically no more than five seconds. As a result, the message must be short and to the point. Outdoor advertisers must consider the type of traffic passing a billboard location as well as the volume of traffic going by (slower is better). Outdoor advertising copy cannot be as detailed or as informative as ads in other media.

Legal restrictions. Outdoor billboards are subject to strict regulations and to a high degree of standardization. At the federal level, the Highway Beautification Act of 1965 requires signs and billboards to be a standard size and to be attractive. At the local level, many cities place limitations on the number and type of signs and billboards allowed along the roadside. Recently, several major cities have severely restricted or banned the construction of new outdoor signs.

Lack of prominence. This clutter of billboards and signs tends to reduce the effectiveness of a single ad, which loses its prominence in the crowd of billboards.

Using Outdoor Ads. Because the outdoor ad is stationary and the viewer is in motion, the small business owner must pay special attention to its design. An outdoor ad should:

- Identify the product and the company clearly and quickly.
- Use a simple background. The background should not compete with the message.
- Rely on large illustrations that jump out at the viewer.
- Include clear, legible type. All lowercase or a combination of upper- and lowercase letters is best. Very bold or very thin type faces become illegible at a distance.
- Use black-and-white designs. Research shows that black-and-white outdoor ads are more effective than color ads. If color is important to the message, pick color combinations that contrast in both hue and brightness (e.g., black on yellow).
- Emphasize simplicity; short copy and short words are best. Don't try to cram too much onto a billboard. One study found that ads with fewer than eight words were most effective, and those containing more than 10 words were least effective.
- Use sharp, eye-catching graphics. Many billboards now use three-dimensional features or extensions that capture viewers' attention.
- Be located on the right-hand side of the highway. Studies show that ads located there draw higher recall scores than those located on the left-hand side.
- Use billboards as a reinforcement for other methods of advertising and to remind prospects of where you are and what you do.[18]

Transit Advertising. Transit advertising includes advertising signs inside and outside some 70,000 public transportation vehicles throughout the country's urban areas. The medium is likely to grow as more cities look to public transit systems to relieve transportation problems.

Transit ads offer a number of *advantages*:

Wide coverage. Transit advertising offers advertisers mass exposure to a variety of customers. The message literally goes to where the people are. This medium also reaches people with a wide variety of demographic characteristics. Orbital Science Corporation and Itec Entertainment Corporation have teamed up to produce material for television on public transportation. The product is a blend of entertainment and advertising. The pilot project is operating on select city buses in Orlando, Florida.[19]

Repeat exposure. Transit ads provide repeated exposure to a message. This gives advertisers ample opportunity to present their messages to transit riders.

Low cost. Even small business owners with limited budgets can afford transit advertising. Many transit systems offer discounts for long-term contracts.

Flexibility. Transit ads come in a wide range of sizes, numbers, and durations. With transit ads, an owner can select an individual market or any combination of markets across the country.

Transit ads also have several *disadvantages*:

Generality. Even though a small business can choose the specific transit routes on which to advertise, it cannot target a particular segment of the market through transit advertising. The effectiveness of transit ads depends on the routes that public vehicles travel and on the people they reach. Unfortunately, the advertiser cannot control either of those factors.

Limited appeal. Unlike many media, transit ads are not beamed into the potential customer's residence or business. The result is that customers cannot keep them for future reference. Also, these ads do not reach with great frequency the upper income, highly educated portion of the market.

Brief message. Transit ads do not permit the small advertiser to present a detailed description or a demonstration of the product or service for sale. Although inside ads have a relatively long exposure (the average ride lasts 22.5 minutes), outside ads must be brief and to the point.

Directories. Directories are an important advertising medium for reaching customers who have already made purchase decisions. The directory simply helps these customers locate the specific product or service they have decided to buy. Directories include telephone books, industrial or trade guides, buyer's guides, annuals, catalog files, and yearbooks that list various businesses and the products they sell.

Directories offer several *advantages* to advertisers:

Prime prospects. Directory listings reach customers who are prime prospects, since they have already decided to purchase an item. The directory just helps them find what they are looking for.

Long life. Directory listings usually have long lives. A typical directory may be published annually.

However, there are certain *disadvantages* to using directories:

Lack of flexibility. Listings and ads in many directories offer only a limited variety of design features. Business owners may not be as free to create unique ads as in other printed media.

Obsolescence. Because directories are commonly updated only annually, some of their listings become obsolete. This is a problem for a small firm that changes its name, location, or phone number.

Using Directories. When choosing a directory, the small business owner should evaluate several criteria:

- *Completeness.* Does the directory include enough listings that customers will use it?

- *Convenience.* Are the listings well organized and convenient? Are they cross-referenced?
- *Evidence of use.* To what extent do customers actually use the directory? What evidence of use does the publisher offer?
- *Age.* Is the directory well established, and does it have a good reputation?
- *Circulation.* Do users pay for the directory, or do they receive complimentary copies? Is there an audited circulation statement?

IN THE FOOTSTEPS OF AN ENTREPRENEUR
A Tough Market to Reach

About 33 percent of American men and 36 percent of American women are considered overweight. For years, marketers ignored this plus-sized segment of the population, acting as if the typical customer were shaped like models selling *haute couture* on the runways of the world's greatest fashion houses. That left larger customers with little choice but to try to squeeze into clothing styles and designs made for smaller people. More recently, however, businesses have begun to realize the potential for catering to this growing market. In fact, since 1980, there has been a 9 percent increase in the number of overweight people in this country. Increasingly, companies of all sizes have been providing products and services aimed at this target audience. In 1989, Jan Herrick began publishing Royal Resources, a directory of companies offering plus-sized products and services. The first edition contained just 137 entries. Today, Royal Resources lists in more than 50 categories more than 1,200 companies selling everything from dating services and toilet seats to wigs and motorcycle gear.

One small company focusing on the plus-sized market is Anne Kelly's Junonia Ltd., a maker of active wear that sells its products through a mail-order catalog. Kelly, herself a full-figured person, says that she got the idea for her business when she had difficulty finding active wear for her workouts at the gym. Kelly's direct mail catalog carries items such as bike shorts, swimsuits, sports bras, ski jackets, leggings, and many others. Within three years, Junonia's mailing list topped 350,000, and sales surged past $2 million.

Like Kelly, many companies targeting the plus-sized market have discovered that direct mail is an excellent avenue for reaching their customers. For many large people, shopping in retail stores can be frustrating, embarrassing, and painful. "Who wants to schlep around to stores looking for [clothes] when you know they don't carry your size?" says Bill Fabrey. "And big people get really insensitive treatment from salespeople." Fabrey launched his own mail-order catalog, Amplestuff, featuring home furnishings, closet and bath items, and other gadgets for large people in 1988.

Companies selling to the plus-sized market must exercise caution, however. The problem stems from America's obsession with thinness: No one, not even an overweight person, likes to think of himself as "fat." "Do you know how people react when they receive a mailing for large-sized people?" asks Fabrey. "They're insulted and annoyed." Few advertisements succeed by insulting the very people they are targeting, so advertisers must find other ways to reach this target market. One way many have found to work well is by placing ads in magazines such as *BBW, Radiance,* and *Dimension* and other media that invite customers to write, fax, call, or e-mail for a catalog. Magazines, however, reach only a portion of the total market, leaving advertisers searching for creative ways to reach their target audience. "We're really pioneers in this market," says Fabrey. "It's like the Wild West used to be."

1. Working with a team of your classmates, develop at least five methods small companies targeting the plus-sized market could use to reach their customers.

2. What kinds of unique selling propositions should they consider?

Source: Adapted from Frances Huffman, "Living Large," *Entrepreneur,* October 1997, pp. 156–159.

Trade shows. Trade shows provide manufacturers and distributors with a unique opportunity to advertise to a preselected audience of potential customers who are inclined to buy. Thousands of trade shows are sponsored each year. Business owners need to begin by carefully defining their goals regarding what a specific trade show might contribute to sales. Next, evaluate the alternative shows based on both cost and size and type of audience. The third component is to staff your booth with the right people. Individuals must be willing to be on their feet and work hard. Finally, create a "lead" retrieval system that ensures your capability to continue communications with them in the future.[20]

Trade shows offer the following *advantages*:

A natural market. Trade shows bring together buyers and sellers in a setting where products can be explained, demonstrated, and handled. Comparative shopping is easy, and the buying process is efficient.

Preselected audience. Trade exhibits attract potential customers with a specific interest in the goods or services being displayed. There is a high probability that these prospects will make a purchase.

New customer market. Trade shows offer exhibitors a prime opportunity to reach new customers and to contact people who are not accessible to sales representatives. Plus, there is no better place to introduce new products (or a new company) than at a trade show, where all of the people there are interested in what's new and exciting.

Industry information. Trade shows provide excellent opportunities for entrepreneurs to find out what is happening in their industries and to size up their competitors—all in one place. Observant entrepreneurs can spot key trends in the industry and find out which products or services will be the next hot sellers.

International contacts. Many small companies make their first international sales at trade shows, which are extremely popular with foreign businesses. Michigan State University's Center for International Business Education and Research (www.ciber.msu.edu/busrestradshow.htm) includes listings of trade shows and expos around the world.

Cost advantage. As the cost of making a field sales call continues to escalate, more companies are realizing that trade shows are an economical method for making sales contacts and presentations. Studies show that the cost per visitor reached at trade shows is still well below the average cost of a personal sales call. For making a connection with the best sales prospects, trade shows provide good value for every dollar spent.

There are, however, certain *disadvantages* associated with trade shows:

Increasing costs. The cost of exhibiting at trade shows is rising quickly. Registration fees, travel and setup costs, sales salaries, and other expenditures may be a barrier to some small firms. The largest expenses at most trade shows are the cost of the display and booth rental.

Wasted effort. A poorly planned exhibit ultimately costs the small business more than its benefits are worth. Too many firms enter exhibits in trade shows without proper preparation, and they end up wasting their time, energy, and money on unproductive activities.

Specialty Advertising. As advertisers have shifted their focus to "narrow casting" their messages to target audiences and away from "broadcasting," specialty advertising has grown in popularity. Advertisers now spend more than $3 billion annually on specialty items. This category includes all customer gift items imprinted with the company's name, address, telephone number, and slogan. Specialty items are best used as reminder ads to supplement other forms of advertising and to help create goodwill with existing and potential customers.

Specialty advertising offers several *advantages*:

Reaching select audiences. Advertisers can reach specific audiences with well-planned specialty items.

Personalized nature. By carefully choosing a specialty item, business owners can personalize their advertisements. A small business owner should choose items that are unusual, related to the nature of the business, and meaningful to customers.

Versatility. The rich versatility of specialty advertising is limited only by the business owner's imagination. Advertisers print their logos on everything from pens and scarves to wallets and caps. When choosing advertising specialties, entrepreneurs should use items that are unusual and related to the nature of the business.

There are *disadvantages* to specialty advertising:

Potential for waste. Unless the owner chooses the appropriate specialty item, he will be wasting his time and money. The options are virtually infinite.

Costs. Some specialty items can be quite expensive. Plus, some owners have a tendency to give advertising materials to anyone—even people who are not potential customers.

Special Events and Promotions. A growing number of small companies are finding that special events and promotions attract a great deal of interest and provide a lasting impression of the company. As customers become increasingly harder to reach through any single advertising medium, companies of all sizes are finding that sponsoring special events and promotions—from wine tastings and beach volleyball tournaments to fitness walks and rock climbs—is an excellent way to reach their target audiences. The more creative the entrepreneur the higher the probability that the event will both attract potential customers and earn excellent coverage in the media.

Point-of-Purchase Ads. In the last several years, in-store advertising has become more popular as a way of reaching the customer at a crucial moment—the point of purchase. Research suggests that consumers make two thirds of all buying decisions at the point of sale. Self-service stores are especially well suited for in-store ads as they remind people of the products as they walk the aisles. These in-store ads are not just bland signs or glossy photographs of the product in use. Some businesses use in-store music interspersed with household hints and, of course, ads. Another ploy involves tiny devices that sense when a customer passes by and triggers a prerecorded sales message.

In sum, small business owners have an endless array of advertising tools, techniques, and media available to them. Even postage stamps, bathroom walls, sides of cows, and parking meters offer advertising space!

PREPARING AN ADVERTISING BUDGET

One of the most challenging decisions confronting a small business owner is how much money to invest in advertising. The amount the owner wants to spend and the

4. Identify four basic methods for preparing an advertising budget.

amount the firm can afford to spend on advertising usually differ significantly. There are four methods of determining an advertising budget: what is affordable, matching competitors, percentage of sales, and objective-and-task.

Under the *what-is-affordable method,* the owner sees advertising as a luxury. He or she views advertising completely as an expense, not as an investment that produces sales and profits in the future. Therefore, as the name implies, management spends whatever it can afford on advertising. Too often, the advertising budget is allocated funds only after all other budget items have been financed. The result is an inadequate advertising budget. This method also fails to relate the advertising budget to the advertising objective.

Another approach is to *match* the advertising expenditures of the firm's competitors, either in a flat dollar amount or as a percentage of sales. This method assumes that a firm's advertising needs and strategies are the same as those of its competitors. Competitors' actions can be helpful in establishing a floor for advertising expenditures, but relying on this technique can lead to blind imitation instead of a budget suited to the small firm's circumstances.

The most commonly used method of establishing an advertising budget is the simple *percentage-of-sales approach.* This method relates advertising expenditures to actual sales results. Tying advertising expenditures to sales is generally preferred to relating them to profits because sales tend to fluctuate less than profits. A useful rule of thumb when establishing an advertising budget: 10 percent of projected sales the first year in business; 7 percent the second year; and at least 5 percent each year after that. Relying totally on such broad rules can be dangerous, however. They may not be representative of a small company's advertising needs.

The *objective-and-task method* is the most difficult and least used technique for establishing an advertising budget. It also is the method most often recommended by advertising experts. With this method, an owner links advertising expenditures to specific objectives. Whereas the other three methods break down the total amount of funds allocated to advertising, the task method builds up the advertising funds by analyzing what it will cost to accomplish the specific objectives. For example, suppose that a manager wants to boost sales of a particular product 10 percent by attracting local college students. He may determine that a nearby rock radio station would be the best medium to use. Then he must decide on the number and frequency of the ads and estimate their costs. Entrepreneurs simply follow this same process for each advertising objective. A common problem with the method is that managers tend to be overly ambitious in setting advertising objectives, and, consequently, they set unrealistically high advertising expenditures. The manager may be forced to alter objectives, or the plans to reach them, to bring the advertising budget back to a reasonable level. However, the plan can still be effective.

Most small companies find it useful to plan in advance their advertising expenditures on a weekly basis. This short-term planning ensures a consistent advertising effort throughout the year. A calendar like the one pictured in Figure 11.4 can be one of the most valuable tools in planning a small company's advertising program. The calendar enables owners to prepare for holid´ys and special events, to monitor actual and budgeted expenditures, and to ensure that ads are scheduled on the appropriate media at the proper times.

HOW TO ADVERTISE BIG ON A SMALL BUDGET

The typical small business does not have the luxury of an unlimited advertising budget. Most cannot afford to hire a professional ad agency. This does not mean, how-

Figure 11.4
A Sample Advertising Calendar

October

Sun	Mon	Tue	Wed	Thu	Fri	Sat
Advertising Budget for October: 9% of Sales = $2,275 Co-op Ads = $ 550 Total = $2,825		October Advertising Expenditures: $2,845 Under/(Over) Budget: $20 Remaining Balance: $6,400		**1** WPCC Radio 5 spots, $125 Billboard, $350	**2** <u>The Chronicle</u> 140 lines, $100	**3**
4	**5**	**6**	**7**	**8**	**9** <u>The Chronicle</u> 140 lines, $100	**10**
11	**12**	**13** Meet w/ Leslie re: November ad campaigns, 2 p.m.	**14**	**15** Envelope "Stuffer" in invoices: Halloween Sale, $175	**16** <u>The Chronicle</u> 140 lines, $100	**17** WPCC Radio, 5 spots, $100
18	**19**	**20** WPCC Radio, 5 spots, $125	**21**	**22** Direct Mail, Halloween Sale Promo "Preferred Customers," $120	**23** <u>The Chronicle</u> 140 lines, $100	**24** WPCC Radio, 5 spots, $100
25	**26** WPCC Radio, 5 spots, $125	**27** WPCC Radio, 5 spots, $125	**28** WPCC Radio, 5 spots, $125	**29** WPCC Radio, 5 spots, $125	**30** <u>The Chronicle</u> Half-page spread, Sale, $300	Halloween Sale **31** WPCC Radio, Live remote broadcast, $425

5. Explain practical methods for stretching a small business's advertising budget.

ever, that the small company should assume a second-class advertising posture. Most advertising experts say that, unless a small company spends more than $10,000 a year on advertising, it probably doesn't need an ad agency. For most, hiring free-lance copywriters and artists on a per-project basis is a much better bargain. With a little creativity and a dose of ingenuity, small business owners can stretch their advertising dollars and make the most of what they spend. Three useful techniques to do this are cooperative advertising, shared advertising, and publicity.

Cooperative Advertising

In **cooperative advertising,** a manufacturing company shares the cost of advertising with a retailer if the retailer features its products in those ads. Both the manufacturer and the retailer get more advertising per dollar by sharing expenses. This is an opportunity that is too often overlooked by small retailers. Cooperative advertising not only helps small businesses stretch their advertising budgets; it also offers another source of savings: the free advertising packages that many manufacturers supply to retailers. These packages usually include photographs and illustrations of the product as well as professionally prepared ads to use in different media.

Shared Advertising

In **shared advertising,** a group of similar businesses forms a syndicate to produce generic ads that allow the individual businesses to dub in local information. The technique is especially useful for small businesses that sell relatively standardized products or services such as legal assistance, autos, and furniture. Because the small firms in the syndicate pool their funds, the result usually is higher-quality ads and significantly lower production costs.

Publicity

The press can be either a valuable friend or a fearsome foe to a small business, depending on how well the owner handles his or her firm's publicity. Too often, entrepreneurs take the attitude, "My business is too small to be concerned about public relations." However, wise small business managers recognize that investing time and money in public relations (publicity) benefits both the community and the company. The community gains the support of a good business citizen, and the company earns a positive image in the marketplace.

Many small businesses rely on media attention to get noticed, and getting that attention takes a coordinated effort. Publicity doesn't just happen; business owners must work at getting their companies noticed by the media. Although such publicity may not be free, it definitely can lower the company's advertising expenditures and still keep its name before the public. Because small companies' advertising budgets are limited, publicity takes on significant importance.

One successful publicity technique is cause marketing, in which a small business sponsors and promotes fund-raising activities of nonprofit groups and charities while raising its own visibility in the community. In most cases, the cost of sponsorship is modest in comparison with the excellent exposure the business receives as participants now view the sponsoring companies in a favorable fashion.

Other Ways to Save

Other cost-saving suggestions for advertising expenditures include the following:

Repeat ads that have been successful. In addition to reducing the cost of ad preparation, repetition may create a consistent image in a small firm's advertising program.

Use identical ads in different media. If a billboard has been an effective advertising tool, an owner should consider converting it to a newspaper or magazine ad or a direct mail flier.

Hire independent copywriters, graphic designers, photographers, and other media specialists. Many small businesses that cannot afford a full-time advertising staff buy their advertising services a la carte. They work directly with independent specialists and usually receive high-quality work that compares favorably with that of advertising agencies without paying a fee for overhead.

Concentrate advertising during times when customers are most likely to buy. Some small business owners make the mistake of spreading an already small advertising budget evenly—and thinly—over a 12-month period. A better strategy is to match advertising expenditures to customers' buying habits.

CHAPTER SUMMARY

1. Describe the steps in developing an advertising strategy.
   - Define the purpose of the company's advertising program by creating specific, measurable objectives.
   - Analyze the firm and its target audience.
   - Decide what to say and how to say it, making sure to build the message around the company's unique selling proposition (USP).
   - Evaluate the ad campaign's effectiveness.
2. Explain the differences among promotion, publicity, personal selling, and advertising.
   - Promotion is any form of persuasive communication designed to inform consumers about a product or service and to influence them to purchase those goods or services.
   - Publicity is any commercial news covered by the media that boosts sales but for which the small business does not pay.
   - Personal selling is the personal contact between salespeople and potential customers resulting from sales efforts.
   - Advertising is any sales presentation that is non-personal in nature and is paid for by an identified sponsor.
3. Describe the advantages and disadvantages of the various advertising media.
   - The medium used to transmit an advertising message influences the consumer's perception—and reception—of it.
   - Media options include newspapers, radio, television, magazines, direct mail, the World Wide Web, outdoor advertising, transit advertising, directories, trade shows, special events and promotions, and point-of-purchase ads.
4. Identify four basic methods for preparing an advertising budget.
   - Establishing an advertising budget presents a real challenge to the small business owners. There are four basic methods: what is affordable, matching competitors, percentage of sales, and objective-and-task.
5. Explain practical methods for stretching a small business's advertising budget.
   - Despite their limited advertising budgets, small businesses do not have to take a second-class approach to advertising. Three techniques that can stretch a small company's advertising dollars are cooperative advertising, shared advertising, and publicity.

DISCUSSION QUESTIONS

1. What are the three elements of promotion? How do they support one another?
2. What factors should a small business manager consider when selecting advertising media?
3. What is a unique selling proposition? What role should it play in a company's advertising strategy?
4. Create a table to summarize the advantages and disadvantages of the following advertising media:
   Newspapers
   Radio
   Television
   Magazines
   Specialty advertising
   Direct mail
   Outdoor advertising
   Transit advertising
   Directories
   Trade shows
5. What are fixed spots, preemptible spots, and floating spots in radio advertising?
6. Describe the characteristics of an effective outdoor advertisement.
7. Briefly outline the steps in creating an advertising plan. What principles should the small business owner follow when creating an effective advertisement?
8. Describe the common methods of establishing an advertising budget. Which method is most often used? Which technique is most often recommended? Why?
9. What techniques can small businesses use to stretch their advertising budgets?

1. Contact a small retailer, a manufacturer, and a service firm, and interview each one about his or her advertising program.
   a. Are there specific advertising objectives?
   b. What media does the owner employ? Why?
   c. How does the manager evaluate an ad's effectiveness?
   d. What assistance does the manager receive in designing ads?
2. Contact several small business owners and determine how they establish their advertising budgets. Why do they use the method they do?
3. Collect two or three advertisements for local small businesses and evaluate them on a scale of 1 (low) to 10 (high) using the following criteria: attention-getting, distinctive, interesting, concise, appealing, credible, USP-focused, convincing, motivating, and effective. How would you change the ads to make them more effective?
4. Browse through a magazine and find two ads that use sex to sell a good or service—one that you consider effective and one that you consider offensive. Compare your ads and reasoning with those of your classmates. What implications does your discussion have for advertisers?

TAKE IT TO THE NET

Visit the Scarborough/Zimmerer home page at **www.prenhall.com/scarborough** for updated information, online resources, Web-based exercises, and sample business plan.

ENDNOTES

1. Bob Weinstein, "A Golden Opportunity," *Business Start-Ups*, November 1997, pp. 63–65.
2. Lin Grensing-Pophal, "Who Are You?" *Business Start-Ups*, September 1997, pp. 38–44,
3. Meg Whittemore, "Partner with a Charity for Profits," *Your Company*, August/September 1997, p. 24.
4. Lynn Beresford, "Going My Way?" *Entrepreneur*, February 1996, p. 32.
5. Elizabeth Jensen, "Rosie and Friends Make Drake's Cakes a Star," *Wall Street Journal*, February 10, 1997, pp. B1, B7.
6. Cassandra Cavanah, "High-Tech Handshakes," *Entrepreneur*, August 2000, pp. 52–54.
7. "Meeting Customer Needs," *In Business*, May/June 1989, p. 14.
8. "Ad Suggestions from New Study," *Communication Briefings*, June 1995, p. 2.
9. Mike Langberg, "Adman's Delight," *SBC*, June 2001, p. 12
10. Jennifer Rewick, "Brand Awareness Fuels Strategies for Online Advertising Next Year," *Wall Street Journal*, December 28, 2000, p. B2.
11. Ron Cheek, Michelle Kunz, and Peggy Osborne, "Web Advertising: A Look at Types and Cost," *www.sbaer.uca.edu/Research2000/2001/ACME/52acme01.htm.*

12. Jim Sterne, "In Praise of E-Mail," *Inc., Tech 2000*, No. 2, pp. 149–150.
13. *The Dynamics of Change in Markets and Media*, from a Magazine Publishers Association
14. Lea Goldman, "Junk-Mail Junkie," *Forbes*, October 15, 2000, p. 98.
15. Gayle Sato Stodder, "Getting Noticed," *Entrepreneur*, October 1997, p. 33.
16. Anna Kelly, "Doing Business South of the Border," *Region Focus*, Spring 1998, p. 8.
17. *www.signweb.com/buy-guides/july97/outdoor1b.html.*
18. *The Big Outdoor* (New York Institute of Outdoor Advertising), p. 15; "Outdoor Ads That Work Best," *Communication Briefings*, October 1993, p. 6; Lynn Beresford, "The Big Picture," *Entrepreneur*, July 1996, p. 38.
19. Robert Johnson , "Ad-Packed TVs May Soon Be Boarding City Buses," *Wall Street Journal*, February 21, 2001, p. B1.
20. Maira Allen, "Showing the World," *Entrepreneur*, November, 2000, p. 48.

Chapter 12

Global Marketing Strategies for Entrepreneurs

> *Nothing Sucks Like an Electrolux*
>
> —Scandinavian Translation of English Product Slogan

> *Pepsi Bring Your Ancestors Back from the Grave*
>
> —Chinese Translation of "Pepsi Comes Alive"

Upon completion of this chapter, you will be able to:

1. Explain why "going global" has become an integral part of many entrepreneurs marketing strategies.

2. Describe the principal strategies for going global.

3. Explain how to build a thriving export program.

4. Discuss the major barriers to international trade and their impact on the global economy.

5. Describe the trade agreements that will have the greatest influence on foreign trade in the twenty-first century.

It is no longer a surprise to entrepreneurs that they face global competition in the marketplace. The new economic world order is the result of the interaction of dynamic forces. Culture, politics, and the basic social fabric of nations are evolving at unprecedented pace as change is facilitated by technology and challenged by global economic and competitive forces. Twenty-first-century entrepreneurs recognize that the markets of today are small in comparison to the market potential of tomorrow. The world market for goods and services continues to expand, fueled by a global economy that welcomes consumers with new wealth. Technology, which continues to become increasingly affordable and powerful, links trading partners whether they are giant corporations or single individuals with a small business.

The interdependency of nations is highlighted daily as billions of dollars in trade takes place with little or no national interference. Global business is accepted as a natural phenomenon, and new entries join daily. The tools of global business are not beyond the reach of any entrepreneur. This chapter cannot delve into great depth in any specific area, but is designed to demonstrate the nature and scope of the opportunities available to entrepreneurs who accept the challenge to "go global."

WHY GO GLOBAL?

1. Explain why "going global" has become an integral part of many entrepreneurial marketing strategies.

The answer to why go global is not unlike the response given by the legendary bank robber, Willie Sutton, who, when asked why he robbed banks, simply replied, "That's where the money is." The same is true for global business today. Failure to cultivate global markets can be a lethal mistake for modern businesses, whatever their size. Increasingly, small businesses will be under pressure to expand into international markets, to consider themselves businesses without borders.

Going global can put tremendous strain on a small company, but entrepreneurs who take the plunge into global business can reap the following benefits:

- *Offset sales declines in the domestic market.* Markets in foreign countries may be booming when those in the United States are sagging. In this way, global business acts as a counter-cyclical balance.
- *Increase sales and profits.* Two forces are working in tandem to make global business increasingly attractive: income rising to levels where potential sales are now possible and the realization that 96 percent of the planet's population is outside of the United States.
- *Extend their products' life cycle.* Some companies have been able to take products that had reached the maturity stage of the product life cycle in the United States and sell them successfully in foreign markets.
- *Lower manufacturing costs.* In industries characterized by high levels of fixed costs, businesses that expand into global markets can lower their manufacturing costs by spreading those fixed costs over a larger number of units.
- *Improve competitive position and enhance reputation.* Going up against some of the toughest competition in the world forces a company to hone its competitive skills.
- *Raise quality levels.* Customers in many global markets are much tougher to satisfy than those in the United States. One reason Japanese products have done so well worldwide is that Japanese companies must build products to satisfy their customers at home, who demand extremely high quality and are sticklers for detail. Businesses that compete in global markets learn very quickly how to boost their quality levels to world-class standards.

IN THE FOOTSTEPS OF AN ENTREPRENEUR
Blasting Their Way into International Markets

Anna Chong and her husband, Eric Kelly, are co-owners of Engineered Demolition, a family business with 20 employees that operates in a unique niche market that spans the globe: explosive demolition. The Minneapolis-based company is one of just a handful of businesses worldwide that uses implosion to destroy old buildings in metropolitan areas to make way for new ones. Implosion destroys a building by causing it to burst inward (compared with an explosion, which causes things to burst outward) as a result of carefully planned and precisely timed explosives placed at strategic points in the structure.

Imploding a building costs about 20 percent less than tearing it down the old-fashioned way. Still, Chong and Kelly spend a great deal of time educating clients about the implosion process, dispelling the misconceived images people have of debris shooting out for hundreds of yards from the work site. To emphasize the safety of Engineered Demolition's work, Chong often shows videotapes of demolitions from the company's portfolio. One of the company's most challenging jobs was to implode a building that was actually touching another building that had to be saved! Chong and Kelly also successfully imploded an old refrigeration plant in Montreal that left a 236-year-old home just 15 feet away untouched.

Imploding a typical 10-story building requires about 300 pounds of explosives and costs about $250,000. After studying the blueprints of the target building, Engineered Demolition workers plan the blast, emphasizing four key elements: the direction of the fall, how straight the fall is, the material structure of the building, and the proximity and location of adjoining buildings. Taking these factors into account, demolition experts develop a schematic of the number, placement, and size of the explosives needed to do the job. After a contractor "preps" the building by gutting as much of it as possible, the team of demolitionists go inside to insert the explosives, a process called loading. The team attaches blasting caps to touch off the explosions and wires the whole network together with miles of wire connected to a plunger on a detonating device located several hundred feet away.

As one might imagine, implosion is a highly specialized field that requires extensive training. Both Kelly and Chong hold blaster's licenses valid in the United States and internationally. In fact, Chong is one of the few women to hold such a license. Engineered Demolition currently averages about 75 jobs a year, but business is doubling about every four years. Chong says that the number of jobs from international customers is increasing rapidly. Currently, about one third of the company's contracts come from international clients, but Chong expects that number to accelerate. "What we are seeing is an increased worldwide demand to make more efficient use of costly and limited land space by removing old structures," she says. As nations around the globe upgrade their infrastructure to spur economic growth, Engineered Demolition is discovering new opportunities to market its unique service. "In Asia, it's very common for the land costs to be higher than the value of the structures (currently sitting on the land), and the buildings are so close together that it's impossible to use a wrecking ball without damaging adjoining structures," says Chong. The only alternative is implosion.

Although used for years in the United States and Canada, demolition by implosion has caught on in Asia, Europe, and Latin America only recently. "Canada is our largest and most accessible market outside of the United States because of its proximity, similarity of culture, and ways of doing business," says Chong. Implosion jobs in congested cities in Asia, Europe, and Latin America are on the rise, however. Performing an implosion in these countries is more difficult because of the time required to get the necessary permits. "We tend to rely on the local labor as much as possible when doing our work internationally because it's more cost-effective for both parties in arranging handling, sales, transportation, and simple things like getting a local permit. They understand the culture and have the right connections to get the job done."

As their international clientele increases, Chong and Kelly have learned to be more sensitive to their customers' cultural preferences and customs. "In countries like Japan and Korea," says Chong, "the number 4 means death. We won't demolish a structure on the fourth of the month, and we often avoid loading explosives on the fourth floor of a building."

(continued)

Chong also steps into the background in many jobs in Asia because "clients don't always feel comfortable about a woman pushing down the plunger on the detonating device because they believe it might bring bad luck."

Engineered Demolition is actively pursuing business in European markets. Chong was one of 22 women who participated in a recent Women in Trade mission to Europe led by the U.S. Commerce Department. "These missions are great for that kind of exposure on your own, " says Chong. The exposure has already paid off. Not long after Chong returned from the trip, Engineered Demolition landed one of its most unusual jobs in Europe. "We found an old power plant they wanted destroyed," she recalls, "but officials did not want us to use explosives even though it was the best way to go. So we actually had our people go in and hand-cut all the key supporting beams, a lengthy and involved process." The last person out of the building? Chong's husband, Eric, who made the final cut that began the building's collapse.

Not only are Chong and Kelly successful, but they also love their work. "It's something beautiful to start and complete a project to the finish," she says. "You have to be gutsy and a risk taker, but how many people can say their work is a real blast?" she says with a smile.

1. What factors are contributing to the growth of Engineered Demolition international business? Which countries should be the company's target? Why?
2. Work with a team of your classmates to brainstorm ways that Engineered Demolition can locate international customers.

Source: Adapted from Curtice K. Cultice, "Blasting a Path to World Markets: U.S. Demolition Exporter Levels Playing Field," *Business America*, January–February 1997, pp. 21–26.

- *Become more customer oriented.* Delving into global markets teaches business owners about the unique tastes, customs, preferences, and habits of customers in many different cultures. Responding to these differences imbues businesses with a degree of sensitivity toward their customers, both domestic and foreign.

Becoming a global entrepreneur does require a modification in the mindset of the firm. Success in the global economy also requires constant innovation; staying nimble enough to use speed as a competitive weapon; maintaining a high level of quality and constantly improving it; being sensitive to foreign customers' unique requirements; adopting a more respectful attitude toward foreign habits and customs; hiring motivated, multilingual employees; and retaining a desire to learn constantly about global markets. In short, the path to success requires businesses to become "insiders" rather than just "exporters."

As with any new venture, the entrepreneur needs to prepare. In this case, it is critical to ask, and answer, the following questions about our business:

1. Is there a profitable market in which our firm has the potential to be successful for an extended period of time?
2. Does our firm have the specific resources, skills, and commitment to succeed in this venture?
3. Are there pressures domestically that are forcing the firm to seek global opportunities?
4. Do we know the culture, history, economics, value system, and so on, of the country(s) we are considering?
5. Is there a viable "exit strategy" if the conditions change or the new venture is not successful?

STRATEGIES FOR GOING GLOBAL

2. Describe the principal strategies for going global.

Entrepreneurs have a variety of strategic options to choose among. Many of these strategies can be combined. The principal strategies are: The World Wide Web, trade intermediaries, joint ventures, foreign licensing, franchising, counter-trading, bartering, exporting, and the establishment of international locations. Whatever the single or combination of strategic options the entrepreneur selects, the mindset of the organization's leadership must be broadened. Becoming a global business depends on instilling a global culture throughout the organization that permeates *everything* the company does. Entrepreneurs who routinely conduct international business have developed a global mindset for themselves and their companies.

In reality, an entrepreneur must understand the needs of the customers in the new marketplace. Consider the case of Pentaura Ltd., a Greenville, South Carolina, manufacturer of high-quality, handmade furniture, who sought assistance from the Japan External Trade Organization who, in addition to providing help with exporting issues, recommended that the firm modify the height of its tables to accommodate the smaller stature and compact living space of Japanese customers.[1] In this case, product acceptance was improved through product modification to the physical needs of the customer (see Figure 12.1)

Employing a Presence on the World Wide Web

Perhaps in our technology-rich global environment the fastest, least expensive, and lowest cost strategic option to creating a global business presence is the creation of a

Figure 12.1
Eight Strategies
for Going Global

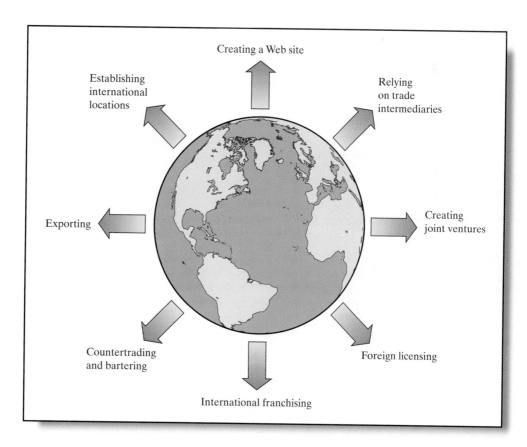

Creating a Web site

Establishing international locations

Relying on trade intermediaries

Exporting

Creating joint ventures

Countertrading and bartering

Foreign licensing

International franchising

IN THE FOOTSTEPS OF AN ENTREPRENEUR
Overcoming Barriers Online

The Internet has opened up international borders to many entrepreneurs, but language and cultural barriers still exist. One company, based in the rolling hills of wine country in Northern California, has learned this lesson first hand. Next Wine is a four-person operation that has successfully tapped into the global market—without breaking its small bank.

Dain Dunston, Next Wine President, knows first-hand that it is folly to assume any company can slap up a Web site and become a global player overnight. Dunston notes, "It's the little things—like someone sending you a document in Microsoft Word from France and a spellchecker that suddenly doesn't work." Other "little things" like working with people who are nine hours ahead of you makes the reality of a global economy hit home.

Even though most of Next Wine's products are sold via the Internet, Dunston says, "We're not a dot-com. We're a company selling wine on the Internet." The decision was made in the beginning not to add .com to the corporate masthead. Sometimes the ordering process gets a little 'hairy.'" Web customers order wine that must be shipped from two or three different countries. Can Next Wine deliver? Yes. But the regulatory burden is greater and international restrictions sometimes mean that wine can't always ship together. Dunston notes that tweaking the software isn't nearly as hard as getting the customer to understand the shipping issues.

Many of the logistical barriers have been overcome by the acquisition of software that allows the company to maintain Web content in several different languages, setting different rules for each version of its site. Dunston also made sure the software would grow with the company.

Aside from logistical barriers, perhaps the most common and vexing problem is language. Small businesses often miss out on global opportunities because they cannot converse with foreign associates in their native dialect.

As with other issues, the Internet is starting to make it easier to surmount language barriers. For example, SDL International offers translation services for those on a budget using software and the Internet. For one cent per word, a business owner can log on to *www.plustranslation.com* and upload an entire document and have it "roughly" translated into English in a few minutes. For a few cents more, SDL will run the document past a real person for the final clean up. Why bother with this process? One language says, "You can't have everything in English and then ship it over to your Japanese subsidiary and say 'translate this to Japanese.'"

For small businesses like Next Wine, expanding globally can be challenging, but with the help of the Internet and some innovative software, it can be done.

1. What will be the improvements in computer software that will make it possible for smaller firms to more effectively conduct business on a global basis via the Internet.

Source: Michael Grebb, "Business Without Borders," *Destinationsoho.com*, September 2001, pp. 36–41.

Web site. The reach of the Web is global. With a well-designed Web site, an entrepreneur can extend its reach to customers anywhere in the world—and without breaking the budget! A company's Web site is available to anyone anywhere in the world and provides exposure 24 hours a day to its products or services seven days a week. For many small companies, the Web has become a tool that is as essential to doing business as the telephone and the fax machine.

Establishing a presence on the Web has become an important part of a company's strategy for reaching customers outside the United States. A study by the International Development Conference estimates the number of World Wide Web users to be 320 million worldwide. Approximately 136 million of them live in the United States, leaving 184 million potential Web customers outside this country's

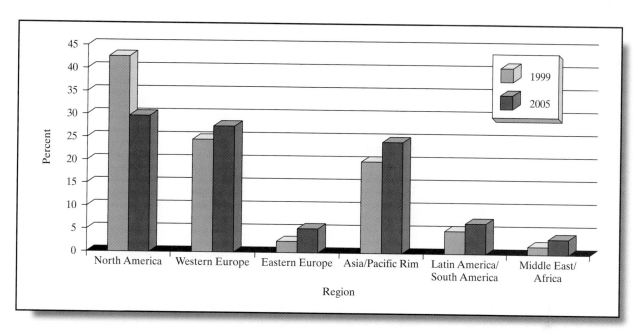

Figure 12.2
Internet Users by World Region, 1999 and 2005

Source: Computer Industry Almanac.

borders.[2] Figure 12.2 provides a comparison of the Web-using population by region for 1999 (actual) and 2005 (projected).

Most small companies follow a three-step evolutionary approach to conducting global business on the Web.

Step 1. Connecting to e-mail. Even though it lacks the ability to provide the engaging images, sounds, and animation available on the Web, e-mail gives entrepreneurs the ability to communicate with customers anywhere in the world quickly and easily. E-mail correspondence often is the first step to establishing lasting relationships with international customers. Not only is e-mail communication less expensive than international telephone calls, but it also overcomes many of the problems associated with different time zones.

James Cantor, CEO of Eastern Avionics International, a small company that markets navigation and communication equipment to private pilots, has used e-mail to boost his company's sales in foreign markets. Because he speaks only English, Cantor relies on a Web-based translation program to help him translate the e-mail orders and inquiries he often gets from customers written in French, German, Spanish, Italian, and Portuguese into English. In just 10 weeks, Eastern Avionics' international sales had climbed 60 percent.[3]

Step 2. Using the Web to conduct international market research. Entrepreneurs quickly recognize the power of the Internet to generate sales leads by researching customers and market characteristics in other countries.

Step 3. Building a globally accessible Web site. This step allows the business to both educate potential customers about the specific products of the firm, as well as generate inquires and hopefully orders. With the introduction in recent years of highly secure transaction software, orders can be quickly and safely accepted.

Without question, the Internet has provided the entrepreneur with the quickest and easiest way to go global. For greater detail on the use of the Internet for opening international markets, see Chapter 13.

Trade Intermediaries

Another relatively easy way to break into international markets is by using a trade intermediary. **Trade intermediaries** are domestic agencies that serve as distributors in foreign countries for domestic companies of all sizes. They rely on their networks of contacts, their extensive knowledge of local customs and markets, and their experience in international trade to market products effectively and efficiently all across the globe. Although a broad array of trade intermediaries is available, the following are ideally suited for small businesses:

Export Management Companies. Export management companies (EMCs) are an important channel of foreign distribution for small companies just getting started in international trade or for those lacking the resources to assign their own people to foreign markets. Most EMCs are merchant intermediaries, working on a buy-and-sell arrangement with domestic small companies. They provide small businesses with a low-cost, efficient, independent, international marketing department, offering services ranging from market research and advice on patent protection to arranging financing and handling shipping. More than 1,000 EMCs operate across the United States, and many of them specialize in particular products or product lines.

Export Trading Companies. Another tactic for getting into international markets with a minimum of cost and effort is through export trading companies (ETCs), which have been an important vehicle in international trade throughout history. The Hudson's Bay Company and the East India Company were ETCs that were dominant powers in world trade in the sixteenth, seventeenth, and eighteenth centuries.[4] **Export trading companies** are businesses that buy and sell products in a number of countries, and they typically offer a wide range of services such as exporting, importing, shipping, storing, distributing, and others to their clients. Unlike EMCs, which tend to focus on exporting, ETCs usually perform both import and export trades across many countries' borders. However, like EMCs, ETCs lower the risk of exporting for small businesses. Some of the largest ETCs in the world are based in the United States and Japan. In fact, many businesses that have navigated successfully Japan's complex system of distribution have done so with the help of ETCs.

In 1982, Congress passed the Export Trading Company Act to allow producers of similar products to form ETC cooperatives without the fear of violating antitrust laws. The goal was to encourage U.S. companies to export more goods by allowing businesses in the same industry to band together to form ETCs.

Manufacturer's Export Agents. Manufacturer's export agents (MEAs) act as international sales representatives in a limited number of markets for various noncompeting domestic companies. Unlike the close, partnering relationship formed with most EMCs, the relationship between the MEA and a small company is a short-term one, and the MEA typically operates on a commission basis.

Export Merchants. Export merchants are domestic wholesalers who do business in foreign markets. They buy goods from many domestic manufacturers and then market them in foreign markets. Unlike MEAs, export merchants often carry competing lines, which means they have little loyalty to suppliers. Most export merchants specialize in particular industries: office equipment, computers, industrial supplies, and others.

Resident Buying Offices. Another approach to exporting is to sell to a **resident buying office,** a government-owned or privately owned operation of one country established in another country for the purpose of buying goods made there. Many foreign governments and businesses have set up buying offices in the United States. Selling to them is just like selling to domestic customers because the buying office handles all the details of exporting.

Foreign Distributors. Some small businesses work through foreign distributors to reach international markets. Domestic small companies export their products to these distributors, who handle all of the marketing, distribution, and service functions in the foreign country. *Ed Anderson, founder of Lil' Orbits, a Minnesota-based company that makes doughnut machines, sold his machinery only in the United States for nearly 15 years with great success. Then he began to wonder why his doughnut-making hardware wouldn't sell in international markets as well. In 1987, he placed a $40 ad in a U.S. Department of Commerce publication and was flooded with inquiries from foreign distributors. Today, Lil' Orbits has 42 long-time foreign distributors who sell the company's line of seven machines around the world. The company collects more than 60 percent of its $10 million annual revenue from abroad.*[5]

The Value of Using Trade Intermediaries. Trade intermediaries such as these are becoming increasingly popular among businesses attempting to branch out into world markets because they make that transition much faster and easier. Most small businesses simply do not have the knowledge, resources, or confidence to go global alone. Intermediaries' global networks of buyers and sellers allow their small business customers to build their international sales much faster and with fewer hassles and mistakes.

The key to establishing a successful relationship with a trade intermediary is conducting a thorough screening to determine what type of intermediary—and which one in particular—will best serve a small company's needs. A company looking for an intermediary should compile a list of potential candidates using some of the sources listed in Table 12.1. The 50 World Trade Centers (most of which are affiliated with the U.S. government) and the 15 Export Assistance Centers located across the United States offer valuable advice and assistance to small companies wanting to get started in conducting global business. In addition, entrepreneurs can find reliable intermediaries by using their network of contacts in foreign countries and by attending international trade shows while keeping an eye out for potential candidates.

Joint Ventures

Joint ventures, both domestic and foreign, lower the risk of entering global markets for small businesses. They also give small companies more clout in foreign lands. In a **domestic joint venture,** two or more U.S. small businesses form an alliance for the purpose of exporting their goods and services. For export ventures, participating companies get antitrust immunity, allowing them to cooperate freely. The businesses share the responsibility and the costs of getting export licenses and permits, and they split the venture's profits. Establishing a joint venture with the right partner has become an essential part of maintaining a competitive position in global markets for a growing number of industries.

Table 12.1
Resources for Locating a Trade Intermediary

Trade intermediaries make doing business around the world much easier for small companies, but finding the right one can be a challenge. Fortunately, several government agencies offer a wealth of information to businesses interested in reaching into global markets with the help of trade intermediaries. Entrepreneurs looking for help in breaking into global markets should contact the International Trade Administration, the U.S. Commerce Department, and the Small Business Administration first to take advantage of the following services:

- *Agent/Distributor Service (ADS).* Provides customized searches to locate interested and qualified foreign distributors for a product or service. (Search cost, $250 per country)

- *Commercial Service International Contacts (CSIC) List.* Provides contact and product information for more than 82,000 foreign agents, distributors, and importers interested in doing business with U.S. companies.

- *Country Directories of International Contacts (CDIC) List.* Provides the same kind of information as the CSIC List but is organized by country.

- *Industry Sector Analyses (ISAs).* Offers in-depth reports on industries in foreign countries, including information on distribution practices, end-users, and top sales prospects.

- *International Market Insights (IMIs).* Includes reports on specific foreign market conditions, upcoming opportunities for U.S. companies, trade contacts, trade show schedules, and other information.

- *Trade Opportunity Program (TOP).* Provides up-to-the-minute, prescreened sales leads around the world for U.S. businesses, including joint venture and licensing partners, direct sales leads, and representation offers.

- *International Company Profiles (ICPs).* Commercial specialists will investigate potential partners, agents, distributors, or customers for U.S. companies and will issue profiles on them.

- *Commercial News USA.* A government-published magazine that promotes U.S. companies' products and services to 259,000 business readers in 152 countries at a fraction of the cost of commercial advertising. Small companies can use *Commercial News USA* to reach new customers around the world for as little as $395.

- *Gold Key Service.* For a small fee, business owners wanting to target a specific country can use the Department of Commerce's Gold Key Service, in which experienced trade professionals arrange meetings with prescreened contacts whose interests match their own.

- *Matchmaker Trade Delegations Program.* Helps small U.S. companies establish business relationships in major markets abroad by introducing them to the right contacts.

- *Multi-State/Catalog Exhibition Program.* Working with state economic development offices, the Department of Commerce presents companies' product and sales literature to hundreds of interested business prospects in foreign countries.

- *International Fair Certification Program.* Promotes U.S. companies' participation in foreign trade shows that represent the best marketing opportunities for them.

- *National Trade Data Bank (NTDB).* Most of the information listed above is available on the NTDB, the U.S. government's most comprehensive database of world trade data. With the NTDB, small companies have access to information that only *Fortune* 500 companies could afford.

- *Economic Bulletin Board (EBB).* Provides online trade leads and valuable market research on foreign countries compiled from a variety of federal agencies.

- *U.S. Export Assistance Centers.* The Department of Commerce has established 19 export centers (SEACs) around the country to serve as one-stop shops for entrepreneurs needing export help. Call (800) 872-8723.

- *Trade Information Center.* Helps locate federal export assistance, provides export assistance, and offers a 24-hour automated fax retrieval system that gives entrepreneurs free information on export promotion programs, regional market information, and international trade agreements. Call USA-TRADE.

- *Office of International Trade.* The Small Business Administration provides a variety of export development assistance, how-to publications, and information on foreign markets.

- *Export Hotline.* Provides no-cost trade information on more than 50 industries in 80 countries. Call (800) 872-9767.

- *Export Opportunity Hotline.* Trade specialists have access to online databases and reports from government and private agencies concerning foreign markets. Call (202) 628-8389.

GAINING THE COMPETITIVE EDGE
What Advice Would You Give?

Specialty Building Supplies is a small company with $6.4 million in annual sales that manufactures and sells a line of building supply products such as foundation vents, innovative insulation materials, and fireplace blowers to building supply stores in the northeastern United States. The eight-year-old company, founded by Tad Meyers, has won several awards for its unique and innovative products and has earned a solid reputation among its supply store customers and the builders and homeowners who ultimately buy its products. Before launching the company, Meyers had been a home builder. As he watched the price of home heating fuels climb dramatically over time, Meyers began to incorporate into the houses he built simple, inexpensive ways to help homeowners save energy. He began tinkering with existing products, looking for ways to improve them. The first product he designed (and the product that ultimately led him to launch Specialty Building Supplies) was an automatic foundation vent that was thermostatically controlled (no electricity needed). The vent would automatically open and close based on the outside temperature, keeping cold drafts from blowing under a house. Simple and inexpensive in its design, the Autovent was a big hit in newly constructed homes in the Northeast because it not only saved energy, it also avoided a major headache for homeowners in cold climates: water pipes that would freeze and burst. Before long, Meyers stopped building houses and focused on selling the Autovent. Its success prompted him to add other products to the company's line.

Specialty's sales have been lackluster for more than a year now, primarily due to a slump in new home construction in its primary market. Tad Meyers recently met the company's top marketing managers and salespeople to talk about their options for getting Specialty's sales and profit growth back on track. "What about selling our products in international markets?" asked Dee Rada, the company's marketing manager. "I read an article just last week about small companies doing good business in other countries, and many of them were smaller than we are."

"Interesting idea," Meyers said, pondering the concept. "I've never really thought about selling anything overseas. In fact, other than my years in the military, I've never traveled overseas and don't know anything about doing business there."

"It's a big world out there. Where should we sell our products?" said Hal Milam, Specialty's sales manager. "How do we find out what the building codes are in foreign countries? Would we have to modify our designs to meet foreign standards?"

"I don't know," shrugged Meyers. "Those are some good questions."

"How would we distribute our products?" asked Rada. "We have an established network of distributors here in the United States, but how do we find foreign distributors?"

"I wonder if exporting is our only option," asked Meyers. "There must be other ways to get into the global market besides exporting. What do you think? Where do we start?"

1. What advice would you offer Meyers and the other managers at Specialty Building Supplies about their prospects of going global?

2. How would you suggest these managers go about finding the answers to the questions they have posed? What other questions would you advise them to answer?

3. Outline the steps these managers should take to assemble an international marketing plan.

In a **foreign joint venture,** a domestic small business forms an alliance with a company in the target nation. The host partner brings to the joint venture valuable knowledge of the local market and its method of operation as well as of the customs and the tastes of local customers, making it much easier to conduct business in the foreign country. Sometimes foreign countries place certain limitations on joint ventures. Some nations, for example, require host companies to own at least 51 percent of the venture.

The most important ingredient in the recipe for a successful joint venture is choosing the right partner. A productive joint venture is much like a marriage,

GAINING THE COMPETITIVE EDGE
Hello Havana . . . Soon???

Have the entrepreneurs of the United States been out-flanked by their Canadian and European competitors? Over the past few years as the world watches the evolution of economic policy in Cuba, aggressive Canadian and European business interests have begun to stake their claims on what they hope will be a revitalized Cuban economy when its president, Fidel Castro, steps aside. These competitors have established over 400 joint ventures in Cuba.

Prior to the revolution, Cuba was a country with a strong agricultural and tourism base. Today, tourism is returning, although it is illegal for American citizens to travel to Cuba. Slowly, the U.S. government is modifying our economic relation-ship with Cuba. In the short term, American policy is not likely to make a major deviation from current policy.

Currently, the government in Cuba is the entity foreign businesses are dealing with. If Cuba becomes open to U.S. entrepreneurs and the economic system of Cuba becomes more free market in its behavior, how will they proceed?

1. Will Cuba be a viable new market for U.S. goods and services? Some estimate that Cuba could represent $20 billion per year in revenue for U.S. companies. Should we pursue this opportunity? If so, do you believe the $20 billion forecast?

Source: Abby Ellin, "The Next Revolution: Thinking of Doing Business with Cuba," *Fuse*, December 2000, pp. 106–110.

---

requiring commitment and understanding. In addition to picking the right partners, a second key to creating a successful alliance is to establish common objectives. Defining *exactly* what each party in the joint venture hopes to accomplish at the outset will minimize the opportunity for misunderstandings and disagreements later on. One important objective should always be to use the joint venture as a learning experience, which requires a long-term view of the business relationship.

Often joint ventures fail because the entrepreneur didn't do the following:

- Define at the outset important issues such as each party's contributions and responsibilities, the distribution of earnings, the expected life of the relationship, and the circumstances under which the parties can terminate the relationship.
- Understand in depth their partner's reasons and objectives for joining the venture.
- Select a partner who shares their company's values and standards of conduct.
- Spell out in writing exactly how the venture will work and where decision-making authority lies.
- Select a partner whose skills are different from but compatible with those of their own companies.
- Prepare a "prenuptial agreement" that spells out what will happen in case of a business "divorce."

Foreign Licensing

Rather than sell their products or services directly to customers overseas, some small companies enter foreign markets by licensing businesses in other nations to use their patents, trademarks, copyrights, technology, processes, or products. In return for

Section IV   Small Business Marketing Strategies

licensing such assets, the small company collects royalties from the sales of its foreign licenses. Licensing is a relatively simple way for even the most inexperienced business owner to extend his reach into global markets. The alternative is to license—to find someone who can capture the market for you who is already at home in that market. Licensing is ideal for companies whose value lies in unique products or services, a recognized name, or proprietary technology. Although many businesses consider licensing only their products to foreign companies, the licensing potential for intangibles such as processes, technology, copyrights, and trademarks often is greater. You often make more money from licensing your know-how for production or product control than you could from actually selling your finished product in a highly competitive market. Foreign licensing enables a small business to enter foreign markets quickly, easily, and with virtually no capital investment. Risks to the company include the potential of losing control over its manufacturing and marketing and creating a competitor if the license gains too much knowledge and control. Securing proper patent, trademark, and copyright protection beforehand can minimize those risks, however.

International Franchising

Over the past decade, a growing number of franchises have been attracted to international markets to boost sales and profits as the domestic market has become increasingly saturated with outlets and much tougher to wring growth from. International franchisors sell virtually every kind of product or service imaginable—from fast food to child day care—in international markets. In some cases, the products and services sold in international markets are identical to those sold in the United States. However, most franchisors have learned that they must modify their products and services to suit local tastes and customs. As you travel the world, you will discover that American fast-food giants like McDonalds and Domino's make significant modifications in their menu to remain attractive to the demands of local customers. For example, Big Macs share the menu with Vegetable McNuggets in India, teriyaki burgers in Japan, and McHuevos in Uruguay.

Although franchise outlets span the globe, Canada is the primary market for U.S. franchisors, with Japan and Europe following. These markets are most attractive to franchisors because they are similar to the U.S. market: rising personal incomes, strong demand for consumer goods, growing service economies, and spreading urbanization. There is little doubt that franchising is becoming a two-way street and that globalization will continue to be a powerful driving force in the growth of the strategic marketing option. Early entry into emerging markets with cultural sensitivity to national values and taste may be a key to the achievement of long-term success.

Countertrading and Bartering

Countertrade involves a transaction in which a company selling goods in a foreign country agrees to promote investment and trade in that country. The goal of the transaction is to help offset the capital drain from the foreign country's purchases. As entrepreneurs enter more and more developing countries, they will need to develop skills at implementing this strategy. In some cases, small and medium-sized businesses find it advantageous to work together with large corporations who have experience in the implementation of this marketing strategy.

Countertrading does suffer numerous drawbacks. Countertrade transactions can be complicated, cumbersome, and time consuming. They also increase the chances

GAINING THE COMPETITIVE EDGE
The Secret Language of International Business

When U.S. businesspeople enter international markets for the first time, they often are amazed at the differences in foreign cultures' habits and customs. Understanding and heeding these often subtle cultural differences is one of the most important keys to international business success. The maze of cultural variables from one country to another can be confusing, but with proper preparation and a little common sense, any manager can handle international transactions successfully. In short, before packing your bags, do your homework. In most cases, conducting international business successfully requires managers to have unlimited patience, a long-term commitment, and a thorough knowledge of the local market, business practices, and culture. The key for entrepreneurs is learning to be sensitive to the business cultures in which they operate. Consider these pointers.

- Patience is a must for doing business in Spain. Like the French, Spaniards want to get to know business associates before working with them. In the United States, business comes before pleasure, but in Spain business is conducted after dinner, when the drinks and cigars are served. "I've known American businessmen who have shocked their Spanish host by pulling out their portfolios and charts before dinner is even served," says one expert. In Spain, women should avoid crossing their legs; it is considered unladylike. Men usually cross their legs at the knees.

- Appearance and style are important to Italian businesspeople; they judge the polish and the expertise of the company's executives as well as the quality of its products and services. Italians expect presentations to be organized, clear, and exact. A stylish business wardrobe also is an asset in Italy. Physical contact is an accepted part of Italian society. Don't be surprised if an Italian businessperson uses a lingering handshake or touches you occasionally when doing business.

- In Great Britain, businesspeople consider it extremely important to conduct business "properly"—with formality and reserve. Boisterous behavior such as backslapping or overindulging in alcohol and ostentatious displays of wealth are considered ill mannered. The British do not respond to hard-sell tactics but do appreciate well-mannered executives. Politeness and impeccable manners are useful tools for conducting business successfully here.

- In Mexico, making business appointments through a well-connected Mexican national will go a long way toward assuring successful business deals. "People in Mexico do business with somebody they know, they like, or they're related to," says one expert. Because family and tradition are top priorities for Mexicans, entrepreneurs who discuss their family heritages and can talk knowledgeably about Mexican history are a step ahead. In business meetings, making extended eye contact is considered impolite.

- In China, entrepreneurs will need an ample dose of the "three Ps": patience, patience, patience. Nothing in China—especially business—happens fast! In conversations and negotiations, periods of silence are common; they are a sign of politeness and contemplation. The Chinese view personal space much differently than Americans; in normal conversation, they will stand much closer to their partners.

- In the Pacific Rim, entrepreneurs must remember that each country has its own unique culture and business etiquette. Starting business relationships with customers in the Pacific Rim usually requires a third-party contact because Asian executives prefer to do business with people they know. Also, building personal relationships is important. Many business deals take place over informal activities in this part of the world.

  American entrepreneurs doing business in the Pacific Rim should avoid hard-sell techniques, which are an immediate turnoff to Asian businesspeople. Harmony, patience, and consensus make good business companions in this region. It is also a good idea to minimize the importance of legal documents in negotiations. Although getting deals and trade agreements down in writing always is advisable, attempting to negotiate detailed contracts (as most American businesses tend to do) would insult most Asians, who base their deals on mutual trust and benefits.

- Japanese executives conduct business much like the British: with an emphasis on formality, thoughtfulness, and respect. Don't expect to hear Japanese executives say no, even during a negotiation; they don't want to offend or to appear confrontational. Instead of "no" the Japanese negotiator will say, "It is very difficult," "Let us think about that," or "Let us get back to you on that." Similarly, "yes" from a Japanese executive doesn't necessarily mean that. It could mean, "I understand," "I hear you," or "I don't understand what you mean, but I don't want to embarrass you."

- In Japan and South Korea, exchanging business cards, known in Japan as *meishi*, is an important business function (unlike Great Britain, where exchanging business cards is less popular). A Western executive who accepts a Japanese companion's card and then slips it into his pocket or scribbles notes on it has committed a major blunder. Tradition there says a business card must be treated just as its owner would be—with respect. Travelers should present their own cards using both hands with the card positioned so the recipient can read it. (The flip side should be printed in Japanese, an expected courtesy.)

Greeting a Japanese executive properly includes a bow and a handshake—showing respect for both cultures. In many traditional Japanese businesses, exchanging gifts at the first meeting is appropriate. Also, a love of golf (the Japanese are crazy about the game) is a real plus for winning business in Japan.

1. What can an entrepreneur do to avoid committing cultural blunders when conducting global business?

Sources: Adapted from Laura Fortunato, "Japan: Making It in the USA," *Region Focus,* Fall 1997, p. 15; David Stamps, "Welcome to America," *Training,* November 1996, p. 30; Barbara Pachter, "When in Japan, Don't Cross Your Legs," *Business Ethics,* March–April 1996, p. 50; Tom Dunkel, "A New Breed of People Gazers," *Insight,* January 13, 1992, pp. 10–14; M. Katherine Glover, "Do's and Taboos," *Business America,* August 13, 1990, pp. 2–6; Deidre Sullivan, "An American Businesswoman's Guide to Japan," *Overseas Business,* Winter 1990, pp. 50–55; Stephanie Barlow, "Let's Make a Deal," *Entrepreneur,* May 1991, p. 40; "Worldly Wise," *Entrepreneur,* March 1991, p. 40; David Altany, "Culture Clash," *Industry Week,* October 2, 1989, pp. 13–20; Edward T. Hall, "The Silent Language of Overseas Business," *Harvard Business Review,* May–June 1960, pp. 5–14; John S. McClenahen, Andrew Rosenbaum, and Michael Williams, "As Others See U.S.," *Industry Week,* January 8, 1990, pp. 80–82; James Bredin, "Japan Needs to Be Understood," *Industry Week,* April 20, 1992, pp. 24–26; David L. James, "Don't Think about Winning," *Across the Board,* April 1992, pp. 49–51; "When in Japan," *Small Business Reports,* January 1992, p. 8; Bernie Ward, "Other Climates, Other Cultures," *Sky,* March 1992, pp. 72–86; Roger E. Axtell, *Gestures: The Do's and Taboos of Body Language Around the World,* New York: John Wiley and Sons, 1991; Suzanne Kreiter, "Customs Differ Widely from Those in the U.S., " *Greenville News,* September 26, 1993, p. 15D; Bradford W. Ketchum, "Going Global: East Asia–Pacific Rim," *Inc.* (Special Advertising Section), May 20, 1997; Valerie Frazee, "Getting Started in Mexico," *Global Workforce,* January 1997, pp. 16–17.

that a company will get stuck with merchandise that it cannot move. They can lead to unpleasant surprises concerning the quantity and quality of products required in the countertrade. Still, countertrading offers one major advantage: Sometimes it's the only way to make a sale!

Entrepreneurs must weigh the advantages against the disadvantages for their company before committing to a countertrade deal. Because of its complexity and the risks involved, countertrading is not the best choice for a novice entrepreneur looking to break into the global marketplace.

Bartering, the exchange of goods and services for other goods and services, is another way of trading with countries lacking convertible currency. In a barter exchange, a company that manufactures electronics components might trade its products for the coffee that a business in a foreign country processes, which it then sells to a third company for cash. Barter transactions require finding a business with complementary needs, but they are much simpler than countertrade transactions.

Exporting

3. Explain how to build a thriving export program.

Until recently, small businesses were reluctant to undertake exporting because of the perception that the process was overly complex and required sophisticated skills. Approximately 100,000 U.S. companies currently export; however, experts estimate that at least twice as many are capable of exporting but are not doing so.[6] The biggest barrier facing companies that have never exported is not knowing where or how to start. The following steps provide guidance to an entrepreneur on how to establish an exporting program:

1. *Recognize that even the tiniest companies and least experienced entrepreneurs have the potential to export.* The size of the firm has nothing to do with the demand for its products. If the products meet the needs of global customers, there is a potential to export.
2. *Analyze your product or service.* Is it special? New? Unique? High quality? Priced favorably because of lower costs or exchange rates? In which countries would there be sufficient demand for it? In many foreign countries, products from America are in demand because they have an air of mystery about them! Exporters quickly learn the value foreign customers place on quality.
3. *Analyze your commitment.* Are you willing to devote the time and the energy to develop export markets? Does your company have the necessary resources? Export start-ups can take from six to eight months (or longer), but entering foreign markets isn't as tough as most entrepreneurs think. Table 12.2 summarizes key issues managers must address in the export decision.
4. *Research markets and pick your target.* Before investing in a costly sales trip abroad, entrepreneurs should make a trip to the local library or the nearest branch of the Department of Commerce. Exporters can choose from a multitude of guides, manuals, books, newsletters, videos, and other resources to help them research potential markets. Armed with research, small business owners can avoid wasting a lot of time and money on markets with limited potential for their products and can concentrate on those with the greatest promise. Research shows export entrepreneurs whether they need to modify their existing products and services to suit the tastes and preferences of their foreign target customers. Sometimes foreign customers' lifestyles, housing needs, body size, and cultures require exporters to make alterations in their product lines. Such modifications can sometimes spell the difference between success and failure in the global market. Table 12.3 offers questions to guide entrepreneurs conducting export research.
5. *Develop a distribution strategy.* Should you use an export middleperson or sell directly to foreign customers? Small companies just entering international markets may prefer to rely on export middlepersons to break new ground.
6. *Find your customer.* Small businesses can rely on a host of export specialists to help them track down foreign customers. (Refer to Table 12.1 for a list of some of the resources available from the government.) The U.S. Department of Commerce and the International Trade Administration should be the first stops on an entrepreneur's agenda for going global. These agencies have the market research available for locating the best target markets for a particular company and specific customers in those markets. Industry Sector Analyses (ISAs), International Market Insights (IMIs), and Customized Market Analyses (CMAs) are just some of the reports and services global entrepreneurs find most useful. They also have knowledgeable staff specialists experienced in the details of global trade and in the intricacies of foreign cultures. *Jimmy Kaplanges, head of GP66 Chemical Corporation, a small producer of industrial degreasers, had led his*

Table 12.2
Management
Issues in the
Export Decision

I. Experience

1. With what countries has your company already conducted business (or from what countries have you received inquiries about your product or service)?
2. What product lines do foreign customers ask about most often?
3. Prepare a list of sale inquiries for each buyer by product and by country.
4. Is the trend of inquiries or sales increasing or decreasing?
5. Who are your primary domestic and foreign competitors?
6. What lessons has your company learned from past export experience?

II. Management and Personnel

1. Who will be responsible for the export entity's organization and staff? (Do you have an export "champion"?)
2. How much top management time
   a. Should you allocate to exporting?
   b. Can you afford to allocate to exporting?
3. What does management expect from its exporting efforts? What are your company's export goals and objectives?
4. What organization structure will your company require to ensure that it can service export sales properly? (Note the political implications, if any.)
5. Who will implement the plan?

III. Production Capacity

1. To what extent is your company using its existing production capacity? Is there any excess? If so, how much?
2. Will filling export orders hurt your company's ability to make and service domestic sales?
3. What will additional production for export markets cost your company?
4. Are there seasonal or cyclical fluctuations in your company's workload? When? Why?
5. Is there a minimum quantity foreign customers must order for a sale to be profitable?
6. To what extent would your company need to modify its products, packaging, and design specifically for its export targets? Is your product quality adequate for foreign customers?
7. What pricing structure will your company use? Will prices be competitive?
8. How will your company collect payment on its export sales?

IV. Financial Capacity

1. How much capital will your company need to begin exporting? Where will it come from?
2. How will you allocate the initial costs of your company's export effort?
3. Does your company have other expansion plans that would compete with an exporting effort?
4. By what date do you expect your company's export program to pay for itself?
5. How important is establishing a global presence to your company's future success?

Source: Adapted from *A Basic Guide to Exporting*, Washington, DC: U.S. Department of Commerce, 1986, p. 3.

---

company into exporting its products to Brazil, Spain, France, and Greece. He also saw plenty of opportunity for the company's products in China, but Kaplanges knew that cracking that market was more than GP66 Chemical could accomplish on its own. That's when Kaplanges turned to the Export Assistance Center in the company's home-town of Baltimore, Maryland. Kaplanges credits the trade specialist there, Nasir

Table 12.3

Questions
to Guide
International
Market Research

- Is there an overseas market for your company's products or services?
- Are there specific target markets that look most promising?
- Which new markets abroad are most likely to open up or expand?
- How big is the market your company is targeting, and how fast is it growing?
- What are the major economic, political, legal, social, technological, and other environmental factors affecting this market?
- What are the demographic and cultural factors affecting this market (e.g., disposable income, occupation, age, gender, opinions, activities, interests, tastes, and values)?
- Who are your company's present and potential customers abroad?
- What are their needs and desires? What factors influence their buying decisions: price, credit terms, delivery terms, quality, brand name, and the like?
- How would they use your company's product or service? What modifications, if any, would be necessary to sell to your target customers?
- Who are your primary competitors in the foreign market?
- How do competitors distribute, sell, and promote their products? What are their prices?
- What are the best channels of distribution for your product?
- What is the best way for your company to gain exposure in this market?
- Are there any barriers such as tariffs, quotas, duties, or regulations to selling your product in this market? Are there any incentives?
- Are there any potential licensing or joint venture partners already in this market?

Source: Adapted from *A Basic Guide to Exporting,* Washington, DC: Department of Commerce, 1986, p. 11.

Abbasi, with helping his company enter the Chinese market successfully. Sales to Chinese customers have climbed from $3 million to more than $12 million.[7]

7. *Find financing.* One of the biggest barriers to small business exports is lack of financing. Access to adequate financing is a crucial ingredient in a successful export program because the cost of generating foreign sales often is higher and collection cycles are longer than in domestic markets. The trouble is that bankers and other sources of capital don't always understand the intricacies of international sales and view financing them as excessively risky. Also, among major industrialized nations, the U.S. government spent the least per capita to promote exports.

Several federal, state, and private programs are operating to fill this export financing void, however. Programs such as the Small Business Administration's Export Working Capital Program (90 percent loan guarantees up to $750,000), the Export–Import Bank (www.exim.gov), the Overseas Private Investment Corporation, and a variety of state-sponsored programs offer export-minded entrepreneurs both direct loans and loan guarantees. (A list of all state foreign trade assistance offices is available in the Commerce Department's National Export Directory.) In recent years, the Export–Import Bank has emphasized loans and loan guarantees for small exporters; 81 percent of its lending volume has gone to small companies.[8] The Bankers Association for Foreign Trade (telephone number, 1-800-49-AXCAP) is an association of 450 banks that matches exporters needing foreign trade financing with interested banks. *When Robert Cavallarin was traveling in Europe in 1989, he realized that he and partner Steve Macri, co-owners of S&S Seafood, could export Maine lobsters to Europe. Unfortunately, Cavallarin and Macri could not get the $100,000 in financing necessary* *to start their export venture, despite the fact that they had orders from seafood importers in hand. Macri turned to a trade consultant for help, and soon S&S Seafood had a business plan for its proposed export business and a contact at the Export–Import Bank. With a 90 percent loan guarantee from the Export–Import Bank, S&S Seafood was able to secure a $100,000 bank loan and begin exporting. Today, the company has eight employees and generates annual sales of $12 million, 95 percent of which comes from exports to Europe and Asia.[9]*

8. *Ship your goods.* Export novices usually rely on international freight forwarders and custom-house agents—experienced specialists in overseas shipping—for help in navigating the bureaucratic morass of packaging requirements and paperwork demanded by customs. These specialists, also known as transport architects, are to exporters what travel agents are to passengers and normally charge relatively small fees for a valuable service. They move shipments of all sizes to destinations all over the world efficiently, saving entrepreneurs many headaches. "(A freight forwarder) is going to be sure that his client conforms with all the government regulations that apply to export cargo," explains the owner of an international freight-forwarding business. "He acts as an agent of the exporter, and, in most circumstances, is like an extension of that exporter's traffic department." *The Johnson Sweeper Company, a manufacturer of street sweepers, ships its 20,000-pound pieces of equipment worldwide with the help of an international freight forwarder.[10]* (See Table 12.4 for shipping terms.)

9. *Collect your money.* Collecting foreign accounts can be more complex than collecting domestic ones, but by picking their customers carefully and checking their credit references closely, entrepreneurs can minimize bad-debt losses. Financing foreign sales often involves special credit arrangements such as letters of credit and bank (or documentary) drafts. A **letter of credit** is an agreement between an exporter's bank and the foreign buyer's bank that guarantees payment to the exporter for a specific shipment of goods. In essence, a letter of credit reduces the financial risk for the exporter by substituting a bank's creditworthiness for that of the purchaser (see Figure 12.3). A **bank draft** is a document the seller draws on the buyer, requiring the buyer to pay the face amount (the purchase price of the goods) either on sight (a sight draft) or on a specified date (a time draft) once the goods have been shipped. Rather than use letters of credit or drafts, some exporters simply require cash in advance or cash on delivery (COD). Insisting on cash payments up front, however, may cause some foreign buyers to reject a deal. The parties to an international deal should always come to an agreement in advance on an acceptable method of payment.

Planned carefully and taken one step at a time, exporting can be a highly profitable route for small businesses. Many small companies are forming **foreign sales corporations (FSCs,** pronounced "fisks") to take advantage of a tax benefit that is designed to stimulate exports. Although large companies have used the tax advantages of FSCs for many years, a rapidly growing number of small exporters is beginning to catch on. More than 5,000 U.S. corporations have created FSCs in the past decade, and the number is growing by 25 percent a year. By forming an FSC, a company can shelter about 15 percent of its profits on foreign sales from federal—and in some cases state—income taxes. Setting up an FSC requires a company to establish a shell corporation in the Virgin Islands, Barbados, or one of another 40 tax-friendly offshore locations that have tax treaties with the United States. The company also must have fewer than 25 shareholders and one non-U.S. resident board member.

Table 12.4

Common International Shipping Terms and Their Meaning

SHIPPING TERM	SELLER'S RESPONSIBILITY	BUYER'S RESPONSIBILITY	SHIPPING METHOD(S) USED
FOB ("Free on Board"), Seller	Deliver goods to carrier and provide export license and clean on-board receipt. Bear risk of loss until goods are delivered to carrier.	Pay shipping, freight, and insurance charges. Bear risk of loss while goods are in transit.	All
FOB ("Free on Board"), Buyer	Deliver goods to the buyer's place of business and provide export license and clean on-board receipt. Pay shipping, freight, and insurance charges.	Accept delivery of goods after documents are tendered.	All
FAS ("Free Along Side"), Vessel	Deliver goods alongside ship. Provides an "alongside" receipt.	Provide export license and proof of delivery of the goods to the carrier. Bear risk of loss once goods are delivered to the carrier.	Ship
CFR ("Cost and Freight")	Deliver goods to carrier, obtain export licenses, and pay export taxes. Provide buyer with clean bill of lading. Pay freight and shipping charges. Bear risk of loss until goods are delivered to buyer.	Pay insurance charges. Accept delivery of goods after documents are tendered.	Ship
CIF ("Cost, Insurance, and Freight")	Same as CFR plus pay insurance charges and provide buyer with insurance policy.	Accept delivery of goods after documents are tendered.	Ship
CPT ("Carriage Paid to . . .")	Deliver goods to carrier, obtain export licenses, and pay export taxes. Provide buyer with clean transportation documents. Pay shipping and freight charges.	Pay insurance charges. Accept delivery of goods after documents are tendered.	All
CIP ("Carriage and Insurance Paid to . . .")	Same as CPT plus pay insurance charges and provide buyer with insurance policy.	Accept delivery of goods after documents are tendered.	All
DDU ("Delivered Duty Unpaid")	Obtain export license, pay insurance charges, and provide buyer documents for taking delivery.	Take delivery of goods and pay import duties.	All
DDP ("Delivered Duty Paid")	Obtain export license and pay import duty, pay insurance charges, and provide buyer documents for taking delivery.	Take delivery of goods.	All

Source: Adapted from *Guide to the Finance of International Trade*, edited by Gordon Platt (HBSC Trade Services, Marine Midland Bank, and the Journal of Commerce), <infoserv2.ita.doc.gov/efm/efm.nsf/503d177e3c63f0b48525675900112e24/6218a8703573b32985256759004c41f3/$FILE/Finance_.pdf>, pp. 6–10.

Figure 12.3
How a Letter of
Credit Works

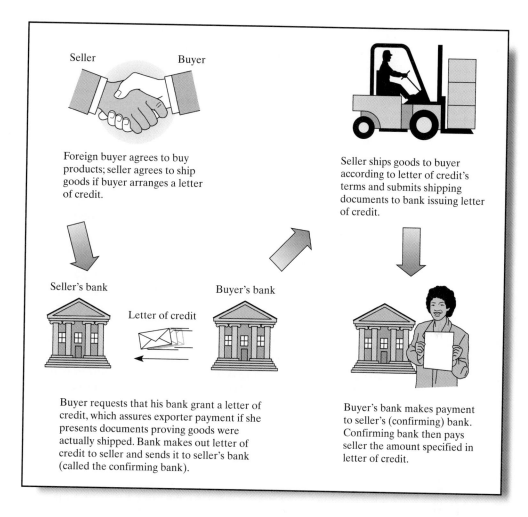

Seller Buyer

Foreign buyer agrees to buy products; seller agrees to ship goods if buyer arranges a letter of credit.

Seller ships goods to buyer according to letter of credit's terms and submits shipping documents to bank issuing letter of credit.

Seller's bank   Buyer's bank

Letter of credit

Buyer requests that his bank grant a letter of credit, which assures exporter payment if she presents documents proving goods were actually shipped. Bank makes out letter of credit to seller and sends it to seller's bank (called the confirming bank).

Buyer's bank makes payment to seller's (confirming) bank. Confirming bank then pays seller the amount specified in letter of credit.

Because it costs about $2,500 to establish an FSC and about $1,500 a year to maintain one, a business should earn at least $50,000 a year to make the savings from an FSC worthwhile. For help on setting up an FSC, contact the FSC/DISC Tax Association at (914) 642-8924.

Establishing International Locations

Once established in international markets, some small businesses set up permanent locations there. Establishing an office or a factory in a foreign land can require a substantial investment reaching beyond the budgets of many small companies. Plus, setting up an international office can be an incredibly frustrating experience in some countries. Business infrastructures are in disrepair or are nonexistent. Getting a telephone line installed can take months in some places, and finding reliable equipment to move goods to customers is nearly impossible. Securing necessary licenses and permits from bureaucrats often takes more than filing the necessary paperwork; in some nations, bureaucrats expect payments to "grease the wheels." Finding the right person to manage an international office is crucial to success; it also is a major challenge, especially for small businesses. Small companies usually have lean management staffs and cannot afford to send key people abroad without running the risk of losing their focus.

The major advantages to establishing an international location can be the combination of lower production and marketing costs, as well as development of an intimate knowledge of customer preferences.

BARRIERS TO INTERNATIONAL TRADE

4. Discuss the major barriers to international trade and their impact on the global economy.

Governments have always used a variety of barriers to block free trade among nations in an attempt to protect businesses within their own borders. The benefit of protecting their own companies, however, comes at the expense of foreign businesses, which face limited access to global markets. Numerous trade barriers—domestic and international—restrict the freedom of businesses in global trading. Even with these barriers, international trade has grown 26-fold to more than $7.0 *trillion* over the past 30 years.[11]

Domestic Barriers

Sometimes the biggest barriers potential exporters face are right here at home. Three major domestic roadblocks are common: attitude, information, and financing. Perhaps the biggest barrier to small businesses exporting is the attitude "I'm too small to export. That's just for big corporations." The first lesson of exporting is "Take nothing for granted about who can export and what you can and cannot export." The first step to building an export program is recognizing that the opportunity to export exists. Another reason entrepreneurs neglect international markets is a lack of information about how to get started. The key to success in international markets is choosing the correct target market and designing the appropriate strategy to reach it. That requires access to information and research. Although a variety of government and private organizations make volumes of exporting and international marketing information available, many small business owners never use it. A successful global marketing strategy also recognizes that not all international markets are the same. Companies must be flexible, willing to make adjustments to their products and services, promotional campaigns, packaging, and sales techniques.

An additional obstacle is the inability of small firms to obtain adequate export financing. Financial institutions that serve smaller firms are often not experienced with this type of financing and are unwilling to accept the perceived higher risk.

International Barriers

Domestic barriers aren't the only ones export-minded entrepreneurs must overcome. Trading nations also erect obstacles to free trade. Two types of international barriers are common: tariff and nontariff.

Tariff Barriers. A **tariff** is a tax, or duty, that a government imposes on goods and services imported into that country. Imposing tariffs raises the price of the imported goods—making them less attractive to consumers—and protects the makers of comparable domestic products and services. Established in the United States in 1790 by Alexander Hamilton, the tariff system generated the majority of federal revenues for about 100 years.

Nontariff Barriers. Many nations have lowered the tariffs they impose on products and services brought into their borders, but they rely on other nontariff structures as protectionist trade barriers.

Quotas. Rather than impose a direct tariff on certain imported products, nations often use quotas to protect their industries. A **quota** is a limit on the amount of a product imported into a country. Worried about the Japanese economic juggernaut, the European Union has limited Japanese automakers' share of the European market to just 16 percent. In the U.S. auto market, the Japanese have agreed to "voluntary quotas," limiting the number of autos shipped here.

Japan, often criticized for its protectionist attitude toward imports, traditionally used tariffs and quotas to keep foreign competitors out. Japan's tariffs are now among the world's lowest—averaging just 2 percent—but quotas still exist on many products.

Embargoes. An **embargo** is a total ban on imports of certain products. The motivation for embargoes is not always economic. For instance, because of South Africa's history of apartheid policies, many nations have embargoes imports of Krugerrands (gold coins). Traditionally, Taiwan, South Korea, and Israel have banned imports of Japanese autos.

Dumping. In an effort to grab market share quickly, some companies have been guilty of **dumping** products: selling large quantities of them in foreign countries below cost. The United States has been a dumping target for steel, televisions, shoes, and computer chips in the past. Under the U.S. Antidumping Act, a company must prove that the foreign company's prices are lower here than in the home country and that U.S. companies are directly harmed.

Political Barriers

Entrepreneurs who go global quickly discover a labyrinth of political tangles. Although many U.S. business owners complain of excessive government regulation in the United States, they are often astounded by the complex web of governmental and legal regulations and barriers they encounter in foreign countries.

Companies doing business in politically risky lands face the very real dangers of government takeovers of private property; attempts at coups to overthrow ruling parties; kidnapping, bombings, and other violent acts against businesses and their employees; and other threatening events. Their investments of millions of dollars may evaporate overnight in the wake of a government coup or the passage of a law nationalizing an industry (giving control of an entire industry to the government).

Business Barriers

American companies doing business internationally quickly learn that business practices and regulations in foreign lands can be quite different from those in the United States. Simply duplicating the practices they have adopted (and have used successfully) in the domestic market and using them in foreign markets is not always a good idea. Perhaps the biggest shock comes in the area of human resources management, where international managers discover that practices common in the United States, such as overtime, women workers, and employee benefits are restricted, disfavored, or forbidden in other cultures. Business owners new to international business sometimes are shocked at the wide range of labor costs they encounter and the accompanying wide range of skilled labor available. In some countries, what appear to be "bargain" labor rates turn out to be excessively high after accounting for the quality of the labor force and the benefits their governments mandate: from company-sponsored housing, meals, and clothing to profit-sharing and extended vacations. In many nations, labor unions are present in almost every company, yet they play a very different role from the unions in the United States. Although management–union relations are not as hostile as in the United States and strikes are not as common, unions can greatly complicate a company's ability to compete effectively.

Cultural Barriers

The culture of a nation includes the beliefs, values, views, and mores that its inhabitants share. Differences in cultures among nations create another barrier to international trade. The diversity of languages, business philosophies, practices, and traditions make international trade more complex than selling to the business down the street. Consider the following examples:

- A U.S. entrepreneur, eager to expand into the European Union, arrives at his company's potential business partner's headquarters in France. Confidently, he strides into the meeting room, enthusiastically pumps his host's hand, slaps him on the back, and says "Tony, I've heard a great deal about you; please, call me Bill." Eager to explain the benefits of his product, he opens his briefcase and gets right down to business. The French executive politely excuses himself and leaves the room before negotiations ever begin, shocked by the American's rudeness and ill manners. Rudeness and ill manners? Yes—from the French executive perspective.
- Another American business owner flies to Tokyo to close a deal with a Japanese executive. He is pleased when his host invites him to play a round of golf shortly after he arrives. He plays well and manages to win by a few strokes. The Japanese executive invites him to play again the next day, and again he wins by a few strokes. Invited to play another round the following day, the American asks, "But when are we going to start doing business?" His host, surprised by the question, says, "But we have been doing business."

When American businesspeople enter international markets for the first time, they often are amazed at the differences in foreign cultures' habits and customs. In the first scenario above, for instance, had the entrepreneur done his homework, he would have known that the French are very formal (backslapping is *definitely* taboo!) and do not typically use first names in business relationships (even among long-time colleagues). In the second scenario, a global manager would have known that the Japanese place a tremendous importance on developing personal relationships before committing to any business deals. Thus, he would have seen the golf games for what they really were: an integral part of building a business relationship.

Understanding and heeding these often subtle cultural differences is one of the most important keys to international business success. Conducting a business meeting with a foreign executive in the same manner as one with an American businessperson could doom the deal from the outset. Business customs and behaviors that are acceptable, even expected, in this country may be taboo in others.

Entrepreneurs who fail to learn the differences in the habits and customs of the cultures in which they hope to do business are at a distinct disadvantage. The stories of business executives who unknowingly insulted their foreign counterparts are both lengthy, legendary, and a continuing reminder of the cost associated with a failure to prepare for dealing in a culture different from one's own.

INTERNATIONAL TRADE AGREEMENTS

With the fundamental assumption that free trade among nations results in enhanced economic well-being for all who participate the last five decades have witnessed a

5. Describe the trade agreements that will have the greatest influence on foreign trade in the twenty-first century.

gradual opening of trade among nations. Hundreds of agreements have been negotiated among nations in this time frame, with each contributing to free trade across the globe.

GATT

Created in 1947, the General Agreement on Tariffs and Trade (GATT) became the first global tariff agreement. It was designed to reduce tariffs among member nations to facilitate trade across the globe. Originally signed by the United States and 22 other nations, GATT has grown to include 124 member countries today. Together, they account for nearly 90 percent of world trade. The latest round of GATT negotiations, called the Uruguay Round, was completed in December 1993 and took effect on July 1, 1995. Before the Uruguay Round, the trade agreement had been successful in reducing trade barriers around the world by 90 percent since its inception. Average tariffs in industrial countries had fallen to just 4.7 percent, down from an average of 40 percent in 1947.

The Uruguay Round continues this trend. Negotiators reduced the remaining industrial tariffs by 40 percent, established new rules governing dumping goods at unfairly low prices, strengthened the global protection of patents, and cut the level of government subsidies on agricultural products. In addition, negotiators agreed to form a World Trade Organization with more power than GATT to settle trade disputes among member nations.

WTO

The World Trade Organization (WTO) came into being in January 1995 and replaced GATT. Currently, the WTO has more than 140 member countries, including the newest member, China. These member countries represent over 97 percent of all world trade. An additional 30 nations are actively seeking membership. The rules and agreements of the WTO are the result of negotiations among its members. The WTO actively implements the rules established by GATT and continues to negotiate additional trade agreements. Through the agreements of the WTO, members commit themselves to nondiscriminatory trade practices. These agreements spell out the rights and obligations of each member country. Each member country receives guarantees that its exports will be treated fairly and consistently in other member countries' markets. Specifically addressed have been banking, insurance, telecommunications, and tourism under the WTO's General Agreement on Trade in Services, (GATS). In addition, the WTO's intellectual property agreement, which covers patents, copyrights, and trademarks, amounts to the rules for trade and investment in ideas and creativity.

In addition to the development of agreements among members, the WTO is involved in the resolution of trade disputes among members. The WTO system is designed to encourage dispute resolutions through consultation. If this approach fails, the WTO has a stage-by-stage procedure that can culminate in a ruling by a panel of experts.

NAFTA

The North American Free Trade Agreement (NAFTA) created a free trade area among Canada, Mexico, and the United States. A **free trade area** is an association of countries that have agreed to knock down trade barriers, both tariff and nontariff, among partner nations. Under the provision of NAFTA, these barriers were eliminated for trade among the three countries, but each remained free to set its own tariffs on imports from nonmember nations.

NAFTA forged a unified United States–Canada–Mexico market of 380 million people with a total annual output of more than $6.5 trillion dollars of goods and services. This important trade agreement binds together the three nations on the North American continent into a single trading unit stretching from the Yukon to the Yucatan. Because Canada and the United States already had a free-trade agreement in effect, the businesses that will benefit most from NAFTA are those already doing business, or those wanting to do business, with Mexico. Before NAFTA took effect on January 1, 1994, the average tariff on U.S. goods entering Mexico was 10 percent. Under NAFTA, these tariffs will be reduced to zero on most goods over the next 10 to 15 years. NAFTA's provisions will encourage trade among the three nations, make that trade more profitable and less cumbersome, and open up new opportunities for a wide assortment of companies.

Among NAFTA's provisions are:

- *Tariff reductions.* Immediate reduction, then gradual phasing out, of most tariffs on goods traded among the three countries.
- *Elimination of nontariff barriers.* Most nontariff barriers to free trade are to be eliminated by 2008.
- *Simplified border processing.* Mexico, in particular, opens its border and interior to U.S. truckers and simplifies border processing.
- *Tougher health and safety standards.* Industrial standards involving worker health and safety are to become more stringent and more uniform.

CONCLUSION

To remain competitive, businesses must assume a global posture. Global effectiveness requires managers to be able to leverage workers' skills, company resources, and customer know-how across borders and throughout cultures across the world. Managers also must concentrate on maintaining competitive cost structures and a focus on the core of every business—the *customer!* Although there are no surefire rules for going global, small businesses wanting to become successful international competitors should observe these guidelines[12]:

- Make yourself at home in all three of the world's key markets: North America, Europe, and Asia. This triad of regions is forging a new world order in trade that will dominate global markets for years to come.
- Appeal to the similarities within the various regions in which you operate but recognize the differences in their specific cultures. Although the European Union is a single trading bloc composed of 15 countries, smart entrepreneurs know that each country has its own cultural uniqueness and do not treat them as a unified market.
- Develop new products for the world market. Make sure your products and services measure up to world-class quality standards.
- Familiarize yourself with foreign customs and languages; constantly scan, clip, and build a file on other cultures: their lifestyles, values, customs, and business practices.
- Learn to understand your customers from the perspective of *their* culture, not your own. Bridge cultural gaps by being willing to adapt your business practices to suit their preferences and customs.

- "Glocalize": Make global decisions about products, markets, and management but allow local employees to make tactical decisions about packaging, advertising, and service.
- Train employees to think globally, send them on international trips, and equip them with state-of-the-art communications technology.
- Hire local managers to staff foreign offices and branches.
- Do whatever seems best wherever it seems best, even if people at home lose jobs or responsibilities.
- Consider using partners and joint ventures to break into foreign markets you cannot penetrate on your own.

By its very nature, going global can be a frightening experience. Most entrepreneurs who have already made the jump, however, have found that the benefits outweigh the risks and that their companies are much stronger because of it.

CHAPTER SUMMARY

1. Explain why "going global" has become an integral part of many entrepreneurs marketing strategies.
   - Companies that move into international business can reap many benefits, including offsetting sales declines in the domestic market's increasing sales and profits; extending their products' life cycles; lowering manufacturing costs; improving competitive position; raising quality levels; and becoming more customer oriented.

2. Describe the principal strategies for going global.
   - Perhaps the simplest and least expensive way for a small business to begin conducting business globally is to establish a site on the World Wide Web. Companies wanting to sell goods on the Web should establish a secure ordering and payment system for online customers.
   - Trade intermediaries such as export management companies, export trading companies, manufacturer's export agents, export merchants, resident buying offices, and foreign distributors can serve as a small company's "export department."
   - In a domestic joint venture, two or more U.S. small companies form an alliance for the purpose of exporting their goods and services abroad. In a foreign joint venture, a domestic small business forms an alliance with a company in the target area.

- Some small businesses enter foreign markets by licensing businesses in other nations to use their patents, trademarks, copyrights, technology, processes, or products.
- Franchising has become a major industry for the United States. The International Franchise Association estimates that more than 20 percent of the nation's 4,000 franchisors have outlets in foreign countries.
- Some countries lack a hard currency that is convertible into other currencies, so companies doing business there must rely on countertrading or bartering. A countertrade is a transaction in which a business selling goods in a foreign country agrees to promote investment and trade in that country. Bartering involves trading goods and services for other goods and services.
- Although small companies account for 97 percent of the companies involved in exporting, they generate only 33 percent of the dollar value of the nation's exports. However, small companies, realizing the incredible profit potential it offers, are making exporting an ever-expanding part of their marketing plans. Nearly half of the U.S. companies with annual revenues under $100 million export goods.
- Once established in international markets, some small businesses set up permanent locations there. Although they can be very expensive to establish and maintain, international locations give businesses the

opportunity to stay in close contact with their international customers.

3. Explain how to build a thriving export program.
   - Building a successful export program takes patience and research. Steps include: Realize that even the tiniest firms have the potential to export; analyze your product or service; analyze your commitment to exporting; research markets and pick your target; develop a distribution strategy; find your customer; find financing; ship your goods; and collect your money.

4. Discuss the major barriers to international trade and their impact on the global economy.
   - Three domestic barriers to international trade are common: the attitude that "we're too small to export," lack of information on how to get started in global trade, and a lack of available financing.
   - International barriers include tariffs, quotas, embargoes, dumping, and political business and cultural barriers.

5. Describe the trade agreements that will have the greatest influence on foreign trade into the twenty-first century.
   - Created in 1947, the General Agreement on Tariffs and Trade (GATT), the first global tariff agreement, was designed to reduce tariffs among member nations and to facilitate trade across the globe.
   - The World Trade Organization (WTO) was established in 1995 to implement the GATT tariff agreements. The WTO has over 140 member nations and represents over 97 percent of all global trade. The WTO is the governing body that resolves trade disputes among members.
   - The North American Free Trade Agreement (NAFTA) created a free trade area among Canada, Mexico, and the United States. The agreement created an association that knocked down trade barriers, both tariff and nontariff, among these partner nations.

DISCUSSION QUESTIONS

1. Why must entrepreneurs learn to think globally?
2. What forces are driving small businesses into international markets?
3. What advantages does going global offer a small business owner? Risks?
4. Outline the eight strategies that small businesses can use to go global?
5. Describe the various types of trade intermediaries small business owners can use. What functions do they perform?
6. What is a domestic joint venture? A foreign joint venture? What advantages does taking on an international partner through a joint venture offer? Disadvantages?
7. What mistakes are first-time exporters most likely to make? Outline the steps a small company should take to establish a successful export program.
8. What are the benefits of establishing international locations? Disadvantages?
9. Describe the barriers businesses face when trying to conduct business internationally. How can a small business owner overcome these obstacles?
10. What is a tariff? A quota? What impact do they have on international trade?
11. What impact have the GATT, WTO, and NAFTA trade agreements had on small companies wanting to go global? What provisions are included in these trade agreements?
12. What advice would you offer an entrepreneur interested in launching a global business effort?

STEP INTO THE REAL WORLD

1. Go to lunch with a student from a foreign country. Discuss what products and services are most needed. How does the business system there differ from ours? How much government regulation affects business? What cultural differences exist? What trade barriers has the government erected?
2. Review several current business publications and prepare a brief report on which nations seem to be the most promising for U.S. entre-

preneurs. What steps should a small business owner take to break into those markets? Which nations are the least promising? Why?

3. Select a nation that interests you and prepare a report on its business customs and practices. How are they different from those in the United States? How are they similar?

TAKE IT TO THE NET

Visit the Scarborough/Zimmerer home page at **www.prenhall.com/scarborough** for updated information, online resources, Web-based exercises, and sample business plan.

ENDNOTES

1. Rudolph Bell, "Japanese Connection," *Upstate Business,* September 5, 1999, pp. 1, 8–9.
2. Larry Pearl and Sandeep Thakrar, "Taking Your Business Worldwide," *FSB,* March 23, 2000, *www.esb.com/foortunesb/articles/o,2227, 634.00, html.*
3. Emily Esterson, "United Nations," *Inc. Technology,* No. 2, 1998, p. 88.
4. Larry M. Greenberg, "Besieged Hudson's Bay Company Starts to Blaze New Trails," *Wall Street Journal,* February 13, 1998, pp. B1, B9.
5. John R. Engen, "Rolling in Dough," *Success,* June 1997, p. 29.
6. Roger Axtell, "The Do's and Taboos of International Trade," New York: John Wiley & Sons, 1994, p. 10.
7. Roberta Maynard, "A Simplified Route to Markets Abroad," *Nation's Business,* November 1997, pp. 46–48.
8. J. Russell Boner, "Tap American's Top Export Leaders to Expand Abroad," *Your Company,* October–November 1997, p. 28.
9. Ibid., p. 28.
10. Charlotte Mulhern, "Fast Forward," *Entrepreneur,* October 1997, p. 34.
11. World Trade Organization, *www.wto/org/wto/ intltrad/internet.html.*
12. Frank Beeman, "Selling Around the World," *Selling Power,* November–December 1996, pp. 82–83; "Going Global: Focus on Western Europe," *Inc.* (Special Advertising Section), March 1997; Jeremy Muin, "How to Go Global—and Why," *Fortune,* August 1989, pp. 70–76.

13

E-Commerce and Entrepreneurship

> *If you don't believe deeply, wholly, and viscerally that the 'Net is going to change your business, you're going to lose. And if you don't understand the advantages of starting early and learning fast, you're going to lose.*

—GARY HAMEL AND JEFF SAMPLER

> *In the mental geography of e-commerce, distance has been eliminated. There is only one economy and one market.*

—PETER DRUCKER

Upon completion of this chapter, you will be able to:

1. Describe the benefits of selling on the World Wide Web.
2. Understand the factors an entrepreneur should consider before launching into e-commerce.
3. Explain the 12 myths of e-commerce and how to avoid falling victim to them.
4. Discuss the five basic approaches available to entrepreneurs wanting to launch an e-commerce effort.
5. Explain the basic strategies entrepreneurs should follow to achieve success in their e-commerce efforts.
6. Learn the techniques of designing a killer Web site.
7. Explain how companies track the results from their Web sites.
8. Describe how e-businesses ensure the privacy and security of the information they collect and store from the Web.

As a student studying business, you are fortunate to witness the emergence of an event that is reshaping the way companies of all sizes do business: e-commerce. E-commerce is creating a new economy, one that is connecting producers, sellers, and customers via technology in ways that have never been possible before. The result is a whole new set of companies built on business models that are turning traditional methods of commerce and industry on their heads. Companies that ignore the impact of the Internet on their markets run the risk of becoming as relevant to customers as a rotary-dial telephone. The most successful companies are embracing the Internet, not as merely another advertising medium or marketing tool but as a mechanism for transforming their companies and changing *everything* about the way they do business. As these companies discover new, innovative ways to use the Internet, computers, and communications technology to connect with their suppliers and to serve their customers better, they are creating a new industrial order. In short, e-commerce has launched a revolution. Just as in previous revolutions in the business world, some old, established players are being ousted, and new leaders are emerging. The winners are discovering new business opportunities, new ways of designing work, and new ways of organizing and operating their businesses.

Perhaps the most visible changes are occurring in the world of retailing. Although e-commerce will not replace traditional retailing, no retailer, from the smallest corner store to industry giant Wal-Mart, can afford to ignore the impact of the World Wide Web on their business models. Companies can take orders at the speed of light from anywhere in the world and at any time of day. The Internet enables companies to collect more information on customers' shopping and buying habits than any other medium in history. This ability means that companies can focus their marketing efforts like never before—for instance, selling garden supplies to customers who are most likely to buy them and not wasting resources trying to sell to those who have no interest in gardening. The capacity to track customers' Web-based shopping habits allows companies to personalize their approaches to marketing and to realize the benefits of individualized (or one-to-one) marketing (refer to Chapter 7). Ironically, the same Web-based marketing approach that allows companies to get so personal with their customers also can make shopping extremely impersonal. Entrepreneurs who set up shop on the Web will likely never meet their customers face-to-face or even talk to them. Yet, those customers, who can live anywhere in the world, will visit the online store at all hours of the day or night and expect to receive individual attention. Making a Web-based marketing approach succeed requires a business to strike a balance, creating an e-commerce strategy that capitalizes on the strengths of the Web while meeting customers' expectations of convenience and service.

In this fast-paced world of e-commerce, size no longer matters as much as speed and flexibility do. One of the Web's greatest strengths is its interactive nature, the ability to provide companies with instantaneous customer feedback, giving them the opportunity to learn and to make necessary adjustments. Businesses, whatever their size, that are willing to experiment with different approaches to reaching customers and are quick to learn and adapt will grow and prosper; those that cannot will fall by the wayside. The Internet is creating a new industrial order, and companies that fail to adapt to it will soon become extinct.

E-commerce start-ups are redefining even the most traditional industries. *Ted Farnsworth's company, Farmbid.com, is revolutionizing what for centuries had been a low-tech business—farming. Every day, some 90,000 farmers from around the globe visit Farmbid's Web site to check the latest commodity news, weather forecasts, futures prices, information about more than 20,000 farm products and farm legislation, and even jokes. Farmers also can participate in online auctions of a wide range of products; Farmbid takes a*

Figure 13.1
Internet Users by
World Region

Source: Nua Internet
Surveys,
*www.nua.ie/surveys/how
_many_online/*

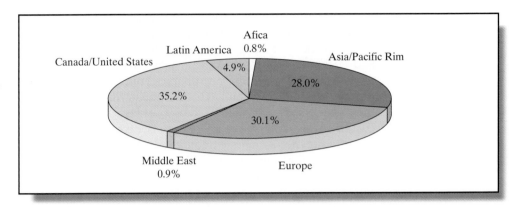

High-volume, low-margin, commodity products are best suited for selling on the Web. Indeed, the items purchased most often online are travel services, computer hardware, clothing, books, and consumer electronics. However, companies can—and do—sell practically anything over the Web, from antiques and pharmaceuticals to popcorn and drug-free urine. The most commonly cited reasons among owners of small and mid-sized companies for taking their companies to the Web are: (1) to reach new customers, (2) to sell goods and services, (3) to disseminate information more quickly, (4) to keep up with competitors, and (5) to reach global markets.[2]

5 percent commission on every sale. Farnsworth, the nephew of a dairy farmer, decided to target a niche that other entrepreneurs were ignoring and raised $4 million in start-up capital from family members and friends. His idea is paying off. The site generates 7 million hits a month! "At one time, the most important piece of farm equipment was a tractor. Today, it's a laptop and the 'Net," says Farnsworth.[1] By using an innovative approach to create an all-in-one, easy-to-use, online farming site, Farmbid.com has established a unique position in the market and changed the way farmers operate their businesses.

Companies of all sizes are establishing a presence on the Web because that's where their customers are. The number of Internet users worldwide now stands at more than 500 million, up from 147 million at the end of 1998 (see Figure 13.1).[3] In 1999, e-commerce made up 0.8 percent of U.S. gross domestic product (GDP); in 2003, that percentage had climbed to 8.9 percent![4] Although this torrid pace of growth will not last indefinitely, the Web represents a tremendous opportunity that businesses simply cannot afford to ignore.

BENEFITS OF SELLING ON THE WEB

1. Describe the benefits of selling on the World Wide Web.

Although a Web-based sales strategy does not guarantee success, the companies that have pioneered Web-based selling have realized many benefits, including the following:

- *The opportunity to increase revenues.* For many small businesses, launching a Web site is the equivalent of opening a new sales channel. Companies that launch e-commerce efforts soon discover that their sites are generating additional sales from new customers.
- *The ability to expand their reach into global markets.* The Web is the most efficient way for small businesses to sell their products to the millions of potential customers who live outside the borders of the United States. Tapping into these global markets through more traditional methods would be too complex and too costly for the typical small business. Yet, on the Web, a small company can

sell its products efficiently to customers anywhere in the world at any time of day.

- *The ability to remain open 24 hours a day, seven days a week.* More than half of all retail sales occur after 6 P.M., when many traditional stores close. Extending the hours a brick-and-mortar store remains open can increase sales, but it also takes a toll on the business owner and the employees. With a Web site up and running, however, a small company can sell around the clock without having to incur additional staffing expenses. Customers never have to worry about whether or not an online store is "open."

- *The capacity to use the Web's interactive nature to enhance customer service.* Although selling on the Web can be highly impersonal because of the lack of human interaction, companies that design their sites properly can create an exciting, interactive experience for their online visitors. Customers can contact a company at any time of the day, can control the flow of information they get, and in some cases can interact with company representatives in real time. In addition, technology now allows companies to "personalize" their sites to suit the tastes and preferences of individual customers. Drawing on a database containing information customers have provided in the past, modern Web sites can customize themselves, displaying content that appeals to an individual visitor. For instance, a site selling clothing can greet a returning customer by name and ask if she is shopping for herself or for someone on her personal shopping list. Based on her response, the site can recall appropriate sizes and favorite styles and colors and can even make product recommendations.

- *The power to educate and to inform.* Far more than most marketing media, the Web gives entrepreneurs the power to educate and to inform customers. Women and members of Generation Y, especially, crave product information before they make purchases. The Web allows business owners to provide more detailed information to visitors than practically any other medium. For instance, a travel company advertising an Alaskan tour in a newspaper or magazine might include a brief description of the tour, a list of the destinations, a telephone number, the price, and perhaps a photo or two. A Web-based promotion for the same tour could include all of the information above as well as a detailed itinerary with dozens of breath-taking photographs; descriptions and photographs of all accommodations; advice on what to pack; airline schedules, seating configurations, and availability; information on optional side trips; comments from customers who have taken this tour before; and links to other Web sites about Alaska, the weather, and fun things to do in the region.[5]

- *The ability to lower the cost of doing business.* The Web is one of the most efficient ways of reaching both new and existing customers. Properly promoted, a Web site can reduce a company's cost of generating sales leads, providing customer support, and distributing marketing materials. For instance, sending customers an e-mail newsletter is much less expensive than paying the printing and postage costs of sending the same newsletter by "snail mail." By integrating its Web site with its inventory control system, a company also can reduce its inventory costs by shortening the sales cycle. Finally, linking Web sales activity to suppliers enables a business to cut its purchasing costs.

- *The ability to spot new business opportunities and to capitalize on them.* E-commerce companies are poised to give customers just what they want when they want it. As the number of dual-career couples rises and the amount of available leisure time shrinks, consumers are looking for ways to increase the convenience of shopping, and the Web is fast becoming the solution they seek. Increasingly, customers view shopping as an unpleasant chore that cuts into already scarce leisure time, and they are embracing anything that reduces the amount of time they must spend shopping. Entrepreneurs who tap into customers' need to buy goods more conveniently and with less hassle are winning the battle for market share. New opportunities to serve customers' changing needs and wants are constantly arising, and the Web is the birthplace of many of them.

- *The power to track sales results.* The Web gives businesses the power to track virtually any kind of activity on their Web sites, from the number of visitors to the click-through rates on their banner ads. Because of the Web's ability to monitor traffic continuously, entrepreneurs can judge the value their sites are generating for their companies.

Men's clothier Jos. A. Bank is reaping many of these benefits. In 1998, the company began a market test to see whether or not customers would purchase its clothing over the Web. The company hired a third-party hosting site that took customers' orders and faxed them to Jos. A. Bank, who then shipped the merchandise. When this decidedly low-tech approach proved to be successful, Jos. A. Bank brought the operation of its Web site in-house. With the help of a local Web development company, Jos. A. Bank created a site featuring a handy search engine, an easy checkout process, and a customized "build-a-suit" feature. The company, which has 128 brick-and-mortar stores nationwide, says that its online store generates the largest volume of sales and accounts for 20 percent of the company's revenue![6]

FACTORS TO CONSIDER BEFORE LAUNCHING INTO E-COMMERCE

2. Understand the factors an entrepreneur should consider before launching into e-commerce.

Despite the many benefits the Web offers, not every small business owner is ready to embrace e-commerce. Recent surveys by SuperPages.com and the National Federation of Independent Businesses found that only 27 percent of U.S. companies with fewer than 50 employees have Web sites and that only 7 percent of small companies actually sell merchandise online.[7] Although small companies account for more than half of all retail sales in the United States, they generate only 6 percent of online retail sales.[8] Why are so many small companies hesitant to use the Web as a business tool? For many entrepreneurs, the key barrier is not knowing where or how to start an e-commerce effort, while for others cost concerns are a major issue. Other roadblocks include the fear that customers will not use the Web site and the problems associated with ensuring online security.

Whatever their size, traditional companies must realize that selling their products and services on the Web is no longer a luxury. Business owners who are not at least considering creating a Web presence or integrating the Web creatively into their operations are putting their companies at risk. However, before launching an e-commerce effort, business owners should consider the following important issues:

- How a company exploits the Web's interconnectivity and the opportunities it creates to transform relationships with its suppliers and vendors, its customers, and other external stakeholders is crucial to its success.
- Web success requires a company to develop a plan for integrating the Web into its overall strategy. The plan should address issues such as site design and maintenance, creating and managing a brand name, marketing and promotional strategies, sales, and customer service.
- Developing deep, lasting relationships with customers takes on even greater importance on the Web. Attracting customers on the Web costs money, and companies must be able to retain their online customers to make their Web sites profitable.

- Creating a meaningful presence on the Web requires an ongoing investment of resources—time, money, energy, and talent. Establishing an attractive Web site brimming with catchy photographs of products is only the beginning.
- Measuring the success of its Web-based sales effort is essential to remaining relevant to customers whose tastes, needs, and preferences are always changing.

Doing business on the Web takes more time and energy than many entrepreneurs think. Answering the following questions will help entrepreneurs make sure they are ready to do business on the Web and avoid unpleasant surprises in their e-commerce efforts:

- What exactly do you expect a Web site to do for your company? Will it provide information only, reach new customers, increase sales to existing customers, improve communication with customers, enhance customer service, or reduce your company's cost of operation? Will customers be able to place orders from the site, or must they call your company to buy?
- How much can you afford to invest in an e-commerce effort?
- What rate of return do you expect to earn on that investment?
- How long can you afford to wait for that return?
- How well suited are your products and services for selling on the Web?
- How will the "back office" of your Web site work? Will your site be tied into your company's inventory control system?
- How will you handle order fulfillment? Can your fulfillment system handle the increase in volume you are expecting?
- What impact, if any, will your Web site have on your company's traditional channels of distribution?
- What mechanism will your site use to ensure secure customer transactions?
- How will your company handle customer service for the site? What provisions will you make for returned items?
- How do you plan to promote the site to draw traffic to it?
- What information will you collect from the visitors to your site? How will you use it? Will you tell visitors how you intend to use this information?
- Have you developed a privacy policy? Have you posted that policy on your company's Web site for customers?
- Have you tested your site with real, live customers to make sure that it is easy to navigate and easy to order from?
- How will you measure the success of your company's Web site? What objectives have you set for the site?

TWELVE MYTHS OF E-COMMERCE

3. Explain the 12 myths of e-commerce and how to avoid falling victim to them.

Although many entrepreneurs have boosted their businesses with e-commerce, setting up shop on the Web is no guarantee of success. Scores of entrepreneurs have plunged unprepared into the world of e-commerce only to discover that there is more to it than merely setting up a Web site and waiting for the orders to start pouring in. Make sure that you do not fall victim to one of the following e-commerce myths.

Myth 1. Setting up a business on the Web is easy and inexpensive. A common misconception is that setting up an effective Web site for an online business is easy and inexpensive. Although practically anyone with the right software can post a static page in just a few minutes, creating an effective, professional, and polished Web site can be an expensive, time-consuming project. Most small businesses set up their Web pages as simple "electronic flyers," pages that post product information, a few photographs, prices, and telephone and fax numbers. Although these simple sites lack the capacity for true electronic commerce, they do provide a company with another way of reaching both new and existing customers.

Establishing a true transactional Web site will require several months and an investment ranging from $10,000 up to nearly $1 million, depending on the features and capacity it incorporates. The average initial investment a small company makes in setting up a Web site is $8,500.[9] According to a study by Jupiter Communications, setting up an e-commerce site takes most companies at least six months to complete. The study also revealed that setting up the site was only the first investment required. Companies cited these follow-up investments: (1) redesign Web site, (2) buy more hardware to support Web site, (3) automate or expand warehouse to meet customer demand, (4) integrate Web site into inventory control system, and (5) increase customer call center capacity.[10]

Myth 2. If I launch a site, customers will flock to it. Some entrepreneurs think that once they set up their Web sites, their expenses end there. Not true! Without promotional support, no Web site will draw enough traffic to support a business. With more than two billion Web pages in existence and the number growing daily, getting a site noticed has become increasingly difficult. Even listing a site with popular Web search engines cannot guarantee that customers surfing the Web will find your company's site. Just like traditional retail stores seeking to attract customers, virtual companies have discovered that drawing sufficient traffic to a Web site requires promotion— and lots of it! "No one will know you're on the Web unless you tell them and motivate them to visit," explains Mark Layton, owner of a Web-based distributor of computer supplies and author of a book on e-commerce.[11]

Entrepreneurs with both physical and virtual stores must promote their Web sites at every opportunity by printing their URLs on everything related to their physical stores—on signs, in print and broadcast ads, on shopping bags, on merchandise labels, and anywhere else their customers will see. Virtual shop owners should consider buying ads in traditional advertising media as well as using banner ads, banner exchange programs, and cross-marketing arrangements with companies selling complementary products on their own Web sites. Other techniques include creating a Web-based newsletter, writing articles that link to the company's site, hosting a chat room that allows customers to interact with one another and with company personnel, or sponsoring a contest. For instance, Williams Nursery, an 81-year-old family business, has been successful in promoting its Web site and its retail store with a variety of creative contests, from scarecrow building to Halloween costumes.[12]

The key to promoting a Web site is networking, building relationships with other companies, customers, trade associations, online directories, and other Web sites your company's customers visit. "You need to create relationships with the businesses and people with whom you share common customers," says Barbara Ling, author of a book on e-commerce. "Then you need to create links between sites to help customers find what they are looking for."[13]

Myth 3. Making money on the Web is easy. Promoters who hawk "get-rich-quick" schemes on the Web lure many entrepreneurs with the promise that making money on the Web is easy. It isn't. One recent study by SuperPages.com reports that 55 percent of small businesses say their Web sites have either broken even or are profitable.[14] Making money on the Web is possible, but it takes time and requires an upfront investment. As hundreds of new sites spring up every day, getting a company's site noticed requires more effort and marketing muscle than ever before. One study by a management consulting firm, Boston Consulting Group, and shop.org, an

Internet retailing trade association, found that Web retailers invested 65 percent of their revenues in marketing and advertising, compared to their off-line counterparts, who invested just 4 percent.[15]

Myth 4. Privacy is not an important issue on the Web. The Web allows companies to gain access to almost unbelievable amounts of information about their customers. Many sites offer visitors "freebies" in exchange for information about themselves. Companies then use this information to learn more about their target customers and how to market to them most effectively. Concerns over the privacy of and the use of this information has become the topic of debate by many interested parties, including government agencies, consumer watchdog groups, customers, and industry trade associations.

Companies that collect information from their online customers have a responsibility to safeguard their customers' privacy, to protect that information from unauthorized use, and to use it responsibly. That means that businesses should post a privacy statement on their Web sites, explaining to customers how they intend to use the information they collect. One of the surest ways to alienate online customers is to abuse the information collected from them by selling it to third parties or by spamming customers with unwanted solicitations.

Businesses that publish privacy policies and then adhere to them build trust among their customers, an important facet of doing business on the Web. A study by Jupiter Communications found that 64 percent of Web customers distrust Web sites.[16] According to John Briggs, director of e-commerce for the Yahoo! Network, "customers need to trust the brand they are buying and believe that their online purchases will be safe transactions. They need to feel comfortable that [their] personal data will not be sold and that they won't get spammed by giving their e-mail address. They need to know about shipping costs, product availability, and return policies up front."[17] Privacy *does* matter on the Web, and businesses that respect their customers' privacy will win their customers' trust. Trust is the foundation on which the long-term customer relationships that are so crucial to Web success are built.

Myth 5. The most important part of any e-commerce effort is technology. Although understanding the technology of e-commerce is an important part of the formula for success, it is *not* the most crucial ingredient. What matters most is the ability to understand the underlying business and to develop a workable business model that offers customers something of value at a reasonable price while producing a reasonable return for the company. The entrepreneurs who are proving to be most successful in e-commerce are those who know how their industries work inside and out and then build an e-business around that knowledge. They know that they can hire Webmasters, database experts, and fulfillment companies to design the technical aspects of their online businesses, but that nothing can substitute for a solid understanding of their industry, their target market, and the strategy needed to pull the various parts together. The key is seeing the Web for what it really is: another way to reach and serve customers with an effective business model and to minimize the cost of doing business.

Dell Computer, the pioneer of the online build-to-order computer, has integrated the Web into its business strategy very effectively. Dell allows shoppers to customize their PCs at Dell.com, get a delivery date, and track the status of their orders at any time. Dell also uses the Web to control one of the most challenging aspects of its business: managing inventory. Dell's component suppliers log onto a special site to get instructions about which parts to deliver, how many to ship, and where and when to deliver them. Using the Web to tie together its supply chain, Dell keeps its inventory levels so low that it turns its inventory an amazing 60 times a year![18]

The key to Dell's success on the Web is the company's knowledge of the computer industry to which it then applied the technology of the Web. Unfortunately, many entrepreneurs tackle e-commerce by focusing on technology first and then determine how that technology fits their business idea. "If you start with technology, you're likely going to buy a solution in search of a problem," says Kip Martin, Program Director of META Group's Electronic Business Strategies. Instead, he suggests, "Start with the business and ask yourself what you want to happen and how you'll measure it. *Then* ask how the technology will help you achieve your goals. Remember: Business first, technology second."[19]

Myth 6. "Strategy? I don't need a strategy to sell on the Web! Just give me a Web site, and the rest will take care of itself." Building a successful e-business is no different than building a successful brick-and-mortar business, and that requires a well-thought-out strategy. Building a strategy means that an entrepreneur must first develop a clear definition of the company's target audience and a thorough understanding of those customers' needs, wants, likes, and dislikes. To be successful, a Web site must be appealing to the customers it seeks to attract just as a traditional store's design and décor must draw foot traffic. Before your Web site can become the foundation for a successful e-business, you must create it with your target audience in mind.

Myth 7. On the Web, customer service is not as important as it is in a traditional retail store. A study conducted by Jupiter Research found that 72 percent of online buyers cite customer service as a critical factor in their online shopping satisfaction; yet, only 41 percent say they are satisfied with the service they receive from online merchants.[20] The fact is that many Web sites treat customer service as an after-thought, and this attitude costs businesses plenty. A report by Datamonitor estimates that online stores lose more than $6 billion in sales because of poor customer service.[21] Sites that are difficult to navigate, slow to load, offer complex checkout systems, or are confusing will turn customers away quickly, never to return. Online merchants must recognize that customer service is just as important (if not more so) on the Web as it is in traditional bricks-and-mortar stores.

There is plenty of room for improvement in customer service on the Web. Research by BizRate.com found that 75 percent of Web shoppers who fill their online shopping carts become frustrated and leave the site before checking out.[22] The most common reasons for leaving a site without purchasing include the following: (1) customers could not find the items they were looking for, (2) the shopping cart was too hard to find, (3) checking out took too long, (4) the site did not look trustworthy, and (5) shipping charges were too high.[23]

In an attempt to improve the level of service they offer, many sites provide e-mail links to encourage customer interaction. Unfortunately, e-mail takes a very low priority at many e-businesses. One study by Jupiter Communications found that 42 percent of business Web sites took longer than five days to respond to e-mail inquiries, never replied at all, or simply were not accessible by e-mail![24] The lesson for e-commerce entrepreneurs is simple: Devote time, energy, and money to developing a functional mechanism for providing superior customer service. Those who do will build a sizeable base of loyal customers who will keep coming back. Perhaps the most significant actions online companies can take to bolster their customer service efforts are providing a quick online checkout process, creating a well-staffed and well-trained customer response team, offering a simple return process, and providing an easy order-tracking process so customers can check the status of their orders at any time.

Myth 8. Flash makes a Web site better. Businesses that fall into this trap pour most of their e-commerce budgets into designing flashy Web sites with all of the "bells and whistles." The logic is that to stand out on the Web, a site really has to sparkle. That logic leads to a "more is better" mentality when designing a site. On the Web, however, "more" does *not* necessarily equate to "better." Although fancy graphics, bright colors, playful music, and spinning icons can attract attention, they also can be quite distracting and very slow to download. Sites that download slowly may never have the chance to sell because customers will click to another site. Keep the design of your site simple.

Myth 9. It's what's up front that counts. Designing an attractive Web site is important to building a successful e-business. However, designing the back office, the systems that take over once a customer places an order on a Web site, is just as important as designing the site itself. If the behind-the-scenes support is not in place or cannot handle the traffic from the Web site, a company's entire e-commerce effort will come crashing down. Although e-commerce can lower many costs of doing business, it still requires a basic infrastructure somewhere in the channel of distribution to process orders, maintain inventory, fill orders, and handle customer service. Many entrepreneurs hoping to launch virtual businesses are discovering the need for a "clicks-and-mortar" approach to provide the necessary infrastructure to serve their customers. "The companies with warehouses, supply-chain management, and solid customer service are going to be the ones that survive," says Daryl Plummer, head of the Gartner Group's Internet and new media division.[25]

To customers, a business is only as good as its last order, and many e-companies are not measuring up. One study suggests that only 30 percent of e-commerce Web sites feature real-time inventory look-up, which gives online shoppers the ability to see if an item they want to purchase is actually in stock.[26] In addition, only 7 percent of Web sites are linked to the back office.[27] These figures will increase as software to integrate Web sites with the back office becomes easier to use and more affordable, but in the meantime customers will have to endure late shipments, incorrect orders, and poor service.

Web-based entrepreneurs often discover that the greatest challenge their businesses face is not necessarily attracting customers on the Web but creating a workable order fulfillment strategy. Order fulfillment involves everything required to get goods from a warehouse into a customer's hands and includes order processing, warehousing, picking and packing, shipping, and billing. Some entrepreneurs choose to handle order fulfillment in-house with their own employees, while others find it more economical to hire specialized fulfillment houses to handle these functions. Finding a fulfillment house willing to handle a relatively small volume of orders at a reasonable price can be difficult for some small businesses, however. Major fulfillment providers include FedEx, UPS, NewRoads, and NFI Interactive.

Myth 10. E-commerce will cause bricks-and-mortar retail stores to disappear. The rapid growth of e-commerce does pose a serious threat to some traditional retailers, especially those who fail to find ways to capitalize on the opportunities the Web offers them. However, it is unlikely that Web-based shopping will replace customers' need and desire to visit real stores selling real merchandise that they can see, touch, and try on. Some products simply lend themselves to selling in real stores more naturally than in online shops. For instance, furniture stores and supermarkets have struggled for success online. On the other hand, other items, particularly standard commodity products for which customers have little loyalty, are ideally suited for online sales. Virtual stores have, and will, continue to drive out of existence some traditional companies that resist creating new business models or are too slow to change. To remain competitive, traditional bricks-and-mortar stores must find ways to transform themselves into flexible clicks-and-mortar operations that can make the convenience, the reach, and the low transaction costs of the Web work for them.

REI, Inc., a retailer of outdoor gear and apparel with 60 stores, integrates its Web presence into its retail outlets using in-store kiosks that give customers access to more than 178,000 items from its Web site. Both online and in-store customers can access more than 400 how-to articles and clinics to help them evaluate and select the right product for their needs. REI.com's "Learn and Share" section gives (and takes) valuable advice on a variety of topics ranging from rock climbing to fly fishing. Customers' response to in-store Web access has been phenomenal. REI says that the revenue generated by its in-store kiosks is equivalent to that generated by a 25,000-square-foot store![28]

Myth 11. The greatest opportunities for e-commerce lie in the retail sector. As impressive as the growth rate and total volume for on-line retail sales are, they are dwarfed by those in the on-line business-to-business (B2B) sector, where businesses sell to one another rather than to retail customers. In fact, B2B sales account for 90 percent of e-commerce transactions.[29] Entrepreneurs who are looking to sell goods to other businesses on the Web will find plenty of opportunities available in a multitude of industries.

Business-to-business e-commerce is growing so rapidly (see Figure 13.2) because of its potential to boost productivity, slash costs, and increase profits. This brand of e-commerce is transforming the way companies design and purchase parts, supplies, and materials as well as the way they manage inventory and process transactions. The Web's power to increase the speed and the efficiency of the purchasing function represents a fundamental departure from the past. Experts estimate that transferring purchasing to the Web can cut total procurement costs by 10 percent and transaction costs by as much as 90 percent.[30] For instance, Chris Cogan, CEO of GoCo-op, an Internet purchasing site for hotels, restaurants, and health care companies, explains, "We estimate [that] the average cost of executing a paper purchase order is $115." Businesses using his company's Web-based purchasing system "get that cost down to $10," he says.[31]

Business-to-business e-commerce is growing because of the natural link that exists with business-to-consumer e-commerce. As we have seen, one of the greatest challenges Web-based retailers face is obtaining and delivering the goods their customers order fast enough to satisfy customers' expectations. Increasingly, Web-based retailers are connecting their front office sales systems and their back office purchas-

Figure 13.2
B2B E-Commerce Sales

Source: Gartner Research, 2001.

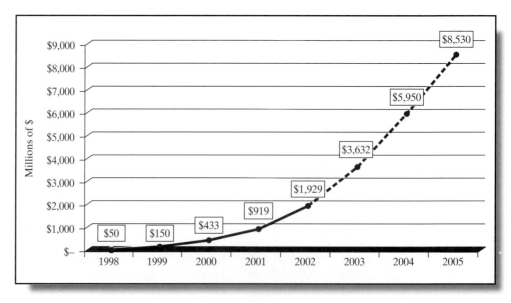

ing and order fulfillment systems with those of their suppliers. The result is a faster, more efficient method of filling customer orders. So far, the most successful online business-to-business companies are those that have discovered ways of tying their front offices, their back offices, their suppliers, and their customers together into a single, smoothly-functioning, Web-based network. *Cisco Systems, a maker of computer routers, switches, and other hardware, provides a good example of a fully integrated B2B company. Customers go to the Cisco Web site to check out product specifications and to place orders. Cisco then uses the Internet to transfer those orders directly to its suppliers, who then ship the necessary raw materials to Cisco, or, in many cases, ship products directly to customers. (About 65 percent of Cisco's orders go directly from the supplier to the customer without Cisco ever handling them!) The efficiency of this system minimizes the amount of raw materials inventory that Cisco must carry and allows customers to check on the status of their orders over the Web as well. Cisco keeps its costs low and its customers happy with its innovative Web-based strategy.*[32]

Myth 12. It's too late to get on the Web. A common myth, especially among small companies, is that those businesses that have not yet moved onto the Web have missed a golden opportunity. The reality is that the Internet is still in its infancy, and companies are still figuring out how to succeed on the Web. Recall that just half of small businesses's Web sites are profitable. For every e-commerce site that exists, many others have failed. An abundance of business opportunities exist for those entrepreneurs insightful enough to spot them and clever enough to capitalize on them.

One fact of e-commerce that has emerged is the importance of speed. Companies doing business on the Web have discovered that those who reach customers first often have a significant advantage over their slower rivals. "The lesson of the Web is not how the big eat the small, but how the fast eat the slow," says a manager at a venture capital firm specializing in Web-based companies.[33]

Succumbing to this myth often leads entrepreneurs to make a fundamental mistake once they finally decide to go online: They believe they have to have a "perfect" site before they can launch it. Few businesses get their sites "right" the first time. In fact, the most successful e-commerce sites are constantly changing, removing what does not work and adding new features to see what does. Successful Web sites are much like a well-designed flower garden, constantly growing and improving, yet changing to reflect the climate of each season. Their creators worry less about creating the perfect site at the outset than about getting a site online and then fixing it, tweaking it, and updating it to meet changing customer demands.

APPROACHES TO E-COMMERCE

4. Discuss the five basic approaches available to entrepeneurs wanting to launch an e-commerce effort.

A successful e-commerce effort requires much more than merely launching a Web site; entrepreneurs must develop a plan for integrating the Web into their overall business strategy. Many entrepreneurs choose to start their e-commerce efforts small and simple and then expand them as sales grow and their needs become more sophisticated. Others make major investments in creating full-blown, interconnected sites at the onset. The cost of setting up a Web site varies significantly, depending on which options an entrepreneur chooses. Generally, Web experts identify three basic pricing categories for creating a Web site: less than $10,000, between $10,000 and $30,000, and more than $30,000. When it comes to choosing an approach to e-commerce, there are no "right" or "wrong" answers; the key is creating a plan that fits into the small company's budget and meets its e-commerce needs as it grows and expands. Entrepreneurs looking to launch an e-commerce effort have five basic choices:

(1) online shopping malls, (2) storefront-building services, (3) Internet service providers (ISPs), (4) hiring professionals to design a custom site, and (5) building a site in-house.

Online Shopping Malls. In the under-$10,000 category, the simplest way for entrepreneurs to get their businesses online is to rent space for their products at an online shopping mall (also called a shopping portal). Online shopping malls are the equivalent of an electronic strip mall because they list on one site the product offerings from many different small companies. The primary advantages they offer are their simplicity and their low cost. To join an online mall, entrepreneurs simply provides descriptions and photographs of the products they sell. For a low monthly fee, the mall creates and maintains a virtual storefront for the company and funnels customer orders from it to the company. Another advantage of this approach is the increased customer exposure it offers an online business.

The major disadvantages of using an online shopping mall are an individual store's lack of prominence and the lack of control entrepreneurs have over their sites. Most malls host dozens of businesses in a multitude of industries, and standing out in the crowd can be a challenge because all of the sites follow a similar (or the same) design. In addition, some malls are much more effective than others at promoting their resident businesses.

Storefront-Building Services. Also in the under-$10,000 category are storefront-building services that help entrepreneurs create online shops that include features such as Web-hosting services, the ability to handle secure credit card transactions, databases for order fulfillment and customer tracking, advertising placement, and search engine registration—all for as little as $100 to $500 per month. Some storefront-building services offer to handle a limited number of transactions for free, although most businesses quickly outgrow the free service and end up paying the service the monthly fee for site hosting and operation. Most Internet portals such as Yahoo! *(www.store.yahoo.com/)* and e-commerce service companies such as Bigstep.com *(www.bigstep.com)*, FreeMerchant.com *(www.freemerchant.com)*, Microsoft's bcentral.com *(wwwbcentral.com)*, Storesense.com *(www.storesense.com/)* or BizLand.com *(www.bizland.com)*, offer these e-commerce services.

The major advantages of using these storefront-building services is their simplicity and their low cost. Setting up a store can take as little as a few hours, and the hosting company shoulders the burden of setting up and running the cyberstore, creating minimal headaches for the entrepreneur behind it. The downside of these services is that most of their sites look as though they came out of the same cookie-cutter approach because they rely on a limited number of templates to create store sites. It is extremely difficult to make a company's Web store stand out when every storefront is stamped from the same mold. Plus, most services limit the number of products they will handle at the base price on these sites and charge extra for credit card processing.

Despite its drawbacks, using a storefront-building service offers a fast and easy way to create a virtual store that is open 24 hours a day, seven days a week. *Jules Mahabir, founder of a cosmetics company that targets African-Americans, knew that his company needed to be online. Given his limited budget, Mahabir opted to build an online store using StoreSense.com's storefront system. For just $500 a month, Mahabir has a site, BlackCosmetics.com, that draws 3,000 hits a day. Because StoreSense uses standard HTML templates, Mahabir can customize the site and update it as often as he needs to.*[34]

Internet Service Providers. Another e-commerce option in the under-$10,000 category is using an Internet service provider (ISP) or an application service provider (ASP) to create an online store. ISPs and ASPs provide many of the same features as

IN THE FOOTSTEPS OF AN ENTREPRENEUR
Rafting the Web to Success

Your trip down California's Stanislaus River offers panoramic views of the beautifully rugged Sequoia country, scenic stair-step waterfalls, and exhilarating stretches of whitewater. Yet you manage to remain completely dry because you are not actually there! You are taking a virtual 3-D tour of the river over the Web from the All-Outdoors Whitewater Rafting Company's site, *www.aorafting.com.* AO Rafting is a second-generation family business founded in 1961 by George Armstrong, then a public school teacher in Concord, California. Armstrong formed an outdoor activities club and, using borrowed equipment, began taking his students to nearby rivers. The kids loved it, and soon Armstrong's whole family was involved in guiding various groups on whitewater river trips.

The company grew slowly throughout the 1970s, mostly by word-of-mouth. As AO Rafting's customer base grew and repeat customers returned, revenues climbed, reaching $750,000 in the 1980s. When the company's sales crossed the $1 million mark, George's sons, Gregg and Scott, were running the business on a daily basis. The Armstrongs were spending about $150,000 a year on their marketing effort, which consisted of glossy print catalogs, Yellow Pages ads, direct mail campaigns, and discount programs for corporate groups. The brothers were overwhelmed by the time and energy required to coordinate the multiple marketing effort and run the remainder of the business. "I was managing a whole train of marketing programs," says Gregg. "Instead of 10 avenues, I wished there was one way to reach everyone."

Having made a decision to focus on growing their company, the Armstrongs began to explore the World Wide Web, which at the time was just emerging as a business tool. They approached Jamie Low, one of their guides who had studied marketing in college and had worked as a graphic designer with an offer: "Our future is on the Internet, and you're the guy who is going to take us there." Low accepted the challenge. AO Rafting immediately registered its URL and gave Low the go-ahead to set up a Web site. "The Internet could express everything we were trying to pack into all of the other marketing materials," says Gregg. The Internet was much easier to update [than our print brochures]. It could replace this marketing monster we had built."

The company's basic approach to designing its Web site was one of simplicity—easy to find, easy to navigate, and easy to book trips. Because they understood the importance of search engines to the typical

AO Rafting customers enjoy an exciting trip down a California river. Eighty-four percent of the company's business comes through its award-winning Web site.
Courtesy of rapidshooters.com.

(continued)

Web browser, the Armstrongs made sure they registered the site on every major search engine and received good placement. That proved to be a wise decision because 70 percent of the company's new business comes from customers using search engines to locate their site.

AO Rafting has been through several revisions of its site, but the basic architecture of its current site was launched in 1997. The payoff was almost immediate. In just a few months, 55 percent of the company's revenue was coming through its Web site! The Web site also lowered AO Rafting's marketing costs. "We had been spending 20 to 25 percent of our revenues on marketing," says Gregg. "With the Web it's now about 5 to 10 percent," adds Scott. In addition to lowering the company's marketing costs, the Web site also produces results that are much easier to track. Today, the Armstrongs generate reports that provide details on how customers found the AO Rafting site and what they are looking for once they get there. Today, 84 percent of the company's business comes through its Web site, and sales have grown to more than $2 million. "It's well worth the investment of resources [we made]," says Gregg. "It's the best investment AO has ever made."

1. What benefits has AO Rafting gained from its Web site?

2. The Armstrongs developed their company's Web site internally, using one of their own employees. What are the advantages and the disadvantages of this approach? What other options do small companies have for developing a Web site?

3. What steps can AO Rafting take to promote its Web site to attract new customers and generate more business?

Source: Adapted from Michael Warshaw, "A Web Strategy Runs Through It," *Inc.*, November 2001, pp. 134–138.

storefront-design services except they offer their small business customers more design flexibility and the ability to customize their Web sites. ISP packages such as EarthLink Entrepreneur Packages or VerioStore are not as easy to use as the templates from storefront-design services and typically require the entrepreneurs using them to know some basics of the hypertext markup language (HTML) used to design most Web sites. Although most ISPs provide basic design templates, experienced HTML users can modify them easily. ISP templates usually include shopping cart and catalog features as well as secure order and payment processing and report generation capabilities. ASPs' packages provide these same features. However, rather than requiring users to purchase e-commerce software, ASPs "rent" a variety of e-commerce applications, from site building and hosting to purchasing automation and accounting, to their customers on an as-needed basis.

In addition to hosting and running a company's virtual store, ISPs offer the ability to grow with a small company as its online store's sales volume climbs. Most base their fees on the number of visitors a site attracts and the amount of space it takes up on their server, so start-up stores offering a small product line can spend as little as $100 a month (plus initial setup costs). Before choosing an ISP, entrepreneurs should investigate its operating history (specifically the amount of downtime the provider has experienced), the quality of its backup systems (in case of a crash), and its remaining capacity for hosting sites.

Hiring Professionals to Design a Custom Site. Businesses that are able to spend between $10,000 and $30,000 (or more) can afford to hire professionals to create their sites. The primary benefit this option offers is the unlimited ability to customize a site, making it anything an entrepreneur wants, including complete front-office and back-office integration. Just like building a custom-designed house, hiring professionals to design a site from the ground up gives entrepreneurs a high degree of control over the final result. Also, most Web development companies offer complete e-commerce solutions, including consulting and design services, Web hosting, site registration, and listings with search engines and directories.

Because custom-built sites require custom programming, they are much more expensive to create than sites based on preformatted templates. The Gartner Group estimates that building and launching an e-commerce site with complete front-office and back-office integration now costs more than $500,000![35] Expenses in that range are out of the question for most e-commerce entrepreneurs.

Building a Web Site In-House. Building a Web site in-house gives an entrepreneur complete control over the site and its design, operation, and maintenance. However, hiring and supporting an in-house staff of Web designers can quickly run up the cost of creating and maintaining a custom Web site into the $250,000 to $500,000 range. Because of the high costs involved in hiring professional Web development companies or in maintaining a staff of Web designers, most entrepreneurs wanting to establish a Web presence do so by using either online shopping malls, storefront-building services, or Internet service providers.

STRATEGIES FOR E-SUCCESS

5. Explain the basic strategies entrepreneurs should follow to achieve success in their e-commerce efforts.

The typical Web user spends an average of 5 hours and 52 minutes online each week. (Figure 13.3 shows the volume of Internet traffic by day of the week and by hour of the day.) Across a lifetime, the average baby boomer will spend 5 years and 6 months online; the average Generation Xer will spend 9 years and 11 months online; and the average Generation Y user will spend 23 years and 2 months online, almost one third of their lives![36] However, converting these Web surfers into online customers requires a business to do more than merely set up a Web site and wait for the hits to start rolling up. Doing business from a Web site is like setting up shop on a dead-end street or a back alley. You may be ready to sell, but no one knows you are there! Building sufficient volume for a site takes energy, time, money, creativity, and, perhaps most importantly, a well-defined strategy.

Although the Web is a unique medium for creating a company, launching an e-business is not much different from launching a traditional off-line company. The basic drivers of a successful business are the same on the Web as they are on Main Street. To be successful, both off-line and online companies require solid planning and a well-formulated strategy that emphasizes customer service. The goals of e-commerce are no different from traditional off-line businesses—to increase sales, improve efficiency, and boost profits. Yet, the Web has the power to transform businesses, industries, and commerce itself. How a company integrates the Web into its overall business strategy determines how successful it ultimately will become. Following are some guidelines for building a successful Web strategy for a small e-company.

Focus on a Niche in the Market. Rather than try to compete head-to-head with the dominant players on the Web who have the resources and the recognition to squash smaller competitors, entrepreneurs should consider focusing on serving a market niche. Smaller companies' limited resources usually are better spent serving niche markets than trying to be everything to everyone (recall the discussion of the focus strategy in Chapter 2). The idea is to concentrate on serving a small corner of the market the giants have overlooked. Niches exist in every industry and can be highly profitable, given the right strategy for serving them. A niche can be defined in many ways, including by geography, by customer profile, by product, by product usage, and many others. *Rather than try to sell a complete line of sporting goods, JustBalls!*

Figure 13.3
Daily Internet Traffic

Source: Nielsen/NetRatings, 2001.

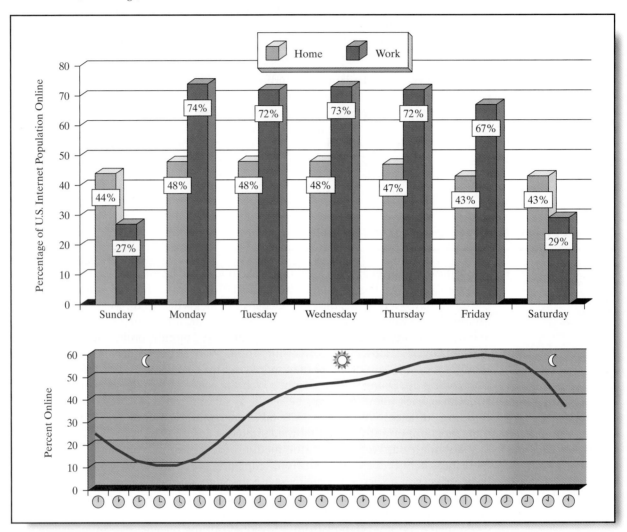

(www.justballs.com) *focuses on (as its name suggests) just balls! This e-tailer sells every kind of sports ball imaginable, from autographed collectible balls and cricket balls to tennis balls and balls used to play sepak takraw (a game known as the "sport of kings" in Southeast Asia).*[37] Because of its broad reach, the Web is the ideal mechanism for implementing a focus strategy because small companies can reach large numbers of customers with a common interest.

Develop a Community. On the Web, competitors are just a mouse click away. To attract customers and keep them coming back, e-companies have discovered the need to offer more than just quality products and excellent customer service. Many seek to develop a community of customers with similar interests, the nucleus of which is their Web site. The idea is to increase customer loyalty by giving customers the chance to interact with other like-minded visitors or with experts to discuss and learn more about topics they are passionate about. E-mail lists and chat rooms are powerful tools for building a community of visitors at a site. *David Rogelberg, founder* *of Studio B, a literary agency that specializes in representing authors of computer books, uses mailing list software that circulates ongoing e-mail discussions among subscribers to his site. Rogelberg set up his site (www.studiob.com) with two goals: providing a forum for both published and aspiring authors to ask and answer questions about the publishing business and, of course, attracting clients to his agency. He has succeeded on both counts. Rogelberg's site is now considered to be one of the major resources in the computer book publishing industry and has helped him land 150 new clients for his literary agency.*[38] Like Studio B, companies that successfully create a community around their Web sites turn mere customers into loyal fans who keep coming back and, better yet, invite others to join them.

Attract Visitors by Giving Away "Freebies." One of the most important words on the Internet is "free." Many successful e-merchants have discovered the ability to attract visitors to their site by giving away something free and then selling them something else. One e-commerce consultant calls this cycle of giving something away and then selling something "the rhythm of the Web."[39] The "freebie" must be something customers value, but it does *not* have to be expensive nor does it have to be a product. In fact, one of the most common giveaways on the Web is *information.* (After all, that's what most people on the Web are after!) Creating a free online or e-mail newsletter with links to your company's site, of course, and to others of interest is one of the most effective ways of attracting potential customers to a site. Meaningful content presented in a clear, professional fashion is a must. Experts advise keeping online newsletters short—no more than about 600 words. *Poor Richard's E-Mail Publishing* by Chris Pirillo (Top Floor Publishing) offers much useful advice on creating online newsletters.

Paul Cline, who sells upscale men's clothing to his busy clients by calling on them in their offices, uses an e-mail newsletter to offer his customers informative fashion tips and to tell them about the latest season's offerings and special sales. Customers see the newsletter, a smooth blend of both fashion advice and salesmanship, as a valuable and informative service, which helps Kline boost sales of his clothing line.

Make Creative Use of E-Mail, but Avoid Becoming a "Spammer." Used properly and creatively, e-mail can be an effective way to build traffic on a Web site. Just as with any newsletter, the e-mail's content should offer something of value to recipients. Supported by online newsletters or chat rooms, customers welcome well-constructed permission e-mail that directs them to a company's site for information or special deals, unlike unsolicited and universally despised e-mails known as "spam."

Companies often collect visitors' e-mail addresses when they register to receive a "freebie." To be successful at collecting a sufficient number of e-mail addresses, a company must make clear to customers that they will receive messages that are meaningful to them and that the company will not sell e-mail addresses to others (which should be part of its posted privacy policy). Once a company has a customer's permission to send information in additional e-mail messages, it has a meaningful marketing opportunity to create a long-term customer relationship.

Make Sure Your Web Site Says "Credibility." A joint study by Shop.org and the Boston Consulting Group concluded that trust and security issues are the leading inhibitors of online shopping.[40] Unless a company can build among customers *trust* in its Web site, selling is virtually impossible. Visitors begin to evaluate the credibility of a site as soon as they arrive. Does the site look professional? Are there misspelled words and typographical errors? If the site provides information, does it note the sources of that information? If so, are those sources legitimate? Are they trustworthy? Is the presentation of the information fair and objective, or is it biased? Does the company include a privacy policy posted in an obvious place?

One of the simplest ways to establish credibility with customers is to use brand names they know and trust. Whether a company sells nationally recognized brands or its own well-known private brand, using those names on its site creates a sense of legitimacy. People buy brand names they trust, and online companies can use that to their advantage. Another effective way to build customer confidence is by joining an online seal program such as TRUSTe or BBBOnLine. The online equivalent of the Underwriter Laboratories stamp or the Good Housekeeping Seal of Approval, these seals mean that a company meets certain standards concerning the privacy of customers' information and the resolution of customer complaints. Finally, providing a street address, an e-mail address, and a toll-free telephone number sends a subtle message to shoppers that a legitimate business is behind a Web site. Many small companies include photographs of their bricks-and-mortar stores and of their employees to combat the Web's anonymity and to give shoppers the feeling that they are supporting a friendly small business.

Consider Forming Strategic Alliances. Most small companies seeking e-commerce success lack the brand and name recognition that larger, more established companies do. Creating that sort of recognition on the Web requires a significant investment of both time and money, two things that most small companies find scarce. If building name recognition is one of the keys to success on the Web, how can small companies with their limited resources hope to compete? One option is to form strategic alliances with bigger companies that can help a small business achieve what it could not accomplish alone. One expert says, "The question is no longer, 'Should I consider an alliance?' Now the questions are 'What form should the alliance take?' and 'How do I find the right partner?' "[41] *Jonathan Carson, co-founder of FamilyEducation Network* (www.familyeducation.com), *an education-oriented Web site that attracts more than 2.5 million visitors a month, relied on strategic alliances to promote the company and establish it as a leader in its field. Thanks to alliances with much larger organizations such as the National Education Association, the American Association of School Administrators, America Online, and Intel, the company has grown rapidly, attracting customers it never would have been able to land on its on.*[42]

Before plunging into a strategic alliance with a larger partner, however, entrepreneurs must understand their dark side. Research shows that the success rate of Internet strategic alliances is just 55 percent.[43] The most common reasons for splitting up? One study found the following causes: incompatible corporate cultures (75 percent), incompatible management personalities (63 percent), and differences in strategic priorities (58 percent).[44]

Make the Most of the Web's Global Reach. Despite the Web's reputation as an international marketplace, many Web entrepreneurs fail to utilize fully its global reach. Although 85 percent of the Web's pages are in English, only 43 percent of Web users speak English (and that percentage is declining)![45] It does not make sense for entrepreneurs to limit their Web sites to less than half the world because of a language barrier. A top manager at Travelocity, a travel planning Web site, says that whenever his company adds country-specific features to its site, sales in that country typically double![46]

E-companies wanting to draw significant sales from foreign markets must design their sites with customers from other lands and cultures in mind. A common mechanism is to include several "language buttons" on the opening page of a site that take customers to pages in the language of their choice. Virtual companies trying to establish a foothold in foreign markets by setting up Web sites dedicated to them run the same risk that actual companies do: offending international visitors by using the business conventions and standards they are accustomed to using in the

United States. Business practices, even those used on the Web, that are acceptable, even expected, in the United States may be taboo in other countries. A little research into the subtleties of a target country's culture and business practices can save a great deal of embarrassment and money! Creating secure, simple, and reliable payment methods for foreign customers also will boost sales.

When translating the content of their Web pages into other languages, e-companies must use extreme caution. This is *not* the time to pull out their notes from an introductory Spanish course and begin their own translations. Hiring professional translation and localization services to convert a company's Web content into other languages minimizes the likelihood of a company unintentionally offending foreign customers.

Promote Your Web Site Online and Off-line. E-commerce entrepreneurs have to use every means available—both online and off-line—to promote their Web sites and to drive traffic to it. In addition to using traditional online techniques such as registering with search engines, creating banner ads, joining banner exchange programs, Web entrepreneurs must promote their sites off-line as well. Ads in other media such as direct mail or newspapers that mention a site's URL will bring customers to it. It is also a good idea to put the company's Web address on *everything* a company publishes, from its advertisements and letterhead to shopping bags and business cards. A passive approach to generating Web site traffic is a recipe for failure. On the other hand, entrepreneurs who are as innovative at promoting their e-businesses as they are at creating them can attract impressive numbers of visitors to their sites.

DESIGNING A KILLER WEB SITE

6. Learn the techniques of designing a killer Web site.

World Wide Web users are not a patient lot. They sit before their computers, surfing the Internet, their fingers poised on their mouse buttons, daring any Web site to delay them with files that take a long time (according to one study, that's anything more than 8 seconds) to load.[47] Slow-loading sites or sites that don't deliver on their promises will cause a Web user to move on faster than a bolt of lightning can strike. With more than 4 million Web sites online, how can an entrepreneur design a Web site that will capture and hold potential customers' attention long enough to make a sale? What can they do to keep customers coming back on a regular basis? There is no surefire formula for stopping surfers in their tracks, but the following suggestions will help.

Start with Your Target Customer. Before launching into the design of their Web sites, entrepreneurs must paint a clear picture of their target customers. Only then are they ready to design a site that will appeal to their customers. The goal is to create a design in which customers see themselves when they visit. Creating a site in which customers find a comfortable fit requires a careful blend of market research, sales know-how, and aesthetics. The challenge for a business on the Web is to create the same image, style, and ambiance in its online presence as in its off-line stores.

Select a Domain Name That Is Consistent with the Image You Want to Create for Your Company and Register It. Entrepreneurs should never underestimate the power of the right domain name or universal resource locator (URL), which is a company's address on the Internet. It not only tells Web surfers where to find a company, but it also should suggest something about the company and what it does. Even the casual Web surfer could guess that the "toys.com" name belongs to a company selling children's toys. (It does; it belongs to eToys Inc., which also owns "etoys.com," "e-toys.com," and several other variations of its name). The ideal domain name should be:

- *Short.* Short names are easy for people to remember, so the shorter a company's URL is, the more likely potential customers are to recall it.
- *Memorable.* Not every short domain name is necessarily memorable. Some business owners use their companies' initials as their domain name (e.g., *www.sbfo.com* for Stanley Brothers Furniture Outlet). The problem with using initials for a domain name is that customers rarely associate the two, which makes a company virtually invisible on the Web.
- *Indicative of a company's business or business name.* Perhaps the best domain name for a company is one that customers can guess easily if they know the company's name. For instance, mail order catalog company L.L. Bean's URL is *www.llbean.com;* and New Pig, a maker of absorbent materials for a variety of industrial applications, uses *www.newpig.com* as its domain name. (The company carries this concept over to its toll-free number, which is 1-800-HOT-HOGS.)
- *Easy to spell.* Even though a company's domain name may be easy to spell, it is usually wise to buy several variations of the correct spelling simply because some customers are not likely to be good spellers!

Just because an entrepreneur comes up with the perfect URL for his company's Web site does not necessarily mean that he can use it. Domain names are given on a first-come, first-served basis. Before business owners can use a domain name, they must ensure that someone else has not already taken it. The simplest way to do that is to go to a domain name registration service such as Network Solutions at *www.net worksolutions.com/* or NetNames at *www.netnames.com* to conduct a name search. Entrepreneurs who find the domain name they have selected already registered to someone else have two choices: They can select another name, or they can try to buy the name from the original registrant. Some entrepreneurs buy the rights to their name relatively cheaply, but not every Web start-up is as fortunate. Business incubator eCompanies purchased the rights to the domain name "business.com" from an individual for $7.5 million![48]

Finding unregistered domain names can be a challenge, but several new top-level domain names recently became available: .aero (airlines), .biz (any business site), .coop (business cooperatives), .info (any site), .museum (museums), .name (individuals' sites), and .pro (professionals' sites). Once an entrepreneur finds an unused name that is suitable, he or she must register it (plus any variations of it)—and the sooner, the better! Registering is quite easy: simply use one of the registration services listed above to fill out a form and pay $70, which registers the name for two years. The registration renewal fee is $35 per year. The next step is to register the domain name with the U.S. Patent and Trademark Office at a cost of $245. The USPTO's Web site *(www.uspto.gov/web/menu/tm.html#)* not only allows users to register a trademark online, but it also offers useful information on trademarks and the protection they offer.

Be Easy to Find. With more than two billion pages already on the Web and more coming on every day, making your site easy for people to find is a real challenge. Because the Web is so expansive, many Web users rely on search engines to help them locate sites. In fact, one recent study found that 92 percent of Web surfers use search engines regularly.[49] Smart Web site designers embed codes called meta tags into their home pages that move their sites to the top of the most popular search engines such as Yahoo!, AltaVista, Lycos, Excite, Google, WebCrawler, and others. Search Engine Watch *(www.searchenginewatch.com)* offers many useful tips on search engine placement and registration as well as on using meta tags to increase the likelihood that a search engine will list a particular site.

Listing a site with the major search engines' indexes can also yield more hits. Entrepreneurs can go to each search engine's Web site to find the instructions for submitting their companies' URLs in the index. Crosslinkz Search Engine site (*www.crosslinkz.com*) provides links to nine of the leading Search engine submission sites. Rather than spend time themselves submitting their companies' URLs to search engine sites, entrepreneurs can hire submission services such as Microsoft's SubmitIt (*www.submit-it.com/*), which will submit a site's address to more than 400 search engines for just $99 a year. Registering with multiple search engines is critical because even the largest ones cover less than 20 percent of the Web![50]

Give Customers What They Want. Although Web shoppers are price conscious, they rank fast, reliable delivery high on their list of criteria in their purchase decisions. Studies also show that surfers look for a large selection of merchandise available to them immediately. Remember that the essence of selling on the Web is providing convenience to customers. Sites that allow them to shop whenever they want, to find what they are looking for easily, and to pay for it conveniently and securely will keep customers coming back. Furniture maker Herman Miller's Web site not only makes it easy for shoppers to browse and to buy its products, but the site also offers research on the benefits of ergonomic designs and allows visitors to try various furniture layouts in rooms created with a special 3-D design tool.[51]

Establish Hyperlinks with Other Businesses, Preferably Those Selling Products or Services That Complement Yours. Listing the Web addresses of complementary businesses on a company's site and having them list its address on their sites offers customers more value and can bring traffic to your site that you otherwise would have missed. For instance, the owner of a site selling upscale kitchen gadgets should consider a cross-listing arrangement with sites that feature gourmet recipes, wines, and kitchen appliances.

Include an E-Mail Option, an Address, and a Telephone Number in Your Site. Customers appreciate the opportunity to communicate with your company. If you include e-mail access on your site, however, be sure to respond to it promptly. Nothing alienates cyber-customers faster than a company that is slow to respond or fails to respond to their e-mail messages. Also, be sure to include an address and a toll-free telephone number for customers who prefer to write or call with their questions. Unfortunately, many companies either fail to include their telephone numbers on their sites or bury them so deeply within the sites' pages that customers never find them.

Give Shoppers the Ability to Track Their Orders Online. Many customers who order items online want to track the progress of their orders. One of the most effective ways to keep a customer happy is to send an e-mail confirmation that your company received the order and another e-mail notification when you ship the order. The shipment notice should include the shipper's tracking number and instructions on how to track the order from the shipper's site. Order and shipping confirmations instill confidence in even the most Web-wary shoppers.

Offer Web Shoppers a Special All Their Own. Give Web customers a special deal that you don't offer in any other advertising piece. Change your specials often (weekly, if possible) and use clever "teasers" to draw attention to the offer. Regular special offers available only on the Web give customers an incentive to keep visiting a company's site. Also, provide product prices and shipping charges early in the transaction. Customers do not like to be surprised by high charges at checkout.

Follow a Simple Design. Catchy graphics and photographs are important to snaring customers, but designers must choose them carefully. Designs that are overly complex take a long time to download, and customers are likely to move on before they appear. Web Site Garage *(http://websitegarage.netscape.com/)*, a Web site maintenance company, offers companies a free evaluation of how their sites measure up in terms of speed.

Specific design tips include:

- Avoid clutter. The best designs are simple and elegant with a balance of both text and graphics.
- Avoid huge graphic headers that must download first, prohibiting customers from seeing anything else on your site as they wait (or more likely, *don't* wait). Use graphics judiciously so that the site loads quickly.
- Include a menu bar at the top of the page that makes it easy for customers to find their way around your site.
- Make the site easy to navigate by including navigation buttons at the bottom of pages that enable customers to return to the top of the page or to the menu bar. This avoids "the pogo effect," where visitors bounce from page to page in a Web site looking for what they need. Without navigation buttons or a site map page, a company runs the risk of customers getting lost in its site and leaving.
- Incorporate meaningful content in the site that is useful to visitors, well organized, easy to read, and current. The content should be consistent with the message a company sends in the other advertising media it uses. Although a Web site should be designed to sell, providing useful, current information attracts visitors, keeps them coming back, and establishes a company's reputation as an expert in the field.
- Include a "frequently asked questions (FAQ)" section. Adding this section to a page can reduce dramatically the number of telephone calls and e-mails customer service representatives must handle. FAQ sections typically span a wide range of issues—from how to place an order to how to return merchandise—and cover whatever topics customers most often want to know about.
- Be sure to include privacy and return policies as well as product guarantees the company offers.
- Avoid fancy typefaces and small fonts because they are too hard to read.
- Be vigilant for misspelled words, typographical errors, and formatting mistakes; they destroy a site's credibility in no time.
- Don't put small fonts on "busy" backgrounds; no one will read them!
- Use contrasting colors of text and graphics. For instance, blue text on a green background is nearly impossible to read.
- Be careful with frames. Using frames that are so thick that they crowd out text makes for a poor design.
- Test the site on different Web browsers and on different size monitors. A Web site may look exactly the way it was designed to look on one Web browser and be a garbled mess on another. Sites designed to display correctly on large monitors may not view well on small ones.
- Use your Web site to collect information from visitors, but don't tie up visitors immediately with a tedious registration process. Most will simply leave the site never to return. Offers for a free e-mail newsletter or a contest giveaway can give visitors enough incentive to register with a site.
- Avoid automated music that plays continuously and cannot be cut off.
- Make sure the overall look of the page is appealing. "When a site is poorly designed, lacks information, or cannot support customer needs, that [company's] reputation is seriously jeopardized," says one expert.[52]
- Remember: Simpler usually is better.

Assure Customers That Their Online Transactions Are Secure. If you are serious about doing business on the Web, make sure that your site includes the proper security software and encryption devices. Computer-savvy customers are not willing to divulge their credit card numbers on sites that are not secure.

GAINING THE COMPETITIVE EDGE
Climbing to the Top

Chris Warner, founder of Earth Treks, Inc., a company that offers rock- and ice-climbing trips as well as one of the largest indoor climbing gyms in the country, wanted a way to connect with his customers and to create a sense of community built around his company. Warner knew that climbing enthusiasts are fascinated by the challenges of a climb, even if it's not *their* journey, but the question he faced was how to take his customers along on a climb while bringing them together. Then, in 1999, Warner discovered that the answer to his problem was the World Wide Web.

Warner hired his sister-in-law to create a Web site for Earth Treks (*www.earthtreksclimbing.com*) that Warner has used in a creative fashion to pump up sales at the company he founded in 1990. For instance, the guides on the company's climbing expeditions regularly post journal entries on Earth Treks' Web site via satellite phones from the peaks of some of the world's most challenging summits, including Ecuador's Cotopaxi volcano and the Himalayas' Mount Everest. The journals have proved to be extremely popular among climbing enthusiasts, many of whom visit the Earth Treks site to read about the climbers' adventures. On Warner's last trip to Mount Everest, for example, more than 50,000 visitors logged on to the site the day the expedition reached the summit!

Earth Treks also uses its Web site to cultivate its next generation of customers through its Shared Summits program, an online program that allows students aged 6 to 18 to earn academic credit as they learn about geography, weather, various cultures, teamwork, and leadership through the climbing expeditions the company hosts. Students can view digital photographs and real-time videos and can e-mail climbers with questions about the climb. (One of the most commonly asked questions is "How do you go to the bathroom up there?" Answer: "We use suits with front-to-back zippers for easy access," says

Warner.) The unique nature of the Shared Summits program has brought Earth Treks a great deal of publicity, both in magazines and national newspapers.

In addition to building camaraderie among its customer base, Warner also uses the Web site for more mundane applications such as promoting the company's climbing center, its mountaineering trips, and its climbing instruction. Since the Web site's launch, sales have climbed rapidly to more than $1.4 million. Earth Treks is now receiving a record number of e-mails from people who want to schedule a climb to one of the world's most challenging summits, and revenues for its indoor climbing center have increased by 40 percent. The climbing center also hosts climbing parties for children's birthdays and is the center for the Youth Rox climbing program in which kids aged 10 to 14 learn to scale the center's most basic mountains with trained instructors.

Warner is thrilled with the tremendous return his company has earned on the $3,000 he spent to launch and the $7,200 it spends for its part-time Webmaster. He constantly updates the site's content, keeping it fresh so that customers have a reason to return to it. Most importantly, Earth Treks' Web site has enabled the company to connect with its customers in a way that otherwise would be impossible. Warner expects the payoff from creating a community of customers with a common passion to continue many years into the future.

1. In what ways is Earth Treks' use of the Web different from other companies' approaches?

2. Review the "Designing a Killer Web Site" section in this chapter and then visit the Earth Treks Web site at *www.earthtreksclimbing.com*. How well does the company's site meet the criteria explained in this chapter? Can you offer any suggestions for improving the Web site?

Source: Adapted from Constance Loizos, "Traffic Magnets," *Inc.*, November 2001, pp. 140–142.

Keep Your Site Updated. Customers want to see something new when they visit stores, and they expect the same when they visit virtual stores as well. Delete any hyperlinks that have disappeared and keep the information on your Web site current. One sure way to run off customers on the Web is to continue to advertise your company's "Christmas Special" in August! On the other hand, fresh information and new specials keep customers coming back.

Consider Hiring a Professional to Design Your Site. Pros can do it a lot faster and better than you can. However, don't give designers free rein to do whatever they want to with your site. Make sure it meets your criteria for an effective site that can sell.

Entrepreneurs must remember that on the World Wide Web every company, no matter how big or small it is, has the exact same screen size for its site. What matters most is not the size of your company but how you put that screen size to use.

TRACKING WEB RESULTS

Software Solutions

7. Explain how companies track the results from their Web sites.

As they develop their Web sites, entrepreneurs seek to create sites that generate sales, improve customer relationships, or lower costs. How can entrepreneurs determine the effectiveness of their sites? **Web analytics,** tools that measure a Web site's ability to attract customers, generate sales, and keep customers coming back, help entrepreneurs know what works—and what doesn't—on the Web. In the early days of e-commerce, entrepreneurs strived to create sites that were both "sticky" and "viral." A **sticky site** is one that acts like electronic flypaper, capturing visitors' attention and offering them useful, interesting information that makes them stay at the site. The premise of stickiness is that the longer customers stay in a site, the more likely they are to actually purchase something and to come back to it. A **viral site** is one that visitors are willing to share with their friends. This "word-of-mouse" advertising is one of the most effective ways of generating traffic to a company's site. As the Web has matured as a marketing channel, however, the shortcomings of these simple measures have become apparent, and other e-metrics continue to emerge. E-businesses now focus on **recency,** the length of time between a customer's visits to a Web site. The more frequently customers visit a site, the more likely they are to become loyal customers. Another important measure of Web success is the **conversion** (or **browse-to-buy) ratio,** which measures the proportion of visitors to a site who actually make a purchase.

How can online entrepreneurs know if their sites are successful? Answering that question means that entrepreneurs must track visitors to their sites, the paths within the site, and the activity they generate while there. A variety of methods for tracking Web results are available, but the most commonly used ones include counters and log-analysis software. The simplest technique is a **counter,** which records the number of "hits" a Web site receives. Although counters measure activity on a site, they do so only at the broadest level. If a counter records 10 hits, for instance, there is no way to know if those hits came as a result of 10 different visitors or as a result of just one person making 10 visits. Plus, counters cannot tell Web entrepreneurs where visitors to their sites come from or which pages they look at on the site.

A more meaningful way to track activity on a Web site is through **log-analysis software,** which has the goal of helping entrepreneurs understand visitors' online behavior. Server logs record every page, graphic, audio clip, or photograph that visitors to a site access, and log-analysis software analyzes these logs and generates reports describing how visitors behave when they get to a site. With this software, entrepreneurs can determine how many unique visitors come to their site and how often repeat visitors return. Owners of e-stores can discover which FAQ customers click on most often, which part of a site they stayed in the longest, which site they came from, and how the volume of traffic at the site affected the server's speed of operation. The result is the ability to infer what visitors think about a Web site, its products, its content, its design, and other features. Feedback from log-analysis software helps entrepreneurs redesign their sites to eliminate confusing navigation, unnecessary graphics, meaningless content, incomplete information, and other problems that can cause visitors to leave.

Other tracking methods available to owners of e-businesses include:

- **Clustering.** This software observes visitors to a Web site, analyzes their behavior, and then groups them into narrow categories. Companies then target each category of shoppers with products, specials, and offers designed to appeal to them.
- **Collaborative filtering.** This software uses sophisticated algorithms to determine visitors' interests by comparing them to other shoppers with similar tastes. Companies then use this information to suggest products an individual customer would most likely be interested in, given his or her profile.
- **Profiling systems.** These programs tag individual customers on a site and note their responses to the various pages in the site. Based on the areas a customer visits most, the software develops a psychographic profile of the shopper. For instance, a visitor who reads an article on massage techniques might receive an offer for a book on alternative medicine or a magazine focusing on environmental issues.
- **Artificial intelligence (AI).** This software, sometimes called neural networking, is the most sophisticated of the group because it actually learns from users' behavior. The more these programs interact with customers, the "smarter" they become. Over time, they can help online marketers know which special offers work best with which customers, when customers are most likely to respond, and how to present the offer.

Return on Investment

Just like traditional businesses, e-businesses must earn a reasonable return on an entrepreneur's investment. The difficulty, however, is much of the total investment required to build, launch, maintain, and market a Web site is not always obvious. Plus, the payoffs of a successful site are not easy to measure and do not always fit neatly into traditional financial models that calculate return on investment (ROI). For instance, how can a business with both a clicks-and-bricks presence determine exactly how many customers come into its retail store as a result of having visited its Web site? Can it quantify the increase in customer loyalty as a result of its e-commerce efforts? Many companies have discovered that the payoff from their online sales efforts are long-term and sometimes intangible.

Owners of e-businesses are developing new models to evaluate the performances of their companies. Ipswitch Inc., a software development company, examines its Web site from three perspectives: what it costs, what it generates in revenues, and what savings it produces for the company. Managers have determined that for every dollar they spend on their Web site, Ipswitch generates $22 in online sales. They also know that if they had produced those sales through sales representatives, the company would have incurred an additional $2.3 million in costs![53]

ENSURING WEB PRIVACY AND SECURITY

Privacy

8. Describe how e-businesses ensure the privacy and security of the information they collect and store from the Web.

The Web's ability to track customers' every move naturally raises concerns over the privacy of the information companies collect. E-commerce gives businesses access to tremendous volumes of information about their customers, creating a responsibility to protect that information and to use it wisely. A recent survey by Forrester Research discovered that just 6 percent of online customers trust Web sites with their personal information.[54] Yet, the Federal Trade Commission estimates that 97 percent of commercial Web sites collect personal information from their customers.[55] The potential for breaching customers' privacy is present in any e-business. To make sure they are using the information they collect from visitors to their Web sites legally and ethically and safeguarding it adequately, companies should take the following steps:

Take an Inventory of the Customer Data Collected. The first step to ensuring proper data handling is to assess exactly the type of data the company is collecting and storing. How are you collecting it? Why are you collecting it? How are you using it? Do visitors know how you are using the data? Do you need to get their permission to use it in this way? Do you use all of the data you are collecting?

Develop a Company Privacy Policy for the Information You Collect. A **privacy policy** is a statement explaining the nature of the information a company collects online, what it does with that information, and the recourse customers have if they believe the company is misusing the information. *Every* online company should have a privacy policy, but research firm Computer Economics estimates that only half of online U.S. businesses have developed one.[56] Several online privacy firms such as TRUSTe *(www.truste.org)*, BBBOnLine *(www.bbbonline.com)*, and BetterWeb *(www.betterweb.com)* offer Web "seal programs," the equivalent of a good housekeeping seal of privacy approval. To earn a privacy seal of approval, a company must adopt a privacy policy, implement it, and monitor its effectiveness. Many of these privacy sites also provide online policy wizards, automated questionnaires that help e-business owners create comprehensive privacy statements.

Post Your Company's Privacy Policy Prominently on Your Web Site and Follow It. Creating a privacy policy is not sufficient; posting it in a prominent place on the Web site (it should be accessible from every page on the site) and then abiding by it make a policy meaningful. Whether or not a company has a privacy policy posted prominently often determines whether or not a customer will do online business with it. One of the worst mistakes a company can make is to publish its privacy policy online and then fail to follow it. Not only is this unethical, but it also can lead to serious damage awards if customers take legal action against the company.

KBKids.com, an online retailer of children's toys, games, and videos (www.kbkids.com), *positions its privacy policy in a highly prominent position on its site using a large tab that links to a separate page. The page provides a comprehensive description of its policy, the way it collects information, how customers can view the information the company collects, and its affiliation with BBBOnLine. "We established a security and privacy policy to assure our customers that we respect the information they provide to us and that its only use is to help us serve them better," says KBKids.com's marketing vice-president.[57]*

Security

A company doing business on the Web faces two conflicting goals: to establish a presence on the Web so that customers from across the globe can have access to its site and the information maintained there and to preserve a high level of security so that the business, its site, and the information it collects is safe from hackers and intruders intent on doing harm. Companies have a number of safeguards available to them, but hackers with enough time, talent, and determination usually can beat even the most sophisticated safety measures. If hackers manage to break into a system, they can do irreparable damage, stealing programs and data, modifying or deleting valuable information, changing the look and content of sites, or crashing sites altogether. For instance, hackers recently broke into one company's e-commerce site, stealing information on more than 15,000 customers' credit card accounts, including their credit card numbers. Other hackers flooded Amazon.com's Web site with so many hits that legitimate users were locked out (a denial-of-service attack), costing the company an estimated $244,000 in lost sales every hour it was out of service.[58]

To minimize the likelihood of invasion by hackers, e-companies rely on several tools, including virus detection software, intrusion detection software, and firewalls. Perhaps the most basic level of protection, **virus detection software** scans computer drives for viruses, nasty programs written by devious hackers and designed to harm computers and the information they contain. The severity of viruses ranges widely, from relatively harmless programs that put humorous messages on a user's screen to those that erase a computer's hard drive or cause the entire system to crash. Because hackers are *always* writing new viruses to attack computer systems, entrepreneurs must keep their virus detection software up-to-date and must run it often. An attack by one virus can bring a company's entire e-commerce platform to a screeching halt in no time! The "I love you" virus infected computer systems across the globe, leaving companies with an estimated $15 billion in damages and downtime.

Intrusion detection software is essential for any company doing business on the Web. These packages constantly monitor the activity on a company's network server and sound an alert if they detect someone breaking into the company's computer system or if they detect unusual network activity. Intrusion detection software not only can detect attempts by unauthorized users to break into a computer system while they are happening, but it also can trace the hacker's location. Most packages also have the ability to preserve a record of the attempted break-in that will stand up in court so that companies can take legal action against cyber-intruders.

A **firewall** is a combination of hardware and software operating between the Internet and a company's computer network that allows authorized employees to have access to the Internet but keeps unauthorized users from entering a company's network and the programs and data it contains. Establishing a firewall is essential for any company operating on the Web, but entrepreneurs must make sure that their firewalls are set up properly. Otherwise, they are useless! One recent study of more than 2,000 Web sites by ICSA.net, a security consulting firm, found even though every site had a firewall in place, more than 80 percent were vulnerable to attack with commonly available software because they were not properly designed.[59] Even with all of these security measures in place, it is best for a company to run its Web page on a separate server from the network that runs the business. If hackers break into the Web site, they still do not have access to the company's sensitive data and programs.

The Computer Security Institute *(www.gocsi.com/)* offers articles, information, and seminars to help business owners maintain computer security. The *Business Security e-Journal (www.lubrinco.com)* is a free monthly newsletter on computer security, and *Information Security* magazine *(www.infosecuritymag.com/)*, published by the International Computer Security Association *(www.icsa.net/)*, also offers helpful advice on maintaining computer security. For entrepreneurs who want to test their sites' security, ICSA offers its Security Snapshot system (free of charge) that runs various security tests on a site and then e-mails a "Risk Index" score in six different categories, including the site's risk of hacker intrusion.

In e-commerce just as in traditional retail, sales do not matter unless a company gets paid! On the Web, customers demand transactions they can complete with ease and convenience, and the simplest way to allow customers to pay for e-commerce transactions is with credit cards. From a Web customer's perspective, however, one of the most important security issues is the security of their credit card information. To ensure the security of their customers' credit card information, online retailers typically use **secure sockets layer (SSL) technology** to encrypt customers' transaction information as it travels across the Internet. By using secure shopping cart features from storefront-building services or Internet service providers, even the smallest e-commerce stores can offer their customers secure online transactions.

Processing credit card transactions requires a company to obtain an Internet merchant account from a bank or financial intermediary. Setup fees for an Internet merchant account typically range from $500 to $1,000, but companies also pay monthly access and statement fees of between $40 and $80 plus a transaction fee of 10 to 60 cents per transaction. Once an online company has a merchant account, it can accept credit cards from online customers.

Online credit card transactions also pose a risk for merchants; online companies lose an estimated $1 billion a year to online payment fraud each year.[60] The most common problem is **chargebacks,** online transactions that customers dispute. Unlike credit card transactions in a retail store, those made online involve no signatures, so Internet merchants incur the loss when a customer disputes an online credit card transaction. Experts estimate that payment fraud online is 5 to 10 times greater than in bricks-and-mortar stores.[61] A thief in Romania recently tried to use a stolen credit card to purchase eight handbags from Velma Handbags, a small company founded by Margaret Cobbs, but the company that handles her credit card transactions discovered the attempt and stopped the $380 transaction.[62]

One way to prevent fraud is to ask customers for their card verification value (CVV or CVV2), the three-digit number above the signature panel on the back of the credit card, as well as their card number and expiration date. Online merchants also can subscribe to a real-time credit card processing service that authorizes credit card transactions, but the fees can be high. Also, using a shipper that provides the ability to track shipments enables online merchants to prove that the customer actually received the merchandise can help minimize the threat of payment fraud.

CHAPTER SUMMARY

E-commerce is creating a new economy, one that is connecting producers, sellers, and customers via technology in ways that have never been possible before. In this fast-paced world of e-commerce, size no longer matters as much as speed and flexibility do. The Internet is creating a new industrial order, and companies that fail to adapt to it will soon become extinct.

1. Describe the benefits of selling on the World Wide Web.

    Although a Web-based sales strategy does not guarantee success, the companies that have pioneered Web-based selling have realized many benefits, including the following:
    - The opportunity to increase revenues
    - The ability to expand their reach into global markets

- The ability to remain open 24 hours a day, seven days a week
- The capacity to use the Web's interactive nature to enhance customer service
- The power to educate and to inform
- The ability to lower the cost of doing business
- The ability to spot new business opportunities and to capitalize on them
- The power to track sales results

2. Understand the factors an entrepreneur should consider before launching into e-commerce.

   Before launching an e-commerce effort, business owners should consider the following important issues:
   - How a company exploits the Web's interconnectivity and the opportunities it creates to transform relationships with its suppliers and vendors, its customers, and other external stakeholders is crucial to its success.
   - Web success requires a company to develop a plan for integrating the Web into its overall strategy. The plan should address issues such as site design and maintenance, creating and managing a brand name, marketing and promotional strategies, sales, and customer service.
   - Developing deep, lasting relationships with customers takes on even greater importance on the Web. Attracting customers on the Web costs money, and companies must be able to retain their online customers to make their Web sites profitable.
   - Creating a meaningful presence on the Web requires an ongoing investment of resources—time, money, energy, and talent. Establishing an attractive Web site brimming with catchy photographs of products is only the beginning.
   - Measuring the success of its Web-based sales effort is essential to remaining relevant to customers whose tastes, needs, and preferences are always changing.

3. Explain the twelve myths of e-commerce and how to avoid falling victim to them.

   The 12 myths of e-commerce are:
   - Myth 1. Setting up a business on the Web is easy and inexpensive.
   - Myth 2. If I launch a site, customers will flock to it.
   - Myth 3. Making money on the Web is easy.
   - Myth 4. Privacy is not an important issue on the Web.
   - Myth 5. The most important part of any e-commerce effort is technology.
   - Myth 6. "Strategy? I don't need a strategy to sell on the Web! Just give me a Web site, and the rest will take care of itself."
   - Myth 7. On the Web, customer service is not as important as it is in a traditional retail store.
   - Myth 8. Flash makes a Web site better.
   - Myth 9. It's what's up front that counts.
   - Myth 10. E-commerce will cause bricks-and-mortar retail stores to disappear.
   - Myth 11. The greatest opportunities for e-commerce lie in the retail sector.
   - Myth 12. It's too late to get on the Web.

4. Discuss the five basic approaches available to entrepreneurs wanting to launch an e-commerce effort.

   Entrepreneurs looking to launch an e-commerce effort have five basic choices: (1) online shopping malls, (2) storefront-building services, (3) Internet service providers (ISPs), (4) hiring professionals to design a custom site, and (5) building a site in-house.

5. Explain the basic strategies entrepreneurs should follow to achieve success in their e-commerce efforts.

   Following are some guidelines for building a successful Web strategy for a small e-company:
   - Consider focusing on a niche in the market.
   - Develop a community of online customers.
   - Attract visitors by giving away "freebies."
   - Make creative use of e-mail, but avoid becoming a "spammer."
   - Make sure your Web site says "credibility."
   - Consider forming strategic alliances with larger, more established companies.
   - Make the most of the Web's global reach.
   - Promote your Web site online and off-line.

6. Learn the techniques of designing a killer Web site.

   There is no surefire formula for stopping surfers in their tracks, but the following suggestions will help:
   - Select a domain name that is consistent with the image you want to create for your company and register it.
   - Be easy to find.
   - Give customers want they want.

- Establish hyperlinks with other businesses, preferably those selling products or services that complement yours.
- Include an e-mail option and a telephone number in your site.
- Give shoppers the ability to track their orders online.
- Offer Web shoppers a special all their own.
- Follow a simple design for your Web page.
- Assure customers that their online transactions are secure.
- Keep your site updated.
- Consider hiring a professional to design your site.

7. Explain how companies track the results from their Web sites.

     The simplest technique for tracking the results of a Web site is a counter, which records the number of "hits" a Web site receives. Another option for tracking Web activity is through log-analysis software. Server logs record every page, graphic, audio clip, or photograph that visitors to a site access, and log-analysis software analyzes these logs and generates reports describing how visitors behave when they get to a site.

8. Describe how e-businesses ensure the privacy and security of the information they collect and store from the Web.

     To make sure they are using the information they collect from visitors to their Web sites legally and ethically, companies should take the following steps:
- Take an inventory of the customer data collected.
- Develop a company privacy policy for the information you collect.
- Post your company's privacy policy prominently on your Web site and follow it.

To ensure the security of the information they collect and store from Web transactions, companies should rely on virus and intrusion detection software and firewalls to ward off attacks from hackers.

DISCUSSION QUESTIONS

1. In what ways have the Internet and e-commerce changed the ways companies do business?
2. Explain the benefits a company earns by selling on the Web.
3. Discuss the factors entrepreneurs should consider before launching an e-commerce site.
4. What are the 12 myths of e-commerce? What can an entrepreneur do to avoid them?
5. Explain the five basic approaches available to entrepreneurs for launching an e-commerce effort. What are the advantages, the disadvantages, and the costs associated with each one?
6. What strategic advice would you offer an entrepreneur about to start an e-company?
7. What design characteristics make for a successful Web page?
8. Explain the characteristics of an ideal domain name.
9. Describe the techniques that are available to e-companies for tracking results from their Web sites. What advantages does each offer?
10. What steps should e-businesses take to ensure the privacy of the information they collect and store from the Web?
11. What techniques can e-companies use to protect their banks of information and their customers' transaction data from hackers?
12. Why does evaluating the effectiveness of a Web site pose a problem for online entrepreneurs?

BEYOND THE CLASSROOM

1. Work with a team of your classmates to come up with an Internet business you would be interested in launching. Come up with several suitable domain names for your hypothetical e-company. Once you have chosen a few names, go to a domain name registration service such as Network Solutions' Internic at *www.networksolutions.com/* or Netnames at *www.netnames.com* to conduct a name search. How many of the names your team came up with were already registered to someone? If an entrepreneur's top choice for a domain name is already registered to someone else, what options does he or she have?
2. Select 5 to 10 online companies with which you are familiar and visit their Web sites.

What percentage of them have privacy policies posted on their sites? How comprehensive are these policies? What percentage of the sites you visited belonged to a privacy watchdog agency such as TRUSTe or BBBOnLine? How important is a posted privacy policy for e-companies? Explain.

3. Visit five e-commerce sites on the Web and evaluate them on the basis of the Web site design principles described in this chapter. How well do they measure up? What suggestions can you offer for improving the design of each site? If you were a customer trying to make a purchase from each site, how would you respond to the design?

TAKE IT TO THE NET

Visit the Scarborough/Zimmerer home page at **www.prenhall.com/scarborough** for updated information, online resources, Web-based exercises, and sample business plan.

ENDNOTES

1. Pamela Rohland, "Milk It," *Business Start-Ups,* September 2000, p. 71.
2. Andrew Raskin, "Setting Your Sites," *Inc. Technology,* No. 2 1999, p. 20.
3. Nua Internet Surveys, *www.nua.ie/surveys/how_many_online/.*
4. "Internet at a Glance," *Business 2.0,* January 23, 2001, p. 112.
5. "Marketing on the World Wide Web," Alaska Internet Marketing, *www.alaskaoutdoors.com/Misc/info.html.*
6. Lorraine Farquharson, "The Web @ Work: Jos. A. Bank," *Wall Street Journal,* October 29, 2001, p. B5.
7. George Mannes, "Don't Give Up on the Web," *Fortune,* March 5, 2001, pp. 184[B]–184[L]; Douglas Gantenbein, "The Tender Digital Trap," *Small Business Computing,* May 1, 2001, *www.sbcmag.com.*
8. David G. Propson, "Small Biz Gets Small Piece of the Pie," *Small Business Computing,* November 1999, p. 24; "Survival of the Fastest," *Inc. Technology,* No. 4, 1999, pp. 44–57.
9. Mannes, "Don't Give Up on the Web."
10. "Reality Bites," *Wall Street Journal,* May 1, 2000, p. B18.
11. Robert McGarvey, "Connect the Dots," *Entrepreneur,* March 2000, pp. 78–85.
12. Joe Dysart, "Promote Your Site," *Emerging Business,* Summer 2001, pp. 29–32; Williams Nursery, *www.williams-nursery.com/.*
13. Claire Tristram, "Many Happy Returns," *Small Business Computing,* May 1999, p. 73.
14. Gantenbein, "The Tender Digital Trap."
15. Melissa Campanelli, "E-Business Busters," *Entrepreneur,* January 2000, pp. 46–50.
16. Jodi Mardesich, "The Web Is No Shopper's Paradise," *Fortune,* November 8, 1999, pp. 188–198.
17. "Survival of the Fastest," *Inc. Technology,* No. 4, 1999, p. 57.
18. "The Smart Business 50: Dell Computer," *Smart Business,* September 2001, p. 74.
19. Steve Bennett and Stacey Miller, "The E-Commerce Plunge," *Small Business Computing,* February 2000, p. 50.
20. Amanda C. Kooser, "Ring My Bell," *Entrepreneur,* December 2000, p. 24.
21. "Web-Based Customer Service," *Success,* November 2000, p. 12.
22. Alice Hill, "5 Reasons Customers Abandon Their Shopping Carts (and What You Can Do About It)," *Smart Business,* March 2001, pp. 80–84.
23. Ibid.
24. Bronwyn Fryer, "When Something Clicks," *Inc. Technology,* No. 1, 2000, pp. 62–72; Tristram, "Many Happy Returns," pp. 70–75; Mardesich, "The Web Is No Shopper's Paradise."
25. Fred Vogelstein, "A Cold Bath for Dot-Com Fever," *U.S. News & World Report,* September 13, 1999, p. 37.
26. Mardesich, "The Web Is No Shopper's Paradise."
27. Bethany McLean, "More Than Just Dot-Coms," *Fortune,* December 6, 1999, pp. 130–138.
28. "The Smart Business 50: REI," *Smart Business,* September 2001, p. 73.
29. Lori Enos, "The Biggest Myths of E-Tail," *E-Commerce Times,* September 26, 2001, *www.ecommercetimes.com/perl/story/13722.html*
30. Robert McGarvey, "From: Business To: Business," *Entrepreneur,* June 2000, pp. 96–103.
31. Ibid.
32. "The Smart Business 50: Cisco Systems," *Smart Business,* September 2001, p. 80; William J. Holstein, "Rewiring the 'Old Economy,'" *U.S. News & World Report,* April 10, 2000, pp. 38–40.

33. Bronwyn Fryer and Lee Smith, ".com or Bust," *Forbes Small Business*, December 1999/January 2000, p. 41.

34. Jason Compton, "Case Study: Tapping the Market," *Smart Business*, February 2001, p. 147.

35. Anne Ashley Gilbert, "Going Small Time," *Fortune,* September 27, 1999, pp. 262[A]–262[F].

36. Michelle Prather, "Life Online," *Business Start-Ups,* May 2000, p. 17.

37. Just Balls, *http://www.justballs.com/.*

38. J. W. Dysart, "Think Big," *Entrepreneur's Netpreneur,* June 2000, pp. 34–38.

39. Ralph F. Wilson, "The Five Mutable Laws of Web Marketing," *Web Marketing Today, www.wilsonweb. com/wmta/basic-principles. htm,* April 1, 1999, pp. 1–7.

40. Giesla M. Pedroza, "Do Or Die," *Start-Ups,* October 2000, p. 17.

41. Jan Gardner, "10 Ideas for Growing Business Now," *Inc.,* October 29, 2001, *www2.inc.com/search/ 23629.html.*

42. Jonathan Carson, "The Art of Effective Alliance," *EntreWorld.org,* August 16, 2000, *www.entreworld.org.*

43. David Ernst, Tammy Halevy, Jean-Hugues Monire, and Higo Sazzarin, "A Future for e-Alliances," *The McKinsey Quarterly,* Number 2, 2001, *www.mckin seyquarterly.com/article_page.asp?tk=440472:1039: 24&ar=1039&L2=24&L3=47.*

44. Robert McGarvey, "Irreconcilable Differences," *Entrepreneur,* February 2000, p. 75.

45. Dylan Tweney, "Think Globally, Act Locally," *Business 2.0,* November 2001, pp. 120–121.

46. Ibid.

47. "Design Matters," *Fortune Tech Guide,* 2001, pp. 183–188.

48. "Virtual Estate," *Entrepreneur,* May 2001, p. 28; Robert A. Mamis, "The Name Game," *Inc.'s The State of Small Business 2000,* pp. 141–144; "Name Your Price," *Start-Ups,* January 2001, p. 14.

49. Amy Austin, "Making Your Site Stand Out," *Small Business Computing,* October 1999, advertising insert.

50. Ibid.

51. Herman Miller, *www.hermanmiller.com;* "Design Matters," *Fortune Tech Guide,* 2001, pp. 183–188.

52. Carol Stavraka, "There's No Stopping E-Business. Are You Ready?" *Forbes,* December 13, 1999, Special Advertising Section.

53. Kathleen Dooher, "Many Happy Returns," *Inc.,* November 2001, pp. 150–152; Anne Stuart, "The Best Small Business Sites in America, *Inc.,* November 2001, pp. 129–130.

54. Ann Harrison, "Privacy? Who Cares," *Business 2.0,* June 12, 2001, pp. 48–49.

55. Alix Nyberg, "Privacy Matters," *CFO,* July 2001, p. 22.

56. Ibid.

57. J. D. Tuccille, "Don't Be Big Brother," *Small Business Computing,* July 1999, pp. 42–43; Kbtoys, *www.kbtoys.com.*

58. Michael Bertin, "The New Security Threats," *Smart Business,* February 2001, pp. 78–86.

59. Melissa Campanelli, "A Wall of Fire," *Entrepreneur,* February 2000, pp. 48–49.

60. "Insane Stat," *Business 2.0,* March 6, 2001, p. 30.

61. Yie-Yun Lee, "Wrong Number," *Entrepreneur,* March 2001, pp. 84–85; Paul Kraaijvanger, "Don't Get Slammed if Your Business Takes Credit Cards Online," *Success,* February 2000, pp. 62–63.

62. Susan Greco, "The Fraud Bogeyman," *Inc.,* February 2001, pp. 103–104.

Chapter 14

Sources of Equity Financing

> *Rule # 1: You can never have too much equity. Rule # 2: You can never have too much capital. Rule # 3: When Rules 1 and 2 conflict, choose Rule #2.*
>
> —PEG WYANT, VENTURE CAPITALIST

> *If you don't know who the fool is in a deal, it's you.*
>
> —MICHAEL WOLFF

Upon completion of this chapter, you will be able to:

1. Explain the differences in the three types of capital small businesses require: fixed, working, and growth.

2. Describe the various sources of equity capital available to entrepreneurs, including personal savings, friends and relatives, angels, partners, corporations, venture capital, and public stock offerings.

3. Describe the process of "going public," as well as its advantages and disadvantages and the various simplified registrations and exemptions from registration available to small businesses wanting to sell securities to investors.

4. Explain the various simplified registrations, exemptions from registration, and other alternatives available to entrepreneurs wanting to sell shares of equity to investors.

Raising the money to launch a new business venture has always been a challenge for entrepreneurs. Capital markets rise and fall with the stock market, overall economic conditions, and investors' fortunes. These swells and troughs in the availability of capital make the search for financing look like a wild roller coaster ride. For instance, during the late 1990s, founders of "dot-com" companies were able to attract mountains of cash from private and professional investors, even if their businesses existed only on paper! Investors flocked to initial public offerings from practically any dot-com company. The market for capital became bipolar: easy-money times for dot-coms and tight money times for "not-coms." Even established, profitable companies in "old economy" industries such as manufacturing, distribution, real estate, and bricks-and-mortar retail had difficulty raising the capital they needed to grow. Then, early in 2000, the dot-com bubble burst, and financing an Internet business also became extremely challenging. During both the boom and the bust of Internet companies, not-com companies, especially those in low-tech industries, found attracting capital very difficult.

Entrepreneurs, especially those in less glamorous industries or those just starting out, soon discover the difficulty of finding outside sources of financing. Many banks shy away from making loans to start-ups, venture capitalists are looking for ever-larger deals, private investors have grown cautious, and making a public stock offering remains a viable option for only a handful of promising companies with good track records and fast-growth futures. The result has been a credit crunch for entrepreneurs looking for small to moderate amounts of start-up capital. Entrepreneurs and business owners needing between $100,000 and $3 million are especially hard hit because of the vacuum that exists at that level of financing.

In the face of this capital crunch, businesses's need for capital has never been greater. Experts estimate the small business financing market to be $170 billion a year; yet, that still is not enough to satisfy the capital appetites of entrepreneurs and their cash-hungry businesses.[1] When searching for the capital to launch their companies, entrepreneurs must remember the following "secrets" to successful financing:

- *Choosing the right sources of capital for a business can be just as important as choosing the right form of ownership or the right location.* It is a decision that will influence a company for a lifetime, so entrepreneurs must weigh their options carefully before committing to a particular funding source.
- *The money is out there; the key is knowing where to look.* Entrepreneurs must do their homework *before* they set out to raise money for their ventures. Understanding which sources of funding are best suited for the various stages of a company's growth and then taking the time to learn how those sources work is essential to success.
- *Creativity counts.* To find the financing their businesses demand, entrepreneurs must use as much creativity in attracting financing as they did in generating the ideas for their products and services.
- *The World Wide Web puts at entrepreneurs' fingertips vast resources of information that can lead to financing.* The Web often offers entrepreneurs, especially those looking for relatively small amounts of money, the opportunity to discover sources of funds that they otherwise might be missing. The Web site created for this book *(www.prenhall.com/scarborough)* provides links to many useful sites related to raising both start-up and growth capital. The Web also provides a low-cost, convenient way for entrepreneurs to get their business plans into potential investors' hands anywhere in the world. When searching for sources of capital, entrepreneurs must not overlook this valuable tool!

- *Be thoroughly prepared before approaching potential lenders and investors.* In the hunt for capital, tracking down leads is tough enough; don't blow a potential deal by failing to be ready to present your business idea to potential lenders and investors in a clear, concise, convincing way. That, of course, requires a solid business plan.
- *Entrepreneurs cannot overestimate the importance of making sure that the "chemistry" between themselves, their companies, and their funding sources is a good one.* Too many entrepreneurs get into financial deals because they needed the money to keep their businesses growing only to discover that their plans do not match those of their financial partners.

Rather than rely primarily on a single source of funds as they have in the past, entrepreneurs must piece together capital from multiple sources, a method known as **layered financing.** They have discovered that raising capital successfully requires them to cast a wide net to capture the financing they need to launch their businesses. *While earning his MBA at Carnegie Mellon University, Cormac Kinney came up with an idea for software that would enable stock traders to track stocks at a glance using color squares of different hues and intensities that appear on their computer monitors. Kinney convinced Marc Graham, a research scientist at the university, to create the software in exchange for part ownership in the company, NeoVision Hypersystems. To get the business up and running, both Kinney and Graham invested thousands of dollars of their own money, but they needed more. With business plan in hand, they turned to family and friends for $100,000 and convinced one of Kinney's former bosses to put in another $100,000. Then, using a network of connections, Kinney and Graham found three private investors who put up an additional $800,000 and helped the young company acquire a bank loan. One of the private investors introduced the entrepreneurs to a partner in a venture capital firm that ultimately invested $2 million in NeoVision. The company continues to grow, and the co-founders are considering another round of venture capital and perhaps making an initial public offering to meet NeoVision's appetite for capital.*[2]

This chapter and the next will guide you through the myriad of financing options available to entrepreneurs, focusing on both sources of equity (ownership) and debt (borrowed) financing.

PLANNING FOR CAPITAL NEEDS

1. Explain the differences among the three types of capital small businesses require: fixed, working, and growth.

Becoming a successful entrepreneur requires one to become a skilled fund raiser, a job that usually requires more time and energy than most business founders think. In start-up companies, raising capital can easily consume as much as one half of the entrepreneur's time and can take many months to complete. Most entrepreneurs are seeking less than $1 million (indeed, most need less than $100,000), which may be the toughest money to secure. Where to find this seed money depends, in part, on the nature of the proposed business, and on the amount of money required. For example, the creator of a computer software firm would have different capital requirements than the founder of a coal mining operation. Although both entrepreneurs might approach some of the same types of lenders or investors, each would be more successful targeting specific sources of funds best suited to their particular financial needs.

Capital is any form of wealth employed to produce more wealth. It exists in many forms in a typical business, including cash, inventory, plant, and equipment. Entrepreneurs need three different types of capital:

Fixed Capital. **Fixed capital** is needed to purchase a business's permanent or fixed assets such as buildings, land, computers, and equipment. Money invested in these fixed assets tends to be frozen since it cannot be used for any other purpose. Typically, large sums of money are involved in purchasing fixed assets, and credit terms usually are lengthy. Lenders of fixed capital expect the assets purchased to improve the efficiency and, thus, the profitability of the business, and to create improved cash flows that ensure repayment.

Working Capital. Working capital represents a business's temporary funds; it is the capital used to support a company's normal short-term operations. Accountants define working capital as current assets minus current liabilities. The need for working capital arises because of the uneven flow of cash into and out of the business due to normal seasonal fluctuations. Credit sales, seasonal sales swings, or unforeseeable changes in demand will create fluctuations in *any* small company's cash flow. Working capital normally is used to buy inventory, pay bills, finance credit sales, pay wages and salaries, and take care of any unexpected emergencies. Lenders of working capital expect it to produce higher cash flows to ensure repayment at the end of the production/sales cycle.

Table 14.1
Equity Capital Sources at Various Stages of Company Growth

	Start-Up	*Early*	*Expansion*	*Profitability*
Characteristics	Business is in conceptual phase and exists only on paper.	Business is developing one or more products or services but is not yet generating sales.	Business is selling products or services and is generating revenue and beginning to establish a customer base.	Company has established a customer base and is profitable.
Possible Sources of Funding	*Likelihood of using each source: H = Highly likely; P = Possible; U = Unlikely*			
Personal savings	H	H	H	H
Retained earnings	U	U	U	H
Friends and relatives	H	H	P	P
Angel investors	H	H	P	U
Partners	H	H	P	U
Corporate venture capital	P	H	H	H
Venture capital	U	P	H	H
Initial public offering (IPO)	U	U	P	H
Regulation S-B Offering	U	U	P	H
Small Company Offering Registration (SCOR)	U	P	P	H
Private placements	U	P	P	H
Intrastate offerings (Rule 147)	U	P	P	H
Regulation A	U	P	P	H

Growth Capital. **Growth capital,** unlike working capital, is not related to the seasonal fluctuations of a small business. Instead, growth capital requirements surface when an existing business is expanding or changing its primary direction. For example, a small manufacturer of silicon microchips for computers saw his business skyrocket in a short time period. With orders for chips rushing in, the growing business needed a sizable cash infusion to increase plant size, expand its sales and production workforce, and buy more equipment. During times of such rapid expansion, a growing company's capital requirements are similar to those of a business start-up. Like lenders of fixed capital, growth capital lenders expect the funds to improve a company's profitability and cash flow position, thus ensuring repayment.

Although these three types of capital are interdependent, each has certain sources, characteristics, and effects on the business and its long-term growth that entrepreneurs must recognize. Table 14.1 shows the various stages of a company's growth and the sources of capital most suitable in each stage.

SOURCES OF EQUITY FINANCING

2. Describe the various sources of equity financing available to entrepreneurs.

Equity capital represents the personal investment of the owner (or owners) in a business and is sometimes called *risk* capital because these investors assume the primary risk of losing their funds if the business fails. *For instance, private investor Victor Lombardi lost the $3.5 million he invested in a start-up called NetFax, a company that was developing the technology to send faxes over the Internet. However, when NetFax's patent application stalled, the company foundered. Just three years after its launch, NetFax ceased operations, leaving Lombardi's investment worthless.*[3]

If a venture succeeds, however, founders and investors share in the benefits, which can be quite substantial. The founders of and early investors in Yahoo!, Sun Microsystems, Federal Express, Intel, and Microsoft became multimillionaires when the companies went public and their equity investments finally paid off. To entrepreneurs, the primary advantage of equity capital is that it does not have to be repaid like a loan does. Equity investors are entitled to share in the company's earnings (if there are any) and usually to have a voice in the company's future direction.

The primary disadvantage of equity capital is that the entrepreneur must give up some—perhaps *most*—of the ownership in the business to outsiders. Although 50 percent of something is better than 100 percent of nothing, giving up control of your company can be disconcerting and dangerous. Many entrepreneurs who give up majority ownership in their companies in exchange for equity capital have found themselves forced out of the businesses they started! Entrepreneurs are most likely to give up more equity in their businesses in the startup phase than in any other.

We now turn our attention to nine common sources of equity capital.

Personal Savings

The *first* place entrepreneurs should look for startup money is in their own pockets. It's the least expensive source of funds available! Entrepreneurs apparently see the benefits of self-sufficiency; the most common source of equity funds used to start a small business is the entrepreneur's pool of personal savings. *Before David and Robin Penn launched their preschool, The Learning Center, their business plan helped them determine that they would need $125,000. The Penns invested everything they could into the business—$13,000—before raising $12,000 from family and friends. The couple also managed to secure a bank loan of $100,000 guaranteed by the Small Business Administration to fulfill their company's capital requirements.*[4]

"I need 80 million dollars to develop a plan of a concept of a vision of the seed of an idea."

Lenders and investors *expect* entrepreneurs to put their own money into a business start-up. If an entrepreneur is not willing to risk his own money, potential investors are not likely to risk their money in the business either. Further, failing to put up sufficient capital of their own means that entrepreneurs must either borrow an excessive amount of capital or give up a significant portion of ownership to outsiders to fund the business properly. Excessive borrowing in the early days of a business puts intense pressure on its cash flow, and becoming a minority shareholder may dampen a founder's enthusiasm for making a business successful. Neither outcome presents a bright future for the company involved.

Friends and Family Members

Although most entrepreneurs look to their own bank accounts first to finance a business, few have sufficient resources to launch their businesses alone. In fact, three out of four people who start businesses do so with capital from outside sources.[5] After emptying their own pockets, entrepreneurs should look to friends and family members who might be willing to invest in a business venture. Because of their relationships with the founder, these people are most likely to invest. *When Tony and Freddie Seba founded PrintNation.com, an online supplier of printing equipment, they turned to their mother, who invested $100,000 of her retirement money in their new business. Their business grew rapidly, and eventually the Sebas were able to attract $5.75 million from a prominent venture capital firm, which later invested another $25.5 million in the business. Mrs. Seba's investment has paid off handsomely; PrintNation.com is now the largest online supplier to the commercial printing industry.[6]*

A recent study of *Inc.* magazine's 500 fastest growing companies found that 30 percent of these business founders relied on relatives and friends for start-up capital.[7] Often, family members and friends are more patient than other outside investors and are less meddlesome in a business's affairs than many other types of investors. Investments from family and friends are an excellent source of seed capital and bridge financing, the money that gets a young business far enough along to attract money from private investors or venture capital companies. Inherent dangers lurk in family business investments, however. Unrealistic expectations or misunderstood

IN THE FOOTSTEPS OF AN ENTREPRENEUR
In Search of Capital

In 1991, Lori Bonn Gallagher launched her jewelry design and manufacturing business, Lori Bonn Design, in Oakland, California with $1,000 from her personal savings. Her company's mid- to upper-priced jewelry has found a market, and sales have climbed to more than $3 million a year. The company has been profitable since its first year of operation. As her company grew, Gallagher used a variety of funding sources, including the retained earnings of the company and bank loans. Once she landed a few major retailers such as Nordstrom and Sak's Fifth Avenue, she started factoring the company's accounts receivable. Currently, Gallagher has a six-figure line of credit at a bank that she draws on primarily for working capital.

The line of credit and the other sources of capital that Lori Bonn Designs has relied on in the past are not enough to fuel the growth Gallagher sees for her company, however. "My product is selling really, really well right now," she says. "I can't produce enough to meet the demand from my customers. There's so much opportunity. We could get to [$10 million in annual sales] much faster, but to do that I need significantly more capital than I've gotten so far."

Gallagher wants to hire someone to manage the financial aspects of the business, freeing her to focus on what she does best: jewelry design and marketing. She also wants to launch an aggressive national marketing campaign, to expand into international markets, and to improve the company's inventory control procedures. "What I really need is a couple million dollars and a smart person or two to serve on my board," quips Gallagher. She still owns 100 percent of the company's stock, and she would prefer not to give up a large stake in the company to outsiders.

1. Assume the role of financial consultant to Gallagher. What steps should she take to prepare her company before she begins her search for capital?

2. Where would you recommend she search for the capital to accomplish the goals she has established for her business? Explain your reasoning.

Sources: Adapted from Jill Andresky Fraser, "Money Hunt: Plans for Growth," *Inc.,* March 2001, pp. 56–57.

---

risks have destroyed many friendships and have ruined many family reunions. To avoid this problem, an entrepreneur must honestly present the investment opportunity and the nature of the risks involved to avoid alienating friends and family members if the business fails. On the other hand, some investments return more than friends and family members ever could have imagined. In 1995, Mike and Jackie Bezos invested $300,000 into their son Jeff's start-up business, Amazon.com. Today, Mike and Jackie own 6 percent of Amazon.com's stock, and their shares are worth billions of dollars![8]

Angels

After dipping into their own pockets and convincing friends and relatives to invest in their business ventures, many entrepreneurs still find themselves short of the seed capital they need. Frequently, the next stop on the road to business financing is private investors. These **private investors** (or **"angels"**) are wealthy individuals, often entrepreneurs themselves, who invest in business start-ups in exchange for equity stakes in the companies. In many cases, angels invest in businesses for more than purely economic reasons (because they have a personal interest in the industry), and they are willing to put money into companies in the earliest stages, long before venture capital firms and institutional investors jump in. Angel financing, the fastest-growing segment of the small business capital market, is ideal for companies that have outgrown the capacity of investments from friends and family but are still too small to attract the interest of venture capital companies. For instance, after raising the money to launch Amazon.com from family and friends, Jeff Bezos turned to angels because venture capital firms were not interested in a business start-up. Bezos attracted $1.2 million from a dozen angels before landing $8 million from venture capital firms a year later.[9]

Angels are a primary source of start-up capital for companies in the embryonic stage through the growth stage, and their role in financing small businesses is significant. Experts estimate that 400,000 angels invest $50 billion a year in 50,000 small companies, most of them in the start-up phase.[10] Angels finance 15 to 20 times the number of companies that institutional venture capital firms do. Former Beatle Paul McCartney has joined the ranks of angel investors, putting an undisclosed amount of money into Magex, a company that encrypts digital material on the World Wide Web.[11] Because the angel market is so fragmented, we may never get a completely accurate estimate of its investment in business startups. However, experts concur on one fact: angels are a vital source of external equity capital for small businesses.

Angels fill a significant gap in the seed capital market. They are most likely to finance startups with capital requirements in the $10,000 to $2 million range, well below the $3 million to $10 million minimum investments most professional venture capitalists prefer. Because a $500,000 deal requires about as much of a venture capitalist's time to research and evaluate as a $5 million deal does, venture capitalists tend to focus on big deals, where their returns are bigger. Angels also tolerate risk levels that would make venture capitalists shudder; as many as 90 percent of angel-backed companies fail.[12] One angel investor, a former executive at Oracle Corporation, says that of the 10 companies he has invested in, seven have flopped. Three of the start-ups, however, have produced 50-fold returns![13] Because of the inherent risks in startup companies, many venture capitalists have shifted their investment portfolios away from start-ups toward more established firms. That's why angel financing is so important: Angels often finance deals that no venture capitalist will consider. *When Jim Miller co-founded a company to provide broadband Internet services, he was able to attract $250,000 in equity from a small group of angels. Miller turned to angel investors because his deal was far too small to interest venture capital firms.*[14]

Because angels prefer to maintain a low profile, the real challenge lies in *finding* them. Most angels have substantial business and financial experience, and many of them are entrepreneurs or former entrepreneurs. The typical angel invests in companies at the start-up or infant growth stage and accepts 30 percent of the investment opportunities presented; makes an average of two investments every three years; and has invested an average of $150,000 of equity in 3.5 firms.[15] When evaluating a proposal, angels look for a qualified management team ("We invest in people," says one angel), a business with a clearly defined niche, the potential to dominate the market, and a competitive advantage. They also want to see market research that proves the existence of a sizeable and profitable customer base.

Because angels frown on "cold calls" from entrepreneurs they don't know, locating them boils down to making the right contacts. Asking friends, attorneys, bankers, stockbrokers, accountants, other business owners, and consultants for suggestions and introductions is a good way to start. Networking is the key. One entrepreneur who has successfully raised an average of $120,000 a month for his growing business has developed a list of more than 100 potential angels through an extensive network of contacts in the industry.[16] Angels almost always invest their money locally, so entrepreneurs should look close to home for them—typically within a 50- to 100-mile radius. Angels also look for businesses they know something about and most expect to invest their knowledge, experience, and energy as well as their money in a company. In fact, the advice and the network of contacts that angels bring to a deal can sometimes be as valuable as their money! *John McCallum, founder of VetExchange, an Internet-based service provider for veterinarians, found that the contacts and the advice angel investors brought to his company to be invaluable. "Our angels are networked across the country," says McCallum. "They have relationships you can't imagine." One angel, a former entrepreneur, gave McCallum valuable advice on a key strategic issue recently. "He's dealt with the same issue five times before," he says.*[17]

Angels tend to invest in clusters as well, many of them through one of the nation's 150 angel capital networks. With the right approach, an entrepreneur can attract an angel who might share the deal with some of his cronies. *In 1995, Hans Severiens, a professional investor, created the Band of Angels, a group of about 150 angels (mostly Silicon Valley millionaires) who meet monthly in Portola Valley, California to listen to entrepreneurs pitch their business plans. The Band of Angels reviews about 30 proposals each month before inviting a handful of entrepreneurs to make brief presentations at their monthly meeting. Interested members often team up with one another to invest in the businesses they consider most promising. The Band of Angels' average investment is $600,000, which usually nets them between 15 percent and 20 percent of a company's stock. Since its inception, the Band of Angels has invested more than $74 million in 122 companies.*[18]

The Internet has expanded greatly the ability of entrepreneurs in search of capital and angels in search of businesses to find one another. Dozens of angel networks have opened on the World Wide Web, including AngelMoney.com, Business Angels International, Garage Technology Ventures, CommonAngels.com, The Capital Network, WomenAngels.net, and many others.

Angels are an excellent source of "patient money," often willing to wait five to seven years or longer to cash out their investments. They earn their returns through the increased value of the business, not through dividends and interest. For example, more than 1,000 early investors in Microsoft Inc. are now millionaires, and the original investors in Genentech Inc. (a genetic engineering company) have seen their investments increase more than 500 times.[19] Angels' return-on-investment targets tend to be lower than those of professional venture capitalists. Although venture capitalists shoot for 60 percent to 75 percent returns annually, private investors usually settle for 20 percent to 50 percent (depending on the level of risk involved in the venture). The average rate of return for angels is 30 percent a year.[20] Private investors typically take less than 50 percent ownership leaving the majority ownership to the company founder(s). The lesson: If an entrepreneur needs relatively small amounts of money to launch a company, angels are a primary source.

Table 14.2 offers useful tips for attracting angel capital.

Partners

As we saw in Chapter 3, entrepreneurs can take on partners to expand the capital base of a business. *When Lou Bucelli and Tim Crouse were searching for the money to launch CME Conference Video, a company that produces and distributes videotapes of educational conferences for physicians, they found an angel willing to put up $250,000 for 40 percent of the business. Unfortunately, their investor backed out when some of his real estate investments went bad, leaving the partners with commitments for several conferences but no cash to produce and distribute the videos. With little time to spare, Bucelli and Crouse decided to form a series of limited partnerships with people they knew, one for each videotape they would produce. Six limited partnerships produced $400,000 in financing, and the tapes generated $9.1 million in sales for the year. As the general partners, Bucelli and Crouse retained 80 percent of each partnership. The limited partners earned returns of up to 80 percent in just*

Table 14.2
Tips for Attracting Angel Financing

Although they are an important source of small business financing, angels can be extremely difficult to locate. You won't find them listed under "Angels" in the Yellow Pages of the telephone directory. Patience and persistence—and connections—pay off in the search for angel financing, however. How does an entrepreneur needing financing find an angel to help launch or expand a company and make the deal work?

- *Start early.* Finding private investors takes a lot longer than most entrepreneurs think.

- *Have a business plan ready.* Once you find a potential private investor, don't risk his or her losing interest while you put together a business plan. Have the plan ready to go *before* you begin your search.

- *Look close to home.* Most angels prefer to invest their money locally, so conduct a thorough search for potential angels within a 50- to 100-mile radius of your business.

- *Canvass your industry.* Angels tend to specialize in particular industries, usually ones they know a lot about.

- *Recognize that, in addition to the money they invest, angels also want to provide their knowledge and expertise.* Indeed, angels' experience and knowledge can be just as valuable as their money *if* entrepreneurs are willing to accept it.

- *Remember that angels invest for more than just financial reasons.* Angels want to earn a good return on the money they invest in businesses, but there's usually more to it than that. Angels often invest in companies for personal reasons.

- *Join local philanthropic organizations, chambers of commerce, nonprofit organizations, and advisory boards.* Potential investors often are involved in such organizations.

- *Ask business professionals such as bankers, lawyers, stockbrokers, accountants, and others for names of potential angels.* They know people who have the money and the desire to invest in business ventures.

- *Network, network, network.* Finding angel financing initially is a game of contacts—getting an introduction to the right person from the right person.

- *Investigate the investors and their past deals.* Never get involved in a deal with an angel you don't know or trust. Be sure you and your investors have a common vision of the business and the deal.

- *Summarize the details of the deal in a letter of intent.* Although a letter of intent is not a legal document, it outlines the basic structure of the deal and exposes the most sensitive areas being negotiated so that there are no surprises. What role, if any, will the angel play in running the business? Angels can be a source of valuable help, but some entrepreneurs complain of angels' meddling.

- *Keep the deal simple.* The simpler the deal is, the easier it will be to sell to potential investors. Probably the simplest way to involve angels is to sell them common stock.

- *Nail down the angel's exit path.* Angels make their money when they sell their ownership interests. Ideally, the exit path should be part of structuring the deal. Will the company buy back the angels' shares? Will the company go public so the angels can sell their shares on the market? Will the owners sell out to a larger company? What is the time frame for doing so?

- *Avoid intimidating potential investors.* Most angels are turned off by entrepreneurs with an attitude of "I have someone else who will do the deal if you don't." In the face of such coercion, many private investors simply walk away from the deal.

- *Always be truthful.* Overpromising and underdelivering will kill a deal and spoil future financing arrangements.

- *Develop alternative financing arrangements.* Never back an angel into a corner with "take this deal or leave it." Have alternative plans prepared in case the investor balks at the outset.

- *Don't take the money and run.* Investors appreciate entrepreneurs who keep them informed—about how their money is being spent and the results it shows. Prepare periodic reports for them.

- *Stick to the deal.* It's tempting to spend the money where it's most needed once it is in hand. Resist! If you promised to use the funds for specific purposes, do it. Nothing undermines an angel's trust as quickly as violating the original plan.

six months. Within two years, their company was so successful that venture capitalists started calling. To finance their next round of growth, Bucelli and Crouse sold 35 percent of their company to a venture capital firm for $1.3 million.[21]

Before entering into any partnership arrangement, however, entrepreneurs must consider the impact of giving up some personal control over operations and of sharing profits with others. Whenever entrepreneurs give up equity in their businesses (through whatever mechanism), they run the risk of losing control over it. As the founder's ownership in a company becomes increasingly diluted, the probability of losing control of its future direction and the entire decision-making process increases.

Corporate Venture Capital

Large corporations have gotten into the business of financing small companies. Today, 900 large corporations across the globe, including Intel, Motorola, Cisco Systems, Nokia, UPS, and General Electric, invest in start-up companies. According to the National Venture Capital Association, 30 percent of all venture capital investments comes from corporations.[22] Start-up companies not only get a boost from the capital injections large companies give them, but they also stand to gain many other benefits from the relationship. The right corporate partner may share technical expertise, distribution channels, marketing know-how, and provide introductions to important customers and suppliers. Another intangible yet highly important advantage an investment from a large corporate partner gives a start-up is credibility. Doors that otherwise would be closed to a small company magically open when the right corporation becomes a strategic partner. *When Lisa and Mark Hammitt needed expansion capital for their fast-growing enterprise software business, Black Pearl, the venture capital firms that had invested in the business in earlier rounds were caught up in the dot-com frenzy and were not interested. The Hammitts took their business plan to Intel, which invested $8.4 million in Black Pearl. Using the strength of Intel's name, the Hammitts attracted other venture funds that have invested an additional $14 million! Black Pearl also was able to land new customers with Intel's help. "When you're a partner with Intel," says Lisa, "it gives you an ear that you normally wouldn't have if you were just a small company banging on doors."*[23]

Foreign corporations are also interested in investing in small U.S. businesses. Often, these corporations are seeking strategic partnerships to gain access to new technology, new products, or access to lucrative U.S. markets. In return, the small companies they invest in benefit from the capital infusion as well as from their partners' international experience and connections. In other cases, small companies are turning to their customers for the resources they need to fuel their rapid growth. Recognizing how interwoven their success is with that of their suppliers, corporate giants such as AT&T, JCPenney, and Ford now offer financial support to many of the small businesses they buy from.

Venture Capital Companies

Venture capital companies are private, for-profit organizations that purchase equity positions in young businesses they believe have high-growth and high-profit potential, producing annual returns of 300 to 500 percent over five to seven years. More than 3,000 venture capital firms operate across the United States today, investing in promising small companies in a wide variety of industries (see Figure 14.1). Seeking to boost the returns they earn on their endowments, colleges and universities have entered the venture capital business. More than 100 colleges across the nation now have venture funds designed to invest in promising businesses started by their students, alumni, and faculty.[24] Even the Central Intelligence Agency (CIA) has launched a venture capital firm called In-Q-Tel that invests in companies that are

Figure 14.1
Venture Capital Financing

Source: PricewaterhouseCoopers Moneytree Report, *www.pwc.moneytree.com*.

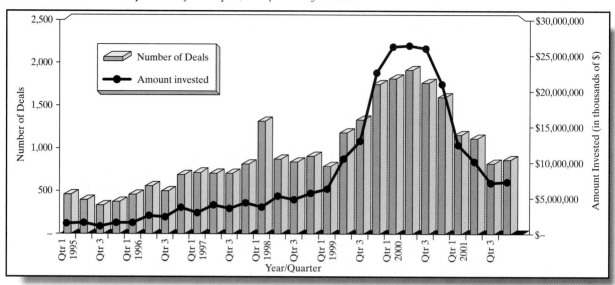

developing new technologies that could benefit the CIA. One of In-Q-Tel's investments is in a company that is developing a three-dimensional Web browser that allows users to see "live" versions of the Web sites they visit.[25]

Venture capital firms, which provide about 7 percent of all funding for private companies, have invested billions of dollars in high potential small companies over the years, including such notable businesses as Apple Computer, Microsoft Inc., Intel, and Data General. Although companies in high-tech industries such as the Internet, communications, computer hardware and software, medical care, and biotechnology are the most popular targets of venture capital, a company with extraordinary growth prospects has the potential to attract venture capital, whatever its industry. Table 14.3 offers a humorous look at how venture capitalists decipher the language of sometimes overly optimistic entrepreneurs.

Policies and Investment Strategies. Venture capital firms usually establish stringent policies to implement their overall investment strategies.

Investment Size and Screening. Depending on the size of the venture capital corporation and its cost structure, minimum investments range from $50,000 to $5 million. Investment ceilings, in effect, do not exist. Most firms seek investments in the $3 million to $10 million range to justify the cost of investigating the large number of proposals they receive.

The venture capital screening process is *extremely* rigorous. The typical venture capital company invests in less than 1 percent of the applications it receives! For example, the average venture capital firm screens about 1,200 proposals a year, but over 90 percent are rejected immediately because they do not match the firm's investment criteria. The remaining 10 percent are investigated more thoroughly at a cost ranging from $2,000 to $3,000 per proposal. At this time, approximately 10 to 15 proposals will have passed the screening process, and these are subjected to comprehensive review. The venture capital firm will invest in three to six of these remaining proposals.

Ownership. Most venture capitalists prefer to purchase ownership in a small business through common stock or convertible preferred stock. The share of ownership

Table 14.3
Deciphering the Language of the Venture Capital Industry

By nature, entrepreneurs tend to be optimistic. When screening business plans, venture capitalists must make an allowance for entrepreneurial enthusiasm. Here's a dictionary of phrases commonly found in business plans and their accompanying venture capital translations.

Exploring an acquisition strategy—Our current products have no market.

We're on a clear P2P (pathway to profitability)—We're still years away from earning a profit.

Basically on plan—We're expecting a revenue shortfall of 25 percent.

Internet business model—Potential bigger fools have been identified.

A challenging year—Competitors are eating our lunch.

Considerably ahead of plan—Hit our plan in one of the last three months.

Company's underlying strength and resilience—We still lost money, but look how we cut our losses.

Core business—Our product line is obsolete.

Currently revising budget—The financial plan is in total chaos.

Cyclical industry—We posted a huge loss last year.

Entrepreneurial CEO—He is totally uncontrollable, bordering on maniacal.

Facing challenges—Our sales continue to slide, and we have no idea why.

Facing unprecedented economic, political, and structural shifts—It's a tough world out there, but we're coping the best we can.

Highly leverageable network—No longer works but has friends who do.

Ingredients are there—Given two years, we might find a workable strategy.

Investing heavily in R&D—We're trying desperately to catch the competition.

Limited downside—Things can't get much worse.

Long sales cycle—Yet to find a customer who likes the product enough to buy it.

Major opportunity—It's our last chance.

Niche strategy—A small-time player.

On a manufacturing learning curve—We can't make the product with positive margins.

Passive investor—She phones once a year to see if we're still in business.

Positive results—Our losses were less than last year.

Refocus our efforts—We've blown our chance, and now we have to fire most of our employees.

Repositioning the business—We've recently written off a multimillion-dollar investment.

Selective investment strategy—The board is spending more time on yachts than on planes.

Solid operating performance in a difficult year—Yes, we lost money and market share, but look how hard we tried.

Somewhat below plan—We expect a revenue shortfall of 75 percent.

Expenses were unexpectedly high—We grossly overestimated our profit margins.

Strategic investor—One who will pay a preposterous price for an equity share in the business.

Strongest fourth quarter ever—Don't quibble over the losses in the first three quarters.

Sufficient opportunity to market this product no longer exists—Nobody will buy the thing.

Too early to tell—Results to date have been grim.

A team of skilled, motivated, and dedicated people—We've laid off most of our staff, and those who are left should be glad they still have jobs.

Turnaround opportunity—It's a lost cause.

Unique—We have no more than six strong competitors.

Volume-sensitive—Our company has massive fixed costs.

Window of opportunity—Without more money fast, this company is dead.

Work closely with the management—We talk to them on the phone once a month.

A year in which we confronted challenges—At least we know the questions even if we haven't got the answers.

Sources: Adapted from Scott Herhold, "When CEOs Blow Smoke," *e-company*, May 2001, pp. 125–127; Suzanne McGee, "A Devil's Dictionary of Financing," *Wall Street Journal*, June 12, 2000, p. C13; John F. Budd Jr., "Cracking the CEO's Code," *Wall Street Journal*, March 27, 1995, p. A20; "Venture-Speak Defined," *Teleconnect*, October 1990, p. 42; Cynthia E. Griffin, "Figuratively Speaking," *Entrepreneur*, August 1999, p. 26.

a venture capital company purchases may be less than 5 percent for a profitable company to possibly 100 percent for a financially unstable firm. Usually, venture capital firms do not buy a majority of a company's shares; instead, a typical venture capital company seeks to purchase 20 percent to 40 percent of a business. Anything more incurs the risk of draining the entrepreneur's dedication and enthusiasm for managing the firm. Still, entrepreneurs must weigh the positive aspects of receiving needed financing against the negative features of owning a smaller share of the business.

Stage of Investment. Most venture capital firms invest in companies that are either in the early stages of development (called early stage investing) or in the rapid-growth phase (called expansion stage investing). Others specialize in acquisitions, providing the financing for managers and employees of a business to buy it out. On average, 91 percent of all venture capital goes to businesses in these stages, although some venture capital firms are showing more interest in companies in the start-up phase because of the tremendous returns that are possible by investing then.[26] Most venture capital firms do not make just a single investment in a company. Instead, they invest in a company over time across several stages, where their investments often total $10 to $15 million.

Control. In exchange for the financing they receive from venture capitalists, entrepreneurs must give up a portion of their businesses, sometimes surrendering a majority interest and control of its operations. Venture capitalists usually join the boards of directors of the companies they invest in or send in new managers or a new management team to protect their investments. Sometimes venture capitalists serve as financial and managerial advisors, while others take an active role in the managing of the company—recruiting employees, providing sales leads, choosing attorneys and advertising agencies, and making daily decisions. A recent study by the Stanford Business School found that entrepreneurs who financed their businesses with venture capital were more than twice as likely to be replaced as CEO than those who relied on other forms of financing.[27] One cautionary note for every entrepreneur seeking venture capital is to find out before the deal is done *exactly* how much control and "hands-on" management investors plan to assume.

Investment Preferences. The venture capital industry has undergone important changes over the past decade. Venture capital funds are larger, more numerous, and more specialized. As the industry grows, more venture capital funds are focusing their investments in niches—everything from low-calorie custards to the Internet. Some will invest in almost any industry but prefer companies in particular stages, including the start-up phase. Traditionally, however, only about 9 percent of the companies receiving venture capital financing are in the start-up (seed) stage when entrepreneurs are forming a company or developing a product or service. Most of the start-up businesses that attract venture capital are technology companies.

What Venture Capitalists Look For. Small business owners must realize that it is very difficult for any small business, especially start-ups, to pass the intense screening process of a venture capital company and qualify for an investment. Venture capital firms finance an average of about 3,000 deals in a typical year.[28] Two factors make a deal attractive to venture capitalists: high returns and a convenient (and profitable) exit strategy. When evaluating potential investments, venture capitalists look for the following features:

Competent Management. The most important ingredient in the success of any business is the ability of the management team, and venture capitalists recognize this. To venture capitalists, the ideal management team has experience, managerial skills, commitment, and the ability to build teams.

Competitive Edge. Investors are searching for some factor that will enable a small business to set itself apart from its competitors. This distinctive competence may range from an innovative product or service that satisfies unmet customer needs to a unique marketing or R&D approach. It must be something with the potential to make the business a leader in its field.

Growth Industry. Hot industries attract profits—and venture capital. Most venture capital funds focus their searches for prospects in rapidly expanding fields because they believe the profit potential is greater in these areas. Venture capital firms are most interested in young companies that have enough growth potential to become at least $100 million businesses within three to five years. Venture capitalists know that most of the businesses they invest in will flop, so their winners have to be *big* winners.

Viable Exit Strategy. Venture capitalists not only look for promising companies with the ability to dominate a market, but they also want to see a plan for a feasible exit strategy, typically to be executed within three to five years. Venture capital firms realize the return on their investments when the companies they invest in either make an initial public offering or sell out to another business.

Intangible Factors. Some other important factors considered in the screening process are not easily measured; they are the intuitive, intangible factors the venture capitalist detects by gut feeling. This feeling might be the result of the small firm's solid sense of direction, its strategic planning process, the chemistry of its management team, or a number of other factors.

Entrepreneurs in search of financing must understand the implications of accepting venture capital. *When Mark Fasciano and Ari Kahn launched FatWire, a company that enables businesses to maintain and continuously update their Web sites, venture capital firms came calling, offering the young entrepreneurs between $5 and $10 million to finance the young company's growth. Realizing that their software product was not fully developed, however, Fasciano and Kahn refused the venture capitalists' offers. "It was tempting," admits Fasciano. Two years later, with their product, UpdateEngine, complete, the entrepreneurs presented their business plan at a forum of venture capitalists, where more than a dozen firms took an interest. Within months, FatWire had closed a deal with two venture capital firms for $9.25 million. As the company grew and prospered, other venture capital firms have provided additional growth capital.*[29]

Despite its many benefits, venture capital is not suited for every entrepreneur. "VC money comes at a price," warns one entrepreneur. "Before boarding a one-way money train, ask yourself if this is the best route for your business and personal desires, because investors are like department stores the day after Christmas—they expect a lot of returns in a short period of time."[30]

Public Stock Sale ("Going Public")

4. Describe the process of "going public" as well as its advantages and disadvantages and the various simplified registrations and exemptions from registration available to small businesses.

In some cases, entrepreneurs can "go public" by selling shares of stock in their corporations to outside investors. In an **initial public offering (IPO)**, a company raises capital by selling shares of its stock to the general public for the first time. A public offering is an effective method of raising large amounts of capital, but it can be an expensive and time-consuming process filled with regulatory nightmares. "An IPO can be a wonderful thing," says one investment banker, "but it's not all sweetness and light."[31] Once a company makes an IPO, *nothing* will ever be the same again. Managers must consider the impact of their decisions not only on the company and its employees but also on its shareholders and the value of their stock.

GAINING THE COMPETITIVE EDGE
Campus Venture Capital

You may not realize it, but you could be sitting in the midst of an entrepreneurial trend. Drawn by colleges' and universities' ability to create and incubate new businesses, venture capital firms are searching campuses across the nation for promising companies in which to invest. Buoyed by the success of many businesses that were launched on college campuses by students and faculty members such as Dell Computer, Yahoo! Inc., and Akamai Technologies, venture capital firms such as ITU Ventures, Silicon Ivy Ventures, and University Angels.com are investing capital in early-stage companies, many of which are built on cutting-edge technology. "Universities are a constant source of innovation. They're a good place for us to be," explains Jonah Schnel, confounder of ITU Ventures. With a capital base of more than $50 million, ITU Ventures is aggressively investing in businesses born on campuses, including the California Institute of Technology, Stanford University, the Massachusetts Institute of Technology, and others.

Founded in 2000 by Schnel and two other twenty-something friends, Adam Winnick and Chad Brownstein, ITU operates by finding at each school "campus partners," typically regular students who serve as scouts for promising ideas and as liaisons with ITU. In addition to doing their normal coursework, campus partners use their knowledge of their campuses and their networks of contacts to search out the most promising business ideas. Just like any venture capitalist, they review business plans, listen to entrepreneurs pitch their ideas, and evaluate the prospects of the business ideas they find. In his first two months as a campus partner for ITU at the University of California at Berkeley, Matthew Fogarty read 200 business plans and heard 30 pitches from prospective entrepreneurs. Fogarty and ITU's other campus partners also analyze the proposals they see before passing on the hottest prospects to ITU's investment committee. They also serve as consultants to the start-up companies in which ITU has invested,

helping them hone their strategies, recruit key employees, and prepare for their next round of financing. ITU's campus partners receive a stipend and the chance to get equity shares in ITU and in the companies in which ITU invests.

Although most venture capital firms shy away from investments in early stage businesses, those focusing on colleges and universities embrace them. Recognizing that the risks they encounter are higher, these venture capital firms see their investments as an opportunity to latch on to promising technologies and businesses before any one else does. ITU, for instance, typically makes investments of $100,000 to $1 million in exchange for up to 25 percent of the equity in the businesses it funds. Some of the most promising businesses ITU has bankrolled include OEwaves, SkyFlow, and OnWafer. OEwaves is a company founded at Cal Tech that has developed technology with important applications in the optical and wireless communications industries. SkyFlow was founded by a University of California at Berkeley professor and a graduate student and is based on technology that gives people easy access to the Internet over their cell phones. The entrepreneurs behind OnWafer have developed a new technology that increases the productivity of makers of semiconductors and has the potential to save chipmakers billions of dollars. "We believe the amount of intellectual capital that is germinated on these campuses is tremendous," says Schnel.

1. What advantages do venture capital firms that focus on finding promising business ventures on college and university campuses gain? What challenges do they face?

2. Assume that you are one of ITU's campus partners. What characteristics would you look for in a prospective business venture before recommending it to ITU's investment committee? Explain.

Sources: Adapted from Emily Barker, "The VC in My Dorm Room," *Inc.*, October 2001, pp. 42–48; Matthew DeBellis, "Universities and VCs Are Getting Cozy," *Red Herring*, March 16, 2000, *www.redherring,com/vc/2000/0316/vc-school031600.html*; Debora Vrana, "Fund Bolsters University Ideas," *L.A. Times*, December 18, 2000, *www.itu.com/la_times.html*; Erika Gonzales, "Wanted: A Few Good Ideas," *Rocky Mountain News*, April 21, 2001, *www.itu.com/rocky_mountain.html*; Stephanie Franken, "At CMU, A Meeting of Money and Minds," May 10, 2001, Post-Gazette.com, *www.post-gazette.com/businessnews/20010510cmu4.asp*.

Going public isn't for every business. In fact, most small companies do not meet the criteria for making a successful public stock offering. In a typical year, only about 550 companies manage to make IPOs of their stock, and only 20,000 companies in the United States—less than 1 percent of the total—are publicly held. Few companies with less than $10 million in annual sales manage to go public successfully. It is extremely difficult for a start-up company with no track record of success to raise money with a public offering. Instead, the investment bankers who underwrite public stock offerings typically look for established companies with the following characteristics:

- Consistently high growth rates (usually at least 20 percent a year)
- Strong record of earnings
- Three to five years of audited financial statements
- A solid position in rapidly growing markets
- A sound management team and a strong board of directors

Figure 14.2 shows the number of IPOs since 1981, along with the amount of capital raised during that time.

Entrepreneurs who are considering taking their companies public should first consider carefully the advantages and the disadvantages of an IPO. The *advantages* include the following:

Ability to raise large amounts of capital. The biggest benefit of a public offering is the capital infusion the company receives. After going public, the

Figure 14.2
Initial Public Offerings
Source: Thomson Financial Securities Data, 2001.

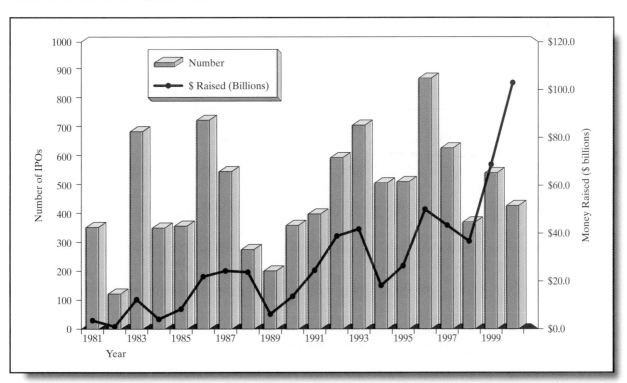

corporation has the cash to fund research and development (R&D) projects, expand plant and facilities, repay debt, or boost working capital balances without incurring the interest expense and the obligation to repay associated with debt financing. *For instance, when the World Wrestling Federation went public recently, the sale of 10 million shares at $17 per share generated more than $170 million for the company (before subtracting the expenses of making the offering).*[32]

Improved corporate image. All of the media attention a company receives during the registration process makes it more visible. Plus, becoming a public company in some industries improves its prestige and enhances its competitive position, one of the most widely recognized, intangible benefits of going public.

Improved access to future financing. Going public boosts a company's net worth and broadens its equity base. Its improved stature and financial strength make it easier for the firm to attract more capital—both debt and equity—and to grow.

Attracting and retaining key employees. Public companies often use stock-based compensation plans to attract and retain quality employees. Stock options and bonuses are excellent methods for winning employees' loyalty and for instilling a healthy ownership attitude among them. Employee stock ownership plans (ESOPs) and stock purchase plans are popular recruiting and motivational tools in many small corporations, enabling them to hire top-flight talent they otherwise would not be able to afford.

Using stock for acquisitions. A company whose stock is publicly traded can acquire other businesses by offering its own shares rather than cash. Acquiring other companies with shares of stock eliminates the need to incur additional debt.

Listing on a stock exchange. Being listed on an organized stock exchange, even a small regional one, improves the marketability of a company's shares and enhances its image. The World Wrestling Federation's stock trades on the New York Stock Exchange, giving it more clout in its market. Most small companies' stocks, however, do not qualify for listing on the nation's largest exchanges—the New York Stock Exchange (NYSE) and the American Stock Exchange (AMEX). However, the AMEX offers a market for small-company stocks, The Emerging Company Marketplace. Most small companies' stocks are traded on either the National Association of Securities Dealers Automated Quotation (NASDAQ) system's National Market System (NMS) and its emerging small-capitalization exchange or one of the nation's regional stock exchanges. The most popular regional exchanges include the Midwest (MSE), Philadelphia (PHLX), Boston (BSE), and Pacific (PSE).

Despite these advantages, many factors can spoil a company's attempted IPO. In fact, only 5 percent of the companies that attempt to go public ever complete the process.[33]

The *disadvantages* of going public include the following:

Dilution of founder's ownership. Whenever entrepreneurs sell stock to the public, they automatically dilute their ownership in their businesses. Most owners retain a majority interest in the business, but they may still run the risk of unfriendly takeovers years later after selling more stock.

Loss of control. If enough shares are sold in a public offering, a founder risks losing control of the company. If a large block of shares falls into the hands of dissident stockholders, they could vote the existing management team (including the founder) out.

Loss of privacy. Taking their companies public can be a big ego boost for owners, but they must realize that their companies are no longer solely theirs. Information that was once private must be available for public scrutiny. The initial prospectus and the continuous reports filed with the Securities and Exchange Commission (SEC) disclose a variety of information about the company and its operations—from financial data and raw material sources to legal matters and patents to *anyone*—including competitors. One study found that loss of privacy and loss of control were the most commonly cited as the reasons that CEOs choose not to attempt IPOs.[34]

Reporting to the SEC. Operating as a publicly held company is expensive. Publicly held companies must file periodic reports with the SEC, which often requires a more powerful accounting system, a larger accounting staff, and greater use of attorneys and other professionals. Complying with the SEC's accounting and filing requirements alone can cost $150,000 a year.

Filing expenses. A public stock offering usually is an expensive way to generate funds for start-up or expansion. For the typical small company, the cost of a public offering is around 12 percent of the capital raised. On small offerings, costs can eat up as much as 40 percent of the capital raised, while on offerings above $20 million, just 5 percent will go to cover expenses.[35] Once an offering exceeds $10 million, its relative issuing costs drop. The largest cost is the underwriter's commission, which is typically 7 percent of the proceeds on offerings less than $10 million and 13 percent on those over that amount.

Accountability to shareholders. The capital that entrepreneurs manage and risk is no longer just their own. The manager of a publicly held firm is accountable to the company's shareholders. Indeed, the law requires that he recognize and abide by a relationship built on trust. Profit and return on investment become the primary concerns for investors. If the stock price of a newly public company falls, shareholder lawsuits are inevitable. Investors whose shares decline in value often sue the company's managers for fraud and the failure to disclose the potential risks to which their investment exposes them. After the technology company in which he purchased stock failed, one investor, rather than filing a lawsuit, turned his now worthless stock certificates (that at one point were worth $8.5 million) into placemats for his kitchen table![36]

Pressure for short-term performance. In privately held companies, entrepreneurs are free to follow their strategies for success, even if those strategies take years to produce results. When a company goes public, however, entrepreneurs quickly learn that shareholders are impatient and expect results immediately. Founders are under constant pressure to produce growth in profits and in market share, which requires them to maintain a delicate balance between short-term results and long-term strategy.

Loss of focus. As impatient as they can be, entrepreneurs often find the time demands of an initial public offering frustrating and distracting. Managing the IPO takes time away from managing the company.

Working on an IPO can consume as much as 75 percent of top managers' time, robbing top managers of their ability to manage the business effectively.

Timing. While it prepares its offering, a company also runs the risk that the market for IPOs or for a particular issue may go sour. Factors beyond managers' control, such as declines in the stock market and potential investors' jitters, can quickly slam shut a company's "window of opportunity" for an IPO. *For instance, Divine interVentures, an Internet incubator, filed for an IPO just before the market for high-tech stocks soured. Founder Flip Filipowski initially planned to raise $300 million in the offering. Seven months later, Divine interVentures managed to complete its IPO, but the company raised just $129 million. Divine interVentures was fortunate in some respects; many companies planning IPOs were forced to withdraw their proposed stock offerings altogether.[37]*

The Registration Process. Taking a company public is a complicated, bureaucratic process that usually takes several months to complete. Many experts compare the IPO process to running a corporate marathon, and both the company and its management team must be in shape and up to the grueling task. The typical entrepreneur *cannot* take his company public alone. It requires a coordinated effort from a team of professionals, including company executives, an accountant, a securities attorney, a financial printer, and at least one underwriter. The key steps in taking a company public follow.

Choose the Underwriter. The single most important ingredient in making a successful IPO is selecting a capable **underwriter** (or **investment banker**). The underwriter serves two primary roles: helping to prepare the registration statement for the issue and promoting the company's stock to potential investors. The underwriter works with company managers as an advisor in preparing the registration statement that must be filed with the SEC, promoting the issue in a road show, pricing the stock, and providing after-market support. Once the registration statement is finished, the underwriter's primary job is selling the company's stock through an underwriting syndicate of other investment bankers it develops.

Negotiate a Letter of Intent. To begin an offering, the entrepreneur and the underwriter must negotiate a **letter of intent,** which outlines the details of the deal. The letter of intent covers a variety of important issues, including the type of underwriting, its size and price range, the underwriter's commission, and any warrants and options included. It almost always states that the underwriter is not bound to the offering until it is executed—usually the day before or the day of the offering. However, the letter usually creates a binding obligation for the company to pay any direct expenses the underwriter incurs relating to the offer.

The letter of intent covers a variety of important issues, including the type of underwriting, its size and price range, the underwriter's commission, and any warrants and options included. There are two types of underwriting agreements: firm commitment and best effort. In a **firm commitment agreement,** the underwriter agrees to purchase all of the shares in the offering and then resells them to investors. This agreement *guarantees* that the company will receive the required funds, and most large underwriters use it. In a **best efforts agreement,** the underwriter merely agrees to use its best efforts to sell the company's shares and does not guarantee the company will receive the needed financing. The managing underwriter acts as an agent, selling as many shares as possible through the syndicate. Some best-effort contracts are all or nothing—if the underwriter cannot sell all of the shares, the offering is withdrawn. Another version of the best efforts agreement is to set a minimum number of shares that must be sold for the issue to be completed. These methods are riskier because the company has no guarantee of raising the required capital.

The company and the underwriter must decide on the size of the offering and the price of the shares. To keep the stock active in the aftermarket, most underwriters prefer to offer a *minimum* of 400,000 to 500,000 shares. A smaller number of shares inhibits sufficiently broad distribution. Most underwriters recommend selling 25 percent and 40 percent of the company in the IPO. They also strive to price the issue so that the total value of the offering is at least $8 million to $15 million (Although there are exceptions; some underwriters, especially regional ones, are interested in doing IPOs in the $2 million to $5 million range). To meet these criteria and to keep interest in the issue high, the underwriter usually recommends an initial price between $10 and $20 per share.

Most letters of intent include a **lock-up agreement** that prevents the sale of insider. shares, those owned by directors, managers, founders, employees, and other insiders, for 12 to 36 months. The sale of these shares early in a company's public life could send negative signals to investors, eroding their confidence in the stock and pushing its price downward.

Prepare the Registration Statement. After a company signs the letter of intent, the next task is to prepare the **registration statement** to be filed with the SEC. This document describes both the company and the stock offering and discloses information about the risks of investing. It includes information on the use of the proceeds, the company's history, its financial position, its capital structure, any risks it faces, its managers, and many other details. The statement is extremely comprehensive and may take months to develop. To prepare the statement, entrepreneurs must rely on their team of professionals.

File with the SEC. When the statement is finished (with the exception of pricing the shares, proceeds, and commissions, which cannot be determined until just before the issue goes to market), the company officially files the statement with the SEC and awaits the review of the Division of Corporate Finance. The Division sends notice of any deficiencies in the registration statement to the company's attorney in a comment letter. The company and its team of professionals must cure all of the deficiencies in the statement noted by the comment letter. Finally, the company files the revised registration statement, along with a pricing amendment (giving the price of the shares, the proceeds, and the commissions).

Wait to Go Effective. While waiting for the SEC's approval, the managers and the underwriters are busy. The underwriters are building a syndicate of other underwriters who will market the company's stock. (No sales can be made prior to the effective date of the offering, however.) The SEC also limits the publicity and information a company may release during this quiet period (which officially starts when the company reaches a preliminary agreement with the managing underwriter and ends 90 days after the effective date).

Securities laws do permit a **road show**, a gathering of potential syndicate members sponsored by the managing underwriter. Its purpose is to promote interest among potential underwriters in the IPO by featuring the company, its management, and the proposed deal. The managing underwriter and key company officials barnstorm major financial centers at a grueling pace. *During the road show for Ashford.com, an online retailer of luxury goods that raised $75 million in its IPO, top managers courted potential investors on two continents, hitting 24 cities in just 14 days! "In one day, we had a breakfast meeting in Frankfurt, flew to Paris for lunch meetings, then to New York, and* finally to Baltimore," says David Gow, Ashford's chief financial officer. "We kept gaining hours. It was the never-ending day."[38]

On the last day before the registration statement becomes effective, the company signs the formal underwriting agreement. The final settlement, or closing, takes place a few days after the effective date for the issue. At this meeting the underwriters receive their shares to sell and the company receives the proceeds of the offering.

Typically, the entire process of going public takes from 60 to 180 days, but it can take much longer if the issuing company is not properly prepared for the process.

Meet State Requirements. In addition to satisfying the SEC's requirements, a company also must meet the securities laws in all states in which the issue is sold. These state laws (or "blue-sky" laws) vary drastically from one state to another, and the company must comply with them.

Simplified Registrations and Exemptions

The IPO process described above (called an S-1 filing) requires maximum disclosure in the initial filing and discourages most small businesses from using it. Fortunately, the SEC allows several exemptions from this full-disclosure process for small businesses. Many small businesses that go public choose one of these simplified options the SEC has designed for small companies. The SEC has established the following simplified registration statements and exemptions from the registration process:

Regulation S-B. Regulation S-B is a simplified registration process for small companies seeking to make initial or subsequent public offerings. Not only does this regulation simplify the initial filing requirements with the SEC, but it also reduces the ongoing disclosure and filings required of companies. Its primary goals are to open the doors to capital markets to smaller companies by cutting the paperwork and the costs of raising capital. Companies using the simplified registration process have two options: Form SB-1, a "transitional" registration statement for companies issuing less than $10 million worth of securities over a 12-month period and Form SB-2, reserved for small companies seeking more than $10 million in a 12-month period.

To be eligible for the simplified registration process under Regulation S-B, a company must:

- Be based in the U.S. or Canada
- Have revenues of less than $25 million
- Have outstanding publicly held stock worth no more than $25 million
- Not be an investment company
- Provide audited financial statements for two fiscal years

The goal of Regulation S-B's simplified registration requirements is to enable smaller companies to go public without incurring the expense of a full-blown registration. Total costs for a Regulation S-B offering are approximately $35,000.

Regulation D (Rule 504): Small Company Offering Registration (SCOR). Created in the late 1980s, the Small Company Offering Registration (also known as the Uniform Limited Offering Registration, ULOR) now is available in 47 states. A little-known tool, SCOR is designed to make it easier and less expensive for small companies to sell their stock to the public by eliminating the requirement for registering the offering with the SEC. The whole process typically costs less than half of what a traditional public offering costs. Entrepreneurs using SCOR will need an attorney and an accountant to help them with the issue, but many can get by without a securities lawyer, which can save tens of thousands of dollars. Some entrepreneurs even choose to market their companies' securities themselves (e.g., to customers), saving the expense of hiring a broker. However, selling an issue is both time and energy consuming, and most SCOR experts recommend hiring a professional securities or brokerage firm to sell the company's shares. The SEC's objective in creating SCOR was to give small companies the same access to equity financing that large companies have via the stock market while bypassing many of the same costs and filing requirements.

The capital ceiling on a SCOR issue is $1 million, and the price of each share must be at least $5. That means that a company can sell no more than 200,000 shares (making the stock less attractive to stock manipulators). A SCOR offering requires only minimal notification to the SEC. The company must file a standardized disclosure statement, the U-7, which consists of 50 fill-in-the-blank questions. The form, which asks for information such as how much money the company needs, what the money will be used for, what investors receive, how investors can sell their investments, and other pertinent questions also serves as a business plan, a state securities offering registration, a disclosure document, and a prospectus. Entrepreneurs using SCOR may advertise their companies' offerings and can sell them directly to any investor with no restrictions and no minimums. An entrepreneur can sell practically any kind of security through a SCOR, including common stock, preferred stock, convertible preferred stock, stock options, stock warrants, and others.

Dwayne Fosseen, founder of Mirenco, Inc., a company that has developed patented technology to improve the fuel economy, reduce the emissions, and lower the maintenance costs associated with cars and trucks, relied on a SCOR offering to secure an early round of outside capital for his business. After launching Mirenco with his own funds, Fosseen obtained patents for his technology and then landed a grant from the Department of Energy. Needing more capital for expansion, Mirenco raised money through both SB-2 and SCOR offerings. Based in tiny Radcliffe, Iowa, Mirenco, whose shares trade on the OTC Bulletin Board, used the proceeds of its offerings to build a new headquarters, to fund more research and development, and to expand the market for its innovative products.[39]

Dwayne Fosseen, founder of Mirenco, Inc., used multiple sources of financing, including both SB and SCOR offerings, to raise the capital to develop and market this device that improves vehicles' fuel economy.

A SCOR offering offers entrepreneurs needing equity financing several *advantages*:

- Access to a sizeable pool of equity funds without the expense of full registration with the SEC. Companies often can complete a SCOR offering for less than $25,000.
- Few restrictions on the securities to be sold and on the investors to whom they can be sold.
- The ability to market the offering through advertisements to the public.
- Young or start-up companies can qualify.
- No requirement of audited financial statements for offering less than $500,000.
- Faster approval of the issue from regulatory agencies.
- The ability to make the offering in several states at once.

There are, of course, some *disadvantages* to using SCOR to raise needed funds:

- Not every state yet recognizes SCOR offerings.
- Partnerships cannot make SCOR offerings.
- A company can raise no more than $1 million in a 12-month period.
- An entrepreneur must register the offering in every state in which shares of stock will be sold, although current regulations allow simultaneous registration in multiple states.
- The process can be time consuming, distracting an entrepreneur from the daily routine of running the company. A limited secondary market for the securities may limit investors' interest. Currently, SCOR shares must be traded through brokerage firms that make small markets in specific stocks. However, the Pacific Stock Exchange and the NASDAQ's electronic bulletin board recently began listing SCOR stocks, so the secondary market for them has broadened.

Regulation D (Rules 505 and 506): Private Placements. Rules 505 and 506 are exemptions from federal registration requirements that give emerging companies the opportunity to sell stock through private placements without actually going public. In a private placement, the company sells its shares directly to private investors without having to register them with the SEC. *For example, Will Mullin, founder of Longport Inc., a company that makes a high-frequency portable scanner for medical use, made a private equity placement to finance the company's early growth. Longport used the money to expand its sales and marketing efforts and to reach new markets. Longport's stock now trades on the Over-the-Counter Bulletin Board.*[40]

A *Rule 505* offering has a higher capital ceiling than a SCOR offering ($5 million) in a 12-month period but imposes more restrictions (no more than 35 nonaccredited investors, no advertising of the offer, and more stringent disclosure requirements).

Rule 506 imposes no ceiling on the amount that can be raised, but, like a Rule 505 offering, it limits the issue to 35 "nonaccredited" investors and prohibits advertising the offer to the public. There is no limit on the number of accredited investors, however. Rule 506 also requires detailed disclosure of relative information, but the extent depends on the size of the offering.

These Regulation D Rules minimize the expense and the time required to raise equity capital for small businesses. Fees for private placements typically range from 1 to 5 percent rather than the 7 to 13 percent underwriters normally charge for managing a public offering. Offerings made under Regulation D do impose limitations and demand certain disclosures, but they only require a company to file a simple form (Form D) with the SEC within 15 days of the first sale of stock.

IN THE FOOTSTEPS OF AN ENTREPRENEUR
Financing Healthy Growth

In 1996, Rosemary Deahl launched HeartWise Express, a Chicago restaurant that features healthy, high-quality fast food. With its menu of salads, sandwiches, and vegetarian dishes, HeartWise offers diners a healthier alternative to traditional fast food. The menu even lists the calories, fat, cholesterol, sodium, and fiber content of each one of the more than 55 offerings available to diners. HeartWise's high-volume location in the Loop takes a big bite out of the company's revenues (about 17 percent), but it also produces enough customers to keep the company profitable. Deahl manages to generate an impressive sales volume even though the restaurant is open only from 6:30 A.M. to 6 P.M. Monday through Friday and caters only to the breakfast and lunch crowd. Deahl has experimented with evening hours, but they did not prove to be cost effective.

Deahl and her husband have invested $2.5 million of their own money in the restaurant, which now boasts sales of more than $1 million a year and a net profit margin of about 5 percent. Their goal ultimately is to build HeartWise Express into a national chain. To get there, however, the Deahls need $5 million to develop eight stores that will serve as a springboard for future growth. Two major questions face the Deahls:

- Can a national chain of healthy fast-food restaurants be successful?

- If so, where can they get the financing to build the eight restaurants and, ultimately, a chain of restaurants?

The National Restaurant Association (NRA) reports that diners have expressed greater interest in more nutritional menu items in the last several years. Half of the NRA's members say that they have seen increased interest in low-fat menu items from their customers. Forty percent of all restaurants promote menu items because of their health and nutritional benefits according to the NRA. Still, most fast-food outlets thrive by offering menus loaded with fat, calories, and cholesterol.

The Deahls are considering their financing options. Their first task is to raise enough capital to build the eight restaurants so they can prove their concept has national appeal.

1. Use the National Restaurant Association's Web site *(www.restaurant.org)* and Web search engines to research trends in the restaurant industry. On a scale of 0 (low) to 10 (high), how would you rate HeartWise Express's chances of successfully expanding into a national chain? Explain.

2. Assume the role of consultant to the Deahls. Where would you recommend they search for the capital to build eight restaurants? Explain your reasoning.

3. Assume that the Deahls are successful with their eight new restaurants. How should they finance the expansion of their restaurant chain to the national level? Explain.

Sources: Adapted from Cynthia E. Griffin, "Mass Appeal," *Entrepreneur,* July 2001, pp. 53–54; Neil D. Rosenberg, "It's Fast, It's Trendy, and (Surprise) . . . It's Healthy," *Milwaukee Journal Sentinel, www.jsonline.com/alive/nutrition/aug99/food-fat23082299.asp*; National Restaurant Association, *www.restaurant.org*.

Section 4(6). Section 4(6) covers private placements and is similar to Regulation D, Rules 505 and 506. It does not require registration on offers up to $5 million if they are made only to accredited investors.

Intrastate Offerings (Rule 147). Rule 147 governs intrastate offerings, those sold only to investors in a single state by a company doing business in that state. To qualify, a company must be incorporated in the state, maintain its executive offices there, have 80 percent of its assets there, derive 80 percent of its revenues from the state, and use 80 percent of the offering proceeds for business in the state. There is no ceiling on the amount of the offering. *Gary Hoover put up just $5,000 of his own money and* *convinced several private investors to purchase $850,000 worth of preferred stock to launch TravelFest, a retail store that caters to travelers. As the company grew, Hoover decided to make an intrastate offering under Rule 147 to raise the money he needed for expansion. He registered the offering in TravelFest's home state of Texas, where resident investors purchased $5.6 million in convertible preferred stock.*[41]

Regulation A. Regulation A, although currently not used often, allows an exemption for offerings up to $5 million over a 12-month period. Regulation A imposes few restrictions, but it is more costly than the other types of exempted offerings, usually running between $80,000 and $120,000. The primary difference between a SCOR offering and a Regulation A offering is that a company must register its SCOR offering only in the states where it will sell its stock; in a Regulation A offering, the company also must file an offering statement with the SEC. Like a SCOR offering, a Regulation A offering allows a company to sell its shares directly to investors. *For instance, when Blue Fish Clothing Inc, an all-natural women's clothing company, needed money to fuel its rapid growth, founder Jennifer Barclay decided to make a direct public offering under Regulation A, selling 800,000 shares at $5 each. "Banks wouldn't provide the funds, and venture capital firms wanted a huge percentage of the company," says Barclay. Blue Fish publicized its $4 million offering through mailings, advertisements, fish-shaped hanging tags on its garments, and word-of-mouth among its base of 30,000 loyal customers and supporters. Blue Fish, whose shares are traded on the Chicago Stock Exchange, used the offering's proceeds to build new retail stores, to install a computerized information system, and to expand its management team.*[42]

Direct Stock Offerings. Many of the simplified registrations and exemptions discussed above give entrepreneurs the power to sidestep investment bankers and sell their companies' stock offerings directly to investors and, in the process, save themselves thousands of dollars in underwriting fees. By going straight to Main Street instead of through underwriters on Wall Street, entrepreneurs cut out the underwriter's commission, many legal expenses, and most registration fees. Entrepreneurs willing to handle the paperwork requirements and to market their own shares can make direct public offerings (DPOs) for about 6 percent of the total amount of the issue, compared with 13 percent for a traditional stock offering. *Thanksgiving Coffee Company, a business that sells organically grown coffee and related products, recently engineered a successful direct public offering. Founders Paul and Joan Katzeff targeted their base of loyal customers and those who supported their company's focus on social responsibility. In addition to a notice of the offering on the Thanksgiving Coffee's Web site, the company included announcements in customers' orders, in strategic locations throughout the store, and in some magazines and newspapers. Within a few months, Thanksgiving Coffee had sold all of the shares in its offering.*[43]

The World Wide Web has opened a new avenue for direct public offerings and is one of the fastest-growing sources of capital for small businesses. Much of the Web's appeal as a fund-raising tool stems from its ability to reach large numbers of prospective investors very quickly and at a low cost. The Web enables a small company to make its investment prospectus available to the world at a minimal cost. Companies making direct stock offerings on the Web most often make them under either Regulation A or Regulation D and usually generate between $300,000 and $4 million for the company.

Direct public offerings work best for companies that have a single product or related product lines, a base of customers who are loyal to the company, good name recognition, and annual sales between $3 million and $25 million. The first company to make a successful DPO over the Internet was Spring Street Brewing, a microbrewery founded by Andy Klein. Klein raised $1.6 million in a Regulation A offering in 1996. Companies that make successful DPOs of their stock over the Web must meet the same standards as companies making stock offerings using more traditional methods. Experts caution Web-based fund seekers to make sure their electronic prospectuses meet SEC and state requirements. Table 14.4 provides a brief quiz to help entrepreneurs determine whether their companies would be good candidates for a DPO.

Foreign Stock Markets

Sometimes, foreign stock markets offer entrepreneurs access to equity funds more readily than U.S. markets. The United Kingdom's Unlisted Securities Market and the Off Exchange (OFEX) as well as the Vancouver Stock exchange are especially attractive to small companies. Both encourage equity listings of small companies, and the costs of offerings are usually lower than in the United States. *Thomas Burnham, founder of South Beach Cafe, turned to OFEX to raise the $700,000 he needed to open his third cafe in London. After opening two successful locations in Michigan, Burnham decided to take his gourmet cafe concept international and to use foreign capital to finance the expansion. After submitting a business plan and a fairly simple prospectus, he had made a successful public offering on OFEX, raising $750,000. Five months after the offering, the first South Beach Cafe in London opened its doors. Burnham's first foreign offering proved so successful that he returned a year later and raised $3 million to fuel the company's expansion into Europe.*[44]

Table 14.4

Is a Direct Public Offering for You?

Drew Field, an expert in direct public offerings, has developed the following 10-question quiz to help entrepreneurs decide whether their companies are good candidates for a DPO.

1. Does your company have a history of consistently profitable operations under the present management?
2. Is your company's present management team honest, socially responsible, and competent?
3. In 10 words or fewer, can you explain the nature of your business to laypeople new to investing?
4. Would your company excite prospective investors, making them want to share in its future?
5. Does your company have natural affinity groups, such as customers with strong emotional loyalty?
6. Do members of your natural affinity groups have discretionary cash to risk for long-term gains?
7. Would your company's natural affinity groups recognize your company's name and consider your offering materials?
8. Can you get the names, addresses, and telephone numbers of affinity group members, as well as some demographic information about them?
9. Can a high-level company employee spend half-time for six months as a DPO project manager?
10. Does your company have—or can you obtain—audited financial statements for at least the last two fiscal years?

Sources: Drew Field Direct Public Offers, Screen Test for a Direct Public Offering *www.dfdpo.com/screen.htm*; Stephanie Gruner, "Could You Do a DPO?" *Inc.*, December 1996, p. 70.

CHAPTER SUMMARY

1. Explain the differences in the three types of capital small businesses require: fixed, working, and growth.
   - Capital is any form of wealth employed to produce more wealth. Three forms of capital are commonly identified: fixed capital, working capital, and growth capital.
   - Fixed capital is used to purchase a company's permanent or fixed assets; working capital represents the business's temporary funds, and is used to support the business's normal short-term operations; growth capital requirements surface when an existing business is expanding or changing its primary direction.
2. Describe the various sources of equity capital available to entrepreneurs, including personal savings, friends and relatives, angels, partners, corporations, venture capital, and public stock offerings.
   - The most common source of financing a business is the owner's personal savings. After emptying their own pockets, the next place entrepreneurs turn for capital is family members and friends. Angels are private investors who not only invest their money in small companies, but they also offer valuable advice and counsel to them. Some business owners have success financing their companies by taking on limited partners as investors or by forming an alliance with a corporation, often a customer or a supplier. Venture capital companies are for-profit, professional investors looking for fast-growing companies in "hot" industries. When screening prospects, venture capital firms look for competent management, a competitive edge, a growth industry, and important intangibles that will make a business successful. Some owners choose to attract capital by taking their companies public, which requires registering the public offering with the SEC.
3. Describe the process of "going public," as well as its advantages and disadvantages.
   - Going public involves: (1) choosing the underwriter, (2) negotiating a letter of intent, (3) preparing the registration statement, (4) filing with the SEC, and (5) meeting state requirements.
   - Going public offers the advantages of raising large amounts of capital, improved access to future financing, improved corporate image, and gaining listing on a stock exchange. The disadvantages include dilution of the founder's ownership, loss of privacy, reporting to the SEC, filing expenses, and accountability to shareholders.
4. Explain the various simplified registrations and exemptions from registration available to small businesses wanting to sell securities to investors.
   - Rather than go through the complete registration process, some companies use one of the simplified registration options and exemptions available to small companies: Regulation S-B, Regulation D (Rule 504) Small Company Offering Registration (SCOR), Regulation D (Rule 505, and Rule 506) Private Placements, Section 4(6), Rule 147, Regulation A, direct stock offerings, and foreign stock markets.

DISCUSSION QUESTIONS

1. Why is it so difficult for most small business owners to raise the capital needed to start, operate, or expand their ventures?
2. What is capital? List and describe the three types of capital a small business needs for its operations.
3. Define equity financing. What advantage does it offer over debt financing?
4. What is the most common source of equity funds in a typical small business? If an owner lacks sufficient equity capital to invest in the firm, what options are available for raising it?
5. What guidelines should an entrepreneur follow if friends and relatives choose to invest in her business?
6. What is an "angel"? Assemble a brief profile of the typical private investor. How can entrepreneurs locate potential angels to invest in their businesses?

7. What advice would you offer an entrepreneur about to strike a deal with a private investor to avoid problems?
8. What types of businesses are most likely to attract venture capital? What investment criteria do venture capitalists use when screening potential businesses? How do these compare to the typical angel's criteria?
9. How do venture capital firms operate? Describe their procedure for screening investment proposals?
10. Summarize the major exemptions and simplified registrations available to small companies wanting to make public offerings of their stock.

BEYOND THE CLASSROOM

1. Interview several local business owners about how they financed their businesses. Where did their initial capital come from? Ask the following questions:
   a. How did you raise your starting capital? What percent did you supply on your own?
   b. What percent was debt capital and what percent was equity capital?
   c. Which of the sources of funds described in this chapter do you use? Are they used to finance fixed, working, or growth capital needs?
   d. How much money did you need to launch your businesses? Where did subsequent capital come from? What advice do you offer others seeking capital?
2. Contact a local private investor and ask him or her to address your class. (You may have to search to locate one!) What kinds of businesses does this angel prefer to invest in?

What screening criteria does he or she use? How are the deals typically structured?
3. Contact a local venture capitalist and ask him or her to address your class. What kinds of businesses does his or her company invest in? What screening criteria does the company use? How are deals typically structured?
4. Invite an investment banker or a financing expert from a local accounting firm to address your class about the process of taking a company public. What do they look for in a potential IPO candidate? What is the process, and how long does it usually take?
5. Interview the administrator of a financial institution offering a method of financing with which you are unfamiliar, and prepare a short report on its method of operation.
6. Contact your state's business development board and prepare a report on the financial assistance programs it offers small businesses.

TAKE IT TO THE NET

Visit the Scarborough/Zimmerer home page at **www.prenhall.com/scarborough** for updated information, online resources, Web-based exercises, and sample business plan.

ENDNOTES

1. Paul DeCeglie, "What About Me?" *Business Start-Ups,* June 2000, pp. 45–51.
2. Elaine Pofeldt, "Six Degrees of Capitalization," *Success,* January 2000, pp. 16, 57.
3. Silva Sansoni, "Burned Angels," *Forbes,* April 19, 1999, pp. 182–185.
4. Jacquelyn Lynn, "Secret to My Financing," *Entrepreneur,* May 2000, http://www.Entrepreneur.com/article/o,4621,2718 5,00.html.
5. Carrie Coolidge, "The Bootstrap Brigade," *Forbes,* December 28, 1998, pp. 90–91.
6. Simeon Furman, "Blood Is Thicker Than Ink," *Success,* September 2000, p. 22.
7. "Starting Up," *The Inc. 500,* October 31, 2001, pp. 78–79.
8. Paul Kvinta, "Frogskins, Shekels, Bucks, Moolah, Cash, Simoleans, Dough, Dinero: Everybody Wants It. Your Business Needs It. Here's How to Get It," *Smart Business,* August 2000, pp. 74–89.

9. Pamela Sherrid, "Angels of Capitalism," *U.S. News & World Report,* October 13, 1997, pp. 43–45.

10. Joanne Gordon, "Wings," *Forbes,* October 30, 2001, pp. 299–300.

11. "Is He an Angel or a Beatle?" *FSB,* October 2000, p. 39.

12. Wendy Taylor and Marty Jerome, "Pray," *Smart Business,* July 2000, p. 45; John Heylar, "The Venture Capitalist Next Door," *Fortune,* November 13, 2000, pp. 293–312.

13. Sansoni, "Burned Angels," pp. 182–185.

14. Juan Hovey, "Harley's Angels," *Success,* September 2000, pp. 66–68.

15. Jennifer Keeney and Ron Orol, "Touched by an Angel," *FSB,* April 2001, p. 34.

16. Jennifer Lawton, "Making Friends: The Name of the Angel Game," *EntreWorld.org,* February 1, 2000, *www.entreworld.org.*

17. Kvinta, "Frogskins, Shekels, Bucks, Moolah, Cash, Simoleans, Dough, Dinero: Everybody Wants It. Your Business Needs It. Here's How to Get It," p. 78.

18. Loren Fox, "Heaven Can't Wait," *Business 2.0,* March 20, 2001, pp. 123–124; Anne Ashby Gilbert, "Small Stakes in Small Business," *Fortune,* April 12, 1999, p. 162[H]; Sherrid, "Angels of Capitalism"; Heylar, "The Venture Capitalist Next Door."

19. Bruce J. Blechmna, "Step Right Up," *Entrepreneur,* June 1993, pp. 20–25.

20. Heylar, "The Venture Capitalist Next Door."

21. Nancy Scarlato, "Money," *Business Start-Ups,* December 1995, pp. 50–51; Gianna Jacobson, "Raise Money Now," *Success,* November 1995, pp. 39–50.

22. Ian Springsteel, "Need More Money? Find a Big White Knight," *FSB,* September 2000, pp. 33–36.

23. Geoff Williams, "Supersize It," *Entrepreneur,* August 2001, p. 49.

24. Arlyn Tobias Gajilan, "Big Money on Campus," *Your Company,* October 1999, p. 34.

25. Warren P. Strobel, "The Spy Who Funded Me (and My Start-Up)," *U.S. News & World Report,* July 17, 2000, pp. 38–39.

26. PricewaterhouseCoopers MoneyTree Survey, *www.pwcmoneytree.com/stage.asp?year=3 ; National Venture Capital Association,* www.nvca.org.

27. D. M. Osborne, "Dear John," *Inc.,* May 2001, pp. 44–48.

28. PricewaterhouseCoopers MoneyTree Survey, *www.pwcmoneytree.com/PDFS/mt_q3_2001.pdf.*

29. Hilary Stout, "Two Start-Up Partners Turn Down Millions, and Are Happier for It," *Wall Street Journal,* May 2, 2001, p. B2.

30. Dave Pell, "What's Old Is New Again," *FSB,* July/August 2000, p. 122.

31. Kvinta, "Frogskins, Shekels, Bucks, Moolah, Cash, Simoleans, Dough, Dinero: Everybody Wants It. Your Business Needs It. Here's How to Get It," p. 87.

32. IPO.com, *www.ipo.com*

33. David R. Evanson, "Tales of Caution in Going Public," *Nation's Business,* June 1996, p. 58.

34. Roberta Maynard, "Are You Ready to Go Public?" *Nation's Business,* January 1995, pp. 30–32.

35. Philip W. Taggart, Roy Alexander, and Robert M. Arnold, "Deciding Whether to Go Public," *Nation's Business,* May 1991, p. 52.

36. Sally McGrane, "The Crash's Silver Lining," *Forbes,* September 10, 2001, p. 26.

37. "The Little IPO That Couldn't," *Fortune,* September 4, 2000, p. 358; IPO.com, *www.ipo.com.*

38. Kvinta, "Frogskins, Shekels, Bucks, Moolah, Cash, Simoleans, Dough, Dinero: Everybody Wants It. Your Business Needs It. Here's How to Get It," p. 88.

39. Mirenco, Inc., *www.mirenco.com/Company/SECFilings.asp;* Tom Stewart-Gordon, SCOR-Report, *www.scor-report.com.*

40. David R. Evanson and Art Beroff, "Board Games," *Entrepreneur,* January 2000, *www.entrepreneur.com/Magazines/Copy_of_MA_SegArticle/0,4453,232490——1-,00.html.*

41. Toni Mack, "They Stole My Baby," *Forbes,* February 12, 1996, pp. 90–91.

42. Drew Field Direct Public Offerings: Client Summaries, Blue Fish Clothing, *www.dfdpo.com/clientsum9.htm;* "A Fishy Success," *Business Ethics,* July/August 1996, p. 6; Paul DeCeglie, "Public Enemy?" *Business Start-Ups,* November 1999, pp. 38–48.

43. Drew Field Public Offerings: Client Summaries, Thanksgiving Coffee Company, *www.dfdpo.com/clientsum11.htm;* Thanksgiving Coffee Company, *www.thanksgivingcoffee.com/*

44. "Go Public Overseas," *Success,* September 1997, pp. 89–96.

Chapter 15

Sources of Debt Financing

> *Capital is to the progress of society what gas is to a car.*

—JAMES TRUSLOW ADAMS

> *Don't ever borrow a little bit of money because when you borrow a little bit of money, you have a serious creditor if you run short. And, if you borrow a lot of money, you have a partner when you get into trouble.*

—FRED SMITH, FOUNDER, FEDERAL EXPRESS

Upon completion of this chapter, you will be able to:

1. Describe the various sources of debt capital and the advantages and disadvantages of each.
2. Explain the types of financing available from nonbank sources of credit.
3. Identify the sources of government financial assistance and the loan programs these agencies offer.
4. Describe the various loan programs the Small Business Administration offers.
5. Discuss state and local economic development programs.
6. Discuss valuable methods of financing growth and expansion internally with bootstrap financing.
7. Explain how to avoid becoming a victim of a loan scam.

Debt financing involves the funds that the small business owner borrows and must repay with interest. Lenders of capital are more numerous than investors, although small business loans can be just as difficult (if not more difficult) to obtain. Although borrowed capital allows entrepreneurs to maintain complete ownership of their businesses, it must be carried as a liability on the balance sheet as well as be repaid with interest at some point in the future. In addition, because small businesses are considered to be greater risks than bigger corporate customers, they must pay higher interest rates because of the risk–return trade-off—the higher the risk, the greater the return demanded. Most small firms pay the **prime rate,** the interest rate banks charge their most creditworthy customers, *plus* two or more percentage points. Still, the cost of debt financing often is lower than that of equity financing. Because of the higher risks associated with providing equity capital to small companies, investors demand greater returns than lenders. Also, unlike equity financing, debt financing does not require an entrepreneur to dilute her ownership interest in the company.

The need for debt capital can arise from a number of sources, but financial experts identify the following reasons business owners should consider borrowing money[1]:

- *Increasing the company's workforce and/or inventory to boost sales.* Sufficient working capital is the fuel that feeds a company's growth.
- *Gaining market share.* Businesses often need extra capital as their customer bases expand and they incur the added expense of extending credit to customers.
- *Purchasing new equipment.* Financing new equipment that can improve productivity, increase quality, and lower operating expenses often takes more capital than a growing company can generate internally.
- *Refinancing existing debt.* As companies become more established, they can negotiate more favorable borrowing terms compared to their start-up days, when entrepreneurs take whatever money they can get at whatever rate they can get. Replacing high-interest loans with loans carrying lower interest rates can improve cash flow significantly.
- *Taking advantage of cash discounts.* Suppliers sometimes offer discounts to customers who pay their invoices early. As you will learn in Chapter 17, "Purchasing, Quality Management, and Vendor Analysis," business owners should take advantage of cash discounts in most cases.
- *Buying the building in which the business is located.* Many entrepreneurs start out renting the buildings that house their businesses; however, if location is crucial to their success, it may be wise to purchase the location.
- *Establishing a relationship with a lender.* If a business has never borrowed money, taking out a loan and developing a good repayment and credit history can pave the way for future financing. Smart business owners know that bankers who understand their businesses play an integral role in their companies' ultimate success.
- *Retiring debt held by a "nonrelationship" creditor.* Entrepreneurs find that lenders who have no real interest in their companies' long-term success or do not understand their businesses can be extremely difficult to work with. They prefer to borrow money from lenders who are willing to help them achieve their business mission and goals.
- *Foreseeing a downturn in business.* Establishing access to financing before a business slowdown hits insulates a company from a serious cash crisis and protects it from failure.

Entrepreneurs seeking debt capital are quickly confronted with an astounding range of credit options varying greatly in complexity, availability, and flexibility. Not all of these sources of debt capital are equally favorable, however. By understanding the various sources of capital—both commercial and government lenders—and their characteristics, entrepreneurs can greatly increase the chances of obtaining a loan. We now turn to the various sources of debt capital.

SOURCES OF DEBT CAPITAL

Commercial Banks

1. Describe the various sources of debt capital and the advantages and disadvantages of each.

Commercial banks are the very heart of the financial market, providing the greatest number and variety of loans to small businesses. One study by the Federal Reserve concluded that commercial banks provide about 54 percent of the traditional financing available to small businesses and that 80 percent of all loans to existing businesses come from banks![2] For small business owners, banks are lenders of *first* resort, especially as their companies grow (see Figure 15.1).

Banks tend to be conservative in their lending practices and prefer to make loans to established small businesses rather than to high-risk start-ups. One expert estimates that only 5 to 8 percent of business start-ups get bank financing.[3] Bankers want to see evidence of a company's successful track record before committing to a loan. They are concerned with a firm's operating past and will scrutinize its records to project its position in the immediate future. They also want proof of the stability of the firm's sales and about the ability of the product or service to generate adequate cash flows to ensure repayment of the loan. If they do make loans to a startup venture, banks like to see significant investment from the owner, sufficient cash flows to repay the loan, ample collateral to secure it, or a Small Business Administration (SBA) guarantee to insure it. Studies suggest that small banks (those with less than $300 million in assets) are most likely to lend money to small businesses.[4]

Figure 15.1
Financing from Commercial Banks by Company Size by Number of Employees
Source: Small Business Administration Office of Advocacy.

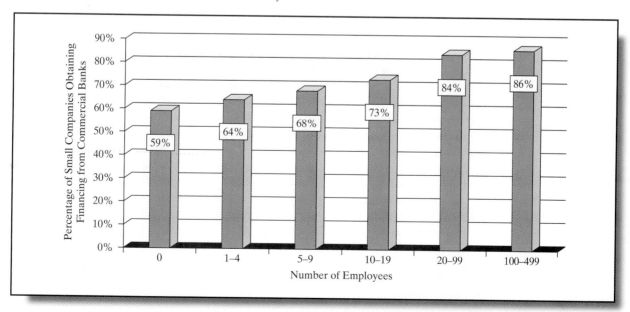

After banks refused to lend him $500,000 to purchase the rights to five Blimpie franchises in Michigan because of the risk involved, Todd Recknagel developed a plan to give bankers exactly what they wanted. He convinced four wealthy friends to guarantee the bank loan in exchange for 32 percent of his company's stock. A bank accepted his loan proposal, lending the money at just 0.5 percent above the prime rate and paving the way for Recknagel's success. He now owns eight Blimpie franchises, has repaid the original loan, repurchased the investor's stock, and has an SBA-guaranteed fixed-rate loan to finance growth.[5]

When evaluating a loan application, banks focus on a company's capacity to create positive cash flow because they know that's where the money to repay their loans will come from. The first question in most bankers' minds when reviewing an entrepreneur's business plan is "Can this business generate sufficient cash to repay the loan?" Even though they rely on collateral to secure their loans, the last thing banks want is for a borrower to default, forcing them to sell the collateral (often at "fire sale" prices) and use the proceeds to pay off the loan. *That's* why bankers stress cash flow when analyzing a loan request, especially for a business start-up. "Cash is more important than your mother," jokes one experienced borrower.[6]

Short-Term Loans

Short-term loans, extended for less than one year, are the most common type of commercial loan banks make to small companies. These funds typically are used to replenish the working capital account to finance the purchase of inventory, boost output, finance credit sales to customers, or take advantage of cash discounts. As a result, an owner repays the loan after converting inventory and receivables into cash. There are several types of short-term loans.

Commercial Loans (or "Traditional Bank Loans"). The basic short-term loan is the commercial bank's specialty. It is usually repaid as a lump sum within three to six months and is unsecured because secured loans are much more expensive to administer and maintain. In other words, the bank grants a loan to the small business owner without requiring him to pledge any specific collateral to support the loan in case of default. The owner is expected to repay the total amount of the loan at maturity. Sometimes the interest due on the loan is prepaid—deducted from the total amount borrowed. Until a small business is able to prove its financial strength and liquidity (cash flow) to the bank's satisfaction, it will probably not qualify for this kind of commercial loan.

Lines of Credit. One of the most common requests entrepreneurs make of banks is to establish a **line of credit,** a short-term loan with a preset limit that provides much-needed cash flow for day-to-day operations. With an approved line of credit, a business owner can borrow up to the predetermined ceiling at any time during the year quickly and conveniently by writing himself a loan. Banks usually limit the open line of credit to 40 to 50 percent of the firm's present working capital, although they will lend more for highly seasonal businesses. It is usually extended for one year (or more) and is secured by collateral, although some banks offer unsecured lines of credit to small companies with solid financial track records. A business typically pays a small handling fee (1 to 2 percent of the maximum amount of credit) plus interest on the amount borrowed—usually prime-plus-three points or more. One study of small businesses with lines of credit found that 76 percent used them; the remaining 24 percent have established their lines as a safety net but had not activated them.[7]

Rich McElaney, CEO of Micromarketing, a company that helps retailers prepare targeted direct mail campaigns, recently landed his company's first bank line of credit to finance its rapid growth and to diversify its customer base. Because of Micromarketing's track record of *success and its solid cash flow, McElaney had no trouble securing the $3 million line of credit.*[8]

Floor Planning. Floor planning is a form of financing frequently employed by retailers of "big ticket items" that are easily distinguishable from one another (usually by serial number), such as automobiles, boats, and major appliances. For example, a commercial bank finances Auto City's purchase of its inventory of automobiles and maintains a security interest in each car in the order by holding its title as collateral. Auto City pays interest on the loan monthly and repays the principal as the cars are sold. The longer a floor-planned item sits in inventory, the more it costs the business owner in interest expense. Banks and other floor planners often discourage retailers from using their money without authorization by performing spot checks to verify prompt repayment of the principal as items are sold.

Intermediate- and Long-Term Loans

Banks primarily are lenders of short-term capital to small businesses, although they will make certain intermediate- and long-term loans. Intermediate- and long-term loans are extended for one year or longer and are normally used to increase fixed- and growth-capital balances. Commercial banks grant these loans for starting a business, constructing a plant, purchasing real estate and equipment, and other long-term investments. Loan repayments are normally made monthly or quarterly.

Term Loans. Another common type of loan banks make to small businesses is a **term loan.** Typically unsecured, banks grant these loans to businesses whose past operating history suggests a high probability of repayment. Some banks make only secured term loans, however. Term loans impose restrictions (called **covenants**) on the business decisions an entrepreneur makes concerning the company's operations. For instance, a term loan may set limits on owners' salaries, prohibit further borrowing without the bank's approval, or submit financial reports and analyses on a particular schedule. An entrepreneur must understand all of the terms attached to a loan before accepting it.

Installment Loans. These loans are made to small firms for purchasing equipment, facilities, real estate, and other fixed assets. In financing equipment, a bank usually lends the small business from 60 to 80 percent of the equipment's value in return for a security interest in the equipment. The loan's amortization schedule typically coincides with the length of the equipment's usable life. When financing real estate (commercial mortgages), banks typically will lend up to 75 to 80 percent of the property's value and will allow a lengthier repayment schedule of 10 to 30 years.

Discounted Installment Contracts. Banks will also extend loans to small businesses when the owner pledges installment contracts as collateral. The process operates in the same manner as discounting accounts receivable (discussed later). For example, Acme Equipment Company sells several pieces of heavy equipment to General Contractors Inc. on an installment basis. To obtain a loan, Acme pledges the installment contract as collateral and receives a percentage of the contract's value from the bank. As Acme receives installment payments from General Contractors, it transfers the proceeds to the bank to satisfy the loan. If the installment contract is with a reliable business, the bank may lend the small firm 100 percent of the contract's value.

Character Loans. Banking regulatory changes intended to create jobs by increasing the credit available to small- and medium-sized companies now allow banks to make **character loans.** Rather than requiring entrepreneurs to prove their creditworthiness with financial statements, evaluations, appraisals, and tax returns, banks making

Too often, entrepreneurs communicate with their bankers only when they find themselves in a tight spot needing money. Unfortunately, that's not the best way to manage a working relationship with a bank. "Businesspeople have a responsibility to train their bankers in their businesses," says one lending advisor. "A good banker will stay close to the business, and a good business will stay close to the banker."

How can business owners develop and maintain a positive relationship with their bankers? The first step is picking the right bank and the right banker. Some banks are not terribly enthusiastic about making small business loans, and others target small businesses as their primary customers. It's a good idea to visit several banks—both small, community banks and large, national banks—and talk with a commercial loan officer about your banking needs and the bank's products and services. After finding the right banker, an entrepreneur must focus on maintaining effective *communication*. The best strategy is to keep bankers informed—*of both good news and bad.*

Tim Chen, owner of Keys Fitness Products, knows that's the secret to keeping bankers in his company's corner. He is always finding ways to show his bank that his company has proper financial controls in place. The former financial analyst makes it a point to explain to his bankers the intricate details of his company. He calls them twice each month to discuss "our supply sources, our pricing strategy, our marketing channels. We want them to be confident about our long-term growth prospects as well as our short-term results," says Chen. That means he also lets them know when problems arise in his wholesale exercise equipment business.

Chen's approach has impressed his bankers so much that they have raised his firm's line of credit from $50,000 to $4 million! What else can entrepreneurs do to manage their banking relationships?

- *Invite the banker to visit your company.* An on-site visit gives the banker the chance to see exactly what a company does and how it does it. It's also a great opportunity to show the bank where and how its money is put to use.

- *Make a good impression.* A company's physical appearance can go a long way toward making either a positive (or a negative) impression on a banker. Lenders appreciate clean, safe, orderly work environments and view sloppily maintained facilities (such as spills, leaks, and unnecessary clutter) as negatives.

- *Send customer mailings to the banker as well.* "Besides the numbers, we try to give our bankers a sense of our vision for the business," says Mitchell Goldstone, president of Thirty-Minute Photos Etc. Goldstone sends customer mailings to his bankers "so they know we're thinking about opportunities to generate money."

- *Send the banker samples of new products.* "I try to make my banker feel as if he's a partner," says Drew Santin, president of a product-development company. "Whenever we get a new machine, I go out of my way to show the banker what it does."

- *Show off your employees.* Bankers know that one of the most important components of building a successful company is a dedicated team of capable employees. Giving bankers the opportunity to visit with employees and ask them questions while touring a company can help alleviate fears that they are pumping their money into a high-risk "one-person show."

- *Know your company's assets.* Almost always interested in collateral, bankers will want to judge the quality of your company's assets—property, equipment, inventory, accounts receivable, and others. Be sure to point them out. "As you walk the lender through your business," says one experienced banker, "it's always a good idea to identify assets the banker might not think of."

- *Be prepared to personally guarantee any loans the bank makes to your business.* Even though many business owners choose the corporate form of ownership for its limited liability benefits, some are surprised when a banker asks them to make personal guarantees on business loans. It's a common practice, especially on small business loans.

(continued)

- *Keep your business plan up-to-date and make sure your banker gets a copy of it.* Bankers lend money to companies that can demonstrate that they will use the money wisely and productively. They also want to make sure that the company offers a high probability of repayment. The best way to provide bankers with that assurance is with a solid business plan.

- *Know how much money you need and how you will repay it.* When a banker asks "How much money

do you need?" the correct answer is not "How much can I get?"

1. What advantages do entrepreneurs gain by communicating openly with their bankers?

2. Why do so few entrepreneurs follow Tim Chen's example when dealing with their bankers?

3. What are the consequences of an entrepreneur failing to communicate effectively with a banker?

Sources: Adapted from Maggie Overfelt, "How to Raise Cash During Crunch Time," *FSB*, March 2001, pp. 35–36; Jenny McCune, "Getting Banks to Say 'Yes'," Bankrate.com, March 19, 2001, *www.bankrate.com/brm/news/biz/Capital_borrowing/200010319a.asp*; Joan Pryde, "Lending a Hand with Financing," *Nation's Business*, January 1998, pp. 53–59; Joseph W. May, "Be Frank with Your Bank," *Profit*, November/December 1996, pp. 54–55; "They'll Up Your Credit If . . ." *Inc.*, April 1994, p. 99; Jane Easter Bahls, "Borrower Beware," *Entrepreneur*, April 1994, p. 97; Jacquelyn Lynn, "You Can Bank on It," *Business Start-Ups*, August 1996, pp. 56–61; Stephanie Barlow, "Buddy System," *Entrepreneur*, March 1997, pp. 121–125; Carlye Adler, "Secrets from the Vault," *FSB*, June 2001, p. 33.

character loans base their lending decisions on the borrower's reputation and reliability (i.e., "character"). *Two entrepreneurs who co-founded a river touring business received a character loan from a small local bank. Because of their solid reputations in the community and their overall business experience, they were able to borrow $20,000 to purchase canoes, supplies, and safety equipment and to hire guides without even pledging any collateral. "We simply signed our names on the loan agreement and got the money to launch the company," says one of the partners.*

The accompanying *Gaining the Competitive Edge* feature describes how small business owners can maintain positive relationships with their bankers.

Nonbank Sources of Debt Capital

2. Explain the types of financing available from nonbank sources of credit.

Although they are usually the first stop for entrepreneurs in search of debt capital, banks are not the only lending game in town. We now turn our attention to other sources of debt capital that entrepreneurs can tap to feed their cash-hungry companies.

Asset-Based Lenders

Asset-based lenders, which are usually smaller commercial banks, commercial finance companies, or specialty lenders, allow small businesses to borrow money by pledging otherwise idle assets such as accounts receivable, inventory, or purchase orders as collateral. This form of financing works especially well for manufacturers, wholesalers, distributors, and other companies with significant stocks of inventory, accounts receivable, equipment, real estate, or other assets. Even unprofitable companies whose income statements could not convince loan officers to make traditional loans can get asset-based loans. These cash-poor but asset-rich companies can use normally unproductive assets—accounts receivable, inventory, equipment, and purchase orders—to finance rapid growth and the cash crises that often accompany it.

Although asset-based lenders consider a company's cash flow, they are much more interested in the quality of the assets pledged as collateral. The amount a small business can borrow through asset-based lending depends on the **advance rate,** the percentage of an asset's value that a lender will lend. For example, a company pledging $100,000 of accounts receivable might negotiate a 70 percent advance rate and qualify for a $70,000 asset-based loan. Advance rates can vary dramatically depending on the quality of the assets pledged and the lender. Because inventory is an illiquid asset (i.e., hard to sell), the advance rate on inventory-based loans is quite low, usually 10 to 50 percent. Steven Melick, CEO of the Sycamore Group, an e-business software developer, gets an 85 percent advance rate on his company's loans from GE Capital by pledging high-quality accounts receivable as collateral.[9] The most common types of asset-based financing are discounting accounts receivable and inventory financing.

Discounting Accounts Receivable. The most common form of secured credit is accounts receivable financing. Under this arrangement, a small business pledges its accounts receivable as collateral; in return, the lender advances a loan against the value of approved accounts receivable. The amount of the loan tendered is not equal to the face value of the accounts receivable, however. Even though the bank screens the firm's accounts and accepts only qualified receivables, it makes an allowance for the risk involved because some will be written off as uncollectible. A small business usually can borrow an amount equal to 55 to 80 percent of its receivables, depending on their quality. Generally, lenders will not accept receivables that are past due.

Many commercial finance companies engage in accounts receivable financing. *Kyle Jodice, founder of Milnucorp, a small distributor of products ranging from hula hoops to tank parts, uses accounts receivable financing from Action Capital, a commercial finance company in Atlanta, to get the cash he needs to purchase inventory. Action Capital advances money based on Milnucorp's accounts receivable. After Action Capital collects payment from Milnucorp's customers, typically within 40 to 60 days, the commercial finance company remits the payments to Jodice after subtracting the amount of the loan and the interest it charges.[10]*

Inventory Financing. Here, a small business loan is secured by its inventory of raw materials, work in process, and finished goods. If an owner defaults on the loan, the lender can claim the firm's inventory, sell it, and use the proceeds to satisfy the loan (assuming the bank's claim is superior to the claims of other creditors). Because inventory usually is not a highly liquid asset and its value can be difficult to determine, lenders are willing to lend only a portion of its worth, usually no more than 50 percent of the inventory's value. Most asset-based lenders avoid inventory-only deals; they prefer to make loans backed by inventory *and* more secure accounts receivable.

Jeffrey Martinez-Malo, president of Ocean World Fisheries USA, a company that imports shrimp and crab from Latin America to the United States, uses inventory financing from Gerber Trade Finance to avoid cash flow problems. Ocean World Fisheries' suppliers demand payment as soon as they ship an order of seafood. However, because the company's customers are scattered across the country, collecting its accounts takes time. Martinez-Milo now has a $600,000 line of credit secured by the company's inventory at 2 percent above the prime rate.[11]

Asset-based financing is a powerful tool. A small business that could obtain a $1 million line of credit with a bank would be able to borrow as much as $3 million by using accounts receivable as collateral. It is also an efficient method of borrowing because a small business owner has the money he needs when he needs it. In other words, the business pays only for the capital it actually needs and uses.

However, asset-based loans are more expensive than traditional bank loans because of the cost of originating and maintaining them and the higher risk involved. To ensure the quality of the assets supporting the loans they make, lenders must monitor borrowers' assets, perhaps as often as weekly, making paperwork requirements on these loans intimidating, especially to first-time borrowers. Rates usually run from two to eight percentage points (or more) above the prime rate. Because of this rate differential, small business owners should not use asset-based loans over the long term; their goal should be to establish their credit through asset-based financing and then to move up to a line of credit. Figure 15.2 shows the upward trend in asset-based borrowing since 1980.

Trade Credit

Because of its ready availability, trade credit is an extremely important source of financing to most entrepreneurs. When banks refuse to lend money to a start-up business because they see it as a bad credit risk, an entrepreneur may be able to turn to trade credit for capital. Getting vendors to extend credit in the form of delayed payments (e.g., "net 30" credit terms) usually is much easier for small businesses than obtaining bank financing. Essentially, a company receiving trade credit from a supplier is getting a short-term, interest-free loan for the amount of the goods purchased.

It is no surprise that businesses receive three dollars of credit from suppliers for every two dollars they receive from banks as loans.[12] Vendors and suppliers usually are willing to finance a small business owner's purchase of goods from 30 to 90 days, interest free. *For instance, Gus Walboldt, owner of AMCAL, a fine-art publishing company, uses supplier financing as an integral part of his company's 20-year growth plan. Because calendars represent a large portion of AMCAL's sales, its business is highly seasonal, which creates significant cash flow problems. "We would spend half the year flush with cash [and the other half] cash poor," says Walboldt. Walboldt worked out a financing arrangement with the companies that print the calendars. AMCAL pays the printers' labor and material costs when the calendars are printed during the summer months and then covers their profit margins when its cash flow swells in the fall.[13] The key to maintaining trade credit as a*

Figure 15.2
Asset-Based Loans (in Millions of $)
Source: Commercial Finance Association

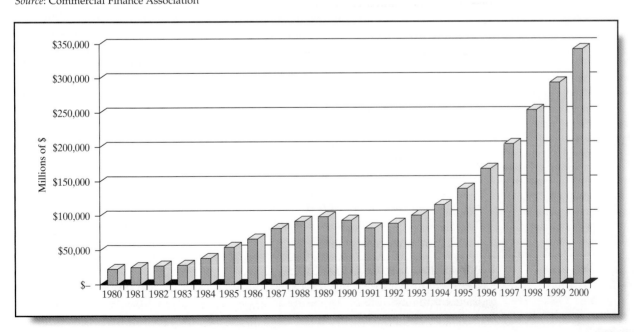

source of funds is establishing a consistent and reliable payment history with every vendor.

Equipment Suppliers

Most equipment vendors encourage business owners to purchase their equipment by offering to finance the purchase. This method of financing is similar to trade credit, but with slightly different terms. Usually, equipment vendors offer reasonable credit terms with only a modest down payment with the balance financed over the life of the equipment (often several years). In some cases, the vendor will repurchase equipment for salvage value at the end of its useful life and offer the business owner another credit agreement on new equipment. Start-up companies often use trade credit from equipment suppliers to purchase equipment and fixtures such as counters, display cases, refrigeration units, machinery, and the like. It pays to scrutinize vendors' credit terms, however; they may be less attractive than those of other lenders.

Commercial Finance Companies

When denied a bank loan, small business owners often look to commercial finance companies for the same type of loan. Commercial finance companies are second only to banks in making loans to small businesses and unlike their conservative counterparts, are willing to tolerate more risk in their loan portfolios.[14] Of course, their primary consideration is collecting their loans, but finance companies tend to rely more on obtaining a security interest in some type of collateral, given the higher-risk loans that make up their portfolios. Because commercial finance companies depend on collateral to recover most of their losses, they do not require the complete financial projections of future operations that most banks do. However, this does *not* mean that they do not carefully evaluate a company's financial position before making a loan.

Approximately 150 large commercial finance companies such as AT&T Small Business Lending, GE Capital, CIT Group, and others make a variety of loans to small companies, ranging from asset-based loans and business leases to construction and Small Business Administration loans. Dubbed "the Wal-Marts of finance," commercial finance companies usually offer many of the same credit options as commercial banks do, including intermediate- and long-term loans for real estate and fixed assets as well as short-term loans and lines of credit. However, because their loans are subject to more risks, finance companies charge higher interest rates than commercial banks (usually at least prime plus 2 percent). Their most common methods of providing credit to small businesses are asset based—accounts receivable financing and inventory loans. Specific rates on these loans vary, but can be as high as 20 to 30 percent (including fees), depending on the risk a particular business presents and the quality of the assets involved. Entrepreneurs whose companies bankers shun because of their short track records, less-than-perfect credit ratings, or fluctuating earnings often find the loans they need at commercial finance companies.

When their bank balked at their loan application for their established auto body repair shop, Leticia and Tony Bucio turned to CIT Group for the capital they needed to finance their company's rapid growth. In just two weeks, the giant commercial finance company approved a loan for $820,000 secured by the company's equipment and real estate holdings at a favorable interest rate.[15]

Savings and Loan Associations

Savings and loan associations (S&Ls) specialize in loans for real property. In addition to their traditional role of providing mortgages for personal residences, S&Ls offer financing on commercial and industrial property. In the typical commercial or industrial loan, the S&L will lend up to 80 percent of the property's value with a repayment schedule of up to 30 years. Minimum loan amounts are typically $50,000, but most S&Ls hesitate to lend money for buildings specially designed for a particular customer's needs. S&Ls expect the mortgage to be repaid from the firm's future profits.

Stockbrokerage Houses

Stockbrokers are getting into the lending business, too, and many of them offer loans to their customers at lower interest rates than banks. These **margin loans** carry lower rates because the collateral supporting them—the stocks and bonds in the customer's portfolio—is of high quality and is highly liquid. Moreover, brokerage firms make it easy to borrow. Usually, brokers set up a line of credit for their customers when they open a brokerage account. To tap that line of credit, a customer simply writes a check or uses a debit card. Typically, there is no fixed repayment schedule for a margin loan; the debt can remain outstanding indefinitely, as long as the market value of the borrower's portfolio of collateral meets minimum requirements. Aspiring entrepreneurs can borrow up to 50 percent of the value of their stock portfolios, up to 70 percent of their bond portfolios, and up to 90 percent of the value of their government securities. *For example, one woman borrowed $60,000 to buy equipment for her New York health club, and a St. Louis doctor borrowed $1 million against his brokerage account to help finance a medical clinic.*[16]

There is risk involved in using stocks and bonds as collateral on a loan. Brokers typically require a 30 percent cushion on margin loans. If the value of the borrower's portfolio drops, the broker can make a **margin call**—that is, the broker can call the loan in and require the borrower to provide more cash and securities as collateral. Recent swings in the stock market have translated into margin calls for many entrepreneurs, requiring them to repay a significant portion of their loan balances within a matter of days—or hours. If an account lacks adequate collateral, the broker can sell off the customer's portfolio to pay off the loan.

Insurance Companies

For many small businesses, life insurance companies can be an important source of business capital. Insurance companies offer two basic types of loans: policy loans and mortgage loans. **Policy loans** are extended on the basis of the amount of money paid through premiums into the insurance policy. It usually takes about two years for an insurance policy to accumulate enough cash surrender value to justify a loan against it. Once he accumulates cash value in a policy, an entrepreneur may borrow up to 95 percent of that value for any length of time. Interest is levied annually, but repayment may be deferred indefinitely. However, the amount of insurance coverage is reduced by the amount of the loan. Policy loans typically offer very favorable interest rates, sometimes below the prime rate. Only insurance policies that build cash value—that is, combine a savings plan with insurance coverage—offer the option of borrowing. These include whole life (permanent insurance), variable life, universal life, and many corporate-owned life insurance policies. Term life insurance, which offers only pure insurance coverage, has no borrowing capacity.

Insurance companies make **mortgage loans** on a long-term basis on real property worth a minimum of $500,000. They are based primarily on the value of the real property being purchased. The insurance company will extend a loan of up to 75 or 80 percent of the real estate's value, and will allow a lengthy repayment schedule over 25 or 30 years so that payments do not strain the firm's cash flows excessively. Many large real estate developments such as shopping malls, office buildings, and theme parks rely on mortgage loans from insurance companies.

Credit Unions

Credit unions, nonprofit financial cooperatives that promote saving and provide loans to their members, are best known for making consumer and car loans. However, many are also willing to lend money to their members to launch businesses, especially since many banks have restricted loans to higher-risk start-ups. Of the 11,000 state- and federally chartered credit unions operating in the United States, about 1,600 are actively making business loans, those of more than $25,000 granted without personal collateral for the purpose of starting a business, to their members. Credit unions make more than $3 billion in small business loans each year.[17]

Credit unions don't make loans to just anyone; to qualify for a loan, an entrepreneur must be a member. Lending practices at credit unions are very much like those at banks, but they usually are willing to make smaller loans. Entrepreneurs around the globe are turning to credit unions to finance their businesses, sometimes borrowing tiny amounts of money. *After quitting their jobs in government-owned plants, Ion Constantine and his brother decided to open a pastry shop in Bucharest, Romania. The Constantines turned to a local credit union for a small loan (about $2,300) to purchase their start-up equipment and supplies. As their business grew, the brothers took out another loan to move to a location in a bustling section of Bucharest. Their success in their new location already has them planning for another loan to refurbish their store and train their employees.*[18]

Bonds

Bonds, which are corporate IOUs, have always been a popular source of debt financing for large companies, but few small business owners realize that they can also tap this valuable source of capital. Although the smallest businesses are not viable candidates for issuing bonds, a growing number of small companies are finding the funding they need through bonds when banks and other lenders say no. Because of the costs involved, issuing bonds usually is best suited for companies generating annual sales between $5 million and $30 million and have capital requirements between $1.5 million and $10 million. Although they can help small companies raise

Ion Constantine (center) and two employees show off some of the equipment purchased for his pastry shop in Bucharest, Romania with a loan from a credit union.

much-needed capital, bonds have certain disadvantages. The issuing company must follow the same regulations that govern businesses selling stock to public investors. Even if the bond issue is private, the company must register the offering and file periodic reports with the SEC.

Small manufacturers needing money for fixed assets with long repayment schedules have access to an attractive, relatively inexpensive source of funds in **industrial development bonds (IDBs).** A company wanting to issue IDBs must get authorization from the appropriate municipality and the state before proceeding. Typically, the amount of money small companies issuing IDBs seek to raise is at least $1 million, but some small manufacturers have raised as little as $500,000 using a minibond program created in 1999 that offers a simple application process and short closing times. Companies raising money through minibonds typically work with a local or state economic development agency to win approval for a bond issue. Each state has its own criteria, such as job creation, expansion of the tax base, and others, that companies must meet to be eligible to issue minibonds. *Ned Golterman used minibonds to finance the expansion of building materials company in St. Louis, Missouri. Working with the St. Louis County Economic Authority, Golterman was able to close the deal in about the same time it would have taken to close a bank loan, and he was able to borrow money at 2 percent below the bank's best interest rate! "My minibond [issue] gave me the money I needed for expansion, [and] it allowed me to pay over a much longer period than any commercial bank would allow," says Golterman.*[19]

To open IDBs up to even smaller companies, some states pool the industrial bonds of several small companies too small to make an issue. By joining together to issue composite industrial bonds, companies can reduce their issuing fees and attract a greater number of investors. The issuing companies typically pay lower interest rates than they would on conventional bank loans, often below the prime interest rate.

Private Placements

In the previous chapter, we saw how companies can raise capital by making private placements of their stock (equity). Private placements are also available for debt instruments. A private placement involves selling debt to one or a small number of investors, usually insurance companies or pension funds. Private placement debt is a hybrid between a conventional loan and a bond. At its heart, it is a bond, but its terms are tailored to the borrower's individual needs, as a loan would be.

Privately placed securities offer several advantages over standard bank loans. First, they usually carry fixed interest rates, rather than the variable rates banks often charge. Second, the maturity of private placements is longer than most bank loans: 15 years, rather than five. Private placements do not require hiring expensive investment bankers. Finally, because private investors can afford to take greater risks than banks, they are willing to finance deals for fledgling small companies. *For example, Longview Fibre, a timber company and paper products maker, has tapped the private placement market repeatedly in recent years, borrowing to buy everything from timberland to pulp machines. The company cites the speed and ease of getting the financing it needs as major advantages.*[20]

Small Business Investment Companies (SBICs)

The Small Business Investment Company program was started after Russia's successful launch of the first space satellite, Sputnik, in 1958. Its goal was to accelerate the United States' position in the space race by funding high-technology start-ups. Created by the 1958 Small Business Investment Act, **small business investment companies (SBICs),** are privately owned financial institutions that are licensed and regulated by the SBA. The 396 SBICs operating across the United States use a combination of private capital and federally guaranteed debt to provide long-term capital to small businesses. There are two types of SBICs: regular SBICs and specialized SBICs (SSBICs). Approximately 60 SSBICs provide credit and capital to small businesses that are at least 51 percent owned by minorities and socially or economically disadvantaged people. Since their inception in 1969, SSBICs have helped finance more than 19,500 minority-owned companies with investments totaling $1.9 billion. Most SBICs prefer later round financing (mezzanine financing) and leveraged buyouts (LBOs) over funding raw start-ups. Because of changes in their financial structure made a few years ago, however, SBICs now are better equipped to invest in start-up companies. In fact, more than 50 percent of SBIC investments go to companies that are no more than three years old.[21] Funding from SBICs helped launch companies such as Apple Computer, Federal Express, America Online, Sun Microsystems, and Outback Steakhouse.

Since 1960, SBICs have provided more than $26.5 billion in long-term debt and equity financing to some 90,000 small businesses, adding many thousands of jobs to the American economy.[22] Both SBICs and SSBICs must be capitalized privately with a minimum of $5 to $10 million, at which point they qualify for up to four dollars in long-term SBA loans for every dollar of private capital invested in small businesses. As a general rule, both SBICs and SSBICs may provide financial assistance only to small businesses with a net worth of less than $18 million and average after-tax earnings of $6 million during its past two years. However, employment and total annual sales standards vary from industry to industry. SBICs are limited to a maximum investment or loan amount of 20 percent of their private capital to a single client, while SSBICs may lend or invest up to 30 percent of their private capital in a single small business.

SBICs operate as government-backed venture capitalists, providing both debt and equity financing to small businesses. The average amount of SBIC financing in a company is $1,041,682.[23] Because of SBA regulations affecting the financing arrangements an SBIC can offer, many SBICs extend their investments as loans with an option to convert the debt instrument into an equity interest later. Most SBIC loans are between $100,000 and $5 million and carry interest rates that can be as high as 17 or 18 percent, but the loan term is longer than most banks allow. When they make equity investments, SBICs are prohibited from obtaining a controlling interest in the companies in which they invest (no more than 49 percent ownership). The most common forms of SBIC financing (in order of their frequency) are equity-only investments (43.5%), debt instruments combined with equity investments (31.5%), and straight debt (25.0%).[24]

Fran Lent and her husband launched Fran's Healthy Helpings, a company that makes frozen meals specifically for kids, with $100,000 from their savings. The meals, with fun names such as Lucky Ducky Chicken and Twinkle Star Fish, sold well, and within two years, the Lents were looking for expansion capital. With a proven track record and a solid business plan in hand, the Lents were able to secure $2.6 million from Bank of America SBIC, financing that vaulted the young company to success.[25]

Small Business Lending Companies

Small business lending companies (SBLCs) make only intermediate- and long-term SBA-guaranteed loans. They specialize in loans that many banks would not consider and operate on a nationwide basis. For instance, most SBLC loans have terms extending for at least 10 years. The maximum interest rate for loans of seven years or longer is 2.75 percent above the prime rate; for shorter-term loans, the ceiling is 2.25 percent above prime. Another feature of SBLC loans is the expertise the SBLC offers borrowing companies in critical areas.

SBLCs also screen potential investors carefully, and most of them specialize in particular industries. The result is a low loan default rate of roughly 4 percent. Corporations own most of the nation's SBLCs, giving them a solid capital base.

FEDERALLY SPONSORED PROGRAMS

3. Identify the sources of government financial assistance and the loan programs these agencies offer.

Federally sponsored lending programs have suffered from budget reductions in the past several years. Current trends suggest that the federal government is reducing its involvement in the lending business, but many programs are still quite active and some are actually growing.

Economic Development Administration

The Economic Development Administration (EDA), a branch of the Commerce Department, offers loan guarantees to create new business and to expand existing businesses in areas with below-average income and high unemployment. Focusing on economically distressed communities, the EDA finances long-term investment projects needed to stimulate economic growth and to create jobs by making loan guarantees. The EDA guarantees up to 80 percent of business loans between $750,000 and $10 million. Entrepreneurs apply for loans through private lenders, for whom an EDA loan guarantee significantly reduces the risk of lending. Start-up companies must supply 15 percent of the guaranteed amount in the form of equity, and established businesses must make equity investments of at least 15 percent of the guaranteed amount. Small businesses can use the loan proceeds in a variety of ways, including supplementing working capital and purchasing equipment to buying land and renovating buildings.

EDA business loans are designed to help replenish economically distressed areas by creating or expanding small businesses that provide employment opportunities in local communities. To qualify for a loan the business must be located in the disadvantaged area, and its presence must directly benefit local residents. Some communities experiencing high unemployment or suffering from the effects of devastating natural disasters have received EDA Revolving Loan Fund Grants to create loan pools for local small businesses. Since 1972, the EDA has funded nearly 600 Revolving Loan Funds that have, in turn, made loans to more than 7,200 private businesses.[26]

Department of Housing and Urban Development (HUD)

The Department of Housing and Urban Development (HUD) sponsors several loan programs to assist qualified entrepreneurs in raising needed capital. Community Development Block Grants (CDBGs) are extended to cities and towns that, in turn, lend or grant money to entrepreneurs to start small businesses that will strengthen the local economy. Grants are aimed at cities and towns in need of revitalization and economic stimulation. Some grants are used to construct buildings and plants to be leased to entrepreneurs, sometimes with an option to buy. Others are earmarked for revitalizing a crime-ridden area or making start-up loans to entrepreneurs or expansion loans to existing business owners. No ceilings or geographic limitations are placed on CDBG loans and grants, but projects must benefit low- and moderate-income families.

CDBG loan and grant terms are negotiated individually between a town and an entrepreneur. An entrepreneur might negotiate a low-interest, long-term loan, while another might arrange for a grant in return for a promise to share a portion of the company's profits for several years with the town.

U.S. Department of Agriculture's Rural Business-Cooperative Service

The U.S. Department of Agriculture provides financial assistance to certain small businesses through the Rural Business-Cooperative Service (RBS). The RBS program is open to all types of businesses (not just farms) and is designed to create nonfarm employment opportunities in rural areas—those with populations below 50,000 and not adjacent to a city where densities exceed 100 people per square mile. Entrepreneurs in many small towns, especially those with populations below 25,000, are eligible to apply for loans through the RBS program, which makes about $850 million in loan guarantees each year. *Frederick James and Sanco Rembert received financing from the RBS to expand and improve their church furnishings business, Church Manufacturing Corporation. The company, which builds and installs pews, pulpits, and other furnishings in churches across the country, used the funding to earn ISO 9000 certification and to upgrade its equipment and facilities.*[27]

The RBS does make a limited number of direct loans to small businesses, but the majority of its activity is in loan guarantees. The RBS will guarantee as much as 90 percent of a bank's loan up to $25 million (although actual guarantee amounts are almost always far less) for qualified applicants. Entrepreneurs apply for loans through private lenders, who view applicants with loan guarantees much more favorably than those without such guarantees. The RBS guarantee reduces the lender's risk dramatically because the guarantee means that the government agency would pay off the loan balance (up to the ceiling) if the entrepreneur defaults on the loan.

To make a loan guarantee, the RBS requires much of the same documentation as most banks and most other loan guarantee programs. Because of its emphasis on developing employment in rural areas, the RBS requires an environmental-impact statement describing the jobs created and the effect the business has on the area.

Local Development Companies

The federal government encourages local residents to organize and fund **local development companies (LDCs)** on either a profit or nonprofit basis. After raising initial capital by selling stock to at least 25 residents, the company seeks loans from banks and from the SBA. Each LDC can qualify for up to $1 million per year in loans and guarantees from the SBA to assist in starting small businesses in the community. Most LDCs are certified to operate locally or regionally, but each state may have one LDC that can operate *anywhere* within its boundaries. LDCs enable towns to maintain a solid foundation of small businesses even when other attractive benefits such as trade zones and tax breaks are not available.

Three parties are involved in providing the typical LDC loan—the LDC, the SBA, and a participating bank. An LDC normally requires the small business owner to assist by supplying about 10 percent of a project's cost, and then arranges for the remaining capital through SBA guarantees and bank loans. LDCs finance only the fixed assets of a small business—acquiring land or buildings and modernizing, renovating, or restoring existing facilities and sites. They cannot provide funds for working capital to supply inventory, supplies, or equipment, but they can help arrange loans from banks for working capital. LDCs usually purchase real estate, refurbish or construct buildings and plants, equip them, and then lease the entire facility to the small business. The lessee's payments extend for 20 to 25 years to allow repayment of SBA, bank, and LDC loans. When the lease expires, the LDC normally gives the small business owners an option to purchase the facility, sometimes at prices well below market value.

Small Business Innovation Research Program

Started as a pilot program by the National Science Foundation in the 1970s, the Small Business Innovation Research (SBIR) program has expanded to 10 federal agencies, ranging from NASA to the Department of Defense, and has an annual budget of $1.2 billion. These agencies award cash grants or long-term contracts to small companies wanting to initiate or to expand their research and development (R&D) efforts. SBIR grants give innovative small companies the opportunity to attract early-stage capital investments *without* having to give up significant equity stakes or taking on burdensome levels of debt. The SBIR process includes three phases. Phase I grants, which determine the feasibility and commercial potential of a technology or product, last for up to six months and have a ceiling of $100,000. Phase II grants, designed to develop the concept into a specific technology or product, run for up to 24 months with a ceiling of $750,000. Approximately 40 percent of all Phase II applicants receive funding. Phase III is the commercialization phase, in which the company pursues commercial applications of the research and development conducted in phases I and II and must use private or non-SBIR federal funding to bring a product to market.

Competition for SBIR funding is intense; only 12 percent of the small companies that apply receive funding. So far, more than 30,000 SBIR awards totaling in excess of $7 billion have gone to small companies, who traditionally have had difficulty competing with big corporations for federal R&D dollars. The government's dollars have been well invested. About one in four small businesses receiving SBIR awards have achieved commercial success for their products.[28] *Charles Chalfant, president of Space Photonics, has received more than $2 million in SBIR funds to help his company develop numerous optical fiber communications products and services for the aerospace industry. Space Photonics went on to apply the technology it developed through the SBIR program to consumer-oriented products that greatly expand the bandwidth and the speed at which information travels across communication networks.*[29]

The Small Business Technology Transfer Program

The Small Business Technology Transfer (STTR) program complements the SBIR Program. Whereas the SBIR focuses on commercially promising ideas that originate in small businesses, the STTR uses companies to exploit the vast reservoir of commercially promising ideas that originate in universities, federally funded R&D centers, and nonprofit research institutions. Researchers at these institutions can join forces with small businesses and can spin off commercially promising ideas while remaining employed at their research institutions. Five federal agencies award grants of up to $500,000 in three phases to these research partnerships. The STTR's annual budget is approximately $5 million.

SMALL BUSINESS ADMINISTRATION

The Small Business Administration (SBA) has several programs designed to help finance both startup and existing small companies that cannot qualify for traditional loans because of their thin asset base and their high risk of failure. In its nearly 50 years of operation, the SBA has helped more than 14.5 million companies get the financing they need for startup or for growth. To be eligible for SBA funds, a business must be within the SBA's criteria for defining a small business. Also, some types

4. Describe the various loan programs available from the Small Business Asministration.

of businesses, such as those engaged in gambling, pyramid sales schemes, or real estate investment, among others, are ineligible for SBA loans.

The loan application process can take from between three days to many months, depending on how well prepared the entrepreneur is and which bank is involved. To speed up processing times, the SBA has established a Certified Lender Program (CLP) and a Preferred Lender Program (PLP). About 850 lenders across the United States are certified lenders, and another 500 qualify as preferred lenders.[30] Both are designed to encourage banks and other lenders to become frequent SBA lenders. When a lender makes enough good loans to qualify as a **certified lender,** the SBA promises a fast turnaround time for the loan decision—typically 3 to 10 business days. When a lender becomes a **preferred lender,** it makes the final lending decision itself, subject to SBA review. In essence, the SBA delegates the application process, the lending decision, and other details to the preferred lender. The SBA guarantees up to 75 percent of PLP loans in case the borrower fails and defaults on the loan. The minimum PLP loan guarantee is $100,000, while the maximum is $500,000. Using certified or preferred lenders can reduce the processing time for an SBA loan considerably.

To further reduce the paperwork requirements involved in its loans, the SBA recently instituted the **Low Doc** (for "low documentation") **Loan Program,** which allows small businesses to use a simple one-page application for all loan applications. Before the Low Doc Program, a typical SBA loan application required an entrepreneur to complete at least 10 forms, and the SBA often took 45 to 90 days to make a decision about an application. Under the Low Doc Program, response time is just three days.

To qualify for a Low Doc loan, a company must have average sales below $5 million during the previous three years and employ fewer than 100 people. The maximum loan amount is $150,000, and businesses can use Low Doc loans for working capital, machinery, equipment, and real estate. The SBA guarantees 80 percent of loans up to $100,000 and 75 percent of loans over that amount. Borrowers must be willing to provide a personal guarantee for repayment of the loan principal. Interest rates are prime-plus-2.75 percent on loans of seven years or longer and prime-plus-2.25 percent on loans of less than seven years. The average Low Doc loan is $79,500.

Richard Smith, owner of a whitewater rafting business, needed money to expand his 20-year-old company and to buy new equipment. Smith, however, was hesitant to approach the SBA because he wanted to avoid "myriads of paperwork." At his banker's urging, Smith decided to try the Low Doc Program, and within days of submitting his application, he received a $100,000 loan.[31]

Another program designed to streamline the application process for SBA loan guarantees is the **SBA***Express* **Program,** in which participating lenders use their own loan procedures and applications to make loans of up to $150,000 to small businesses. Because the SBA guarantees up to 50 percent of the loan, banks are often more willing to make smaller loans to entrepreneurs who might otherwise have difficulty meeting lenders' standards. Loan maturities on SBA*Express* loans typically are between 5 and 10 years but can go as long as 25 years.

SBA Loan Programs

7(A) Loan Guaranty Program. The SBA works with local lenders (both bank and nonbank) to offer a variety of loan programs all designed to help entrepreneurs who cannot get capital from traditional sources gain access to the financing they need to launch and grow their businesses. By far, the most popular SBA loan program is the **7(A) loan guaranty program** (see Figure 15.3), which makes loans up to $2 million to

Figure 15.3
SBA 7(A) Guaranteed Loans

Source: U.S. Small Business Administration.

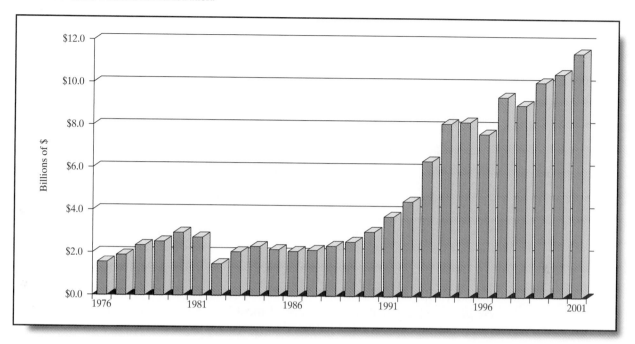

small businesses. Private lenders actually extend these loans to companies, but the SBA guarantees them (80 percent of loans up to $100,000; 75 percent of loans above $100,000 up to the loan guarantee ceiling of $1 million). In other words, the SBA does not actually lend any money; it merely acts as an insurer, guaranteeing the lender this much repayment in case the borrower defaults on the loan. Because the SBA assumes most of the credit risk, lenders are more willing to consider riskier deals that they normally would refuse. In a typical year, the SBA guarantees loans to about 43,000 small businesses that would have difficulty getting loans without the help of the SBA guarantee. *Years ago, two young entrepreneurs, Ben Cohen and Jerry Greenfield, secured an SBA-guaranteed loan for their young ice cream business. From humble beginnings in a converted gas station in Burlington, Vermont, the duo used the loan to build Ben & Jerry's Homemade into a business that today sells gourmet ice cream around the globe!*

Qualifying for an SBA loan guarantee requires cooperation among the entrepreneur, the participating bank, and the SBA. The participating bank determines the loan's terms and sets the interest rate within SBA limits. Contrary to popular belief, SBA guaranteed loans do *not* carry special deals on interest rates. Typically, rates are negotiated with the participating bank, with a ceiling of prime-plus-2.25 percent on loans of less than 7 years and prime-plus-2.75 percent on loans of 7 to 25 years. Interest rates on loans of less than $25,000 can run up to prime-plus-4.75 percent. The average interest rate on SBA-guaranteed loans is prime-plus-2 percent (compared to prime-plus-1 percent on conventional bank loans). The SBA also assesses a one-time guaranty fee of up to 3.875 percent for all loan guarantees.

The mean loan through the 7(A) guaranty program is $232,500, and the average duration of an SBA loan is 12 years—longer than the average commercial small business loan. In fact, longer loan terms are a distinct advantage of SBA loans. At least half of all bank business loans are for less than one year. By contrast, SBA real estate loans can extend for up to 25 years (compared to just 10 to 15 years for a conventional loan), and working capital loans have maturities of seven years (compared with 2 to 5 years at most banks). These longer terms translate into lower payments, which are better suited for young, fast-growing, cash-strapped companies.

The CAPLine Program. In addition to its basic 7(a) loan guarantee program (through which the SBA makes about 85 percent of its loans), the SBA provides guarantees on small business loans for start-up, real estate, machinery and equipment, fixtures, working capital, exporting, and restructuring debt through several other methods. About two thirds of all SBA's loan guarantees are for machinery and equipment or working capital. The **CAPLine Program** offers short-term capital to growing companies needing to finance seasonal buildups in inventory or accounts receivable under five separate programs, each with maturities up to five years: seasonal line of credit (provides advances against inventory and accounts receivable to help businesses weather seasonal sales fluctuations), contract line of credit (finances the cost of direct labor and materials costs associated with performing contracts), builder's line of credit (helps small contractors and builders finance labor and materials costs), standard asset-based line of credit (an asset-based revolving line of credit for financing short-term needs), and small asset-based line of credit (an asset-based revolving line of credit). CAPLine is aimed at helping cash hungry small businesses by giving them a credit line to draw on when they need it. These loans built around lines of credit are what small companies need most because they are so flexible, efficient, and, unfortunately, so hard for small businesses to get from traditional lenders.

Loans Involving International Trade. For small businesses going global, the SBA has the **Export Working Capital (EWC) Program,** which is designed to provide working capital to small exporters by providing loan guarantees of 90 percent of the loan amount up to $1 million. The SBA works in conjunction with the Export–Import Bank to administer this loan guarantee program. Applicants file a one-page loan application, and the response time normally is 10 days or less. Loan proceeds must be used to finance small business exports. *Crown Products Inc., a small company generating more than $16 million in annual sales by exporting grocery products to more than 70 countries, typifies the small companies that benefit most from the EWC program. In its early years, Crown's retained earnings and its owners financed the company's growth. But as its growth accelerated, the company's cash needs began to outstrip its internal funding sources. With the help of the Hibernia National Bank, owners Kee Lee, Sun Kim, and Jeffrey Teague were able to land a $750,000 line of credit that fueled its international growth.*[32]

The **International Trade Program** is for small businesses that are engaging in international trade or are adversely affected by competition from imports. The SBA allows global entrepreneurs to combine loans from the EWC Program with those from the International Trade Program for a maximum guarantee of $1,250,000. Loan maturities range from one to 25 years.

Section 504 Certified Development Company Program. Established in 1980, the SBA's Section 504 program is designed to encourage small businesses to expand their facilities and to create jobs. Section 504 loans provide long-term, fixed-asset financing to small companies to purchase land, buildings, or equipment. Three lenders play a role in every 504 loan: a bank, the SBA, and a **certified development company (CDC).** A CDC is a nonprofit organization licensed by the SBA and designed to promote economic growth in local communities. Some 270 CDCs now operate across the United States. An entrepreneur generally is required to make a down payment of just 10 percent of the total project cost. The CDC puts up 40 percent at a long-term fixed rate, supported by an SBA loan guarantee in case the entrepreneur defaults. The bank provides long-term financing for the remaining 50 percent, also supported by an SBA guarantee. The major advantages of Section 504 loans is their fixed rates and terms, their 10- to 20-year maturities, and the low down payment required.

When Marilyn Kohl needed money to relocate company headquarters to the South City section of St. Louis, she turned to a CDC for a $270,000 loan with a 20-year repayment term and a fixed interest rate that is adjustable in 2008. Kohl says the SBA's loan programs have been instrumental in the success of her business, Pipe Fittings and Industrial Supplies, which makes industrial conveyor belts. "Over the past six years, I've raised $365,000 in SBA-backed loans," she says. "I'm not sure my business would be around if I didn't have that support."[33]

As attractive as they are, 504 loans are not for every business owner. The SBA imposes several restrictions on 504 loans:

- For every $35,000 the CDC loans, the project must create at least one new job or achieve a public policy goal such as rural development, expansion of exports, minority business development, and others.
- Machinery and equipment financed must have a useful life of at least 10 years.
- The borrower must occupy at least two thirds of a building constructed with the loan, or the borrower must occupy at least half of a building purchased or remodeled with the loan.
- The borrower must qualify as a small business under the SBA's definition and must not have a tangible net worth in excess of $6 million and must not have an average net income in excess of $2 million after taxes for the preceding two years.

Because of strict equity requirements, existing small businesses usually find it easier to qualify for 504 loans than do start-ups.

Microloan Program. Recall from the previous chapter that about three fourths of all entrepreneurs need less than $100,000 to launch their businesses. Indeed, research suggests that most entrepreneurs require less than $50,000 to start their companies. Unfortunately, loans of that amount can be the most difficult to get. Lending these relatively small amounts to entrepreneurs starting businesses is the purpose of the SBA's Microloan Program. Called **microloans** because they range from just $100 to as much as $35,000, these loans have helped thousands of people take their first steps toward entrepreneurship. Banks typically have shunned loans in such small amounts because they considered them to be unprofitable. In 1992, the SBA began funding microloan programs at 96 private nonprofit lenders in 44 states in an attempt to "fill the void" in small loans to start-up companies, and the program has expanded from there. Since its inception, the microloan program has made loans totaling more than $110 million! The average microloan is $10,500 with a maturity of 37 months (the maximum term is six years), and lenders' standards are less demanding than those on conventional loans. All microloans are made through nonprofit intermediaries approved by the SBA such as Trickle Up and ACCION International. Although microloans are available to anyone, the SBA hopes to target those entrepreneurs who have the greatest difficulty getting start-up and expansion capital: women, minorities, and people with low incomes.

Sharon Johnson, a New York City–based jewelry artisan, recently received a $1,500 microloan from ACCION International to buy a printer and design software for her business. With her purchases, Johnson was able to boost her production and launch a Web site, opening the door to e-commerce. Today, her jewelry designs are sold in 10 New York stores, and her company now employs three part-time workers.[34]

Prequalification Loan Program. The **Prequalification Loan Program** is designed to help disadvantaged entrepreneurs such as those in rural areas, minorities, women, the disabled, those with low incomes, veterans, and others, prepare loan applications and "prequalify" for SBA loan guarantees before approaching banks and lending institutions for business loans. Because lenders are much more likely to approve loans that the SBA has prequalified, these entrepreneurs have greater access to the capital they need. The maximum loan under this program is $250,000, and loan maturities range from seven to 25 years. A local Small Business Development Center usually helps entrepreneurs prepare their loan applications at no charge.

Lola Howerton, owner of a small funeral home in Virginia, had to turn down several large funerals because she did not have the facilities to accommodate them. When she approached two banks for a $225,000 loan to expand her business, both rejected her application. Then Howerton learned about the SBA's prequalification program. She met with a representative from a local Small Business Development Center who helped her prepare a business plan and then received a letter from the SBA prequalifying her for a loan guarantee. With her business plan and the prequalifying letter, Howerton found banks very receptive to her loan request. Four banks offered to lend her the money she needed, and the terms were better than Howerton expected.[35]

Disaster Loans. As their name implies, **disaster loans** are made to small businesses devastated by some kind of financial or physical losses from hurricanes, floods, tornadoes, and other disasters. Business physical disaster loans are designed to help com-

---

IN THE FOOTSTEPS OF AN ENTREPRENEUR
The Search Continues

Hal Galvin, owner of AlumiPlate Inc., a metal-plating company holding several patents on its processes, is in a tight spot, one in which many entrepreneurs find themselves. He recently received a huge order from a large customer, but his company lacks the plant capacity to fill it. "You need the customer to get big, but you're not big enough to have the customer," he says. To accept the order, Galvin would have to expand his plant from its present size by a factor of 20 at a cost of $10 million, money he doesn't have. Although his capital needs are bigger than those of most entrepreneurs, Galvin has run the numbers on the project and is confident that the money would take his company to the next level. "If we had the $10 million, we could get a 30 percent return annually on it," he says. His company would be able to sell to the giants in the auto industry as well as to makers of semiconductors for the computer and electronics industries.

Still, Galvin has had no luck convincing lenders or investors to put up the $10 million in expansion capital. The bankers he has approached have refused his requests. "Banks weren't interested at all in a project like this because the company was too small and didn't have a history of operating a plant of that scale," he explains. As anxious as he is to get the financing to expand his business, Galvin recognizes the dangers of choosing the wrong source of capital. He has seen other entrepreneurs lose control of their companies and wants to avoid making that same mistake. For now, Galvin is focusing on growing his company slowly while he continues his search for capital. "Eventually," he says, "somebody is going to give us the money, and we'll find that big market."

1. Assume the role of financial consultant to Galvin. Where would you recommend he search for the capital he needs to expand his business? Explain your reasoning.

2. What risks does Galvin face if he is successful in securing the $10 million he needs for expansion? What can he do to minimize these risks?

Sources: Adapted from Mark Henricks, "It's a Stretch," *Inc.*, January 2002, pp. 48–53.

---

panies repair or replace damage to physical property (buildings, equipment, inventory, etc.) caused by the disaster, and economic injury loans provide working capital for businesses throughout the disaster period. The maximum disaster loan usually is $500,000, but Congress often raises that ceiling when circumstances warrant. Disaster loans carry below-market interest rates (often as low as four percent) and long payback periods. Loans for physical damage above $10,000 and financial damage of more than $5,000 require the entrepreneur to pledge some kind of collateral, usually a lien on the business property. In the aftermath of the terrorist attacks on September 11, 2001, that destroyed, damaged, or disrupted an estimated 14,000 businesses in lower Manhattan alone, the SBA approved more than $200 million in disaster loans.[36]

SBA's 8(a) Program. The SBA's 8(a) Program is designed to help minority-owned businesses get a fair share of federal government contracts. Through this program, the SBA directs about $4 million each year to small businesses with "socially and economically disadvantaged" owners. Once a small business convinces the SBA that it meets the program's criteria, it finds a government agency needing work done. The SBA then approaches the federal agency that needs the work done and arranges for a contract to go to the SBA. The agency then subcontracts the work to the small business. Government agencies cooperate with the SBA in its 8(a) program because the law requires them to set aside a portion of their work for minority-owned firms.

STATE AND LOCAL LOAN DEVELOPMENT PROGRAMS

5. Discuss state and local economic development programs.

Just when many federally funded programs are facing cutbacks, state-sponsored loan and development programs are becoming more active in providing funds for business start-ups and expansions. Many states have decided that their funds are better spent encouraging small business growth rather than "chasing smokestacks"—trying to entice large businesses to locate in their boundaries. These programs come in a wide variety of forms, but they all tend to focus on developing small businesses that create the greatest number of jobs and economic benefits. For example, South Carolina's Jobs Economic Development Authority (JEDA) is a direct lending arm of the state, offering low-interest loans to manufacturing, industrial, and service businesses. JEDA also provides financial and technical assistance to small companies seeking to develop export markets.

Although each state's approach to economic development is somewhat special, one common element is some kind of small business financing program: loans, loan guarantees, development grants, venture capital pools, and others. One approach many states have had success with is **Capital Access Programs (CAPs).** First introduced in Michigan in 1986, twenty-two states now offer CAPs that are designed to encourage lending institutions to make loans to businesses that do not qualify for traditional financing. Under a CAP, the bank and the borrower each pay an upfront fee (a portion of the loan amount) into a loan-loss reserve fund at the participating bank, and the state matches this amount. The reserve fund, which normally ranges from 6 to 14 percent of the loan amount, acts as an insurance policy against the potential loss a bank might experience on a loan and frees the bank to make loans that it otherwise might refuse. One study of CAPs found that 55 percent of the entrepreneurs who received loans under a CAP would not have been granted loans without the backing of the program.[37]

Even cities and small towns have joined in the effort to develop small businesses and help them grow. More than 7,500 communities across the United States operate revolving loan funds (RLFs) that combine private and public funds to make loans to small businesses, often at below-market interest rates. As money is repaid into the funds, it is loaned back out to other entrepreneurs. A study by the Corporation for Enterprise Development of RLFs in seven states found that the median RLF loan was $40,000 with a maturity of five years.[38] *Arlis Hanson, owner of Ag Services, a soybean-processing business in Huffton, South Dakota, received a $150,000 loan from a revolving loan fund, Rural Electric Economic Development Inc (REED). Hanson used the loan to purchase new equipment and inventory and to increase his company's production of soybean oil.[39]*

INTERNAL METHODS OF FINANCING

6. Discuss valuable methods of financing growth and expansion internally with bootstrap financing.

Small business owners do not have to rely solely on financial institutions and government agencies for capital. Instead, the business itself has the capacity to generate capital. This type of financing, called **bootstrap financing,** is available to virtually every small business and encompasses factoring, leasing rather than purchasing equipment, using credit cards, and managing the business frugally.

Factoring Accounts Receivable. Instead of carrying credit sales on its own books (some of which may never be collected), a small business can sell outright its accounts receivable to a factor. A **factor** buys a company's accounts receivable and pays for them in two parts. The first payment, which the factor makes immediately, is for 50 to 80 percent of the accounts' agreed-upon (and usually discounted) value. The factor makes the second payment of 15 to 18 percent, which makes up the balance, less the factor's service fees, when the original customer pays the invoice. Because factoring is a more expensive type of financing than loans from either banks or commercial finance companies, entrepreneurs should view factors as lenders of last resort. However, for businesses that cannot qualify for those loans, factoring may be the only choice!

Begun by American colonists to finance their cotton trade with England, factoring has become an important source of capital for many small businesses (see Figure 15.4). Factoring deals are either with recourse or without recourse. Under deals arranged with recourse, a small business owner retains the responsibility for customers who fail to pay their accounts. The business owner must take back these uncollectible invoices. Under deals arranged without recourse, however, the owner is relieved of the responsibility for collecting them. If customers fail to pay their accounts, the factor bears the loss. Because the factoring company assumes the risk of collecting the accounts, it normally screens the firm's credit customers, accepts those judged to be creditworthy, and advances the small business owner a portion of the value of the accounts receivable. Factors will discount anywhere from 5 to 40 percent of the face value of a company's accounts receivable, depending on a small company's:

- Customers' financial strength and credit ratings
- Industry and its customers' industries because some industries have a reputation for slow payments
- History and financial strength, especially in deals arranged with recourse
- Credit policies

Factoring is a source of quick cash and is ideally suited for fast-growing companies, especially start-ups that cannot qualify for bank loans. *For example, when Phil Nagel, founder of firstPro, a temporary staffing company in Atlanta, needed cash to finance*

Figure 15.4
Factoring Volume (in millions)

Source: Commercial Finance Association.

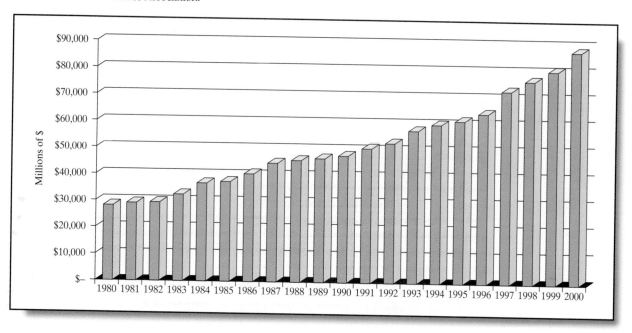

his business's rapid growth, he began selling his accounts receivable to a factor each week. Short-term financing is crucial to Nagel because of the gap between paying his temporary workers and collecting payment from his customers, but in the early days, his asset-poor fledgling firm could not qualify for a bank loan. Nagel used factoring as his primary source of capital for a decade before his company "graduated" to bank financing. "Factoring allowed me to grow at a faster pace than would have been possible otherwise," he says. "It was perfect for us."[40]

Leasing. Leasing is another common bootstrap financing technique. Today, small businesses can lease virtually any kind of asset—from office space and telephones to computers and heavy equipment. By leasing expensive assets, a small business owner is able to use them without tying up valuable capital for an extended period of time. In other words, entrepreneurs can reduce the long-term capital requirements of their businesses by leasing equipment and facilities, and they are not investing their capital in depreciating assets. Also, because no down payment is required and because the cost of the asset is spread over a longer time (lowering monthly payments), the firm's cash flow improves.

Credit Cards. Unable to find financing elsewhere, some entrepreneurs have launched their companies using the fastest and most convenient source of debt capital available: credit cards! A survey by Arthur Andersen and National Small Business United found that 50 percent of the owners of small and medium-sized businesses used credit cards as a source of funds.[41] Putting business start-up costs on credit cards charging 21 percent or more in annual interest is expensive, risky, and can lead to severe financial woes, but some determined entrepreneurs have no other choice. Credit cards are a ready source of temporary financing that can carry a company through the start-up phase until it begins generating positive cash flow. *After* *banks rejected his loan application for a Luxury Bath Systems franchise, Bernie Mexicotte used 27 credit cards to cover his start-up and operating expenses for eight months. He constantly juggled balances from one card to another to capitalize on low interest rates. Fortunately, his store's sales took off, and Mexicotte was able to repay the $75,000 credit card debt within two years. Today, Mexicotte's franchise is a thriving business that owes its early success to a very simple form of financing.[42]*

WHERE *NOT* TO SEEK FUNDS

7. Explain how to avoid becoming a victim of a loan scam.

Entrepreneurs searching for capital must be wary of con artists whose targets frequently include financially strapped small businesses. The swindle usually begins when the con man scours an area for "DEs"—Desperate Entrepreneurs—in search of quick cash injections to keep their businesses going. Usually, the small business scheme follows one of two patterns (although a number of variations exist). Under one scheme, the small business owner is guaranteed a loan for whatever amount he needs from a nonexistent bank with false credentials. The con man tells the owner that loan processing will take time, and that in the meantime he must pay a percentage of the loan amount as an advance fee. Of course, the loan never materializes, and the small business owner loses his deposit, sometimes several hundred thousand dollars. *Richard Gould, owner of a small chain of drive-through restaurants, believed that his business was an ideal candidate for franchising, but he needed the money to finance the expansion. He answered an ad in an industry trade journal from a company claiming to have capital to invest in growing businesses. When the company officials told Gould that he would have to pay a $60,000 fee up front, he refused. Ultimately, however, he paid the company $18,000 for the promise of attracting as much as $3 million from investors it supposedly represented. Gould never received a dime in investments from the company.[43]*

Another common scam begins with a con artist who claims to be a representative of the Small Business Administration. He promises the cash-hungry small business owner an SBA loan if he pays a small processing fee. Again, the loan never appears, and the small business owner loses his deposit.

Unfortunately, scams by con artists preying on unsuspecting business owners in need of capital are more common than ever. The World Wide Web has made crooks' jobs easier. On the Web, they can establish a legitimate-looking presence, approach their targets anonymously, and vanish instantly—all while avoiding mail fraud charges if they happen to get caught. These con artists move fast, cover their trails well, and are extremely smooth. The best protection against such scams is common sense and remembering "If it sounds too good to be true, it probably is." Experts offer the following advice to business owners:

- Be suspicious of anyone who approaches you—unsolicited—with an offer for "guaranteed financing."
- Watch out for red flags that indicate a scam: "guaranteed" loans, credit, or investments; up-front fees; pitches over the World Wide Web; Nigerian letter scams (promises to cut you in for a share if you help transfer large amounts of money from distant locations, such as Nigeria. Of course, the con artists will need the numbers for your account, which they promptly clean out).
- Conduct a thorough background check on any lenders, brokers, or financiers you intend to do business with. Does the company have a listing in the telephone book? Does the Better Business Bureau have a record of complaints against the company? Does the company have a physical location? If so, visit it.

- Ask the lender or broker about specific sources of financing. Then call them to verify the information.
- Make sure you have an attorney review all loan agreements before you sign them.
- Never pay advance fees for financing, especially on the World Wide Web, unless you have verified the lender's credibility.

CHAPTER SUMMARY

1. Describe the various sources of debt capital and the advantages and disadvantages of each: banks, asset-based lenders, vendors (trade credit), equipment suppliers, commercial finance companies, savings and loan associations, stock brokers, insurance companies, credit unions, bonds, private placements, Small Business Investment Companies (SBICs), and Small Business Lending Companies (SBLCs).
   - Commercial banks offer the greatest variety of loans, although they are conservative lenders. Typical short-term bank loans include commercial loans, lines of credit, discounting accounts receivable, inventory financing, and floor planning.
   - Trade credit is used extensively by small businesses as a source of financing. Vendors and suppliers commonly finance sales to businesses for 30, 60, or even 90 days.
   - Equipment suppliers offer small businesses financing similar to trade credit, but with slightly different terms.
   - Commercial finance companies offer many of the same types of loans that banks do, but they are more risk oriented in their lending practices. They emphasize accounts receivable financing and inventory loans.
   - Savings and loan associations specialize in loans to purchase real property—commercial and industrial mortgages—for up to 30 years.
   - Stock-brokerage houses offer loans to prospective entrepreneurs at lower interest rates than banks because they have high-quality, liquid collateral—stocks and bonds in the borrower's portfolio.
   - Insurance companies provide financing through policy loans and mortgage loans. Policy loans are extended to the owner against the cash surrender value of insurance policies. Mortgage loans are made for large amounts and are based on the value of the land being purchased.
   - Small Business Investment Companies are privately owned companies licensed and regulated by the SBA that qualify for SBA loans to be invested in or loaned to small businesses.
   - Small Business Lending Companies make only intermediate- and long-term loans that are guaranteed by the SBA.
2. Identify the various federal loan programs aimed at small businesses.
   - The Economic Development Administration, a branch of the Commerce Department, makes loan guarantees to create and expand small businesses in economically depressed areas.
   - The Department of Housing and Urban Development extends grants (such as Community Development Block Grants) to cities that, in turn, lend and grant money to small businesses in an attempt to strengthen the local economy.
   - The Department of Agriculture's Rural Business-Cooperative Service loan program is designed to create nonfarm employment opportunities in rural areas through loans and loan guarantees.
   - Local development companies receive loans from banks and guarantees from the SBA and then make loans to small businesses for fixed assets. The goal is to stimulate economic growth and to create jobs in the local communities.
   - The Small Business Innovation Research Program involves 10 federal agencies that award cash grants or long-term contracts to small companies wanting to initiate or to expand their research and development (R&D) efforts.

- The Small Business Technology Transfer Program allows researchers at universities, federally funded R&D centers, and non-profit research institutions to join forces with small businesses and develop commercially promising ideas.

3. Describe the various loan programs available from the Small Business Administration.
   - Almost all SBA loan activity is in the form of loan guarantees rather than direct loans. Popular SBA programs include: LowDoc program, the SBA*Express* program, the 7(A) loan guaranty program, the CAPLine program, the Export Working Capital program, the Section 504 Certified Development Company program, the Microloan program, the Prequalification Loan Program, the Disaster Loan program, and the 8(a) program.
   - Many state and local loan and development programs such as Capital Access Programs and Revolving Loan Funds complement those sponsored by federal agencies.

4. Discuss state and local economic development programs.
   - In an attempt to develop businesses that create jobs and economic growth, most states offer small business financing programs, usually in the form of loans, loan guarantees, and venture capital pools.

5. Discuss valuable methods of financing growth and expansion internally with bootstrap financing.
   - Small business owners may also look inside their firms for capital. By factoring accounts receivable, leasing equipment instead of buying it, and by minimizing costs, owners can stretch their supplies of capital.

6. Explain how to avoid becoming a victim of a loan scam.
   - Entrepreneurs hungry for capital for their growing businesses can be easy targets for con artists running loan scams. Entrepreneurs should watch out for promises of "guaranteed" loans, up-front fees, pitches over the World Wide Web, and Nigerian letter scams.

DISCUSSION QUESTIONS

1. What role do commercial banks play in providing debt financing to small businesses? Outline and briefly describe the major types of short-, intermediate-, and long-term loans commercial banks offer.
2. What is trade credit? How important is it as a source of debt financing to small firms?
3. Explain how asset-based financing works. What is the most common method of asset-based financing? What are the advantages and disadvantages of using this method of financing?
4. What is trade credit? How important is it as a source of financing for small businesses?
5. What function do SBICs serve? How does an SBIC operate? What methods of financing do SBICs rely on most heavily?
6. Briefly describe the loan programs offered by the following:
   a. The Economic Development Administration
   b. The Department of Housing and Urban Development
   c. The Department of Agriculture
   d. Local development companies
7. Explain the purpose and the methods of operation of the Small Business Innovation Research Program and the Small Business Technology Transfer Program.
8. Which of the Small Business Administration's loan programs accounts for the majority of its loan activity? How does the program work?
9. Explain the purpose and the operation of the SBA's microloan program.
10. How can a firm employ bootstrap financing to stretch its current capital supply?
11. What is a factor? How does the typical factor operate? Explain the advantages and the disadvantages of factoring. What kinds of businesses typically use factors?

BEYOND THE CLASSROOM

1. Interview several local business owners about how they financed their businesses. Where did their initial capital come from? Ask the following questions:

a. How did you raise your starting capital? What percent did you supply on your own?

b. What percent was debt capital and what percent was equity capital?

c. Which of the sources of funds described in this chapter do you use? Are they used to finance fixed, working, or growth capital needs?

d. How much money did you need to launch your businesses? Where did subsequent capital come from? What advice do you offer others seeking capital?

2. After a personal visit, prepare a short report on a nearby factor's operation. How is the value of the accounts receivable purchased determined? Who bears the loss on uncollected accounts?

3. Interview the administrator of a financial institution program offering a method of financing with which you are unfamiliar, and prepare a short report on its method of operation.

4. Contact your state's economic or business development board and prepare a report on the financial assistance programs it offers small businesses.

5. Use the resources of the World Wide Web to research microloan programs. Develop a plan for establishing a microloan program in your community. Which organizations, groups, banks, and individuals would you contact for help? How would you establish lending criteria?

TAKE IT TO THE NET

Visit the Scarborough/Zimmerer home page at **www.prenhall.com/scarborough** for updated information, online resources, Web-based exercises, and sample business plan.

ENDNOTES

1. Cynthia E. Griffin, "Something Borrowed," *Entrepreneur,* February 1997, p. 26; Business Lenders Inc., *www.businesslenders.com/q&a.htm.*

2. *Small Business Lending in the United States,* Small Business Administration Office of Advocacy (Washington, DC), June 2000, p. i, *www.sba.gov/advo/stats/lending.*

3. Karen Axelton, "Don't Bank on It," *Business Start-Ups,* May 1998, p. 116.

4. Cynthia E. Griffin, "Money in the Bank," *Entrepreneur,* July 2000, pp. 84–89; *Small Business Lending in the United States,* pp. i–iii.

5. Paul DeCeglie, "Funny Money," *Entrepreneur's Be Your Own Boss,* January 2001, pp. 141–146.

6. Daniel M. Clark, "Banks and Bankability," *Venture,* September 1989, p. 29.

7. "Lines of Credit," *Inc.,* July 1990, p. 96.

8. "Dispatches," *Inc.,* December 31, 2001, pp. 92–94.

9. Juan Hovey, "Want Easy Money? Look for Lenders Who Say Yes," *FSB,* November 2000, pp. 41–44.

10. Anne Ashby Gilbert, "Where to Go When the Bank Says No," *Fortune,* October 12, 1998, pp. 188[C]–188[F].

11. Jane Applegate, "Inventory-Based Lines of Credit," *Entrepreneur,* July 16, 2001, *www.entrepreneur.com/article/0,4621,291071,00.html.*

12. "What Is Business Credit?" National Association of Credit Management, *www.nacm.org/aboutnacm/what.html;* "Financing Small Business," *Small Business Reporter,* C3, p. 9.

13. Jill Andresky Fraser, "When Supplier Credit Helps Fuel Growth," *Inc.,* March 1995, p. 117.

14. *Small Business Lending in the United States,* p. 1.

15. Hovey, "Want Easy Money? Look for Lenders Who Say Yes," pp. 41–44.

16. Scott McMurray, "Personal Loans from Brokers Offer Low Rates," *Wall Street Journal,* January 7, 1986, p. 31.

17. Cynthia E. Griffin, "Give 'Em Credit," *Entrepreneur,* July 1999, p. 26.

18. "Spotlights on Development: Romania," World Council of Credit Unions, *www.woccu.org/development/docs/rom_spt.pdf.*

19. Sean P. Melvin, "Itsy-Bitsy Bonds," *Entrepreneur,* January 2002, pp. 78–81.

20. Robert McGough, "Money to Burn," *FW,* June 26, 1990, p. 18; Longview Fibre Company, *www.longviewfibre.com/.*

21. "SBIC Program Statistical Package," U.S. Small Business Administration, *www.sba.gov/INV/stat/2001a.html.*

22. "Success Stories," National Association of Small Business Investment Companies, *www.nasbic.com/success.cfm.*

23. Ibid.

24. Ibid.

25. Carla Vincent, "Found Money," *Emerging Business,* Summer 2001, pp. 186–191; Fran's Healthy Helpings, *www.frans.com/company.htm.*

26. "Economic Development Fact Sheet," *www.doc.gov/eda/pdf/1a5_1_99factsheet.pdf.*

27. Sarah Zajaczek, "Local Manufacturer Gets Minority Ownership Funding," *Clinton Chronicle,* July 25, 2001, p. 4A.

28. "SBA Technology: Small Business Innovation Research Program (SBIR), *www.sba.gov/SBIR/sbir.html; Charles Stein,* "A Sugar Daddy for Hungry Start-Ups," *FSB,* May/June 2000, pp. 41–42.

29. "Tibbetts Award Winners," SBA Office of Technology, SBIR/STTR, www.sba.gov/SBIR/index-tibbetts-2001winners.html; "Space Photonics Takes Flight," *ScienceDaily,* February 18, 2000, *www.sciencedaily.com/releases/2000/02/000218060115.htm.*

30. Art Beroff and Dwayne Moyers, "SBA Guaranteed Loans," *Entrepreneur, www.entrepreneur.com/article/0,4621,261896,00.html.*

31. Laura M. Litvan, "Some Rest for the Paperwork Weary," *Nation's Business,* June 1994, pp. 38–40; Robert W. Casey, "Getting Down to Business," *Your Company,* Summer 1994, pp. 30–33.

32. Roberta Reynes, "Borrowing Tailored for Exporters," *Nation's Business,* March 1999, pp. 29–30.

33. Lori Ioannou, "Loan Docs: When the Economy Says No, the SBA Says Yes," *FSB,* February 2001, pp. 35–37.

34. Brian O'Connell, "Brother, Can You Spare $10,000?" *Entrepreneur,* December 2000, *www.entrepeneur.com/article/0,4621,284219,00.html.*

35. Anna Barron Billingsley, "Dream Weavers," *Region Focus,* Fall 1999, pp. 20–23.

36. "SBA Disaster Loan Assistance in NYC Reaches $200 Million Following September 11 Attack," Small Business Administration, *www.sba.gov/news/index-headline.html*; Susan Hansen, "Ground Zero: The State of Small Business," *Inc.,* October 8, 2001, *www.inc.com/search/23503.html.*

37. Ziona Austrian and Zhongcai Zhang, "An Inventory and Assessment of Pollution Control and Prevention Financing Programs," Great Lakes Environmental Finance Center, Levin College of Urban Affairs, Cleveland State University, *www.csuohio.edu/glefc/inventor.htm#sba.*

38. Sharon Nelton, "Loans That Come Full Circle," *Nation's Business,* June 1999, pp. 35–36.

39. Ibid.

40. Roberta Reynes, "A Big Factor in Expansion," *Nation's Business,* January 1999, pp. 31–32.

41. Phaedra Hise, "Don't Start a Business Without One," *Inc.,* February 1998, pp. 50–53.

42. DeCeglie, "Funny Money."

43. Jill Andresky Fraser, "Business Owners, Beware!" *Inc.,* January 1997, pp. 86–87.

Chapter **16**

Location, Layout, and Physical Facilities

Upon completion of this chapter, you will be able to:

1. Explain the stages in the location decision.
2. Describe the location criteria for retail and service businesses.
3. Outline the basic location options for retail and service businesses.
4. Explain the site selection process for manufacturers.
5. Discuss the benefits of locating a start-up company in a business incubator.
6. Describe the criteria used to analyze the layout and design considerations of a building, including the Americans with Disabilities Act.
7. Explain the principles of effective layouts for retailers, service businesses, and manufacturers.
8. Evaluate the advantages and disadvantages of building, buying, and leasing a building.

467

Most new entrepreneurs discover quickly that maintaining their business is less than glamorous.

What are the barriers that entrepreneurs face in choosing where to locate their businesses? The answer is few, if any. What every entrepreneur must do is look beyond the personal "comfort zone" and use the Internet and the library to uncover the locations that are best suited to the new venture. Where is the strongest concentration of individuals that fit the profile of the target market? Among the various potential locations, where are the competitors weakest? What, if any, are the barriers to operating in the potential locations? The answers to these questions come only from doing the legwork.

It is not possible to determine how many businesses with positive potential fail because of the entrepreneur's failure to find a location compatible with the business. The choice of location can make or break any business venture. *One entrepreneur, known to the author, decided to fulfill a lifelong dream when he was "downsized" from his corporate position. This entrepreneur had all of the skills and education necessary to make a success of his auto parts store. His all-consuming love of automobiles—especially muscle cars—his expertise in sales, a background in bookkeeping, and his excellent reputation for honesty and fair treatment seemed like more than enough to guarantee success. He positioned his business to compete with the larger chain parts stores by offering hard-to-find parts and offering delivery service. What could be wrong with this picture? What finally forced the business into bankruptcy? Location! The entrepreneur located his store in an economically depressed city on a blind curve. It was virtually impossible to see the business in one direction until well past the store, and only at risk to life and limb could anyone maneuver in or out of the small parking area.* Sadly, this is a familiar scenario that leads to the failure of many a small business. The first section of this chapter serves as a guide to help the entrepreneur qualify his choices among various location alternatives.

THE LOGIC OF LOCATION: FROM REGION TO STATE TO CITY TO SITE

An entrepreneur's ultimate location goal is to locate the company at a site that will maximize the likelihood of success. The more entrepreneurs invest in researching

1. Explain the stages in the location decision.

potential locations, the higher is the probability that they will find the spot that is best suited for their company. The trick is to keep an open mind about where the best location might be. Just as with most decisions affecting a business, the customer drives the choice of the "best" location for a business. Choosing an appropriate location is essentially a matter of selecting the site that best serves the needs of the business's target market. Is there a location where the new business will have the greatest number of customers that need, want, and can afford the products or services your business provides? The better entrepreneurs know and understand their target customers' characteristics, demographic profiles, and buying behavior, the greater are their chances of identifying the right location from which to serve them.

The search for the ideal location involves research that entrepreneurs can conduct in libraries, by telephone, in person, and on the World Wide Web. The logic of location selection is to begin with a broad regional search and then to systematically narrow the focus of the site selection process (see Figure 16.1).

Figure 16.1
The Identification of Regional and Local Market Areas

Source: From Dale M. Lewison and M. Wayne DeLozier, *Retailing* (Columbus, OH: Merrill/Macmillan Publishing, 1984), p. 341. Used with permission.

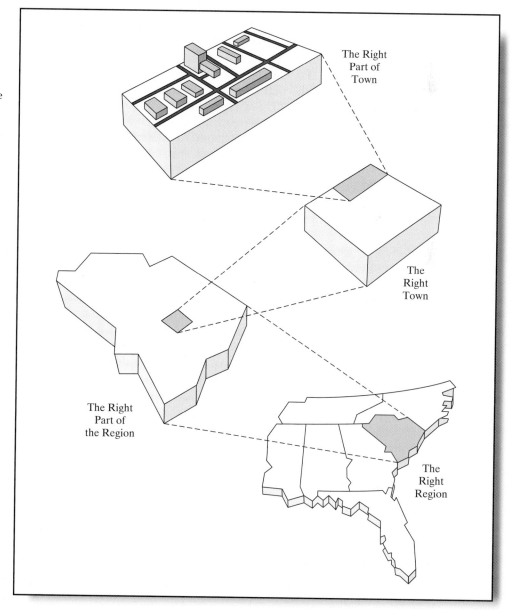

The Right Part of Town

The Right Town

The Right Part of the Region

The Right Region

Selecting the Region

The first step in selecting the best location is to focus at the regional level. Which region of the country has the characteristics necessary for a new business to succeed? Common requirements include rapid growth in the population of a certain age group, rising disposable incomes, the existence of specific infrastructure, a nonunion environment, and low operating costs.

At the broadest level of the location decision, entrepreneurs usually identify regions of the country that are experiencing substantial growth. Every year, many popular business publications prepare reports on which regions of the nation are growing, which are stagnant, and which are declining. Studying shifts in population and industrial growth will give an entrepreneur an idea of where the action is—and isn't. For example, how large is the population? How fast is it growing? What is the demographic makeup of the overall population? Which segments are growing fastest? Slowest? What is the population's income? Is it increasing or decreasing? Are other businesses moving into the region? If so, what kind of businesses? In general, owners want to avoid dying regions; these regions simply cannot provide a broad base of potential customers. A firm's customers will be people, businesses, and industry, and if it is to be successful, the business must locate in a place that is convenient to them.

One of the first stops entrepreneurs should make when conducting a regional evaluation is the U.S. Census Bureau. The Census Bureau produces many publications to aid entrepreneurs in their search for the best location. The Census Bureau publishes a monthly newsletter, *Census and You,* which is especially helpful to business owners. In addition, the Census Bureau makes most of the information contained in its valuable data banks available to entrepreneurs through its easy-to-use World Wide Web site *(www.census.gov/).* At this site, entrepreneurs can find vital demographic information for specific locations. Sorting through each report's 92 fields, entrepreneurs can prepare customized profiles of the sites they are considering.

Oregon State University also has compiled much of the data from the Census Bureau, the Bureau of Economic Analysis, the National Center for Education Statistics, and the Mesa Group into the World Wide Web's Government Information Sharing Project *(http:/govinfo.kerr.orst.edu/).* This Web site gives users an easy and powerful system for mining information from the vast and valuable resources the U.S. government has collected and compiled. These Web resources give entrepreneurs instant access to important site location information that only a few years ago would have taken many hours of intense research to compile. *American Demographics* magazine is an exceptional source for information on current demographic trends that impact our society. This publication provides in-depth articles that allow the entrepreneur to gain valuable insights into the changes in our society that produce valuable business opportunities. AmeriStat *(www.ameristat.org),* provides a detailed breakdown of much of the most relevant data collected from Census 2000.

Other helpful publications merit mention as well. *Demographics USA Series* is a three-edition series covering the United States, its counties, and zip code areas. This publication provides market surveys on the various segments of the United States demographics, including purchasing power, consumption, and economic conditions of the various geographic levels. *Lifestyle Market Analyst,* an annual publication, matches population demographics with lifestyle interests. Section 1 gives demographics and lifestyle information by "Areas of Dominant Influence." Section 2 gives demographic and geographic information according to 57 lifestyle interests. Section

3 lists areas of dominant influence and lifestyles according to 42 demographic segments. It is wise to consult the introductory material on how to use this source.

Markets of the U.S. for Business Planners features "Omigraphics," a comprehensive market tool, which provides current and historical profiles of the 183 U.S. urban economies by major section and industry. It includes regional maps, graphics, and economic commentary. *Rand McNally Commercial Atlas & Marketing Guide* is an annual publication that features maps, transportation, communication, and population data, and includes a variety of economic data. For example, it has population, income, and sales data for many areas of the United States. It also lists the largest U.S. firms in a variety of industries. Each state map includes an analysis of business and manufacturers by county, and a list of banking facilities. The *Sourcebook of County Demographics* is another annual publication that provides up-to-date estimates for economic and demographic characteristics such as age distribution, population, education, employment, housing, income distribution, race, household income, and potential demand. Data are presented alphabetically by state and county. Similar summary data are given for states, and metropolitan statistical areas.

Sales and Marketing Management's Survey of Buying Power, published annually, provides a detailed breakdown of population, retail sales, spendable income, and other characteristics for census regions, states, metropolitan areas, countries, and cities. The survey includes highlights and summary sections, analyses of changes in metro markets, and summaries of sales of certain merchandise. The *Editor and Publisher Market Guide* is similar to the *Survey of Buying Power,* but provides additional information on markets. The guide includes detailed information on key cities. The *Zip Code Atlas and Market Planner* is also an extremely useful location and market-planning tool. It combines a breakdown of zip codes (often the basis of psychographic customer profiles) with maps featuring physical features such as mountains, rivers, and major highways. The planner contains loose-leaf, full-color maps, each with a reusable acetate overlay showing five-digit zip code boundaries. It includes detailed maps of all 50 states, plus 85 specific inset maps and 11 vicinity maps.

Finally, the Small Business Administration's Small Business Development Center (SBDC) program also offers location analysis assistance to entrepreneurs. Some 600 centers nationwide provide training, counseling, research, and other specialized assistance to entrepreneurs and existing business owners on a wide variety of subjects—all at no charge! They are an important resource, especially for entrepreneurs who may not have access to a computer. (To locate the SBDC nearest you, contact the SBA office in your state or go to the SBA's home page at *www.sba.gov/.*)

The task of analyzing potential locations—gathering and synthesizing data on a wide variety of demographic and geographic variables—is one ideally suited for a computer. In fact, a growing number of entrepreneurs are relying on geographic information systems (GISs), powerful software programs that combine map drawing with database management capability, to pinpoint the ideal location for their business. These programs enable users to search through virtually *any* database and plot the relevant findings on a detailed map of the country, an individual state, a specific city, or even a single city block. The visual display highlights what otherwise would be indiscernible business trends. "The most significant benefit of GIS may be its ability to take the results of an analysis and display them in a visually powerful way," says the head of one GIS consulting firm.[1] The days when managers stuck colored pins into maps taped on a wall to analyze population characteristics are gone!

Using a GIS program, an entrepreneur could plot her existing customer base on a map, with various colors representing the different population densities. Then she could zoom in on the areas with the greatest concentration of customers, mapping a detailed view of Zip Code borders or even city streets. Geographic information system street files originate in the U.S. Census Department's TIGER (Topological Integrated Geographic Encoding Referencing) file, which contains map information broken down for every street in the country and detailed block statistics for the 345 largest urban areas. In essence, TIGER is a computerized map of the entire United States, and, when linked with a database, gives small business owners incredible power to pinpoint existing and potential customers. The accompanying *In the Footsteps of an Entrepreneur* feature describes how one entrepreneur uses a GIS program to determine the best locations for his company's franchised restaurants.

Selecting the State

Every state has a business development office to recruit new businesses to that state. Even though the publications produced by these offices will be biased in favor of locating in that state, they still are an excellent source of facts and can help entrepreneurs assess the business climate in each state. Some of the key issues to explore include the laws, regulations, and taxes that govern businesses and any incentives or investment credits the state may offer to businesses locating there. Other factors to consider include proximity to markets, proximity to raw materials, quantity and quality of the labor supply, general business climate, and wage rates.

Proximity to Markets. Locating close to markets that manufacturing firms plan to serve is extremely critical when the cost of transportation of finished goods is high relative to their value. Locating near customers is necessary to remain competitive. Service firms often find that proximity to their clients is essential. If a business is involved in repairing equipment used in a specific industry, it should be located where that industry is concentrated. The more specialized the business or the greater the relative cost of transporting the product to the customer, the more likely it is that proximity to the market will be of critical importance in the location decision. *After German automaker BMW chose upstate South Carolina as the site for its first assembly plant in North America, the counties near the plant immediately became the locations of choice for many BMW suppliers. Because BMW wanted quick deliveries with minimal inventory investment, many of its suppliers decided to set up plants close to the assembly operation.*

Proximity to Needed Raw Materials. A business that requires raw materials that are difficult or expensive to transport may need a location near the source of those raw materials. For example, fish-processing plants are almost always located close to ports. Some companies locate close to the source of raw materials because of the cost of transporting heavy low-value materials over long distances. *For instance, the owner of a small company making kitty litter chose a location near a large vein of kaolin, a highly absorbent clay and the basic raw material in his finished product. Transporting the heavy, low-value material over long distances would be impractical—and unprofitable.* In situations in which bulk or weight is not a factor, locating close to suppliers can facilitate quick deliveries and reduce inventory holding costs. The value of products and materials, their cost of transportation, and their unique functions all interact in determining how close a business needs to be to its sources of supply.

Labor Supply. Two distinct factors are important for entrepreneurs analyzing the labor supply in a potential location: the number of workers available in the area and their level of education, training, and experience. Business owners want to know how many qualified people are available in the area to do the work required in the business. The size of the local labor pool determines a company's ability to fill jobs at reasonable wages. However, employment and labor cost statistics can be misleading if a company needs people with specific qualifications. Some states have attempted to attract industry with the promise of cheap labor. Unfortunately, businesses locating in those states found exactly what the term implied: unskilled, low-wage labor. Unskilled laborers can be difficult to train.

Knowing the exact nature of the labor needed and preparing job descriptions and job specifications in advance will help business owners determine whether there is a good match between their company and the available labor pool. Checking educational statistics in the state to determine the number of graduates in relevant fields of study will provide an idea of the local supply of qualified workers. Such planning will result in choosing a location with a steady source of quality workers.

For instance, North Carolina's Research Triangle, an area defined by the surrounding communities of Raleigh, Durham, and Chapel Hill, has become a mecca for companies in high-tech industries such as computer software, semiconductors, communications, drugs, and biotech because of the area's pool of highly skilled labor. Major colleges such as Duke University, the University of North Carolina, and North Carolina State University funnel talented graduates trained in fields such as virtual reality and market research into local companies. For example, *Centennial Campus* is NC State's vision of the campus of the future. The 12-building complex (with 13 additional buildings in design or construction) forms a "technopolis" of university, corporate and government research and development (R&D) facilities, and business incubators. In addition, the master plan for the campus features a hotel/conference center complex and a town center on Lake Raleigh, a golf course and residential neighborhoods. This facility exemplifies a national trend in which universities are redesigning education and research efforts to include faculty spin-off companies, real-world experience for students, and closer ties to the industries that translate research into quality-of-life improvements for the public.[2]

As witnessed in the above example, what occurs over time is the creation of "clusters" of companies and a pool of highly trained employees. It is very common to find new entrepreneurial ventures among these industry or technology clusters because of this pool of highly qualified employees. It is possible, with some basic demographic research, to map these clusters of technology and identify the depth of the pool of skilled employees.

Wage Rates. Wage rates provide another measure for comparison among states. Entrepreneurs should determine the wage rates for jobs that are related to their particular industry or company. In addition to published government surveys, local newspapers will give entrepreneurs an idea of the wages local companies must pay to attract workers. What trends have emerged in wage rates over time? How does the rate of increase in wage rates compare among states? Another factor influencing wage rates is the level of union activity in a state. How much union organizing activity has the state seen within the past two years? Is it increasing or decreasing? Which industries have unions targeted in the recent past?

The issue becomes the nature of the employee that the business needs, the availability of workers with those skills and the current—and anticipated future—wage rates for the specific skills needed. Additionally, the issue of availability of skilled employees in the case of rapid growth should be considered. Is the depth of the workforce sufficient to supply the needs of the business under the condition of rapid expansion without resulting in an unacceptable increase in wages? In some cases, what looks positive today could prove to be either a barrier to growth in the future or a source of higher costs.

Business Climate. What is the state's overall attitude toward your kind of business? Has it passed laws that impose restrictions on the way a company can operate? Does the state impose a corporate income tax? Is there an inventory tax? Are there "blue laws" that prohibit certain business activity on Sundays? Does the state offer small business support programs or financial assistance to entrepreneurs? Some states are more "small business friendly" than others.

Table 16.1 is an abbreviated example of an evaluation matrix that can be constructed by an entrepreneur to assist in the state-to-state evaluation process. Because of the unique nature of each business venture, the entrepreneur would need to modify the table to include the location criteria that are relevant to the specific business and then weight each criteria in the appropriate manner. Such a simple evaluation tool can add objectively to the search for the most attractive state.

Selecting the City

This final stage in the location process involves greater hands-on, or maybe "feet-on" activities. The numbers will provide the entrepreneur with the leads as to potential locations, but the locations need to be investigated close up and in person. This investigation needs to be done thoroughly and on several occasions at different times of the day and night. Get to know your potential neighbors! Once you've signed the lease, it's too late to find out that a local biker gang known as "Nobody's Angels" uses the vacant building next door as an after-hours gathering place. In addition, the entrepreneur will need to factor into his or her decision the population density and growth trends, the nature of competition, the location's potential to attract customers, the cost of the location, and many other factors.

Population Trends and Density. An entrepreneur should know more about a city and its various neighborhoods than do the people who live there. By analyzing pop-

Table 16.1
State Evaluation
Matrix

LOCATION CRITERION	WEIGHT	SCORE	STATE WEIGHTED SCORE (WEIGHT X SCORE)		
			FLORIDA	ALABAMA	SOUTH CAROLINA
Quality of labor force		1 2 3 4 5			
Wage rates		1 2 3 4 5			
Union activity		1 2 3 4 5			
Energy costs		1 2 3 4 5			
Tax burden		1 2 3 4 5			
Educational/ training assistance		1 2 3 4 5			
Start-up incentives		1 2 3 4 5			
Quality of life		1 2 3 4 5			
Availability of raw materials		1 2 3 4 5			
Other		1 2 3 4 5			
Other		1 2 3 4 5			
Total score					

Assign to each location criterion a weight that reflects its relative importance. Then score each state on a scale of 1 (low) to 5 (high). Calculate the weighted score (weight X score) for each state. Finally, add up the total weighted score for each state. The state with the highest total weighted score is the best location for your business.

Not many people would believe that restaurants employ sophisticated geographic information systems (GISs), to assist in the determination of ideal locations. Sonny's Bar-B-Q restaurants use GIS technology on maps to superimpose color-coded representations of virtually any characteristic of an area's population—from income levels, traffic counts on local highways, to eating habits. The ability to display complex combinations of data in a simple, visual way makes GIS the perfect tool for selecting and evaluating potential sites for new restaurants. "Combining maps and data makes it easy for people to quickly understand a lot of information," says the head of one marketing research company.

Managers look for regions where people are already familiar with barbecue (primarily the South) but that do not have a high concentration of competing barbecue restaurants. They all also cull specific data from the Census Bureau's database and then combine it with census maps to get a picture (literally) of a site's potential for a new restaurant. The company's analysis includes a traffic count at the site, the area's total population, its population distribution and density, and the median age and household incomes of its residents. The GIS compiles all of the data and superimposes them graphically onto a map of a site. With just a few mouse clicks, Sonny Tillman, the company's founder, can display a map showing each population characteristics separately, or he can show them in any combination. Tillman can set the minimum criteria for each characteristic and let the BIS display the area that meet those criteria, or he can outline a geographic area the company is interested in developing and the system will display the traits of the population in it.

Tillman establishes strict criteria for locations. "We try not to have restaurants closer than seven miles from each other," he says. "In each new area we open, we like to have . . . territories with populations of 70,000 that match the characteristics we look for." Once Tillman finds an area that meets the basic criteria, he then analyzes specific sites within that area to determine whether it will be able to support a franchise.

Putting together a smoothly functioning GIS was neither easy nor inexpensive for a small company such as Sonny's Bar-B-Q. Says Tillman; "We developed the whole system, including the database, for $30,000." Although some of the money went for hardware, the majority of it paid for GIS software and the database of information that drives the entire system. For what the company gets, however, its GIS is a bargain at that price. "Five years ago, it was impossible to do this," says Tillman, referring to the fact that only the largest companies with the most powerful computers could handle such a large volume of information. "If you did this work the traditional way, with a large computer, it would cost from $200,000 to $500,000." Sonny's uses a desktop computer that costs about $2,500 and a basic GIS package from MapInfo selling for about $1,300.

In just a short period of time, the system has paid for itself many times over. "We [recently] franchised a county in Florida," says Tillman, "and the original projection was that it would hold four restaurants. After we ran the mapping program, we found out it would hold eight. We ended up franchising on the basis of seven. Just that one [application] has paid back everything we've put in over this year, and it's an ongoing payoff." Although many companies for whom finding the right location is key to success might consider GIS a luxury, others disagree. One location consultant explains, "It can be absolutely essential. You can't afford to make major investments that deal with extensive populations without having that kind of information or being able to do that kind of analysis."

1. What advantages does GIS give Sonny's in franchising?

2. What other types of businesses would benefit from using a GIS program? What other business applications can you think of for GIS? Explain.

Source: Adapted from Tony Seidman, "You Gotta Know the Territory," *Profit*, October 1996, pp. 21–24.

ulation and other demographic data, an entrepreneur can examine a city in detail, and the location decision becomes more than "a shot in the dark." Studying the characteristics of a city's residents, including population sizes and density, growth trends, family size, age breakdowns, education, income levels, job categories, gender, religion, race, and nationality gives an entrepreneur the facts she needs to make an informed location decision. In fact, using only basic census data, entrepreneurs can determine the value of the homes in an area, how many rooms they contain, how many bedrooms they contain, what percentage of the population own their homes, and how much residents' monthly rental or mortgage payments are. Imagine how useful such information would be to someone about to launch a home accessories store!

A company's location should match the market for its products or services, and assembling a demographic profile will tell an entrepreneur how well a particular site measures up to her target market's profile. For instance, an entrepreneur planning to open a fine china shop would likely want specific information on family income, size, age, and education. Such a shop would need to be in an area where people appreciate the product and have the discretionary income to purchase it.

Trends or shifts in population components may have more meaning than total population trends. For example, if a city's population is aging, its disposable income may be decreasing and the city may be gradually dying. On the other hand, a city may be experiencing rapid growth in the population of high-income, professional young people. For example, Atlanta, where the average age of inhabitants is 29, has seen an explosion of businesses aimed at young people with rising incomes and hearty appetites for consumption.

Population density can be another important factor in determining the optimal business location. In many of the older cities in the eastern United States, people live or work in very high-density areas. Businesses that need high traffic volume would benefit by locating in high-density areas, and the entrepreneur can benefit from an understanding of daily ebbs and flows of population movement within the selected area.

Knowing the population density within a few miles of a potential location can give entrepreneurs a clear picture of whether the city can support their business and can even help them develop the appropriate marketing strategies to draw customers. Fitness club owners have discovered that population density is one of the most important factors in selecting a suitable location. Experience has taught them that customers are willing to drive or walk only so far to visit a fitness club. Information on population density and other important demographic characteristics is available from magazines such as *American Demographics (www.demographics.com/ Publications/AD/index.htm)* and from market research companies.

Competition. For some retailers, locating near competitors makes sense because having similar businesses located near one another may increase traffic flow. **Clustering,** as this location strategy is known, works well for products for which customers are most likely to comparison shop. Michael Porter defines clustering as "geographic concentrations of interconnected companies and institutions in a particular field that encompass an array of linked industries and other entities important to competition."[3] From a practical perspective, most of us are familiar with auto dealers who locate next to one another in a "motor mile," in an effort to create a shopping magnet for customers. The convenience of being able to shop for dozens of brands of cars, all within a few hundred yards of one another, draws customers from a sizable trading area. *According to one expert, "Those areas that have embraced clustering and rejected old-line sprawl strategies that promoted hollowing of the core, growth by* *accretion, minimal synergies and shared vision in contrast promote a regional focus, revitalization of the core, growth by renewal, maximum synergy, and shared vision."*[4]

Of course, this strategy has limits. Overcrowding of businesses of the same type in an area can create an undesirable impact on the profitability of all competing firms. Consider the specific nature of the competing businesses in the area. Do they offer the same quality merchandise or comparable services? The products or services of a business may be superior to those that competitors presently offer, giving it the potential to create a competitive edge.

Lack of competition may also have merit in certain situations. Consider Enrique's Mexican Restaurant, which is located miles from Ponca City, Oklahoma. Enrique Avila's 100-seat restaurant, located at a local airport, attracts customers from across the Midwest and produces over a million dollars in revenue each year.[5] Enrique's is a destination location for hungry travelers, private pilots, and others throughout the region.

Studying the size of the market for a product or service and the number of existing competitors will help entrepreneurs determine whether they can capture a sufficiently large market share to earn a profit. Again, Census Bureau reports can be a valuable source of information. The Bureau's *County Business Patterns Economic Profile* shows the breakdown of businesses in manufacturing, wholesale, retail, and service categories and estimates companies' annual payrolls and number of employees. The *Economic Census*, which covers 15 million businesses and is published in years that end in 2 and 7, gives an overview of the businesses in an area, including their sales (or other measure of output), employment, payroll, and form of organiza-

GAINING THE COMPETITIVE EDGE
Everybody Has an Opinion

Okay, where are the best cities in America to locate a business? That depends on who's opinion (and research) you prefer. The following lists contain examples of "the best":

Forbes/Milken Institute	*Fortune*	*Entepreneur*	*Inc.*
1. San Jose, CA	1. New York, NY	1. Fort Worth/Arlington, TX	1. Las Vegas, NV
2. Austin, TX	2. San Francisco, CA	2. West Palm Beach, FL	2. Fargo, ND–Moorhead, MN
3. San Francisco, CA	3. Chicago, IL	3. Raleigh/Durham, NC	3. Sioux Falls, SD
4. Boulder, CO	4. Washington, D.C.	4. Atlanta, GA	4. Reno, NV
5. Dallas, TX	5. San Jose, CA	5. Charlotte, NC	5. Austin, TX
6. Santa Rosa, CA		6. Dallas, TX	6. Charleston, SC
7. Boise, ID		7. Las Vegas, NV	7. Wilmington–Jacksonville, NC
8. San Diego, CA		8. Orlando, FL	8. Montgomery, AL
9. Phoenix, AZ		9. New York, NY	9. Columbia, SC
10. Oakland, CA		10. Austin, TX	10. Baton Rouge, LA

Why would experts disagree? Based on your readings or experience, how would you rate the top ten cities?

Sources: *Forbes*, May 28, 2001, pp. 138–146; *Fortune*, November 27, 2000, pp. 218–231; *Entrepreneur*, October 2000, pp. 84–94; *Inc.*, December 2000, pp. 45–65.

tion. It covers eight industry categories including retail, wholesale, service, manufacturing, and construction and gives statistics at not only the national level but also by state, MSA (metropolitan statistical area; the 255 MSAs are subdivided into census tracts), county, places with 2,500 or more inhabitants, and zip code. The *Economic Census* is a useful tool for helping entrepreneurs determine whether the areas they are considering as a location are already saturated with competitors.

The Index of Retail Saturation. The index of retail saturation (IRS) is a measure of the potential sales per square foot of store space for a given product within a specific trading area. This measure combines the number of customers in a trading area, their purchasing power, and the level of competition. The index is the ratio of a trading area's sales potential for a particular product or service to its sales capacity:

$$IRS = \frac{C \times RE}{RF} \tag{1}$$

where:

    C = Number of customers in the trading area
    RE = Retail expenditures (the average expenditure per person [\$] for the product in the trading area)
    RF = Retail facilities (the total square feet of selling space allocated to the product in the trading area)

This computation is an important one for any retailer to make. Locating in an area already saturated with competitors results in dismal sales volume and often leads to failure.

To illustrate the index of retail saturation, let's suppose that an entrepreneur looking at two sites for a shoe store finds that he needs sales of \$175 per square foot to be profitable. Site 1 has a trading area with 25,875 potential customers, each of whom spends an average of \$42 on shoes annually; the only competitor in the trading area has 6,000 square feet of selling space. Site 2 has 27,750 potential customers spending an average of \$43.50 on shoes annually; two competitors occupy 8,400 square feet of space. The IRS of site 1 is:

$$IRS = \frac{25,875 \times 42}{6,000} \tag{2}$$

$$= \$181.12 \text{ sales potential per square foot}$$

The IRS of site 2 is:

$$IRS = \frac{27,750 \times 43.50}{8,400} \tag{3}$$

$$= \$143.71 \text{ sales potential per square foot}$$

Although site 2 appears to be more favorable on the surface, site 1 is supported by the index; site 2 fails to meet the minimum standard of \$175 per square foot.

The amount of available data on the population of any city or town is staggering. These statistics allow a potential business owner to compare a wide variety of cities or towns and to narrow the choices to those few that warrant further investigation. The mass of data may make it possible to screen out undesirable locations, but it does not make a decision for an entrepreneur. The owner needs to see the locations firsthand. Only by personal investigation will the owner be able to add that intangible factor of intuition into the decision-making process.

Costs. For many businesses, the cost of locating and operating is always critical to success. Some entrepreneurs search for locations that possess a spirit of revitalization and locate when the entry cost is very low. Consider two examples: *Sabra and Bill Nickas located their gourmet restaurant near downtown Anderson, South Carolina. The past few decades had been hard on their textile-dependent community, yet the owners saw opportunity where others did not. They purchased the century-old Sullivan Hardware building and opened Sullivan's Metropolitan Grill. Across the country in the busy city of Los Angeles, entrepreneurs took a risk on what was a rapidly declining section of the city to open shops, which are now becoming a West Coast fashion center.* In both examples, entrepreneurs saw opportunities where others did not and located their businesses at the "right place at the right time" and at dramatically lower cost.[6]

A growing number of small cities are establishing special technology zones that offer tax exemptions and reduced fees and licensing costs in an attempt to attract high-tech businesses. *For instance, Winchester, Virginia, a town of 23,000 residents, recently established a technology zone in the heart of its 100-acre downtown district that drew in TeleGrafix Communications, an Internet multimedia company.* The cities that have been most successful in transforming Main Street into Cyberstreet are those that offer other amenities that start-up and growing companies need, such as capable workforces, management consultant services, and access to capital. "Tax breaks provide a good field [for a company] to take root in, but you need capital for fertilizer," says Pat Clawson, CEO of TeleGrafix.[7]

Local Laws and Regulations. Before selecting a particular site within a city, small business owners must explore the local zoning laws to determine if there are any ordinances that would place restrictions on business activity or that would prohibit establishing a business altogether. **Zoning** is a system that divides a city or county into small cells or districts to control the use of land, buildings, and sites. Its purpose is to contain similar activities in suitable locations. For instance, one section of a city may be zoned industrial to house manufacturing operations. Before choosing a site, an entrepreneur must explore the zoning regulations governing it to make sure it is not out of bounds. In some cases, an entrepreneur may appeal to the local zoning commission to rezone a site or to grant a **variance** (a special exception to a zoning ordinance), but this tactic is risky and could be devastating if the board disallows the variance.

Compatibility with the Community. One of the intangibles that an entrepreneur can determine only by visiting a particular city is the degree of compatibility a business has with the surrounding community. In other words, a company's image must fit in with the character of the town and the needs and wants of its residents. Consider the costs associated with opening a retail business in an upscale, high-income community. To succeed, the business would have to match the flavor of the surrounding businesses and create an image that would appeal to upscale customers. Rents, along with fixtures and other decor items, would likely be expensive. Is there an adequate markup in your merchandise to justify such costs?

Quality of Life. One of the most important, yet most difficult to measure, criteria for a city is the quality of life it offers. Entrepreneurs have the freedom and the flexibility to locate their companies in cities that suit not only their business needs but also their personal preferences. When choosing locations for their companies, entrepreneurs often consider factors such as cultural events, outdoor activities, entertainment opportunities, safety, and the city's "personality." *Software retailer Egghead Inc. recently moved its corporate headquarters to Spokane, Washington, primarily because of the area's quality of life. A key factor in the company's decision was the desire to locate in an area* *that gave employees a chance to enjoy the family values that sometimes get lost in larger urban areas.*[8]

Transportation Networks. Manufacturers and wholesalers in particular must investigate the quality of local transportation systems. If a company receives raw materials or ships finished goods by rail, is a location with railroad access available in the city under consideration? What kind of highway access is available? Does the city have smoothly flowing highways that will make transporting materials and products efficient? Will transportation costs be reasonable? In some situations, double or triple handling of merchandise and inventory causes transportation costs to skyrocket. For retailers, the availability of loading and unloading zones is an important feature of a suitable location. Some downtown locations suffer from a lack of space for carriers to unload deliveries of merchandise.

Police and Fire Protection. Does the community in which you plan to locate offer adequate police and fire protection? Inadequate police and fire services will be reflected in the cost of the company's business insurance.

Public Services. Some governmental unit that provides water and sewer services, trash and garbage collection, and other necessary utilities should serve the location. The streets should be in good repair with adequate drainage. Locating in a jurisdiction that does not provide these services will impose higher costs on a business over time.

The Location's Reputation. Like people, a city or parts of a city can have a bad reputation. In some cases, the reputation of the previous business will lower the value of the location. Sites where businesses have failed repeatedly create negative impressions in customers' minds; customers often view any business locating there as just another one that will soon be gone. They carry negative impressions based on previous experiences and simply never give the new business a try. *One restaurateur struggled early on to overcome the negative image his new location had acquired over the years, as one restaurant after another had failed there. He eventually established a base of loyal customers and succeeded, but it was a slow and trying process.*

The Final Site Selection Decision

Successful entrepreneurs develop a site evaluation system that is both detailed and methodical. Each type of business has different evaluation criteria and experience has taught successful entrepreneurs to analyze the facts and figures behind each potential location in search of the best possible site. A manufacturer's prime consideration may be access to raw materials, suppliers, labor, transportation, and customers. Service firms need access to customers but can generally survive in lower-rent properties. A retailer's prime consideration is customer traffic. The one element common to all three is the need to locate where customers want to do business.

Site location draws on the most precise information available on the makeup of the area. By using the published statistics mentioned earlier in this chapter, an owner can develop valuable insights regarding the characteristics of people and businesses in the immediate community. Two additional Census Bureau reports entrepreneurs find especially useful when choosing locations are *Summary Population,* which provides a broad demographic look at an area, and *Housing Characteristics,* which offers a detailed breakdown of areas as small as city blocks. The data are available on CD-ROM and on the World Wide Web at the Census Bureau's home page. Any small business owner with a properly equipped personal computer can access this incredible wealth of data with a few clicks of a mouse.

LOCATION CRITERIA FOR RETAIL AND SERVICE BUSINESSES

2. Describe the location criteria for retail and service businesses.

Because their success depends on a steady flow of customers, retail and service businesses must locate with their target customers' convenience and preferences in mind. The following are important considerations.

Trade Area Size

Every retail business should determine the extent of its trading area: the region from which a business can expect to draw customers over a reasonable time span. The primary variables that influence the scope of a trading area are the type and size of the operation. If a retailer is a specialist with a wide assortment of products, he may draw customers from a great distance. In contrast, a convenience store with a general line of merchandise may have a small trading area because it is unlikely that customers would drive across town to purchase what is available within blocks of their homes or businesses. As a rule, the larger the store and the greater its selection of merchandise, the broader its trading area.

For instance, the typical movie theater draws its customers from an area of five to seven miles; however, the AMC Grand, a collection of 24 screens under one roof in Dallas, Texas, draws customers from as far as 25 miles away. This "megaplex" has expanded the normal theater trading area and attracts an amazing 3 million moviegoers a year. AMC Grand's attendance per screen is 38 percent higher than what AMC Entertainment's traditional theaters average; its revenue per customer is 10 percent higher; and its profit margins are 12.5 percent higher.[9]

The following environmental factors influence the retail trading area size.

- *Retail compatibility.* Shoppers tend to be drawn to clusters of related businesses. That's one reason shopping malls and outlet shopping centers are popular destinations for shoppers and are attractive locations for retailers. The concentration of businesses pulls customers from a larger trading area than a single freestanding business does. Retail compatibility describes the benefits a company receives by locating near other businesses selling complementary products and services. *Not long after the AMC Grand opened, for instance, seven new restaurants popped up within easy walking distance of the theaters.* Clever retailers choose their locations with an eye on the surrounding mix of businesses.
- *Degree of competition.* The size, location, and activity of competing businesses also influence the size of the trading area. If a business will be the first of its kind in a location, its trading area might be extensive. However, if the area already has eight or ten nearby stores that directly compete with a business, its trading area might be very small. How does the size of your planned operation compare with those that presently exist? Your business may be significantly larger and have more drawing power, giving it a competitive advantage.
- *Transportation network.* The transportation networks are the highways, roads, and public service routes that presently exist or are planned. An inconvenient location reduces the business's trading area. Entrepreneurs should check to see if the transportation system works smoothly and is free of barriers that might prevent customers from reaching their store. Is it easy for customers traveling in the opposite direction to cross traffic? Do signs and lights allow traffic to flow smoothly?
- *Physical, cultural, or emotional barriers.* Physical barriers may be parks, rivers, lakes, or any other obstruction that hinders customers' access to the area.

Locating on one side of a large park may reduce the number of customers who will drive around it to get to the store. In urban areas, new immigrants tend to cluster together, sharing a common culture and language. These trading areas are defined by cultural barriers, where inhabitants patronize only the businesses in their neighborhoods. The Little Havana section of Miami or the Chinatown sections of San Francisco, New York, and Los Angeles are examples. One powerful emotional barrier is fear. If high-crime areas exist around a site, most of a company's potential customers will not travel through those neighborhoods to reach the business. The mayors of many large cities in the United States have recognized that economic viability depends on the attitudes of both entrepreneurs and customers. The leaders of these cities are focusing their efforts on reducing crime and eliminating barriers to potential shoppers.

- *Political barriers are creations of law.* Federal, state, county, or city boundaries—and the laws within those boundaries—can influence the size of a company's trading area. For instance, in South Carolina, some counties have outlawed video poker machines while others allow them. In the counties where betting on video poker is legal, hundreds of small video parlors have sprung up, especially near the borders of the counties that no longer permit the practice. State laws also create conditions where customers cross over to the next state to save money. For instance, North Carolina imposes a very low cigarette tax, and shops located on its borders do a brisk business in the product.

Customer Traffic

Perhaps the most important screening criteria for a potential retail (and often for a service) location is the number of potential customers passing by the site during business hours. To be successful, a business must be able to generate sufficient sales to surpass its breakeven point, and doing that requires an ample volume of traffic. One of the key success factors for a convenience store, for instance, is a high-traffic location with easy accessibility. Entrepreneurs should know the traffic counts (pedestrian and auto) at the sites they are considering. *Shoeshine stands in airports are an example of service businesses in which the customer comes directly to the entrepreneur. The high volume of persons traveling on business is their prime customer base.*

Adequate Parking

If customers cannot find convenient and safe parking, they are not likely to stop in the area. Many downtown areas have lost customers because of inadequate parking. Although shopping malls typically average five parking spaces per 1,000 square feet of shopping space, many central business districts get by with 3.5 spaces per 1,000 square feet. Customers generally will not pay to park if parking is free at shopping centers or in front of competing stores. Even when a business provides free parking, some potential customers may not feel safe on the streets, especially after dark. Many large city business districts become virtual ghost towns at the end of the business day. A location where traffic vanishes after 6 P.M. may not be as valuable as mall and shopping center locations that mark the beginning of the prime sales at 6 P.M.

Room for Expansion

A location should be flexible enough to provide for expansion if success warrants it. Failure to consider this factor can force a successful business to open a second store when it would have been better to expand in its original location.

Visibility

No matter what a retailer sells or how well it serves customers' needs, it cannot survive without visibility. Highly visible locations simply make it easy for customers to make purchases. A site lacking visibility puts a company at a major disadvantage before it even opens its doors. In a competitive marketplace, customers seldom wish to search for a business when equally attractive alternatives are easy to locate.

Some service businesses, however, can select sites with less visibility if the majority of their customer contacts are by telephone, fax, or the Internet. For example, customers usually contact plumbers by telephone; so rather than locating close to their customer bases, plumbers have flexibility in choosing their locations. Similarly, businesses that work at their customers' homes, such as swimming pool services, can operate from their homes and service vans.

LOCATION OPTIONS FOR RETAIL AND SERVICE BUSINESSES

3. Outline the basic location options for retail and service businesses.

There are six basic areas where retailers and service business owners can locate: the central business district, neighborhoods, shopping centers and malls, near competition, outlying areas, and at home. For any specific business, some options are not relevant. The location criteria discussed above can be applied in the evaluation of most reasonable location options.

Central Business District

The central business district (CBD) is the traditional center of town: the downtown concentration of businesses established early in the development of most towns and cities. Small business owners derive several advantages from a downtown location. Because their businesses are centrally located, they attract customers from the entire trading area of the city. Plus, they benefit from the traffic generated by other stores clustered in the district. However, locating in a CBD does have certain disadvantages. Intense competition, high rental rates, traffic congestion, and inadequate parking facilities characterize some CBDs. In addition, many cities have experienced difficulty in preventing the decay of their older downtown business districts as a result of "mall withdrawal." Downtown districts withered as shoppers who preferred the convenience of modern shopping malls drifted away from the unique atmosphere of the traditional downtown.

Revitalization of the central business districts has been the rallying cry for the past three decades. In some cases, revitalization has been very successful, and although the business mix has changed the CBD is alive and economically viable. The success stories may vary, but the common theme is the vision of the CBD as a unique shopping experience. Convenient and safe parking, attractive landscaping, preserved historic buildings, and an open friendly environment of specialty shops that are compatible with the targeted shopper.

Joel Kotkin, author of the book, *The New Geography: How the Digital Revolution Is Reshaping the American Landscape,* traces the decline and now reemergence of the central business districts in many American cities, both large and small. "Securing a long-term role for a geographic place depends on the recognition by local merchants, developers, and property owners, as well as by the citizenry, that the success of an area depends precisely on maintaining and cultivating that place's unique characteristics as a marketplace. . . . As shoppers have become more interested in preserving their downtown districts, retailers have returned to Main Street. Even large retailers such as Talbots, The Gap, J. Crew, Williams Sonoma, Eddie Bauer, Starbucks, and others are opening locations in traditional CBDs."[10]

Neighborhood Locations

Small businesses that locate near residential areas rely heavily on the local trading areas for business. For example, many grocers and convenience stores located just outside residential subdivisions count on local clients for successful operations. One study of food stores found that the majority of the typical grocer's customers live within a five-mile radius. The primary advantages of a neighborhood location include relatively low operating costs and rents and close contact with customers.

Shopping Centers and Malls

Shopping centers and mall have experienced explosive growth over the last four decades. Shopping centers now offer an amazing 20 square feet of shopping space per U.S. resident.[11] The Forum Shops of Caesar's Palace in Las Vegas records an amazing $1,300 of revenue per square foot.[12] Put another way, at this level of sales per square foot, a 15,000 square foot store would produce revenues of $19,500,000!

Malls vary in size and the complexity of nonretail activities. At the lower end of the spectrum is what has been described as neighborhood shopping centers. At the upper end of the spectrum would be the malls, which are virtually destinations in themselves. The following are four broad categories of malls:

1. *Neighborhood or lifestyle shopping centers.* The typical neighborhood shopping center is relatively small, containing from three to twelve stores and serving a population of up to 40,000 people that live within a 10-minute drive. The anchor store in these centers is usually a supermarket or a drugstore.
2. *Community shopping centers.* The community shopping center contains from 12 to 50 stores and serves a population ranging from 40,000 to 150,000 people. The leading tenant is a department or variety store.
3. *Regional shopping malls.* The regional shopping mall serves a much larger trading area, usually from 10 to 15 miles or more in all directions. It contains from 50 to 100 stores and serves a population in excess of 150,000 people living within a 20- to 40-minute drive. The anchor is typically one or more major department stores.
4. *Power centers.* A power center combines the drawing strength of a large regional mall with the convenience of a neighborhood shopping center. Anchored by large specialty retailers, these centers target older, wealthier baby boomers that want selection and convenience. Anchor stores usually account for 80 percent of power center space, compared with 50 percent in the typical strip shopping center. Small companies must be careful in choosing power center locations to avoid being overshadowed by their larger neighbors. Spillover traffic from the anchor stores, although not guaranteed, is the primary benefit to small businesses locating in power centers.

Because the cost of locating in a shopping center or mall can be quite high, it is important for an entrepreneur to consider these questions:

- Is there a good fit with other products and brands sold in the mall or center?

- Who are the other tenants? Which stores are the "anchors" that will bring people into the mall or center?
- Demographically, is the center a good fit for your products or services? What are its customer demographics?
- How much foot traffic does the mall or center generate? How much traffic passes the specific site you are considering?
- How much vehicle traffic does the mall or center generate? Check its proximity to major population centers, the volume of tourists it draws, and the volume of drive-by freeway traffic. A mall or center that scores well on all three is probably a winner.
- What is the vacancy rate? The turnover rate?
- Is the mall or center successful? How many dollars in sales does it generate per square foot? Compare its record against industry averages.

The experts who predicted that malls would lose their appeal and fall from the retail scene have certainly been proven wrong. New alternatives have emerged, but the mall space per shopper continues to expand.

Near Competitors

One of the most important factors in choosing a retail or service location is the compatibility of nearby stores with the retail or service customer. For example, stores selling high-priced goods such as cars or merchandise that requires comparisons such as antiques, find it advantageous to locate near competitors to facilitate comparison shopping. Locating near competitors might be a key factor for success in businesses that sell goods that customers compare on the basis of price, quality, color, and other factors.

Although some small business owners seek to avoid locations near direct competitors, others want to locate near rivals. The advantage to locating near competitors is found in the behavior of consumers. When a potential buyer can conveniently visit a number of stores before making a final decision, the area becomes a magnet to these shoppers. In other cases, an area can become known for its collection of businesses. In some cities, restaurants will cluster together to achieve a location advantage base not only on the quality of their restaurant, but also those of its competitors.

There are limits to locating near competitors, however. Clustering too many businesses of a single type into a small area ultimately will erode their sales once the market reaches the saturation point. As the number of gourmet coffee shops has exploded in recent years, many have struggled to remain profitable, often competing with three or four similar shops, all within easy walking distance of one another. When an area becomes saturated with competitors, the stores cannibalize sales from one another, making it difficult for all of them to survive.

Outlying Areas

In general, it is not advisable for a small business to locate in a remote area because accessibility and traffic flow are vital to retail and service success, but there are exceptions. Some small firms have turned their remote locations into trademarks. One small gun shop was able to use its extremely remote location to its advantage by incorporating this into its advertising to distinguish itself from its competitors.

Outlying locations become a distinct disadvantage when potential customers cannot find your location; if they believe that there is no overriding reason to travel to your location; or if they fear for their safety either at your location or on the way to and from your location.

Home-Based Businesses

For some 20 million Americans, home-based businesses have become an opportunity to actively participate in our entrepreneurial economy while remaining at home. Although there have always been home-based businesses, the availability of affordable computing and communication technology have been the major factor in the creation of these new ventures. If current trends continue, the number of home-based businesses will surpass 25 million by the year 2003. Entrepreneurs who are technically savvy have created sophisticated networks of suppliers who can support what, in effect, is a virtual store. Home-based Internet business can actually sell goods that they do not have physical possession of, or even title to, and ship directly to the customer from the suppliers' warehouse. Electronic data interconnectivity allows a home-based business to operate like a larger business.

Choosing a home location has certain disadvantages for entrepreneurs, however. Interruptions are frequent, the refrigerator is all too handy, work is always just a few steps away, and isolation can be a problem. Presenting a professional image to clients can also be a challenge for some home-based entrepreneurs. Another problem for some entrepreneurs running businesses from their homes involve zoning laws. As their businesses grow and become more successful, entrepreneurs' neighbors often begin to complain about the increased traffic, noise, and disruptions from deliveries, employees, and customers who drive through their residential neighborhoods to conduct business. After a dispute arose over zoning violations in a residential area, one small town in New York recently passed an ordinance outlawing home-based businesses![13] Many cities now face the challenge of passing updated zoning laws that reflect the reality of today's home-based businesses while protecting the interests of residential homeowners. Refer to Table 1.2 in Chapter 1 for advice on issues to consider before setting up a home-based business.

THE LOCATION DECISION FOR MANUFACTURERS

4. Explain the site selection process for manufacturers.

The criteria for the location decision for manufacturers is very different from those of retailers and service businesses; however, the decision can have just as much impact on the company's success. In some cases, a manufacturer has special needs that influence the choice of a location. In other cases the decision is influenced by municipal regulations.

Local zoning ordinances will limit a manufacturer's choice of location. If the manufacturing process creates offensive odors or noise, the business may be even further restricted in its choices. City and county planners will be able to show potential manufacturers the area of the city or county set aside for industrial development. Some cities have developed industrial parks in cooperation with private industry. These industrial parks typically are equipped with sewage and electrical power sufficient for manufacturing. Many locations are not so equipped, and it can be extremely expensive for a small manufacturer to have such utilities brought to an existing site.

The type of transportation facilities needed can dictate location of the plant. Some manufacturers may need to locate on a railroad siding; others may only need reliable trucking service. If raw materials are purchased by the carload for economies of scale, the location must be convenient to a railroad siding. Bulk materials are sometimes shipped by barge and, consequently, require a facility convenient to a navigable river or lake. The added cost of using multiple shipping (e.g., rail-to-truck or barge-to-truck) can significantly increase shipping costs and make a location unfeasible for a manufacturer.

In some cases the perishability of the product dictates location. Vegetables and fruits must be canned near the fields in which they are harvested. Fish must be processed and canned at the water's edge. Location is determined by quick and easy access to the perishable products. Needed utilities, zoning, transposition, and special requirements may also work together to limit the number of locations that are suitable for a manufacturer.

Foreign Trade Zones

Foreign trade zones can be an attractive location for many small manufacturers that are engaged in global trade and are looking to lower the tariffs they pay on the materials and parts they import and on the goods they export. A **foreign trade zone** is a specially designated area that allows resident companies to import materials and components from foreign countries; assemble, process, package, or manufacture them; and then ship finished products out while incurring low tariffs and duties or, in some cases, paying no tariffs or duties at all. For instance, a bicycle maker might import parts and components from around the world and assemble them onto frames made in the United States. If located in a foreign trade zone, the manufacturer pays no duties on the parts it imports or on the finished bicycles it exports. The only duty the manufacturer would pay is on bicycles it sells in the United States (see Figure 16.2).

Empowerment Zones

Originally created to encourage companies to locate in economically blighted areas, **empowerment zones** offer entrepreneur's tax breaks on investments they make within zone boundaries. Companies can get federal tax credits for hiring workers living in empowerment zones and for investments they make in plant and equipment in the zones. Before becoming an empowerment zone, downtown Detroit had become a virtual ghost town, littered with crumbling buildings and unsightly vacant lots. With the tax incentives available through the empowerment zone, businesses came back to the downtown, investing more than $2 billion in 80 new projects in just the first two years. Projects ranged from a Chrysler engine factory and retail stores to housing developments and an art museum.[14]

Figure 16.2
How a Foreign Trade Zone (FTZ) Works

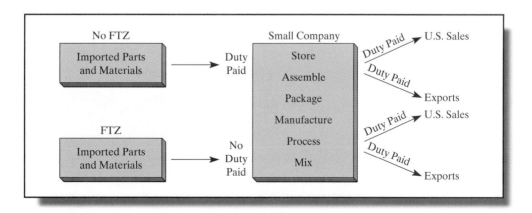

5. Discuss the benefits of locating a start-up company in a business incubator.

Business Incubators

For many start-up companies, a business incubator may make the ideal initial location. A **business incubator** is an organization that combines low-cost, flexible rental space with a multitude of support services for its small business residents. The overwhelming reason for establishing an incubator is to enhance economic development in an area and to diversify the local economy. Common sponsors of incubators include government agencies (49 percent); colleges or universities (13 percent); partnerships among government agencies, nonprofit agencies, and private developers (18 percent); and private investment groups (12 percent). Business and technical incubators vary to some degree as to the types of clients they attempt to attract, but most incubator residents are engaged in light manufacturing, service businesses, and technology- or research-related fields (see Figure 16.3).[15] For additional information on incubators, contact the National Business Incubator Association at their World Wide Web address *(wnn.nbia.org/).*

The shared resources incubators typically provide their tenants include secretarial services, a telephone system, a computer and software, fax machines, meeting facilities, and, sometimes, management consulting services. An incubator will normally have entry requirements that are tied to its purpose and that detail the nature and scope of the business activities to be conducted. Incubators also have criteria that establish the conditions a business must meet to remain in the facility as well as the expectations for "graduation."

Business incubators have been around for four decades and have spawned over 20,000 successful businesses. Today, incubators have evolved into many specialty types based on the goals of its sponsor. As an example, the San Francisco-based Women's Technology Cluster *(www.womenstechcluster.orb)* claims to be the first high-tech incubator for women entrepreneurs.[16]

In addition to shared services, incubators offer their fledgling tenants reduced rents and another valuable resource: access to the early-stage capital that young companies need to grow. A recent survey by the National Business Incubation Association found that 83 percent of incubators provide some kind of access to seed capital, ranging from help with obtaining federal grants to making connections with angel investors.[17] Some incubators also provide assistance to resident businesses interested in exporting.

More than 900 active incubators operate across the United States, and a new incubator opens, on average, every week. Most receive some type of financial assistance from their sponsors to continue operations. The investment that supports the incubator is generally a wise one because firms that graduate from incubators have only an 11 percent failure rate. The average incubator houses 17 ongoing businesses employing 55 people.[18]

Figure 16.3
Business
Incubator Tenants
by Industry

Source: National
Business Incubation
Association, Athens,
OH, 1998

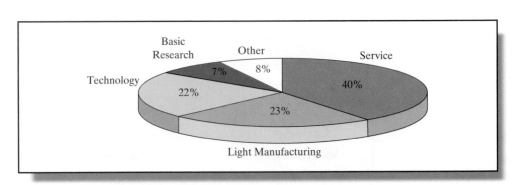

LAYOUT CONSIDERATIONS: ANALYZING THE BUILDING

6. Describe the criteria used to analyze the layout and design considerations of a building, including the Americans with Disabilities Act.

Once an entrepreneur finds the right location for her business, the next question deals with the physical facility and the layout of the facility. The building where the business will operate and the physical arrangement within the building both contribute to the success of the business. In planning the layout of a building, the goal is to maximize employees' and customers' safety and comfort, the business's effectiveness and efficiency, and, in retail settings, sales. Wise small business owners understand that attention to detail is crucial when designing a proper layout for a business. The following layout and design factors have a significant impact on a building's influence on the business.

Size

A building must be large enough to accommodate a business's daily operations comfortably. If it is too small at the outset of operations, efficiency will suffer. There must be room enough for customers' movement, inventory, displays, storage, work areas, offices, and restrooms. Haphazard layouts undermine employee productivity and create organizational chaos. Too many small business owners start their operations in locations that are already overcrowded and lack room for expansion. The result is that the owner is forced to make a costly move to a new location within the first few years of operation.

If an owner plans any kind of expansion, will the building accommodate it? Will hiring new employees, purchasing new equipment, expanding production areas, or increasing service areas require a new location? How fast is the company expected to grow over the next three to five years? Inadequate room may become a limitation on the growth of the business. Most small businesses wait too long before moving into larger quarters, and they fail to plan the new space arrangements properly. Some experts recommend that, to avoid such problems, new businesses should plan their space requirements one to two years ahead and update the estimates every six months. When preparing the plan, managers should include the expected growth in the number and location of branches to be opened.

Construction and External Appearance

Is the construction of the building sound? It pays to have an expert look it over before buying or leasing the property. Beyond the soundness of construction, does the building have an attractive external and internal appearance? The physical appearance of the building provides customers with their first impression of a business and contributes significantly to establishing its identity in the customer's mind. This is especially true in retail businesses. Is the building's appearance consistent with the entrepreneur's desired image for the business? Small retailers must recognize the importance of creating the proper image for their store and how their shop's layout and physical facility influence this image. In many ways the building's appearance sets the tone for what the customer can expect in the way of quality and service. The appearance should, therefore, reflect the business's "personality." Should the building project an exclusive image or an economical one? Is the atmosphere informal and relaxed or formal and businesslike? Externally, the storefront, its architectural style and color, signs, entrances, and general appearance give important clues to customers about a business's image.

IN THE FOOTSTEPS OF AN ENTREPRENEUR
When It Comes to Store Layout, She Keeps 'Em Guessing

About the only thing that Atchison, Kansas, is famous for is that it is the birthplace of Amelia Earhart. So what makes people drive up to three hours to this quaint little railroad town about 50 miles north of Kansas City that is surrounded by nothing but farmland? Most of the people who go to Atchison are looking to buy some home furnishings from Mary Carol Garrity's unique shop named Nell Hill's (after Garrity's grandmother). Garrity's unique little shop sells an eclectic mix of European antiques and less expensive home decorating items ranging from baskets and pottery to dinnerware and pillows. Twenty percent of the inventory is antique; 80 percent is new. Sixteen years ago, Nell Hill's began as a gourmet shop, but, over time, the shop evolved into the unique home furnishings store it is today.

A significant part of the store's success is due to its unique layout and Garrity's effective use of her inventory and props to create a wonderfully warm and friendly environment that makes customers want to linger and shop—and buy. Housed in an old bank building, Nell Hill's gives shoppers the impression that they are in someone's tastefully decorated home rather than a retail shop. The colors are soft, warm, and inviting. Ornaments and greenery hang from the ceiling; lamps, candles, and vases are displayed on tables and desks; framed paintings cover the walls; and everywhere there is furniture, so much so that customers can barely turn around without seeing something that they want to buy. Practically everything the customers see is for sale.

In addition to the store's welcoming ambiance, Nell Hill's offers customers something new every time they come in. Garrity is constantly changing the store layout. Even customers whose visits are just days apart will see a layout that is completely different! For many, shopping at Nell Hill's has become a game; they can hardly wait to see what Garrity will come up with next. Because she sells merchandise straight off the shop floor, the store's merchandise is never the same. Not only is the inventory changing, but Garrity also repaints every room in the store at least once a year. The primary reason Garrity is constantly changing the layout of the store is to keep her customers interested and coming back frequently. "If they are going to drive all the way from town to get here," she says, "I'm going to make sure they're happy and see something they haven't seen before." Many of Nell Hill's items are one-of-a-kind pieces that Garrity picks up at auctions and estate sales. Even the new items she stocks are unique and not run-of-the-mill pieces that customers could find in a mall. Prices range from as little as a few dollars for candles and small "sit-around" items to $7,875 for a gorgeous French carved walnut antique hutch.

Garrity is so busy working the floor and helping customer that she doesn't even have an office or a desk; she says that keeping in such close contact with her customers helps her to know which items to stock and how to display them in the store. "People bring in magazines, fabrics, and pictures, and we do what they want at a really good value," she says. Garrity's husband, Dan, who quit his law practice several years ago to help run the business, takes care of the company's finances and handles the furniture selection.

Garrity's recipe for Nell Hill's is a success. The company's net profit margin of 10 percent is well above that of similar shops and is growing at an amazing 20 percent a year. She recently opened a second store in Atchison—G. Dieboldt's (named after her father)—that focuses on bedroom furnishings and fabrics, which had formerly occupied the top floor at Nell Hill's. Garrity's plan is to open four or five stores, all with different themes, but with the same spirit as Nell Hill's—all in Atchison. "I have no visions of expanding outside Atchison," says Garrity. "I just want to keep it small and personal, and I want to keep the romance to it."

1. Why is layout such an important component in stores, such as Garrity's, that sell home furnishings and decorations?

2. Use the World Wide Web to develop a demographic profile of the residents of Atchison, Kansas. On the basis of your analysis, discuss the importance of Garrity's approach to store layout and her overall sales strategy for Nell Hill's.

Source: Adapted from Maria Atanasov, "Meet the Best Little Merchant in Kansas," *Your Company*, February/March 1998, pp. 54–56.

A glass front enables a retail business to display merchandise easily and to attract potential customers' attention. Passersby can look in and see attractive merchandise displays or, in some cases, employees busily working. *Krispy Kreme, a chain of doughnut shops along the Atlantic seaboard, attracts attention—and customers—by prominently displaying its doughnut-making equipment behind a glass wall. Most customers are mesmerized as they watch the machine turn out a batch of those tasty golden circles, which it then coats with molten icing. After watching the machine go through its doughnut-making cycle, viewers can hardly resist buying a doughnut. The smell of fresh-baked doughnuts wafting through the air doesn't hurt business either!*

A window display can be a powerful selling tool if used properly. Often, a store's display window is an afterthought, and many business owners change their displays too infrequently. For maximum eye-catching potential, businesses should display small merchandise such as jewelry, cosmetics, or shoes in windows with elevations of at least 36 inches. Displays of larger merchandise can start lower: just 12, 18, or 24 inches from the ground. The following tips will help business owners create window displays that will sell:

- *Keep displays simple.* Simple, uncluttered arrangements of merchandise will draw the most attention and will have the greatest impact on potential customers. Avoid taping posters on display windows; it cheapens a store's look.
- *Keep displays clean and up to date.* Dusty, dingy displays or designs that are outdated send the wrong message to customers.
- *Promote local events.* Small companies can show their support of the community by devoting part of the display window to promote local events.
- *Change displays frequently.* Customers don't want to see the same merchandise every time they visit a store. Experts recommend changing window displays at least quarterly. Businesses that sell fashionable items, however, should change their displays at least twice a month, if not weekly.
- *Get expert help, if necessary.* Some business owners have no aptitude for design! In that case, their best bet is to hire a professional to design window and in-store displays. If a company cannot afford a professional designer's fees, the entrepreneur should check with the design departments at local colleges and universities. There, he might be able to locate a faculty member or a talented student willing to work on a freelance basis.
- Contact the companies whose products you sell to see if they offer design props and assistance.

Entrances

All entrances to a business should invite customers in. Wide entryways and attractive merchandise displays that are set back from the doorway can draw customers into a business. Retailers with heavy traffic flows such as supermarkets or drugstores often install automatic doors to ensure a smooth traffic flow into and out of their stores. Retailers should remove any barriers that interfere with customers' easy access to the storefront. Broken sidewalks, sagging steps, mud puddles, and sticking or heavy doors not only create obstacles that might discourage potential customers, but they also create legal hazards for a business if they cause customers to be injured. Entrances should be lighted to create a friendly atmosphere that invites customers to enter a business.

The Americans with Disabilities Act

The **Americans with Disabilities Act (ADA),** passed in July 1990, requires practically all businesses to make their facilities available to physically challenged customers and employees. In addition, the law requires businesses with 15 or more employees to accommodate physically challenged candidates in their hiring practices. The rules of the ADA's Title III are designed to ensure that mentally and physically challenged customers have equal access to a firm's goods or services. For instance, the act requires business owners to remove architectural and communication barriers when "readily achievable." The ADA allows flexibility in how a business achieves this equal access, however. For example, a restaurant could either provide menus in braille or offer to have a staff member read the menu to blind customers. Or a small dry cleaner might not be able to add a wheelchair ramp to its storefront without incurring significant expense, but the owner could comply with the ADA by offering curbside pickup and delivery services for disabled customers at no extra charge.

Although the law allows a good deal of flexibility in retrofitting existing structures, buildings that were occupied after January 25, 1993, must be designed to comply with all aspects of the law. For example, buildings with three stories or more must have elevators; anywhere the floor level changes by more than one-half inch, an access ramp must be in place. In retail stores, checkout aisles must be wide enough—at least 36 inches—to accommodate wheelchairs. Restaurants must have 5 percent of their tables accessible to wheelchair-bound patrons.

Complying with the ADA does not necessarily require businesses to spend large amounts of money. Companies with $1 million or less in annual sales or with 30 or fewer full-time employees that invest in making their locations more accessible to all qualify for a tax credit. The credit is 50 percent of their expenses exceeding $250 but not more than $10,250.

The ADA also prohibits any kind of employment discrimination against anyone with a physical or mental disability. A physically challenged person is considered to be "qualified" if he or she can perform the essential functions of the job. The employer must make "reasonable accommodation" for a physically challenged candidate or employee without causing "undue hardship" to the business. The following are some of the specific provisions of Title III of the act:

- Restaurants, hotels, theaters, shopping centers and malls, retail stores, museums, libraries, parks, private schools, day care centers, and other similar places of public accommodation may not discriminate on the basis of disability.
- Physical barriers in existing places of public accommodation must be removed if readily achievable (i.e., easily accomplished and able to be carried out without much difficulty or expense). If not, alternative methods of providing services must be offered, if those methods are readily achievable.
- New construction of places of public accommodation and commercial facilities (nonresidential facilities affecting commerce) must be accessible.
- Alterations to existing places of public accommodation and commercial facilities must be done in an accessible manner. When alterations affect the utility of or access to a "primary function" area of a facility, an accessible path of travel must be provided to the altered areas, and the restrooms, telephones, and drinking fountains serving the altered areas must also be accessible, to the extent that the cost of making these features accessible does not exceed 20 percent of the cost of the planned alterations. The additional accessibility requirements for alterations to primary function areas do not apply to measures taken solely to comply with readily achievable barrier removal.
- Elevators are not required in newly constructed or altered buildings under three stories or with less than 3,000 square feet per floor, unless the building is a shopping center; shopping mall; professional office of a health care provider; terminal, depot, or station used for public transportation; or an airport passenger terminal.

Most businesses have found that making these reasonable accommodations for customers and employees have proven to create a more pleasant environment and have attracted new customers, as well as qualified employees.

Signs

One of the lowest-cost and most effective methods of communicating with customers is a business sign. Signs tell potential customers what a business does, where it is, and what it is selling. America is a very mobile society, and a well-designed, well-placed sign can be a powerful tool for reaching potential customers.

A sign should be large enough for passersby to read it from a distance, taking into consideration the location and speed of surrounding traffic arteries. To be most effective, the message should be short, simple, and clear. A sign should be legible both in daylight and at night; proper illumination is a must. Contrasting colors and simple typefaces are best. Because signs become part of the surrounding scenery over time, business owners should consider changing their features to retain their effectiveness. Animated parts and unusual shapes can attract interest.

The most common problems with business signs are that they are illegible, poorly designed, improperly located, poorly maintained, and have color schemes that are unattractive or are hard to read. Most communities have sign ordinances. Before investing in a sign, an entrepreneur should investigate the local community's ordinance. In some cities and towns, local regulations impose restrictions on the size, location, height, and construction materials used in business signs.

Interiors

Like exterior considerations, the functional aspects of building interiors are very important and require careful evaluation. Designing a functional, efficient interior is not easy. Technology has changed drastically the way employees, customers, and the environment interact with one another.

Piecing together an effective layout is *not* a haphazard process. **Ergonomics,** the science of adapting work and the work environment to complement employees' strengths and to suit customers' needs, is an integral part of a successful design. For example, chairs, desks, and table heights that allow people to work comfortably can help employees perform their jobs faster and more easily. Design experts claim that proper lighting, good acoustics, a comfortable climate, and properly designed equipment and work spaces benefit the company as well as employees. An ergonomically designed work space can improve workers' productivity significantly and lower days lost due to injuries and accidents. Unfortunately, not many businesses use ergonomics to design their layouts, and the result is costly. The Occupational Safety and Health Administration (OSHA) estimates that poor design in the work environment results in more than $20 billion in workers' compensation claims every year. One OSHA study found that 62 percent of all workplace injuries are musculoskeletal injuries, most of which could have been prevented by ergonomic designs.[19]

When planning store, office, or plant layouts, business owners too often focus on minimizing costs. Although staying within a budget is important, enhancing employees' productivity or maximizing sales with an effective layout should be the overriding issues. Ergonomics experts are convinced that a properly designed work environment not only reduces accidents, injuries, and absenteeism but also increases productivity and morale. Plus, retailers know that an effective store layout can increase traffic in their shops and boost sales and profits.

When evaluating an existing building's interior, an entrepreneur must be sure to determine the integrity of its structural components. Are the building's floors strong enough to hold the business's equipment, inventory, and personnel? Strength is an especially critical factor for manufacturing firms that use heavy equipment. Are the upper floors anchored as solidly as the primary floor? Can inventory be moved safely and easily from one area of the plant to another? Is the floor space ideal for safe and efficient movement of goods and people? Consider the cost of maintaining the floors. Hardwood floors may be extremely attractive but require expensive and time-consuming maintenance. Carpeted floors may be extremely attractive in a retail business but may be totally impractical for a manufacturing firm. The small business manager must consider both the utility and durability of flooring materials as well as their maintenance requirements, attractiveness, and, if important, effectiveness in reducing noise.

Like floors, walls and ceilings must be both functional and attractive. On the functional side, walls and ceilings should be fireproof and soundproof. Are the colors of walls and ceilings compatible, and do they create an attractive atmosphere? Retail stores should have a light and bright appearance. Ceilings should therefore be done in light colors to reflect the store's lighting. Walls may range from purely functional, unpainted cement block in a factory to wallpapered showpieces in expensive restaurants and exclusive shops. Wall coverings are expensive and should be considered only when the additional cost will enhance the sale of goods or services.

Lights and Fixtures

Good lighting allows employees to work at maximum efficiency. Proper lighting is measured by what is ideal for the job being done. Proper lighting in a factory may be quite different from that required in an office or a retail shop. Retailers often use creative lighting to attract customers to a specific display. Jewelry stores provide excellent examples of how lighting can be used to display merchandise effectively.

Modern advances in lighting technology give small businesses more options for lighting their stores, factories, and offices. New lighting systems offer greater flexibility, increased efficiency, and lower energy consumption.

Lighting is often an inexpensive investment when considering its impact on the overall appearance of the business. Few people seek out businesses that are dimly lit because they convey an image of untrustworthiness. The use of natural and artificial light in combination can give a business an open and cheerful look. Many restaurant chains have added greenhouse glass additions to accomplish this.

LAYOUT: MAXIMIZING REVENUES, INCREASING EFFICIENCY, AND REDUCING COSTS

7. Explain the principles of layouts for retailers, service businesses, and manufacturers.

Layout is the arrangement of the physical facilities in a business. The ideal layout contributes to efficient operations, increased productivity, and higher sales. What is ideal depends on the type of business and on the entrepreneur's strategy for gaining a competitive edge. Retailers design their layouts with the goal of maximizing sales revenue; manufacturers design theirs to increase efficiency and productivity and to lower costs.

Layout for Retailers

Retail layout is the arrangement and method of display of merchandise in a store. A retailer's success depends, in part, on a well-designed floor display. It should pull customers into the store and make it easy for them to locate merchandise; compare price, quality, and features; and, ultimately, make a purchase. In addition, the floor plan should take customers past displays of other items that they may buy on impulse.

Retailers have always recognized that some locations within a store are superior to others. Customers' traffic patterns give the owner a clue to the best location for the items with the highest gross margin. Merchandise purchased on impulse and convenience goods should be located near the front of the store. Items people shop around for before buying and specialty goods will attract their own customers and should not be placed in prime space. Prime selling space should be restricted to products that carry the highest markups. Table 16.2 offers suggestions for locating merchandise in a small retail store.

Layout in a retail store evolves from a clear understanding of customers' buying habits. If customers come into the store for specific products and have a tendency to walk directly to those items, it will benefit retailers to place complementary products in their path. Observing customer behavior can help the owner identify the "hot spots" where merchandise sells briskly and the "cold spots" where it may sit indefinitely. By experimenting with factors such as traffic flow, lighting, aisle size, display location, sounds, signs, and colors, an owner can discover the most productive store layout.

Retailers have three basic layout patterns to choose from: the grid, the free-form layout, and the boutique. The **grid layout** arranges displays in rectangular fashion so that aisles are parallel. It is a formal layout that controls the traffic flow through the store. Most supermarkets and many discount stores use the grid layout because it is well suited to self-service stores. This layout uses the available selling space efficiently, creates a neat organized environment, and facilitates shopping by standardizing the location of items. Figure 16.4 shows a typical grid layout.

Unlike the grid layout, the **free-form layout** is informal, using displays of various shapes and sizes. Its primary advantage is the relaxed, friendly shopping atmosphere it creates, which encourages customers to shop longer and increases the number of impulse purchases they make. Still, the free-form layout is not as efficient as the grid layout in using selling space, and it can create security problems if not properly planned. Figure 16.5 illustrates a free-form layout.

Table 16.2

Classification and Arrangement of Merchandise in a Small Retail Store

Merchandise Type	How or Why Bought	Placement in Store
Impulse goods	As result of attractive visual merchandising displays	Small store: near entrance Larger store: on main aisle
Convenience goods	With frequency in small quantities	Easily accessible feature locations along main aisle
Necessities or staple goods	Because of need	Rear of one-level stores, upper floors of multilevel stores (not a hard-and-fast rule)
Utility goods	For home use: brooms, dust-pans, similar items	As impulse items, up front or along main aisle
Luxury and major expense items	After careful planning and considerable "shopping around"	Some distance from entrance

Source: U.S. Small Business Administration, "Small Business Location and Layout," *Administrative Management Course Program, Topic 13* (Washington, DC: SBA, 1980), p. 6.

Figure 16.4
The Grid Layout

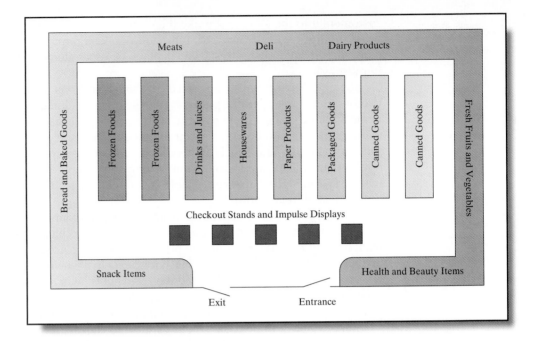

The **boutique layout** divides the store into a series of individual shopping areas, each with its own theme. It is like building a series of specialty shops into a single store. The boutique layout is informal and can create a unique shopping environment for the customer. Small department stores sometimes use this layout to create a distinctive image. Figure 16.6 shows a boutique layout for a small department store.

Business owners should display merchandise as attractively as their budgets will allow. Customers' eyes focus on displays, which tell them the type of merchandise the business sells. It is easier for customers to relate to one display than to a rack or shelf of merchandise. Open displays of merchandise can surround the focal display, creating an attractive selling area. Retailers can boost sales by displaying together items that complement each other. For example, displaying ties near dress shirts or handbags next to shoes often leads to multiple sales.

Spacious displays provide shoppers an open view of merchandise and reduce the likelihood of shoplifting. An open, spacious image is preferable to a cluttered appearance. Display height is also important because customers won't buy what they cannot see or reach. When planning displays, retailers should remember the following:

- The average man is 68.8 inches tall, and the average woman is 63.6 inches tall.
- The average person's normal reach is 16 inches, and the extended reach is 24 inches.
- The average man's standing eye level is 62 inches from the floor, and the average woman's standing eye level is 57 inches from the floor.[20]

Retailers must remember to separate the selling and nonselling areas of a store. They should never waste prime selling space with nonselling functions (storage, office, dressing area, etc.). Although nonselling activities are necessary for a successful retail operation, they should not take precedence and occupy valuable selling space. Many retailers place their nonselling departments in the rear of the building,

Figure 16.5
The Free-Form
Layout

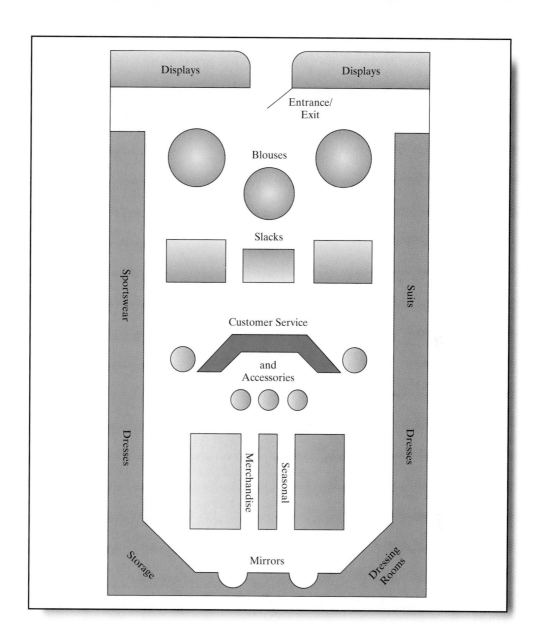

recognizing the value of each foot of space in a retail store and locating their most profitable items in the best selling areas.

Clearly, the portions of a small store's interior space are not of equal value in generating sales revenue. Certain areas contribute more to revenue than others. The value of store space depends on floor location in a multistory building, location with respect to aisles and walkways, and proximity to entrances. Space values decrease as distance from the main entry-level floor increases. Selling areas on the main level contribute a greater portion to sales than do those on other floors because they offer greater exposure to customers than either basement or higher-level locations. Therefore, main-level locations carry a greater share of rent than other levels. Figure 16.7 offers one example of how rent and sales could be allocated by floors.

The layout of aisles in the store has a major impact on the customer exposure that merchandise receives. Items located on primary walkways should be assigned a

Figure 16.6
The Boutique Layout

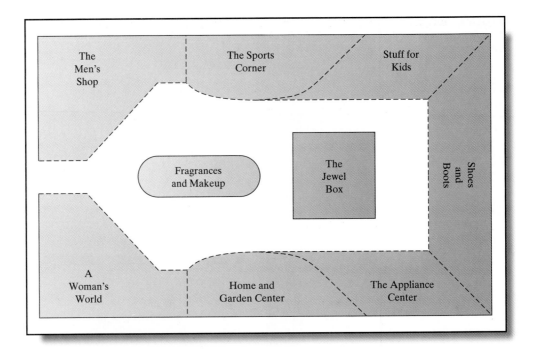

higher share of rental costs and should contribute a greater portion to sales revenue than those displayed along secondary aisles. Figure 16.8 shows that high-value areas are exposed to two primary aisles.

Space values also depend on the space's relative position to the store entrance. Typically, the farther away an area is from the entrance, the lower its value. Another consideration is that most shoppers turn to the right when entering a store and will move around it counter-clockwise, Finally, only about one fourth of a store's customers will go more than halfway into the store. Using these characteristics, Figure 16.9 illustrates space values for a typical small-store layout.

Understanding the value of store space ensures proper placement of merchandise. The items placed in the high-rent areas of the store should generate adequate

Figure 16.7
Rent Allocation by Floors

Source: From Dale M. Lewison, *Retailing,* 4th ed. (New York: Macmillan, 1991), p. 287. Used with permission.

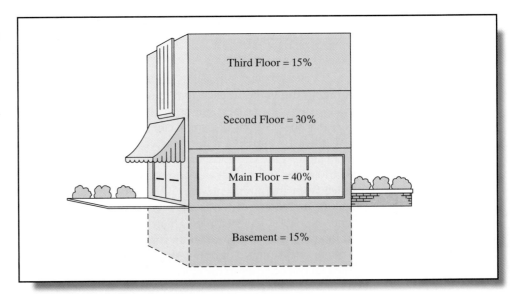

Figure 16.8
Rent Allocated by
Traffic Aisle

Source: From Dale M.
Lewison, *Retailing*, 4th
ed. (New York:
Macmillan, 1991), p.
289. Used with permis-
sion.

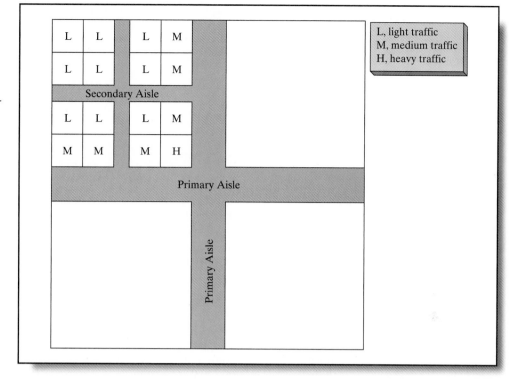

sales and contribute enough profit to justify their high-value locations. The decline
in value of store space from front to back of the shop is expressed in the 40-30=20-10
rule. This rule assigns 40 percent of a store's rental cost to the front quarter of the
shop, 30 percent to the second quarter, 20 percent to the third quarter, and 10 percent
to the final quarter. Similarly, each quarter of the store should contribute the same
percentage of sales revenue.

Figure 16.9
Space Values for
a Small Store

Source: From Dale M.
Lewison, *Retailing*, 4th
ed. (New York:
Macmillan, 1991), p.
288. Used with permis-
sion.

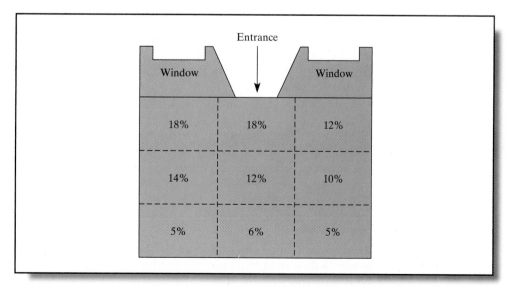

For example, suppose that the owner of a small department store anticipates $120,000 in sales this year. Each quarter of the store should generate the following sales volume:

Front quarter	$120,000 \times 0.40 / = $48,000
Second quarter	$120,000 \times 0.30 / = $36,000
Third quarter	$120,000 \times 0.20 / = $24,000
Fourth quarter	$120,000 \times 0.10 / = $12,000
Total	$120,000

Layout for Manufacturers

Manufacturing layout decisions take into consideration the arrangement of departments, workstations, machines, and stock-holding points within a production facility. The general objective is to arrange these elements to ensure a smooth work flow (in a production area) or a particular traffic pattern (in a service area).

Manufacturing facilities have come under increased scrutiny as firms attempt to improve quality, decrease inventories, and increase productivity through facilities that are integrated, flexible, and controlled. Facility layout has a dramatic effect on product mix, product processing, materials handling, storage, control, and production volume and quality. Some manufacturers are using 3-D simulation software (based on the same technology as the 3-D video games people play) to test the layout of their factory and its impact on employees and their productivity *before* they ever build them. The highly realistic simulations tell designers how well a particular combination of people, machinery, and environment interact with one another. The software can identify potential problem areas, such as layouts that force workers into awkward positions that would cause injuries, equipment designs that cause workers to reach too far for materials, and layouts that unnecessarily add extra time to the manufacturing process by requiring extra materials handling or unneeded steps.[21]

Factors in Manufacturing Layout. The ideal layout for a manufacturing operation depends on several factors, including the following:

- *Type of product.* Product design and quality standards; whether the product is produced for inventory or for order; and physical properties such as the size of materials and products, special handling requirements, susceptibility to damage, and perishability.
- *Type of production process.* Technology used; types of materials handled; means of providing a service; and processing requirements in terms of number of operations involved and amount of interaction between departments and work centers.
- *Ergonomic considerations.* To ensure worker safety; to avoid unnecessary injuries and accidents; and to increase productivity
- *Economic considerations.* Volume of production; costs of materials, machines, workstations, and labor; pattern and variability of demand; and length of permissible delays
- *Space availability within the facility itself.*

Types of Manufacturing Layouts. Manufacturing layouts are categorized either by the work flow in a plant or by the production system's function. There are three basic types of layouts that manufacturers can use separately or in combination—product, process, and fixed position—and they differ in their applicability to different levels of manufacturing volume.

In a **product** (or **line**) **layout,** a manufacturer arranges workers and equipment according to the sequence of operations performed on the product (see Figure 16.10).

Conceptually, the flow is an unbroken line from raw materials input to finished goods. This type of layout is applicable to rigid-flow, high-volume, continuous or mass-production operations or when the product is highly standardized. Automobile assembly plants, paper mills, and oil refineries are examples of product layouts.

Product layouts offer the advantages of lower materials-handling costs; simplified tasks that can be done with low-cost, lower-skilled labor; reduced amounts of work-in-process inventory; and relatively simplified production control activities. All units are routed along the same fixed path, and scheduling consists primarily of setting a production rate.

Disadvantages of product layouts include their inflexibility, monotony of job tasks, high fixed investment in specialized equipment, and heavy interdependence of all operations. A breakdown in one machine or at one workstation can idle the entire line. Such a layout also requires the owner to duplicate many pieces of equipment in the manufacturing facility; duplication can be cost-prohibitive for a small firm.

In a **process layout,** a manufacturer groups workers and equipment according to the general function they perform, without regard to any particular product (see Figure 16.11).

Process layouts are appropriate when production runs are short, when demand shows considerable variation and the costs of holding finished goods inventory are high, or when the product is customized.

Process layouts have the advantages of being flexible for doing customer work and promoting job satisfaction by offering employees diverse and challenging tasks. Its disadvantages are the higher costs of materials handling, more skilled labor, lower productivity, and more complex production control. Because the work flow is intermittent, each job must be individually routed through the system and scheduled at the various work centers, and its status must be monitored individually.

In **fixed-position layouts,** materials do not move down a line as in a product layout; because of the bulk or weight of the final product, materials are assembled in

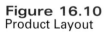

Figure 16.10
Product Layout

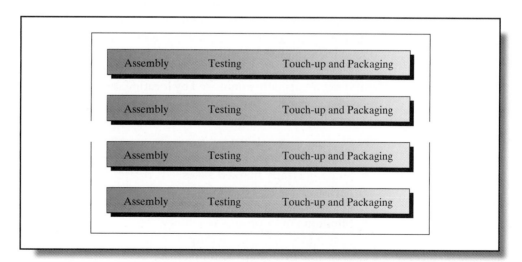

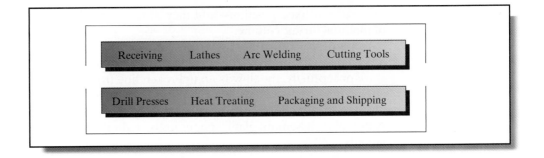

Figure 16.11
Process Layout

one spot. In other words, workers and equipment go to the materials rather than having the materials flow down a line to them. Aircraft assembly shops and shipyards typify this kind of layout.

Designing Layouts. The starting point in layout design is determining how and in what sequence product parts or service tasks flow together. One of the most effective techniques is to create an overall picture of the manufacturing process using assembly charts and process flowcharts. Given the tasks and their sequence, plus knowledge of the volume of products to be produced, an owner can analyze space and equipment needs to get an idea of the facility's demands. When a product layout is being used, these demands take precedence, and manufacturers must arrange equipment and workstations to fit the production tasks and their sequence. If a process layout is used, different products place different demands on the facility. Rather than having a single best flow, there may be one flow for each product, and compromises will be necessary. As a result, any one product may not get the ideal layout.

Analyzing Production Layouts. Although there is no general procedure for analyzing the numerous interdependent factors that enter into layout design, specific layout problems lend themselves to detailed analysis. Two important criteria for selecting and designing a layout are worker effectiveness and materials-handling costs.

Designing layouts ergonomically so that they maximize workers' strengths is especially important for manufacturers. Creating an environment that is comfortable and pleasant for workers will pay big benefits over time in the form of higher productivity, lower absenteeism and tardiness, and fewer injuries. Designers must be sure that they match the environment they create to workers' needs rather than trying to force workers to adapt to the environment.

Manufacturers can lower materials-handling costs by using layouts designed to automate product flow whenever possible and to minimize flow distances and times. The extent of automation depends on the level of technology and amount of capital available, as well as behavioral considerations of employees. Flow distances and times are usually minimized by locating sequential processing activities or interrelated departments in adjacent areas. The following features are important to a good manufacturing layout:

- Planned materials flow pattern
- Straight-line layout where possible
- Straight, clearly marked aisles
- Backtracking kept to a minimum
- Related operations close together
- Minimum of in-process inventory
- Easy adjustment to changing conditions
- Minimum materials-handling distances

- Minimum of manual handling
- No unnecessary rehandling of material
- Minimum handling between operations
- Materials delivered to production employees quickly
- Use of gravity to move materials whenever possible
- Materials efficiently removed from the work area
- Material handling done by indirect labor
- Orderly materials handling and storage
- Good housekeeping

BUILD, BUY, OR LEASE?

8. Evaluate the advantages and disadvantages of building, buying, and leasing a building.

Evaluate the advantages and disadvantages of building, buying, and leasing a building.

Another important decision business owners must make involves the ownership of the building. The ability to obtain the best possible physical facilities given the cash the owner has available may depend largely on whether the entrepreneur decides to build, buy, or lease a building.

The Decision to Build

If a business had unlimited funds, the owner could design and build a perfect facility. However, few new business owners have this luxury. Constructing a new facility can project a positive image to potential customers. The business looks new and consequently creates an image of being modern, efficient, and of top quality. A new building can incorporate the most modern features during construction, which can significantly lower operating costs. In addition, by constructing a new building, a business owner can incorporate into the layout features that meet the business's unique design needs such as loading docks, laboratories, or refrigeration units. Building a new facility can also improve a company's long-term productivity and efficiency.

In some rapidly growing areas, there are only a few or sometimes no existing buildings to buy or lease that match an entrepreneur's requirements. In these situations, a business owner must consider the cost of constructing a building as a significant factor in her initial estimates of capital needs and breakeven point. Constructing a building imposes a high initial fixed cost that an owner must weigh against the facility's ability to generate revenue and to reduce operating expenses. Building a new structure also requires more time than either buying or leasing an existing one.

The Decision to Buy

In many cases, there may be an ideal building in the area where an entrepreneur wants to locate. Buying the facility allows her to remodel it without seeking permission from anyone else. As can building, buying can put a drain on the business's financial resources, but the owner knows exactly what her monthly payments will be. Under a lease, rental rates can (and usually do) increase over time. If an owner believes that the property will actually appreciate in value, a decision to purchase may prove to be wise. In addition, the owner can depreciate the building each year, and both depreciation and interest are tax-deductible business expenses.

When considering the purchase of a building, the owner should use the same outline of facilities requirements developed for the building option to ensure that

The Lion's Head, a popular Greenwich Village restaurant and bar, recently closed its doors after three decades as the favorite gathering place of writers, artists, and actors. "It was a great place to meet and talk," says Mike Reardon, who once owned the Lion's Head. The restaurant and bar had its ups and downs over the years, but its base of loyal customers kept it going. Then, a series of steep increases in the Lion's Head's lease payments put the restaurant in a precarious financial situation. A five-year lease negotiated in 1989 raised the company's monthly rent from $5,000 to $8,000. Severe cash flow problems, due in part to the higher lease payments, forced the Lion's Head into chapter 11 bankruptcy. Reardon and two partners bought the business and reorganized it. When the lease came up for renewal in 1994, however, the monthly rent jumped up to $10,000. The Lion's Head's monthly overhead costs skyrocketed to $40,000, making it extremely difficult for the company to break even. Reardon began looking for a new location, but before he could find one, fate struck another blow: the neighboring Circle Repertory Theater moved, taking with it a steady stream of theater customers. Shortly thereafter, the Lion's Head closed. "New Yorkers go to the newest, hottest areas, and right now those are the Upper East Side and Soho," says one restaurateur. "[Greenwich] Village restaurants rely more on local clientele. It's hard to make it if you have a heavy rent."

Rent or lease payments represent one of the largest expenses many business owners pay. As the Lion's Head proves, failing to negotiate a satisfactory lease can push a company's operating expenses so high that ultimately the company fails. What can a business owner do to avoid lease nightmares? The following tips will help:

- *Read the lease agreement before you sign it.* Amazingly, some small business owners simply sign their leases without even reading them, often because they fear losing out on a great location. One attorney specializing in leases says, "Take your time and read every word of the lease, no matter how many would-be tenants are behind you."

- *Ask an experienced attorney to review the lease before you sign it.* At one time, leases were relatively simple contracts. Today, however, it is not uncommon for a lease to be a "40- to 60-page document filled with very complex issues many tenants are not always equipped to deal with on their own," says a real estate broker.

- *Incorporate (or form an LLC) before you sign a lease.* Otherwise, if the business cannot make the lease payments, the landlord has the right to make the business owner personally responsible for them.

- *Try to negotiate a lease term that is as short as possible at the outset.* Many landlords ask business owners to personally guarantee lease payments. To reduce the risk of getting stuck with long-term payments, try to get a short-term lease that you can renew rather than agreeing to a 5- or 10-year term.

- *Deal only with a reputable leasing company.* Check their references.

- *Demand full disclosure of all financial aspects of the deal.*

- *Have your attorney and/or accountant review all the documents prior to signing.*

- *Get everything in writing.* Under the Statute of Frauds, courts require all contracts that transfer interest in land [such as a lease] to be in writing and be enforceable. Those oral promises from a landlord don't mean a thing if a dispute arises! The owners of a small medical consulting firm learned this lesson the hard way when they relied on their landlord's verbal promises to renew the company's lease. Within a few months, they were looking for a new location.

- *Pay close attention to the details.* Make sure the lease agreement doesn't contain any unpleasant surprises. The owner of a small flower shop was amazed when his landlord told him he would be responsible for the damage a broken pipe in his part of the building had caused in other businesses. "If you're moving into [an older] building, you could be partially liable for large future

(continued)

repair bills for items such as the air-conditioning system or roof if you don't structure your lease carefully," says one expert.

- *Make sure you have good insurance to cover any damage to property.* Renter's insurance is usually very inexpensive and can be a company's salvation if something goes wrong.

- *Verify that the lease's provision on such issues as parking spaces, improvements, operating hours, air conditioning and heating, cleaning and other services, and maintenance suit your business and its financial situation.* Too often, business owners overlook these small but important matters.

- *Ask for the availability to sublease (with the landlord's approval, of course).* Otherwise, if your company folds you may be committed to making large lease payments for many years out of your own pocket.

- *Retailers who lease spaces in shopping centers should try to include a clause that guarantees the landlord will not lease to another competing business (called an "exclusive").* They should also include an *occupancy clause*, which states that they do not pay rent until the center has a specific level of occupancy.

Source: Adapted from Paul DeCeglie, "Beauty and the Lease," *Start-Ups*, November 2000, p. 32; Jan Norman, "How to Negotiate a Lease," *Business Start-Ups*, March 1998, pp. 48–52; Kitty Barnes, "Rising Costs, Changing Tastes Lead to Last Call at Legendary Tavern," *Inc.*, March 1997, p. 26; Barbara Etchieson, "Shutting the Door on Lease Problems," *Nation's Business*, March 1996, pp. 24–25; Susan Hodges, "Getting a Grip on Your Lease," *Nation's Business*, December 1997, pp. 48–49.

this property will not be excessively expensive to modify for his use. Remodeling can add a significant initial expense. The layout of the building may be suitable in many ways, but it may not be ideal for a particular business. Even if a building housed the same kind of business, its existing layout may be completely unsuitable for the way the new owner plans to operate.

Building or buying a building greatly limits an entrepreneur's mobility, however. Some business owners prefer to stay out of the real estate business to retain maximum flexibility and mobility. Plus, not all real estate appreciates in value. Surrounding property can become run-down and consequently can lower a property's value despite the owner's efforts to keep it in excellent condition. Many downtown locations have suffered from this problem.

The Decision to Lease

The major advantage of leasing is that it requires no large initial cash outlay, so the business's funds are available for purchasing inventory or for supporting current operations. Also, lease expenses are tax deductible. Firms that are short on cash usually end up leasing their facilities. Because leasing is usually the least expensive option, most start-up businesses lease their buildings.

Additional advantages of leasing includes:

- The value of maintenance and repair provided by the lessor
- The ability to upgrade equipment to meet your changing needs
- The improved appearance of your balance sheet (if leased assets are excluded)
- No restrictions on your ability to borrow additional funds

Then there's the other side of the leasing coin (even beyond the higher costs that a thorough cash analysis will reveal):

- You have no equity in leased equipment—although you might consider negotiating a purchase option, crediting part of the lease payments toward the purchase price.

- You probably can't cancel the agreement, so you're committed to making payments for the entire period, whether you use the equipment or not.
- While you may write off payments, you can't deduct the depreciation.

Bottom line: Leasing is more expensive over the life of the asset, but you have immediate access to equipment with little upfront investment, thereby freeing up cash for other expenses and investments. Carefully weigh the benefits and the drawbacks before signing that lease.[22]

One major disadvantage of leasing is that the property owner might choose not to renew the lease. A successful business might be forced to move to a new location, and relocation can be extremely costly and could result in a significant loss of established customers. In many cases, it is almost like starting the business again. Also, if a business is successful, the property owner may ask for a significant increase in rent when the lease renewal is negotiated. The owner of the building is well aware of the costs associated with moving and has the upper hand in the negotiations. In some lease arrangements, the owner is compensated, in addition to a monthly rental fee, by a percentage of the tenant's gross sales. This practice is common in shopping centers.

Still another disadvantage to leasing is the limitation on remodeling. A building owner who believes that modifications will reduce the future rental value of the property, will likely require a long-term lease at a higher rent or might not allow the modifications to be made. In addition, all permanent modifications of the structure become the property of the building owner.

CHAPTER SUMMARY

1. Explain the stages in the location decision.
   - The location decision is one of the most important decisions an entrepreneur will make, given its long-term effects on the company. An entrepreneur should look at the choice as a series of increasingly narrow decisions: Which region of the country? Which state? Which city? Which site?
   - Demographic statistics are available from a wide variety of sources, but government agencies such as the Census Bureau have a wealth of detailed data that can guide an entrepreneur in her location decision.
2. Describe the location criteria for retail and service businesses.
   - For retailers and many service businesses, the location decision is especially crucial. They must consider the size of the trade area, the volume of customer traffic, number of parking spots, availability of room for expansion, and the visibility of a site.
3. Outline the basic location options for retail and service businesses.
   - Retail and service businesses have six basic

location options: central business districts (CBDs), neighborhoods, shopping centers and malls, near competitors, outlying areas, and at home.
4. Explain the site selection process for manufacturers.
   - A manufacturer's location decision is strongly influenced by local zoning ordinances. Some areas offer industrial parks designed specifically to attract manufacturers. Two crucial factors for most manufacturers are the accessibility to (and the cost of transporting) raw materials and the quality and quantity of available labor.
5. Discuss the benefits of locating a start-up company in a business incubator.
   - Business incubators are locations that offer flexible, low-cost rental space to their tenants as well as business and consulting services. Their goal is to nurture small companies until they are ready to "graduate" into the larger business community. Many government agencies and universities offer incubator locations.

6. Describe the criteria used to analyze the layout and design considerations of a building, including the Americans with Disabilities Act.
   - When evaluating the suitability of a particular building, an entrepreneur should consider several factors: size (is it large enough to accommodate the business with some room for growth?); construction and external appearance (is the building structurally sound, and does it create the right impression for the business?); entrances (are they inviting?); legal issues (does the building comply with the Americans with Disabilities Act? If not, how much will it cost to bring it up to standard?); signs (are they legible, well located, and easy to see?); interior (does the interior design contribute to our ability to make sales? Is it ergonomically designed?); lights and fixtures (is the lighting adequate for the tasks workers will be performing, and what is the estimated cost of lighting?).
7. Explain the principles of effective layouts for retailers, service businesses, and manufacturers.
   - Layout for retail stores and service businesses depends on the owner's understanding of her customers' buying habits.

Retailers have three basic layout options from which to choose: grid, freeform pattern, and boutique. Some areas of a retail store generate more sales per square foot and are, therefore, more valuable than others.
   - The goal of a manufacturer's layout is to create a smooth, efficient work flow. Three basic options exist: product layout, process layout, and fixed position layout. Two key considerations are worker productivity and materials-handling costs.
8. Evaluate the advantages and disadvantages of building, buying, and leasing a building.
   - Building a new building gives an entrepreneur the opportunity to design exactly what he wants in a brand-new facility; however, not every small business owner can afford to tie up significant amounts of cash in fixed assets. Buying an existing building gives a business owner the freedom to renovate as needed, but this can be an expensive alternative. Leasing a location is a common choice because it is economical, but the business owner faces the uncertainty of lease renewals, rising rents, and renovation problems.

DISCUSSION QUESTIONS

1. How do most small business owners choose a location? Is this wise?
2. What factors should a manager consider when evaluating a region in which to locate a business? Where are such data available?
3. Outline the factors entrepreneurs should consider when selecting a state in which to locate a business.
4. What factors should a seafood-processing plant, a beauty shop, and an exclusive jewelry store consider in choosing a location? List factors for each type of business.
5. What intangible factors might enter into the entrepreneur's location decision?
6. What are zoning laws? How do they affect the location decision?
7. What is the trade area? What determines a small retailer's trade area?
8. Why is it important to discover more than just the number of passersby in a traffic count?
9. What types of information can an entrepreneur collect from census data?
10. Why may a cheap location not be the best location?
11. What function does a small firm's sign serve? What are the characteristics of an effective business sign?
12. Explain the statement: "The portions of a small store's interior space are not of equal value in generating sales revenue." What areas are most valuable?
13. What are some of the major features that are important to a good manufacturing layout?
14. Summarize the advantages and disadvantages of building, buying, and leasing a building.

STEP INTO THE REAL WORLD

1. Ask your librarian to help you with a search of government documents to gain additional insight about a city or town you are familiar with. What did you learn about the area and its residents? What kind of businesses would be most successful there? Least successful?
2. Visit a successful retail store and evaluate its layout. What, if anything, struck you about the layout of the store? What suggestions can you make for improving it?
3. Locate the most recent issue of either *Entrepreneur* or *Fortune* describing the "best cities for (small) business." (For *Entrepreneur*, it is usually the October issue, and for *Fortune*, it is normally an issue in November.) Which cities are in the top 10? What factors did the magazine use to select these cities? Pick a city and explain what makes it an attractive destination for locating a business.
4. Spend some time researching the details of creating an attractive window display. On the basis of your research, develop a simple rating system to evaluate the effectiveness of window displays. Then visit an area of your town or city where there is a cluster of small retail shops. Evaluate the window displays you see using your rating scale. Which ones are most effective? Least effective? Why?

TAKE IT TO THE NET

Visit the Scarborough/Zimmerer home page at **www.prenhall.com/scarborough** for updated information, online resources, Web-based exercises, and sample business plan.

ENDNOTES

1. Srikumar S. Rao, "Corporate Treasure Maps," *FW*, June 20, 1995, p. 61.
2. Kevin Potter, "NC State's Centennial Campus Doubles Corporate Partners in 1998–99," *Hot News—Press Release*, July 9, 1999. Available at *www.centennial.ncsu.edu/news/releases/Doubled.htm*.
3. Michaele Porter, *The Competitive Advantage of Nations* (New York: Simon & Schuster, 1990).
4. Labor, Speed and Business Clustering: Speakers Address Challenges at Alabama Business Conference," *Online Insider—Special Report*, January 15, 2001. Available at *www.conway.com/ssinsider/special/010115a.htm*.
5. Scott McCartney, "Out of the Way Cafes Rely on Fly-In Trade from Hungry Pilots," *Wall Street Journal*, July 26, 2001, p. A1.
6. Chad Terhune, "Anderson SC, Reborn in the 90s Maintains Its Cool in Slowdown," *Wall Street Journal*, July 11, 2001; and Beth Kwon, "LA Renaissance," *FSB*, November 2000, pp. 110–114.
7. Cynthia E. Griffin, "Tech It to the Streets," *Entrepreneur*, October 1997, p. 15.
8. James A. Schriner, "Where Will Employees Want to Live?" *Industry Week*, March 3, 1997, p. 62.
9. Kevin Helliker, "Monster Movie Theaters Invade the Cinema Landscape," *Wall Street Journal*, May 13, 1997, pp. HI, Bl3.
10. Joel Kotkin, "It Takes a Village," *Inc.*, November 2000, p. 77.
11. Vital Statistics," *U.S. News & World Report*, February 12, 2001, p. 21.
12. Dean Storkman, "Mall Developers Envision Shopping Paradise: It's Called Las Vegas," *Wall Street Journal*, July 11, 2001, p. B1.
13. Ellen Wojahn, "They Can't Shut Us Down," *Business@Home*, Summer 1997, pp. 16–23.
14. Veronica Byrd, "Getting into a Zone Could Be This Year's Smart Move," *Your Company*, April/May 1997, pp. 8–10; Cynthia E. Griffin, "In the Zone," *Entrepreneur*, May 1998, pp. 16–17.
15. National Busine ncubation Association, Athens, OH, *www.nbia.org*.
16. Mark Hedricks, "Incubate Your Biz," *Emerging Business*, Summer 2001, pp. 180–184.
17. David R. Evanson, ""Fertile Ground," *Entrepreneur*, August 1997, pp. 55–56.
18. National Business Incubation Association.
19. Sit Up Straight—OSHA Is Watching," *Business Ethics*, May/June 1994, p. 12.
20. Tom Stevens, "Practice People," *Industry Week*, March 17, 1997, pp. 33–36.
21. "Release Me," *Entrepreneur*, January 1998, pp. 48–49.
22. Paul DeCeglie, "Beauty and the Lease," *Start-Up*, November 2000, p. 32.

Chapter

17

Purchasing, Quality Management, and Vendor Analysis

You never know what is enough until you know what is more than enough.

—WILLIAM BLAKE

*Quality is never an accident; it is always the result of high intention,
sincere effort, intelligent direction, and skillful execution;
it represents the wise choice of many alternatives.*

—WILLIAM A. FOSTER

Upon completion of this chapter, you will be able to:

1. Understand the components of a purchasing plan.
2. Explain the principles of total quality management (TQM) and its impact on quality.
3. Conduct economic order quantity (EOQ) analysis to determine the proper level of inventory.
4. Differentiate among the three types of purchase discounts vendors offer.
5. Calculate a company's reorder point. Develop a vendor rating scale.
6. Describe the legal implications of the purchasing function.

This chapter introduces the topics of purchasing, quality management, and vendor analysis, none of which are generally perceived as exciting. However, when understood and effectively implemented in practice these areas can consistently produce higher profitability. Purchasing involves obtaining the right merchandise or services, of the proper quality at an acceptable price. Entrepreneurs quickly learn that if they have not purchased the goods or services they need in adequate volume or the proper quality and at a competitive price, they cannot be competitive. Selecting the proper vendors or suppliers is consequently critical to the success of any business venture. For this reason, an entrepreneur needs to create a purchasing plan, establish well-defined measures of product/service quality, and select vendors/suppliers based on objectively determined variables.

THE PURCHASING PLAN

1. Understand the components of a purchasing plan.

Purchasing involves the acquisition of needed materials, supplies, services, and equipment of the right quality, in the proper quantities, for reasonable prices, at the appropriate time, from the right vendor or supplier. A major objective of purchasing is to acquire enough (but not too much!) stock to ensure smooth, uninterrupted production or sales and to see that the merchandise is delivered on time. Companies large and small are purchasing goods and supplies from all across the globe, and coordinating the pieces of the global puzzle requires a comprehensive purchasing plan. The plan must identify a company's quality requirements, its cost targets, and the criteria for determining the best supplier, considering such factors as reliability, service, delivery, and cooperation.

The purchasing plan is closely linked to the other functional areas of managing a small business: production, marketing, sales, engineering, accounting, finance, and others. A purchasing plan should recognize this interaction and help integrate the purchasing function into the total organization. A small company's purchasing plan should focus on the five key elements of purchasing; quality, quantity, price, timing, and vendor selection (see Figure 17.1).

Figure 17.1
The Key
Components of a
Purchasing Plan

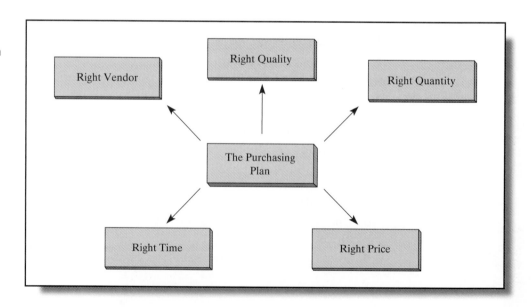

QUALITY

2. Explain the principles of total quality management (TQM) and its impact on quality.

Not long ago businesses saw quality products and services as luxuries for customers who could afford them. Many companies mistakenly believed that producing, and therefore purchasing, high-quality products and services was too costly. The last few decades, however, have taught every businessperson that quality goods and services are absolutely *essential* to staying competitive. The benefits companies earn by pursuing quality products, services, and processes come not only in the form of fewer defects but also as lower costs, higher productivity, reduced cycle time, greater market share, increased customer satisfaction, and higher customer retention rates. W. Edwards Deming, one of the founding fathers of the modern quality movement, always claimed that higher quality actually resulted in lower cost. Internally, companies with a quality focus report significant improvements in work-related factors such as increased employee morale, lower employee turnover, and enhanced quality of work life. Benefits such as these can result in earning a significant competitive advantage over rivals of *any* size.

Total quality companies believe in and manage with the attitude of continuous improvement, a concept the Japanese call *kaizen*. The kaizen philosophy holds that small improvements made continuously over time accumulate into a radically reshaped and improved process. *The Alexander Doll Company of New York City knows the value of improving quality through continuous improvement. The company fell into such bad financial shape that it declared bankruptcy before managers decided to try to turn it around with kaizen. Managers began by setting up a cross-functional team (a team of workers from different functional areas of the business) to identify problems with the production process and to make suggestions for solving them. The first problem the team tackled was the manufacturing process itself, which was spread out over three floors, causing a high breakage rate. The team recommended moving the production process onto one floor and rearranging it to minimize handling. Alexander created more teams, which went to work on 65 projects covering all phases of its operation. The results: The distance dolls traveled during manufacturing decreased from 630 feet to just 40 feet. The inventory of unfinished doll pieces dropped from 29,000 to 34, and productivity went from eight dolls per person per day to 25! In addition, the lead time to produce a doll went from 90 days to just 90 minutes. Managers cannot credit any single change with producing such dramatic results; rather, they are the outcome of many small changes teams of creative workers came up with over time.*[1]

Companies that did not respond to the challenge to improve the quality of their products did not survive. In our market-driven competitive environment, consumers have made their preferences clear and quality products and competitive prices are essential to survival.

Total Quality Management

Under the total quality management (TQM) philosophy, companies define a quality product as one that conforms to predetermined standards that satisfy customers' demands. That means getting *everything*—from delivery and invoicing to installation and follow-up—right the first time. Although these companies know that they may never reach their targets of perfect quality, they never stop striving for perfection, recognizing that even a 99.9 percent level of quality is not good enough (see Table 17.1). The businesses, both large and small, that have effectively implemented these programs understand that the process involves a total commitment from strategy to practice from the top of the organization to the bottom.

IN THE FOOTSTEPS OF AN ENTREPRENEUR
Why Certify?

It took LabChem more than nine months and cost the small specialty chemical manufacturer more than $50,000, but, according to vice-president Mike Semon, it was definitely worth it. "It was like winning our Stanley Cup," says Semon. LabChem has seen costs drop, productivity rise, and more customers come on board, many of whom had never considered buying from the small, 25-employee company. What caused the transformation? LabChem earned ISO 9000 certification!

Once a concern only for major corporations, ISO 9000 certification has attracted the attention of a growing number of small businesses who see the benefits of certification. Established by the International Organization for Standards (ISO) in 1979, ISO 9000 certification established a uniform set of standards that are designed to improve a company's quality, productivity, and efficiency. Rather than certify the quality of a company's finished products or services, ISO's standards verify that it has established a functional quality control process and consistently follows it. The logic is that if a company's quality processes are appropriate and it follows them consistently, high-quality products and services will result. More than 100 countries have adopted ISO 9000 as their national quality standard.

Why are small companies such as LabChem spending thousands of dollars to become ISO 9000 certified? One fourth of all the corporations around the globe require their suppliers to be ISO 9000 certified. In other words, these companies are telling their suppliers, large and small, who want to keep their business that they must prove their quality by meeting the ISO's requirements. One survey by the *Quality Systems Update* newsletter of all ISO 9000–certified companies found that 83 percent encourage their suppliers also to become certified. "The pressure for companies to become certified . . . is increasing and will continue to increase," says one ISO consultant. Many of the companies that are discovering the benefits of becoming certified are small businesses. The *Quality Systems Update* newsletter survey found that 58 percent of all registered companies had annual sales of less than $4 million. "The growth among smaller firms seeking ISO 9000 registration in the past several years has been phenomenal," says the head of an ISO consulting firm.

The benefits of ISO 9000 certification are both internal and external. A quality survey of ISO 9000–certified companies found that 95 percent had derived internal benefits such as improved quality, more efficient systems, and higher productivity. Nearly 85 percent cited higher quality awareness among workers as an advantage. Externally, ISO certification opens the door to more customers. After losing a customer because their company lacked certification, managers at Arizona Calibration and Electronics Corporation, an eight-person company that repairs and calibrates mechanical testing equipment, set gaining ISO certification as a top priority. Now that the company is certified, "We're getting a lot of new interest all of a sudden from people who didn't even know we existed before," says president Frank Havelock. At Sub-Tronics, a 25-employee manufacturer of magnetic devices, keeping a major customer, 3M Corporation, was the incentive to earn ISO 9000 certification. "3M notified us (that) it (preferred) its vendors to be ISO certified," says Nancy Peck, the company's quality assurance manager. "We didn't want to lose them (as a customer)."

Gaining ISO 9000 certification, like most things that are worthwhile, takes time, money, and effort. The average cost for a small business (those with less than $1 million in sales) to earn certification is $71,000: $51,000 for internal expenses and $20,000 for external expenses such as quality consultants and trainers. The average time required to pass the final ISO 9000 audit is 15 months. Despite the cost and time involved, companies see the payoff of becoming certified. Nancy Peck of Sub-Tronics says that her company now has the processes—and the credentials—to go head to head with any competitor anywhere in the world. LabChem's Mike Semon says, "There will be some firms that won't need ISO 9000 certification. But for many firms that don't have it, they need to ask themselves one question: "Do I want my company to be in business five years from now?"

1. What benefits does a small company derive from becoming ISO certified? What are the costs?

(continued)

Rather than trying to inspect quality into products and services after they are completed, TQM instills the philosophy of doing the job right the first time. Although the concept is simple, implementing such a process is a challenge that requires a very different kind of thinking and very different culture than most organizations are comfortable with. Because the changes TQM requires are so significant, patience is a must for companies adopting the philosophy. Consistent quality improvements rarely occur overnight. Yet too many small business managers think, "We'll implement TQM today and tomorrow our quality will soar." TQM is *not* a "quick-fix," short-term program that can magically push a company to world-class status overnight. Because it requires such fundamental, often drastic, changes in the way a company does business, TQM takes time both to implement and to produce results. Patience is a must. Although some small businesses that use TQM begin to see some improvements within just a matter of weeks, the *real* benefits take longer to realize. Studies show that it takes at least 3 or 4 years before TQM principles gain acceptance among employees, and that 8 to 10 years are necessary to fully implement TQM in a company.[2]

To implement TQM successfully, a small business owner must rely on 10 fundamental principles:

1. *Shift from a management-driven culture to a participative, team-based one.* Two basic tenets of TQM are employee involvement and teamwork. Business owners must be willing to push decision-making authority down the organization to where the real experts are. Teams of employees working together to identify and solve problems can be a powerful force in an organization of any size. Experience with TQM has taught entrepreneurs that the combined knowledge, and especially experience of the total workforce, is much greater than that of only one person. Tapping into the problem-solving capabilities of the team produces profitable results.

Table 17.1
Why 99.9% Quality
Isn't Good Enough

Most companies willingly accept a certain percentage of errors and defects. Usually, the range is 1% to 5%. In some companies, it is regarded as a routine part of daily operations.

However, quality consultants say that even 99.9% isn't good enough. To improve their own quality, many companies are relying on a single supplier for their raw materials and components. Partnering between suppliers and customers in such a close relationship means that those sole-source suppliers have to shoot for 100% quality and performance! One small maker of fabrics used in the paper industry forged such a partnership with a single supplier but made it clear that just one late or poor-quality shipment would terminate the relationship.

2. *Modify the reward system to encourage teamwork and innovation.* Because the team—not the individual—is the building block of TQM, companies often have to modify their compensation systems to reflect team performance. Traditional compensation methods pit one employee against another, undermining any sense of cooperation. Often, they are based on seniority rather than on how much an employee contributes to the company. Compensations systems under TQM usually rely on incentives, linking pay to performance. However, rather than tying pay to individual performance, these systems focus on team-based incentives. Each person's pay depends on whether the entire team (or, sometimes, the entire company) meets a clearly defined, measurable set of performance objectives. *For instance, when Laitram Corporation, a small manufacturing company, implemented TQM, it determined employees' base pay on their "market value," using regional and local surveys. Managers also set up a profit-sharing incentive system based on overall company and team performances. Workers have input into the system because they evaluate their co-workers' performance as well as those of their managers. "Employees were skeptical of the whole system," says human resource manager, James Evens, "until they started getting checks."*[3]

3. *Train workers constantly to give them the tools they need to produce quality and to upgrade the company's knowledge base.* One of the most important factors in making long-term, constant improvements in a company's processes is teaching workers the philosophy and the tools of TQM. Admonishing employees to "produce quality" or offering them rewards for high quality is futile unless a company gives them the tools and know-how to achieve that end. Managers must be dedicated to making their companies "learning organizations" that encourage people to upgrade their skills and give them the opportunities and incentives to do so. The most successful companies spend anywhere from 1 to 5 percent of their employees' time on training, most of it invested in workers, not managers. To give employees a sense of how the quality of their job fits into the big picture, many TQM companies engage in **cross-training,** teaching workers to do other jobs in the company.

4. *Train employees to measure quality with the tools of statistical process control (SPC).* The only way to ensure gains in quality is to measure results objectively and to trace the company's progress toward its quality objectives. That requires teaching employees how to use statistical process control techniques such as fishbone charts, Pareto charts, control charts, and measures of process capability.[*] Without knowledgeable workers using these quantitative tools, TQM cannot produce the intended results.

5. *Use Pareto's Law to focus TQM efforts. One of the toughest decisions managers face in companies embarking on TQM for the first time is "where do we start?"* The best way to answer that fundamental question is to use Pareto's Law (also called the 80/20 Rule), which states that 80 percent of a company's quality problems arise from just 20 percent of all causes. By identifying this small percentage of causes and focusing quality improvement efforts on them, a company gets maximum returns for minimum efforts. This simple, yet powerful rule forces workers to concentrate resources on the most significant problems first, where payoffs are likely to be biggest, and helps build momentum for a successful TQM effort. *For instance, when one company's customers began complaining about their product losses during shipment, a team of salespeople used Pareto analysis to*

---

[*] To learn more about the tools of statistical quality control, look in modern statistics or production management textbooks or visit the following Web sites: *http://deming.eng.clemson.edu/pub/tutorials/qctoosl qct.htmPCHART* and *www.enlac.com/whitepap/project6htm.*

identify the small percentage of shippers who were responsible for the bulk of the losses. They collected the data they needed, analyzed them, and solved the problem with just a few telephone calls and visits.[4]

6. *Share information with everyone in the organization.* Asking employees to make decisions and to assume responsibility for creating quality necessitates that the owner share information with them. Employees cannot make sound decisions consistent with the company's quality initiative if managers are unwilling to give them the information they need to make those decisions.

7. *Focus quality improvements on astonishing the customer.* The heart of TQM is customer satisfaction—better yet, customer astonishment. Unfortunately, some companies focus their quality improvement efforts on areas that never benefit the customer. Quality improvements with no customer focus (either internal or external) are wasted.

8. *Don't rely on inspection to produce quality products and services.* The traditional approach to achieving quality was to create a product or service and then to rely on an army of inspectors to "weed out" all of the defectives. Not only is such a system a terrible waste of resources (consider the cost of scrap, rework, and no-value-added inspections), but it gives managers no opportunity for continuous improvement. The only way to improve a process is to discover the cause of poor quality, fix it (the sooner, the better), and learn from it so that workers can *avoid* the problem in the future. Using the statistical tools of the TQM approach allows a company to learn from its mistakes with a consistent approach to constantly improving quality.

9. *Avoid using TQM to place blame on those who make mistakes.* In many firms, the only reason managers seek out mistakes is to find someone to blame for them. The result: a culture based on fear and an unwillingness of workers to take chances to innovate. The goal of TQM is to improve the processes in which people work, *not* to lay blame on workers. Searching out "the guilty party" is fruitless! The TQM philosophy sees each problem that arises as an opportunity for improving the company's system.

10. *Strive for continuous improvement in processes as well as in products and services.* There is no finish line in the race for quality. A company's goal must be to improve the quality of its processes, products, and services constantly, no matter how high it currently stands!

Many of these principles are evident in quality guru W. Edwards Deming's 14 points, a capsulized version of how to build a successful TQM approach (see Table 17.2).

Implementing a TQM program successfully begins at the top. If the owner or chief executive of a company doesn't actively and visibly support the initiative, the employees who must make it happen will never accept it. TQM requires change—in the way a company defines quality, in the way it sees its customers, in the way it treats employees, and in the way it sees itself. Successful implementation involves the modification in the organization's operational culture as much as in the work processes. What is being changed in the mindset of everyone involved? World-class organizations in the twenty-first century have continuous improvement as a fundamental element in all their competitive strategic initiatives.

QUANTITY: THE ECONOMIC ORDER QUANTITY

The typical small business has its largest investment in inventory. But an investment in inventory is not profitable because dollars spent return nothing until the inventory

Table 17.2
Deming's 14 Points

Total quality management cannot succeed as a piecemeal program or without true commitment to its philosophy. W. Edwards Deming, the man most visibly connected to TQM, drove home these concepts with his 14 points, the essential elements for integrating TQM successfully into a company. Deming's message was straightforward: Companies must transform themselves into customer-oriented, quality-focused organizations in which teams of employees have the training, the resources, and the freedom to pursue quality on a daily basis. The goal is to track the performance of a process, whether manufacturing a clock or serving a bank customer, and to develop ways to minimize variation in the system, eliminate defects, and spur innovation. The 14 points are:

1. *Constantly strive to improve products and services.* This requires total dedication to improving quality, productivity, and service—*continuously.*

2. *Adopt a total quality philosophy.* There are no shortcuts to quality improvement; it requires a completely new way of thinking and managing.

3. *Correct defects as they happen,* rather than relying on mass inspection of end products. Real quality comes from improving the process, not from inspecting finished products and services. At that point, it's too late. Statistical process control charts can help workers detect when a process is producing poor-quality goods and services. Then they can stop it, make corrections, and get the process back on target.

4. *Don't award business on price alone.* Rather than choosing the lowest-cost vendor, businesses should work toward establishing close relationships with the vendors who offer the highest quality.

5. *Constantly improve the system of production and service.* Managers must focus the entire company on customer satisfaction, must measure results, and must make adjustments as necessary

6. *Institute training.* Workers cannot improve quality and lower costs without proper training to erase old ways of doing things.

7. *Institute leadership.* The supervisor's job is not to boss workers around; it is to lead. The nature of the work is more like coaching than controlling.

8. *Drive out fear.* People often are afraid to point out problems because they fear the repercussions. Managers must encourage and reward employee suggestions.

9. *Break down barriers among staff areas.* Departments within organizations often erect needless barriers to protect their own turf. Total quality requires a spirit of teamwork and cooperation across the entire organization.

10. *Eliminate superficial slogans and goals.* These only offend employees because they imply that workers could do a better job if they would only try.

11. *Eliminate standard quotas.* They emphasize quantity over quality. Not everyone can move at the same rate and still produce quality.

12. *Remove barriers to pride of workmanship.* Most workers want to do quality work. Eliminating "de-motivators" frees them to achieve quality results.

13. *Institute vigorous education and retraining.* Managers must teach employees the new methods of continuous improvement, including statistical process control techniques.

14. *Take demonstrated management action to achieve the transformation.* Although success requires involvement of all levels of the organization, the impetus for change must come from the top.

These 14 interrelated elements contribute to a chain reaction effect. As a company improves its quality, costs decline, productivity increases, the company gains additional market share due to its ability to provide high-quality products at competitive prices, and the company and its employees prosper.

Source: The W. Edwards Deming Institute, *www.deming.org/deminghtmll/wedi.html.*

3. Conduct economic order quantity (EOQ) analysis to determine the proper level of inventory.

is sold. In a sense, the small firm's inventory is its largest non–interest-bearing "account." The owner must focus on controlling this investment and on maintaining proper inventory levels.

A primary objective of this portion of the purchasing plan is to generate an adequate turnover of merchandise by purchasing proper quantities. Tying up capital in the maintenance of extra inventory limits the firm's working capital and exerts pressure on its cash flows. Also, the firm risks the danger of being stuck with spoiled or obsolete merchandise, an extremely serious problem for many small businesses. Excess inventory also takes up valuable store or selling space that could be used for items with higher turnover rates and more profit potential. On the other hand, maintaining too little inventory can be extremely costly. An owner will be forced to reorder merchandise frequently, escalating total inventory costs. Also, inventory stockouts will occur when customer demand exceeds the firm's supply of merchandise, causing customer ill will. Persistent stockouts are inconvenient for customers, and many will eventually choose to shop elsewhere.

Clearly the small business must maintain enough inventory to meet customer orders, but not so much that storage costs and inventory investment are excessive. The analytical techniques used to determine **economic order quantities (EOQs)** will help the manager compute the amount of stock to purchase with an order or to produce with each production run to minimize total inventory costs. To compute the proper amount of stock to order or to produce, the small business owner must first determine the three principal elements of total inventory costs: the cost of the units, the holding (or carrying) cost, and the setup (or ordering) cost.

Cost of Units

The cost of the units is simply the number of units demanded for a particular time period multiplied by the cost per unit. Suppose that a small manufacturer of lawn mowers forecasts demand for the upcoming year to be 100,000 mowers. He needs to order enough wheels at $1.55 each to supply the production department. So he computes:

$$\text{Total annual cost of units} = D \times C \tag{1}$$

where:

D = Annual demand (in units)
C = Cost of a single unit ($)

In this example,

D = 100,000 mowers $\times$ 4 wheels per mower = 400,000 wheels
C = $1.55/wheel

$$\begin{aligned} \text{Total annual cost of units} &= D \times C \tag{2}\\ &= 400{,}000 \text{ wheels} \times \$1.55 \\ &= \$620{,}000 \end{aligned}$$

Holding (Carrying) Costs

The typical costs of holding inventory include the costs of storage, insurance, taxes, interest, depreciation, spoilage, obsolescence, and pilferage. The expense involved in physically storing the items in inventory is usually substantial, especially if the inventories are large. The owner may have to rent or build additional warehousing facilities, pushing the cost of storing the inventory even higher. The firm may also incur expenses in transferring items into and out of inventory. The cost of storage also includes the expense of operating the facility (e.g., heating, lighting, refrigeration), as well as the depreciation, taxes, and interest on the building. Most small business owners purchase insurance on their inventories to shift the risk of fire, theft, flood, and other disasters to the insurer. The premiums paid for this coverage are also included in the cost of holding inventory. In general, the larger the firm's average inventory, the greater its storage cost.

Many small business owners fail to recognize the interest expense associated with carrying large inventories. In many cases the interest expense is evident when the firm borrows money to purchase inventory. But a less obvious interest expense is the opportunity cost associated with investing in inventory. In other words, the owner could have used the money invested in inventory (a non–interest-bearing investment) for some other purpose, such as plant expansion, research and development, or reducing debt. Thus, the cost of independent financing of inventory is the cost of forgoing the opportunity to use those funds elsewhere. A substantial inventory investment ties up a large amount of money unproductively.

Depreciation costs represent the reduced value of inventory over time. Some businesses are strongly influenced by the depreciation of inventory. For example, a small auto dealer's inventory is subject to depreciation because he must sell models left over from one year at reduced prices.

Spoilage, obsolescence, and pilferage also add to the costs of holding inventory. Some small firms, especially those that deal in fad merchandise, assume an extremely high risk of obsolescence. For example, a fashion merchandiser with a large inventory of the latest styles may be left with worthless merchandise when styles suddenly change. Small companies selling perishables must always be aware of the danger of spoilage. For example, the owner of a small fish market must plan purchases carefully to ensure a fresh inventory. Unless the owner establishes sound inventory control procedures, the business will suffer losses from employee theft and shoplifting.

The lawn mower manufacturer example illustrates the cost of holding inventory:

$$\text{Total annual holding (carrying) costs} = \frac{Q}{2} \times H$$

(3)

where:

Q = Quantity of inventory ordered
H = Holding cost per unit per year

The greater the quantity ordered, the greater the inventory carrying costs. This relationship is shown in Table 17.3, assuming that the cost of carrying a single unit of inventory for 1 year is $1.25.

Setup (Ordering) Costs

The various expenses incurred in actually ordering materials and inventory or in setting up the production line to manufacture them determine the level of setup or ordering costs of a product. The costs of obtaining materials and inventory typically include preparing purchase orders; analyzing and choosing vendors; processing, handling, and expending orders; receiving and inspecting items; and performing all the required accounting and clerical functions. Even if the small company produces its own supply of goods, it encounters most of these same expenses. Ordering costs are usually relatively fixed, regardless of the quantity ordered.

Table 17.3

Carrying Costs

If Q Is . . .	$Q/2$ Average Inventory Is . . .	$Q/2 \times H$, Carrying Cost Is . . .
500	250	$ 312.50
1,000	500	625.00
2,000	1,000	1,250.00
3,000	1,500	1,875.00
4,000	2,000	2,500.00
5,000	2,500	3,125.00
6,000	3,000	3,750.00
7,000	3,500	4,375.00
8,000	4,000	5,000.00
9,000	4,500	5,625.00
10,000	5,000	6,250.00

Setup or ordering costs are found by multiplying the number of orders made in a year (or the number of production runs in a year) by the cost of placing a single order (or the cost of setting up a single production run). In the lawn mower manufacturing example, the annual requirement is 400,000 wheels per year and the cost to place an order is $9.00, so the ordering costs are as follows:

$$\text{Total annual setup (ordering) cost} = \frac{D}{Q} \times S \quad \text{(4)}$$

where:

D = Annual demand
Q = Quantity of inventory ordered
S = Setup (ordering) costs for a single run (or order)

The greater the quantity ordered, the smaller the number of orders placed. This relationship is shown in Table 17.4, assuming an ordering cost of $9.00 per order.

Solving for EOQ

Clearly, if carrying costs were the only expense involved in obtaining inventory, the small business manager would purchase the smallest number of units possible in each order to minimize the cost of holding the inventory. For example, if the lawn mower manufacturer purchased four wheels per order, carrying cost would be minimized:

$$\text{Carrying cost} = \frac{Q}{2} \times H \quad \text{(5)}$$

$$= \frac{4}{2} \times \$1.25$$

$$= \$2.50$$

but his ordering cost would be outrageous

$$\text{Ordering cost} = \frac{D}{Q} \times S \quad \text{(6)}$$

$$= \frac{100,000 \times \$9}{4}$$

$$= \$2,250,000$$

Table 17.4
Setup Cost

If Q Is . . .	D/Q, Number of Orders per Year, Is . . .	$D/Q \times S$, Ordering (Setup) Cost, Is . . .
500	800	$7,200.00
1,000	400	3,600.00
5,000	80	720.00
10,000	40	360.00

Obviously, this is not the small manufacturer's ideal inventory solution.

Similarly, if ordering costs were the only expense involved in procuring inventory, the small business manager would purchase the largest number of units possible in order to minimize the ordering cost. In our example, if the lawn mower manufacturer purchased 400,000 wheels per order, ordering cost would be minimized:

$$\text{Ordering cost} = \frac{D}{Q} \times S$$

$$= \frac{400,000}{400,000} \times \$9 \qquad \textbf{(7)}$$

$$= \$9$$

but his carrying cost would be tremendously high:

$$\text{Carrying cost} = Q \times H$$

$$= \frac{400,000}{2} \times \$1.25 \qquad \textbf{(8)}$$

$$= \$250,000$$

Figure 17.2
Inventory Costs

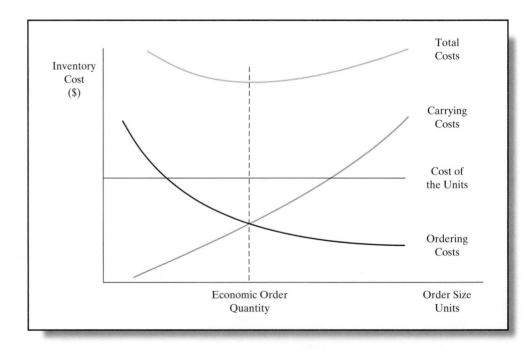

A quick inspection shows that neither of those solutions minimizes the total cost of the manufacturer's inventory. Total cost is composed of the cost of the unit, carrying cost, and ordering costs:

$$\text{Total cost} = (D \times C) + \left(\frac{Q}{2} \times H\right) + \left(\frac{D}{Q} \times S\right) \tag{9}$$

These costs are graphed in Figure 17.2. Notice that as the quantity ordered increases, the ordering costs decrease and the carrying costs increase.

The EOQ formula simply balances the ordering cost and the carrying cost of the small business owner's inventory so that total costs are minimized. Table 17.5 summarizes the total costs for various values of Q for our lawn mower manufacturer.

As Table 17.4 and Figure 17.2 illustrate, the EOQ formula locates the minimum point on the total cost curve, which occurs where the cost of carrying inventory ($Q/2 \times H$) equals the cost of ordering inventory ($DIQ \times S$). If the small business places the smallest number of orders possible each year, its ordering cost is minimized but its carrying cost is maximized. Conversely, if the firm orders the smallest number of units possible in each order, its carrying cost is minimized, but its ordering cost is maximized. Total inventory cost is minimized when carrying cost and ordering costs are balanced.

Let us return to our lawn mower manufacturer and compute its EOQ, using the following formula:

$$S = \$9.00 \text{ per order}$$
$$C = \$1.55 \text{ per wheel} \tag{10}$$

$$EOQ = \sqrt{\frac{2 \times D \times S}{H}}$$

$$= \sqrt{\frac{2 \times 400{,}000 \times 9.00}{1.25}}$$

$$= 2{,}400 \text{ wheels}$$

To minimize total inventory cost, the lawn mower manufacturer should order 2,400 wheels at a time. Further

$$\text{Number of orders per year} = \frac{D}{Q}$$

$$= \frac{400{,}000}{2{,}400} \tag{11}$$

$$= 166.67 \text{ orders}$$

Table 17.5
Economic Order Quantity and Total Cost

If Q Is . . .	$D \times C$, Cost of Units, Is . . .	$Q/2 \times H$, Carrying Cost, Is . . .	$D/Q \times S$, Ordering Cost, Is . . .	TC, Total Cost, Is . . .
500	$620,000	$ 312.00	$7,200.00	$627,512.00
1,000	$620,000	$ 625.00	$3,600.00	$624,225.00
2,400	**$620,000**	**$1,500.00**	**$1,500.00**	**$613,000.00**
5,000	$620,000	$3,125.00	$ 720.00	$623,845.00
10,000	$620,000	$6,250.00	$ 360.00	$626,610.00

This manufacturer will place approximately 167 orders this year at a minimum total cost of $623,000, computed as follows:

$$\text{Total cost} = (D \times C) + \left(\frac{Q}{2} \times H\right) + \left(\frac{D}{Q} \times S\right) \tag{12}$$

$$= (400,000 \times 1.55) + \left(\frac{2,400}{2} \times 1.25\right) + \left(\frac{400,000}{2,400} + 9.00\right)$$

$$= \$620,000 \qquad + \$1,500 \qquad + \$1,500$$

$$= \$623,000$$

EOQ with Usage

The preceding EOQ model assumes that orders are filled instantaneously; that is, fresh inventory arrives all at once. Because that assumption does not hold true for many small manufacturers, it is necessary to consider a variation of the basic EQQ model that allows inventory to be added over a period of time rather than instantaneously. In addition, the manufacturer is likely to be taking items from inventory for use in the assembly process over the same time period. For example, the lawn mower manufacturer may be producing blades to replenish his supply, but, at the same time, assembly workers are reducing the supply of blades to make finished mowers. The key feature of this version of the EQQ model is that inventories are used while inventories are being added.

Using the lawn mower manufacturer as an example, we can compute the EOQ for the blades. To make the calculation, we need two additional pieces of information: the usage rate for the blades, U, and the plant's capacity to manufacture the blades, P. Suppose that the maximum number of lawn mower blades the company can manufacture is 480 per day. We know from the previous illustration that annual demand for mowers is 100,000 units (therefore, 100,000 blades). If the plant operates 5 days per week for 50 weeks (250 days), its usage rate is

$$U = \frac{100,000 \text{ units per year}}{250 \text{ days}} = 400 \text{ units per day} \tag{13}$$

It costs $325 to set up the blade manufacturing line and $8.71 to store one blade for 1 year. The cost of producing a blade is *$4.85*. To compute *EOQ* we modify the basic formula to get:

$$EOQ = \sqrt{\frac{2 \times D \times S}{H \times \left(1 - \dfrac{U}{P}\right)}} \tag{14}$$

For the lawn mower manufacturer,

$$D = 100,000 \text{ blades}$$
$$S = \$325 \text{ per production run}$$
$$H = \$8.71 \text{ per blade per year}$$
$$U = 400 \text{ blades per day}$$
$$P = 480 \text{ blades per day}$$

$$EOQ = \sqrt{\frac{2 \times 100{,}000 \times 325}{8.71 \times \left(1 - \dfrac{400}{480}\right)}}$$

$$= 6{,}691.50 \text{ blades} = 6{,}692 \text{ blades}$$

Therefore, to minimize total inventory cost, the lawn mower manufacturer should produce 6,692 blades per production run. Also,

$$\text{Number of production runs per year} = \frac{D}{Q}$$

$$= \frac{100{,}000 \text{ blades}}{6{,}692 \text{ blades/run}} \qquad \textbf{(15)}$$

$$= 14.9 = 15 \text{ runs}$$

The manufacturer will make 15 production runs during the year at a total cost of:

$$\text{Total cost} = (D \times C) + \left(\frac{1 - \dfrac{U}{P} \times Q}{2} \times H\right) + \left(\frac{D}{Q} \times S\right) \qquad \textbf{(16)}$$

$$= (100{,}000 \times \$4.85) + \left(\frac{1 - \dfrac{400}{480} \times 6.692}{2} \times 8.71\right) + \left(\frac{100{,}000}{6{,}692} \times \$325\right)$$

$$= \$485{,}000 + \$4{,}857 + \$4{,}857$$

$$= \$494{,}714$$

Small business managers must remember that the EOQ analysis is based on estimations of cost and demand. The final result is only as accurate as the input used. Consequently, this analytical tool serves only as a guideline for decision making. The final answer may not be the ideal solution because of intervening factors, such as opportunity costs or seasonal fluctuations. Knowledgeable entrepreneurs use EOQ analysis as a starting point in making a decision and then will use managerial, judgment to produce a final ruling.

PRICE

For the typical small business owner, price is always a substantial factor in purchasing inventory and supplies. In many cases, an entrepreneur can negotiate price with potential suppliers on large orders of frequently purchased items. In other instances, perhaps when small quantities of items are purchased infrequently, the small business owner must pay list price.

The typical small business owner shops around and then orders from the supplier offering the best price. Still, this does not mean the small business manager should always purchase inventory and supplies at the lowest price available. The best purchase price is the lowest price at which the owner can obtain goods and services *of acceptable quality*. This guideline usually yields the best value more often than simply purchasing the lowest-priced goods.

IN THE FOOTSTEPS OF AN ENTREPRENEUR
Fewer Surprises Are a Good Thing

Tom Thornbury, CEO of Softub, a $15 million maker of hot tubs, understands just how important the right vendors can be to a small company's success. In fact, he learned the hard way that one bad supplier can threaten the health of a growing business. Several years ago, Softub purchased from an outside supplier the motor, pump, and assembly unit that provide the jet action in its hot tubs. Thornbury met with the company's owner and heard other customers rave about its quality. " That was back when I was the purchasing department," says Thornbury. "That might have been the problem." Before long, defective jet assemblies turned up in Softub's factory and in customers' homes. Then the supplier went out of business. Thornbury scrambled to repair all of the faulty assemblies and to try to keep its network of distributors from defecting. He estimates the entire episode cost his company about $500,000. "If we had done a better job of surveying our suppliers," he says, "this might not have happened."

The odds of its happening again are slim. Because two thirds of Softub's products cost is in materials—from sheet metal to nuts and bolts—that the company purchases from outside suppliers, managers saw the need to evaluate vendors more thoroughly before inviting them to become a crucial link in its production process. Under the direction of Gary Anderson, Softub's purchasing agent, cross-functional teams of 10 employees visit potential vendors on site and use a checklist Anderson developed to evaluate them. The checklist covers everything from safety devices and cleanliness to preventive maintenance and quality processes. "(The checklist) forces the team to focus on specific areas so we don't forget anything when we're on a visit," says Anderson.

Team visits may take as little as two hours or as long as two days, and team members delve into every aspect of the prospective supplier's business. They interview everyone from the president to the factory workers and ask lots of questions. Before going on site, every team member receives a packet of information about the company, including any articles about it from trade journals.

Back in Softub's offices, the checklist generates a great deal of discussion about critical issues such as quality and on-time delivery. Anderson also verifies the accuracy of every potential vendor's claims by contacting at least three of its customers. When all the information is in, the team makes its recommendation to the management team, who selects one vendor. "The payoff is that we're recruiting a better breed of supplier," says Thornbury. Since beginning to use the forms, Softub is getting fewer defective products from its suppliers, and its vendor turnover rate has been cut in half. Plus, Softub has discovered one more unexpected benefit: closer relationships with quality suppliers. On several occasions, suppliers have given employees at Softub ideas and suggestions on how to solve production problems. "We're developing partnerships in which we have a pretty free exchange of information," says Thornbury. "Also, as we've gotten to know our vendors better, there are fewer surprises. In a manufacturing operation, surprises can be lethal."

1. Why is using a vendor evaluation scale important to companies such as Softub?

2. What benefits can companies that conduct vendor audits expect to gain?

Source: Adapted from Stephanie Gruner, "The Smart Vendor-Audit Checklist," *Inc.*, April 1995, pp. 93–95.

Recall that one of Deming's 14 points is "End the practice of awarding business on the basis of price tag." Without proof of quality, an item with the lowest initial price may produce the highest total cost. Deming condemned the practice of constantly switching suppliers in search of the lowest initial price because it increases the variability of a process and lowers its quality. Instead, he recommended that businesses establish long-term relationships built on mutual trust and cooperation with a single supplier. *For instance, when New Pig Inc., a small manufacturer of contained absorbents (socklike bundles of absorbent materials used to soak up industrial leaks and spills), set out to improve quality, reduce the time required to introduce new products, and innovate new product development, it turned to its suppliers for help. New Pig depends on its suppliers for some element of every one of the 3,000 items it sells, so establishing closer supplier relationships was one of management's top priorities. The company began forming strategic alliances with its 30 largest-volume suppliers, improving communication with them and involving them in product development and quality improvement efforts. One joint project resulted in changing a shipping method that produced savings of hundreds of thousands of dollars. "We've developed a synergy and are moving forward together (with our suppliers) to cut costs, be more efficient, and increase profits," says Doug Evans, New Pig's director of strategic purchasing.[5]*

When evaluating a supplier's price, small business owners must consider not only the actual price of the goods and services but also the selling terms accompanying them. In some cases the selling terms can be more important than the price itself. Sometimes a vendor's terms might include some type of purchase discount. Vendors typically offer three types of discounts: trade discounts, quantity discounts, and cash discounts.

Trade Discounts

4. Differentiate among the three types of purchase discounts that vendors offer.

Trade discounts are established on a graduated scale and depend on a small firm's position in the channel of distribution. In other words, trade discounts recognize the fact that manufacturers, wholesalers, and retailers perform a variety of vital functions at various stages in the channel of distribution and compensate them for providing these needed activities. Figure 17.3 illustrates a typical trade discount structure.

Quantity Discounts

Quantity discounts are designed to encourage businesses to order large quantities of merchandise and supplies. Vendors are able to offer lower prices on bulk purchases because the cost per unit is lower than for handling small orders. Quantity discounts normally exist in two forms: noncumulative and cumulative. Noncumulative quantity discounts are granted only if a large enough volume of merchandise is purchased

Figure 17.3
Trade Discount
Structure

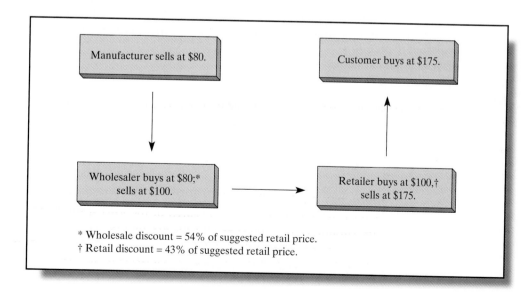

Manufacturer sells at $80.

Customer buys at $175.

Wholesaler buys at $80;* sells at $100.

Retailer buys at $100,† sells at $175.

* Wholesale discount = 54% of suggested retail price.
† Retail discount = 43% of suggested retail price.

Table 17.6
Noncumulative
Quanity Discount
Structure

ORDER SIZE	PRICE
1–1,000 units	List price
1,001–5,000 units	List price—2%
5,001–10,000 units	List price—4%
10,001 units and above	List price—6%

in a single order. For example, a wholesaler may offer a small retailer a 3 percent discount only if he or she purchases 10 gross of Halloween masks in a single order. Table 17.6 shows a typical noncumulative quantity discount structure.

Cumulative quantity discounts are offered if a firm's purchases from a particular vendor exceed a specified quantity or dollar value over a predetermined time period. The time frame varies, but a yearly basis is most common. For example, a manufacturer of appliances may offer a small firm a 3 percent discount on subsequent orders if its purchases exceed $10,000 per year.

Some small business owners who normally buy in small quantities and are unable to qualify for quantity discounts can earn such discounts by joining buying groups, purchasing pools, or buying cooperatives. *For instance, Edward Reagan, owner of Performance Audio, joined a purchasing pool in an attempt to cut his company 's health insurance costs. By joining with more than 4,300 other small business owners in California's state-sponsored Health Insurance Plan of California, Reagan was able to cut health insurance costs for himself and his eight employees by 42 percent.*[6]

Cash Discounts

Cash discounts are offered to customers as an incentive to pay for merchandise promptly. Many vendors grant cash discounts to avoid being used as an interest-free bank by customers who purchase merchandise and then neglect to pay within the invoice due date. To encourage prompt payment of invoices, many vendors allow customers to deduct a percentage of the purchase amount if payment is remitted within a specified time. Cash discount terms "2/10, net 30" are common in many industries. This notation means that the total amount of the invoice is due 30 days after its date, but if the bill is paid within 10 days, the buyer may deduct 2 percent from the total. A discount offering "2/10, EOM" (EOM means "end of month") indi-

Figure 17.4
A Cash Discount

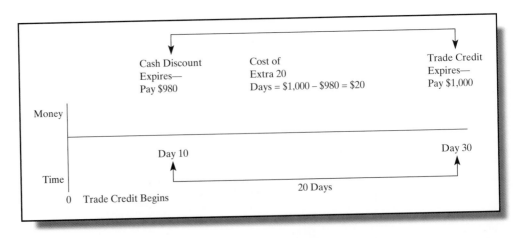

Section VII   Managing a Small Business: Techniques for Enhancing Profitability

cates that the buyer may deduct 2 percent if the bill is paid by the tenth of the month after purchase.

In general, it is sound business practice to take advantage of cash discounts. The money saved by paying invoices promptly is freed up for use elsewhere. Conversely, there is an implicit (opportunity) cost of forgoing a cash discount. By forgoing a cash discount, the small business owner is, in effect, paying an annual interest rate to retain the use of the discounted amount for the remainder of the credit period. For example, suppose the Print Shop receives an invoice for $1,000 from a vendor offering a cash discount of 2/10, net 30. Figure 17.4 illustrates this situation and shows how to compute the cost of forgoing the cash discount.

Actually, it costs the Print Shop $20 to retain the use of its $980 for an extra 20 days. Translate this into an annual interest rate:

$$I = P \times R \times T \qquad \text{(17)}$$

where:

$I =$ Interest ($)
$P =$ Principle ($)
$R =$ Rate of interest (%)
$T =$ Time (number of days/360)

So, to compute R, the annual interest rate,

$$R = \frac{I}{P \times T} \qquad \text{(18)}$$

In our example,

$$R = \frac{\$20}{980 \times \dfrac{20}{360}} \qquad \text{(19)}$$

$$= 36.735\%$$

The cost to the Print Shop of forgoing the cash discount is 36.735 percent per year! If there is $980 available on day 10 of the trade credit period, the owner should pay the invoice unless he is able to earn a return greater than 36.735 percent on it. If the owner does not have $980 on day 10 but can borrow it at less than 36.735 percent, he should do so to take advantage of the cash discount. Table 17.7 summarizes the cost of forgoing cash discounts offering various terms.

Although it is a good idea for business owners to take advantage of cash discounts, it is not a wise practice to stretch accounts payable to suppliers beyond the payment terms specified on the invoice. Letting payments become past due can destroy the trusting relationship a small company has built with its vendors. *When*

Table 17.7

Cost of Forgoing Cash Discounts

CASH DISCOUNT TERMS	COST OF FORGOING (ANNUALLY)
2/10, net 30	36.735%
2/30, net 60	34.490%
2/10, net 60	13.693%
3/10, net 30	55.670%
3/10, net 60	22.268%

GAINING THE COMPETITIVE EDGE
A Funny Thing Happened on the Way to Your Business

Every year, U.S. companies spend an amount equivalent to 10.5 percent of the nation's gross domestic product (GDP)—more than $700 billion—just to package and transport goods from one place to another. With so much at stake, it is little wonder that distribution, or logistics, has become an important part of companies' competitive strategies. "You have far more opportunities to get cost out of the supply chain than you do out of manufacturing," says one CEO. Streamlining a company's ordering and distribution process can reduce delivery times and its investment in inventory as well as cut costs and avoid costly mistakes. Consider, for example, the following (true) distribution horror stories.

The shipping manager at a plant in China is struggling to ready a rush order of men's and women's athletic shoes for shipment to a retailer in the United States. He runs into a snag when trying to load the cartons containing the shoes into 40-foot shipping containers. He places a call to the retailer's logistics manager to ask how many shoes to put in each container. "As many as you can fit," comes the reply. "Please don't bother me with such silly questions."

The Chinese shipping manager complies with the customer's request. He has workers take the shoes out of the cartons, remove them from their individual shoe boxes, and put them into the shipping containers. When the shipment arrives in the United States, the retailer's warehouse manager gets an even bigger surprise. The Chinese workers didn't even tie the shoes in pairs. The containers are filled with thousands of pairs of shoes—all floating around loose! The retailer has already advertised a big sale on these shoes and quickly arranges for workers to go to the warehouse, where they match and box thousands of pairs of shoes. The company incurs thousands of dollars of unplanned labor expenses and eventually sells the shoes at close to its cost.

A dock worker is handling a shipment of margarine traveling from Denmark to Tacoma, Washington, when he notices a leak in one of the shipping containers. The cargo is loaded onto a truck headed for a warehouse, but as the driver rolls down the highway, he looks in his rearview mirror and notices yellow blobs flying from the back of his truck. At the warehouse, workers open the containers to find 2,000 cartons of margarine that have experienced a complete meltdown. "Anyone got any popcorn?" asks one worker. The shipping document from the company in Denmark failed to specify a temperature setting for the cargo.

One freight company that has contracts with two movie studios mistakenly switches their shipments. Of course, one shipment contains X-rated films, and the other contains family films. The manager at the adult video store is sorely disappointed in the mild films he receives, and the nuns at the convent expecting to watch *The Sound of Music* really get a surprise!

How can business owners avoid shipping problems such as these? Although some shipping foul-ups are inevitable, the following tips can help minimize them:

- Communicate clearly with vendors, suppliers, and shipping companies. Never assume that the other party will do what you expect.

- Specify special shipping instructions when required.

- Make sure all shipping labels and instructions are legible and firmly attached to the package.

- Use pressure-sensitive packing tape to seal packages. Masking tape and cellophane tape are not strong enough to do the job.

- Try to use single shipments rather than multiple shipments. Items sent at different times or in multiple containers are more likely to go astray.

- On international shipments, verify that the shipper is familiar with the customs regulations of the destination country and knows how to negotiate them. Otherwise, your shipment could founder indefinitely in customs.

- When in doubt about a shipment, contact a shipping professional for advice.

Source: Adapted from Steve Bates, "The Dog Ate My Shipment," *Nation's Business*, December 1997, pp. 36–37.

David Brent took over the Nutty Bavarian, a small company that sells cinnamon-glazed almonds and pecans from kiosks, the company was growing rapidly and was experiencing cash flow problems. Brent soon discovered that the company owed more than $100,000 to its nut suppliers, almost all of it past due. To make matters worse, the previous managers had ignored past due notices and telephone calls from suppliers seeking payment. Brent took an honest, straightforward approach to solving the problem. "I went to my suppliers to ask for longer credit terms and worked out a payment plan that we could meet," he says. Although it took more than a year, Brent eventually paid off all of the company's past-due bills. "Instead of lying and saying the check's in the mail, tell suppliers what's happening and what you propose to do about it," he advises. "If you have a bill that's due, you call them, instead of waiting for them to call you. If you owe them, suppliers are eager to find a way to work with you." Thanks to his forthright approach with the Nutty Bavarian's suppliers, Brent has maintained close partnerships with all of the company's suppliers.[7]

TIMING—WHEN TO ORDER

5A. Calculate a company's reorder point.

Timing the purchase of merchandise and supplies is also a critical element of any purchasing plan. The owner must schedule delivery dates so that the firm does not lose customer goodwill from stockouts. Also, the owner must concentrate on maintaining proper control over the firm's inventory investment without tying up an excessive amount of working capital. There is a trade-off between the cost of running out of stock and the cost of carrying additional inventory.

When planning delivery schedules for inventory and supplies, the owner must consider the **lead time** for an order, the time gap between placing an order and receiving it. In general, business owners cannot expect instantaneous delivery of merchandise. As a result, the manager must plan its reorder points for inventory items with lead time in mind.

To determine when to order merchandise for inventory, a small business manager must calculate the reorder point for key inventory items. Developing a reorder point model involves determining the lead time for an order, the usage rate for the item, the minimum level of stock allowable, and the EOQ. The lead time for an order is the time gap between placing an order with a vendor and actually receiving the goods. It may be as little as a few hours or as long as several weeks to process purchase requisitions and orders, contact the supplier, receive the goods, and sort them into the inventory. Obviously, owners who purchase from local vendors encounter shorter lead times than those who rely on distant suppliers.

The usage rate for a particular product can be determined from past inventory and accounting records. The small business owner must estimate the speed at which the supply of merchandise will be depleted over a given time. The anticipated usage rate for a product determines how long the supply will last. For example, if an owner projects that she will use 900 units in the next six months, the usage rate is five units per day (900 units/180 days). The simplest reorder point model assumes that the firm experiences a linear usage rate; that is, depletion of the firm's stock continues at a constant rate over time.

The small business owner must determine the minimum level of stock allowable. If the firm runs out of a particular item (i.e., incurs stockouts), customers may lose faith in the business, and customer ill will may develop. To avoid stockouts, many firms establish a minimum level of inventory greater than zero. In other words, they build a cushion, called **safety stock,** into their inventories in case demand runs ahead of the anticipated usage rate. In such cases the owner can dip into the safety stock to fill customer orders until the stock is replenished.

To compute the reorder point for an item, the owner must combine this inventory information with the product's EOQ. The following example will illustrate the reorder point technique:

$$L = \text{Lead time for an order} = 5 \text{ days}$$
$$U = \text{Usage rate} = 18 \text{ units/day} \qquad \textbf{(20)}$$
$$S = \text{Safety stock (minimum level)} = 75 \text{ units}$$
$$EOQ = \text{Economic order quantity} = 540 \text{ units}$$

The formula for computing the reorder point is:

$$\text{Reorder point} = (L \times U) + S \qquad \textbf{(21)}$$

In this example,

$$\text{Reorder point} = (5 \text{ days} \times 18 \text{ units/day}) + 75 \text{ units} \qquad \textbf{(22)}$$
$$= 165 \text{ units}$$

Thus, this owner should order 540 more units when inventory drops to 165 units. Figure 17.5 illustrates the reorder point situation for this small business.

The simple reorder technique makes certain assumptions that may not be valid in particular situations. First, the model assumes that the firm's usage rate is constant, when in fact for most small businesses demand varies daily. Second, the model assumes that lead time for an order is constant, when, in fact, few vendors deliver precisely within lead-time estimates. Third, in this sample model, the owner never taps safety stock; however, late deliveries or accelerated demand may force the owner to dip into this inventory reserve. More advanced models relax some of these assumptions, but the simple model can be a useful inventory guideline for making inventory decisions in a small company.

Another popular reorder point model assumes that the demand for a product during its lead time is normally distributed (see Figure 17.6). The area under the normal curve at any given point represents the probability that that particular demand level will occur. Figure 17.7 illustrates the application of this normal distribution to the reorder point model *without* safety stock. The model recognizes that three different demand patterns can occur during a product's lead time. Demand pattern 1 is an example of below-average demand during lead time; demand pattern 2 is an exam-

Figure 17.5
Reorder Point
Model

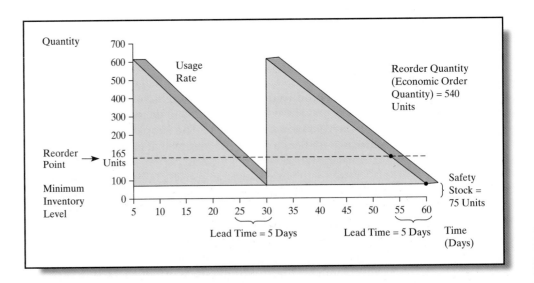

Section VII   Managing a Small Business: Techniques for Enhancing Profitability

Figure 17.6
Demand During
Lead Time

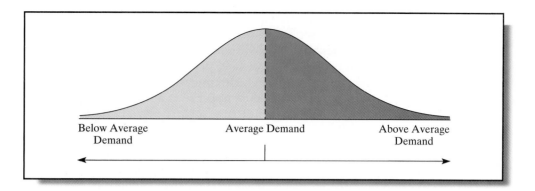

ple of average demand during lead time; and demand pattern 3 is an example of an above-average demand during lead time.

If the reorder point for this item is the average demand for the product during lead time, 50 percent of the time, demand will be below average (note that 50 percent of the area under the normal curve lies below average). Similarly, 50 percent of the time, demand during lead time will exceed the average, and the firm will experience stockouts (note that 50 percent of the area under the normal curve lies above average).

To reduce the probability of inventory shortage, the small business owner can increase the reorder point above $\overline{D}_L$ (average demand during lead time). But how much should the owner increase the reorder point? Rather than attempt to define the

Figure 17.7
Reorder Point Without Safety Stock

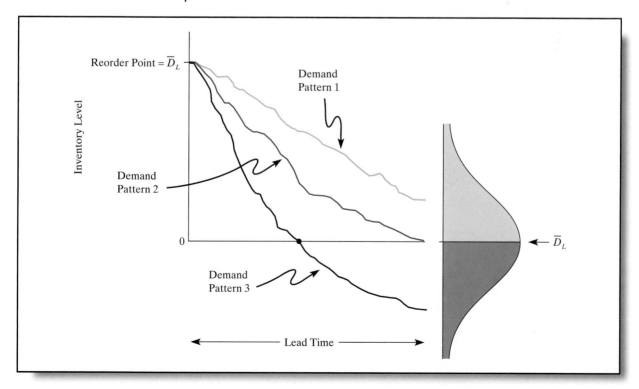

actual costs of carrying extra inventory versus the costs of stockouts (remember the trade-off described earlier), this model allows the small business owner to determine the appropriate reorder point by setting a desired customer level. For example, the owner may wish to satisfy 95 percent of customer demand for a product during lead time. This service level determines the amount of increase in the reorder point. In effect, these additional items serve as a safety stock:

$$\text{Safety stock} = SLF \times SD_L \tag{23}$$

where:

SLF = Service level factor (the appropriate Z score)
SD_L = Standard deviation of demand during lead time

Table 17.8 shows the appropriate service level factor (Z score) for some of the most popular target customer service levels.

Figure 17.8 shows the shift to a normally distributed reorder point model with safety stock. In this case the manager has set a 95 percent customer service level; that is, the manager wants to meet 95 percent of the demand during lead time. The normal curve in the model without safety stock (from Figure 17.7) is shifted up so that 95 percent of the area under the curve lies above the zero inventory level. The result is a reorder point that is higher than the original reorder point by the amount of the safety stock:

$$\text{Reorder point} = \bar{D}_L + (SLF \times SD_L) \tag{24}$$

where:

$\bar{D}_L$ = Average demand during lead time (original reorder point)
SLF = Service level factor (the appropriate Z score)
SD_L = Standard deviation of demand during lead time

To illustrate, suppose that the average demand for a product during its lead time (1 week) is 325 units with a standard deviation of 110 units. If the service level is 95 percent, the service level factor (from Table 17.7) would be 1.645. The reorder point would be:

$$R = 325 + (1.645 \times 110) = 325 + 181 = 506 \text{ units} \tag{25}$$

Figure 17.9 illustrates the shift from a system without safety stock to one with safety stock for this example. With a reorder point of 325 units (D_L), this small business owner will experience inventory shortages during lead time 50 percent of the time. With a reorder point of 506 units (i.e., a safety stock of 181 units), the business owner will experience inventory stockouts during lead time only 5 percent of the time.

Table 17.8

Service Level Factors and Z Scores

Target Customer Service Level	Z Score[a]
99%	2.33
97.5%	1.96
95%	1.645
90%	1.275
80%	0.845
75%	0.675

[a]Any basic statistics book will provide a table of areas under the normal curve, which will give the appropriate Z score for *any* service level factor.

Figure 17.8
Reorder Point with Safety Stock

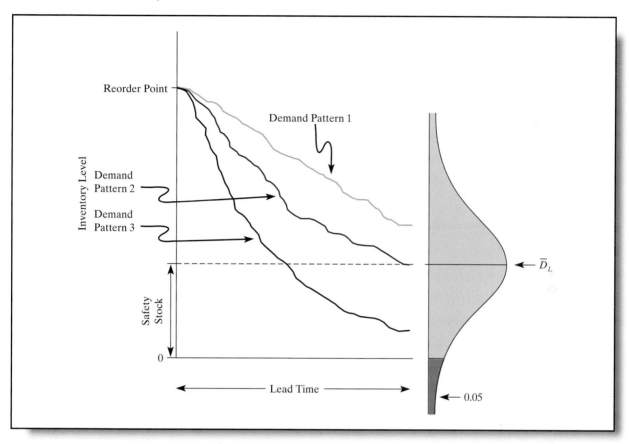

VENDOR ANALYSIS

5B. Develop a vendor rating scale.

Experienced business owners realize the importance of finding vendors that can supply them with quality merchandise, equipment, supplies, and services at reasonable prices in a timely manner. Selecting the right vendors or suppliers for a business can have an impact well beyond simply obtaining goods and services at the lowest costs. Although searching for the best price will always be an important factor, successful small business owners must always consider other factors in vendor selection such as reliability, reputation, quality, support services, and proximity.

Vendor Certification

To add some objectivity to the selection process, many firms are establishing vendor certification programs: agreements to give one supplier the majority of their business once that supplier meets rigorous quality and performance standards. Today, businesses of all sizes and types are establishing long-term "partnering" arrangements with vendors that meet their certification standards. When creating a vendor certification program, a business owner should remember the three Cs: commitment, communication, and control. *Commitment* to consistently meeting the quality standards of the company must be paramount. No company can afford to do business with

Figure 17.9
Shift from a No-
Safety Stock
System to a
Safety Stock
System

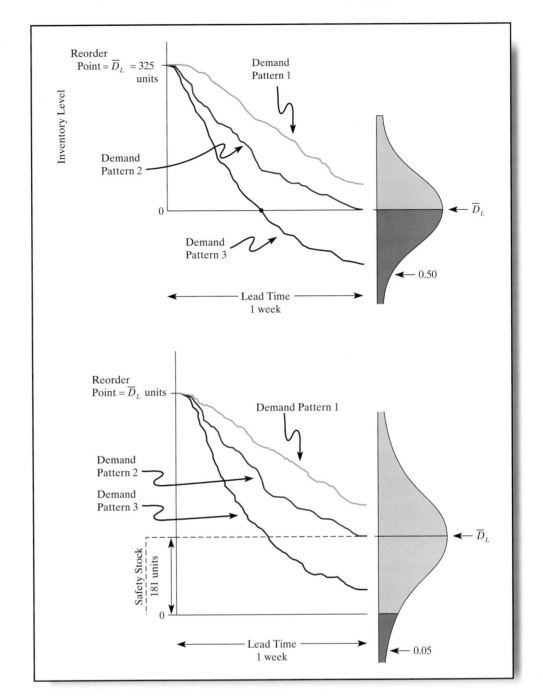

vendors that cannot meet its quality targets. Second, a company must establish two-way *communication* with vendors. Communication implies trust, and trust creates working relationships that are long-term and mutually beneficial. Treating suppliers like partners can reveal ways to boost quality and lower costs for both parties. Finally, a company must make sure that its vendors and suppliers have in place the *controls* that enable them to produce quality results and to achieve continuous improvements in their processes. In today's competitive marketplace, an entrepreneur should expect that every vendor be able to demonstrate that they operate a con-

GAINING THE COMPETITIVE EDGE
Step-by-Step Process to Building a Base of Competent Suppliers

Many small firms pay prices for goods and services that are too high, and they find that their options are limited by the lack of a base of competent suppliers. The broader the base of potential suppliers a business has, the stronger the likelihood they will have greater options and find the best price. The following steps in the process of scanning potential vendors is never ending:

- *Be assertive.* Ask tough questions and be a knowledgeable buyer. Don't allow the supplier to do their typical "sales pitch."

- *Get referrals.* Demand that all potential vendors supply a list of referrals of businesses that they have served over the past five years or more. Then make the necessary contacts.

- *Don't fixate on price.* Look for value in what they sell. If your only message is "what's your lowest price?", the vendor will push their lowest priced (and often lowest quality) product line.

- *Attend trade shows.* Work the room. It's not a vacation, it's pure business. You may find in the next booth a valuable new vendor who has the potential to increase your profits!

- *Work with the vendors.* Tell your suppliers what you like and don't like about their products and service. In many cases, they can resolve your concerns. Most vendors want to build a long-term relationship. Give them a chance to do this.

- *Do unto others.* Treat your vendors right. Be selective, but pay on time and treat them with respect.

1. Why do so many firms focus solely on lowest price?

2. Develop a list of ten questions you would ask a potential vendor on a product you select.

Source: Jan Norman, "How to Find Suppliers," *Business Start-Ups*, October 1998, pp. 44–47.

tinuous improvement process, which has proven to be proactive in assessing product quality.

Creating a vendor certification program requires an entrepreneur to develop a vendor rating scale that allows the company to evaluate the various advantages and disadvantages of each potential vendor. The scale allows managers to score each vendor on some measure of those purchasing criteria that are most important to their companies' success. The first step in developing a scale is to determine which criteria are most important in selecting a vendor (e.g., price, quality, prompt delivery). The next step is to assign weights to each criterion to reflect its relative importance. The third step involves developing a grading scale for comparing vendors on the criteria. Developing a usable scale requires that the owner maintain proper records of past vendor performances. Finally, the owner must compute a weighted total score for each vendor and select the vendor that scores the highest on the set of criteria. Consider the following example. Bravo Bass Boats, Inc., is faced with choosing from among several suppliers of a critical raw material. The company's owner has decided to employ a vendor rating scale to select the best vendor using the following procedure.

Step 1: Determine important criteria. The owner of Bravo has selected the following criteria:

Quality
Price
Prompt delivery
Service
Assistance

Step 2: Assign weights to each criterion to reflect its relative importance.

Criterion	Weight
Quality	35
Price	30
Prompt delivery	20
Service	10
Assistance	5
Total	100

Step 3: Develop a grading scale for each criterion.

Criterion	Grading Scale
Quality	Number of acceptable lots from Vendor X / Total number of lots from Vendor X
Price	Lowest quoted price of all vendors / Price offered by Vendor X
Prompt delivery	Number of on-time deliveries from Vendor X / Total number of deliveries from Vendor X
Service	A subjective evaluation of the variety of services offered by each vendor
Assistance	A subjective evaluation of the advice and assistance provided by each vendor

Step 4: Compute a weighted score for each vendor.

Criterion	Weight	Grade	Weighted Score (weight × grade)
Vendor 1			
Quality	35	9/10	31.5
Price	30	12.5/12.5	30.0
Prompt delivery	20	10/10	20.0
Service	10	8/10	8.0
Assistance	5	5/5	5.0
Total weighted score			94.5
Vendor 2			
Quality	35	8/10	28.0
Price	30	12.5/12.5	27.8
Prompt delivery	20	8/10	16.0
Service	10	8/10	8.0
Assistance	5	4.5	4.0
Total weighted score			83.8
Vendor 3			
Quality	35	7/10	24.5
Price	30	12.5/12.5	30.0
Prompt delivery	20	6/10	12.0
Service	10	7/10	7.0
Assistance	5	1/5	1.0
Total weighted score			74.5

On the basis of this analysis of the three suppliers, Bravo should purchase the majority of its raw material from Vendor 1.

This vendor analysis procedure assumes that business owners have a detailed working knowledge of the suppliers' network. Start-up companies seldom will. Owners of start-up companies must focus on finding suppliers and then gathering data to conduct the vendor analysis. One of the best ways to do that is to ask potential vendors for references. If the references provided by the potential vendor are not potential competitors, they may be willing to verify the claims of the vendor.

In some cases, the industry trade association will have knowledge regarding the integrity of suppliers or vendors. Start-up companies can be viewed as vulnerable to scams by unethical vendors. Research about the history of every potential vendor may reduce the likelihood of being victimized by the handful of unethical vendors who prey on inexperienced entrepreneurs. New entrepreneurs may have difficulty locating ethical suppliers of inventory and materials to start their businesses. One obvious way for entrepreneurs to find vendors for their products is to approach established businesses selling similar lines and interview the managers. Clearly, local competitors are not likely to be very cooperative with new competitors, but a beginning entrepreneur can get the necessary information from businesses outside the immediate trading area.

Other sources for information on vendors include trade association and shows, the local chamber of commerce, and certain publications. These publications include library reference books that list national distributors and their product lines and publications such as *McRae's Blue Book* and the *Thomas Register of American Manufacturers (www.thomas register.com)*. Both of these sources provide lists of products and services along with names, addresses, telephone numbers, and ratings of manufacturers.[8]

The *U.S. Industrial Directory* is similar to the *Thomas Register,* although its coverage is not as broad. Business owners also should consult the U.S. Chamber of Commerce publication *Sources of State Information and State Industrial Directories,* which lists state directories of manufacturers. Entrepreneurs whose product lines have an international flair may look to *Kelly's Manufacturers and Merchants Directory, Marconi's International Register,* or *Trade Directories of the World* for information on companies throughout the world dealing in practically every type of product or service.

The World Wide Web is another rich source of information on potential suppliers. Purchasing agents in companies of all size are stepping up their use of the Internet as a tool for locating and buying merchandise, equipment, and supplies. The volume of Web-based purchasing activity will continue to grow in the future as more business owners discover its power to reduce the cost of placing an order and the time required to get it delivered.

The Final Decision

Once business owners identify potential vendors and suppliers, they must decide which one (or ones) to do business with. Entrepreneurs should consider the following factors before making the final decision about the right supplier.

Number of Suppliers. One important question the small business owner faces is "Should I buy from a single supplier or from several different sources?" Concentrating purchases at a single supplier gives the individual attention from the sole supplier, especially if orders are substantial. Second, the firm may receive quantity discounts if its orders are large enough. Finally, the firm is able to cultivate a closer, more cooperative relationship with the supplier. Suppliers are more willing to assist companies they consider to be their loyal customers. The result of such a partnership can be better quality goods and services.

However, using a single vendor also has disadvantages. The small firm may experience shortages of critical materials if its only supplier suffers a catastrophe, such as a fire, strike, or bankruptcy. *For instance, one small clothing maker experienced an interruption in its supply of fabric when its primary supplier's textile factory was damaged by a tornado. The textile manufacturer resumed production one month later, but the clothing maker's output suffered because it was unable to purchase material in sufficient quantities from other suppliers on such short notice.*

The advantages of developing close, cooperative relationships with a single supplier outweigh the risks of sole sourcing in most cases. A business owner must exercise great caution in choosing a supplier to make sure he or she picks the right one, however. Otherwise, the outcome could be disastrous.

Reliability. The business owner must evaluate the potential vendor's ability to deliver adequate quantities of quality merchandise when it is needed. One common complaint small businesses have against suppliers is late delivery. Late deliveries or shortages cause lost sales and create customer ill will. If you are a small customer sometimes you are the last to be served.

Proximity. The small firm's physical proximity is an important factor in choosing a vendor. Costs for transporting merchandise can substantially increase the cost of merchandise to the buyer. *For example, one East Coast glass manufacturer found that to obtain proper-quality sand for its production operation it had to make its purchases from a*

GAINING THE COMPETITIVE EDGE
Is There Room at the Bottom?

After unprecedented growth in the 1990s, many online retailers are being faced with new "cyber-realities" as we move into the new millenium. In 2000 alone, at least 130 Internet companies shut down. Nearly 100 of these companies catered to the consumer. Business-to-business (B2B) companies did not escape the downward trend either. Twenty-six B2B sites closed down in 2000. What is left in the aftermath? For some companies, all that remains is unused equipment, customer lists, and warehouses filled with merchandise. Enter the bottom feeders.

Individuals, such as Patrick Byrne of Over stock.com, are building successful businesses on the demise of others. Overstock.com employs about 70 people and buys goods from distressed Web start-ups, manufacturers, and other sources for 30 to 50 percent of their wholesale costs. Inventory liquidators are not necessarily a bad thing in the retail market-place, but exist to "move" the merchandise that others were unable to sell.

The key issue is how to know when it's time to find a strategic partner who has the capability to move the inventory that is unsold through traditional channels. There will always be a need in the retail arena for "bottom feeders" who have the capability to scoop up and sell inventory that was someone else's mistake.

1. How would you determine when it is time to put unsold inventory through a liquidator? How do you go about determining what went wrong in your ability to sell the unsold inventory through traditional channels?

2. Using the Internet, identify five or six firms whose strategic competence is the liquidation of unsold inventory.

Source: Nick Winfield, "New Breed of Vulture Gets Fat on Remains of Experienced E-tailers," *Wall Street Journal*, November 14, 2000.

midwestern supplier. The cost of transporting the sand was greater than the cost of the sand itself! Also, some vendors offer better service to local small businesses because they know the owners. In addition, a small business owner is better able to solve coordination problems with nearby vendors than with distant vendors.

Services. The small business owner must evaluate the range of services vendors offer. Do salespeople make regular calls on the firm, and are they knowledgeable about their product line? Will the sales representatives assist in planning store layout and in creating attractive displays? Will the vendor make convenient deliveries on time? Is the supplier reasonable in making repairs on equipment after installation and in handling returned merchandise? Are sales representatives able to offer useful advice on purchasing and other managerial functions? Before choosing a vendor, the small business owner should answer these and other relevant questions about suppliers.

LEGAL ISSUES AFFECTING PURCHASING

6. Describe the legal implications of the purchasing function.

When a small business purchases goods from a supplier, ownership passes from seller to buyer. But when does title to the goods pass from one party to the other? The answer is important because any number of things could happen to the merchandise after it has been ordered but before it has been delivered. When they order merchandise and supplies from their vendors, small business owners should know when the ownership of the merchandise—and the risk associated with it—shifts from supplier to buyer.

Title

Before the Uniform Commercial Code (UCC) was enacted, the concept of title—the right to ownership of goods—determined where responsibility for merchandise fell. Today, however, the UCC has replaced the concept of title with three other concepts: identification, risk of loss, and insurable interest.

Identification

Identification is the first requirement that must be met. Before title can pass to the buyer, the goods must already be in existence and must be identifiable from all other similar goods. Specific goods already in existence are identified at the time the sales contract is made. For example, if Graphtech, Inc. orders a Model 477-X computer and a plotter, the goods are identified at the time the contract (oral or written) is made. Generic goods are identified when they are marked, shipped, or otherwise designated as the goods in the contract. For example, an order of fuel oil may not be identified until it is loaded into a transfer truck for shipment.

Risk of Loss

Risk of loss determines which party incurs the financial risk if the goods are damaged, destroyed, or lost before they are transferred. Risk of loss does *not* always pass with title. Three particular rules govern the passage of title and the transfer of risk of loss:

> *Rule 1: Agreement.* A supplier and a small business owner can agree to the terms under which title passes. Similarly, the two parties can agree

(preferably in writing) to shift the risk of loss at any time during the transaction. In other words, any explicit agreement between buyer and seller determines when title and risk of loss will pass. Without an agreement, title and risk of loss pass when the seller delivers the goods under the contract.

Rule 2: FOB seller. Under a sales contract designated FOB (free on board) seller, title passes to the buyer as soon as the seller delivers the goods into the care of a carrier or shipper. Similarly, risk of loss transfers to the small business owner when the supplier delivers the goods to the carrier. In addition, an **FOB seller contract** (also a **shipment contract**) requires that the buyer pay all shipping and transportation costs. For example, a North Carolina manufacturer sells 100,000 capacitors to a buyer in Ohio with terms "FOB North Carolina." Under this contract the Ohio firms pays all shipping costs, and title and risk of loss pass from the manufacturer as soon as the carrier takes possession of the shipment. If the goods are lost or damaged in transit, the buyer suffers the loss. Of course, the buyer has legal recourse against the carrier.

Rule 3: FOB buyer. A sales contract designated FOB buyer requires that the seller deliver the goods to the buyer's place of business (or to an agent of the buyer). Title and risk of loss are transferred to the small business when the goods are delivered there or to another designated destination. Also, an **FOB buyer contract** (also called a **destination contract**) requires the seller to pay all shipping and transportation costs. In the example above, if the contract were "FOB Ohio," the North Carolina manufacturer would pay the cost of shipping the order, and title and risk of loss would pass to the Ohio company when the shipment was delivered to its place of business. In this case losses due to goods lost or damaged in transit are borne by the seller.

Who bears the risk of lost or damaged goods? Too often, buyers and sellers ignore such details in their sales contracts. The Uniform Commercial Code offers three rules to allocate the risk of loss: the parties' agreement, shipment contract terms, and destination contract terms.

Insurable Interest

Insurable interest ensures the right to either party to the sales contract to obtain insurance to protect against lost, damaged, or destroyed merchandise as long as that party has "sufficient interest" in the goods. In general, if goods are identified, the buyer has an insurable interest in them. The seller has a sufficient interest as long as he retains title to the goods. However, under certain circumstances both the buyer and the seller have insurable interests even after title has passed to the buyer.

Receiving Merchandise

Once the merchandise is received, the buyer must verify its identity and condition. When the goods are delivered, the owner should check the number of cartons unloaded against the carrier's delivery receipt so that none are overlooked. It is also a good idea to examine the boxes for damage; if shipping cartons are damaged, the carrier should note this on the delivery receipt. The owner should open all cartons immediately after delivery and inspect the merchandise for quality and condition and also check it against the invoices to eliminate discrepancies. If merchandise is

GAINING THE COMPETITIVE EDGE
Internet-Based Supply Chain Management: A Look at the Future

A competitive advantage is seldom a free gift, but it is almost always the product of an investment of time, effort, strategic thinking, and a talent for creating a process vastly superior to the industry operational norm. The current reality of the competitive world is that many successful companies in almost every industry have used the technology of the Internet to compress the supply chain to squeeze ever-increasing efficiencies from a continually evolving supply chain.

Industry leaders know before their competitors the actual behavior of customers. They are electronically connected to customers and suppliers and this allows them to respond rapidly to buyer preferences with modifications in the inventory purchased in real time. In turn, suppliers can make the necessary adjustments in production scheduling to produce what the customer has chosen and the buyer is demanding. Time compression and seamless integration of the purchasing process from the consumer to the retailer to the supplier cuts the cost of producing and stocking unwanted and unsold merchandise.

The Internet has enabled organizations to connect to one another in novel ways, creating new partners and greater efficiencies. "Until recently, too many companies depended almost entirely on ERP (enterprise resource planning) systems to manage supply chain issues," notes one research director for supply chain management. He goes on to say, "The Web has changed everything. It is pushing organizations away from an enterprise-centric approach and toward a collaborative model."

What should be remembered is that the process is still a matter of an entrepreneur making decisions, not a machine! Information is more time sensitive but still must be interpreted and utilized by the entrepreneur. Profits are earned only through the process of quality decision making. The technological tools and communication devices are more sophisticated and more affordable. However, what must be created in the process of utilizing the tools is data that the entrepreneur can use to make the proper strategic decisions.

1. How has the small business evolved into a worthy competitor for larger, more established firms through the utilization of Internet-based supply chain analysis?

2. What, if any, are the barriers to the application of the Internet for the small business owner?

Sources: Ian Mount and Brian Caulfield, "The Missing Link: What You Need to Know About Supply Chain Technology," *www.ecompany.com*, May 2001, pp. 81–88; Samuel Greengard, "Using the Web to Link Supply Chains," *Beyond Computing*, March 2001, pp. 26–37.

damaged or incorrect, the buyer should contact the supplier immediately and follow up with a written report. The owner should never destroy or dispose of tainted or unwanted merchandise unless the supplier specifically authorizes it. Proper control techniques in receiving merchandise prevent the small business owner from paying for suppliers' and shippers' mistakes.

Selling on Consignment

Small business owners who lack the necessary capital to invest or are unwilling to assume the risk of investing in inventory may be able to sell the goods on consignment. Selling on consignment means that the small business owner does not purchase the merchandise carried from the supplier (called the consignor); instead, the owner pays the consignor only for the merchandise actually sold. For providing the supplier with a market for his goods, the small business owner normally receives a portion of the revenue on each item sold. The business owner (called the consignee) may return any unsold merchandise to the supplier without obligation. Under a consignment agreement, title and risk of loss do not pass to the consignee unless the contract specifies such terms. In other words, the supplier (consignor) bears the financial costs of lost, damaged, or stolen merchandise. The small business owner who sells merchandise on a consignment basis realizes the following advantages:

- The owner does not have to invest money in these inventory items, but the merchandise on hand is available for sale.
- The owner does not make payment to the consignor until the item is sold.
- Because the consignment relationship is founded on the law of agency, the consignee never takes title to the merchandise and does not bear the risk of loss for the goods.
- The supplier normally plans and sets up displays for the merchandise and is responsible for maintaining it.

Before selling items on consignment, the small business owner and the supplier should create a workable written contract, which should include the following items:

- A list of items to be sold and their quantities
- Prices to be charged
- Location of merchandise in store
- Duration of contract
- Commission charged by the consignee
- Policy on defective items and rejects
- Schedule for payments to consignor
- Delivery terms and merchandise storage requirements
- Responsibility for items lost to pilferage and shoplifting
- Provision for terminating consignment contract

If managed properly, selling goods on consignment can be beneficial to both the consignor and the consignee.

CHAPTER SUMMARY

1. Understand the components of a purchasing plan.
   - The purchasing function is vital to every small business's success because it influences a company's ability to sell quality goods and services at reasonable prices. Purchasing is the acquisition of needed materials, supplies, services, and equipment

of the right quality, in the proper quantities, for reasonable prices, at the appropriate time, and from the right suppliers.

2. Explain the principles of total quality management (TQM) and its impact on quality.
   - Under the total quality management (TQM) philosophy, companies define a quality product as one that conforms to predetermined standards that satisfy customers' demands. The goal is to get delivery and invoicing to installation and follow-up— right the first time.
   - To implement TQM successfully, a small business owner must rely on 10 fundamental principles: Shift from a management-driven culture to a participative, team-based one; modify the reward system to encourage teamwork and innovation; train workers constantly to give them the tools they need to produce quality and to upgrade the company's knowledge base; train employees to measure quality with the tools of statistical process control (SPC); use Pareto's Law to focus TQM efforts; share information with everyone in the organization; focus quality improvements on astonishing the customer; don't rely on inspection to produce quality products and services; avoid using TQM to place blame on those who make mistakes; and strive for continuous improvement in processes as well as in products and services.

3. Conduct economic order quantity (EOQ) analysis to determine the proper level of inventory.
   - A major goal of the small business is to generate adequate inventory turnover by purchasing proper quantities of merchandise. A useful device for computing the proper quantity is economic order quantity (EOQ) analysis, which yields the ideal order quantity: the amount that minimizes total inventory costs. Total inventory costs consist of the cost of the units, holding (carrying) costs, and ordering (setup) costs. The EOQ balances the costs of ordering and of carrying merchandise to yield minimum total inventory cost.

4. Differentiate among the three types of purchase discounts vendors offer.
   - Trade discounts are established on a graduated scale and depend on a small firm's position in the channel of distribution.
   - Quantity discounts are designed to encourage businesses to order large quantities of merchandise and supplies.
   - Cash discounts are offered to customers as an incentive to pay for merchandise promptly.

5. Calculate a company's reorder point.
   - There is a time gap between the placing of an order and actual receipt of the goods. The reorder point model tells the owner when to place an order to replenish the company's inventory.

6. Develop a vendor rating scale.
   - Creating a vendor analysis model involves four steps: Determine the important criteria (i.e., price, quality, prompt delivery, service, etc.); assign a weight to each criterion to reflect its relative importance; develop a grading scale for each criterion; compute a weighted score for each vendor.

7. Describe the legal implications of the purchasing function.
   - Important legal issues involving purchasing goods involve title, or ownership of the goods; identification of the goods; risk of loss and when it shifts from seller to buyer; and insurable interests in the goods. Buyer and seller can have an insurable interest in the same goods at the same time.

DISCUSSION QUESTIONS

1. What is purchasing? Why is it important for the small business owner to develop a purchasing plan?
2. What is TQM? How can it help small business owners achieve the quality goods and services they require?
3. One top manager claims that to implement total quality management successfully, "You have to change your company culture as much as your processes." Do you agree? Explain.

4. List and briefly describe the three components of total inventory costs.
5. What is the economic order quantity? How does it minimize total inventory costs?
6. Should a small business owner always purchase the products with the lowest prices? Why or why not?
7. Briefly outline the three types of purchase discounts. Under what circumstances is each the best choice?
8. What is lead time? Outline the procedure for determining a product's reorder point.
9. Explain how an entrepreneur launching a company could locate suppliers and vendors.
10. What factors are commonly used to evaluate suppliers?
11. Explain the procedure for developing a vendor rating scale.
12. Explain briefly the three concepts that have replaced the concept of title. When do title and risk of loss shift under an FOB seller contract and under an FOB buyer contract?
13. What should a small business owner do when merchandise is received?
14. Explain how a small business would sell goods on consignment. What should be included in a consignment contract?

STEP INTO THE REAL WORLD

1. Interview a number of small business owners and attempt to discover if they have implemented any of the following:
   a. a purchasing plan
   b. a quality management program
   c. a vendor analysis program
   On the basis of their responses, how would you rate the effectiveness of their programs?
2. Interview two or three retailers and ask about the nature and type of their purchase discounts. Do they normally take advantage of the discounts that are offered? If not, why? Do the businesses you interviewed have a formal vendor analysis program? If not, what steps should they take to create one?
3. Contact the owner of a small retail shop in your area. How does the owner determine

inventory levels? How does he or she know how many items to keep in stock? Are there certain items that move much faster than others? Does the owner purchase all of a particular type of item from a single vendor or from several vendors? Why?
4. Interview the owner of a small manufacturing company. What percentage of the components in the company's finished product comes from outside vendors and suppliers? How does the owner select those vendors? What problems does he or she normally encounter when buying from vendors? Does the owner use a checklist or vendor rating scale to select vendors? How does the owner judge the quality of incoming shipments from vendors?

TAKE IT TO THE NET

Visit the Scarborough/Zimmerer home page at **www.prenhall.com/scarborough** for updated information, online resources, Web-based exercises, and sample business plan.

ENDNOTES

1. Roberta Maynard, "A Company Is Turned Around through Japanese Principles," *Nation's Business,* February 1996, p. 9.
2. "Patience Pays Off,"' *Industry Week,* April 4, 1994, p. 9.
3. Michael Barrier, "Who Should Get How Much—and Why?" *Nation's Business,* November 1995, pp. 58–59.
4. Mark Henricks, "80/20 Vision," *Entrepreneur,* April 1996, pp. 68–71.
5. Roberta Maynard, "Striking the Right Match," *Nation's Business,* May 1996, pp. 18–28.
6. Roberta Maynard, "The Power of Pooling," *Nation's Business,* March 1995, pp. 16–22.
7. "The Nuts and Bolts of Supplier Relations," *Nation's Business,* August 1997, p. 11.
8. Joel Kurtzman, "These Days, Small Manufacturers Can Play on a Level Field," *Fortune,* July 20, 1998, p. 156[F].

Chapter 18

Managing Inventory

> *The craft of the merchant is this: bringing a thing from where it abounds to where it is costly.*

—EMERSON

> *J am the world's worst salesman; therefore J must make it easy for people to buy.*

—F. W. WOOLWORTH

Upon completion of this chapter, you will be able to:

1. Explain the various inventory control systems and the advantages and disadvantages of each.
2. Describe how just-in-time (JIT) and JIT II inventory control techniques work.
3. Describe some methods for reducing loss from slow-moving inventory.
4. Discuss employee theft and shoplifting and how to prevent them.

In the previous chapter, we saw the impact entrepreneurs' purchasing decisions have on their company's bottom line. This chapter focuses on the procedures designed to maximize the value of a company's inventory and to reduce both the costs and the risks of owning inventory. For most businesses, especially retailers, the largest expenditure most companies make is for inventory. Properly managing inventory can be a key factor in increased operational efficiency and profitability.

Managing inventory effectively requires an entrepreneur to implement the following seven interrelated steps:

1. *Develop an accurate sales forecast.* The proper inventory levels for each item are directly related to the demand for that item. A business can't sell what it does not have, and conversely, an owner does not want to carry what will not sell.

2. *Develop a plan to make inventory available when and where customers want it.* Inventory will not sell if customers have a difficult time finding it. If a company is constantly running out of items customers expect to find, its customer base will dwindle over time as shoppers look elsewhere for those items.

3. *Build relationships with your most critical suppliers to ensure that you can get the merchandise you need when you need it.* Business owners must keep suppliers and vendors aware of how their merchandise is selling and communicate their needs to them. Vendors and suppliers can be an entrepreneur's greatest allies in managing inventory. Increasingly, the word that describes the relationship between world-class companies and their suppliers is *partnership*.

4. *Set realistic inventory turnover objectives.* Keeping in touch with their customers' likes and dislikes and monitoring their inventory enables owners to estimate the most likely buying patterns for different types of merchandise. As we learned in Chapter 7, one of the factors having the greatest impact on a company's sales, cash flow, and ultimate success is its inventory turnover ratio.

5. *Compute the actual cost of carrying inventory.* Holding inventory in stock is expensive! Carrying costs include such items as interest on borrowed money, insurance expenses associated with the inventory, inventory-related personnel expenses, and all other related operating costs. In the fast-paced computer business, for example, the onrush of new technology causes the value of a personal computer held in inventory to drop by about 1 percentage point each week![1] That gives computer makers big incentives to move their inventories quickly. Without an accurate cost of carrying inventory, it is impossible to determine an optimal inventory level.

6. *Use the most timely and accurate information system the business can afford to provide the facts and figures necessary to make critical inventory decisions.* Computers and modern point-of-sale terminals that are linked to a company's inventory records enable business owners to know exactly which items are selling and which ones are not. *For example, the owner of a chain of baby products stores uses a computer network to link all of his stores to the computer at central headquarters. Every night, after the stores close, the point-of-sale terminals in each store download the day's sales to the central computer, which compiles an extensive sales and inventory report. When he walks into his office every morning, the owner reviews the report and can tell exactly which items are moving fastest, which are moving slowest, and which are not selling at all. He credits the system with the company's above-average inventory turnover ratio—and much of his chain's success.*

7. *Teach employees how inventory control systems work so that they can contribute to managing the firm's inventory on a daily basis.* All too often, the employees on the floor have no idea of how the various information systems and inventory control techniques operate or interact with one another. Consequently, the people

closest to the inventory contribute little to controlling it. Well-trained employees armed with information can be one of an entrepreneur's greatest weapons in the battle to control inventory.

The goal is to find and maintain the proper balance between the cost of holding inventory and the requirements to have the merchandise when the customer demands it. Either extreme can be costly. If entrepreneurs focus solely on minimizing cost, they will undoubtedly lose sales and generate ill will because they cannot satisfy their customer's needs. On the other hand, entrepreneurs who attempt to hold inventory to meet every peak customer demand will find that inventory costs have diminished their chances of remaining profitable. Walking this inventory tightrope is never easy, but the following inventory control systems can help business owners strike a reasonable balance between the two extremes.

Today, a small growing company can improve their working relationships with both suppliers and customers through the application of electronic data interchange (EDI). Aroma National, Inc., has grown from $80,000 in sales to over $5 million in four years. As their relationship between themselves, suppliers, and customers became more complex, they found that their EDI system made the company a great deal more efficient.[2]

INVENTORY CONTROL SYSTEMS

1. Explain the various inventory control systems and the advantages and disadvantages of each.

Regardless of the type of inventory control system business owners choose, they must recognize the importance of Pareto's Law (or the 80/20 rule), which holds that about 80 percent of the value of the firm's sales revenue is generated by 20 percent of the items kept in stock. Some of the firm's items are high-dollar volume goods, while others account for only a small portion of sales volume. Because most sales are generated by a small percentage of times, owners should focus the majority of their inventory control efforts on this 20 percent. Observing this simple principle ensures that entrepreneurs will spend time controlling only the most productive—and, therefore, most valuable—inventory items. With this technique in mind, we now examine three basic types of inventory control systems: perpetual, visual, and partial.

Perpetual Inventory Systems

Perpetual inventory systems are designed to maintain a running count of the items in inventory. Although a number of different perpetual inventory systems exist, they all have a common element: They all keep a continuous tally of each item added to or subtracted from the firm's stock of merchandise. The basic perpetual inventory system uses a perpetual inventory sheet that includes fundamental product information such as the item's name, stock number, description, economic order quantity (EOQ), and reorder point.

These perpetual inventory sheets are usually placed next to the merchandise in the warehouse or storage facility. Whenever a shipment is received from a vendor, the quantity is entered in the receipt column and added to the total. When the item is sold and taken from inventory, it is simply deducted from the total. As long as this procedure is followed consistently, the owner can quickly determine the number of each item on hand.

Although consistent use of the system yields accurate inventory counts at any moment, sporadic use creates problems. If managers or employees take items out of stock or place them in inventory without recording them, the perpetual inventory sheet will yield incorrect totals and can foul up the entire inventory control system.

Another disadvantage of this system is the cost of maintaining it. Keeping such records for a large number of items and ensuring the accuracy of the system can be excessively expensive. Therefore, these systems are used most frequently and most successfully in controlling high-dollar volume items that require strict monitoring. Management must watch these items closely and ensure that inventory records are accurate.

Technical advances in computerized cash registers have overcome many of the disadvantages of using the basic perpetual inventory system. Small businesses now are able to afford computerized **point-of-sale (POS) systems** that perform all of the functions of a traditional cash register and maintain an up-to-the-minute inventory count. Although POS systems are not new (major retailers have been using them for more than 25 years), their affordable prices are. Not so long ago, most systems required mini- or mainframe computers and cost $20,000 or more. Today, small business owners can set up POS systems on personal computers for less than $1,000! Combining a POS system with Universal Product Code (bar code) labels and high-speed scanners gives a small business a state-of-the art checkout system that feeds vital information into its inventory control system. These systems rely on an inventory database; as items are run up on the register, product information is recorded and inventory balances are adjusted. Using the system, business owners can tell how quickly each item is selling and how many items are in stock at any time. Plus, their inventory records are accurate and always current. They also can generate instantly a variety of reports to aid in making purchasing decision. The system can be programmed to alert owners when the supply of a particular item drops below a predetermined reorder point or even to print automatically a purchase order for the EOQ indicated. Computerized systems such as these make it possible for the owner to use a basic perpetual inventory system for a large number of items—a task that, if performed manually, would be virtually impossible.[3]

Spanish clothing retailer, ZARA, may be located in the small town of La Coruna, Spain, but its inventory control system is sophisticated enough to integrate the movement of merchandise among its suppliers and its 400 stores in 25 countries. Supply-chain management, information sharing, and speed to market are more than catch phrases, they are the source of ZARA's competitive advantage.[4]

Specific Perpetual Inventory Control Systems. Perpetual inventory systems operate in a number of ways, but three basic variations are particularly common: the sales ticket method, the sales stub method, and the floor sample method.

The Sales Ticket Method. Most small businesses use sales tickets to summarize individual customers' transactions. These tickets serve two major purposes: They provide the customer with a sales receipt for the merchandise purchased, and they provide the owner with a daily record of the number of specific inventory items sold. The **sales ticket method** operates by gathering all the sales tickets at the end of each day and transcribing the data onto the appropriate perpetual inventory sheet. By posting inventory deductions to the perpetual inventory system from sales tickets, the small business manager can monitor sales patterns and keep close control on inventory. The primary disadvantage of using such a system is the time required to make it function properly. Most managers find it difficult to squeeze in the time needed to post sales tickets to the perpetual inventory system.

The Sales Stub Method. The principle behind the **sales stub method** of inventory control is the same as that underlying the sales ticket method, but its mechanics are slightly different. Retail stores often attach a ticket with two or more parts containing relevant product information to each inventory item in stock. When an employee sells an item, he removes a portion of the stub and places it in a container. At the end of the day, the owner posts the inventory deductions recorded by the stubs to the proper perpetual inventory sheet.

The Floor Sample Method. The **floor sample method** of controlling inventory is commonly used by businesses selling big-ticket items with high unit cost. In many cases, these items are somewhat bulky and are difficult to display in large numbers. For example, the owner of a small furniture store might receive a shipment of 15 roll-top desks in a particular style. A simple technique for maintaining control of these items is to attach a small pad to the display desk with sheets numbered in descending order from 15 to 1. Whenever an employee sells a rolltop desk, she removes a sheet from the pad. As long as the system is followed consistently, the owner is able to determine accurate inventory levels with a quick pass around the sales floor. When the supply of a particular item dwindles, the owner simply calls the vendor to replenish the inventory. The procedure is simple and serves its purpose.

Visual Inventory Control Systems

The most common method of controlling inventory in a small business is the **visual control system,** in which managers simply conduct periodic visual inspections to determine the quantity of various items they should order. As mentioned earlier, manual perpetual inventory systems can be excessively costly and time consuming. Such systems are impractical when the business stocks a large number of low-value items with low dollar volume. Therefore, many owners rely on the simplest, quickest inventory control method: the visual system. Unfortunately, this method is also the least effective for ensuring accuracy and reliability. Oversights of key items often lead to stockouts and resulting lost sales. The biggest disadvantage of the visual control system is its inability to detect and to foresee shortages of inventory items.

GAINING THE COMPETITIVE EDGE
Unloading Overstocks Online

The Internet's business-to-business merchants of unsold inventory are finding ways to unload some of the $332 billion a year (that's correct, billion) goods that failed to sell. About 11 percent of the current Internet sites are involved in selling excess inventory. One of the most interesting aspects of this Web marketplace is the greater number of buyers who now comparison shop on the Web sites in search of the "best deal." Web sites such as Retail Exchange.com, iSolve.com, TradeOut.com, and OVERSTOCK.com are new high-volume entrepreneurial ventures, with the oldest being formed in 1999. Inventory surplus Web sites allow a variety of transaction methods: auctions, barter, private sale, listing, and negotiation.

Although the Web is only a new vehicle for an old established business, it is predicted to grow from its present 1 percent of excess inventory to 14 percent (or $22 billion) in sales by 2004.

1. Are established retailers and manufacturers creating their own Web sites to sell off excess inventory? If yes, please provide some examples.

2. Do you see any problem with established retailers selling deeply discounted items online? Discuss the possibility of "cannibalization" of the click-and-mortar store of the existing bricks-and-mortar distribution network.

Source: Adapted from Carol Pickering, "The Price of Excess," *Business2.com*, February 6, 2001, pp. 38–42.

In general, a visual inventory control system works best in firms where daily sales are relatively consistent, the owner is closely involved with the inventory, the variety of merchandise is small, and items can be obtained quickly from vendors. For example, small firms dealing in perishable goods use visual control systems very successfully, and rarely, if ever, rely on analytical inventory control tools. For these firms, shortages are not likely to occur under a visual system; when they do occur, they are not likely to create major problems. Still, the manager who uses a visual inventory control system should leave reminders to make regular inspections and should be alert to shifts in customer buying patterns that alter required inventory levels.

Partial Inventory Control Systems

For small business owners with limited time and money, the most viable option for inventory management is a partial inventory control system. Such a system relies on the validity of the 80/20 rule. For example, if a small business carries 5,000 different items in stock, roughly 1,000 of them account for about 80 percent of the firm's sales volume. Experienced business owners focus their control efforts on those 1,000 items. Still, many managers seek to maintain tight control over the remaining 4,000 items, a frustrating and wasteful practice. Smart small business owners design their inventory control systems with this principle in mind. One of the most popular partial inventory control systems is the ABC system.

The ABC Method of Inventory Control. Too many managers apply perpetual inventory control systems universally when a partial control system would be much more practical. Partial inventory systems minimize the expense involved in analyzing, processing, and maintaining records, a substantial cost of any inventory control system. The ABC method is one such approach, focusing control efforts on that small percentage of items that account for the majority of the firm's sales. The typical **ABC system** divides a firm's inventory into three major categories:

A items account for a high-dollar usage volume.
B items account for a moderate-dollar usage volume.
C items account for low-dollar usage volume.

The **dollar usage volume** of an item measures the relative importance of that item in the firm's inventory. Note that value is not necessarily synonymous with high unit cost. In some instances, a high-cost item that generates only a small dollar volume can be classified as an A item. But, more frequently, A items are those that are low to moderate in cost and high volume by nature.

The initial step in establishing an ABC classification system is to compute the annual dollar usage volume for each product (or product category). **Annual dollar usage volume** is simply the cost per unit of an item multiplied by the annual quantity used. For instance, the owner of a stereo shop may find that she sold 190 pairs of a popular brand of speaker during the previous year. If the speakers cost her *$75* per unit, their annual dollar usage volume would be as follows:

$$190 \times \$75 = \$14{,}250 \qquad \text{(1)}$$

The next step is to arrange the products in descending order on the basis of the computed annual dollar usage volume. Once so arranged, they can be divided into appropriate classes by applying the following rule:

A items: Roughly the top 15 percent of the items listed
B items: Roughly the next 35 percent
C items: Roughly the remaining 50 percent

For example, Florentina's, a small retail shop, is interested in establishing an ABC inventory control system to lower losses from stockouts, theft, or other hazards. Florentina has computed the annual dollar usage volume for the store's merchandise inventory, as shown in Table 18.1. (For simplicity, we show only 12 inventory items.)

The ABC inventory control method divides the firm's inventory items into three classes depending on the items' value. Figure 18.1 graphically portrays the segmentation of the items listed in Table 18.1.

The purpose of classifying items according to their annual dollar usage volume is to establish the proper degree of control over each item held in inventory. Clearly, it is wasteful and inefficient to exercise the same level of control over C items and A items. Items in the A classification should be controlled under a perpetual inventory system with as much detail as necessary. Analytical tools and frequent counts may be required to ensure accuracy, but the extra cost of tight control for these valuable items is usually justified. Managers should not retain a large supply of reserve or safety stock because doing so ties up excessive amounts of money in inventory, but they must monitor the stock closely to avoid stockouts and lost sales.

Control of B items should rely more on periodic control systems and basic analytical tools such as EOQ and reorder point analysis (discussed in Chapter 17). Managers can maintain moderate levels of safety stock for these items to guard against shortages and can afford monthly or even bimonthly merchandise inspections. Because B items are not as valuable to the business as A items, less rigorous control systems are required.

C items typically constitute a minor proportion of the small firm's inventory value and, as a result, require the least effort and expense to control. These items are

Figure 18.1
ABC Inventory
Control

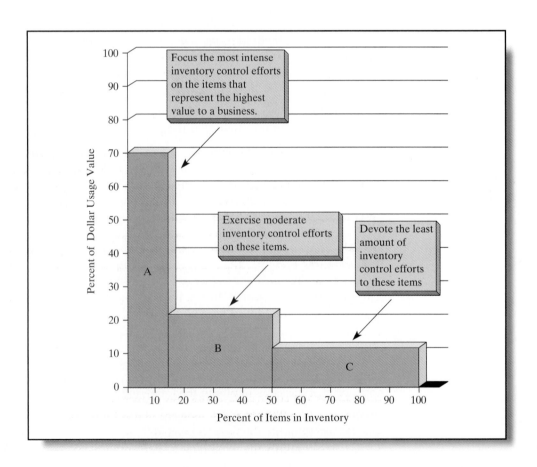

Section VII   Managing a Small Business: Techniques for Enhancing Profitability

Table 18.1

Calculating Annual Dollar Usage Volume and an ABC Inventory Analysis for Florentina's

ITEM	ANNUAL DOLLAR USAGE VOLUME	% OF ANNUAL DOLLAR USAGE
Paragon	$374,100	42.0
Excelsior	294805	33.1
Avery	68,580	7.7
Bardeen	54,330	6.1
Berkeley	27,610	3.1
Tara	24,940	2.8
Cattell	11,578	1.3
Faraday	9,797	1.1
Humboldt	8,016	0.9
Mandel	7,125	0.08
Sabot	5,344	0.06
Wister	4,453	0.05
Total	$890,678	100.0

CLASSIFICATION	ITEMS	ANNUAL DOLLAR USAGE	% OF TOTAL
A	Paragon, Excelsior	$668,905	75.1
B	Avery, Bardeen, Berkeley, Tara	175,460	19.7
C	Cattell, Faraday, Humboldt, Mandel, Sabot, Wister	46,313	5.2
Total		$890,678	100.0

usually large in number and small in total value. The most practical way to control them is to use uncomplicated records and procedures. Large levels of safety stock for these items are acceptable because the cost of carrying them is usually minimal. Substantial order sizes often enable the business to take advantage of quantity discounts without having to place frequent orders. The cost involved in using detailed record keeping and inventory control procedures greatly outweighs the advantages gleaned from strict control of C items.

One practical technique for maintaining control simply is the **two-bin system,** which keeps two separate bins full of material. The first bin is used to fill customer orders, and the second bin is filled with enough safety stock to meet customer demand during the lead time. When the first bin is empty, the owner places an order with the vendor large enough to refill both bins. During the lead time for the order, the manager uses the safety stock in the second bin to fill customer demand.

When storage space or the type of item does not suit the two-bin system, the owner can use a **tag system.** Based on the same principles as the two-bin system, which is suitable for many manufacturers, the tag system applies to most retail, wholesale, and service firms. Instead of placing enough inventory to meet customer demand during lead time into a separate bin, the owner marks this inventory level with a brightly colored tag. When the supply is drawn down to the tagged level, the owner reorders the merchandise. Figure 18.2 illustrates the two-bin and tag systems of controlling C items.

In summary, business owners minimize total inventory costs when they spend time and effort controlling items that represent the greatest inventory value. Some inventory items require strict, detailed control techniques; others cannot justify the cost of such systems. Because of its practicality, the ABC inventory system is commonly used in industry. In addition, the technique is easily computerized, speeding

Figure 18.2
The Two-Bin and
Tag Systems of
Inventory Control

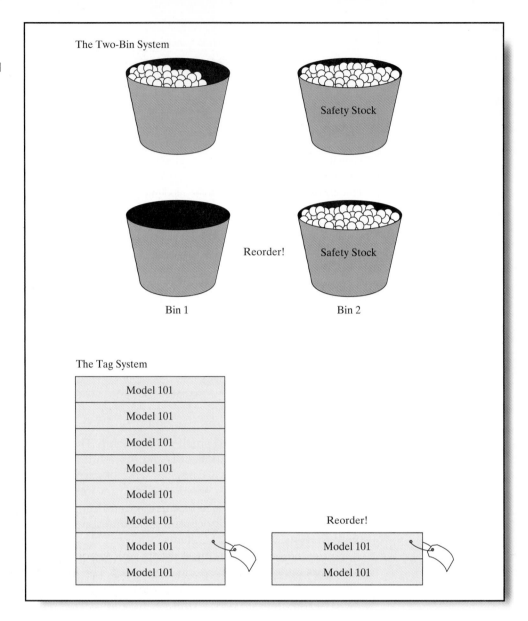

The Two-Bin System

Safety Stock

Reorder!   Safety Stock

Bin 1   Bin 2

The Tag System

| Model 101 |
| Model 101 |
| Model 101 |
| Model 101 |
| Model 101 |
| Model 101 |
| Model 101 |
| Model 101 |

Reorder!

| Model 101 |
| Model 101 |

up the analysis and lowering its cost. Table 18.2 summarizes the use of the ABC control system.

Physical Inventory Count

Regardless of the type of inventory control system used, every small business owner must conduct a periodic physical inventory count. Even when a company uses a perpetual inventory system, the owner must still count the actual number of items on hand because of the possibility of human error. A physical inventory count allows owners to reconcile the actual amount of inventory in stock with the amount reported through the inventory control system. These counts give managers a fresh start in determining the actual number of items on hand and enable them to evaluate the effectiveness and the accuracy of their inventory control systems.

Table 18.2

ABC Inventory Control Features

FEATURE	A ITEMS	B ITEMS	C ITEMS
Level of control	Monitor closely and maintain tight control.	Maintain moderate control.	Maintain loose control.
Reorder	Based on forecasted requirements.	Based on EOQ calculations and past experience.	When level gets low, reorder.
Record keeping	Keep detailed records of receipts and disbursements.	Use periodic inspections and control procedures.	No records required.
Safety stock	Keep low levels of safety stock.	Keep moderate levels of safety stock.	Keep high levels of safety stock.
Inspection frequency	Monitor schedule changes frequently.	Check on changes in requirements periodically.	Make few checks on requirements.

The typical method of taking inventory involves two employees; one calls out the relevant information for each inventory item, and the other records the count on a tally sheet. There are two basic methods of conducting a physical inventory count. One alternative is to take inventory at regular intervals. Many businesses take inventory at the end of the year. In an attempt to minimize counting, many managers run special year-end inventory reduction sales. This periodic physical count generates the most accurate measurement of inventory. The other method of taking inventory, called **cycle counting,** involves counting a number of items on a continuous basis. Instead of waiting until year-end to tally the entire inventory of items, the manager counts a few types of items each week and checks the numbers against the inventory control system. Such a system allows for continuous correction of mistakes in inventory control systems and detects inventory problems sooner than an annual count would.

Once again, technology can make the job of taking inventory much easier for the small business owner. Electronic data interchange systems enable business owners to track their inventories and to place orders with vendors quickly and with few errors by linking them to their vendors electronically. These systems often rely on handheld computer terminals equipped with a scanning wand. An employee runs the wand across a bar code label on the shelf that identifies the inventory item; then he counts the items on the shelf and enters that number using the number pad on the terminal. Then, by linking the handheld terminal to a personal computer, he can download the physical inventory count into the company's inventory control software in seconds.

In the past, suppliers simply manufactured a product, shipped it, and then sent the customer an invoice. To place an order, employees or managers periodically would estimate how much of a particular item they would need and when they would need it. Today, however, in many EDI systems, the vendor is tied directly into a company's POS system, monitoring it constantly; when the company's supply of a particular item drops to a preset level, the vendor automatically sends a shipment to replenish its stock to an established level. Information that once traveled by mail (or was never shared at all), such as shipping information, invoices, inventory balances, sales, even funds, now travels instantly between businesses and their suppliers. The result is a much more efficient system of purchasing, distribution, and inventory control. *For example, when one of Ideal Supply Company's top customers asked the small supplier of industrial pipes and valves to set up an EDI system in 1990, General Manager*

IN THE FOOTSTEPS OF AN ENTREPRENEUR
The Best Hardware Store in the World

Customers walking to Harvey's Hardware in Needham, Massachusetts, for the first time have a tendency to be overwhelmed by what they see; a modest-sized store loaded with wall-to-wall and floor-to-ceiling inventory. As far as the eye can see, there is hardware . . . and more hardware. Most customers are also taken aback by the squadron of salespeople stationed at the front door. All decked out in flannel and hardware aprons and ranging from age 16 to 70, these devotees of hardware stand ready to guide customers through the store's crowded aisles and multiple floors. Its devoted following of extremely loyal customers are not joking when they tell the uninitiated that Harvey's is simply the best hardware store in the world. First-time customers soon begin to understand why.

Harvey Katz started the hardware store shortly after he returned from the Korean War. In the early days, Harvey had very little money to invest in the business, and he couldn't afford much inventory. To make his store look well stocked, he scattered his meager inventory of hardware around the shelves and then filled in the gaps with empty boxes he had taped shut. Business picked up gradually, and Harvey noticed that quite a few customers came in looking for odd items that none of the hardware stores in town—including his own—carried. He also observed that when he did happen to have a hard-to-find item, the customer seemed to be especially pleased and usually came back repeatedly to buy other items. Harvey's competitive strategy was born! Stock as much merchandise as you possibly can, and you can build a large base of loyal customers.

Today, Harvey's strategy lives on through his two sons, Gary and Jeff, who now manage the store. One customer describes the store this way: "Every square inch of shelf and wall space, and the vast majority of floor space—even a significant percentage of ceiling space—is crammed with a riotous melange of wares. The lighting is on the dim side. There are no aisle placards or any other store navigational aids; nor does any logical scheme of organization suggest itself!"

The cornerstone of Harvey's strategy for success led to the second factor that puts the store so far ahead of the competition. (Although competitors are scarce, seven hardware stores folded in 1993.) The second pillar on which Harvey's success is built is customer service. "This is not a self-service store," explains Gary. "We have people here to help you find what you're looking for." Years ago, not long after he began stocking so much hardware, Harvey realized that he either had to move to a much larger building where he could spread his merchandise out so customers could help themselves or he had to hire workers to serve customers. He really didn't want to move, and besides that, there weren't any places in town big enough to spread that much inventory out! Soon, superior customer service became another hallmark of Harvey's. "When you get to know your customers and build a relationship with them, it creates a sense of loyalty and trust," explains Gary. (A customer once recognized Gary from a restaurant window and called to him as the hardware retailer floated down a canal in Venice, Italy!)

Gary and Jeff installed a computer system several years ago to help them maintain control over their extensive inventory, but they found that they didn't need most of the features it offered. The sales staff knows and watches the inventory so closely that they know they need to order duct tape before the computer tells them to! Stocking and displaying such a volume of merchandise provides a challenge, but the Katz brothers use the store's crowded look to their advantage as well. Harvey's packs $135 worth of inventory per square foot into its building, whereas the typical hardware store carries just $35 worth of goods per square foot. "The trick is to keep everything organized," says Harvey. "Not too neat—but organized."

Customers apparently love the overcrowded look because it seems to encourage them to buy, buy, buy. Harvey's sales are more than three times the average for hardware stores: $503 per square foot verses $129 per square foot at the average hardware store. "When someone comes in and finds what they're looking for and tells me they've been to eight other places looking for it, I say to them, 'Maybe you'll come here first next time,'" says Gary. The sheer volume of merchandise offers customers an almost subliminal invitation to engage in a hardware

(continued)

shopping spree. The average sale at a typical hardware store is $12; at Harvey's, it is $17.

Retail experts know that the key to success is rapid inventory turnover. With such a huge stockpile of inventory, much of it admittedly slow-moving, one would suspect that Harvey's average inventory turnover ratio would be dangerously low. Not so! Those slow-moving items in the store's stock seem to draw customers from far and wide who buy lots of fast-moving merchandise. The result is an inventory turnover ratio of 4.5 times per year, compared with just 3.7 times per year at the typical hardware store.

Gary and Jeff have built a highly successful hardware department for appliances and other items, and they have turned Harvey's into one of the nation's leading distributors of Weber gas grills. But, for the most part, they have kept their father's basic strategy intact. After all, why tinker with the strategy that built the best hardware store in the world?

1. What factors set Harvey's Hardware apart from its competitors? What role have these factors played in the company's success?

2. What dangers does the company face as a result of its unique retail strategy?

Source: Adapted from David H. Freedman, "Best Hometown Business in America," *Inc.*, July 1997, pp. 57–66.

Michael Fidenza decided that doing so would give his company an edge over its rivals. "Our industry is old-fashioned," says Fidenza. "We tend to lag behind the times." Ideal Supply not only forged an even closer relationship with its big customer; it also reaped benefits from its suppliers. Because Ideal Supply was one of the few companies in the industry with EDI capability, Fidenza was able to negotiate higher discounts from its suppliers because of increased efficiencies in the purchasing process. "One of our vendors offered us an extra 5 percent in discounts," he says. "Another plugs in an extra $10,000 worth of product with every $50,000 purchase—just because we're EDI." Ideal Supply has earned an impressive return on its original investment of $5,000 for EDI hardware and software. Today, 80 percent of the company's purchases and 15 percent of its sales are processed through its EDI system.[5]

JUST-IN-TIME INVENTORY CONTROL TECHNIQUES

2. Describe how just-in-time (JIT) and JIT II inventory control techniques work.

Many U.S. manufacturers have turned to a popular inventory control technique called **just-in-time (JIT)** to reduce costly inventories and turn around their financial fortunes. Until recently, these firms had accepted and practiced without question the following long-standing principles of manufacturing: Long production runs of standard items are ideal; machines should be up and running as much as possible; machines must produce a large number of items to justify long setup times and high costs; similar processes should be consolidated into single departments; tasks should be highly specialized and simplified; and inventories (raw materials, work-in-process, and finished goods) should be large enough to avoid emergencies such as supply interruptions, strikes, and breakdowns.

The just-in-time philosophy, however, views excess inventory as a blanket that masks problems and as a source of unnecessary costs that inhibit a firm's competitive position. Under a JIT system, materials and inventory should flow smoothly through the production process without stopping. They arrive at the appropriate location just in time instead of becoming part of a costly inventory stockpile. Just-in-time is a manufacturing philosophy that seeks to improve a company's efficiency. The key measure of manufacturing efficiency is the level of inventory maintained; the lower the level of inventory, the more efficient the production system.

IN THE FOOTSTEPS OF AN ENTREPRENEUR
Hog Heaven

Armand Schaubroeck's business, the House of Guitars, caters to guitarists of all skill levels—from beginning amateurs to professionals in rock bands. A few years ago, when the rock band Metallica performed a concert in a nearby town, band members wanted to shop at "the HOG" (as its fans affectionately call it), but their only free time was after their concert. Schaubroeck, who normally closes at 9 P.M., reopened the shop at 11 P.M. so that band members could browse through the store's extensive collection of guitars. He and his employees were treated to a miniconcert of their own as the musicians tried out the guitars and other musical instruments the store carries. HOG's customer list includes not only Metallica but also bands such as Motley Crue, Aerosmith, and a host of lesser known groups as well as individual performers such as Ozzy Osbourne and Matthew Sweet.

Although HOG sells everything from CDs and drums to amplifiers and keyboards, its specialty is guitars. The business occupies an old feed store, which is connected to its five cavernous warehouses by a labyrinth of passages so complex that employees sometimes get lost. Ozzy Osbourne says the House of Guitars has "a great vibey feel." Mountains of T-shirts and CDs fill one room. Autographs of famous musicians decorate a wall in another warehouse, and rock 'n' roll memorabilia, such as a pair of Elvis Presley's leather pants, are everywhere. But what sets the House of Guitars apart from other musical instruments stores is its inventory and the way it is displayed. Rather than keep his guitars locked in glass cases, Schaubroeck puts them out in the open and encourages customers to try them out. He has even built small, soundproof rooms so that customers can hook guitars up to amplifiers and play as loudly as they like.

The huge selection of guitars the HOG offers attracts many customers. The business stocks practically every make of instrument (and what the store doesn't stock, it can get), whereas other instrument stores specialize in a single brand. Schaubroeck estimates that he has 9,000 guitars in stock. After taking a guest on a tour, however, he revises his estimate upward to 11,000 guitars. "It is total guitar heaven and the high point of any tour," says alternative musician Matthew Sweet. Sweet once missed a preconcert sound check because he couldn't tear himself away from the HOG. He bought three guitars, spending several thousand dollars. The House of Guitars has 20 employees, all musicians, and racks up sales of $7 million a year. Andy Babiuk, a salesperson at HOG for 17 years, is a member of a local heavy-metal band call the Chesterfield Kings. Wading through a knee-deep collection of vintage amplifiers, Babiuk marvels, "You can't walk into any music store and get this," waving his hand.

Schaubroeck's accountant almost panicked when he saw the inventory level the House of Guitars maintains. On paper, it looks like a recipe for disaster. In person, at first glance, the disarray looks like a disaster. Then, the beauty of Schaubroeck's strategy begins to emerge. The HOG, says Schaubroeck's accountant, "doesn't turn its inventory as fast as it should, but they carry older things—so once they become out of stock at other places, (HOG's) prices go up." One of the store's prize pieces, for instance, is a 1947 D'Angelico New York, which Schaubroeck calls "the Stradivarius of guitars." The valuable collector's item is worth more than $50,000! Although Schaubroeck's investment in inventory is what most musical instrument store owners would consider excessive, it is actually an important part of the company's success. Guitarists and musicians across the country plan their tours so they can shop there. "When asked about the HOG, one rock star says simply, "All the pros know it."

1. What benefits does maintaining a large inventory offer the House of Guitars? What costs are associated with holding a large inventory?

2. What advice would you offer Armand Schaubroeck about controlling his company's inventory more effectively?

Source: Emily Nelson, "Meet the Master of the House of Guitars," *Wall Street Journal*, June 12, 1997, pp. B1, B7.

In the past, only large companies could reap the benefits of computerized JIT and inventory control software, but now a proliferation of inexpensive programs designed for personal computers gives small companies that ability. The most effective businesses know that what is required is not simply the technology but the critical strategic alliances with suppliers who are themselves technologically sophisticated enough to interact on a real time basis to deliver what is needed when it is needed. The ultimate goal is to drive the inventory to zero.

Jason and Matthew Olim did exactly that when they created CD Now. The company built working partnerships with producers of compact discs (CDs) that allow CD Now to make the sale and have the company who produced the CD supply the requested selection only after the sale was made. As such, no inventory. The Olim brothers parlayed their $20,000 investment into a successful business that was acquired by Columbia House, a subsidiary of Time Warner and Sony. The founder retained a 20 percent stake in the new venture Columbia House/CD Now.[6]

Today, many suppliers recognize that extremely high quality and absolutely on-time delivery are essential elements of remaining competitive. Just-in-time systems work because suppliers recognize that if they are unable to meet the demands their customers set forth, some other company surely will. *Cisco Systems, a manufacturer of computer hardware, ships thousands of sophisticated computer routers to customers in Europe each week. Cisco's customers expect to know where their shipments are at all times, which also is important information for Cisco because it may have to reroute a shipment to meet a customer's urgent request. To be able to meet these rather exacting demands, Cisco hired UPS Worldwide Logistics to design a computerized system to schedule and track all of its shipments. Before Cisco implemented its new system, deliveries to its European customers took up to three weeks; now, those same deliveries arrive in just four days. Deliveries are much faster and more reliable; customers are more satisfied; and Cisco has saved a bundle on its inventory investment.*

Advocates claim that when JIT is successfully implemented, companies experience five positive results:

1. Lower investment in inventory
2. Reduced inventory carrying and handling costs
3. Reduced costs from obsolescence of inventory
4. Lower investment in space for inventories and production
5. Reduced total manufacturing costs from the better coordination needed between departments to operate at lower inventory levels

For JIT systems to be most productive, small business owners must consider the human component of the equation as well. The two primary human elements on which successful JIT systems are built are:

1. *Mutual trust and teamwork.* Managers and employees view each other as equals, have a commitment to the organization and its long-term effectiveness, and are willing to work as a team to find and solve problems.
2. *Empowerment.* Effective organizations provide their employees with the authority to take action to solve problems. The objective is to have the problems dealt with at the lowest level and as quickly as possible.

At a technical level, JIT is most effective in repetitive manufacturing operations where there are significant inventory levels, where production requirements can be forecast accurately, and where suppliers are an integral part of the system. Experience shows that companies with the following characteristics have the greatest success with JIT:

- Reliable deliveries of all parts and supplies
- Short distance between client and vendors

- Consistently high quality of vendors' products
- Stable and predictable product demand that allows for accurate production schedules

Just-in-Time II Techniques

In the past, some companies that adopted JIT techniques discovered an unwanted side effect: increased hostility resulting from the increased pressure they put on their suppliers to meet tight, often challenging schedules. To resolve that conflict, many businesses have turned to an extension of JIT, **just-in-time II (JIT II),** which focuses on creating a close, harmonious relationship with a company's suppliers so that both parties benefit from increased efficiency. Lance Dixon, who created the JIT II concept when he was a manager at Bose Corporation, a manufacturer of audio equipment, calls it "empowerment of the supplier within the customer's organization."[7] To work successfully, JIT II requires suppliers and their customers to share what was once closely guarded information in an environment of trust and cooperation. Under JIT II, customers and suppliers work hand-in-hand, acting more like partners than mere buyers and sellers. *For instance, Dell Computer Corporation uses the Internet and modern Web-based software to link its suppliers' manufacturing systems with its own. Sharing information with suppliers over the Internet has allowed Dell to reduce its inventory investment significantly and to speed its inventory turnover.*[8]

In many businesses practicing JIT II, suppliers' employees work on site at the customer's plant, factory, or warehouse almost as if they were its employees: These on-site workers are responsible for monitoring, controlling, and ordering inventory from their own companies. While at Bose, Dixon decided to try JIT II because it offered the potential to reduce sharply the company's inventories of materials and components, to cut purchasing costs, and to generate cost-cutting design and production tips from suppliers who understood Bose's process. This new alliance between suppliers and their customers would form a new supply chain that would lower costs at every one of its links. To protect against leakage of confidential information, Dixon had all of the employees from Bose's suppliers who would work in its plant sign confidentiality agreements. Dixon also put a ceiling on the amount each supplier's employee could order without previous authorization from Bose.

Growing numbers of small companies are forging JIT II relationships with their suppliers and customers. *For instance, Northern Polymer Corporation, a seven-person plastics maker, sells plastic resin to G & F Industries, a 170-employee injection molding company in Sturbridge, Massachusetts, under a JIT II arrangement. Northern employees visit G & F's plant several times each month to check its inventory and consumption levels. Northern has set up a resin storage facility near G & F's plant so that it can restock its resin supply within just a few hours, if necessary. The arrangement "secures that piece of business for a long period," says Northern's founder, Joseph St. Martin.* As Northern Polymer's experience with G & F Industries indicates, an EDI system such as those mentioned earlier in this chapter allows many companies to operate JIT II systems without having an employee from the supplier in-house. G & F Industries, in turn, has a JIT II relationship with one of its biggest customers, Bose Corporation, and G & F does keep an employee in Bose's plant on a full-time basis.[9]

Manufacturers are not the only companies benefiting from JIT II. In a retail environment, the concept is more commonly known as **efficient consumer response (ECR),** but the principles are the same. Rather than build inventories of merchandise that might sit for months before selling (or worse, never sell at all), retailers using ECR replenish their inventories constantly on an as-needed basis. Because vendors

GAINING THE COMPETITIVE EDGE
Can "The Goal" Be Perfection?

Eliyahu Goldratt, an Israeli physicist, in his book, *The Goal*, presents to manufacturers and others the concept of the Theory of Constraints (TOC). In this book, Goldratt states that every business has at least one resource that prevents it from making infinite profits. Identify and remove the constraints, and the result is increased productivity and profitability. In a market that is changing at today's frantic pace, innovations may last less than a year before new innovation occurs. Speed to respond to the demands of the marketplace makes time a critical constraint. With TOC, reduction in the time it takes to manufacture and deliver translates into faster throughput and higher revenues. TOC can help any entrepreneur discover where in their operations constraints are occurring and how working through

these problems will result in higher productivity, and correspondingly, higher profitability.

Can we ever reach a level where no constraints exist? Likely not, but entrepreneurs are becoming aware that tools like TOC have the power to improve performance in all areas of the operation and result in superior performance.

1. One constraint that can create a serious bottleneck for business owners is obsolete inventory. No one wants the goods available and the demand is for newer, more technologically savvy merchandise. Discuss ways that a business owner can avoid this pitfall in a *proactive* manner.

Source: Karen Kroll, "The Theory of Constraints Revisted," *Industry Week*, April 20, 1998, p. 20.

are linked electronically to the retailer's POS system, they can monitor the company's inventory and keep it stocked with the right merchandise mix in the right quantities. Both parties reduce the inventories they must carry and experience significant reductions in paperwork and ordering costs. Just-in-time II works best when two companies transact a significant amount of business that involves many different parts or products. Still, trust is the biggest barrier the companies must overcome.

TURNING SLOW-MOVING INVENTORY INTO CASH

3. Describe some methods for reducing loss from slow-moving inventory.

Managing inventory effectively requires a business owner to monitor the company's inventory turnover ratio and to compare it with that of other firms of similar size in the same industry. As you recall, the inventory turnover ratio is computed by dividing the firm's cost of goods sold by its average inventory. This ratio expresses the number of times per year the business turns over its inventory. In most cases, the higher the inventory turnover ratio, the better the small firm's financial position will be. A very low inventory turnover ratio indicates that much of the inventory may be stale and obsolete or that inventory investment is too large.

Slow-moving items carry a good chance of loss resulting from spoilage or obsolescence. Firms dealing in trendy fashion merchandise or highly seasonal items often experience losses as a result of being stuck with unsold inventory for long periods of time. Some small business owners are reluctant to sell these slow-moving items by cutting prices, but it is much more profitable to dispose of this merchandise as quickly as possible than to hold it in stock at the regular prices. The owner who postpones marking down stale merchandise, fearing it would reduce profit and hoping that the goods will sell eventually at the regular price, is making a huge mistake. The longer the merchandise sits, the dimmer the prospects of ever selling it, much less selling it at a profit. Pricing these items below regular price or even below cost is difficult, but it is much better than having valuable working capital tied up in unproductive assets.

The most common technique for liquidating slow-moving merchandise is the markdown. Not only is the markdown effective in eliminating slow-moving goods, but it also is a successful promotional tool. Advertising special prices on such merchandise helps the small business garner a larger clientele and contributes to establishing a favorable business image. Using special sales to promote slow-moving items helps create a functional program for turning over inventory more quickly. To get rid of a large supply of out-of-style neckties, one small business offered a "one cent sale" to customers purchasing neckware at the regular price. One retailer of stereos and sound equipment chooses an unusual holiday—George Washington's birthday—to sponsor an all-out blitz, including special sales, prices, and promotions to reduce its inventory. Other techniques that help eliminate slow-moving merchandise include the following:

- Middle-of-the-aisle display islands that attract customer attention
- One-day-only sales
- Quantity discounts for volume purchases
- Bargain tables with a variety of merchandise for customers to explore
- Eye-catching lights and tickets marking sale merchandise

PROTECTING INVENTORY FROM THEFT

4. Discuss employee theft and shoplifting and how to prevent them.

Small companies are a big target for crime. Security experts estimate that businesses lose $400 billion annually to criminals, although the actual loss may be even greater because so many business crimes go unreported. Whatever the actual loss is, its effect is staggering, especially on small companies. Smaller companies sometimes lack the sophistication to identify early on the illegal actions of employees or professional thieves. When the losses are detected, it often results in a crippling loss to a business venture that may be battling cash flow problems. When a firm has fewer assets to operate with, a loss from theft can become a major setback.

If you ask some naive entrepreneurs, they may respond that the sources of theft are external to the business. In reality, most firms are victimized by their own employees.

Employee Theft

The greatest criminal threat to small businesses, ironically, comes from inside. Employee theft accounts for the greatest proportion of the criminal losses businesses suffer. One of the problems is that small business owners simply don't want to believe that the people who work for them would steal from them! One U.S. Justice Department study reports that approximately 30 percent of all employees are "hardcore pilferers." The study also estimates that without preventive security measures in place, 80 percent of employees will become involved in theft.[10] These employees steal from the companies that employ them simply because the opportunity presents itself. Many thefts by employees involve "nickel-and-dime" items (nails for a home repair job, a box of pencils for personal use), but a significant number of them involve large sums of money.

IN THE FOOTSTEPS OF AN ENTREPRENEUR
Where Has Civility Gone?

In an era of economic prosperity in America, especially relatively well-off Americans, are behaving like low-class common thieves. How can we explain the number of people who drive through toll booths or fill up with gasoline and simply drive off? Why would you believe you are entitled to self-upgrade yourself to first-class on a flight when you purchased a coach ticket? Restaurants are reporting that everything from silverware to bottles of wine are routinely stolen. Aureole, a Las Vegas restaurant, reported that $10,000 in Limoges ashtrays alone were stolen in the first two weeks of its operations.

What's the motive for such behavior? Do some people believe that they are entitled to more without paying? Is it because few are caught and consequently seldom punished? Businesses are now recognizing that people do not steal from need, but for a new societal force that reflects a lack of respect for the property rights of others. Who will pay for this criminal behavior? You know who—us. Entrepreneurs have little choice but to raise prices to cover the additional cost created by Americans who have lost civility in our society.

1. What would you recommend in the following scenario: You are the owner of a very private, very upscale chalet that caters to known celebrities and political figures who wish to escape the "paparazzi" for a quiet retreat. After one popular film star leaves, you notice that several thousand dollars in original artwork is missing. What would you do?

2. Assume that you decide to simply write off the loss as "shrinkage." Discuss the ethics of passing this cost on to other guests.

Source: Eileen Daspin, "The Cheater Principles," *Wall Street Journal*, August 25, 2000, pp. W1–17.

How can thefts go undetected? Most thefts occur when employees take advantage of the opportunities to steal that small business owners give them. Typically, small business owners are so busy building their companies that they rarely even consider the possibility of employee theft—until disaster strikes. Also, small companies are not likely to have adequate financial, audit, and security procedures in place. Add into that mix the high degree of trust most small business owners place in their employees, and you have a perfect recipe for employee theft. A recent study by the Association of Certified Fraud Examiners found that small companies (those with fewer than 100 employees) "were the most vulnerable to fraud and abuse." The study found that the median loss per fraud was $120,000, nearly as large as that for firms with more than 10,000 workers (median of $126,000 per fraud). Although no business can afford such large losses, crimes of that magnitude can drive a small company out of existence because they lack the financial resources to absorb such devastating losses. Survey participants estimated that their companies lose about 6 percent of their annual revenues to employee theft and fraud.[11]

What Causes Employee Theft? Employees steal from their companies for any number of reasons. Some may have a grudge against the company; others may have a drug, alcohol, or gambling addiction to support. "Employees take from the company for four reasons: need, greed, temptation, and opportunity," says one security expert. "A company can control the last two."[12] To minimize their losses to employee theft, business owners must understand how both the temptation and the opportunity to steal creep into their companies. The following are conditions that lead to major security gaps in small companies.

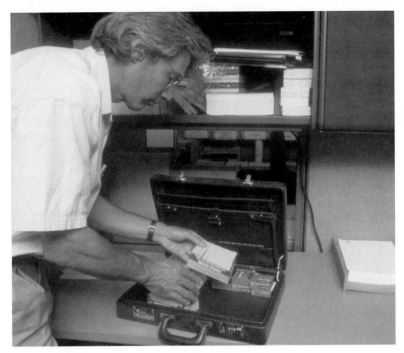

The latest National Retail Security Survey reports that losses from employee theft have reached record levels and that total inventory shrinkage cost U.S. retailers $32.3 billion last year, up from $29 billion the year before.

The Trusted Employee. The fact is that any employee could be a thief, although most are not. Studies show that younger, less devoted employees steal from their companies most often, but long-time employees can cause more damage. In many small businesses, the owner views employees, especially long-time workers, almost as partners, operating the business in a family atmosphere. Such a feeling, although not undesirable, can develop into a security breach. Many owners refuse to believe that their most trusted employees present the greatest security threat, but these workers have the greatest accessibility to keys, cash registers, records, and even safe combinations. Because of their seniority, these employees hold key positions and are quite familiar with operations, so they know where weaknesses in control and security procedures lie.

Small business owners should also be wary of "workaholic" employees. Is this worker really dedicated to the company, or is he working so hard to cover up theft? Employee thieves are unwilling to take extended breaks from their jobs for fear of being detected. As long as the dishonest employee remains on the job, he can cover up theft. As a security precaution, business owners should require every employee to take vacations long enough so that someone else has to take over their responsibilities (at least five consecutive business days). Most schemes are relatively simple and require day-to-day maintenance to keep them going. Business failure records are filled with stories of firms in which the "ideal" employee turned out to be a thief. "In 90 percent of the cases in which people steal from their companies, the employer would probably have described this person, right up to the time the crime was discovered, as a trusted employee," says one expert.[13]

Disgruntled Employees. Small business managers must also monitor the performance of disgruntled employees. Employees are more likely to steal if they believe that their company treats employees unfairly, and the probability of their stealing goes even higher if they believe they themselves have been treated unfairly. Employees dissatisfied with their pay or their promotions may retaliate against an employer by stealing. Dishonest employees will make up the difference between what they are paid and what they believe they are worth by stealing. Many believe pilfering is a well-deserved "perk."

Organizational Atmosphere. Many entrepreneurs unintentionally create an atmosphere that encourages employee dishonesty. Failing to establish formal controls and procedures invites theft. Nothing encourages dishonest employees to steal more than knowing they are unlikely to be caught. Four factors encourage employee theft:

1. The need or desire to steal (e.g., to support a habit or to cope with a sudden financial crisis)
2. A rationalization for the act ("They owe me this.")
3. The opportunity to steal (e.g., access to merchandise, complete control of financial functions)
4. The perception that there is a low probability of being caught ("Nobody will ever know.")

The owner must recognize that he sets the example for security and honesty in the business. Employees place more emphasis on what the owner does than on what he says. A business owner who installs a complete system of inventory control and then ignores it is telling employees that security in unimportant. No one should remove merchandise, materials, or supplies from inventory without recording them properly. There should be no exceptions to the rules, even for the boss and his relatives. Managers should develop clear control procedures and establish penalties for violations. The single biggest deterrent to employee theft is a strong, top-down policy that is well communicated to all employees that theft will not be tolerated and that anyone caught stealing will be prosecuted—no exceptions.

Managers must constantly emphasize the importance of security. Small business owners must use every available opportunity to lower the temptation to steal. One business owner relies on payroll inserts to emphasize to employees how theft reduces the funds available for growth, expansion, and higher wages. Another has established a written code of ethics, spelling out penalties for violations. Workers must know that security is a team effort. Security rules and procedures must be reasonable, and the owner must treat the workers equitably. Unreasonable rules are no more effective—and may even be more harmful—than poorly enforced procedures. A work environment that fosters honesty at every turn serves as an effective deterrent to employee theft.

Physical Breakdowns. Another major factor contributing to employee theft is weak physical security. The owner who pays little attention to the distribution of keys, safe combinations, and other entry devices is inviting theft. Also, owners who fail to lock doors and windows or to install reliable alarm systems are literally leaving their businesses open to thieves both inside and outside the organization.

Open windows give dishonest employees a prime opportunity to slip stolen merchandise out of the plant or store. A manufacturer of small appliances discovered that several employees were dropping crates of finished products out of an unlocked window, picking them up after work, and reselling them. By the time the perpetrators were detected, the owner had lost nearly $10,000 worth of merchandise and supplies.

Unlocked or unmonitored doors represent another security leak for many small businesses. The greater the number of doors in a plant or store, the greater the chance of employee theft. Every unnecessary door should be locked (while still conforming to fire regulations), and all regularly used doors should be monitored. Many thefts occur as workers load and unload merchandise. If the owner allows the same employee who prepares purchase orders and handles invoices to check shipments in or out, the temptation to alter documents and steal merchandise may be too great.

Many businesses find that their profits go out with the trash, literally. When collecting trash, a dishonest employee may stash valuable merchandise in with the refuse and dump it in the receptacle. After the store closes, the thief returns to collect the loot. One drugstore owner lost more than $7,000 in merchandise in just six months through trash thefts.

Improper Cash Control. Many small business owners encourage employee theft by failing to implement proper cash control procedures. Without a system of logical, practical audit controls on cash, a firm will likely suffer internal theft. Dishonest employees quickly discover there is a low probability of detection and steal cash with impunity.

Cashiers clearly have the greatest accessibility to the firm's cash and, consequently, experience the greatest temptation to steal. The following scenario is all too common: A customer makes a purchase with the exact amount of cash and leaves quickly. The cashier fails to ring up the purchase and pockets the cash without anyone's knowledge. Some small business owners create a cash security problem by allowing too many employees to operate cash registers and handle customer payments. If a cash shortage develops, the manager is unable to trace responsibility.

A daily inspection of the cash register tape can point out potential employee theft problems. When tapes indicate an excessive amount of voided transactions or no-sale transactions, the owner should investigate. A no-sale transaction could mean the register was opened to give a customer change or to steal cash. A large number of incorrect register transactions also are a sign of foul play. Clerks may be camouflaging cash thefts by voiding transactions or by underringing sales amounts. Shortages

IN THE FOOTSTEPS OF AN ENTREPRENEUR
It's an Inside Job

Over the past few years, the National Retail Federation has begun to report the disturbing trend in the increase in merchandise stolen by employees. "Over the past three years, U.S. stores total losses from employee theft have jumped 34 percent to roughly $12.85 billion a year, while shoplifting losses have risen a modest 14 percent to $10.15 billion." What should be an even more alarming statistic to any entrepreneur is that the average "insiders" theft is now over $1,000.

Even large sophisticated retailers like Wal-Mart, discover that those they trust most often take the greatest advantage of their position to steal. A New England Wal-Mart store manager was alerted by employees that the store's detective was loading merchandise into his car. The search of the employee's home uncovered $30,000 in stolen goods.

Retailers are beginning to strike back. The United States Mutual Association was formed recently to serve as a clearinghouse for individuals who are known thieves. The organization maintains a "blacklist" of about 750,000 people who have been dismissed by store owners for thievery. Members can now screen potential applicants to determine if they are listed by this new organization.

1. Interview a small business owner and a retail store manager in regards to the amount of estimated loss from employee theft. How does the individual or business pass on the costs of this type of shrinkage? Has either prosecuted an employee for theft? If so what was the result?

Source: Calmetta Coleman, "As Thievery by Insiders Overtakes Shoplifting, Retailers Crack Down," *Wall Street Journal*, September 8, 2000, p. 1.

and overages are also clues that alert the manager to possible theft. All small business owners are alarmed by cash shortages, but few are disturbed by cash overages. However, cash discrepancies in either direction are an indication of inept cashiering or of poor cash controls. The manager who investigates all cash discrepancies can greatly reduce the opportunity for cashiers to steal.

Preventing Employee Theft. Many incidents of employee theft go undetected, and of those employees who are caught stealing, only a small percentage are prosecuted. The burden of dealing with employee theft falls squarely on the owner's shoulders. Although business owners cannot eliminate the possibility of employee theft, they can reduce its likelihood by using some relatively simple procedures and policies that are cost-effective to implement.

Screen Employees Carefully. Perhaps a business owner's greatest weapon against crime is a thorough preemployment screening process. The best time to weed out prospective criminals is before hiring them! Although state and federal regulations prohibit employers from invading job applicants' privacy and from using discriminatory devices in the selection process, employers have a legitimate right to determine job candidates' integrity and qualifications. A comprehensive selection process and reliable screening devices greatly reduce the chances that an entrepreneur will hire a thief. Smart entrepreneurs verify the information applicants provide on their résumés because they know that some of them will either exaggerate or misrepresent their qualifications. A thorough background check with references and previous employers also is essential. (One question that sheds light on a former employer's feelings toward a one-time employee is "Would you hire this person again?".)

Some security experts recommend the use of integrity tests, paper-and-pencil tests that offer valuable insight into job applicants' level of honesty. Business owners can buy integrity tests for $20 or less that are already validated (to avoid charges of discrimination) and that they can score on their own. Because drug addictions drive many employees to steal, employers also should administer drug tests consistently to all job applicants. The most reliable drug tests cost the company from $35 to $50 each, a small price to pay given the potential losses that can result from hiring an employee with a drug habit.

Create an Environment of Honesty. Creating an environment of honesty and integrity starts at the top. That requires business owners to set an impeccable example for everyone else in the company. In addition to creating a standard of ethical behavior, business owners should strive to establish high morale among workers. A positive work environment where employees see themselves as an important part of the team is an effective deterrent to employee theft. Establishing a written code of ethics and having new employees sign "honesty clauses" offers tangible evidence of a company's commitment to honesty and integrity.

Establish a System of Internal Controls. The basis for maintaining internal security on the job is establishing a set of reasonable internal controls designed to prevent employee theft. An effective system of checks and balances goes a long way toward deterring internal crime; weak or inconsistently enforced controls are an open invitation for theft. The most basic rule is to separate among several employees related duties that might cause a security breach if assigned to a single worker. For instance, owners should avoid letting the employee who issues checks reconcile the company's bank statement. Similarly, the person who orders merchandise and supplies should not be the one who also approves those invoices for payment. Spreading these tasks among a number of employees makes organizing a theft more difficult. The owner of a small retail art shop learned this lesson the hard way. After conducting an inventory audit, he discovered that more than $25,000 worth of art supplies were missing. The owner finally traced the theft to the company's bookkeeper, who was creating fictional invoices and then issuing checks to herself for the same amounts.

Business owners should insist that all company records be kept up to date. Sloppy record keeping makes theft difficult to detect. All internal documents—shipping, ordering, billing, and collecting—should be numbered. Missing numbers should arouse suspicion. One subtle way to test employees' honesty is to commit deliberate errors occasionally to see if employees detect them. If you send an extra case of merchandise to the loading dock for shipment, does the foreman catch it, or does it disappear?

Finally, business owners should demonstrate zero tolerance for theft. They must adhere strictly to company policy when dealing with employees who violate the company's trust. When business owners catch an employee thief, the best course of action is to fire the perpetrator and to prosecute. Too often, owners take the attitude: "Resign, return the money, and we'll forget it." Letting thieves off, however, only encourages them to move on to other businesses where they will steal again. Prosecuting a former employee for theft is never easy, but it does send a clear signal about how the company views employee crime.

The written policies and management talks about honesty and integrity have a great deal more meaning when employees know from past experience that the owner will prosecute and testify. Think about what the casino owners in Las Vegas do. They share information among themselves on problem employees. They have strict policies regarding theft. They have constant surveillance of employees while at

IN THE FOOTSTEPS OF AN ENTREPRENEUR
Now That's a Nice Jacket—Is It Authentic?

All Kyu Sik Han did was steal the logos of athletic teams; how could you make money doing that? In fact, this form of product counterfeiting can yield millions of dollars. The International Anti-Counterfeiting Coalition estimates the losses to the rightful holders of these trademarks at $200 billion a year.

Mr. Han, who avoided apprehension, was purchasing jackets produced in Korea using counterfeit logos for $17 per jacket and selling each item for as much as $80. The counterfeit merchandise business has, for years, gone unchallenged. However, now manufacturers such as Nike, Oakley, Tommy Hilfiger, and Louis Vuitton are hiring private investigators to track down those individual manufacturing, wholesaling and retailing, counterfeit goods. Local police and the U.S. Customs Service use this information to supplement their own investigations and have begun

to crack down on this illegal business. But it's a contest; counterfeiters who fear legal retribution have begun avoiding personal financial loss by leasing vehicles and equipment and even buying homes in the names of relatives. Paying fines is viewed as just another cost of doing business.

1. Discuss your opinion on what, if anything, should be done to consumers who buy merchandise that is *obviously* a counterfeit (e.g., purchasing a "Hermes" scarf for $20 at a flea market when the scarf usually retails for several hundred dollars in an upscale shop should be a tip-off to authenticity!). Should the penalty be the same as for receiving stolen merchandise? Why or why not?

Source: William Greene and Katherine Bruce, "Riskless Crime?", *Forbes*, August 11, 1997, pp. 100–102.

work. Finally, they prosecute when theft occurs. Despite these efforts, employees still try to steal. If the owners of these casinos are willing to invest as much as they do in security, an entrepreneur should question what steps he is taking to protect the assets of the firm.

Shoplifting

The most frequent business crime is shoplifting, Businesses lose an estimated $17 billion to $20 billion to shoplifters each year, and small businesses, especially retailers, suffer a significant share of those losses. Shoplifting takes an especially heavy toll on small businesses because they usually have the weakest lines of defense against shoplifters. Shoplifting losses, which ultimately are passed on to the consumer, account for approximately 3 percent of the average price tag.[14]

Types of Shoplifters. Anyone who takes merchandise from a store without paying for it, no matter what the justification, is a shoplifter. Shoplifters look exactly like other customers. They can be young children in search of a new toy or elderly people who are short of money. Anyone can be a shoplifter, given the opportunity, the ability, and the desire to steal.

Fortunately for small business owners, most shoplifters are amateurs who steal because the opportunity presents itself. Many steal on impulse, and the theft is the first criminal act. Many of those caught have the money to pay for their "five-finger discounts." Observant business owners supported by trained store personnel can spot potential shoplifters and deter many shoplifting incidents; however, they must understand the shoplifter's profile. Experts identify five types of shoplifters.

Juveniles. Juveniles account for approximately one half of all shoplifters. Many juveniles steal as a result of peer pressure. Most have little fear of prosecution, assuming they can hide behind their youth. When owners detect juvenile shoplifters, they must not let sympathy stand in the way of good judgment. Many hard-core criminals began their careers as shoplifters, and small business owners who fail to prosecute the youthful offender do nothing to discourage a life of crime. Juvenile offenders should be prosecuted through proper legal procedures just as any adult shoplifter would be.

Impulse Shoplifters. Impulse shoplifters steal on the spur of the moment when they succumb to temptation. These shoplifters do not plan their thefts, but when a prime opportunity to shoplift arises, they take advantage of it. For example, a salesperson may be showing a customer pieces of jewelry. If the salesperson is called away, the customer might pocket an expensive ring and leave the store before the employee returns.

Many well-respected individuals are impulse shoplifters. The perpetrator might even be a regular customer. Impatient customers after a hectic shopping day might be unwilling to wait to pay for merchandise, or a disgruntled customer may be seeking revenge against a company; whatever the case, shoplifting is the result.

The most effective method of fighting impulse shoplifting is prevention. To minimize losses, the owner should remove the opportunity to steal by implementing proper security procedures and devices.

Alcoholics, Vagrants, and Drug Addicts. Shoplifters motivated to steal to support a drug or alcohol habit are usually easy to detect because their behavior is usually unstable and erratic. One shoplifter recently apprehended was supporting a $100-a-day heroin habit by stealing small items from local retailers and then returning the merchandise for refunds. (The stores almost never asked him for sales receipts.)

Small business owners should exercise great caution in handling these shoplifters because they can easily become violent. Criminals deranged by drugs or alcohol might be armed and could endanger the lives of customers and employees if they are detained. It is best to let the police apprehend these shoplifters.

Kleptomaniacs. Kleptomaniacs have a compulsive need to steal even though they have little, if any, need for the items they shoplift. In many cases, these shoplifters could afford to purchase the merchandise they steal. Kleptomaniacs account for less than 5 percent of shoplifters, but their "disease" costs business owners a great deal.[15] They need professional psychological counseling, and the owner only helps them by seeing that they are apprehended.

Professionals. Although only about 15 percent of shoplifters are professionals, they can severely damage a business.[16] Because the professional shoplifter's business is theft, he is very difficult to detect and deter. Career shoplifters tend to focus on expensive merchandise they can sell quickly to their "fences," such as stereo equipment, appliances, guns, or jewelry. Usually, the fences don't keep the stolen goods long, often selling them at a fraction of their value. Thus, apprehending and prosecuting professional shoplifters is quite difficult. Police have apprehended profes-

IN THE FOOTSTEPS OF AN ENTREPRENEUR
An Error in Judgment?

Patricia Caldwell was shopping in a retail store. A store security employee became suspicious when he saw that she was carrying a large purse and was handling many small items. As she shopped, Caldwell went into several departments and bent down out of sight of the security guard. She says she bent down to look at items displayed on low shelves. She also removed her glasses to read labels and returned them to her purse several times. The guard, believing he had seen Caldwell put some items in her purse, followed her into the parking lot and accused her of shoplifting. He asked Caldwell to open her purse. She did, but the guard found none of the store's merchandise inside.

Rather than releasing her, he told Caldwell to return to the store with him, where he escorted her back to areas where she had been shopping. They walked around the store for approximately 15 minutes, during which time the guard told her six or seven times that he had seen her conceal merchandise in her purse. No one touched Caldwell or searched her. With no evidence of stolen merchandise, another employee told Caldwell she could leave the store.

Caldwell brought a lawsuit against the retailer for slander, making false defamatory statements about another, and false imprisonment depriving a person of his liberty without justice. The court allowed the retailer's loss prevention manual to be introduced as evidence. The manual spelled out the company's guidelines for employees in making shoplifting arrests. For instance, the manual stated that before apprehending a suspected shoplifter, an employee "must see the shoplifter take our property." It also stated than an employee should watch the suspect continuously and should apprehend him after he has had the opportunity to pay for the merchandise and is outside the store. The manual said that apprehension should be made in the presence of a witness and that any interrogation should be done in the privacy of the Loss Prevention Office.

The jury in the case awarded Caldwell $75,000 in total damages, and the retailer appealed. The appellate court affirmed the lower court's ruling.

1. What did the retailer in this case do wrong?
2. What guidelines should store employees follow when dealing with a suspected shoplifter?

Source: *Caldwell v. K-Mart Corporation*, No. (17) (S.C. Ct. App. filed October 14, 1991).

sional shoplifters with detailed maps of a city's shopping districts, showing target stores and the best times to make a "hit." Furthermore, many professional shoplifters are affiliated with organized crime, and they are able to rely on their associates to avoid detection and prosecution.

Detecting Shoplifters. Although shoplifters can be difficult to detect, small business owners who know what to look for can spot them in action. They must always be on the lookout for shoplifters, but merchants should be especially vigilant on Saturdays and around Christmas, when shoplifters can hide their thefts more easily in the frenzy of a busy shopping day.

Shoplifters can work alone or in groups. In general, impulse shoplifters prefer solitary thefts, whereas juveniles and professionals operate in groups. A common tactic for group shoplifters is for one member of the gang to create some type of distraction while other members steal the merchandise. Business owners should be wary of loud, disruptive gangs that enter their stores.

Solitary shoplifters are usually quite nervous. They avoid crowds and shy away from store personnel, preferring privacy to ply their trade. To make sure they avoid detection, they constantly scan the store for customers and employees. These shoplifters spend more time nervously looking around the store than examining merchandise. Also, they shop when the store is most likely to be understaffed, during early morning, lunch, or late evening hours. Shoplifters frequently linger in the same area for an extended time without purchasing anything. Customers who refuse the help of sales personnel or bring in large bags and packages (especially empty ones) also arouse suspicion.

Shoplifters have their own arsenal of tools to assist them in plying their trade. They often shop with booster boxes, shopping bags, umbrellas, bulky jackets, baby strollers, or containers disguised as gifts. These props often have hidden compartments that can be tripped easily, allowing the shoplifter to fill them with merchandise quickly.

Some shoplifters use specially designed coats with hidden pockets and compartments that can hold even large items. Small business owners should be suspicious of customers wearing out-of-season clothing (heavy coats in warm weather, rain gear on clear days) that could conceal stolen goods. Hooked belts also are used to enable the shoplifter to suspend items from hangers without being detected.

Another common tactic is "ticket switching"; the shoplifter exchanges price tickets on items and pays a very low price for an expensive item. An inexperienced or unobservant cashier may charge $9.95 for a $30.00 item that the shoplifter re-marked while no one was looking.

One variation of traditional shoplifting techniques is the "grab-and-run," in which a shoplifter grabs an armload of merchandise located near an exit and then dashes out the door into a waiting getaway car. The element of surprise gives these thieves an advantage, and they are often gone before anyone in the store realizes what has happened.

Deterring Shoplifters. The problem of shoplifting is worsening. Every year, business losses due to customer theft increase, and many companies are declaring war on shoplifting. Their funds allocated for fighting shoplifting losses are best spent on *prevention*. By focusing on preventing shoplifting rather than on prosecuting violators after the fact, business owners take a stronger stand in protecting their firms' merchandise. Of course, no prevention plan is perfect. When violations occur, owners must prosecute; otherwise, the business becomes known as an easy target. Merchants say that when a store gets a reputation for being tough on shoplifters, thefts drop off.

Knowing what to look for improves dramatically a business owner's odds in combating shoplifting:

- *Watch the eyes.* Amateurs spend excessive time looking at the merchandise they're to steal. Their eyes, however, are usually checking to see who (if anyone) is watching them.
- *Watch the hands.* Experienced shoplifters, like good magicians, rely on sleight of hand.
- *Watch the body.* Amateurs' body movements reflect their nervousness; they appear to be unnatural.
- *Watch the clothing.* Loose, bulky clothing is the uniform of the typical shoplifter.
- *Watch for devices.* Anything a customer carries is a potential concealing device.
- *Watch for loiterers.* Many amateurs must work up the nerve to steal.
- *Watch for switches.* Working in pairs, shoplifters will split duties; one will lift the merchandise, and, after a switch, the other will take it out of the store.

Store owners can take other steps to discourage shoplifting, including the following.

Train Employees to Spot Shoplifters. One of the best ways to prevent shoplifting is to train store personnel to be aware of shoplifters' habits and to be alert for possible theft. In fact, most security experts agree that alert employees are the best defense against shoplifters. Employees should look for nervous, unusual customers and monitor them closely. Shoplifters prefer to avoid sales personnel and other customers, and when employees approach them, shoplifters know they are being watched. Even when all salespeople are busy, an alert employee should approach the customer and mention, "I'll be with you in a moment." Honest customers appreciate the clerk's politeness, and shoplifters are put off by the implied surveillance.

All employees should watch for suspicious people, especially those carrying the props of concealment. Employees in clothing stores must keep a tally of the items being taken into and out of dressing rooms. Some clothing retailers prevent unauthorized use of dressing rooms by locking them. Customers who want to try on garments must check with a store employee first.

An alert cashier can be a tremendous boon to the store owner attempting to minimize shoplifting losses. A cashier who knows the store's general pricing policy and is familiar with the prices of many specific items is the best insurance against the ticket-switching shoplifter. A good cashier also should inspect all containers being sold; tool boxes, briefcases, and other containers could conceal stolen merchandise.

Employees should be trained to watch for group shoplifting tactics. A group of shoppers that enters the store and then disperses in all directions may be attempting to distract employees so that some gang members can steal merchandise. Sales personnel should watch closely the customer who lingers in one area for an extended time, especially one who examines a lot of merchandise but never purchases anything.

The sales staff should watch for individuals who consistently shop during the hours when most personnel are on breaks. Managers can help eliminate this cause of shoplifting by ensuring that their stores are well staffed at all times. Coordinating work schedules to ensure adequate coverage of customers is a simple but effective method of discouraging shoplifting.

The cost of training employees to be alert to shoplifting "gimmicks" can be regained many times over in preventing losses from retail theft. The local police department or chamber of commerce may be able to conduct training seminars for local small business owners and their employees, or security consulting firms might sponsor a training course on shoplifting techniques and protective methods.

Refresher courses every few months can help keep employees sharp in spotting shoplifters.

Pay Attention to the Store Layout. A well-planned store layout also can be an effective obstacle in preventing shoplifting losses. Proper lighting throughout the store makes it easier for employees to monitor shoppers, whereas dimly lit areas give dishonest customers a prime opportunity to steal without detection. Also, display cases should be kept low, no more than three or four feet high, so store personnel can have a clear view of the entire store. Display counters should have spaces between them; continuous displays create a barrier between customers and employees.

Business owners should keep small expensive items such as jewelry, silver, and pocket calculators behind display counters or in locked cases with a salesclerk nearby. Valuable or breakable items also should be kept out of customer reach and should not be displayed near exits, where shoplifters can pick them up and quickly step outside. All merchandise displays should be neat and organized so that it will be noticeable if an item is missing.

Cash registers should be located so that cashiers have an unobstructed view of the entire store. Other protective measures include prominently posting antishoplifting signs describing the penalties involved and keeping unattended doors locked (within fire regulations). Exits that cannot be locked because of fire regulations should be equipped with noise alarms to detect any attempts at unauthorized exit.

Install Mechanical Devices. Another option a small business owner has in the attempt to reduce shoplifting losses is to install mechanical devices. A complete deterrence system can be expensive, but failure to implement one is usually more expensive. Tools such as two-way mirrors allow employees at one end of the store to monitor a customer at the other end, and one-way viewing windows enable employees to watch the entire store without being seen.

Other mechanical devices, such as closed-circuit TV cameras, convex wall mirrors, and peepholes, also help the owner protect the store from shoplifters. Not every small business can afford to install a closed-circuit camera system, but one clever entrepreneur got the benefit of such a system without the high cost. He installed one "live" camera and several "dummy" cameras that did not work. The cameras worked because potential shoplifters thought they were all live. Another high-tech weapon used against shoplifters is a mannequin named Anne Droid, who is equipped with a tiny camera behind one eye and a microphone in her nose!

An owner can deter ticket-switching shoplifters by using tamper-proof price tickets: perforated gummed labels that tear away if a customer tries to remove them or price tags attached to merchandise by hard-to-break plastic strips. Some owners use multiple price tags concealed on items to deter ticket switchers. One of the most effective weapons for combating shoplifting is the electronic article surveillance system, small tags that are equipped with electronic sensors that set off sound and light alarms if customers take them past a store exit. These tags are attached to the merchandise and can be removed only by employees with special shears. Owners using these electronic tags must make sure that all cashiers are consistent in removing them from items purchased legitimately; otherwise, they may be liable for false arrest or, at the very least, may cause customers embarrassment.

Apprehending Shoplifters. Despite all of the weapons business owners use to curtail shoplifting, the sad reality is that about 98 percent of the time shoplifters are successful at plying their trade! Of the more than 60 million estimated shoplifting incidents that occur in a typical year, business owners detect only 1.2 million. Of those shoplifters who do get caught, less than half are prosecuted. The chance that any shoplifter will actually go before a judge is just one in 100![17] Building a strong case against a shoplifter is essential; therefore, small business owners must determine beforehand the procedures to follow once they detect a shoplifter. The store owner has to be certain that the shoplifter has taken or concealed the merchandise and has left the store with it. Although state laws vary, owners must do the following to make the charges stick:

1. See the person take or conceal the merchandise.
2. Identify the merchandise as the store's.
3. Testify that it was taken with the intent to steal.
4. Prove that the merchandise was not paid for.

Most security experts agree that an owner should never apprehend the shoplifter if he or she has lost sight of the suspect even for an instant. In that time, the person may have dumped the merchandise.

Another primary consideration in apprehending shoplifters is the safety of store employees. In general, employees should never directly accuse a customer of shoplifting and should never try to apprehend the suspect. The wisest course of action when a shoplifter is detected is to alert the police or store security personnel and let them apprehend the suspect. Apprehension *outside* the store is safest. This tactic strengthens the owner's case and eliminates unpleasant in-store scenes that upset other customers or that might be dangerous. Of course, if the stolen merchandise is very valuable, or if the criminal is likely to escape once outside, the owner may have no choice but to apprehend in the store.

Once business owners detect and apprehend a shoplifter, they must decide whether to prosecute. Many small business owners fail to prosecute because they fear legal entanglements or negative publicity. However, failure to prosecute encourages shoplifters to try again and gives the business the image of being an easy target. Of course, each case is an individual matter. For example, the owner may choose not to prosecute elderly or senile shoplifters or those who are mentally incompetent. But in most cases, prosecuting the shoplifter is the best option, especially for juveniles and first-time offenders. The business owner who prosecutes shoplifters consistently soon develops a reputation for toughness that most shoplifters hesitate to test. Read over the *In the Footsteps of an Entrepreneur* and discuss with your classmates the ways to enforce prosecution of shoplifters without making fatal mistakes.

CONCLUSION

Inventory control is one of those less-than-glamorous activities that business owners must perform if their businesses are to succeed. Although it doesn't offer the flash of marketing or the visibility of customer service, inventory control is no less important. In fact, business owners who invest the time and the resources to exercise the proper degree of control over their inventory soon discover that the payoff is huge!

CHAPTER SUMMARY

1. Explain the various inventory control systems and the advantages and disadvantages of each.
   - Inventory represents the largest investment for the typical small business. Unless prop-

erly managed, the cost of inventory will strain the firm's budget and cut into its profitability. The goal of inventory control is to balance the cost of holding and maintaining inventory with meeting customer demand.

- Regardless of the inventory control system selected, business owners must recognize the relevance of the 80/20 rule, which states that roughly 80 percent of the value of the firm's inventory is in about 20 percent of the items in stock. Because only a small percentage of items account for the majority of the value of the firm's inventory, managers should focus control on those items.

- Three basic types of inventory control systems are available to the small business owner: perpetual, visual, and partial. Perpetual inventory control systems are designed to maintain a running count of the items in inventory. Although they can be expensive and cumbersome to operate by hand, affordable computerized point-of-sale (POS) terminals that deduct items sold from inventory on hand make perpetual systems feasible for small companies. The visual inventory system is the most common method of controlling merchandise in a small business. This system works best when shortages are not likely to cause major problems. Partial inventory control systems are most effective for small businesses with limited time and money. These systems operate on the basis of the 80/20 rule.

- The ABC system is a partial system that divides a firm's inventory into three categories depending on each item's dollar usage volume (cost per unit multiplied by quantity used per time period). The purpose of classifying items according to their value is to establish the proper degree of control over them. A items are most closely controlled by perpetual inventory control systems; B items use basic analytical tools; and C items are controlled by very simple techniques such as the two-bin system, the level control method, or the tag system.

2. Describe how just-in-time (JIT) and JIT II inventory control techniques work.
- The just-in-time system of inventory control sees excess inventory as a blanket that masks production problems and adds unnecessary costs to the production operation. Under a JIT philosophy, the level of inventory maintained is the measure of effi-

ciency. Materials and parts should not build up as costly inventory. They should flow through the production process without stopping, arriving at the appropriate location just in time.

- JIT II techniques focus on creating a close, harmonious relationship with a company's suppliers so that both parties benefit from increased efficiency. To work successfully, JIT II requires suppliers and their customers to share what was once closely guarded information in an environment of trust and cooperation. Under JIT II, customers and suppliers work hand-in-hand, acting more like partners than mere buyers and sellers.

3. Describe some methods for reducing loss from slow-moving inventory.
- Managing inventory requires monitoring the company's inventory turnover ratio; slow-moving items result in losses from spoilage or obsolescence.

- Slow-moving items can be liquidated by markdowns, eye-catching displays, or quantity discounts.

4. Discuss employee theft and shoplifting and how to prevent them.
- Employee theft accounts for the majority of business losses due to theft. Most small business owners are so busy managing their companies' daily affairs that they fail to develop reliable security systems. Thus, they provide their employees with prime opportunities to steal.

- The organizational atmosphere may encourage employee theft. The owner sets the organizational tone for security. A complete set of security controls, procedures, and penalties should be developed and enforced. Physical breakdowns in security invite employee theft. Open doors and windows, poor key control, and improper cash controls are major contributors to the problem of employee theft. Employers can build security into their businesses by screening and selecting employees carefully. Orientation programs also help the employee to get started in the right direction. Internal controls, such as division of responsibility, spot checks, and audit procedures, are useful in preventing employee theft.

- Shoplifting is the most common business crime. Fortunately, most shoplifters are amateurs. Juveniles often steal to impress their friends, but prosecution can halt their criminal ways early on. Impulse shoplifters steal because the opportunity suddenly arises. Simple prevention is the best defense against these shoplifters. Alcoholics, vagrants, and drug addicts steal to supply some need and are usually easiest to detect. Kleptomaniacs have a compelling need to steal. Professionals are in the business of theft and can be very difficult to detect and quite dangerous.

- Three strategies are most useful in deterring shoplifters. First, employees should be trained to look for signs of shoplifting. Second, store layout should be designed with theft deterrence in mind. Finally, antitheft devices should be installed in the store.

DISCUSSION QUESTIONS

1. Describe some of the incidental costs of carrying and maintaining inventory for the small business owner.
2. What is a perpetual inventory system? How does it operate? What are the advantages and disadvantages of using such a system?
3. List and describe briefly the four versions of a perpetual inventory system.
4. Give examples of small businesses that would find it practical to implement the four systems described in question 3.
5. What advantages and disadvantages does a visual inventory control system have over other methods?
6. For what type of business product line is a visual control system most effective?
7. What is the 80/20 rule, and why is it important in controlling inventory?
8. Outline the ABC inventory control procedure. What is the purpose of classifying inventory items using this procedure?
9. Briefly describe the types of control techniques that should be used for A, B, and C items.
10. What is the basis for the JIT philosophy? Under what condition does a JIT system work best?
11. What is JIT II? What is its underlying philosophy? What risks does it present to businesses?
12. Outline the two methods of taking a physical inventory count. Why is it necessary for every small business manager to take inventory?
13. Why are slow-moving items dangerous to the small business? What can be done to liquidate them from inventory?
14. Why are small companies more susceptible to business crime than large companies?
15. Why is employee theft a problem for many small businesses? Briefly describe the reasons for employee theft.
16. Construct a profile of the employee most likely to steal goods or money from an employer. What four elements must be present for employee theft to occur?
17. Briefly outline a program that could help the typical small business owner minimize losses due to employee theft.
18. List and briefly describe the major types of shoplifters.
19. Outline the characteristics of a typical shoplifter that should arouse a small business manager's suspicions. What tools and tactics is a shoplifter likely to use?
20. Describe the major elements of a program designed to deter shoplifters.
21. How can proper planning of store layout reduce shoplifting losses?
22. What must an owner do to have a good case against a shoplifter? How should a suspected shoplifter be apprehended?

STEP INTO THE REAL WORLD

1. Contact a local small business owner and interview him or her to get answers to the following questions: What type of inventory control system is used? How well does it work? Does the 80/20 rule apply to the entrepreneur's inventory? Does the owner's inventory control system reflect the 80/20 rule? How does the owner liquidate slow-moving merchandise?
2. Visit a small manufacturer and ask if the company is using a JIT or JIT II system to integrate inventory and production. If it is, what

have the results been? What problems has the company encountered? How did the company solve those problems? What improvements, if any, has the business experienced by using JIT?

3. Interview a local small business owner who has been a victim of shoplifting or employee theft. What security breaches contributed to the theft? How can the owner prevent a recurrence of the theft? What changes has the owner made in the business since the theft occurred?

4. Contact an attorney and interview him or her about the laws governing the apprehension of suspected shoplifters in your state. What should the small business owner who suspects someone of shoplifting do? Write a policy spelling out the proper procedure.

5. Invite a security consultant, police officer, or security agent from a local business to speak to your class about preventing employee theft and shoplifting. How extensive is the problem? What techniques does he or she recommend to prevent losses due to theft?

TAKE IT TO THE NET

Visit the Scarborough/Zimmerer home page at **www.prenhall.com/scarborough** for updated information, online resources, Web-based exercises, and sample business plan.

ENDNOTES

1. Evan Ramstead, "Compaq Stumbles as PCs Weather New Blow," *Wall Street Journal*, March 9, 1998, pp. B1, B8.
2. Leanne Italie, "Candle, Candle Burning Bright," *SBC*, July 2001, p. 23.
3. Tim McCollum, "A Cutting Edge for Small Stores," *Nation's Business*, February 1998, pp. 43–46.
4. Jane M. Folpe, "Zara Has Made-to-Order Plan for Success," *Fortune*, September 4, 2001, p. 80.
5. Phaedra Hise, "Early Adoption Pays Off," *Inc.*, August 1996, p. 101.
6. Jay Akasie, "Imagine, No Inventory," *Forbes*, November 17, 1997, pp. 144–145, and IPO Central, August 10, 1999.
7. Mark Henricks, "On the Spot," *Entrepreneur*, May 1997, p. 80.
8. John H. Sheridan, "Pushing the Envelope," *Industry Week*, August 17, 1998, pp. 84–90.
9. Henricks, "On the Spot," pp. 80–82.
10. Seth Kantor, "How to Foil Employee Crime," *Nation's Business*, July 1983, p. 38
11. Lori Ioannou, "Are Your Employees Robbing You Blind?", *Your Company*, August/September 1996, pp. 23–28; see also Heather Page, "Easy Target," *Entrepreneur*, May 1996; John R. Emshwiller, "Small Business Is the Biggest Victim of Theft, Survey Shows," *Wall Street Journal*, October 25, 1995.
12. Kantor, "How to Foil Employee Crime."
13. Robert T. Gray, "Clamping Down on Employee Crime," *Nation's Business*, April 1997, p. 44.
14. William Ecenbarger, "They're Stealing You Blind," *Reader's Digest*, June 1996, pp. 97–103.
15. Ibid., p. 99.
16. Ibid., p. 98.
17. Ecenbarger, "They're Stealing You Blind," p. 101.

Chapter 19

Staffing and Leading a Growing Company

Quotes taken from actual resumes:
"I have a bachelorette degree in computers."
"Served as assistant sore manager."
"Married, eight children. Prefer frequent travel."
"Objective: To have my skills and ethics challenged on a daily basis."
"Special skills: Thyping."
"Skills: Operated Pitney Bones machine."
"Education: College, August 1880–May 1984."

Upon completion of this chapter, you will be able to:

1. Explain the challenges involved in the entrepreneur's role as leader and what it takes to be a successful leader.
2. Describe the importance of hiring the right employees and how to avoid making hiring mistakes.
3. Explain how to build the kind of company culture and structure to support the entrepreneur's mission and goals and to motivate employees to achieve them.
4. Understand the potential barriers to effective communication and describe how to overcome them.
5. Discuss the ways in which entrepreneurs can motivate their employees to achieve higher levels of performance.

THE ENTREPRENEUR'S ROLE AS LEADER

1. Explain the challenges involved in the entrepreneur's role as leader and what it takes to be a successful leader.

Once a business begins to grow and the entrepreneur becomes dependent on the productive energies of others to achieve results, leadership becomes the critical variable that fuels success.

Leadership is the process of influencing and inspiring others to work to achieve a common goal and then giving them the power and the freedom to achieve it. Without leadership ability, entrepreneurs—and their companies—never achieve the full potential of the organization or that of the employees. There exists no simple or recent formula for leadership. In today's rapidly changing business environment, an entrepreneur is required to modify her leadership skills as employee's change. People of multiple generations and differing ethnic and cultural backgrounds have differing personal and professional needs, as well as expectation regarding the style and behavior of persons that they accept as leaders. Knowledge workers in a high-tech firm who are in their 20s and 30s can be expected to define effective leadership a few dimensions differently than 50 and 60 year olds from traditional manufacturing industries. Effective leadership requires the entrepreneur to know each person as an individual, as well as the unique conditions that impact the employees and the firm. Becoming and remaining an effective leader requires a willingness to remain open to the changes in both people and "things," a deep commitment to the long-term well-being of employees, to the needs of the firm's employees, and a high level of sensitivity. Leaders are always "on stage" in the sense that employees continually judge their actions, as well as their words.

Until recently, experts compared the leader's job to that of a symphony orchestra conductor. Like the symphony leader, a small business manager made sure that everyone was playing the same score, coordinated individual efforts to produce harmony, and directed the members as they played. The conductor (manager) retained virtually all of the power and made all of the decisions about how the orchestra would play the music without any input from the musicians themselves. Today's successful small business leader, however, is more like the leader of a jazz band, which is known for its improvisation, innovation, and creativity. Max DePree, former head of Herman Miller, Inc., a highly successful office furniture manufacturer, explains the connection this way:

> Jazz band leaders must choose the music, find the right musicians, and perform—in public. But the effect of the performance depends on so many things—the environment, the volunteers playing in the band, the need for everybody to perform as individuals and as a group, the absolute dependence of the leader on the members of the band, the need for the followers to play well. . . . The leader of the jazz band has the beautiful opportunity to draw the best out of the other musicians. We have much to learn from jazz bandleaders, for jazz, like leadership, combines the unpredictability of the future with the gifts of individuals.[1]

In short, management and leadership are not the same; yet both are essential to a small company's success. Leadership without management is unbridled; management without leadership is uninspired. Leadership gets a small business going; management keeps it going. Stephen Covey, author of *Principle-Centered Leadership,* explains the difference between management and leadership this way:

> Leadership deals with people; management deals with things. You manage things; you lead people. Leadership deals with vision; management deals with logistics toward that vision. Leadership deals with doing the right

things; management focuses on doing things right. Leadership deals with examining the paradigms on which you are operating; management operates within those paradigms. Leadership comes first, then management, but both are necessary.[2]

Leadership and management are intertwined; a small business that has one but not the other will go nowhere.

Effective leaders exhibit certain behaviors. They:

- *Create a set of values and beliefs for employees and passionately pursue them.* Employees look to their leaders for guidance in making decisions. Leaders should be like beacons in the night, constantly shining light on the principles, values, and beliefs on which they founded their companies.
- *Respect and support their employees.* To gain the respect of their employees, leaders must first respect those who work for them.
- *Set the example for their employees.* A leader's words ring hollow if he fails to "practice what he preaches." Few signals are transmitted to workers faster than the hypocrisy of a leader who sells employees on one set of values and principles and then acts according to a different set.
- *Focus employees' efforts on challenging goals and keep them driving toward those goals.* Effective leaders have a clear vision of where they want their companies to go, and they are able to communicate their vision to those around them. Leaders must repeatedly reinforce the goals they set for their companies.
- *Provide the resources employees need to achieve their goals.* Effective leaders know that workers cannot do their jobs well unless they have the tools they need. They provide workers with not only the physical resources they need to excel but also the necessary intangible resources such as training, coaching, and mentoring.
- *Communicate with their employees.* Leaders recognize that helping workers see the company's overarching goal is just one part of effective communication; encouraging employee feedback and then listening is just as vital. In other words, they know that communication is a two-way street.
- *Value the diversity of their workers.* Smart business leaders recognize the value of their workers' varied skills, abilities, backgrounds, and interests. When channeled in the right direction, such diversity can be a powerful weapon in achieving innovation and maintaining a competitive edge.
- *Celebrate their workers' successes.* Effective leaders recognize that workers want to be winners and do everything they can to encourage top performance among their people. The rewards they give are not always financial; in many cases, a reward may be as simple as a handwritten congratulatory note.
- *Encourage creativity among their workers.* Rather than punish workers who take risks and fail, effective leaders are willing to accept failure as a natural part of innovation and creativity. They know that innovative behavior is the key to future success and do everything they can to encourage it among workers.
- *Maintain a sense of humor.* One of the most important tools a leader can have is a sense of humor. Without it, work can become dull and unexciting for everyone.
- *Keep their eyes on the horizon.* Effective leaders are never satisfied with what they and their employees accomplished yesterday. They know that yesterday's successes are not enough to sustain their companies indefinitely. They see the importance of building and maintaining sufficient momentum to carry their companies to the next level.
- *Set clear goals, shares their vision, and rewards employees who meet or exceed the firm's performance targets.*
- *Behave with integrity in all situations and at all times.*

IN THE FOOTSTEPS OF AN ENTREPRENEUR
Hiring the Wrong Executive

Everybody makes decisions that turn out to be wrong, but when it's the employment of an executive in a key position in a small business that is experiencing the pressures of growing, it can be devastating!! Ask Brian Geisel, CEO of Alogent Corporation (a Norcross, Georgia, firm that designs and installs payment processing software), who recalls the error and its consequences. "It was a desperation move," says Brian Geisel, when the new executive he hired turned out to be a bad fit with the organization. In many ways, the error was not uncommon among rapidly growing firms who do not know how to perform the necessary due diligence about applicants for key positions. Brian Geisel recognized that he lacked anyone in human resources, nor did he have either a board of directors nor an experienced management team to use as a

sounding board. Geisel did not do a comprehensive check of the applicant's references or background and discovered too late that the individual could simply not handle the task of the position.

The consequences were, as you expect, a complete mismatch between the CEO and the new executive. The new executive left the company but time and the momentum of growth were lost.

1. What are alternative sources for identifying potential executive talent?

2. Was the lack of a board of directors a critical error in this situation? If so, what could a board have done to assist the CEO in making his decision?

Source: Rifka Rosenwein, "CEO's Regret #5: "Hiring the Wrong Executive," *Inc.,* October 15, 2000.

"Leader" is not a title that you can bestow upon yourself. A manager's employees, the followers, are the individuals who determine if you have demonstrated the qualities of leadership. *Without followers, there are no leaders.* Followers need a leader who can clarify the vision for the organization, define what must be achieved, motivate all involved, provide the resources needed, and empower the employees to act with confidence and courage. When all these elements are in place, employees produce results, organizations prosper, and leadership exists!

Leaders must staff their organization with the right people and then create the most appropriate work environment. These two functions are interrelated and remain a continuing challenge to achieve.

HIRING THE RIGHT EMPLOYEES

2. Describe the importance of hiring the right employees and how to avoid making hiring mistakes.

The decision to hire a new employee is an important one for every business, but its impact is magnified many times in a small company. Every "new hire" a business owner makes determines the heights to which the company can climb—or the depths to which it will plunge. "Bad hires" are incredibly expensive, and no organization, especially a small one, can afford too many of them. One study concluded that an employee hired into a typical entry-level position who quits after six months costs a company about $17,000 in salary, benefits, and training. In addition, the intangible costs—time invested in the new employee, lost opportunities, reduced morale among co-workers, and business setbacks—are seven times the direct costs of a bad hire. In other words, the total price tag for this bad hire is about $136,000![3]

With these costs involved, it's easy to make a solid case for entrepreneurs investing time in attracting, hiring, and retaining the best-qualified employees. Some of the causes of poor hiring can be traced to sloppy business practices. When the new ven-

GAINING THE COMPETITIVE EDGE
Hiring Smart

Wayne Outlaw, in his book *Smart Staffing* (Upstart Publishing), emphasizes the importance of finding new employees who "fit" with the values and mission of your organization. Outlaw suggest you start with a list of the responsibilities and qualifications. Next, develop a recruiting plan that details how to reach and attract the type of people you need. Third, screen the applicants thoroughly. Finally, interview and select.

Outlaw goes on to say that staffing doesn't end there. He includes career counseling, job enrichment, and benefits management as ways to retain the employees who perform. The following are Outlaw's seven reasons why it's critical to hire smart:

1. Choosing the wrong person costs you money.
2. Low turnover makes your firm a better financial risk for investors.
3. Every employee in a small firm makes a significant impact.
4. You are legally accountable for your employees' actions.
5. Bad employees chase away good customers.
6. Good employees make your job as a manager easier.
7. Hiring right is good preventive care for your organization.

Source: Soundview Executive Book Summaries, "The Smart Way to Hire," *Inc.*, January 1, 1999, p. 23.

ture was being developed, the entrepreneur often depended on people she knew and had worked with previously. The initial employees had proven themselves before and the entrepreneur knew their accomplishments. As the business grows and the need for additional employees arises, often there is no effort made to establish human resources policies and procedures.

The following guidelines can help small business managers avoid making costly hiring mistakes.

Create Practical Job Descriptions and Job Specifications

Small business owners must recognize that what they do *before* they ever start interviewing candidates for a position determines to a great extent how successful they will be at hiring winners. The first step is to perform a **job analysis,** the process by which a firm determines the duties and nature of the jobs to be filled and the skills and experience required of the people who are to fill them. The first objective of a job analysis is to develop a job description, a written statement of the duties, responsibilities, reporting relationships, working conditions, and materials and equipment used in a job. A results-oriented **job description** explains what a job entails and the duties the person filling it is expected to perform.

Preparing job descriptions may be one of the most important parts of the hiring process because it creates a "blueprint" for the job. Without this blueprint, a manager tends to hire the person with experience whom she likes the best. Useful sources of information for writing job descriptions include the manager's knowledge of the job, the workers currently holding the job, and the *Dictionary of Occupational Titles (DOT)*, available at most libraries. The *DOT*, published by the Department of Labor, lists more than 20,000 job titles and descriptions and serves as a useful tool for getting a small business owner started when writing job descriptions. Table 19.1 provides an example of the description drawn from the *DOT* for an unusual job.

Table 19.1
A Sample Job
Description from
the Dictionary of
Occupational Titles

Worm picker: Gathers worms to be used as fish bait; walks about grassy areas, such as gardens, parks, and golf courses and picks up earthworms (commonly called dew worms and nightcrawlers). Sprinkles chlorinated water on lawn to cause worms to come to the surface, and locates worms by use of lantern or flashlight. Counts worms, sorts them, and packs them into containers for shipment.

The second objective of a job analysis is to create a **job specification,** a written statement of the qualifications and characteristics needed for a job stated in such terms as education, skills, and experience. A job specification shows the small business manager what kind of person to recruit and establishes the standards an applicant must meet to be hired. When writing job specifications, some managers define the traits a candidate needs to do a job well. Does the person have to be a good listener, empathetic, well-organized, decisive, a "self starter"? A business owner about to hire a new employee who will be telecommuting from home, for instance, would look for someone with excellent communication skills, problem-solving ability, a strong work ethic, and the ability to use technology comfortably. Table 19.2 provides an example that links the tasks for a sales representative's job (drawn from a job description) to the traits or characteristics a small business owner identified as necessary to succeed in that job.

Plan an Effective Interview

Once the manager knows what she must look for in a job candidate, then she can develop a plan for conducting an informative job interview. Too often, small business owners go into an interview unprepared, and, as a result, they fail to get the information they need to judge the candidate's qualifications, qualities, and suitability for the job. Conducting an effective interview requires a small business owner to know what she wants to get out of the interview in the first place and to develop a series of questions to extract that information. The following guidelines will help an owner develop interview questions that will give her meaningful insight into an applicant's qualifications, personality, and character.

- *Develop a series of core questions and ask them of every candidate.* To give the screening process consistency, smart business owners rely on a set of relevant ques-

Table 19.2
Linking Tasks from
a Job Description
to the Traits
Necessary to
Perform the Job

JOB TASK	TRAIT OR CHARACTERISTIC
Generate and close new sales.	Outgoing, persuasive, friendly
Make 15 "cold calls" per week.	A self-starter, determined, optimistic, independent, confident
Analyze customers' needs and recommend proper equipment.	Good listener, patient, empathetic
Counsel customers about options and features needed.	Organized, polished speaker, other oriented
Prepare and explain financing methods; negotiate finance contracts.	Honest, numbers oriented, comfortable with computers
Retain existing customers.	Customer oriented, relationship builder

What do we really learn from the initial interview?

tions they ask in every interview. Of course, they also customize each interview using impromptu questions based on an individual's responses.

- *Ask open-ended questions rather than questions calling for "yes or no" answers.* Open-ended questions are most effective because they encourage candidates to talk about their work experience in a way that will disclose the presence or the absence of the traits and characteristics the business owner is seeking.

- *Create hypothetical situations candidates would be likely to encounter on the job and ask how they would handle them.* Building the interview around such questions gives the owner a preview of the candidate's work habits and attitudes. Rather than telling interviewers about what candidates might do, these scenarios give them an idea of what candidates would do (or have done) in a job-related situation.

- *Probe for specific examples in the candidate's work experience that demonstrate the necessary traits and characteristics.* A common mistake interviewers make is failing to get candidates to provide the detail they need to make an informed decision.

- *Ask candidates to describe a recent success and a recent failure and how they dealt with them.* Smart entrepreneurs look for candidates who describe them both with equal enthusiasm because they know that peak performers put as much into their failures as they do their successes and usually learn something valuable from their failures.

- *Arrange a "noninterview" setting that allows several employees to observe the candidate in an informal setting.* Taking candidates on a plant tour or setting up a coffee break gives everyone a chance to judge a candidate's interpersonal skills and personality outside the formal interview process. These informal settings can be very revealing. One business owner was ready to extend a job offer to a candidate for a managerial position until he saw how the man mistreated a waitress who had made a mistake in his lunch order.

Table 19.3 shows an example of some interview questions one manager uses to uncover the traits and characteristics he seeks in a top-performing sales representative.

Table 19.3

Interview
Questions for
Candidates for a
Sales
Representative
Position

TRAIT OR CHARACTERISTIC	QUESTION
Outgoing, persuasive, friendly, a self-starter, determined, optimistic, independent, confident	How do you persuade reluctant prospects to buy?
Good listener, patient, empathetic, organized, polished speaker, other oriented	What would you say to a fellow salesperson who was getting more than his share of rejections and was having difficulty getting appointments?
Honest, customer-oriented, relationship builder	How do you feel when someone questions the truth of what you say? What do you do in such situations?

Other questions:

If you owned a company, why would you hire yourself?

If you were head of your department, what would you do differently? Why?

How do you acknowledge the contributions of others in your department?

Conduct the Interview

An effective interview contains three phases: breaking the ice, asking questions, and selling the candidate on the company.

Breaking the Ice. In the opening phase of the interview the manager's primary job is to diffuse the tension that exists because of the nervousness of both parties. Many skilled interviewers use the job description to explain the nature of the job and the company's culture to the applicant. Then, they use icebreakers—questions about a hobby or special interest—to get the candidate to relax. *For instance, to loosen up one very tense but promising candidate, one entrepreneur asked about his hobby, military history. "He launched into a description of the Battle of Midway that was so enthralling, I told him, 'Since you can come across like that, I'm going to give you a shot,'" recalls the business owner. "He went on to be a star salesman."*[4]

Asking Questions. During the second phase of the interview, the employer asks the questions from her question bank to determine the applicant's suitability for the job. Her primary job at this point is to *listen*. Effective interviewers spend about 25 percent of the interview talking and about 75 percent listening. They also take notes during the interview to help them ask follow-up questions based on a candidate's comments and to evaluate a candidate after the interview is over. Experienced interviewers also pay close attention to a candidate's nonverbal clues, or body language, during the interview. They know that candidates may be able to say exactly what they want with their words but that their body language does not lie! Be sensitive to the behavior of the candidate and if you are uncomfortable with his or her body language, follow up with additional questions. Some unusual body language may be only a result of interview nervousness. Some of the most valuable interview questions attempt to gain insight into the candidate's ability to reason and be logical and even creative.

Entrepreneurs must be careful to make sure they avoid asking candidates illegal questions. At one time, interviewers could ask wide-ranging questions covering just about every area of an applicant's background. Today, interviewing is a veritable minefield of legal liabilities, waiting to explode in the unsuspecting interviewer's face. Companies are more vulnerable to job discrimination lawsuits now than ever before. Although the Equal Employment Opportunity Commission (EEOC), the

IN THE FOOTSTEPS OF AN ENTREPRENEUR
What Would You Answer?

Inc. magazine asked a number of entrepreneurs the most innovative questions that they use during employee interviews and why they ask the questions. The following are a few of the questions and whys:

1. Jim Sheward (Fiberlink, Blue Bell, Pennsylvania)
   Question: "What's the biggest career mistake you've made so far?"
   Why: "I've found that those who can't think of anything either don't take risks or aren't telling me the truth."

2. John Discerni (Physicians Formulation International, Phoenix, Arizona)
   Question: "What's the last book you've read?"
   Why: "It's not what they read so much as the amount of time it takes them to answer the question: If they have to think a long time, they probably aren't that well read."

3. Tony Petrucciani (Single Source Systems, Fisher, Indiana)
   Question: "Why do they make manhole covers round?"

Why: "We ask this of potential developers to see if they get flustered, and how they think on their feet."

4. Robert Baden (Rochester Software Associates, Rochester, New York)
   Question: "If I stood you next to a skyscraper and gave you a barometer, how could you figure out how tall the building was?"
   Why: "The answer: Well, there really isn't one. Baden just wants to see how creative people are."

5. Doug Chapiensky (Center Point Solutions, Denver, Colorado)
   Question: "If you had your own company, what would it do?"
   Why: "I want to see if they've got that certain entrepreneurial spirit it takes to succeed in a small software company."

Source: "101 Great Ideas for Managing People from America's Most Innovative Small Companies," *Inc.*, October 21, 1999.

government agency responsible for enforcing employment laws, does not outlaw specific interview questions, it does recognize that some questions can result in employment discrimination. If a candidate files charges of discrimination against a company, the burden of proof shifts to the employer to prove that all preemployment questions were job related and nondiscriminatory. In addition, many states have passed laws that forbid the use of certain questions or screening tools in interviews. To avoid trouble, a business owner should keep in mind why he is asking a particular question. The goal is to find someone who is qualified to do the job well. By steering clear of questions about subjects that are peripheral to the job itself, employers are less likely to ask questions that will land them in court. Wise business owners ask their attorneys to review their bank of questions before using them in an interview. Table 19.4 offers a quiz to help you understand which kinds of questions are most likely to create charges of discrimination, and Table 19.5 describes a simple test for determining whether an interview question might be considered discriminatory.

Selling the Candidate on the Company. In the final phase of the interview, the employer tries to sell her company to desirable candidates. This phase begins by allowing the candidate to ask questions about the company, the job, or other issues. Again, experienced interviewers note the nature of these questions and the insights they give into the candidate's personality. This part of the interview offers the employer a prime opportunity to explain to the candidate why her company is an

Table 19.4
Is It Legal?

Some interview questions can land an employer in legal hot water. Review the following interview questions and then decide whether you think each one is legal or illegal.

Legal	Illegal	
❏	❏	1. Are you currently using illegal drugs?
❏	❏	2. Have you ever been arrested?
❏	❏	3. Do you have any children or are you planning to have children?
❏	❏	4. When and where were you born?
❏	❏	5. Is there any limit on your ability to work overtime or to travel?
❏	❏	6. How tall are you? How much do you weigh?
❏	❏	7. Do you drink alcohol?
❏	❏	8. How much alcohol do you drink each week?
❏	❏	9. Would your religious beliefs interfere with your ability to do this lob?
❏	❏	10. What contraceptive practices do you use?
❏	❏	11. Are you HIV positive?
❏	❏	12. Have you ever filed a lawsuit or a workers' compensation claim against a former employer?
❏	❏	13. Do you have any physical or mental disabilities that would interfere with your doing this job?
❏	❏	14. Are you a U.S. citizen?

Answers: 1. Legal. 2. Illegal. Employers cannot ask about an applicant's arrest record, but they can ask if a candidate has ever been *convicted* of a crime. 3. Illegal. Employers cannot ask questions that could lead to discrimination against a particular group (e.g., women, physically challenged, etc.). 4. Illegal. The Civil Rights Act of 1964 bans discrimination on the basis of race, color, sex, religion, or national origin. 5. Legal. 6. Illegal. Unless a person's physical characteristics are necessary for job performance (e.g., lifting 100-pound sacks of mulch), employers cannot ask candidates such questions. 7. Legal. 8. Illegal. Notice the fine line between question 7 and question 8; this is what makes interviewing challenging. 9. Illegal. This question would violate the Civil Rights Act of 1964. 10. Illegal. What relevance would this have to an employee's job performance? 11. Illegal. Under the Americans with Disabilities Act, which prohibits discrimination against people with disabilities, people that are HIV positive or have AIDS are considered "disabled." 12. Illegal. Workers who file such suits are protected from retribution by a variety of federal and state laws. 13. Illegal. This question also would violate the Americans with Disabilities Act. 14. Illegal. This question violates the Civil Rights Act of 1964.

attractive place to work. Remember: The best candidates will have other offers, and it's up to you to make sure they leave the interview wanting to work for your company. Finally, before closing the interview, the employer should thank the candidate and tell him or her what happens next (e.g., "We'll be contacting you about our decision within two weeks.").

Table 19.5
A Guide for Interview Questions

Small business owners can use the **"OUCH"** test as a guide for determining whether an interview question might be considered discriminatory:

- Does the question **O**mit references to race, religion, color, sex, or national origin?
- Does the question **U**nfairly screen out a particular class of people?
- Can you **C**onsistently apply the question to every applicant?
- Does the question **H**ave job relatedness and business necessity?

GAINING THE COMPETITIVE EDGE
Avoiding Legal Pitfalls in Hiring

As businesses grow, entrepreneurs must actively work at hiring employees whose talents and performance are compatible with their vision for the business. The mistakes an entrepreneur can make in the hiring process are many, but almost all can be avoided through knowledge of the law and proper preparation.

Step 1: Know the laws that regulate employment practices. Most laws are federal, but some are state; make a list of what *not* to do during the interview process. Avoiding a mistake is valuable. For example, know what questions you can ask potential applicants (and which ones are illegal). You may not ask interview questions that elicit information about an applicant's membership in any of the categories protected by antidiscrimination laws.

Step 2: Select employees who you believe have demonstrated in the interview process, back-

ground checks, or testing to be trustworthy, possessing the skills required for the position and motivated to perform. Do the research to verify your "gut level" instincts.

Step 3: Develop and follow your employment policies. Be absolutely sure that each and every employment policy meets the legal standards and then follow your policies without deviation. Employment policies cover a vast array of topics from orientation to termination. Be sure that every person knows the policies and every supervisor follows these policies to the letter. A policy that is not rigidly adhered to has no value and will eventually lead to serious organizational conflicts and potential legal difficulties.

Step 4: When in doubt, consult an attorney who specializes in employment law.

Source: Stan Soper, "Avoid Hiring Mistakes," *Inc.,* June 22, 2001, p. 8.

Check References

Small business owners should take the time to check *every* applicant's references. Although many business owners see checking references as a formality and pay little attention to it, others realize the need to protect themselves (and their customers) from hiring unscrupulous workers. Is a reference check really necessary? Yes! According to the American Association for Personnel Administration, approximately 25 percent of all résumés and applications contain at least one *major* fabrication.[5] Checking references thoroughly can help an employer uncover false or exaggerated information. Failing to do so can be costly. *One small company became the subject of an expensive lawsuit when it failed to check the references of a newly hired sales representative. While driving to a sales call, the employee, who was intoxicated, caused an accident that severely injured a person. The lawsuit came about when the injured party discovered that the sales representative had been fired from his three previous jobs for drunkenness, which a reference check would have revealed.*[6] Rather than contacting only the references listed, experienced employers call an applicant's previous employers and talk to his or her immediate supervisors to get a clear picture of the applicant's job performance, character, and work habits.

Conduct Employment Tests

Although various state and federal laws have made using employment tests as screening devices more difficult in recent years, many companies find them quite useful. To avoid charges of discrimination, business owners must be able to prove that the employment tests they use are both valid and reliable. A **valid test** is one that measures what it is intended to measure (e.g., aptitude for selling, creativity,

Everyone knows that a workplace is for work, but can an entrepreneurial firm build an organization culture that includes fun in the workplace and some firms believe that in today's competitive environment for high-quality employees a workplace that's fun is an intangible benefit. Example of firms that do simple things that convey a message that work and fun are not incompatible include the following:

FIRMANIC AND ASSOCIATES

Let's go to the movies!! In fact, the staff all go together four times per year. Not a big thing, but they look forward to their visits to the movies.

HOT TOPICS

This California music-related apparel and accessories company reimburses employees for tickets to rock concerts. To get the reimbursement, the employee reports on the fashions that the band and the fans were wearing.

KAUFER MILLER COMMUNICATIONS

Periodically, David Kaufer rents a bus and, without notice, takes the entire staff to a baseball game or to other forms of amusement and fun.

Many firms now have special meals catered for employees to make them feel that they are all part of one team. Another hired high school students to surprise each employee by washing every car in the company parking lot. The king of fun must be the former CEO of Southwest Airlines who, over his career, appeared one evening at the maintenance department dressed as Elvis Presley. On another occasion, he arm-wrestled another CEO to settle a dispute over the company's slogan. Many entrepreneurs believe that an organizational culture, which blends hard work and fun is the most profitable combination.

Sources: Christopher Caggiano, "Perks You Can Afford," *Inc.*, November 1997; Bob Nelson, "Fun at Work: Enliven Your Culture," *Nelson Motivational*, May 1999; Stephanie L. Grung, "Have Fun, Make Money," *Inc.*, May 1998.

integrity). A **reliable test** is one that measures consistently over time. Employers must also be sure that the tests they use measure aptitudes and factors that are job related. Many testing organizations offer ready-made tests that have been proved to be both valid and reliable, and business owners can use these tests safely. In today's environment, if a test has not been validated, proven to be reliable, or not job related, it's best not to use it.

Experienced small business owners don't rely on any one element in the employee selection process. They look at the total picture painted by each part of a candidate's portfolio. They know that the hiring process provides them with one of the most valuable raw materials their companies count on for success—capable, hard-working people. They also recognize that hiring an employee is not a single event but the beginning of a long-term relationship. The accompanying *Gaining the Competitive Edge* feature describes how to hire and keep great employees.

BUILDING THE RIGHT CULTURE AND STRUCTURE

Culture

Company culture is the distinctive, unwritten code of conduct that governs the behavior, attitudes, relationships, and style of an organization. It is the essence of "the way we do things around here." In many small companies, culture plays as important a part in gaining a competitive edge as strategy does. In others, it adds

3. Explain how to build the kind of company culture and structure to support the entrepreneur's mission and goals and to motivate employees to achieve them.

practically nothing to the business's competitive position because managers fail to give employees a sense of ownership in the company. A company's culture has a powerful impact on the way people work together in a business, how they do their jobs, and how they treat their customers. Company culture manifests itself in many ways—from how workers dress and act to the language they use.

The culture of the organization reflects the deep-seated philosophy of the founder or executives on how the people in the organization should behave toward the customers or clients, as well as toward themselves. There is no one best or correct organizational culture. The culture that evolves must reflect the philosophy and values of the organization. Investment firms that serve corporate executives and involve large financial dealings many create a formal and very professional culture that displays sophistication and seriousness. In contrast, a firm like Amy's Ice Cream has a work culture that reflects its founder's (Amy Miller) belief that visiting one of their stores should be fun. Employees perform a variety of activities to entertain the customer, as well as serve gourmet ice cream. In many companies, the culture creates its own language. At Disney, for instance, workers are not "employees"; they are "cast members." They don't merely go to work; their jobs are "parts in a performance." Disney's customers are "guests." When a cast member treats someone to lunch, it's "on the mouse." Anything negative—such as a cigarette butt on a walkway—is "a bad Mickey," and anything positive is "a good Mickey."

Nurturing the right culture in a company can enhance a company's competitive position by improving its ability to attract and retain quality workers and by creating an environment in which workers can grow and develop. In fact, as a younger generation of employees enters the workforce, companies are finding that offering a more open and relaxed culture gives them an edge in attracting the best workers. Like Amy's Ice Creams, these companies embrace nontraditional, relaxed, fun cultures that incorporate concepts such as casual dress, virtual teams, telecommuting, flexible work schedules, on-site massages, cappuccinos in company cafeterias, and other cutting-edge concepts. Today's organizational culture does reinforce some basic principles that are fundamental to the creation of a productive workplace:

- Respect for the quality of work and a balance between work life and home life
- A sense of purpose that reflects a connection between the behavior of each employee and the mission of the organization
- Respect for diversity in all forms
- Integrity in *all* behaviors and a commitment to ethical and socially responsible actions by all employees
- A learning environment that encourages and supports lifelong learning
- Empowerment of employees to make decisions and take actions that further the objective of the organization

Retaining and Modifying the Organization's Culture During the Growth Cycle. As companies grow from seedling businesses into leggy saplings and beyond (perhaps into giants in the business forest), they often experience dramatic changes in their culture. Procedures become more formal, operations grow more widespread, jobs take on more structure, communication becomes more difficult, and the company's personality begins to change. As more workers come on board, employees find it more difficult to know everyone in the company and what their jobs are. Unless an entrepreneur works hard to maintain her company's unique culture, she may wake up one day to find that she has sacrificed that culture—and the competitive edge that went with it—in the name of growth.

Ironically, growth can sometimes be a small company's biggest enemy, causing a once successful business to spiral out of control into oblivion. The problem stems from the fact that the organizational structure (or lack of it!) and the style of management that makes an entrepreneurial start-up so successful often cannot support the business as it grows into adolescence and maturity. As a company grows, not only does its culture tend to change but so does its need for a management infrastructure capable of supporting that growth. Compounding the problem is the entrepreneur's tendency to see all growth as good. After all, who wouldn't want to be the founder of a small company whose rapid growth makes it destined to become the next rising star in the industry? Yet, achieving rapid growth and *managing* it are two distinct challenges. Entrepreneurs must be aware of the challenges rapid growth brings with it; otherwise, they may find their companies crumbling around them as they reach warp speed. *Looking back, one entrepreneur whose specialty-food business "crashed into the wall" sees fast, uncontrolled growth as the primary cause of his company's troubles. In just five years, James Bildner took his business from start-up to a publicly held company with 20 retail stores, 1,250 employees, and $48 million in sales. Uncontrolled growth, which magnified J. Bildner and Sons' other problems, sent the company careening into "the wall." Bildner says, "Rapid growth itself—too many locations, new products, new people; too much or too little capital; and always too little investment up front in financial systems and controls—makes everything worse." Like many entrepreneurs, Bildner never saw (or chose to ignore) the signs of trouble—diminishing cash flow, rapid turnover of good people, expanding general and administrative expenses, and increasing distance from the core of the business—until it was too late. The company survived, but, according to Bildner, it is "a shadow of its former self."[7]*

In many cases, small companies achieve impressive growth because they bypass the traditional organizational structures, forgo rigid policies and procedures, and maintain maximum flexibility. Small companies often have the edge over their larger rivals because they are naturally quick to respond; they concentrate on creating new product and service lines; and they are willing to take the risks necessary to conquer new markets.

But growth brings with it change: changes in management style, organizational strategy, and methods of operations. Growth produces organizational complexity. In this period of transition, the entrepreneur's challenge is to walk a fine line between retaining the small-company traits that are the seeds of the business's success and incorporating the elements of the infrastructure essential to supporting and sustaining the company's growth.

Management Style, Organizational Culture, and Organizational Structure

Growth and acceptance of the business is always reinforcement that the business concept and its implementation were correct. Yet, the very nature of organizational growth produces a new set of challenges to the entrepreneur's style of management and the structure of the organization. In short, what was effective when the business was small may become ineffective in a period of growth.

Entrepreneurs have traditionally relied on six different management styles to guide their companies as they grow. The first three (craftsman, classic, and coordinator) involve running a company without any management assistance and are best suited for small companies in the early stages of growth; the last three (entrepreneur-plus-employee team, small partnership, big-team venture) rely on a team approach to run the company as its growth speeds up.[8] In recent years entrepreneurs whose companies are growing have been turning more and more to a formerly big-business strategy: team-based management.

IN THE FOOTSTEPS OF AN ENTREPRENEUR
How Do You Manage Generation X?

Everyone has heard the stereotypes of Generation X, those born between 1965 and 1977: They are lazy, anti-authority slackers with brief attention spans and absolutely no loyalty to their employees. But are these stereotypes true? Not necessarily.

The key lies in knowing what Gen X workers expect in the workplace. Pamela Hamilton, founder of Collaborative Communications, a public relations agency with 13 employees (12 of whom are Generation Xers) says, "It is a challenge to manage them, but if you do, you'll get terrific results." Indeed, learning to manage Generation X workers is essential; they make up 34 percent of the workforce! The problem is that most managers (many of whom sit squarely in the baby boomer generation) assume that Generation X workers are just like themselves, with the same goals and aspirations. As a result, they treat their Generation X workers the way they themselves want to be treated and are befuddled when their attempts fail.

How can business owners motivate, stimulate, and reward their Generation X employees? The following suggestions will help:

- *Don't rely on the traditional career motivators such as fancy job titles and more pay.* "What gets these folks up in the morning is very different from why baby boomers wake up, " says Pamela Hamilton. "They are not interested in climbing the conventional job ladder. Offer them an additional $10,000 a year, and they won't necessarily hop jobs." Gen X workers prefer instead jobs that challenge them, require diverse skills, and contribute to the company's success. They want to have an impact on the company's overall mission.

- *Give them challenging assignments that allow them to learn more skills.* Generation X workers value education and want to continuously upgrade their knowledge. Lee Hunt, founder of a creative design firm, has had tremendous success in attracting and retaining Generation X employees by emphasizing the educational benefits his company offers them. "When I talk to them, I say, 'You can probably make more money at a bigger company, but I'll give you a chance to try a lot of different things at once,'" he says.

- *Treat them as individuals.* One hallmark of Generation X employees is their desire to be treated as individuals. Business owners who set up reward systems that take into account their employees' unique tastes and preferences will be more successful than those who don't. One entrepreneur found that concert tickets and CDs were effective motivators for some of his Generation X employees. Also, Generation X employees are drawn to companies that offer flextime, telecommuting, and casual dress codes—all features that allow them to express their individuality. "Provide a degree of choice, and members of this generation flourish," says one employer.

- *Avoid an authoritarian approach.* The surest way to alienate Gen X employees is to manage with the attitude "It's my way or the highway." These employees expect managers to explain the "whats" and the "whys"—but *not* the "hows"—of their assignments. They thrive on a participative approach coupled with plenty of two-way communication.

- *Trust them.* Another turnoff for Generation X employees is a manager who is constantly checking up on them to make sure they are doing their job. These workers call it "parenting," and they hate it! Of course, managers must have control systems in place, but they must learn to trust employees to do their jobs without constant intervention and supervision. One expert advises, "Don't check to see if they are doing the job right—that sends the wrong parental signal—but check to see if they need any support or guidance."

- *Offer them varied assignment.* Gen Xers thrive on multiple challenges. "They are happy doing three things at once," says one business owner. "A job with plenty of variety keeps them challenged."

- *Say what you mean and mean what you say.* Generation X workers also value companies that have principles and stand for integrity. If they sense a streak of insincerity or hypocrisy in a business owner, they are likely to leave the company. They judge their managers not so much by what they say but by what they do.

(continued)

- *Offer frequent rewards.* Annual performance appraisals and salary adjustments don't click with Generation Xers. They want lots of feedback on their performance, and they want it frequently. Offbeat awards such as a special parking space, a day off, or a massage often have as much impact as financial rewards. They key is to recognize top performers frequently.

Small companies are ideally suited for Generation X employees because they offer workers the chance to get involved in many different aspects of the company and because workers can make a difference in the company's future, both of which rank high on Gen Xers' list of priorities. Indeed, many of those who choose not to work for small companies start their own! One fifth of all small business owners in the United States are Generation Xers, and this generation has the highest business start-up rate among all the others.

1. How would you respond to a manager who used the technique described above? Explain.

2. Write a one-page paper describing a job you have held in which your manager did not use effective management and motivational techniques. What impact did the manager's style have on your level of motivation? On job performance? On morale? What suggestions would you make to improve the situation?

Sources: Adapted from Roberta Maynard, "A Less-Stressed Work Force," *Nation's Business,* November 1996, pp. 50–51; Robert McGarvey, "X Appeal," *Entrepreneur,* May 1997, pp. 87–89; "Who Is Generation X?" *Business News,* Summer 1996, pp. 31–34; Susan Caminiti, "Young and Restless," *Your Company,* February/March 1998, pp. 36–47.

The Craftsman. One of the earliest management styles to emerge was the craftsman. These entrepreneurs literally run a one-man (or one-woman) show; they do everything themselves because their primary concern is with the quality of the products or services they produce. Woodworkers, cabinetmakers, glassblowers, and other craftsmen rely on this style of management. The benefits of this style include minimal operating expenses (no employees to pay), very simple operations (no workers' compensation, incentive plans, or organization charts), no supervision problems, and the entrepreneur's total control over both the business and its quality.

Of course, one disadvantage of the craftsman management style is that the entrepreneur must do *everything* in the business, including those tasks that she does not enjoy. The biggest disadvantage of this style, however, is the limitations it puts on a company's ability to grow. A business can grow only so big before the craftsman has to take on other workers and delegate authority to them. Before choosing this management style, a craftsman must decide: "How large do I want my business to become?"

The Classic. As business opportunities arise, craftsmen quickly realize that they could magnify the company's capacity to grow by hiring other people to work. Classic entrepreneurs bring in other people but do not delegate any significant authority to them, choosing instead to "watch over everything" themselves. They insist on tight supervision, constantly monitor employees' work, and perform all of the critical tasks themselves. Classic entrepreneurs do not feel comfortable delegating the power and the authority for making decisions to anyone else; they prefer to keep a tight rein on the business and on everyone who works there.

Even though this management style gives a business more growth potential than the craftsman style, there is a limit to how much an entrepreneur can accomplish. Therefore, entrepreneurs who choose to operate this way must limit the complexity of their business if they are to grow at all. An inherent danger of this style is entrepreneurs' tendency to "micromanage" every aspect of the business rather than spend their time focusing on those tasks that are most important and most productive for the company.

The Coordinator. The coordinator style of management gives an entrepreneur the ability to create a fairly large company with very few employees. In this type of business (often called a virtual corporation because the company is actually quite "hollow"), the entrepreneur farms out a large portion of the work to other companies and then coordinates all of the activities from "headquarters." By hiring out at least some of the work (in some cases, most of the work), the entrepreneur is free to focus on pumping up sales and pushing the business to higher levels. Some coordinators hire someone to manufacture their products, pay brokers to sell them, and arrange for someone to collect their accounts receivable! With the help of just a few workers, a coordinator can build a multimillion-dollar business!

Although the coordinator style sounds like an easy way to build a business, it can be very challenging to implement. The business's success is highly dependent on its suppliers and their ability to produce quality products and services in a timely fashion. Getting suppliers to perform on time is one of the hardest tasks. Plus, if the entrepreneur hires someone else to manufacture the product, he or she loses control over its quality.

The Entrepreneur-plus-Employee Team. As their companies grow, many entrepreneurs see the need to shift to a team-based management style. The entrepreneur-plus-employee team gives an entrepreneur the power to grow the business beyond the scope of the manager-only styles. In this style, the entrepreneur delegates authority to key employees, but she retains the final decision-making authority in the company. Of course, the transition from a management style in which the entrepreneur retains almost total authority to one based on delegation requires some adjustments for employees and especially for the entrepreneur! Employees have to learn to make decisions on their own, and the manager must learn to give workers the authority, the responsibility, and the information to make them. Delegating requires a manager to realize that there are several ways to accomplish a task and that sometimes employees will make mistakes. Still, delegation allows managers to get the maximum benefit from each employee while freeing themselves up to focus on the most important tasks in the business.

The Small Partnership. As the business world grows more complex and interrelated, many entrepreneurs find that there is strength in numbers. Rather than manage a company alone, they choose to share the managerial responsibilities with one or more partners (or shareholders). As we saw in Chapter 3, the benefits are many. Perhaps the biggest advantage is the ability to share responsibility for the company with others who have a real stake in it and are willing to work hard to make it a success. Some of the most effective partnerships are those in which the owners' skills complement one another, creating natural lines for dividing responsibilities. Of course, the downside to this management style includes the necessity of giving up total control over the business and the potential for personality conflicts and disputes over the company's direction.

The Big-Team Venture. The broadest-based management style is the big-team venture, which typically emerges over time as a company grows larger. The workload demands on a small number of partners can quickly outstrip the time and energy they can devote to them, even if they are effective delegators. Once a company reaches this point, managers must expand the breadth of the management team's experience to handle the increasing level of responsibility that results from the sheer size of the company. If the company's operations have become global in scope, the need for such a big management team is even more pronounced; the big-team venture is almost a necessity.

Any of these management styles can be successful for an entrepreneur if it matches his or her personality and the company's goals. The key is to plan for the company's growth and to lay out a strategy for managing the changes the company will experience as it grows. "Ask yourself whether your management style is really effective for a business of this particular size, shape, and complexity," advises Ronald Merrill and Henry Sedgwick, the authors of *The New Venture Handbook*. "If the answer is no, modify your plan."[9]

Team-Based Management. Large companies have been using self-directed work teams for years to improve quality, increase productivity, raise morale, lower costs, and boost motivation; yet team-based management is just now beginning to catch on in small firms. In fact, a team approach may be best suited for small companies. Even though converting a traditional company to teams requires a major change in management style, it is usually relatively easy to implement with a small number of workers. A **self-directed work team** is a group of workers from different functional areas of a company who work together as a unit largely without supervision, making decisions and performing tasks that once belonged only to managers. Some teams may be temporary, attacking and solving a specific problem, but many are permanent components of an organization's structure. As their name implies, these teams manage themselves, performing such functions as setting work schedules, ordering raw materials, evaluating and purchasing equipment, developing budgets, hiring and firing team members, solving problems, and a host of other activities. The goal is to get people working together to serve customers better.

Managers in companies using teams don't just sit around drinking coffee, however. In fact, they work just as hard as before, but the nature of their work changes dramatically. Before teams, managers were bosses who made most of the decisions affecting their subordinates alone and hoarded information and power for themselves. In a team environment, managers take on the role of coaches who empower those around them to make decisions affecting their work and share information with workers. As facilitators, their job is to support and to serve the teams functioning in the organization and to make sure they produce results.

Companies have strong competitive reasons for using team-based management. Companies that use teams effectively report significant gains in quality, reductions in cycle time, lower costs, increased customer satisfaction, and improved employee motivation and morale. A team-based approach is not for every organization, however. Teams are *not* easy to start, and switching from a traditional organization structure to a team-based one is filled with potential pitfalls. Teams work best in environments where the work is interdependent and people must interact to accomplish their goals. Although a team approach might succeed in a small plant making gas grills, it would most likely fail miserably in a real estate office, where salespeople work independently with little interaction required to make a sale. Table 19.6 describes some of the transitions a company must make as it moves from a traditional organizational structure to a team-based style.

In some cases, teams have been a company's salvation from failure and extinction; in others, the team approach has flopped. What made the difference? What causes teams to fail? The following errors are common:

- Assigning a team an inappropriate task, one in which the team members may lack the necessary skills to be successful (lack of training and support)
- Creating work teams but failing to provide the team with meaningful performance targets
- Failure to deal with known underperformers and assuming that being part of a group will solve the problem (it doesn't)
- Failure to compensate the members of the team equally

Table 19.6

Making the
Transition from a
Traditional
Organization to a
Team-Based One

TRADITIONAL ORGANIZATION	TEAM-BASED ORGANIZATION
Management driven	Customer driven
Isolated specialists	Multiskilled workforce
Many job descriptions	Few job descriptions
Information limited	Information shared
Many management levels	Few management levels
Departmental focus	Whole-business focus
Management controlled	Team regulated
Policy and procedure based	Values and principles based
Selection-based employment	Training-based employment
Temporary changes	Ongoing changes
Seemingly organized	Seemingly chaotic
Incremental improvement	Continuous improvement
High management commitment	High worker commitment

Source: Kenneth P. De Meuse and Thomas J. Bergmann, "Managers Must Relinquish Control if They Are to Establish Effective Work Teams," *Small Business Forum,* Spring 1996, p. 86.

In so many cases in which teams prove to be ineffective, the answer can be found in an entrepreneur who did not structure and create teams that could be expected to succeed. Teams can be powerfully effective in terms of performance when their mission and performance targets are realistic and known to the team members; when the team has the needed skill; when the nature of the work is compatible with the use of teams; when management actively supports the work of the team; and, lastly, when there is a linkage between the performance achieved by the team and the compensation of the team.

Figure 19.1 illustrates the four stages teams go through on their way to performing effectively and accomplishing goals.

The remainder of this chapter will focus on the role of the entrepreneur as communicator and motivator. These skills can be learned and must be mastered if the entrepreneur hopes to achieve maximum performance from the employees of the firm.

COMMUNICATING EFFECTIVELY

4. Understand the potential barriers to effective communication and describe how to overcome them.

Like all leaders, entrepreneurs constantly confront dilemmas as they operate their business. Frequently, they must walk the fine line between the chaos involved in encouraging creativity and maintaining control over their companies. At other times, they must steer their companies around those questionable actions that might produce large short-term gains into those that are ethical. As leaders, an important and highly visible part of their jobs is to communicate the values, beliefs, and principles for which their business stands. A leader must be the communicator of the company's vision. It is a job that never ends. "The essence of leadership today is to make sure that the organization knows itself," says one entrepreneur when asked about his job as a leader. "There are certain durable principles that underlie an organization. The leader should embody those values. They're fundamental."[10] One of the first skills successful leaders must acquire is the ability to communicate. Nowhere is this skill more important than among entrepreneurs, whose organizations are predicated on their founders' ability to communicate a vision and a set of values that everyone in the company can embrace.

Figure 19.1
The Stages of Team Development

Source: Adapted from Mark A. Frohman, "Do Teams . . . But Do Them Right," Industry Week, April 3, 1995, p. 22; "The Stages of a Group," *Communication Briefings,* October 1997, p. 6.

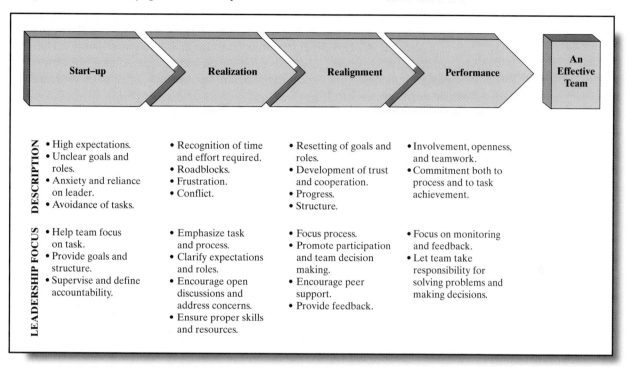

Improving Communication

Research shows that managers spend about 80 percent of their time in some form of communication: 30 percent talking, 25 percent listening, 15 percent reading, and 10 percent writing.[11] To some managers, however, communicating means only one thing: sending messages to others. Although talking to people both inside and outside the organization is an important part of an entrepreneur's job, so is the other aspect of an entrepreneur's job as chief communicator—listening.

Sending Messages. One of the most frustrating experiences for entrepreneurs occurs when they ask an employee to do something and nothing happens! Although entrepreneurs are quick to perceive the failure to respond as the employee's lack of motivation or weak work ethic, often the culprit is improper communication. The primary reasons employees usually don't do what they are expected to do have little to do with their motivation and desire to work. Instead, workers often fail to do what they are suppose to because they didn't understand what was expected or they felt that they would be punished if they told the owner that they were confused about the assignment or lacked the skills to perform the task. Before communications can be improved, the causes of failed communications must be recognized and dealt with. The most common barriers to effective communications include the following:

- *Managers and employees don't always feel free to say what they really mean.* CEOs and top managers in companies of any size seldom hear the truth about problems and negative results from employees. This less-than-honest feedback results from the hesitancy of subordinates to tell "the boss" bad news. Over time, this tendency can paralyze the upward communication in a company.

- *Ambiguity blocks real communication.* The same words can have different meanings to different people, especially in modern companies, where the workforce is likely to be highly diverse. For instance, a business owner may tell an employee to "take care of this customer's problem as soon as you can." The owner may have meant "solve this problem by the end of the day," but the employee may think that fixing the problem by the end of the week will meet the owner's request.
- *Information overload causes the message to get lost.* With information from mail, telephone, faxes, e-mail, face-to-face communication, and other sources, employees in modern organizations are literally bombarded with messages. With such a large volume of information washing over workers, it is easy for some messages to get lost.
- *Selective listening interferes with the communication process.* Sometimes, people hear only what they want to hear, selectively tuning in and out on a speaker's message. The result is distorted communication.
- *Defense mechanisms block a message.* When people are confronted with information that upsets them or conflicts with their perceptions, they immediately put up defenses. Defense mechanisms range from verbally attacking the source of the message to twisting perceptions of reality to maintain self-esteem.
- *Conflicting verbal and nonverbal messages confuse listeners.* Nonverbal communication includes a speaker's mannerisms, gestures, posture, facial expressions, and other forms of "body language." When a speaker sends conflicting verbal and nonverbal messages, research shows that listeners will believe the nonverbal message almost every time.

How can entrepreneurs overcome these barriers to become better communicators? The following tips will help:

- *Clarify your message before you attempt to communicate it.* Before attempting to communicate your message, identify exactly what you want the receiver to think and do as a result of the message. Then focus on getting that point across clearly and concisely.
- *Use face-to-face communication whenever possible.* Although not always practical, face-to-face communication reduces the likelihood of misunderstandings because it allows for immediate feedback and nonverbal clues.
- *Be empathetic.* Try to put yourself in the place of those who will receive your message, and develop it accordingly. Be sure to tell your audience up front what's in it for them.
- *Match your message to your audience.* A business owner would be very unlikely to use the same words, techniques, and style to communicate his company's financial position to a group of industry analysts as he would to a group of workers on the factory floor.
- *Be organized.* Effective communicators organize their messages so that their audiences can understand them easily.
- *Encourage feedback.* Allow listeners to ask questions and to offer feedback. Sometimes, employees are hesitant to ask the boss any questions for fear of "looking stupid." One useful technique, especially when giving instructions, is to ask workers to repeat the message to make sure they understand it correctly.
- *Tell the truth.* The fastest way to destroy your credibility as a leader is to lie.

- *Don't be afraid to tell employees about the business, its performance, and the forces that affect it.* Too often, entrepreneurs assume that employees don't care about such details.
- *Listening.* When you think about communications, listening does not necessarily come to mind. Too often, managers never develop effective listening skill. When an entrepreneur does develop excellent listening skills, they discover clues to improved performance and profitability. Entrepreneurs need to be conscious of what employees who are on the "firing line" are learning about the customers' needs and demands.

The employees who perform the work in the company and serve its customers are the real experts in its day-to-day activities and are in closer contact with potential problems and opportunities at the operating level. By encouraging employees to develop creative solutions to problems and innovative ideas and then listening to and acting on them, business owners can make their companies more successful. *For instance, the manager of a plant making toothpaste found that the frequent need to wash out the steel holding tank interrupted the company's production schedule. One day the manager was talking to one of the operators, who suggested that the company put in a second tank. "That way we can use one tank while we wash the second one, and we don't have to stop production to do it."* This simple, yet effective, solution that was so obvious to the worker because he dealt with the problem every day had never occurred to the plant's managers.

Such improvements depend on an owner's ability to listen. To improve listening skills, one management consultant suggests managers use the "PDCH formula": identify the speaker's *purpose;* recognize the *details* that support that purpose; see the *conclusions* they can draw from what the speaker is saying; and identify the *hidden* meanings communicated by body language and voice inflections.[12]

That Informal Communication Network: The "Grapevine"

Despite all of the modern communication tools available, the grapevine—the informal lines of communication that exist in every company—remains an important link in a company's communication network. The grapevine carries vital information—and sometimes rumors—through every part of the organization with incredible speed. One researcher describes the grapevine this way: "With the rapidity of a burning powder trail, information flows like magic out of the woodwork, past the water fountain, past the manager's door and the janitor's mop closet. As elusive as a summer zephyr it filters through steel walls, bulkheads, or glass partitions, from office boy to executive."[13] In one classic study, researchers found that when management made an important change in the organization, most employees would hear the news first by the grapevine. A supervisor and an official memorandum ran a poor second and third, respectively.[14] In a more recent study, 96 percent of executives said their employees routinely use the company grapevine to communicate and that their workers consider the grapevine to be a reliable source of information.[15]

THE CHALLENGE OF MOTIVATING EMPLOYEES

Motivation is the degree of effort an employee exerts to accomplish a task; it shows up as excitement about work. Motivating workers to higher levels of performance is one of the most difficult and challenging tasks facing a small business manager. Few things are more frustrating to a business owner than an employee with a tremendous amount of talent who lacks the desire to use it. This section discusses four aspects of motivation: empowerment, job design, rewards and compensation, and feedback.

Empowerment

One of the principles underlying the team-based management style is empowerment. **Empowerment** involves giving workers at every level of the organization the authority, the freedom, and the responsibility to control their own work, to make decisions, and to take action to meet the company's objectives. Competitive forces and a more demanding workforce challenge business owners and managers to share power with everyone in the organization, whether they use a team-based approach or not.

Empowering employees requires a different style of management and leadership from that of the traditional manager. Many old-style managers are unwilling to share power with anyone because they fear that doing so weakens their authority and reduces their influence. In fact, exactly the *opposite* is true! Business owners who share information, responsibility, authority, and power soon discover that their success (and their company's success) is magnified many times over. Empowered workers become more successful on the job, which means the entrepreneur also becomes more successful.

Empowerment builds on what real business leaders already know: that the people in their organizations bring with them to work an amazing array of talents, skills, knowledge, and abilities. Workers are willing—even anxious—to put these to use; unfortunately, in too many small businesses, suffocating management styles and poorly designed jobs quash workers' enthusiasm and motivation. Enlightened business owners recognize their workers' abilities, develop them, and then give workers the freedom and the power to use them. Empowered employees are more likely to display creativity and initiative in problem solving when they feel that management respects their ideas and talents.

When implemented properly, empowerment can produce impressive results, not only for the small business but also for newly empowered employees. For the business, benefits typically include significant productivity gains, quality improvements, more satisfied customers, improved morale, and increased employee motivation. *When Rheacom, a supplier of parts to the aerospace industry, switched to empowered work teams, workers unleashed a torrent of new ideas aimed at improving the company's performance. One suggestion led to a reduction in the machine time required for a brake shoe the company had been making for 25 years from more than three and a half hours to less than one hour.*[16]

For workers, empowerment offers the chance to do a greater variety of work that is more interesting and challenging. Empowerment challenges workers to make the most of their creativity, imagination, knowledge, and skills. This method of management encourages them to take the initiative to identify and solve problems on their own and as part of a team. As empowered workers see how the various parts of a company's manufacturing or service systems fit together, they realize their need to acquire more skills and knowledge to do their jobs well. Entrepreneurs must realize that empowerment and training go hand-in-hand.

Not every worker *wants* to be empowered, however. Some will resist, wanting only to "put in their eight hours and go home." One expert estimates that companies moving to empowerment can expect to lose about 5 percent of their workforce. "Out of every 100 employees, five are diehards who will be impossible to change," he says. Another 75 percent will accept empowerment and thrive under it, if it is done properly. The remaining 20 percent will pounce eagerly on empowerment because it is something they "have been waiting to do their whole [work] lives," he says.[17] Empowerment works best when a business owner[18]:

- *Is confident enough to give workers all the authority and responsibility they can handle.* Early on, this may mean giving workers the power to tackle relatively simple assignments. But as their confidence and ability grow, most workers are eager to take on more responsibility.

- *Plays the role of coach and facilitator, not the role of meddlesome boss.* One surefire way to make empowerment fail is to give associates the power to attack a problem and then to hover over them, criticizing every move they make. Smart owners empower their workers and then get out of the way so they can do their jobs!

- *Recognizes that empowered employees will make mistakes.* The worst thing an owner can do when empowered employees make mistakes is to hunt them down and punish them. That teaches everyone in the company to avoid taking risks and to always play it safe—something no innovative small business can afford.

- *Hires people who can blossom in an empowered environment.* Empowerment is not for everyone. Owners quickly learn that as costly as hiring mistakes are, such errors are even more costly in an empowered environment. Ideal candidates are high-energy self-starters who enjoy the opportunity to grow and to enhance their skills.

- *Trains workers continuously to upgrade their skills.* Empowerment demands more of workers than traditional work methods. Managers are asking workers to solve problems and make decisions they have never made before. To handle these problems well, workers need training, especially in effective problem-solving techniques, communication, teamwork, and technical skills.

- *Trusts workers to do their jobs.* Once workers are trained to do their jobs, owners must learn to trust them to assume responsibility for their jobs. After all, they are the real experts; they face the problems and challenges every day.

- *Listens to workers when they have ideas, solutions, or suggestions.* Because they are the experts on the job, employees often come up with incredibly insightful, innovative ideas for improving them—if business owners give them the chance. Failing to acknowledge or to act on employees' ideas sends them a clear message: Your ideas really don't count.

- *Recognizes workers' contributions.* One of the most important tasks a business owner has is to recognize jobs well done. Some businesses reward workers with monetary awards; others rely on recognition and praise; still others use a combination of money and praise. Whatever system an owner chooses, the key to keeping a steady flow of ideas, improvements, suggestions, and solutions is to recognize the people who supply them.

- *Shares information with workers.* For empowerment to succeed, business owners must make sure workers get adequate information, the raw material for good decision making. Some companies have gone beyond sharing information to embrace **open-book management,** in which employees have access to *all* of a company's records, including its financial statements. The goal of open-book management is to enable employees to understand why they need to raise productivity, improve quality, cut costs, and improve customer service. Under open-book management, employees: (1) see and learn to understand the company's financial statements and other critical numbers in measuring its performance; (2) learn that a significant part of their jobs is making sure those critical numbers move in the right direction; and (3) have a direct stake in the company's success through profit sharing, employee stock ownership plans (ESOPs), or performance-based bonuses. In short, open-book management establishes the link between employees' knowledge and their performance. One expert writes, "Instead of telling employees how to cut defects, open-book management asks them to boost profits—and lets them figure out how. Instead of giving them a reengineered job, it turns them into businesspeople. They experience the challenge—and the sheer fun and excitement—of matching wits with the marketplace, toting up the score, and sharing in the proceeds . . . There's no better motivation."[19]

Job Design

Over the years, managers have learned that the job itself and the way it is designed can be a source of motivation (or demotivation!) for workers. In some companies, work is organized on the principle of **job simplification,** breaking the work down into its simplest form and standardizing each task, as in some assembly line operations. The scope of jobs organized in such a way is extremely narrow, resulting in impersonal, monotonous, and boring work that creates little challenge or motivation for workers. Job simplification invites workers to "check their brains at the door" and offers them little opportunity for excitement, enthusiasm, or pride in their work. The result can be apathetic, unmotivated workers who don't care about quality, customers, or costs.

To break this destructive cycle, some companies have redesigned jobs so that they offer workers intrinsic rewards and motivation. Three strategies are common: job enlargement, job rotation, and job enrichment.

Job enlargement (or **horizontal job loading**) adds more tasks to a job to broaden its scope. For instance, rather than having an employee simply mount four screws in computers as they come down an assembly line, the worker might assemble, install, and test the entire motherboard (perhaps as part of a team). The idea is to make the job more varied and to allow employees to perform a more complete unit of work.

Job rotation involves cross-training employees so they can move from one job in the company to others, giving them a greater number and variety of tasks to perform. As employees learn other jobs within an organization, both their skills and their understanding of the company's purpose and processes rise. Cross-trained workers are more valuable because they give a company the flexibility to shift workers from low-demand jobs to those where they are most needed.[20] As an incentive for workers to learn to perform other jobs within an operation, some companies offer **skill-based pay,** a system under which the more skills workers acquire, the more they earn.

Job enrichment (or **vertical job loading**) involves building motivators into a job by increasing the planning, decision-making, organizing, and controlling functions (i.e., traditional managerial tasks) workers perform. The idea is to make every employee a manager—at least a manager of his own job. Notice that empowerment is based on the principle of job enrichment.

To enrich employees' jobs, a business owner must build five core characteristics into them:

1. *Skill variety.* The degree to which a job requires a variety of different skills, talents, and activities from the worker. Does the job require the worker to perform a variety of tasks that demand a variety of skills and abilities, or does it force him to perform the same task repeatedly?
2. *Task identity.* The degree to which a job allows the worker to complete a whole or identifiable piece of work. Does the employee build an entire piece of furniture (perhaps as part of a team), or does he merely attach four screws?
3. *Task significance.* The degree to which a job substantially influences the lives or work of others—employees or final customers. Does the employee get to deal with customers, either internal or external? One effective way to establish task significance is to put employees in touch with customers so that they can see how customers use the product or service they make.
4. *Autonomy.* The degree to which a job gives a worker freedom, independence,

and discretion in planning and performing tasks. Does the employee make decisions affecting his work, or must he rely on someone else (e.g., the owner, a manager, or a supervisor) to "call the shots"?

5. *Feedback.* The degree to which a job gives the worker direct, timely information about the quality of his performance. Does the job give employees feedback about the quality of their work, or does the product (and all information about it) simply disappear after it leaves the worker's station?

As the nation's workforce and the companies employing them continue to change, business is changing the way people work, moving away from a legion of full-time employees in traditional 8-to-5, on-site jobs. Organizational structures, even in small companies, are flatter than ever before, as the lines between traditional "managers" and "workers" get blurrier. Rather than resembling the current pyramid, the organization of tomorrow will more closely resemble a spider's web, with a network of interconnected employee specialists working in teams and using lightning-fast communication to make decisions without having to go through three or four layers of management. Changes in workplace design and the integration of technology have resulted in an economy in which productivity per employee continues to grow. The nature of how work is done has also changed. Flextime, job sharing, and flexplace are all relatively new concepts that, for some firms, have proven to be beneficial.

Flextime is an arrangement under which employees build their work schedules around a set of "core hours"—such as 11 A.M. to 3 P.M.—but have flexibility about when they start and stop work. For instance, one worker might choose to come in at 7 A.M. and leave at 3 P.M. to attend her son's soccer game, while another may work from 11 A.M. to 7 P.M. A recent study by the Society for Human Resources Management found that 46 percent of companies with fewer than 500 workers offered flextime programs.[21]

Flextime not only raises worker morale, but it also makes it easier for companies to attract high-quality young workers who want rewarding careers without sacrificing their lifestyles. In addition, companies using flextime schedules often experience lower levels of tardiness and absenteeism.

Job sharing is a work arrangement in which two or more people share a single full-time job. For instance, two college students might share the same 40-hour-a-week job, one working mornings and the other working afternoons. Although job sharing affects a relatively small portion of the nation's workforce, it is an important job design strategy for some companies that find it difficult to recruit capable, qualified, full-time workers.

Flexplace is a work arrangement in which employees work at a place other than the traditional office, such as a satellite branch closer to their homes or, in some cases, at home. Flexplace is an easy job design strategy for companies to use because of **telecommuting.** Using modern communication technology such as e-mail, fax machines, and laptop computers, employees have more flexibility in choosing where they work. Today, it is quite simple for workers to hook up electronically to their workplaces (and to all of the people and the information there) from practically anywhere on the planet!

Telecommuting not only makes it easier for employees to strike a balance between their work and home lives, but it also leads to higher productivity. Studies show that workers say they are from 5 percent to 20 percent more productive when working at home because they encounter fewer distractions.[22]

Before attempting to switch to an organizational setting with a significant flexplace component it would be worthwhile to answer the following questions about the nature of the work under consideration:

- *Does the nature of the work fit telecommuting?* Obviously, some jobs are better suited for telecommuting than others. Positions in which employees work independently, use computers frequently, or spend a great deal of time calling on customers and clients are good candidates for telecommuting.
- *Can you monitor compliance with federal wage and hour laws for telecommuters?* In general, employers must keep the same employment records for telecommuters that they do for traditional office workers.
- *Which workers are best suited for telecommuting?* Those who are self-motivated, are disciplined, and have been around long enough to establish solid relationships with co-workers make the best telecommuters.
- *Can you provide the equipment and the technical support telecommuters need to be productive?* Telecommuting often requires an investment in portable computers, fax machines, extra telephone lines, and software. Workers usually need technical training as well because they often assume the role of their own technical support staff.
- *Are you adequately insured?* Employers should be sure that the telecommuting equipment employees use in their homes is covered under their insurance policies.
- *Can you keep in touch?* Telecommuting works well as long as long-distance employees stay in touch with headquarters. Frequent telephone conferences, regular e-mail messages, and occasional personal appearances in the office will prevent employees from losing contact with what's happening "at work."

A variation of telecommuting that is growing in popularity is **hoteling,** in which employees who spend most of their time away from the office anyway use the same office space at different times, just as travelers use the same hotel rooms on different days. Businesses that use hoteling have been able to reduce the cost of leasing office space, sometimes by as much as 50 percent. Workers can connect their laptops into the company's computer network and e-mail system, forward their telephone calls to their temporary offices, and even move mobile file cabinets in when they need them. Flexible office designs and furnishings allow workers to configure these "hot offices" (so called because they turn over so quickly that the seats are still hot from the previous user) to suit their individual needs.

Rewards and Compensation

The rewards an employee gets from the job itself are intrinsic rewards, but managers have at their disposal a wide variety of extrinsic rewards to motivate workers. The key to using rewards to motivate involves tailoring them to the needs and characteristics of the workers. If we expect to motivate employees to perform, it is essential that rewards follow closely after the performance we wish to reinforce and that the nature of the reward be relevant to the individual. The attempted reward that the employee does not perceive as a reward will not motivate further performance.

One of the most popular rewards is money. Cash is an effective motivator—up to a point. Over the last 20 years, many companies have moved to **pay-for-performance compensation systems,** in which employees' pay depends on how well they perform their job. In other words, extra productivity equals extra pay. By linking employees' compensation directly to the company's financial performance, a business owner increases the likelihood that workers will achieve performance targets that are in their best interest and in the company's best interest.

Such systems work only when employees see a clear connection between their performance and their pay. That's where small companies actually have an advantage over large businesses. Because they work for small companies, employees can see more clearly the impact their performance has on the company's profitability and ultimate success than their counterparts at large corporations. To be successful, however, pay-for-performance systems should meet the following criteria:

- Employees' incentive pay must be clearly and closely linked to their performances. That's where most compensation systems based on simple annual raises lose their effectiveness.
- Entrepreneurs must set up the system so that employees see the connection between what they do every day on the job—selling to customers, producing a product, or anything else—and the rewards they receive under the system.
- The system must be simple enough so that employees understand and trust it. Complex systems that employees have difficulty understanding will not produce the desired results.
- Employees must believe the system is fair.
- The system should be inclusive. Entrepreneurs are finding creative ways to reward all employees, no matter what their jobs might be.
- The company should make frequent payouts to employees. A single annual payout is the worst schedule because employees have long since forgotten what they did to earn the incentive pay. Many companies pay employees the week after they have achieved an important goal. Regular and frequent feedback is an essential ingredient in any incentive-pay program.

For example, Mark Swepston, owner of Atlas Butler Heating and Cooling, was looking for a way to increase sales and to improve his company's cash flow, so he decided to enlist the help of his sales force. Swepston switched to a pay-for-performance system under which his six full-time sales representatives receive sales commissions rather than salaries. A salesperson gets 50 percent of a job's net income, but only after the company receives the customer's payment. Since the switch, Atlas receives customer payments four times faster than before, and its bad debt losses have dropped from 2.7 percent to just 0.3 percent. In addition to improving the company's financial performance, the new compensation system is also producing better customer service. "It's made [the sales representatives] pay more attention to the customers' needs. . . . This practice brings them one step closer to customers because their pocketbooks are affected," says Swepson.[23]

Money isn't the only motivator business owners have at their disposal, of course. In fact, nonfinancial incentives can be more important sources of employee motivation than money! After its initial motivational impact, money loses its impact; it does not have a lasting motivational effect (and for small businesses, with their limited resources, a lasting effect is a plus.) Often, the most meaningful motivating factors are the simplest ones—praise, recognition, respect, feedback, job security, promotions, and others—things that any small business, no matter how limited its budget, can do. Praise, recognition, and daily demonstrations of respect for an individual can be displayed on a regular basis at absolutely no cost. When an employee has done an exceptional job, the entrepreneur needs to be the first to recognize that accomplishment and the first to say "thank you." Praise is simple, yet a powerful, motivational too. People enjoy getting praise—it's human nature. As Mark Twain once said, "I can live for two months on a good compliment." Praise is an easy and inexpensive reward for employees producing extraordinary work.

One of the surest ways to kill high performance is simply to fail to recognize it and the employees responsible for it. Failing to praise good work eventually conveys the message that the owner either doesn't care about exceptional performance or cannot distinguish between good work and poor work. In either case, through inaction, the manager destroys employees' motivation to excel.

Because they lack the financial resources of bigger companies, small business owners must be more creative when it comes to giving rewards that motivate workers. In many cases, however, using rewards other than money gives small businesses an advantage because they usually have more impact on employee performance over time.

In short, rewards do *not* have to be expensive to be effective, but they should be creative and should have a direct link to employee performance. Consider how the following rewards for exceptional performance both recognize the employee's contribution while also building a positive organizational culture:

- The company CEO washes the top performing employee's car at lunchtime in front of the building.
- A small firm that historically suffered from high levels of tardiness created a poker game with a weekly $20 prize. Employees that were on time every morning received a card. Best hand on Friday won the prize.
- Best employee suggestion, as judged by an employee team, wins an evening for two with a limo and dinner.

Whatever system of rewards they use, managers will be most successful if they match rewards to employees' interests and tastes. For instance, the ideal reward for one employee might be tickets to a hockey game; to another, it might be tickets to a musical show. Once again, because they know their employees so well, this is an area in which small business owners have an advantage over large companies. The better you know your employees' interest and taste, the more effective will be the matching of reward to performance.

In the future, managers will rely more on nonmonetary rewards—praise, recognition, car washes, letters of commendation, and others—to create a work environment where employees take pride in their work, enjoy it, are challenged by it, and get excited about it: in short, act like owners of the business themselves. The goal is to let employees know that every person is important and that excellent performance is noticed, appreciated, and recognized.

Feedback

Business owners not only must motivate employees to excel in their jobs, but they must also focus their efforts on the right targets. Providing feedback on progress toward those targets can be a powerful motivating force in a company. To ensure that the link between her vision for the company and its operations is strong, an entrepreneur must build a series of specific performance measures that serve as periodic monitoring points. For each critical element of the organization's performance (e.g., product or service quality, financial performance, market position, productivity, employee development), the owner should develop specific measures that connect daily operational responsibilities with the company's overall strategic direction. These measures become the benchmarks for measuring employees' performance and the company's progress. The adage "what gets measured and monitored gets done" is true for most organizations. By connecting the company's long-term strategy to its daily operations and measuring performance, an entrepreneur makes it clear to everyone in the company what is most important. Jack Stack, CEO of Springfield Remanufacturing Corporation, explains the importance of focusing every employee's attention on key performance targets:

> To be successful in business, you have to be going somewhere, and everyone involved in getting you there has to know where it is. That's a basic

rule, a higher law, but most companies miss . . . the fact that you have a much better chance of winning if everyone knows what it takes to win.[24]

In other words, getting or giving feedback implies that business owners have established meaningful targets that serve as standards of performance for them, their employees, and the company as a whole. One characteristic successful people have in common is that they set goals and objectives, usually challenging ones, for themselves. Business owners are no different. Successful entrepreneurs usually set targets for performance that make them stretch to achieve, and then they encourage their employees to do the same. The result is that they keep their companies constantly moving forward.

The linkage between an effective feedback system and employee maturation is highlighted in Figure 19.2, the feedback loop.

Deciding What to Measure. The first step in the feedback loop is deciding what to measure. Every business is characterized by a set of numbers that are critical to its success, and these "critical numbers" are what the entrepreneur should focus on. Obvious critical numbers include sales, profits, profit margins, cash flow, and other standard financial measures. However, running beneath these standard and somewhat universal measures of performance is an undercurrent of critical numbers that are unique to a company's operations. In most cases, these are the numbers that actually drive profits, cash flow, and other financial measures and are the company's *real* critical numbers. Does each employee know these critical factors that drive the success (or failure) of the business? Do they know the nature of the interrelationship among these critical factors? If not, the first step is to demonstrate to every employee how their performance impacts the success or failure of the business.

Deciding How to Measure. Once a business owner identifies his company's critical numbers, the issue of how to best measure them arises. In some cases, identifying the critical numbers defines the measurements the owner must make, and measuring

Figure 19.2
The Feedback Loop

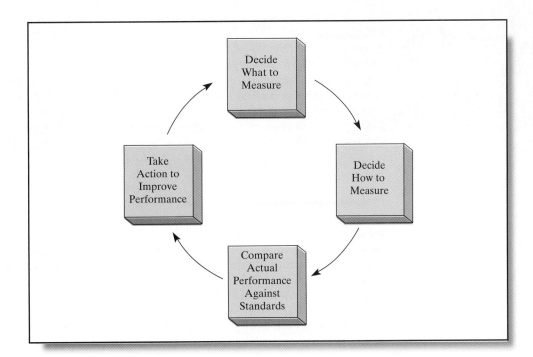

them simply becomes a matter of collecting and analyzing data. In other cases, the method of measurement is not as obvious—or as tangible. For instance, in some businesses, social responsibility is a key factor, but how should a manager measure his company's performance on such an intangible concept? One of the best ways to develop methods for measuring such factors is to use brainstorming sessions involving employees, customers, and even outsiders. For example, one company used this technique to develop a "fun index," which used the results of an employee survey to measure how much fun employees had at work (and, by extension, how satisfied they were with their work, the company, and their managers).

Comparing Actual Performance Against Standards. In this stage of the feedback loop, the idea is to look for deviations *in either direction* from the performance standards the company has set for itself. In other words, opportunities to improve performance arise when there is a gap between "what should be" and "what is." The most serious deviations usually are those where actual performance falls far below the standard. Managers and employees must focus their efforts on figuring out why actual performance is substandard. The goal is not to hunt down the guilty party (or parties) for punishment, but to discover the cause of the subpar performance and fix it! Managers should not ignore deviations in the other direction, however. When actual performance consistently exceeds the company's standards, it is an indication that the standards are set too low. The company should look closely at "raising the bar another notch" to spur motivation.

Taking Action to Improve Performance. When managers or employees detect a performance gap, their next challenge is to decide on a course of action that will eliminate it. Typically, several suitable alternatives to solving a performance problem exist; the key is finding an acceptable solution that solves the problem quickly, efficiently, and effectively.

John Westrum, founder of Westrum Development Company, a home-building business, was concerned about his employees' ability to maintain quality standards in the face of rapid growth. He was afraid his company was losing sight of the four principles on which the business was founded: quality construction, customer satisfaction, on-time delivery, and cost control. Westrum and his 30 employees developed an 11-point plan designed to measure the company's performance on those principles. Workers then set specific, measurable objectives in each of the four areas, including scores on a 178-point checklist for construction quality. If the company met its objectives, employees would receive incentive pay and set new objectives. Westrum tracked performance on an Excel spreadsheet and posted graphs of the company's progress for all to see. "Employees started focusing not so much on the dollars but on the results," says Westrum. "The company's goal-driven incentives have worked. Employees are earning more, and the company's scores have improved dramatically. [The system] has boosted quality, financial controls, and customer satisfaction and has cultivated a team spirit that is second to none," says Westrum.[25]

Performance Appraisal. One of the most common methods of providing feedback on employee performance is through performance appraisal, the process of evaluating an employee's actual performance against desired performance standards. Most performance appraisal programs strive to accomplish three goals: (1) to give employees feedback about how they are doing their jobs, which can be an important source of motivation; (2) to provide a business owner and an employee the opportunity to create a plan for developing the employee's skills and abilities and for improving his performance; and (3) to establish a basis for determining promotions and salary increases. Although the primary purpose of performance appraisals is to encourage and to help employees improve their performances, too often they turn into uncomfortable confrontations that do nothing more than upset the employee, aggravate the business owner, and destroy trust and morale. Why? Because most business owners don't understand how to conduct an effective performance appraisal. Although American businesses have been conducting performance appraisals for about 75 years, most companies, their managers, and their employees are dissatisfied with the entire process. Common complaints include unclear standards and objectives; managers who lack information about employees' performances; managers who are unprepared or who lack honesty and sincerity; and managers who use general, ambiguous terms to describe employees' performances.[26]

Perhaps the biggest complaint concerning appraisals is that they happen only periodically: in most cases, just once a year. Employees do not have the opportunity to receive any ongoing feedback on a regular basis. All too often, a manager saves up all of the negative feedback to give an employee and then dumps it on him in the annual performance review. Not only does it destroy the employee's motivation, but it does *nothing* to improve the employee's performance. What good does it do to tell an employee that six months before, he botched an assignment that caused the company to lose a customer? Lack of ongoing feedback is like asking employees to bowl in the dark. They can hear some pins falling, but they have no idea which ones are left standing for the next frame. How motivated would you be to keep bowling? Managers should address problems when they occur rather than wait until the performance appraisal session. Continuous feedback, both positive and negative, is a much more effective way to improve employees' performances and to increase their motivation.

If done properly, performance appraisals can be effective ways to provide employee feedback and to improve workers' performances. However, it takes some planning and preparation on the business owner's part. The following guidelines can help a business owner create a performance appraisal system that actually works:

- *Link the employees performance criteria to the job description discussed earlier in this chapter.* To evaluate an employee's performance effectively, a manager must understand the job he is in very well.
- *Establish meaningful, job-related, observable, measurable, and fair performance criteria.* The criteria should describe behaviors and actions, not traits and characteristics. What kind of behavior constitutes a solid performance in this job?
- *Prepare for the appraisal session by outlining the key points you want to cover with the employee.* Important points to include are the employee's strengths and weaknesses and developing a plan for improving his performance.
- *Invite the employee to provide an evaluation of his own job performance based on the performance criteria.*
- *Be specific.* One of the most common complaints employees have about the appraisal process is that managers' comments are too general to be of any value. Offer employees specific examples of their desirable or undesirable behavior.
- *Keep a record of employees' critical incidents—both positive and negative.* The most productive evaluations are those based on a manager's direct observation of their employees' on-the-job performances. Such records also can be vital in case legal problems arise.
- *Discuss an employee's strengths and weaknesses.* An appraisal session is not the time to "unload" about everything an employee has done wrong over the past year. Use it as an opportunity to design a plan for improvement and to recognize employees' strengths, efforts, and achievements.

- *Incorporate employees' goals into the appraisal.* Ideally, the standard against which to measure an employee's performance is the goal he has played a role in setting. Workers are likely to be motivated to achieve goals that they have helped establish.
- *Keep the evaluation constructive.* Avoid the tendency to belittle employees. Do not dwell on past failures. Instead, point out specific things they should do better and help them develop meaningful goals for the future and a strategy for getting there.
- *Focus on behaviors, actions, and results.* Problems arise when managers move away from tangible results and actions and begin to critique employees' abilities and attitudes. Such criticism creates a negative tone for the appraisal session and undercuts its primary purpose.
- *Avoid surprises.* If a business owner is doing her job well, performance appraisals should contain no surprises for employees or the business owner. The ideal time to correct improper behavior or slumping performance is when it happens, not months later. Managers should provide employees with continuous feedback on their performances and use the appraisal session to keep employees on the right track.
- *Plan for the future.* Smart business owners use appraisal sessions as gateways to workers' future success. They spend only about 20 percent of the time discussing past performance; they use the remaining 80 percent of the time to develop goals, objectives, and a plan for the future.

Many companies are encouraging employees to evaluate each others' performance in **peer reviews** or to evaluate their boss's performance in **upward feedback,** both part of a technique called **360-degree feedback.** Peer appraisals can be especially useful because an employee's coworkers see his on-the-job performance every day. As a result, peer evaluations tend to be more accurate and more valid than those of some managers. Plus, they may capture behavior that managers might miss. Disadvantages of peer appraisals include potential retaliation against co-workers who criticize, the possibility that appraisals will be reduced to "popularity contests," and the refusal of some workers to offer any criticism because they feel uncomfortable evaluating others. Some bosses using upward feedback report similar problems, including personal attacks and extreme evaluations by vengeful subordinates.

CHAPTER SUMMARY

1. Explain the challenges involved in the entrepreneur's role as leader and what it takes to be a successful leader.
   - Leadership is the process of influencing and inspiring others to work to achieve a common goal and then giving them the power and the freedom to achieve it.
   - Management and leadership are not the same; yet both are essential to a small company's success. Leadership without management is unbridled; management without leadership is uninspired. Leadership gets a small business going; management keeps it going.

2. Describe the importance of hiring the right employees and how to avoid making hiring mistakes.
   - The decision to hire a new employee is an important one for every business, but its impact is magnified many times in a small company. Every "new hire" a business owner makes determines the heights to which the company can climb or the depths to which it will plunge.
   - To avoid making hiring mistakes, entrepreneurs should: develop meaningful job descriptions and job specifications; plan

and conduct an effective interview; and check references before hiring any employee.

3. Explain how to build the kind of company culture and structure to support the entrepreneur's mission and goals and to motivate employees to achieve them.
   - Company culture is the distinctive, unwritten code of conduct that governs the behavior, attitudes, relationships, and style of an organization. Culture arises from an entrepreneur's consistent and relentless pursuit of a set of core values that everyone in the company can believe in. Small companies' flexible structures can be a major competitive weapon.
   - Entrepreneurs rely on six different management styles to guide their companies as they grow. The first three (craftsman, classic, and coordinator) involve running a company without any management assistance and are best suited for small companies in the early stages of growth; the last three (entrepreneur-plus-employee team, small partnership, big-team venture) rely on a team approach to run the company as its growth speeds up.

4. Understand the potential barriers to effective communication and describe how to overcome them.
   - Research shows that managers spend about 80 percent of their time in some form of communication; yet their attempts at communicating sometimes go wrong. Several barriers to effective communication include: managers and employees don't always feel free to say what they really mean; ambiguity blocks real communication; information overload causes the message to get lost; selective listening interferes with the communication process; defense mechanisms block a message; and conflicting verbal and nonverbal messages confuse listeners.
   - To become more effective communicators, business owners should: clarify their messages before attempting to communicate them; use face-to-face communication whenever possible; be empathetic; match their messages to their audiences; be organized; encourage feedback; tell the truth; not be afraid to tell employees about the business, its performance, and the forces that affect it.

5. Discuss the ways in which entrepreneurs can motivate their workers to higher levels of performance.
   - Motivation is the degree of effort an employee exerts to accomplish a task; it shows up as excitement about work. Four important tools of motivation are empowerment, job design, rewards and compensation, and feedback.
   - Empowerment involves giving workers at every level of the organization the power, the freedom, and the responsibility to control their own work, to make decisions, and to take action to meet the company's objectives.
   - Job design techniques for enhancing employee motivation include job enlargement, job rotation, job enrichment, flextime, job sharing, and flexplace (which includes telecommuting and hoteling).
   - Money is an important motivator for many workers, but not the only one. The key to using rewards such as recognition and praise to motivate involves tailoring them to the needs and characteristics of the workers.
   - Giving employees timely, relevant feedback about their job performance through a performance appraisal system can also be a powerful motivator.

DISCUSSION QUESTIONS

1. What is leadership? What is the difference between leadership and management?
2. What behaviors do effective leaders exhibit?
3. Why is it so important for small companies to hire the right employees? What can small business owners do to avoid making hiring mistakes?
4. What is a job description? A job specification? What functions do they serve in the hiring process?
5. Outline the procedure for conducting an effective interview.
6. What is company culture? What role does it play in a small company's success? What

threats does rapid growth pose for a company's culture?

7. Explain the six different management styles entrepreneurs rely on to guide their companies as they grow (craftsman, classic, coordinator, entrepreneur-plus-employee team, small partnership, and big-team venture).

8. What mistakes do companies make when switching to team-based management? What can they do to avoid these mistakes? Explain the four phases teams typically go through.

9. What is empowerment? What benefits does it offer workers? The company? What must a small business manager do to make empowerment work in a company?

10. Explain the differences among job simplification, job enlargement, job rotation, and job enrichment. What impact do these different job designs have on workers?

11. Is money the "best" motivator? How do pay-for-performance compensation systems work? What other rewards are available to small business managers to use as motivators? How effective are they?

12. Suppose that a mail-order catalog company selling environmentally friendly products identifies its performance as a socially responsible company as a "critical number" in its success. Suggest some ways for the owner to measure this company's "social responsibility index."

13. What is performance appraisal? What are the most common mistakes managers make in performance appraisals? What should small business managers do to avoid making those mistakes?

STEP INTO THE REAL WORLD

1. One leadership development program demonstrates how leaders can overcome resistance within a work group by using the following exercise. Participants are organized into groups and are assigned to a table. At each table, one person is assigned to be the change agent, another to be a change supporter, and two others to be change resisters. On the table sits an unopened carton of buttermilk. The change agent must convince the other members of the group to taste the buttermilk. Only when the change agent opens the carton does the full challenge of the task become apparent. The buttermilk has been injected with a harmless, but *green* food coloring. Set up your own buttermilk experiment. How would you convince other members of your group to taste the green buttermilk? What does this experiment say about your leadership style?

2. Visit a local business that has experienced rapid growth in the past three years and ask the owner about the specific problems he or she had to face that were caused by the organization's growth. How did the owner handle these problems? Looking back, what would he or she do differently?

3. Contact a local small business with at least 20 employees. Does the company have job descriptions and job specifications? What process does the owner use to hire a new employee? What questions does the owner typically ask candidates in an interview?

4. Using a search engine such as InfoSeek, Yahoo!, or Excite, conduct a search on the various employment tests that are available to companies as screening devices. The American Psychological Association's Web site (*www.apa.org*) may be a good place to begin. Write a one-page summary of what you learn about employment tests.

5. Ask the owner of a small manufacturing operation to give you a tour of his or her operation. During your tour, observe the way jobs are organized. To what extent does the company use the following job design concepts: Job simplification? Job enlargement? Job rotation? Job enrichment? Flextime? Job sharing? On the basis of your observations, what recommendations would you make to the owner about the company's job design?

Take It to the Net

Visit the Scarborough/Zimmerer home page at **www.prenhall.com/scarborough** for updated information, online resources, Web-based exercises, and sample business plan.

Endnotes

1. Max DePree, *Leadership Jazz* (New York: Currency Doubleday, 1992), pp. 8–9.
2. Francis Huffman, "Taking the Lead," *Entrepreneur*, November 1993, p. 101.
3. Michael Barrier, "Hiring the Right People," *Nation's Business*, June 1996, pp. 18–27.
4. "Making the Most of Job Interviews," *Your Company*, Spring 1993, p. 6.
5. David K. Lindo, "Hiring Strategies," *Business Start-Ups*, November 1997, pp. 66–69; Greg Norred, "Weeding Out the Bad Apples," *Small Business Reports*, November 1993, pp. 58–61; Emma Fluker, "Checking Employee References," *Small Business Digest* (Premier Issue 1990), p. 7.
6. Peter Weaver, "Ignoring a Résumé Can Prove Costly," *Nation's Business*, September 1997, pp. 32–34.
7. James L. Bildner, "Hitting the Wall," *Inc.*, July 1995, pp. 21–22.
8. Ronald E. Merrill and Henry D. Sedgwick, "To Thine Own Self Be True," *Inc.*, August 1994, pp. 50–56.
9. Ibid., p. 56.
10. Mort Meyerson, "Everything I Know about Leadership Is Wrong," *Fast Company's Handbook of the Business Revolution*, 1997, p. 9.
11. "Message Methods for Managers," *Communication Briefings*, February 1997, p. 5.
12. Robert McGarvey, "Now Hear This," *Entrepreneur*, June 1996, p. 89.
13. E. Rogers and R. Agarwala Rogers, *Communication in Organizations* (New York: Free Press, 1976), p. 82.
14. Eugene Walton, "How Efficient Is the Grapevine?", *Personnel*, March–April 1961, pp. 45–49.
15. Janean Huber, "In the Loop," *Entrepreneur*, December 1994, p. 23.
16. Michael Barrier, "Beyond the Suggestion Box," *Nation's Business*, July 1995, pp. 34–37.
17. Theodore B. Kinni, "The Empowered Workforce," *Industry Week*, September 19, 1994, p. 37.
18. Robert McGarvey, "More Power to Them," *Entrepreneur*, February 1995, p. 73.
19. John Case, "The Open-Book Revolution," *Inc.*, June 1995, pp. 26–43.
20. Thomas Love, "Keeping the Business Going When an Executive Is Absent" *Nation's Business*, March 1998, p. 10.
21. Laura Koss-Feder, "Motivate Your Staff with a Flextime Plan," *Your Company* (Forecast 1997), pp. 64–65.
22. Melanie Warner, "Working at Home—The Right Way to Be a Star in Your Bunny Slippers," *Fortune*, March 3, 1997, pp. 165–166.
23. Harvey R. Meyer, "Linking Payday to Cash in Hand," *Nation's Business*, May 1996, pp. 36–35.
24. Jack Stack, "That Championship Season," *Inc.*, July 1996, p. 27.
25. Roberta Maynard, "Hammering Home Performance Incentives," *Nation's Business*, May 1996, p. 10; Donna Fenn, "Goal-Driven Incentives," *Inc.*, August 1996, p. 91.
26. Gina Imperato, "How to Give Good Feedback," *Success*, September 1998, pp. 144–156.

Chapter

Management Succession and Risk Management Strategies in the Family Business

*Success in a family business can be measured in two ways: How well
the business is doing and how well the family is doing.*

—JOHN MOLINA

*When it works right, nothing succeeds like a family firm. The roots run
deep, embedded in family values. The flash of the fast buck is replaced
with long-term plans. Tradition counts.*

—ERIC CALONIUS

Upon completion of this chapter, you will be able to:

1. Explain the factors necessary for a strong family business.
2. Understand the exit strategy options available to an entrepreneur.
3. Discuss the stages of management succession.
4. Explain how to develop an effective management succession plan.
5. Understand the four risk management strategies.
6. Discuss the basics of insurance for small businesses.

FAMILY BUSINESSES

1. Explain the factors necessary for a strong family business.

More than 80 percent of all companies in the United States are family owned. Yet, family-owned businesses are often overlooked by the media, who focus most of their attention on the larger firms in our economy. In reality, family businesses generate 50 percent of the U.S. gross domestic product, account for 60 percent of all employment and 78 percent of job creation, and pay 65 percent of all wages.[1] Not all family businesses are small, however; more than one third of the *Fortune* 500 companies are family businesses.

When a family business works right, it is a thing of beauty. Family members share deeply rooted values that guide the company and give it a sense of harmony. Family members understand and support one another as they work together to achieve the company's mission. That harmony can produce a significant financial payoff. A study by the Family Business Center at California State University at Northridge comparing the financial performances of similar sets of family and non-family businesses concluded that "firms controlled by the founding family have greater value, are operated more efficiently, and carry less debt than other firms."[2]

Family businesses also have a dark side, and it stems from their lack of continuity. Sibling rivalries, fights over control of the business, and personality conflicts often lead to nasty battles that can tear families apart and destroy once-thriving businesses. Family relationships can be difficult, and when mixed with business decisions and the wealth family businesses can create, the result can be explosive. Unfortunately, 80 percent of first-generation businesses fail to survive into the second generation, and of those that do, only 13 percent make it to the third generation.[3] The stumbling block is management succession. Just when they are ready to make the transition from one generation of leaders to the next, family businesses are most vulnerable. As a result, the average life expectancy of a family business is 25 years, although some last much longer (see Table 20.1).[4]

Table 20.1
The World's Oldest Family Businesses

William O'Hara, director of the Institute for Family Enterprise at Bryant College, has compiled a list of some of the world's oldest family businesses.

COMPANY	COUNTRY	NATURE OF BUSINESS	YEAR ESTABLISHED
Kongo Gumi	Japan	Temple construction	578
Hoshi Hotel	Japan	Hotel	718
Barovier & Toso	Italy	Artistic glassmaking	1295
Antinori	Italy	Wine	1385
Fabbrice D'Armi Beretta	Italy	Firearms production	1526
Akerblads	Sweden	Hotel	1539
John Brooke & Sons	Great Britain	Textiles	1541
Glasshutte	Germany	Glass making	1568
R. Durtnell & Sons	Great Britain	Building restoration	1591
Mellerio dits Meller	France	Jeweler	1613
Zildjian Cymbal	Turkey	Cymbal maker	1623
Tuttle Farm	United States	Farm and food store	1635
Hugel Corporation	France	Wine	1639

Source: Rachel Emma Silverman, "An 11-Generation Farm Seeks a 12th," *Wall Street Journal*, November 17, 1999, pp. B1, B4.

The best way to avoid deadly turf battles and conflicts is to develop a succession plan for the company. Although business founders inevitably want their businesses to survive them and almost 80 percent intend to pass them on to their children, they seldom support their intentions by a plan to accomplish that goal. About 54 percent of all family business owners do not have a formal management succession plan![5] Many entrepreneurs dream of their businesses continuing in the family but take no significant steps to make their dreams a reality.

David Bork, founder of the Aspen Family Business Conference, has identified several qualities that are essential to a successful family business: shared values, shared power, tradition, a willingness to learn, family behavior, and strong family ties.[6]

Shared Values. The first, and probably most overlooked, quality is a set of shared values. What family members value and believe about people, work, and money shapes their behavior toward the business. All members of a family business should talk openly to determine, in a nonjudgmental fashion, each one's values. Without shared values, it is difficult to create a future direction for a business.

Individual family members may share the values of the family but may be motivated to achieve personal goals that are different from those of their parents or siblings. In many cases this is an advantage when there are many children in the family. One or two of the children may elect to work in the business while the others select alternative careers.

To avoid the problems associated with conflicting values and goals, the family should consider taking the following actions:

- *Make it clear to every family member that they are not required to join the business on a full-time basis.* Family members' goals, ambitions, and talents should be foremost in their career decisions.
- *Do not assume that a successor must always come from within the family.* Simply being born into a family does not guarantee that a person will make a good business leader.
- *Give family members the opportunity to work outside the business first to learn firsthand how others conduct business.* Working for others will allow them to develop knowledge, confidence, and credibility before stepping back into the family business.

Shared Power. Shared power is not necessarily equal power. Rather, shared power is based on the simple idea that the skills and talents of each family member may run in different directions. Shared power is based on the idea that family members should allow those with the greatest expertise, ability, and knowledge in particular areas to handle decisions in those areas. Dividing responsibilities along the lines of expertise is an important way of acknowledging respect for each family member's talents and abilities. *For instance, when Thad Garner invented a concoction of red peppers and vinegar called Texas Pete Hot Sauce during the Great Depression, he and his brothers, Harold and Ralph, built a business, T. W. Garner Food Company, around the product. Each assumed responsibilities in a different area of the company based on his talents and interests. Thad (known as "Mr. Texas Pete") took over the sales and marketing side of the business, while Harold managed its financial and operational aspects, and Ralph handled production. Working together, the brothers built the company into a very successful business, selling millions of dollars' worth of Texas Pete a year.*[7]

Tradition. Tradition is necessary for a family business because it serves to bond family members and to link one generation of business leaders to the next. However, founders must hold tradition in check when it becomes a barrier to change. The key is to select those traditions that provide a solid foundation for positive behavior while taking care not to restrict the future growth of the business. "The companies that are successful change their strategy after each generation," says Joachim Schwass, a professor of family business at Switzerland's IMD business school. "Bringing in the new generation and saying, 'Son, do as I did,' will not work."[8]

A Willingness to Learn. A willingness to learn and grow is the hallmark of any successful firm, and it is essential to a family business. The family business that remains open to new ideas and techniques is likely to reduce its risk of obsolescence. The current generation of leadership must set the stage for new ideas involving the next generation in today's decisions. In many cases, a formalized family council serves as a mechanism through which family members can propose new ideas. Perhaps more important than a family council is fostering an environment in which family members trust one another enough to express their ideas, thoughts, and suggestions openly and honestly. Open discussion of the merits of new ideas is a tradition that has proved valuable for many family business's ability to sustain their competitive advantages.

Behaving Like Families. Families that play together operate family businesses that are more likely to stay together. Time spent together outside the business creates the foundation for the relationships family members have at work. Too often, life in a family business can degenerate into nothing but day after day of work and discussions of work at home. In some cases, work is the only way some parents interact with their children. But when a family adds activities outside the scope of the business, new relationships develop in a different arena. A family should not force members to "play together," but instead should create an environment that welcomes every member into fun family activities. Planned activities should be broad enough in scope to involve all family members. In time, trust, respect, openness, and togetherness will lead to behavior that communicates genuine caring and concern for the well-being of each family member, and that spills over into the working relationship as well.

Strong Family Ties. Strong family ties grow from one-on-one relationships. Shared time conveys the message that the family business is *more* than just a business; it is a group of people who care for one another working together for a common goal. The bond that a family business creates among relatives can be strong and enduring. "There's a love and a trust and a respect that can be very powerful when they are brought into a business environment," says Ross Nager, director of the Arthur Andersen Center for Family Business.[9]

The same emotions that hold family businesses together can also rip them apart if they run counter to the company's and the family's best interest. Emotions run deep in family businesses, and the press is filled with examples of once-successful companies that have been ruined by family feuds over who controls the company and how to run it. Conflict is a natural part of any business but can be especially powerful in family businesses because family relationships magnify the passions binding family members to the company. *Unfortunately, the successful business Thad Garner and his brothers built around Texas Pete Hot Sauce was not immune to a family battle. Problems began when the founding brothers handed the reins of the T. W. Garner Food Company over to the next generation of family managers. Thad Garner managed to hold the company and the family together until he developed Alzheimer's disease. Shortly afterwards, several family members who worked in the business staged a coup, firing the elderly Thad as president and removing his daughter Kathryn from the company as well. After Thad died, lawsuits erupted among family members over who was to control the company. Only when a court-appointed arbitrator handed down a decision did the battle finally end, but by that time, the rift had split the family for good.*[10]

Exit Strategies

2. Understand the exit strategy options available to an entrepreneur.

Most family business founders want their companies to stay within their families although in some cases, maintaining family control is not practical. Sometimes no one in the next generation of family members has an interest in managing the company or has the necessary skills and experience to handle the job. Under these circumstances, the founder must look outside the family for leadership if the company is to survive. Whatever the case, entrepreneurs must confront their mortality and plan for the future of their companies. Having a solid management succession plan in place well before retirement is near is absolutely critical to success. Entrepreneurs should examine their options once they decide it is time to step down from the businesses they have founded. Three options are available to entrepreneurs planning to retire: sell to outsiders, sell to (nonfamily) insiders, or pass the business on to the family members with the help of a management succession plan. We turn now to these three exit strategies.

Selling to Outsiders

As you learned in Chapter 5, selling a business to an outsider is no simple task. Done properly, it takes time, patience, and preparation to locate a suitable buyer, strike a deal, and make the transition. Advance preparation, maintaining accurate financial records, and timing are the keys to a successful sale. Too often, however, business owners, like some famous athletes, stay with the game too long until they and their businesses are well past their prime. They postpone selling until the last minute—when they reach retirement age or when they face a business crisis. Such a "fire sale" approach rarely yields the maximum value for a business.

A straight sale may be best for those entrepreneurs who want to step down and turn the reins of the company over to someone else. However, selling a business outright is not an attractive exit strategy for those who want to stay on with the company or for those who want to surrender control of the company gradually rather than all at once.

The financial terms of a sale also influence the selling price of the business and the number of potential bidders. Does the owner want "clean, cash-only, 100 percent at closing" offers, or is he willing to finance a portion of the sale? The 100 percent, cash-only requirement dramatically reduces the number of potential buyers. On the other hand, the owner can exit the business "free and clear" and does not incur the risk that the buyer may fail to operate the business in a profitable fashion and not be able to complete the financial transition.

Selling to Insiders

When entrepreneurs have no family members to whom they can transfer ownership or who want to assume the responsibilities of running a company, selling the business to employees is often the preferred option. In most situations, the options available to owners are: (1) sale for cash plus a note, (2) a leveraged buyout, and (3) an employee stock ownership plan (ESOP).

A Sale for Cash Plus a Note. Whether entrepreneurs sell their businesses to insiders, outsiders, or family members, they often finance a portion of the sales price. The buyer pays the seller a lump-sum amount of cash up front and the seller holds a promissory note for the remaining portion of the selling price, which the buyer pays off in installments. Because of its many creative financial options, this method of selling a business is popular with buyers. They can buy promising businesses without having to come up with the total purchase price all at one time. Sellers also appreciate the security and the tax implications of accepting payment over time. They receive a portion of the sale up front and have the assurance of receiving a steady stream of income in the future. Plus, they can stretch their tax liabilities from the capital gains on the sale over time rather than having to pay them in a single year. In many cases, sellers' risks are lower because they may even retain a seat on the board of directors to ensure that the new owners are keeping the business on track.

When Jim and Lorraine Hudson decided to retire from the successful auto dealership they had operated for 26 years, they decided to sell the business to their daughter Lynne and her husband Chad Millspaugh. The founding couple were confident in turning over the decision making to Lynne and Chad, but they needed help structuring the sale so that it would give them the retirement income they sought but would not put the new owners in a difficult financial position. Because the land on which the dealership sat had become so valuable, they separated it from the business. They sold the dealership to the Millspaughs for $2 million, accepting a down payment and financing the balance. The Hudsons kept the real estate and will receive lease payments from it, providing them with a healthy retirement income.[11]

Leveraged Buyouts. In a **leveraged buyout (LBO),** managers and/or employees borrow money from a financial institution and pay the owner the total agreed-upon price at closing; then they use the cash generated from the company's operations to pay off the debt. The drawback of this technique is that it creates a highly leveraged business. Because of the high levels of debt they take on, the new management has very little room for error. Too many management mistakes or a slowing economy has led many highly leveraged businesses into bankruptcy.

If properly structured, LBOs can be attractive to both buyers and sellers. Because they get their money up front, sellers do not incur the risk of loss if the buyers cannot keep the business operating successfully. The managers and employees who buy the company have a strong incentive to make sure the business succeeds because they own a piece of the action and some of their capital is at risk in the business. The result can be a highly motivated workforce that works hard and makes sure that the company operates efficiently. *In one of the most successful LBOs in recent years, Jack Stack and a team of managers and employees purchased an ailing subsidiary of International Harvester. The new company, Springfield Remanufacturing Corporation (SRC), which specializes in engine remanufacturing for the automotive, trucking, agricultural, and construction industries, began with a debt-to-equity ratio that was astronomically high, but the team of motivated managers and employees turned the company around. Today, SRC has more than 1,000 employees and $140 million in sales.*[12]

Employee Stock Ownership Plans. Unlike LBOs, **employee stock ownership plans (ESOPs)** allow employees and/or managers (i.e., the future owners) to purchase the business gradually, which frees up enough cash to finance the venture's future growth. With an ESOP, employees contribute a portion of their earnings over time toward purchasing shares of the company's stock from the founder until they own the company outright. (Although in leveraged ESOPs, the ESOP borrows the money to buy the owner's stock up front. Then, using employees' contributions, the ESOP repays the loan over time. It is a long-term exit strategy that benefits everyone

Over the past decade, the France family's business has become one of the most popular and most successful businesses in the United States. The Frances are the owners of NASCAR, the National Association for Stock Car Auto Racing, which is the centerpiece of one of the hottest sports in the nation. Founded in 1947 by Bill France, Sr., NASCAR had humble beginnings. France, who owned a gas station in Daytona Beach, Florida, began promoting dirt-track car races on the side to indulge his passion for the sport. He tapped into America's postwar love affair with the automobile and fascination with speed, putting American-made cars on the track and letting the drivers determine which one was fastest. Recognizing the need to organize the sport, France launched NASCAR and held the first NASCAR-sanctioned race on the beach/road course in Daytona Beach in February 1948. The fledgling business truly was a family operation in the early days. France organized the races and recruited drivers while his young sons distributed posters promoting events. His wife, Anne, sold tickets and handled the money. After each race, the Frances would tally the day's profits and soon were amazed at how lucrative racing could be.

In 1972, Bill, Sr. handed the reins of NASCAR over to his son, Bill, Jr., who managed the family business for the next 28 years, guiding it to new heights. NASCAR recently closed a television deal worth nearly $2.8 billion, and despite having the highest average ticket prices of any sport ($80), consistently sells out each race. NASCAR's Winston Cup races average more than 135,000 fans, and television ratings are climbing rapidly, unlike those of other professional sports, which are declining. Television ratings, of course, attract advertisers, and sponsors pay as much as $15 million to racing teams to get their names and logos emblazoned on a stock car. Sales of NASCAR-related products now exceed $1 billion a year.

In addition to the revenue the France family receives as the owners of NASCAR is money that comes in from their position as majority owners of International Speedway Corporation (ISC), a publicly held company that owns 13 racetracks around the country and hosts nearly half of the races on the NASCAR circuit. NASCAR and ISC have proved to be extremely lucrative for the France family. Although they reveal little about their finances, *Forbes* magazine lists Bill France, now in his 70s, and his brother Jim,

NASCAR's executive vice-president and secretary, as billionaires on their list of the world's wealthiest people. Bill's son, Brian, is senior vice-president of marketing and communications for NASCAR.

For the first time in its history, NASCAR has a president whose last name is not France. Although he named an outsider, Mike Helton, as president of NASCAR in 2000, Bill France still calls the shots in the business. He remains chairman of the board of directors, and the France family holds four of the five seats on the company's board, remaining firmly in control of the fastest-growing spectator sport in the nation.

1. In what ways is NASCAR a typical family business? In what ways is it unique?

2. Explain the qualities that are necessary for a successful family business.

3. What advice would you offer the France family about keeping their family business in the family?

Sources: Adapted from Liz Clarke and Thomas Heath, "NASCAR's Owner Does It His Way," *Greenville News*, July 8, 2001, pp. 1G, 4G; "History of NASCAR," *Chatham Journal*, July 2000, *www.chathamjournal.com/700nascarhistory.html*; Mike Harris, "NASCAR's France Resigns," *Witchita Eagle*, November 29, 2000, *web.wichitaeagle.com/content/wichitaeagle/2000/11/29/racing/nascar1128_txt.htm*.

---

involved. The owner sells the business to the people he can trust the most—his managers and employees. The managers and employees buy a business they already know how to run successfully. Plus, because they own the company, the managers and employees have a huge incentive to see that it operates effectively and efficiently.

The third exit strategy available to company founders is transferring ownership to the next generation of family members with the help of a comprehensive management succession plan.

MANAGEMENT SUCCESSION

3. Discuss the stages of management succession.

Experts estimate that between 2001 and 2017, $12 trillion in wealth will be transferred from one generation to the next, representing the greatest transfer of wealth ever and much of it funneled through family businesses.[13] Most of the family businesses in existence today were started after World War II, and their founders, many of whom are now in their 70s and 80s, are ready to pass the torch of leadership on to the next generation. For a smooth transition from one generation to the next, these companies need a succession plan. Without a succession plan, family businesses face an increased risk of faltering or failing in the next generation. Those businesses with the greatest probability of surviving are the ones whose owners prepare a succession plan well before it is time to "pass the torch of leadership" to the next generation. Succession planning also allows business owners to minimize the impact of taxes on their businesses, their estates, and their successors' wealth as well. With tax rates on gifts and estates as high as 55 percent, a plan that reduces the bite taxes take out of a business transfer is no small matter.

Why, then, do so many entrepreneurs postpone succession planning until it is too late? One barrier to succession planning is that, in planning the future of the business, owners are forced to accept the painful reality of their own mortality. Also, many business founders hesitate to let go of their businesses because their personal identities are so wrapped up in their companies. Over time, the founder's identity becomes so intertwined in the business that, in the entrepreneur's mind, there is no distinction between the two. Plus, turning over the reins of a business they have sacrificed for, fretted over, and dedicated themselves to for so many years is extremely difficult to do—even if the successor is a son or daughter! Paul Snodgrass, son of the founder of Pella Products, a maker of apparel for work and outdoor activities, who accepted leadership of the company from his father, explains, "Dad loves you and wants you to take over the business, but he also put heart and soul into that business, and he's not going to let anybody screw it up—not even you."[14] Finally, many family business founders believe that controlling the business also gives them a degree of control over family members and family behavior.

David Molina started Molina Health Care, a hospital and insurance company, in 1980 with just $5,000. Although the company grew to be a huge success with hundreds of millions of dollars in sales, Molina never got around to preparing a succession plan for the business. When he died in 1996, the family business faced a serious challenge. "Dad had not expressed what he wanted to happen to the company should he not be here," says son John, one of five children who worked for the family business. Ultimately, the board of directors selected Molina's oldest son, Mario, to assume the helm. The family rallied around Mario to maintain the company's success and have created a family council that has put in place a succession plan for the next generation of ownership.[15]

Planning for management succession protects not only the founder's, successor's, and company's financial resources, but it also preserves what matters most in a successful business: its heritage and tradition. "Real succession planning involves developing a strategy for transferring the trust, respect, and goodwill built by one generation to the next," explains Andy Bluestone, who took over as president of the financial services company his father founded.[16] Management succession planning requires, first, an attitude of trusting others. It recognizes that other family members have a stake in the future of the business and want to participate in planning its future. Planning is an attitude that shows that decisions made with open discussion are more constructive than those without family input. Second, management succession as an evolutionary process must reconcile an entrepreneur's inevitable anguish and even pain with her successors' desire for autonomy. Owners' emotional ties to their businesses usually are stronger than their financial ties. On the other side are the successors, who desire or even crave the autonomy to run the business their way. These inherent conflicts can—and often do—result in skirmishes.

Succession planning reduces the tension and stress created by these conflicts by gradually "changing the guard." A well-developed succession plan is like the smooth, graceful exchange of a baton between runners in a relay race. The new runner still has maximum energy; the concluding runner has already spent her energy by running at maximum speed. The athletes never come to a stop to exchange the baton; instead, the handoff takes place on the move. The race is a skillful blend of the talents of all team members—an exchange of leadership is so smooth and powerful that the business never falters, but accelerates, fueled by a new source of energy at each leg of the race.

Management succession involves a lengthy series of interconnected stages that begin very early in the life of the owner's children and extend to the point of final ownership transition (see Figure 20.1). If management succession is to be effective, it is necessary for the process to begin early in the successor's life (stage I). For instance, the owner of a catering business recalls putting his son to work in the family-owned company at age 7. On weekends, the boy would arrive at dawn to baste turkeys and was paid in his favorite medium of exchange—doughnuts![17] In most cases, family business owners involve their children in their businesses while they are still in junior high or high school. In this phase, the tasks are routine, but the child is learning the basics of how the business operates. Young adults begin to appreciate the role the business plays in the life of the family. They learn firsthand about the values and responsibilities of running the company.

Figure 20.1
Stages in Management Succession

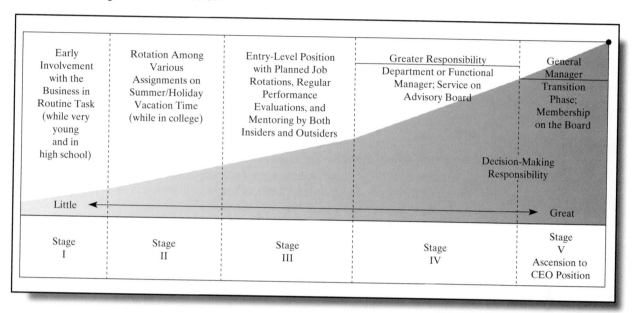

While in college, the successor moves to stage II of the continuum. During this stage, the individual rotates among a variety of job functions to both broaden his base of understanding of the business and to permit the parents to evaluate his skills. Upon graduation from college, the successor enters stage III. At this point, the successor becomes a full-time worker and ideally has already begun to earn the respect of co-workers through his or her behavior in the first two stages of the process. Stage III focuses on the successor's continuous development, often through a program designed to groom the successor using both family and nonfamily managers as mentors. In some cases, the successor may work for a time outside of the family business to gain experience and to establish a reputation for competency that goes beyond "being the boss's kid." *For example, after graduating from college, David Katz went to work in his father Arnold's photography studio, and quickly discovered that was a mistake. David quit and went to work for a competitor, serving his apprenticeship in the business there. When he did return to his father's company, David used his knowledge of digital photography (which his father had shied away from) to take the business in a new direction and to open the many opportunities the technology offered. Arnold was wise enough and confident enough to allow his son the freedom to make the move, which has paid off handsomely in increased sales and profits and lower costs.*[18]

As the successor develops his skills and abilities, he moves to stage IV, in which real decision-making authority grows rapidly. Stage IV of the succession continuum is the period when the founder makes a final assessment of the individual's abilities to take full and complete control over the firm. The skills the successor will need include:

- *Financial abilities.* Understanding the financial aspect of a business, what its financial position is, and the managerial implications of that position are crucial to success.
- *Technical knowledge.* Every business has its own body of knowledge, from how the distribution system works to the trends shaping the industry, that an executive must master.

- *Negotiating ability.* Much of business, whether buying supplies and inventory or selling to customers, boils down to negotiating, and a business owner must be adept at it.
- *Leadership qualities.* Leaders must be bold enough to stake out their company's future and then give employees the resources, the power, and the freedom to pursue it.
- *Communication skills.* Business leaders must communicate the vision they have for their businesses; good listening skills also are essential for success as a top manager.
- *Juggling skills.* Business owners must be able to handle multiple projects effectively. Like a juggler, they must maintain control over several important assignments simultaneously.
- *Commitment to the business.* It helps if a successor has a genuine passion for the business. Leaders who have enthusiasm for what they do create a spark of excitement throughout the entire organization.[19]

The final stage in the management succession process involves the ultimate transition of organizational leadership. It is during this stage that the founder's role as mentor is most crucial. *When Debbie Bailey joined Delta Dallas Staffing, the staffing and temporary services company her mother founded, she was concerned that working for the family business might damage their mother–daughter relationship. It didn't happen. The move worked out well for mother, daughter, and the company, which under Debbie's guidance has diversified and has grown to sales of more than $11.5 million a year. "The biggest advantage of taking over a family business," says Debbie, "is that you have a built-in mentor."*[20]

In stage IV, the successor may become the organization's CEO while the former CEO retains the title of chairman of the board. In other cases, the best solution is for the founder to step out of the business entirely and give the successor the chance to establish his own identity within the company. "Any leader's final legacy is building the next generation," says one business consultant.[21]

DEVELOPING A MANAGEMENT SUCCESSION PLAN

4. Explain how to develop an effective management succession plan.

Families that are most committed to ensuring that their businesses survive from one generation to the next exhibit four characteristics:

1. They believe that owning the business helps achieve their families' missions.
2. They are proud of the values their businesses are built on and exemplify.
3. They believe that the business is contributing to society and makes it a better place to live.
4. They rely on management succession plans to assure the continuity of their companies.[22]

Developing a plan takes time and dedication, yet the benefits are well worth the cost. It is important to start the planning process early, well before the founder's retirement. Succession planning is not the kind of activity an entrepreneur can do in a hurry, and the sooner an entrepreneur starts, the easier it will be. Unfortunately, too many entrepreneurs put it off until it's too late. "Succession works best when parents have enough fortitude to discuss everything with their kids and resolve these issues while they're still alive," says one expert.[23] Creating a succession plan involves the following steps:

Step 1: Select the Successor

The average tenure of the founder of a family business has remained constant at 25 years for the past decade.[24] Yet, there comes a time for even the most dedicated founder to step down and hand the reins of the company to the next generation. Entrepreneurs should never assume that their children want to take control of the business, however. Above all, they should not be afraid to ask the question: "Do you really want to take over the family business?" Too often, children in this situation tell Mom and Dad what they want to hear out of loyalty, pressure, or guilty feelings. It is critical to remember at this juncture in the life of a business that children do not necessarily inherit their parents' entrepreneurial skills and desires. By leveling with the children about the business and their options regarding a family succession, the owner will know which heirs, if any, are willing to assume leadership of the business.

One of the worst mistakes entrepreneurs can make is to postpone naming a successor until just before they are ready to step down. One study by Arthur Andersen and MassMutual found that nearly one third of family business owners age 61 or older have not yet designated a successor![25] The problem is especially acute when more than one family member works for the company and is interested in assuming leadership of it. Sometimes founders avoid naming successors because they don't want to hurt the family members who are not chosen to succeed them. However, both the business and the family will be better off if, after observing family members as they work in the business, the founder picks a successor based on skill and ability. When naming a successor, merit is a better standard to use than birth order. The key is to establish standards of performance, knowledge, education, and ability and then to identify the person who best meets those standards. As part of his company's succession plan, Joe De La Torre selected his daughter Gina to take over Juanita's Foods rather than his two sons because her financial skills and her ability to solve problems were what the company needed most.[26]

When considering a successor, an entrepreneur should consider taking the following actions:

- Make it clear to all involved that they are not required to join the business on a full-time basis. Family members' goals, ambitions, and talents should be foremost in their career decisions.
- Do not assume that a successor must always come from within the family. Simply being born into a family does *not* guarantee that a person will make a good business leader.
- Give family members the opportunity to work outside the business first to learn firsthand how others conduct business. Working for others will allow them to develop knowledge, confidence, and credibility before stepping back into the family business.
- Involve siblings in the process of identifying the successor. This can alleviate some of the hard feelings that might otherwise surface among those not chosen.

Step 2: Create a Survival Kit for the Successor

Once he or she identifies a successor, the entrepreneur should prepare a survival kit and then brief the future leader on its contents, which should include all of the company's critical documents (wills, trusts, insurance policies, financial statements, bank accounts, key contracts, corporate bylaws, etc.). The founder should be sure that the successor reads and understands all the relevant documents in the kit. Other important steps the owner should take to prepare the successor to take over leadership of the business include:

- Create a strategic analysis for the future. Working with the successor, entrepreneurs should identify the primary opportunities and the challenges facing the company and the requirements for meeting them.
- On a regular basis, share with the successor their vision of the business's future direction, describing key factors that have led to its success and those that will bring future success.
- Be open and listen to the successor's views and concerns.
- Teach and learn at the same time.
- Identify the industry's key success factors.
- Tie the key success factors to the company's performance and profitability.
- Explain the company's overall strategy and how it creates a competitive advantage.
- Discuss the values and philosophy of the business and how they have inspired and influenced past actions.
- Discuss the people in the business and their strengths and weaknesses.
- Discuss the philosophy underlying the firm's compensation policy and explain why employees are paid what they are.
- Make a list of the firm's most important customers and its key suppliers or vendors and review the history of all dealings with the parties on both lists.
- Discuss how to treat these key players to ensure the company's continued success and its smooth and error-free ownership transition.
- Develop a job analysis by taking an inventory of the activities involved in leading the company. This analysis can show successors those activities on which they should be spending most of their time.
- Document as much process knowledge—"how we do things"—as possible. After many years in their jobs, business owners are not even aware of their vast reservoirs of knowledge. For them, making decisions is a natural part of their business lives. They do it effortlessly because they have so much knowledge and experience. It is easy to forget that a successor will not have the benefit of those years of experience unless the founder communicates it.

Step 3: Groom the Successor

The process by which business founders transfer their knowledge to the next generation is gradual and often occurs informally as they spend time with their successors. Grooming the successor is the founder's greatest teaching and development responsibility, and it takes time, usually 5 to 10 years. To implement the succession plan, the founder must be:

- Patient, realizing that the transfer of power is gradual and evolutionary and that the successor should earn responsibility and authority one step at a time until the final transfer of power takes place
- Willing to accept that the successor will make mistakes
- Skillful at using the successor's mistakes as a teaching tool
- An effective communicator and an especially tolerant listener
- Capable of establishing reasonable expectations for the successor's performance
- Able to articulate the keys to successor's performance

Teaching is in reality the art of assisting discovery and requires letting go rather than controlling. When a problem arises in the business, the founder should consider delegating it to the successor-in-training. If so, he must resist the tendency to wade in and fix the problem unless it is beyond the scope of the successor's ability. Most great teachers and leaders are remembered more for the success of their students and followers than for their own.

Step 4: Promote an Environment of Trust and Respect

Another priceless gift a founder can leave a successor is an environment of trust and respect. Trust and respect on the part of the founder and others fuel the successor's desire to learn and excel and build the successor's confidence in making decisions. Empowering the successor by gradually delegating responsibilities creates an environment in which all parties can objectively view the growth and development of the successor. Customers, creditors, suppliers, and staff members can gradually develop confidence in the successor. The final transfer of power is not a dramatic, wrenching change but a smooth, coordinated passage.

A problem for some founders at this phase is the meddling retiree syndrome, in which they continue to show up at the office after they have officially stepped down and get involved in business issues that no longer concern them. This tendency merely undermines the authority of the successor and confuses employees as to who really is in charge. *Helen Dragas, who succeeded her father at The Dragas Company, a residential construction business, praises her father for handing the reins of the company over to her and then trusting her to handle them. "He gave me the authority and then he stepped back," she says of the successful transfer of leadership.*[27]

Step 5: Cope with the Financial Realities of Estate and Gift Taxes

The final step in developing a workable management succession plan structuring is the transition to minimize the impact of estate, gift, and inheritance taxes on family members and the business. Entrepreneurs who fail to consider the impact of these taxes may force their heirs to sell a successful business just to pay the estate's tax bill. Still, a survey by consulting firm Regeneration Partners found that 25 percent of senior-generation owners had done no estate planning at all![28] *Ella Perkins, co-owner of Perkins Flowers, and her son Gordon saw the need to develop an estate plan to minimize the impact of estate and gift taxes on the company, which Gordon was running. Each year, Ella gave Gordon $10,000 worth of stock in the company, the maximum amount the law allows without triggering gift taxes. She also transferred majority ownership in the company to Gordon using other estate planning tools so that estate taxes would be smaller on her minority share of the business. Gordon also purchased enough life insurance for his mother to pay the estimated estate tax bill. When Ella died at age 83, Gordon discovered that despite their attempts at estate planning, the amount of tax due was more than he had expected. "At the very least," he says, "it's going to repress the growth of my business for some significant amount of time." He says that he may have to sell a 43-acre tree farm the company owns to pay the full tax bill.*[29]

Although tax laws currently allow individuals to pass up to $1 million of assets to their heirs without incurring any estate taxes, the tax rate on transfers above that amount starts at 37 percent! The tax rate climbs to 55 percent for estates valued at more than $3 million. Although Congress has overhauled the estate and gift tax (see Table 20.2), without proper estate planning, an entrepreneur's family members will incur a painful tax bite when they inherit the business. Entrepreneurs should be actively engaged in estate planning no later than age 45; those who start businesses early in their lives or whose businesses grow rapidly may need to begin as early as

Table 20.2

Changes in the Estate and Gift Taxes

After years of complaints from family business owners, Congress finally overhauled the often punishing structures of estate and gift taxes. The federal estate tax is actually interwoven with the gift tax, but under the modified law, the impact of the two taxes will differ starting in 2004. The estate tax is scheduled to be repealed in 2010, but under current provisions, it will reappear in 2011! The following table shows the exemptions and the minimum tax rates for the estate and gift taxes as they currently stand:

YEAR	ESTATE TAX EXEMPTION	GIFT TAX EXEMPTION	MAXIMUM TAX RATE
2001	$675,000	$675,000	55%
2002	$1 million	$1 million	50%
2003	$1 million	$1 million	49%
2004	$1.5 million	$1 million	48%
2005	$1.5 million	$1 million	47%
2006	$2 million	$1 million	46%
2007	$2 million	$1 million	45%
2008	$2 million	$1 million	45%
2009	$3.5 million	$1 million	45%
2010	Tax repealed	$1 million	35% (gifts only)
2011	$1 million	$1 million	55%

Sources: "Need for Good Estate Plans Undiminished by New Law," *In the Vanguard,* Autumn 2001, p. 11; Lynn Asinof, "Changes in Estate Tax Could Bring About a Bad Heir Day," *Wall Street Journal,* August 30, 2001, pp. C1, C11.

age 30. A variety of options exist that may prove to be helpful in reducing the estate tax liability. Each operates in a different fashion, but their objective remains the same: to remove a portion of business owners' assets out of their estates so that when they die, those assets will not be subject to estate taxes. Many of these estate planning tools need time to work their magic, so the key is to put them in place early on in the life of the business.

Buy/Sell Agreement. One of the most popular estate planning techniques is the buy/sell agreement. One survey by the Chartered Life Underwriters and the Chartered Life Financial Consultants found that 76 percent of small business owners who have estate plans have created buy/sell agreements.[30] A **buy/sell agreement** is a contract that co-owners often rely on to ensure the continuity of a business. In a - typical arrangement, the co-owners create a contract stating that each agrees to buy the others out in case of the death or disability of one. That way, the heirs of the deceased or disabled owner can "cash out" of the business while leaving control of the business in the hands of the remaining owners. The buy/sell agreement specifies a formula for determining the value of the business at the time the agreement is to be executed. One problem with buy/sell agreements is that the remaining co-owners may not have the cash available to buy out the disabled or deceased owner. To resolve this issue, many businesses buy life and disability insurance for each of the owners in amounts large enough to cover the purchase price of their respective shares of the business.

Partners Ray Ellis, Scott Hopkins, and John Leimbach spent six months creating a buy/sell agreement to protect themselves and their business, Mailing Concepts Inc., a direct marketing agency, in the event of the death or disability of a partner. "When we got it done," says Leimbach, "we knew we had guaranteed the long-term survival of the company." The agreement is supported by two disability and two life insurance policies on each partner, giv-

ing them the income security they need for their families and providing the remaining part-ners the financial resources to buy the shares of the missing partner.[31] Without the support of adequate insurance policies, a buy/sell agreement offers virtually no protection.

Lifetime Gifting. The owners of a successful business may transfer money to their children (or other recipients) from their estate throughout the parents' lives. Current federal tax regulations allow individuals to make gifts of $10,000 per year, per par-ent, per recipient, that are exempt from federal gift taxes. Each child would be required to pay income taxes on the $10,000 gift they receive, but the children are usually in lower tax brackets than those of the giver. For instance, husband-and-wife business owners could give $1.2 million worth of stock to their three children and their spouses over a period of 10 years without incurring any estate or gift taxes at all.

Setting Up a Trust. A **trust** is a contract between a grantor (the founder) and a trustee (generally a bank officer or an attorney) in which the grantor gives to the trustee legal title to assets (e.g., stock in the company), which the trustee agrees to hold for the beneficiaries (children). The beneficiaries can receive income from the trust, or they can receive the property in the trust, or both, at some specified time. Trusts can take a wide variety of forms, but two broad categories of trusts are avail-able: revocable trusts and irrevocable trusts. A **revocable trust** is one that the grantor can change or revoke during his lifetime. Under present tax laws, however, the only trust that provides a tax benefit is an **irrevocable trust,** in which the grantor cannot require the trustee to return the assets held in trust. The value of the grantor's estate is lowered because the assets in an irrevocable trust are excluded from the value of that estate. However, an irrevocable trust places severe restrictions on the grantor's control of the property placed in the trust. Business owners use several types of irrev-ocable trusts to lower their estate tax liabilities:

- *Bypass trust.* The most basic type of trust is the bypass trust, which allows a business owner to put $1,300,000 into trust naming his spouse as the beneficiary upon his death. The spouse receives the income from the trust throughout her life, but the principal in the trust goes to the couple's heirs free of estate taxes upon the spouse's death.
- *Irrevocable life insurance trust.* This type of trust allows a business owner to keep the proceeds of a life insurance policy out of his estate and away from estate taxes, freeing up that money to pay the taxes on the remainder of the estate. To get the tax benefit, business owners must be sure that the business or the trust (rather than themselves) owns the insurance policy. The disadvantage of an irrevocable life insurance trust is that if the owner dies within three years of establishing it, the insurance proceeds do become part of his estate and are sub-ject to estate taxes.
- *Irrevocable asset trust.* An irrevocable asset trust is similar to a life insurance trust except that it is designed to pass the assets in the parents' estate on to their chil-dren. The children do not have control of the assets while the parents are still living, but they do receive the income from those assets. Upon the parents' death, the assets in the trust go to the children without being subjected to the estate tax.
- *Grantor retained annuity trust (GRAT).* A GRAT is a special type of irrevocable trust and has become one of the most popular tools for entrepreneurs to transfer ownership of a business while maintaining control over it and minimizing estate taxes. Under a GRAT, an owner can put property in an irrevocable trust for a maximum of ten years. While the trust is in effect, the grantor (owner)

retains the voting power and receives the interest income from the property in the trust. At the end of the trust (not to exceed 10 years), the property passes to the beneficiaries (heirs). The beneficiaries are required to pay the gift tax on the value of the assets placed in the GRAT but no estate tax on them. However, the IRS taxes GRAT gifts only according to their discounted present value because the heirs did not receive use of the property while it was in trust. The primary disadvantage of using a GRAT in estate planning is that if the grantor dies during the life of the GRAT, its assets pass back into the grantor's estate. These assets then become subject to the full estate tax.

Establishing a trust requires meeting many specific legal requirements and is not something business owners should do on their own. It is much better to hire experienced attorneys, accountants, and financial advisors to assist in creating them. Although the cost of establishing a trust can be high, the tax savings they generate are well worth the expense.

Estate Freeze. An **estate freeze** attempts to minimize estate taxes by having family members create two classes of stock for the business: (1) preferred voting stock for the parents and (2) nonvoting common stock for the children. The value of the preferred stock is frozen while the common stock reflects the anticipated increased market value of the business. Any appreciation in the value of the business after the transfer is not subject to estate taxes. However, the parent must pay gift tax on the value of the common stock given to the children. The value of the common stock is the total value of the business less the value of the voting preferred stock retained by the parent. The parents also must accept taxable dividends at the market rate on the preferred stock they own.

Family Limited Partnership. Creating a **family limited partnership (FLP)** allows business-owning parents to transfer their company to their children (thus lowering their estate taxes) while still retaining control over it for themselves. To create a family limited partnership, the parents (or parent) sets up a partnership among themselves and their children. The parents retain the general partnership interest, which can be as low as 1 percent, and the children become the limited partners. As general partners, the parents control both the limited partnership and the family business. In other words, nothing in the way the company operates has to change. Over time, the parents can transfer company stock into the limited partnership, ultimately passing ownership of the company to their children. One of the principal tax benefits of an FLP is that it allows discounts on the value of the shares of company stock the parents transfer into the limited partnership. Because a family business is closely held, shares of ownership in it, especially minority shares, are not as marketable as those of a publicly held company. As a result, company shares transferred into the limited partnership are discounted at 20 to 50 percent of their full market value, producing a large tax savings for everyone involved. The average discount is 40 percent, but that amount varies based on the industry and the individual company involved. A business owner should consider an FLP as part of a succession plan "when there has been a buildup of substantial value in the business and the older generation has a substantial amount of liquidity," says one expert.[32] Because of their ability to reduce estate and gift taxes, family limited partnerships have become one of the most popular estate planning tools in recent years.

Developing a succession plan and preparing a successor requires a wide variety of knowledge and skills, some of which the business founder will not have. That's why it is important to bring experts into the process when necessary. Entrepreneurs often call on their attorneys, accountants, insurance agents, and financial planners to

IN THE FOOTSTEPS OF AN ENTREPRENEUR
A Vintage Business

Founded by brothers Ernest and Julio Gallo in 1933 in Modesto, California, E. & J. Gallo Winery has grown into the largest wine producer in the world with sales of more than $1.4 billion in 90 countries across the globe. To satisfy its thirst for the grapes from which it makes its wines, the company consumes 30 percent of California's annual wine grape harvest! Now selling more than 64 million cases of wine a year, the winery remains a privately owned and operated family business. Currently, the third generation of the Gallo family (they call themselves "G3s") is running the thriving winery. In all, 13 of the founders' 20 grandchildren, all raised among the vineyards, are climbing the ranks of the family business. "It's a very exciting time," says Ernest Gallo, 26, namesake of one of the co-founders. "The company is slowly undergoing a transition from an entrepreneurial to a professional company." Ernest Gallo, now in his 90s, has been transferring ownership in the company to both the second and third generations of Gallos through trusts and through gifts. (Co-founder Julio Gallo was killed in a truck accident in 1993.)

Much of the credit for the winery's recent success goes to good planning and the ability to select and train the most talented family members to manage the company. Julio's granddaughter, Gina, has taken on the challenge her grandfather gave her: to update the Gallo image. Although wine retailing for less than $4 a bottle accounts for 70 percent of Gallo's sales, Gina has made great strides in accomplishing her assignment. Under her guidance, Gallo has introduced successfully two top-label wines, Gallo Estate and Gallo of Sonoma County. Estate wines sell for $35 to $65 a bottle, and Sonoma County sells for slightly less. Both wines have won numerous awards at prestigious wine contests.

Running the company is truly a family affair. Gina is the principal winemaker ("She is the only other person in this organization who has my taste," brags Ernest) and appears in the company's ads. Her brother Matt heads operations in Sonoma and spends most of his time in the vineyards. Stephanie Gallo manages the Turning Leaf label, which sells wines in the $7 to $10 per bottle range. Theodore Coleman is an apprentice to Gina, and Caroline Coleman is in charge of marketing for the Sonoma brand and is the company spokesperson. Other G3s are in charge of Gallo bottling and printing operations.

(continued)

Photo by Daniel Bosler / Getty Images, Inc.

For now, the second generation of Gallos is in charge of the company, which sells one out of every four bottles of wine consumed in the United States. Three G2s share the responsibility of overseeing daily operations, as they have been doing for several years. Ernest Gallo still takes a role in steering the company, however. "Nonno," which his grandchildren call him (it means "grandfather" in Italian), is likely to stay involved in the company he founded as long as he lives. Caroline Coleman expresses the Gallo clan's relationship with the winery when she says, "My business is my family, and my family is my business."

1. What challenges does the Gallo family face in terms of management succession?

2. What steps should the Gallos take to ensure that control of their family business passes smoothly to the G3s?

3. Explain some of the tools the Gallos can use to minimize the impact of estate taxes on their family business.

Sources: Adapted from Ann Marsh, "Here's to the Kids," *Forbes*, December 13, 1999, pp. 168–174; Susan Caminit, "Mixing It Up," *FSB*, November 1999, pp. 20–21; E. & J. Gallo Winery, *www.gallo.com*.

help them build a succession plan that works best for their particular situations. Because the issues involved can be highly complex and charged with emotion, bringing in trusted advisors to help improves the quality of the process and provides an objective perspective. Table 20.3 provides an estate planning checklist for entrepreneurs.

RISK MANAGEMENT STRATEGIES

5. Understand the four risk management strategies.

Insurance is an important part of creating a management succession plan because it can help business owners minimize the taxes on the estates they pass on to their heirs and can provide much-needed cash to pay the taxes the estate does incur. However, insurance plays an important role in many other aspects of a successful business—from covering employee injuries to protecting against natural disasters that might shut a business down temporarily. When most small business owners think of risks such as these, they automatically think of insurance. However, insurance companies are the first to point out that insurance does not solve all risk problems. Instead, dealing with risk successfully requires a combination of four risk management strategies: avoiding, reducing, anticipating, and transferring (or spreading) risk.

Avoiding risk requires a business to take actions to shun risky situations. For example, you could substantially reduce the risk of an automobile accident if you sold your car, refused to ride with others, walked to work, and carefully looked both ways before crossing the street. Such actions would be possible, but not practical, because in our busy society people depend on transportation by car or bus. However, businesspeople can avoid risk by thoughtful business practices. For instance, conducting credit checks of customers can help decrease losses from bad debts. Wise managers know that they can avoid some risks simply by taking positive management actions. Workplace safety improves when business owners implement programs designed to make all employees aware of the hazards of their jobs and how to avoid being hurt. Business owners who have active risk identification and prevention programs can reduce their potential insurance costs as well as create a safer, more attractive work environment for their employees. Because avoiding risk altogether usually is not practical, however, a strategy of reducing risk becomes necessary.

Table 20.3
Estate Planning
Checklist

Would your estate be in order if you died unexpectedly? Would your family suffer because you hadn't planned? Would your estate be socked with high taxes? Would your business be able to continue? Answer these 10 questions to measure how well you have done your estate planning.

1. Do you have a will?
2. Has your will been updated within the past three years?
3. Do you know your net worth?
4. Do you know the value of your business?
5. Do you know who would acquire ownership of your business if you were to die tomorrow?
6. Do you know who would run your business if you were to die tomorrow?
7. Would your business be likely to survive under the ownership and leadership of the people named in questions 5 and 6?
8. Have you groomed your successor properly to take over the management of the business?
9. Have you cultivated a team of people to support your successor in running the business successfully?
10. Do you know how your estate would finance the applicable estate taxes if you were to die tomorrow?
11. Do you know how the new owner of your business would finance its purchase?
12. Has an attorney, an accountant, and other professionals who specialize in estate planning reviewed your estate plan?

Scoring:

Give yourself 10 points for every question you answered "yes." If your score is:

- Between 100 and 120—Your estate is in secure hands. You should talk with an estate-planning professional periodically to adjust your plan as your needs change.
- Between 70 and 90—Your estate is exposed to more risk than it should be. Your family is likely to incur unnecessary expenses and trouble with your estate. See an estate planning professional for advice soon.
- Between 0 and 80—Your estate is in imminent danger! You should call an estate planning professional immediately and develop a sound plan to make sure your business survives you.

Sources: Adapted from Carole Matthews, "Choosing a Successful Successor," *Inc.,* October 17, 2001, *www.inc.com/search/23550.html;* Randy Myers, "Where There's a Will . . ." *Nation's Business,* April 1997, p. 26.

A risk-reducing strategy takes actions that build an extra degree of safety into a situation with an identified level of risk. Businesses can reduce risk by following common safety practices, such as installing a sprinkler system to lower the threat of damage from fire. The sprinkler system cannot guarantee that a fire will not occur, but it may minimize the damage that results. Risk-reduction strategies do not eliminate the source of the risk, but they lessen the impact of its occurrence. Even with avoidance and reduction strategies, the source of the risk is still present; thus, losses can occur.

Risk anticipation strategies promote self-insurance. Knowing that some element of risk still exists, a business owner puts aside money each month to cover any losses that might occur. For example, suppose that a business owner checks each customer's credit very carefully. She takes all reasonable steps to ensure that the customer can pay the bill and has a sound history of prompt payment. Shortly after the sale, however, a fire completely destroys the customer's business, and the merchandise, unpaid for, also was destroyed. The business owner also discovers that the customer's business was not insured and that the loss will cause him to declare bankruptcy. She may have done all she could to determine that the customer's credit was solid, but that did not prevent the financial loss caused by the fire and subsequent bankruptcy. In this case, the owner's loss would be less devastating to the company if she had put aside cash periodically to cover such losses.

Sometimes, a self-insurance fund set aside may not be large enough to cover the losses from a particular situation. When this happens, the business or individual stands to lose despite the best efforts to anticipate risk, especially in the first few years when the fund may be insufficient to cover large losses. Most individuals and businesses therefore include in their risk strategies some form of insurance to transfer risk. *For instance, Jay Goltz, owner of Artists' Frame Service in Chicago, grew tired of watching the cost of health care coverage for his 125 employees climb every year and decided to establish a self-insurance fund to cover his employees' health care benefits. If employees' claims were low in a given year, he would save money over what he would have paid in insurance premiums. If several workers suffered catastrophic illnesses at once, however, his company could face a cash crisis. Recognizing that a self-insurance strategy alone could be risky, Goltz purchased a "stop-loss" policy, which takes over payment of all claims that exceed a certain level. In the 10 years he has been self-insuring, Goltz says the strategy has saved his company tens of thousands of dollars, despite two years of high claims. "Occasionally, you're going to get the $5,000 to $10,000 claim that you have to pay yourself," he says. "But your premiums are $2,000 to $3,000 a month less because you're self-insured."*[33]

Self-insurance is not for every business owner, however. For businesses with fewer than 50 employees, self-insurance is usually not a wise choice because there is so much variation in the number of annual claims. Also, companies using self-insurance should be financially secure with a relatively stable workforce and should see it as a long-term strategy for savings. Self-insuring also is more time consuming, requiring a business owner to take a more active role in managing the company's insurance needs. *James Meier, co-owner of Herzog-Meier, a Beaverton, Oregon, car dealership, discovered the disadvantages of being small and trying to self-insure. Major illnesses among several employees in two consecutive years drained the company's self-insurance fund, forcing the dealership to dig into other accounts to pay employees' claims. Even with its stop-loss coverage, the dealership spent $280,000 in just one year, an amount much higher than its health insurance premiums would have been with full insurance coverage. The company is now fully insured again, and its owners are much more comfortable with their limited exposure.*[34] Table 20.4 provides a self-test for entrepreneurs to determine whether or not self-insurance is the best option for their companies.

Risk transfer strategies depend on the use of insurance. Insurance is a risk transfer (or risk spreading) strategy because an individual or a business transfers some of the costs of a particular risk to an insurance company, which is set up to spread out the financial burdens of risk. During a specific time period, the insured business or individual pays money (a premium) to the insurance carrier (either a private company or a government agency). In return, the carrier promises to pay the insured a certain amount of money in the event of a loss.

THE BASICS OF INSURANCE

Insurance is the transfer of risk from one entity (an individual, a group, or a business) to an insurance company. Without insurance, many of the activities and services we take for granted would not be possible because the risk of overwhelming

Table 20.4

A Self-Test for Self-Insurers

The Self-Funding Academy, a professional association in Winston-Salem, North Carolina, offers the following test for companies considering self-insuring their health care benefits. If you can answer "yes" to all seven questions, then your company probably is ready to self-insure.

1. Do you have at least 50 employees among whom you can spread the risk of high claims, or do you have the assets to withstand some unpredictability year-to-year for claims? Are you financially able to withstand an occasional year when employee health care claims may be higher than anticipated?

2. Are your top managers comfortable leaving behind the month-to-month cost stability of a fully insured plan? Are they prepared to withstand more volatility under a self-funded plan?

3. Do you want to self-fund because you are committed to the idea of being in greater control of your company's benefits and their costs? Remember: The primary motivation for self-funding should not be to gain some minimal savings over the insurance premiums your company is paying currently.

4. Do you have partners such as insurance consultants or risk brokers you can trust to help you create and administer the plan?

5. Do you have access to reasonably priced stop-loss coverage to prevent serious cash flow problems in those years when employees' claims will exceed what you expect (and those years will occur)? Does that plan include specific coverage (claims from any one person's illness) as well as aggregate coverage (which protects the company in case all employees' claims exceed a particular amount)?

6. Are you aware of the many options your company has under a self-insurance plan? For instance, companies can pay claims as they come in or they can set aside money in a trust fund. Self-insured businesses can limit employees to a specific group of health care providers, or they can let them choose any provider.

7. Have you thought through any concerns that your employees have about self-funding? Are your employees comfortable with the idea?

Source: Laura M. Litvan, "Are You Ready to Self-Fund?" *Nation's Business*, March 1996, p. 21.

6. Discuss the basics of insurance for small businesses.

financial loss would be too great for a business to assume. Yet many small business owners ignore their companies' insurance needs. A survey by *Entrepreneur* magazine found that just 55 percent of business owners believed that they had adequate insurance coverage for essentials—property damage, fire, theft, and liability.[35] Home-based business owners are less well covered. According to the Independent Insurance Agents of America, only 40 percent of home-based business owners have adequate insurance coverage![36]

How can insurance companies assume so much risk? On the surface, it may seem that insurance companies are themselves in a risky situation. If a business pays $1,000 each year in premiums and has a claim of $150,000, it would not take long for insurance companies to go bankrupt. But what is actually operating here is the law of large numbers. A business owner's premiums of $1,000 per year for fire insurance are pooled with those of thousands of other business owners. Out of this pool, the insurance company pays out benefits to what it expects will be only a fraction of those paying premiums. Occasionally, insurance companies experience an unprecedented disaster that strains the entire insurance system. For instance, the terrorist attacks of September 11, 2001, cost insurance companies an estimated $60 billion, breaking the record of $20 billion set by Hurricane Andrew.[37] Even if in one year the benefits paid out occasionally are greater than the premiums paid in, the law of large numbers says that in the long run, the insurance company will have a surplus of premiums.

To be insurable, a situation or hazard must meet the following requirements:

1. It must be possible to calculate the actual loss being insured. For example, it would probably not be possible to insure an entire city against fire because too many variables are involved. It is possible, however, to insure a specific building.
2. It must be possible to select the risk being insured. No business owner can insure against every potential hazard, but insurance companies offer a wide variety of policies. One company even offers an alien abduction policy ($150 a year for $150 million of coverage) and has actually paid one claim! Another offers werewolf insurance, but the policy pays only if the insured turns into a werewolf.[38]
3. There must be enough potential policyholders to assume the risk. If you are a tightrope walker specializing in walking between tall downtown buildings, you probably cannot be insured because there are simply not enough people engaging in this activity to spread the risk sufficiently.

The risk management pyramid (see Figure 20.2) can help business owners decide how they should allocate their risk management dollars. Begin by identifying the

Figure 20.2
The Risk Management Pyramid
Source: Adapted from "Tote Up Potential Hazards in a Totem Pole," *Journal of Business Strategy,* April 1997, p. 12.

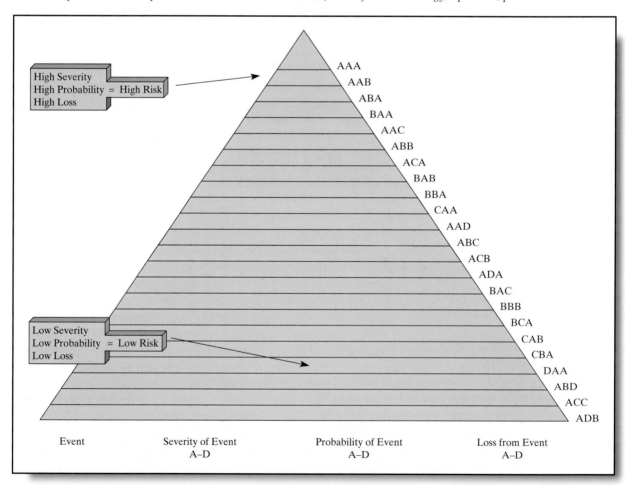

primary risks your company faces: for example, a fire in a manufacturing plant, a lawsuit from a customer injured by your company's product, an earthquake, and so on. Then rate each event on three factors:

1. *Severity.* How much would the event affect your company's ability to operate?
2. *Probability.* How likely is the event to occur?
3. *Cost.* How much would it cost your company if the event occurred?

Rate the event on each of these three factors using a simple scale: A (high) to D (low). For instance, a small company might rate a fire in its manufacturing plant as ABA. On the other hand, that same company might rank a computer system crash as CBA. Using the risk management pyramid, the business owner sees that the event rated ABA is higher on the risk scale than the event rated CBA. Therefore, this company would focus more of its risk management dollars on preventing a fire in its plant than on dealing with a computer system crash.

Types of Insurance

No longer is cost of insurance a small and inconsequential part of doing business. Now the ability to get adequate coverage and to pay the premiums is a significant factor in starting and running a small business. Sometimes, just finding coverage for their businesses is a challenge for entrepreneurs. *When J. Linwood Paul and Leslie Bourne launched Fulcrum Learning Systems Inc. in Redondo Beach, California, they had an extremely difficult time finding a company willing to sell them liability insurance because of the risk involved in their business. Fulcrum Learning Systems is an adventure training company that provides customers with training experiences that magnify real-life situations, such as navigating a high-ropes course or scaling a vertical rock cliff. Unfortunately, that makes the company an extremely high insurance risk. "Without insurance, there is no business," says Bourne. The entrepreneurs finally found a company willing to insure them, but for the first six years of business, Fulcrum had six different insurance companies. Although Fulcrum had a perfect safety record for its 80,000 clients and had made no claims, each insurance company decided to get out of the adventure training industry. Finally, the entrepreneurs were able to secure a policy from a more stable insurance company, and their business continues to boom.*[39]

A wide range of business, individual, and group insurance is available to small business owners, and deciding which ones are necessary can be difficult. Some types of insurance are essential to providing a secure future for the company; others may provide additional employee benefits. The four major categories of insurance are property and casualty insurance, life and disability insurance, health insurance and workers' compensation coverage, and liability insurance. Each category is divided into many specific types, each of which has many variations offered by insurance companies. Business owners should begin by purchasing a basic **business owner's policy (BOP),** which typically includes basic property and casualty insurance and liability insurance coverage. BOPs alone are not sufficient to meet most small business owners' insurance needs, however. Entrepreneurs should start with BOPs and then customize their insurance coverage to suit their companies' special needs by purchasing additional types of coverage.

Property and Casualty Insurance. Property and casualty insurance covers a company's tangible assets, such as buildings, equipment, inventory, machinery, signs, and others that might be damaged, destroyed, or stolen. Business owners should be sure that their policies cover the replacement cost of their property, not just its value at the time of the loss, even if it costs extra. One business owner whose policy covered the replacement cost of his company's building was glad he had purchased the extra coverage when he suffered a devastating fire loss. When he began rebuilding, he discovered that the cost to comply with current building code regulations was $1 million, much higher than merely replacing the previous structure. "Without this extra coverage, he never would have made it," says his insurance agent.[40]

Specific types of property and casualty insurance include property, surety, marine and inland marine, crime, liability, business interruption, motor vehicle, and professional liability insurance.

Property insurance protects a company's assets against loss from damage, theft, or destruction. It applies to automobiles, boats, homes, office buildings, stores, factories, and other items of property. Some property insurance policies are broadly written to include all of an individual's property up to some maximum amount of loss, whereas other policies are written to cover only one building or one specific piece of property, such as a company car. Many natural disasters such as floods and earthquakes are not covered under standard property insurance; business owners must buy separate insurance policies for those specific causes of loss. Within the past decade, business owners across the United States have suffered billions of dollars in losses from natural disasters, including floods in the Midwest, hurricanes on the East Coast, and earthquakes in California. Many of those businesses without proper insurance coverage were forced to close, and others are still struggling to recover.

A company's BOP may insure the buildings and contents of a factory for loss from fire or natural disaster, but the owner may also buy insurance, called extra expense coverage, to cover expenses that occur while the destroyed factory is being rebuilt. **Extra expense coverage** pays for the costs of temporarily relocating workers and machinery so that a business can continue to operate while it rebuilds or repairs its factory. A similar type of insurance, called **business interruption insurance,** covers business owners' lost income and ongoing expenses in case their companies cannot operate for an extended period of time. As devastating as such interruptions can be to a small company, studies show that nearly half of all business owners do not purchase business interruption coverage. Yet 40 percent of businesses whose operations are interrupted because of a disaster never recover.[41] *Dottie Bourgeois was glad she had purchased business interruption insurance for her small clothing and gift shop, Pierre Crawdeaux Company, Inc. When a runaway freighter slammed into the Riverwalk Mall in New Orleans where her store was located, the damage forced her company to close for six weeks. Because she had adequate property and business interruption insurance, Bourgeois was able to recover all of the losses her company sustained.*[42]

Machinery and equipment insurance is a common addition for many businesses and covers a wide range of problems with equipment such as production machinery; electrical systems; heating, ventilating, and air conditioning (HVAC) systems; and others. For instance, a restaurant that loses thousands of dollars' worth of food when a freezer breaks would be covered for its loss under machinery and equipment insurance.

Electronic data processing (EDP) insurance covers losses from the theft or loss of computers and data, the impact of computer viruses and computer system failures, intrusion by hackers, and problems with the privacy of customer information stored in databases. EDP insurance has become more important as businesses have moved their operations online and engage in increasing volumes of e-commerce. *Thomas Shipley, whose company sells business accessories, generates 30 percent of his sales from the company's Web site. Shipley recently purchased an EDP policy that protects his business from, among other things, hackers and viruses. The policy costs $14,000 a year, but Shipley says it is well worth the price to protect his company that now brings in more than $10 million in sales a year.*[43]

A business may also purchase **surety insurance,** which protects against losses to customers that occur when the company fails to complete a contract on time or completes it incorrectly. Surety protection guarantees customers that they will get either the products or services they purchased or the money to cover losses from contractual failures.

Businesses also buy insurance to protect themselves from losses that occur when either finished goods or raw materials are lost or destroyed while being shipped. **Marine insurance** is designed to cover the risk associated with goods in transit. The name of this insurance goes back to the days when a ship's cargo was insured against high risks associated with ocean navigation. Today, business owners can purchase marine insurance to cover property in transit and property still under their care.

Crime insurance does not deter crime, but it can reimburse the small business owner for losses from the three Ds: dishonesty, disappearance, and destruction. Business owners should ask their insurance brokers or agents exactly what their crime insurance policies do and do not cover; after-the-fact insurance coverage surprises are seldom pleasant. Premiums for such policies vary depending on the type of business, store location, number of employees, maximum cash value, quality of the business's security system, and the business's history of losses. Specific coverage may include fidelity bonds, which are designed to reimburse the business owner for losses due to embezzlement and employee theft. Forgery bonds reimburse the business owner for any loss sustained from the forgery of business checks.

Life and Disability Insurance. Unlike most forms of insurance, life insurance does not pertain to avoiding risk because death is a certainty for everyone. Rather, **life insurance** protects families and businesses against loss of income, security, or personal services that results from an individual's untimely death. Life insurance policies are usually issued in a face amount payable to a beneficiary upon the death of the insured. Life insurance for business protection, though not as common as life insurance for family protection, is becoming more popular. Many businesses insure the lives of key executives to offset the costs of having to make a hurried and often unplanned replacement of important managerial personnel.

When it comes to assets that are expensive to replace, few are more costly than the key people in a business, including the owner. What would it take to replace a company's top sales representative? Its production supervisor? Clearly, money alone would not be the answer, but it would provide the business with the funds necessary to find and train their replacements and to cover the profits lost because of their untimely deaths or disabilities. That's what key-person insurance does. It provides valuable working capital to keep a business on track while it reorganizes and searches for the right person to replace the loss of someone in a key position in the company.

Pensions and annuities are special forms of life insurance policies that combine insurance with a form of saving. With an annuity or pension plan, the insured person's premiums go partly to provide standard insurance coverage and partly to a fund that is invested by the insurance company. The interest from the invested portion of the policy is then used to pay an income to the policyholder when she reaches a certain age. If the policyholder dies before reaching that age, either the policy converts to income for the spouse or family of the insured or the insurance proceeds (plus interest) go to the beneficiary as they would in ordinary life insurance.

Disability insurance, like life insurance, protects an individual in the event of unexpected and often very expensive disabilities. Because a sudden disability limits a person's ability to earn a living, the insurance proceeds are designed to help make up for the loss of what that person could have expected to earn if the accident had not occurred. Sometimes called income insurance, these policies usually guarantee a stated percentage of an individual's income—usually around 60 percent—while he or she is recovering and is unable to run a business. Short-term disability policies cover the 90-day gap between the time a person is injured and when workers' compensation payments begin. Long-term disability policies pay for lost income after 90 days or longer. In addition to the portion of income a policy will replace, another important factor to consider when purchasing disability insurance is the waiting period, the time gap between when the disability occurs and the disability payments begin. Although many business owners understand the importance of maintaining adequate life insurance coverage, fewer see the relevance of maintaining proper coverage for disabilities. For most people, disability represents a greater risk than death.

Health Insurance and Workers' Compensation. One of small business owners' greatest concerns in recent years has been the skyrocketing cost of health insurance. A recent study by the Kaiser Family Foundation revealed that 76 percent of small firms not offering health plans cited cost as the reason.[44] As health care costs have climbed and the average age of the workforce has risen, health insurance has become an extremely important benefit to most workers. Companies that offer thorough health coverage often find that it gives them an edge in attracting and retaining quality workers. Four basic options are available to employers:

1. *Traditional indemnity plans.* Under these plans, employees choose their own health care providers, and the insurance company either pays the provider directly or reimburses employees for the covered amounts.
2. *Managed care plans.* As part of employers' attempts to put a lid on escalating health care costs, these plans have become increasingly popular. Two variations, the health maintenance organization (HMO) and the preferred provider organization (PPO), are most common. An HMO is a prepaid health care arrangement under which employees must use health care providers who are employed by or are under contract with the HMO their company uses. Although they lower health care costs, employees have less freedom in selecting physicians under an HMO. Under a PPO, an insurance company negotiates discounts for health care with certain physicians and hospitals. If employees choose a health care provider from the approved list, they pay only a small fee for each office visit (often just $10 to $25). The insurance company pays the remainder. Employees may select a provider outside the PPO, but they pay more for the service.
3. *Medical savings accounts (MSAs).* MSAs are similar to individual retirement accounts (IRAs) except employees' contributions are used for medical expenses rather than for retirement. An MSA is a special savings account coupled with a high-deductible insurance policy (usually $3,000 to $4,500). Employees or employers contribute pretax dollars from their paychecks into the fund and use them as they need to. Withdrawals from an MSA are not taxed as long as the money is used for approved medical expenses. Unused funds can accumulate indefinitely and earn tax-free interest. Currently, only self-employed individuals or those who work for companies with 50 or fewer employees qualify for MSAs. MSAs offer employees incentives to contain their health care costs, but the employer must choose both an insurance carrier to provide coverage and a custodial firm to manage employees' accounts. *When Roger Stewart's PPO raised his company's health care premiums 26 percent in one year, the owner of RJR Manufacturing Inc., decided to set up an MSA for his 20 employees. Costs of the program remained the same, and employees use the money in their MSAs to cover the higher deductible on their health care expenses.*[45]

4. *Self-insurance.* As you learned earlier in this chapter, some business owners choose to insure themselves for health coverage rather than to incur the costs of fully insured plans offered by outsiders. The benefits of self-insurance include greater control over the plan's design and the coverage it offers, fewer paperwork and reporting requirements, and, in some cases, lower costs. The primary disadvantage, of course, is the possibility of having to pay large amounts to cover treatments for several employees' major illnesses at the same time, which can strain a small company's cash flow. Many self-insured businesses limit their exposure to such losses by purchasing stop-loss insurance.

Another type of health-related coverage is **workers' compensation,** which is designed to cover employees who are injured on the job or who become sick as a result of their work environment. Before passage of workers' compensation legislation, any employee injured on the job could bring a lawsuit to prove the employer was liable for the worker's injury. Because of the red tape and expenses involved in these lawsuits, many employees were never compensated for job-related accidents and injuries. Although the details of coverage vary from state to state, workers' compensation laws require employers to provide benefits and medical and rehabilitation costs for employees injured on the job. The amount of compensation an injured employee will receive is determined by a fixed schedule of payment benefits based on three factors: the wages or salary that the employee was earning at the time of the accident or injury, the seriousness of the injury, and the extent of the disability to the employee. *For instance, the producers of the hit Broadway musical* The Phantom of the Opera *experienced a large workers' compensation claim when a maintenance worker was injured on the set. The worker was polishing the show's huge chandelier as it sat on the floor when another employee unknowingly hit the switch to retract the chandelier into the ceiling. The chandelier knocked the worker into the orchestra pit, seriously injuring him. That one claim ran "well into six figures," says the agent representing the insurance company.*[46]

Only three states—New Jersey, South Carolina, and Texas—do not require companies to purchase workers' compensation coverage once they reach a certain size. Usually, the state sets the rates businesses pay for workers' compensation coverage, and business owners purchase their coverage from private insurance companies. Rates vary by industry, business size, and the number of claims a company's workers make. For instance, workers' compensation premiums are higher for a typical timber cutting business than for a retail gift store. Whatever industry they are in, business owners can reduce their worker's compensation costs by improving their employees' safety records. *Alan Layton, CEO of Layton Construction Company, set up a safety training program and a reward system to lower the number of accidents employees suffered on job sites. The company works with its workers' compensation insurance company to improve safety. "Our [insurance] carrier gives us training and shares information about new developments or techniques we can use," says Layton. Although his business is in a relatively dangerous industry with high workers' compensation costs, Layton has managed to improve his company's safety record, lower his insurance costs, and boost worker productivity.*[47]

Liability Insurance. One of the most common types of insurance coverage is liability insurance, which protects a business against losses resulting from accidents or injuries people suffer on the company's property, from its products or services, and damage the company causes to others' property. Most BOPs include basic liability coverage; however, the limits on the typical policy are not high enough to cover the potential losses many small business owners face. For example, one "slip-and-fall" case involving a customer who is injured when he slips and falls on a wet floor could easily exceed the standard limits on a basic BOP. Claims from customers injured by a company's product or service are also covered by its liability policy. With jury

GAINING THE COMPETITIVE EDGE
What Kind of Coverage?

"Pizza's here!" announced Lars as he pushed open the door to the offices of WebMedia Inc.

"Great! Just in time for the board of directors meeting," laughed Chase. "Let's set it up in the boardroom. Come on, Stephanie."

WebMedia's office was a converted warehouse, and the boardroom consisted of the corner nearest the foosball table with an old door set up on two sawhorses—not exactly deluxe accommodations, but the founders of the small Web design and hosting company weren't interested in fancy offices. Lars, Chase, and Stephanie wanted to make sure their company succeeded. In the early days of their business, they were more interested in conserving cash than in surrounding themselves with symbols of power and accomplishment.

"Okay, what's first on the agenda?" asked Lars, scooping up a slice of pizza.

"We need to talk about risk exposure," said Stephanie.

"Don't we have an insurance policy—a BOP?" asked Chase. "I thought that took care of our insurance needs."

"That gives us some basic coverage," said Stephanie. "But I was reading an article yesterday that really opened my eyes to some of the risk our business—and we—are exposed to."

"Like what?" asked Lars. "Doesn't the policy we have cover our computers and other equipment?"

"Yes, it provides some basic coverage, but what happens if lightning or a power surge takes out our servers? Our clients' Web sites would be shut down, and we'd be out of business—fast," said Stephanie. "It would take quite a while to get new equipment in here and running again."

"Or viruses . . ." Chase added. "As much as we guard against them, you can never be 100 percent protected. And what about hackers? Oh man! If somebody decided to hack our site or our clients' sites, there's no telling what could happen. Hackers might post unauthorized links to some of our clients' sites . . ." His voice trailed off as he thought of the problems that could cause.

"What kind of insurance coverage do we need?" asked Lars. "Insurance isn't our thing. We know the Web and how to design and manage Web sites."

"I don't know, but it sounds as though we need to find out," Chase said.

"I'm with you two on this one," said Stephanie. "I'll call our insurance agent first thing tomorrow and ask some questions. Pass me a piece of pizza. What's next on the agenda?"

1. What types of risk does WebMedia face? Use the risk pyramid described in this chapter to assess the risks you identify.

2. Does a basic BOP provide adequate coverage for WebMedia? Explain.

3. What types of insurance policies do you suggest Lars, Chase, and Stephanie purchase for their company? Explain.

awards in product liability cases often reaching into the millions of dollars (the median product liability claim settlement cost is $7.4 million), business owners who fail to purchase sufficient liability coverage may end up losing their businesses.[48] Most insurance experts recommend at least $1 million of liability coverage for businesses. As a result, many business owners find it necessary to purchase additional liability coverage for their companies.

Auto insurance policies offer liability coverage that protects against losses resulting from injuries, damage, or theft involving the use of company vehicles. A typical BOP does not include liability coverage for automobiles; business owners must purchase a separate policy for auto insurance. Autos a business owns must be covered by a commercial policy, not a personal one.

Another important type of liability insurance for many small businesses is **professional liability insurance** or **"errors and omissions" coverage.** This insurance protects against damage a business causes to customers or clients as a result of an error an employee makes or an employee's failure to take proper care and precautions. For instance, a land surveyor may miscalculate the location of a customer's property line. If the landowner relies on that property line to build a structure on what he thinks is his land and it turns out to be on his neighbor's land, the surveyor would be liable for damages. Doctors, dentists, attorneys, and other professionals protect themselves through a similar kind of insurance, malpractice insurance, which protects them against the risk of lawsuits arising from errors in professional practice or judgment.

Employment practices liability insurance (EPLI) provides protection against claims arising from charges of employment discrimination, wrongful termination, sexual harassment, and violations of the Americans with Disabilities Act, the Family and Medical Leave Act, and other employment legislation. Because the number of lawsuits from these sources has climbed so dramatically in the past several years, this is one of the fastest-growing forms of insurance coverage. Although most violations of these employment laws are not intentional but are the result of either carelessness or lack of knowledge, the company that violates them is still liable. Because they often lack full-time human resources professionals, small companies are especially vulnerable to charges of improper employment practices, making this type of insurance coverage all the more important to them. *Frank Buckley, president of Banna Bungalow Management Inc., a chain of youth hostels and hotels, recently purchased EPLI, and the decision saved the company from major losses after it was hit with two wrongful termination lawsuits from former employees. The policy paid for the out-of-court settlements and for legal fees Banna Bungalow incurred.*[49]

Every business's insurance needs are somewhat unique, requiring owners to customize insurance coverage they purchase. Entrepreneurs also must keep their insurance coverage updated as their companies grow; when companies expand, so do their insurance needs. *Davin Wedel, founder of Global Protection Corporation, a company that makes condoms, purchased a simple BOP that gave him adequate coverage for his tiny business. As sales grew and the company took on more customers and moved into foreign markets, Wedel recognized that the company's risk exposure also had changed. Today, in addition to an expanded BOP, Wedel has insurance policies that cover product liability, increased limits on general liability, and employment practices liability.*[50]

Controlling Insurance Costs

Small business owners face constantly rising insurance premiums. Business owners can take steps to lower insurance costs, however. In the property and casualty insurance area, owners should take the following steps:

1. *Pursue a loss-control program by making risk-reduction a natural part of all employees' daily routine.* As discussed earlier in the chapter, risk reduction minimizes claims and eventually lowers premiums. Loss-control programs means taking steps such as installing modern fire alarms, safety programs, and sophisticated security systems.
2. *Increase their policies' deductibles.* If a business can afford to handle minor losses, the owner can save money by raising the deductible to a level that protects the business against catastrophic events but, in effect, self-insures against minor losses. Business owners must determine the amount of financial exposure they can reasonably accept.
3. *Work with qualified professional insurance brokers or agents.* Business owners should do their homework before choosing insurance brokers or agents. This includes checking their reputation, credentials, and background by asking them to supply references.

4. *Work actively with brokers to make sure they understand the business owners' particular needs.* Brokers need to know about an entrepreneur's business and objectives for insurance coverage. They can help only if they know their clients' needs and the degree of risk they are willing to take.

5. *Work with brokers to find competitive companies that want small companies' insurance business and have the resources to cover losses when they arise.* The price of the premium should never be an entrepreneur's sole criterion for selecting insurance. The rating of the insurance company should always be a primary consideration. What good is it to have paid low premiums if, after a loss, a business owner finds that the insurance company is unable to pay? Many small business owners learned costly lessons when their insurance companies, unable to meet their obligations, filed for bankruptcy protection.

6. *Conduct a periodic insurance audit.* Reviewing your company's coverage annually can ensure that insurance coverage is adequate and can lead to big cost savings as well. *Keith Alper, owner of Creative Products Group (CPG), a business that produces videos for* Fortune *500 companies, was surprised to discover that CPG was wasting thousands of dollars on policies it did not need. Many employees were classified incorrectly for workers' compensation coverage, several policies duplicated the coverage of others, and the company was paying for auto insurance on four cars when it had only three! In all, Alper was able to shave more than $10,000 off of CPG's $75,000 annual insurance bill.*[51]

When it comes to the cost of health insurance, the sky seems to be the limit for costs. The popular press and every national political candidate have debated the need to balance health services with the cost of providing them. Traditionally, businesses have been and continue to be the principal suppliers of health insurance in our society. To control the cost of health insurance, the small business owners should consider the following:

- *Increase the dollar amount of employee contributions and the amount of the employee's deductibles.* Neither option is desirable, but rising medical costs will inevitably result in individuals becoming, to some degree, self-insured in order to cover the high deductibles.
- *Switch to HMOs or PPOs.* Higher premium costs have encouraged some small business owners to reevaluate HMOs and PPOs as alternatives to traditional health insurance policies. Although some employees resent being told where they must go to receive treatment, the number of businesses offering the HMO and PPO options to employees is rising.
- *Consider joining an insurance pool.* Small businesses can lower their insurance premiums by banding together to purchase coverage. In many states, chambers of commerce, trade associations, and other groups form insurance pools that small businesses can join, spreading risk over a larger number of employees. In Pennsylvania, for example, two dozen chambers of commerce have formed an insurance pool that covers 30,000 people employed at small businesses at rates well below those that the owners could negotiate separately.[52]
- *Conduct a yearly utilization review.* A review may reveal that your employees' use of their policies is statistically lower, which may provide you leverage to negotiate lower premiums or to switch to an insurer that wants a business with your track record and offers lower premiums.
- *Make sure your company's health plan fits the needs of your employees.* One of the best ways to keep health care costs in check is to offer only those benefits that employees actually need. Getting employee input is essential to the process.

- *Create a wellness program for all employees.* We have all heard the old adage that an ounce of prevention is worth a pound of cure, but when it comes to the high cost of medical expenses, this is true! Companies that have created wellness programs report cost savings of $6 for every $1 they invest. Furthermore, it makes good sense to include not only employees but their families as well. Providing a wellness program does not mean building a gym, however. Instead, it may be as simple as providing routine checkups from a county nurse, incentives for quitting smoking, or after-work athletic games that involve as many employees as possible.
- *Conduct a safety audit.* Reviewing the workplace with a safety professional to look for ways to improve its safety has the potential for saving some businesses thousands of dollars a year in medical expenses and workers' compensation claims. The National Safety Council offers helpful information on creating a safe work environment.
- *Create a safety manual and use it.* Incorporating the suggestions for improving safety into a policy manual and then using it will reduce the number of on-the-job accidents. Training employees, even experienced ones, in proper safety procedures is also effective.
- *Create a safety team.* Assigning the responsibility for workplace safety to workers themselves can produce amazing results. When one small manufacturer turned its safety team over to employees, the plant's lost time due to accidents plummeted to zero for three years straight! The number of accidents is well below what it was when managers ran the safety team, and managers say that's because employees now "own" safety in the plant.

The key to controlling insurance costs is aggressive prevention. Entrepreneurs who actively manage the risks that their companies are exposed to find that they can provide the insurance coverage their businesses need at a reasonable cost. Finding the right insurance coverage to protect their businesses is no easy matter for business owners. The key to dealing with those differences is to identify the risks that represent the greatest threat to a company and then to develop a plan for minimizing their risk of occurrence and insuring against them if they do.

CHAPTER SUMMARY

1. Explain the factors necessary for a strong family business.
   - More than 80 percent of all companies in the United States are family owned. Family businesses generate 50 percent of the U.S. gross domestic product, employ more than 40 million people, and pay 65 percent of all wages. Several factors are important to maintaining a strong family business, including: shared values, shared power, tradition, a willingness to learn, behaving like families, and strong family ties.
2. Understand the exit strategy options available to an entrepreneur.
   - Family business owners wanting to step down from their companies can sell to out-

siders, sell to insiders, or transfer ownership to the next generation of family members. Common tools for selling to insiders (employees or managers) include: sale for cash plus a note, leveraged buyouts (LBOs), and employee stock ownership plans (ESOPs).
   - Transferring ownership to the next generation of family members requires a business owner to develop a sound management succession plan.
3. Discuss the stages of management succession.
   - Unfortunately, seventy percent of first-generation businesses fail to survive into the second generation, and of those that do, only 13 percent make it to the third genera-

tion. One of the primary reasons for this lack of continuity is poor succession planning. Planning for management succession protects not only the founder's, successor's, and company's financial resources, but it also preserves what matters most in a successful business: its heritage and tradition. Management succession planning can ensure a smooth transition only if the founder begins the process early on.

4. Explain how to develop an effective management succession plan.
   - A succession plan is a crucial element in transferring a company to the next generation. Preparing a succession plan involves five steps: (1) Select the successor. (2) Create a survival kit for the successor. (3) Groom the successor. (4) Promote an environment of trust and respect. (5) Cope with the financial realities of estate taxes.
   - Entrepreneurs can rely on several tools in their estate planning, including buy/sell agreements, lifetime gifting, trusts, estate freezes, and family limited partnerships.

5. Understand the four risk management strategies.
   - Four risk strategies are available to the small business: avoiding, reducing, anticipating, and transferring risk.

6. Discuss the basics of insurance for small businesses.
   - Insurance is a risk transfer strategy. Not every potential loss can be insured. Insurability requires that it be possible to estimate the amount of actual loss being insured against and identify the specific risk and that there be enough policyholders to spread out the risk.
   - The four major types of insurance small businesses need are property and casualty insurance, life and disability insurance, health insurance and workers' compensation coverage, and liability insurance.
   - Property and casualty insurance covers a company's tangible assets, such as buildings, equipment, inventory, machinery,

signs, and others that have been damaged, destroyed, or stolen. Specific types of property and casualty insurance include extra expense coverage, business interruption insurance, surety insurance, marine insurance, crime insurance, fidelity insurance, and forgery insurance.
   - Life and disability insurance also comes in various forms. Life insurance protects a family and a business against the loss of income and security in the event of the owner's death. Disability insurance, like life insurance, protects an individual in the event of unexpected and often very expensive disabilities.
   - Health insurance is designed to provide adequate health care for business owners and their employees. Workers' compensation is designed to cover employees who are injured on the job or who become sick as a result of a work environment.
   - Liability insurance protects a business against losses resulting from accidents or injuries people suffer on the company's property, from its products or services, and damage the company causes to others' property. Typical liability coverage includes professional liability insurance or "errors and omissions" coverage, which protects against damage a business causes to customers or clients as a result of an error an employee makes or an employees' failure to take proper care and precautions. Doctors, dentists, attorneys, and other professionals protect themselves through a similar kind of insurance, malpractice insurance, which protects them against the risk of lawsuits arising from errors in professional practice or judgment. Employment practices liability insurance provides protection against claims arising from charges of employment discrimination, sexual harassment, and violations of the Americans with Disabilities Act, the Family and Medical Leave Act, and other employment legislation.

DISCUSSION QUESTIONS

1. What factors must be present for a strong family business?

2. Discuss the stages of management succession in a family business.

3. What steps are involved in building a successful management succession plan?
4. What exit strategies are available to entrepreneurs wanting to step down from their businesses?
5. What strategies can business owners employ to reduce estate and gift taxes?
6. Can insurance eliminate risk? Why or why not?
7. Outline the four basic risk management strategies and give an example of each.
8. What problems occur most frequently with a risk anticipating strategy?
9. What is insurance? How can insurance companies bear such a large risk burden and still be profitable?
10. Describe the requirements for insurability.
11. Briefly describe the various types of insurance coverage available to small business owners.
12. What kinds of insurance coverage would you recommend for the following businesses?
  a. A manufacturer of steel sheets
  b. A retail gift shop
  c. A small accounting firm
  d. A limited liability partnership involving three dentists
13. What can business owners do to keep their insurance costs under control?

STEP INTO THE REAL WORLD

1. Interview two local business owners about their companies' management succession plans. Do the owners have succession plans? If so, how are they structured? Who have they designated to take over their businesses? What is the timetable for implementing the plan? What impact will estate and gift taxes have on the transfer of ownership? What provisions have they made to minimize the impact of those taxes? Write a two-page report on what you learned from your experience.
2. Contact an attorney and an accountant and ask them what steps they recommend small business owners take to plan for management succession. Are their small business clients well prepared to deal with management succession issues? Why or why not? What are the implications for those who are not well prepared?
3. a. Interview two small business owners in the local community and report on the types of insurance coverage each carries. Did they have difficulty finding insurance coverage?
   b. Contact an insurance agent and ask about the insurance coverage he or she would recommend for the types of businesses whose owners you interviewed. Do you see any gaps? If so, how much would the additional coverage cost? If the business owners are underinsured, what are the potential consequences of incurring losses?

TAKE IT TO THE NET

Visit the Scarborough/Zimmerer home page at **www.prenhall.com/scarborough** for updated information, online resources, Web-based exercises, and sample business plan.

ENDNOTES

1. Nicholas Stein, "The Age of the Scion," *Fortune*, April 2, 2001, pp. 121–128; MassMutual Family Business Network, *www.massmutual.com/fbn/index.htm*.
2. Ibid.
3. Ibid.
4. Wayne Tomkins, "Early Planning Helps Businesses Remain in the Family," *The Courier-Journal*, January 1, 2001, pp. D1–D2.
5. Sharon Nelton, "Preparing for a Loss of Leadership," *Nation's Business*, April 1997, p. 8.
6. Sharon Nelton, "Ten Keys to Success in Family Business," *Nation's Business*, April 1991, pp. 44–45.
7. "Family Members Fight Over Control of Texas Pete Hot Sauce Empire," *Greenville News*, May 17, 1997, p. 11D.
8. Stein, "The Age of the Scion," p. 124.

9. Ibid.

10. "Family Members Fight Over Control of Texas Pete Hot Sauce Empire," p. 11D.

11. Lori Ioannou, "Keeping the Business All in the Family," *FSB*, November 2001, p. 75.

12. Springfield Remanufacturing Corporation, *www.screman.com/index/htm.*

13. Paul J. Lim, "Putting Your House in Order," *U.S. News & World Report*, December 10, 2001, p. 38.

14. TCPN Quotations Center, *www.cyber-nation.com/victory/quotations/subject/quotes_subjects_f_to_h.html#f.*

15. Karen Fuller, "Healthy Transition," *Success*, June 2000, pp. 52–53.

16. Andy Bluestone, "Succession Planning Isn't Just About Money," *Nation's Business*, November 1996, p. 6.

17. Shelly Branch, "Mom Always Liked You Best," *Your Company*, April/May 1998, pp. 26–38.

18. Lee Smith, "The Next Generation," *Your Company*, October 1999, pp. 36–46.

19. Patricia Schiff Estess, "Heir Raising," *Entrepreneur*, May 1996, pp. 80–82.

20. Linda Thieman, "When Gen-X Takes Over," *Success*, February/March 2001, pp. 44–45.

21. Jacquelyn Lynn, "What Price Successor?" *Entrepreneur*, November 1999, p. 146.

22. Craig E. Aronoff and John L. Ward, "Why Continue Your Family Business," *Nation's Business*, March 1998, pp. 72–74.

23. Gordon Williams, "Passing the Torch," *Financial World*, January 21, 1997, p. 78.

24. Smith, "The Next Generation."

25. Donna Fenn, "Could Your Kids Run Your Company?" *Inc.*, July 1998, pp. 121–122.

26. Annetta Miller, "You Can't Take It With You," *Your Company*, April 1999, pp. 28–34.

27. Sharon Nelton, "Why Women Are Chosen to Lead," *Nation's Business*, April 1999, p. 51.

28. Miller, "You Can't Take It With You."

29. Ibid.; Joan Pryde, "The Estate Tax Toll on Small Firms," *Nation's Business*, August 1997, pp. 20–24.

30. Amanda Walmac, "Get an Estate Plan to Protect Your Family," *Your Company*, Forecast 1997, pp. 48–54.

31. Juan Hovey, "The Ultimate Assurance of Buy-Sell Agreements," *Nation's Business*, March 1999, pp. 24–26.

32. Joan Szabo, "Spreading the Wealth," *Entrepreneur*, July 1997, pp. 62–64.

33. Pamela Rohland, "Quick Guide to Insurance," *Entrepreneur*, September 2000, pp. 33–38; Dale D. Buss, "Cost-Saving Tips for Health Plans," *Nation's Business*, May 1999, pp. 30–33.

34. Stephen Blakely, "The Backlash Against Managed Care," *Nation's Business*, July 1998, pp. 16–24.

35. Robert McGarvey, "Take Coverage," *Entrepreneur*, September 1999, pp. 24–30.

36. Jan Norman, "How To: Insure Your Home-based Business," *Business Start-Ups*, May 1998, pp. 46–49.

37. Russ Banham, "Under Cover?" *CFO*, November 2001, pp. 49–56.

38. Kimberly Lankford, "Weird Insurance," *Kiplinger's Personal Finance Magazine*, October 1998, pp. 113–116.

39. Elaine W. Teague, "Risky Business," *Entrepreneur*, May 1999, pp. 104–107.

40. Barbara Etchieson, "Does Your Policy Have You Covered?" *Nation's Business*, August 1996, p. 43.

41. McGarvey, "Take Coverage."

42. Jacquelyn Lynn, "A Quick Guide to Insurance," *Entrepreneur*, June 1997, pp. 29–32.

43. Ilan Mochari, "A Security Blanket for Your Web Site," *Inc.*, December 2000, pp. 133–134.

44. Mark Henricks, "Sickening, Isn't It?" *Entrepreneur*, October 2001, pp. 83–84.

45. Carla Vincent, "Cut Your Health Coverage Costs," *Emerging Business*, Summer 2001, pp. 127–130; Buss, "Cost-Saving Tips for Health Plans," pp. 30–33; Joan Szabo, "An Ounce of Prevention," *Entrepreneur*, February 1999, pp. 76–79.

46. Leslie Scism, "If Disorder Strikes This 'Titanic,' Chubb Could Lose Millions," *Wall Street Journal*, April 9, 1997, pp. A1, A4.

47. Jacquelyn Lynn, "Why Workers' Comp?" *Entrepreneur*, June 1997, p. 31.

48. Banham, "Under Cover?" pp. 49–56.

49. Emily Barker, "Taking the Sting Out of the Courtroom," *Inc.*, June 2001, pp. 75–76.

50. Mie-Yun Lee, "Pile It On," *Entrepreneur*, February 2001, pp. 82–84.

51. Ilan Mochari, "Bug Your Broker," *Inc.*, August 2000, pp. 127–128.

52. Buss, "Cost-Saving Tips for Health Plans," pp. 30–33.

Chapter 21

Ethics, Social Responsibility, and the Entrepreneur

> *Ethics is a code of values which guide our choices and actions and determine the purpose and course of our lives.*
>
> —AYN RAND

> *Values are like fingerprints. Nobody's are the same, but you leave 'em all over everything you do.*
>
> —ELVIS PRESLEY

Upon completion of this chapter, you will be able to:

1. Define business ethics and describe the three levels of ethical standards.
2. Determine who is responsible for ethical behavior and why ethical lapses occur.
3. Explain how to establish and maintain high ethical standards.
4. Define social responsibility.
5. Understand the nature of business's responsibility to the environment.
6. Describe business's responsibility to employees.
7. Explain business's responsibility to customers.
8. Discuss business's responsibility to investors.
9. Describe business's responsibility to the community.

Business operates as an institution in our complex and interrelated society. As such, every entrepreneur is expected to behave in ways that are compatible with the value system of our society. It is society that imposes the rules of conduct for all business owners in the form of ethical standards of behavior and responsibilities to act in ways that benefit the long-term interest of all. It is assumed and expected that business owners strive to earn a profit on their investment. Ethics and social responsibility simply set behavioral boundaries for decision makers. Ethics is a branch of philosophy that studies and creates theories about the basic nature of right and wrong, duty, obligation, or virtue. In the next section, we will investigate the differences in ethical theory and, hopefully, develop an appreciation of the various ways ethical behavior is operationalized.

Social responsibility involves how an organization responds to the needs of the many elements in society, including shareholders, lenders, employees, consumers, governmental agencies, and the environment. Because business is allowed to operate in society, it has an obligation to behave in ways that benefit all of society.

AN ETHICAL PERSPECTIVE

1. Define business ethics and describe three levels of ethical standards.

Business ethics consist of the fundamental moral values and behavioral standards that form the foundation for the people of an organization as they make decisions and interact with stakeholders. Business ethics is a sensitive—and highly complex—issue, but it is not a new one. It is rare to find executives who explicitly use the views of Plato and Aristotle, Mill, and Kant to explain and justify their actions. But ethical theory does inform our judgments and actions. Any time we explain why we decided to act as we did, we appeal to certain standards. These standards must be grounded in a deep understanding of ethical values if they are to have any lasting and beneficial effect on how we live. Business is a human activity. As such, it is subject to moral evaluation, just like any other activity that we engage in. The old adage that the sole purpose of business is to maximize profits has never been relevant. It is becoming rare to find anyone who takes this view seriously. Increasingly, success in business requires an understanding of ethical theory. Because business is generally not yet structured to handle these questions and managers have not been trained to do so, there is a demand to find a way to determine what values ought to guide a business and to set up procedures for employees to handle these issues.

Unlike the natural sciences, with their highly refined methods and well-defined theories and laws, ethical issues and positions are complex. This has caused some to think that moral values are merely the reflection of our personal opinions and feelings, nothing more. Others view them as the standards of the culture within which one lives. However one conceives of moral values, clearly there is some apprehension as to whether it is possible for a person in business to master the knowledge necessary to understand ethics. It is important, at this point, to recall Aristotle's advice:

> We must be content then, in speaking of such subjects and with such premises to indicate the truth roughly and in outline, and in speaking about things which are only for the most part true, and with premises of the same kind, to reach conclusions that are no better. In the same spirit, therefore, should each type of statement be received; for it is the mark of an educated man to look for precision in each class of things just so far as the nature of the subject admits; it is evidently foolish to accept probably reasoning from a Mathematician and to demand from a rhetorician demonstrative proofs." (Aristotle, *Nicomachean Ethics*, book 1, part 3)

It is not hard to understand the source of the complexity in explaining our moral values. From childhood onward, our values have been shaped by a variety of direct and indirect influences. However, even in our democratic society where there is a great deal of diversity in religious, social, and moral outlooks, there is a broad consensus concerning certain moral values. This is partly due to the fact that family, religious, and other social institutions have shaped and reinforced these values. But ethical theories have played an important part in shaping our underlying moral ethos. As we begin to understand the role that these theories have played in developing an individual's moral values, the study of ethical theory becomes easier for us. What is right (and wrong), good (and bad), and required (or optional) in our behaviors has been learned and reinforced. Except for individuals whose rational capabilities have become diminished, all persons form individual value systems that are reinforced (and sometimes altered) by life's experiences.

Consequently, an individual's decisions and actions are rarely out of alignment with his or her philosophical value system. It is easy to imagine the psychological damage to people if they consistently act in opposition to their philosophical orientation. The personal conflict could be psychologically crippling and result in serious personal problems. Consequently, managers and executives attempt to make decisions and take actions consistent with their individual value system. Entrepreneurs must recognize that actions taken that conflict with society's ethical standards incur a very high price. The reputation of a business can be harmed severely by the actions of a single employee. Trust, once broken, is difficult to mend. Customers are not likely to do business with a firm that they feel treated them in an unethical fashion. In reality, some businesses fail due to being publicly identified as acting in an unethical fashion.

An entrepreneur should communicate to each employee that there are three levels of ethical performance standards. The first are the laws that govern the behaviors of all persons in our society. As we know, the laws define what we "must not do." Laws, therefore, set a minimum standard. Simply obeying the law is insufficient as a guide for ethical behavior as ethical behavior requires more. The second level is the clearly written and inclusive set of organizational policies and procedures that serve as specific guidelines for decision making. The third level is the moral stance the entrepreneur wishes each employee to take when they encounter a situation that is not governed under levels one and two. The ethical stance reflects the values of the entrepreneur. Successful entrepreneurs know that they must begin during the employee's orientation to make absolutely clear how they expect every employee to judge right from wrong and good from bad. Employees must know exactly what you expect them to do when faced with an ethical dilemma. As the organization grows, the employees have greater opportunities to come face-to-face with ethical dilemmas that require them to act (make decisions) in ways that reflect the values of the entrepreneur and the organization.

As an entrepreneur, it is important that you have an absolutely clear understanding of your personal philosophical orientation and that you clarify how your philosophical orientation influences what actions should be taken by all employees under specific circumstances. *Consequentialists* hold that the value of an act should be judged solely on the basis of that act's effects on others. In contrast, *deontologists* hold that the rightness of an act is derived from its logical consistency and universalizability. For deontologists, the right action is obligatory without regard to its consequences. *Objectivists* believe that moral values can be objectively true independent of individual, subjective feelings. In contrast, *relativists* do not believe in the existence of universal moral truth and hold that right and wrong must be defined within the context of the cultural norms and mores.

Organizations need to hire employees who have a more advanced level of personal moral development. Lawrence Kohlberg[1] describes three levels of individual moral development, with each level having two stages. The last and highest stage is that of moral conscience. The moral development of individuals is generally related to growth and maturity.

Kohlberg terms the first level of moral development the *preconventional level.* This level deals with the motivation of small children. In the first stage, Kohlberg notes that children typically do not have any notion of right and wrong. They are usually guided in their actions by their aversion to punishment. So in the first stage they act in order to avoid being scolded or spanked. In the second stage, however, they realize that often their good behavior is rewarded, usually by the praise of their parents. So they are then motivated by a desire to receive a reward.

The second level of moral development is the *conventional level.* The first stage is known as the Good Boy/Nice Girl stage. Here, young people conform to social expectations and roles because they begin to understand the importance of rules and moral norms. It is more complex than the praise that we receive from our parents in the earlier stages. Here, it is a process of socialization where we enter the social world. We do what parents, peers, and teachers expect of us. The second stage is one in which we develop an understanding of our culture and legal structure. Here, we come to identify with the laws of our society. There is an understanding of what a good citizen is and what actions one must perform.

The final level is the *postconventional* or *principled level* of moral development. Here, people find themselves conforming to principles not because of the demands and expectations of others, but because it is the right thing to do. We are able to give a rational defense of our principles and do not require the encouragement of society to motivate us. In fact, sometimes we find ourselves compelled to reject social norms because they are inconsistent with moral principles. The first stage of this level is one that is governed by the ideal of the social contract. We understand the importance of living up to agreements through a "golden rule" mentality. At the final stage, though, we act on principles that we accept as our principles.

For a long time there has been the perception that business is not properly concerned with ethics. This has fostered a corporate culture in the past that has not concerned itself too much with fostering ethical reasoning and sensibility, believing that such matters are best left to individuals to sort out for themselves. To this extent, corporate culture has been criticized for its narcissistic tendencies. This is evident in such controversial issues as plant closings and exploiting labor in developing countries. But there is a recent trend that suggests that corporate culture is changing, that it is taking this ethical dimension more seriously in its policies and practices. Businesses do see themselves as human activities and that they must address the quality of life that they foster for their employees and their customers. Entrepreneurs need to provide management and employee training in ethics, as well as in shaping corporate policies and practices to reflect the importance of the ethical dimension in today's corporate culture and guidance in identification of specific areas of opportunity.

Establishing an Ethical Framework

To cope successfully with the myriad ethical decisions they face, entrepreneurs must develop a workable ethical framework to guide them. Although many such frameworks exist, the following four-step process can work quite well.

Step 1. Recognize the Ethical Dimensions Involved in the Dilemma or Decision. Before entrepreneurs can make an informed ethical decision, they must recognize

GAINING THE COMPETITIVE EDGE
Ethical Choices: A Case Study of RU 486

Entrepreneurs, as each of us, have an underlying philosophical orientation that is likely based on one of the more traditional ethical viewpoints. The utilitarian approach holds that ethical actions are those that provide the greatest balance of good over evil. The good would be to choose the course of action, which provides the greatest good for the greatest number. The right approach focuses on the individual's right to choose for himself or herself. People have dignity based on their ability to choose freely what they will do with their lives, and that they have a fundamental moral right to have these choices respected. The question this approach poses is whether the action in question respects the moral rights of everyone? The justice approach simply suggests that equals should be treated equally and unequals unequally. For those holding this viewpoint, the ethical question is how fair is any action? Does it treat everyone in the same way, or does it show favoritism or discrimination? The common-good approach respects and values the freedom of individuals to pursue their own goals, but challenges us to also recognize and further those goals that we share in common. Finally, the virtue approach asks us to make a value decision based on answers to questions such as "What kind of person should I be?" or "What will promote the development of character within myself and my community?"

Employing the five philosophical orientations we may find it valuable to evaluate an action or a decision after answering the following questions about the action or decision:

- What benefit and what harms will each course of action produce, and which alternative will lead to the best overall consequences?

- What moral rights do the affected parties have, and which course of action best respects those rights?

- Which course of action advances the common good?

- Which course of action develops moral virtues?

With this brief groundwork laid, consider the dilemma that faced Dr. Edouard Sakiz, the chairman of the small French pharmaceutical firm Rouseel-Uclaf, in the late 1980s. Rouseel-Uclaf had developed a new product, RU-486, which was between 90 and 95 percent effective in causing a miscarriage during the first five weeks of pregnancy. The sides in the debate over the sale and distribution of RU-486 quickly formed. Dr. Sakiz was faced with a dilemma of enormous proportion. Fifty-five percent of Rouseel-Uclaf was owned by the German firm Hoechst, whose chairman was fundamentally opposed to abortion. The French government owned 36 percent of Rouseel-Uclaf, and the French Ministry of Health closely regulated the company and, consequently, had great influence over the firm's future business opportunities. The French government insisted that Rouseel-Uclaf go forward with the sale and distribution of RU-486. Beyond the direct financial and governmental stakeholders were the antiabortion advocates who threatened to boycott both Rouseel-Uclaf and Hoechst, and some among them threatened violence against company personnel. China, a major potential customer, was demanding that RU-486 be sold to them. Groups in support of women's rights to choose were also aggressively advocating the distribution of the product. In short, both sides in this dispute have the power to harm the organization and its chairman.

1. Using the five philosophical orientations presented, analyze the situation and advise Dr. Sakiz as to his best (most ethical) options and why.

Sources: "Thinking Ethically: A Framework for Moral Decision Making," *Ethics,* Winter 1996, pp. 2–5; Manueal Velasquez, Claire Andre, Thomas Shanks, S.J., and Michael J. Meyer, "Defining Moments: When Managers Must Choose Between Right and Right," *Harvard Business School Press,* Joseph L. Badaracco, Jr., Boston, 1997.

that an ethical situation exists. Only then is it possible to define the specific ethical issues involved. Too often, business owners fail to take into account the ethical impact of a particular course of action until it is too late. To avoid ethical quagmires, entrepreneurs must consider the ethical forces at work in a situation—honesty, fairness, respect for community, concern for the environment, trust, and others—to have a complete view of the decision.

Step 2. Identify the Key Stakeholders Involved and Determine How the Decision Will Affect Them. Every business influences, and is influenced by, a multitude of stakeholders. Frequently, the demands of these stakeholders conflict with one another, putting a business in the position of having to choose which groups to satisfy and which to alienate. Before making a decision, managers must sort out the conflicting interests of the various stakeholders by determining which ones have important stakes in the situation. Although this analysis may not resolve the conflict, it will prevent the company from inadvertently causing harm to people it may have failed to consider.

Step 3. Generate Alternative Choices and Distinguish Between Ethical and Unethical Responses. Small business managers will find the questions in Table 21.1 to be helpful.

Step 4. Choose the "Best" Ethical Response and Implement It. At this point, there likely will be several ethical choices from which managers can pick. Comparing these choices with the "ideal" ethical outcome may help managers make the final decision. The final choice must be consistent with the company's goals, culture, and value system as well as those of the individual decision makers.

WHO IS RESPONSIBLE FOR ETHICAL BEHAVIOR?

1. Determine who is responsible for ethical behavior and why ethical lapses occur.

Although companies may set ethical standards and offer guidelines for employees, the ultimate decision on whether to abide by ethical principles rests with the *individual.* In other words, companies really are not ethical or unethical; individuals are. Managers, however, can greatly influence individual behavior within the company. And that influence must start at the *top.* A chief executive officer who practices ethical behavior establishes the moral tone for the entire organization. Table 21.2 summarizes the characteristics of the three ethical styles of management: immoral, amoral, and moral management.

Gaining the Benefits of Moral Management

Over the past few decades, business leaders have, in general, become more proactive in terms of implementing the organizational characteristics of moral management as outlined in Table 21.2. Entrepreneurs know that these positive organizational practices avoid the extremely damaging effects on the firm's reputation from unethical behaviors. Additionally, ethical company practice earns the respect of both customers and employees. Although the "ethics factor" is intangible, it is both recognized and appreciated by all of the firm's stockholders. A company's ethical philosophy has an impact on its ability to provide value for its customers and job security for its employees. Increasingly, entrepreneurs are recognizing ethical behavior as an investment in the company's future rather than a cost of doing business.

Why Ethical Lapses Occur

When faced with an ethical dilemma, not every manager or employee will make the correct decision. In fact, many unethical acts are committed by normally decent people who believe in moral values. What then causes these ethical lapses to occur?[2]

Table 21.1

Questions to Help Identify the Ethical Dimension of a Situation

Principles and Codes of Conduct
- Does this decision or action meet my standards for how people should interact?
- Does this decision or action agree with my religious teachings or beliefs (or with my personal principles and sense of responsibility)?
- How will I feel about myself if I do this?
- Do we (or I) have a rule or policy for cases like this?
- Would I want everyone to make the same decision and take the same action if faced with these circumstances?
- What are my true motives for considering this action?

Moral Rights
- Would this action allow others freedom of choice in this matter?
- Would this action involve deceiving others in any way?

Justice
- Would I feel this action was just (right) if I were on the other side of the decision?
- How would I feel if this action were done to me or someone close to me?
- Would this action or decision distribute benefits justly?
- Would it distribute hardships or burdens justly?

Consequences and Outcomes
- What will be the short- and long-term consequences of this action?
- Who will benefit from this course of action?
- Who will be hurt?
- How will this action create good and prevent harm?

Public Justification
- How would I feel (or how will I feel) if (or when) this action becomes public knowledge?
- Will I be able to explain adequately to others why I have taken the action?
- Would others feel that my action or decision is ethical or moral?

Intuition and Insight
- Have I searched for all alternatives? Are there other ways I could look at this situation? Have I considered all points of view?
- Even if there is sound rationality for this decision or action, and even if I could defend it publicly, does my inner sense tell me it is right?
- What does my intuition tell me is the ethical thing to do in this situation? Have I listened to my inner voice?

Source: Sherry Baker, "Ethical Judgment," *Executive Excellence*, March 1992, pp. 7–8.

The "Bad Apple." Ethical decisions are individual decisions, and some people are corrupt. Try as they might to avoid them, organizations occasionally find that they have hired a bad apple. Eliminating unethical behavior requires the elimination of these bad apples.

The "Bad Barrel." In some cases, the company culture has been poisoned with an unethical overtone; in other words, the problem is not the bad apple but the bad barrel. Pressure to prosper produces an environment that creates conditions that reward unethical behavior, and employees act accordingly.

Table 21.2
Approaches to Management Ethics

ORGANIZATIONAL CHARACTERISTICS	IMMORAL MANAGEMENT	AMORAL MANAGEMENT	MORAL MANAGEMENT
Ethical norms	Management decisions, actions, and behavior imply a positive and active opposition to what is moral (ethical). Decisions are discordant with accepted ethical principles. An active negation of what is moral is implicit.	Management is neither moral nor immoral; decisions are not based on moral judgments. Management activity is not related to any moral code. A lack of ethical perception and moral awareness may be implicit.	Management activity conforms to a standard of ethical, or right, behavior. Management activity conforms to accepted professional standards of conduct. Ethical leadership is common-place.
Motives	Selfish. Management cares only about its or the company's gains.	Well-intentioned but selfish in the sense that the impact on others is not considered.	Good. Management wants to succeed but only within the confines of sound ethical precepts (fairness, justice, due process).
Goals	Profitability and organizational success at any price.	Profitability. Other goals are not considered.	Profitability within the confines of legal obedience and ethical standards.
Orientation toward law	Legal standards are barriers that management must overcome to accomplish what it wants.	Law is the ethical guide, preferably the letter of the law. The central question is what we can do legally.	Obedience toward letter and spirit of the law. Law is a minimal ethical behavior. Prefer to operate well above what law mandates.
Strategy	Exploit opportunities for corporate gain. Cut corners when it appears useful.	Give managers free rein. Personal ethics may apply but only if managers choose. Respond to legal mandates if caught and required to do so.	Live by sound ethical standards. Assume leadership position when ethical dilemmas arise. Enlightened self-interest.

Source: Archie B. Carroll, "In Search of the Moral Manager," reprinted from *Business Horizons,* March/April, 1987. Copyright 1987 by the Foundation for the School of Business at Indiana University. Used with permission.

Moral Blindness. Sometimes, fundamentally ethical people commit ethical blunders because they are blind to the ethical implications of their conduct. Moral blindness may be the result of failing to realize that an ethical dilemma exists, or it may arise from a variety of mental defense mechanisms. One of the most common mechanisms is rationalization:

- "Everybody does it."
- "If they were in my place, they'd do it too?"
- "Being ethical is a luxury I cannot afford right now."
- "The impact of my decision/action on (whoever or whatever) is not my concern."
- "I don't get paid to be ethical; I get paid to produce results."

Training in ethical thinking and creating an environment that encourages employees to consider the ethical impact of their decisions can reduce the problem of moral blindness.

Competitive Pressures. If competition is so intense that a company's survival is threatened, managers may begin to view what were once unacceptable options as

GAINING THE COMPETITIVE EDGE
Doing the Right Things Pays Off

Entrepreneurs are now more than ever willing to come forward and express their belief that acting in ethical and socially responsible ways produces positive outcomes. Behaving in an ethical and socially responsible fashion has the following positive outcomes:

- Improved capability of attracting and retaining high-quality productive employees

- Builds long-lasting relationships with customers or clients

- Helps employees focus on positive behaviors knowing that management supports their decisions and actions

Good Corporate citizenship begins with the establishment and enforcement of positive internal policies which include the basics such as:

- Always, and in every way, obey the law.

- Treat all employees fairly and with respect.

- Be honest and fair to employees, customers, and suppliers.

- Be aware of the impact of your actions on others and the environment.

- Design your products to deliver what you promise.

- Ensure high-quality and safe products.

1. Can you suggest how a company could quantify the "bottom line" value of these policies? How?

Source: Rhonda Abrams, "Companies Strive to Do Well by Doing Good," *Business,* August 12, 2001, p. 3.

acceptable. Managers and employees are under such pressure to produce that they may sacrifice their ethical standards to reduce the fear of failure or the fear of losing their jobs. A study conducted by the Ethics Resource Center found that 30 percent of employees admitted to feeling pressure to compromise their company's ethical standards because of deadlines, overly aggressive objectives, concerns about the company's survival, and other factors.[3] They begin to believe that attaining objectives is their only task and what they do to reach their target is of little consequence. *For example, the high-pressure environment at Chambers Development Company, once a rising star in the solid waste disposal industry, ultimately led employees to use inappropriate accounting practices, overstating company profits. Former employees say that company founder John Rangos, Sr., pushed so hard for sales growth and for meeting his lofty profit objectives that manipulating the numbers was not only tolerated but also encouraged. "John Rangos would not tolerate the presence of someone who would not give him the answers he wanted," says one former consultant. The result was numerous violations of generally accepted accounting principles (GAAP) and grossly overstated earnings. (Although company records were reporting record profits, the company was actually losing money!) As a result, Chambers Development Company became the target of numerous lawsuits. The company survived, but has yet to recover fully from the problem stemming from its ethical violations.[4]*

Opportunity Pressures. When the opportunity to "get ahead" by taking some unethical action presents itself, some people cannot resist the temptation. The greater the reward or the smaller the penalty for unethical acts, the greater is the probability that such behavior will occur. If managers, for example, condone or even encourage unethical behavior, they can be sure it will occur. Those who succumb to opportunity pressures often make one of two mistakes: They overestimate the cost of doing the right thing, or they underestimate the cost of doing the wrong thing. Either error can lead to disaster.

IN THE FOOTSTEPS OF AN ENTREPRENEUR
"Double Bottom Line": The Next Generation of Socially Responsible Businesses

David Griswald of Sustainable Harvest, Seth Goldman of Honest Tea, Inc., Daniel Grossman of Wild Plant Toys Inc., Nick Gleason of City Soft Inc., Aaron Lamstein of Worldwise, Inc., Mark Deutschmann of Village Real Estate Services, and Jeff Mendelsohn of New Leaf Paper LLC are each examples of the new generation of entrepreneurs who are committed to what is termed the *double bottom line.* The concept of double bottom line simply places at its core the equality of environmental and social issues on par with economic performance. What seems to be fundamentally different between the socially and environmentally sensitive entrepreneurs listed above and their predecessors, such as Ben Cohen and Jerry Greenfield of Ben and Jerry's Homemade, Anita Roddick of the Body Shop International, Paul Hawken of Smith and Hawken, and Yvon Chouinard of Patagonia, is the recognition of the absolute necessity that the business ventures they start are fundamentally strong businesses and a willingness to become, or hire, business-educated professionals. The younger entrepreneurs acknowledge the contribution of the pioneers as highly visible mentors who loudly proclaimed the gospel of social responsibility and equality among stockholders.

The average age of the new breed of socially responsible corporate founders listed at the beginning of this section is 37. They began their new ventures between 1990 and 1998 and have reported revenues of between $1.2 million and $30 million, with all but one profitable at the time of this writing. These new entrepreneurs are proud to be in business and recognize that their ideals alone will not result in a successful business venture. The product and revenues they market must met or exceed the quality of their competitors, and the price they charge must be attractive enough to develop an adequate customer base.

The pioneers of socially responsible entrepreneurship looked negatively upon those trained in the skills of business, whereas this new breed recognizes the need to embrace the knowledge and skills of effective management. This new breed is as dedicated to building viable, profitable businesses as they are to the social and environmental concerns that motivated them to create the business.

1. Using the Internet, research briefly three or four of the seven firms highlighted in this section. Based on your initial research, do you believe that these firms have the potential of remaining competitive?

2. In your opinion, will customers remain attracted to firms with a strong social and environmental commitment when economic conditions result in dramatic price competition? Why or why not?

Source: Thea Singer, "Can Business Still Save the World?", *Inc.*, April 2001, pp. 58–71.

Globalization of Business. The globalization of business has intertwined what once were distinct cultures. This cultural cross-pollination has brought about many positive aspects, but it has created problems as well. Companies have discovered that there is no single standard of ethical behavior applying to all business decisions in the international arena. Practices that are illegal in one country may be perfectly acceptable, even expected, in another. Actions that would send a businessperson to jail in Western nations are common ways of working around the system in others. *For example, as part of Russia's move to privatize formerly government-owned businesses, government officials decided to sell the 1,777-room Cosmos Hotel, originally built for the 1980 Olympics. The hotel generates revenues of $100 million a year (in hard currency) and produces profits of $10 million each year. Although such a business would sell for at least $100 million in the United States or in Western Europe, Mikhail Kharshan bought a 25 percent interest in the Cosmos for a mere $2.5 million! Getting the property at just 10 percent of its value was no easy task. As an insider, Kharshan knew the hotel would be put up for sale before most people did, and he used the extra time to scare off rival bidders for the popular hotel. He* bribed journalists from two influential business papers to publish negative financial reports about the Cosmos. Then he arranged to be interviewed on Russian television, where he talked about the poor state of the Russian hotel industry. He bribed government officials to limit the Cosmos auction to just two locations and then bribed two other likely bidders not to participate in the auction. The result: Kharshan was the only serious bidder at the auction; that's how he managed to get the hotel at such a bargain. Kharshan says that his actions, although unethical by U.S. business standards, "are normal business practices in Russia. We didn't shoot anyone and we didn't violate any laws."[5]

ESTABLISHING ETHICAL STANDARDS

3. Explain how to establish and maintain high ethical standards.

Although there is no single standard for ethical behavior, managers must encourage employees to become familiar with the various ethical tests for judging behavior.

> *The utilitarian principle.* Choose the option that offers the greatest good for the greatest number of people.
> *Kant's categorical imperative.* Act in such a way that the action taken under the circumstances could be a universal law or rule of behavior.
> *The professional ethic.* Take only those actions that a disinterested panel of professional colleagues would view as proper.
> *The Golden Rule.* Treat other people the way you would like them to treat you.
> *The television test.* Would you and your colleagues feel comfortable explaining your actions to a national television audience?
> *The family test.* Would you be comfortable explaining to your children, your spouse, and your parents why you took this action?[6]

Although these tests do not offer universal solutions to ethical dilemmas, they do help employees identify the moral implications of the decisions they face. People must be able to understand the ethical impact of their actions before they can make responsible decisions.

Table 21.3 describes 10 ethical principles that differentiate between right and wrong, thereby offering a guideline for ethical behavior.

Implementing and Maintaining Ethical Standards

Establishing ethical standards is only the first step in an ethics-enhancing program; implementing and maintaining those standards is the real challenge facing management. What can managers do to integrate ethical principles into their companies?

Create a Company Credo. A **company credo** defines the values underlying the entire company and its ethical responsibilities to its stakeholders. It offers general guidance in ethical issues. The most effective credos capture the elusive essence of a company—what it stands for and why it's important—and can be an important ingredient in the company's competitive edge. A company credo is especially important for a small company, where the entrepreneur's values become the values driving the business. A credo is an excellent way to transform those values into employees' ethical behavior.

Develop a Code of Ethics. A **code of ethics** is a written statement of the standards of behavior and ethical principles a company expects from its employees. Codes of ethics do not ensure ethical behavior, but they do establish minimum standards of behavior throughout the organization. A code of ethics spells out what kind of behav-

Table 21.3

Ten Ethical
Principles to Guide
Behavior

The study of history, philosophy, and religion reveals a strong consensus about certain universal and timeless values that are central to leading an ethical life.

1. **Honesty.** Be truthful, sincere, forthright, straightforward, frank, candid; do not cheat, lie, steal, deceive, or act deviously.
2. **Integrity.** Be principled, honorable, upright, and courageous, and act on convictions; do not be two-faced or unscrupulous or adopt an ends-justifies-the-means philosophy that ignores principle.
3. **Promise-keeping.** Be worthy of trust, keep promises, fulfill commitments, and abide by the spirit as well as the letter of an agreement; do not interpret agreements in a technical or legalistic manner in order to rationalize noncompliance or to create excuses for breaking commitments.
4. **Fidelity.** Be faithful and loyal to family, friends, employers, and country; do not use or disclose information earned in confidence; in a professional context, safeguard the ability to make independent professional judgments by scrupulously avoiding undue influences and conflicts of interest.
5. **Fairness.** Be fair and open-minded, be willing to admit error, and, when appropriate, change positions and beliefs and demonstrate a commitment to justice, the equal treatment of individuals, and tolerance for diversity; do not overreach or take undue advantage of another's mistakes or adversities.
6. **Caring for others.** Be caring, kind, and compassionate; share, be giving, serve others; help those in need and avoid harming others.
7. **Respect for others.** Demonstrate respect for human dignity, privacy, and the right to self-determination for all people; be courteous, prompt, and decent; provide others with the information they need to make informed decisions about their own lives; do not patronize, embarrass, or demean.
8. **Responsible citizenship.** Obey just laws (if a law is unjust , openly protest it); exercise all democratic rights and privileges responsibly by participation (voting and expressing informed views), social consciousness, and public service; when in a position of leadership or authority, openly respect and honor democratic processes of decision making, avoid secrecy or concealment of information, and ensure others have the information needed to make intelligent choices and exercise their rights.
9. **Pursuit of excellence.** Pursue excellence in all matters; in meeting personal and professional responsibilities, be diligent, reliable, industrious, and committed; perform all tasks to the best of your ability, develop and maintain a high degree of competence, and be well informed and well prepared; do not be content with mediocrity, but do not seek to win "at any cost."
10. **Accountability.** Be accountable; accept responsibility for decisions, for the foreseeable consequences of actions and inactions, and for setting an example for others. Parents, teachers, employers, many professionals, and public officials have a special obligation to lead by example and to safeguard and advance the integrity and reputation of their families, companies, professions, and the government; avoid even the appearance of impropriety and take whatever actions are necessary to correct or prevent inappropriate conduct by others.

Source: Michael Josephson, "Teaching Ethical Decision Making and Principled Reasoning," *Ethics: Easier Said Than Done*, Winter 1988, pp. 28–29.

ior is expected (and what kind will not be tolerated) and offers everyone in the company concrete guidelines for dealing with ethics every day on the job. Although creating a code of ethics does not guarantee 100 percent compliance with ethical standards, it does tend to foster an ethical atmosphere in a company. Workers who will be directly affected by the code should have a hand in developing it.

Enforce the Code Fairly and Consistently. Managers must take action whenever they discover ethical violations. If employees learn that ethical breaches go unpunished, the code of ethics becomes meaningless. Enforcement of the code of ethics demonstrates to everyone that you believe that ethical behavior is mandatory.

Conduct Ethics Training. Instilling ethics in an organization's culture requires more than creating a code of ethics and enforcing it. Managers must show employees that the organization truly is committed to practicing ethical behavior. One of the most effective ways to display that commitment is through ethical training designed to raise employees' consciousness of potential ethical dilemmas. Ethics training programs not only raise employees' awareness of ethical issues, but they also communicate to them the core of the company's value system.

Hire the Right People. Ultimately, the decision in any ethical situation belongs to the individual. Hiring people with strong moral principles and values is the best insurance against ethical violations. To make ethical decisions, people must have: (1) *ethical commitment*—the personal resolve to act ethically and do the right thing; (2) *ethical consciousness*—the ability to perceive the ethical implications of a situation; and (3) *ethical competency*—the ability to engage in sound moral reasoning and develop practical problem-solving strategies.[7]

Perform Periodic Ethical Audits. One of the best ways to evaluate the effectiveness of an ethics system is to perform periodic audits. These reviews send a signal to employees that ethics is not just a passing fad.

Establish High Standards of Behavior, Not Just Rules. No one can legislate ethics and morality, but managers can let people know the level of performance they expect. It is crucial to emphasize to *everyone* in the organization the importance of ethics. All employees must understand that ethics is *not* negotiable.

Set an Impeccable Ethical Example at All Times. Remember that ethics starts at the top. Far more important than credos and codes are the examples the company's leaders set. If managers talk about the importance of ethics and then act in an unethical manner, they send mixed signals to employees. Workers believe managers' *actions* more than their words.

Create a Culture That Emphasizes Two-Way Communication. A thriving ethical environment requires two-way communication. Employees must have the opportunity to report any ethical violations they observe. Such a two-way system is integral to a whistle-blowing program, in which employees anonymously report breaches of ethical behavior through proper channels.

Involve Employees in Establishing Ethical Standards. Encourage employees to offer feedback on how standards should be established. Involving employees improves the quality of a firm's ethical standards and increases the likelihood of employee compliance.

THE ISSUE OF SOCIAL RESPONSIBILITY

4. Define social responsibility.

The concept of social responsibility has evolved from a nebulous "do-gooder" image to one of "social steward" with expectations of specific organizational behaviors that benefit the environments in which the business operates. Society has continually redefined its expectations of business owners and now holds all enterprise to high behavioral standards.

In a free enterprise system, companies that fail to respond to their customers' needs and demands soon go out of business. Today, customers are increasingly

IN THE FOOTSTEPS OF AN ENTREPRENEUR
Following Nature's Example

Ray Anderson had spent most of his career working for major textile companies; then, in the early 1970s, he traveled to Europe, where he saw computer rooms furnished in square "tiles" of carpeting. Upon his return to the United States, he launched his own company, Interface, Inc., which soon became the leading manufacturer of modular carpeting in the country. Twenty years later, however, Interface was struggling as its cost had gotten out of control and its customers began to question the company's impact on the environment. An employee gave Anderson a copy of Paul Hawken's *The Ecology of Commerce,* which chronicles a thoughtful plan for business success without sacrificing the environment. Based on the model of nature itself, Hawken's book calls for controlling the creation of harmful wastes rather than focusing on their disposal. Hawken's book envisions a business system that copies nature, where everything's waste is food for something else. Nothing is wasted. Anderson says that, after reading the book, he thought about his grandchildren's future, and he wept. "It was like a spear in my chest," he recalls. Anderson decided to launch his company on a new mission: to create zero pollution and to consume zero oil without sacrificing the interests of investors, employees, or customers. Anderson took the concepts in *The Ecology of Commerce* to heart and used nature itself as the model for conducting business. He hired environmental consultants and created teams of employees to study every process in the company to find ways to "ecologize' them. Winning ideas earned employees bonuses. A new yarn tufting method reduced the use of nylon by 10 percent. Interface now combines carpet yarns with natural fibers from hemp and flax to create carpeting that is both "harvestable" and "compostable." Water from the plant is treated and recycled to irrigate a local golf course. Massive electric motors are jump-started with gravity-fed systems rather than with huge jolts of electricity. "Looking at waste really forces you to look at how your systems are designed," says one top Interface manager. The changes not only have helped the environment, but they also have saved the company more than $75 million in just three years!

Still, some of the biggest benefits of Interface's new method of doing business come in its marketing efforts. Doing business with a "green" vendor, especially a low-cost green vendor, is an attractive feature to many companies. Interface has attracted the attention of other companies with an interest in the environment as potential customers. The Gap, Inc., ordered carpet for its new headquarters because they were the low bidder; however, Gap invited Interface to bid only because of its impressive environmental record. Managers say that Interface has landed several contracts because of its ecological approach to business that it otherwise would not have.

Employees benefit from the company's natural approach as well. The typical carpet mill is a noisy, dusty place, where lint particles can be seen floating in malodorous air. Not so at Interface. The factory is not dusty, and the air is free of both odors and lint particles. Sunlight bathes the entire factory through three-story windows. Rather than a manicured and chemical-filled lawn, the plant is landscaped naturally, with wild grasses and wildflowers. Joyce LaValle, plant manager, takes about 1,000 potential customers through the plant each year. "If they come into this building, I've got them hands down," she says, "especially if they've been to other plants."

Although Interface has a long way to go to reach its environmental goals, the company has come a long way. It is once again the world leader in its market segment, and, more importantly, Interface has discovered that it is possible to create business success and a renewable future at the same time by following nature's example.

1. What benefits does conducting business according to nature's model offer companies such as Interface? What is the impact on a company's stakeholders?

2. What future do you predict for this management philosophy? Explain.

Source: Adapted from Thomas Petzinger, Jr., "Business Achieves Greatest Efficiencies When at Its Greenest," *Wall Street Journal,* July 11, 1997, p. B1.

demanding the companies they buy goods and services from to be socially responsible. When customers shop for "value," they no longer consider only the price–performance relationship of the product or service; they also consider the company's stance on social responsibility. In a recent survey by the Walker Group, nearly 90 percent of consumers said that when price, service, and quality are equal among competitors, they will buy from the company that has the best reputation for social responsibility. The survey also revealed that 70 percent of consumers would not buy, at any price, from a company that was not socially responsible.[8]

Putting Social Responsibility into Practice

One problem facing businesses is defining just what social responsibility is. Is it manufacturing environmentally friendly products? Is it donating a portion of profits to charitable organizations? Is it creating jobs in inner cities plagued by high unemployment levels? The specific nature of a company's social responsibility efforts will depend on how its owners, employees, and other stakeholders define what it means to be socially responsible. Typically, businesses have responsibilities to several key stakeholders, including the environment, employees, customers, investors, and the community. **Social responsibility** is the awareness by a company's managers of the social, environmental, political, human, and financial consequences their actions produce.

BUSINESS'S RESPONSIBILITY TO THE ENVIRONMENT

5. Understand the nature of business's responsibility to the environment.

Driven by their customers' interest in protecting the environment, companies have become more sensitive to the impact their products, processes, and packaging have on the planet. Environmentalism has become and will continue to be one of the dominant issues for companies worldwide because consumers have added another item to their list of buying criteria: environmental safety. Companies have discovered that sound environmental practices make for good business. In addition to lowering their operating costs, environmentally safe products attract environmentally conscious customers and can give a company a competitive edge in the marketplace. Socially responsible business owners focus on the three Rs: reduce, reuse, recycle.

- *Reduce* the amount of materials used in your company, from the factory floor to the copier room.
- *Reuse* whatever you can.
- *Recycle* the materials that you must dispose of.

Progressive companies are taking their environmental policies a step further, creating redesigned, "clean" manufacturing systems that focus on *avoiding* waste and pollution. That requires a different manufacturing philosophy. These companies design their products, packaging, and processes from the start with the environment in mind, working to eliminate hazardous materials and by-products and looking for ways to turn what had been scrap into salable products. Such an approach requires an ecological evaluation of every part of the process—from the raw materials put into the product to the disposal or reuse of the packaging that surrounds it. Table 21.4 offers a list of questions environmentally responsible entrepreneurs should ask themselves.

Table 21.4
Environmentally
Responsible
Questions

Industry Week challenged Jonathan Schorsch, environmental research director at the Council on Economic Priorities, to describe what companies can do to be environmentally responsible. Schorsch came up with the following questions for managers to ask themselves.

- Are we trying to reduce the volume of our packaging?
- How do we deal with disposal?
- Are we recycling in the office?
- Can we get beyond the concept of volume sales to build products that last?
- Are we reducing waste and substituting toxic substances with nontoxic ones?
- Are we reformulating waste for resale?
- Do we have a formal environmental policy?
- Do we go beyond compliance?
- Are we uniformly stringent environmentally in operations outside, as well as inside, the United States?
- Do we educate employees about the hazards of working with toxic materials?
- Do we encourage employees to submit proposals on how to reduce waste?
- Do we conserve energy?
- Are we avoiding paying taxes, when those tax dollars might go to support environmental programs?
- How do our operations affect the communities they're in, including indigenous people in other countries?

Source: Therese R. Welter, "A Farewell to Arms," *Industry Week,* August 20, 1990, p. 42. Copyright 1990 Penton Publishing Company, Inc., reprinted with permission from *Industry Week.*

BUSINESS'S RESPONSIBILITY TO EMPLOYEES

6. Describe business's responsibility to employees.

Few other stakeholders are as important to a business as its employees. It is common for managers to *say* their employees are their most valuable resource, but the truly excellent ones *treat* them that way. Employees are at the heart of increases in productivity and they add the personal touch that puts the passion in customer service. In short, employees produce the winning competitive advantage for the entrepreneur. As such, employees really are the firm's most valuable asset.

Entrepreneurs who are sensitive to the value of their employees follow a few simple procedures; they:

- Listen to employees and respect their opinions.
- Ask for their input; involve them in the decision-making process.
- Provide regular feedback—positive and negative—to employees.
- Tell them the truth—always.
- Let them know exactly what's expected of them.
- Reward employees for performing their jobs well.
- Trust them; create an environment of respect and teamwork.

One highly successful entrepreneurial company that places extensive energy on its employees is Starbucks. *Starbucks Coffee Company, the successful Seattle-based coffee retailer, recognizes the special role its employees (partners) play in keeping customers coming back to its retail locations, and it shows employees that it appreciates their contribution. Reflecting on the importance of having satisfied partners interacting with customers in the*

Successful small businesses recognize their employees as their most valuable resource and treat them that way. At Starbucks, employees are such an integral part of the company's success that they are called "partners" rather than "employees."

retail business, CEO Howard Schultz explains, "We recognized (from the onset that) we had to build trust and confidence with customers and shareholders. But first and foremost, we had to build this trust with employees." At Starbucks, employee-partners come first. Great benefits, constant training, respect, and a team approach keep costs low and employee turnover down: just one eighth of the industry average.[9]

Several important issues face small business managers trying to meet their social responsibility to employees. Although not complete, this chapter will address the topics of cultural diversity, drug testing, AIDs, sexual harassment, and privacy. Each of these are areas where a firm has a responsibility to its employees; both through policies and procedures and proactive implementation.

Cultural Diversity in the Workplace

The United States has always been a nation of astonishing cultural diversity, a trait that has imbued it with an incredible richness of ideas and creativity. Indeed, this diversity is one of the driving forces behind the greatest entrepreneurial effort in all the world, and it continues to grow. The United States, in short, is moving toward a "minority majority," and significant demographic shifts will affect virtually every aspect of business. Although at this writing the employment data by gender or national origin from the U.S. Census for 2000 has not yet been released, it is anticipated that diversity within the U.S. population has continued to expand. The trend of increased women entrepreneurs is well documented, with 1997 Bureau of the Census data indicating that 5.4 million U.S. businesses were owned by women (this is greater than those owned by males). In 1998, women-headed households with a business had an average income level 2.5 times that of those without a business; similarly, those with a business had an average net worth nearly six times those without.[10]

Employment statistics released in 1999 showed the following data related to employment by race, ethnic group, and gender[11]:

Total Employment in Private Industry	100%
A. Male	52.8%
Female	47.2%

B. White male	38.4%
White female	33.2%
C. African-American	14.0%
D. Hispanic	9.7%
E. Asian/Pacific	4.1%

This rich mix of cultures within the workforce presents both opportunities and challenges to employers. One of the chief benefits of a diverse workforce is the rich blend of perspectives, skills, talents, and ideas employees have to offer. Also, the changing composition of the nation will change the customer base. What better way is there for an entrepreneur to deal with culturally diverse customers than to have a culturally diverse workforce?

Managing a culturally diverse workforce presents a real challenge for employers, however. Molding workers with highly varied beliefs, backgrounds, and biases into a unified team takes time and commitment. Stereotypes, biases, and prejudices will present barriers that workers and managers must constantly overcome. Communication may require more effort because of language differences. In many cases, dealing with diversity causes a degree of discomfort for entrepreneurs because of the natural tendency to associate with people who are similar to ourselves. These reasons and others cause some entrepreneurs to resist the move to a more diverse workforce, a move that threatens their ability to create a competitive edge.

How can entrepreneurs achieve unity through diversity? The only way is by *managing* diversity in the workforce: That is, entrepreneurs must create an environment in which all types of workers—men, women, Hispanic, African-American, white, disabled, homosexual, elderly, and others—can flourish and can give top performance to their companies. Managing a culturally diverse workforce requires a different way of thinking, however, and that requires training. In essence, diversity training will help make everyone aware of the dangers of bias, prejudice, and discrimination, however subtle or unintentional they may be. Managing a culturally diverse workforce successfully requires a business owner to:

Assess your company's diversity needs. The starting point for an effective diversity management program is an assessment of the company's needs and problems. Surveys, interviews, and informal conversations with employees can be valuable tools. Several organizations offer more formal assessment tools—"cultural audits," questionnaires, and diagnostic forms—that also might be useful.

Learn to recognize and correct your own biases and stereotypes. One of the best ways to identify your own cultural biases is to get exposure to people who are not like you! By spending time with those who are different from you, you will learn quickly that stereotypes simply don't hold up.

Avoid making invalid assumptions. Decisions based on faulty assumptions are bound to be flawed. Potential employers' false assumptions made on the basis of inaccurate perceptions has kept many qualified women and minorities from getting jobs and promotions.

Push for diversity in your management team. To get maximum benefit from a culturally diverse workforce, a company must promote nontraditional workers into top management. A culturally diverse top management team that can serve as mentors and role models provides visible evidence that nontraditional workers can succeed.

Concentrate on communication. Any organization, especially a culturally diverse one, will stumble if lines of communication break down.

Frequent training sessions and regular opportunities for employees to talk with one another in a nonthreatening environment can be extremely helpful.

Make diversity a core value in the organization. For a cultural diversity program to work, top managers must "champion" the program and take active steps to integrate diversity throughout the entire organization.

Continue to adjust your company to your workers. Rather than pressure workers to conform to the company, those entrepreneurs with the most successful cultural diversity programs are constantly looking for ways to adjust their businesses to their workers. Flexibility is the key.

Table 21.5 compares the traditional management assumptions that companies must change and the diversity management assumptions needed to replace them.

Drug Testing

One of the realities of our society is the use of illegal drugs. The second reality, which entrepreneurs now must face head-on, is that this problem does affect the workplace. Drug and alcohol abuse by employees results in reduced productivity and increased medical costs, as well as higher rates of accidents and absenteeism. Individuals with drug and alcohol problems are working in our businesses. What should concern entrepreneurs the most is that these individuals seek organizations that do not understand the nature of the problem and, consequently, have no related policy in place. Because the practice of drug testing is controversial, due to the employee's right to privacy, its random use can result in employees' taking legal action against the firm. Extreme care must be exercised to ensure absolute privacy and avoidance of public disclosure.

An effective proactive drug program should include the following four elements:

1. *A written substance abuse policy.* The first step in the war against drugs is creating a written policy that spells out the company's position on drugs. The policy should state its purpose, prohibit the use of drugs on the job (or off the job if it

Table 21.5
The Traditional Paradigm Versus the Valuing Diversity Paradigm

TRADITIONAL PARADIGM	VALUING DIVERSITY PARADIGM
Expectations, standards, and explicit and implicit rules shaped by the needs of those at the top.	Expectations, standards, and explicit and implicit rules shaped by diverse customers and employees.
Success linked to assimilation.	Success linked to unique contribution.
Limited range of appropriate communication, work, and leadership styles.	Expanded range of styles.
No strategic business linkage.	Diversity is a competitive business strategy.
Diversity equals a potential liability	Diversity equals a unique asset.
No human resources system alignment.	Human resources system in alignment.
Token gender and/or racial diversity at middle management level.	Visible diversity at all management levels.
Uncommitted and uninformed leadership.	Aware and committed leadership.
Underlying assumption: Change the people and preserve the culture.	Underlying assumption: Modify the culture to support the people.

Source: Marilyn Loden, *Implementing Diversity* (Homewood, IL: Irwin, 1996), p. 28.

affects job performance), specify the consequences of violating the policy, explain any drug testing procedures to be used, and describe the resources available to help troubled employees.

2. *Training for supervisors to detect drug-using workers.* Supervisors are in the best position to identify employees with drug problems and to encourage them to get help. The supervisor's job, however, is not to play "cop" or "therapist." The supervisor should identify problem employees early and encourage them to seek help. The focal point of the supervisor's role is to track employees' performances against their objectives to identify the employees with performance problems.

3. *A drug testing program, when necessary.* Experts recommend that business owners seek the advice of an experienced attorney before establishing a drug testing program. Preemployment testing of job applicants generally is a safe strategy to follow, as long as it is followed consistently. Testing current employees is a more complex issue.

4. *An employee assistance program (EAP).* No drug-battling program is complete without a way to help addicted employees. An **employee assistance program (EAP)** is a company-provided benefit designed to help reduce workplace problems such as alcoholism, drug addiction, a gambling habit, and other conflicts and to deal with them when they arise. Although some troubled employees may balk at enrolling in an EAP, the company controls the most powerful weapon in motivating them to seek and accept help: *their job.* The greatest fear that substance-abusing employees have is losing their jobs, and the company can use that fear to help workers recover.

AIDS

One of the most serious health problems to strike the world is AIDS (acquired immune deficiency syndrome). This deadly disease, for which no cure yet exists, poses an array of ethical dilemmas for businesses, ranging from privacy to discrimination. AIDS has had an impact on our economy in the form of billions of dollars in lost productivity and increased health care cost.

Unlike other health-related problems, AIDS is a disease that, for the vast majority of employees, causes fear and is surrounded by misunderstanding. What often occurs is a "knee-jerk" reaction to the disease, with the infected employee being fired. Too many entrepreneurs are unaware of their legal obligation to employees with AIDS. AIDS is considered a disability and, as such, is covered by the Americans with Disabilities Act (ADA). This legislation prohibits discrimination against any person with a disability, including AIDS, in hiring, promoting, discharging, or compensation. In addition, employers are required to make "reasonable accommodations" that will allow an AIDS-stricken employee to continue working. Some examples of these accommodations include job sharing, flexible work schedules, job reassignment, sick leave, and part-time work.

Despite the fact that AIDS is becoming more common in the workplace; few businesses are adequately prepared to deal with it. Yet coping with AIDS in a socially responsible manner requires a written policy and an educational program, ideally implemented *before* the need arises. Decisions on dealing with AIDS must be based on facts rather than on emotions, so owners must be well informed.

As with drug testing, it is important to ensure that a company's AIDS policies are legal. In general, a company's AIDS policy should include the following:

Employment. Companies must allow employees with AIDS to continue working as long as they can perform the job.

"AIDS in my company? No way! I'm just a small business owner. It's the large companies that need policies and procedures to deal with AIDS-stricken employees." That's the response many small business owners offer when questioned about their readiness to cope with AIDS. Unfortunately, *it's just not true*. Small companies are not exempt from this devastating problem, and it won't just go away if owners close their eyes or turn their backs. In a small business, the impact of AIDS can be incredibly destructive. One writer explains:

> The AIDS virus itself presents a perfect metaphor for its effect on relationships and institutions. People with AIDS do not die from the virus itself, which destroys the body's immune system, but from the petty ubiquitous infections the body can no longer fight. Likewise, AIDS attacks the immune system of personal relationships, and organizations like businesses, making them even more vulnerable to weakness already there, turning commonplace threats into legal toxins. By the same token, AIDS can bring out the strengths of people and organizations. . . . A company that already treats its employees well will respond compassionately when one of its own has AIDS; a company that doesn't, won't.

Here's a story of one company's response to an AIDS-stricken employee: After returning from another extended bout with illness, Paul asked to meet privately with the managers of Circle Solutions, Inc., a small research and consulting firm. He told them that he was HIV positive. Paul's revelation prompted a host of questions about HIV, and managers needed answers fast. Were Paul's co-workers in danger of infection? What were the company's legal responsibilities to Paul? What would happen if Paul could no longer perform his duties?

Managers saw an immediate need for an AIDS education program and called in a local expert to counsel managers first and then to conduct a half-day AIDS education program for all Circle Solutions' employees. Managers also hired this expert to provide counseling to Paul, who decided to tell his co-workers about his disease.

Managers met with employees in small groups to tell them about Paul's illness. AIDS education sessions quickly followed, and management gave employees the chance to meet privately with the doctor directing the employee assistance program (EAP), "Amazingly, the response was overwhelmingly one of concern, sympathy, and support for Paul," says the company's human resources manager. "Not one person came forward to object, resign, or ask to be moved from Paul's work area." Explaining that positive response, one employee cited management's concern and Paul's openness. "We wanted to return Paul's trust by doing whatever we could for him," he said.

Circle Solution's managers also brought in an attorney specializing in AIDS discrimination cases to avoid legal problems. The attorney's advice: Keep Paul's medical information private, provide him with the same benefit as those with any life-threatening illness, allow him to work as long as he is able, and ensure that the company did not discriminate against him in any way. Managers made a commitment to living up to their legal and ethical obligations to Paul. That commitment soon was put to the test as Paul's health began to deteriorate and he missed work frequently. Managers first modified his job duties to accommodate his condition. As Paul grew weaker, managers allowed him to work whenever he could, filling in the gaps with vacation and sick leave to keep regular paychecks coming. Several of Paul's co-workers picked up the slack caused by his condition. When Paul's leave was depleted, Circle Solutions' president sent employees a memo announcing the creation of a "leave bank," to which any employee could donate a vacation day and a sick day. The memo created an outpouring of support from co-workers, who donated a total of six months' paid time. The company also arranged for a pharmacist to provide Paul's costly medications and then picked up the tab and completed the necessary paperwork. When Paul could no longer report to work, his co-workers arranged for someone in the company to contact him at least once a week to boost his morale and to keep him in touch with workplace activities.

Paul died one year after he was diagnosed. The staff held a memorial service, and several employees created a square for an AIDS quilt in his honor. What managers learned about AIDS through Paul's experience proved to be valuable when two other Circle Solutions employees contracted the HIV virus. The company is well prepared for this unfortunate reality.

1. What steps should a small company take to deal effectively with AIDS?

2. Evaluate Circle Solutions' response to AIDS.

Sources: Adapted from Tom Ehrenfield, "The Business Lesson of AIDS," *Inc.*, April 1994, pp. 29–30; Marilyn B. Ayres, "When AIDS Hits Home," *Small Business Reports*, July 1994, pp. 14–19.

Discrimination. Because AIDS is a disability, employers cannot discriminate against qualified people with the disease who can meet job requirements.

Employee benefits. Employees with AIDS have the right to the same benefits as those with any other life-threatening illness.

Confidentiality. Employers must keep employees' medical records strictly confidential.

Education. An AIDS education program should be a part of every company's AIDS policy. The time to create and implement one is before the problem arises. As part of its AIDS program, one small company conducted informational seminars, distributed brochures and booklets, established a print and video library, and even set up individual counseling for employees.

"Reasonable accommodations." Under the ADA, employers must make reasonable accommodations for employees with AIDS. These may include extended leaves of absence, flexible work schedules, restructuring a job to require less-strenuous duties, purchasing special equipment to assist affected workers, and other modifications.

Sexual Harassment

One of the historical ugly truths about the working environment in some businesses was the silent acceptance of sexual harassment. Such behaviors were often ignored and, as such, allowed to continue without consequence. Society, through its legal system, has clearly spoken out that such practices are unquestionably wrong and contrary to its values. Sexual harassment is a violation of Title VII of the Civil Rights Act of 1964 and is considered to be a form of sex discrimination.

Sexual harassment is any unwelcome sexual advance, request for sexual favors, and other verbal or physical sexual conduct made explicitly or implicitly as a condition of employment. Women bring about 90 percent of all sexual harassment charges. Jury verdicts reaching into the millions of dollars are not uncommon. *For instance, a jury awarded a woman who had been a secretary in a law firm for three months $7.1 million (later reduced to $3.5 million) because, among other things, one attorney touched her inappropriately while pouring M&Ms into her shirt pocket. The jury concluded that the law firm knew about the harassment and had not done enough to prevent it.*[12] Several types of behavior may result in charges of sexual harassment.

Pro Quo Harassment. The most blatant, and most potentially damaging, form of sexual harassment is *quid pro quo* ("something for something"), in which a superior conditions the granting of a benefit (promotion, raise, etc.) upon the receipt of sexual favors from a subordinate. Only managers and supervisors, not co-workers, can engage in *quid pro quo* harassment. Unfortunately, this form of harassment is all too common.

Hostile Environment. Behavior that creates an abusive, intimidating, offensive, or hostile work environment also constitutes sexual harassment. A hostile environment usually requires a *pattern* of offensive sexual behavior rather than a single, isolated remark or display. In judging whether a hostile environment exists, courts base their decisions on how a "reasonable woman" would perceive the situation. (The previous standard was that of a "reasonable person.") Although not easily defined, a hostile work environment is one in which continuing unwelcome sexual conduct in the workplace interferes with an employee's work performance. Most sexual harassment charges arise from claims of a hostile environment.

Do you know sexual harassment when you see it? Consider the following true case:

Catherine was exposed to nude photographs posted in various areas of the plant in which she worked. She eventually complained about the pictures to the plant manager, who (1) made inappropriate personal and sexual remarks to her, (2) addressed her as "honey" and "dear," and (3) insinuated that she was a troublemaker. Thereafter, some, but not all, of the pictures were removed, despite the employer's policy to remove sexually explicit materials upon discovery.

When Catherine's immediate supervisor heard of her complaint, he indicated that he disapproved of "women's liberation" and recited a story to Catherine about employees who had quit their jobs after the jobs were made intolerable. Other employees (including another supervisor) also expressed to Catherine their annoyance over her complaint, and she was subjected to catcalls and harassing whistles. These instances of harassment were also reported by Catherine to her immediate supervisor and the plant manager, who indicated to her that she was somehow encouraging the harassment. Management failed to put an end to the whistling and catcalls.

In its defense, the company cited the fact that it had instituted a policy of using gender-neutral terms in its job titles.

Did Catherine have a legitimate sexual harassment complaint? Explain.

Yes, although the company had a mechanism for employees to complain about sexual harassment, managers failed to take any action to stop the harassment. Indeed, the managers to whom she complained participated in the harassment. Catherine prevailed in court.

One of the primary causes of sexual harassment in the workplace is the lack of education concerning what constitutes harassment. The following quiz asks you to assume the roles of an employee and of a manager when answering the questions. Perhaps these statements can help you avoid problems with sexual harassment on the job.

A. TEST FOR EMPLOYEES

Answer each question as true or false.

1. If I just ignore unwanted sexual attention, it will usually stop.

2. If I don't mean to sexual harass another employee, there's no way my behavior can be perceived by him or her as sexually harassing.

3. Some employees don't complain about unwanted sexual attention from another worker because they don't want to get that person in trouble.

4. If I make sexual comments to someone and that person doesn't ask me to stop, then I guess my behavior is welcome.

5. To avoid sexually harassing a woman who comes to work in a traditionally male workplace, the men simply should not haze her.

6. A sexual harasser may be told by a court to pay part of a judgment to the employee he or she harassed.

7. A sexually harassed man does not have the same legal rights as a woman who is sexually harassed.

8. About 90 percent of all sexual harassment in today's workplace is done by males to females.

9. Sexually suggestive pictures or objects in a workplace don't create a liability unless someone complains.

10. Displaying "girlie" pictures can constitute a hostile work environment even though most workers in the workplace think they are harmless.

11. Telling someone to stop his or her unwanted sexual behavior usually doesn't do any good.

Answers: (1) False, (2) False, (3) True, (4) False, (5) False, (6) True, (7) False, (8) True, (9) False, (10) True, (11) False.

A TEST FOR MANAGERS

Answer each question as true or false.

1. Men in male-dominated workplaces usually have to change their behavior when a woman begins working there.

2. Employers are not liable for the sexual harassment of one of their employees unless that employee loses specific job benefits or is fired.

3. Supervisors can be liable for sexual harassment committed by one of their employees against another.

(continued)

4. Employers can be liable for the sexually harassing behavior of management personnel even if they are unaware of that behavior and have a policy forbidding it.

5. It is appropriate for a supervisor, when initially receiving a sexual harassment complaint, to determine if the alleged recipient overreacted or misunderstood the alleged harasser.

6. When a supervisor is telling an employee that an allegation of sexual harassment has been made against the employee, it is best to ease into the allegation instead of being direct.

7. Sexually suggestive visuals or objects in a workplace don't create a liability unless an employee complains about them and management allows them to remain.

8. The lack of sexual harassment complaints is a good indication that sexual harassment is not occurring.

9. It is appropriate for supervisors to tell an employee to handle unwelcome sexual behavior if they think that the employee is misunderstanding the behavior.

10. The *intent* behind employee A's sexual behavior is more important than the *impact* of that behavior on employee B when determininng if sexual harassment has occurred.

11. If a sexual harassment problem is common knowledge in a workplace, the courts assume that the employer has knowledge of it.

Answers: (1) False, (2) False, (3) True, (4) True, (5) False, (6) False, (7) False, (8) False, (9) False, (10) False, (11) True.

Sources: Reprinted with permission from *Industry Week,* November 18, 1991, p. 40. Copyright Penton Publishing, Cleveland, Ohio; *Sexual Harassment Manual for Managers and Supervisors* (Chicago: Commerce Clearing House), 1992, p. 22: Andrea P. Brandon and David R. Eyler, *Working Together* (New York: McGraw-Hill), 1994.

Harassment by Nonemployees. An employer can be held liable for third parties (customers, sales representatives, and others) who engage in sexual harassment if the employer has the ability to stop the improper behavior. *For example, one company required a female elevator operator to wear an extremely skimpy, revealing uniform. She complained to her boss that the uniform encouraged members of the public to direct offensive comments and physical contact toward her. The manager ignored her complaints, and later she refused to wear the uniform, resulting in her dismissal. The court held the company accountable for the employee's sexual harassment by nonemployees because it required her to wear the uniform after she complained of the harassment.*[13]

No business wants to incur the cost of defending itself against charges of sexual harassment, but those costs can be devastating for a small business. Multimillion-dollar jury awards in such cases are becoming increasingly common because the Civil Rights Act of 1991 allows victims to collect punitive damages and emotional distress awards.

In recent rulings, the United States Supreme Court changed the nature of an employer's liability for sexual harassment, rejecting the previous standard that the employer had to be negligent somehow to be liable for a supervisor's improper behavior toward employees. In *Burlington Industries v. Ellerth,* the court ruled that an employer can be held liable *automatically* if a supervisor takes a "tangible employment action" such as failing to promote or firing an employee whom he has been sexually harassing. The employer is liable even if he was not aware of the supervisor's conduct. If a supervisor takes no tangible employment action against an employee but engages in sexually harassing behavior such as offensive remarks, inappropriate touching, or sexual advances, the employer is not *automatically* liable for the supervisor's conduct. An employer would be liable for such conduct if, for example, he knew (or should have known) about the supervisor's behavior and failed to stop it.[14]

A company's best weapons against sexual harassment are education, policy, and procedures:

Education. Preventing sexual harassment is the best solution, and the key to prevention is educating employees about what constitutes sexual harassment. Training programs are designed to raise employees' awareness of what might be offensive to other workers and how to avoid sexual harassment altogether. Table 21.6 offers guidelines for battling sexual harassment in the workplace.

Policy. Another essential ingredient is a meaningful policy against sexual harassment that management can enforce. The policy should:

- Clearly define what behaviors constitute sexual harassment.
- State in clear language that harassment will not be tolerated in the workplace.
- Identify the responsibilities of supervisors and employees in preventing harassment.
- Define the sanctions and penalties for engaging in harassment.
- Spell out the steps to take in reporting an incident of sexual harassment.

In another case, the United States Supreme Court ruled that an employer was liable for a supervisor's sexually harassing behavior even though the employee never reported it. The company's liability stemmed from its failure to communicate its sexual harassment policy throughout the organization. This ruling makes employers' policies and procedures on sexual harassment the focal point of their defense.[15]

Procedure. Socially responsible companies provide a channel for all employees to express their complaints. Choosing a person inside the company (perhaps someone in the human resources area) and one outside the company (a close adviser or attorney) is a good strategy. At least one of these should be a woman. When a complaint arises, managers should:

- Listen to the complaint carefully without judging. Taking notes is a good idea. Tell the complainant what the process involves. Never treat the complaint as a joke.

Table 21.6
Guidelines for Battling Sexual Harassment

Before you speak or act, ask . . .	To keep the workplace harassment free . . .
• Would you say it or do it in front of your spouse, parent, or child?	• Have a clear, written policy prohibiting sexual harassment.
• Would you say it or do it if your remark or action were going to be quoted on the front page of the newspaper or televised?	• Have mandatory training programs.
• Would you say it or do it to a member of your same sex?	• Ensure that your workplace is free of offensive materials.
• Would you behave the same way with a member of your same sex?	• Establish a program outlining the steps to take to file a complaint.
• Does it need to be said or done at all?	• Keep informed of all complaints and their resolution.

Sources: Ann Meyer, "Getting to the Heart of Sexual Harassment," *HRMagazine*, July 1992, p. 82; Jan Bohren, "Six Myths of Sexual Harassment," *Management Review*, May 1993, p. 62.

- Investigate the complaint *promptly,* preferably within 24 hours. Failure to act quickly is irresponsible and illegal.
- Interview the accused party and any witnesses who may be aware of a pattern of harassing behavior *privately* and separately.
- Keep findings confidential.
- Decide what action to take, relying on company policy as a guideline.
- Inform both the complaining person and the alleged harasser of the action taken.
- Document the entire investigation.[16]

Privacy

Modern technology has given business owners the ability to monitor workers' performances as they never could before, but where is the line between monitoring productivity and invasion of privacy? At the touch of a button, it's possible to view e-mail messages employees send to one another, listen to voice-mail or telephone conversations, and actually see what's on their monitors while they're sitting at their computer terminals. Managers use electronic monitoring to track customer service representatives, word processing clerks, data entry technicians, and other workers for speed, accuracy, and productivity. Even truck drivers, long the lone rangers of the road, are not immune to electronic tracking. Almost two thirds of the major trucking companies now have communications devices in their trucks. Companies use these devices to monitor drivers' exact locations at all times, to regulate their speed, to make sure they stop only at approved fueling points, and to ensure that they take the legally required hours of rest.

Electronic communication technology also poses ethical problems for employers. Increasingly, workers are using voice-mail and electronic-mail systems to communicate with others; however, few know just what the rules governing their use and their privacy are. A study by the Society for Human Resource Management found that, although 80 percent of all organizations communicate via e-mail, only 34 percent have written policies governing the privacy of e-mail messages.[17] Most employees simply do not know that their bosses can legally monitor their e-mail and voice-mail messages, often without notification. To avoid ethical problems, a business owner should establish a clear policy for monitoring employees' communications and establish guidelines for the proper use of the company's communication technology. The policies should be reasonable and should reflect employees' reasonable expectations of privacy.

BUSINESS'S RESPONSIBILITY TO CUSTOMERS

7. Explain business's responsibility to customers.

One of the most important groups of stakeholders that a business must satisfy is its *customers.* Building and maintaining a base of loyal customers is no easy task, however. It requires more than just selling buyers a product or a service; the key is to build relationships with customers. Socially responsible companies recognize their duty to abide by the Consumer Bill of Rights, first put forth by President John Kennedy. This document gives consumers the following rights.

Right to Safety

The right to safety is the most basic consumer right. Companies have the responsibility to provide their customers with safe, quality products and services. The greatest breach of trust occurs when businesses produce products that, when properly used, injure customers. Product liability cases can be controversial, such as the McDonald's hot coffee litigation in which the jury found that the coffee was "too hot" and resulted in serious injury when the store patron dropped the coffee in her lap. In many other situations, the evidence was clear that the product purchased had fundamental flaws in either design or construction and resulted in injury to its user when operated properly. Industry associations often take action to identify products, which they find to be unsafe in an attempt to make the buyer aware of unsafe products.

Right to Know

Consumers have the right to honest communication about the products and services they buy and the companies they buy them from. In a free market economy, information is one of the most valuable commodities available. Customers often depend on companies for the information they need to make decisions about price, quality, features, and other factors. As a result, companies have a responsibility to customers to be truthful in their advertising.

Unfortunately, not every business recognizes its social responsibility to be truthful in advertising. Consider the following examples of unethical ads from small businesses.[18]

- A "universal coat hanger" for just $3.99. The product: a 10-penny nail.
- A "solid-state compact food server" for $39.95. The product: a spoon.
- A new "vision dieter." The product: a pair of glasses with one red lens and one blue lens; the lenses were supposed to make food look unappetizing (or at least purple).
- "Hide-a-Swat," guaranteed to kill flies and pests, for $9.95. The product: a rolled-up newspaper.

Businesses that rely on such unscrupulous tactics may profit in the short-term, but they will not last in the long-run!

Right to Be Heard

The right to be heard suggests that the channels of communication between companies and their customers run in both directions. Socially responsible businesses provide customers with a mechanism for resolving complaints about products and services. Some companies have established a consumer ombudsman to address customer questions and complaints. Others have created customer hotlines, toll-free numbers designed to serve customers more effectively. Another effective technique for encouraging two-way communication between customers and companies is the customer report card. *The Granite Rock Company relies on an annual report card from its customers to learn how to serve them better.* Although the knowledge a small business owner gets from customer feedback is immeasurable for making improvements, only 1 in 12 small companies regularly schedules customer satisfaction surveys such as Granite Rock's.[19] It's a tool that can boost a company's profitability significantly.

Right to Education

Socially responsible companies give customers access to educational programs about their products and services and how to use them properly. The goal is to give customers enough information to make informed purchase decisions. A product that is the wrong solution to the customer's need will only result in a disappointed customer who is likely to blame the manufacturer or retailer for the mistake. Consumer education is an inexpensive investment in customer satisfaction and the increased probability that a satisfied customer is a repeat buyer.

Right to Choice

Inherent in the free enterprise system is the consumer's right to choose among competing products and services. Socially responsible companies do not restrict competition, and they abide by the United States' antitrust policy, which promotes free trade and competition in the market. The foundation of this policy is the Sherman Antitrust Act of 1890, which forbids agreements among sellers that restrain trade or commerce and outlaws any attempts to monopolize a market.

BUSINESS'S RESPONSIBILITY TO INVESTORS

8. Discuss business's responsibility to investors.

Companies have the responsibility to provide investors with an attractive return on their investment. Although earning a profit may be a company's *first* responsibility, it is not its *only* responsibility; meeting its ethical and social responsibility goals is also a key to success. Business owners have discovered that investors wish to know what actions the organization is taking that encourage and support ethical decision making and acts of social responsibility. Investors know that such proactive steps reduce the risk of future economic loss. Ethical and socially responsible businesses seldom loose legal challenges. Maintaining high social and ethical standards translates into an environment where the stability of long-term profitability is more safely assured.

Companies also have the responsibility to report their financial performances in an accurate and timely fashion to their investors. Firms that misrepresent or falsify their financial and operating records are guilty of violating the fiduciary relationship with their investors. *For example, investors in Bre-X Minerals, a tiny mineral exploration company in Calgary, Canada, saw the value of their stock skyrocket when the company announced that it had made the richest gold find of the century in its Busang mine in Borneo, Indonesia. Within two years, however, the value of the company's stock collapsed when an independent consulting firm discovered that drilling samples from the mine had been doctored with gold dust from other sources. Angry investors saw billions of dollars of their wealth evaporate when it became apparent that Bre-X's mine contained only planted gold. That none of the 268 holes that Bre-X had drilled over three years contained any gold amounts to what experts say is a scam "without precedent in the history of mining." Investors immediately filed several class-action lawsuits against the company, claiming that Bre-X executives had committed fraud and had misled shareholders about the Busang mine's potential. Within three months of the discovery, Bre-X was in bankruptcy.*[20]

BUSINESS'S RESPONSIBILITY TO THE COMMUNITY

As corporate citizens, businesses have a responsibility to the communities in which they operate. In addition to providing jobs and creating wealth, companies contribute to the local community in many different ways. Socially responsible businesses are aware of their duty to put back into the community some of what they take out as they generate profits; their goal is to become a neighbor of choice.

9. Discuss business's responsibility to the community.

The following are just a few examples of ways small businesses have found to "give back" to their community:

- Managers and employees act as volunteers for community groups such as the American Red Cross, United Way, literacy programs, or the community food bank.
- Work on projects that aid the elderly or economically disadvantaged.
- Adopt a highway near the business to promote a clean community.

Employees, as well as the community, respond positively to an employer who actively supports the community in which it operates.

CONCLUSION

Businesses must do more than merely earn profits; they must act ethically and in a socially responsible manner. Establishing and maintaining high ethical and socially responsible standards must be a top concern of every business owner. Managing ethics and social responsibility presents a tremendous challenge, however. There is no universal definition of ethical behavior, and what is considered ethical may change over time or may be different in other cultures. Many companies are tackling the problem with education and the establishment of clearly written standards of behavior, which are consistently reinforced.

Finally, business owners and managers must recognize the key role they play in influencing their employees' ethical and socially responsible behavior. What owners and managers *say* is important, but what they *do* is even more vital! Employees throughout a small company look to the owner and managers as models; therefore, these owners and managers must commit themselves to following the highest ethical standards if they expect their organizations to do so.

CHAPTER SUMMARY

1. Define business ethics and describe the three levels of ethical standards.
   - Business ethics involves the fundamental moral values and behavioral standards that form the foundation for the people of an organization as they make decisions and interact with organizational stakeholders. Small business managers must consider the ethical and social as well as the economic implications of their decisions.
   - The three levels of ethical standards are (1) the law, (2) the policies and procedures of the company, and (3) the moral stance of the individual.
2. Determine who is responsible for ethical behavior and why ethical lapses occur.
   - Managers set the moral tone of the organization. There are three ethical styles of management: immoral, amoral, and moral.

Although moral management has value in itself, companies that operate with this philosophy discover other benefits, including a positive reputation among customers and employees.
   - Ethical lapses occur for a variety of reasons:
     Some people are corrupt ("the bad apple").
     The company culture has been poisoned ("the bad barrel").
     Competitive pressures push managers to compromise.
     Managers are tempted by an opportunity to "get ahead."
     Managers in different cultures have different views of what is ethical.
3. Explain how to establish and maintain high ethical standards.
   - Philosophers throughout history have developed various tests of ethical behavior:

the utilitarian principle, Kant's categorical imperative, the professional ethic, the Golden Rule, the television test, and the family test.

- A small business manager can maintain high ethical standards in the following ways:

  Create a company credo.
  Develop a code of ethics.
  Enforce the code fairly and consistently.
  Hire the right people.
  Conduct ethical training.
  Perform periodic ethical audits.
  Establish high standards of behavior, not just rules.
  Set an impeccable ethical example at all times.
  Create a culture emphasizing two-way communication.
  Involve employees in establishing ethical standards.

4. Define social responsibility.
   - Social responsibility is the awareness of a company's managers of the social, environmental, political, human, and financial consequences of their actions.
5. Understand the nature of business's responsibility to the environment.
   - Environmentally responsible business owners focus on the three Rs: reduce, reuse, recycle: *reduce* the amount of materials used in the company from the factory floor to the copier room; *reuse* whatever you can; and *recycle* the materials that you must dispose of.

6. Describe business's responsibility to employees.
   - Companies have a duty to act responsibly toward one of their most important stakeholders: their employees. Businesses must recognize and manage the cultural diversity that exists in the workplace; establish a responsible strategy for combating substance abuse in the workplace (including drug testing) and dealing with AIDS; prevent sexual harassment; and respect employees' right to privacy.
7. Explain business's responsibility to customers.
   - Every company's customers have a right to safe products and services; to honest, accurate information; to be heard; to education about products and services; and to choices in the marketplace.
8. Discuss business's responsibility to investors.
   - Companies have the responsibility to provide investors with an attractive return on their investments and to report their financial performances in an accurate and timely fashion to their investors.
9. Describe business's responsibility to the community.
   - Increasingly, companies are seeing a need to go beyond "doing well" to "doing good"—being socially responsible community citizens. In addition to providing jobs and creating wealth, companies contribute to the local community in many different ways.

DISCUSSION QUESTIONS

1. What is ethics? Discuss the three levels of ethical standards.
2. In any organization, who determines ethical behavior? Briefly describe the three ethical styles of management. What are the benefits of moral management?
3. Why do ethical lapses occur in businesses?
4. Describe the various methods for establishing ethical standards. Which is most meaningful to you? Why?
5. What can business owners do to maintain high ethical standards in their companies?
6. What is social responsibility?

7. Describe business's social responsibility to each of the following areas:
   a. The environment
   b. Employees
   c. Customers
   d. Investors
   e. The community
8. What can businesses do to improve the quality of our environment?
9. Should companies be allowed to test employees for drugs? Explain. How should a socially responsible drug testing program operate?
10. Many owners of trucking companies use electronic communications equipment to monitor

their drivers on the road. They say that the devices allow them to remain competitive and to serve their customers better by delivering shipments of vital materials exactly when their customers need them. They also point out that the equipment can improve road safety by ensuring that drivers get the hours of rest the law requires. Opponents argue that the surveillance devices work against safety. "The drivers know they're being watched," says one trucker. "There's an obvious temptation to push." What do you think? What ethical issues does the use of such equipment create? How should a small trucking company considering the use of such equipment handle these issues?

11. What rights do customers have under the Consumer Bill of Rights? How can businesses ensure those rights?

STEP INTO THE REAL WORLD

1. Search the current literature (e.g., periodicals such as *Business Ethics, Inc., Entrepreneur, Fortune, Forbes*, the *Wall Street Journal*, and other business publications) to find examples of companies using each of the three ethical styles of management: immoral, amoral, and moral. Prepare a brief report summarizing each and explaining the consequences of management's behavior.

2. Obtain copies of codes of ethics from several companies or associations and compare them. What are the similarities and differences among them? Do you think these codes would be useful to an employee facing an ethical dilemma? Explain.

3. Contact several local business owners. How do they view their responsibility to society? Have they altered their management styles and their companies to reflect society's changing demands for responsible companies? What methods do they use to meet their responsibility to the stakeholders discussed in this chapter?

4. "Job safety and performance are more important than the slight invasion of privacy caused by drug testing," says one plant manager. Another, who refuses to test employees, claims, "Drug testing is an outright invasion of employee privacy." Conduct a debate in your class on these two positions.

5. Working in a team with another student, interview the owners of two small businesses with at least 10 employees about their experience with employee substance abuse in the workplace. Do the owners use drug tests? If so, what is their policy? If not, why not? Do the owners have formal drug policies? Why? Write a two-page report on your findings and include at least five specific recommendations you would make to these business owners about preventing substance abuse in their workplaces.

6. Consider the following actual case. Working with teammates, decide how you would handle the situation. What ethical and socially responsible principles guided you?

David is a former drug user who has spent time in jail. For the past three years he has been straight, and he now operates a forklift at a small construction company. Lately, however, he's begun having seizures, or "flashbacks," as a result of his earlier use of the drug PCP. He has been carefully evaluated by Employee Assistance Program (EAP) professionals and found to be clean of current drug use; indeed, they say flashbacks of this nature are quite common in ex-addicts. Mishandling of David's machine could be dangerous to him and his coworkers. However, he has already had flashbacks while at the controls, and in each case the seizure caused him to release a handle, which simply stopped the machine. It is the only work he is qualified to do within this company.*

---

* *Source:* Minda Zetlin, "Combating Drugs in the Workplace," *Management Review,* August 1991, pp. 7–24.

TAKE IT TO THE NET

Visit the Scarborough/Zimmerer home page at **www.prenhall.com/scarborough** for updated information, online resources, Web-based exercises, and sample business plan.

ENDNOTES

1. Lawrence Kohlberg, *The Psychology of Moral Development: The Nature and Validity of Moral Stages* (New York: Harper & Row, 2000).
2. C. Farrell and John Fraedrich, "Understanding Pressures That Cause Unethical Behavior in Business," *Business Insights,* Spring/Summer 1990, pp. 1–4.
3. Lori A. Tansey, "Right vs. Wrong," *Managing Your Career,* Spring/Summer 1994, pp. 11–12.
4. Gabriella Stern, "Polluted Numbers," *Wall Street Journal,* October 21, 1992, pp. Al, A7.
5. Paul Klebnikov, "Russia—The Ultimate Emerging Market," *Forbes,* February 14, 1994, pp. 88–94.
6. Gene Laczniak, "Business Ethics: A Manager's Primer," *Business,* January–March, 1983, pp. 23–29.
7. Michael Josephson, "Teaching Ethical Decision Making and Principled Reasoning," *Ethics: Easier Said Than Done,* Winter 1988, p. 28.
8. Gayle Sato Stodder, "Goodwill Hunting," *Entrepreneur,* July 1998, pp. 118–125.
9. Mary Scott, "Howard Schultz," *Business Ethics,* November/December 1995, pp. 26–29.
10. "Women in Business—2001," U.S. Small Business Administration, Office of Advocacy, the Office of Economic Research, 2001.
11. *www.eeoc.gov/stats/jobpat/1999/National.html.*
12. Alexandra Alger and WIlliam G. Flanagan, "Sexual Politics," *Forbes,* May 6, 1996, pp. 106–110; Gary Schweikhart, "Sexual Harassment," *Business News,* Fall 1995, pp. 30–36.
13. *Sexual Harassment Manual for Managers and Supervisors* (Chicago: Commerce Clearing House, 1992), pp. 25–26.
14. *Burlington Industries v. Ellerth* (97-569), 123 F.3d 490; William H. Floyd III and Eric C. Schweitzer, "Sexual Harassment Rules Change," *South Carolina Business Journal,* August 1998, pp. 1, 8.
15. Floyd and Schweitzer, "Sexual Harassment Rules Change."
16. Nicole P. Cantey, "High Cost Rules Same Sex Harassment Is Against the Law," *South Carolina Business Journal,* April 1998, p. 3; Jack Corcoron, "Of Nice and Men," *Success,* June 1998, pp. 64–67.
17. Samuel Greengard, "Policy Matters," *Personnel Journal,* May 1996, p. 75.
18. Dennis G. Bates, "Fraud by Mail," *Modern Maturity,* April–May, 1991, p. 33.
19. Elyse Mall, "Make Sure That Your Customers Love You," *Your Company,* Forecast 1997, pp. 23–29.
20. Peter Waldman and Jay Solomon, "Gold-Fraud Recipe? Bre-X Workers Saw Mine Samples Mixed," *Wall Street Journal,* May 6, 1997, pp. Al, A12; "All That Glitters Now Is the Whodunit," *Atlanta Journal/Constitution,* May 6, 1997, p. F2; Suzanne McGee and Mark Heinzl, "How Bre-X Holders Passed Warnings, Got Lost in Glitter," *Wall Street Journal,* May 16, 1997, pp. Cl, C13; Rachard Behar, "Jungle Fever," *Fortune,* June 9, 1997, pp. 116–128.

Chapter 22

The Legal Environment: Business Law and Government Regulation

A verbal contract isn't worth the paper it's written on.

—Samuel Goldwyn

Governments tend not to solve problems, only to rearrange them.

—Ronald Reagan

Upon completion of this chapter, you will be able to:

1. Explain the basic elements required to create a valid, enforceable contract.
2. Outline the major components of the Uniform Commercial Code governing sales contracts.
3. Discuss the protection of intellectual property rights using patents, trademarks, and copyrights.
4. Explain the basics of the law of agency.
5. Explain the basics of bankruptcy law.
6. Explain some of the government regulations affecting small businesses, including those governing trade practices, consumer protection, consumer credit, and the environment.

The legal environment in which small businesses operate is becoming more complex, and entrepreneurs must understand the basics of business law if they are to avoid legal entanglements. Particularly in the United States, situations that present potential legal problems arise every day in most businesses, although the majority of small business owners never recognize them. Routine transactions with customers, suppliers, employees, government agencies, and others can develop into costly legal battles. For example, a manufacturer of lawnmowers might face a lawsuit if a customer injures himself while using the product. Or a customer who slips on a wet floor while shopping could sue the retailer for negligence. A small manufacturer who reneges on a contract for a needed raw material when he finds a better price elsewhere may be open to a breach of contract suit. Even when they win a lawsuit, small businesses often lose because the costs of defending themselves can run quickly into thousands of dollars. Lawsuits also are bothersome distractions that prevent entrepreneurs from focusing their energy on running their businesses. Plus, one big judgment against a small company in a legal case could force it out of business. *After years of fighting a losing battle against product liability suits, Cessna Aircraft stopped manufacturing small airplanes. Jury awards held Cessna responsible for accidents involving its planes, no matter how old they were or what the competence or condition of the pilot was. Only after Congress in 1994 passed the General Aviation Revitalization Act, which limited product liability claims to planes no more than 18 years old, did Cessna reenter the small aircraft business.*[1] The best way for entrepreneurs to avoid legal problems that can threaten their companies is to equip themselves with a basic understanding of the principles of business law.

This chapter is not designed to make you an expert in the business law or the regulations that govern business but to make you aware of the fundamental legal issues of which every business owner should be aware. Business owners should consult their attorneys for advice on legal questions involving specific situations.

THE LAW OF CONTRACTS

1. Explain the elements required to create a valid, enforceable contract.

Contract law governs the rights and obligations among the parties to an agreement (contract). It is a body of laws that affects virtually every business relationship. A **contract** is simply a legally binding agreement. It is a promise or a set of promises for the breach of which the law gives a remedy, or the performance of which the law in some way recognizes as a duty. A contract arises from an agreement, and it creates an obligation among the parties involved. Although almost everyone has the capacity to enter into a contractual agreement (freedom of contract), not every contract is valid and enforceable. A *valid* contract has four separate elements:

1. *Agreement.* A valid offer by one party that is accepted by the other.
2. *Consideration.* Something of legal value that the parties exchange as part of a bargain.
3. *Contractual capacity.* The parties must be adults capable of understanding the consequences of their agreement.
4. *Legality.* The parties' contract must be for a legal purpose.

In addition, a contract must meet two supplemental requirements: genuineness of assent and form. *Genuineness of assent* is a test to make sure that the parties' agreement is genuine and not subject to problems such as fraud, misrepresentation, or mistakes. *Form* involves the writing requirement for certain types of contracts. Although not every contract must be in writing to be enforceable, the law does require some contracts to be evidenced by a writing.

Agreement

Agreement requires a "meeting of the minds" and is established by an offer and an acceptance. One party must make an offer to another, who must accept that offer. Agreement is governed by the objective theory of contracts, which states that a party's intention to create a contract is measured by outward facts—words, conduct, and circumstances—rather than by subjective, personal intentions. In settling contract disputes, courts interpret the objective facts surrounding the contract from the perspective of an imaginary reasonable person. *For instance, Klick-Lewis, a car dealership, offered a new Chevrolet Beretta as a prize to any person who hit a hole-in-one on the ninth hole of a golf tournament. It displayed the car at the tee box of the ninth hole with a sign saying, "HOLE-IN-ONE Wins this 1988 Chevrolet Beretta GI Courtesy of Klick-Lewis Buick-Chevrolet-Pontiac $49.00 OVER FACTORY INVOICE in Palmyra." Amos Carbaugh was playing in the East End Open Golf Tournament and scored a hole-in-one on the ninth hole, but when he attempted to claim the prize, Klick-Lewis refused to sell him the car at $49.00 over invoice. The dealer said that it had offered the car as a prize in another golf tournament that had taken place two days earlier and that it had simply neglected to remove the car and the sign before the tournament in which Carbaugh was playing. Carbaugh filed a lawsuit against Klick-Lewis and won the right to buy the car at $49.00 over invoice. The court said that, based on the objective theory of contracts, an imaginary reasonable person in Carbaugh's position would have believed that the dealership was making an offer, citing the presence of the sign, the car, and no mention of a specific golf tournament. Klick-Lewis's subjective intent was irrelevant.*[2] Agreement requires that one of the parties to a contract make an offer and the other an acceptance.

Offer. An **offer** is a promise or commitment to do or refrain from doing some specified thing in the future. For an offer to stand, there must be an intention to be bound by it, reasonably certain terms, and communication of the offer. The party making the offer must genuinely intend to make an offer, and the offer's terms must be definite, not vague. The following terms must either be expressed or be capable of being implied in an offer: the parties involved; the identity of the subject matter (which goods or services); and the quantity. Other terms offerors should specify include price, delivery terms, payment terms, timing, and shipping terms. Although these elements are not required, the more terms a party specifies, the more likely it is that an offer exists.

Courts often supply missing terms in a contract when there is a reliable basis for doing so. For instance, the court usually supplies a time term that is reasonable for the circumstances. It supplies a price term (a reasonable price at the time of delivery) if a readily ascertainable market price exists; otherwise, a missing price term defeats the contract. On rare occasions, the court supplies a quantity term, but a missing quantity term usually defeats a contract. For example, the small retailer who mails an advertising circular to a large number of customers is not making an offer because one major term—quantity—is missing. Similarly, price lists and catalogs sent to potential customers are not offers.

An offer must always be communicated to the other party because one cannot agree to a contract unless he or she knows it exists. The offeror may communicate an offer by verbal expression, written word, or implied action.

Acceptance. Only the person to whom the offer is made (the offeree) can accept an offer and create a contract. The offeree must accept voluntarily, agreeing to the terms exactly as the offeror presents them. When the offeree suggests alternative terms or conditions, he is implicitly rejecting the original offer and making a counteroffer. Common law requires that the offeree's acceptance exactly match the offer. This is called the **mirror image rule,** which says that an offeree's acceptance must be the mirror image of the offeror's offer.

Generally, silence by the offeree cannot constitute acceptance, even if the offer contains statements to the contrary. For instance, when an offeror claims, "If you do not respond to this offer by Friday at noon, I conclude your silence to be your acceptance," no acceptance exists even if the offeree does remain silent. The law requires an offeree to act affirmatively to accept an offer in most cases.

An offeree must accept an offer by the means of communication authorized by and within the time limits specified by the offeror. Generally, offers accepted by alternative media or after specified deadlines are ineffective. If the offeror specifies no means of communication, the offeree must use the same medium used to extend the offer (or a faster method). According to the **mailbox rule,** if an offeree accepts by mail, the acceptance is effective when the letter is dropped in the mailbox, even if it never reaches the offeror. Also, all offers must be properly dispatched; that is, they must be properly addressed, noted, and stamped.

Consideration

Contracts are based on promises, and because it is often difficult to distinguish between promises that are serious and those that are not, courts require that consideration be present in virtually every contract. **Consideration** is something of *legal* value (*not* necessarily economic value) that the parties to a contract bargain for and exchange as the "price" for the promise given. Consideration can be money, but parties most often swap promises for promises. For example, when a buyer promises to buy an item and a seller promises to sell it, valuable consideration exists. The buyer's promise to buy and the seller's promise to sell constitute the consideration for their contract. To comprise valuable consideration, a promise must impose a liability or create a duty.

For a contract to be binding, the two parties involved must exchange valuable consideration. The absence of consideration makes a promise not binding. A promise to perform something one is already legally obligated to do is not valuable consideration. Also, because consideration is what the promisor requires in exchange for his promise, it must be given after the promisor states what is required. In other words, past consideration is not valid. Also, under the common law, new promises require new consideration. For instance, if two businesspeople have an existing contract for performance of a service, any modifications to that contract must be supported by new consideration. Also, promises made in exchange for "love and affection" are not enforceable because this does not constitute valuable consideration.

One important exception to the requirement for valuable consideration is **promissory estoppel.** Under this rule, a promise that induces another party to act can be enforceable without consideration if the promisee substantially and justifiably relies on the promise. Suppose, for example, that Singleton promises to sell a franchise to Barlow once Barlow purchases a tract of land in a nearby town. Barlow sells some of her personal assets to purchase the land, but Singleton refuses to grant her the franchise. If Barlow sues Singleton on the basis of promissory estoppel, she would be awarded damage even though she gave Singleton no consideration. Thus, promissory estoppel is a substitute for consideration.

In most cases, courts do not evaluate the adequacy of consideration given for a promise. In other words, there is no legal requirement that the consideration the parties exchange be of approximately equal value. Even if the value of the consideration one party gives is small compared with the value of the consideration to the other party, the bargain stands. Why? The law recognizes that people have the freedom to contract and that they are just as free to enter into "bad" bargains as they are to enter into "good" ones. Only in extremes cases (e.g., cases affected by mistakes, misrepresentation, fraud, duress, undue influence) will the court examine the value of the consideration provided in a trade.

Contractual Capacity

The third element of a valid contract requires that the parties involved in it must have contractual capacity for it to be enforceable. Not every individual who enters into a contract has the capacity to do so. Under the common law, minors, intoxicated people, and insane people lack contractual capacity. As a result, contracts these people enter into are considered to be voidable—that is, the party can annul or disaffirm the contract at his option.

Minors. Minors constitute the largest group of individuals without contractual capacity. In most states, anyone under age 18 is a minor. With a few exceptions, any contract make by a minor is voidable at the minor's option. In addition, a minor can avoid a contract during minority and for "a reasonable time" afterwards. The adult involved in the contract cannot avoid it simply because he is dealing with a minor.

If a minor receives the benefit of a completed contract and then disaffirms that contract, she must fulfill her duty of restoration by returning the benefit. In other words, the minor must return any consideration she has received under the contract to the adult, and she is entitled to receive any consideration she gave the adult under the contract. The minor must return the benefit of the contract no matter what form or condition it is in. For instance, suppose that Brighton, a 16-year-old minor, purchases a mountain bike for $415 from Cycle Time, a small bicycle shop. After riding the bike for a little more than a year, Brighton decides to disaffirm the contract. Under the law, all he must do is return the mountain bike to Cycle Time, whatever condition it is in (pristine, used, wrecked, or rubble), and he is entitled to get all of his money back. In most states, he does not have to pay Cycle Time for the use of the bike or the damage done to it. Adults enter into contracts with minors at their own risk.

Parents are usually not liable for any contracts made by their children, although a co-signer is bound equally with the minor. Small business owners can protect themselves in dealing with minors by requiring an adult to co-sign. If the minor disaffirms the contract, the adult co-signer remains bound by it.

Intoxicated People. A contract entered into by an intoxicated person can be either voidable or valid, depending on the person's condition when entering into the contract. If reason and judgment are impaired so that the person does not realize he is making a contract, the contract is voidable (even if the intoxication was voluntary) and the benefit must be returned. However, if the intoxicated person understands that he is forming a contract, although it may be foolish, the contract is valid and enforceable.

Insane People. A contract entered into by an insane person can be void, voidable, or valid, depending on the mental state of the person. Those who have been judged to be so mentally incompetent that a guardian is appointed for them cannot enter into a valid contract. If such a person does make a contract, it is void (i.e., it does not exist). An insane person who has not been legally declared insane nor appointed a guardian (e.g., someone suffering from Alzheimer's disease) is bound by a contract if he was lucid enough at the time of the contract to comprehend its consequences. On the other hand, if at the time of entering the contract, that same person was so mentally incompetent that he could not realize what was happening or could not understand the terms, the contract is voidable. Like a minor, he must return any benefit received under the contract.

Legality

The final element required for a valid contract is legality. The purpose of the parties' contract must be legal. Because society imposes certain standards of conduct on its members, contracts that are illegal (criminal or tortuous) or against public policy are void. Despite the power the Internet gives businesses to sell products to customers efficiently anywhere at anytime, some small companies cannot use it to sell their products. *When Congress passed the Twenty-First Amendment Enforcement Act in October 2000, it gave the states the power to control the marketing and sale of alcoholic beverages over the Internet within their borders. Twenty-eight states now prohibit out-of-state sellers from making direct sales of alcoholic beverages to residents that circumvent these states' three-tiered system (manufacturer → wholesaler → distributor). For example, an out-of-state winery that ships a bottle of wine to a customer in Florida is creating an illegal contract and could face a $3,000 fine and jail time.*[3]

If a contract contains both legal and illegal elements, the courts will enforce the legal parts as long as they can separate the legal portion from the illegal portion. However, in some contracts, certain clauses are so unconscionable that the courts will not enforce them. Usually, the courts do not concern themselves with the fairness and equity of a contract between parties because individuals are supposed to be intelligent. But in the case of unconscionable contracts, the terms are so harsh and oppressive to one party that the courts often rule the clause to be void. These clauses, called **exculpatory clauses,** frequently attempt to free one party of all responsibility and liability for an injury or damage that might occur. For instance, suppose that Miguel Sancho signs an exculpatory clause when he leaves his new BMW with the attendant at a parking garage. The clause states that the garage is "not responsible for theft, loss, or damage to cars or articles left in cars due to fire, theft, or other causes." The attendant leaves Miguel's car unattended with the keys in the ignition, and a thief steals the car. A court would declare the exculpatory clause void because the garage owes a duty to its customers to exercise reasonable care to protect their property, a duty it breached because of gross negligence.

Genuineness of Assent and the Form of Contracts

A contract that contains the four elements just discussed—agreement, consideration, capacity, and legality—is valid, but a valid contract may still be unenforceable because of two possible defenses against it: genuineness of assent and form. **Genuineness of assent** serves as a check on the parties' agreement, verifying that it is genuine and not subject to mistakes, misrepresentation, fraud, duress, or undue influence. The existence of a contract can be affected by mistakes that one or both parties to the contract make. Different types of mistakes exist, but only mistakes of *fact* permit a party to avoid a contract. Suppose that a small contractor submits a bid on the construction of a bridge, but the bidder mistakenly omits the cost of some materials. The client accepts the contractor's bid because it is $12,000 below all others. If the client knew or should have known of the mistake, the contractor can avoid the contract; otherwise, he must build the bridge at the bid price.

Fraud also voids a contract because no genuineness of assent exists. **Fraud** is the intentional misrepresentation of a material fact, justifiably relied on, that results in injury to the innocent party. The misrepresentation with the intent to deceive can result from words or conduct. Suppose a small retailer purchases a new security system from a dealer who promises it will provide 20 years of reliable service and lower the cost of operation by 40 percent. The dealer knowingly installs a used, unreliable system. In this case, the dealer has committed fraud, and the retailer can either rescind the contract with his original position restored or enforce it and seek damages for injuries.

Duress, forcing an individual into a contract by fear or threat, eliminates genuineness of assent. The innocent party can choose to carry out the contract or to avoid it. For example, if a supplier forces the owner of a small video arcade to enter a contract to lease his machines by threat of personal injury, the supplier is guilty of duress. Blackmail and extortion used to induce another party to enter a contract also constitute duress.

Generally, the law does not require contracts to follow a prescribed form; a contract is valid whether it is written or oral. Most contracts do not have to be in writing to be enforceable, but for convenience and protection, a small business owner should insist that every contract be in writing. If a contract is oral, the party attempting to enforce it must first prove its existence and then establish its actual terms. Although each state has its own rules, the law, called the Statute of Frauds, generally requires the following contracts to be in writing:

- Contracts for the sale of land
- Contracts involving lesser interests in land (e.g., rights-of-way or leases lasting more than one year)
- Contracts that cannot by their terms be performed within one year
- Collateral contracts such as promises to answer for the debt or duty of another
- Promises by the administrator or executor of an estate to pay a debt of the estate personally
- Contracts for the sale of goods (as opposed to services) priced above $500

Breach of Contract

The majority of contracts are discharged by both parties fully performing the terms of their agreement. Occasionally, however, one party fails to perform as agreed. This failure is called breach of contract, and the injured party has certain remedies available. *For instance, Ronald Leek, owner of a drag strip, entered into a contract with Randy Folk to resurface the 25-year-old surface of the raceway and to build several retaining walls required by Leek's insurance company. After Folk had completed the job, Leek refused to pay for the work, claiming that it was of poor quality and would have to be redone. At trial, several experts testified that the surface was uneven, that it contained large dips, and that it was unsafe. One race official attended a race at which the track's poor condition caused several racecars to lose control with one crashing. The court ruled that Folk had failed to perform his obligations under the contract and ruled in Leek's favor.*[4]

Generally, the nonbreaching party is entitled to sue for **compensatory damages,** the monetary damages that will place him in the same position he would have been in had the contract been performed. In addition to compensatory damages, the nonbreaching party may also be awarded **consequential damages** (also called special damages) that arise as a consequence of the breach. For the nonbreaching party to recover consequential damages, the breaching party must have known the consequences of the breach. Suppose a fireworks manufacturer fails to deliver a shipment of merchandise by June 30 in anticipation of the busy July 4 holiday celebration. The retailer can sue for the profits lost because of the late delivery since the manufacturer could have foreseen the damages late delivery would cause. Of course, the injured party has the duty to mitigate the damages incurred. In other words, the nonbreaching party must make a reasonable effort to minimize the damages incurred by the breach.

In some cases, monetary damages are inadequate to compensate the injured party for the breach of contract. The only remedy that would compensate the non-breaching party might be specific performance of the act promised in the contract. *Specific performance* is usually the remedy for breached contracts dealing with unique items (antiques, land, animals). For example, if an antique auto dealer enters a contract to purchase a rare Dusenberg and the other party breaches the contract, the dealer may sue for specific performance. That is, she may ask the court to order the breaching party to sell the antique car. Courts rarely invoke the remedy of specific performance. Generally, contracts for performance of personal services are not subject to specific performance.

THE UNIFORM COMMERCIAL CODE

2. Outline the major components of the Uniform Commercial Code governing sales contracts.

For many years, sales contracts relating to the exchange of goods were governed by a loosely defined system of rules and customs called the *Lex Mercatoria* (Merchant Law). Many of these principles were assimilated into the U.S. common law through court opinions, but they varied widely from state to state and made interstate commerce difficult and confusing for businesses. In the 1940s, a group of legal scholars compiled the **Uniform Commercial Code** (or the **UCC** or the **Code**) to replace the hodgepodge collection of confusing, often conflicting state laws that govern basic commercial transactions with a document designed to provide uniformity and consistency. The UCC replaced numerous statutes governing trade when each of the states, the District of Columbia, and the Virgin Islands adopted it. (Louisiana has adopted only articles 1, 3, 4, and 5.) The Code does not alter the basic tenets of business law established by the common law; instead, it unites and modernizes them into a single body of law. In some cases, however, the Code changes some of the specific rules under the common law. The Code consists of 10 articles:

1. General Provisions
2. Sales
2A. Leases
3. Negotiable Instruments
4. Bank Deposits and Collections
5. Letters of Credit
6. Bulk Transfers
7. Documents of Title, Warehouse Receipts, Bills of Lading, and Others
8. Investment Securities
9. Secured Transactions
10. Effective Date and Repealer

This section covers some of the general principles relating to sales (UCC Article 2), but small business owners should also become familiar with the basics of the other parts of the Code. The UCC creates a "caste system" of merchants and non-merchants and requires merchants to have a higher degree of knowledge and understanding of the Code.

Sales and Sales Contracts

Every sales contract is subject to the basic principles of law that govern all contracts—agreement, consideration, capacity, and legality. But when a contract involves the sale of goods, the UCC imposes rules that may vary slightly or substantially from basic contract law. Article 2 governs *only* contracts for the *sale of goods*. To be considered "goods," an item must be personal property that is tangible and moveable (e.g., not real estate), and a "sale" is the "passing of title from the seller to the buyer for a price" (UCC Sec. 2-106[1]). The UCC does not cover the sale of services, although certain "mixed transactions," such as the sale by a garage of car parts (goods) and repairs (a service) will fall under the Code's jurisdiction if the goods are the dominant element of the contract.

In addition to the rules it applies to the sale of goods in general, the Code imposes special standards of conduct in certain instances when merchants sell goods to one another. Usually, a person is considered a professional **merchant** if he "deals in goods of the kind" involved in the contract and has special knowledge of the business or of the goods; employs a merchant agent to conduct a transaction for him; or holds himself out to be a merchant.

Although the UCC requires that the same elements outlined in common law be present in forming a sales contract, it relaxes many of the specific restrictions. For example, the UCC states that a contract exists even if the parties omit one or more terms (price, delivery date, place of delivery, quantity), as long as they intended to make a contract and there is a reasonably certain method for the court to supply the missing terms. Suppose a manufacturer orders a shipment of needed raw materials from her usual supplier without asking the price. When the order arrives, the price is substantially higher than she expected, and she attempts to disaffirm the contract. The Code verifies the existence of a contract and assigns to the shipment a price that was reasonable at the time of delivery.

Common law requires acceptance of an offer to be exactly the same as the offer; an acceptance that adds some slight modification is no acceptance at all, and no contract exists. Any modification constitutes a counteroffer. But the UCC states that as long as an offeree's response (words, writing, or actions) indicates a sincere willingness to accept the offer, it is judged as a legitimate acceptance even though varying terms are added. In dealings between buyers and sellers, these added terms become "proposals for addition." Between merchants, however, these additional proposals automatically become part of the contract unless they materially alter the original contract, the offer expressly states that no terms other than those in the offer will be accepted, or the offeror has already objected to the particular terms. Unless the offeror objects to the added terms, they will become part of the contract. For example, suppose an appliance wholesaler offers to sell a retailer a shipment of appliances for $5,000 plus freight. The retailer responds with acceptance but adds "Price is $5,100 including freight." A contract exists, and the addition will become part of the contract unless the wholesaler objects within a reasonable time. If the wholesaler objects, a contract still exists, but it is formed on the wholesaler's original terms of $5,000 plus freight.

The UCC significantly changes the common law requirement that any contract modification requires new consideration. Under the Code, modifications to contract terms are binding without new consideration if they are made in good faith. For example, suppose a small building contractor forms a contract to purchase a supply of lumber for $1,200. After the agreement but before the lumber is delivered, a hurricane forces the price of the lumber to double, and the supplier notifies the contractor that he must raise the price of the lumber shipment to $2,400. The contractor reluctantly agrees to the additional cost but later refuses to pay. According to UCC, the contractor is bound by the modification because no new consideration is required.

The Code also has its own Statute of Frauds provision relating to the form of contracts for the sale of goods. If the price of the goods is $500 or more, the contract must be written to be enforceable. Of course, the parties can agree orally and then follow it with a written memorandum. The Code does not require both parties to sign the written agreement, but it must be signed by the party against whom enforcement is sought (which is impossible to tell before a dispute arises, so it's a good idea for *both* parties to sign the agreement).

The UCC includes a special provision involving the writing requirement in contracts between merchants. If merchants form a verbal contract for the sale of goods priced at more than $500 and one of them sends a written confirmation of the deal to the other, the merchant receiving the confirmation must object to it *in writing* within 10 days. Otherwise, the contract is enforceable against *both* merchants, even though the merchant receiving the confirmation has not actually signed anything.

Once the parties create a sales contract, they are bound to perform according to its terms. Both the buyer and the seller have certain duties and obligations under the contract. Generally, the Code assigns the obligations of "good faith" (defined as "honesty in fact in the conduct or transaction concerned") and "commercial reasonableness" (commercial standards of fair dealing) to both parties.

The seller must make delivery of the items involved in the contract, but "delivery" is not necessarily physical delivery. The seller simply must make the goods available to the buyer. The contract normally outlines the specific details of the delivery, but occasionally the parties omit this provision. In this instance, the place of delivery will be the seller's place of business, if one exists; otherwise, it is the seller's residence. If both parties know the usual location of the identified goods, that is the place of delivery (e.g., a warehouse). In addition, the seller must make the goods available to the buyer at a reasonable time and in a reasonable manner, and the buyer must give the seller proper notice of the goods' availability. Unless otherwise noted, all goods covered in the contract must be tendered in one delivery.

A buyer must accept the delivery of conforming goods from the buyer. Of course, the buyer has the right to inspect the goods in a reasonable manner and at any reasonable time or place to ensure that they are conforming goods before making payment. However, cash on delivery (COD) terms prohibit the right to advance inspection unless the contract specifies otherwise. Under the perfect tender rule in Section 2-601 of the Code, "if goods or tender of delivery fail, in any respect, to conform to the contract," the buyer is not required to accept them.

A buyer can indicate his acceptance of the goods in several ways. Usually, the buyer indicates acceptance by an express statement that the goods are suitable. This expression can be by words or by conduct. For example, suppose a small electrical contractor orders a truck to use in her business. When she receives it, she equips it to suit her trade, including a company decal on each door. Later, the contractor attempts to reject the truck and return it. By customizing the truck, the buyer has indicated her acceptance of the truck. Also, the Code assumes acceptance if the buyer has a reasonable opportunity to inspect the goods and has failed to reject them within a reasonable time.

A buyer has the duty to pay for the goods on the terms stated in the contract when they are received. A seller cannot require payment before the buyer receives the goods. Unless otherwise stated in the contract, payment must be in cash.

Breach of Sales Contracts

As we have seen, when a party to the sales contract fails to perform according to its terms, that party is said to have breached the contract. The law provides the innocent (nonbreaching) party numerous remedies, including damage awards and the right to retain possession of the goods. The object of these remedies is to place the innocent party in the same position as if the contract had been carried out. The parties to the contract may specify their own damages in case of breach. These provisions, called **liquidated damages,** must be reasonable and cannot be in the nature of a penalty. For example, suppose that Alana Mitchell contracts with a local carpenter to build a booth from which she plans to sell crafts. The parties agree that if the booth is not completed by September 1, Mitchell will receive $500. If the liquidated damages had been $50,000, they would be unenforceable because such a large amount of money is clearly a penalty.

An unpaid seller has certain remedies available under the terms of the Code. Under a seller's lien, every seller has the right to maintain possession of the goods until the buyer pays for them. In addition, if the buyer uses a fraudulent payment to obtain the goods, the seller has the right to recover them. If the seller discovers the buyer is insolvent, the seller can withhold delivery of the goods until the buyer pays in cash. If goods are shipped to an insolvent buyer, the seller can require their return within 10 days after receipt. In some cases, the buyer breaches a contract while the goods are still unfinished in the production process. When this occurs, the seller must use "reasonable commercial judgment" in deciding whether to sell them for scrap or complete them and resell them elsewhere. In either case, the buyer is liable for any loss the seller incurs. Of course, the seller has the right to withhold performance when the buyer breaches the sales contract.

When the seller breaches a contract, the buyer also has specific remedies available. For instance, if the goods do not conform to the contract's terms, the buyer has the right to reject them. Or, if the seller fails to deliver the goods, the buyer can sue for the difference between the contract price and the market price at the time the breach became known. When the buyer accepts goods and then discovers they are defective or nonconforming, he must notify the seller of the breach. In this instance, damages amount to the difference between the value of the goods delivered and their value if they had been delivered as promised. If a buyer pays for goods that the seller retains, he can take possession of the goods if the seller becomes insolvent within 10 days after receiving the first payment. If the seller unlawfully withholds the goods from the buyer, the buyer can recover them. Under certain circumstances, a buyer can obtain specific performance of a sales contract; that is, the court orders the seller to perform according to the contract's terms. As mentioned earlier, specific performance is a remedy only when the goods involved are unique or unavailable on the market. Finally, if the seller breaches the contract, the buyer has the right to rescind the contract; if the buyer has paid any part of the purchase price, it must be refunded.

Whenever a party breaches a sales contract, the innocent party must bring suit within a specified period of time. The Code sets the statute of limitations at four years. In other words, any action for a breach of a sales contract must begin within four years after the breach occurred.

Sales Warranties and Product Liability

The U.S. economy once promulgated the philosophy of "let the buyer beware," but today the marketplace enforces a policy of "let the seller beware." Small business owners must be aware of two general categories involving the quality and reliability of the products sold: sales warranties and product liability.

Sales Warranties. Simply stated, a **sales warranty** is a promise or a statement of fact by the seller that a product will meet certain standards. Because a breach of warranty is a breach of promise, the buyer has the right to recover damages from the seller. Several different types of warranties can arise in a sale. A seller creates an **express warranty** by making statements about the condition, quality, and performance of the good that the buyer substantially relies on. Express warranties can be created by words or actions. For example, a vendor selling a shipment of cloth to a customer with the promise that "it will not shrink" clearly is creating an express warranty. Similarly, the jeweler who displays a watch in a glass of water for promotional purposes creates an express warranty that "this watch is waterproof" even though no such promise is ever spoken. Generally, an express warranty arises if the seller indicates that the goods conform to any promises of fact the seller makes, to any description of them (e.g., printed on the package or statements of fact made by salespersons), or to any display model or sample (e.g., a floor model used as a demonstrator).

Whenever someone sells goods, the UCC automatically implies certain types of warranties unless the seller specifically excludes them. These **implied warranties** take several forms. Every seller, simply by offering goods for sale, implies a **warranty of title,** which promises that his title to the goods is valid (i.e., no liens or claims exist) and that transfer of title is legitimate. A seller can disclaim a warranty of title only by using very specific language in a sales contract.

An implied **warranty of merchantability** applies to every merchant seller, and the only way to disclaim it is by mentioning the term "warranty of merchantability" in a conspicuous manner. An implied warranty of merchantability assures the buyer that the product will be of average quality—not the best and not the worst. In other words, merchantable goods are "fit for the ordinary purposes for which such goods are used" (UCC Sec. 2-314[1-C]). For example, a refrigeration unit that a small food store purchases should keep food cold.

Webster, a long-time New England resident, ordered a bowl of fish chowder at the Blue Ship Tea Room, a Boston restaurant that overlooked the ocean. After eating three or four spoonfuls, Webster felt something caught in her throat. It turned out to be a fish bone that was in the bowl of chowder she had ordered. Webster had to undergo two surgical procedures to remove the bone from her throat, and she filed a lawsuit against the restaurant, claiming that it had breached the implied warranty of merchantability. The Supreme Court of Massachusetts ruled in favor of the Blue Ship Tea Room, stating that "the occasional presence of [fish bones] in chowders is . . . to be anticipated and . . . [does] not impair their fitness or merchantability." Because the fish bone in the fish chowder was not a foreign object, but one that a person could reasonably expect to find in chowders on occasion, the court decided that the restaurant had not breached a warranty of merchantability.[5]

An implied **warranty of fitness for a particular purpose** arises when a seller knows the particular reason for which a buyer is purchasing a product and knows that the buyer is depending on the seller's judgment to select the proper item. For example, suppose a customer enters a small hardware store requesting a chemical to kill poison ivy. The owner hands over a gallon of chemical, but it fails to kill the weed; the owner has violated the warranty of fitness for a particular purpose.

The Code also states that the only way a merchant can disclaim an implied warranty is to include the words "sold as is" or "with all faults," stating that the buyer purchases the product as it is, without any guarantees. The following statement is usually sufficient to disclaim most warranties, both express and implied: "Seller hereby disclaims all warranties, express and implied, including all warranties of merchantability and all warranties of fitness for a particular purpose." Such statements must be printed in bold letters and placed in a conspicuous place on the product or its package.

Product Liability. At one time, only the parties directly involved in the execution of a contract were bound by the law of sales warranties. Today, the UCC and the states have expanded the scope of warranties to include any person (including bystanders) incurring personal or property damages caused by a faulty product. In addition,

Stella Liebeck, 79, was sitting in the passenger seat of her grandson's car when they pulled up to the drive-in window at a McDonald's in Albuquerque, New Mexico. Her grandson stopped the car so she could add cream and sugar to the cup of coffee she had just ordered. Liebeck put the Styrofoam cup between her knees to remove the lid, but when she did, the coffee spilled into her lap, soaked into her sweatpants, and burned her severely. She received third-degree burns over 6 percent of her body, was hospitalized for eight days, and had to undergo skin grafts and other treatments.

Liebeck sued McDonald's under product liability law. During the trial, McDonald's documents showed more than 700 claims filed between 1982 and 1992 by people burned by its coffee. McDonald's testified that, at a consultant's advice, it held its coffee at temperatures between 180 and 190 degrees to maintain optimum taste but that it had not studied the safety implications of serving coffee at that temperature. A quality assurance manager for the chain testified that the company actively enforces a requirement that coffee be kept and served at that temperature. Evidence also revealed that other restaurants typically serve their coffee at much lower temperatures and that coffee made at home typically is between 135 and 140 degrees. In addition, attorneys pointed to a warning to the franchise industry from the Shriner's Burn Institute in Cincinnati that some chains were causing unnecessarily serious burns by serving beverages at temperatures above 130 degrees.

An expert witness for Mrs. Liebeck testified that at 180 degrees liquids that come into contact with human skin will cause third-degree burns within two to seven seconds. Liquids at 155 degrees also can produce third-degree burns but the time required to do so is about 60 seconds.

McDonald's claimed that its customers buy coffee on their way to work or home with the intent of drinking it when they arrive at their destinations. The company admitted that it did not warn customers of the risk of incurring severe burns in case of spilled coffee served at McDonald's required temperature. McDonald's argued that its customers know that its coffee is hot and that they prefer it that way. (The company sells about $1.3 million of coffee a day.)

The jury awarded Mrs. Liebeck $200,000 in compensatory damages for her injuries, but that amount was reduced to $160,000 because the jury ruled that Liebeck was 20 percent responsible for the accident. The jury also awarded her $2.7 million in punitive damages, roughly the equivalent of two days' worth of McDonald's coffee sales, but that amount was reduced to $480,000. Ultimately, McDonald's and Mrs. Liebeck entered into a secret postverdict settlement.

1. On what grounds could Mrs. Liebeck have brought her product liability suit against McDonald's?

2. Do you agree or disagree with the jury's verdict in this case? Explain.

3. What advice would you give to a restaurant owner about serving coffee to customers and wanting to avoid legal liabilities?

Sources: Adapted from "The McDonald's Scalding Coffee Case," The Association of Trial Lawyers of America, *www.atlanet.org/CJFacts/other/mcdonald.ht*; "The Actual Facts About the McDonald's Coffee Case," 'Lectric Law Library, *www.lectlaw.com/files/cur78.htm*; "Mythbuster! The 'McDonald's Coffee Case' and Other Fictions," Center for Justice and Democracy, *www.centerjd.org/free/mythbusters-free/MB_mcdonalds.htm*.

most states allow an injured party to sue any seller in the chain of distribution for breach of warranty. A company that might shoulder just a small percentage of the responsibility for a person's injury may end up bearing the majority of the damage award in the case. Courts have awarded billions of dollars to consumers who incur loss of injury from products that break, are improperly designed, are improperly inspected, are incorrectly labeled, contain faulty instructions, or have other dangerous faults. The average size of jury verdicts in product liability cases is $1.8 million![6]

Many customers who file suits under product liability laws base their claims on **negligence,** when a manufacturer or distributor fails to do something that a "reasonable" person would do. Typically, negligence claims arise from one or more of the following charges[7]:

Negligent design. In claims based on negligent design, a buyer claims an injury occurred because the manufacturer designed the product improperly. To avoid liability charges, a company does not have to design products that are 100 percent safe, but it must design products that are free of "unreasonable" risks.

Negligent manufacturing. In cases claiming negligent manufacturing, a buyer claims that a company's failure to follow proper manufacturing, assembly, or inspection procedures allowed a defective product to get into the customer's hands and cause injury. A company must exercise "due care" (including design, assembly, and inspection) to make its products safe when they are used for their intended purpose.

Failure to warn. Although manufacturers do not have to warn customers about obvious dangers of using their products, they must warn them about the dangers of normal use and of foreseeable misuse of the product. (Have you ever read the warning label on a stepladder?) Many businesses hire attorneys to write the warning labels they attach to their products and include in their instructions.

Another common basis for product liability claims against businesses is **strict liability,** which states that a manufacturer is liable for its actions no matter what its intentions or the extent of its negligence. Unlike negligence, a claim of strict liability does not require the injured party to prove that the company's actions were unreasonable. The injured person must prove only that the company manufactured or sold a product that was defective and that it caused the injury. For instance, suppose the head of an axe flies off its handle, injuring the user. To sue the manufacturer under strict liability, the customer must prove that the defendant sold the axe, the axe was unreasonably dangerous to the customer because it was defective, the customer incurred physical harm to a person or to property, and the defective axe was the proximate cause of the injury or damage. If these allegations are true, the axe manufacturer's liability is virtually unlimited.

PROTECTION OF INTELLECTUAL PROPERTY RIGHTS

3. Discuss the protection of intellectual property rights involving patents, trademarks, and copyrights.

Entrepreneurs excel at coming up with innovative ideas for creative products and services. Many entrepreneurs build businesses around intellectual property, products, and services that are the result of the creative process and have commercial value. New methods of teaching foreign languages at an accelerated pace, hit songs, books that bring a smile, and new drugs that fight diseases are just some of the ways intellectual property makes our lives better or more enjoyable. Entrepreneurs can protect their intellectual property from unauthorized use with the help of three important tools: patents, trademarks, and copyrights.

Patents

A **patent** is a grant from the federal government's Patent and Trademark Office (PTO) to the inventor of a product, giving the exclusive right to make, use, or sell the invention in this country for 20 years from the date of filing the patent application. The purpose of giving an inventor a 20-year monopoly over a product is to stimulate creativity and innovation. After 20 years, the patent expires and cannot be renewed. Most patents are granted for new product inventions, but **design patents,** extending for 14 years beyond the date the patent is issued, are given to inventors who make new, original, and ornamental changes in the design of existing products that enhance their sales. Inventors who develop a new plant can obtain a **plant patent,** provided they can reproduce the plant asexually (e.g., by grafting or cross-breeding rather than planting seeds). To be patented, a device must be new (but not necessarily better!), not obvious to a person of ordinary skill or knowledge in the related field, and useful. A device cannot be patented if it has been publicized in print anywhere in the world or if it has been used or offered for sale in this country prior to the date of the patent application. A U.S. patent is granted only to the true inventor, not a person who discovers another's invention. No one can copy or sell a patented invention without getting a license from its creator. A patent does not give one the right to make, use, or sell an invention, but the right to exclude others from making, using, or selling it.

In recent years, the PTO has awarded companies, primarily Web-based businesses, patents on their business methods. Rather than giving them the exclusive rights to a product or an invention, a business method patent protects the way a company conducts business. For instance, Amazon.com earned a patent on its "1-Click" Web-based checkout process, precluding other e-tailers from using it. Priceline.com has a patent on its business model of "buyer-driven commerce," in which customers name the prices they are willing to pay for airline tickets, hotel rooms, and other items.

Although inventors are never assured of getting a patent, they can enhance their chances considerably by following the basic steps suggested by the PTO. Before beginning the often lengthy and involved procedure, inventors should obtain professional assistance from a patent practitioner—a patent attorney or a patent agent—who is registered with the PTO. Only attorneys and agents who are officially registered may represent an inventor seeking a patent. Approximately 98 percent of all inventors rely on these patent experts to steer them through the convoluted process.[8]

The Patent Process. Since George Washington signed the first patent law in 1790, the U.S. Patent and Trademark Office has issued patents on everything imaginable (and some unimaginable items, too), including mouse traps (of course!), animals (genetically engineered mice), games, and various fishing devices. To date, the PTO has issued more than 60 million patents, and it receives more than 300,000 new applications each year (see Figure 22.1). Because of the high volume of applications it receives, processing a patent application now takes the PTO an average of 25 months.[9] To receive a patent, an inventor must follow these steps:

1. *Establish the invention's novelty.* An invention is not patentable if it is known or has been used in the United States or has been described in a printed publication in this or a foreign country.
2. *Document the device.* To protect his patent claim, inventors should be able to verify the date on which they first conceived the idea for their inventions. Inventors can document a device by keeping dated records (including drawings) of their progress on the invention and by having knowledgeable friends witness these records. Inventors also can file a disclosure document with the PTO—a process that includes writing a letter describing the invention and sending a check for $10 to the PTO.
3. *Search existing patents.* To verify that the invention truly is new, nonobvious, and useful, inventors must conduct a search of existing patents on similar

Figure 22.1
Patent Applications and Patents Granted

Source: U.S. Patent and Trademark Office.

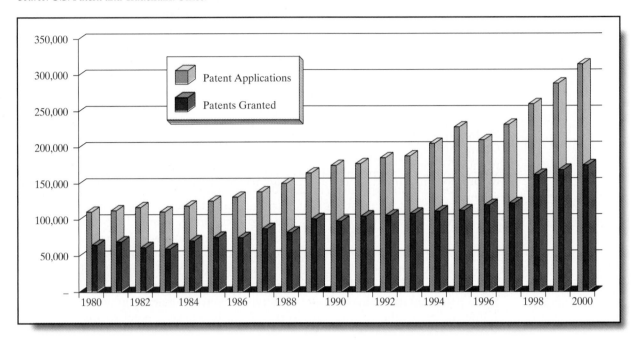

products. The purpose of the search is to determine whether or not the inventor has a chance of getting a patent. Most inventors hire professionals trained in conducting patent searches to perform the search.

4. *Study search results.* Once the patent search is finished, inventors must study the results to determine their chances of getting a patent. To be patentable, a device must be sufficiently different from what has been used or described before and must not be obvious to a person having ordinary skill in the area of technology related to the invention.

5. *Submit the patent application.* If an inventor decides to seek a patent, he must file an application describing the invention with the PTO. This description, called the patent's claims, should be broad enough so that others cannot easily engineer around the patent, rendering it useless. However, they cannot be so narrow as to infringe on patents that other inventors already hold.

6. *Prosecute the patent application.* Before the PTO will issue a patent, one of its examiners studies the application to determine whether or not the invention warrants a patent. If the PTO rejects the application, the inventor can amend his application so that the PTO can accept it.

Defending a patent against "copycat producers" can be expensive and time consuming but often is necessary to protect an entrepreneur's interest. Phony products, most of them made outside U.S. borders, include everything from Beanie Babies and Rolex watches to birth control pills and helicopter parts.[10] The average cost of a patent infringement lawsuit is about $1.5 million if the case goes to trial (about half that if the parties settle before going to trial), but the odds of winning are in the patent holder's favor. More than 60 percent of those holding patents win their infringement suits.[11]

Section IX   Legal Aspects of Small Business

Trademarks

A **trademark** is any distinctive word, phrase, symbol, design, name, logo, slogan, or trade dress that a company uses to identify the origin of a product or to distinguish it from other goods on the market. (A **service mark** is the same as a trademark except that it identifies and distinguishes the source of a service rather than a product.) A trademark serves as a company's "signature" in the marketplace. A trademark can be more than just a company's logo, slogan, or brand name; it can also include symbols, shapes, colors, smells, or sounds. For instance, Coca Cola holds a trademark on the shape of its bottle, and NBC owns a trademark on its three-toned chime. Motorcycle maker Harley-Davidson has applied for trademark protection for the shape of its oil tanks and the throaty rumbling sound its engines make![12] Components of a product's identity such as these are part of its **trade dress,** the unique combination of elements that a company uses to create a product's image and to promote it. For instance, a Mexican restaurant chain's particular décor, color schemes, design, and overall "look and feel" would be its trade dress. To be eligible for trademark protection, trade dress must be inherently unique and distinctive to a company, and another company's use of that trade dress must be likely to confuse customers. *Joshua Wesson created Best Cellars Inc., a chain of retail stores, to make buying wine much simpler and less intimidating, and customers responded. Selling only 100 labels, all for less than $10 per bottle, the company grew quickly, thanks to its unique displays and eye-catching layout. Wesson was stunned when he learned that a competitor, Grape Finds, had created a wine store that was virtually identical to Best Cellars' shops. Wesson filed a lawsuit, charging that Grape Finds had copied his company's trade dress; the court agreed, ruling in favor of Best Cellars and ordering Grape Finds to change its stores to avoid copying the distinctive look of Best Cellar's stores.*[13]

There are 1.5 million trademarks registered in the United States, 900,000 of which are in actual use. Federal law permits a manufacturer to register a trademark, which prevents other companies from employing a similar mark to identify their goods. Before 1989, a business could not reserve a trademark in advance of use. Today, the first party who either uses a trademark in commerce or files an application with the PTO has the ultimate right to register that trademark. Unlike patents and copyrights, which are issued for limited amounts of time, trademarks last indefinitely as long as the holder continues to use it. However, a trademark cannot keep competitors from producing the same product and selling it under a different name. It merely prevents others from using the same or confusingly similar trademark for the same or similar products.

Many business owners are confused by the use of the symbols ™ and ®. Anyone who claims the right to a particular trademark (or servicemark) can use the ™ (or ^SM) symbols without having to register the mark with the PTO. The claim to that trademark or servicemark may or may not be valid, however. Only those businesses that have registered their marks with the PTO can use the ® symbol. Entrepreneurs do not have to register trademarks or servicemarks to establish their rights to those marks; however, registering a mark with the PTO does give entrepreneurs greater power in protecting their marks. Filing an application to register a trademark or servicemark is relatively easy, but it does require a search of existing names. *When Barbara Allen launched a business selling an old family recipe of oils and vitamins that prevented pets from shedding, she named her product Mrs. Allen's SHED-STOP. Rather than applying for a patent for her product, however, Allen chose to register its name as a trademark. "If we went the patent route," she explains, "we'd have to divulge the formula. So we decided on the 'Coca-Cola' approach—trademark the name and keep the formula secret."*[14]

An entrepreneur may lose the exclusive right to a trademark if it loses its unique character and becomes a generic name or if the company abandons its trademark by failing to market the brand adequately. Aspirin, escalator, thermos, brassiere, super glue, yo-yo, and cellophane all were once enforceable trademarks that have become common words in the English language. These generic terms can no longer be licensed as a company's trademark. *Mark O'Brien, owner of The Pizza Maker Inc., a company known for its low-calorie "take-and-bake" pizzas, trademarked his company's name and logo in 1990. Then, in 1997, the PTO voided his trademarks, saying that he had abandoned them by failing to support the trademarks with an adequate marketing effort. Food industry giant Sysco Corporation then registered "The Pizza Maker" as its trademark.*[15]

Copyrights

A **copyright** is an exclusive right that protects the creators of original works of authorship such as literary, dramatic, musical, and artistic works (e.g., art, sculptures, literature, software, music, videos, video games, choreography, motion pictures, recordings, and others). The internationally recognized symbol © denotes a copyrighted work. A copyright protects only the form in which an idea is expressed, not the idea itself. A copyright on a creative work comes into existence the moment its creator puts that work into a tangible form. Just as with a trademark, obtaining basic copyright protection does not require registering the creative work with the U.S. Copyright Office; doing so, however, gives creators greater protection over their work. *When author J. K. Rowling wrote the manuscripts for the immensely popular* Harry Potter *series, she automatically had a copyright on her creation. To secure her works against infringement, however, Rowling registered the copyright with the U.S. Copyright Office.* Copyright applications must be filed with the Copyright Office in the Library of Congress for a fee of $30 per application. A valid copyright on a work lasts for the life of the creator plus 50 years after his or her death. (A copyright lasts 75 to 100 years if the copyright holder is a business.) When a copyright expires, the work becomes public property and can be used by anyone free of charge.

Because they are so easy to duplicate, computer software programs and videotapes are among the most-often pirated items by copyright infringers. PC Data, a research organization, estimates that one out of every four software programs running in the United States is a pirated copy, a problem that costs software manufacturers $11 billion a year![16] Movie makers fare no better. Hollywood loses $2 billion to those who forge counterfeit videotapes and sell them. In one New York City raid of a video warehouse, police confiscated $500,000 worth of tapes, including many titles that had not yet been released in movie theaters, on their way to dishonest rental stores.[17]

Protecting Intellectual Property

Acquiring the protection of patents, trademarks, and copyrights is useless unless an entrepreneur takes action to protect those rights in the marketplace. Unfortunately, not every businessperson respects others' rights of ownership to products, processes, names, and works and infringes on those rights with impunity. In other cases, the infringing behavior simply is the result of a lack of knowledge about others' rights of ownership. The primary weapon an entrepreneur has to protect patents, trademarks, and copyrights is the legal system. The major problem with relying on the legal system to enforce ownership rights is the cost of infringement lawsuits, which can quickly exceed the budget of most small businesses.

If an entrepreneur has a valid patent, trademark, or copyright, stopping an infringer often requires nothing more than a stern letter from an attorney threatening a lawsuit. Often, offenders don't want to get into expensive legal battles and agree to stop their illegal behavior. If that tactic fails, the entrepreneur may have no choice but to bring an infringement lawsuit.

Legal battles can be expensive. Before bringing a lawsuit, an entrepreneur must consider the following issues:

- Can the opponent afford to pay if you win?
- Do you expect to get enough from the suit to cover the costs of hiring an attorney and preparing a case?
- Can you afford the loss of time, money, and privacy from the ensuing lawsuit?

THE LAW OF AGENCY

4. Explain the basics of the law of agency.

An **agent** is one who stands in the place of and represents another in business dealings. Although he has the power to act for the principal, an agent remains subject to the principal's control. Many small business managers do not realize that their employees are agents while performing job-related tasks, but the employer is liable only for those acts that employees perform within the scope of employment. For example, if an employee loses control of a flower shop's delivery truck while making a delivery and crashes into several parked cars, the owner of the flower shop (the principal) and the employee (the agent) are liable for any damages caused by the crash. Even if the accident occurred while the employee was on a small detour of his own (e.g., to stop by his house), the owner is still liable for damages as long as the employee is "within the scope of his employment." Normally, an employee is considered to be within the scope of his employment if he is motivated in part by the principal's action and if the place and time for performing the act is not significantly different from what is authorized.

Any person, even those lacking contractual capacity, can serve as an agent, but a principal must have the legal capacity to create contracts. Both the principal and the agent are bound by the requirements of a fiduciary relationship, one characterized by trust and good faith. In addition, each party has specific duties to the other. An agent's duties include the following:

- *Loyalty.* Every agent must be faithful to the principal in all business dealings.
- *Performance.* An agent must perform his duties according to the principal's instructions.
- *Notification.* The agent must notify the principal of all facts and information concerning the subject matter of the agency.
- *Duty of care.* An agent must act with reasonable care when performing duties for the principal.
- *Accounting.* An agent is responsible for accounting for all profits and property received or distributed on the principal's behalf.

A principal's duties include the following:

- *Compensation.* Unless a free agency is created, the principal must pay the agent for his or her services.
- *Reimbursement.* The principal must reimburse the agent for all payments made for the principal or any expenses incurred in the administration of the agency.
- *Cooperation.* Every principal has the duty to indemnify the agent for any authorized payments or any loss or damages incurred by the agency, unless the liability is the result of the agent's mistake.

- *Safe working conditions.* The law requires a principal to provide a safe working environment for all agents. Workers' compensation laws cover an employer's liability for injuries agents receive on the job.

As agents, employees can bind a company to agreements, even if the owner did not intend for them to do so. An employee can create a binding obligation, for instance, if the business owner represents her as authorized to perform such transactions. As an example, the owner of a flower shop who routinely permits a clerk to place orders with suppliers has given that employee *apparent authority* for purchasing. Similarly, employees have *implied authority* to create agreements when performing the normal duties of their jobs. For example, the chief financial officer of a company has the authority to create binding agreements when dealing with the company's bank.

BANKRUPTCY

5. Explain the basics of bankruptcy law.

Bankruptcy occurs when a business is unable to pay its debts as they come due. Filing for bankruptcy was once akin to contracting a social disease. Today, however, bankruptcy has become an accepted business strategy.

Forms of Bankruptcy

Many of those filing for bankruptcy are small business owners seeking protection from creditors under one of the eight chapters of the Bankruptcy Reform Act of 1978. Under the act, three chapters (7, 11, and 13) govern the majority of bankruptcies related to small business ownership (see Figure 22.2). Usually, small business own-

Figure 22.2
Bankruptcy Filings by Chapter

Source: Judicial Business: 2000, p. 31, *www.uscourts.gov/judbus2000/front/2000artext.pdf.*

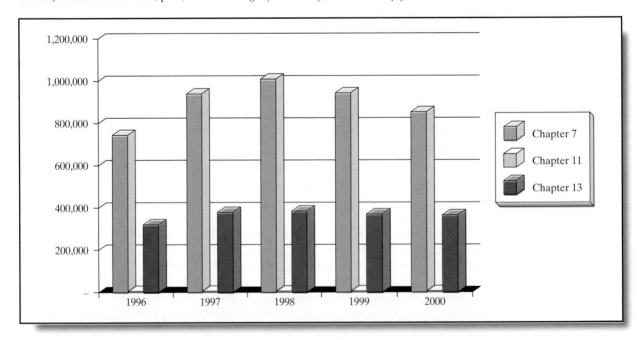

ers in danger of failing can choose from two types of bankruptcies: **liquidation** (once the owner files for bankruptcy, the business ceases to exist) and **reorganization** (after filing for bankruptcy, the owner formulates a reorganization plan under which the business continues to operate).

Chapter 7: Liquidations. The most common type of bankruptcy is filed under chapter 7 (called straight bankruptcy), which accounts for 70 percent of all filings. Under chapter 7, a debtor simply declares all of his firm's debts; he must then turn over all assets to a trustee, who is elected by the creditors or appointed by the court. The trustee sells the assets and distributes all proceeds first to secured creditors and then to unsecured creditors (which include stockholders). Depending on the outcome of the asset sale, creditors can receive anywhere between 0 and 100 percent of their claims against the bankrupt company. Once the bankruptcy proceeding is complete, any remaining debts are discharged, and the company disappears.

Straight bankruptcy proceedings can be started by filing either a voluntary or an involuntary petition. A voluntary case starts when the debtor files a petition with a bankruptcy court, stating the names and addresses of all creditors, the debtor's financial position, and all property the debtor owns. On the other hand, creditors start an involuntary petition by filing with the bankruptcy court. If there are 12 or more creditors, at least three of them whose unsecured claims total $10,000 or more must file the involuntary petition. If a debtor has fewer than 12 creditors, only one of them having a claim of $10,000 or more is required to file. As soon as a petition (voluntary or involuntary) is filed in a bankruptcy court, all creditors' claims against the debtor are suspended. Called an automatic stay, this provision prevents creditors from collecting any of the debts the debtor owed them before the petition was filed. In other words, no creditor can begin or continue to pursue debt collection once the petition is filed.

Not every piece of property the individual bankrupt debtor owns is subject to court attachment. According to the Code, certain assets are exempt, although each state establishes its own exemptions. Most states make an allowance for equity in a home, interest in an automobile, interest in a large number of personal items, and other personal assets. Federal law allows a $15,000 exemption for a home, $4,000 exemption for household items and clothing, a $3,750 ($7,500 for a married couple) exemption for equity in a house, and a $400 exemption for other property.

The law does not allow a debtor to transfer the ownership of property to others to avoid its seizure in a bankruptcy. If a debtor transfers property within one year of the filing of a bankruptcy petition, the trustee can ignore the transfer and claim the assets. In addition, any transfer of property made for the express purpose of avoiding repayment of debts (called fraudulent conveyance) will be overturned. The new law also enables a judge to dismiss a chapter 7 bankruptcy petition if it is a "substantial abuse" of the bankruptcy code.

Chapter 11: Reorganization. For a small business weakened by a faltering economy or management mistakes, chapter 11 provides a second chance for success. The philosophy behind this form of bankruptcy is that ailing companies can prosper again if given a fresh start with less debt. Under chapter 11, a company is protected from creditors' legal actions while it formulates a plan for reorganization and debt repayment or settlement. In most cases, the small firm and its creditors negotiate a settlement in which the company repays its debts and is freed of the remainder. The business continues to operate under the court's direction, but creditors cannot foreclose on it, nor can they collect any prebankruptcy debts the company owes.

A chapter 11 bankruptcy filing can be either voluntary or involuntary. Once the petition is filed, an automatic stay goes into effect and the debtor has 120 days to file a reorganization plan with the court. Usually, the court does not replace management with an appointed trustee; instead, the bankrupt party, called the debtor in possession, serves as trustee. If the debtor fails to file a plan within the 120-day limit, any party involved in the bankruptcy, including creditors, may propose a plan. The plan must identify the various classes of creditors and their claims, outline how each class will be treated, and establish a method to implement the plan. It also must spell out which debts cannot be paid, which can be paid, and what methods the debtor will use to repay them.

Once the plan is filed, the court must decide whether or not to approve it. A court will approve a plan if a majority of each of the three classes of creditors—secured, priority, and unsecured—votes in favor of it. The court will confirm a plan if it has a reasonable chance of success, is submitted in good faith, and is "in the best interest of the creditors." If the court rejects the plan, the creditors must submit a new one for court approval. *After several attempts to streamline its operations and cut its costs, Regal Cinemas, which operates movie theaters both in the United States and abroad, filed for chapter 11 bankruptcy in an attempt to reorganize and stay in business. With its filing, Regal joined a dozen other theater chains that already had declared bankruptcy, all suffering from market saturation and a precipitous drop in ticket sales.*[18]

Filing under chapter 11 offers a weakened small business a number of advantages, the greatest of which is a chance to survive (although most of the companies that file under chapter 11 ultimately are liquidated). In addition, employees keep their jobs, and customers get an uninterrupted supply of goods and services. But there are costs involved in bankruptcy proceedings. Customers, suppliers, creditors, and often employees lose confidence in the firm's ability to succeed. Creditors frequently incur substantial losses in chapter 11 bankruptcies.

Chapter 13: Individual's Repayment Plans. Chapter 13 bankruptcy is the consumer version of chapter 11 proceedings. Individual debtors (not businesses) with a regular income who owe unsecured debts of less than $250,000 or secured debts under $750,000 may file for bankruptcy under chapter 13. Many proprietors who have the choice of filing under chapter 11 or 13 find that chapter 13 is less complicated and less expensive. Chapter 13 proceedings must begin voluntarily. Once the debtor files the petition, creditors cannot start or continue legal action to collect payment. Under chapter 13, only the debtor can file a repayment plan, whose terms cannot exceed five years. If the court approves the plan, the debtor may pay off the obligations— either in full or partially—on an installment basis. The plan is designed with the debtor's future income in mind, and when the debtor completes the payments under the plan, all debts are discharged.

GOVERNMENT REGULATION

Although most entrepreneurs recognize the need for some government regulation of business, most believe the process is overwhelming and out of control. Government regulation of business is far from new; in fact, Congress created the Interstate Commerce Commission in 1887. The Great Depression of the 1930s triggered a great deal of regulation of business. From the 1930s forward, laws regulating business practices and government agencies to enforce the regulations have expanded continuously. Not to be outdone by the federal regulators, most states have created their own regulatory agencies to create and enforce a separate set of rules and regulations. In many instances, small business owners are overwhelmed by the paperwork required to respond to all the governmental agencies trying to regulate and protect them.

1. Explain some of the government regulations affecting small business, including those governing trade practices, consumer protection, consumer credit, and the environment.

The major complaint small business owners have concerning government regulation revolves around the cost of compliance. The National Federation of Independent Businesses (NFIB) says that businesses spend $721 billion a year to comply with government regulations.[19] For small companies, regulatory compliance cost per employee is significantly higher than those of large businesses with whom they must compete. One study found that companies with fewer than 20 employees pay two to three times more per employee than larger companies to comply with government regulations![20] In a competitive market, small companies cannot simply pass these additional costs forward to their customers and, consequently, they experience a squeeze on their profit margins. A 1996 law, the Small Business Regulatory Enforcement and Fairness Act, offers business owners some hope. Its purpose is to require government agencies to consider the impact of their regulations on small companies and gives business owners more input into the regulatory process.

Most business owners agree that some government regulation is necessary. There must be laws governing working safety, environmental protection, package labeling, consumer credit, and other relevant issues because some dishonest, unscrupulous managers will abuse the opportunity to serve the public's interest. It is not the regulations that protect workers and consumers and achieve social objectives that businesses object to, but those that produce only marginal benefits relative to their costs. Owners of small firms, especially, seek relief from wasteful and meaningless government regulations, charging that the cost of compliance exceeds the benefits gained.

Trade Practices

Sherman Antitrust Act. Contemporary society places great value on free competition in the marketplace, and antitrust laws reflect this. The notion of laissez-faire—that the government should not interfere with the operation of the economy—that once dominated U.S. markets no longer prevails. One of the earliest trade laws was the Sherman Antitrust Act, which was passed in 1890 to promote competition in the U.S. economy. This act is the foundation on which antitrust policy in the United States is built and was aimed at breaking up the most powerful monopoly of the late nineteenth century, John D. Rockefeller's Standard Oil Trust. Although its language is very general, the Sherman Antitrust Act contains two primary provisions affecting growth and trade among businesses.[21]

Section I forbids "every contract combination in the form of trust or otherwise, or conspiracy, in restraint of trade or commerce among the several states, or with foreign nations." This section outlaws any agreement among sellers that might create an unreasonable restraint on free trade in the marketplace. For example, a group of small and medium-size regional supermarkets formed a cooperative association to purchase products to resell under private labels only in restricted geographic regions. The U.S. Supreme Court ruled that their action was an attempt to restrict competition by allocating territories and had "no purpose except stifling of competition."[22]

Section II of the Sherman Antitrust Act makes it illegal for any person to "monopolize or attempt to monopolize any part of the trade or commerce among the several states, or with foreign nations." The primary focus of Section II is on preventing the undesirable effects of monopoly power in the marketplace.

Clayton Act. Congress passed the Clayton Act in 1914 to strengthen federal antitrust laws by spelling out specific monopolistic activities. The major provisions of the Clayton Act forbid the following activities:

GAINING THE COMPETITIVE EDGE
Are Your Ads Setting You Up for Trouble?

When a Florida auto dealer offered a "free four-day, three-night vacation to Acapulco" to any customer purchasing a new car or van, he had no idea of the legal problems his advertisement would create. A customer who bought a van from the dealer felt cheated when he discovered that the "free vacation" was actually a sales promotion for a time-share condominium and was overrun with restrictions, conditions, and qualifications. Believing the ad was deceptive, the customer filed a lawsuit against the dealer. The jury ruled against the car dealer and awarded the customer $1,768 in compensatory damages and $667,000 in punitive damages!

Entrepreneurs sometimes run afoul of the laws concerning advertising because they do not know how to comply with legal requirements. The Federal Trade Commission (FTC) is the federal agency that regulates advertising and deals with problems created by deceptive ads. Under federal and state laws, an advertisement is unlawful if it misleads or deceives a reasonable customer, even if the business owner responsible for it had no intention to deceive. Any ad containing a false statement is in violation of the law, although the entrepreneur may not know that the statement was false. The FTC judges an ad by the overall impression it creates and not by the technical truthfulness of its individual parts.

What can entrepreneurs do to avoid charges of deceptive advertising? The following guidelines will help:

- *Make sure your ads are accurate.* Avoid creating ads that promise more than a product or service can deliver. Take the time to verify the accuracy of every claim or statement in your ads. If a motor oil protects an engine from damage, don't claim that it will repair damage that already exists in an engine—unless you can prove that it actually does!

- *Get permission to use quotations, pictures, and endorsements.* Never use material in an ad from an outside source unless you get written permission to do so. One business owner got into trouble when he inserted a photograph of a famous athlete without his permission into an ad for his company's service.

- *Be careful when you compare competitors' products or services to your own.* False statements that harm the reputation of a competitor's business, products, or services not only may result in charges of false advertising but also in claims of trade libel. Make sure that any claims in your ads comparing your products to competitors' are fair and accurate.

- *Stock sufficient quantities of advertised items.* Businesses that advertise items for sale must be sure to have enough units on hand to meet anticipated demand. If you suspect that demand may outstrip your supply, state in the ad that quantities are limited.

- *Avoid "bait and switch" advertising.* This illegal technique involves advertising an item for sale at an attractive price when a business has no real intention of selling that product at that price. Companies using this technique often claim to have sold out of the advertised special. Their goal is to lure customers in with the low price and then switch them over to a similar product at a higher price.

- *Use the word "free" carefully and accurately.* Every advertiser knows that one of the most powerful words in advertising is "free." However, anything you advertise as being free must actually be free! For instance, suppose a business advertises a free paintbrush to anyone who buys a gallon of a particular type of paint for $11.95. If the company's regular price for this is less than $11.95, the ad is deceptive because the paintbrush is not really free.

- *Be careful of what your ad does not say.* Omitting information in an ad that leaves customers with a false impression about a product or service and its performance is also a violation of the law.

- *Describe sale prices and "savings" carefully.* Business owners sometimes get into trouble with false advertising when they advertise items at prices that offer huge "savings" over their "regular" prices. One jeweler violated the law by advertising a bracelet for $299, a savings of $200 from the item's regular $499 price. In reality, the

(continued)

jeweler had never sold the item at its $499 "regular" price; the item's normal price was the $299 he advertised as the "sale" price.

1. Visit the Web site for the Federal Trade Commission at *www.ftc.gov/*. Use the information you find there to compile a list of five suggestions to help entrepreneurs avoid charges of deceptive advertising.

2. Get a copy of a local paper and look for advertisements that you suspect may be false or misleading.

Sources: Adapted from *Guides Against Bait Advertising,* Federal Trade Commission (Washington, DC), *www.ftc.gov/bcp/guides/baitads-gd.htm;* Frequently Asked Advertising Questions: A Guide for Small Business, Federal Trade Commission (Washington, DC), *www.ftc.gov/bcp/conline/pubs/buspubs/ad-faqs.htm;* Carlotta Roberts, "The Customer's Always Right," *Entrepreneur,* November 20, 2000, *www.entrepreneur.com/article/0,4621,284044,00.html;* "Seven Rules for Legal Advertising," *Inc.* (no date), *www.inc.com/search/20153.html;* "Consumer Protection Laws," *Inc.* (no date), *www.inc.com/search/19691.html.*

1. *Price discrimination.* A firm cannot charge different customers different prices for the same product, unless the price discrimination is based on an actual cost savings, is made to meet a lower price from competitors, or is justified by a difference in grade, quality, or quantity sold.
2. *Exclusive dealing and tying contracts.* A seller cannot require a buyer to purchase only her product to the exclusion of other competitive sellers' products (an exclusive dealing agreement). Also, the act forbids sellers to sell a product on the condition that the buyer agrees to purchase another product the seller offers (a tying agreement). For example, a computer manufacturer could not sell a computer to a business and, as a condition of the sale, require the firm to purchase software as well.
3. *Purchasing stock in competing corporations.* A business cannot purchase the stock or assets of another business when the effect may be to substantially lessen competition. This does not mean that a corporation cannot hold stock in a competing company; the rule is designed to prevent horizontal mergers that would reduce competition. The Federal Trade Commission (FTC) and the Antitrust Division of the Justice Department enforce this section, evaluating the market shares of the companies involved and the potential effects of a horizontal merger before ruling on its legality.
4. *Interlocking directorates.* The act forbids interlocking directorates—a person serving on the board of directors of two or more competing companies.

Federal Trade Commission Act. To supplement the Clayton Act, Congress passed the Federal Trade Commission Act in 1914, which created its namesake agency and gave it a broad range of powers. Section 5 gives the FTC the power to prevent "unfair methods of competition in commerce and unfair or deceptive acts or practices in commerce." Recent amendments have expanded the FTC's powers. The FTC's primary targets are those businesses that engage in unfair trade practices, often brought to the surface by consumer complaints. In addition, the agency has issued a number of trade regulation rules defining acceptable and unacceptable trade practices in various industries. Its major weapon is a "cease and desist order," commanding the violator to stop its unfair trade practices.

The FTC Act and the Lanham Trademark Act of 1988 (plus state laws) govern the illegal practice of deceptive advertising. In general, the FTC can review any advertisement that might mislead people into buying a product or service they would not buy if they knew the truth. For instance, if a small business advertised a "huge year-end inventory reduction sale" but kept its prices the same as its regular prices, it is violating the law.

Robinson–Patman Act. Although the Clayton Act addressed price discrimination and the FTC forbade the practice, Congress found the need to strengthen the law because many businesses circumvented original rules. In 1936, Congress passed the Robinson–Patman Act, which further restricted price discrimination in the marketplace. The act forbids any seller "to discriminate in price between different purchases of commodities of like grade and quality" unless there are differences in the cost of manufacture, sale, or delivery of the goods. Even if a price-discriminating firm escaped guilt under the Clayton Act, it violated the Robinson–Patman Act. Traditionally, the FTC has had the primary responsibility of enforcing the Robinson–Patman Act.

Other Legislation. The Celler–Kefauver Act of 1950 gave the FTC the power to review certain proposals for mergers so it could prevent too much concentration of power in any particular industry.

Congress created the Miller–Tydings Act in 1937 to introduce an exception to the Sherman Antitrust Act. This act made it legal for manufacturers to use fair trade agreements that prohibit sellers of the manufacturer's product from selling it below a predetermined fair trade price. This form of price fixing was outlawed when Congress repealed the Miller–Tydings Act in 1976. Manufacturers can no longer mandate minimum or maximum prices on their products to sellers.

Consumer Protection

Since the early 1960s, legislators have created many laws aimed at protecting consumers from unscrupulous sellers, unreasonable credit terms, and mislabeled or unsafe products. Early laws focused on ensuring that food and drugs sold in the marketplace were safe and of proper quality. The first law, the Pure Food and Drug Act, passed in 1906, regulated the labeling of various food and drug products. Later amendments empowered government agencies to establish safe levels of food additives and to outlaw carcinogenic (cancer-causing) additives. In 1938, Congress passed the Food, Drug, and Cosmetics Act, which created the Food and Drug Administration (FDA). The FDA is responsible for establishing standards of safe over-the-counter drugs; inspecting food and drug manufacturing operations; performing research on food, additives, and drugs; regulating drug labeling; and other related tasks.

Congress has also created a number of laws to establish standards pertaining to product labeling for consumer protection. Since 1976, manufacturers have been required to print accurate information about the quantity and content of their products in a conspicuous place on the package. Generally, labels must identify the raw materials used in the product, the manufacturer, the distributor (and its place of business), the net quantity of the contents and the quantity of each serving if the package states the number of servings. The law also requires labels to be truthful. For example, a candy bar labeled "new, bigger size" must actually be bigger. These requirements, created by the Fair Packaging and Labeling Act of 1976, were designed to improve the customers' ability to comparison shop. A 1970 amendment to the Fair Packaging and Labeling Act, the Poison Prevention Packaging Act, required manufacturers to install childproof caps on all products that are toxic.

With the passage of the Consumer Products Safety Act in 1972, Congress created the Consumer Products Safety Commission (CPSC) to control potentially dangerous products sold to consumers, and it has broad powers over manufacturers and sellers of consumer products. For instance, the CPSC can set safety requirements for consumer products, and it has the power to ban the production of any product it considers hazardous to consumers. It can also order vendors to remove unsafe products from their shelves. In addition to enforcing the Consumer Product Safety Act, the CPSC is also charged with enforcing the Refrigerator Safety Act, the Federal Hazardous Substance Act, the Child Protection and Toy Safety Act, the Poison Prevention Package Act, and the Flammable Fabrics Act.

The Magnuson–Moss Warranty Act, passed in 1975, regulates written warranties that companies offer on the consumer goods they sell. The act does not require companies to offer warranties; it only regulates the warranties companies choose to offer. It also requires businesses to state warranties in easy-to-understand language and defines the conditions warranties must meet before they can be designated as "full warranties."

Consumer Credit

Another area subject to intense government regulation is consumer credit. This section of the law has grown in importance since credit has become a major part of many consumer purchases. The primary law regulating consumer credit is the Consumer Credit Protection Act (CCPA), passed in 1968. More commonly known as the Truth-in-Lending Act, this law requires sellers who extend credit and lenders to fully disclose the terms and conditions of credit arrangements. The FTC is responsible for enforcing the Truth-in-Lending Act. The law outlines specific requirements that any firm that offers, arranges, or extends credit to customers must meet. The two most important terms of the credit arrangement that lenders must disclose are the finance charge and the annual percentage rate. The finance charge represents the total cost—direct and indirect—of the credit, and the annual percentage rate (APR) is the relative cost of credit stated in annual percentage terms.

The Truth-in-Lending Act applies to any consumer loan for less than $25,000 (or loans of any amount secured by mortgages on real estate) that includes more than four installments. Merchants extending credit to customers must state clearly the following information, using specific terminology:

- The price of the product
- The down payment and any trade-in allowance made
- The unpaid balance owed after the down payment
- The total dollar amount of the finance charge
- Any prepaid finance charges or required deposit balances, such as points, service charges, or lenders' fees
- Any other charges not include in the finance charge
- The total amount to be financed
- The unpaid balance
- The deferred payment price, including the total cash price and finance and incidental charges
- The date on which the finance charge begins to accrue
- The APR of the finance charge
- The number, amounts, and due dates of payments
- The penalties imposed in case of delinquent payments
- A description of any security interest the creditor holds
- A description of any penalties imposed for early repayment of principal

Another provision of the Truth-in-Lending Act limits the credit card holder's liability in case the holder's card is lost or stolen. As long as the holder notifies the company of the missing card, she is liable for only $50 of any amount that an unauthorized user might charge on the card (or zero if the holder notifies the company before any unauthorized use of the card).

In 1974, Congress passed the Fair Credit Billing Act, an amendment to the Truth-in-Lending Act. Under this law, a credit card holder may withhold payment on a faulty product, providing she has made a good faith effort to settle the dispute first. A credit card holder can also withhold payment to the issuing company if she believes her bill is in error. The cardholder must notify the issuer within 60 days but is not required to pay the bill until the dispute is settled. The creditor cannot collect any finance charge during this period unless there was no error.

Another credit law designed to protect consumers is the Equal Credit Opportunity Act of 1974, which prohibits discrimination in granting credit on the basis of race, religion, national origin, color, sex, marital status, or whether the individual receives public welfare payment.

In 1971, Congress created the Fair Credit Reporting Act to protect consumers against the circulation of inaccurate or obsolete information pertaining to credit applications. Under this act, the consumer can request the nature of any credit investigation, the type of information assembled, and the identity of those persons receiving the report. The law requires that any obsolete or misleading information contained in the file be updated, deleted, or corrected.

Congress enacted the Fair Debt Collection Practices Act in 1977 to protect consumers from abusive debt collection practices. The law does not apply to business owners collecting their own debts, but only to debt collectors working for other businesses. The act prevents debt collectors from doing the following:

- Contacting the debtor at his workplace if the employer objects
- Using intimidation, harassment, or abusive language to pester the debtor
- Calling on the debtor at inconvenient times (before 8 A.M. or after 9 P.M.).
- Contacting third parties (except parents, spouses, and financial advisers) about the debt
- Contacting the consumer after receiving notice of refusal to pay the debt (except to inform the debtor of the involvement of a collection agency)
- Making false threats against the debtor

Environmental Law

In 1970, Congress created the Environmental Protection Agency (EPA) and gave it the authority to create laws that would protect the environment from pollution and contamination. Although the EPA administers a number of federal environmental statutes, three in particular stand out: the Clean Air Act, the Clean Water Act, and the Resource Conservation and Recovery Act.

The Clean Air Act. To reduce the problems associated with acid rain, the Greenhouse Effect, and airborne pollution, Congress passed the Clean Air Act in 1970 (and several amendments since then). The act targets everything from coal-burning power plants to automobiles. The Clean Air Act assigned the EPA the task of developing a national air-quality standard, and the agency works with state and local governments to enforce compliance with these standards.

The Clean Water Act. The Clean Water Act, passed in 1972, set out to make all navigable waters in the United States suitable for fishing and swimming by 1983 and to eliminate the discharge of pollutants into those waters by 1985. Although the EPA has made progress in cleaning up many bodies of water, it has yet to achieve these goals. The Clean Water Act requires the states to establish water-quality standards and to develop plans to reach them. The act also prohibits the draining, dredging, or filling of wetlands without a permit. The Clean Water Act also addresses the issues of providing safe drinking water and cleaning up oil spills in navigable waters.

The Resource Conservation and Recovery Act. Congress passed the Resource Conservation and Recovery Act (RCRA) in 1976 to deal with solid waste disposal. The RCRA sets guidelines by which solid waste landfills must operate, and it establishes rules governing the disposal of hazardous wastes. The RCRA's goal is to prevent solid waste from contaminating the environment. But what about those waste disposal sites that are already contaminating the environment? In 1980, Congress passed the Comprehensive Environmental Response, Compensation, and Liability Act (CERCLA) to deal with those sites. The act created the Superfund, a special federal fund set up to finance and to regulate the cleanup of solid-waste disposal sites that are polluting the environment.

CHAPTER SUMMARY

1. Explain the basic elements required to create a valid, enforceable contract.
   - A valid contract must contain these elements: agreement (offer and acceptance), consideration, capacity, and legality. A contract can be valid and yet unenforceable because it fails to meet two other conditions: genuineness of assent and proper form.
   - Most contracts are fulfilled by both parties performing their promised actions; occasionally, however, one party fails to perform as agreed, thereby breaching the contract. Usually, the nonbreaching party is allowed to sue for monetary damages that would place her in the same position she would have been in had the contract been performed. In cases where money is an insufficient remedy, the injured party may sue for specific performance of the contract's terms.
2. Outline the major components of the Uniform Commercial Code governing sales contracts.
   - The Uniform Commercial Code (UCC) was an attempt to create a unified body of law governing routine business transactions. Of the 10 articles in the UCC, Article 2 on the sale of goods affects many business transactions.
   - Contracts for the sale of goods must contain the same four elements of a valid contract, but the UCC relaxes many of the specific restrictions the common law imposes on contracts. Under the UCC, once the parties

create a contract, they must perform their duties in good faith.
   - The UCC also covers sales warranties. A seller creates an express warranty when he makes a statement about the performance of a product or indicates by example certain characteristics of the product. Sellers automatically create other warranties—warranties of title, implied warranties of merchantability, and, in certain cases, implied warranties of fitness for a particular purpose—when they sell a product.
3. Discuss the protection of intellectual property rights using patents, trademarks, and copyrights.
   - A patent is a grant from the federal government that gives an inventor exclusive rights to an invention for 20 years. To submit a patent, an inventor must: establish novelty, document the device, search existing patents, study the search results, submit a patent application to the U.S. Patent and Trademark Office, and prosecute the application.
   - A trademark is any distinctive word, symbol, or trade dress that a company uses to identify its product or to distinguish it from other goods. It serves as the company's "signature" in the marketplace.
   - A copyright protects original works of authorship. It covers only the form in which an idea is expressed and not the idea itself and lasts for 50 years beyond the creator's death.

4. Explain the basic workings of the law of agency.
   - In an agency relationship, one party (the agent) agrees to represent another (the principal). The agent has the power to act for the principal but remains subject to the principal's control. While performing job-related tasks, employees play an agent's role.
   - An agent has the following duties to a principal: loyalty, performance, notification, duty of care, and accounting. The principal has certain duties to the agent: compensation, reimbursement, cooperation, indemnification, and safe working conditions.
5. Explain the basics of bankruptcy law.
   - Entrepreneurs whose businesses fail often have no other choice but to declare bankruptcy under one of three provisions: chapter 7 liquidations, in which the business sells its assets, pays what debts it can, and disappears; chapter 11, reorganizations, in which the business asks that its debts be forgiven or restructured and then reemerges; and chapter 13, straight bankruptcy, which is for individuals only.
6. Explain some of the government regulations affecting small businesses, including those governing trade practices, consumer protection, consumer credit, and the environment.
   - Businesses operate under a multitude of government regulations governing many areas, including trade practices, where laws forbid restraint of trade, price discrimination, exclusive dealing and tying contracts, purchasing controlling interests in competitors, and interlocking directorates.
   - Other areas subject to government regulations include consumer protection (the Food, Drug, and Cosmetics Act and the Consumer Product Safety Act) and consumer credit (the Consumer Credit Protection Act [CCPA], the Fair Debt Collection Practices Act, and the Fair Credit Reporting Act), and the environment (the Clean Air Act, the Clean Water Act, and the Resource Conservation and Recovery Act [RCRA]).

DISCUSSION QUESTIONS

1. What is a contract? List and describe the four elements required for a valid contract. Must a contract be in writing to be valid?
2. What constitutes an agreement?
3. What groups of people lack contractual capacity? How do the courts view contracts that minors create? Intoxicated people? Insane people?
4. What circumstances eliminate genuineness of assent in the parties' agreement?
5. What is breach of contract? What remedies are available to a party injured by a breach?
6. What is the Uniform Commercial Code? To which kinds of contracts does the UCC apply? How does it alter the requirements for a sale contract?
8. Under the UCC, what remedies does a seller have when a buyer breaches a sales contract? What remedies does a buyer have when a seller breaches a contract?
9. What is a sales warranty? Explain the different kinds of warranties sellers offer.
10. Explain the different kinds of implied warranties the UCC imposes on sellers of goods.
Can sellers disclaim these implied warranties? If so, how?
11. What is product liability? Explain the charges that most often form the basis for product liability claims. What must a customer prove under these charges?
12. What is intellectual property? What tools do entrepreneurs have to protect their intellectual property?
13. Explain the differences among patents, trademarks, and copyrights. What does each protect? How long does each last?
14. What must an inventor prove to receive a patent?
15. Briefly explain the patent application process.
16. What is an agent? What duties does an agent have to a principal? What duties does a principal have to an agent?
17. Explain the differences among the three major forms of bankruptcy: chapter 7, chapter 11, and chapter 13.
18. Explain the statement "For each benefit gained by regulation, there is a cost."

1. Interview a local attorney about contract law. What is the difference between a valid contract, a void contract, a voidable contract, and an enforceable contract? What elements must be present for a valid contract to exist? What are the most common mistakes business owners make when creating contracts? What advice does the attorney offer to avoid making these mistakes?

2. Go to the U.S. Patent and Trademark Office's Web site at *www.uspto.gov/*. Select a product that interests you and search through some of the patents the office has granted for that product. Write a one-page summary of your search results. Do you see any ways to improve upon existing patents?

3. Contact the Small Business Development Center in your area or a local attorney and ask about the "real world" problems of obtaining a patent and enforcing your rights once it has been granted.

4. Visit a small manufacturing company in your area and interview the owner or manager about the federal and state regulations with which the company must comply. Ask to see some of the paperwork required to comply with federal and state regulations. Which government agencies regulate the company's activities? How much does it cost the company to comply with these regulations? Which regulations make the most sense to the owner? The least? Why? Write a two-page summary of your interview.

TAKE IT TO THE NET

Visit the Scarborough/Zimmerer home page at **www.prenhall.com/scarborough** for updated information, online resources, Web-based exercises, and sample business plan.

ENDNOTES

1. Philip Siekman, "Cessna Tackles Lean Manufacturing," *Fortune,* May 1, 2000, *www.fortune.com/indexw.jhtml?channel=artcol.jhtml&d oc_id=00001351.*
2. *Carbaugh v. Klick-Lewis,* 561 A.2d 1248 (Pa 1989).
3. Cora Nucci, "Can't Ship That Wine if It's Bought Online," *TechWeb,* February 12, 2001, *content.techweb.com/wire/story/TWB20010212S0019;* Lori Enos, "Battle Intensifies Over Net Alcohol Sales," *E-Commerce Times,* March 1, 2001, *www.ecommercetimes.com/perl/story/?id=7819;* Pul Kanoho, "Restrictions on Alcohol Sales on the Internet: Issues of Safety and Freedom," *The Internet Law Journal,* April 16, 2001, *www.internetlawjournal.com/content/ecomhead-line04140102.htm.*
4. *Folk v. Central National Bank and Trust Company,* 210 Ill. App (1991).
5. *Webster v. Blue Ship Tea Room,* 198 N.E. 2d 309 (Mass. 1964); 347 Mass 421.
6. "Juries Handing Out Bigger Product Liability Awards," February 2, 2001, Overlawyered.com, *www.overlawyered.com/archives/01/feb1.html#0202b.*
7. "Product Liability Basics," *Inc.,* February 22, 2000, *www.inc.com/search/17249.html.*
8. Tomima Edmark, "Finders Keepers," *Entrepreneur,* July 1998, pp. 100–103.
9. Carol Pickering, "Patently Absurd," *Business 2.0,* May 29, 2001, pp. 28–30.
10. Richard Behar, "Beijing's Phony War on Fakes," *Fortune,* October 30, 2000, pp. 189–208.
11. Ibid.; Tomima Edmark, "On Guard," *Entrepreneur,* August 1997, pp. 92–94; Tomima Edmark, "On Guard," *Entrepreneur,* February 1997, pp. 109–111.
12. Nina Munk, "The Smell of This Magazine Is a Registered Trademark," *Forbes,* May 5, 1997, pp. 39–40.
13. Rodney Ho, "Best Cellars Inc Doesn't Think Imitation Is Flattering," *Wall Street Journal,* April 18, 2000, p. B1.
14. Lance Frazer, "A Small Biz Guide to Trademarks, Patents, and Copyrights," *E-Merging Business,* Fall/Winter 2000, pp. 112–115.
15. Ibid.
16. Joel Enos, "Sega Is Seething from Swarmy Swash-bucklers," *Forbes ASAP,* November 27, 2000, p. 44.

17. Phillip E. Ross, "Cops Versus Robbers in Cyberspace," *Forbes,* September 9, 1996, pp. 134–139.

18. Bill Brewer, "Regal Cinemas to Restructure in Chapter 11 Bankruptcy," *Naples Daily News,* September 7, 2001, *www.marconews.com/01/09/business/d675956a.htm.*

19. Phillip Harper, "Warning: Government Regulations Ahead," Microsoft bCentral, *www.bcentral.com.articles/harper/109.asp?format=print.*

20. Ibid.

21. John Steele Gordon, "Read Your History, Janet," *Forbes,* February 23, 1998, pp. 92–95.

22. *United States v. Topco Associates Inc.,* 405 U.S. 596 (1972).

INDEX

ratios, net profit on sales, 241, 245

ratios, net sales to total assets, 240, 245

ratios, sales to working capital, 240–41, 245

Uniform Commercial Code, 688–94

warranties, 691–92

World Wide Web, 376, 378, 395

Sales and Marketing Management's Survey of Buying Power, 471

Salesforce.com (computer software), 319

Sales Proposal-Architect (computer software), 319

Salsatheque, 190

Sampler, Jeff, 374

Santin, Drew, 442

Santos, Willie, 186

Savings and loan associations (S&Ls), 71, 446–47

SBA. *See* Small Business Administration

Scams/con artists, debt financing and, 462–63

Schaefer, Ulf, 93

Schapansky, Mike, 207

Schaubroeck, Armand, 558

Schnatter, John, 11

Schnel, Jonah, 422

Schwartz, Howard/Edna, 166

Schwass, Joachim, 617

S corporations, 71, 84–86

Scott, Wayne/Marty, 55–56

Screening employees, 567

Seal programs, online, 392

Search engine placement/registration and Web site design, 394–95

Search Engine Watch, 394

Seba, Tony/Freddie, 412

Secure sockets layer (SSL) technology, 402

Securities and Exchange Commission (SEC), 84, 272, 425

Security, fear and loss of, 427

Security and employee theft, 565–66

Security issues on the Web, 391, 397, 400–2

Self-insurance, 633–34, 635*t*, 641

Seller's side and buying an existing business, 147–51

Semon, Mike, 512

Serial entrepreneurs, 7

Service industry/firms

customer satisfaction, marketing and, 205–7

growth in entrepreneurship, 14–15

location decisions/issues, 481–86

plans, business, 164–66

prices/pricing, 303–5

vendor analysis, 539

Service marks, 697

Service Quality Institute, 207

Setup costs, inventory and, 518–19

Severiens, Hans, 415

Sexual harassment, 670–74, 673*t*

Shared advertising, 342

Shawe, Paul, 14–15

SHED-STOP, 697

Sherman, Aliza, 256–57

Sheward, Jim, 586

Shipping

cash flow/management, 283

contracts, 293, 540

foul-ups, minimizing, 528

global issues/marketing, 363, 364*t*

See also Distribution, product/service

Shoplifting, 569–74

Shop.org, 380–81, 391

Shopping centers as business locations, 484–85

Shopping malls, online, 387

Short-term loans, 440

Shriner's Burn Institute, 693

Signs as layout consideration/issue, 493

Silent partners, 75

Silicon Ivy Ventures, 422

Singapore, 111

Singer, Isaac M., 93

Site selection, franchising and, 99–100

See also Location decisions/issues

Size as layout consideration/issue, 489

Skimming pricing strategy, 292

SkyFlow, 422

Small Business Administration (SBA), 22, 23–24, 362, 411, 439, 453–59, 462, 471

Small Business Development Center (SBDC), 471

Small businesses, contributions of, 21–22, 204–5

See also individual subject headings

Small Business Innovation Research (SBIR), 453

Small business investment companies (SBICs), 449–50

Small business lending companies (SBLCs), 450–51

Small business technology transfer (STTR), 453

Small company offering registration (SCOR), 428–30

Smilor, Ray, 40

Smith, Greg, 242, 252

Smith and Hawken, 658

Snodgrass, Paul, 621–22

Soapworks, 208

Social responsibility, company's

advertising, truth in, 675

AIDS (acquired immune deficiency syndrome), 668–70

case example (Circle Solutions), 669

case example (Interface Inc.), 662

to the community, 676–77

conclusions/chapter summary, 677–78

to customers, 674–76

defining terms, 650, 663

discussion questions, 679

drug testing, 667–68

to employees, 664–70, 672–74

to the environment, 663, 664*t*

exercises, practice/review, 679

to investors, 676

new breed of socially responsible corporate founders, 658

objectives, chapter, 649

overview, 661, 663

privacy, workplace, 674

sexual harassment, 670–74, 673*t*

society, opportunity to contribute to, 11

See also Ethics

Soderstrom, Mark, 206

Softub, 524

Software, computer

copyright infringement, 698

personal selling, 319

security, World Wide Web, 401–2

tracking Web results, 398–99

viruses, detecting computer, 401

Sole proprietorship, 67, 69–70, 72

Sony's Bar-B-Q, 475

Sourcebook of County Demographics, 471

Sources of State Information, 537

South Beach Cafe, 433

South Carolina

BMW, 472

loan programs, debt financing and, 459

trade area size, politics and, 482

workers' compensation, 641

South of the Border, 334

Southstream Seafoods, 206

Space Adventures, 5–6

Space Photonics, 453

Space values, layout decisions/issues and, 498–500, 499*f*

Spain, 358

Spam on the Web, 391

Specialized small business investment companies (SSBICs), 450

Specialty Building Supplies, 355

Speed as a major competitive weapon, 208–9

Spill 911 Inc., 211

Spoilage and costs of holding inventory, 518

Sports Illustrated, 10

Spouses, companies co-owned by, 20–21

Springfield Remanufacturing Corporation (SRC), 606, 619

Spring Street Brewing, 432–33

S&S Seafood, 362–63

St. Louis County Economic Authority, 448

Stack, Jack, 606, 619

Staffing. *See* Employee/staffing issues

Stallion Manufacturing, 279

Stamp, Ronald, 5

Standard Industrial Classification (SIC) code, 224

Standardization and franchising, 93–94, 97, 101

Standard Oil Trust, 703

Stanford University, 422

Stanley, Thomas, 11

Starbucks, 664–65

Start-up capital, 66

See also Capital/financing

State, location decisions/issues and selecting the, 472–74, 474*t*

State Industrial Directories, 537

Statement of cash flows, 222–24

quality, 514
service, superior, 207
shoplifters, spotting, 572–73
Transferable ownership, corporations and, 83
Transfers, franchise, 113
Transit advertising, 335–36
Transition, entrepreneurial, 26–27
TransPerfect Translations, 14–15
Transportation networks and location decisions/issues, 480
TransUnion, 272
Travel agencies, threats facing, 43–44
Travelocity, 44
TRUSTe, 392, 400
Trusts, 629–30
Truth and advertising, 675, 704–6
Truth and effective communication, 598
Tschol, John, 207
Turnover rate, franchisee, 108
Twain, Mark, 605
Two-bin method of inventory control, 553, 554f

U

Undercapitalization, 24
Underwriters and companies going public, 426
Uniform Commercial Code (UCC), 135, 539, 688–94
Uniform Franchise Offering Circular (UFOC), 104–8
Uniform Limited Offering Registration (ULOR), 428–30
Unions and international trade, 367–68
Uniqueness, marketing and, 197–98
Unique selling proposition (USP), 314–15
United States Mutual Association, 566
Universities/colleges and business plan competitions, 178–79
University Angels, 422
University of California at Berkeley, 422
University of North Carolina, 473
Uproar Entertainment, 20–21
UPS Worldwide, 559
Upward feedback, 610
U.S. Industrial Outlook Handbook, 164
Usage rates and reorder point model, 529
Utilitarian ethical viewpoint, 653

V

Valuation, business
adjusted balance sheet technique, 140–43
balance sheet technique, 139, 141t
earnings approach, 142–46
market approach, 146–47
overview, 138–39
Values, family businesses and shared, 616
Value test and business plan, 175
Valvoline Instant Oil Change Franchising Inc., 98
van Stolk, Peter, 186

Vanstory, Randy, 200
Variable costing, 300–1, 301t
Variable expenses, 248
Vasos, Michael, 290
Velma Handbags, 402
Vendor analysis, purchasing and, 533–39, 534f
Venezuela, 115
Venture capital companies, 417–18, 419t, 420–22
Verbal and nonverbal messages, conflicting, 598
Veritas, 266
Vernon, Lillian, 14, 27
Vest Pocket Guide to Financial Ratios, 243
VetExchange, 415
Videotapes and copyright infringement, 698
Village Real Estate Services, 658
Viral Web sites, 398
Virtue approach (ethical viewpoint), 653
Virus detection software, 401
Visa, 305
Visibility and location decisions/issues, 483
Vision, developing a clear, 40–41
Visual inventory control systems, 550–51
VoteHere, 43
Vylene Enterprises, 100

W

Wages, 282, 473, 604–5
Walboldt, Gus, 445
Wal-Mart, 566
Wanamaker's Department Store, 23
Warner, Chris, 397
Warning customers, product liability cases and, 694
Warranties, sales, 691–92
Watson, Tom, 117
Weaknesses/strengths, assessing the company's, 42–43
Web, the. *See* World Wide Web
Wedel, Davin, 643
Wellness programs, 645
Wendy's, 116
Wesson, Joshua, 697
Western, T. J., 93
WestJet, 45
Westrum (John) and Westrum Development Company, 608
Whitehall Consultants, 266
Wild Plant Toys Inc., 658
Win² (computer software), 319
Window displays, 491
Winnick, Adam, 422
Wolff, Michael, 407
WomenAngels.net, 415
Women entrepreneurs, 16, 17f
Women's Technology Cluster, 488
Women's Travel Club, 197
Woodendipity, 333
Woolworth, F. W., 546
Workers' compensation, 641
Working capital, 410
World Trade Organization (WTO), 369

World Wide Web (WWW)
advertising, 327–28, 328t
alliances, strategic, 392
approaches to e-commerce, 385–86, 388–89
barter exchanges, 280
benefits of selling on the web, 376–78
business-to-business e-commerce, 384–85
capital/financing, 415
case example (AO Rafting), 387–88
case example (Earth Treks), 397
community, developing, 390–91
conclusions/chapter summary, 402–4
credibility, Web site, 391–92
credit and collection policy, establishing a, 272
credit cards, 307–8
direct stock offerings, 432–33
discussion questions, 404
exercises, practice/review, 404–5
freebies, attracting visitors by giving away, 391
global issues/marketing, 349–52, 351f, 376–77, 392–93
growth in entrepreneurship, 15
in-house, building a Web site, 388
Internet service providers as e-commerce option, 386, 388
inventory, 550
before launching into e-commerce, 378–79
location decisions/issues, 469–70
marketing, 209–11, 389–90
myths of e-commerce, twelve, 379–85
niche marketing, 389–90
objectives, chapter, 374
overview, 375–76
privacy, 381, 400
professionals to design custom sites, hiring, 388–89, 398
promotion, Web site, 393
prototyping, business, 167
sales, increasing and tracking, 376, 378, 395
security issues, 391, 397, 400–2
shopping malls, online, 387
spammer, avoid becoming a, 391
storefront-building services, 387
success, strategies for, 389–93
supply chain management, 541
tracking Web results, 378, 389–99
traffic, daily, 390f
users by world region, 376f
utilization of global reach, 392–93
vendor analysis, 537
Web sites, designing, 388–89, 393–98
World Wrestling Federation, 424
Worlwise Inc., 658
Writing requirements and contracts, 682, 687, 690
WWW. *See* World Wide Web
Wyant, Peg, 407
Wynn, Steve, 252

X

X PRIZE Foundation, 5